GUNSMOKE

GUNSMOKE

A COMPLETE HISTORY
AND ANALYSIS
OF THE LEGENDARY
BROADCAST SERIES

*With a Comprehensive Episode-by-Episode Guide
to Both the Radio and Television Programs*

by SuzAnne Barabas *and*
Gabor Barabas

McFarland & Company, Inc., Publishers
Jefferson, North Carolina, and London

Frontispiece: James Arness, as Matt Dillon, administering justice.

Photographs from the television program series Gunsmoke, *originally broadcast over the CBS Television Network, are used with the permission of the copyright proprietor, CBS Inc. All rights reserved.*

British Library Cataloguing-in-Publication data are available

Library of Congress Cataloguing-in-Publication Data

Barabas, SuzAnne, 1949–
    Gunsmoke : the complete history and analysis of the legendary broadcast series with a comprehensive episode-by-episode guide to both the radio and television programs / by SuzAnne Barabas and Gabor Barabas.
    p. cm.
    [Includes index.]
    Includes bibliographical references.
    ISBN 0-89950-418-3 (lib. bdg.; 50# acid-free natural and
      60# sterling gloss alk. papers) ∞
    1. Gunsmoke (Radio program) 2. Gunsmoke (Television program)
I. Barabas, Gabor. II. Title.
PN1991.77.G86B36   1990
791.44′72—dc20   89-42703
                                                               CIP

© 1990 SuzAnne Barabas and Gabor Barabas. All rights reserved

Manufactured in the United States of America

McFarland & Company, Inc., Publishers
  Box 611, Jefferson, North Carolina 28640

To the memory of
John Meston • Norman Macdonnell
Amanda Blake • Milburn Stone
Georgia Ellis • Howard McNear
and all the
inhabitants of Dodge City
who are no longer
with us

TABLE OF CONTENTS

Acknowledgments ix

Part I. The History of *Gunsmoke*
    Introduction   3
    The Real Dodge City   7
    The Western Genre   13
    Radio — The Pioneers   23
    Television — The New Frontier   73
    Reflections by Guest Stars   157
    Postscripts   201
    Which Way'd They Go?   225

Part II. Photographs   229

Part III. The Programs, Episode-by-Episode
    The Radio Programs   357
    The Television Programs   443

Part IV. Appendices
    Appendix A: Quotes from *Gunsmoke*   729
    Appendix B: The Television Directors   742
    Appendix C: The Radio and Television Writers   745
    Appendix D: The Television Producers   747
    Appendix E: The Radio and Television Awards   748

TABLE OF CONTENTS

Appendix F: The Television Time Schedule 752
Appendix G: The Television Actors 753
Appendix H: The Radio Performers 767
Appendix I: The Television Production Staff 769
Appendix J: The Principal Performers' Credits 774
Appendix K: Gunsmoke 2 781

References 783
Bibliography 787
Index 793

ACKNOWLEDGMENTS

We are indebted to many individuals and organizations whose kind assistance and cooperation have made this book possible. We learned very early in our journey through Dodge City that for the individuals acknowledged here *Gunsmoke* was generally a labor of love, and we hope that we have done justice to their sentiments.

We would like to thank in particular James Arness, Amanda Blake, Ken Curtis, Dennis Weaver, Buck Taylor, Burt Reynolds, Roger Ewing, Parley Baer, Mary Ann Hooper Meston, Harry Ackerman, Harry Bartell, Guy della Cioppa, Larry Dobkin, Paul F. Edwards, Kathleen Hite, Ray Kemper, Rex Koury, Lou Krugman, Philip Leacock, Vic Perrin, Herb Purdum, Denver Pyle, William Robson, Robert Totten, Paul Savage, George Walsh, Charles Marquis Warren, and Morgan Woodward for giving generously of their time and sharing memories and thoughts with us.

A special thanks to John Mantley for his assistance and for opening his home to us so that we could at leisure study his comprehensive collection of *Gunsmoke* material that included logs, journals and contemporary critiques.

We express our appreciation to Sue Ane Langdon, Neil Summers, Link Wyler, Charles Aidman, Morey Amsterdam, John Anderson, Richard Anderson, Tige Andrews, Michael Ansara, Herb Armstrong, R.G. Armstrong, Edward Asner, Val Avery, Donna Bacalla, Bonnie Bartlett, Jeanne Bates, Richard Beals, Ralph Bellamy, Nellie Bellflower, Richard Bradford, John Brandon, Foster Brooks, Joshua Bryant, Gary Busey, Owen Bush, Lillian Buyeff, Joseph Campanella, Harry Carey, Jr., Stephen Carlson, Paul Carr, David Carradine, Mary Carver, Eunice Christopher, Julie Cobb, William Conrad, Ben Cooper, Jeanne Cooper, Alex Cord, Jeff Corey, Royal Dano, June Dayton, John Dehner, George Di Cenzo, Lieux Dressler, Don Dubbins, Val Dufour, Jane Dulo, John Dunkel, Robert Easton, Sam Edwards, Jack Elam, Richard Evans, John Fiedler, Eddie Firestone, Fionnula Flanagan, Med Flory, Nina Foch, Michael Fox, Anne Francis, Victor

French, Allen Garfield, Beverly Garland, Jack Ging, Leo Gordon, Karen Grassle, Dabbs Greer, James Griffith, Mariette Hartley, Eileen Heckart, Katherine Helmond, Darryl Hickman, Pat Hingle, John Hoyt, Kim Hunter, Anne Jackson, Bill James, Clifton James, Graham Jarvis, Salome Jens, Russell Johnson, Ted Jordan, DeForest Kelley, George Kennedy, Helen Kleeb, Robert Lansing, Louise Latham, Cloris Leachman, Michael Learned, Ruta Lee, Joanne Linville, June Lockhart, Tyler McVey, Irving J. Moore, Ed Nelson, Mayf Nutter, Carroll O'Connor, Paul Picerni, Robert Pine, Laurie Prange, Tom Reese, Madlyn Rhue, Peter Mark Richman, Fran Ryan, John Saxon, William Schallert, Hal Smith, William Smith, Julie Sommars, James Stacy, Craig Stevens, Guy Stockwell, Leonard Stone, Loretta Swit, Jess Walton, Clyde Ware, William Windom, and Ben Wright for contributing their time, insights and reminiscences.

John Hickman provided invaluable assistance and material on the radio show. His interviews with John Meston, Norman Macdonnell and others chronicled the creation of the program. He shared with us hours of taped interviews that did not appear in his classic five-hour analysis of *Gunsmoke* on his radio program.

A network of individuals monitored television episodes of *Gunsmoke* for us around the United States. We would like to thank Dave Kempton, Tom Wesseler, Marc Lowy, and Monica Lowy in Ohio, Kim Barabas in Michigan, Phillip Lieberman in Pennsylvania, Lauren Schwarz Siwoff and Ron Siwoff in New Jersey, and Guy McMillin in New Hampshire. Richard D. Arnold and John Hickman were among those who provided radio tapes.

CBS opened up its archives to us so that we could analyze original logs, scripts and news releases with Frank Carra's assistance. Virginia Frey consistently guided us in accessing this valuable information. We would like to thank the CBS Department of Photography and Martin Silverstein for allowing us to look though the most definitive collection of photographs on *Gunsmoke* and for permitting us to reproduce some of the photos that appear in our book.

Around the country there are various libraries and archives that have collections of rare *Gunsmoke* materials. They opened their doors to us and shared their expertise. At the Huntington Library we were able to study over a hundred original radio scripts, assisted by Sue Hodson and Sara Hodkins. The University of Oregon Special Collections Department and Hillary Cummings provided us with television scripts. At the Library of Congress we viewed *Gunsmoke* tapes and other materials with the guidance of Barbara Humphries and Katharine Loughney. Tim Hawkins at the Wisconsin Center for Film and Theater Research provided photographs. The Boot Hill Museum in Dodge City and Darlene Clifton Smith assisted us in our study of the history of Dodge City.

Acknowledgments

The *TV Guide* Readers' Service shared articles written over the years on *Gunsmoke,* and the A.C. Nielsen Company provided comprehensive statistics related to ratings. *Emmy Magazine* shared additional background information.

We would also like to thank Actor's Equity, the American Federation of Television and Radio Artists, the Producers Guild of America, the Writers Guild of America, the Directors Guild of America, Tony Phipps and the Screen Actors Guild, Hal Ross, David Gershenson, Jay Hickerson and Friends of Old Time Radio, Alice Weaver, Brendon Boone, Beau Bridges, Anne Nelson, Lonny Chapman, Judith Macdonnell, Joanna Moore, Bev Tondreau Feldman, Vonnie Crutchfield, Mrs. James Nusser, Mrs. Ronald Bishop, Etta McPeters, Sheila Tucker, Mrs. Dorothy I. Devine, Mrs. Ed Begley, Mary Brako Cobb, Fay M. O'Malley, Karl Puttfarkin, Jane Garrison Stone, Min Strange, Kit McNear, Gregg del Valle, Judith Oates, Jan P. Ellis O'Hare, Jack Weston, Wayne Rogers, Rory Calhoun, John Chandler, Betty Conner, Michael Constantine, Gretchen Corbett, Gene Evans, Brett Halsey, Elliott Lewis, Suzanne Lloyd, Anna Navarro, Lois Nettleton, Jeanette Nolan, Katharine Ross, Harry Townes, Van Williams, Don Aston, Paul Kochanski, Gary Yoggy, Roger Crowley, and our publishers for their support and assistance.

We would especially like to thank Larry Gassman, John Gassman, Chris Lembesis, Don Haefele and all the members of S.P.E.R.D.V.A.C. (Society to Perserve and Encourage Radio Drama, Variety and Comedy) for their assistance and encouragement.

We would also like to thank Bernard Press, Jayne Fields, and Anne Ochester for their assistance in research and secretarial functions. A special thanks to Howard Lewis who made late night trips to keep our computer operational, and to Merek Press for his help in editing.

The *Gunsmoke* photographs used in this book are by permission of CBS, Inc., and Viacom, and have been provided by CBS, Inc., the Wisconsin Center for Film and Theater Research, John Hickman, Neil Summers, Georgia Ellis Puttfarkin, and the authors' private collection. The photos by Harry Bartell are courtesy of Mr. Bartell. The photos in Dodge City have been provided by the Boot Hill Museum, Inc., Dodge City, Kansas. Additional photos are courtesy of the interviewed subjects or their estates.

The summaries for the radio shows have been obtained by listening to the original programs and reading scripts, and in a few instances from the recollections of authors or actors. The titles for the shows were obtained from Norman Macdonnell's radio log.

The summaries for the television episodes were obtained by viewing original programs and reading scripts, and from CBS press releases through the assistance of CBS, Inc. The titles for the shows were obtained through CBS and the television logs of Norman Macdonnell and John Mantley.

PART I.
THE HISTORY
OF *GUNSMOKE*

INTRODUCTION

Gunsmoke represents the rarest of phenomena in the annals of radio and television. It not only ran for decades, but also introduced to the public a cast of characters that gradually took on mythic proportions and forever became part of the popular consciousness. Like Sherlock Holmes and Doctor Watson, the imaginary inhabitants of Dodge City gradually became as real as any individuals born by more conventional means. Even the cynical are soon convinced that U.S. Marshal Matt Dillon, crotchety Doc Adams, sultry saloon-owner Kitty Russell, gamey-legged Chester, and scruffy Festus walked the dusty streets of Dodge City in the 1870s. In fact, the Chamber of Commerce of Dodge City once stated that "as near as we can determine, Matt lived here at one time."

This rare phenomenon did not occur by happenstance, but because of the unique vision of its creators, John Meston and Norman Macdonnell. It continued to evolve under the masterful guidance of Macdonnell and subsequent producers, Charles Marquis Warren, Philip Leacock, and John Mantley, with each producer adding his own distinctive contribution.

The magical touch of directors such as Mark Rydell, Vincent and Bernard McEveety, Andrew V. McLaglen, Irving J. Moore, and Harry Harris, Jr., helped perfect *Gunsmoke*. Talented writers, whose numbers have included Kathleen Hite, Les Crutchfield, John Dunkel, Marian Clark, Ron Bishop, Paul Savage, Calvin Clements, Clyde Ware, Jim Byrnes, and Sam Peckinpah, consistently found that *Gunsmoke* was the show to write for. It fully challenged their creativity and imaginations by giving them the opportunity and the freedom to write about complex issues where frequently there was no answer or resolution.

The actors also rose to the occasion and jealously guarded their characters throughout the years. All of the principal actors (William Conrad, Parley Baer, Howard McNear, Georgia Ellis on radio, and James Arness, Milburn Stone, Amanda Blake, Ken Curtis, Dennis Weaver, and Buck

Taylor on television) devoted a major part of their careers to the show. They nurtured the characters they were entrusted with, and allowed them to blossom into living, breathing, "real" people.

The inhabitants of Dodge City became three-dimensional and developed complex interpersonal relationships. They became a close-knit family and their audience was made to feel a part of that family each week. Producers, directors, writers, actors and administrators would come and go, each bringing a new dimension to the show, yet still retaining the honesty and integrity of the original concept throughout the nine years that *Gunsmoke* was broadcast on radio and the 20 years that it aired on television.

Gunsmoke demanded of its audience thoughtful reflection. It transcended mere entertainment and dealt with the stuff of life. Even Marshal Dillon, its larger-than-life hero, was fallible. As in Greek tragedies, we are constantly reminded of his mortality. In the world of *Gunsmoke*, the innocent are all too often victimized, and the guilty frequently escape earthly retribution. However, we generally sense that there is a higher order and justice, and though this may not always be physically apparent, the spirit of this higher order pervades the world of Dodge City.

The stories are primarily morality plays and Marshal Dillon and his friends struggle against fate and against forces frequently beyond their control. Matt makes the best decisions he can and lives with their consequences. Amidst evil and lawlessness he clings faithfully to his simple principles and tenaciously upholds the law that he is willing to die for.

Gunsmoke speaks against condescension. It assumes that its audience consists of mature and intelligent individuals. It applies no pat formulas and does not pander to a "popular taste." The radio show, which opened in 1952, was without a sponsor after almost a year of successful programming. It was considered a "prestige program," intelligently conceived and produced, and aimed at an audience with a high level of intelligence. *Time* magazine noted in its March 23, 1953, issue, that such shows are "seldom sponsored, for any intelligent sponsor knows that reasonably intelligent audiences are hardly worth spending money on."[1] Norman Macdonnell and CBS persisted, however, and Macdonnell indicated that he was not especially worried about the lack of a sponsor, explaining that: "There would be problems. We'd have to clean the show up. Kitty would have to be living with her parents on a sweet little ranch.... And Matt, he'd have to wear buckskin and swagger around with his guns blazing. He'd even have to ride a pure white charger."[2] A major sponsor finally did pick up the show, which became one of the most successful radio programs of all time. It eventually went off the air on June 18, 1961, as television gained predominance. During those nine years, however, Matt never did take to wearing buckskin or riding a pure white charger, and Kitty clung stubbornly to the Long Branch Saloon.

Introduction

The television program, which ran for a record-breaking 20 years, from 1955 to 1975, is still widely aired around the world, attesting to its universal relevance and appeal. In Great Britain, under the title *Gun Law,* it enjoyed similar popularity. In 1987, after a 12-year silence, a made-for-television movie, *Gunsmoke: Return to Dodge,* was aired on CBS. Produced by John Mantley, written by Jim Byrnes, and directed by Vincent McEveety, it starred James Arness, Amanda Blake, and Buck Taylor and was favorably received by *Gunsmoke* fans old and new.

This book is a journey to discover what has made *Gunsmoke* the unique and rare phenomenon that it has become, and to understand how a fictitious Dodge City could evolve into a metaphor for the world and the human condition. It also explains how *Gunsmoke* soared above most other shows in the popular media to become an achievement against which all others must be measured.

THE REAL DODGE CITY

In creating *Gunsmoke*, both John Meston and Norman Macdonnell emphasized authenticity. Meston was an ardent student of the frontier and his depiction of Dodge City in the 1870s reveals an intimate knowledge of the times. He was not interested in every historical detail but sought to capture the vitality and energy of "the wickedest little city in America" so as to heighten the realism of his stories.

The Opening of the Frontier

In 1865, Fort Dodge was established in southwest Kansas to guard the flow of traffic on the Santa Fe Trail. The Trail extended from Missouri to New Mexico and 500 of its 750 miles were located in Kansas. By 1862 it carried a trade of $40 million and the United States Government was committed to protecting it from the Indians and to encouraging white settlements. The land opened up when Cyrus K. Holliday decided to build the Atchison, Topeka & Santa Fe Railroad that traversed Kansas and followed the Santa Fe Trail. Started in 1868, the rails finally reached Dodge in 1872. The first house built on land that was ultimately to become Dodge City was that of Henry L. Sitler who settled northwest of the Fort in 1871. With the railroad came traders, hunters, settlers and fortune-seekers. Some were escaping from their past, others from the law, while still others, with no past to speak of, were pursuing dreams of a better future. The early trains brought in liquor and took out buffalo hides and meat. Mrs. Calvina Anthony, an early settler, describes the times:

> ...the town of Dodge City was started on what might be called the borders of the Sahara. Very few families had yet shown the courage to locate in this frontier town. The morning I arrived I looked around in vain for a woman's face, and did not see one until I was taken to the Dodge House

and introduced to the landlady. We sat down to our breakfast with a great crowd of long haired hunters, with their buckskin suit and pistols. All was excitement and trading. A man stood by the door as they went out and collected a dollar from each one for their meal.[3]

The first bar in town was a makeshift tent erected by George Hoover and his partner John McDonald. George "Hoodoo" Brown and his associate, Charley Stewart, built the first saloon and catered to the growing number of buffalo hunters and adventurers. The going rate for a drink of whiskey was 25 cents. By 1873 Dodge was a settlement on the edge of an economic and social explosion. Various businesses sprung up in quick succession and included Webster's dry goods and clothing store, Evans' grocery store, Peacock's Billiard Hall and saloon, Hoover and McDonald's wholesale liquor store and saloon, Collar's clothing store, Zimmerman's hardware store, Fringer's drug store, Colonel Isaac Young's harness and saddle shop, and a post office.[4] The key businesses were on Front Street and many of these early merchants became wealthy catering to the transients who sought refuge from the prairie and the wilderness. There was no lack of brothels and saloons to choose from.

In 1872 the population of Dodge was 500 and its economy was totally dependent on buffalo. Charles Rath built a mercantile business dealing in buffalo hides, bones and meat and his company made Dodge into the "Buffalo City." The meat was a delicacy and the bones were used for utensils, buttons, fertilizer, and in sugar refining. Hunters came by the thousands to stalk the great herds that carpeted the prairies of western Kansas and Texas. A man could become wealthy within a year, and the Government greatly encouraged hunting because it was felt that by depriving the Indian of his food source he could be vanquished and destroyed once and for all. The strategy succeeded beyond anyone's imaginings, and in ten years over three million buffalo were slaughtered. The great herds were no more and the starving Indians were forced to live on reservations in order to survive. When the buffalo trade collapsed the boom did not end. It was quickly supplanted by the cattle trade and Texan cowboys made Dodge into the "Queen of the Cowtowns."

By 1875 Dodge had become the main shipping point for cattle destined for Eastern and Northwest markets. Every spring the town prepared for the coming deluge of tired, thirsty and bored drovers who had spent months on the lonesome trail. A cattle drive arriving from Texas on the Western Trail could traverse fifteen hundred dangerous miles, and a cowboy made $30 a month for that difficult journey. Up to three thousand head of cattle, and a hundred working horses would be fording the Red River, the North Canadian River and the Cimarron south of Dodge.

A trail boss with ten to twelve hands, a cook and a wrangler could spend 16 hours in the saddle each day. No wonder that when the boys hit Dodge

The Real Dodge City

there was no stopping them. Shooting up the "Cowboy Capital" was an honored diversion for those weary of the dust and the saddle. The first place they stormed was the tonsorial parlor to clean up and get a shave and a haircut. After putting on a new suit it was time to carouse with the women, to gamble, and to drink oneself into oblivion. The "beautiful, bibulous Babylon of the frontier"[5] catered readily to all these needs.

The cattle trade changed the face of Dodge. In the spring, when the cowboys came, the population of Dodge would double. There were great stockyards and up to 100,000 head could be found grazing outside of town. Large sums were exchanged and fortunes were made and lost. The Bank of Dodge City was organized to accommodate the cattle buyers and sellers and to handle the large flow of cash. The Dodge House was the largest hotel. It had 38 rooms, a restaurant, a bar, and a billiard hall. There were theaters that boasted the likes of Dora Hand and Fannie Garrettson. One could see Eddie Foy at The Comique, where he developed the acts that later brought him vaudeville fame. In one year, up to 300 barrels of whiskey were consumed. In 1877, George Hoover, who ran a wholesale business, received 5,000 cigars a week.

One could forget the trail in saloons with exotic names such as the Alamo, Long Branch, Alhambra, Saratoga, Occident, Nueces, Crystal Palace, Lone Star, Oasis, and the St. James. Some were one-room shanties with dirt floors and a few creaky beds in the back, while the most grand offered elegant decor, billiard tables, gambling and the usual rooms in the back. The Long Branch was the fanciest saloon in town and was frequented by gamblers and cattlemen. Although it allowed no dancing, it had a five to eight piece orchestra. One of its owners, Chalk Beeson, was a musician. It even had a room in the back where drunks were locked up for the night until they sobered up.

Dodge City quickly developed a reputation throughout the nation as the wildest and most sinful of all Western towns. The *Oskaloosa (Iowa) Herald* offered the anecdote of a drunken cowboy boarding a train. When the conductor confronts him and asks for his ticket he responds, "hint got none." When questioned as to where he is going he replies, "Goin' to-hic-Hell." To which the conductor replies, "All right, give me fifty cents and get off at Dodge."[6] It is said that in 1879, when the population was 700, there were almost 50 prostitutes plying their trade. These soiled doves and fallen frails entertained the cowboys in dance halls and saloons. A ten-minute dance with one of the girls was 75 cents. Confidence men, gamblers, merchants and whores preyed on the unwary victims. The *Hays Sentinel* described Dodge at the time:

> The town is full of prostitutes and every other house is a brothel...the street is brilliantly lighted and thronged with gaudily dressed women, and

men whose garb betokens the cow-boy. From many saloons proceeds rollicking strains of music...the dance halls are crowded with lewd women and rough men who plunge into the intimacies of the dance with a reckless abandon and inflamed with drink, they make the night hideous with their boisterous revelry...The employment of many citizens is gambling, her [Dodge's] virtue is prostitution and her beverage is whiskey. She is a merry town, and the only visible means of support of a great number of her citizens is jocularity. Here rowdyism has taken its most aggravated forms.[7]

In Dodge, a man could "break all ten commandments in one night, die with his boots on, and be buried on Boot Hill in the morning."[8]

The Law

In 1872 there was no formal law in Dodge. A vigilance committee took care of horse thieves and other "criminals." On other occasions, citizens hired private "lawmen" to administer justice. Most frequently, however, the law was arbitrarily determined by the gun. To John Meston, the Dodge of this period was "a kind of arena for frustrated gladiators." It was here that "homicidal psychopaths gathered...and had themselves a real circus with little or nothing to stop them from happily mowing one another down."[9]

As the town grew, a marshal was appointed by the mayor and the city council. This was primarily a political post, and it was the deputy marshal who was directly responsible for maintaining the peace. The marshal and deputy marshal operated within the city limits while the sheriff of Ford County was responsible for enforcing the law outside of Dodge. Their activities, however, frequently overlapped. In 1876 Lawrence Deger was marshal and Wyatt Earp was deputy marshall of Dodge City. Charles Bassett became the first sheriff of Ford County. These were hard men who met the challenge and the violence of their positions with an enthusiasm that made them suspect. Those who became lawmen were sometimes more worthy of jail or hanging than the men they faced. For their labors they earned about $75 a month. They played an important role in bringing some semblance of order to Dodge. In the final analysis, *Gunsmoke's* Matt Dillon is a fictional synthesis of these real life characters. Commenting on the character he immortalized on television, James Arness stated:

> To me, Matt Dillon is a fictional character in name only. He is something of a composite of the real-life lawman: the Bat Mastersons, the Pat Garretts and the Wyatt Earps. I've been reading every historical account I've been able to get my hands on and I know I'm not only getting the feel of the role but now I'm familiar with the temper of the times and atmosphere

The Real Dodge City

of that period in American history. Dillon...after all, is truly a product of dramatic retrospect.[10]

Unlike Matt, the lawmen of Dodge shot first and asked questions later. Those who did not learn this simple rule did not survive for long. There was very little of the "etiquette" that we see on *Gunsmoke*. Ed Masterson, Bat's eldest brother, was an exception. He was a chivalrous marshal who allowed his opponents to draw first. For him it was but a matter of time, and when he was killed the whole town mourned. Violence was rampant. In a typical year, in 1878, Bat Masterson and his posse captured two train robbers; Bat's brother, Marshal Ed Masterson was murdered, and Deputy Marshal H.T. McCarty was killed in the Long Branch; some months later, cowboy George Hoy was killed by Assistant Marshal Wyatt Earp, and Dora Hand, the dance hall singer and darling of Dodge, was killed, a case of mistaken identity. The year then ended with Dull Knife and his band of Cheyennes fleeing through Kansas and panicking the countryside.

Horse thefts, shoot-outs, fights and jail breaks were daily occurrences in Dodge. Between 1872 and 1873 there were 17 killings in a town with a population of 300. The first burial on Boot Hill was in 1872. The site was not selected through civic planning, but became the infamous cemetery after some unknown transient was gunned down on the hill and was left there for the buzzards. It soon became the burial place for the destitute, and for desperados, and other unsavory characters that graced Dodge with their presence.

Boot Hill was a barren and treeless place that got its name because most of the men buried there had died with their boots on. It quickly found its way into the romantic imagination as seen in a popular cowboy ballad of the time: "...take me to Boot Hill and cover me with roses, I'm just a young cowboy and I know I done wrong."[11] It became so famous that, according to the *Dodge City Times*, "...our graveyard is considered almost as great a curiosity as the grave of Shakespeare."[12] When years later the property became too valuble to house the bones of these victims of Dodge's raucous days, they were disinterred and removed to Prairie Grove Cemetery to join the good folk of Dodge. When developing *Gunsmoke* for television, Charles Marquis Warren chose Boot Hill as the opening scene for his early shows. Each week Matt stood atop the barren hill, surrounded by simple grave markers, reflecting on the fates of the men buried there. The monologue was different with each episode and was reminiscent of William Conrad's opening monologue on the radio show. Writers for the program took this opportunity to give Matt a chance to moralize since at other times he tended to be a man of but few words. An example is the prologue to *Stage Hold-Up* written by Les Crutchfield:

MATT: I've seen a lot of men buried up here on Boot Hill and most of them really earned what they got. They cheated at cards, robbed banks, stole horses, murdered innocent men, picked fights with friend and enemy alike. They lived and died as though they'd never heard of the law, and they treated me like a trespasser, like someone who had no right to interfere with their bloody little games. But I shot it out with them anyway. I guess I'll go right on doing it as long as I last. Matt Dillon, U.S. Marshal.

On another occasion, John Meston had Matt reflect on his own mortality in the prologue to *Young Love.*

MATT: You know, there must be easier ways to die than most of the men up here took, like passing away in one's sleep, or gently dissolving in old age, or even being carried off by some disease of some kind. But getting stabbed, shot, hung, kicked to death all the violent ways we have of dying out here they leave a man without any dignity at all. And, it's worse when it happens suddenly, when a man hasn't time to prepare himself. It's something I, myself, have to face everyday. Matt Dillon, U.S. Marshal.

The Coming of Civilization

Dodge City's reputation as a wild frontier town was established during a remarkably short period of time. In the feverish decade from 1872–1882 it developed the dubious distinction of becoming the "hell-hole" of the West. By 1883, however, signs of "civilization" were appearing. There were attempts to do away with the brothels, businesses were now closed on Sundays, policeman took to wearing uniforms and church attendance was at an all time high. Temperance committees, ministers and good folk banded together to rend the fiber of sin and violence that had characterized Dodge in its infancy. The great lawmen were fast fading into the sunset and shady characters, whose names would have done John Meston proud, such as Mysterious Dave Mather, Cock-Eyed Frank, Eat-'em up Jake, Emporia Belle, Scar-faced Lillie, Three-Fingered Dave, Black Jack Bill, Dynamite Sam, Dirty Sock Jack and Dark Alley Jim were no more.

In reflecting on this period it would seem that "the West" was not just a particular place, but also a moment in America's history where two conflicting modes of life converged: the law of the jungle which was the law of the West, with its violence, its anarchy, its heroic elements and spirited characters, versus civilization, with its impersonal institutions, codified laws and tamed and timid middle-class citizenry.[13]

THE WESTERN GENRE

The Western has been viewed as the quintessential story of America. It is the archetypal morality play expressed in American terms. In order to fully appreciate the remarkable achievement of *Gunsmoke,* it is important to have some understanding of the history of the Western genre. For the past 150 years this genre has found its outlet in various media including literature, cinema, radio, and television. It is in *Gunsmoke* that this most purely American art form achieves its greatest heights.

J. Fred MacDonald in his book, *Who Shot the Sheriff? The Rise and Fall of the Television Western,* describes the Western as "a thriving cultural attraction whose symbols and rhetoric helped define American society for almost a century."[13] On television its popularity was greatest during the late 1950s. MacDonald viewed this phenomenon in political terms and related it to the East-West confrontation. He noted that "Western stories and symbols fit the temper of the time. Their political, military, social, economic, and spiritual implications were most appropriate...many Americans understood themselves and their civilization in terms of the genre...a militaristic art form, the Western spoke especially well the language of Cold War America."[14]

The Western in Literature

John G. Cawelti, in his book, *The Six-Gun Mystique,* views James Fenimore Cooper as the creator of the Western.[15] His books enjoyed great popularity in the nineteenth century and included works such as *The Pioneers* (1823), *The Last of the Mohicans* (1826), *The Pathfinder* (1840), and *The Deerslayer* (1841). Other writers who wrote fictional accounts of the West included Bret Harte (*The Luck of Roaring Camp and Other Sketches,* 1870) Mark Twain (*Roughing It,* 1872), Frank Norris (*The Octopus,* 1901), and Emerson Hough (*The Story of the Cowboy,* 1897). Owen Wister's *The Virginian* (1902) was a bestseller that created a character and type of story that some consider to be the basis of the modern Western. Stephen Crane wrote highly artistic Western stories including *The Bride Comes to Yellow Sky* and *The Blue Hotel*. By the turn of the century these men had provided a special fictional view of the settling of the frontier and had contributed to the developing myth of the West. Subsequent writers such as Willa Cather (*O Pioneers!*, 1913), Eugene Manlove Rhodes (*Good Men and True*, 1910, *West Is West*, 1917), and Zane Grey (*The Spirit of the Border*, 1905, *Riders of the Purple Sage*, 1910) continued this tradition.

Wild West Shows

An individual who contributed greatly to the evolving myth of "the Wild West" was William F. Cody (Buffalo Bill). During the 1870s he toured the country with dramas and outdoor extravaganzas, and his "Rough Riders of the World Wild West Show" was complete with horses, wagons, cowboys, Indians and assorted frontier characters. While these portrayals did not give a realistic view of the West, they did generate tremendous excitement about the frontier and a pride in the history and growth of the nation.

The Western in Films

Early filmmakers found that stories of the West were ideal for their new medium, for they provided them with the opportunity to portray action scenes in motion pictures. *The Great Train Robbery* in 1903 starred Gilbert Anderson, who later became the first Western movie star. In 1907 he played Broncho Billy in the popular two-reeler, *The Bandit Makes Good*. Over the next ten years he was the director and star of hundreds of episodes featuring this character. He languished in obscurity for many years until the Academy of Motion Pictures awarded him a special Oscar in 1957 to recognize his "contributions to the development of motion pictures as entertainment."

William S. Hart started in films in 1914 when he was already 44. He had been a successful Shakespearean actor on Broadway and also appeared in productions of *Ben-Hur*, *The Virginian*, and *The Trail of the Lonesome Pine*. He loved the West and was supposedly a personal friend of Wyatt Earp and Bat Masterson. Some claim that he was the first to develop the "adult" Western in films. His films included *The Man from Nowhere* (1915), *The Devil's Double* (1916), *The Apostle of Vengeance* (1916), and the classic *Tumbleweeds* (1925). Hart encouraged authenticity in costumes and settings and frequently played characters who were neither good nor bad. His pony, Fritz, was his constant companion, and an ad for one of his films, *The Narrow Trail*, trumpeted the homily, "Better a painted pony than a painted woman."

The Western Genre

Tom Mix was also a legendary cowboy star, and made his debut in 1910 in *Ranch Life in the Great Southwest*. He had been in the Texas Rangers and was a member of the "Miller Brothers 101 Ranch Wild West Show." In 1909 he won the national riding and rodeo championship. Mix made numerous one- and two-reelers and was the silent screen's most popular Western star. His character was geared toward kids and his movies religiously ignored serious issues. Mix was resolute, virtuous and unswerving, and never displayed ordinary human weaknesses. He was everything a boy could aspire to.

The scope of the Western continued to grow, and in 1923 James Cruze presented *The Covered Wagon*, which can be considered to be the first epic Western film. John Ford followed in 1924 with *The Iron Horse*, and Raoul Walsh's *The Big Trail* in 1930 featured John Wayne in a "talkie." During the Depression, B Westerns ("budget" Westerns) were extremely popular and kids flocked to the movie houses in droves to escape their oppressive environment. These films were populated by two-dimensional heroes and singing cowboys.

The Western in Radio

At the same time that films were exploring the possibilities of the Western, radio was introduced to the nation amidst great excitement. Early programs were geared toward children and included *Red Ryder, Straight Arrow, Tom Mix, The Cisco Kid,* and *The Lone Ranger*. This last program was first aired on January 30, 1933, on WXYZ Radio in Detroit. Created by Fran Striker, it was an immediate success. For decades its popularity was uncontested and it is one of the few radio Westerns that can rival *Gunsmoke's* longevity, having been presented in 2,956 episodes over two decades. The adventures of the masked man and Tonto finally came to an end on radio on September 3, 1954. *Death Valley Days* was another very popular program that was presented on radio and television for a total of 35 years. Its creator was Mrs. Ruth Woodman, who was an authority on Death Valley history. The stories were supposed to be based on true incidents.

The Adult Western

While most films and radio programs were simplistic in their approach to the West, there was a serious undercurrent in all the media that ultimately gave rise to the "adult" Western. These works explored more carefully how the frontier was settled and strove for authenticity. They also presented complex characters. On occasion, they portrayed lawmen who were beset with doubts. At other times they explored the psychological backgrounds of outlaws to illuminate the nature of their criminality. Some even had the temerity to suggest that the Indian may have had a legitimate grudge against the white man. They analyzed the events and upheavals that accompanied the growth of the nation. They presented more realistically the hardships encountered by the settlers and the psychological toll upon those fool enough to challenge the elements and the frontier.

In literature, novels such as B. Traven's *The Treasure of Sierra Madre,* Jack Schaefer's *Shane* and Walter Van Tilburg Clark's *The Oxbow Incident* explored adult elements and were powerful works ultimately translated to cinema. In films, John Ford's *Stagecoach* (1939), focused on characterization, and William Bowers' *The Gunfighter* (1950), presented the archetypal story of the confrontation between an aging gunfighter and a young challenger anxious to make a name for himself. Delmer Dove's *Broken Arrow* dealt with the love affair of a white scout and an Indian girl. Other "adult" films included *Duel in the Sun* (1948), *High Noon* (1952), and *Giant* (1955).

When *Gunsmoke* aired on radio for the first time in 1952, the stage was already set. There had been an evolutionary movement toward the "adult" Western and *Gunsmoke* was the end-point along this continuum. Although there were other serious Westerns on radio, none ever developed as complex a world as that of *Gunsmoke* nor the rich characters and characterizations that became the trademark of the program. These other shows included *The Six-Shooter* with James Stewart (1953), *Dr. Six-Gun* (1955), and *Fort Laramie,* starring Raymond Burr (1956). Macdonnell was the producer and director of *Fort Laramie* and brought four years of his experience on *Gunsmoke* to the program. The show featured stories of the Wyoming frontier and its cast was composed of regulars from the *Gunsmoke* stock-company. Vic Perrin played Sergeant Goerss, Harry Bartell was Lieutenant Seiberts, and Jack Moyles played Major Daggett. The soundmen were those who created the revolutionary sound of *Gunsmoke*. Other serious Westerns on radio were *Luke Slaughter of Tombstone* with Sam Buffington (1958), and *Frontier Gentleman* (1958), which opened with the lines:

> Herewith, an Englishman's account of life and death in the West. As a reporter for the London *Times,* he writes his colorful and unusual accounts. But as a man with a gun, he lives and becomes a part of the violent years in the new territories. Now, starring John Dehner, this is the story of J.B. Kendall, Frontier Gentleman.

It was the last important program to open on radio and presented stories of the highest caliber. Once again, it featured the regulars who made up the supporting cast on *Gunsmoke,* such as John McIntire, Jeanette Nolan, Lawrence Dobkin, Harry Bartell, Virginia Gregg, Jack Moyles, Joe Kearns and Jack Kruschen. The series was created by Antony Ellis, a frequent contributor to

The Western Genre

Gunsmoke. Another program, *Have Gun, Will Travel,* was somewhat of an anomaly on radio for it first premiered on television and then it was introduced on radio. The time-honored pattern was to introduce a show on radio and then transfer it to television. On television, it starred Richard Boone as the hired gun, Paladine, and premiered in 1957. It opened in 1958 on radio and featured John Dehner. His Oriental sidekick, Heyboy, was played by Ben Wright, and his girlfriend, Missy Wong, was portrayed by Virginia Gregg. All three were noted supporting actors on *Gunsmoke.* Norman Macdonnell was also an occasional director.

Despite the creation of programs such as those listed above, radio was already a doomed medium by the time *Gunsmoke* aired in 1952. The final irony is that just as radio was about to achieve a certain artistic, creative, and technical sophistication, its evolution was rudely interrupted by the introduction of television.

The Revival of the B Western on Television

Although the tradition of the "adult" Western had already been well established in radio, during its infancy on television the Western genre was still viewed as children's entertainment. Early presentations were vintage B Westerns packaged for television. These films that had been gathering dust for decades and which had been mostly forgotten provided a great library for the revolutionary new medium to draw from. Television was starving for material, and by appropriating these films, programming hours could be quickly expanded with a minimum of production expense. More sponsors could be courted to publicize their wares and services on the home screen.

Once again, a new generation of children (and adults), thrilled to the adventures of such forgotten cowboy stars as Ken Maynard (*Cheyenne,* 1929; *Texas Gunfighter,* 1932), Kermit Maynard (*Galloping Dynamite,* 1937; *The Night Riders,* 1939), Wild Bill Elliott (*Taming of the West,* 1939; *King of Dodge City,* 1941), Hoot Gibson (*The Galloping Kid,* 1922; *King of the Rodeo,* 1919), Tom Mix (*The Range Riders,* 1910; *Hard Boiled,* 1926; *Destry Rides Again,* 1932), Bob Steele (*The Mojave Kid,* 1927; *The Great Train Robbery,* 1941), Tim McCoy (*The Westerner,* 1935; *Phantom Ranger,* 1938), and the Durango Kid, Charles Starrett (*The Man from Sundown,* 1939; *Pardon My Gun,* 1942).

William Boyd (Hopalong Cassidy), was in the forefront of this movement. He had been a star of the silent screen and was one of Cecil B. De Mille's favored actors. His first role was as an extra in De Mille's *Why Change Your Wife?* (1920). Later films included *The Volga Boatman* (1926) and *King of Kings* (1927). In 1935 he was cast as the star of the Western, *Hop-A-Long Cassidy.* The movie was tremendously successful and made him a star. Boyd played in 54 Hopalong episodes and in the process went from being a poor rider to an accomplished horseman. When the producer finally dropped the series, Boyd took over himself. Later on, he had the foresight to purchase all rights to the Hoppy character as well as the television rights to his old Hopalong Cassidy films. When he realized the potential of his property, he leased some of the old films to a Los Angeles television station in 1948. The demand for his films was so great that he produced an additional 52 "Hoppy" films expressly for television and quickly became a multimillionaire.

Other stars of the silver screen who also capitalized on this trend were Roy Rogers and Gene Autry. Once again they were emulated figures throughout households in America. In the early 1940s, Roy Rogers had been billed as the "King of the Cowboys" and his companion, Dale Evans was the "Queen of the West." Numbered among his screen credits were films such as *Tumbling Tumbleweeds* (1935), *Billy the Kid Returns* (1938), *Red River Valley* (1941), *The Yellow Rose of Texas* (1944), and *My Pal Trigger* (1946). When television was introduced, he started his own production company and made over 100 half-hour films. Children tuned in to watch the *Roy Rogers Show* (1951-1957) as Roy and Dale battled evil forces with the help of Roy's horse, Trigger, dog, Bullet, sidekick Pat and his jeep, Nellybelle. Their faithful young audience put both Roy and Dale into The Cowboy Hall of Fame, and Roy into his extremely lucrative restaurant business.

Gene Autry followed a similar path. He had been a singer and a cowboy when Will Rogers heard him and encouraged him to enter show business in the 1920s. He appeared on radio, and was a phenomenally prolific songwriter composing two hundred songs including "Here Comes Santa Claus." Autry appeared in various movies and was Republic's star in the 1930s. His films include *In Old Santa Fe* (1934), *Tumbling Tumbleweeds* (1935), *The Singing Vagabond* (1935), *The Singing Cowboy* (1937), and *Cowboy Serenade* (1942). With television's advent he formed the "Flying A productions" and produced *The Gene Autry Show* (1950–56). He, too, had a trusty horse, Champion, as well as a comic sidekick, Pat Buttram, who provided comic relief with his antics and predicaments. Gene's famous theme was "Back in the Saddle" and he needed little prompting to launch into song. He and Roy Rogers were the epitome of the "singing cowboy."

The Children's Western on Television

By 1949, an NBC survey found that children preferred Westerns above all programming including *Howdy Doody, Milton Berle, Lucky Pup, Small Fry Club,* and *Kukla, Fran and Ollie.* It is ironic that with the success of the television Western came the demise of the genre in cinema. In their book, Les

The Western Genre

Adams and Buck Rainey note that in their heyday (1930-1941), 1,345 Western commercial films were made which represented 39.8 percent of all films produced during that period. In the early years of television (1950-55), there were 592 Westerns made, constituting only 17.5 percent of the total. By the time that the Western reigned supreme on television (1956-59), 244 Western films were made for cinema, representing only 7.2 percent of the total.[16]

In response to this growing popularity, more and more Westerns were developed specifically for television. Producers hired staff with experience in B Westerns. During television's early years, these programs included such famous shows as *The Lone Ranger* (1949-57), played by stuntman Clayton Moore. Astride his noble horse, Silver, he terrorized the villains of the West. Moore's contract stipulated that he could not make public appearances without his full outfit and disguise. His Indian companion was Jay Silverheels who was featured as his faithful friend, Tonto. They had their work cut out for them, for the Lone Ranger had sworn that he would not rest until all the outlaws in the West were vanquished.

Other programs included *The Cisco Kid* (1950-56), which featured Duncan Renaldo in his foppish embroidered shirts, and his bumbling companion, Pancho, played by Mexican actor Leo Carrillo. At the time that filming began Renaldo was already in his fifties and Carrillo in his seventies. They gasped and wheezed their way through 156 episodes accompanied by their equine assistants, Diablo and Loco.

Another program was *The Range Rider* (1951-52), and its hero was played by Jock Mahoney, a six-foot-four stuntman. *Sky King* (1951-54) featured Kirby Grant as the owner of the Flying Crown Ranch. Unfortunate criminals, despite all their posturings to the contrary, were at great disadvantage as Sky swooped down on them in his plane, The Songbird, accompanied by his niece, Penny, and nephew, Clipper.

The Adventures of Kit Carson (1951-55), also glossed over historical accuracy. It featured Bill Williams and Don Diamond played his comic companion, El Toro. Interestingly, Diamond was no authentic Latino but hailed from Brooklyn. *The Adventures of Wild Bill Hickock* (1951-58), featured the heartthrob of bobby-soxers, Guy Madison. Corpulent Andy Devine, with his grating and high-pitched voice played Jingles, his deputy. Together they roamed disconnected portions of the West, with Madison astride his horse, Buckshot, and Devine riding an unfortunate, but seemingly uncomplaining, Joker. *Annie Oakley* (1954-57), was produced by Gene Autry's company and featured the perky blond actress Gail Davis. The fringed heroine kept the peace in the town of Diablo through 81 episodes.

These early television programs provided great entertainment to countless children and probably to many adults as well who got caught up in the simple adventures. George W. Trendle, the producer of *The Lone Ranger*, was one of the key individuals who set the standard for "kiddie" Westerns. He avoided violence and stressed that his hero embody patriotic and conservative sentiments. His "Kemo Sabe" was polite, gallant and devoid of flaws. The Lone Ranger was fearless in the face of great odds and when using his gun he was careful not to kill but only to teach a painful lesson. Gene Autry's "Cowboy Code" stressed a similar approach to Westerns. The philosophy articulated in this code clearly applied to his young viewers as well as to his hero. He said that a cowboy:

> ...never takes unfair advantage, even of an enemy; never betrays a trust; always tells the truth; is kind to small children, to old folks, and to animals; is free from racial and religious prejudice; is always helpful, and when anyone's in trouble he lends a hand; is a good worker; is clean about his person;... respects womanhood, his parents, and the laws of his country; [and] is a patriot.[17]

The Adult Western on Television

The adult Western started to make its appearance in transitional programs that were slightly more sophisticated than their predecessors. These programs were still not "adult" per se, but their formulas were geared to provide good entertainment for the entire family, and their plots and scripts were of a higher caliber. A famous example is *Davy Crockett, Indian Fighter* (1954-1955), which was presented on *Disneyland*. The program was followed by such a Crockett craze that kids all across the nation felt that their lives were devoid of meaning unless they possessed a fringed jacket and coonskin cap, matching underwear and pajamas, and assorted Crockett paraphernalia including lunch pails, watches and ukeleles. The show attracted such a large adult audience that even the most torpid network executive could not fail but take note.

Clearly, what had been learned on radio also applied to television: there was indeed an adult audience out there somewhere. These transitional programs included *The Adventures of Rin Tin Tin* (1954-1958), which featured a cerebral German shepherd that was adopted along with his master, Rusty, by a cavalry unit. Rusty was made a corporal and "Tinny" earned his private stripes as he kept hostile Indians and other unsavory characters at bay. *Sergeant Preston of the Yukon* (1955-1956), starred Richard Simmons. Keeping him company in the snowy wilderness were his horse, Rex, and his canine partner, King. *Tales of the Texas Rangers* (1955-1958), starred Willard Parker and Harry Lauter.

Zorro (1957-1959) was another product from Disney Studios. The masked swordsman from Spanish California had originally appeared in a comic strip

The Western Genre

created by Johnston McCulley in 1919 and was seen subsequently in various films. On television, Don Diego de la Vega once again donned the famous disguise so he could battle the evil commandant and his forces. Guy Williams played the masked hero, whose true identity was known only to his mute servant, Bernardo. Although he had the somewhat irritating habit of carving his initial on his hapless foes, all was forgiven as he sacrificed his safety in order to help the wretched, and the innocent.

Intimations of a truly adult Western were found in *The Death of Billy the Kid* (*"The Philco Television Playhouse"*) in 1955, which featured Paul Newman. *Stories of the Century* was another program that portrayed the West in a documentary format and won the Emmy in 1954 as Best Western or Adventure Series. It was into this television arena that *Gunsmoke* entered in 1955. Over the next 20 years it was to set the standard for all other Westerns. This was also the year that three other adult Westerns were introduced to television audiences. In September 1955, *Frontier* premiered on NBC, and *Cheyenne* and *The Life and Legend of Wyatt Earp* aired on ABC. Not everyone was pleased, however, with this trend toward adult Westerns. Mack Brown, star of B Westerns, lamented:

> ...the films we made had a good plot and a lot of action. We had people tumbling over cliffs and swimming rivers. TV does the whole thing in a room...They just let their characters talk. We really showed them riding to the pass...In TV all you've got is talk. You got New York actors in Western hats who don't know what a cow is...Where's the flying, riding, falling-the thrills of the Old West?[18]

Critic John Lardner also echoed these sentiments in *The New Yorker*. He felt that the "writers of adult Westerns have become too adult for their own good, and their world, like the Roman Empire, is crumbling around them."[19] *TV Guide's* Cleveland Amory quipped that nowadays on Westerns "there are not only good guys and bad guys, but also in-between guys."[20]

Despite these occasional misgivings, the evolutionary course of the genre was clear and set. The Western was becoming the dominant story form through which our American heritage could be explored. It embodied in a strange way the subconscious aspirations of an entire nation. The Western presented in a distilled form the morality and ethics that Americans hold dear. It transported a people beset with doubts into a world where life indeed was uncertain and brutal, but was confronted with certitude. Given the audience's fascination with the Western, some even found that it was the ideal forum within which to explore contemporary issues. The popularity of the Western in the 1950s and early 1960s as a story form remains unequalled in American history. *Gunsmoke* represents the highest point in its evolution. In order to appreciate this achievement, it is necessary to go back to the days of radio.

RADIO — THE PIONEERS

On Saturday, April 26, 1952, radio history was made. It was on this day that *Gunsmoke* was broadcast for the first time over the CBS radio network at station KNX in Hollywood. It opened with the once famous lines:

ANNOUNCER: Around Dodge City and in the territory on West, there's just one way to handle the killers and the spoilers, and that's with a U.S. Marshal and the smell of *Gunsmoke! Gunsmoke,* starring William Conrad. The transcribed story of the violence that moved West with young America, and the story of a man who moved with it.

DILLON: I'm that man. Matt Dillon, United States Marshal, the first man they look for, and the last they want to meet. It's a chancy job, and it makes a man watchful, and a little lonely.

There was already an established tradition of Westerns on radio that included *Tom Mix, Red Ryder, The Lone Ranger,* and *Hopalong Cassidy.* These were all successful programs geared toward adolescents with simple story lines. They were the shoot-'em-up and chase type Westerns, with sarsaparilla drinking, six-gun toting, horse-kissing, singing cowboys. *Gunsmoke* was unique in that it was the first "adult Western." Although there had been a previous Western with an adult audience in mind, *Hawk Larabee,* the show was unsuccessful and ran but briefly. Produced by CBS in 1947, five years before the premiere of *Gunsmoke,* it starred Barton Yarborough as a Texan cowboy. While it was not as ambitious as *Gunsmoke,* its producer, Peabody Award winner William Robson found that at least, "Hawk didn't kiss his horse."

The Creation of Gunsmoke

The seeds of *Gunsmoke* were sown several years before it ever premiered. On CBS radio, between 1946 and 1952 there were many successful programs and the same actors, producers, writers, and directors kept working together until a kind of "stock company" developed. They all came to know one another's styles and nuances and ultimately brought this invaluable experience with them to *Gunsmoke.* Prior to collaborating on *Gunsmoke,* Norman Macdonnell and John Meston had worked together on a successful radio suspense-drama series *Escape,* directed by Robson. Macdonnell was initially assistant director of *Escape* and subsequently its director. Listeners were treated to the finest stories, many of which have become radio classics.

Escape premiered with Kipling's *The Man Who Would Be King* on CBS July 7, 1947. Other segments featured tales adapted from Joseph Conrad, Edgar Allan Poe, H. Ryder Haggard, Jack London and Daphne du Maurier. Audiences were mesmerized, entertained and frightened out of their wits. Despite the high quality of the program it was mostly sustained by the network and never had a permanent sponsor. It had a cadre of experienced and talented radio actors. Included in this group were Parley Baer, who became Chester, Howard McNear, who became Doc, and Georgia Ellis, who played Kitty. Also appearing were many actors who would play frequent supporting roles on *Gunsmoke.* These included John Dehner, Lawrence Dobkin, Virginia Gregg, Vivi Janiss, Jack Kruschen, Sam Edwards, Ben Wright, and Byron Kane. William Conrad, who was to become radio's Matt Dillon, was heard every week as the opening voice of *Escape,* announcing: "Tired of the every day grind? Ever dream of a life of...romantic adventure? Want to get away from it all? We offer you—*ESCAPE!*"

Some of the key writers on *Gunsmoke* developed their craft by writing for *Escape.* Les Crutchfield, Kathleen Hite, and Antony Ellis adapted stories. Writer John Dunkel, who penned *Gunsmoke* scripts for both radio and television, was a story editor. John Meston was in charge of continuity acceptance for CBS and functioned as head censor for the network. He was responsible for all transcontinental programs originating in Hollywood. Meston took over as story editor when John Dunkel left to free-lance. The first radio script that Meston wrote was for *Escape* and was titled *Crossing Paris.* Its success led him to write another episode, a Western entitled, *Wild Jack Rhett.* Rhett was played by John Dehner, and also in the cast were Parley Baer, Howard McNear, and William Conrad.

It was during this time that Meston and Macdonnell started to formulate their ideas for an "adult Western." They both felt that there was an adult audience somewhere out there, an audience ready for the true, grim reality of the old West, and the rugged individuals who through grit and fortitude forged a new world out of a wilderness.

In 1951, they worked together once again on a Western story titled *Pagosa,* for the radio series *Romance. Romance* opened on CBS in 1947 and was directed by Albert Ward and Charles S. Monroe. It presented light romances and comedies and by the 1950s was guided by producer-director Norman Macdonnell. Its writers included Kathleen Hite and Antony Ellis. Radio stars such as John Dehner, Jack Moyles, Virginia Gregg, Jack Kruschen, Lawrence Dobkin, Harry Bartell and Ben Wright were frequently featured. They later graced the microphones of *Gunsmoke*. The main character in *Pagosa* was Jeff Spain, who later became the model for Matt Dillon. Spain was played by William Conrad in a blunt, laconic style.

At the same time that Macdonnell and Meston were formulating their ideas for an "adult Western," CBS was in the process of developing a similar project. William S. Paley, the founder and chairman of the board at CBS was a great fan of the radio program, *The Adventures of Philip Marlowe*. He suggested to Hubbell Robinson, who was the network executive in charge of programming for CBS in New York, that CBS develop a "Philip Marlowe of the early West." Robinson in turn phoned Harry Ackerman, vice president in charge of programs on the West Coast, and Ackerman quickly pulled his staff together to develop the idea. Ackerman notes that, "I called into action all of the creative people," and became "the architect of the show's development."

According to one source, Ackerman and his assistant, Guy della Cioppa, decided that the new Western should be titled "Gunsmoke," a name they supposedly stumbled upon while leafing through a book of titles put out by the Academy of Motion Picture Arts and Sciences. Enamoured with the title, they bought the name from Universal. However, both Ackerman and della Cioppa claim the name was entirely a brainchild of Ackerman's. In a recent interview, Ackerman recalled that: "It just popped into my head one day. To the best of my knowledge nothing was ever purchased."

When Macdonnell and Meston approached CBS executives with their ideas for a new "adult Western," they were surprised to learn that CBS was already developing such a program. They suggested the title *Jeff Spain* from *Pagosa*, but Ackerman felt that *Jeff Spain* sounded too much like the name of a villain rather than of a hero. In addition, CBS had already produced two audition acetate disks of *Gunsmoke*, and Ackerman wanted to pursue these further. The first, recorded on June 11, 1949, featured Rye Billsbury as "Mark" Dillon in *Mark Dillon Goes to Gouge Eye* and was directed by Ralph Rose. The story was developed by Mort Fine and David Friedkin. It was re-recorded on July 15, 1949, with Howard Culver as Dillon, who years later played Howie the hotel clerk on television's *Gunsmoke*. Neither "pilot" ever got on the air. Despite urgings, CBS executives could not be moved to put the show on.

For a while it appeared as if Macdonnell and Meston would not be the ones to develop the first adult Western. However, there was an unexpected turn of events when a popular spy show on CBS, *Operation Underground*, produced by Bill Robson, faltered for lack of a sponsor. The network needed a quick replacement and Ackerman asked Macdonnell to produce and direct the *Gunsmoke* project. He was given a generous week to come up with a script, find its star, and develop a musical theme.

Years later, Macdonnell looked back upon this hectic week and recalled:

> We got Walter Brown Newman to come in, one of the better writers in town. We gave him an acetate disk of *Pagosa* and *Wild Jack Rhett* and said, "This is the style, this is the color, this is the feel." We laid out no other guidelines except we told him how we felt Dillon should be written, and the kind of character he was, and sent Walter away...That was on a Monday.[21]

Newman busily worked on the first script, *Billy the Kid*, using the guidelines laid down by Meston and Macdonnell. Meston immediately renamed the main character "Matt" explaining that "Mark" was too modern. With the script underway, Macdonnell turned his attention to the enormous problem of casting. CBS wanted to hire a big name for Matt and Raymond Burr was among the many actors considered for the job. Guy della Cioppa recalls that, "We were looking for somebody that sounded like Orson Welles. A totally different voice and not a Western drawler." William Conrad was not even considered at first for radio executives were concerned with his "overexposure" in the medium, as well as with his image as a villain in a recent film, *The Killers*. Conrad had a long tradition of playing villains, and had been featured as the "heavy extraordinaire" in such classic films as *Body and Soul* and *Sorry Wrong Number*. Reflecting years later, Conrad recounted, "I think that when they started casting, somebody said, 'Good Christ, let's not get Bill Conrad. We're up to you know where with Bill Conrad.'"[22] Macdonnell and Meston, however, having worked with him on many radio programs were impressed with Conrad's range as an actor and finally prevailed. He was given a chance to read and as he recalls:

> They auditioned everybody in town, and as a last resort, they called me and said, "Okay, we give up. Come on in." And I went in and read about two lines and they said, "Okay, thank you." And I walked out. Then the next day they called me and said, "You have the job."[23]

Present at the audition were Meston, Macdonnell, della Cioppa, and Anne Nelson, who was in charge of business affairs for CBS radio and later held the same position in television.

Soon after Conrad got the part of Dillon, Howard McNear and Parley Baer were cast as Doc and Chester. They both became running characters, although it is not entirely clear whether this was the intention at first. Georgia Ellis was in the first show as a saloon girl, but the actual character of Kitty was not invented until several episodes into the series. Writer Herb Purdum, who wrote five of the early *Gunsmoke* scripts, recently stated, "I think I did the first radio show that used the name Kitty."

Confident that the script and the casting were well in hand, Macdonnell focused on the musical score. A top CBS executive approached composer Rex Koury, who agreed to talk to Macdonnell. Koury had started as an organist on radio and had done many shows for CBS. He later became the musical director on the West Coast at ABC and was also doing some free lancing at the time he was approached for *Gunsmoke*. Although he had never composed for a Western before, Koury said, "I'm game to tackle anything." He met with Macdonnell and "was immediately charmed." He found Macdonnell to be a man "with a magnetic personality [who] knew what he wanted.... Something that had a big, wide, open sound to it.... Something that suggested the open spaces."[24] When Koury asked to see the script, he was surprised to learn that it was not yet written. Undaunted, he took up the challenge and started to collect his ideas. Koury had little time to work on the theme. He confessed later that it:

> ...was written under rather frantic circumstances because I had gone to bed the night before...feeling that I knew pretty well what I wanted, and figuring I could do it rather quickly in the morning...At 8:00 o'clock in the morning I'm in the middle of shaving and I suddenly realize we haven't written the theme. So I grabbed a magazine, a piece of manuscript, and a pencil, and sat down in the most convenient spot, and that is where the *Gunsmoke* theme was actually composed.[25]

When the theme was finally recorded, an 18-piece orchestra was utilized. The music for subsequent episodes was played by a six to seven piece orchestra consisting of an accordion, guitar, french horn, trumpet, clarinet and tympani. Koury often played an electric accordion which William Conrad called an "electronic urinal." On occasion, Koury would place paper-clips on piano strings to give them a player-piano sound for barroom scenes, or a harmonica would be added to the guitar to heighten the "Western" atmosphere. When recently interviewed, Koury indicated that he travels widely today as a concert organist. He always marvels that despite the intervening years, hardly a performance goes by that someone in the audience does not request the theme from *Gunsmoke*.

With his one week time limit drawing to an end, Walter Brown Newman rose to the occasion and delivered his script to Macdonnell and Meston in time. It is ironic that the author of the first episode never wrote another *Gunsmoke* script despite the fact that he was held in high esteem by Meston.

With the premiere of *Billy the Kid* the *Gunsmoke* saga began. Macdonnell later recalled that despite favorable reviews, "nobody was quite sure upstairs whether we had a hit or a miss because our leading man didn't sound like a leading man. Conrad was not playing Matt as a warm, understanding, paternal figure whatsoever."[26] Years later Macdonnell attributed the survival of the show during the first critical year to a rave review in the *New York Times* by Jack Gould. Gould was an influential critic whose support reassured the executives at CBS that they had a viable product.

The program gained support over the next two years, and finally achieved full "legitimacy" when in 1954 Liggett/Myers and L&M cigarettes became the sponsors. Those were the days when there were no restrictions on advertising cigarettes on the air. George Fenneman was the announcer who did the Chesterfield commercials, and George Walsh did the ones for L&M. The same program was broadcast twice a week, first on Sunday night and then the following Saturday morning. *Gunsmoke* quickly captured the popular imagination and William Conrad once fancifully estimated the weekly audience at an incredible 50,000,000 listeners.

Along with the critical praise and audience adulation came a series of awards that included for several years the annual Radio-Television Mirror Daily Award.

Kansans were especially proud of their hero, Matt Dillon. The Honorable Edward F. Arn, governor of the state, announced:

> It's a real pleasure for me on behalf of Kansans everywhere, to congratulate the CBS radio network, the writers, producers, directors, actors, and technicians, on their splendid job...with *Gunsmoke*. Here is real adult Western drama without the usual horse-opera cliches, portraying an era and community of Kansas that graphically marked the formative years of our great state."

Arn was careful to disavow the violence, however, saying:

> ...that the Dodge City of today is a far cry from the Dodge City so vividly brought to life in *Gunsmoke*. From those early pioneer and frontier days, Dodge City has developed into one of the fine cities of our state, industrially, agriculturally, and historically. The folks of Dodge City, and indeed all the people of this Sunflower State, thank you for a good job well done.[27]

Gunsmoke, even made an appearance in the *Congressional Record.* During one heated debate, a particular individual stated as a point or argument that Matt Dillon "would never have done such a thing." When it was pointed out in rebuttal that Matt had never lived, the man expressed surprise, saying, "No? But he was so real, it seemed as though he really existed."

What was it that kept *Gunsmoke* so honest and authentic that people believed Matt Dillon and the inhabitants of Dodge City were not a fictional creation, but real? So real that the governor of Kansas felt obliged to stress that Dodge City was no longer an unsettled frontier town, and made the congressman shake his head in disbelief when told that Matt Dillon never existed? What elements contributed to the continued success of *Gunsmoke?* First, there were the writers, a cross-section of the best talent of the time that included Les Crutchfield, Marian Clark, Kathleen Hite, Antony Ellis, and John Dunkel. But it was John Meston who was most responsible for creating the world of *Gunsmoke* and who set the standard of authenticity that distinguished it from other programs.

John Meston

Meston grew up in Pueblo, Colorado. He knew cowboys and was familiar with their way of life and their vernacular. Mary Ann Hooper Meston, John's wife recalls:

> John's father, who was from Boston, fell in love with a lovely Colorado lady and they got married and raised three children. John was the youngest and since he was a small child he lived on horses. As he grew older he became a bronco rider and performed in rodeos...At 16 his father said, "This boy is going to end up a bum if we don't get him educated." So they sent him off to Exeter and Dartmouth and then Harvard. So he ended up being quite a literary cowboy. His specialty was James Joyce. John was also a poet...His great love was poetry. He started writing when he was quite young.

Meston also studied at the Sorbonne in Paris and later taught in Cuba for a year. He then travelled to Mexico where he met the poet, Robert Penn Warren, and the two became close friends. He returned to the States and entered the Army where he became a censor, little knowing that this would lead him later into a career in radio. Meston was stationed in the Aleutian Islands and after his discharge became the network censor at CBS. As the head of "continuity acceptance" he had access to all scripts to be aired. Bored with the position, Meston began writing and when John Dunkel quit as story editor in 1950, Meston took over.

Although until this time Meston had not thought of himself as a writer for radio, his first script, *Crossing Paris,* received critical acclaim. It was several months later that he wrote the Western, *Wild Jack Rhett,* which was an adaptation. As he explained, he tried to make the style different, and unlike "the usual B movie crap." He developed a style where much of the narration that was characteristic of radio writing was eliminated. This was quite innovative at the time.

There was a simplicity to Meston's style. He wrote spare dialogue with few embellishments. He always "wrote short" and "never wrote speeches." In the early years he went to all the readings and rehearsals in order to have the actors teach him "how to write dialogue." He recalled that: "If they couldn't read a line they'd let me know with great pleasure and they were generally right."[28]

GUNSMOKE — I. THE HISTORY

Meston explored a wide range of issues that only later became political and social concerns. He was truly ahead of his time, writing stories about the exploitation of women, Indians, and Orientals. He looked beneath the glorified veneer of the fictitious West and story after story attempted to present "what the West was really like." Though various writers were hired over the years, it was John Meston who dominated the early programs and set the tone and atmosphere. He presented the privations suffered by the early settlers, and the violence of a frontier town where man's basest instincts were frequently unbridled. Reflecting on Meston's talents, Norman Macdonnell explained:

> To try and analyze John Meston's contributions to the writing style of *Gunsmoke* would be difficult...John's writing is not flashy, it's not filled with purple prose....If anything it's understated and simple...Good Western writing doesn't necessarily mean double negatives...It really requires research and understanding of the cowboy...John was an avid researcher...A great deal of the language came from cowboys he had known...For instance, there was one phrase that John loved particularly...A cowboy was talking to another cowboy about his mare... When asked if the mare was a fast runner, the first cowboy looked for a moment and said, "Yes, she's swift. She could run a hole in the wind, she set her mind to it." This was the kind of phrase that John loved because it was the man of the earth...using things that he knew and...saw around him for descriptions. This gave the dialogue...a richness and fullness with a strange combining of words and a strange combining of emotions that...was hard for anyone else to duplicate. Meston always had a feeling about names, too. He felt that a name was a whole indication of the character...A friend of Matt's arrives in town...An ex-lawman Meston called Nick Search, a marvelous way of painting the man's whole background with just a couple of words...A funny, pathetic little crook...was Joe Phy...A doctor who...got in trouble...was professor Lute Bone...or the buffalo hunter called Gatluf. John never gave Gatluf any other name because he felt Gatluf was enough, but he did mention that he was a man with speckled eyes like a turkey egg...which is a beautiful way of describing a man...A family that lived out on the prairie in a sod hut...was called the Beedles.[29]

Macdonnell also noted that:

> Running through many of John's scripts is a thread of the dignity of man, and yet at the same time, of man's inhumanity to man...One of the things that John did in his scripts was to paint the difficult position of women. Nowadays we're inclined to say, "Well, if life's that difficult, why didn't they go somewhere else?" And, as John had his characters explain, "Where was there to go?" They had no money. The household probably consisted of one mule, and you can't ride too far on one mule...And if

a woman did get into town, what was she going to do? She couldn't suddenly find work in a boutique. She either was a dance hall girl or something less...The frontier life was a hard and unforgiving sort of life as John pictured it, and I think quite accurately.[30]

Parley Baer, reflecting on Meston's early, critical contributions to *Gunsmoke* explains that:

> John Meston was a thorough technician and a writer of great integrity and accuracy...Since that era was probably the most colorful in Western history, he strove to create and paint the most accurate image of the times that he could. And I think he succeeded.

Baer went on to say:

> Matt Dillon was so faithfully written...that at one time we had a letter from the secretary or president of the Chamber of Commerce in Dodge City. He wanted to know, since they had already determined that Matt Dillon had lived in Dodge City, did we have accurate knowledge as to when...But so far as we knew, and so far as John Meston knew, Matt Dillon was completely a brain-child.[31]

Baer felt that Meston had an uncanny ability to conjure up the West the way it really was, however tragic it might seem and noted,

> People came West for a variety of reasons...chiefest among them...was a tragedy that had occurred either back East or in Europe...Or people came West to forget, or hide something...I think the West as it developed...was a result of disappointment elsewhere and his pen had the ability to pick that up.

Baer loved the way Meston captured a man's character, his life, and his way of speech. He recalled that on one occasion:

> Chester and Matt were talking and Matt asked Chester why he got up so early. "Well, I can't sleep," he said, "It's a trait I have, that as soon as the sun's up, my feet start to sweat, and then I get uncomfortable and get up." John knew a person who said that, some old codger he had met. Humanisms...John did those things. Chester acquired this dog that he loved dearly...and, the dog liked everybody but Chester. And after he had bitten him soundly, Chester's only comment was, "He'll come around." John Meston wrote realism. You could see the mud. You could see the slue...You could see the filth...it was adroitly painted in.[32]

William Conrad also admired the humanism in Meston's work. He stated that:

> He is a great bleeder. He bleeds for everybody, and perhaps that is the key to the success of the show...that it is so filled with the repulsion of

man's inhumanity to man, seasoned and highlighted by red streaks of magnificent violence...and yet, the final total compassion... You add all those up and they spell "Mother."[33]

Another trademark of a Meston script was his realistic treatment of the plight of the American Indian. Meston stated:

As I recall, we were about the first show to treat Indians as human beings, not just red skins or "the only good Indians are dead ones"...We did a number of shows about...intermarriage, and of course the buffalo... The way the white man treated the Indian was a national disgrace. It still is...Most of the white men out there were not nice guys. They were a bunch of nuts who went West.[34]

Meston detested the stereotype of the Western hero. In a letter to the *New York Herald Tribune* he explained his approach to writing:

It isn't often that a writer or any man is given an opportunity to destroy a figure he's always hated...a character that all his life has cluttered his landscape like a slum. And to be able to do so, and get paid for it to boot, is to be doubly blessed. My hated figure is the Western hero who rides along looking like a transvestite, strumming his guitar, nasally singing a synthetic ballad, and looking for all the world like a fugitive from a cheap circus. I spit in his milk, and he'll have to go elsewhere to find somebody to pour the lead for his golden bullets.

Now the best way to destroy something is to ride it down with something better. And I've got a guy I think outclasses any of these phony big-hats. His name's Matt Dillon, and his hair is probably red, if he's got any left. He'd be handsomer than he is if he had better manners but life and his enemies have left him looking a little beat up, and I suppose having seen his mother (back about 1840) trying to take a bath in a wooden washtub without fully undressing left his soul a little warped. Anyway, there'd have to be something wrong with him or he wouldn't have hired on as a United States Marshal in the heyday of Dodge City, Kansas. Dodge at that time was the wildest town in America, and it was populated by men just as warped, and more so than Matt Dillon.

...the West just after the Civil War was, in a sense, a kind of arena for frustrated gladiators. Homicidal psychopaths gathered along the Frontier and had themselves a real circus, with little or nothing to stop them from happily mowing one another down. That more men didn't die in this senseless slaughter may be laid to their comparatively primitive weapons and certainly not to any civilized tendencies on their part. It ended, finally, and the murderers killed one another off and gradually disappeared from this section of the American scene. But the end was finally hastened by a few strangers who happened to get their satisfaction killing on the side of the law—sheriffs, marshals, and the like. Sure a few of these men had a hazy sense of what the coming of law-and-order meant, but for the most part they looked on their role in the play of Progress simply as a job, and they went ahead and did their job, often in the face of unbelievable odds, and then picked up their pay-checks and went their way. Heroes? To us they were heroes, but to their contemporaries the biggest hero was he who, by whatever means, murdered the greatest number of his fellow men. The rules were childishly simple: if the other man went for his gun before you did, you were free to kill him with immunity. And anyway, if there weren't too many unfriendly witnesses about, you could always claim he did, and probably get by with it just as easily. Matt Dillon, because of obvious reasons, is a cut above the usual lawman I've described. But he's not, I trust, so far above the real thing as to be pure fiction. And the hardest thing for me, the writer, is to keep him — on paper — from goofing off into the never-never land of pure heroism; and the hardest thing for Norman Macdonnell, the producer-director, and Bill Conrad, the star, is to translate the script's attempt at authenticity into the living character of Matt Dillon. But we try, and try, and keep trying. Our attempt to create as realistic and entertaining a program as possible is not, of course, the only one of its kind. But we did precede and were on the air, trying, before the release of such pictures as *High Noon* and *Shane*. And we're still on the air, and we're still trying.[35]

Given his disdain for heroes Meston strove to eliminate cliches. He and Macdonnell once compiled a list of all the Western cliches they could think of and swore never to fall into their trap.

At first, Meston was the story editor on *Gunsmoke*. Years later, he could not recall why he did not write the first script himself. After six months, however, he was writing almost all of the scripts. It was Meston who best captured the essence of the West that was portrayed on *Gunsmoke*.

He had a great reverence for language. He found that cowboys had a wonderful facility for language and for unique turns of phrase. He once claimed that "the cowboys back in Colorado are now using phrases that I made up [on *Gunsmoke*] that they didn't think of."[36]

Meston was able to conjure the hardships, the defeats, the small triumphs, the brutality and hope of those times. Most of Meston's stories dealt with a moral conflict and plot was only secondary. Although many of his stories were violent they were never gratuitously so. He created hundreds of memorable characters and his vision was like that of Charles Dickens in its scope.

Meston strove constantly for authenticity and realism, and viewed life in the Old West as being violent and tragic. Compared to other Westerns that tended to sanitize this violence, he had a dark vision of life and found that:

> Most stories do end tragically...despite the propaganda in the great United States of America...Most people those days had sad endings... Jesus, it was a hard life. They didn't live very long...while they lived it was

pretty rough. Then the brutality and violence. You talk about violence these days...Of course this stuff they put on television is terrible...but violence in those days was rampant. My God, the violence! And the poor way of life...no medicine, no sanitation...not much of anything...a little water and not much food. It wasn't a great life. It's been romanticized fairly well, but...I didn't romanticize it....[37]

Radio broadcaster John Hickman, aptly sums up Meston's particular brand of genius:

> ...legends, facts, and fantasies were brilliantly blended by writer John Meston in his portrayal of Dodge City, Kansas in the 1870s. Meston's cow-town was a microcosm of the American West, and in the center of it was Marshal Matt Dillon. We met and came to know him, his friends, and his enemies, and we learned of his life in a town referred to by historian Lucius Beebee as a "suburb of Hell." The picture that Meston painted of Kansas is remarkably accurate. There really was a Front Street in Dodge City. You actually could buy a drink at the Long Branch Saloon, the same saloon where Wyatt Earp and Bat Masterson called the bluff of psychopathic killer, Clay Allison, driving him out of town. Chances are there was a doctor similar to Meston's. Most likely the buffalo steaks served in the restaurants of the period did taste like shoe-leather. And I can guarantee you that there were many Kittys in that Babylon of the Plains...Looking back, it seems strange that it took from 1926, when network radio began, to 1952, a total of 26 years, for someone to offer an adult portrayal of the American West.[38]

Mary Ann Hooper Meston in a recent interview provided a rare insight into the unique relationship that existed between Meston and his creation. She recalled that:

> When I met John I realized he was very much like Matt Dillon. He listened a great deal. He was a natural wit...When John was at Harvard he had a close friend there who was Japanese, and a few years before John passed away he met this friend after many years. And the friend said, "John, we see *Gunsmoke* all the time and there's just one thing I'd like to know. Why did you write yourself into Matt Dillon?" Maybe it was unconscious. Matt Dillon was a man that if he couldn't change things, he accepted them...John was a man of letters...A man who was basically a philosopher and poet and somehow got involved with *Gunsmoke*. He wrote as he thought. Everything was simple. If Matt had something to say, he said it. After a few lines you knew the character. This was his brain...his philosophy.

John Meston was an enormously talented and prolific writer and yet his achievements have gone relatively unrecognized. Even his contribution to *Gunsmoke* has never fully been acknowledged despite the fact that of the 413 radio episodes he wrote 183 and of the 635 television episodes he penned 196.

Macdonnell was disturbed by this lack of recognition of Meston's role as writer-creator of *Gunsmoke*. Commenting on it he said:

> I think it should be known, that perhaps the most deserving award...was never passed out...(It) was the one that should have gone to John Meston, who wrote hundreds of these scripts, and to the best of my knowledge, received no specific award, which I think is rather a tragedy and an oversight.[39]

Although official recognition never came, those who worked most closely with Meston greatly appreciated his talents. John Dunkel noted that Meston, "Knew what he was writing about, and was generally a helluva writer." Kathleen Hite found that, "He influenced me without ever trying to...he taught me not by telling me anything but just by admiring his work."

In the final analysis, Meston was the master and preeminent *Gunsmoke* writer. He left *Gunsmoke* shortly after Philip Leacock became producer of the television show, after which he took a well deserved rest. He did several television pilots and screenplays, none of which made it. Mrs. Meston remembers, "He didn't like writing for T.V. because it was all done by committee." When Meston died, in 1979, he was working on a screenplay for film director John Frankenheimer.

As for Meston's own appraisal of his achievement, Mrs. Meston recalls, "He didn't really think it was all that important." Meston once commented, "I did a good job...I did the best I could. Whatever I wrote was usually the best I could do...So *Gunsmoke* happened to be a great success. That doesn't make a person a great writer...If I would have known it would last this long, I would never have created the darn thing."[40]

The Writers

Various other writers developed scripts for *Gunsmoke*. During the first year these writers included Herb Purdum, Les Crutchfield, and Antony Ellis. Meston supervised the development of these scripts and many hours were spent discussing the characters and stories.

As time went on, other writers climbed aboard the *Gunsmoke* bandwagon. They included Marian Clark, John Dunkel, and Kathleen Hite. They became especially active during the fifth season when Meston started to write for the television show. The writers who contributed to *Gunsmoke* were the best radio writers of the time. On occasion Macdonnell himself would pen a script as would the sound men Tom Hanley and Ray Kemper. Vic Perrin,

Harry Bartell and William Conrad were among the actors who wrote an occasional story as did Frank Paris, the assistant director.

Les Crutchfield

A major contributor to radio's and subsequently television's *Gunsmoke*, was Les Crutchfield, who was working as an engineer at Cal Tech when he first met Macdonnell around 1946. Prior to becoming a writer he studied engineering and majored in mining and metallurgy. He did graduate work in physical chemistry, psychology and mathematics, then worked as a mine foreman and as an explosives consultant.

Somehow his interest turned to writing and by 1948-1949 he was providing scripts for *Escape* and *Romance*. When Macdonnell moved to *Gunsmoke*, Crutchfield became part of the family. Macdonnell described him as a "warm and very funny...very charming man. He was his own man, and he did what he wanted, when he wanted. If you needed him desperately to do a script, he might be available or he might have been on his way to Africa, and you never really knew. But when he was in town he wrote well and he was dependable."[41] Meston found that his plots were "sound and original; his characterizations true, sharp and subtle; his dialogue superbly playable; and his backgrounds accurate, colorful, and apparently inexhaustible..." Crutchfield's scripts were "easily adaptable to TV because of the highly visual quality with which he writes and presents his stories."

William Robson noted that Crutchfield wrote

> his way to the very top rank of radio writers...An exceptionally fine dramatist, his characters are sensitively developed and his plays never lack a quiet and warming sense of humor. In a medium which is of necessity "blind," his scripts are almost unique in the degree to which they visualize the action for the listener.

Crutchfield wrote 81 *Gunsmoke* radio scripts, and Macdonnell recalled that he was:

> ...One of the solid contributors to *Gunsmoke*...Perhaps Les did more of the light or comedy shows than John Meston. One in particular that I've always enjoyed was *Colleen So Green* in which this attractive girl comes to town and completely befuddles Doc, and Chester, and everybody else in town, including Mr. Bodkin at the bank. But one of Les' scripts that I remember particularly and perhaps personifies the kind of writing that made him such a valuable piece of manpower for *Gunsmoke,* was a script that he wrote called, *Tag, You're It.*[42]

Like Meston, Crutchfield's stories were sometimes dark, but they were more forgiving. Crutchfield concentrated on character and nature, and often moralized on how man should observe animals and adapt to the elements rather than struggle against them. He believed that man had a lot to learn from nature, when to fight and when to give up. In his own life, Crutchfield lost a valiant battle against cancer in 1966.

Marian Clark

Marian Clark was one of *Gunsmoke's* most prolific writers. She ultimately wrote over 75 scripts for *Gunsmoke*. Clark was introduced to Macdonnell by another writer, Kathleen Hite, who had taken her under her wing. Clark was confined to a wheel chair, and Hite suggested that it might be good therapy for her to write a script. Macdonnell was sufficiently impressed with her early efforts to give her further assignments. Clark offered a marvelous insight into the woman's side of the story and wrote sad, and often wistful stories such as *The Piano,* a tragic tale about an old Southern Belle. However, she had just as much insight into the male point of view. Her characters often have a tragic flaw, such as pride or stubbornness, or just plain ignorance, that leads to their ultimate destruction.

John Dunkel

John Dunkel was the story editor for CBS Radio in Hollywood from 1946 to 1949. In 1954 he returned to CBS as a freelance writer. *Gunsmoke* was already a successful show when Macdonnell asked him to write for it. Dunkel "refused, pleading no knowledge of the form, the West, or cowboys." Later on, however, he became a student of the West by "reading, as well as visiting and riding in western ranch country." Interestingly, he started to write scripts for television Westerns first. Commenting on Western writing he found that:

> Like any other historical fiction, it required research and interest in the time, place and way of life, and some empathy with the people and how they thought and felt. I think perhaps the writers most successful in the genre also had some experience in the outdoors and some love for nature and the "land."

Antony Ellis

Antony Ellis wrote for *Gunsmoke* both on radio and television. His style at times approximates poetry. Ellis could combine humor and pathos, and painted characters you could love and hate at the same time. He wrote wonderfully distinctive stories such as *The Ride Back,* which featured Matt and only one other character, which was quite daring for a radio drama at the time. This particular episode was eventually made into a screenplay. Ellis frequently created melancholy characters who were haunted by their tragic past as in *Shakespeare* and *Christmas Story*. Ellis was also responsible for the Western radio series, *Frontier Gentleman*. For television Ellis wrote for *Zane Grey Theater* and was also the producer of a television Western called *Black Saddle* that aired first on NBC and later on ABC in 1959-60. At one time he was married to Georgia Ellis, Miss Kitty.

Kathleen Hite

Another important writer for *Gunsmoke* was Kathleen Hite. She wrote only seven scripts for radio but she became an active contributor to the television show during its first decade. Hite was one of the few women writers to break into the male-dominated field of script writing. She had worked with both Meston and Macdonnell on various projects before *Gunsmoke,* such as *Escape* and *Romance,* and they admired her abilities. Hite was a very accomplished writer with a distinctive style, and her scripts focusing on women are especially admired. Actor/director Larry Dobkin found that "she would lay back a layer of skin... and the male and female relationships would glitter." Hite later went on to write the scripts for *Fort Laramie* starring Raymond Burr. Her research on cavalry life in the West was meticulous and *Fort Laramie* stands as one of radio's mostly forgotten classics. Kathleen Hite died of emphysema in 1989.

Herb Purdum

Herb Purdum graduated from U.S.C. and received a masters degree from Tulane. He planned to be a teacher but changed his mind and decided to try his hand at writing. "I got started in radio, because radio was the only thing to write for at the time," he recalls. "I wrote a script on speculation for Dick Powell and he bought it, and that started me." Purdum became a member of the small group of writers that provided CBS with scripts for its dramatic series. He wrote for *Romance, Suspense,* and "a half dozen other shows." He was one of the first writers to join the *Gunsmoke* staff and found that, "We worked together and we all tried to contribute, to make the characters real and three-dimensional... to make it fundamentally good and solid so that those writers who followed us had no problems writing for it."

Table 1. The Radio Writers

YEAR	1	2	3	4	5	6	7	8	9	TOTAL
John Meston	30	47	46	45	0	0	3	1	11	183
Les Crutchfield	17	0	2	2	36	20	4	0	0	81
Marian Clark	0	0	0	0	0	14	28	23	12	77
Norman Macdonnell	4	4	2	0	1	0	0	1	0	12
John Dunkel	0	0	1	5	1	2	3	0	0	12
Tom Hanley	0	0	0	1	2	1	2	2	0	8
Antony Ellis	8	0	0	0	0	0	0	0	0	8
Kathleen Hite	1	0	0	0	0	0	0	6	0	7
Herb Purdum	5	0	0	0	0	0	0	0	0	5
Ray Kemper	0	0	0	0	0	0	0	2	1	3
Vic Perrin	0	0	0	0	0	0	1	2	0	3
Frank Paris	0	0	0	0	0	0	0	0	2	2
Perrin & Bartell	0	0	0	0	0	0	0	0	2	2
Robert Mitchell	0	0	0	0	0	2	0	0	0	2
Walter B. Newman	1	0	0	0	0	0	0	0	0	1
Joel Murcott	1	0	0	0	0	0	0	0	0	1
Lou Houston	1	0	0	0	0	0	0	0	0	1
David Ellis	1	0	0	0	0	0	0	0	0	1
William Conrad	1	0	0	0	0	0	0	0	0	1
William Leicester	0	0	0	0	1	0	0	0	0	1
Gil Doud	0	0	0	0	1	0	0	0	0	1
Fonda & Macdonnell	0	0	0	0	0	1	0	0	0	1
TOTAL	70	51	51	53	42	40	41	37	28	413

The Actors and Their Characters

In the same manner that the writers developed a strong foundation for *Gunsmoke,* the actors used that foundation as the basis for shaping their characters permitting them to evolve into multifaceted "real" people rather than the cardboard caricatures so often associated with Westerns.

Matt, Doc, Kitty, and Chester became complex people who related to one another on many levels. They supported each other through thick and thin, and risked their lives for one another. However, they were not perfect, far from it. They bickered, criticized, argued, and made mistakes that were sometimes fatal. They occasionally held grudges, told bad jokes as well as good ones, and lashed out when they were not in the best of moods. Over the years they matured and grew as we listened. They changed and continued to change. The four wonderful citizens of Dodge City had strong, solid foundations, but they were also full of surprises, nuances, mannerisms, actions and reactions. They mellowed, and became a comfortable shoe or sometimes a thorn in our sides. One came to love and accept them despite, or perhaps because of their faults, just as they accepted one another. And the individual who drew them and the audience together was the cornerstone, the pillar of Dodge City, U.S. Marshal Matt Dillon, impeccably portrayed by William Conrad.

William Conrad and Matt Dillon

William Conrad not only had the perfect voice for radio, but he also brought a certain quality to the character of Dillon that ultimately led to the development of an intricate persona. Conrad was born in Louisville, Kentucky, in 1920. His family moved to Los Angeles when he was seven. He started in radio in 1938 at the age of 17, when he approached the news director of KMPC in Beverly Hills and announced that he was looking for a job. Clete Roberts, in a *TV Guide* interview (February 21, 1976), remembers that "He had this big voice. It reminded me of Orson Welles."

In 1946 Conrad appeared in the movie, *The Killers*. Other films were *Sorry, Wrong Number*, *The Naked Jungle* and *Johnny Concho*. Because of his weight he was generally cast in the role of the villain, but on radio he could capitalize on his wonderful voice and play any character. In the 1940s and 1950s he appeared in over 7,500 radio productions and as we have seen was the host of *Escape* as well as the *CBS Radio Workshop*. His greatest radio role, however, was as Matt Dillon. When the radio program ended he found limited opportunities as an actor on television so he developed a new career as a producer and director of such shows as *Bat Masterson* and *Klondike*. He even directed two episodes of *Gunsmoke*. On television, off camera, he was the narrator of *The Bullwinkle Show*, *The Fugitive*, and of *Tales of the Unexpected*. In recent years he has once again become a star playing the lead in such television programs as *Cannon*, *Nero Wolfe*, and *Jake and the Fat Man*. Conrad's career is that of a survivor paralleling that of his alter ego, Matt Dillon.

Conrad's Dillon represents a unique characterization in the annals of the radio Western. Perhaps it comes closest to Meston's intent. Matt is a man with a job to do. A job that is often unpleasant, but has to be done. Unfortunately for Dillon, he does it well. As Conrad plays him, Matt is a man with a short fuse who is frequently abrasive to others, including his friends. He is not above snapping at Chester without provocation when he is in a foul mood. His voice and words are harsh. To his audiences he provides comfort not because he is an infallible hero, but because despite all his faults he is basically a moral man. We sense that there is a deep vein of brutality in Matt, and that he must constantly struggle to keep this in check. He is a man divided. A man frequently forced to be brutal who must kill in the name of the law. We sense the constant tension of a man who walks a thin line, a line that separates the law from the lawless. Matt carries a tremendous burden on his shoulders and we can feel and hear the physical and emotional fatigue. Death's hand is constantly on his shoulder and his is indeed, as Meston described it, a "chancy job." The brutal confrontations have scarred him. The tremendous pain and exploitation Matt has witnessed have isolated him from others. Kitty, Doc, and Chester are his lifeline and his final link to his fellow men.

In commenting on Dillon and Conrad's portrayal, Parley Baer found:

> ...a tremendously pathetic quality to Dillon...Dillon trusted Chester, Doc and Kitty as much as he dared to trust anyone. He knew that if he needed someone to stand at his back, Chester would be there. But I'm sure that in the back of his mind, he wasn't sure that Chester would function all the time...He had the same feeling about Doc. Doc was dependable. But every now and then he'd get soused...and maybe at the moment of removing an appendix, Doc was a little bit snockered. Chester was dishonest with many people, but had to be completely honest with Dillon. There was Dillon's strength. Everybody had to be honest with Dillon, because in so far as human beings are concerned, I think probably of the whole cast, Dillon was the one who was most completely honest in his dealings with lawbreakers...with the town...with everyday associates.[43]

George Walsh, the announcer for both the radio and television shows, felt that Conrad set the pace for Matt and that James Arness adopted this pace later for his television role. "Conrad had a great ability in establishing character in your mind, and could be tough, hard, or sentimental."[44]

To writer John Dunkel, Conrad's Matt Dillon was a "very compassionate man, probably the ideal lawman."[45]

For Macdonnell, Matt was "a lonely, sad, tragic man...a quiet, unhappy, confused Marshal; these days we'd send him to an analyst."[46]

Meston simply felt that Matt was "an honest guy...A guy with a sense of tragedy...A guy who didn't particularly enjoy the job. He did it."[47] He felt Conrad played him well because he took the time to let Matt evolve.

Conrad, with his characteristic self-assurance, reflected on the success of his portrayal:

> The success of any series has to do with the charisma that the leading character has. You can give it the best stories and the best production in the world, and the best support in the world, and if the guy or the gal does not have it, it isn't going to make it...It's charisma...I can't define it. I stand back and look at it. I've been on the other side for so long that I can evaluate it quite clearly without being involved emotionally, or ego wise. There was great character development[48]

GUNSMOKE — I. THE HISTORY

Without a doubt, Conrad had the charisma he spoke about, and so did three other remarkable actors who held their own beside him. They were Parley Baer, Howard McNear and Georgia Ellis.

Parley Baer and Chester Proudfoot

Radio's Chester was played by Parley Baer. A prolific actor, he got his radio start at KSL in Salt Lake City and went on to appear in over 10,000 network radio shows. In the original script of *Gunsmoke,* Chester was known only as the "Townsman." However, Conrad did not feel comfortable calling him "Townsman," and he complained about it to Macdonnell. Baer recalls that Conrad suddenly said, "Call him Chester, or something like that," and so, Chester he became. Chester's last name, "Proudfoot," was conjured by Baer. After several weeks on the air, Baer had a speech that read, "Well, as sure as...," and he started to flounder with his lines. Conrad just let him flounder, something they did to each other quite a bit. Baer was finally forced to ad lib his way out of the dilemma, adding, "Well, as sure as my name is Chester Wesley Proudfoot." Thus the full name was born, along with a very complicated radio personality full of foibles and folly.

Although John Mantley, the producer of television's *Gunsmoke* for its final nine years, once referred to Chester as a "dim-witted, town loafer," Baer disagreed. He found that, "although Chester was lazy, he still did his work, and he spun his hooves a great deal and kicked a lot of gravel." Baer describes Chester as a "dependable non-thinker." Elaborating on this, he explains:

> If we had a hypothetical case with nine desperadoes holed up, and Matt Dillon had said, "Chester you watch the back door, and as they come out you plug number one, three, five and seven," Chester would have said, "Yessir." And as they came out, he would have said, "One," bang! He'd have let two go, and he'd have gotten three, and he'd let four go and he'd have gotten five. Even though two and four were bearing down on him, he would have said, "Mister Dillon said to shoot them others, so thems the one's I'm gonna shoot." Chester was energetic. He was loyal. At times put upon by everybody but Dillon...As we played it, Chester was not really deputized. Chester got Dillon out of scrapes every now and then. There was a pathetic tone...Chester realized his shortcomings. I remember one script we did...Chester saved Dillon. They went back to town and he said, "You best not tell anybody about that, Mister Dillon, because that could embarrass you, if people was to know that I saved you. We just don't talk about that..." I think that was basically Chester. He was a loyal, sensitive man, who, much to Dillon's annoyance, put sugar in his rye whiskey, and was overly fond of jelly...One time when Dillon said that chewing tobacco was a filthy habit, he confessed that he really

didn't chew tobacco, it was licorice. That was Chester, simple but not a simpleton, loyal but not intelligent. The economy of the day got to him. Chester was never affluent. His family would have been sharecroppers, or tenant farmers. I don't think they were ever great land owners. But Chester was fiercely proud of his family, and defended them, and had an absolute adulation for Dillon. Dillon was the ultimate so far as he was concerned.[49]

On television, Baer has been on numerous programs including *The Golden Girls, Night Court, The Addams Family, Twilight Zone, Simon & Simon* and *The A-Team*. In addition, he was a regular on *The Adventures of Ozzie and Harriet, The Andy Griffith Show*, and *Double Life of Henry Phyfe*. He had parts in various movies such as *Gypsy, Those Calloways*, and *Dr. Detroit*. He is also heard as the voice of the famous Keebler elf. Besides acting, Baer has had an active career in circus, appearing frequently as the ring-master.

Howard McNear and Doc Adams

Radio's Doc was played by Howard McNear. Although he is best known for his portrayal of Floyd on television's *Andy Griffith Show*, his greatest characterization was that of Doc on radio's *Gunsmoke*. McNear's background was in legitimate theater and he was a versatile character actor who appeared in various films including *Irma La Douce, Bell, Book, and Candle*, and *Anatomy of a Murder*. He was a featured guest on numerous television series and made an occasional appearance on television's *Gunsmoke*. Anyone who came in contact with McNear had a great affection for him as can be seen in Baer's reminiscences:

> ...When you talk about Howard, all the adjectives like wonderful, unique, magnificent come to mind...for he was one of the truly delightful people I've ever known, ever met, and I have never heard anyone who didn't like him. Everybody loved him, and he was an absolute asset to anything and everything he did...And I can truthfully say that some of the happiest hours of my life were spent in his company...Not only our business, but the world suffered a great loss when he was taken, and I don't know of anyone who is remembered more fondly by our profession than Howard.[50]

William Conrad also remarked that:

Howard McNear probably was the most fascinating human being I have ever known in my life. He was a consummate actor. He was a consummate human being, and all of this wrapped up in a pixie-like body, a wonderful comic mind that would make a laugh out of anything in the world...He was the life of our cast. He and Parley combined were unbelievable in their making lightness and happiness, and joy, out of a common everyday experience. Howard and Parley are two people that everybody should know in their lives.[51]

Baer recalls that Conrad came up with the name for Doc after a caustic cartoonist on the staff of the *New Yorker* magazine. At first "he was just Doc...and Howard McNear, who was so delightful in that role, played him with just a trickle of blood dripping from his fangs, and you got the feeling that Mephistophiles was looking over his shoulder a little bit...Bill Conrad christened him Dr. Charles Addams...after the cartoonist."[52]

McNear played Doc as a "bloodthirsty little man," quite unlike the sympathetic, yet garrulous character he finally became under Milburn Stone on television. On radio, Doc was sometimes a mercenary, insensitive member of the medical profession who was occasionally ignorant of the Hippocratic Oath. As time went on, however, he became under McNear a cranky-skeptical-cynical-loveable-compassionate Doc, brilliantly played. To Meston, Doc was a "cantankerous old guy who didn't know too much medicine...who didn't believe much in anybody but his friends...But he was not a cynic."[53]

McNear died in 1969; he left behind, however, a legacy in the minds and hearts of all the people whose lives he had touched.

Georgia Ellis and Kitty Russell

The fourth member of the *Gunsmoke* "family" was Kitty played by Georgia Ellis. Ellis had attended UCLA but left to work at the Pasadena Playhouse. Her first acting role was in 1942 in a *Hopalong Cassidy* movie. She was already a well-established actress on radio when she got the part of Kitty. She had appeared on various radio programs and played ingenue parts on *Escape* and *Philip Marlowe*. On *Rogers of the Gazette* she played the girlfriend of Will Rogers, Jr.

Macdonnell said of Kitty's character that she was "just someone Matt has to visit every once in a while." Ellis, who lovingly developed the role, saw Kitty as:

> ...a very generous, loving human being. She adored the men in her life, Matt predominately, and then Chester and Doc. Not to say that she didn't have a certain kind of ambivalent feeling toward Matt. I do think that she considered him, sort of the boss-man, but she adored him dearly. And I'm quite sure they were very compatible. They were lovers. The best kind, because they truly understood one another, so there wasn't need for too much talk. I don't think there was any forgiveness to be done because I

don't think Kitty was available to anybody else but Matt. Undoubtedly, she had wild dreams from time to time, which she realized were completely unrealistic, but doing what? Who knows? 'Cause Matt would never be happy doing anything but what he was doing, and she knew she would never be happy with Matt if he were not happy. So, she was resigned to serving booze and saying, "Be careful, Matt.". . . She didn't have anything left in the East, or wherever she came from, to go back to, so what the hell, she was stuck in Dodge. She was a good girl. She made a lot of it.[54]

In later years Ellis retired from the industry, unlike Conrad, McNear, and Baer, who went on to successful careers in television. She lived in quiet anonymity in Woodland Hills, California with her husband, and was known as Georgia Puttfarkin. She rarely attended show business functions and radio's Miss Kitty gradually became more and more distant and eventually faded from our minds as television's Miss Kitty took over. Amanda Blake in a recent interview, reflected on her radio counterpart, "Georgia had the wonderful voice... the great whiskey voice, which was terrific!" Georgie Ellis Puttfarkin died in March, 1988.

The Supporting Cast

A great deal of the credit for *Gunsmoke's* success must also go to its strong supporting cast. Radio acting was a special craft and made specific demands on an actor. There was a need for fluency that required certain technical abilities such as scanning a line and speed reading a script. One had to scan as one read and the actor had to free himself from the reading pattern and the printed word. Larry Dobkin, who was a frequent member of *Gunsmoke's* illustrious supporting cast, finds that today:

> ...there are many actors who can read very fluently but can never make you believe they are doing anything but reading. They cannot free themselves from the particular rhythm and placement that indicates that what they are saying is being read. They can't get out of it until they have memorized the dialogue.

This was a luxury that was not available to radio actors who had little time to look over the script before taping.

Radio actors were cast according to their "voices." Each had his or her own specialty but each sought to master as many voices and dialects as possible in order to be more competitive. Even animal noises and other sound effects were listed on actors' cards and were a part of everyone's bag of tricks. When cast, one might frequently play more than one part and would "double" or "triple," for that might be the only way of making the budget. Most everyone worked for scale. Dobkin estimates that "the whole radio community [in Hollywood] did not number more than 70 or 80 people who worked enough to call it a livelihood."

Macdonnell was a very loyal individual and tended to use the same actors over and over again. The "stock company" of performers that made up *Gunsmoke's* supporting cast included Larry Dobkin, Vic Perrin, Harry Bartell, Jeanette Nolan, Virginia Gregg, Ben Wright, Ralph Moody, Jack Kruschen, Lou Krugman, and John Dehner.

John Dehner

John Dehner was one of the actors in Macdonnell's "elite Repertory Company." Early in his career he struggled through Broadway and summer stock productions but was generally hungry and broke. Tired of the uncertainties of acting he became an animator and worked on Disney's *Fantasia,* and *Bambi,* and various Mickey Mouse, Donald Duck, and Goofy cartoons. He drifted back to acting and appeared on radio in *Suspense, Sam Spade, The Lone Ranger, Escape, Romance,* and *Gunsmoke.* Dehner became a star on radio playing the principal roles on *The Judge* and *Frontier Gentleman.* He was Paladin on *Have Gun, Will Travel,* a show that came to radio after it debuted on television.

In movies, Dehner generally appeared in supporting roles as the sadistic villain or laconic cop. A tall, attractive, often moustachioed actor, with sharp distinguished features, Dehner occasionally played leads, but he never made the leap to superstardom. His long list of films include *The Left-Handed Gun, Cast a Long Shadow, Slaughterhouse-Five, The Day of the Dolphin, The Boys from Brazil,* and *The Right Stuff.*

On television, Dehner appeared as a regular on several shows including *The Westerner, The Roaring Twenties, The Don Knotts Show,* and *The Doris Day Show.* He was also a frequent visitor on television's *Gunsmoke,* where he played a variety of characters. More recently he has been seen in made-for-television movies and miniseries such as *The Missiles of October* and *The Winds of War.*

With a career spanning over half a century, the multifaceted Dehner has done it all. Whoever has gone to the movies, watched television, or listened to radio, has been exposed at one time or another to the talents of John Dehner.

When the role of radio's Dillon was being cast, John Dehner was one of the actors who was seriously considered. However, Dehner was looking for greener pastures, and did not want to be typecast as a cowboy.

Radio — The Pioneers

Vic Perrin

Vic Perrin was another integral member of the supporting cast. He attended the University of Wisconsin and got his start acting on the school's radio station. After graduation he had the "choice of starving in New York or starving in Hollywood" and chose to go West. With two letters of introduction from his professor he pounded the pavement and finally got a job at NBC working in the parking lot. He was assured, however, that when there was an opening he would be given an audition. After parking cars for six weeks an audition finally materialized and he won his first professional job as a junior announcer at NBC in 1941. He was also accepted into Charles Laughton's Shakespearean workshop, which consisted of a group of actors who met regularly with Laughton to work on classic plays. Laughton had a house in the Pacific Palisades but purchased a house in Hollywood with a large studio for the express purpose of being near his acting troupe. They met on Mondays, Wednesdays and Fridays for two hours to work on Shakespeare and Chekhov and it was a great opportunity for the young actor to develop the talents that would make him a successful radio actor. There were about a dozen actors in the group, including Shelley Winters, Robert Ryan, and Jane Wyatt. Laughton told Perrin that "he had never had a family of his own, and this was going to be his family." According to Perrin, Laughton "gave completely of himself." At the end of rehearsals his wife, Elsa Lanchester, would come in with the key to the liquor cabinet and would take out one bottle and set it down in front of the group. Laughton insisted that, "Actors should drink together."

Perrin went on to play Ross Farnsworth for seven years on *One Man's Family*. Soap operas on radio were as popular as they are on television today and Perrin had continuing roles in *Dr. Paul*, *Aunt Mary* and *The Story of Holly Sloan*. He was Clyde Beatty on *The Clyde Beatty Show* and Sergeant Gorse in Raymond Burr's *Fort Laramie*. For years he was a stock company regular on *Gunsmoke* and *Dragnet*. On *Gunsmoke* Perrin found that he generally played a "very wimpish little guy or some poor sucker who was being beaten by bullies." He also played his share of heavies.

Perrin was fascinated with the character of Chester and wrote several scripts for *Gunsmoke* sometimes collaborating with his close friend, Harry Bartell. They would get together and improvise scenes and then type the dialogue. By this time they were so familiar with the characters that they knew their nuances and language.

Starting in 1958 Perrin began to make appearances on television including *Dragnet*, *Mission: Impossible*, *Gunsmoke*, *Star Trek*, *Big Valley*, and *The Untouchables*. He was the control voice and narrator for *The Outer Limits* and warned millions of viewers each week not to touch their television dials. His melodic voice was heard on the Porsche commercials.

Perrin attributed much of his success in the industry to the principles that he had learned working with Charles Laughton who said, "Let the words do the work. Don't inject too much emotion into them, just let them come out." Vic Perrin died July 4, 1989.

Larry Dobkin

Larry Dobkin was also one of the radio "regulars." Writer Herb Purdum recently confessed, "Larry Dobkin was the only actor I ever wrote a fan letter to. It was in the early days when I was quite impressionable. I got very upset with many actors who did not seem to care much about their characterisation, but I was so impressed with his talent, that I sat down and wrote him a fan letter."

Dobkin had been a child actor in New York and did some radio while still in high school. During World War II he was assigned to a radio propaganda unit in the Air Force. After the War he auditioned for ABC and won the title role on *Ellery Queen*. When ABC decided to move the show to Hollywood, Dobkin moved to the West Coast. Unfortunately, the show was soon cancelled and Dobkin found himself without a job in a strange city.

The West Coast stock company was difficult to break into but he finally came to Macdonnell's attention and started to work for CBS. He was a frequent guest on *Gunsmoke,* and found that since there was only one hero and one assistant, "You made a very good living playing villains." He recalls that one day he showed up at the studio to rehearse a new script and when he arrived he asked Macdonnell, "Where the hell is everybody?" And was told, "Everybody's here. It's just you and Bill." He had been called in to do *The Ride Back,* the rare episode that was written for only two characters.

Later on in television Dobkin appeared in *Playhouse 90, Matinee Theater* and *Climax* and did live comedy on Red Skelton's and Lucille Ball's programs. In 1960 he started directing and did the pilot and the first six episodes of *The Munsters.* One day while directing a television program that required an actor to play an animal trainer, he had an unexpected reunion. Impatient, waiting for the actor to appear, Dobkin called out, "Where the hell is the animal trainer?" His assistant replied, "He's coming." But the actor was still not on the set after it had been lit. An exasperated Dobkin finally yelled out, "Animal trainer where the hell are you?" To which a vaguely familiar voice answered, "I'm coming." Dobkin recalls, "When Parley came out we both looked at each other and burst into tears."

Dobkin has worked in all aspects of television including writing screenplays. He was the narrator for *Naked City* and earned an Emmy Award Nomination as Best Supporting Actor for *Do Not Go Gentle into That Good Night*. His film credits include *Patton, Ten Commandments, Twelve O'Clock High* and *The Defiant Ones*.

Dobkin looks back on his radio days with a special fondness. "The few of us who are left," he commented, "keep telling each other that we never had it so good."

Harry Bartell

Harry Bartell became involved in radio in 1930 in Houston, Texas. A friend of his was an announcer on KPRC and they started to do shows late at night. He was involved in college drama and little theater. He drifted to California and started to work at the Pasadena Playhouse. After doing some commercial radio he went to New York in 1940 but "froze to death" and "ran out of money." He decided that "if it was going to be starving time it would be better in a warmer climate."

Once back in California Bartell became a disc jockey and then a station announcer. Finding this to be a dead end he started to freelance in 1943 and this ultimately led to appearances in "about 10,000 shows" on radio.

Bartell became involved in *Gunsmoke* when he was called for the audition record that was aired as the first show, *Billy the Kid*. He played Mr. Hightower, who was a newspaper editor and telegrapher. "Well, this has got to be a lifelong career," he thought to himself, but found that Hightower did not appear again until a year later.

In the meantime, Bartell played other characters on *Gunsmoke*. "I played all sorts of things. I played heavies. I played goodies... I had a wider variety of characters on there than I can ever recall having done." Quite often when he played the heavy he was paired off with his good friend Vic Perrin. Whoever had the first speech had the choice of whether he was going to do the low-voiced villain or the high-voiced villain so the audience could discriminate between the two. He commented on his collaboration with Perrin in writing scripts: "It was fairly late in the *Gunsmoke* run.... The themes, the actual plot lines that had been written primarily by John Meston and Kathleen Hite were beginning to poop out a little bit, they were getting tired.... Vic and I were coming from a different angle."

Besides radio, Bartell has acted in various films including *Johnny Concho, Voice in the Mirror* and *The Decks Ran Red*. On television, he, too made the guest circuit on numerous shows including *Gunsmoke*. To this day, a stock line in the Bartell household is, "Be careful, Matt."

GUNSMOKE — I. THE HISTORY

Lou Krugman

Lou Krugman first began in radio while still in high school. In 1929 he had his own show on WODA in Paterson, New Jersey, and later went to New York. He did some theater and radio there and finally moved to the West Coast. He appeared in numerous radio programs including *Escape* and because of his rough, heavy voice was frequently cast as the villain.

On *Gunsmoke,* Krugman recalled, "I was a character actor. I did mostly heavies and utility... A lot of actors were expected to double and triple. The triple might be a line or a half a line... No one felt they were part of anything historic at the time. It was a job. You did it and went on. But instincts told you that it was far better than the average show."

In movies Krugman appeared in 1948 in *To the Ends of the Earth* and in 1958 he was in the classic film *I Want to Live* with Susan Hayward.

Krugman also was featured in several television series and guest starred on *Gunsmoke*. When asked to compare the radio and television versions he replied, "How do you compare the father to the son? Same genes. Radio awakens the dormant sights and sounds of the mind, while television titillates the eye as well as the ear, which unfortunately in turn, turns off the imaginative mind."

Jack Kruschen

Canadian-born Jack Kruschen, who according to Harry Bartell, "was an excellent dialectician," a "very steady actor," and a "good double" on *Gunsmoke,* started acting in radio at the age of 16. He eventually moved on to films where the burly actor landed a variety of character roles ranging from the comedic to the dramatic. He appeared in such features as *The War of the Worlds, The Angry Red Planet, McLintock!,* and *Freebie and the Bean.* In 1960 he was nominated for an Academy Award as Best Supporting Actor for his performance in *The Apartment.*

In more recent years, Kruschen has turned his attention to television. In addition to numerous made-for-television movies, he was a regular on *Hong Kong, Busting Loose* and *Webster.*

Ben Wright

Ben Wright started in radio working for the B.B.C. before World War II. He also did some early television in 1938–39. During the War he served in the British Army as a captain in the Kings Royal Rifle Corps and was stationed in India. He came to the States in 1946 and got involved in radio. He finally came to Macdonnell's attention and worked on *Romance* and *Escape* and later, *Gunsmoke.* He recalled,

> Norman took a chance on me as an actor...thanks to some very kind remarks about my work by Jack Kruschen...I then became fortunate enough to join Norman Macdonnell's Elite Repertory Company...I was fortunate enough to work with actors and actresses of remarkable talent — and am still in awe of them!

Wright considered himself a "dialectician" and was generally cast as "the old German gunsmith, an occasional Scot...or an occasional Irish priest, if called for." He commented that, "They were all over the place!" in those days. On *Have Gun, Will Travel,* another CBS radio Western, he played the Chinese houseboy, Hey Boy, opposite Virginia Gregg's Missy Wong and John Dehner's Paladin.

In reflecting on his experience with *Gunsmoke,* Wright related, "I think that to have *Gunsmoke* as a credit meant that one was 'worth one's salt' as an actor or actress." Ben Wright died on July 2, 1989.

Sam Edwards

Sam Edwards' parents were dramatic stock performers. He played kid parts and sang as a child on WOAI in San Antonio, Texas, in the 1930s. A light tenor, in later years he was usually cast as a teenager or "the wild young man." On KTSA San Antonio his family produced a radio show called *The Adventures of Sonny and Buddy,* and Edwards and his brother played the primary roles. When the family moved to California to produce the show he started to act in radio programs there. He ultimately came to Macdonnell's attention and worked on various CBS programs. He worked on the audition show of *Gunsmoke* and recalls playing "in about 60 to 70 percent of all *Gunsmoke* shows from beginning to end." Edwards found that *Gunsmoke* "was the most relaxing show" on which he ever appeared and felt that it was "the best, most true to life Western of its time." Reflecting on the program, he comments:

> Most radio westerns were shoot-em-up gunfights and chases on horses with the lead character portrayed as a super-sheriff or super-marshall or super-gunfighter. Matt Dillon was first of all a human being, with human virtues and human faults. He tried to do his job as marshall without having to use violence or gunplay. Bill Conrad's portrayal of Dillon was so believable that I could have imagined his having been a real Marshall Dillon of the era. The other members of the cast were no less wonderful in the portrayals. I considered them to be among the best of the radio performers. And John Meston's writing was superb. His dialogue was so natural and easy to read that the cast could read through a script one time

and be ready to go on the air. In fact, many times I believe the cast could have gone on the air without a dialogue rehearsal.

Richard Beals

Beals majored in radio at Michigan State. As a senior he began his professional career in Detroit on the *Lone Ranger, Green Hornet* and *Challenge of the Yukon* shows. Because of his high-pitched voice he generally played kids. He moved to Hollywood in 1952. Macdonnell cast him as Billy the Kid in the pilot program of *Gunsmoke* and he was an active member of the cast until the end of the radio show. Reminiscing recently about the show Beals commented:

> Bill, Parley, Georgia and Howard were perfectly cast. And Norman only cast the top voices in town, and it showed. It was the first show I worked on that was taped. All others were either "live" or recorded on disc. Because of the pros working the show we seldom had pickups. The "guiding force" behind the show was the director, but a close second was Bill Conrad. He added so much strength to his role. He was so believable. *Gunsmoke* was number one. The best radio show in Hollywood. My favorite show to work on. It was a study in perfection... It was such a joy just getting the call. I looked forward to being around the regulars. At the break we all went to Nicodells for lunch, then back for the dress and show... It was always a most enjoyable experience.

Jeanette Nolan

Gunsmoke was fortunate in having one of Hollywood's greatest character actresses among its cadre of performers, Jeanette Nolan. Equally at home on radio, television, stage and film, she gave a classic performance as Lady Macbeth in Orson Welles' *Macbeth*. An incredibly versatile performer, Nolan appeared frequently on radio, and on *Gunsmoke* could play anything from a toothless old woman from the Ozarks to a sophisticated socialite from Philadelphia's Main Line. As *Maw Hawkins* (May 8, 1959) she played a spirited mother who wanted her son to follow in her husband's lawless footsteps. "Mrs. Junius Chamberlain" from *Dowager's Visit* (May 10, 1959) was the widow of a prominent senator. On *Wagon Show* (May 24, 1959) she jumped into action as "Dainty Margarita," the strongest woman in the world. Nolan is especially admired by the actors she has worked with, and her coworker, Harry Bartell, considers her to be "one of the finest actresses in America." Nolan also appeared in many movies including *Abandoned, The Big Heat, The Rabbit Trap, The Man Who Shot Liberty Valance, Tribute to a Bad Man,*

Radio — The Pioneers

My Blood Runs Cold, and *The Winds of Autumn.* On television she was a regular on *The Richard Boone Show, The Virginian* featuring her husband, John McIntire, and was the star of *Dirty Sally,* a spin-off from television's *Gunsmoke.*

Virginia Gregg

Another grande dame of *Gunsmoke* was Virginia Gregg, a character actress extraordinaire. Born in Harrisburg, Illinois, she moved to California at the age of six. She started as a musician and played double bass viol with the Pasadena Symphony Orchestra and later with a group called the "Singing Strings" that performed on CBS and at Mutual Radio Network. While there, she started to do commentaries, emceeing, and small parts on various shows. She ultimately decided to give up music for acting, and explained, "I sold my bass that night so I could never go back to it." Like Nolan, Gregg had a successful career in all aspects of the industry. Georgia Ellis considered her to be one of Hollywood's "great radio voices" with a range that enabled her to play any character from the sublime to the ridiculous. She frequently played more than one character in a show and her radio credits include *One Man's Family* (Betty), *Let George Do It* (Claire), *Dr. Kildare* (Nurse Parker), *Have Gun, Will Travel* (Missy Wong), *Lum and Abner* (Charity), and many others. Although she was quite youthful during her radio days, she was frequently summoned to play old cronies on *Gunsmoke* such as "Della Bass" from *Old Fool* (August 7, 1960), or feisty frontier women like *Nettie Sutton* (May 1, 1960). Her cavalcade of motley characters also included bigamist murderess "Bertha Housecavitz" of *Marryin' Bertha* (May 22, 1960), homely spinster "Emma Crown" from *Homely Girl* (June 19, 1960), and *Minnie* (December 25, 1960), the wife of a jealous buffalo hunter, which she later recreated on television's *Gunsmoke.* Gregg was featured in many movies including *Dragnet, I'll Cry Tomorrow, The Hanging Tree* and *Spencer's Mountain.* William Conrad provided her first motion picture role in *Body and Soul,* starring John Garfield. Her face was as versatile as her voice. On television she guest-starred on various series and was a regular on the dramatic series *Little Women.* (Biography courtesy of Ms. Gregg's son, Gregg del Valle.)

Many other performers appeared frequently on *Gunsmoke* including Barney Phillips, Joseph Kearns, Ralph Moody, Virginia Christine, Vivi Janiss, Lillian Buyeff, Jeanne Bates, Helen Kleeb and James Nusser.

James Nusser

Nusser struggled with alcoholism throughout much of his life, and most directors were reluctant to cast him except for Norman Macdonnell. Macdonnell gave him fairly steady employment during the nine and a half years of the radio show. When Macdonnell became producer of *Gunsmoke* on television, Nusser was sometimes seen in bit parts. Ironically, in later years Nusser joined the cast as Louie Pheeters, Dodge City's resident drunk, and gave his most brilliant performance in a role he was born to play.

Barney Phillips

Barney Phillips was seen on television's *Dragnet* as Sergeant Ed Jacobs and also appeared in *Johnny Midnight, Twelve O'Clock High, Felony Squad,* and *The Betty White Show.* In films he appeared among others in *Eight Iron Men, Blueprint for Murder* and *Cry Terror.* On radio's *Gunsmoke,* his strong baritone voice led to roles as classic villains.

Joseph Kearns

Joseph Kearns is probably best known as television's George Wilson in *Dennis the Menace.* He also played in *Our Miss Brooks.* In films he appeared in *Hard, Fast and Beautiful, The Gift of Love* and *Anatomy of a Murder.*

Ralph Moody

On radio, Ralph Moody specialized in old Indian chiefs, old settlers, and old buffalo hunters. In films he acted in *Red Mountain, I Died a Thousand Times, The Last Hunt* and *The Outsider.*

Virginia Christine, Helen Kleeb, Jeanne Bates, and Lillian Buyeff played the various and sundry saloon girls, victimized Indian maidens, forsaken prairie wives and battered women that populated Dodge and its environs.

Virginia Christine

Virginia Christine is best known to today's audiences as Mrs. Olson in the Folger's coffee commercial. She has had an active career in show-business. During the forties she made B movies for Warner Bros. and later appeared in Stanley Kramer's features including *High Noon* and *Judgement at Nuremberg.* In 1944 she played the unconscious damsel carried by Lon Chaney, Jr., in *The Mummy's Curse.* She almost got the part of Kitty Collins in *The Killers* but lost out to Ava Gardner. The producer, however, was so impressed with her work, he wrote in a part for her. Christine appeared in later films such as *The*

Prize and *Guess Who's Coming to Dinner?* On television she was a regular on *Wells Fargo*.

Helen Kleeb

Kleeb did her first radio work in 1932 at the old KGW studios in Portland, Oregon. She was trained as an actress and worked in theater in the Northwest starting in 1928. During the Depression, work was scarce and KGW was just beginning to do dramatic shows. One of the first was *Covered Wagon Days* and she started to do parts on this program. As she recalls, "The pay was small but it proved to be valuable experience. In about 1935 I was called from Portland to go to San Francisco to audition for a show called *Dr. Kate*, a daytime serial. I won the role of 'Miss Sarah,' the head nurse, and continued doing it for the next nine years. Of course, I did many other radio shows as well. NBC was a beehive of activity then. *One Man's Family* originated there. In 1950 I left San Francisco and went to Los Angeles where I began working on such radio shows as *Dr. Christian, Dragnet* and eventually *Gunsmoke*... Perhaps working on *Gunsmoke* was unique in that there was a camaraderie in the cast that was exceptional, a relaxed atmosphere and energy that was remarkable. It was also fun. Radio actors were mostly bright, talented, versatile, witty people. I look back on those days of radio with delight. We loved what we were doing."

Kleeb has appeared in films and television, including *The Manchurian Candidate, The Fortune Cookie, Friendly Persuasion,* and *Seven Days in May*. On television she was in *Harrigan and Son* and on *The Waltons* she played Mamie Baldwin from 1972–81.

Jeanne Bates

Jeanne Bates started in radio soaps for NBC and CBS, then moved to the West Coast when one of her shows, *Whodunit*, a murder mystery, became a hit and was transferred to Hollywood under the title, *Murder Will Out*. She recalls that her roles over the years included ingenues, "sincere young mothers in distress" and "sometimes bad girls." In 1944 she made two films, *Shadows in the Night* and *The Soul of a Monster*. On television Bates played Nurse Will on *Ben Casey,* and Anne Peters on the NBC soap opera, *Days of Our Lives*.

Lillian Buyeff

Buyeff was working in a little theater group in Hollywood in 1944 when her director, who worked at KNX told her that the radio program *I Was There* was looking for someone with a Polish accent. She recalls how she broke into radio:

> I said I could do a Russian accent, but I'd never done Polish. He laughed and said, "They'll never know the difference." Apparently they didn't because I got the job. My first professional radio job. Playing my husband was Hans Conreid and the local announcer was Chet Huntley. I was mighty impressed and thrilled...

She, too, found that:

> There was a "special-ness" about working on *Gunsmoke* which is not easy to explain. There was a feeling of family about the group and great pride in being part of a quality production. I didn't know anyone in the upper echelon or powers that be... *Gunsmoke* was definitely a cut above most of the other shows being aired at the time. It had class. It was especially different from other radio westerns which were generally predictable and peopled with cardboard characters. There was joy and a great deal of laughter and good-natured ribbing... Someone dubbed Parley Baer as "Barely Par." All of us roared, especially Parley.

There were many other great voices on *Gunsmoke*. Richard Crenna appeared on the program, as did character actor John McIntire. Paul DuBov was a frequent guest and ultimately left acting to become a writer. Vivi Janiss became "Myrtle Davis" on television's *Father Knows Best*.

John Dunkel, in commenting on the overall performance of the actors on *Gunsmoke* said, "The people involved were simply excellent. It was a kind of culmination that had been building all through the Forties."

The Role of Sound on Gunsmoke

The high quality of *Gunsmoke* was only partly due to the caliber of the writing and acting. There was meticulous emphasis on music and sound which reached artistic and technical heights as the program developed. Our society today is dominated by the visual media and so it is difficult for us today to imagine how important the quality of sound was in radio drama. Sound was a highly technical field and the quality and credibility of a program relied heavily on the talents of the sound men. The finest technicians were recruited as sound artists, and the realism, that was the primary goal of the program, was greatly enhanced and furthered by their magic. The best crews were in great demand and were utilized on several shows at the same time. When the advent of audio tape let the soundmen move from the restrictions of the studio acetate disc to the more portable and practical medium of recorded tapes, whole avenues opened up for sound artistry.

Radio — The Pioneers

There was a lot of time spent on sound effects recognizing that sound was one of the critical factors that gave *Gunsmoke* its unique color. There was great care given to detail. As Macdonnell explained:

> It had always been a rule of thumb in radio that there should be no "dead air," that people must keep talking. Well, we changed that. Not because we deliberately set out to change it, but because the people we were working with didn't talk all the time. So we had to fill it with sound patterns.[55]

Gunsmoke was revolutionary in its use of sound. It utilized "exaggerated sound patterns," and although there was a lot of dead air it seemed to work. If someone walked across a room he was allowed to walk without dialogue cluttering the scene, and the audience would hear a door close. If someone crossed a street he was given the time. There were three sound men, Bill James, Tom Hanley, and Ray Kemper, and Macdonnell felt that they "contributed more to the show than anybody could ever imagine." For example, when the sound men realized that there was trouble with live gunshots, they went on a Saturday with their own equipment to the woods and recorded shots on tape with a .45, a .38, a .32, and a .22. As George Walsh humorously puts it, "They made sure that in most of the shows the villain had a nine millimeter pistol, while Matt had a 155 millimeter Howitzer."

Macdonnell appreciated this "above and beyond the call of duty" attitude on the part of his soundmen. He commented that:

> These effects could then be played directly through the lines so that it didn't flatten out and become just a dull pop on the air... We always used a .45 for Matt, and for the other heavies there would be a .38 or a .32. This is the kind of thing that the boys did in order to make the sound better... They also worked on the smallest possible details like Matt getting up and walking to the stove to get a cup of coffee. The boys knew exactly how many steps it was from Matt's desk to the stove, or how many steps it was from the front of Matt's office to the jail-cell. The one place where we cheated a bit was on the walk from Matt's office down to the Long Branch. If we were running short on time it was two steps across from the boardwalk, five steps across the street, one step up on the other side, and then the doors. If we wanted to stretch a little bit, that walk sometimes became considerably longer. But the boys made the walk work, because they used spurs for Matt. Whoever was walking with him would be without spurs. So you could differentiate between two people, Matt and Chester, for instance, walking down the street. They went into the whole bit of the squeak of the leather, when Matt would mount a saddle. You could hear the stirrup leathers stretch and squeak, and we took time to play the sound patterns. This I think contributed in great part to the color and the feel of authenticity, if you will.[56]

Sound could be used not only to enhance the drama, but could provide the drama itself. In one episode Matt and Chester happen upon a man who has just been lynched, and one can hear the slow, steady, terrifying creak of his lifeless body swaying in the wind. The staff was not afraid to experiment. They cut out much of the narration that was so prevalent in the radio shows of the day. They were not intimidated by silence and used it effectively to heighten dramatic effects.

Timing was very important with sound and the soundmen would work on every subtle nuance. Ray Kemper would get so involved with his work that he would unconsciously stick out his tongue. Macdonnell recalled that:

> ...the more involved he got the farther his tongue would come out... Farther and farther, much to the annoyance and dismay of his co-workers. But the result would be a beautiful sound pattern and he would look up to wonder why everyone would be smiling.[57]

Parley Baer was equally impressed with the quality of the sound. He reflected on the great pains that were taken to enhance its richness:

> When they did horses' hooves, I remember Bill would use one set of coconuts to depict our horses, which were shod, and another set for an Indian horse. Probably to the listener there was no difference, but to them there was a vast difference... They would change background noises from one saloon to another... and they had a different set of street sounds for the day and for the night.[58]

It is unfortunate that at a time when the technology of sound was on the verge of a major advance, radio drama was eclipsed by television and its applied potential was never fully realized.

Norman Macdonnell

The individual who integrated the writing, acting, sound, and music into a cohesive whole, and who ultimately guided *Gunsmoke* through nine years of radio and nine years of television was Norman Macdonnell. Despite his great contributions, Macdonnell was a self-effacing man. A reminiscence by John Dunkel is illustrative:

> Macdonnell used to say very often that the success of *Gunsmoke* was a three-way effort, the script, the actors and the music. He was very generous in saying this because, of course, he was also a very able director and the direction should have been thrown in there as well.[59]

Norman Macdonnell, the producer and director of *Gunsmoke* was born in Pasadena, California, in 1916. He got started in radio in 1938 when he went to KNX. He aspired to be another Tony Marvin, a well-known announcer, but had to settle for being a tour guide for CBS Radio Network in Hollywood for two to three years. He founded the Columbia Radio Players, a workshop for CBS Radio employees, and it was with this group that he gained experience as a radio actor and director.

Macdonnell left for the Service during World War II and took part in the D-Day invasion of Normandy. After returning to the States in 1946 he was a "contact man" or assistant director for CBS Radio. In 1947 he advanced from assistant director to producer-director when Bill Robson put in a good word for him. At the time, Robson was producing and directing *Escape* at CBS, which aired on Thursdays. The network decided that it also wanted to air the show on Saturday mornings. Robson guarded his weekends jealously and informed CBS that he was not about to get up early on Saturdays just to rehash the show and suggested Macdonnell, saying, "Let the young guy do it." This was a perfect opportunity for a fledgling director, for all Macdonnell had to do was to redirect what Robson had done earlier in the week, and to edit five minutes out to make room for more sponsors. He had a cast that already knew the script and so under minimum pressure he could develop his skills. He worked closely with John Dunkel, who was the story editor and was in charge of all programs coming out of CBS on the West Coast. Macdonnell worked with Dunkel for a number of years, until Meston took over.

As we have seen, Macdonnell gathered about himself a stock company including John Dehner, Larry Dobkin, Ben Wright, Dick Crenna, John and Jeanette McIntire, and Jack Webb all of whom appeared on *Escape*.

By 1948 Macdonnell was producing *Doorway to Life, Escape, The Adventures of Philip Marlowe,* and *Suspense.* He directed and produced two to four transcontinental shows per week, which is why he developed a stock company. On a Monday he might need John Dehner as an English cavalryman, on Wednesday as a Southern cook, and on Friday as an 80-year-old wino. That was the beauty of radio. One could get 40 or 50 character parts out of eight actors. When Macdonnell became the producer-director of *Gunsmoke,* he translated Meston's vision and that of other writers to the program. Later on, he was also to do this for television. He had a great talent for seeing talent in others. He provided the protective umbrella for creative writers, actors, and directors to grow. John Dunkel found that his creative freedom "was all but complete" on both radio and television "as long as Norman Macdonnell was producer and John Meston editor."

Those who worked with Macdonnell provide the best testimonials regarding his contributions. Georgia Ellis found that Macdonnell conjured a protective environment within which the actors could reflect and develop. She noted that:

> Whereas most of the radio shows were done with a sense of hurry and time, there was time to pause and think. There was time to establish in the minds of the people...And Norman was so good. Norman had that beautiful sense of timing a show, so that he was never pressed, and you never felt pressed as an actor....[60]

The actors were gently guided by Macdonnell, and they used this freedom to its greatest advantage.

Vic Perrin also observed that *Gunsmoke* owed its spirit to Macdonnell. He felt that "he was not a director, but a sort of master of ceremonies."

Harry Bartell found that Macdonnell "was essentially a very artistic man...a very sensitive man. He had wonderful taste and a sense for drama." And to Lou Krugman he was "the guiding force hands down."

The vibrant and inventive atmosphere that characterized *Gunsmoke* was made possible by Norman Macdonnell's paternal and self-assured approach to creativity. He was a director who loved his actors and staff and they reciprocated in turn.

Dirty Saturdays

It is evident that *Gunsmoke's* success depended on the complex coalescence of many factors. In addition to the creative and technical aspects, there was also a unique bond of affection and comaraderie that developed between the cast and staff, so that each week they looked forward to working together on the next show. Rehearsals were on Saturdays and ad libbing was frequently engaged in and was calculated to crack up a fellow actor. Baer describes these times as "happy and halcyon." The atmosphere was friendly and greatly conducive to creativity. Conrad recalls that those days were:

> An absolute ball. We'd do two shows on Saturday. We'd do one in the morning. Go to lunch, and then do one in the afternoon. We'd probably start at 11:00 and be through by 3:30 or 4:00...It was joyful. It really was. Everybody looked forward to coming to work...God, we used to go in with eleven page scripts and take all the time in the world to do it, and the production values of really paying attention to the sound effects, and playing them for what they were and realistically. And John's [Meston's] contribution of taking an incident and making it a story, instead of doing a full-fledged, full-blown opening and closing, with a middle and contrapuntal characterization. We all really felt very firmly that we had something, and I think we all treated it very carefully.[61]

Reflecting on this further, Baer recalled:

> We had some high old times. For years, Bill (Conrad) and I had a running gag where he'd say, "Hand me those handcuffs," or, "Hand me this, it's

in the drawer." I don't know what started it really, but it became a running gag. As you heard the sound effects of a drawer opening, I said, "Here...Well, there's my...I've been looking all over for that...How did that get there?"...And after this had been going on for many, many years, Bill said to me one day, "For nearly ten years we've been playing this show and you've been looking for something. Now for heaven's sake what is it?" And, I said, "It's right here in my pocket, and you can have it." He said, something appropriately pithy in his comment...but I couldn't have told you what it was. It just seemed like a good gimmick at the time.[62]

Howard McNear used to refer to their Saturday rehearsals as "dirty Saturdays." According to Baer,

Somebody would make an inflection in a line that would come out slightly spiked and colored, and from then on, no matter what you said, the most innocuous line became really a bunch of dirty words, when they were not intended so." The sound men would spend hours "working up a ribald sound effect, or something of the sort," recalls Baer. "And then, we would all dutifully collapse...We were lucky people. We really were. This became a labor of love with everybody on the show. Some of those Saturday recording sessions seem as though they were just yesterday, and I wish they were tomorrow. We had more of ourselves put into that show than almost any other series. I know that I never felt the same about any other series...or loved it as much.[63]

Vic Perrin found that "any resemblance to what was on the page and what came out at the first reading was purely coincidental." Perrin was the butt of one of the many pranks that were played on unsuspecting victims. One Saturday, he made the mistake of wearing a pair of jeans with a rubber waistband. Perrin recalled with a smile that he was at the mike doing a scene when Georgia Ellis "just walked up behind me and pulled the pants all the way down which of course stopped the taping."

Larry Dobkin felt that there was a healthy "irreverence." "We would do these terrible things to each other," he said in a recent interview. "Just as Rex [Koury] was ready to play the organ you would hear a horse fart just off mike, and you better not break up. It was a challenge."

Frank Paris, the assistant director, struggled through this party atmosphere with good humor and somehow kept track of the time. Announcer George Walsh recalls:

Anne Gaffney, Macdonnell's secretary, was noted for bringing in a cigar box full of very sharp pencils every Saturday morning, and she passed these out like a school teacher. And with all their seriousness, she and Frank Paris had one thing in common, once the crew got them laughing Anne and Frank were practically gone for the rest of the day.

GUNSMOKE — I. THE HISTORY

It is clear that there was something infectious and magical about these mornings. Macdonnell found that:

> One of the nicest things about the Saturday morning table readings, was when Parley Baer would arrive with two enormous boxes of goodies from Benishes Bakery, and of course everyone would always complain that Parley brought the wrong kind of tarts...which would drive Parley up the wall, and Howard McNear would laugh...But anyway, it was a pleasant way to start out...All of the members of both the casual and the regular cast were such professionals that they could kid as they worked without losing emphasis.[64]

Sam Edwards recalls:

> Once bets were made that Bill Conrad could not lose enough weight on his diet to be able to wear my coat in a given period of time. We are about the same height, but at the time my weight was about 130 pounds. Bill won the bet and wore my coat without splitting the seams.

The technicians and musicians also contributed to the merriment and mayhem of these Saturday mornings. "The sound-effects men would do everything to break Conrad up," Macdonnell recalled:

> On one occasion a stranger came into the saloon and asked Matt where Kitty was. Matt replied, "She's up in her room," then continued his conversation with Chester. In the background a stranger's footsteps could be heard walking up the stairs and down the hallway. This was followed by a door opening and closing and then suggestive sounds. On another occasion, Chester was to ride up to Matt on his horse. The hoofbeats, however, kept on going and Conrad was speechless. At times, when the horses were standing still, instead of making appropriate horse-noises, they occasionally made less than delicate sounds as well.[65]

Ray Kemper offered his own unique perspective on these irreverent times in a recent interview.

> And now we get to your question, "Was there mischief sometimes emanating from the sound technicians?" Well...yes, there was, indeed there was. Constantly. Most of it Tom [Hanley] and I did on the spur of the moment but some of it we went to great lengths to accomplish...Keep in mind that it was known by cast and crew as "dirty Saturday." With that in mind please forgive the following crudeness but I know of no delicate way of wording it. I could use the word flatulence but somehow it just doesn't paint the same picture. You see, Tommy and I built a fart machine. We then transferred these embarrassingly realistic sounds to a tape cartridge complete with electronic cue marks, labeled it FX and kept it always at the ready in the multiple deck we used for gunshots and

other sound effects. During dress rehearsal we would wait for an opportune moment — usually a dramatic, semiromantic scene between Matt and Kitty — then we would cut loose with one of those terrible sounds. The whole purpose was to break up the cast and that almost always succeeded. Bill Conrad, however, took great pride in being able to pick up on anything we did and would usually make some remark such as, "You gotta quit eatin' at the beanery, Kitty," always in perfect Matt Dillon character. Georgia Ellis never made it — she always fell on the floor, as did Norm Macdonnell in the booth and the rest of the cast. How they ever timed that show is beyond me. I will tell you this, though, when we went on the air we were all dead serious and practically never had to do a retake.

There was another thing we really got Bill Conrad with. Tommy and I found an old bass drum in the sound department. We hauled it up to the shop and kept it hidden behind the prop table. Remember I told you that Matt Dillon's footsteps were unique-heavy and with spurs. Once again, forgive my crudeness but our idea was to denote how "well hung" Matt Dillon was so with every step we added a subtle ka-boom, ka-boom of the bass drum. That one got Bill every time and he would choke and chuckle through the next several pages of script.

Another thing that comes to mind was cooked up between Tommy and Bill. Picture us now in the Long Branch with Doc and Chester — through the batwing doors comes Matt who queries, "Where's Kitty?" Chester says, "Why, she's upstairs, Mr. Dillon." Now we hear Matt's heavy footsteps and spurs ascending the stairs, walking down the hall — a door opens, footsteps in, door close, Matt says, "C'mere Kitty." We hear bed springs, some grunting and panting, the springs begin to move faster and faster (complete with spurs). The springs get very fast then suddenly stop. The spurs and boots get down on the floor, walk to the door, open it and Kitty calls out one word in disgust — "Rabbit!" End of sequence. Norm is on the floor in the booth and the rest of the cast is not worth much for a long time.

There is one other story I must relate to you that demonstrates the pixy humor of Tom Hanley. Bill Conrad came in one Saturday morning with a terrible hangover or the flu bug or something. He was feeling awful and during a break decided to go over to Stearns' drug store to get something to help him. Now the drug store was owned by a gentle person we all affectionately called Ma Stearns. Her hands were gnarled, she always wore a funny looking apron and a green sun visor. She definitely looked more like an old-fashioned faro dealer than a pharmacist. Nevertheless she whomped up a concoction for Conrad and gave it to him. Tommy found out about all this and watched closely until Bill had swallowed a good slug of Ma Stearns' snake oil. Hanley then signaled a page who came bursting into the studio with a note presumably from Ma Stearns but which in reality had been written with shaky hand by Tom Hanley. The note said, "Mr. Conrad, do not take the medicine I gave you. I made a mistake. Call me immediately!" and it was signed Mrs. Stearns. Bill's face turned a little white and he headed for the phone, but we could contain ourselves no longer and broke out laughing. Bill did a slow take, then looked at Tommy and said, "You son-of-a-bitch, I'll get you for that!" Later, he came over to us and said, "Damn, if I'd had my wits about me I'd have faked a heart attack—that woulda gotcha." Obviously, we were all very fond of one another or we could never have done all those silly things.

Everyone joined in the romp. While taping a classic rehearsal of the *New Hotel*, Rex Koury surprised everyone by playing as background music, "I Don't Want to Set the World on Fire," as the hotel goes up in a dramatic conflagration. He ended the show with another surprise: "There's a Small Hotel" from *Pal Joey*.

Ben Wright remembered a particular rehearsal:

> When my daughter Conista was born, I was a little late for rehearsal from the hospital...and only too anxious to show the card with the small footprint of my daughter. With one accord the cast brought out, each one, a drawing of a gigantic foot—each of which had seven toes! A cake followed. It was dear and typical of old friends. Then the rehearsal went on.

"All I can say," Georgia Ellis reflected, "is that it was ten years of having a ball every Saturday morning, not only of enjoying the drama of it, but of laughing, of humor, and of having your wits exercised a little bit."[66]

Perhaps Vic Perrin best expressed what it meant to be a part of the *Gunsmoke* family in those "halcyon" years when he voiced, "I would rather have gone to a *Gunsmoke* session than the Academy Awards or the greatest nightclub."

The Decline of Radio Drama

Gunsmoke had been on radio for only one year when it became apparent that television was becoming a competing force. It is ironic that at the very time that the program was enjoying all this success, radio, as the dominant form of mass communication and entertainment, was on the verge of collapse. Dramatic radio from the West Coast was drying up and *Gunsmoke* had almost appeared too late. Macdonnell once commented that: "Dramatic radio may be one of the shortest-lived industries in the American theater. It blossomed, bore fruit and died in a matter of 15 or 20 years."[67]

Macdonnell and Meston recognized the potential of television and approached CBS executives about developing their program for the new medium. They found to their surprise, however, that this was already in the works. They understandably assumed that they would be producing and

Radio — The Pioneers

writing the television show but they were to be greatly disappointed. Motion picture producer-director Charles Marquis Warren had already been called in to organize the television series and Macdonnell had to content himself with being the associate producer.

Another disappointment came when to his great consternation, Macdonnell found that the radio cast was not even being considered for the television roles. Help came from an unexpected quarter. A Los Angeles newspaperman, Hal Humphries, who was a great fan of *Gunsmoke* and its cast, took up their cause and started to campaign in his column. He petitioned day after day in the *Los Angeles Times* to secure auditions for the radio principals.

This was also a time when CBS was undergoing some organizational changes. Ackerman recalls that "the radio portion and the television portion of the network were broken in two." Paley felt that the operation was "becoming too immense" for one individual to handle and Ackerman assumed the responsibility of developing television programs. His assistant, della Cioppa, became the head of CBS' radio operations, and found that as time went on "the television division was stripping the radio division of as many shows as they could switch over." Besides *Gunsmoke,* this included other classic programs such as *Our Miss Brooks,* and *December Bride.*

For the next several years della Cioppa struggled to keep the radio division alive and "to keep *Gunsmoke* from disappearing into the maw of television." On one occasion, when *Gunsmoke* was already making television history, he approached the executive vice president in charge of radio for CBS in New York and said, "At least get us a royalty." This resulted in an unprecedented arrangement within the network that della Cioppa always viewed as a "great triumph." For several years the television division paid the radio division $800 per *Gunsmoke* episode. Della Cioppa knew, however, that he was fighting a losing battle.

As the key advocate for CBS' radio division, della Cioppa was among those who objected "vociferously to not having the radio cast considered" for television. As he recalls, Harry Ackerman finally "agreed and had a photographic session in Knott's Berry Farm with the cast of the radio show dress in authentic Western costumes." Vic Perrin notes that the principal cast "got all rigged out and...posed in front of a saloon and they looked like authentic tin-types of the West."

Finally, the radio cast was given its chance. The audition took place in Studio 43 at Television City, and Conrad curtailed his gastronomic tendencies so that he could lose weight for the event. A pleased Humphrey wrote in his February 9, 1955 *Mirror-News* column:

> There's a chance, but a very slim one, that TV audiences may soon get a Western series which has some resemblance to reality...In typical

GUNSMOKE — I. THE HISTORY

> Hollywood fashion the bigdomes at CBS have tested four hero types for the role of U.S. Marshal Matt Dillon. Last week they finally got around to making a test of William Conrad...If CBS will just let Macdonnell and John Meston do for TV what they've done for radio, it will have another hit. And Bill Conrad and Parley Baer will be hailed as "discoveries" in their new TV roles.[68]

Macdonnell later recalled that the results of the audition were all right but not "staggering."[69] Some have said that none of the network's executives ever saw the tape, for it was apparently a token audition to keep the radio cast satisfied, and to keep resentment down. Others, however, have indicated that the radio cast was afforded fair consideration.

There were probably several reasons why the radio cast was not seriously considered for the television program. First of all, CBS had a hit radio show and it did not want to jeopardize a successful project. Another reason was that it was felt that Conrad was visually wrong for the part. Although his marvelous voice captured Matt on radio, CBS felt that it needed someone else to portray him on television. Whether audiences would have been disappointed in seeing the hero of their imaginations take material form will never be known. Conrad himself felt that the radio audience thought him to be tall and handsome and would have been disappointed with his appearance.

After the unsuccessful auditions, the radio cast and staff continued on for another seven years, and ultimately many were able to transfer their talents to television. It is clear from interviews that the cast was disappointed in having been overlooked for television.

With the passage of time, however, Macdonnell conceded that Warren had made the right casting decisions, but he was unable to appreciate this at first. Others, however, including John Dunkel were never quite convinced. In a recent interview, Dunkel reflected that these events were:

> ...a sore point with all of us who loved the radio show. Not only were the radio characters richer and stronger — they were played by better actors and were a lot more fun to write for...Not only the four principals...but the whole gang of superb supporting actors...

Harry Bartell voiced similar sentiments when he commented that:

> In my estimation the radio program was far superior. The television version was adapted to the styles of the actors while the radio show grew with the actors as a part of it. I believe that the radio characters were a great deal more legitimate to the time they portrayed. The television show became the Hollywood version of the adult western. The stamp of moviemaking was heavy upon it. I believe there was more honesty in the radio show especially in the early years before anyone tired of it.

Radio — The Pioneers

Perrin reflected that, "I don't think there every really was a six-foot-seven marshal in the west. They were fat and kind of rough like Bill Conrad."

For some time feelings ran high, and reflecting years later on this transition, Macdonnell indicated that in the first few months he had great difficulty in hearing the television cast say their lines in rehearsals. In fact, he found that it was an effort for him to watch "big Jim" Arness playing Matt in the beginning. He offered as explanation that on radio:

> I'd had my own private Matt Dillon, my own sexy particular Kitty, my own bumbling Doc, and my own nutty Chester and they all did things and looked exactly the way I wanted them to look.[70]

With time, two factions have developed. There are those who feel that the radio show was more honest and that the acting was more pure, while there are those who maintain that the television version was more complex and developed beyond the "cliche" that the radio program ultimately became. This debate over the relative merits of radio versus television, and over the strength of the radio cast versus the television cast must take into account that each program was a unique creation and that each stands as a great achievement in its own right. As Ben Wright explains, "One cannot compare aural performances with visual ones. Two different methods are employed. In one, the actor creates a mental image to the listener. In the other, the viewer is asked to accept what he or she sees — i.e. the image is presented — take it or leave it."

Lou Krugman recently reflected on this issue and offered the following as a comparison:

> Many actors have played Hamlet and played it brilliantly. In the final analysis there is only one Hamlet, the one that Shakespeare created. Actors add their own personality and nuances. But the characters that Meston and Macdonnell brought to the screen and radio are their creation. Ergo, they are basically the same.

Besides the advent of television, other factors also hastened the demise of radio. By the late 1950s those with programming experience were leaving the field or were retiring. In the 1940s and 1950s, executives at CBS generally understood the creative aspects of radio. As time went on, however, economics mattered more and more and it was now businessmen and accountants who ran the show, and they generally had scant knowledge of these creative elements. Macdonnell found that during the 1940s and 1950s it was extremely easy for him to arrange for a meeting with CBS brass. He just had to walk in the door and sit down and talk to Ackerman or one of his charges. Macdonnell recalled that on one occasion when he wanted to do a "female version" of *Gunsmoke* starring Joan Fontaine, it took him but six minutes to present it to Ackerman and to get his approval. There were no committees. One man had the power to say, "Yes" or "No." Later on he found that it took him "longer to ride up the elevator to get to one of the executive's offices to ask for an appointment."[71] Macdonnell produced an audition record with Fontaine but the concept never got off the ground. However, this is the type of experimentation that was encouraged.

The radio executives of the Golden Age were individuals with experience in the theatrical end of radio rather than the business end. Macdonnell noted that "there was a wonderful meeting of the minds."[72] Over ten years ago, however, he observed that in the new environment, the typical executive knew primarily demographics, and frequently did not have a feel for the creative and intuitive aspects of production. As evidence, he pointed to the use of audience research by the networks so that an executive could be relieved of having to make a decision. Macdonnell lamented that "a lot of the heart had gone out of production and product."[73] When he offered these reflections, he was talking not only about radio but about television as well, and he played a major role in the first ten years of television. In this environment of economic pressures, when the sponsor, Liggett-Myers, finally pulled out in 1957, a severe blow was dealt to *Gunsmoke*. Network radio had been losing ground for some time and when various shows were now cancelled there were no replacements in the works. *Gunsmoke* was the last network drama to be produced on the West Coast.

Looking back, Parley Baer noted that he was glad he did not know when he was doing the last episode. "It would have been terribly depressing to know that this was the last time," he commented. "As it is, we went blithely on our way. We did the last show, and I think I was working on *Petticoat Junction* when I got word that it had been taken off the air."[74]

The final radio broadcast of *Gunsmoke* was in June of 1961, and it came so abruptly that the cast had not even been informed. The last program ended with the understated lines, "This concludes the current series of *Gunsmoke* on CBS radio."

Looking Back

Years later, those who had been most intimately involved with the radio program reflected on what had made *Gunsmoke* such a success. Although no one can ever quite capture the essence of fame, they sorted through their memories and tried to explain the *Gunsmoke* phenomenon. John Meston noted that:

> ... It was fairly new, the style, the form, the approach to a Western. Also I think it was Goddamm well done. I mean great actors. And Norm did

Radio — The Pioneers

> a helluva job... And sound... God what they did with sound is marvelous. People... you never know what they're going to like. Maybe they enjoyed the characters. In Chicago... they had a club that would meet every week or ten days, and discuss *Gunsmoke*, and the scripts and the ideas. But you know, when you write something, and send it in... you kind of forget there's an audience out there, and these people sit around and discuss what has gone on, the moral aspects, or whatever. I suppose that's the one reason it was popular... But you never know how to approach them. You do what you want to do, and if you like it, and if somebody else likes it, you're in luck.[75]

Soundman Bill James observes:

> Of all the hundreds of different shows and thousands of episodes on which I appeared *Gunsmoke* was the stand-out. It had everything: drama, heart, action, outstanding acting, direction, music, and above all the dedication of everyone involved. It was the first attempt to capture an adult audience with this genre. It came at a time when many of the old taboos were passing into well-deserved oblivion. It was the right show at the right time. The best people... I can only say that it was the best time of my life. And even after all these years I have never been able to bring myself to watch even one episode of the TV version. To me, those performers are nothing but imposters.

Georgia Ellis commented:

> The people were human beings. Kitty was human, and some of them had very homey touches like, perhaps a dress fitting, or Howard fussing about how to kill a pain in the tooth, which consumed a minute or two. It was not continuous action or blood-letting, or mystery or anything. It had a sense of continuity. You could almost taste the dust in the streets. Perhaps the beer wasn't very cold, but at least it was beer.[76]

She wistfully added:

> ...In radio, the magic of it, is to give a visual feeling to the listener. The writers were brilliant... The sound men were the greatest... The sounds were imaginative, and they were inspired.[77]

To John Dunkel *Gunsmoke* was an instant success:

> ...because it was different. Westerns up to that time had all been pretty much... simple stories that appealed to youngsters of all ages. I think even today's Westerns tend to be fairly simple story lines. As they say there are about four basic plots and you change the names. *Gunsmoke* came along with stories that were not necessarily the typical Western. They were emotional stories... more adult, more sophisticated, more far-reaching... It was something that hadn't been presented to the American public before. I think that it gave the listener the benefit of respect.

GUNSMOKE — I. THE HISTORY

John Dehner recalls that his days with *Gunsmoke:*

> ...were the most happy, because for one thing, we all knew each other, and once this show was established and we were established as a group, we worked so well together. We knew what the other's reactions were going to be, and we felt at ease personally with each other. For instance we'd come to work in the morning and we wouldn't get down to the first reading for an hour. We'd be sitting around with danish and coffee jabbering and having a marvelous time. And I mention it only because it is this kind of intimate relationship with the other actors...that allowed you a tremendous inner freedom, a relaxation, a feeling of comfort. There was no tension at all.[78]

Dehner further recalled that suggestions from the actors regarding the program were welcomed. Some even did research out of an interest in the West. "I still have in my library a number of books dealing with United States history in and around Dodge City and Western Kansas and Eastern Colorado," he stated. "None of us could have written like John Meston, or the other writers, but if there was a detail that was inaccurate or a period of time...that was not painted we would all say, 'No, that is not right.' And we weren't above bringing some of our reference books in and saying, 'Look...I'm right.'"[79]

George Walsh recently commented, "I felt ashamed to take money for it because I enjoyed it so much. It was a wonderful experience...it was a very special time as we sat around the table and started the reading of each program."

The experiences of the radio cast and staff had been so rich that each participant was forever marked by it. Few of them suspected while working on *Gunsmoke* that they were creating a part of history. Reflecting on it years later confirmed for them that it was not just the momentary flush of success that had colored their perspective, but that indeed, *Gunsmoke* was meeting the test of time.

The Lights Fade

It is difficult for us today to imagine how vibrant and creative a medium radio was during its Golden Age from the 1930s to the 1950s. Today, when most stations are dominated by disc jockeys spinning records and by talk shows, we are hard put to imagine the great diversity of programs that were aired and the enthusiasm with which these programs were received. Since so much was left to the imagination, there was an exciting element to radio that cannot be replaced by television. Parley Baer was intrigued by its possibilities. He felt that, "It was the ideal medium for both the performer and

Radio — The Pioneers

the auditor. If there were ten million people listening, you were giving ten million performances." He recalls that Hans Conried once said, "Wouldn't it be wonderful if radio was coming in and television was on its way out."

In an interview, only a few years prior to his death, Macdonnell noted that radio as an art form was not being used to its true fulfillment today. He indicated that radio drama was being overlooked and was a neglected "orphan," and he had hopes of resurrecting his beloved medium. He felt that even in today's environment radio could serve as a way of giving newcomers in the acting, directing and writing fields the opportunity to perfect their crafts. Macdonnell found that because of the terrible expense of doing television shows producers and executives are understandably reluctant to take chances on new faces or scripts. They are fearful of playing a hunch and there is less opportunity to explore and experiment. Radio on the other hand, was a fertile arena in which experimentation was frequently encouraged. It is perhaps Macdonnell who has provided the most fitting obituary for radio when he stated:

> I would truly enjoy going back to the old days of being completely involved in radio. There was a marvelous feeling which doesn't exist anymore...The marvelous feeling of going home after you'd finished your day's work, and indeed, finished your program and sitting down and saying, "Boy, I like what happened today. I liked the show we did. I feel good about it." And being able to sit there sometimes if it was taped delay, and hear your own show...No committees, no groups, you as the director handled the music, and the sound, and the announcer, and the cast, and you were completely involved...You worked in a control booth with your assistant director to your right and your engineer to your left and you had earphones set up so you could talk while the show was on the air...to the sound men or to Rex Koury...If you wanted to enlarge, or slow down or speed up even while on the air, this could be done because every unit of the show could hear what you wanted to do. When the show was off the air at 29:30 you left with a feeling that you had done something quite special...It had been done over a course of six or eight hours from conception to completion. It was a very satisfying way to work with a minimal crew. The engineer put it all together with some 8–10 mikes servicing the show...The beauty, of course, was that the next morning you got up and started on the script for the following day, or two days later, or five days later. And you were starting a whole new world all over again, which you wanted to deliver in three days and had to be confined to 29 minutes and 30 seconds. Now this, I think, was the beauty of radio. Each member of the audience, however big or small, had a chance to exercise his own imagination, and to draw his own pictures and add it to what he heard. Bill Robson said that, "America may well have forgotten how to listen," and I think this well might be true. So many of us are apt to sit in front of the television set, whether we really absorb anything or

not...And we sit and we watch. In radio, which has been called the "theater of the mind," your imagination worked and drew for you whatever pictures you wanted. The theater of the mind has been dark for nearly fifteen years now, and I think perhaps it is time somebody turned the lights up again.[80]

TELEVISION: THE NEW FRONTIER

Transition to Television

On August 11, 1955, Hubbell Robinson, Jr., vice-president in charge of network programs for CBS Television Network announced that the acclaimed radio program would be dramatized on television. The show would be aired from 10:00 p.m. to 10:30 p.m. EDT, and would be sponsored by Liggett & Myers Tobacco Company for Chesterfield Cigarettes.

On Saturday, September 10, 1955, *Gunsmoke* made its debut, as people turned their sets on expecting to see but one more "run-of-the-mill" Western. A hero dressed in white, would stand in relief in the sunlight, with his six-shooters blazing, and would earn the audience's admiration by rescuing some pure and innocent maiden from a moustachioed scoundrel dressed in black. His pearly white teeth would glisten and his hair would remain unruffled as he administered justice to the outlaw. There would probably be a wise-cracking sidekick, an old-timer with a quick draw and a mouth full of chewing tobacco, and a noble horse unequalled in this world or the next.

The followers of the radio program already knew what not to expect, but the vast majority of television viewers were shocked. Instead of the hero saving the day, Matt Dillon was gunned down. He was left lying in the dusty streets of Dodge ministered to by a cheap dance hall girl and a seedy-looking doctor, while his crippled deputy stood by. A far cry from the fairytale Westerns the public had been used to. Dillon was human and three dimensional, and the audience gravitated to his vulnerable character. The dance hall girl — a fallen woman — was wise, loving, and beautiful. The crotchety doctor may not be able to save every patient, but he was sincere and caring. And the faithful, gamey-legged deputy would risk his life to defend his friends.

Gunsmoke debuted during the "Golden Age" of television when it was dominated by programs featuring live dramas and anthology programming as well as by various comedians hosting their own variety shows. Another "adult Western," *The Life and Legend of Wyatt Earp,* starring Hugh O'Brian, aired the same year. This was a time characterized by a creative surge perhaps unequalled in television history. It was also a period when shows were becoming too expensive for one advertiser to produce, and networks started to assume the dominant role in production.

The Regime of Charles Marquis Warren

When the decision was made to transfer *Gunsmoke* to television, William Paley once again turned to Harry Ackerman to direct the venture. One would have thought that Macdonnell and Meston would have been given the responsibility of re-creating the program on television. After all, it was their creation and Macdonnell was greatly respected for his accomplishments on radio. The executives at CBS, however, did not feel that this was sufficient credit for television and the job was given to Charles Marquis Warren. Warren had impressive credentials in directing films, especially Westerns.

Warren was born in Baltimore, Maryland, on December 16, 1912, and was the son of a real estate broker. He attended Baltimore High School where he distinguished himself in football and was a star athlete at Baltimore City College where he developed an interest in writing. While still in college, he wrote a play, *No Sun, No Moon,* which was produced at Princeton. When M-G-M took an option on the play in 1933, Warren decided to go to Hollywood. He landed a job at M-G-M as a staff writer, a position he received when F. Scott Fitzgerald, his godfather, intervened on his behalf. He worked on the script for *Mutiny on the Bounty,* starring Clark Gable and Charles Laughton, after which M-G-M "loaned" him out to RKO where he collaborated on the Fred Astaire-Ginger Rogers musical, *Top Hat.*

Warren left Hollywood for a time and went to New York, where he wrote pulp fiction for various magazines and ultimately for the *Saturday Evening Post.* Two of his serials were published as books and became best sellers. During World War II he joined the Navy and was wounded. While recovering in Guadalcanal, he learned that Warner Bros. had purchased the screen rights to his novel, *Only the Valiant.* After he was discharged, he returned to Hollywood and became a successful writer and director of Westerns.

Warren's works include *Only the Valiant* (1950) with Gregory Peck, *Beyond Glory* (1948) with Alan Ladd, *Streets of Laredo* (1949) with William Holden, and *Springfield Rifle* (1952) with Gary Cooper. He was the writer and director of *Little Big Horn* (1951), after which he formed the Commander Films Corporation, which produced *Hellgate* in 1952, a movie that featured James Arness. Warren then went to work at Paramount writing the screenplay for

Television — The New Frontier

Pony Express (1953), featuring Charlton Heston and Forrest Tucker. Also in 1953, Warren wrote and directed *Arrowhead* (1953) with Charlton Heston and Jack Palance. One of the actors in this movie was Milburn Stone, who would later become Doc on television. Warren also wrote and directed *Flight to Tangier* in 1953. For Allied Artists he directed *Seven Angry Men* (1955) with Raymond Massey, in which Dennis Weaver, television's Chester, had a prominent part.

The decision at CBS to hand the reins over to Warren was a difficult one but it made sense. Here was a man with tremendous experience in Westerns, while Macdonnell had no experience at all in films. Warren approached the project with a fresh vision. He felt little commitment to the radio cast or the creators of the radio show. Macdonnell, on the other hand, was fiercely loyal to his cast and staff and could not have made the crucial decisions regarding casting that Warren ultimately made. When Warren was first given the opportunity to bring *Gunsmoke* to television, he was reluctant to take it. Television was in its infancy and those in film tended to look on the new medium with disdain. "When I started shooting *Gunsmoke* I didn't even have a television," Warren explained in a recent interview. "We looked down on television ... and we wouldn't even spit on radio." He went on to elaborate further:

> John Wayne lived near me and we met at his bar and sat around reviling television. He hated TV and I hated TV. Tiny little motion pictures. What is that? We thought it had something to do with the telephone. The budgets were ridiculous. When I first started, *Gunsmoke* cost $25,000 an episode, and that included everything, even the salaries. I was doing big budget films for one to two million. Television? What is this upstart? We despised it. It was a threat to us but we didn't understand that.

CBS was persistent, however, and it made Warren an offer he found difficult to turn down. They wooed him away from Paramount and when Warren confided in John Wayne, "the Duke" warned him without mincing words: "Look, you bastard, don't sell out. Don't go into TV." The offer, however, was irresistible and as Warren explained to Wayne, "They offered me $7000 a week." He recalls that "at that time even John Wayne had to look around for that kind of money."

Warren accepted CBS' generous offer and a new chapter in *Gunsmoke's* history was to be written. Macdonnell was made associate producer of the television show at the same time that he continued to produce and direct the radio program. This gave CBS the unique opportunity of producing the radio and television programs concurrently.

The two producers never developed a working relationship. While Warren found that Macdonnell "was very handsome, with a wonderful sense of humor," he couldn't stand him. "I never allowed him on the set," he recalls.

I felt his resentment. You couldn't blame him. He must have thought, "I'm the guy that put this together with Meston and Ackerman." And he did. And he thought, rightly so, that he knew the characters. After all, he had invented them, and I changed them. Maybe it was pure vanity. I changed them, saying, "I'm going to put my mark on it. Make it mine. After all, why did they hire me?"...I felt his resentment, and I resented him back. I wasn't big enough to take him for a drink and say, "What can I do for you? Let's work this out."...I'm glad he produced it later on after I left. I'm really glad. That makes me happy.

Warren immersed himself in the project with enthusiasm and was both the director and producer of the first 26 episodes. He is the one who visually conjured the "Babylon of the West." He created its saloons, boardwalks, and jail. He brought before the audience in a concrete and material form what had been but an ephemeral place in their imagination for so many years on radio. He conjured the desolate prairies, the dust-swept plains, the lonely homesteads and ranches. Warren was painfully meticulous, and personally supervised everything from the sagebrush on the prairie to the wardrobes for his actors.

As we have seen, when *Gunsmoke* was transferred to television many campaigned for the radio cast. After all, the voices of radio's Matt, Chester, Doc and Kitty had been heard for three years throughout millions of living rooms and their following was tremendous. The show was even broadcast to G.I.s during the Korean War. It was only natural to give the radio cast the chance to remain in Dodge as it relocated to television. While these emotional sentiments were understandable, Warren hesitated. Reflecting on it years later he said:

> Who was I to argue, they had all been successful. They were all nice people, and it's tough when you like them. But they all expected to be considered automatically and I'll never understand that. Well, maybe I can. I gave them a fair chance, though. Just like all the others. I filmed their audition, then I said, "I'm not going to judge it." I sent it over to Robinson and Dozier at CBS and said, "You choose." I got back a brief message with one sentence, "We think that you have better."

Coming from a film background, Warren readily recognized that although the radio cast's voices gave life to the wonderful characters in our imaginations, their physical appearances may not be able to sustain their creations in a visual medium. Warren was a filmmaker. He sought not voices but faces. When CBS asked him to listen to the radio show he thought it was terrible. "I didn't like Bill Conrad's voice," he commented. "It was Shakespeare, not Dodge City." Conrad later said that he had been overlooked for the part because "I didn't look like Gary Cooper." Warren also found problems with the radio dialogue. "I couldn't get used to it," he stated. As a motion picture man he had difficulty relating to characters who would describe the setting and the action, when he was so used to painting this broadly with the brush of cinematography.

It seems that none of the radio actors were seriously considered for a principal role on television. In the final analysis this may have been fortunate for if the radio cast had moved on to television the radio program would most likely have folded. As it happened, the show ran an additional six years after the television series debuted.

The Search for Matt

For the plum part of Dillon, Warren auditioned many actors. He recalls,

> Raymond Burr came, who I like. But I couldn't use him because when he got out of the chair, the chair came with him. I wrote a ten page script for the audition with all the four characters...Dick Boone read but he was too ugly...Everyone at CBS had two cousins and two young actors that they wanted me to see.

A young actor named John Pickard was seriously considered; his love scene with Kitty, however, did not turn out well. Denver Pyle was also a strong candidate for Dillon, and Pyle remembers his audition with Amanda Blake and Rayford Barnes, "who played a marvelous heavy." He and Blake had rehearsed their scene and came prepared. "It was taped, and Bill Warren came down from his booth," Pyle recalls, "He was out of breath," and said, "This is it. We found them." The only thing left was to make a tape for New York and have some individuals there look at it and approve it. Then Warren took Pyle and Blake to dinner. As Pyle recalls, "Amanda and I were in heaven. We finally had a job." After dinner they went back to the studio and taped the scene again for the executives in New York. Subsequently they heard from Warren that the top brass was very happy with the test and they were invited to Warren's house that Sunday so that they could look at scripts together and select the first episode for *Gunsmoke*. When they met that Sunday, Pyle remembers Warren assuring him, "There's just one more guy we have to see. But, he won't look good because he's too tall." The "guy" turned out to be James Arness. The next Monday Pyle got a call from Warren who said "I'm sorry. They want him." Sometime later, Warren approached Pyle saying, "Listen, I want you to play a part in the first episode. In case they don't like James Arness I can say, 'Well, what about the heavy?'"

The story as to how Arness became Matt Dillon is a complicated one. He was reluctant to audition and even when he already had the part he considered backing out. Arness did not want the role because he wanted to make his mark in films, and his agent, Kurt Frings, was also less than enthusiastic.

GUNSMOKE — I. THE HISTORY

There were other film actors who also shied away from auditioning for Matt, and who considered television professional suicide. At the time, however, Arness had limited credits and had played primarily obscure roles. His one claim to fame was his portrayal of the misanthropic plant from outer space who is accidently thawed out of his tomb of ice and runs amok in the cult classic, *The Thing*.

Arness' recruitment began with a phone call. It appears that Harry Ackerman, who was integrally involved with Warren in developing the program, was contacted by a CBS associate who told him to expect a call. That afternoon the phone rang and a voice said at the other end:

> Mr. Ackerman, this is Duke Wayne. I understand you're having some problems finding a good leading man for your *Gunsmoke* television series, and I want you to know I have under personal contract a guy who is so tall and handsome that most of the male stars in town won't work with him. His name is Jim Arness, and I would appreciate your meeting with him.

As Ackerman explains:

> I'd like to say the rest is history, but it wasn't quite that easy. My programming advisor, Hal Hudson and I, did meet with Arness and offered him a screen test. What I did not know until quite recently when I spent an evening in the company of Pat Wayne (one of John's sons) is that Arness after the meeting said he didn't want to tie himself to a television series and be unavailable for movies. According to Pat, the Duke said, "This may be the best shot you'll ever have in this town. Now get your ass over to CBS and do that test for Ackerman!"

It is interesting to note that Warren probably had Arness in mind all along, having worked with him in *Hellgate* (1952). In a recent interview Arness recalled that:

> In about the fall of '54 I got a call from Charles Marquis Warren...He said that he was going to be doing *Gunsmoke* and they were starting out looking at some big name actors, and all that. But he said he had me in mind, and he said don't worry about all the stuff you read. I'll get a hold of you at the right point, and I'd like to have you come in and we'll talk it over. So he really was the first man that contacted me on it and was interested in me. Subsequently two, three, four months went by and in the interim I went and did this picture. Then I got another picture. I was down in the Bahamas making the film when they called me from CBS and asked me how soon I was getting home, because they wanted me to make a test. And then, when I did get home I really wasn't all that sure that that was what I wanted to do right at that moment. And I sort of expressed that to the network and that's when John Wayne called me in and kinda

leaned on me. He said he thought I'd be crazy not to do it. And he surely as hell turned out to be right.

At a *Gunsmoke* retrospective held in March 1988 in Los Angeles, Arness offered further insights. "I think I was... the last guy they tested," he recalled. "It was about two weeks before they were going to make the pilot... I made the test, got the part, and we were shooting... I'd say in about a week to ten days after that. It happened kind of fast." It did happen fast, but Arness needed a lot of convincing and vacillated back and forth. In a recent interview Burt Reynolds, who played blacksmith Quint Asper on *Gunsmoke,* related a story he was told by Arness about his reluctance to accept the part,

> I remember Jim telling me... he didn't want to do this show, and John Wayne was the one who talked him into doing it. Got him drunk actually... Got him smashed... and made him sign the contract. And when I came on the show Jim had made more money in that amount of time... than Wayne had made in his entire motion picture career.

So, according to Burt Reynolds, Arness was "snockered" when he signed the most important contract of his career.

Now that *Gunsmoke* was signed, sealed and delivered, all seemed well in Dodge City. However, the night before wardrobe fittings, Arness was once again having second thoughts, and was about to back out of the contract. When CBS got wind of this, William Dozier called and bluntly told Arness, "You don't know me, but I want to tell you that you are about to do something very unprofessional." Arness replied, "Something unprofessional? What's that?" Seeing that he could not argue on the phone, Dozier invited Arness to his house so as to "Pump some sunshine up his ass."[81] Exactly what was said at that meeting may never be known, but clearly, Arness heeded Dozier's advice.

These reflections should lay to rest a widely circulated myth. As this story goes, it was John Wayne who was initially offered the part of Matt Dillon by CBS over Norman Macdonnell's objections. It was felt that in the public's eye Wayne epitomized, more than any other actor, the rugged individualism of those who tamed the "Wild West." William Dozier, CBS vice president in charge of programming, was elected to talk to Wayne, and when Wayne declined the offer, he suggested Arness for the role. In a recent interview, however, Warren maintained that this story is pure fantasy:

> Some critic started the myth about Wayne, so I wrote him a long letter saying that if I had asked John Wayne to play Matt Dillon he would have broken my neck. It was never offered to him. Not that I wouldn't have loved him to do it, but one day when we were sitting at his bar I jokingly asked Wayne if he would consider doing Dillon. He turned, grabbed me by the neck, and he took this triple size martini and poured it on my head.

And yet, as a favor to me he introduced the first show. "John, no one will ever see it," I said, "and we haven't got enough money to pay you!"

Wayne, as a gesture of support for his protégé, made an unprecedented appearance on television and introduced the first episode of *Gunsmoke* with these words:

> ...I've been kicking around Hollywood a long time. I made a lot of pictures out here, all kinds. Some of them have been Westerns and that's what I'm here to tell you about tonight, a Western, a new television show called *Gunsmoke*. No, I'm not in it. I wish I were though, 'cause I think it's the best thing of its kind to come along and I hope you'll agree with me. It's honest, it's adult, it's realistic. When I first heard about the show *Gunsmoke*, I knew there was only one man to play in it, James Arness. He's a young fella, and may be new to some of you, but I've worked with him and I predict he'll be a big star. So you might as well get used to him, like you've had to get used to me. Now I'm proud to present my friend, Jim Arness, and *Gunsmoke*.

James Arness and Matt Dillon

James Arness was born "Aurness" in Minneapolis and grew up in a big frame house on the outskirts of the city. He changed the spelling of his last name in 1946. His brother, Peter Graves, also changed his name so that he would not be confused with his elder brother. Graves also became a television star, playing Mr. Phelps in *Mission: Impossible.* Arness tended to be shy as a youngster partly because of his height. At six-foot-six he towered above his friends. Coaches eyed him constantly in school as a candidate for their teams but Arness preferred noncompetitive sports. Minnehaha Creek ran through a little valley behind his house and he and his friends would float rafts during the summer and would skate on its frozen waters in the winter. "It was a real Huckleberry Finn existence," he recalled.[82] He also dreamed of becoming a boat designer and had a love of poetry. Even then he enjoyed solitude.

The young Arness was restless and skipped classes. He had a wanderlust and enjoyed hopping freight trains. "Some of my happiest memories are riding the freight in winter and summer—riding them to harvest the fields in the Dakotas or to logging camps in Idaho," he reminisced. "Railroad cops used to toss me off...but I was fascinated by the romance of the old steam engines. That's all gone now. I was part of a time that's dead now."[83] Arness was a drifter and at the age of 18 he left home. Graves once commented on his brother's adventurous spirit: "In my mind there's no question Jim would have been with Marco Polo or Lewis and Clark if he had been born in earlier times."[84] Arness confirms this, saying, "There's probably an awful lot of the old Westerner in me. If I'd been born a hundred years ago, I imagine I'd be one of the men moving West."[85] He once attributed his independence to his Norwegian heritage.

After leaving home, Arness attended Beloit University for a year but dropped out to join the Army. During World War II he was shipped overseas and landed in Anzio. Since he was the tallest man in his company, his commander ordered him to be the first one out of the landing craft and into the water so that he could gauge its depths. Two weeks later he was wounded severely in the right leg. He lay for hours while the battle raged around him. He was finally found lying in a freezing stream 18 hours later. He was placed on a stretcher but the medics accidently dropped him and he rolled down an embankment. He lay in a cast for over a year, his recovery hampered by osteomyelitis, a serious bone infection. The incident left him with a visible limp that could be seen occasionally on television. He disguised it well at first, but over the years his limp became more noticeable especially as he developed associated back problems.

In 1945 Arness was discharged from the Army and entered the University of Minnesota. He found that his "grades were lousy"[86] and it was clear that he was not cut out for the academic life. When a friend, Dick Bremicker, suggested that they pick up and go to Hollywood, Arness needed little prompting. Bremicker had a burning desire to become an actor, while Arness had a "burning desire to go someplace."[87] He had little ambition at the time and once again sought adventure. "I wasn't interested in acting," he noted, but he could also rationalize that his leg was bothering him "in the frigid winter weather."[88] And so, the future Matt Dillon quit school and was off to seek his destiny.

In California, Arness spent his days at the beach. As a "flatlander" he was fascinated with the ocean and his long and constant love affair with the Pacific Ocean began. When Bremicker joined a little theater group, Arness occasionally accompanied him to rehearsals. Finally, the director suggested that he take a part. "I didn't have anything better to do," Arness explained, "and it looked like fun, so I said, 'Yes.'"[89] Ten days after his play opened, an agent, Leon Lance "discovered" him and asked if they could meet at RKO studios the following morning. The next day Arness arrived at the studios and landed a role as one of Loretta Young's three brothers in *The Farmer's Daughter*. The other brothers were played by Lex Barker and Keith Andes. At $400 a week he was able to put away $3000 and found himself a "rich" man. "I spent like a wild man," he recalls.[90] After the show closed he decided to retire temporarily from acting and take "a well-earned" vacation. He spent the next nine months in Mexico until his money ran out and then returned to Hollywood broke but optimistic.

Arness was in for a rude awakening, however, and it took him another year and a half to land an acting job. In the meantime he took odd jobs and joined the "52-20 club." As a veteran of the War he was eligible to collect $20 a week for 52 weeks while unemployed. Finally, in 1949 he got a role in the M-G-M movie *Battleground,* directed by Dore Schary. This was followed by roles in other M-G-M features such as *The People Against O'Hara* (1951) and *Hellgate* (1952), where he met Charles Marquis Warren. Despite these successes Arness found it difficult to get roles. Leading men felt uncomfortable working with him and considered him a threat because of his height. He recalls that, "None of the leading men at the studio wanted to be in the same picture with me." Arness felt stifled and recognized that he had no future at M-G-M. As a consequence, he and the studio came to a mutual decision to part ways.

It was sometime later that one of those fortuitous meetings came about that would forever change his life. Arness was appearing in a small theater production one night and John Wayne was in the audience. The Duke, who was not intimidated by tall men, was immediately impressed with Arness and signed him to a personal contract with his production company, the Wayne-Fellows Company. This association was to last three years and led to roles in *Big Jim McLain* (1952), *Island in the Sky* (1953), *Hondo* (1954), and *The Sea Chase* (1955). He was now rated as a $1500-a-week actor. As he recalls, "I used to sit around the house until the agent called that we had a job. Then I'd go up to town and get into a suit of western clothes and make a few thousand bucks." During his best year Arness earned $30,000. He also found that in Hollywood, "You can earn good money and have a good life...and be almost completely unknown."[91] All told, Arness made about 20 films during eight years before he got a chance to play Matt Dillon. At the time he was virtually unknown, except for the role he had played in *The Thing* (1951) for which he was "loaned out" to RKO. At the age of 31, however, he suddenly became a television star.

He soon found, however, that it was not enough to land the part of Matt. "I was suddenly faced with having to come up with a performance," he notes. "And that turned out to be something more than I had really anticipated.... To try and really stand up in front of a camera and try to make this a believable character.... It turned out to be a heck of a hard job and I wanted to get all the help I could." For help Arness turned to the radio shows. "I went over many of those shows and tried to get the feeling of the character as much as I could," he recalls.

> And of course listening to the old radio shows was tremendously helpful in establishing the feel of the guy and so forth...Norman Macdonnell and John Meston were right there on hand and we spoke practically on a daily basis in the first year or two. We spent many an evening over a glass of beer after work talking about the characters and going through that sort of creative process...

Conrad's Matt was a hard act to follow. In an early interview Arness stated, "I'm well aware of the mental image that many listeners have of Matt Dillon through Bill Conrad's voice. I don't intend to change it."[92] Ultimately, however, Arness did change the character and created a distinctive and classic portrayal.

The work schedule in the early years of *Gunsmoke* was gruelling. Every four days a half-hour episode was filmed. Matt was the central character and most stories revolved around him or his presence was required in most of the scenes. Arness put in ten to fourteen hours a day during that period and carried much of the acting load. This would go on for nine months each season and would be followed by a brief hiatus before filming would commence again. Eventually, Arness asked for more time away from the set. As his influence grew the shooting schedule was tailored more and more to his schedule. He once told Macdonnell, "If we can't schedule it this way, let's forget the whole thing. I'm going to have some time with my children. Period."[93]

With time there also developed an interesting struggle within Arness. Intellectually, he was committed to Meston and Macdonnell's original vision that Matt must never become a superhero and that he must remain vulnerable. Emotionally, however, the actor could be insecure and insisted that Matt be infallible. At one point Amanda Blake commented that, "He didn't want Matt to make a mistake. It certainly didn't hurt the show but I remember thinking sometimes, 'Why doesn't he let Matt be wrong once?'"[94] Arness had his own ideas as to how Matt should be portrayed and sometimes there were arguments. With time he also stopped doing promotional activities. The other primary characters came to shoulder more of the acting burden and specific episodes were written for Stone, Weaver, and Blake. While in the beginning most of the shows centered around Matt, later he became less visible although he always remained the main character. Initially, he was involved in most of the primary conflicts while later he would sometimes be returning from Hayes City at the end of the episode to witness what had occurred. During the Mantley years there were even occasional episodes that did not include Matt. But even in these stories the strong presence of the Marshal of Dodge City was palpable.

Commenting on these changes, Arness observes that:

> It certainly had my support all the way. Just from a personal standpoint, after so many years of being right up front and being most visible throughout each episode, I felt that it could be overdone. You over stay your welcome... I felt that he [Matt] should be de-emphasized and used a little less so that we don't run out of steam... My feeling was that that would help to give it longevity. And besides I had other things in my life that I was doing. If I could get a little time off here and there I thought

it was great. And it gave the producers more leeway to get out into other story areas and characters. And as it turned out, it couldn't possibly have been better. I mean that's unquestionably one of the factors that led to the longevity of the show.

Despite this trend, every season for 20 years there were always episodes that featured Arness. Fortunately for the writers and directors all of the principals were strong actors and could carry any episode.

Arness took advantage of his well-earned leisure time. He became an excellent surfer, rifle-shot, skier, and sailor. At one time he had a log cabin in Mammoth, California, and would fly there in his two-engine Beechcraft that he named "The Red Baron." And there he would ski, hike or ride horseback. He also liked to fly down to Baja California and land on some deserted beach and spend days away from civilization and *Gunsmoke*. Arness never lost his love for the ocean. He constantly sought to get away from what he has considered to be the "ecological disaster" of Los Angeles. He has commented that: "The greatest spiritual cleansing I can imagine is to dive into a big surf. Getting into the clean salt water, away from affectation, away from the mixed-up world, and coming to grips with the elements...."[95]

As an actor, Arness has been greatly underrated. He never received an award from the Academy of Television Arts and Sciences and has been taken for granted despite the fact that he developed one of the few timeless characters on television. He did this year after year for two decades and matured in front of the audience as few actors have. But Hollywood stopped watching *Gunsmoke* after the first several years. Familiarity bred a kind of contempt. There was also resentment because he kept a low profile and did no politicking with the public or the press and shunned publicity and popularity. Many could never understand this reticence and reacted personally. Milburn Stone understood and explained that Arness did not "take himself too seriously."[96] Macdonnell commented that: "Jim has never held court as many actors do. There never has been an admiring throng... He'd much rather go to his dressing room and lie down and talk to one of the guys. All he wants is to do the show and get away."[97] One friend reflected that Arness' attitude to acting was, "I'm an actor. I play Matt Dillon. I play Matt Dillon to the very best of my ability." This same friend commented that Arness had a "meat and potatoes attitude" toward acting and "attached no great glamor to it."[98]

In reflecting on his approach to acting and on his early years with *Gunsmoke*, Arness recently stated:

> When I started out in this thing, the way I remembered it is that it controlled me a lot more than I controlled it. In other words, I stepped into this thing and boy, from the time we pressed the start button everything happened so fast. It felt literally like I was being just pulled along at breakneck pace there, just to learn the scenes for the next day's work so I knew

my lines and all. As Spencer Tracy used to say, "I try not to bump into the furniture." I had a heck of a time being ahead of this. I didn't have too much time for that backward reflection really, into the more subtle aspects of the characters. But I think that what did happen was, which I also happen to believe is true with any really good series, is that the actors became this group, where the actors themselves become the characters, and there's a commingling of the personal and the characters. And there's also the family interrelationship thing that exists there, and that chemistry which is a subtle thing but it's vital and it shows. You know, every series has a sort of an inner group or family of central characters, and when those characters gel with the personalities of the actors, if it really comes together you have a series. And if it doesn't come together you don't have a series irregardless of the stories, or the production, or the advertising. All of that means nothing unless the really indefinable chemistry of the people gels. And I think in the case of our show that happened pretty rapidly. Then you have to factor in that they had done it so long on radio that the characters just stepped fully alive right off the page and jumped at you. And then of course, once we got established in people's minds in the living room there, they took us in as their family. Every week you became a sort of guest in their home for that particular night. That's the way I see it. And once they bought the chemistry, then we were really off to the races.

Milburn Stone was convinced that if Arness had been "any other kind of actor the show wouldn't have lasted two years." Stone was also one of the most exacting actors and took his profession very seriously. In some ways he functioned as the conscience of the show and always spoke up for integrity in acting and consistency in characterization. At first, he did not get along well with Arness. There was a significant age difference and Stone found that, "In the beginning Jim was always late and didn't know his lines. He made funny noises with his guns—like a kid. I didn't think he was professional." Yet he also recalled that, "One time I started in on him really screaming and yelling...in a 15-minute tirade." Afterwards, Stone expected that Arness would throw him across the set. After a long silence, however, Arness merely replied, "You're absolutely right," and walked away.[99] As the years passed, Arness became "professional." Vincent McEveety, a director in the later years, called him "the most professional man I've ever worked with."[100] Directors learned to trust his judgment regarding his character and lines. He would sometimes edit down a long speech to a few words when it seemed appropriate. After all, Dillon was a man of action, not words. John Mantley, *Gunsmoke's* producer during its final decade, recalls a lesson that he learned from Arness early on. Mantley started as story consultant on *Gunsmoke* and one of his first assignments was to write in a scene. He recalls:

> I was asked to write a thing where Jim was talking to two desperados and he had to break these guys down to get them to confess... But he was not allowed to brutalize them physically. It was a scene I would normally knock out in 20 minutes, but I worked on that scene for two days. I polished everything. There wasn't a word out of place, and it built beautifully. When I finished I said, "O.K., that's a scene that you can be proud of. That's the first scene that you've ever written on *Gunsmoke* and it's going to blow the audience away." I knew when they were shooting it, and I went down to the set. And Jim read it over and he didn't even read it again and he said, "Well, I don't know why I need all this crap! Why don't I just say, 'Hold it!'" And he was absolutely right.

With regard to his portrayal of Matt, many have tried to understand Arness' success, and to explain why Matt became a mythic character. A character that despite the intervening years still comes across as a timeless portrayal of a man who embodies our most basic ethical precepts. Macdonnell found that "One of the big factors with Jim is an innate honesty that comes through."[101] The audience sensed this honesty, but where Arness begins and ends, and where Matt begins and ends is difficult to say. Matt was witness to great injustices. He was also forced to kill in the name of a greater good, a good that must have sometimes seemed to him elusive. He worked hard and was world-weary. Each confrontation and hardship left its mark on his face, a face that became a map to a difficult life devoted to upholding some dimly visualized justice and law that had to be carved out of Meston's existential void.

Matt was devoted to his fellow men despite the fact that he was often shunned and alienated. There was a strength and at the same time an innocence to Matt Dillon that the audience responded to. One British journalist described him as being "more trigger-sorry than trigger-happy." Actor-director Victor French found that Matt "never had to be fast on the draw. There could be ten men facing him, yet when he says, 'Hold it right there!' Things just stop." Director Ted Post also tried to explain. He stated that:

> This guy's long suit as an actor is the compassion that comes out in the poignant look that I call "Weltschmertz"—world pain. Gary Cooper had it. So did Bogart and Spencer Tracy. Jimmy Stewart and Fonda have it. So has Arness, and he doesn't even know it.[102]

Arness explained more modestly that:

> Matt Dillon was... a guy who not only had to see that the laws were carried out, but had to live by them himself. He had to do the right thing. As a consequence, he always had to hold his own personal feelings or desires in restraint.[103]

It was Stone who ultimately gave Arness his greatest tribute, all the more significant for as we have seen he "spent the first two years on *Gunsmoke* despising" Arness' lack of professionalism. The unsparing Doc Adams conferred his highest accolade when he said that Arness' acting had "reached classical proportions."[104] Despite this, Arness quietly devoted two decades of his live to *Gunsmoke* and never sought to play Hamlet or King Lear. He did not feel the need to venture out into other roles and explained:

> You know, sometimes somebody would say, "My God, year after year the same character!" I never felt that at all. I never really had any desire to rush out on my time off to try to do something else...a lot of actors do that. They can't hardly wait to get out and do some other characters, like they don't like the one they're doing. I never had any feeling of that whatsoever...To me it was a joy playing the role all the way from beginning to end. It was fun.

Dennis Weaver and Chester

When the time came to cast Chester, Warren already had Dennis Weaver in mind, having worked with him in *Seven Angry Men* (1954). Raymond Massey played John Brown, and Weaver played John Brown, Jr., in this feature. "I had done a motion picture with Charles Marquis Warren...three or four months earlier," Weaver recalls. Warren saw something and as Weaver explains, "That made him think that I could be a candidate for Chester...So when I heard they were doing a Western at CBS, I contacted him." Warren asked him to come up and read and as Weaver recalls:

> I read, and after I read he said, "That's good. I would like to test you." And so I tested, and after he saw the test I guess he compared it to the other candidates, and he gave me the part...But I must say, that the first time I read for him, I didn't read with any kind of accent. I didn't use the Chester drawl at all...but my normal speech, which had of course, some mid-Western to it. But it wasn't a heavy "Chester," and I could tell he was a little disappointed...He said, "I was hoping we could get some humor out of the character." When he said that, I remembered that at the University of Oklahoma I used to have a lot of fun at parties doing this dialect, so I said, "Well, let me go out in the hallway, and I'll take another approach to it. If you don't mind, just let me read it once more." And he said, "Fine." Then I came back in and I gave it the "Chester" thang and he jest fell right thar on the floor.

Weaver was the first principal actor to be signed for *Gunsmoke*. The future Chester started acting in Joplin, Missouri, as a boy. He was encouraged by his friend, George Hogroff, who was the local mailman. When he started to take dancing lessons Hogroff built him a plywood base to practice on. His father's involvement in community theater also served to nurture his budding interest in acting. In high school he concentrated on drama and was an accomplished football player, and track and field star. He won a scholarship to Joplin Junior College but was called into the Navy after a year. As a member of the naval track and field team he set various records. After his discharge he went to Oklahoma University to major in drama where he was also a track star and led his team to a Big Six Championship in the two-mile run. Later on he won the Colorado Relays Septathon Championship and after graduating with honors tried out for the Olympic decathlon. He beat Bob Mathias in the 1500-meter run but failed in the over-all competitions. When he was accepted by the Actor's Studio he gave himself over to acting and ended his athletic career. It was there that Shelley Winters apparently discovered him and got him a screen test at Universal International which led to a film contract. During the early 50s Weaver made approximately 19 films prior to his role on *Gunsmoke*. These included *The Lawless Breed* (1952), *The Mississippi Gambler* (1953), *Dangerous Mission* (1954), *Storm Fear* and *Ten Wanted Men* (1955).

There were many who cautioned Warren against casting Weaver opposite Arness for Weaver was six-foot-four. "Everyone warned me that the audience would sympathize with the heavies," he recalls, "If I cast these two brutes, and that made sense." In characteristic fashion, however, Warren followed his own instincts and cast the two giants.

When Warren was first fine tuning the character of Chester he hit upon the idea that he must be given some infirmity. He especially felt that this was necessary because Chester was constantly hanging around Matt and the jail and there had to be some explanation as to why he was so sedentary. "That's why we gave Chester a limp," Warren explains. "This way he wasn't much help." Knowing this could be a delicate situation, Warren waited for the right time to suggest the idea to Weaver and the moment came when they were in the Fairfax Bar across from CBS having martinis. This was before Weaver became a teetotaller. After the fourth drink Warren sprung his idea. He told Weaver that he was bothered by the fact that a healthy looking young man was nothing but "a hanger-on." Could he possibly be crippled? Warren recalls Weaver's response. "He argued, and I didn't blame him. No actor wants to go around and limp all the time. I didn't blame him at all, and I told him so. I said, 'If you can't do it, I understand. We can get someone else.' So he went and did it. . ." They apparently practiced the limp until they were thrown out of the bar. Then they continued to practice in the street until a squad car pulled up. Weaver's recollection of that fateful night is somewhat different and one gets conflicting details depending on who tells the story:

> I actually got the part without using the stiff leg. It was after I had been cast that the director came to me and wondered if I would think about giving Chester a handicap...And I thought about it...And I thought it

would work very well for the character's relationship with the other people... So I came up with the specific handicap of the stiff leg.

Chester became extremely popular and was something of a cult figure. Fans were constantly inquiring after his health, especially of Stone. Warren tells the story that on one occasion Chester forgot to limp and no one noticed this during the filming or editing of the episode. However, "a million viewers spotted it" and Warren received countless letters saying, "Thank God Chester is cured."

In reality, Chester was almost cured after the first episode. Although Paley was very pleased with the characters, he had one objection. "The only critical comment that he made," Ackerman notes, "Is that Chester limped." Paley told Ackerman that he wanted this taken out of the show. "But I didn't tell anybody," Ackerman recalls, "And I took a chance because I had the feeling that it was good. It became the hallmark of the series, and he never said another word about it."

In creating Chester, Weaver explains:

> I drew from my own background, my relatives, and my experience with people that I knew from Oklahoma, from Arkansas, and from Missouri. I really didn't do any extensive background work on the character. I just took what was on the printed page and tried to make the given circumstances in the script reality to me.

He found that Chester changed little over time except that Weaver himself became "a little easier with him" and that this "process maybe softened him a little bit as far as his accent was concerned." He also felt that Chester's "country bumpkin" element diminished with time. When asked if he was influenced at all by Parley Baer's portrayal of Chester on radio, Weaver noted that he "never heard the radio show" and "intentionally did not listen to it" so that he would not be influenced or imitate it. He felt that it "was a very dangerous trap for an actor to imitate someone." For television, his character's name was changed from Chester Wesley Proudfoot to Chester B. Goode. "I know that the reason that they wanted it changed is because it sounded to many people as though it were an Indian name, although Proudfoot is actually an old English name," Weaver recalls. In radio, where the audience "could imagine whatever they wanted to imagine, this did not make any difference." As Weaver explains, "On television when they saw my face some people might say, 'Well, what's his name Proudfoot for? He's not an Indian.'"

Parley Baer also relates a story regarding the reason for changing Chester's name. He explains:

> I was told that one of the officials at CBS said, "We'd better change his name because Parley might have cause for a plagiarism suit." And I saw

> this man in the lobby of the station one day, and I said, "I trust CBS, even though CBS apparently doesn't trust me." They changed his name because they were afraid I would kick up a fuss. What I really should have kicked up a fuss about, as well as Bill, and Howard, and everybody else is, for the first 156 shows they used radio scripts for the television thing almost in toto. And it was a little irritating to hear lines that you'd written, and hear your own ad libs incorporated into the television series. But why joust at windmills?[105]

With regard to Chester's relationship with the other characters Weaver observed that as far as Matt was concerned Chester was "very loyal." Chester felt that "Matt Dillon was the most heroic of people. He idolized him. He was the person that he followed... Matt in his view could do no wrong. Chester was like a puppy dog."

> To Chester, Kitty was somebody that was far out of his reach. He idolized her and had a terrible crush on her, but always from a distance. He just assumed that the fantasy could never materialize. He had great respect for ladies in general... But especially where Miss Kitty was concerned.

With regard to Doc:

> Doc was a thorn in his side in many ways. And he was a little bit jealous of his knowledge and his ability and everything. He just felt that Doc thought he knew more than he really did.

In 1959 Weaver won the Emmy Award for Best Supporting Actor in a Dramatic Series. Despite his great success, however, he was restless and ultimately left the show. He got tired of limping through scene after scene in a part that did not afford him sufficient opportunity to grow as an actor. He tried to leave twice but returned when his projects faltered. He succeeded the third time, however, and left after the ninth season. One of the reasons that Weaver finally left the show was his concern that the longer he stayed with the program the more difficult it would be for him to escape. He recently reflected:

> I felt that if I stayed with it much longer I would have major problems. I recognized that I was doing a very unique character, and that Hollywood had a tendency to typecast and pigeonhole people.

To minimize this, Weaver took various acting jobs during breaks and was careful to "never repeat Chester's character any place else." He would do roles that were "totally different so that the directors and producers would realize that I was an actor that had created a character and that I was not just that character." During these years Macdonnell was sensitive to Weaver's restlessness and tried his best to accommodate him. He was even given the opportunity to direct four *Gunsmoke* episodes; he demonstrated a real flair for it. One of Weaver's favorite episodes is *Marry Me,* a story that he directed. When Weaver left *Gunsmoke* for the last time in 1964, his character was replaced by Festus as portrayed by Ken Curtis. Reflecting on his departure he noted:

> *Gunsmoke* certainly survived 11 years after I left. So that speaks very well for the people that were doing the show at the time. I know that I created a very popular character and people really loved that character, and I would assume that they were somewhat disappointed when I left. But it didn't hurt the ratings particularly.

He did not feel that his departure affected the program to any significant degree although not everyone would agree with his assessment, least of all *TV Guide's* Cleveland Amory, who wrote Chester's poignant eulogy. Amory wrote:

> ...we come to the question of Chester. We have done our best to be philosophical about his departure, and we've tried to make friends with the new-un (we love Burt Reynolds as Quint, and we are growing fond of Festus) but that cold day when Chester gimped off into that settin' sun for Good—Well, it was hard, pard, hard.[106]

Commenting on Weaver's departure, Arness observed:

> I understood that Dennis wanted to move on to other things so I didn't question it at all. He played the heck out of his character for a number of years, and of course he's an exceptionally talented actor. That's why that character came off as tremedously as it did. They loved that character. But he got to a point... where he really did have a desire to get out and try some different things. And I completely understood that. So I didn't have any hesitancy about his moving on. I would have preferred to see him stay myself... because when you have something that good you don't like to see anybody upset the apple cart. But on the other hand, I certainly sympathized with his position and understood it.

Given the tremendous popularity of Chester it speaks to Weaver's talents that he was able to transcend his hobbling shadow. After *Gunsmoke* he went on to create many characters and was the star of *Kentucky Jones* (1964–65), *Gentle Ben* (1967–69), *McCloud* (1970–77) and *Buck James* (1987–88). He never again returned to *Gunsmoke,* although it is said that there was a time when Weaver's agent called to ask if he could return as a guest but the details could not be ironed out. It is always difficult to come home again, but years later, reflecting on his experience with *Gunsmoke* Weaver stated, "It was just a wonderful time... a period in my career which is very, very special to me."

Over the years, Weaver has become a versatile star and has accumulated many credits since he walked off the set of *Gunsmoke* 25 years ago. *Gunsmoke* aficionados, however, would probably agree with Milburn Stone's final volley as Weaver left the show for the last time: "Dennis is a brilliant actor. But he's Chester and, whether he knows it or not, he'll always be Chester."[107]

Milburn Stone and Doc Adams

For the role of Doc Adams, Warren remembered Milburn Stone. They had met on the set of *Arrowhead* (1953) and two years later Warren called Stone in to read. The two had little affection for one another and as Warren explains, "I hated him...[but] damn, he was good." He found that when Stone "...read for Doc, he was the best. And so I sat him down and I said, 'I know you don't like me, and you know I don't like you. But you can do it. I want you to do it.'" Warren "was actually hoping" Stone would say, "No," for he "already had a backup, but he took it..." Elaborating on their relationship Warren explains, "I always went with my actors to wardrobe but I wouldn't go with him. I said, 'You go and pick it out, and you'll look awful in it.' And he went to wardrobe and got himself a jacket, a hat, and stethoscope and he looked great. He made it work."

Stone spent days searching for his outfit in the Western Costume storerooms. He felt that the vest was the most important part of his outfit. Doc would use it to hold his glasses, watch and thermometer. He wanted Doc to look like "nobody paid him, or at least like he was just barely existing." Stone felt that Doc "probably never sent a bill" and "wanted his clothes to show they'd been worn a long time."[108] When Stone was first cast as Doc, Warren asked that his hair be dyed gray and that a moustache be painted on. With time, Stone grew his own moustache and mother nature took care of the rest.

Milburn Stone was born on July 5, 1904, in Burton, Kansas. He grew up in Fort Larned, 50 miles from Dodge. His uncle was Fred Stone, who was a star in his day on Broadway. Stone patterned much of Doc's character after the family doctor of his youth, Doc Hampstead. Stone recalled that the "real" Doc wore a battered black hat and baggy pants. He had dusty old clothes and a shoestring tie. He also interjected some of his grandfather's personality. Joe Stone was apparently a "cantankerous old guy with a great sense of humor ... who loved to tease people."[109] Stone also took note of his grandfather's stooped walk and "brevity of speech."[110] Milburn Stone started his acting career with a three-person tent show in Kansas. He was 18 at the time and earned $35 a week.

Later on, Stone developed a vaudeville act with Smokey Strain called "Stone and Strain" and sang and danced for a living in Denver. Appearing in blazers and straw hats the duo made appearances on KLZ radio and played various theatres in town. In 1932 when the Depression was at its height, a Denver restaurant chain announced that it would tear up the check of any customer who found one of their 24-hour restaurants empty of customers. Stone and his partner took up the challenge and spent many hours trudging from restaurant to restaurant, but they never did get their free meal. During Prohibition he worked Al Capone's speakeasies. On Broadway he was in two short-lived plays, *The Jayhawkers* and *Around the Corner*. The two plays ran for 24 and 16 performances respectively. It was clear that he might starve if he stayed in New York and decided to go to Hollywood.

Stone appeared in over 250 films before he landed the role that was to make him famous. His first movie was *Ladies Crave Excitement* in 1934. He played the villain astride a black horse in at least 100 B Westerns. The closest he ever got to playing a doctor was in the movie *Gung Ho!* (1943), in which he played a Navy doctor. It is evident that when he joined *Gunsmoke* he was the most seasoned of all the principal actors. Amanda Blake explained that: "He was not only Doc, but our technical advisor." Stone was a meticulous and serious actor. Clyde Ware, one of the writers, observed that he was "the consummate actor and an exceptional human being." Every gesture and phrase was wrought with exactness. He carefully developed his character, and small details like a tug at the ear or a particular tilt of the head and click of the tongue became Doc's famous trademarks. Announcer George Walsh observed:

> When Stone bent over a victim that was shot, and he shook his head from side to side, and got that corner of his mouth twitching, that guy was done. On the other hand, when he looked up at Matt and nodded in the affirmative, he was gonna make it. And that saved a page and a half of script right there.

Stone wanted his character to be authentic. He once consulted his personal physician and explained that he was about to do an episode, *Kitty Shot*, where he would have to remove a bullet from Kitty. Stone wanted to know what he should say about Kitty's condition when Matt walked through the door. In trying to explain why Doc wound up in the hinterlands, Stone conjured a fictional past for him. "He was probably a brilliant medical student," Stone reflected. "Perhaps the thing that threw him was that as a kid he was a little too much on fire and too good-looking. He got into some kind of trouble, but it had nothing to do with his medical integrity."[111]

Stone prided himself in developing a professional aura around Doc. Doc was a true healer. He was a compassionate and devoted man who would do anything for his patients including risking his life. The citizens of Dodge looked up to Doc as a "wise man." Although many of his patients did not survive his well-meaning ministrations, the townsfolk were willing to overlook his track record. Doc also enjoyed somewhat of a monopoly being the only physician within a hundred miles. Stone's Doc was quite unlike McNear's radio Doc, who was viewed by Macdonnell as "performing illegal operations in the back room of the Long Branch."[112] Writer Kathleen Hite saw Doc as a "hopeless alcoholic," and while Stone's Doc spent many a halcyon day drinking in the Long Branch, he handled his liquor well and tried to present himself as "a social drinker."

Stone fought anything that would paint Doc in an unfavorable light. It is interesting that the thin line between the actor and the character sometimes blurred. Stone once reflected that, "I never had an identity until Doc. So there was no problem losing my own."[113] He was one of the few layman ever to receive honorary membership in the Kansas Medical Society. He made many personal appearances and once told an interesting story regarding what he learned about his fans during these journeys. At first he would always be friendly and polite signing autographs and acting gracious. The fans, however, always seemed disappointed and Stone was unable to fathom their reaction, until one day in Florida someone called out, "How's Chester!" Since Doc was always snarling at Chester on the air, Stone for a gag yelled out, "Aw, shut up!"[114] This got such a laugh that he finally realized that the fans were not there to see Stone the actor but to lock rapiers with Doc. He was greatly liked and Cleveland Amory reflected, ". . . our game is chess, but we'd even give that up for a session of checkers with Doc."[115]

Of all the principals, he was the most protective of his character. He had no reluctance to suggest changes in dialogue and could be difficult with an unheeding director. He once refused to appear in a scene that he felt was out of character and supposedly told the producer, "I'm too old to scare, and too rich to care."[116] He told one interviewer, "We've had some terrible rows with directors. We won't let them tamper with the characters or the honesty of the show."[117] On one occasion, when a scene called for Doc to call Chester an idiot, Stone refused saying, "I can't call him that. Doc loves Chester too much. . . Chester might think I meant it and it would hurt him badly."[118] The lines were cut and Stone was allowed to deride Chester with a lot of "four syllable medical terms."

In 1968 he won an Emmy Award for Outstanding Performance by an Actor in a Supporting Role in Drama. He won it for the episode *Baker's Dozen,* which was originally written for Dennis Weaver in 1962 but was turned down by the producers at the time. Six years later it was approved as a vehicle for Stone and was rewritten. In the spring of 1971 he had a heart attack and was out recuperating. Pat Hingle replaced him as Dr. Chapman during this period. Chapman was supposedly invited to Dodge by Doc to fill in while he went to Johns Hopkins Medical School for a refresher course to learn new techniques. Stone returned after a 13-week absence in early 1972 and made his "debut" in the only three-part episode ever to be aired in the show's two decades. This was John Mantley's gift to his cantankerous star.

In Jim Byrnes' *Gold Train: The Bullet* Doc was called on to dig a bullet out of Matt that had lodged near his spine. It was in a critical area and surgery in the best of hands would probably be fatal or crippling. Doc's new-found expertise came in handy, however, and the operation was a success. A sign of Stone's recovery was that he once again stood up for his character during the shooting of this story. Mantley supposedly wanted Doc to hit the bottle to steady his nerves for the delicate operation, but Stone refused, saying that Doc would never jeopardize his efficiency by swilling down a few drinks.

On occasion, Stone's reputation could be used to a different effect. One day Norman Macdonnell was summoned to the set by an excited assistant director who told him that there was trouble with Milburn Stone. Expecting the worst, Macdonnell hurriedly vacated his office and rushed to the set wiping the perspiration from his brow. He had visions of the show going down the tubes and braced himself. As he arrived on the set his worst imaginings were confirmed. There was Stone standing jaw to jaw with director John Rich and they were bitterly arguing. The crew stood in stunned silence and turned to see what the hapless Macdonnell would do. Just when it seemed like the two disputants were about to come to blows, they turned to Macdonnell and started to sing "Happy Birthday."

Stone died in 1980 at the age of 75 of heart failure. His portrayal of Doc was a monumental achievement. In some ways it was his character who best summed up Meston's existential vision of the world as he cocked his head saying so many times, "I don't know. I just don't know."

Amanda Blake and Miss Kitty

Amanda Blake was cast as Kitty because of her tenaciousness and persistence. "I wasn't going to see Amanda," Warren recalls:

> ...but she sat outside my office day after day until I gave her an audition. I had wanted other actresses, but I should have known that they were a little too refined, a little too beautiful. But Amanda looked just cheap enough and tough enough to play the part. Her hair was a bit too red. She was just right. I got the message to CBS, "We found Kitty, let's make a deal."

According to Blake they had to give her the part because: "they had no choice," and she had her own recollections:

> I had been working a lot at CBS. It was back when I was doing live television. I had heard that *Gunsmoke* was going to go to television. Since I was

at CBS so much, and knew a lot of the people there I decided that this could be for me. So I talked to the casting people and they said, "We think that you'd be really good for this," so I said, "Well, what do I do now?" At the time, I was working for a show *My Favorite Husband* and they said, "We'll send the producer-director down on the set while you're here, and you can talk to him." And I said, "Fine." So I did the show but I didn't see or hear from anybody or anything. Then I went back to the casting people and said, "I never saw anybody come down. Nobody approached me about *Gunsmoke.*" To make a long story short, I couldn't get an appointment with him. He wouldn't see me. So I called my agent, but he couldn't get an appointment. I talked to the casting people again and they couldn't talk him into seeing me. I said, "What's going on here?" So after a couple of weeks of this, I thought, "God, if they're going to do a pilot and they're going to cast this thing, I better get busy and do something. This is ridiculous." I got myself all done up, and proceeded to march myself over to Warren's office at CBS, but he was not in. So I sat there, and said, "I'm going to wait until he comes in." So that's what I did. And as it turned out, he did come in and his secretary said, "There's this crazy woman sitting here, and she won't leave until she has a chance to talk to you." So he said, "Are you Amanda Blake?" And I said, "Yes." And he said, "Oh!...Well...I've had you mixed up with another one of the girls that was working on *Professional Father!* So we had a nice chat, and he brought in Norman Macdonnell and he said, "Would you be willing to do a test?" "That's why I'm here!" I said. And that's how I got the job.

Amanda Blake was born Beverly Louise Neill in Buffalo. She started her career at the age of seven in a school play. In 1950 she started at M-G-M and was billed as "the young Greer Garson." Later, she worked with Columbia but was unhappy working in what she felt were "dismal pictures." Some of her credits include *Stars in My Crown* (1950), *Smuggler's Gold* (1951), *Cattle Town* (1952), *Lili* (1953), *A Star Is Born* (1954), and *The Glass Slipper* (1955). She even had a bit part in *Battleground* in which Arness appeared as well. *Gunsmoke* made Blake a star and as she stated: "Let's face it. This show has made us all."[119] She was the first woman to be inducted into the Hall of Fame of Great Western Actors and Actresses in Oklahoma City. She was nominated for an Emmy for Best Supporting Actress (Continuing Character) in a Dramatic Series in 1959, but the award went to Barbara Hale for *Perry Mason.*

When she first got the part of Kitty, Blake sat down and tried to envision her character's background. She imagined that Kitty had been defiled at the age of 16 by some no-good rake who "broke her heart and ruined her life." Since in those days "there was little for a destitute girl to do," she could either take in the laundry or take in men. Blake decided that Kitty

> was probably from New Orleans and had worked on the river boats. She came from an unhappy background...Her father left her and she was

literally on her own... And so she just migrated West with the rest of the people and ended up in Dodge earning her way.[120]

As a fan of the radio show, Blake had no illusions about Kitty's profession. She felt that Georgia Ellis had done a wonderful job with her "whiskey voice." She also found that Ellis "could get away with a lot of stuff" on radio that she could not get away with on television. She found that CBS was "very uptight about this saloon-girl thing, even though we were being billed as the 'adult' Western." When Blake was first interviewed and was asked about Kitty's profession, she made the mistake of being honest and saying, "Why, she's a tramp." CBS was appalled and as she recalls, "I almost lost my job." The network was committed to downplaying Kitty's scarlet past and wanted to clean her up for the television program. After a while they no longer allowed the camera to show men going up the stairs at the Long Branch. Blake found that she "had to walk a very narrow line and tread between schoolmarm sweet and saloon hall tough... The guys didn't have this problem." She developed Kitty over the years, applying layer after layer to give her greater depth. Kitty was a woman in love who had to settle for much less than she wanted. There was a certain pathos to her character. She sacrificed a great deal for her love and that is one of the reasons that Doc, Chester, Festus and Newly were always protective of her. Blake found that Kathleen Hite wrote the most challenging scripts for Kitty. "Every day was a challenge." She especially enjoyed her role once Kitty became the owner of the Long Branch. "I loved being the entrepreneur," she explained. "It was a real fantasy for me." With regard to changes in her character, she found that over time:

> Kitty changed with me. As I developed and grew and got older, so did she. An actor has only one source and that's himself.... That's where it comes from when you're creating a character... But I was so comfortable with the whole thing that it just simply took care of itself, more or less. I really didn't have to fight or worry, or mess around, or try to change too much. I just let it come. I just let it evolve and happen.

Commenting on her relationship to the other characters she found that:

> Kitty and Doc was the father-daughter relationship. Kitty goes to Doc if she is having problems and gets straight answers. The relationship between Kitty and Chester, and Kitty and Festus was almost the same. They loved each other, almost like brother and sister. She was dealing here with a couple of strange characters. And Kitty would roll her eyes when Festus would get going about rats or something and blah, blah, blah. And Kitty would say, "Oh, God! Do we have to go through this thing again?"

Kitty was the first major female character to appear in a television Western series. Macdonnell commented that her role was to give "Matt someone to talk to. He can express his inner feelings to her and know he'll be understood. Because of her he takes on another dimension." He felt, however, that they "weren't in love with each other," and that there was "simply a tremendous underlying affection."[121] Blake's Kitty, however, was clearly in love with Matt. This is all the more interesting since they never kissed on the air except for an innocent peck one Christmas. Their relationship was subtly implied, one of "exquisite discretion," but the implications were clear. Macdonnell likened it to a "drawn-out strip tease. We keep hinting that there might be more there than we show."[122] Blake reflected that there were a lot of moments of what she and Arness called "eyeballing scenes." In these scenes there would be "a few subtle words or maybe a cute little thing like, 'Well, if you're not doing anything later, cowboy, why don't you come and have a nightcap?' It wasn't so much the line as the delivery, and Jim and I got very good at that."

Arness commented, "Let's face it. Kitty is a grown-up woman, and Matt's all man. Their relationship is not platonic. The extent of their relationship is up to the viewer's imagination."[123] Fans often asked why they never got married. Blake explained that Matt could not marry Kitty because "He faced death every day. He can't marry her, because he doesn't want to leave her a widow."[124]

There was always a depth of feeling that was evident between Matt and Kitty. This could be seen in various episodes as in *Hostage!,* where she is kidnapped by Jude Bonner and is abused and shot. When Matt returns he holds an overnight vigil by Kitty's bedside cradling her hand and murmuring, "I need you, Kitty." The next day when he sees that she is out of danger he takes off his badge to go after the villain. Doc warns him to do what he must but to do it within the law. Matt, however, who has devoted his life to upholding and living by the law tells a distraught Doc, "If it was anything else, Doc. Anything else."

The rich character that Blake created is the ultimate male fantasy of whore-sister-friend-mother all rolled into one. A whole generation of adolescents and their respective progenitors fantasized about Miss Kitty and longed to be initiated into manhood in her arms. Leslie Raddatz once wrote an open letter to his wife in *TV Guide,* expressing his love for Kitty/Blake.

> ...It was just one of those things—I couldn't help myself. I went out to her house on a routine interview. We had a couple of drinks...a few laughs...And before I knew it, I was in love! Frankly, I am probably just as surprised as you are. I was expecting she would be—well, older. After all, she had been hanging around that Long Branch Saloon for about 10 years now, and she was no spring chicken when *Gunsmoke* went on the air. But Amanda is actually prettier off screen than on—something you can't say about most actresses...I believe that this beautiful...woman needs

me. So, here goes — I'm going to call her now and break the news. Good-by, my best to our seven kids, Your Husband."[125]

Cleveland Amory, that perennial *Gunsmoke* fan also voiced these fantasies when he wrote, "Kitty is from birthmark to marriage threat, the girl we would most...like to be marooned on a TV set with."[126]

Like the other principals Blake was protective of Kitty. She took her cue from Stone who

> was a zealot...which was good. He was just adamant about everything. He was wonderful...We were possessive about the show. We had a property that we loved. Those of us that worked on the show loved the show. It was, "Don't mess around with Miss Kitty." Or, "Miss Kitty wouldn't say that." Or, "Chester wouldn't say that to Matt Dillon." We wanted to keep the character relationships in the right perspective and we just guarded this jealously...

It is clear that Blake greatly loved the show. She was very emotional about it. When it was temporarily cancelled, she recalled that, "I went totally to pieces." George Walsh remembers the going away party:

> They had it on the set at Paramount and I was there. And I saw Norman Macdonnell there. And Amanda Blake had already started to make arrangements to have the bar from the Long Branch Saloon shipped to her home in Arizona.

She felt at home with her coworkers and sometimes went to the set even when she was not filming to spend some time with her friends. As on the radio show, there was a nurturing environment on the set especially when Macdonnell took over after the first year. She found that:

> When they put Norman in charge it really began to blossom. It was his baby and when he grabbed the reins we all sort of relaxed. It was really a super family. Norman was very relaxed. He knew what he wanted to create.

During her years on *Gunsmoke* Blake had many wonderful experiences. She recalled one episode in particular, called *The Jailer*.

> One day the producer...called me in and said, "Amanda, come up to my office. We have something to tell you." And I thought, "Oh, God! I've been fired." When I got there they said, "We're gonna do a show called *The Jailer.*" And they told me what the plot line was and I said, "Oh, God, that sounds wonderful." And then they hit me and they said, "And Bette Davis is going to play the part." And I turned purple and said, "What? You've got to be kidding!" Well, you practically had to carry me down in a gurney. I was a basket case. I couldn't even walk I was so scared. But she was wonderful. She could tell I was nervous and she was nervous as

well, and she turned to me and said, "These first days are bitches, aren't they?" And I said, "You're so right.... They certainly are." And after that we sort of settled down...and we got along great.

Blake saw many young actors pass through Dodge, and she recalled some that especially impressed her at the time like Beau Bridges, Lee Majors, Tom Skerritt, and Loretta Swit.

In her private life Blake was always interested in conservation and maintained a passion for raising cheetahs. She made frequent trips to Kenya and East Africa and had a fascination with and commitment to animals. She called her love an "avocation" but it seemed more a passion and she devoted much of her life to animal rights and advocacy. Most recently she was involved with a desert museum in Arizona that will focus on arthropods and related fauna. "I love bats and cats, and snakes and anything," she explained. "And everybody thinks, 'God, you really are a sicko.'"

During her years on *Gunsmoke,* Blake was married and divorced several times. In later years she made her home in Phoenix, Arizona, and she had to make the long commute to Hollywood. Finally, in the nineteenth year, wearied of commuting, the surprising announcement was made that Kitty was leaving Dodge. "Nineteen years is a hell of a long time for someone to be stuck behind a bar,"[127] she explained. Arness understood. "You do get a little worn trying to repeat it every week," he stated. "She just couldn't seem to go any further with it, and we accepted that. I hated to see her leave but I understood it."

When she left in 1974, many wondered if television's longest running legend could survive. After all, Kitty had kept the characters together and was the "Earth Mother" to them all. Will Henry for the *Los Angeles Times* asked out loud the painful questions that gnawed at the vitals of all *Gunsmoke* fans:

> Will the Long Branch close? Can Marshal Dillon keep his head together? Will Festus finally fester? Will crusty old Doc take to the hard stuff...and...fall...down those damnable second story office stairs? Can anyone envision the squeaky-neat Newly as the "au courant" Matt Dillon? Will a rush message be clicked out over the telegraph key "down to the depot" for ex-deputy Chester, now Marshal McCloud, to limp back to Dodge City? Help, Chester! Forget New York and all that schlepping and slipping around on the pavement. Get shut of those asphalt canyons and come on home!...Veteran fans of Marshal Dillon and Miss Kitty fear the worst. Is a new West a-blowing in the wind? Will they run in a younger filly for Big Matt?...Is it true...That the new Miss Kitty will be a sensitive teen named Misty, pronounced Miz Misty?[128]

Now that the "flamme eternale" of "granite-loined" Dillon was gone who would take her place?

Nineteen years was a long time, however, and Blake had had it. She found herself saying more and more, "God, if I have to put that damn bustle and those curls on one more time I'm gonna snap." Staying with *Gunsmoke* had been safe. "I didn't want to find out what the outside world was like," she said. I felt, "I have my little cocoon here and I really like it." But despite this, she left after having devoted a good part of her career and life to *Gunsmoke*. After she left she had a difficult adjustment. "It was very traumatic," she recalled. "And I did a lot of crying." The Long Branch remained open, however, and as Mantley explained, "Someone has to run the Long Branch because it's such an integral part of the Dodge City scene." Fran Ryan became the new owner, Miss Hannah, and kept the famed saloon open for another year before the final cancellation. Mantley swore, though, never to bring in another Kitty, "For to replace her would be disaster."[129] Mantley truly believed that had the show continued, Blake would have returned.

After *Gunsmoke*, Blake acted in television movies, game shows, and appeared as a guest on various popular shows including *Hart to Hart, The Loveboat, The Quest,* and *Brothers*. In 1988 she was featured in the film *The Boost* which starred James Woods and Sean Young.

Kitty was the epitome of the independent woman, but unlike most other independent women of that period she was reconciled to her condition. In television and movies in the 50s and early 60s women paid a great price for their independence. They usually lost something precious, or their story ended in some tragedy. The message was clear: Those who turn their back on marriage or motherhood are punished. These social pioneers were almost always portrayed as being unhappy, whereas Kitty was content with her lot. It is true that she sometimes questioned her choices but in the final analysis she could look on her life without regret.

Kitty was as self-sufficient as Matt, and yet they supported one another. They were coequals and she was taken seriously by all the men around her. One has but to look at Sam, her loyal bartender, to see in what high regard she was held. Despite her shabby beginnings Kitty pulled herself up to become an integral member of Dodge City even though "good" women shunned her. She had strength and she was able to have a love affair without a marriage bond. And she had integrity, remaining loyal all those years without security or the assurance of a wedding band. She and Matt had a mature relationship. Kitty occasionally tries to escape and take another lover, and Matt sometimes encounters an old girlfriend, but there are no recriminations and no explanations. Kitty was beholden to no one, a life style that Blake emulated in her own private life.

Blake sometimes even lost herself in her character, and as Milburn Stone reflected, with his typical brevity, "Amanda is Kitty." Kitty was her own person at a time when it was an extremely unpopular image for a woman. A time when television was populated by dimwitted blondes, whining housewives and secretaries. A period when women were consistently portrayed as banal characters who got their way either by scheming or by giving up their independence, and when every little girl was encouraged to own a Barbie doll. Although Kitty could not escape being a sex symbol to men, to young women she was one of the few role models of a self-directing and self-reliant woman they could turn to. The most remarkable achievement of Miss Kitty is that she was way ahead of her time, for her character anticipated an entire social movement.

In 1984 President Ronald Reagan presented the annual Courage Award of the American Cancer Society to Amanda Blake. On August 16, 1989, Blake died. She was 60.

The Pilot

Having completed casting, Warren, with characteristic energy set out to write, produce and direct the pilot that was eventually sold to Ligget-Myers for Chesterfield sponsorship. The pilot was *Hack Prine,* featuring besides the regulars, Leo Gordon, George Wallace, Hal Baylor and Wally Cassell. It was adapted from a Meston radio script. Network executives, however, were jittery and requested that another episode be filmed so that they could choose between two films for the opening. The other episode was *Matt Gets It* and was also a Meston script. Featured in the guest cast were Paul Richards, Robert Anderson, Malcolm Atterbury, and Howard Culver, the same Howard Culver who was one of two actors who played "Mark Dillon" in the 1949 radio audition disc *Mark Dillon Goes to Gouge Eye.* It will be forever to the credit of network executives and the production staff that they made the decision to air the more daring episode of the two, *Matt Gets It.* It showed their new hero at his most vulnerable moment as he collapsed in the streets of Dodge bleeding from his myopic opponent's (Dan Grat's) bullet. "It was shocking in those days to have your hero shot down," Warren explains. The episode originally intended to be the premiere, *Hack Prine,* was not aired until May 12, 1956, but it has the distinction of being the film that sold the show to the sponsors.

The Title Scene

CBS originally planned that the opening title would show a smoking gun. Warren, however, insisted on a different opening. He wanted Matt standing on Boot Hill reflecting on the fates of those buried there, for this would give Matt the chance to do a little philosophizing. Warren felt that this was a "beautiful beginning" and it became the title scene for the next several years. The most famous opening scene, the one with Matt walking onto the main street of Dodge to confront his faceless nemesis, was filmed later on. Some have fondly called this the "crotch-shot" and it may be the best-known opening on television. It was first filmed in 1959 and many have wondered who Matt's faceless nemesis was. The original "man in black" was Arvo Ojala, who was billed at one time as "the fastest gun in Hollywood." He was the fast-draw artist who taught Arness to use a gun. It is said that Ojala could draw, fire, and hit his target in six-tenths of a second, which would have made him a formidable opponent for any of the real-life gunslingers from the raucous days of Dodge. Ojala's holsters came into wide use on the sets of all the Westerns in town and became so popular that he ultimately gave up acting to supervise their production.

The title scene was redone once again in 1964 with Fred McDougall cast as the villain. The network had tired of paying Ojala each time he appeared in the title and McDougall was a salaried member of the production staff. The director given the responsibility of reshooting the scene was Vincent McEveety, and little did he know what frightening experience was in store for him on that memorable day. The script called for Matt to face "the man in black" and the villain was to bite the dust as Matt outdrew him. At rehearsal everything went well and the scene was set up. McEveety recalls the moment:

> Jim steps out into the street, draws his gun, shoots right past the hip and — pow! It's timed just right. Except that it's Jim who falls over dead. I ran over in shock at first. He'd secretly exploded a blood capsule in his shirt which made it look frighteningly real. But then some of the crew started laughing. Jim had done this as a joke on me. He'd told the crew to let the camera run and see what I'd do. He's been doing things like this for years to charge me up and make me laugh.[130]

Although stills are available from that scene, Arness unfortunately later ordered that the film be destroyed. One could speculate that Arness in his wisdom insisted on this so that the scene could not be held over his head in case he had a disagreement with the network and they wanted to kill him off.

In 1966 the scene was once again reshot when the show went to color. The famous title was retired in 1970 in response to the antiviolence movement. The new title scene was less "offensive" and showed Matt riding wildly on the plains spurring his horse. In the final years it was replaced by title scenes consisting of cameo or introductory portraits of the principal characters that was more in keeping with the "family" atmosphere CBS was pushing. In general, by viewing the title scene one can date a particular episode as to period of production.

GUNSMOKE — I. THE HISTORY

The Early Scripts

In the first year, Warren had the good fortune of having available to him hundreds of scripts from the radio show. He was able to tap into this great wealth of creative material and except for some minor changes, adapt it to the visual medium. Arness recently commented how critical this was to the success of the television program:

> You know people always ask you, "Well, gee, how did *Gunsmoke* hit so big and last so long and everything?" Well, the simple fact of the matter was that as far as I'm concerned we just stepped into a completely tailor-made beautifully done show, and we had... several hundred scripts there. And the characters were all completely fine-tuned in the scripts. I don't think that any series has ever gone into production with that much of a backlog of great material behind it. And I think that that is really what made the difference...

The early episodes were stark and frequently there was much more unsaid than said. "I got my coterie of writers about me," Warren recalls,

> ...and told them to go down to Room C. There were 50 to 60 scripts in there and I said, "Go through them and pick out the one you like and read it. Then tell me what you want to do with it, and I'll tell you what I want." But they were copying too much. So I told them, "If you pick a radio script you get $450. If you do an original, you get $550." I also said, "Look, this is movies but we only have 26 minutes. So let's not do stories, let's do incidents." We didn't have big plots. We'd begin with a planned hold-up. You didn't need to know where they came from. They wore masks so you knew they were bad. They weren't movies with a plot and a counter plot. We didn't try to pack love and mystery into one episode.

Recreating Dodge

When Warren entered television he brought with him many of his staff from films. He enticed them by explaining, "It's TV but it's regular work. And it's fifty weeks per year instead of eight weeks of filming followed by seven off." This lured everybody and it made Warren's job much easier. "When we were building the set," he recalls, "I told my art director, 'I need a saloon and a hotel. Make it like the one in such and such movie that we did.'" At one point, he even suggested to CBS that they change the title of the program. "*Gunsmoke* sounded too much like a B movie," he noted, "and I wanted another title, *The Outriders,* which has always been my favorite title." For years Warren carried this title with him and when he went to *Rawhide,* he wanted to call it *The Outriders.* By the time he went to Universal to work on *The Virginian,* however, he no longer dared to suggest it.

Television — The New Frontier

Warren also brought some of his writers over from films, and he personally rewrote many of the radio scripts himself. He felt that Meston "was a very fine writer, but he had only written dialogue for radio." However, when Warren returned to films after leaving *Gunsmoke,* he did ask Meston to join him but Meston declined.

Warren preferred to costume his actors himself, including the guest stars. He was known for his Western wardrobes. For example, no one had ever heard of "bugger red." "It was a kind of reddish trouser that people back in the 1870s wore," he explains. "You could break horses in them, roll around in the dirt, and they'd never wear out. I told wardrobe I wanted a lot of them. After that every Western show used them. It was very popular. If I could have gotten one on Kitty, I would have."

As a filmmaker, Warren felt claustrophobic in the studio and wanted to "open things up." He wanted to go out to the mountains and valleys and shoot some of the scenes but found himself confined. He remembered how John Wayne had drummed it into his head that in television he would always be working in some bar or little hotel. "Since I was going to spend most of my time filming indoors, I asked CBS to let me build the town in the studio," he recalls. He got so much resistance, however, that he finally said, "Do it or I walk," and the network reluctantly gave in. His crew set about to build the entire *Gunsmoke* street in the studio. Warren had it built to proportion so that at the end of the street he had the buildings made smaller. This created the illusion that the street was longer. "I didn't want to go racing around to some back lot at Universal or Paramount," he explains. "I saved an awful lot of travel time and an awful lot of money. It was so much easier. You didn't have to stop for a plane."

What We Heard and What We Saw

Although the early television years utilized the scripts from radio there were often significant differences. The radio shows were sometimes darker, and more brutal. There was more of Meston's nightmare vision in them. Perhaps it was felt that the television audience was not yet ready for the grim realism portrayed on radio. Scripts were sometimes toned down for television. An example is *The Guitar.* On radio, Weed Pindle's beloved mule is mutilated when his ear is cut off, but on television this mutilation turns to humiliation as Pindle's tormentors paint his mule with white stripes. In *The Queue* a young Chinese immigrant is strangled with his own pigtail (queue). On television, however, although Chen is severely beaten, he lives to tell about it. In some stories the impact is equally shocking on both radio and television, as in *The Cabin* where in the final scene the villain is impaled on a pitchfork.

There were also differences in character portrayals. Conrad's Matt on radio was a more hardened man than Arness'. He was more of a loner and a pessimist. Not only in his voice but in his mannerisms and attitudes he displayed a fatalism and toughness that could only develop in the merciless world of radio's Dodge. On radio, Matt often makes poor value judgments and mistakes that sometimes cost men's lives. Conrad's Dillon is loud and abrasive. He has a short fuse and snaps at his friends when in a foul mood. Arness' Matt was slow to anger. Although he sometimes got annoyed with Chester, a glance of impatience was all it would usually take to show his displeasure.

Matt on television was more vulnerable, but less fallible. He was more apt to give someone a second chance and less likely to be mistaken about it. Both Matts had a strong disdain for killing. On radio Matt came across as being angry with his lot, angry at having to carry the burden of being the law. On television, Arness came to terms with Matt's chosen profession but there was a profound sadness when he had to kill.

These differences in interpretations also caused alterations in the television scripts. In *Helping Hand* Conrad attempts to assist a young man in going straight who he has saved from lynching. The defiant outlaw, however, turns on him, and so in the radio story Matt has misjudged the recreant. On television, however, it is Kitty who misjudges the man and Matt goes along with helping him only upon her insistance. In another radio story, *Smoking Out the Beedles,* Matt is forced to evict the Beedles who are in the right. He feels justified, however, despite Beedle's protestations, because he is convinced that the man is guilty. At the end the poor man is killed as a direct result of Matt's mistake. On television the episode was retitled *Smoking Out the Nolans* and Matt, believing that Nolan may be innocent all along, averts the killing.

Arness' Matt demonstrates more pity and resignation. In *Gone Straight* on radio Matt and Chester set out in pursuit of a wanted man. They find him in Tascosa where he has become a respected member of the community and is known for his civic zeal. When his past catches up with him he must face his former outlaw partners and is killed. Conrad's Matt reflects that his death is fortunate for despite the man's rehabilitation Matt feels that he probably would have had to take him in. In the television version the man faces his partners and kills them. Matt knows his identity but decides to say that one of the outlaws is the rehabilitated character and so his past is buried.

The relationships that evolved between the characters were also different on the two programs. On radio, although the characters interact and relate, the listener gets the feel that they remain to a great extent alone. It is an existential world of isolated beings. On television, on the other hand, there was a growing feeling of warmth, love and interdependence between the characters. They became more of a family. They nurtured one another to an extent that never developed on radio.

On television they interacted and spent time with one another because they enjoyed each other's company and had a genuine affection for one another. On radio it sometimes seemed that they associated by default, since they were isolated from the rest of the townspeople. While Conrad's Matt clearly displayed a certain deference toward Kitty, one has difficulty in characterizing their relationship as being based on love. On television, however, a deep love evolved. Marriage was out, however, and Arness once commented, "If they ever get married—Pow!—that's all...we're finished. That would be my last show."[131]

On radio, McNear's Doc is sometimes despicable and motivated by greed. The death of an outlaw or even a victim is sometimes viewed in terms of the attendant financial gain as Doc collects his fee for the autopsy. He remains cynical and only occasionally do we see the gentleness that characterized Milburn Stone's Doc on television. Stone's portrayal became the epitome of the paternal country doctor confronting pain and suffering. Despite the limited therapies available in his black bag he confronted epidemics, childbirths gone awry, and inaccessible bullets, and provided comfort to his patients. The town looked to him for wisdom and advice, and his motives were generally above reproach.

Kitty on radio is the victim of man's inhumanity toward woman. She is a whore who frequents all the saloons. What distinguishes her from the others in her trade is that Matt has chosen her to be his confidante. She belittles herself and feels she is unworthy to associate with the good folk of Dodge. This is a far cry from Amanda Blake's Kitty who over time becomes a self-assured entrepreneur running her own saloon. From time to time both Kittys show jealousy when Matt reveals an interest in other women. With Blake's character, however, this tends to be more of a show for she is secure in their relationship. Ellis' Kitty on the other hand, is truly insecure and her position is tenuous. She loves Matt but he does not reciprocate at the same level, while on television their relationship is more balanced and they never have to explain themselves to one another.

Chester, as portrayed on radio by Baer, and on television by Weaver seems to differ least in character. The primary difference is that on radio, Chester was not deputized and did not limp, but he was still Matt's righthand man. As Meston said, "It's tough to limp on radio." Both characterizations were that of a simple but honest man who would perform to the letter, whatever Matt ordered with no questions asked. Television's Chester, however, showed a bit more independent initiative.

GUNSMOKE — I. THE HISTORY

The Public's Response

The response to the new television show was favorable but not everyone was impressed. David Kaufman has enshrined his name in the annals of television history with his comment in *Daily Variety*. He put his boot in his mouth when he reflected that:

> ...it's doubtful whether it *[Gunsmoke]* can seriously edge into the ratings of George Gobel...Gobel probably won't have to worry too much about the opposition...Marshal Matt Dillon.[132]

Gunsmoke, however, quickly rose to prominence and most critics recognized its high quality. Macdonnell once attributed the early success of the show to the three years of prepublicity it received on radio.

Gunsmoke's popularity was tremendous and as Dwight Whitney commented in *TV Guide*, it "transformed its actors from little-known bit players into celebrities mobbed everywhere." It also made "tidy fortunes for its creators, and sold enough cigarettes to stretch several times around the world."[133] *Gunsmoke* was viewed as a "prodigy" among television shows, the most "literate Western,"[134] and was in the vanguard of the "adult" or "psychological" Westerns.[135] It was recognized that the show was unique, concentrating frequently not on the story per se, but rather on character, and psychological and moral conflict.

As *Gunsmoke* pushed *I Love Lucy* out of first place in the Nielsen ratings everyone jumped on the bandwagon. It was widely imitated, and in studios and offices in Hollywood and New York writers and producers were working frantically to create one more Western and one more hero for what appeared to be the public's insatiable appetite. *Gunsmoke* was even the butt of parody in an episode, *Gunshy*, on *Maverick*. In this show James Garner confronts Mort Dooley and all the principal characters had their share of ridicule. While Macdonnell enjoyed the joke, the cast of *Gunsmoke* was apparently not amused.

Westerns were dominant and NBC's *Wagon Train*, starring Ward Bond and Robert Horton, was set to compete against *Disneyland*. It featured guest stars such as Ernest Borgnine, Shelley Winters and Ricardo Montalban. When NBC replaced its ill-fated comedy, *Stanley*, with *Tales of Wells Fargo*, the ratings climbed 29 percent.

ABC launched *Maverick* on Sunday nights with James Garner, to compete against Ed Sullivan and Steve Allen. It also developed *Cheyenne*, with Clint Walker, billed as the first hour-long "adult Western." Other ABC fare featured Michael Ansara as Cochise in *Broken Arrow*, Scott Forbes in *Jim Bowie*, Will Hutchins in *Sugarfoot*, and Ty Hardin in *Bronco*.

Have Gun, Will Travel was CBS' answer to middle-America's plethoric bandmaster, Lawrence Welk. Other shows included *Restless Gun, Colt .45,* and *Tombstone Territory.*

By 1957 there were more than 25 Westerns on television. In addition, there were numerous reruns of old Western movies and yet it seemed that the public could not get enough. It was estimated that advertisers would be spending more than $60 million on Westerns alone. By the spring of 1957, almost 60 television shows had faltered and failed, and it was not lost on television executives, nor on advertisers and producers, that not one of those shows was a Western. The tremendous profusion of shows was remarkable. By October, 1957, so many horse operas were crowding the corral that a viewer could tune in to 64 hours of Westerns each week. One writer commented:

> ...when you and I were kids watching Tom Mix, Tim McCoy and Ken Maynard, a gun was just a piece of equipment supplied by the prop man. Now it's the highest-paid actor in the cast—the title part. Within a couple of weeks, earlier this season, you could have watched *Top Gun, Courage Is a Gun, New Gun in Town, End of a Gun,* and *Return of a Gun.* At the rate things are going, one of these days we're going to get a story about a young killer who learned the business from his father and takes over when the old man retires. And I'm waiting to see what they call that one.[136]

Television was so saturated with Westerns that even Gene Autry was heard to exclaim, "Television Westerns drive me nuts."

Public figures and politicians were also smitten with Westerns. President Eisenhower read Western novels. Vice President Nixon admitted to Washington correspondents that his children were less than impressed with his association with world figures, but when he told them he had met television's Wyatt Earp, he finally earned their admiration. Speaker of the House Sam Rayburn and Senator John McClellan watched Westerns for relaxation. While some of the shows were quality programs, most were quickly developed properties intended to provide good entertainment and designed to exploit the public's passion with the genre. None had the tremendous creative sources to draw upon that characterized *Gunsmoke,* nor, as time would show, the ability to maintain that creative vitality, for they all disappeared from the screen even as *Gunsmoke* developed and evolved. Although *Gunsmoke* was greatly admired by Orson Welles, he expressed concern that the rise of the television Western may be a sign of the decline of television in general.

By the time *Gunsmoke* went off the air on September 1, 1975, there had been 635 episodes consisting of 233 half-hour and 402 one-hour programs. No one could have anticipated this remarkable longevity when Matt first walked out on the dusty streets of Dodge to meet his nemesis, or that it would survive 20 years to become the longest running dramatic program in the history of television.

GUNSMOKE — I. THE HISTORY

The Ratings in the Early Years

Gunsmoke's rise was rapid, and nine months after its first airing, in July 1956, it was in Nielsen's Top Ten. It was the first half-hour Western to achieve this distinction. By July 1957 it was the most popular weekly television series, edging out the formerly invincible *I Love Lucy*. Other Westerns followed close behind and *Wyatt Earp, Broken Arrow, Tales of Wells Fargo* and *Zane Gray Theater* were all successful in the years between 1955 and 1957. At one point, in 1957, there were four Westerns in the Top Ten. *Gunsmoke* was second with a 44.1 rating, *Tales of Wells Fargo* was fifth with 38.6, *Cheyenne* was eighth with 37.3, and *Wyatt Earp* was ninth with 36.3. For the first time in its history the *Ed Sullivan Show* was vanquished by another program, *Maverick*. By January 1958 seven of the Top Ten programs were Westerns. *Gunsmoke* had a rating of 44.6 and was number one. This phenomenal popularity of the Western prompted the appearance of 17 new "oaters" that year. The boom was so overwhelming that one executive was led to remark, "You can be sure if it's a Western." It also prompted one wag to say that this phenomenon was "the second opening of the West."

Warren Exits

Despite the tremendous success of the show and the fact that Warren had at his disposal an inexhaustible supply of scripts, he had his problems. He felt that success was going to everyone's head. According to Warren, "It reached the point where I'd arrive on the set in the morning only to have Arness tell me that 'Matt Dillon wouldn't say a line like that!' Everybody suddenly got to be a self-appointed authority."[137] At the end of a year, due to a combination of fatigue and pressure, Warren left to do a feature and ultimately became producer of the highly successful *Rawhide,* which to this day is his favorite television program. With regard to his involvement with *Gunsmoke* Warren related,

> It was a grueling thing every day. I finally got bored. Day in and day out the same cast, same location, and the movie industry was still out there. I wanted to get out of this little goddam thing, and get back in the movies. When I left, everyone said, "The boss has left." They changed their vest and their clothes. They said, "He didn't create me. I created me." And they made sure I heard about it.

After further reflection he added:

> It was everything a Western shouldn't be. It wasn't gun play, it was talk play. Television wasn't so powerful then. *Gunsmoke* made it powerful. It was popular beyond our thinking. If there hadn't been a radio *Gunsmoke*,

Television — The New Frontier

I would never have created it. After I left, I didn't watch it anymore. I didn't want to be hurt. I was afraid that someone would do it better. At first, when I started with *Gunsmoke* they would ask me, "What are you doing?" and I would answer, "Something dumb called *Gunsmoke.*" But *Gunsmoke* has grown on me, and now I'm very fond of it.

The Old Guard Returns

In the second season Macdonnell once again assumed the role of producing *Gunsmoke* but unlike the radio experience, he declined to direct any of the segments for he felt that combining the two positions was too overwhelming. He stayed with the program through the next nine years, leaving in 1964 in the middle of the tenth season. The cast and staff greeted Macdonnell with enthusiasm. Amanda Blake noted that, "It was the right move on CBS' part because it had been Norman's baby on radio and John Meston's. And I just felt it blossom...."

As he had with the radio show, Macdonnell stressed authenticity. He did point out some deviations, however. Kids and dogs were hardly ever seen on the streets of Dodge, and Macdonnell conceded:

> ...The only place we've fudged is in making Kitty a pretty girl. Actually, the saloon girls were pretty ugly. If we were completely honest, Kitty would be a heavily painted 58-year-old hag who bathed twice a month whether she needed to or not. And Dillon would go around wearing a derby hat and starched collars. You have to make some compromises.[138]

During Macdonnell's tenure the show achieved its greatest popularity and was number one in the Nielsen ratings for the four seasons 1957–1961. Meston dominated *Gunsmoke* during these first ten years and developed 207 of the stories and wrote 196 of the actual scripts for 377 episodes. This intense involvement in television removed him from the radio show and he wrote relatively little for the radio program from its fifth through ninth season. The television staff hardly ever saw Meston for he was travelling through Mexico and Europe and was sending in his scripts by mail. He had married a lady bullfighter and this took him out of the States. The other writers who were active during this period were Les Crutchfield, Kathleen Hite, and John Dunkel. In essence, *Gunsmoke's* radio writers had inherited the television program and were able to rewrite their radio scripts as well as create new ones for the dominant new medium. Herb Purdum, a writer during the first year of the radio show, recently reflected on the transition that was taking place in Hollywood with television's advent. He noted:

> When television came along it was a new challenge and it was also one where radio writers had to prove themselves. It was quite well known

throughout the industry that the people who were doing television shows during the early days made one very serious mistake. They thought that the only writers who could do television were the movie writers. They thought that movie writers were used to writing visual things and they would make better television writers. And of course they found out that this was the kiss of death, for movie writers during those years had what they called "sweet-heart contracts." It was one of those things where they give you two weeks to do the story, ten weeks to do the script, and two weeks to do the polish. And that's just ridiculous for a radio writer who's used to working on a story one day, doing the script in two or three days and polishing with luck. It was inevitable, the movie writers fell on their face... They just couldn't hack it. Couldn't do it. So they finally turned to radio writers rather reluctantly, and found out that radio writers could produce. For a half-hour show, you would take your story in on a Monday and they would expect the script to be delivered by Thursday or Friday. The radio writers could do this with no sweat while the movie writers just stood back and said, "What do you mean?"

Macdonnell had the good fortune of having his old radio writers available who knew the show and the characters intimately, and therefore, he was able to keep the creative momentum going. They were a prolific group and over 70 episodes were aired before *Gunsmoke* ever showed its first rerun. Table 2 summarizes the writing credits.

A new writer on Macdonnell's staff was Sam Peckinpah. After writing nine scripts for *Gunsmoke* he went on to become a director on television and developed his craft on *The Rifleman* and *The Westerner*. In 1969 he surfaced as the director of the classic film western *The Wild Bunch* which many critics have viewed as a movie that reinterpreted and reshaped the cinema Western. Some of his other films were *The Ballad of Cable Hogue* (1970), *Straw Dogs* (1971), *Junior Bonner* (1972), *Pat Garrett and Billy the Kid* (1973), and *The Killer Elite* (1975). An exacting artist with a strong and distinctive vision, Peckinpah's movies tended to be violent and unforgiving. He was a maverick and uncompromising director who became increasingly frustrated by the poor recutting and reediting of his films. He fell into obscurity before his death in 1984.

The directors who were involved during the first decade of *Gunsmoke* were among the finest working in television. Some came from a background of filmmaking, but others were exclusively television directors, and developed their craft on *Gunsmoke*. Their contribution was a communal and evolving recreation of Dodge City and its universe. Besides the writing and the acting, the directing was the third critical element in the success of the program.

Andrew McLaglen directed more *Gunsmoke* episodes than any other individual in its 20 year history. He worked on the show during Macdonnell's tenure but stopped directing during the Leacock and Mantley years. The son of Victor McLaglen, a famous British character actor, he worked as an

Television — The New Frontier

Table 2. The Television Writers — The First Decade: 1955-1965 (Selected List)

YEAR	1	2	3	4	5	6	7	8	9	10	TOTAL
John Meston	4	14	32	29	29	38	19	14	10	7	196
Kathleen Hite	0	0	4	0	0	0	10	12	9	4	39
Les Crutchfield*	2	3	1	10	10	0	0	2	3	6	37
John Dunkel*	9	3	0	0	0	0	4	3	3	1	23
Sam Peckinpah	5	3	1	0	0	0	0	0	0	0	9
Paul Savage*	0	0	0	0	0	0	0	3	4	0	7
Clyde Ware*	0	0	0	0	0	0	0	0	0	3	3
Calvin Clements*	0	0	0	0	0	0	0	0	0	3	3

*Continued to write in the second decade 1965-1975.

assistant director with John Ford then directed his first feature film, *Gun the Man Down*, in 1956. He has directed many films including *McLintock!* (1963), *Shenandoah* (1965), *The Rare Breed* (1966), and *The Wild Geese* (1978). On television he directed numerous episodes for *Have Gun, Will Travel*, *Perry Mason*, *Rawhide* and *The Virginian*.

Another active director during the Macdonnell years was Harry Harris. After McLaglen, he did the most episodes. He has numerous television credits having worked on shows such as *Cagney and Lacey*, *Dallas*, *Eight Is Enough*, *Falcon Crest*, *Fame*, *High Chaparral*, *Lost in Space*, *Rawhide*, and *The Waltons*.

Ted Post, another prolific television director, has among his credits *Baretta*, *Cagney and Lacey*, *Columbo*, *The Desilu Playhouse*, *Perry Mason*, *Peyton Place*, *Rich Man, Poor Man — Book I*, *Route 66*, and *Wagon Train*.

John Rich directed for both Macdonnell and Mantley. He won an Emmy Award for directing *The Dick Van Dyke Show*, and two Emmy Awards for directing and producing *All in the Family*. His feature film credits include *Wives and Lovers* (1963), *The New Interns* (1964), and *Easy Come Easy Go* (1967). Other television credits include *Benson*, *The Brady Bunch*, *Gilligan's Island*, *Our Miss Brooks*, and *The Twilight Zone*.

Richard Whorf has been active in all facets of show-business. At the age of 15 he quit school to join a stage company in Boston. He was an actor for many years then later became a set designer and director for the stage. He worked with the Lunts on Broadway then left for Hollywood where he became a contract player at Warner Bros. and later at M-G-M. He appeared in various films including *Midnight* (1934), *Blues in the Night* (1941), and *Yankee Doodle Dandy* (1942). In 1944 he became a director of films then returned to Broadway to star in *Richard III* in 1949. In the 50s he turned to directing for television.

Table 3. The Television Directors
The First Decade: 1955–1965. (Selected List)

YEAR	1	2	3	4	5	6	7	8	9	10	TOTAL
Andrew McLaglen	0	20	2	8	16	10	11	13	12	3	95
Harry Harris*	0	0	0	0	0	5	12	16	15	12	60
Ted Post	6	14	14	9	1	5	4	2	0	0	55
Charles Warren	26	0	0	0	0	0	0	0	0	0	26
Jesse Hibbs	0	0	0	5	10	5	0	0	0	0	20
Richard Whorf	0	0	6	11	0	0	1	0	0	0	18
John Rich*	0	0	10	0	0	0	0	0	0	0	10
Arthur Hiller	0	0	0	3	4	2	0	0	0	0	9
Robert Stevenson	6	0	0	0	0	0	0	0	0	0	6
Joseph Sargent*	0	0	0	0	0	0	0	3	0	2	5
Buzz Kulik	0	0	3	0	2	0	0	0	0	0	5
Vincent McEveety*	0	0	0	0	0	0	0	0	0	5	5
Mark Rydell*	0	0	0	0	0	0	0	0	0	4	4

*Continued to direct in the second decade 1965–1975.

Arthur Hiller was the director of the hit feature film *Love Story* (1970). He also directed *The Americanization of Emily* (1964), *The Hospital* (1971), *Tobruk* (1967), *The Man in the Glass Booth* (1975), and *Silver Streak* (1976). On television he directed for various well-known shows including *Playhouse 90, Alfred Hitchcock Presents, Naked City,* and *Perry Mason.*

Jesse Hibbs has earned a reputation for making the most of low budgets and poor scripts in films like *Ride Clear of Diablo* (1954), *The Yellow Mountain* (1954), *To Hell and Back* (1955), *Walk the Proud Land* (1956), and *Ride a Crooked Trail* (1958). For television he directed on *The FBI, The Fugitive, Hawaiian Eye, The Invaders,* and *Laramie.*

Joseph Sargent is known in films for his thrillers. His credits include *The Hell With Heroes* (1968), *The Man* (1972), *White Lightning* (1973), *The Taking of Pelham One-Two-Three* (1974), and *MacArthur* (1977).

Burt Reynolds and Quint Asper

One of the most important things that Macdonnell achieved during his term was to introduce two new characters. In 1962, in the eighth season he decided to add a fifth central character. It was felt that there should be a younger member among the closed *Gunsmoke* family who could attract younger audiences. The part of Quint Asper was created by John Meston and was introduced to the television audience on September 29, 1962, in *Quint Asper Comes Home*.

Quint was Burt Reynolds' first major role and his debut was greeted by more fan mail than that of any other new character. Four thousand letters were received within a week after Reynolds first bared his chest as Dodge City's half-breed blacksmith. Reynolds had played other Indian roles prior to this, and his grandmother was a full-blooded Cherokee.

Reynolds needs little introduction. One of the biggest stars of the seventies and eighties he has starred in such well-known films as *Deliverance* (1972), *The Man Who Loved Cat Dancing* (1973), *The Longest Yard* (1974), *Smokey and the Bandit* (1977), *Hooper* (1978), *The Cannonball Run* (1980), *Sharkey's Machine* (1981), *The Best Little Whorehouse in Texas* (1982), and *City Heat* (1984). He established himself as one of the kings of machismo and like Steve McQueen has generally done his own stunt work. He earned especial notoriety when he posed as the first nude male centerfold in *Cosmopolitan* in 1972.

Reynolds was born in Waycross, Georgia, and grew up in Palm Beach, Florida. His father was the town's police chief and had been a cowboy in his youth. Reynolds won a football scholarship to Florida State University and was an All-Star Southern Conference halfback. In 1955 he left school and tried to make it in acting in New York. He spent most of his time, however, washing dishes or being a bouncer at Roseland. His first break came in the New York revival of *Mister Roberts* and this finally led to a television contract with Universal.

Like most others who stepped on the *Gunsmoke* set, Reynolds greatly enjoyed the experience. He notes,

> It was the happiest years of my life in terms of just the working relationship with those people. I was crazy about Jim, and Amanda, what's not to love? And Milburn Stone was like a father to me...and Kenny Curtis...It was a delightful time. It was just a wonderful time.

Macdonnell noted at the time, "He's really made an effort to fit in with us. It's not easy for a newcomer to break into a cast that's been working together like a family all these years."[139]

Despite this, Quint never quite evolved into the character that CBS had been hoping for and Reynolds left after three seasons. He described his role as that of "...a guy who loves physical contact, has no prejudices, is completely independent, takes people at face value, and would just as soon fight as eat." But he perceived that there were limitations for growth in the role and observed that, "It was time for me to move on." He turned to Stone for advice who apparently said to his young protege, "You know, you got to get the hell off this show because I think you got a movie career." Reynolds notes, "I didn't think I had a movie career but I thought he was right." He recently attempted to explain why his character did not work out.

GUNSMOKE — I. THE HISTORY

You can't be a leading man when you're standing next to a guy six-foot-eight and his name is Matt Dillon. I mean, I was the blacksmith and people used to call me a dirty half-breed and spit on me for fifty-eight minutes and then Arness would come back from Hawaii and beat 'em up. So it wasn't a terrific role in terms of really shining.

Ken Curtis and Festus

The other major character introduced by Macdonnell was Festus Haggen played by Ken Curtis. Unlike Quint Asper, Festus stayed with the program until the end. He premiered in the episode *Us Haggens* on December 8, 1962, and was created by Les Crutchfield. Macdonnell and CBS wanted a character to replace Chester when it became apparent that it was but a matter of time until Weaver's departure.

Curtis was selected for the part by Norman Macdonnell and director Andrew V. McLaglen for whom he had played a similar character, Monk, in *Have Gun, Will Travel,* also created by Les Crutchfield. Curtis once described Monk as "an animal skinner who followed the cowherds. Supposedly he smelled so bad that at night the cowboys would tie him to a tree so he couldn't sneak into their camp while they were sleeping."[140] Although Curtis premiered as Festus in the eighth season, the character did not become a regular until the ninth with *Prairie Wolfer* on January 8, 1964. This was a rare episode because it featured Matt, Doc, Kitty, Chester, Festus, Quint, and Sam all in the same story. It was decided that Festus would join the principal characters when Weaver's departure became inevitable and someone had to be found to cover Matt's back, lock horns with Doc, and to show Kitty the respect she had grown accustomed to. Prior to Festus, Curtis had appeared in several *Gunsmoke* episodes playing minor characters. His first role was during the fourth season on January 31, 1959, when he played a drover in *Jayhawkers*. In the fifth season he played an outlaw in *The Ex-Urbanites* and an Indian scout in *Speak Me Fair*. Just before he became a regular he played Kyle Kelly in *Lover Boy*.

Ken Curtis was born Curtis Gates on July 12, 1916, in southeastern Colorado and grew up in Lamar. His father was the sheriff of Bent County and Curtis and his brothers lived for a time in the jail. He helped out as jailkeeper while his mother cooked for the prisoners. Later on he worked on ranches and farms and took up the saxophone. After graduating high school he studied pre-med at Colorado College but left to become a songwriter. He drifted to Hollywood and became a staff singer on NBC Radio. He was the man Tommy Dorsey hired to replace Frank Sinatra when Old Blue Eyes left the orchestra to go it alone. Curtis also sang with the Sons of the Pioneers. After serving in World War II he resumed his career and made many radio appearances. He sang with Johnny Mercer and the Pied Pipers. "I suppose it all started when I sang 'Tumbling Tumbleweeds' on a radio show," he recalls. "The next thing I know I was under contract to Columbia Pictures and riding into the sunset." He usually appeared as a singing cowboy in low-budget Westerns. His early films included *Song of the Prairie* (1945), *Singing on the Trail* (1946), *Over the Santa Fe Trail* (1947), and *Call of the Forest* (1949). John Ford was his father-in-law and encouraged Curtis' career. He started to appear in Ford's films playing nonsinging roles in such classics as *Mister Roberts* (1955), *The Searchers* (1956), *The Wings of Eagles* (1957), and *The Last Hurrah* (1958). In the 50s he produced several movies that have something of a cult status the most notable being *The Killer Shrews*. A lesser "classic" is *The Giant Gila Monster*. On television's *Ripcord* he played the skydiver Jim Buckley and also appeared on *Perry Mason, Rawhide,* and *Have Gun, Will Travel*.

Curtis felt that he had played various characters before Festus that were Festus' "spiritual cousins." On radio he played Dick Swink on the *Lucky U Ranch*. Swink was a bicycle-riding mailman who stuttered. In John Ford's *The Searchers* he played a Texas Ranger who Curtis felt had the seeds of Festus in him. This character had what Curtis considered to be a "dry land" dialect with a drawl similar to Festus'.

When Festus premiered the audience response was positive. *Gunsmoke* die-hards, however, long mourned Chester's departure and it took time for them to transfer their allegiances to Matt's new deputy. But Festus soon squinted and postured his way into their fickle hearts as he became a permanent part of the *Gunsmoke* family.

Curtis approximated Milburn Stone in his well-honed mannerisms. Festus and Doc could stand face to face without saying a word and milk the scene for everything it was worth with a one-eyed squint and a tug at the ear. In 1967 *Newsweek* called him a "scene stealer."[141] Standing in his scruffy stetson on the dusty streets of Dodge, Festus became Matt's sidekick in the tradition of the B Westerns. Working within the confines of this tradition, however, he still "found and developed new facets to the character in each episode." Curtis noted that he was "the only halfway honest member of the Haggen clan—a family of outlaws. But if he shook your hand his word was as good as gold."

When Festus put on his deputy's badge he became the "black sheep" of the family. Curtis found that his character developed over time. "He was practically pure animal in the beginning—but later, due to Doc's influence (though he remained illiterate), he became at least somewhat civilized and more compassionate." He worked hard to keep Festus fresh and "found early on that he worked especially well with children and old folks." Like Chester, "He had a great respect for the ladies." Unlike Chester, however, Festus was more independent. He not only took orders but could take the initiative to help "ol' Math-hew" out of a jam. With time, Festus assumed greater and greater responsibilities until he pretty much kept watch over Dodge whenever Matt was in Hayes City. With regard to Matt, "I admired him tremendously," Curtis explained. "But I remained my own man, and was never afraid to confront him when I felt he was wrong about the situation." When it came to Kitty, Festus:

> ...loved her "harder than a goat could butt a stump" but strictly in a platonic way... He always knew she was a push-over for a free beer. Her great compassion for the under-dog and her deep love for Matthew made her a very special lady to Festus.

Festus' relationship with Doc was a complex one. Beneath the constant exchange of barbs there was a strong bond. "Though their constant bickering would seem to disprove it," he explains:

> Their friendship and mutual admiration grew for each other. How else can a man tell another man he loves him without insulting him? As was proven in several later episodes, either man was willing to die for the other.

On a private level Curtis and Stone toured for a while together making personal appearances at rodeos and fairs. "Those trips were a ball," Curtis commented. "I played the comedy like Festus and then I turned around and sang like myself. It shocked the whey out of everybody."

Curtis appeared on *Gunsmoke* for ten years and played a key role in many episodes. His favorite episode is *Wishbone* for which he and Milburn Stone suggested the story. Written by Paul Savage, Curtis explains that "It was based on a true incident that happened to my mother in Arkansas when she was a young girl." He recalls, "She was bitten by a copperhead and a farmhand killed a chicken-split him open, and applied him to the wound as a poultice, thereby saving her life." In the *Gunsmoke* story Festus' fervent prayer and a fresh-killed chicken combine to save Doc's life.

Curtis was quickly accepted by the other regulars. "We all liked and respected each other," he notes.

> There was great humor on the show and no professional jealousy whatsoever. Every member of the cast was only interested in making the best show possible out of each script and we were all determined never to vary from our own character guidelines.

Curtis felt that this chemistry is what enabled *Gunsmoke* to run for 20 years on television. When asked what Festus would be like today, he commented, "Probably about the same except older, hopefully a little smarter, and a hell of a lot richer."

Television — The New Frontier

Macdonnell's Dismissal

The circumstances surrounding Macdonnell's departure are partly shrouded in mystery. What is clear is that he had no foreknowledge of his dismissal and that he was fired suddenly. One story has it that his successor, Philip Leacock, walked through the door one morning to take his place.

James "the Smiling Cobra" Aubrey was the head of CBS Television at the time. He acquired his reputation because of his management style and the enthusiasm with which he axed his subordinates. Aubrey's representative in Hollywood, Hunt Stromberg, approached Macdonnell with the suggestion that Jack Palance be cast as a continuing heavy opposite Arness to boost the ratings. Macdonnell thought this was absurd and had great difficulty hiding his feelings, and several weeks later he was fired. Whether this had anything to do with his departure is a matter of conjecture, but the man who had always created a sheltered environment for his cast and staff, now found himself without support.

"Tragically, somewhere along the line he found himself outside that protective umbrella and was replaced," observes Paul Savage who was story consultant and writer for television's *Gunsmoke*. Amanda Blake remembers her reaction to Macdonnell's firing. "I was sick," she notes. "I was sick about it. I couldn't understand it. You know, nobody tells you anything. I just felt awful about it. I felt like we were losing the head of the family. I was appalled."

Arness has his own recollections as to why Macdonnell was dismissed. He recently commented that:

> ...When those half-hour shows ultimately began to wear a little thin and times were changing, they decided to make it into one-hour shows. I think everyone assumed that there wouldn't be much difficulty to that...that we would just make a smooth transition into a one-hour show, but it didn't work out that way at all. They found there was a lot of trouble in making that leap...They had a hard time making it work. And there was a period of time there when it was kind of faltering and everybody was feeling their way around...That's when Leacock came in and John Mantley. And along with that they decided to make it in color, which also added something to it. I think when Leacock and Mantley came on board, and ultimately when John (Mantley) took it over...it worked. From that point on it accelerated us out for another ten years. So I think that's what really happened.

Arness was not the only one harboring such sentiments. The ratings had been dropping since the seventh season, and there were some purists who felt that the "Golden Years" of *Gunsmoke* were the first five years. Cecil Smith commented that once the show went to one hour, "The fine, hard, frozen

GUNSMOKE — I. THE HISTORY

moment quality of the Meston half-hour, its jewel-like dramatic impact was gone."[142]

Leacock has his own recollections of that period in *Gunsmoke's* history. "I had been working as a director on *Rawhide,*" he notes,

> ...and Eric Fleming and I had an unfortunate disagreement. I had had four assignments and had done two when they dropped the other two. Then Hunt Stromberg called me and said would I come and see him. And I thought it was about *Rawhide,* and I had a great head of steam up. When I got there he said, "Would you like to produce *Gunsmoke?*" and I was astounded. I had never produced in my life. And after thinking about it I thought it might be something rather interesting. I was a little naive because I didn't know why the previous producer was leaving. And so negotiations were started and I also met with Jim Arness and found out that he was unhappy about the way the show was being run and the direction the stories were taking. And it seemed to me that both these issues could be settled without too much difficulty. Then I met with Norman Macdonnell who was very kind to me, extremely nice, and I began to feel a little worried. By this time the contract was virtually signed, and I did go ahead with it, with some qualms.

Mrs. Judith Macdonnell recently shed some light on Norman Macdonnell and John Meston's feelings about that period:

> I think on the whole they (Macdonnell and Meston) were getting maybe a little weary of it by the time they were finished... Norm never felt it would go in the direction it did, which proved to be wrong perhaps... If you'll notice it *[Gunsmoke]* was far softer in later years than the radio or John Meston's shows... They were always disappointed in what happened to it, because it lost so much of its strength and character... That was their theory.

There are probably many factors that led to Macdonnell's replacement, but whatever the reasons, soon after he left, so did John Meston and Kathleen Hite. Under the new regime they encountered script supervision and rewrites which as former radio writers they were unaccustomed to and which they resented. Kathleen Hite is said to have exited after Leacock turned to her one day and said, "I say, is there really a Dodge City in America?" One has to question this, however, since Leacock had been working in the States for some time. While Dunkel and Crutchfield continued to write an occasional script for the next several years, a new crop of writers was recruited by the producers and soon dominated the creative elements of the program. New directors were also brought in and Andrew McLaglen stopped directing for the show. The creators of *Gunsmoke* were gone and the first chapter of the *Gunsmoke* story was now closed.

In later years, Macdonnell never seemed bitter. In interviews he spoke fondly of the show even though he did not always agree with the direction that it was taking. "Maybe they had just worked together too long," Leacock said in trying to explain the reason for Macdonnell's departure. Or possibly, the drop in ratings suggested to the network that Macdonnell had gotten bored or had lost his creative edge. A gentle man, he was inept at politics and it was probably unrealistic to think that he could survive the increasingly competitive and highly charged environment of Hollywood. He was a product and an inhabitant of another time. Perhaps it is Harry Bartell who provides the best explanation for his departure. He recently reflected:

> I had the greatest respect for that man. I think he was buried unfortunately in a kind of atmosphere in which he couldn't compete. He was essentially a very artistic man. A very sensitive man who had wonderful taste and instinct for drama. And competing in the Hollywood area was very tough.

Philip Leacock

Philip Leacock was born in London in 1917. He was the son of a civil engineer father and an artist mother. After high school he worked for several years with a documentary film unit. In 1938 he joined the British Army and made training films for the Royal Army Ordinance Corps. After leaving the service he stayed in films and ultimately directed *The Little Kidnappers* and *The Brave Don't Cry*. When he came to America he directed movies such as *Let No Man Write My Epitaph*, *13 West Street*, and *Reach for Glory* for Columbia. For television he directed the pilot for *Route 66* on CBS. It was his impressive directing on *The Great Adventure*, *The Alfred Hitchcock Hour*, *The Defenders* and *Rawhide*, that led to his being appointed the producer of *Gunsmoke*. At first, John Mantley was his story consultant and later became his Associate Producer and finally Producer.

When Leacock started producing *Gunsmoke* an actor friend told him to listen to the radio show. He was fascinated. "It had a violence which was really part of the story," he notes, "And the worst thing that ever happened to *Gunsmoke* was the antiviolence thing." As producer, Leacock had a great deal of creative freedom. Unlike in later years, he found that CBS very rarely interfered with the story line and if they did "we just turned Jim on them."

At first, not everyone greeted Leacock with open arms. Some of the cast and staff were still smarting from Macdonnell's sudden departure. He remembers his early interactions with Blake.

> Amanda was very, very emotional, and she and I had terrible rows on the set. Or rather, she did most of the rowing. She cursed me soundly. Then we became very good friends and I really have great, great affection for her."

GUNSMOKE — I. THE HISTORY

One of the first accommodations that he made was to address Arness' concerns. "He was not seeing enough of his kids," Leacock notes.

> He wanted a different schedule which we arranged quite neatly. We would start about six weeks earlier than the show normally started. He would work his butt off for the first ten shows then at some point that suited him, we would have a hiatus for six weeks during which he would see his kids and after that he would do shows where he didn't have a hundred percent involvement. He would always be in every show. And I'm pretty sure it worked well right to the end of the series.

It was during Leacock's tenure that some of the most critical changes in key cast members were made. Burt Reynolds left the show and the rowdies and scum who passed through Dodge no longer had a half-breed blacksmith to kick around any more. Leacock recalls that CBS felt that Quint's part was not working out and he was asked to tell Reynolds. He called Reynolds in and said, "We thought we'd get John Meston to write a script for your farewell." While Leacock really did not understand the network's reasoning at the time, he recalls Milburn Stone's explanation.

> He was a very perceptive and wonderful man. He said that the scripts were not being written correctly for Burt because he had a much stronger bent as a comedian, which subsequent history has proved. He could play drama very well but it wasn't what was needed. And I think if we had slanted him more, if we had made his character more humorous, I think we might have made it work.

The role of the archetypal young man that Quint vacated was rewritten into the character of Thaddeus Greenwood, played by Roger Ewing, and later into the more successful character of Newly O'Brien.

There were many other changes during Leacock's brief term. Ken Curtis became more active as Festus. Color was introduced and the main titles were redone. Guest stars were brought in which drastically altered *Gunsmoke's* format from being dependent primarily on the principal characters to shifting emphasis to transients passing through Dodge. Various stars were employed for this purpose and it was an exciting and vibrant time. Leacock recalls meeting one of these stars.

> The script had been directed towards her but before she would give us an answer she wanted to see the script. And then she asked that Vincent McEveety, who was going to direct it, and I meet her in her apartment in Beverly Hills. It was tea-time when we got there and we sat down to this very charming, rather English sort of tea. And we didn't discuss the show at all but just *Gunsmoke* in general, and lots of other things. Then we left a little bewildered not knowing whether we had made any impression at all. By the time we got back to the office about 25 minutes later

there was a message waiting for us from her agent saying that she would love to do it. Bette Davis was great to work with.

Leacock was intrigued by all the fine actors who passed through Dodge. "Some that you prophesied a great future for disappeared into the woodwork," he recalls. "It's the nature of our business, unfortunately."

He utilized many directors during the two seasons that he was producer. Among those especially active during this juncture were Marc Rydell, Robert Totten, and Vincent McEveety.

Leacock also quickly learned, like all those who had worked on the show that the principal actors "all treasured their characters," and that when it came to the "integrity" of the show Milburn Stone had a formidable temper. "Milburn would hit the roof," he notes.

> But not necessarily over his character. He just wouldn't play the lines if he didn't think they were right. Even if it was Jim's character he would come up to the office screaming, and he was not a man to withhold his feelings. You got it full in the neck. He had a lot to do in a funny way with the show staying on a very steady course. He was sort of an outside factor not involved with the preparation of the scripts but was someone who had an instinctive feeling for the show.

Leacock also observed that although Meston was hardly writing scripts anymore and was soon to depart, "His mark was a very strong one."

Despite the critical changes during his tenure, Leacock's term as producer was short-lived. He was anxious to redirect his creative energies and left temporarily to produce a feature film, *Firecreek*. It was agreed that he and John Mantley would share the responsibilities of producing both the film and *Gunsmoke* until the project was finished. On February 22, 1967, however, the unexpected happened.

A Brief Cancellation

Michael Dann, vice president in charge of programming at CBS, announced that *Gunsmoke* had run its course and would be cancelled next season. The reason given was "program fatigue"[143] but it was obvious that the decision had been brewing for some time. The statisticians and executives at CBS had been carefully watching *Gunsmoke* as it slipped in the ratings between 1963–67. For eight seasons *Gunsmoke* had dominated the choice 10:00 p.m. Saturday slot and had been consistently in Nielsen's Top Ten. Over a three year period, however, it had developed inertia and by 1966–67 it had fallen to 34th place. These cracks in its ratings sent shudders throughout the network for *Gunsmoke* was CBS' flagship program. There were also other reasons for concern. Demographers explained that its original audience had grown older and warned that *Gunsmoke* would no longer be attractive to advertisers who tended to court the younger 18- to 49-year-old segment of the population.

Jay Eliasberg, head of research, and Frank Smith, vice president in charge of sales agreed that the show would be increasingly difficult to sell. CBS wanted to recapture a youthful audience with new programming and prepared to axe *Gunsmoke* to make room for other shows. It is probably no accident that Dann made his fateful announcement while Paley was vacationing in Lynford Cay, his retreat in the Bahamas. The program council did not want to confront him directly about the cancellation of one of his favorite programs.

No one at CBS, however, anticipated the violent reaction to the announcement that would sweep the nation and that would rock the network. The country was up in arms. No cancellation of a television program had ever excited such feelings. The outpouring of sentiment was overwhelming and the perpetrators of the unpopular decision were astounded. The message was clear, life without Matt, Kitty, Doc and Festus was more than most people could stomach. Calls and letters of protest arrived by the thousands. U.S. Senator Byrd, brought up the issue in Congress on March 2, and criticized CBS. The Kansas legislature called for censure. CBS had threatened an integral institution and America was not going to stand for it. CBS remained firm, however, and there was no retraction.

The cast and the crew were stunned. None of them had any inkling of the sudden cataclysm, and it was as if a tornado had hit Dodge. John Mantley recalls that he got a terse call saying, *"Gunsmoke* has been cancelled. Go down and tell your people." Mantley was not as surprised as one would have expected, however, for two days before the cancellation a reporter for *Variety* had warned him of the impending announcement. Mantley of course was incredulous, and to this day he does not know "where that man got his information." Mantley organized a farewell party and corraled Arness into promising to come, but he never showed. "I got into my car five times," Arness later explained. "Once I got as far as six blocks but I just couldn't face those people saying good-bye."[144]

One newspaper story has it that when Arness found out that the show was cancelled, he was on the set and became silent. The next scene called for him to ride a horse. Arness, who was an experienced but cautious rider, spurred his horse and was clocked doing better than 30 miles an hour. The crew was apparently crying at this farewell gesture. Later on, this shot was used as the title scene for several years. As it turned out Arness never had to face his coworkers and say good-bye. Pressure on CBS continued to mount as mid-West affiliates in an unexpected show of force revolted and refused to carry CBS programs unless *Gunsmoke* was reinstated.[145] Even this CBS was willing to weather but the day after the farewell party, Paley finally learned of the threat to his beloved program and of its death throes. Paley hated confrontations and in typical fashion made a discreet call to Tom Dawson, president of the CBS Television Network in New York and made it clear that he wanted *Gunsmoke* back on the air. Dawson pointed out to his boss that the Saturday evening slot for September was already occupied and there was no turning back.

Paley was adamant and could not be dissuaded. He insisted on a solution and asked Dawson to look at the program chart with him. Together they "discovered" that on Monday nights from 7:30 to 8:30 p.m. there was a weak link in the schedule. *Gilligan's Island* and a new comedy, *Doc,* would be cancelled to make room for *Gunsmoke.* In this manner, Paley overruled his program council and the next day *Gunsmoke* was back in the schedule despite the misgivings of many at CBS. Two weeks after the first news release, CBS announced on March 8 that it had "re-evaluated the situation." A spokesman explained, "Our affiliate stations had an affectionate feeling for the program." He went on to elaborate further that, "There was a surprising reaction to our announcement that the program was through. There's feeling that there's life in the old boy yet."[146] Dann recanted later, saying, "All the indications were that the show had run its course. How did we know that we had a mass phenomenon on our hands? We'd all make nothing but hits if we were that smart."[147] John Wayne, however, understood *Gunsmoke's* appeal and said it was no mystery to him. "They always get back on top of the heap," the Duke explained. "They represent our folklore."[148]

Leacock's Departure

After *Gunsmoke* was reinstated in March, Mantley prepared to join Leacock as the line producer of *Firecreek* as they had agreed. CBS, however, in a surprise move approached Mantley and asked him to stay with *Gunsmoke* and to take over the reins as executive producer. Friends urged him not to do it for it was the general feeling that the new Monday night slot for the upcoming 1967-68 season would spell disaster. He went against their well-intentioned remonstrances, however, and now had the dubious honor of having to reconstitute *Gunsmoke* in its vulnerable Monday night position. Those in the know felt that a debacle was in the works and it seems that some of the executives at CBS who had supported the cancellation were awaiting the fulfillment of their "prophecy" and were secretly hoping that *Gunsmoke* would fail.

When the new season opened, however, a television "miracle" occured. In a medium known for its lack of forgiveness, and where resurrections are as rarely encountered as in human history, *Gunsmoke* rapidly climbed to the number four position in the ratings within the first four weeks of the thirteenth season. It was aligned against considerable competition, airing opposite *The Monkees, The Man from U.N.C.L.E.,* and *The Man from Africa.* Paley was vindicated and Mantley was now at the helm of a program that was to remain in the top six for the next several seasons. Many tried to explain this unexpected phenomenon. "For no reason you can imagine," Perry Lafferty, West Coast programming chief reflected, "The show found a new audience waiting for it in the early time period."[149] An entirely new audience "rediscovered" *Gunsmoke.* In addition, *Gunsmoke's* older audience remained faithful and changed its viewing habits. Mantley was also surprised. "I thought the new slot would be a disaster," he said. "But we picked up a lot of kids."[150]

Roger Ewing and Clayton Thaddeus Greenwood

When *Gunsmoke* finished its tenth season (1964-65), it was in 27th place in the ratings. Leacock and Mantley felt there was a need to write in a young deputy to attract new audiences. Burt Reynolds' departure as Quint had left a void in the character slot "of the young man learning from his elders," and Calvin Clements was assigned the role of creating the new character. Roger Ewing was cast as Clayton Thaddeus Greenwood and was supposed to be a "shit-kickin" cowboy who would aid Marshal Dillon. This never quite materialized, however, and Ewing remained only two seasons. Thad made his debut on October 2, 1965, in the beginning of the eleventh season. He played a young man who rides into Dodge to avenge his father's death then settles in town.

Ewing recalls that his first appearance on *Gunsmoke* was in an episode with Theodore Bikel and Lee Majors called *Song for Dying.* "At the time they were looking for somebody in a younger actor category...and they liked what I did in the show and then asked me to appear as a regular." He remembers, "It was at a Christmas party and they asked me if I would like to come on as a regular. I said, 'Well, you don't really need to ask.'"

Prior to *Gunsmoke,* Ewing had worked on the films, *Ensign Pulver,* and *None But the Brave,* directed by Frank Sinatra. On television he appeared in *Eleventh Hour, Room 222,* and *Farmer's Daughter.* He describes Thad as his "first major role" and notes, "I was basically a neophite professionally, as well as personally in the business. All of them lent a lot of help and influence."

Ewing greatly enjoyed his time on the show, and recently reflected on this period in his life.

> I think it was probably the premiere show to work on. Any actor who was working on television at that time would say the best show to work was

Television — The New Frontier

Gunsmoke. The people involved knew what they were doing and there weren't any egos jumping out at you from everywhere. It was just a very easy relaxed atmosphere and everybody was made to feel at home...They were truly the most delightful people to work with. We would laugh...and it would sometimes take us two or three hours to get a ten minute scene done because of the laughing...The craft people as well as the people in front of the camera knew what they were doing. It wasn't as if it was done by rote. It was done professionally by people who knew what they were doing and enjoyed very much what they were doing...It was always a joy. I think any actor that worked the show would say the same thing.

During Ewing's two years, however, Thad's character never quite developed into what Mantley had hoped for. He played a sympathetic young man but never rose to the stature the producers had envisioned. Ewing also sensed this and describes his role:

I was an unofficial official deputy, or official unofficial deputy...a very loose character...He was just there...With Thad's family gone, Matt, Kitty, Doc and Festus sort of adopted him...Anything that needed to be done, you know, an extra hand here, or extra hand there, Thad was always around...He fit in whenever necessary.

When *Gunsmoke* was reinstated after the brief cancellation in 1967, the format was changed and Thad's character no longer appeared. Sometime later the role of the "archetypal young man" was taken over by Buck Taylor as Newly O'Brien.

Soon after leaving *Gunsmoke,* Ewing gave up show-business and travelled extensively throughout Europe, Russia, Mexico and the South Pacific pursuing his love of photography. "I got away from it," he explains. When he recently looked back on his experience with *Gunsmoke* he noted, "It was a lot of fun...a great joy," but, "It's in the past."

John Mantley

John Mantley became the producer of *Gunsmoke* in 1966 and guided the program through its final nine seasons. They were turbulent years marked by great changes in society, and equally great changes in television.

Mantley was born in Toronto in 1920 and aspired as a young boy to be an actor. His parents, who had met on stage while appearing in a play in New York City, were his inspiration. Theater permeated his childhood and his second cousin, who also hailed from Toronto, was Mary Pickford. He has recollections of sitting at the dinner table and asking his father, "Do the line! Do the line!" This was his way of asking his father to recite the most famous line from one of his plays, the memorable line, "Convict's daughter or not, I will marry her!" His parents swore that it brought the audience roaring to its feet each night.

Mantley graduated from the University of Toronto and received a master's degree from Pasadena Playhouse. He ultimately became an actor and made "a reasonable living at it." He toured the States in *Summer and Smoke* and his last role was in *Cyrano de Bergerac* in Kansas City. By this time he had decided that acting was not for him. "I found that acting was really just a kind of vocal exercise for me," he explains. "I loved the rehearsals and the terror of the opening night and so forth. But after that it was just ridiculous." He recognized that the time had come to look for a new profession for he realized, "That this was the wrong psychology for an actor. An actor must always want to perform every time that there's an audience." Acting had become "an empty profession" for him and Mantley retired to become a writer. Reflecting on these early years he noted that his boyhood aspirations were a gesture of love and that "the whole business of acting really came out of an incredible affection for both my parents."

During World War II he was in the Royal Canadian Air Force. After the War he wrote two novels, *The 27th Day* and *The Snow Birch* and started to direct for television in New York. He moved to Rome and directed numerous films, then returned to Hollywood where he became a free-lance writer and wrote scripts for the *Desilu-Westinghouse Playhouse* and for *The Untouchables*. Once he got the formula down for *The Untouchables* he found that it took him about 10 days to write a one-hour show and that each script earned him $3700 which was a "lot of money in those days."

Mantley met Philip Leacock, who directed two of his "all-time favorite features," *Hand in Hand* and *The Little Kidnapper,* while working as story editor on *The Great Adventure* for television. Leacock was one of the directors on the show. "I rewrote a couple of very bad scripts that he had," Mantley recalls, "And he liked them." Several years later when Leacock replaced Macdonnell on *Gunsmoke,* he asked Mantley to be his story editor. Mantley politely refused, however, saying that he was comfortable freelancing. Some time later, Mantley was at CBS' Studio Center with a script that he had written for Clint Eastwood and *Rawhide* when he bumped into Leacock again. "It's funny how life changes by crazy little incidents," he recalls. "I went over to him to tell him that I was sorry that we weren't going to work together." Unwilling to let the matter drop, Leacock asked, "Why won't you come?" To which Mantley replied, "Philip, you and I worked on *The Great Adventure* and I got an ulcer from that show." And Leacock replied, "Well, I never knew that, dear boy. What happened?" Mantley explained,

> I had a producer who couldn't make a decision. He'd go home with his pipe between his teeth on a Friday afternoon and we'd have to shoot a new

show on Monday morning. But we didn't have a script because he would never O.K. any of the ideas that I or anybody else would come up with. Then that night he would O.K. something and I'd be there all night long with the script so it could be xeroxed and shot Monday. And since I'm a responsible guy, that gave me an ulcer.

To this Leacock answered, "Well, my dear boy I do think that I can make a decision. I don't think you'd have that problem with me," but Mantley explained:

It isn't just that Philip. You know I'm making money as a free lance writer now, and I write from seven o'clock in the morning until a little after lunch and that's all. And I'm making a lot of money.

In reply, Leacock innocently asked, "Look here, old boy. If you could make the same amount of money you're making now would you come and be my story editor?" Mantley felt that it was safe to say "yes" knowing full well that there was no way Leacock could come up with that kind of money since story editors at the time were earning between $500 and $600 per week. Mantley returned home and quickly put the matter out of his mind when two hours later the phone rang. It was CBS and they were offering him the position on his terms. "I was trapped," he recalls, "And that's how it happened."

After a year on *Gunsmoke* Leacock made him associate producer, which according to Mantley "didn't mean anything" for he found that he was doing the same thing he had as story editor. The second year he was made producer but told Leacock, "Philip, you're doing everything and I don't want a credit that I didn't earn, so take the credit off." A distressed Leacock replied, "Well you know I can't do that. It would look very bad you know. I think I've been really naughty and you should have some responsibility." After this Mantley became line producer and finally felt involved in the creative process.

It was at this time that Leacock took the job of executive producer of the film *Firecreek*, starring Henry Fonda and James Stewart and asked Mantley to join him as line producer. Mantley now calls their agreement "the dumbest pact ever made by two producers." They agreed to alternate between the movie and *Gunsmoke*, with each taking a turn on a weekly basis. They soon recognized, however, that the arrangement was "insane" and Leacock assumed primary responsibility for the feature while Mantley stayed with *Gunsmoke*.

Mantley also produced other shows during this time. He and Leacock were assigned by CBS to fix an ailing program, *The Wild Wild West* and later on he was called on to work in the same capacity on *MacGyver*, which was also "going down the tubes." These experiences, and similar involvement in other failing shows after *Gunsmoke*, such as *Buck Rogers in the 25th Century*, earned Mantley the unofficial title, "The Fixer."

GUNSMOKE — I. THE HISTORY

When Leacock left *Gunsmoke* and Mantley took over he felt that he was in a secure position as producer. However, the greatest challenge of his career was about to confront him, for the antiviolence movement was casting a long shadow on television and action-adventure series were fighting for their existence.

The Antiviolence Movement

The television antiviolence movement had its beginning in the 1950s. In 1956, Senator Estes Kefauver was conducting congressional hearings into the effect of television violence on society. There was great concern that television was contributing to the rise in juvenile delinquency. Several years later, in October 1959, *The Untouchables* premiered on ABC and became one of the most popular and bloody series in television history. It portrayed the violence of the Prohibition era week after week, and as we have seen John Mantley was ironically one of its writers. ABC's success was not lost on the two other major networks and they started to copy *The Untouchables*. NBC and CBS were so impressed that they hired away key executives from ABC who had been involved in formulating its violent programming. As a consequence, James Aubrey went to CBS and Robert Kinter to NBC and became presidents of these respective networks. Violence on television rapidly escalated as each network sought to go one better in portraying greater and greater mayhem.

In 1961, Senator Thomas J. Dodd of Connecticut took up the cause of the antiviolence movement and pushed for restrictions. One psychologist observed that children exposed to violence on television developed feelings of hostility that could be expressed overtly. For a while it appeared that restrictions would be imposed but then the antiviolence movement lost some of its steam. When John F. Kennedy and Martin Luther King were assassinated, however, the movement regained its momentum and this time threatened television with a vengeance. Television had become the scapegoat for society's ailments and in 1968–69 John Pastore's Senate subcommittee on communications started to look into violence and sex on television.

The writing was on the wall and the networks took heed. They knew that restrictions would be imposed and decided to minimize them by implementing in an anticipatory fashion guidelines and self-regulation. Each network started to develop protocols for limiting violence in its programming. It was a race against time and when the surgeon general became involved directly in the controversy in 1969, it was evident that they had to move expeditiously. Those at CBS felt that the political mood was so hostile that whatever the outcome of the hearings, the findings would not bode well for television. A point system, or "violence quotient" was adopted by the network in 1971. "There were so many points for clean killings, so many for killings with blood, so many for slaps, and so many for kicks and punches," Mantley explained. "If the total was too high, the script was rejected."

In reflecting on the effects of the antiviolence movement on *Gunsmoke,* Arness observed:

> It slowed down a lot of the action, I'm sure of that... The network censors got into the act... I didn't fight that battle out. It was all upstairs. I think that John Mantley had to go up and fight all that out. There was a lot of restriction put on us, which was a pain in the neck. It was particularly galling because they would take out a shoot-out scene saying, "No, you can't shoot this," and, "You can't do that." And then we'd tune in on CBS that night and they'd have some old Western movie on with some movie actor, and they'd be shooting people down every five feet.

Director Robert Totten also found that there was arbitrariness in the implementation of the antiviolence edicts. From behind the camera he observed that:

> The antiviolence movement didn't really cripple things so much as to what we did, as to how we did them. It had to do a lot with staging. The characters did a lot more talking than resorting. They did not resort to violence so quickly. They tried to talk themselves out of it. Sometimes it became a pain in the neck to deal with. Totally unnecessary. It gave people that were not qualified some sort of right to be officious censors... It was another one of our good old American attempts to control entertainment in the worse kind of way. But we survived it, and made some good shows in spite of it.

CBS focused especially on *Gunsmoke,* its banner action-adventure series. Mantley was forced to walk a thin line. As one pundit put it, "What is *Gunsmoke* without gunsmoke?" *Gunsmoke* of course, by its very nature was a violent program and the antiviolence movement threatened its very existence. Mantley, however, was confident that *Gunsmoke* would survive for he felt that he had limitless possibilities. He could eliminate much of the violence and build stories around his versatile and famous characters. He reassured himself and thought:

> Everybody else in this town's in trouble who's got an action-adventure show, but I'm not 'cause I've got four of the best actors in the business and I can write any number of shows around them.

In retrospect, Mantley views this attitude as having been "nearly fatal," and to this day marvels:

> It's really inconceivable to me that I made this mistake because as you know I was born and brought up on what constitutes drama. I mean it

was talked about in my home all the time when I was a child. I was dumb, for the essence of drama is conflict and I couldn't make conflict between these people. They trusted one another implicitly. They loved one another. They thought the same way about everything, and they were all liberals.

To his dismay Mantley found that he was unable to find writers "who could write about conflict between these people." In fact, during a five year period he felt that he was able to do only two shows with "real conflict" between the principals.

Although the antiviolence movement was a greater threat than Mantley had at first anticipated, it ironically provided him with an opportunity that according to him comes to a producer "but once in a life-time." The network people who were usually a constant presence, now pulled away from him. They felt that it was but a matter of time until hostile social forces sounded the death-knell for *Gunsmoke*, and none of them wanted to be anywhere near when it went down. As Mantley notes, "In this business, success has many fathers and failure is an orphan." Mantley recalls "that from that moment on nobody at the network even knew that I existed." This was not just paranoia on the part of the executives but was indeed based on reality, for Paley's management style over the years had made it clear that a failed program was the sign of a failing executive.

Mantley, therefore, was given limitless rope with which to hang himself.

The Solution

When Mantley realized that he was in just as much trouble as every other producer of an adventure series in Hollywood, he made a radical decision that would forever change the format that had been *Gunsmoke's* trademark. He was convinced that changes were necessary for *Gunsmoke's* survival, and he decided to sacrifice the authenticity that had been so carefully developed over the years. At first Mantley did not want to make these modifications, and explained, "The words that can kill this show are, let's do it differently."[151] However, "the show changed because forces forced me to change." He once even complained privately that it got so bad that there were "more children on *Gunsmoke* than...on *Family Affair*."[152] Mantley marvelled that "as the country grows more permissive and freer in dealing with adult themes, television grows more puritanical. We're going backwards."

As part of the necessary changes Mantley decided to do what he had done on *The Untouchables*. "I started to bring outsiders in," he explains,

> ...Guest stars who were real actors and not just images. Ed Asner, Jon Voight, Richard Dreyfuss, and Ellen Burstyn who did their first film ever

on *Gunsmoke*. Bette Davis and Jean Arthur who came because they had stories. And the stories came about because of the terrible tragedies of the Kennedys and Martin Luther King, when a tremendous revulsion to violence developed and television became the scapegoat.

It was this restrictive environment that provided Mantley with the opportunity to explore the story-telling possibilities of *Gunsmoke,* and he found that the possibilities were limitless. Commenting on one of the stories from this period, *This Golden Land,* Mantley says, "Can you imagine in your wildest dreams any network permitting any producer to do a Western about a Jewish patriarch's dedication to the Torah? Just to try and present it would have been crazy." In *The Fires of Ignorance, Gunsmoke* explored compulsory education and a child's need to learn. With *The Deadly Innocent* it presented the travails of a mentally retarded boy. "We were able to do all these things," Mantley reflects.

> We even got carried away and tried to do a show about a midget who conned everyone into thinking that he turned into an elephant at midnight. *[Arizona Midnight]* And it would have worked, too, if we had gotten the right midget.

These divergences from *Gunsmoke's* tradition were greeted favorably by many. *The Deadly Innocent* received an award from the President's Council on Mental Retardation. Another episode, *The Scavengers,* starring Cicely Tyson received the Black Image Award. *This Golden Land* won the mass media "Brotherhood" Award from the National Conference of Christians and Jews. Mantley observes with pride that during his tenure, six consecutive Fame Awards and three Western Heritage Awards were given to *Gunsmoke.*

Mantley found that *Gunsmoke* was weathering what he perceived to be the greatest threat to its existence. The program was singled out and commended for avoiding gratuitous violence. There was a growing emphasis on dramatic rather than physical confrontations. "Forget plot and bring us plays with strong character conflicts," Mantley said to his writers. They were told, "Don't worry about the West, or about Matt, or Kitty, or our characters. We can fit the play to our specifics."[153] Clearly, Mantley was willing to make radical alterations in format, and whatever else was necessary to save *Gunsmoke.* He was forced to turn his back on his earlier sentiments as expressed in a *New York Times* interview,

> It's a grave mistake to make today's sociological comments in a Western drama. The two elements are incompatible. It is invalid to take the problems of today and burden them on another time.[154]

More and more Matt had to keep his gun in its holster and resort to fisticuffs and other forms of persuasion. As Mantley brought in guest stars he relied less and less on the principals and on Matt in particular. "It is true," said Mantley, that we see less and less of him...because of the strong CBS position in regard to violence. He is a marshal with a gun on his hip, and I cannot just have him snoozing in the sun or tipping his hat to the ladies. He is a dramatic hero, and I feel that when he is on the screen he must function as a hero and a lawman.[155]

Arness supported these changes and accepted them graciously. It also gave him the opportunity to spend more time with his family.

Cecil Smith observed in his 1969 article, *Gunsmoke Wins Without a Shootout*,[156] that despite changes the show was able to maintain its quality. In 1971, Dick Kleiner noted that *Gunsmoke* was *Better Without Violence*.[157] While Meston and Macdonnell had portrayed a more authentic Western than had ever been created before, Mantley told contemporary stories within a mythic environment. He created a dramatic anthology of stories incidentally set in the West.

Dennis Weaver, reflecting on these changes, commented:

It became much more epic...It had a broader canvas, a larger canvas. It began to go away from what it really depended on in the beginning...character studies. There was a little more emphasis on the bigness of the show...The show went on many more locations. I think it was a change for the better...because it needed freshening up. That was one thing that I think saved the show...That John Mantley came in and brought a whole new stable of writers with fresh ideas and with a kind of grander look at a more epic style.

Not everyone viewed these changes favorably, however. Macdonnell and those who had created the show and had guided it to its phenomenal successes in the early years, felt that *Gunsmoke* had been tampered with. They felt that it had lost its original purity and intent, and that the authenticity that had distinguished it and that had enabled it to rise above all other shows in its genre was gone. Ken Curtis observed, "Because of the Mantley anthology change we all had less of an impact on each story, which in my opinion lead eventually to the demise of *Gunsmoke.*" When guest stars were first introduced, Milburn Stone grumbled, "We're Matt, Kitty, Doc and Festus. We have no other identity. A Jean Arthur, a James Whitmore, a Betty Hutton are one-shots. Their fans will tune in, but not necessarily again."

Despite the criticisms, *Gunsmoke* lasted while all other westerns rode off into the sunset. It is quite possible that *Gunsmoke* would not have survived the social upheavals of the late sixties and early seventies without drastic changes in its format. It is to Mantley's credit that he had the courage to make difficult decisions and yet, to maintain to a great degree the quality of the program.

Television — The New Frontier

The Writers of the Second Decade

During the last ten years of the program there were many writers who contributed to the constantly evolving world of *Gunsmoke*. At one time John Mantley and his story editor, Calvin Clements, supervised 15 writers in a single season. They were not radio writers as had been the case in the first decade but came from varied backgrounds. Mantley and Clements, however, nurtured their talents and some of them developed their craft as television writers on *Gunsmoke*. Commenting on these writers, Mantley recently stated:

> Earl Wallace had never written any drama. He had been the editor of a newspaper. Jimmy Byrnes had never sold anything, he learned on *Gunsmoke* and wrote *Charlie Noon* and *The Busters*. Bill Kelley who won the Academy Award with Earl Wallace had never written any drama at all. He was a novelist who learned his trade on *Gunsmoke*. We had wonderful writers like Paul Savage, and Calvin Clements who has written more drama than any man alive. When they suddenly realized that we could do anything, Wow! The stories started coming in. There was a new infusion of ideas. The movie, *Witness* came from *Gunsmoke*. The script was called *The Pigman* but it was never done on *Gunsmoke* for the show was cancelled. It was an incredible period. I used to wake up every morning and say, "My God! They're going to pay me to do this again."

Paul F. Edwards is one of the writers who worked on the program during this period. He spent time in Vietnam where he did journalistic and photographic work. When he returned to the States, he wrote several screen plays. One of them, *Dakota Story,* was optioned by Mantley. It was written with George C. Scott in mind but was never produced. However, Mantley was impressed with Edwards' work and took him on as a staff writer in 1969. Edwards wrote some memorable stories including *Chato* and *Hostage!* in which he dealt with American Indians, a subject that has always haunted him. His preoccupation with the subject is reminiscent of John Meston. When questioned as to why, Edwards explained:

> I was born in the middle West and I know that the fate of the American Indian at the hands of American culture has been a disaster. It is probably one of the two major injustices upon which much of the power of this country has been built. The other, of course, being the black experience. We enslaved the one people and committed genocide on the other. I felt incredibly empathic with the Indian, and it was a fertile area for drama.

He found that *Gunsmoke* presented him with a wonderful opportunity to explore various issues as a writer. It had a rich tradition and versatile characters, and Edwards found that:

> It was a kind of classic American fairytale. It had a wonderfully well-rounded established cast of very identifiable people. It was already well-

established by the time I got to it... and so it was like writing in a formula, but it was a formula that was remarkably ample and generous as to what you could do. The show itself was scrupulously produced. The actors knew exactly who they were, and what they would or would not say. And they were right about it. It was like watching an ensemble cast of the Royal Shakespeare Company, only they were doing another kind of genre.

Since Edwards was concerned primarily with moral issues he explored how this could best be presented within *Gunsmoke's* format. He found that the character of Matt was ideally suited to this purpose. Matt was able to give "voice" to ethical concerns through his actions. Edwards notes that:

> Matt Dillon was really a kind of magical Lancelot. A mythological Lone Ranger who had this tremendous innate capacity to sort out what was just, and to come down on the right side of things. Of course, that was his appeal. He had this unerring sense of what was ethically right and a moral aptitude without being a bore, or a pedant, or a person who laid his views off in all directions...

Edwards wrote at the height of the antiviolence movement and like other writers on television at the time, he had to come to terms with this issue. He reflects that:

> There was a kind of tacit understanding that we avoid the misuse of violence. We were never sat down and given a lecture as to how we were supposed to shoot somebody down. In other words, we avoided the Sam Peckinpah school of violence... When I used violence I tried to do one of two things. I tried to show that a good man (Matt) avoided it whenever possible and sometimes at considerable sacrifice to himself. When it was no longer possible to deal with things on any other terms he used it quickly, efficiently, and to a minimum degree to get the job done. When I showed violence on the parts of other people, whether moral or physical, I tried to show that those who do not have a sound humanity, a sound ethical grounding, are the abusers of physical and mechanical agents of violence. I tried to make that reprehensible and ugly.

Edwards created powerful figures for Matt to confront. His villains were frequently the embodiment and distillate of evil and perversion. Their physical and spiritual, albeit evil stature, was equal to that of Matt's. When they came on the screen, even though audiences had always seen Matt triumph before, they could not be certain that Matt would not be vanquished this time. Edwards explains how he crafted these characters so as to challenge Matt to the point where he had to face the very essence of his convictions and morality. He was forced to struggle with the primal and evil forces within himself that are the lot of all men.

> What I tried to do was to put Matt up against moral or ethical dilemmas where it would really stretch him and make him look at his values. And whenever I could, I tried to put him against an adversary who would find some area of his life where he had a weakness or potential weakness, and goes at him where he is most vulnerable.

Edwards was able to find this weakness in the memorable episode, *Hostage!* in which Kitty is abused. Given his love for Kitty, such stories forced Matt to look in the mirror and test his convictions.

The characters on *Gunsmoke* were constantly evolving. They had a history and a background of experiences that approximated real-life individuals. Commenting on the principal actors Edwards notes:

> They succeeded in creating a real family of characters who had a special kind of quality. But qualities which were tremendously, deeply, and mythopoetically American. Americans loved what they were getting. They loved it in the same way they love Huckleberry Finn. It had a folk quality about it that I think was truly remarkable... They were all figures that I think were quintessential Americana. And they were done in such a way that if you set up an archetype, within that archetype there was all kinds of play and room to explore the quirkiness of the individual. It rang a real chord.

In looking back on his career as a writer, Edwards discussed what most writers for television have experienced, a gradual and relentless elimination of the creative elements from the most pervasive medium in the history of mankind. He feels that the demise of the western genre was to a significant degree caused by these changes. "The desire of business to capitalize on the genre," destroyed the Western.

> They really made an awful lot of garbage... real stupid stuff. And the public to some extent overdosed on it from sheer exposure. Plus, they were making all of these junko movies and finally, they became cartoons of themselves... they became parodies. And the public got tired...

In the capacity of story consultant, Edwards found that he was called upon to protect the writing of other authors. He saw how network interference tended to destroy whatever was distinctive, fresh, or visionary in a given writer's work. He tried to buffer and shield these writers from the increasing influence of non-creative business elements in the industry. He recalls:

> Calvin Clements and I would always try to get hold of the writers that we thought were the ones who really brought something to the party... like Ron Bishop... the best writer who ever wrote for *Gunsmoke*. I always tried to appropriate his stuff so I could protect it from the network... To try to maintain the essence of what he wrote. He brought a unique command

GUNSMOKE — I. THE HISTORY

to what the West was all about. He used to say, "Everytime you feed something to the network they stomp it flat and take all the character out of it."

In attempting to sum up the significance of his experiences with *Gunsmoke,* Edwards stated:

> I have never had an experience like the *Gunsmoke* experience and I don't suppose I ever will, because television has become very mechanical and predatory. But *Gunsmoke* was a totally quality show to work on. And I guess because it had so much clout, people did not snipe at you. The accounting and legal types, who really don't know how to do anything, have so much power now that unless your show is extremely successful, they have the power to destroy you with their idiotic input because they have control of the purses. Television is not fun anymore...It's like working in a sweat-shop. The pay may be wonderful...but it doesn't matter that much because the joy of participating is not at all commensurate like it was on *Gunsmoke*...You knew you were reaching for something good and that no one was going to stop you from doing it. There were none of these damn creeps in their black towers, or wherever they lurk, who don't know anything, who can't do anything except say, "No," who have very little judgment about what is good. Nowadays they are so involved they have all the authority and none of the ability. That was not the case on *Gunsmoke*. We did the best we could and fought to keep it the best we could and we succeeded. I've never been able to do it anywhere else again.

A major contributor during the second decade was writer Ron Bishop, who wrote some of the most powerful and memorable scripts on *Gunsmoke*. He died in early 1988 after a stroke. In one classic story, *A Hat,* he quotes a Blackfoot Indian who says "Ash-may, O-may" which translates, "Don't lie and don't quit," a creed for the Blackfoot Indians and perhaps a metaphor for Bishop's work and life. His stories were true Western parables, and his dialogue was rich with the vernacular of its time. The characters Bishop created were larger than life, and transcended their era. In one episode *Balls, Bullets, and Bonnets, and in That Order* (called *Kiowa* when it aired on television) the first thing Bishop says is, "Nobody ever saw Dan Colter smile," which was his way of conjuring the spirit of this hard-as-nails frontiersman. He went on, "Colter's got a wry sense of humor—when involved with a humorous sense of rye. But nobody's ever seen him drunk, and nobody ever will. Because that's just another surrender to Colter. And Colter has never surrendered to anything in his life."

Like all his characters, Bishop's villains breathe the fire of life. They are thoroughly amoral creatures, who just happen to be human. In *Mannon,* Bishop describes Matt's arch-nemesis as "The Devil's temporary victory in its finest focus...(Mannon) knows the West, pussy to posse. To see him is to

Television — The New Frontier

smell smoke." In *Captive* (called *Waco* on television), Bishop paints Waco as "a kind of venal bastard, but cunning enough to be President, even in that day when men ran instead of echoes."

In a 1975 *Los Angeles Times* article, John Mantley called Bishop, "the most unique writer in television today."[158] And at the *Gunsmoke* retrospective held at the Los Angeles County Museum of Art in 1988, Mantley once again affirmed Bishop's status. Bishop's wonderfully rich episode, *Matt's Love Story*, was one of two programs shown at the retrospective, the other being *Matt Gets It* by John Meston.

When *Matt's Love Story* first aired in 1973, as *Gunsmoke* hit the ripe old age of 19, a critic for the *New York Times*, Cyclops, wrote:

> ...the writing was as good as you'll ever get in a Western, gnarled, approximately Elizabethan, a language that was probably never a vernacular but in this instance was so plausibly stylized—a lingual compost of all our ideas about the West, knotty analogies, brutish poems, the inchoate cleverly tortured into expressions of feeling—that myth marched in and made itself at home. Words reacquired some of the magic that our glaze of irony, our evasions of reality, had stolen from them.[159]

Ron Bishop made a literary statement in the way he wrote and a philosophical one in the way he lived. He was a conservationist, a war hero, a black belt in karate, and a man who found that the wide open spaces of Wyoming ideally satisfied his outdoorsman leanings. Bishop was part Indian and Mantley found him to be "the strongest man I ever knew." His friends called him "Bear." Edwards describes him as "a fantastic man and a phenomenon in his own right. He was a maverick and adventuring character, a tremendously vital man with a quirky and wonderful skill." Mantley recounted one of many stories that Bishop's friends tell about him.

> Many, many years ago there was a tremendous blizzard in the West. *LOOK* magazine had an edition devoted to the most extraordinary pictures of frozen cows standing up. People died in their cars who got caught in the blizzard. Helicopters were dropping food to people and hay for the cows. The day before the blizzard started there was a cougar out there that was killing cattle and Ron was a big game hunter. They paid him to come in and take care of the cougar, and the sheriff's posse took him to the head of this valley and dropped him off with his rifle and a small pack and he trudged off into the snow with his snow-shoes. And for the next few days nobody had time to think about Ron Bishop. Suddenly, when the blizzard was over and things were returning to normal, somebody said, "Oh, my God! Bishop!" So they got the posse and they went to the valley. And way down there was Ron with the cougar draped over his shoulder.

GUNSMOKE — I. THE HISTORY

Mantley had many other memories about Bishop but prefaced them by saying that: "The line between reality and fantasy didn't really exist for him at all."

Bishop was larger than life and his vitality came through in his stories and characters. In a 1975 *Los Angeles Times* interview, Bishop said, "People must have something strong to strive for...this country wasn't built on soda pop."[160] A line from one of his stories may serve as his epitaph: "Now there's a man...a good man." (*Mannon*, 1968.)

Paul Savage is a writer whose association with *Gunsmoke* was one of the longest. As a young actor, Macdonnell hired him for the radio shows as an "off-mike-ad-lib-head-nod" performer. He recalls that this literally "paid for my food at the time." Savage started writing in 1957, "when television was relatively young...and well-established writers and directors looked down on it." He recently observed, "It was the bastard industry of Hollywood. That's how I got my foot in the door." A decade after they first met, he once again approached Macdonnell who was now producing the television show, to tell him that he was now a writer. Savage soon found that he was writing stories for the television program and contributed over 20 scripts. He became the story consultant from the twelfth through the fourteenth seasons. One of his stories, *Owney Tupper Had a Daughter*, was nominated for a Writer's Guild Award. It dealt with an old man raising his daughter alone with great love and tenderness. The child is taken from him by the courts because they question whether he can provide her with material comforts. He also wrote *Kitty's Love Affair*, which was one of the few episodes where Kitty strays from Matt, and the powerful, *The Long Night*, where Louie Pheeters is humiliated by a vicious bounty hunter played by Bruce Dern.

Robert Totten recently reflected on the writers he worked with on *Gunsmoke* and in particular Savage. He observed that:

> ...His scripts were always samples of what scripts ought to be. His form, his structure were examples of what we wished all our scripts to be...His characters were always strong and rich...He always got down to the business at hand. He set his characters right up front...He was a student and a fan of classic drama so you know you never got involved with something that was hard to figure out. His scripts followed a logical path of drama development...The best compliment I could say about Paul is that he was consistent. He comes to mind first and foremost...

Looking back over his long involvement with *Gunsmoke*, Savage observes:

> In almost every show there was a statement, obviously many times repeated. We set out to do characters. There was a sameness. The badman is a bad man, but there were almost always fine gradations. And

the good were never shining white, they always had shades of gray. And often times the blacks were not all black...they had shades of gray.

He notes further that:

That's not done today. In fact, it's not done at all. We don't have any westerns. We stick them in outer space and tell the same story. I think it's a tragedy. The young of our country should see dramatizations, albeit glamorized, that depict what it took, what this country came from. It came from the individual...the rugged individualist.

Like Edwards, Savage has been witness to the changes in television and the intrusions on creativity. "The networks, who are strictly business people...make creative decisions," he notes.

Look at what we have on television today. They are copyists. There isn't one single creative entity in the television industry who is left totally alone...The golden age of television, they made a lot of garbage, there's no denying...but the creative talents were left alone...But when the committee system set in, things changed. I think tremendously.

Calvin Clements wrote more scripts for *Gunsmoke* than any other writer in the last decade. Clements was executive story consultant during the fifteenth and sixteenth seasons and guided Mantley's writing staff. In the tradition of Meston and Bishop, Clements had a talent for conjuring characters. He created the character of Thad Greenwood and later on in *The Pillagers* introduced Newly O'Brien. He also created several recurring characters such as the pretty young widow "Abelia" who appeared in several sequels and was especially fond of Festus. A motley hillbilly family, consisting of Merry Florene, Roland Daniel, and Albert Moses, was also his creation. These characters had just the right combination of humor and larceny, and were frequent visitors who stirred things up a bit in Dodge. In addition to *Gunsmoke*, Clements wrote for several other television programs such as *G.E. Theatre*, *The Great Adventure*, *Bonanza*, and *The Greatest Show on Earth*. According to John Mantley, Clements has "probably written more drama than any other man alive."

Jim Byrnes was assistant story consultant for two seasons. He wrote 26 episodes and the recent made-for-television movie, *Gunsmoke: Return to Dodge*. Byrnes also has the distinction of writing the only three-parter for *Gunsmoke*, *Gold Train: The Bullet*. Byrnes had a wonderful knack for finding the vulnerable side of the principal characters. In *The Badge*, Matt is almost fatally wounded and when he is out of danger, Kitty leaves because she is unable to face the prospect that next time he may die. It was a strong statement and CBS executives argued that it was out of character for Kitty and rejected the story. Mantley tendered his resignation to save it and it was reinstated in the

Table 4. The Television Writers — The Second Decade: 1965–1975 (Selected List)

YEAR	11	12	13	14	15	16	17	18	19	20	TOTAL
Calvin Clements*	5	3	6	8	4	1	2	4	4	1	38
Jim Byrnes	0	0	0	2	3	1	4	5	3	8	26
Paul Savage*	4	2	0	3	0	0	0	2	4	2	17
Ron Bishop	0	0	1	5	1	0	2	3	2	1	15
Clyde Ware*	5	7	1	0	0	0	0	0	0	0	13
Jack Miller	0	0	0	0	0	7	3	2	0	0	12
Hal Sitowitz	2	3	3	0	0	0	0	1	1	0	10
William Kelley	0	0	0	0	3	3	2	1	0	0	9
Les Crutchfield*	4	3	0	0	0	0	0	0	0	0	7
Preston Wood	0	2	0	1	1	1	0	0	0	0	5
Paul F. Edwards	0	0	0	0	0	1	0	1	2	0	4

*Also wrote in the first decade: 1955–1965.

Table 5. The Story Consultants

Season	Executive Story Consultant	Story Consultant	Assistant Story Consultant
10th		John Mantley	
11th		John Mantley	
12th		Paul Savage	
13th		Paul Savage	
14th		Paul Savage	Jim Byrnes
15th	Calvin Clements		Jim Byrnes
16th	Calvin Clements		Paul F. Edwards
17th	Jack Miller		Paul F. Edwards
18th	Jack Miller		Paul F. Edwards
19th	Jack Miller		Paul F. Edwards*
20th	Jack Miller		

*Only at the start of the season.

schedule. It remains one of the most powerful episodes aired. In another episode, *Kimbro,* Matt finds the man who inspired him to become a lawman, Adam Kimbro, cleaning out stables for whiskey money. Feeling the need to help his mentor, Matt offers Kimbro the chance to wear a badge once more. The two men share quiet memories, which force Matt to be introspective, and to question his choices in life. The irony is that Matt could be Kimbro in 20 years. Another one of Byrnes' episodes that shakes the foundations of Dodge is *The Foundling.* In that story Matt is given the responsibility of finding a home for an abandoned infant. In the interim he thrusts the baby on Kitty, who considers the child an inconvenience. However, when the time comes to take the baby away, Kitty refuses to give her up. The little girl has triggered Kitty's maternal instincts, and she will do anything to keep her, even sell the Long Branch.

Clyde Ware was also an active writer during the final decade. He was an actor and writer in New York before he moved to Los Angeles. Besides *Gunsmoke* he also wrote for *Rawhide, Airwolf,* and *Alfred Hitchcock Presents.* One of his favorite *Gunsmoke* stories was *Seven Hours Til Dawn.* "I was able to 'kill' Matt Dillon," he recalled.

> ...Even in Kitty's and Festus' eyes; though Doc, of course, was doing it to save Matt's life, [to] give him a chance to recover from gunshot wounds and retake Dodge from John Barrymore, Jr., and gang...

Reflecting on *Gunsmoke* he commented that: "The stories usually strove for high moral values, which always have relevance." As a writer he found that there was something special about creating for Westerns. He noted,

> To me a good story is tell-able in any genre; the Western form was, possibly, the "purest" in a sense, because of the innocence of the period compared to subsequent eras.

In the first decade Macdonnell did not formally use story consultants. However, when Leacock came on as producer he brought John Mantley on as the first story consultant. Table 5 shows the story consultants for the final decade.

The Directors of the Last Decade

There were many directors who worked on the program during the Leacock and Mantley years. The audience saw a different *Gunsmoke* of a more epic dimension. Some of these directors, like Mark Rydell, became best known in movies. Rydell started as an actor then became a television director on shows like *Ben Casey, I Spy,* and *The Wild Wild West.* He made his debut

GUNSMOKE — I. THE HISTORY

in films in 1968 with *The Fox*. His crowning achievement is *On Golden Pond* (1981), starring Katherine Hepburn and Henry Fonda in his last movie. Rydell's other credits include *Cinderella Liberty* (1974), *The Rose* (1979), and *The River* (1984) with Sissy Spacek and Mel Gibson.

Bernard McEveety directed the most *Gunsmoke* episodes during the last ten years and his brother, Vincent followed close behind. Bernard McEveety worked on numerous television programs including *The A-Team, The Big Valley, Charlie's Angels, Marcus Welby* and *The Waltons*. Vincent McEveety directed for Leacock on *Cimarron Strip* as well as on many other programs. His credits include *Dallas, Dirty Sally, Perry Mason, Star Trek,* and *The Untouchables*.

Gunnar Helstrom was very active in the last eight years of the program. He even acted occasionally and was featured in the episode *Dead Man's Law*. He directed for other television programs such as *Dallas, The Wild Wild West* and *The Powers of Matthew Star*.

Other directors included Robert Totten, Philip Leacock, Allen Reisner, and Irving J. Moore. Moore attributed *Gunsmoke's* success to dealing "with basic humanities more than other shows at the time." He had directed hundreds of television shows and was asked by Mantley to direct for *Gunsmoke* after they met on the set of *The Wild Wild West*. When asked to reflect on who the "guiding force" was on *Gunsmoke,* he indicated that, "There were many guiding forces over the years... [and] no one person should get the credit for the success." In looking back on why *Gunsmoke* and other television Westerns disappeared from the scene he attributed it to the fact that they were "very expensive to make."

Robert Totten has won various awards for directing including the George Foster Peabody Broadcasting Award for "The Red Pony," The National Cowboy Hall of Fame Award for "The Sackets," the Emmy for "Huckleberry Finn," and the Golden Lariat for "Excellence in Filmmaking" spanning 25 years. In a recent interview he offered some insights into what it was like to work on *Gunsmoke*. Totten had the unique opportunity of working both behind and in front of the camera.

> I was shooting on a sound stage at Fox Western in Hollywood on Christmas Eve... Working on another episodic series, "Daniel Boone," when I got a call from my agent that right after the holidays I should report to *Gunsmoke*. That was a big thrill for me because I had been wanting to get a job as a director on *Gunsmoke* for some time but had no luck. As it turned out the reason I was suddenly getting lucky is that I was replacing a director who had become ill. It was almost like a life-time dream come true because years before when I was a teenage youngster I had auditioned for two or three of the first episodes, when it was a little half-hour black and white show. I went in, directed, and they liked it. I did a couple of more and they liked them... From there on they kept

trying to hire me to do multiples and I would settle for doing a few at a time...

On the first day of shooting I could immediately feel that it was a more important show than others...The people cared more about it...They had greater pride in what they were doing and you had the feeling that you were working on something worthwhile. It was a classy thing to work on *Gunsmoke*. Like the Cosby stuff today as far as ratings are concerned...The producers cared very much. They didn't work by the hour. They worked until they got the job done, to where they could quit for a little while and have a few moments of privacy and rest. But they were very hard-working guys. And of course, the scripts were really fine. When you got to the directors you had the best directors in episodic television at the time. Then when you came to the crew, you had the finest cameraman because it was either a place where a big name cameraman was doing television to change the pace for himself from features, or it would be a new cameraman that was on his way up to the big time that would be stopping off to do a couple of *Gunsmokes*...When it came to the rest of the crew they were the finest electricians, craft service, props people, and the finest in make-up and cosmetics and hair and wardrobe...And they were the best that you could find in set design, construction, decoration and special effects, and all the things that you need to make movies. When it came to your regular cast it speaks for itself how much they cared...And the guest cast...It was a big deal for an actor to get the guest shot...A very prestigious credit to have...

I remember when Clyde Ware wrote the "Newcomers." I think he first wrote it for a bunch of Greek people and then he changed it...I think he got some Irish involved. Finally we settled on making it Scandinavian because we had seen this actor down in San Diego at the Globe Theater by the name of Jon Voight. And we kind of wanted to see him and Karl Swenson do a father and son thing so let's make them Scandinavian. Of course, who is this kid? Hardly anyone has faith in him. Why are we getting this kid when there's name people we could get? Well, I think you know what happened to Jon Voight. He is the best American actor that we have. He did several shows for *Gunsmoke*. But his first was the "Newcomers." In those days we didn't have videotape auditions that actors could take around to casting agents and directors so he used that 50-millimeter can of film to get him into the Schlesinger film, "Midnight Cowboy" that really made him the big star of that time...It was his *Gunsmoke* episode of the "Newcomers" that did that.

Victor French was an actor who appeared in many *Gunsmoke* episodes and also directed during the last season. He had reflected on his approach to directing and how he got started.

I had done a lot of television, and I found that most of the guys who were directing television, that they were somebody's son and had been second

Table 6. The Directors, The Second Decade: 1965–1975 (Selected List)

YEAR	11	12	13	14	15	16	17	18	19	20	TOTAL
B. McEveety	0	0	1	8	8	9	8	3	9	7	53
V. McEveety*	6	3	3	6	6	8	4	1	4	1	42
G. Hellstrom	0	0	3	1	2	1	1	7	7	9	31
R. Totten	3	7	6	1	2	3	1	0	0	0	23
I. Moore	0	3	3	1	0	0	2	3	2	0	14
P. Leacock	0	0	0	0	7	2	2	1	0	0	12
M. Rydell*	3	3	0	0	0	0	0	0	0	0	6
V. French	0	0	0	0	0	0	0	0	0	5	5
H. Harris*	5	0	0	0	0	0	0	0	0	0	5
J. Rich*	0	0	2	2	0	0	0	0	0	0	4
A. Reisner*	2	2	0	0	0	0	0	0	0	0	4

*Also directed during the first decade.

assistant director or second assistant cameraman and then moved up to directing. And they had no idea how to tell a story. I think you can tell when there's a good director around or a bad one very quick. And so I guess I had done about 25 *Gunsmokes* and I kept saying, "Why don't you let me do one?" I mean, I had directed all this theater. And at that time they were using a whole lot of my students who had studied in my acting class so I said, "Come on here, why don't you let me do one of these?" So I was doing a "Movie of the Week" called *The Tribe,* and while I was filming on the set they sent over a script and said, "We want you to direct this." And it was the worst script I had ever read in my entire life. But I knew how good the people were. John Mantley and his staff were really wonderful and I knew they'd fix it.

And as it turned out, that *Gunsmoke* got more fan mail than any other in the history of the twenty years they were on the air. I enjoyed it. I knew I could do it. I have a lot of trouble saying, "Action" and things, so I never do. I just say, "Do something." But I like actors and I don't believe actors need to be babied. I think they're already big enough babies. They need to be taught some discipline. And that's what I do. I create a wonderful environment for actors to work in. I don't want to play the roles for them. Whenever they're finished they say, "Boy, that was fun to do. Why can't it be like that everywhere?" But you see you can't take one good actor and put him with another good actor and assume that you will have a good scene. If they have different ways of working, the first time they open their mouth they're gonna be at each other's throat. Casting wise you've got to put together a family of people who have a similar way of working. No two actors work exactly alike and there is no "way" to act. There are as many ways as there are actors. So you've got to put together people who have a mutual respect, courtesy, and a way of working that's similar. And then the magic will start out. One guy wants the results at the end, the other one at the beginning...And so I say to myself, "I'm just an actor who directs. I'm not a director."

Victor French died of lung cancer in the summer of 1989.

Buck Taylor and Newly O'Brien

It was during the final decade that the archetypal young man that *Gunsmoke* had been searching for, for 12 years, was finally found. Following on the heels of Quint Asper and Thaddeus Greenwood, it seemed that the character of Newly O'Brien best complemented the *Gunsmoke* family.

Buck Taylor first appeared on *Gunsmoke* as a heavy in a two-part episode, *Vengeance*. Three weeks later when he was asked to play the running character of Newly, the film had to be retired from the rerun shelf. He recalls that at first the producers were looking for a character "Newly Jorgensen," then after he auditioned and was cast, the character was renamed O'Brien to be faithful to Taylor's Irish background and dark looks. His character was designed by Clements and Mantley to be a versatile figure who could be used in different circumstances. Reflecting on the role, Taylor notes:

> I was the wholesome all–American kind of guy who in my estimation was a little too naive at times...But maybe it worked for the show...the public bought it...Kind of bashful around the ladies. The quiet silent type. A little irresponsible at times but, you know, Matt Dillon was the only guy that straightened things out. He had had some education at one point and was going to be a doctor, then came West from Pennsylvania. They made me a gunsmith, and a doctor, and a deputy, and whatever. I did a little bit of everything and they could go in a lot of different directions. I even defended Festus one time as a lawyer.

Newly was unlike any of the other major characters. He was not cast in a narrow mold and was often used as a vehicle that served thematic needs. And yet, Taylor was able to bring some consistency to the character so that Newly became a distinct personality in his own right. Coming from a family of performers he notes, "I was trained the old way. Be early, know your lines, and hit the marks."

Newly was the only major character to get married. In the poignant episode, *Patricia,* Newly takes a wife but she dies of leukemia. A distraught Newly vows to rededicate himself to medicine and to complete his studies under Doc's tutelage. It is said that this episode was written in anticipation of Milburn Stone's failing health in case Dodge needed a new physician.

GUNSMOKE — I. THE HISTORY

Buck Taylor was born Walter Clarence Taylor, III, and was nicknamed by his father when he laid eyes on him soon after birth. He was raised on a small ranch in the San Fernando Valley far from the Hollywood scene. His mother was an acrobatic dancer with the Dean Sisters and his father is the well-known character actor, Dub "Cannonball" Taylor. In high school he was a star gymnast. In 1960 he tried out for the United States Olympic team and was to try again in 1964 but his athletic career was cut short when he injured a shoulder while riding a horse as a stuntman. Taylor aspired to be an illustrator and at the University of Southern California studied art, cinema, and theater. He served in the Navy for two years and upon his return to civilian life decided to become an actor. He appeared in many television shows prior to *Gunsmoke* and drove a truck between jobs. He was generally cast as the villain. He also appeared in films such as *The Wild Angels, The Devil's Angels,* and *Ensign Pulver.*

Taylor has an interesting perspective as to the factors that made *Gunsmoke* a success. Besides the generally cited reasons, he noted that:

> ...part of the success of the show was all the people that especially Milburn [Stone] and Ken [Curtis] reached through the years in the heartland of America. They played at all the fairs and rodeos. And I think that that helped the show because people got to meet us. Milburn Stone told me that movie stars and television stars are two different types. A movie star you'll see in person and you'll kind of look at him and stay away, and kind of stare. Whereas, with television personalities, people come right up to you and say, "Newly, it's so good to see you. How's Doc?" This is because they have allowed you into their homes through the television set. They've allowed you into their bedrooms, into the sanctity of their castles, and that makes you not as big as life but part of their lives. They come up to you like they've known you for years.

The *Gunsmoke* cast did many personal appearances over the years and this supported the popularity of the show. As far back as the Macdonnell years Weaver, Blake, and Stone would travel whenever they could. In the earlier years this sometimes doubled their annual income. Taylor notes that in the final years he sometimes made appearances with Glenn Strange.

Taylor was witness to many of the changes on the show. Like all those involved he was sensitive to the forces that shaped the program. Commenting on these forces he recently observed:

> In one way it took away the action that I think a Western needs. In another way it forced us to come up with more intellectual scripts. But I think we lost most of our audience, the majority of the people that liked the action-packed Western, but oddly, we gained another audience in New York City and in other big cities.

Television — The New Frontier

The Citizens of Dodge

One of the factors that is rarely mentioned, yet contributed greatly to the success of *Gunsmoke,* was the emphasis on continuing "minor" characters. It seemed that much of Dodge was populated with familiar faces. They, too, had their history and contributed to the rich layers of "authenticity" that characterized the show.

Glenn Strange played Sam, the barkeep of the Long Branch. He developed Sam into a major figure around Dodge even though the total of his lines during all those years probably did not equal one decent monologue. Strange was born in New Mexico in 1899 of Irish—Cherokee parentage. His father was, appropriately, a bartender and a rancher. Strange learned to play the fiddle at the age of 12 and was occasionally seen playing it when the local orchestra struck up a tune at some Dodge City sociable. He was a rancher, rodeo performer and sheriff. Strange started in radio in El Paso in 1928. He left for Hollywood and appeared in hundreds of Westerns, usually as the villain confronting cowboy legends such as Hoot Gibson, Tim McCoy, Buck Jones, and Hopalong Cassidy. He made his name, however, playing Frankenstein in some of the greatest horror flicks of all time. Strange inherited Boris Karloff's electrodes and appeared as Mary Shelley's monster in *House of Frankenstein* (1945), *House of Dracula* (1945), and *Abbott and Costello Meet Frankenstein* (1948). He also appeared in obscure creature features such as *The Mad Monster* (1942), and *The Monster Maker* (1944). On television, Strange was the Lone Ranger's first nemesis, and wiped out all the Texas Rangers but one, "Kemo Sabe."

Strange got his chance on *Gunsmoke* when Arness met him in 1959 and asked him when he was going to do an episode. Arness explained that he liked to work with tall guys and at six-foot-four Strange fit the bill.

James Nusser played various roles on radio's *Gunsmoke* but he truly blossomed when he played the role of Louie Pheeters, "Gunsmoke's underrated derelict." With only a line or two Nusser was able to conjure the memorable character of Dodge City's town drunk. Unlike the archetypal drunks in television and cinema who are often comic figures, Louie was pure pathos. His vacant blue eyes staring off into the distance were the eyes of a shipwrecked man. Nusser struggled with alcoholism much of his life, and agents called him "his own worst enemy."[161] Commenting on his character Nusser said, "I don't understand Louie any more than I understand myself."

Ted Jordan played Nathan Burke, the freight agent. Jordan was born in Circleville, Ohio. Before the Second World War he did radio, then joined the See Bees. After he returned to the States he appeared in such movies as *The Wild One,* and *My Six Convicts.* Jordan was in the original Broadway cast of *The Caine Mutiny Court Martial* starring Henry Fonda. He played some

GUNSMOKE — I. THE HISTORY

minor roles on *Gunsmoke* before becoming a regular. Burke was considered the town gossip and was treated like a nuisance. His typical tirades to stir up the Dodge City populace would often be interrupted by Doc with one sentence, "Aw, shut up, Burke."

Hank Patterson played Hank, the stableman. He started out as a piano player for a road show in 1910 then was an actor in tent shows and in vaudeville. He moved to Hollywood and appeared in films like *Duel in the Sun* and *Abilene Town*. On television Patterson played Frank Ziffel on *Green Acres*. He also made appearances on *The Roy Rogers Show* and *Petticoat Junction*.

The stable was originally owned and run by Moss Grimmick as played by George Selk. Selk appeared in the 1953 science fiction classic, *It Came from Outer Space*.

John Harper played Percy Crump, Dodge's busy undertaker. He began his career in college plays and as a magician. Harper appeared in many little theater productions and between jobs worked as a house detective and a busboy. He took riding and fast-draw lessons so that he could audition for Westerns. After *Gunsmoke*, he took a job at the Post Office.

Howard Culver started on radio and played "Mark" Dillon on the original radio "pilot." He was the last Ellery Queen on radio. Culver started on television's *Gunsmoke* in its earliest years as Howie, the hotel clerk of the Dodge House. He also acted in *The Man from Denver* and *The Return of the Beverly Hillbillies*.

Charles Seel played Barney, the telegraph agent. Born in the Bronx, he was working in a glove factory as a young man when one day he saw a silent movie troupe filming in the streets. He landed a bit part and caught the acting bug. Seel appeared in vaudeville and then on radio and in 1937 moved to Hollywood. He is best known for his role on *Dennis the Menace* as Mr. Krinkle.

Woody Chambliss played Mr. Lathrop, the storekeeper. Born in Texas, he studied theater in London then returned to the States. He was a member of Michael Chekhov's repertory company. On television he appeared in *Lassie* and *The New Beginning*.

Dabbs Greer was Mr. Jonas, the owner of the general store. He also appeared on *Dobie Gillis*, *The Ghost and Mrs. Muir*, and *Little House on the Prairie*.

Robert Brubaker started his career doing radio at KMPC in Hollywood. During the 50s he acted on television on *Public Defender* and was the co-star of *US Marshal*. In films he appeared in *The Man of a Thousand Faces, Airport, My Man Godfrey* and *The Sting*. On *Gunsmoke* he played Jim Buck, the stage coach driver, and during the last two seasons he played Floyd, the bartender, after the death of Glenn Strange.

Roy Roberts played Mr. Bodkin, the banker. He first appeared in vaudeville and then played leading men on Broadway. Roberts acted in various films including *The Story of Temple Drake* (1933), *The Trumpet Blows*

(1934), and *The Lady Consents* (1936). A familiar face on television, on *The Gale Storm Show,* he played Captain Huxley, on *Petticoat Junction* he played Norman Curtis, and on *The Beverly Hillbillies* he was John Cushing. He also appeared on *The Lucy Show, Bewitched,* and *McHale's Navy.*

Charles Wagenheim was Halligan, a townsman. He played parts in numerous movies and played the title role in Hitchcock's *The Assassin.*

Sarah Selby appeared as Ma Smalley, who ran Dodge City's boarding House billed as a "clean and affordable alternative to the more expensive Dodge House." She performed in top radio programs, and on television was seen in programs like *Family Affair, My Three Sons* and *Petticoat Junction.* Her movie credits include *The Iron Mistress* (1952), *An Affair to Remember* (1957), and *Stopover Tokyo* (1957).

Tom Brown played Ed O'Connor, the rancher. He started in vaudeville as an infant with his father. Brown acted on Broadway and then did some films. On television's *General Hospital* he was seen as Al Weeks.

In the final year, after Amanda Blake left the series, the proprietor of the Long Branch was Miss Hannah, played by Fran Ryan. On other television programs Ryan appeared as Aggie Thompson of *The Doris Day Show,* Doris Ziffel on *Green Acres,* and Tillie Russell on *The Wizard.*

The Final Years

During the final season of *Gunsmoke* the antiviolence movement continued to dog television's bloody trail. It took three years for the Surgeon General's report on television violence to come out, and in January of 1972 his committee announced that it had found that there was a "modest association between viewing of violence and aggression, among at least children." Senator Pastore and his followers felt betrayed by this lukewarm admonishment and were up in arms. They pressed for more severe censure and demanded clarifications.

Under pressure the Surgeon General finally came out and made a personal statement. He said that he found that there was a "causal relationship between television violence and antisocial behavior." He went on further, to state that the violence was sufficient to "warrant immediate and remedial action." Pastore had won, and CBS quickly developed four guidelines to meet the growing threat. Teaser openings were to be banned and victims of violence were not to be shown at the time of impact. Weaponry was to be kept to a minimum and trailers promoting upcoming episodes would have to keep violence in context.

Mantley had to make compromises but was willing to speak up when he felt that the intrusions on the creative element were excessive. He attempted

Table 7. Gunsmoke Ratings for Twenty Years

DATE	RANK	RATING	SHARE	TELEVISION HOUSEHOLDS SURVEYED, MILLIONS
1955-56	—	—	—	—
1956-57	8	32.7	—	—
1957-58	1	43.1	—	—
1958-59	1	39.6	60	—
1959-60	1	40.3	64.6	44.0
1960-61	1	37.3	62.2	45.2
1961-62	3	28.3	47.3	48.1
1962-63	10	27.0	45.6	49.8
1963-64	20	23.5	39.5	51.3
1964-65	27	22.6	38.1	52.6
1965-66	30	21.3	37.4	53.8
1966-67	34	19.9	34.8	54.9
1967-68	4	25.5	40.3	56.0
1968-69	6	24.9	38.0	57.0
1969-70	2	25.9	39.0	58.5
1970-71	5	25.5	39.0	60.1
1971-72	4	26.0	39.0	62.3
1972-73	8	23.6	35.0	65.1
1973-74	15	22.1	33.0	66.4
1974-75	26	20.7	—	—
1987*	27**	16.6	31.0	88.6

Courtesy A.C. Nielsen Company Northbrook, Illinois

Gunsmoke: Return to Dodge
**For the week

to present his case to the network, but CBS' chief censor, Tom Swafford, put off his arguments by saying that he remained unconvinced that violence begat ratings. As noted in the *Washington Post,* "A touch of innocence has invaded Dodge City."[162]

When one considers this period of transition, it is remarkable that Mantley was able to maintain *Gunsmoke's* standing among the top programs on television. In 1969 it fell from the Number Four position to Number Six but this was due primarily to its competition with the new *Laugh-In*. By 1970 it was back on top once more in the Number Two spot. The program maintained a strong position until the eighteenth season at which time it started to slip, although even then it had a sizeable audience.

Over the years the demographics of *Gunsmoke* were slowly changing. Because of changes in its format new audiences were being picked up as old ones fell by the wayside. In 1967 a Nielsen study revealed that *Gunsmoke* was watched primarily in blue collar households, in households with incomes under $5000, in the South and West, in rural areas, and by those with a grade school education or those above the age of 50. More affluent viewers and those in the Northeast urban centers, as well as younger audiences ages 18-34, tended to watch *Saturday Night Movies,* Dean Martin, Andy Griffith, Jackie Gleason and the Smothers Brothers. As Mantley shifted to anthologies some of the urban audiences started to gravitate toward the show, but its strength was always in the South and Midwest.

The ratings reveal that Mantley's approach of bringing in guest stars and weaving the drama and his principal characters around these central figures seemed to work. Armed with success he even requested a budget increase for the 1969-70 season and as a consequence was able to take the show on location. When he took over in 1966 a single episode cost $178,000 to produce. By 1971 he was receiving almost $250,000.

Mantley's assistant producers and producers aided him in expanding the scope of the program. Joseph Dackow worked with Mantley for four seasons. Dackow had also produced on *The Outlaws* and *Temple Houston.* He was succeeded by Leonard Katzman for five seasons. Katzman went on to fame as the producer of *Dallas, Dirty Sally, The Fantastic Journey, Hawaii Five-O, Logan's Run* and *The Wild Wild West.* In the final years Ron Honthaner also joined Mantley as the associate producer.

With the increased budgets, audiences were now treated to views of the Black Hills of South Dakota, and the beauty of Taos, New Mexico, Sonora, California, Utah and Oregon. A ranch was also opened up in the Simi Valley where barns, corrals, and buildings were constructed for exterior shots. These changes afforded another dimension to the program and greatly enhanced the visual elements of the show. They also encouraged writers to take even greater liberties with authenticity, and the audience found Matt traveling far from Dodge even though a real Dodge City marshal enjoyed but limited jurisdiction and stayed mostly in his backyard. All seemed well in Dodge at the end of the twentieth season and even though there were some cracks in the ratings Mantley and his staff were preparing a new group of scripts for the next season.

The End of an Era

In May 1975, CBS announced the cancellation of *Gunsmoke.* Mantley recalls that he got an unexpected call on April 25th, which happened to be his 55th birthday, informing him that the network had decided to kill the show. At the time, Mantley still felt that the show was evolving in a positive direction. "It had gotten so far away from violence and into rich penetration of character," he observed, "That it could have made it in the family hour."[163]

When cancelled, it was Number 25 on the Nielsen charts. It was replaced in September by *Rhoda* and *Phyllis.* The last new episode aired was *The Sharecroppers,* and the very last episode aired was a rerun of *The Busters.*

Alan Wagner, CBS vice president for program development explained the network's decision.

> The ratings weren't really what killed *Gunsmoke.* The problem was demographics. Because of its setting and its stories the form of the show tended to appeal to rural audiences and older people. Unfortunately, they're not primarily the ones you sell shows to. *Gunsmoke* was still a viable program, but it was a question like this: The Dodgers traded Dixie Walker when he was batting .300. Did they trade him too soon? It's better to get rid of a program one year too soon than one year too late.[164]

Clearly, the statisticians had won out but as Mantley says reflecting on its final ratings, "In today's world it would have been a smash hit."

The executives were clearly playing at fortune-telling in a field where predictions are fraught with uncertainty. At the same time, they could point to the fact that the show was getting very expensive to produce and that the network wanted to shift its emphasis to situation comedies. As Mantley notes, "Fred Silverman never cared about Westerns."

Mantley has expressed certain theories relating to the cancellation and how it affected CBS in general. "It was the gravest mistake ever made," he comments. "Didn't anybody say that this is the filler that starts the whole week?" Some have dated the fall of CBS from its position of uncontested dominance from this period on.

Eulogies were written in all the major publications around the country as critics reflected on the significance of *Gunsmoke* in television's history. One columnist commented: ". . . The first moon colony we establish will be watching *I Love Lucy.* And, probably, *Gunsmoke.* "[165] Cecil Smith fancifully wrote:

> *Gunsmoke* was something quite different. It was the dramatization of the American epic legend of the West, our own *Iliad* and *Odyssey,* created of the standard element of the dime novel and the pulp Western. . . I think that it's interesting that like the gods of the Greeks, the heroes of our legends would have feet of clay, that as puritanical a people as Americans would clasp to their bosom such dubious characters. . . these four were our Zeus, Aphrodite, Bacchus and limping Mercury.[166]

Of course, it had to end some time, for as Steve Allen once noted, the function of any television show is to go off the air. An intuitive adherent to this philosophy, Arness said in an interview in 1957:

Television — The New Frontier

There are very few series that run longer than five years. I have to start thinking of other roles for the future or else I'll be a sitting duck.[167]

Gunsmoke, however, lasted much longer than anyone could have ever imagined. No one could have suspected such a remarkable longevity. What is evident is that by the time *Gunsmoke* went off the air, it had left an indelible mark on television and on American culture. Smith was able to place the program in its historical context in his laudatory farewell article when he wrote:

> *Gunsmoke* changed the face of television. You could almost say the history of television was written in *Gunsmoke*.[168]

REFLECTIONS
BY GUEST STARS

Just about every well-known actor and actress at one time passed through Dodge City on their way to fame. Few actors would want to pass up the opportunity of having a beer at the Long Branch Saloon, getting shot at by Matt Dillon, abducting Kitty, getting patched up by Doc, drinking Chester's coffee, or being baffled by Festus' frontier wisdom. This chapter presents recent reflections by some of the guest stars.

Charles Aidman. *"Gunsmoke* was one of the first shows I did after moving to California from New York in 1958...I played heavies and good guys. I played one poor farmer trying to hold his family together. I don't remember the specifics, but I loved the part...The writing on *Gunsmoke* was superior...It was a terrific series full of warmth, character, and humor...In a segment called *The Money Store* Bill Schallert and I had a lot of fun doing a comical fight scene. Also I rode my first horse on film in my first *Gunsmoke."* Mrs. Betty Aidman adds: *"The Money Store* is the show my husband and I both liked the most. I have it on ¾ inch tape and enjoy it today."

Morey Amsterdam. "I played a drunken bum...It *[Gunsmoke]* was an old fashioned Western...very entertaining, continuing saga of the old West...people loved it. I think the reason for its success was a happy wedding of the right people in front of the cameras and in back of the cameras...It was just another job, but a bigger and successful one! My agent at that time was Jim Molvney. He booked it... Nowadays producers are always looking for something different — without the advice or opinions of the public...The few producers who have done a *Gunsmoke* type series the past few years have had great success but, unfortunately they were not as good as *Gunsmoke* or they might have gotten good ratings."

GUNSMOKE — I. THE HISTORY

John Anderson. "I had a range of roles that was an actor's dream come true... from funky scrofulous characters, to heroic characters — losers, winners. There was almost invariably a moral point to the stories. The scripts were consistently unique and good in one respect or another. There was a sense of fun and family on the set, in part I suppose because I'd done so many. *Gunsmoke* was wonderful entertainment, with a kind of sweetness that made it very appealing. The stories were good, production values first rate, there was an authenticity that made the viewer a believer and some wonderful running roles that were very appealing to an audience. There were values, homilies, moralities that certainly apply today in any society, bearing in mind that there was also by the nature of the medium, an over-simplification...

"However, the trend started by *Gunsmoke,* the so-called 'adult Western,' got so out of hand by imitators, a lot of them good, that the well ran dry on stories and characters... Overdid a good thing... My being cast in a very colorful and dramatic character role in a *Gunsmoke* episode when I first came out from New York in 1957 really kicked off my whole film career. The episode was called *Buffalo Man.* I played the title role. Jack Klugman was my sidekick. *Gunsmoke* was probably the most popular show on the air at the time, and apparently everybody in the business saw the episode the night it aired. My agent, the following Monday, said his phone had been ringing off the hook the entire day. In addition, a clip from the episode with Dillon tied to a wagon wheel and me kicking him in the face... before the antiviolence campaigns... was used several times a day for over a year as a promo, about two seconds short of requiring use payment to me.

"Then for some reason, the excessively long fight sequence between my character and Arness was used by the U.S.C. Film School, as well as many other film schools around the country, in the training of student film editors. It is a fact that most of the cutters under age 50 or so working today learned to cut on all the footage from that sequence, and so far as I know, it is still being used. Klugman said to me recently, 'You know what we're *really* famous for is that damned fight sequence.' The irony of all this is, I was totally inexperienced in film acting or technique when I shot it, and had no encouragement or approval from the director as we filmed, and was absolutely convinced by the end of the shoot, that it was probably my first and last film job. Instead, it lead to an endless string of rich character roles on all the series of that period, Western and non-Western, an actors dream. I could go on..."

Richard Anderson. "I was invited to play an American Indian and the idea intrigued me. The episode defended them [the Indians]... *Gunsmoke* had good acting scenes that allowed one to develop a rounded character... it was first rate. Movie-movie type entertainment. Americana at its allegorical best... I liked acting in Westerns. It was an honor to act in such a dis-

Reflections

tinguished one...My parts had deeper character portrayals. They showed what I could do which surprised a lot of people!"

Tige Andrews. "I worked on the same lot, Republic Studios, on a series called *Robert Taylor Detectives* and years later I got a call to play a heavy on *Gunsmoke*...It was hot, dry and it was my first Western, and except for writing, my last...During a scene I wore a large moustache. While verbally taunting Arness, I put my little finger in my ears, both, and took the wax there in and 'waxed' my moustache. They wanted to cut it out, but didn't. I loved it!"

Michael Ansara. *"Gunsmoke* was better than most...I liked working on a class show...It was a very good series with great care taken...we should have more like it now...more Westerns...I'm tired of auto chases and crashes and dope! I'm tired of half-hour pap nothing, half-hour comedy. So I don't watch series TV anymore. At the risk of sounding old fashioned I think the world needs to distinguish between good and bad. We desperately need values! We have too much gray areas!"

Herb Armstrong. "I had worked many shows from 1959 on in Hollywood. I was submitted for *Gunsmoke* by my agent, interviewed and hired. After that I was hired three more times without an interview...On my last job I had just had eye surgery (cornea transplant) and I had to wear tinted glasses. They re-wrote my character slightly to accommodate me. Very few companies would have done that...*Gunsmoke* was a good solid show that stayed that way because of diligent attention by the producers and the stars. Most successful shows that fail, do so because the people involved get lazy and complacent—not so with this one...As an aside, Dennis Weaver and I started out as young actors in New York together and lived in the same co-op in the Bronx together for awhile."

R.G. Armstrong. "I played powerful ranchers, responsible businessmen, wolfers, leaders of outlaw gangs, and psycho military officers. Usually the characters I played on *Gunsmoke* had to deal with their selfish freewheeling egos wanting wealth and power and being curbed by the socialization process in the wild West...*Gunsmoke* maintained a greater percentage of quality scripts, good stories, and very interesting characters than most other series at the time...There was the feeling of unity and cohesion between the actors—the regulars: James Arness, Amanda Blake, Milburn Stone, Dennis Weaver and later Ken Curtis...a love for one another. Yes, and I was surprised at how funny James Arness could be. It was a class act—first rate and I felt proud to be a part of *Gunsmoke*. It gave me a chance to grow and develop as an actor in films as well as survive. Because of its universal concern, character, and story development, it will always be relevant."

GUNSMOKE — I. THE HISTORY

Edward Asner. "I played heavies in two. On my first episode I played a cavalry sergeant who upon release from jail actually had the temerity and stupidity to try to punch Matt Dillon. The fact that he towered a foot above me didn't phase me...It was a lovely company to be in...an excellent show, excellent resident cast, which did beautiful ensemble work and yet was able to sit back and let the guests do the kind of situations and problems that would be found in an anthology show: Thus giving it its lasting power."

Val Avery. "I was in California, my agent submitted me for a role and they hired me. I've done a few with various parts, mostly heavies. I remember one part was the lead heavy...I was one of—or maybe the only one to beat Marshal Dillon to the draw. I wounded him but, *alas* he got me!...*Gunsmoke* was a good show, a professional show, a smoothly run show. No wasted time—everyone knew what he was doing: cast, crew, make-up, wardrobe—everyone. It had appeal. The good guys vs. the bad guys...the typical Western format, which was done well...and it had James Arness' appeal—The Hero—The John Wayne American. With rock and roll, cynicism, Vietnam, the whole era changed; the modes, the morals, tastes."

Bonnie Bartlett. "I loved doing *Gunsmoke*. Westerns are natural for me. It was my father's favorite show...It's so different from today. *Gunsmoke* is a classic of its day...It was easy to tell the good guys from the bad. It wouldn't work today...We're too corrupt as a country now...Being on *Gunsmoke* made me feel confident getting to L.A. I had been retired as a mom for ten years...I loved getting the beautiful flowers from the producers."

Ralph Bellamy. "As I remember the series the guest was always a 'good guy.' *Gunsmoke* had a very well organized production staff and carefully written scripts...the stories had a feel of accuracy. I had a good time making one of them. All the cross-country riding was filmed on a strip about 500 feet long on the back lot, with varying scenery...The world still has a fondness for Westerns...but there had been too many Westerns, hence their demise. The same thing will probably happen to police stories soon."

Nellie Bellflower. "I auditioned for Pam Polifroni, who was the casting director on the show...It was one of the first shows I guest-starred on, and established me as such...I played a young waitress at the saloon who was in love with a drifter...Even though it was towards the end of the series run, the entire production standards remained high and the excitement was still there for everyone. I was very impressed...Meeting and working with Jack Albertson was and still remains one of the highlights of my professional career."

Richard Bradford. "It was my first TV show. I was a gunfighter, the bad guy...*Gunsmoke* was a high quality show; real, honest, with simple

Reflections

straightforward characters that were easy to identify with; It had a sense of integrity... The stories and problems presented in them are universal issues... I think the networks super-saturated the TV with Westerns. When shows like *Star Trek* came along, people were bored and desperate to see something new."

John Brandon. "I was cast thru Pam Polifroni, the casting director. I played a comic heavy... The show was very professional and easy... It was a nice experience. I worked with Jim Arness, who was completely down-to-earth... There were nice characters, and good honest relationships... *Gunsmoke* was first class!"

Foster Brooks. "When I first came to California in 1961, I lived three doors from a building in which Jim Arness had an apartment. I met him through a gentleman who managed both apartments and, Jim arranged for me to read for the producers of his show. I played a small role after that first reading and appeared in several episodes of *Gunsmoke* after that... I usually was part of the crowd and had one to three lines in the episode... Once I played a telegraph operator and Jim came into the office with a message he wanted me to send. I took the message from him and what Jim had written on the paper was something that could not be put in print for the public to read. I managed to control myself and the show went on... One time I was a deputy who was given the job of guarding Burt Reynolds on the first *Gunsmoke* in which he appeared. He was very happy that day because he had heard he was to get a semi-regular part as the local blacksmith. He's done a little better since... Without a doubt *Gunsmoke* is the finest Western ever on television. If only it could return with as many of the old regulars as possible. I am certain it would make a lot of viewers quite happy... All the main characters had a lot of love and respect for one another. Even Doc and Festus, regardless of their many arguments. Matt and Kitty were definitely in love, but it was played down beautifully. I think everyone wanted to see them get married, but I think if they had the show may not have been as successful... People in 'charge' seem to ignore the fact that, we, the public like to see Westerns. In my opinion, a great Western like *Gunsmoke* would be at or near the top in the ratings. When speaking to friends about television shows, I never fail to hear, 'Whatever happened to all the wonderful Westerns we used to have on TV?' With all the junk and trash on television today, *Gunsmoke* repeats or, a show of its quality would, I think, be most welcome by all... I get a great kick out of saying that, I once had bit roles on *Gunsmoke*. It got me started on a most successful career."

Joshua Bryant. "As I recall, I had no scenes with Jim Arness and was struck by how much his double looked like him, so much that it was him, the stunt double, who did virtually all the scenes in which the character did not speak. The likeness was so close that the man, I don't remember his name, could be photographed three-quarter front and still pass."

Gary Busey. "I appeared in the last one aired, as a bronco buster who was thrown from his horse and was dragged into a fence post, hitting his head and causing a brain injury that will cause death within a week. He had saved enough money to buy a ranch in Montana, fell in love with a dance hall girl, but unbeknownst to him, he was dying. She promised to marry him, then pulled out. As the train to Montana was pulling in he sees the horse that threw him. He mounts and rides out and then dies in the arms of John Beck...I grew up in Tulsa, Oklahoma, watching Doc, Kitty and Matt. I was just frozen in place...couldn't believe I was standing there with Doc. I also studied camera tech with James Best before I ever worked pro, and I went with James everyday to the set. It was my first experience visiting a set. That show had Hal Needham doubling James Arness, Ron Howard playing the kid, all in the desert by Lancaster, California. It was called *Charlie Noon*.

"I was also the last person to die on *Gunsmoke*. We had to come back to film my dying twice because the first time I died it was with my eyes open and with one of them crossed, which was against TV standards at the time...Mr. Lundine, the chief wrangler, put me on a horse that he said, 'Would just buck once.' Lo and behold the mare took off bucking all the way around the corral. I never did get my feet in the stirrups, but he never threw me either. Everyone got a huge laugh and it loosened me up real good. I felt like I belonged. *Gunsmoke* made me feel a real part of the film community, like I had finally 'made it.' It was a classic American morality play. The first in its class...Why did Westerns go off the air? They were replaced with car chases and cops. It's the same formula set in today's society...Also, Strother Martin died."

Owen Bush. "I was doing parts on several Westerns at the time including *Maverick* and *Bonanza*, and I was cast for parts in a couple of *Gunsmokes*...First as one of the townsmen in a scene in the Long Branch, second as Bailiff in a court case in Dodge...In the show in which I was the Bailiff in a court-room trial, Paul Stewart, was playing the half-breed Indian defense lawyer. We finished shooting on Friday with the conclusion to be shot the following Monday. During the weekend Paul suffered a stroke so production was stopped for two weeks. Paul remained partially paralyzed so the crew rigged a platform with skate wheels and only close-ups were taken of him as he was pushed around the court-room giving his final speech to the jury...After 20 years, I guess the interest in Westerns was replaced by detective shows, family shows set in current times and sit coms...The cycle of interest should come around again with new enthusiasm for something we've been without."

Reflections

Joseph Campanella. "I appeared as a trail boss, bank robber and a bounty hunter. The trail boss dealt with the moral issue of 'riding for the brand.' The bounty hunter raised the question of the morality of making a living off others' misfortunes... The authenticity and attention to detail on *Gunsmoke* was so fine that wearing the costumes and walking on the set did a great deal for me as an actor to project me into that time and place. It was an excellent company of actors and all the roles down to the extras were filled with professional, capable people. It was a pleasure talking theater with 'Doc' and music with 'Festus' but, especially talking with the many authentic cowboys and rodeo riders that I worked with in each episode.

"One incident occurred when my wife and first three sons, who were then quite young, came to the studio to pick me up. They were early and were waiting just outside the stage. I was in full western regalia as a trail boss with sidearm and rifle and saddlebags on my shoulder on my way to the dressing room to change. I started to cross the square toward them; neither my wife nor my three little boys recognized me until I got quite close and the expression on their faces will always be magic to me. I felt that the city born and bred man had given a great performance to convince his own family that he really was a cowboy... *Gunsmoke* opened up the Western for me as a vehicle for my work as an actor. I would watch it whenever I could and it made me much more aware of Western lore and legend. The ensemble playing of the winning cast was a treat for this stage trained New York actor to behold. The stories were always interesting and again production details so authentic."

Harry Carey, Jr. "In one episode I played a pig-farmer. It was a great script... It was about a family whose children had been killed by Indians, and they had to take this Indian girl in so she could have her baby. It was outstanding. Robert Totten directed... Mil Stone was an old and dear friend and so was Ken Curtis. Also Jim Arness was a super person and I was in on the very start of his career with *Wagon Master* and *Island in the Sky*.... They were all a big barrel of laughs. Jim had a fantastic sense of humor and at times would get the giggles for so long — we couldn't shoot for a long period of time."

Steve Carlson. "While filming my episode, I had the good fortune to work with Ken Curtis and Milburn Stone, but only for one day. They were very considerate, interesting and made a young actor feel very comfortable. As we talked, it came out that I was from Cheyenne, Wyoming. Well, I found out that these two were great friends and had spent the summers for quite some time, traveling around the country working fairs and rodeos, and that summer they were going back to work one of the largest rodeos in America and Cheyenne's main claim to fame, Cheyenne Frontier Days. They had worked it a few years before and everyone had loved them. I let them know that. We worked and talked the rest of the day, and that was the end of it... I thought.

GUNSMOKE — I. THE HISTORY

"Months later, when Ken and Milburn were in Cheyenne, they remembered this actor they'd worked with briefly from Cheyenne and happened to mention it to someone there. That someone happened to know my family and me, and mentioned that my father had had a heart attack and was currently in the hospital. They called my Dad right then, introduced themselves, told him that they had heard about his attack and hoped that he would soon be better; that they had worked with his son and what a fine young man I was, etc. Well, my Dad couldn't believe it. He was overjoyed, as was my Mom and I. Since my Dad died of this attack, it made it even more special. A couple of things stand out to me about this. First, I didn't really know these guys all that well. What they did was an act of kindness and consideration. They never saw me afterwards to tell me that they 'really made me a big shot in my home town,' or anything like that. They just did it.

"The second thing happened not that long ago. I wanted to thank them, to let them know how much that call meant to all of us, but Milburn, unfortunately, died a few years ago and I never saw Ken Curtis...until last year. We did a celebrity/charity golf-tennis tournament together and I finally got a chance to remind him and thank him. He was very gracious and polite, but I could tell in his eyes that he had no idea what I was talking about. That made it mean even more to me. In their eyes, that little call wasn't that special. They did that sort of thing all the time. That's just the kind of guys they were. They never realized that what was just a moment's kindness to them, could be a highlight in someone else's life. For the moment of happiness and 'specialness' they brought my Dad and my family, I thank them. I also appreciate very much the early lesson on how to utilize celebrity status for 'good.' We lost a wonderful guy when Milburn died, but Ken, fortunately remains one of the great 'good guys.'"

Paul Carr. "At the time I did my first *Gunsmoke* I was working a great deal...I had worked for the director on another show and was requested for *Gunsmoke*. It starred John Dehner as my father. I subsequently did two others over the next few years...On the first one I was the young son of a rancher who marries an Indian woman. I cause the death of my father because of my lust for the woman. In the second one I was the oldest son of a hillbilly family run by John Anderson as the father. This was a goofy comedy where we kidnap Miss Kitty...Abner Biberman was directing. He tried to get me to jump off a water tower onto someone's back. I politely refused, informing him that I wasn't a stunt man. He talked me into jumping onto a double mattress then into a mud pit up to my neck...For the life of me I can't remember the third one, but I'm sure there were three...

"*Gunsmoke* had been around so long and was so successful that there was the feeling that you were doing a classic. Everyone was confident and warm.

Reflections

The crew had been with the show for so long that there was a casual efficiency to the way they worked...The show was done with a care and attention to detail and most of all excellent judgement of script. When I did the show it had been on for at least ten years and these qualities were still evident. The performances, down to smallest were always excellent...the producer was a man of taste and good judgement...the villains were usually men or ladies with some depth, more than one color. That set *Gunsmoke* apart by itself...*Gunsmoke* tried to explore the human spirit with a little more depth than most."

David Carradine. "After I had done my two leads on Broadway, *The Deputy* and *The Royal Hunt of the Sun,* and my own gunfighter Western series, *Shane,* which lasted for 17 segments, I had a dry period, during which I did some guest roles on series. *Gunsmoke* was one of them...I played the youngest of a trio of happy bad guys, casual rustlers and robbers. My buddies in the gang all became important character men, though I can't remember their names...*Gunsmoke* was yet another try at the same old thing; that, because of talent, dedication and good will, managed to go right through the roof into legend status...James Arness was a great star in an archetypal role. The loyalty to him and the other characters was enormous. When I was learning the 'fast draw,' I found out that a lot of the guys practiced by trying to outdraw the marshal on TV. The show always stayed true to the original concept, and had a lot of heart. People could depend on it...

"But kids stopped believing in, or caring about, the mythology. It became a common opinion that Westerns were dead. This feeling is still with us, in spite of some notable successes, largely propagated by wives and children of TV and movie executives. At the time that my series, *Kung Fu* began, the *Laramie* street at Warner had not been used for sometime, and the wranglers and Western supplies were starving...I think that with the countrywide renaissance of John Wayne movies on TV, *Gunsmoke* has great relevance. Jim Arness was as close as the tube ever got to the Duke, apologies to Richard Boone...At the time that I did *Gunsmoke* there was a rush of non-violent censorship on TV. The marshal was not allowed to shoot anyone, and no fighting was allowed. We resolved this by staging a rough-house wherein we still had a lot of rough action, broken tables, etc. but, all in fun. In the end, instead of shooting us down, Dillon got the drop on us and took us to jail. This was late in the series, when Jim pretty much did what he wanted to do, which in this case, consisted of showing up briefly for two days, only for a couple of hours or so. So I didn't get to spend much time with the legend, himself."

Mary Carver. "My first show, *Chester's Mail Order Bride,* in the script I had sent a picture of my pretty sister to Chester and he had sent a picture of

Matt Dillon to me, signing his name. Chester sends Matt to meet me at the station and I'm supposed to run up to him and notice his sheriff's badge. I'm only five feet tall so when I ran up to him my eye level was on his belt buckle, so kiddingly James Arness said, 'That's all right Mary. I can fix that.' And he put the badge on his belt."

Eunice Christopher. "As a transplated actress from N.Y.C. I met with the casting director on a general interview. With my training and background I was promised an audition. With much excitement and anticipation I waited for the call. Two weeks later I read and was cast in my very first television appearance in a dramatic leading role. I still remember the 'thrill.'. . . I played a warm sensitive pioneer woman, a religious woman. . . showing great strength in her convictions and caring for mankind. . . It was a very dramatic role, matter of life and death, giving birth in a covered wagon. As a matter of fact, I believe I was 'giving birth,' weeping and wailing, on both episodes in which I guest-starred. Type casting!. . .

"There was a familial feeling on the set, being out 'on the prairie.' Thinking about what the pioneer days must really have been like as we were attempting to portray them was a marvelous experience. There was a continuity and history to the show and all the characters in it. . . CBS submitted my name for consideration for an EMMY for Best Performance in a Supporting Dramatic Role. A good public relations item; I signed with an influential agent; further work followed, it instilled confidence, but nothing has compared since. For me, it was a highlight! Good women's roles are just not written and opportunities for such roles are given to 'name actors'. . . *Gunsmoke* was a classic Western. Too many others attempted to monopolize on its success, and an abundance of Westerns followed. . . Now it's time for another!. . .

"I remembered meeting James Arness, shaking his immense hand and looking up at him from his belt buckle as he greeted me with genuine warmth. On the TV screen I somehow never perceived the measure of this man. His warm spirit matched his size and some 25 years later, I still recall his open and booming laughter over the 'prairie.' He seemed to be loved by all! The only two TV scripts I have ever saved are those from my two episodes of *Gunsmoke*. . . I wouldn't be portraying 'childbirth' in a forthcoming episode, but how I wish I were about to perform in another classic episode of *Gunsmoke*. . . It was far more than a television show. It was an experience and profound appreciation for the pioneers of our great land."

Julie Cobb. "I was married to Victor French who acted in and directed many episodes. . . I acted in two episodes. The first was a dance hall girl who witnesses a murder or discovers a body and has to testify in court. The second was the fiancée of Dan Travanti and the daughter of the former 'Colonel,' Lee J. Cobb. . . And relationships grew from it that led to other TV work. . .

Reflections

"I loved doing the Western period. The writing was great, the family unit strong, and Arness was so *funny! Gunsmoke* was authentic, heartwarming and unique...the best of TV. Maybe the simplicity of the stories, the rights and wrongs, the ethics didn't seem 'cool' to an apathetic decade and so it disappeared from TV...Today we need heros, people of morals who take action. We need hope. We need inspiration...Being on *Gunsmoke* was a highlight. It stands out because of how special the show was... I had the thrill of working with my father, Lee J. Cobb. We played father and daughter in one of the most moving episodes of the series, *The Colonel*. I think he was as good as he ever was and the experience of performing with him was a gift *Gunsmoke* gave me. He died two years later. Working together was sort of a culmination of our relationship. And I look at the show with such gratitude and such love. Unforgettable!"

Ben Cooper. "In 1960 or '61, I was the guest star for an episode titled, *Apprentice Doc,* a one hour black-and-white. I played a young outlaw who came back to Dodge to 'study medicine' with Doc. We had six or eight scenes of just the two of us and the chemistry was working so well the director saved them for the last two days so we could shoot them in sequence; a very unusual happening in TV. We developed almost a father-son relationship—more than just a student-teacher. I later guest starred on two more...however, *Apprentice Doc* is my *Gunsmoke* memory...[I remember] the selfless interaction, respect and camaraderie among the regulars. They would say, 'This should be his line...' or 'I don't think I'd answer here, let's cut that line.' Unheard of from most TV regulars.

"For an actor, working with Milburn Stone was like someone putting a million dollars in your pocket. At the risk of sounding trite, the very real and mostly comfortable relationship of the characters—due to the writing, production care, direction and playing was a unique combination. The actors were so consumate in their skill, that many thousands of viewers thought they *were* their characters! After my show appeared...they would ask, 'How's Doc?'...My character [in *Apprentice Doc*] was gut shot by a bad guy and left to die. Doc found me and tried to minister to me—The director had saved this scene to be shot last... The moment came when I was to die—Now, Millie and I had refused to rehearse this scene before shooting it—The moment came...I didn't want to die. I held his hand, said 'Doc?' and died. Millie just knelt there looking at me, patting my stomach wound, and all the time I felt his tears dropping onto my hand. I wrote him a letter, thanking him for the wonderful experience of working with and knowing him. I shall always cherish his reply...My love and admiration for Millie Stone and the others will never die."

Jeanne Cooper. "On *Gunsmoke* you were always included as a member of the 'team.' It was the classic television series of all time. It appealed to all ages... High-tech made its entrance on the TV screen, missiles were in — horses out... *Gunsmoke* has a profound effect, even today, for those who are fortunate enough to have seen some of the segments, as it represents — 'at heart' — good, or the attempt thereof, still champions over evil or the noncaring... Film personnel still have a deep respect for you when *Gunsmoke* appears on a resume — and sometimes they have sheer envy."

Alex Cord. "I was born with a love for horses. Cowboys always were, are now, and always will be my heroes. I went to the Saturday matinees to see Hoot Gibson, Johnny Mack Brown, Wild Bill Eliot, Bob Steele, and the very young John Wayne. I never dreamed that I would one day play a part that he made famous... in the remake of *Stagecoach*. It was only natural that I would be a fan of *Gunsmoke*...

"I played a lone mysterious cowboy who takes up residence with an attractive widow and her young son to protect them from the forces of evil. Not unlike *Shane*... It was an opportunity to play a very appealing character. To be tough and capable, yet kind and sensitive. It was an enormously positive experience... I had to have a shootout with the bad guy played by an excellent actor Robert Viharo. The script dictated that I was to win, to vanquish Viharo. In actual fact, his draw was faster than mine and were our conflict real, my life would have been in peril... But... Thanks to the wizardry of cinema I prevailed and laid the villain low. And at the end, rather than stay with the lovely widow and her son, I ride off into the sunset... perhaps... to return another day... Everyone seemed to care deeply about every aspect of the production. I remember us working on location in Tucson, Arizona. Filming in a shallow creek, we were suddenly buzzed by 'The Red Baron,' Jim Arness at the stick. Twenty minutes later he gimped up to the creek and shook my hand. It was great!... For me the 20 seasons weren't long enough. Its beauty was in its honest simplicity. Its totally human values. And those wonderful actors who portrayed them. They were all perfect!... It still has relevance because the values and issues with which it dealt are fast disappearing from our society. We need to get them back."

Jeff Corey. "I believe I was the leader of a 'raiders' group. They alternately made deals with the Union and the Confederacy in the American Civil War... Robert Pine, who played my son, was in opposition to my shifting allegiances. Memory generally serves me well, but I must confess that the details of this segment seem to elude me... James Arness seemed to have been involved with prior commitments of an assorted nature and we would often do scenes with the script supervisor reading Jim's lines off camera. At the end of the day Jim would come in to do all of his close-ups in whatever scenes had already been partially shot... Oddly enough it was not too disconcerting, and as I recall, all of the cast seemed to accommodate the

Reflections

situation. It's part of the mosaic of putting film together. I'm not condemning Jim for it... It appeared to be something that had to be done that way... His character was set...

"*Gunsmoke* was the embodiment of the beguiling myth that good guys prevail. The 'law' was upheld by plain dealing, square shooting, dead-level men and women of principle and courage... no urbane la-de-dah qualities. No affectations, unspoiled. An attractive myth and happily people like that still emerge on the scene from time to time. And, of course, the villains get their comuppance, which we like to believe really should happen... Working on *Gunsmoke* took some getting used to back then, the powerful smell of ammonia fumes generated by the gallons of horsepee that fell on that set daily. But you get used to anything. Particularly if you're paid generously for it."

Royal Dano. "I appeared in 18 to 20 episodes of *Gunsmoke* playing a fairly good variety: minister, miner, sailor, gunman, robber, bully, assailant, victim, etc. *Gunsmoke* was a superior show with friendly concerned regulars. For the most part, the show became a sort of anthology giving lots of leeway to guest performers."

June Dayton. "I did several *Gunsmokes,* but I remember just two. My husband Dean Harens and I did *Laughing Gas.* Needless to say we *laughed* a lot. The other I remember is *Witness*... It was a lovely cast and not too much pressure... a pleasant experience... Today *Gunsmoke* might be a welcome relief."

John Dehner. "I had already been working for Norman Macdonnell when he and John Meston began *Gunsmoke.* I worked on practically all the radio shows as well as on my own show *Have Gun, Will Travel.* The atmosphere surrounding the radio show was, so warm and friendly you couldn't imagine. If ever there was a family, this was it. I remember them all with great affection... *Gunsmoke* was intelligent. The characters, the situations were real... On television Norman Macdonnell became the producer and he had great confidence in my talent. Since both [radio and television treatments] had been produced by Norman Macdonnell they both reflected his steady hand and his imagination and his sense of humor... I appeared in, God knows, 20-plus episodes. My favorite? I can't remember... it was done with Anthony Caruso. There was a mystique about TV's *Gunsmoke*. A 'success' mystique creating a sense that an actor was in an atmosphere of creative security. Hence a sense of freedom."

George Di Cenzo. "I was cast by directors Bernie and Vince McEveety... I played bad, foul, low-life scum... It was fun! Watching Jim Arness memorize a page, crumble it up and stand in front of the camera spitting it out flawlessly!... Doing a series again with Jim Arness was as much fun as *Gunsmoke*. Jim and I got to laugh at each other again in *McLain's Law*. I played *his boss*, Lt. DeNisco."

Lieux Dressler. "I went for a 'reading,' got the part...then was called back other seasons to do two more...I played lusty women — alive and wanting to stay that way...sometimes cunning, sometimes wistful, but always logical...Before one scene, when Jim Arness was supposed to be showing my character how to shoot a rifle, the special effects guys had rigged a 'charge' to go off each time I rehearsed that made it look as though I had hit the target but Jim hadn't. I didn't know this till later. But, what the crew didn't know was that I had been a marksman on the rifle team at school and probably could have shattered the bottles on my own... *Gunsmoke* lead to six years on *General Hospital,* because I was now viewed as a quality performer... *Gunsmoke* was class from the top all the way through. It had integrity, attention to detail — a nurturing of the stories, characters, and anyone connected with the production...it could be counted on to deliver 'above' the average...it was comfortable to be with as an old friend you could trust not to waste your time...I think if those in power had a need to re-promote *Gunsmoke,* you would see the same allegiance emerge to re-enjoy it as has happened with *Star Trek* and others, because the 'good-guys' (Matt et al.) and Kitty were genuine in their beliefs."

Don Dubbins. "I was a hot young actor out of New York — stage — and I was cast in September, 1959 in my first *Gunsmoke, Kitty's Injury*. It's funny to look back now and realize, that even though I was New York born and bred, I played country or hillbillies in all four episodes. A retarded, mean hillbilly in the first, a lecherous hillbilly in the second, a gentle, limited mountain boy in the third and a heavy in the fourth...The regular cast of *Gunsmoke:* i.e. Jim Arness, Amanda Blake, Doc and Chester were like a family. They knew what each of their characters would or could do, or would not do. They embraced members of the guest cast and made us feel a part of them. That's why the show worked for the audience...My favorite show of the four I did, was *Marry Me* which incidentally was sensitively directed by Dennis Weaver. A mountain family came down to Dodge. I played the part of Orkey Cathcart, the oldest son. My younger brother wanted to marry his sweetheart but our father insisted that he couldn't marry until the oldest son did first. They made me go and find someone to marry. Of course I spied Kitty, but she had different ideas and so my brother and I kidnap her. Kitty fought, pleaded, reasoned, and totally frustrated me as I couldn't understand why she didn't want to marry me! Our father, as fate has it, dies and I become head of the family and so give my brother permission to marry. All this was done with great humor, love, and life lesson along the way...I think a great deal of simple love and sacrifice was expressed by 'Orkey' toward his brother and father.

Reflections

Another time, in another show, Milburn Stone as Doc had a line in the script that called for him to call Chester an idiot. Jim, Milburn and Kitty all agreed that Doc would not call Chester an idiot under any circumstance. The producer came down and after some wonderful explanations from this cast, the line was deleted. I thought that was an example of how well the *Gunsmoke* cast knew their characters and kept the integrity of the show alive and beautiful."

Val Dufour. "I can't remember the exact number but I did at least 20 episodes of *Gunsmoke*... Always the bad guy. Mostly I was a murderer or robber of banks. Sometimes I was an outlaw, with justification that is. I killed to protect my land or because my family was threatened. One time I was a very well dressed [for Dodge City] gambler. I did many Westerns in those days. In all of them in fact, the bad guy. *Gunsmoke* had more 'class' it seemed. It usually had better actors. Lynn Stalmaster cast it, and later Stalmaster/Lister. I know that many of the roles I got were the result of having been seen on *Gunsmoke*. Seeing re-runs years later I generally liked what I saw. I did not always like the editing, however. There was a tendency to cut to the actor when *he spoke*. And in drama on film, the story is told thru *re-action* rather than dialogue...

"*Gunsmoke* was my first job in Hollywood. One week after I arrived from New York City Lynn Stalmaster became my biggest booster in my eight years there. I was by no means a beginning actor, having done many Broadway shows and having starred in many New York–based TV shows and soaps. But after reading one page of dialogue for Charles Marquis Warren, he said, 'They're waiting for you at Western costume.' I couldn't believe I had been accepted for a role opposite James Arness, his being so tall and I, six feet. Norm Macdonnell said, 'If we cast only people his size, we'd never get the show on!' When I got on the set I saw adjustments being made on camera. When the camera did my close up it was cranked lower, looking slightly *up* to me. When they shot Jim, it was cranked up and shot *down* on him. The result was we looked the same size. Then of course when we fought in the bar, our stunt men were the same size... Jim always had a pink spotlight on his close-up camera, a 'special treatment' usually given to the great women stars. Being a New York actor and not used to Hollywood ways, the first time we went through my scene with Arness, I knew my lines perfectly and played them 'full hilt'; Jim, on the other hand, read off a script held by the script girl. He didn't know his lines! After we did the scene, he turned to the director, Warren, and asked, 'Is *that* how he's gonna do it?' I was furious being treated as if I weren't there and yelled, 'Hey, *ask me!* What do you think I am, a sack of shit?!' Arness laughed, put out his hand and said, 'I'm sorry.'

"Same day, Dennis W. and I stood at an entrance to start a scene for 20 minutes and he never said a single word to me, not at all friendly. After I did many shows with them, I found out why. Warren and the cast were having a tiff at the time. He left finally and Norm Macdonnell became the producer. They hated Warren and he had said about me, 'Well, we've got a new guy from New York City to play "Chuck," now you'll see what acting is all about!' They hated me on sight. Of course, Hollywood actors are always intimidated by actors from New York. Soon after it became 'Arness & Co.,' and they remembered me as a good actor. So I was used again and again. One year, in the sixties, Milburn and I were nominated for an Emmy. I was not to get one until 1977."

Jane Dulo. "I played a landlady on *Gunsmoke*. It was extremely well organized and pleasant...charming cast, good stories, and talented directors...It was one of the fun shows to do...although my feet did hurt after a day of working on dirt roads...I only did one show, though I wish there were more...We need some good escape entertainment."

Robert Easton. "I became involved with *Gunsmoke* originally through the radio version...Norman Macdonnell, who produced the radio show, had sent for me. Because 'Chester' had been well established as being very bucolic and rural, they got the idea of bringing in Chester's brother, 'Magnus,' an eccentric mountain man who had lived far away from civilization for many years. Because Chester lived in Dodge City he considered himself very worldly and sophisticated. Chester would be ashamed of his uncivilized brother and try to wise him up. As it turned out the naive brother that Chester was trying to protect could, in fact, out-gamble, out-drink and out-womanize Chester. It was essentially an off-beat humorous episode. There was no villain...Later CBS launched the television version...

"I was delighted when Mr. Macdonnell asked me to play 'Magnus' on the TV show. I think I was probably one of the few actors who played the same character on both the radio and TV versions...On radio, Macdonnell had both produced and directed it. So the original concept of the characters and relationships had originated with him and John Meston. When I went to do the TV show it was still being produced by Macdonnell, but it was being directed by Charles Marquis Warren...I was surprised how much it differed from what we had originally done on radio. It seems Mr. Warren had felt that while the *Magnus* episode certainly had a lot of character and color, it didn't follow the classic structure for television drama. There was no villain, no conflict and no dramatic suspense. Then Warren got the idea of introducing a villain into the script. He would be a religious fanatic threatening to kill Miss Kitty because of her loose life style. Then, in addition to Magnus' other unsuspected abilities of being able to hold his own with crooked gamblers etc., there would be a real dramatic twist. Magnus had at one time travelled with an itinerant preacher so he could fake his own religious frenzy, momentarily

Reflections

distracting the crazed religious fanatic. I liked that idea of having conflict and suspense and overcoming a villain in an offbeat way.

"As I commenced the assignment in a state of euphoria, I did not realize there would be two unexpected complications — searing heat and creative conflict. The first was easier to deal with than the second... Macdonnell felt the sudden fiery preacher bit was totally out of character for Magnus and counter-productive to the original concept... he felt it was a gimmick that went beyond believability... Warren felt that the show needed not only comic surprises but an intensely dramatic one as well and he wanted my preaching bit to be electric. Unfortunately, I got caught in the middle... If I did a take electric enough to please Mr. Warren, Mr. Macdonnell would tell me it was totally out of character and that I had lost the lazy, laid-back, low-key quality that had made the radio episode one of his favorites. When I did a take that pleased Macdonnell, Warren would let me know he was unhappy that I had dropped the energy and totally lost the essence of the scene... I was in a no-win situation.... All I could do was try to split the difference between what they wanted and hope neither one would be too disappointed in me.

"The next problem was the heat. We were filming at Gene Autry's ranch in Placerita Canyon... semi-desert country... in an unprecented heat-wave under hot lights. For three days the temperature ran between 112 and 116... the episode was supposed to be taking place in Dodge City, Kansas at Christmas time. Bare-chested prop men drenched in sweat shovelled fake snow... I was wearing a leather shirt and a fur hat... By the end of the week I had lost 12 pounds... Despite all the problems, the episode turned out surprisingly well and has been favorably received in all its reruns over the last 32 years. As I've been on location in many parts of the country, people tell me they've just seen it on their local TV channel, and how much they enjoyed it even though the episode is older than they are."

Jack Elam. "I played in about 26 episodes of *Gunsmoke*. In the first several years, the heavy. In the later years, not a heavy. On each show I did, on my first work day I was presented a fifth of Cutty Sark at 5 p.m.... I remember two hour lunches in a bar across the street from the studio and playing liar's poker with the producers, writers, production managers, actors, etc.... I miss it!"

Richard Evans. "I first became involved with *Gunsmoke* as an actor in an episode called *Moo Moo Raid*. I think it had the highest audience share to date for CBS when *Gunsmoke* was still only a half hour show. Andrew McLaglen directed it... Over the years, averaging one show every two years, I played sons. Good sons of troubled fathers, troubled sons of good fathers. On at least one show, I played the bad son of a bad father. My favorite 'father' was Lew Ayres, because no matter how bad or how crazy when they cast dear old Lew, I knew he was a saint. So did all the others lucky enough to work with him...

"The set cast was truly ensemble in spirit, something that has stuck with me as a way of creating theatre and film, that I believe is very rewarding. There were no star temperaments; the *Gunsmoke* regulars always made the guest actors feel at home and indispensable. I miss this very much today. *Gunsmoke* was a show built around characterization, not so much action. So, of course, we actors loved it...It may have been the only American West many people knew. I'm not sure that that was good, since many liberties were taken with what we know to be historical fact, but the impression seemed intact, of a style, true to its concept, and that is better than no impression at all. Hopefully, *Gunsmoke* opened doors of curiosity for those with no awareness of the Western past...*Gunsmoke* disappeared from television possibly due to the conglomerate or corporate takeover of creative decision making, an area in which men like John Mantley and Philip Leacock were experts, but where the corporate mind is truly out to lunch. They seem to express no sincere esthetic regarding film, no love of the medium.

"Today on TV *empty* cars roll, burst into flame, play loud music, have sex with each other...I guess it's because there *is nobody* at the wheel. *Gunsmoke* had *people,* seemingly real people, not laugh tracks and clothing by Gucci or whoever...*Gunsmoke* helped me land roles in many other TV shows, and at least in a few feature films. And it made me feel part of a kind of legend, a kind of film continuity increasingly rare in Hollywood, or anywhere else in the world, for that matter...In one *Gunsmoke* episode, following a saloon brawl, I was busy dying in Jim Arness' arms. My character's name was Ab, something or other. Arness' dialogue had my name in every other line and it sounded kind of weird. Frustrated with this, Arness, with typical good humor, saw the scene through, let me die, then, cameras still rolling, added: 'Ab what? Abnormal? Abominable? Abyssmal? What *is* this kid's real name?'...

"I was in many shows playing many different roles with usually very good actors. I've forgotten the names of most but a few come to mind: Lew Ayres, Forrest Tucker, Slim Pickens, Bruce Dern, Pat Quinn, Lamont Johnson, who is now a director. I remember doing one of director Mark Rydell's early shows with Frank Silvera...I had a fight scene with Silvera whose acting school was known as the Theater of Being. Frank really threw himself into his work. In this scene, he threw himself out of bed and onto the floor so hard his elbow bone popped through his skin. This was a cue for Arness to throw himself through a locked door, gun drawn, with the familiar, 'Hold it, there!'...Arness took out half the wall, the flat had been secured to the door a bit too well. Frank looked at his elbow, then at Jim and the flying wall, then up at me and said, 'My God, we're good!' And we were."

Reflections

John Fiedler. "I did at least two, as I remember. I played a father with about six kids in one...*Gunsmoke* was a very well done and popular show...The audience liked the characters on it, the regulars and the guest people...It was so long ago, I don't remember much about the details, but it was fun!"

Eddie Firestone. "I first became involved with *Gunsmoke* through the courtesy and help of Paul Savage, story editor at the time. And, if I remember correctly, I replaced Elisha Cook, whose home had burned down a few days before. I must say it was the first time I ever replaced Elisha. He was so good it seems like he kept me unemployed for a hundred years! However, one never really knows how one gets hired in this business. Ever. If I recall, the episode was possibly the first two-parter in the history of *Gunsmoke*, and it was called *Nitro*, directed by Bob Totten...Due to the presence of John Mantley at the top, *Gunsmoke* had become, for me, the best drama in all respects on television, including the so-called 'Golden Years,' during which I also worked. The wonder of the group for me, was Jim, and his ability to walk in, take one look at a page or three or dialogue, and knock it out cold. How I envied him!...

"*Gunsmoke,* like all the successful shows, had an esprit d'corps and aura which made you *want* to work harder...I had had some kind of long career before *Gunsmoke*, starting back in 1932 in radio. By that time I had been connected with about twelve shows that had won major awards such as: *Dragnet, Halls of Ivy, Suspense, The Caine Mutiny Court Martial,* with Henry Fonda on Broadway, etc., etc....but I will say this. I was never prouder of my association with a show than I was with *Gunsmoke*...I recall, truly one of the funniest happenstances I have ever witnessed in almost 60 years of showbiz. The night of the final show *ever,* there was a goodbye party at which damn near everyone finally let down their hair and let everyone else know what they *really* thought of each other after having been penned up together all those years. And then, the next morning, the cancellation was withdrawn, and all those poor people had to report to work again with each other. I wasn't there for that, but I hear it was hilarious."

Fionnula Flanagan. "In 1972 John Mantley, the executive producer, liked my appearance and the audition I did for Pam Polifroni, the casting director, and hired me to guest star in an episode. It was my first Hollywood job!...It made casting directors aware of me in television in Hollywood...In *Gunsmoke* I played a young pioneer woman who had been abducted by the Indians and who had borne a son by an Indian brave...the issues dealt with the social/moral/political aspects of being a young white woman with a half-breed son, now living in a white settlement...John Mantley, James Arness and the other members of the cast all knew exactly

GUNSMOKE — I. THE HISTORY

what they were doing and knew how to do it well. Consequently there was a certain tone set on the production and everyone who guested on the show felt this and benefited by it. They were thoroughly professional and yet very warm and friendly, at least to me they were. This was an atmosphere that originated in the leadership of the show, i.e. among the producer and the principals. It is what was so wonderful for actors to know going in that these people knew their stuff and respected anyone else too who took their work seriously. Yet they were not stuffy—far from it...

"James Arness is probably the tallest and the sweetest actor I ever worked with. Until we worked opposite one another—and we went on to work together several years later in *How the West Was Won*—I had never played a scene at eye-level with a belt buckle!...I thought *Gunsmoke* was a classic of Hollywood's TV era...it was well made, well written and consistent and it didn't upset people...The 1970s, it seems to me brought potential nuclear holocaust to the forefront of European, U.S. and world consciousness in a way never before experienced. Television participated in this to a great degree. Such consciousness hardly had room within the scope of TV to share with costume dramas, which is essentially what Westerns are. They became passe in credibility...The socio-political awareness brought about by the peace movement of the mid to late sixties, the consciousness regarding nuclear war, the advents of Chernoble and AIDS in our world have moved our willingness to suspend disbelief into an intellectual and emotional and psychological place where the mores and philosophy of the good white sheriff and his good white friends simply doesn't wash today."

Med Flory. "I played the part of a drunken private in *Sergeant Holly* starring Forrest Tucker...I played borderline morons to cowardly sheriffs... Being from farmer stock, I immediately sensed the honesty of the scripts, the sets, the regulars, featured players and atmosphere...They were honest professionals from Mantley right down to the grips, thoughtful casting, good writing, a feel for the times...It was great fun for me...Working with the McEveety brothers as directors. Hanging out with Milburn Stone, a nut on the fight game, and Ken Curtis, who sang on Dorsey's Band either just before or just after Sinatra...Jim Arness was congenial and unaffected...The spirit of good will prevailed."

Nina Foch. "My son was a little boy of four and I brought him on the set. It is the only time I let him come *near* the business! I thought he would love the horses. This boy has now graduated from Yale."

Michael Fox. "I was cast after an interview with producer John Mantley. I did several episodes. I was a doctor, a bartender, a gunslinger, and a scrounger...The atmosphere was wonderful. I did over 400 TV shows and

Reflections

Gunsmoke and *Perry Mason* were the best run and enjoyable companies... *Gunsmoke* said something to everybody. Problems were addressed and they were relevant to current life, although they were placed in the old West. Viewers could identify with the characters and the situations... *Gunsmoke* presented a microcosm of life in an exciting setting... I loved it. Jim Arness was a great fellow to work with and the entire company was well disciplined and ran beautifully... At one time I was playing Dick Benjamin's lawyer on *He and She*, a very well dressed, well spoken and unctious character. While playing that role, I was cast as a scroungy dirtfarmer on *Gunsmoke*. At lunch, in wardrobe, in the Commissary, I saw Dick and Paula a few tables away. I walked over, said 'Hello,' and Dick gave me the customary smile, then suddenly recognized me and said, 'My God, Paula, look at our lawyer! It's Mike!'"

Anne Francis. "I played an ex-girlfriend of Matt Dillon's... a strong woman with integrity... In the 70s the old value systems were being attacked. Heroism was out for a while. Rugged individualism was replaced with mass market designer jeans... *Gunsmoke* was a good wholesome show with better than average scripts and a dedicated crew... Working with Jim was a great pleasure... James told me that Lady Bird Johnson had Lyndon Johnson call when the network was planning to ax the show. Her favorite actors were Jim and John Wayne. This was after it had run 13 years or so!"

Victor French. "A large part of my career has been in Westerns. I worked a lot on *Gunsmoke,* acting and directing, and of course *Little House on the Prairie,* but I just don't care a whole lot for what they're directing nowadays. A lot of this stuff I think is just trash. I keep seeing people in films that I wouldn't let in my house, or on my lawn. At what meeting, in what smoke-filled room did someone decide to do this material? It doesn't elate, it doesn't teach, it doesn't guide, it doesn't entertain. Certainly I don't know where their heads are. You can't all do a Western about an anti-hero and expect it to work, and that's what killed the Western more than television. The West and stories about the West should tell about heroic people in a heroic way. I think the Western has been destroyed... The only chance we have to get it back is to put it in the hands of someone who knows how to tell a Western story.

"It was my father, Ted French, who started me on Westerns. He started in B Westerns in 1916. We got to work on a *Gunsmoke* together and that was special for me. He was a wrangler on the San Marcus Ranch in Santa Barbara. So when the Flying-A Studios moved in in 1916 he started doing stunts with all the different Western stars. And so I got to meet a lot of them. All the bad guys used to hang around my house. So I knew them as a kid. As far as young people today go, my advice to them is to watch a lot of B Westerns. They taught me not to cheat, lie or steal, and to respect other people's property. You don't need to swear to get your point over and it's all right to cry. I think it's as good for you as laughing. Buck Jones was everything I ever wanted to be. I wanted to look like him, I wanted to talk like him, I wanted to behave like him, and be as heroic as he was. I think he was probably the best actor of all the guys in B Westerns. I liked his stories because they were very offbeat, and I liked his attitudes about life. You don't lie, or cheat, or steal. And if I could change today, that's who I would like to change into, Buck Jones." (Interviewed at the Riders of the Silver Screen Convention, Knoxville, Tennessee, 1988.)

Allen Garfield. "I played a school teacher from New England who moved to *Gunsmoke*-land, and as an outsider practiced and preached the virtue of basic compulsory education for all children, to prepare them for a better future. He fought against the intolerant townspeople's 'burning of books,' at great jeopardy to his own life, and tried at all costs to safeguard a child's right to an education... The script dealt uniquely with contemporary, relevant issues of society in a yesteryear setting. The show, *The Fires of Ignorance,* which I believe was one of the best dramatic pieces ever on the program, also had its lighter off-screen moments. One day in my scenes with Jim Arness and 'Doc,' Arness and 'Doc' got the giggles so much — and Arness had this robust laugh — that the director Victor French couldn't film for almost an hour, everyone was infected on the set by the laughter...

"*Gunsmoke* was a warm and frank depiction of American and early Americans with all of America's virtues and all of its flaws and imperfections... There is so much corruption and immorality in high places these days that *Gunsmoke* has relevance today, as ever, in terms of lessons still not learned... Appearing on *Gunsmoke* affected my career because folks in the industry saw me for the first time portraying a teacher and a New Englander. And, in any case doing the *Gunsmoke* I did affected my consciousness then and to this day."

Beverly Garland. "All the parts I played on *Gunsmoke* were very strong women, women who were in command in one way or another, or who would take command. The moral issue was always for the good. In the scripts that I did women had rights and were listened to. Of course the bad man got his just rewards. I felt it was a fine show for kids... which made it great for the whole family. There was always a sense of family on that show. No one on it was 'the star.' They were there to make this fine show and we all worked together to find the very best in each other. Of course it was work, but it was always fun because they were the best people. I adored all of them. Even though I was carrying my first child... you could not tell... they wanted me for a certain role. I could not believe it when they got a stunt woman for me because I had to fall down in the street when the bad man kills me. I mean

Reflections

no one does that. You just do your own stunts. At least in those days you did.

"I also remember I had finished my day's work, but they were still shooting, and they said, 'Go on Bev. Take off your costume and then come on back to the set.' When I returned, there was the most beautiful birthday cake you have ever seen...just for me. I can't remember that ever happening on a TV show. I was really touched. My impression...how I wish they were still around. There was a magic there that you cannot find now. The scripts were very good. The people cared. Did it affect my career? Yes. It made it richer!"

Jack Ging. "As a new actor I read for the part of a blind gun fighter...It was a number one show, therefore a good showcase for new and young actors...*Gunsmoke* was one of the best shows ever put on the air...it had simple stories, good acting and superb casting of the regulars on the show...Westerns got worn out. Too many and most not very good. And, of course, the times change...Still I think the relationships between the main characters will always have relevance."

Leo Gordon. "I was among those who tested for the Dillon role. When Jim was chosen, the producers cast me as the heavy in *Hack Prine*. They were right, a hero I'm not. Let's hear it for the heavies!!...The mean, rotten, double dealing, backstabbing, no good fella with a heart of brass shell casings...Westerns are basically morality plays: The good versus the not good. Now there are no such animals. We're all products of our environment, sibling rivalries and lack of parental guidance. In short blameless. It's everyone else's blame, not ours...*Gunsmoke* represented a little piece of land, a stream and homestead—the days of yore when a man could cut out his own path, do what he was able, and to hell with living a life ruled by committee...Returning from location one day during the shooting of the pilot, Amanda mentioned she had an opportunity to pick up a Cad convertible for four thousand dollars. She was concerned about going into debt for so much money, wondering if it was a wise step at that point in her career. I told her to buy it, and to hell with the 'risk.' She did..."

Karen Grassle. "After the pilot for *Little House on the Prairie*, Victor French had his first directing job doing the *Gunsmoke* episode in which I appeared. He was looking forward to our working together again and suggested me for the part...I played a high-spirited prostitute...The unique company that I worked with were not the regular stars but a group of young, excellent actors of unusual dedication. Victor created an atmosphere in which we were encouraged to do our best. The other unique thing was that James Arness appeared only for his own shots in his own scenes. I had never pretended to be acting with someone who wasn't there before. But of course I was new to Hollywood...In the days when I did *Gunsmoke,* it was fashionable for feminist women to let their body hair grow. Thus, I had hair under my arms like a European actress might today. When I put on my saloon dress, which of course was bare above the arms, and went into rehearsal, there was an embarrassed flurry of discussion as to who would tell me or ask me to shave. Although it would have been truer to the character to leave the hair, it was more acceptable to the American audience for me to shave. And I did with no fuss. But I thought it was funny."

Dabbs Greer. "Between 1956 and 1973 I played the character Wilbur Jonas, the storekeeper, in 41 episodes. I also played 'Uncle Wesley Goode' in 1958 and 'Joe Bean' in 1973 for a total of 43 episodes...I enjoyed the company...Today the series seems quite naive."

James Griffith. "I did one or two of the radio episodes when Bill Conrad played the lead...On television I played a snot, a nice-guy-heavy, and a marauder who killed at the slightest pretense. The most fun I had in any part was a Hillbilly opposite William Schallert in *Twelfth Night*...The company totally appreciated actors who got in and got out with the minimum of Actor's Lab students asking, 'What's my motivation?' I always came 'prepared,' with little or no questions for the director...*Gunsmoke* was first class, 'top-of-the-line.'...I always looked forward to working on the show. All the main characters were friends. Family...I remember property men dragging Jim Arness' rocking chair close to the 'work,' so that he could sit in it every chance he had...Over the years the principal characters remained, but the quality standards set by the original and early producers and directors changed. Movie-making got much more expensive and almost all Westerns looked the same, with writers rewriting themselves because they wouldn't let in fresh writing talent. Like, 'Jeepers, let's don't try *that!* I might lose my job!'"

Mariette Hartley. "It was my very first TV show. They had worked together for so long it was like riding on a salt water wave, you simply couldn't sink...We laughed from 4:00 p.m. one afternoon until 10:00 a.m. the next day because of the scene in which I picked up the steak whole with my hands in *Cotter's Girl*...I played a young wild girl who had to be civilized...It started my TV work very positively...*Gunsmoke* was terrific! It gave good actors excellent scripts to work with. Women writers like Kathleen Hite were used. And Arness is an unsung actor."

Eileen Heckart. "*Bonanza* got rid of a skittish, nervous horse. *Gunsmoke* hired it. Festus and I were on the buckboard, and the horse reared back and we came within a foot of going over a cliff. I have never known such terror...I found *Gunsmoke* to be a wonderful show!"

Reflections

Katherine Helmond. "John Mantley saw me in a play called *The House of Blue Leaves* by John Guare and asked me to come read. He read with me and I got the part. He was such a gentleman. He liked actors... I played a very poor farm lady whose husband was in dire straits and Marshal Dillon came to the rescue... It was the first TV show I did. It launched me into TV. It was the most pleasant experience. I learned about something hair raising called *Matching*... My first day at work (I had just finished the play) I had my own dressing room, a dresser, and someone to do my hair and make-up. When I got there I had a big bouquet of flowers, a basket of fruit and a note welcoming me. Shortly after John Mantley came by and asked if anything was wrong and I said, 'How, what could be wrong?' He said, 'Do you need anything?' I went blank. I had never been asked that before. When I got my paycheck I had made as much in one week as I made in six months on stage. I said, 'Gee, I may do this again some day'... I cannot imagine why *Gunsmoke* disappeared from TV... Everyone needs heroes in life and hope. Everyone loves romance and adventure... Nothing has replaced it."

Darryl Hickman. "I don't remember all of them, but I do remember playing a 'Billy the Kid' type killer, threatening everybody in sight... There was an informality on the set, a casualness almost, that set the show apart from other episodic TV of the day... I remember that Jim Arness would often not know his lines and would ask the script supervisor to repeat them for him just before a take. It always surprised me that he could appear so authoritative as Matt Dillon and not know what he was going to say. *Gunsmoke* was a beautifully devised show — a morality play — with appealing characters that the audience came to love. It had good stories, consistency of character, strong producer supervision. I haven't a clue as to why Westerns disappeared. I believe somebody will do one successfully and there will be a rash of them again."

Pat Hingle. "*Gunsmoke* was the best Western TV series ever made, in my opinion. It gave me recognition throughout the country in a way Broadway plays, feature films and other TV never had. In the spring of 1971 my friend, Milburn Stone, contacted me at my home in Suffern, N.Y. *Gunsmoke* had just started shooting episodes for the 71-72 season, and he had to have open heart surgery right away. He asked if I would play the doctor of Dodge City while he was recuperating. I had watched *Gunsmoke* since it had started. Dennis Weaver playing 'Chester' in the early years is a friend. Dennis, in fact, introduced me to Milburn. Anyway, I asked to see the script that would introduce the character I would play. I liked it. Dr. Chapman was a surgeon from New Orleans. Dressed in a brocaded vest, panama hat and linen suit, but cut from the same bolt of cloth as Doc Adams... Which was fortunate since the other scripts I did — 6 — had already been written. We just changed

GUNSMOKE — I. THE HISTORY

the name of the doctor... I had never done a series before. *Gunsmoke* spoiled me. They were in their 17th year, I think, and by far the best organized TV production group I've been associated with in my 37 years as a professional actor."

John Hoyt. "On *Gunsmoke* I played a 'heavy' beyond doubt... I seem to remember a very early call on location somewhere. As in a dream, I went through make-up, went over my lines, wondering if I would deliver the goods... You got the feeling that you were on a 'pioneer' show of its category. 'You're on *Gunsmoke?*, Gosh.' Everyone knew it was 'in the groove'!... *Gunsmoke* was 'the thing' to watch. The star was like one of your family. There was no limit to the ages of the audience... It affected my career perhaps more than I know. I appeared in many Westerns. Did *Gunsmoke* point the way? No reason why not."

Kim Hunter. "Only one memory still stands out, because it's still part of my life, a recipe for beef jerky, from the wardrobe man at that time, Jack Stone. I enclose a copy, to share, since *he* was not shy about sharing."

JACK STONE'S BEEF JERKY
(This recipe requires a gas oven)

2 pounds boneless sirloin or round steak
4 tablespoons Wright's or Colgin's liquid smoke
Salt and freshly ground black pepper

Carefully trim all fat from the meat. This is not a personal idiosyncrasy. It is essential to make good jerky. Live profligately and lose some of the beef rather than goof. Then divide the meat into its natural sections, and trim fat further, if necessary. Marinate the sections in the liquid smoke for about 30 minutes, turning the meat frequently to absorb most of the liquid. Cut the meat into strips, about ¼-inch thick, and lay out on cookie sheet in one layer. Salt and pepper each piece individually, on one side only. Garlic salt or onion salt may be used if you prefer. Put the cookie sheets into the oven, pilot heat only, for three days. After 24 hours, turn each piece to expose the underside. The Jerky is done when thoroughly dry. But *not* crisp. It should be tough, chewy, sort of leathery.

Note: If you have to use your oven for other purposes, remove the cookie sheets and return them only after the oven has cooled completely. Add to the timing slightly.

This recipe also appears in Kim Hunter's autobiographical cookbook, *Loose in the Kitchen,* published in 1975 by Domina Books.

Reflections

Anne Jackson. "I played a lady in a hoop skirt, newly wed and *real* good. Whatever the moral issues were, they were on a high level. For me *Gunsmoke* brought home memories of childhood movies. I had never done a Western before and I was thrilled. My young son was even more thrilled because he would get Arness' autograph and his mommy was going to be on TV with his *hero*. I recall having a really good time. It was playing and dressing up. I had lots of curls cascading down my back and a built in figure in my costume...hoop skirts, I think, or frilly petticoats...a shawl and bonnet...and there was atmosphere on the set...and there were horses and wagons. It was a movie come alive for me...and I was acting with people I had seen in my living room. It was like a dream and they paid me for it!!"

Clifton James. "I was always impressed by Jim Arness' sense of humor and *Gunsmoke's* great producer John Mantley...One time we were filming indoors and the road out of town was painted on the wall and a new horse in town tried to run up the road and knocked himself out."

Graham Jarvis. "I had to drive a wagon...I'd never done that before. I was very glad to have competent 'wranglers'—horsemen or animal handlers—to teach me and keep an eye on me. It was the first Western I did, the first time I drove a wagon, and it was the first time I realized that the main street of the town was *indoors,* on a sound stage, rather than out-of-doors. That was something of a surprise. I thought *Gunsmoke* had a terrific 'mood.' Towards the end I felt that they were sometimes stretching or padding the show, doing lots of sighing and lip-smacking and 'thoughtful' pauses because the dialogue wouldn't quite fill the time allotted, and that bothered me. Still I understand that it was cancelled not because it didn't have an audience, but because the audience didn't have enough women between 19 and 49...It had the 'wrong demographics.' I thought it was a shame to cancel a show for that reason."

Salome Jens. "As I recall the scripts were wonderfully crafted. They always included something magical. In the first script, the guest co-star (Richard Basehart), was a ship's captain building his house like a ship mast—This episode was called *Captain Sligo* and was a beautiful and touching story. *Gunsmoke* was a quality show, beautifully produced and wonderfully acted. We were treated as artists and my experience was that I was participating in worthy television. There were risks taken and time taken...They hired actors and writers and directors who knew about their craft. There was also a deep commitment on the part of the producer to do it well. The stories had to do with courage, commitment, and love—universal and never ending problems. Life was simpler then and the problems are still the same. It is wonderful to see them in that perspective."

GUNSMOKE — I. THE HISTORY

Russell Johnson. "I appeared in four episodes of *Gunsmoke* playing always the bad guy... *Gunsmoke* was first class from start to finish and it had better scripts, as a rule, and better actors than most television shows. In one episode I had to fight Jim Arness. I am 5'9", and Jim is about 8 feet, what a mismatch! But, being a bad guy, I pulled a few tricks on him, before he got me... Dennis Weaver and I were under contract at Universal before he did *Gunsmoke*, so we were good friends. I knew all the others professionally, but Dennis was and is special... John Mantley was one of the 'guiding forces' and those characters [Matt, Kitty, Doc, Chester, Festus] won the hearts of the public... Today, kids and young adults want it *fast* — car crashes — shootings, etc. Even so, a good story well done always has relevance."

Ted Jordan. "I had worked with James as far back as 1945. We became friends for quite some time — twelve years I was on *Gunsmoke* and close friends with his family... When they wrote me in the show as 'Burke,' I didn't want the part... this 'Burke' part was a 'hand out.' I considered it a 'bone' thrown to a dog and told Jim and all involved — I wasn't happy doing it. Burke was a shoeshine boy... who runs around town telling everybody the gossip."

DeForest Kelley. "I only appeared in one episode, titled *Indian Scout*. I do not recall the exact type of character that I played, but he must have been a man with low moral values, for 1955 was the beginning of ten years of my portraying nothing but heavies. What may be of interest is the fact that Charles Marquis Warren saw me portray my first real heavy on *You Are There* in *Gunfight at the OK Corral* and brought me to *Gunsmoke*. He also used me as a lead-heavy in *Rawhide* and... in his motion picture *Tension at Table Rock*... I mention this because he played a big part in my life and I know he played a big part in *Gunsmoke's* life...

"I recall that *Gunsmoke* was the first show in which I worked where there was that over-worked phrase today, 'a feeling of family' with the regular cast. I remember going to lunch one day with the regular cast and was astounded to see Jim Arness put away two huge prime rib steaks — plus dessert. Jim paid the bill for everybody and we in turn each gave him cash for our share. I suppose he was the only one making enough money to save receipts for tax purposes at that early stage. They were a wonderful group and I think it's ironic that *Star Trek* has been referred to as *'Gunsmoke* in Space.'"

George Kennedy. "I appeared in more than a dozen... they helped pay a lot of bills. I played bad guys, mostly... I'll always be grateful. We all became close pals. I used to reminisce with Milburn Stone about old movies, it was very pleasurable... *Gunsmoke* was the best of all TV westerns and it's still as good as it was."

Sue Ane Langdon. "I remember a Christmas goose and a scene that I had in a buckboard with Dennis... I remember James Arness gave me a picture, the ink is faded now, but it says 'A rose by any other name' so we must have had something going on the show about roses. I don't know what it is. Maybe I was wearing rose scented perfume? I remember that Jim was very sweet. He's an awfully nice man; so is Dennis for that matter...I never worked with Amanda, but many years later, we got to meet each other. We appeared at a film festival down in Panama. It was kind of a disorganized festival, but we had a lot of fun...And the fellow who introduced us was very nervous about it. And I remember that he had a Spanish accent and he said, '...a...a...a...and now dat we haf de next person at de fesdival is...a... a... Miss... Sue Ane... a... a... Miss Sue Ane?....Langdon!...Yes, Langdon.' And I said, 'Hello,' and they clapped. And he said, 'And we also haf...a...a... Miss... Miss Margaret... Miss Margaret....a...Miss Margaret....a...Miss Margaret O'Brien...O'Brien.' And she waved and everybody clapped for her. Then it came to Amanda, and he said, 'Next...next we haf Miss Amanda...Miss Amanda?...,' and Amanda said, 'Blake, stupid.' And he said, 'Miss Amanda Blake-Stupid!' And we all laughed, and she just waved. That's Amanda. That's what's best about her. I see her a lot now and I always call her Miss Stupid."

Robert Lansing. "I appeared as lead heavies...There was an attention to period detail in costuming that was unusual. And there was a feeling of professionalism and good will which contributed to a lack of tension and relaxed atmosphere. The show was enjoyable to work. I'm six feet tall, but Jim Arness towers above me at 6'5". It became a bit of a running joke each episode when we had the confrontation scene and I would say, 'Jim, sit down. I have to threaten you.' *Gunsmoke* had quality writing, production, and was a joy to work...I think the quality of the writing didn't keep up with social changes. Write a good Western and they'll be back. Television shows are chronicles of their time. You could do *Gunsmoke* today, but the emphasis, and subtle things about the ethical choices would have to be changed."

Louise Latham. "I played a wide range of ladies from the wife of a lawyer who lived in town, to one who scraped by with her family in a sod house...My characters were always faced with moral choices. One woman was captured by the Indians, bore a half-breed and chose to recognize the child. Another woman was obsessed with social ambition, but freed her children from her own warped values...I think working with good people on good material always enhances one's career...

"I always had a wonderful time on *Gunsmoke* whether it was learning to make biscuits on camera, or how to drive a buggy at full speed...It was an unusually generous close-knit group of people who cared always about the quality of work, from the wranglers to the producer. Jim Arness was marvelous in his high good humor and determination to maintain good work on the set. I believe the star sets the working situation... *Gunsmoke* was a labor of love."

Cloris Leachman. "I played women who were strong and loveable. *Gunsmoke* is black and white and dusty all over. People seemed tall around me. The show ran for 20 years because of guts and thunder... same as mine... but there was always time to stop and share a kindness. It was replaced by sitcoms and short skirts... Short skirts are back in... but don't sell the ranch yet."

Michael Learned. "I played a Western woman named Mike, feisty, living alone, very self-sufficient and quite verbose. I did all the talking and the camera was on James Arness... It was so long ago, first or second year of *The Waltons*. Victor French was in it. Matt has amnesia. I took him in, a love story develops, he gets his memory back and leaves — I was apparently the first woman Matt kisses on the show... I rode a horse, very badly, and felt awfully nervous about being on a show I'd watched as a young girl... James Arness was charming and humble with a great sense of humor."

Ruta Lee. "I listened to the radio show. Later I was signed to play several roles on TV... Working on *Gunsmoke* was very easy — professional but fun in nature — with good directors... A 'family' was built by caring producers. There were good scripts many of which were adapted from radio... In one episode Matt Dillon was to interrupt my seduction of him by picking me up out of the bed, slinging me over his shoulder and taking me down the hall to Miss Kitty. He did so, and in the process slammed my head against the door frame, knocking me out cold. I came to in the arms of big Jim Arness, frantic with worry — tears in his eyes, asking if I was all right. Not everyone could bring tears to Jim's eyes. I loved it!!!"

Joanne Linville. "Everything was done to perfection. This I mean in terms of props, authentic — even when baking — the bread was made in the morning with yeast, so it would rise properly... There was an overall feeling of fun, camaraderie — working hard, but with a sense that this wasn't *Macbeth*. They were all very kind and supportive... It was a good beginning and I loved doing the shows... James Arness had an incredible sense of humor and could find something funny in everything. We were supposed to experience an explosion and we were to shake like we were feeling an earthquake. Well, we began to laugh and could not do the take. Finally the director broke the set till we settled down. I never had that happen before... The work is always so serious because of costs. It was delicious."

June Lockhart. "I appeared with Wayne Morris in an episode called *Crazy Beulah* [Renamed *Dirt*]... and played an alcoholic, nymphomaniac,

Reflections

murderess with the mind of a 12-year-old—but she was sorry!! We shot it in a studio on Melrose in L.A.... The director was Ted Post... It got me two jobs on *Have Gun, Will Travel*. *Gunsmoke* was a great Western—perfect for its time. It was a classic show."

Tyler McVey. "I was called to play a part in the pilot of *Gunsmoke*... having never once been called to work the radio show... I usually played a judge or an attorney, or sheriff. Once I played a husband who killed his wife, the only heavy I played in the series... *Gunsmoke* was a well-done, well written Western. The characters were unique and very consistent. The ratings were always good. So the public liked it. Justice always prevailed... The public today is interested in violence and sex. *Gunsmoke* as produced in the 50s and 60s would have little relevance today...

"My recollection of working on *Gunsmoke* was that the regular cast—with the possible exception of Dennis Weaver—were very clique-y and not particularly cooperative with those of us who came in on a daily basis to play supporting roles. That, of course, was typical of most casts in series. As far as a personal experience is concerned, I recall one scene where I, as the sheriff, was to meet Matt at the bottom of a hill *leading* a posse. As it turned out the posse arrived way ahead of me, because they were horsemen and I was not. Matt and the crew fell on the ground in laughter and the director instructed the posse to please let the sheriff arrive first."

Ed Nelson. "My agent was on good terms with casting and the producers for *Gunsmoke*. The roles I played were sympathetic heavies... young-cowboys-in-trouble who were ignorant, but good... and a good guy who makes bad choices. You always got an extra chance from Matt Dillon and the benefit of the doubt. I liked to work *Gunsmoke*. It was good money, a good cast, always good direction... Andy McLaglen, Harry Harris and others... It had good producers and the input of an intelligent cast. It was very human, with a great balance of comedy, drama and warmth, and the charm and strength of 'Big Jim'... After the antihero 60s, *Gunsmoke's* 'Good Guys' were too good, and its 'Bad Guys' too bad. Can Westerns make a comeback? It's worth a try! There are heroes and kids should know some...

"When *Gunsmoke* went to one-hour from half-hour, I was the Guest Star. During a long monologue while Marshal Dillon and I, Perce McCall, were camping out at night on our way to Dodge, I looked up at the stars... and saw an electrician eating lunch on the walk way above us and reading the newspaper at the same time, paying us no attention. It made me almost laugh in the scene. The big smile turned out to be 'a great idea' the director said, not knowing it was involuntary."

Lois Nettleton. "A wonderful director, Tay Garnett, had directed me in an episode of *Naked City* in New York, and requested me for this particular role in *Gunsmoke*. So they brought me out from New York to do it...It was my first job in Hollywood TV, and I think it opened some doors for me. It also introduced me into the 'movie atmosphere' of TV. The New York TV I had been doing seemed more nitty-gritty, *theatrically* oriented, all of which I loved, of course, since I was basically a theatre actor...*Gunsmoke* was a wonderful, highly professional company, all extremely talented...a dedicated, cooperative and friendly group—aiming for excellence...People got to know and love the central characters. They were familiar and comfortable to the audience, and people cared about them. Also, the humor was delightful...

"I was a newlywed when we were shooting the *Gunsmoke* episode. On a Friday evening, during the filming, I flew back to New York to see my husband's opening in a musical. Since this was my first TV show in Hollywood, I wasn't aware of all the protocol, and didn't think to mention my trip to the producers. I was heading back to California Sunday morning, but there was a huge snowstorm and all the airports were closed for the day. I was due back on the *Gunsmoke* set at 6:30 a.m. Monday. I finally got on a flight out of New York late Sunday to Chicago!—And a flight several hours later from there to California. A frantic and tearful call to my agent had enabled them to reach the *Gunsmoke* people, but it was difficult for them to rearrange a shooting schedule, and it must have cost them dearly in time and money. When I raced onto the set directly from the airport, *several* hours late, in a state of near-hysteria, everyone was cheerful and soothing and good-humored. Except for my constant babbling of apologies, it was as if nothing had happened. Later I learned that everyone had been cautioned not to take note of my tardiness. Now that is *class!!* That's compassion and understanding. That's humanity. I love them all!!"

Mayf Nutter. "I came out from West Virginia and was relatively new in town. I was staying at a $14 a week motel on Ventura Boulevard and had just spent the previous six months trying to get an agent...Finally I got a guy who was breaking away to start his own agency and he signed me. The first interview I got was for Festus' cousin Heathcliff on *Gunsmoke*. So I called a friend of mine, who was starring on *The Virginian,* and he loaned me a pair of bluejeans for the audition...I borrowed his shirt and his cowboy boots. Pam Palifroni was the casting director and I walked in jes talkin' like this and everythin' like that...I mean when I walked in there I said, 'My goodness gracious is this a real television? I never thought I'd be here, 'n may I walk aroun' 'n shake everyone's hand?' And I just kept that character all through and they gave me a script and asked me to read...I just played the hillbilly to the hilt, and the next thing I knew, I was being put into costume...Bo Hopkins and I made our debut on that show.

Reflections

"The thing that strikes me looking back is that it actually felt like the old West to me when I was doing the role... The scenes were very real. To the point where I was no longer aware that there was a camera round. We were just involved in doing whatever it was we were in the scene, like trying to fish an old chest of confederate gold out of a quicksand pile... In acting you can really leave the worldly things behind and really get involved in whatever that scene is and *Gunsmoke* gave me that opportunity... *Gunsmoke* had a life of its own. It wasn't just the actors, but the show itself seemed to have a life, a personality about it and the people on the set... Once you were a character on *Gunsmoke* they kind of opened their arms to you everytime you dropped by the set... If you came by they were glad to see you... And there was a fondness for the characters that you did. I ran into John Rich last year and it had been a good 20 years since we did that episode, and he remembered my character name and the name of the other folk with no fumbling around. 'Mayf Nutter, how have you been? Cousin Heathcliff, *Hard Luck Henry*.'

"As corny as it may sound, *Gunsmoke* was made with a lot of love and personal dedication, and it was a multiplication of the personal dedication that made it something beyond the words that were written on the paper and even the images that were eventually on the still. It became a part of imagination that became reality, first in the minds of the writers and then the producers and directors, then the actors and the editors and then from there the many people who actually watched it... They forgot they were watching a TV show when they were watching *Gunsmoke*. All of a sudden they were in the old West... Since the $14 a week motel room... I ended up buying a place which is up on the mountain overlooking CBS Studios where we did *Gunsmoke*. With a good three wood shot off my roof, I could probably put one into the *Gunsmoke* office down there."

Carroll O'Connor. "I played a rancher and an army officer. Both shows, as I recall, dealt with an unwritten, versus a written code of law. Jim Arness and the other regulars were most pleasant to work with — unusually pleasant... I could not mount to a military saddle, a McClellan, in proper military style."

Paul Picerni. "The stories were well written and well produced... They were based on true to life emotions and situations... It was nice working again with producer John Mantley, who had been a writer on my series *The Untouchables* and with Vince McEveety, who was our assistant director. I also enjoyed working again with Amanda... It was totally enjoyable everytime... An excellent show."

Robert Pine. "The first episode of *Gunsmoke* I appeared in was called *Lyle's Kid,* which was the season debut in September 1968. As I recall they had offered the part to Beau Bridges and he turned it down because he had decided to concentrate on feature films and didn't want to do TV anymore. This was wonderful for me because this was the first big opportunity I had had since leaving Universal, where I had been under contract for three years. I played the title character, that of a fast draw young gun trained by my father, Morgan Woodward, to avenge an old grudge of his. It was a very good piece of TV and one that I am most proud of from my early career.

"I went on to guest three more times. One was called *Jayhawkers* (renamed *The Night Riders*), where I played Jeff Corey's son. In another I played John Payne's son. As you can see they had me typecast. I said 'paw' almost as many times as the Cartwright boys from *Bonanza*. The exciting and gratifying thing about working on *Gunsmoke* were the guest parts. There was always something to get your teeth into, good three dimensional characters with good stories. This is not so true nowadays. The guest parts are usually smaller and less well defined. As far as why *Gunsmoke* lasted for 20 years, that's a difficult question.

"There are so many ingredients that go into a successful TV series. First, I would have to say that good scripts coupled with appealing series regulars are the most important. And, of course, *Gunsmoke* had these virtues in spades... That is what made doing the show so exciting, the high caliber of writing. And Matt, Kitty, Doc, and Festus were as down home and comfy as you could want. But once you have a cast like this assembled it's almost impossible to keep them together for any length of time, much less 20 years. It seems after five, six, or seven years people get antsy and want to move on. That the producers were able to keep three out of the four of the original cast together for 20 years is a tribute to their negotiating ability and to the actors' good sense to appreciate a good thing when they see it. Add to this the many intangibles that go into a successful TV show and you end up with the 20-year miracle that was *Gunsmoke*.

"Westerns waned and disappeared in the 70s I believe because we lost our innocence after the 60s and the Viet Nam War... After our troubles in Viet Nam and the realities of violence depicted on the evening news every night and the complexities that it suggested, it was much harder to accept the simplicities that were TV Westerns. We would no longer identify with these stories and characters... Do I think *Gunsmoke* has relevance today? Yes... as in most classic Westerns, it espouses the traditional values of family, right vs. wrong, hard work, etc. All we have to do is look to none other than Ronald Reagan and George Bush, they won elections trumpeting essentially the same traditional values as those that were presented weekly on *Gunsmoke*... I have managed to rattle on here, but as you can see from this response, I remember my visits to *Gunsmoke* with great affection and it will remain one of the quality experiences of my early career."

Reflections

Laurie Prange. "I had been in the business only a few years when I was cast to make a guest appearance on *Gunsmoke*. The audition was for the role of a young girl who had been raised by wild animals. Because she hadn't any language skills, I showed up for the audition barefoot, filthy, no makeup, and basically trying to present myself as the character. I'm sure I came off quite socially retarded, which was required for the part. At first the director and I just stared at one another across the room. I remember him smiling at me after this long 'stare,' presenting me to the producer John Mantley, and casting me. The director was Bob Totten, one of my very favorite directors...I played a 'wild child,' who as an infant was left in the woods to die and was raised by animals. I made several trips to the zoo to study the behavior of the apes and cats as preparation for the role. I had great fun with this one!...

"What was unique about working on *Gunsmoke* was the kindness of the cast and crew. I felt like I was a welcomed member of a large family. The producer John Mantley ran a very tight group. I liked him very much. Unlike some other producers, one always felt that John loved *Gunsmoke* from his very heart. He didn't just love the idea of a successful series, but took the show very seriously as his beloved child...Everyone was having a wonderful time loving their work, loving the stories. It was a contagious feeling that reached out to those of us fortunate to work on the show and reached out into the living rooms of America...My performance was selected by *Gunsmoke* to be considered for an Emmy nomination for best performance by an actress. The morning after the show aired I got a call from a radio disc jockey who interviewed me live on the air to talk about how I prepared for the character...

"My whole experience with *Gunsmoke* was wonderful! We shot the episode on location in Kanab, Utah. I remember glorious red mountains of sand, the colors were magnificent, and I remember the kindness of James Arness, who I had the pleasure of working with again years later."

Denver Pyle. "I tested with Amanda Blake, she for the part of Kitty and I for the part of Matt. Charles Marquis Warren was the writer, producer, and I guess director. Anyway, we tested on a Friday and Warren said that he thought we were set. We met on Saturday and he told us there was one more guy he had to test but that he wouldn't be good for the part because he was too big and it would be hard to cast around him. As it turned out Jim was perfect for the part and no one, I mean no-body, could have played it better.

"On *Gunsmoke* I played many different parts including heavies, preachers, judges, and a buffalo-hunter Jacob who appeared often...The set was relaxed. Everyone knew their character well and played it perfect. The cast and crew always treated the free-lance actor with great respect. This is a reflection on the producers, who did the same...It survived for twenty years because you never heard a bad word. It was well written, well produced, and good always won out. It appealed to all ages. *Gunsmoke* breached the gap between the people that buy and sell shows. It was an accident really. Jim and Amanda were beautifully cast and it was a very loyal cast...And it had wonderful guest stars like Strother Martin who was a good friend of mine. I also wrote for *Dirty Sally* and some *Gunsmokes*. They bought them, but did not do them."

Tom Reese. "I played mostly villains on *Gunsmoke*...I had just been in Hollywood a few months from New York City and my agent got me an interview on the half-hour, black and white *Gunsmoke*. I went on to work the one-hour color show in later years...It was a warm, friendly company, cast and crew. It was a first class, quality production. I had done a Broadway show with Dennis Weaver in 1951. It was nice to see his success. Also, Jim Arness was easy going and made me feel relaxed and part of the show. Milburn Stone was also nice, as was Amanda Blake...I worked with many fine actors and directors. It was the first of many Westerns that I worked in."

Madlyn Rhue. "I played a sweet young thing...the actors were real and good and moral...they were all lovely...I got my first crush on an actor on *Gunsmoke*. His name was James Drury and he went on to become *The Virginian*."

Peter Mark Richman. "*Gunsmoke* was a fine Western show with excellent actors...One in particular that I remember, I played a bad guy intent on doing Ed Begley in. Ed Begley and I were old friends. It was the third time we had worked together. We both guested on *Gunsmoke*. Ed first appeared with me on an NBC series I had, *Cain's Hundred*."

Fran Ryan. "I was a guest performer on *Gunsmoke* only twice, but I was a regular when cast as 'Miss Hannah.' I was one of several possibilities and was finally awarded the role...It was sheer joy—but I didn't attempt to replace Miss Kitty. The story line was her selling the Long Branch to me. Under the knowledgeable and expert guidance of John Mantley, one was finally in a working part where everything possible was done to elicit your best. I remember the fun and kindness of 'Doc,' Milburn Stone, the fine directors, the pride of being part of a show of this calibre. It was class in a Western...While working *Gunsmoke* I was nominated for Best Supporting Actress for the only time. It also made me feel I would make a living in film, which has followed... [On *Gunsmoke*] I guess we offered the belief that people who harm their fellow man will be punished, that honesty is the best policy, and that the weak in our society must be protected."

John Saxon. "I remember an episode of *Gunsmoke* that I guest starred in vividly because I liked the story so much. It was called *The Whispering Tree*,

Reflections

and I think it was written by John Mantley. It was directed by Vincent McEveety and Edward Asner was a guest star also. I played a poor dirt farmer whose land was so bad he believed he could never offer his wife and sons anything but poverty. He consciously decided to rob a Wells Fargo salary shipment and pay for it by spending eight years in jail. He tells his wife that he is innocent, and secretly buries the money by a certain tree on his land, convinced that this is the only way to provide anything for their future.

"Upon his release from prison, he is joyously reunited with his family. His wife informs him that she has...guess what...while he was in prison?: convinced the bank to loan her the money to have their poor land irrigated. It is now very fertile and parts of it are buried under water; including the tree near which the farmer buried the robbery loot. He is pursued by Asner who plays a Wells Fargo detective convinced that the farmer will lead him to the loot. The farmer can't...and must deal with the regret of losing years of his life when it was unnecessary. I remember the story very fondly."

William Schallert. "I auditioned for the role of 'Chester' in the pilot. Shortly after that I did a play with Dennis Weaver and saw immediately how much more suited for the part he was. Dennis and I became friends and have remained so over the years...Dennis was president of SAG from 1973-1975 and I was elected to the Board of Directors in 1974, so I served with him there for two years. Then, I was elected president from 1979-1981, and Dennis lent me his support...On *Gunsmoke* I played, oddly enough, hillbillies to begin with. Dennis and his wife came from Joplin, Missouri, in the Ozarks, and I picked up the dialect from them. My first part was really the leading role on *Twelfth Night,* still one of my favorites. I was a hillbilly who came down to Dodge City from the mountains to settle a feud. I did a similar guy on one of the hour shows and once played a psychopathic killer who was head of a gang...

"*Gunsmoke* is a classic of television's early to mid years, the apotheosis of the Western of the American frontier...It was unique...For one thing, the intense devotion to and involvement with the show by the cast regulars... And the remarkable quality of the writers. Virtually every script was written by John Meston himself, or adapted from one of his radio scripts by Les Crutchfield or Kathleen Hite. In later years, with John Mantley as producer, *Gunsmoke* became a one-hour dramatic anthology show—treating a wide range of interesting themes and ideas within the Western framework... *Gunsmoke's* success lay in the strong appeal of Jim Arness as Matt Dillon, durable and constant, its outstanding guest casts and directors, its top notch producers like Charles Marquis Warren and Mantley, the ability of the show to adapt and find good cast replacements, the open-ended quality of the Western format for dealing with a wide range of themes and subjects, and finally — and certainly not to be discounted — the time slot, Saturday evenings when serious competition was non-existent. It was the only show worth watching on a Saturday evening, and it suited a Saturday night perfectly...

"One final note: In the second or third season, I wrote a song (words and music) for Amanda Blake to sing on personal appearance tours. It was called *Long Branch Blues,* and she used it for years. Finally, she appeared on *Hee Haw* (I think!) and sang it. As a result I joined ASCAP. For someone who studied composing with Arnold Schoenberg, it was an odd way to achieve a sort of professional status."

Hal Smith. "I appeared in only one episode as I was doing another Western show, *Jefferson Drum,* at the time. I played the hotel clerk...It was delightful...A great experience with fine actors, one of the very best shows on TV...Well written and *fun* to do...I knew many of the actors and had worked with them in other shows. The cast and crew were wonderful pros. Amanda Blake, Jim Arness and the rest were very considerate and happy workers. That makes acting a pleasure. The most vivid experience in my mind was how the prop master reached into his prop box and grabbed a handful of old spectacles and gave them to me saying, 'Here, with all the characters you portray, you might be able to use these.' And I did, and still do. The glasses worked out fine."

William Smith. "There was a feeling of kindredship on the show. I never felt it on any other. It was top knotch in every way and successful because of its reality and tight scripts and the acting was really — real...I remember that Amanda Blake on *Hostage* said, 'Look here you, I've been on this show for 16 years and ain't ever been bred, so do it right!'"

Julie Sommars. "I was fortune to do four *Gunsmokes* very early in my career. One of them marked Bette Davis' television debut. Working with an actress that I admired and still admire was one of the highlights of my career. Bruce Dern, another fine actor, was also in this particular episode, as was Tom Skerritt. Miss Davis was extremely kind to me...Her contract called for her to finish her day at 6 p.m. Since I was low man on the totem pole, my close-ups were saved until the end of the day. Many an evening she stayed late to do her off-camera for me — even though she herself had finished. Ours was never a social relationship and she was always referred to as 'Miss Davis' by me and by the rest of the cast and crew. However, Bruce Dern, always a character, referred to her as 'Hey, Man!' She seemed to enjoy and get a kick out of his familiarity."

James Stacy. "I played a good guy and a gunslinger-good guy...I met my second wife on a two-part *Gunsmoke,* Kim Darby, and during one of my auditions Jon Voight was sitting in the office with me before we read."

Reflections

Craig Stevens. "I remember guest starring as the heavy. The programs were good versus bad... I had not done many Westerns. It was a very professional company, an excellent program, and a good credit at that time."

Guy Stockwell. "The first show was a very small part—two weeks later, or thereabouts, I was back on playing a lead role... *never happens!*... My first starring role was *The Cook*. I miss doing the Western... The smell of a Western set will last forever, fondly in my memory. *Gunsmoke* has images dating to my first listening to it in college—absolute fascination—it seemed so much more *real!*... It never changed, like the Pacific Ocean, you could always tune in for a fix... like visiting the family, safely, for the holidays... I still get a twinge whenever I see Burt. Of the intimacy usually missing in an epic, compare Doc and Kitty to Lone Ranger and Tonto! The Western legend felt like personal history, we were in the bar sharing their thoughts and feelings...

"The impact of *Gunsmoke* cannot be felt today, the broad, young, audience has very little of a reference point. They are twice removed from the Western settlement in this country and the mythology that permeated our literature and movies... I feel we lost the idea of one person having moral power and the ability to vanquish evil. The tragedies of the 60s pushed us to search for the answer more and more in machines; robots, talking cars, etc. We may be trapped in that search now—still!"

Leonard Stone. "The stars—regulars—were most gracious, cooperative, helpful, and professional. It was a pleasure working with them. This cannot be said of all the series I have worked... Bring it back! TV needs shows like *Gunsmoke*..."

Neil Summers. "You got up in the morning and you looked forward to going to work on *Gunsmoke*, because it was like a family of 120 people. I had more fun working on *Gunsmoke* than on any other show I've done. I was involved in the last four years as a stuntman and actor... and most of the time I doubled for the actors. Paul 'Tiny' Nichols started out as Jim Arness' stand-in, way back when the show started and wound up as a first assistant director. He did most of the hiring as far as the stunt-men went. Leonard Katzman was the line producer who was there all the time, but Mantley made all the decisions. The only writer that stayed on location all the time was Jim Byrnes...

"James Arness is a natural wit and kept everyone in stitches with his relaxing humor. I was very fortunate to play a part in an episode called *Matt's Love Story*. It was an episode where Matt Dillon is shot by guest star Victor French and develops amnesia and is nursed back to health by actress Michael Learned. I was one of Keith Andes' gunmen and was shot and killed by Mr.

GUNSMOKE — I. THE HISTORY

French... I did dozens of *Gunsmoke's*... but this particular episode turned out to be the highest rated one in the 20-year run of the show. I am understandably proud to be a part of it."[169]

Loretta Swit. "The two shows I did were such *wonderful* experiences. I remember so much about them so many years later. The first job I had in television was the leading role on *Gunsmoke* so it was very special to me... I read at an audition for John Mantley, Pam Polifroni and Philip Leacock... The role was of a young married trying to help her husband escape from the law, but changes her mind mid-story and does the correct thing for both of them... *Pack Rat* began my career in episodic television in a very prestigious way. Philip Leacock did his usual masterful directing and it was a real plum role for me... It was an extraordinary way to begin in the medium — working with such a wonderful director and a cast of such consumate pros...

"The ensemble of players were wonderful and the quality of work was always high. It was a happy company. Milburn (Millie) Stone made Jim Arness laugh and visa versa. They really enjoyed each other... Milburn was enjoying the work I did on my character, and without my knowledge he called the casting director at Paramount to say some wonderful things about my work. He asked her not to tell me. When I finished the episode on *Gunsmoke* the producers at *Mannix* (Paramount) called me in to read for a leading role... It became my second role on television. Years later, shortly after Millie died, the casting director told me the story of what he had done!"

Jess Walton. "I had an interview with Pam Polifroni and got the job... *Gunsmoke* was the Western among Westerns... the definitive Western TV show... the 'Granddaddy" of them all... Everybody concerned with the show did his or her job not only well, but excellently — Producers, directors, crew, production staff and cast. The show also had a distinct and accurate flavor of the period... There was a feeling of being part of an institution while you were working the show... the costumes and sets were so life like — I felt for a brief time — really a part of the 'old West.' I felt like I went back in time. When I played 'Patricia,' Newly's bride, I discovered that my character was dying of leukemia. So as the character I went outside into the 'yard,' touched the flowers, trees, felt the wind and spun round and round looking up at the sun — appreciating it for the last time — Unfortunately I stared at the sun too long — too many takes — and temporarily burned the retinas of my eyes."

William Windom. "My agent got me a job on the show sometime after April 1961, when I arrived in L.A. from N.Y.C. I played the heavy or the weakling grappling with avarice, lust, cowardice, drunkenness. It was the series most concerned with not showing equine waste matter. I managed to kneel on a dry pie in one shot, to save my knees. I believe it was a unique

Reflections

shot on that series...It was a fun oater. I found out Arness didn't want to appear brutal and would avoid any physical contact with smaller men. Ergo, I could tap him on the chest to make points with impunity...I went after Chester's bad leg with an ax handle once, audio and video. They let it stand. Like the horse puckey, another first for *Gunsmoke?*... Probably just as well that I never got to play with Miss Kitty. Tay Garnett let me create long death scenes. I used to be called: 'Mr. Flip Flop.'"

Morgan Woodward. "I've done more *Gunsmokes* than anyone else. I'm not quite sure how many I've done. I think it's 17. When I first came to Los Angeles I did one of the thirty minute segments. It was probably in the 50s. In 1965 the casting director who had been casting *Gunsmoke* for several years, I believe his name was Jim Lister, died of cancer, and Lister and I did not get along. We had had a little conflict at another studio several years before, and he never invited me in to do another *Gunsmoke*. So for the first ten years I was not a guest star on the show. Anyway, he died in 1965 and was replaced by Pam Polifroni a CBS casting director who knew my work. I came in for the first interview to play a cohort of Ed Begley and I did an interview and a tryout for the part, and I got the part. That's how I was introduced to the series *Gunsmoke*.

"They liked the work that I did very much and in the next ten years I did 17 roles on *Gunsmoke,* more than any other actor in the world. I say in the world because there were some international actors who came here from Europe to do *Gunsmoke* as you know... *Gunsmoke* seemed to be an organization that was incredibly well organized and well put together. The people from the producer right on down to the craft service personnel seemed to be hand picked by the gods because they worked so well together...They were just simply outstanding in what they did from the top to the bottom...highly qualified, I can't think of any *Gunsmoke* that I ever worked on where there was anyone associated with the show that was incompetent or incompetent to any degree. They just had outstanding people. The stories were good and the directors were good.

"A lot of the same actors worked *Gunsmoke*. They had a cache of fine actors, supporting actors, character actors that added to the show. People like Jon Voight and many other fine actors were first introduced on *Gunsmoke* and went on to great fame. Pam Polifroni was an exceptionally fine casting director and there were good line producers and executive producers who cared about the show. During the last ten years, I worked with Philip Leacock as executive producer, John Mantley as executive producer, and Leonard Katzman who now heads *Dallas*. These were extraordinary men...They directed the show the way it should have been directed and produced. *Gunsmoke* had a good solid cast of regulars, and they didn't wear out their welcome because *Gunsmoke* was essentially an anthology.

"The cast of regular characters were the thread that held the show together, and people like me were offered the opportunity to come in and be the star of the show. The regulars were around to lend support, and they were good, solid, interesting characters. Of course, I think that America has always been in love with its image of the Western character, and I think a good Western series today, well done, would do very well. But unfortunately they're so expensive to make, no one wants to try...CBS had considered shelving *Gunsmoke* once before its final cancellation, but they had so many letters and protests that they prolonged it. Why they decided to do away with a popular show like that, I don't know for sure...it could have been something as simple as some executive's wife saying she didn't like it...because believe it or not, things like that do happen...

"I remember well one of my closest friends, one of my dearest friends, Strother Martin, he created some fine performances on *Gunsmoke*. And of course I had the pleasure of working with Jack Elam, who was outstanding on *Gunsmoke,* and Victor French another friend of mine who has gone on *Highway to Heaven* and other shows. I remember working once with Andy Devine on *Gunsmoke,* which was a pleasure...

"I never really thought of it, but if *Gunsmoke* had a message, I suppose it was good over evil. There was always poetic justice in everything, the bad guys always got it in the end and righteousness and virtue always triumphed. For me the message was just damn good entertainment and that's why it survived...The reruns hold up very well over time because they're period pieces and because they were so well done. You know, when you think in terms of Western pictures you can go back and look at Western film, some of the good Western film that was done 30, 35, 40 years ago, and it still holds up. So I think *Gunsmoke* will continue to hold up....

"There was an episode I did called *Lobo* where I played a crazy old mountain man, a wolf hunter. That was my favorite episode. I not only liked the story, but it was the only time in my entire film career that I ever watched myself and forgot that I was watching myself. I was so engrossed...I look back on those shows with affection. I just think what a remarkable achievement it was to have a show on the air and to have been that popular for 20 years. It's extraordinary...Now 12 years after the show closed so many people come up and still talk about *Gunsmoke* saying, 'God, I wish it were still on. I enjoyed your performances so much.' And I say, 'I wish it was on too, it was one of my favorite shows.'"

Link Wyler. "One of the shows I worked on was *The Wild Child* (Retitled *The Lost*). This particular show happened to be Amanda's and Kitty was on a stage coach. The stage coach went over a cliff and she gets amnesia, and ends up running into a little girl that has been running wild living off the land. They are two lost people trying to survive and they come upon a real nasty family. I played one of the mean sons and I had to be kind of rough with Amanda at the end of the show. And then, of course, Matt and the guys come and save her in the end, and we get our just dues.

"It was a very hard show for Amanda. It was very demanding. She had to stay dirty and roughed up, and in this particular episode I guess she and Mantley had had a disagreement about something. It came down to either him going back to Los Angeles and getting out of the way or she would. Robert Totten was directing, so there was a real good possibility of another hit show in the making, if we could just pull everything together and deal with the elements and the hardships. The filming was in Utah and I ended up driving Amanda to the rougher locations with her wardrobe lady, her hair-stylist, and her make-up in this four-wheel drive vehicle. One day we were in a very remote river location where Kitty and the wild child were fighting in the river. I had to have some time to study my script and I'm sitting on a hill trying to study, when I see something out of the corner of my eye every once in a while out in the woods. So I finally put my script down and concentrated real hard on this one area in the woods where the crew was filming on the river. And I'll be damned if it wasn't John Mantley, the executive producer of the number one show on television, having to hide out in the woods to watch his actress work...

"Pam Polifroni was the casting director. Every role was important to Pam whether the actor had only one line or was the guest star. She did an excellent job of casting the show. She not only put people in who she thought could do the part, but also those who looked the part. If you look at the people who were guest stars or who had a small one liner, most of them are successes in the business today. A lot of people who did *Gunsmoke* ended up very successful in the acting profession, or in producing, or directing or writing."

POSTSCRIPTS

During the past few years interviews were conducted with principal actors, producers, directors, writers, and other staff members. Selections from these interviews were interspersed throughout the body of the book. Remaining highlights are included in this section.

James Arness (May, 1988)

Do you recall who was at your screen test and who you tested with?

"Yes. Dennis Weaver was testing to play Chester, and there was another, a third actor. It was kind of a one scene little test...done over at CBS studios."

Who was the guiding force behind Gunsmoke?

"Meston and Macdonnell were the genesis of the whole thing...literally the whole thing came from them...They created this from blank paper and brought these characters to life and made the situation believable and liveable. I think that without any question of a doubt it was our use of their stories in the early years of the show that set *Gunsmoke* immediately apart as a totally different kind of Western story. That was when we had our biggest rating sessions, in those early years with the half-hour shows. The thing just became an incredible shooting rocket."

What was Matt's relationship with Chester?

"I think he really liked the guy. He enjoyed having him around. He was a colorful guy and all, and when it was necessary he could be extremely capable and a good man to have along."

Could you comment on the cast and their possessiveness regarding their characters?

"This was a thing that we all got into in the early seasons...because we all had a sense of having been given a tremendous responsibility with this magnificent, beautiful show that had been so highly accepted by the radio audience for all those years. All these people were out there and they had an image of it in their heads, and now we were the people who were going to have to come on and show it visually. We were all particularly concerned about it, trying to evolve... and to make good what had been given to us. It was only out of concern for that, that all of us I think felt that way, feeling our way around to try and come up with these characters."

When the Arness Production Company started to co-produce the program with CBS how did your role change?

"It didn't really... This was a thing that was done mostly for financial purposes... There were business reasons to form the company, and then I handed it to people who ran it. We tried a couple of pilots... but the company was different from that of an actor who has a company with the full intention of making other shows and becoming a real broad-based company. That was not our intention."

Did you have any warning when CBS temporarily cancelled Gunsmoke?

"No, we didn't have any warning. I think that that's the kind of thing that's difficult to recall accurately so I'm a little hesitant to comment on it. But I remember that somebody at the network had decided that they should cancel it and they made their plans... Of course that wasn't a unique situation. You read everyday about how networks cancel shows without letting people know. We found out one morning that this was going to be the last episode."

Do you have any recollections of William S. Paley?

"Every once in a while when he was visiting the West Coast he would stop by and stop on the set and say, 'Hello'... I always got the sense that it was special to him and he would ask me if everything was going okay, or if there was anything he could do to help me out. I always felt a sort of closeness to him because of that. I felt that he genuinely and sincerely had our best interest at heart and wanted everything to be good."

Could you comment on the directors?

"Charles Marquis Warren was the man who was initially put in charge of the show, and he was a very talented filmmaker and an interesting guy to work with. He's the one who really started the ball rolling for us, and he directed many of those first shows. The memory that I have is of the early guys that worked with us, Andy McLaglen and Harry Harris, and Teddy Post. I remember them as being the guys that probably did the most overall episodes. And of course, the McEveety brothers, through the years. They were all a lovely bunch of guys that really loved doing the show. It was special to them and I think they felt it was kind of a special treat to come over and do *Gunsmoke.*"

Could you comment on the writers?

"There was a whole bunch of them. Ron Bishop did many special ones,

Postscripts

and of course it started out with John Meston who dreamed the whole thing up in the first place. The ones that he wrote were the ones that we relied on most heavily, and they were the ones that catapulted us off into outer space, so to speak."

Do you have any favorite episodes?

"There were so many... In the first two or three years, there were these little gems that Meston had written, which were 30-minute character studies and very intense capsule dramas. I can't remember specific ones but there were just so many... Totally different than any of the Westerns prior to that. It was startling. They were character studies rather than Western action stories and they were just so good that I think there's no question that it set up the show in the early years so that the audience was loyal to it and stayed with it... My personal feeling is that they would probably have stayed with it for a few more years after the 20."

Why do you think Gunsmoke *was finally cancelled? And what were your feelings?*

"I have actually no idea why it was cancelled, except in a general sense, knowing how the network hierarchies go... The newer and younger people come up and they have things that they want to do and directions they want to go in. Ultimately they have their day, and that's it. I fully accepted that. You can't argue with a 20-year run. I was totally ambivalent about it. I would have been perfectly happy to stay, but on the other hand, I couldn't argue after 20 years... I just accepted the way it happened."

Will you be doing another Gunsmoke?

"I haven't been approached... but I'm always willing to talk if they have that feeling about it. I don't know where it will go from here."

What changes have you noticed in the creative process on television?

"I think that because of the cost factor everything has become accelerated... In other words, it's so expensive to make a show, that they have to move everything along so fast, and come up with so much material that it's really harder to come up with anything different or creative... I think a great majority of the evening shows are oriented toward much younger people. I personally wish there was a little different kind of programming some of the time, but on the other hand, what they have seems to be going over, and somebody out there likes it. You can't argue with success, I guess."

What did you do after Gunsmoke? *And why have you concentrated on Westerns?*

"After *Gunsmoke* shut down my outlook was to give the American audience a rest from having to look at my physiognomy up there. I was happy to be off for a while to tell you the truth. I found it very enjoyable to relax and just enjoy life for a while. I genuinely felt, and I still do, that anybody that's been up there week after week, year after year, should give the tube a rest. I think it's good to do. And I was planning to stay away from it but then they came up with *How the West Was Won* almost immediately. It was going to be a single, two-and-a-half hour show and that was going to be it...But it went over so well they decided to go on and make a series out of it. So I was drawn into that. I couldn't escape...But there were many really good shows connected with it...good episodes. When it folded I did take more time off, a couple of years...Then I tried another series...A modern day series, *McClain's Law,* which only stayed on one season. Which was the luck of the draw. I think it was a show that could have probably made it if we had been given a better time-slot...I don't go out seeking something different. I usually go on with my daily life until somebody calls up, and if it sounds good then I get involved. Otherwise, I don't. And it seems that most of the time when somebody calls it's about doing a Western."

Did Gunsmoke *have a message?*

"Well...it's difficult to define it, but it didn't try to have a message in the sense of preaching, which some shows occasionally get trapped into. Meston had a genius for being able to get across an interesting little drama in a half-hour. But it was very intense and often about the human family, the human condition. How human beings relate to each other is pretty much unchanged for the past couple of thousand years. I mean, there's love and hate, happiness and unhappiness, all these basic human conditions. He was able to capture it and make interesting little stories...through a group of citizens who happened to be living in that particular area of the West at that time. I think that's why people enjoy it all over the world. You can be living in God knows what country, in some other part of the world, and if you watch it you recognize things that you yourself went through."

What do your fans most frequently ask you?

"Why aren't you still making it? That's probably the question I'm asked most. People really miss it...They miss that era of television I think."

Amanda Blake (March, 1988)

Who else auditioned for Kitty?

"Listen, I was up against every girl in town. They were testing everybody, but just off-hand I cannot think of anyone's name, but I know they were testing everybody."

Was there any episode that was a particular challenge?

"God...every day was a challenge."

Why do you think Gunsmoke *was so popular?*

"There were so many little things. The relationship between Doc and Chester, the haggling and braggling and carrying on between Doc and Ken Curtis. People looked forward to this each week, to see what Festus and Doc were going to do to each other. And, of course, I think the mysterious

Postscripts

relationship between Matt and Kitty brought people every week saying, 'Well, are they gonna do it this week in this episode?' To this day I will not answer any questions on that...When they ask me, 'What's their relationship?' I say, 'What do you think it was?' That was the whole idea, to let people use their own imaginations...And I think it was handled extremely well...We all liked each other. We got along. We never had too many arguments or fights about anything, and I think because we worked well together and we were easy with each other, the audience could feel that. There was never a time that I remember when there was any professional jealousy whatsoever. We were all very comfortable with what we were doing and we never had any things like, 'Well, he's got more lines than I do,'... and all that crazy stuff. We just didn't have it...and I think that it showed."

What was your reaction when Macdonnell was replaced and Leacock and Mantley took over?

"I was very upset about Norman and I kind of thought, 'Well, they're gonna make all these changes, and they're gonna screw this whole thing up, and they don't know about *Gunsmoke*. We know about *Gunsmoke*. We are *Gunsmoke*...' I was not very flexible, let me put it that way...And Milburn was upset...You know, when you've got an established show like that and all of a sudden people come in with other ideas...I remember digging my heels in with Phil Leacock and Milburn was always digging his heels in...and I remember a session with Phil where there was a line...a terrible line, I can't remember what exactly, but it was not a good scene...And I said, 'I can't say this...Kitty cannot say this to Matt'...Well, Leacock couldn't understand that...He said 'It was supposed to be a joke,' and I said, 'It's a *terrible* joke! And, I'm not going to say it.' I really got defensive about the whole thing..."

What was your reaction when they temporarily cancelled the show?

"I went totally to pieces. I was so angry...and they did it in the typical way that all the networks do. And they still do it. You read it in the paper. Nobody tells you. You just pick up the paper one morning and see '*Gunsmoke* Cancelled.' No warning, no anything...People were calling, and interviews were given and I was spewing forth saying, 'This was the most unfair...blah, blah, blah...and these people, and what are they doing, and how could they treat us this way after all these years?'...It damn near started another American revolution. It was still a top show. What they finally did say was that the demographics were not right. And I had not heard that word before. Demographics...what the hell are demographics?...Some dumb machine was telling us that they don't like us out there...That they're not watching us...That we're not reaching the proper age bracket. That is horse puckey...They were saying they wanted to reach a younger audience...

Like the 35- to 50-year olds don't buy anything...Well, that was what I understood it to be."

Why did you leave the show after 19 years? Was it a difficult choice?

"Yes, it was. I had been commuting...I was living in Phoenix most of the time and I just said, 'My God, I really am tired.' And I felt like I just couldn't go on. You know, every year I was saying I can't go on one more year...I was just tired...tired of racing back and forth..."

Did you miss it after you left?

"Yes I did. And yet, I had a purge really. But it was very traumatic and I did a lot of crying. I did a lot of crying."

Did you ever contribute to any of the scripts or ideas?

"No, for the most part everything was fine with me. But we all had input. We were very fortunate. I'm sure some of the writers didn't like us because we made up words...But we could always change things, improve on a scene...We used to have story conferences. We were in the middle of a scene and we'd say, 'This really isn't working. So what can we do to fix it?' We had conferences down on the set...Norman Macdonnell would come down or John Mantley...and we were able to fix it. We all had a lot of input."

You'd be happy to tackle another Gunsmoke?

"Sure, why not. It was wonderful. It was always wonderful. It's still wonderful. And I really hope CBS sees it in the cards."

You sound like you're one of Gunsmoke's *biggest fans.*

"I am, I am!"

Dennis Weaver (December, 1986)

What was unique about working on Gunsmoke, *compared to your other TV experiences?*

"Well, your first experience of that magnitude or with that kind of success is obviously something that affects you a great deal and that you will always recall as a very wonderful time in your career and a very sweet memory. I was very fortunate to be involved in a strong creative team when we started *Gunsmoke.*"

Do you have a favorite episode you can share with us?

"There are several of them, but the ones that jump out at me the most are obviously the ones that I was more involved in. There's one called *Chesterland.* It was an hour show that I think is an absolute classic of Western humor and an example of Western television in those early days. There was one where Matt Dillon quits, where he turns in his badge *[Bloody Hands].* I think that was the first year or second year. Then there's one that I directed where Amanda Blake is kidnapped by some of these mountain men and taken

Postscripts

off to marry one of these mountaineer type persons *[Marry Me]*. And, that of course sticks in my mind. I can't remember the name of that either, it's been a long time, over 30 years."

What do you think was the major message of Gunsmoke?

"I think that the same general statement, or theme that ran through *Gunsmoke* ran through many television shows...that good conquers evil."

Do you think the show has relevance today?

"Yeah. I think it's a timeless show because it's a period show. I think it certainly has entertainment value today."

Did the cast have any influence on the development of scripts?

"We had a great deal of input. We rewrote dialogue. We rewrote scenes. There was one script that we rewrote almost totally, as far as the structure was concerned. We salvaged some of the lines. But, we had a tremendous impact on what we said because we knew the characters better than anybody else. When you get into a series, you may have anywhere from five to a dozen writers writing different scripts. But you only have one actor playing the part. And all of these writers have their different viewpoints, or slightly different viewpoints, of what the character is, and what kind of words should come out of the character's mouth. But the actor is responsible for maintaining a continuity of character. So we were at liberty to change the dialogue a great deal. This was no reflection on the talent of the writer it was just that everybody had a little different idea of the character."

What was it about Gunsmoke *that enabled it to run for 20 years?*

"It was a first. It created new roots. It opened up a whole new genre as far as television was concerned. It was the first 'adult' Western on the air. And it was a large step away from Gene Autry or Roy Rogers or the kind of late afternoon television shows that were on. I think the fact that we had tremendously creative writers in the beginning was also important. You always have to start with that. And I think the show was cast extremely well, in terms of giving a kind of a balance to the show. There was a chemistry between the four principals that started the show, myself, and Milburn Stone, Amanda Blake, and Jim Arness. It was a wonderful creative time for all of us and we were all very enthused and excited about creating something very special. We put in a lot of time and energy. We gave it our best effort possible. I think the most important thing about that show is that people identified with those characters. They became real. They became a family on television and people wanted to tune in to see what was happening to their friends."

If you had to do it all over, would you make any changes in "Chester"?

"Well, basically I would do him the same way. It's awfully hard to change something that got so much acclaim and won me an Emmy and a couple of nominations and opened up all kinds of doors for me in the Hollywood community. When I see some of those old ones I say to myself sometimes, 'Well,

I probably would have done that scene a little bit differently." And then I see others and I say, 'Man, that was right on. It really holds up.' So while I might sand it down here and there, a couple of the rough edges, basically I would do the same thing."

Ken Curtis (November, 1986)

How did you get the role of Festus?

"I was selected by the producer, Norman Macdonnell and director, Andrew V. McLaglen after having done a similar role for Andy in *Have Gun, Will Travel.*"

How would you characterize Festus' relationship with Doc?

"Doc, being the most learned man in Dodge City, probably tolerated Festus in the beginning because he planned one day to write a paper on him. Though their constant bickering would seem to disprove it — their friendship and mutual admiration grew for each other — How else can a man tell another man he loves him without insulting him? We got up each day with the purpose of destroying each other's day — all in fun, of course, as best friends do. His distaste of having me touch him developed when I took his arm to help him up on the boardwalk one day — that one incident, more than anything else, helped to develop our relationship. As was proven in several later episodes, either man was willing to die for the other."

If you had to do it over, are there any changes you would make in your characterization of Festus?

"None whatsoever."

Do you think Gunsmoke *has relevance today?*

"Yes — all across the Nation people are crying out for simple justice as I feel was portrayed in *Gunsmoke.*"

What special chemistry do you think Gunsmoke *had that enabled it to run for twenty years?*

"We all liked and respected each other — there was great humor on the show and no professional jealousy whatsoever. Every member of the cast was only interested in making the best show possible out of each script and we were all determined to never vary from our own character guidelines."

What impact do you think Gunsmoke *had on television?*

"I think it raised a lot of good kids — entertained *entire* families (not just one segment). Good and evil were very clearly defined, which set an example for children, and I believe helped families stay closer by being entertained together."

Postscripts

Burt Reynolds (January 19, 1988)

How were you cast as Quint Asper?
"At the time Norman Macdonnell was there and it was before John Mantley got there...I went on an interview for an episode of *Gunsmoke*. At the time they weren't thinking of a continuing character. It was just any character, and we did the show. There was a tremendous reaction to the show...Dennis was still there, he had 17 more shows or something like that to do...And they were looking for a replacement for Chester...They were not looking for a leading man by any stretch of the imagination. In essence they were looking for Festus, but they didn't know Festus existed at the time."

How do you think your role on Gunsmoke *ultimately affected your career?*
"It wasn't a career move...I mean, at that time the show had been on about 12 or 13 years and it wasn't the show the industry watched. The first six or seven years of the show would have affected my career enormously. But after a show's been on ten or twelve years, the industry starts looking for what is the next hot show. So it didn't affect my career. It was a nice amount of money and I suppose, out of all the series that I've done, and I've done four, that it was the happiest years of my life in terms of just the working relationship with those people. I was crazy about Jim, and Amanda, what's not to love?...And Milburn Stone was like a father to me, and Kenny Curtis. I started that character with him. It was a delightful time. It was just a wonderful time, but it was time for me to move on."

Who do you think was the guiding force behind the show?
"I think you probably have to give credit to Charles Marquis Warren who originally brought in those characters. Jim was kind of the personification of the quiet, tall, silent cowboy hero, and at that time there wasn't a leading man who was that big. He was huge. He seems to have shrunk lately...Clint Walker, in *Cheyenne* I suppose, was about the only guy that was that tall. And then you had a total relationship kind of show, it wasn't one person. It was the relationship that he had with Kitty and Doc and Chester. And I think you have to go back to the radio show with William Conrad and Parley Baer. The characteristics were about 85% similar to what the television show was."

Is there any particular episode that you recall or were especially fond of?
"I remember a lot of episodes. In particular I remember the first episode that Festus did, and I did quite a few with him, and I cowrote one of the episodes. I remember all those shows very fondly. The shows that were the most fun were the shows in which I had a scene with everybody, and it was a wonderful group of people because in between shots everybody would sit together and tell stories. Milburn would tell stories about vaudeville, and

Fred Stone, who was this great vaudevillian...and I remember one night I got Eddie Foy together with Milburn, it was one of the great evenings, and we all told stories..."

You mentioned the show that you had a hand in writing. How did that opportunity come up?

"They were very open to that. I think in retrospect, I would have probably ended up directing three or four shows, too. I just left before that came up. But they were very open to stories, suggestions, and things like that. And you can imagine after you do a show that many years, that the well runs dry. So they were constantly looking for ideas."

Do you recall the title of the show you wrote?

"No I don't, it was a show about Festus...A cousin, a nephew comes to town looking for Festus. He wants to kill him because Festus bit his earlobe off when he was a child."

Why do you think Westerns have relevance today?

"First of all there are no Westerns today, and everyone sort of misses them. And in Hollywood, being the sort of the town that it is, nobody is going to do a Western until somebody has the courage to do one and it makes money. Then they'll do more Westerns. The last Western that someone did, *Silverado,* didn't make money. I think the reason it didn't make money is because you had four actors who looked like they just got off the subway...The thing about *Gunsmoke* was that the wardrobe was authentic. As authentic as you can get away with in a television show. Because it was black-and-white for such a long time, it had the look of those days, and the sets were wonderful. They were all well done shows. I think part of the fun of that show is that when you look at those old shows you see actors who today are very successful in their careers. I think just about everybody did that show."

What was your impression of the recent two-hour Gunsmoke *special?*

"I thought that it was interesting...The use of the flash-backs and the old fillers were fun...I wish they had used Kenny and I wish they had used Dennis. But I think that Dennis didn't want to do it and there was some argument about money with Kenny. I think they felt that I would be sort of jarring...I talked to Amanda and Jim about it, and we laughed about it. They sort of had the feeling that I wouldn't want to do it, and I don't know if it would have been a real good career move...but I probably would have done it. I like those people so much. It would have been fun."

Looking back what are your general feelings about the show?

"It was a happy time. It was also a strange time in television in those days...there were a tremendous number of Westerns on in those days, so there was a lot of work. Clint was doing *Rawhide* across the street from us. There was a great deal of activity, but the real 'class' show to do was *Gunsmoke.*"

Postscripts

Buck Taylor (September 15, 1987)

How did you get the role of Newly?

"I did a *Gunsmoke* episode with James Stacy in which John Ireland was my father. Kim Darby was also in it. I was the bad gunfighter-kid. Three weeks later I was told they wanted to test me for the part of Newly O'Brien. They tested me with four other actors and I got the part. I was very lucky. Before I did *Gunsmoke* I did a series called *The Monroes* and Michael Anderson, Jr., had been offered the part of Newly Jorgensen on *Gunsmoke*. He told me that they were looking for a Swedish guy. I'm Irish and didn't fit the bill, but when I wound up playing the part they renamed the character O'Brien."

Why do you think the program was cancelled?

"I think that it got too expensive to make and a family situation comedy took one-third the money to make. It got too expensive for the network. The ratings were not that bad but maybe it was time for a change."

Why do you think Gunsmoke *was so successful?*

"I thought it was real good Western entertainment. It was a good dramatic show with a few comic situations thrown in. It got a little hoakey sometimes but it was probably the greatest continuing drama that has ever been on television."

Roger Ewing (May, 1988)

How were you cast?

"Theodore Bikel was the guest star... Lee Majors and I were the co-stars and at the time they were looking for somebody to replace Burt Reynolds. Not necessarily to replace him specifically, but somebody else to come on the show, somebody in a younger actor category... and they liked what I did in the show and asked me to come on as a regular..."

Were there any differences between Gunsmoke *and other shows that you worked on?*

"*Gunsmoke* was probably the premiere show to work on. Any actor who was working on television at that time would say the best show to work was *Gunsmoke*... It was well established, which was a great plus for me. It was already a big hit. And the atmosphere, the creative as well as the working atmosphere was very relaxed, very easy. The people involved knew what they were doing. There weren't any egos jumping out at you from everywhere. It was just a very easy, relaxed atmosphere and everybody was made to feel at home."

What were the shooting schedules and rehearsals like?

"There were never any days set aside for rehearsals like they have today. We got a script a few days in advance, and we'd look it over. If there were any changes that we felt were necessary, we could discuss it with the director and the writer the day of the shoot...Usually there weren't any. The show was extremely well written. And most of the guest actors that came aboard for that particular week already knew in advance what the show was like. So they kind of blended in. And it was a treat for anybody to work on *Gunsmoke*. I mean, people like Bette Davis and Jean Arthur loved to work the show. To them it was a treat. And of course it was a treat for us too."

What was it like working with Bette Davis and Jean Arthur?

"I was terrified. I didn't have that much to do on either of their shows, so I would just come on the set and kind of sit and admire them from afar...When you grow up watching these ladies dominate the screen for so many years, and then you get the chance to meet them and work with them, it's heaven, a dream come true for an aspiring actor. They had so much fun being there...They were a delight..."

Who was the guiding force?

"I would say Jim. Definitely...He was the force behind the show. If something was drastically wrong he would let the powers that be know about it..."

Could you tell us about the temporary cancellation?

"The show was cancelled and there was such a hoop-la that CBS was forced to put it back on again. Unfortunately, they had already slotted the time to a show that Lucille Ball was producing, and so they had to change the time and the format...and with that, I was out. I was still in the business for a while but then I got out of it and got into photography, which is what I do now."

Could you tell us about the cast?

"They were truly the most delightful people to work with. We would laugh...and it would sometimes take us two or three hours to get a ten minutes scene done because of the laughing. There was never any pressure because the craft people as well as the people in front of the camera knew what they were doing. It was a pleasure to come to work regardless of what hour in the morning it was and regardless of what hour you left at the end of the day or evening...It was always a joy. I think any actor that worked the show would say the same thing. Everybody functioned basically as human beings rather than ego, in front of and behind the camera. Everybody just blended in perfectly, and Jim would crack jokes to keep everybody in good spirits...We had a show which was running way over schedule. Jim MacArthur was the guest star, Helen Hayes' son. He and I and a couple of other people were in a covered wagon and it was supposed to blow up. Unfortunately, it ignited too soon, and this was 11:30 at night and we had all been there since 5:00 in the morning. The fire just blew us all out of the wagon...But nobody got seriously hurt...Jim just started cracking a few jokes and within a few minutes everybody was laughing, the scene got done and off we went home. You read about some of these shows today, how they go on and on forever, and how egos get in the way and get bent out of shape...They never allowed that to happen...It's a rarity, a true rarity."

Why do you think Gunsmoke *was so successful?*

"Heart. Simplicity. The success of the show was its heart...the simple basics of life...A humanistic show. I mean you look at what's on TV today or what's in books today and most of it is superficial hype. But I think the reason that *Gunsmoke* was so successful and lasted as long as it did, was because it was just a simple way of looking at life as purely as possible, and not idealistically. If something was good it was good, if it was bad it was bad. There was always gray but there was a basic simplicity...a respect for individual space, which I find lacking today. But the message was heart. It had a heart..."

John Mantley (March, 1988)

Why did Matt always wear a red shirt?

"Because then you could put him in any show that you wanted. You could use his close-ups, you could use his wide shots. If you missed a close-up you could go back and find that close-up in a previous show, reprint it, and cut it into the show. He always had the badge in the same place on his shirt for the same reason."

Could you tell us about the Gunsmoke *set?*

"I could never make the *Gunsmoke* street look as if it was outdoors. I did everything. I grew real grass. I had some grow-lights hidden so that the grass and the bushes would grow. I even had birds in there. Finally, I got Albert Whitlock who does the most beautiful mats in the world to come in. He came with his company and shot 64 shots of the *Gunsmoke* street with Matt walking out of his office across to the Long Branch, and of people making various crosses, and stage coaches coming and going. He also shot the full street and the street at night and in snow. One of the reasons that the street never looked real is because we could never shoot the tops of the buildings. The tops existed but if you shot up at an angle you got the catwalks and the lights and all the rest of it. So what Whitlock did, because he was a magnificent artist, was that he just chopped the tops off the buildings when he shot and then he painted them in and put them against moving clouds of all different kinds. Storm clouds, clouds at night, and little white cirrus clouds. And he put these on prints, and what we would do is start with a shot with the clouds moving in the background and the wind waving the trees, then we would cut down to the street itself."

GUNSMOKE — I. THE HISTORY

What are the problems of doing a Western today?

"We know more about the reality of the West today and so the myth is a lot harder to sell. We know about Wounded Knee, and about Chief Joseph's magnificent march, so we can't have the Indians circling the wagons any more and we can't keep portraying Indians as blood-thirsty savages who scalped everybody. Nor can we portray him as the glorious, brilliant savage, for that has been done, too. A portion of our society now knows the truth about the West and, therefore, is not prepared to accept any part of the myth. I did the myth and I guess it worked. But you've got to remember that the *Gunsmoke* myth and heritage was behind that show. I think it would be damn hard to sell a traditional Western anymore. But I think you could do very good stories still in a Western setting. And if you have the right chemistry with the audience you could succeed. But there are a lot of 'ifs' there."

Robert Totten (September, 1988)

How would you compare the early shows to the later shows?

"I think you have to measure *Gunsmoke* according to mother nature and the maturity of Jim Arness and Amanda Blake. As they grew older the show developed a different kind of maturity. When they started, they were just young people themselves. She was just one of the dance hall girls and he was this young lawman that was kind of out of place, so they stuck him out there and he was working for the federal government. They could stick him most anywhere they wanted. It was as if he were in the military. Now that would suit young people. Then they grew up. She grew into a madam, and he grew into a wise old owl, highly regarded and well-respected, like Earp. But this happened with age. The actors grew older and rather than try to keep them made up to look young, God forbid! they let them age—and they let the scripts, and the stories, and the presentation of the shows age along with them."

Harry Ackerman (April, 1988)

What changes have taken place on television over the years?

"Since television has become so expensive to produce the networks have taken over programming, and with less and less creative executives involved. For the most part, the executives in the past 15 or so years have been people who are out of research or sales, and they become the new program heads at the networks. It's very, very difficult to create a show that is largely owned by the network. They may order you to make changes that make no sense.

Postscripts

I think there is chapter and verse on some of these... where one executive from a network tells you what to do and another one calls you the day after and tells you exactly the opposite. It's very difficult to work with a committee. I think that that's the major difference between the early days and now. In those days you were faced with a challenge. If Bill Paley said, 'I want a western Philip Marlowe,' you went out and got your best people and had weekly meetings and pulled things together until you were satisfied with the final result. But you didn't have to answer to anybody."

What is your general impression of Gunsmoke?

"I think it always was and remains the stand-out show in the Western field. It was the premiere stand-out Western on both radio and television."

Harry Bartell (May, 1988)

Who was the guiding force on Gunsmoke?

"Norm was the guiding force without any question."

What are your general feelings about radio's Gunsmoke?

"I think that it was wonderful. It had an integrity which few of the others did. I think that *Dragnet* had the same kind of thing because of the heavy imprint of Jack Webb. *Gunsmoke* was a real adult Western. It was not done as a trend, or follower of a trend. It was an original at the time. It had an integrity which I attribute to Norman Macdonnell and John Meston. It occasionally lapsed into melodrama but I think it depended largely on characterization which is the real basis of drama."

Could you compare the radio and television programs?

"I believe that the radio characters were a great deal more legitimate to the time they portrayed. The television show became the Hollywood version of the adult Western. The stamp of movie-making was heavy on it. I can't fault them. Certainly, it was the way it should have gone. For example, Weaver suddenly started coming on with a limp. That was pure gimmick. He was looking for something to hang on to. I don't blame him though, for it became his mark and made a great name for him, but again I keep coming back to that word, 'integrity.' I believe there was more honesty in the radio show, especially in the early years before everyone got tired of it."

What are your feelings today about television?

"The only shows that have been able to stay on are the cops and robbers. On television nobody wants to be controversial. This is the most horrible word in the world. And if you start going into different types of psychological phenomena they get scared to death. One day they'll have a great new idea... they'll have a cowboy as a hero."

Parley Baer (June, 1987)

What recollections do you have about the radio show?

"It was probably the happiest time in my professional life and I think it was so with everybody. The whole operation was intact from day one. The same director, the same assistant director, the same script girl, the same engineer, the same sound effects men. We had ample time to rehearse during its formative years. It was a job that any one of us looked forward to. It was a joy to go to work. We had immeasurable fun. The rehearsals were jubilant affairs. Bill and I developed a great rapport with each other, a great empathy. I think that if we had been given an outline of a scene with Georgia as Kitty, Howard as Doc, and Larry Dobkin, John Dehner, Virginia Gregg, Sam Edwards, Harry Bartell, and the people who were frequently on, I think we could have ad libbed a very credible, sincere performance."

Paul Savage (June, 1987)

What recollections do you have about the early days of Gunsmoke?

"*Gunsmoke* has a particularly fond spot in my heart. I came out here in 1946 after the war, as an actor, and in fact, I'm happy to say, I worked *Gunsmoke* radio. Norman Macdonnell gave me jobs that literally paid for my food at the time. I started writing in '57 when television was relatively young out here...And I have been doing nothing but writing, for the last thirty years. I've written for 150-200 credits. Before I started to write I did radio shows. I did little theater, acting work, and I met Norman Macdonnell in a casting session and got a few jobs, crowds, one-liners, two-liners. They paid me $35 a show in those days. When I gave up acting and started to write I went to Norman and told him I was now writing and I would like to do a *Gunsmoke*...This man to me will forever be enshrined as one of the true gentlemen of our business, kind and thoughtful, he gave breaks to new people."

Why do you think Gunsmoke *was so successful?*

"Honesty. The honesty of the show. The honesty of the people behind it. The personal caring. It was more than just a job. The talent, the integrity, the affection, the caring of Norman Macdonnell and John Meston...That's the reason the show became what it did. The Western is the one true, totally American story form, and I think they did it better than anyone else ever could have. The people that followed had the same feeling for it, but never, I don't think, as secure as Norman did...The first year that it went on television, it was given to Charles Marquis Warren. It was a grave disservice, we all felt, to Norman. Of course, he later came in and guided it for several years,

Postscripts

before he was summarily replaced by John Mantley and Philip Leacock. During that time I did nine shows for Norman...nine episodes, and when the network took it away from Norman and brought in the new regime, I was the only writer...the one writer that was the nexus between the two regimes. I say that with no small amount of pride. I have a personal feeling that out of all the things I've done, some of the best I ever did was the *Gunsmoke* show."

How would you, as a writer, characterize and describe the principal characters?

"Matt was the epitome of the lone figure standing against evil, standing against wrong. We don't have this anymore where a lawman says to evil, 'Get out of my town.' Now we have civil libertarians who say, 'You can't say that. He has a right to be here and break this law.' Honesty, integrity...putting his life on the line...if there was ever a treatise against killing, it's the expression on Matt Dillon's face in the opening of *Gunsmoke,* that low angle shot after he's killed that distant badman, and that push up onto the face. He despises killing. But it must be done at certain times. Matt was the lone man standing against the wrong that was being done to the little man, and putting his life on the line."

Do you have any particular episodes that you were especially fond of?

"My ego is going to make me name some of mine...but, Ron Bishop had several...his *Mannon,* his show called *A Hat.* I did one *Zavala,* and *Owney Tupper Had a Daughter,* for which I was nominated for a Writer's Guild Award...The early shows made a statement...a small statement, while entertaining...We don't have that in television anymore, small story themes. You look at the shows that are on the air today and they're automobiles that fly, and crash. And my Lord, the violence that you see on the shows today is totally gratuitous. In our day, they were grimly told 'true stories' of what it took for this Nation to become what it did. It took the strong individual to stand up against evil. That was what *Gunsmoke* was in the early days."

Did the actors on Gunsmoke *have any input in maintaining their characters?*

"Yes. The actors were defensive of their characters. I was very, very close to Milburn Stone...and I can remember Milburn saying things like, he became Doc...Jim was defensive of Matt. If something got by or was wrong for the character, Jim would say, 'You know, I don't think that's right for Matt and how can we change this?'...More important...one of the many, many reasons the show was so good, was that we would write scenes and the actors would sit around and rehearse them, and many times you would hear Doc say, 'God, this would be so much better if this came from Festus. This thought should come from Festus.' In other words, he would say, I'll take a lesser role in this scene because the scene will be stronger. This was just his opinion...and often times we'd change it and make it a Festus scene. Or Jim would say, 'It's so much better if we'd cut Matt's dialogue in half and let me

GUNSMOKE — I. THE HISTORY

play the scene rather than speak the scene.' And so many times it would be stronger. For Christ's sake, you got actors today who count their lines, and if they don't have enough lines in a given scene, not even knowing what the damn scene is about, they'll complain to a producer. We never ever had that on *Gunsmoke*. The cast was concerned about the show. Not to say that there weren't personalities, that there weren't times when someone would get pissed off at somebody else. But that's human nature. But I assure you, they cared about the product. It was a unique spirit."

Did you have more creative freedom in those days?

"Oh, yes, there was always network interference, but you must understand, in the early days when I first worked the show, as an actor, it was sustaining, that means CBS owned it. There was no sponsor in the very, very beginning. They sold spots. Then Chesterfield took over. The evolution of our business is that at one time the advertising agencies owned the hour, and they determined what was going to go in. These creative type people hired creative writers and directors, and left them pretty much alone... Then little, by little, the networks took over, and the networks said who would sponsor what. Then we ended up with four and five and six sponsors per hour. And the networks, who were strictly business people and still are, started to make creative decisions. And look what we have on television today. They are copyists. There isn't one single truly creative individual in the television industry who is left totally alone. When I was on *Gunsmoke* I was the only story editor, and we did 39 shows a year. We hired freelance writers and we winnowed out the good ones, and we gave them multiples, and the bad ones we didn't use anymore. Today they make 22 episodes a year and there are five or six people on staff and network people who are dictating what will be done. Up to 12 minds go into a single story with input to that story. I used to fight. My God, I used to get into arguments when they wanted to change things. All of us did, that cared. We still care, but we know the exigencies of the business today. They want a change, and if you don't change it, they'll get it changed. So that's why you see what you see on television. Some of it is excellent, I'm not saying that everything on TV is terrible, but it's committee work today. The golden era of television, they made a lot of garbage, there's no denying, but the creative talents were left alone...In the early days, *Gunsmoke* had some of that, but when the committee system set in, I think things changed...tremendously."

Did Norman Macdonnell and John Meston understand the significance of their creation?

"I don't think so...It was a labor of love. It obviously was or it wouldn't have turned out like it did. But I don't think that in this kind of field you're totally aware when you are making history. You can feel that maybe you are a part of history, in that it's TV and it's new. But I don't think that anybody is of the mind that we are making history at the moment. You turn around and you look back and you say, 'My God, I knew it was good, but I didn't know it was that good!' That's my personal opinion."

Kathleen Hite (June, 1987)

What was it like working on Gunsmoke?

"Well, we were young for one thing. Most of us connected with the show were either in our twenties or early thirties and we started in radio...We were excited about the idea because there had not been any 'adult' Westerns done. They'd done things like Gene Autry and shows of that nature that just portrayed singing cowboys, but they'd done nothing to indicate the West as it was, especially in the area of Dodge City and the times in which we were writing. So we were excited about it...I was ever so serious about it because it was quite unusual for a young woman to do anything like that. Friends of mine created the series, John Meston and Norman Macdonnell, and so I was given an opportunity to write for it. First in radio and then later in television."

As a writer, how would you describe the principal characters?

"Matt was extremely tall...He took his job seriously and the frontier wasn't exactly a million laughs, but he did enjoy the interplay of the characters. There were sort of jokes between them that were in-jokes to them, but he took his job seriously and he had an utter disdain for anyone who spoiled the settling of the West. Kitty loved Matt, and she was a great comfort to him. I don't know how much you want to infer regarding that comfort, but we always assumed that they were sharing everything but the vow. Doc was an older man. He had a big heart. He gave a lot of time to his work, and was sort of crusty, perhaps because he was often dealing with life and death. But, he was an ingenuous guy and thought well of all the principles. They were a very close knit group."

Would you tell us about your work with John Meston?

"He wrote marvelously. His scripts were very spare, very to the point. He didn't write a lot of elaborate scenes. He didn't write any dialogue that wasn't necessary. He was really a perfect writer for that series. He influenced me without ever trying to. He was the preeminent *Gunsmoke* writer, and he taught me not by telling me anything but by just admiring his work."

What were your feelings about the direction that Gunsmoke *later took?*

"I didn't care for the later years because...it entered areas that we never would have. And, although, ours wasn't a documentary, it was very faithful to the West, and we felt that they were not. I, at least felt that."

Do you have a favorite episode?

"There were two that I liked especially. There was one called *Marry Me*, where a group of hillbilly sort of people kidnap Kitty. And they didn't hurt her or anything, they were just trying to persuade her all the time that she should marry one of them. He wanted to marry her, so he felt that she should want to marry him back. It wasn't a hokey show, we didn't treat the hillbillies as freaks, but more as people who had sort of a limited outlook on things. It was a very effective show. And there was one called *Apprentice Doc*. There were a good many of them that I was quite proud of, but I remember those two especially."

Rex Koury (April 8, 1988)

Could you tell us about your composition, the Gunsmoke *Theme?*
"It was published by Max Herman, who was also my trumpet player on the show. He had a publishing company and wanted to publish it. After we had been on the air for several shows he said, 'We ought to put this on as a popular song,' So I said, 'Well, I don't know if it will have appeal or not.' He suggested, 'Let's get somebody to write some lyrics and we'll put it out as a popular song.' It came out very briefly, but I don't think they ever sold a whole lot of it. But anyway, it came out that the songwriter who wrote the lyrics called it 'Gunsmoke Trail' though we always called it the 'Gunsmoke Theme.' There were something like 32 different people who recorded it and made commercial records, everybody from Fiedler at the Boston Pops all the way down to some Western groups. So there were a lot of records out with the title 'Gunsmoke Trail.'"

What are your feelings about the program?
"I think it has a wide spectrum of appeal for the simple reason that it was based in history... It's based on the early days of the settling of our country and I think it has amazing appeal. It's not the trite type of Western that you watch once and forget. There were some very poignant stories. There were some well-written, really meaty scripts, on both radio and television. I think it has great significance historically. I have every confidence that it's going to be around in syndicated form for a long time, because it's timeless."

William Robson (January, 1989)

What was your opinion of Gunsmoke *on radio?*
"I thought that it was superb. It was a superb show because of the combination of talent and Meston who was a superb writer. And there was Norman who was a superb director... And Bill Conrad. Nobody else was ever Matt Dillon except Bill Conrad. That's my opinion. Then there were

Postscripts

excellent actors...And I know that because they worked for me in *Suspense* and *Escape*. They were part of my regular stock company, so I know how good they were. But on *Gunsmoke,* because of Meston, in a show of superb characters, they became wed to each other in performances that went on week after week."

How would you compare the TV and radio programs?

"I didn't like the obvious selection of a matinee idol for the lead. Nothing was left to the imagination. But it can't be when you're going visual. They were playing for an audience and they got one. But I thought it was relatively dull. In the first place, Bill Conrad was a good friend of mine and I was very annoyed when he didn't get the part. Although I understood the difficulty of management. You can't just put a fat man in there, you've got to have a love interest and so forth. But they should have put him on. And by God! What a show that would have been! That would have been a tremendous show, with Bill Conrad. Though I don't suppose it would have run as long. I only saw one or two of them, and that was later when they weren't even putting what's his name in all the time. I don't mean to be cruel there. It wasn't as good as the radio show because it didn't have Bill Conrad."

Why do you think Conrad stood out?

"Because he had a voice that was unmistakable and couldn't be imitated. Nobody would dare to imitate it. It was just Bill Conrad's. And even now when he's selling fire alarms, that voice is still there. And he was a hell of an actor. But you know I'm such a fan of his it's really unfair."

Why do you think it ran for nine years on radio?

"Well, Bill Conrad and the actors. And John Meston, who was no man's fool. Meston wouldn't be guilty of a cliche. Until his very best work became a cliche itself by being so familiar. The Western itself, the Western movie was a cliche. The good guys, the bad guys and so forth. John introduced in a Western problems in personality and character and human feeling. He avoided the easy way. He did it the hard way. And the hard way is finding another story every week. And that isn't easy. I did a couple of series and I tried to do the same thing John did, but not with the same success. He was...he was...he was John Meston! And Bill Conrad was Bill Conrad. So what's the use of kidding? They were the ones. And Norman Macdonnell was the guy who knew how to get it out of them. These things happened in radio every now and them. In radio it was always remarkable, because every week it's opening night. Remember that...Every week was opening night...And a one night stand. You make a mistake and you can't even repeat it. It's a hell of a challenge. You've got to be with it. And you have to have a lot of stamina to make it work. Most producers in the old days would get a good format and a few good people and would do the same show over, and over, and over again, week after week. But in *Gunsmoke* they put those people through all kinds of human conditions, in that little barroom, in that little town. And they made it work so that it was mature radio theater. That combination was one of the great success stories of the whole history of radio drama."

William Conrad (December 15, 1969)

(Special interview courtesy of Chris Lembesis)

How did you enter radio?
"It's been so long I can hardly remember. I was fascinated with radio when I was a kid. I had to go to work very early. My father died when I was 15. I had a dear friend who was an announcer on one of the local radio stations and I used to hang around with him at night. He'd let me do a commercial every now and then. And I went to a radio station called KNPC and started working. I stayed there for a long, long time. It was the only thing I could figure to do at that point in my life."

How did you get started in dramatic network radio?
"I had never been on a network show and I was in the Army. It was about 1945 and somebody said that they would allow you for the next two or three months to take a job occasionally as long as it did not interfere with your work. And I was in the Armed Forces Radio Service. I went up and auditioned for *The Whistler* on CBS. I hoped to get a small part in it. Much to my amazement I got a call to come and do it that Sunday and that I was doing the lead. It scared the hell out of me. But I did it and I guessed they liked it because they asked me back the next week to do the lead. That was the first network show I ever did."

How much research went into Gunsmoke?
"I think quite a bit. Of course, there was no Matt Dillon. That was a figment of the writer's imagination. But you'd get a lot of fight from a lot of people who will tell you that they know there was. It's pretty funny. I've had several arguments with people about it who will say that they know for a fact that their grandfather was related to him. John Meston and Norman Macdonnell were very meticulous in seeing that everything was as authentic as they could possibly make it. They took complete and deliberate time in setting up the sound effects, which was probably one of the secrets of the show's success... It's still running on television. I guess it's probably the most remarkable series that's ever been on the air in any form."

Would you care to comment on Howard McNear?
"I would be honored to comment on Howard. In all the years that I've been in the business I don't think I have ever worked with a more talented

Postscripts

man, nor have I worked with a nicer human being. Everybody who met Howard, no matter under what condition, loved him. That's all you could do with Howard. He was a zany, wonderful, wild, crazy, beautiful human being. It was such a great shock to us all when he passed away... Parley Baer was asked by Mrs. McNear to give the eulogy at the funeral, and there was no man of the cloth there... The place was filled. It was very, very quiet. And Parley got up and started talking, and there were a lot of tears for a moment, and then the most magical thing happened. He started telling about the wild zaniness of Howard; the beautiful times that we all had together. And for the next 45 minutes, you won't believe this, everybody laughed and loved every minute of it. It was the strangest, most beautiful funeral... I think probably the way all funerals should be."

On television Chester was portrayed as a young man while on radio we always perceived him to be an older character. Could you comment?

"We felt that he was always a middle-aged man who was not too bright... Always getting into jams, and Matt was always saving him... We also felt that because of the name Proudfoot that he had a little Indian blood in him... Incidentally, on Doc there was an interesting reason for giving him the name. This came about one day when we were all sitting around laughing at the ghoulish way that Howard played the part. Doc was always so happy when someone got shot down because then he had a little business. And I said, 'My God, Howard, you know you're like a Charles Adams character. As a matter of fact, that's what you should be called, 'Doc Adams!' And that's how he got his name."

And Georgia Ellis?

"Georgia was a lovely girl who was very, very good in the part. She had a sultry voice and was a great sex symbol in Dodge City."

Any other recollections?

"I do remember one incident... I was walking down the street one day and a nice gentleman stopped me and said, 'I want to say something to you.' And I said, 'Yes?' And he said, 'It's a chancy job, and it makes a man a little lonely.' And I looked at him like he was insane because I said, 'I beg your pardon?' He said, 'You know what that is.' And I said, 'No.' He said, 'Oh, come on, you're being stuffy.' And I said, 'No. I'm not being stuffy. I don't know what that is.' And he said, 'Well, that's ridiculous. A fellow who plays the part and then isn't even nice enough to admit that he wants to 'talk about the show... I'm really annoyed with you.' And he turned and walked away. And I couldn't figure out what in God's name was going on, because you see, that opening was recorded the first week we did the show, which was eight years before, and I had never said those words since... And I had never listened to the show... He was very annoyed with me, and rightfully... He thought I was being a big-shot or something, but I honestly didn't know what he was talking about."

WHICH WAY'D THEY GO?

For half a century the position of the Western in American culture was secure. A dominant genre in films, radio, and television, it seemed that it was invulnerable. By the 1970s, however, its popularity had dimmed. In the period from 1930-1941, 39.8 percent of feature films were Westerns. By 1970-1977, however, Westerns represented only 4.5 percent of all feature films.[170] On television, where Westerns had had their hey-day, the few attempts at resuscitating the genre from 1970-1985 were generally disasterous.

The causes for this collapse are many. Certainly, the antiviolence movement was instrumental in draining some of the vitality from the Western. The growing awareness of the injustices suffered by the American Indian and other minorities at the hands of the "Westerner" also cast an unfavorable light on the genre in general, and on the Western hero in particular. The Vietnam War, and our increasingly belligerent military posture, also caused a large segment of the populace to question the wisdom of emulating the example of the rugged, militant individual. In this period of uncertainty the antihero became a dominant figure and reflected society's ambivalence, and heroes became unfashionable.

As the airwaves were flooded with one Western after another, several generations became satiated with the genre. The vibrant, evolving art form that had given voice to a nation's inner life had turned to self-parody, and when Americans sensed this inertia they turned to something new.

Until recently, statistics pointed uncompromisingly toward a direction that suggested that the Western was dead. Recent developments, however, in film and television, indicate that the Western may have merely entered a period of hibernation.

In a current article, *TV Guide* noted that Westerns were on the comeback trail, and that made-for-television Westerns have been attracting more and more viewers.[171] In a typical week in June, 1988, approximately 30 Western feature films were aired on television including *The Apple Dumpling Gang Rides*

GUNSMOKE — I. THE HISTORY

Again (1979), *The Ballad of Cable Hogue* (1970), *El Dorado* (1967), *The Gunfighter* (1950), *How the West Was Won* (1962), *The Last Wagon* (1956), *Lust in the Dust* (1984), *The Outlaw Josey Wales* (1976), *A Ticket to Tomahawk* (1950), *True Grit* (1969), *Dodge City* (1939), *Winning of the West* (1953), *Wanted: The Sundance Woman* (1976), *Shenandoah, Santee* (1973), *The Gunfighter, The Return of Frank James* (1940), *Run for Cover, San Fernando Valley* (1944), *Shane* (1953), *The Big Land* (1957), *South of the Border* (1939), *The Man Who Shot Liberty Valance* (1962), *Kansas Pacific* (1953), *The Ballad of Josie* (1968), *Bad Man of Deadwood* (1941), *The Big Country* (1958), *Will Penny* (1968), and *The Big Show* (1936). During the same week there were 16 Western series aired from the Golden Age of the television Western. These included *The Rifleman, Last of the Mohicans, Big Valley, Bonanza, Cisco Kid, Sky King, Lone Ranger, Zorro, Iron Horse, Bat Masterson, Broken Arrow, Laredo, Wagon Train, The Monroes, The Wild Wild West,* and *Gunsmoke.*

While it is unlikely that the Western can ever regain the popularity that it once enjoyed, it seems that it will always be a forum for the exploration of America's subconscious aspirations.

Gunsmoke, when viewed in its entirety, is a remarkable and monumental achievement of twentieth century American culture. Reborn week after week, and year after year in an environment increasingly motivated by financial, political, and nonartistic concerns, the creative elements somehow survived and evolved. The producers, directors, writers and actors remained guardians of the germinal vision of Meston and Macdonnell and despite great interference from many sources, to a significant degree kept *Gunsmoke* inviolate.

When *Gunsmoke* aired for the first time on radio and television, the East-West confrontation and Cold War were at their height. There were great fears relating to Soviet expansionism and an increasing realization that in the unleashing of the atom lay the potential for the destruction of mankind. Beneath the sabre-rattling, however, there was a growing feeling of impotence in directing our destiny, and in this atmosphere of fear and paranoia the television Western offered an escape readily embraced by much of the viewing audience.

The role of the Western as a source of escape in American history had been seen previously during a period of profound despair, when during the Great Depression the B Westerns flourished and offered similar comfort. It is almost as if during periods of "crisis" Americans turn to the Western hero to remind them of the indomitable pioneer spirit, and purity of purpose and character, that in our historical myths molded our nation.

Gunsmoke was more than escape, however. It explored the role of ethics in human relationships and how ethical precepts are applied and translated in a society into law. John Meston, in fact, once suggested that the true

Which Way'd They Go?

protagonist of *Gunsmoke* was Dodge City itself, for the fictional Dodge was the prototype of a civilization in evolution.

Gunsmoke dealt with the most basic responsibilities of one man to another. And though in Dodge, good was sometimes vanquished, and the weak were sometimes swept aside, the nature of truth was clear and unassailable, and was never retrospectively determined by outcome. In *Gunsmoke,* evil always stood out in clear relief, and although the program was frequently violent, its intent was to confront the deepest elements of the evil that resides in mankind and to explore the nature and causes of this evil.

Gunsmoke broke new ground in radio and television writing. Many of the writers came from a background where the sanctity of the written word was still upheld. They were craftsmen who sought to chisel from the amorphous lexicon of the English language a crisp, spare, and "authentic" Western vernacular.

Gunsmoke was a testimonial to good acting, and memorable characters were created on both the radio and television programs. There was an epic cavalcade of faces and voices that enriched our culture to an inestimable degree. For decades these characters entered countless homes and became familiar figures. They grew older as we grew older and embodied some of our aspirations, and they validated our beliefs by giving material form to our unformed thoughts.

Gunsmoke is inextricably linked to the Western genre, and was the result of an evolutionary process that encompassed pulp novels, film, radio, and television. It is a luminescent point along this continuum, and perhaps it is the greatest Western story ever told.

Despite its recent somnolence the Western will always play a role in our culture, for it is a form of expression that is distinctly American.

One writer commented that the Western is:

> ...the American morality play, in which Good and Evil, Spirit and Nature, Christian and Pagan fight to the finish on the vast stage of the unbroken prairie. The hero is a Galahad with a six-gun, a Perseus of the purple sage. In his saddlebags he carries a new mythology, an American Odyssey that is waiting for its Homer... And the theme of the epic, hidden beneath the circus glitter of the Wild West Show, is the immortal theme of every myth; man's endless search for the meaning of his life.[172]

Contemporary observers frequently likened the characters on *Gunsmoke* to mythic figures. Robert Lasson wrote:

> ...when Jim Arness rides furiously by in that opening credit, friends, that's not Marshal Dillon. It's Odysseus and Theseus and Siegfried. On Mondays...you can support your local myth.[173]

Gunsmoke tapped into a primal current. It was as if by listening to *Gunsmoke* we were participants in some ancient ritual. In our darkened living rooms we were like our ancestors leaning forward in a half-dream to hear masked actors recite their lines from some classic tragedy or comedy. Sitting in our dens, our faces illuminated by the flickering screen, we were like other audiences from ages past tilting their heads to better hear some lines from Aeschylus or Euripides. In watching *Gunsmoke* words like catharsis and sublimation come to mind. It seemed to draw its source from a primal fount of archetypal truths, and when we watched, we drank deeply of an endless river whose source is that of myth and legend.

Reflecting on *Gunsmoke's* success Robert Totten observed:

> You need to use a cliched, cornball kind of word like Americana. I think that *Gunsmoke* was Americana. Plus it was on television, and television was coming into your home. It was there by the turn of a switch. It was about early pioneer America. It was something that the whole family could make reference to. Grandpa and Grandma, Mom and Dad, and the younger people. Passing it down through generations. American tradition. I guess it was like baseball. It was a part of us. It was a part of our heritage. It was part of our country. It was convenient. It was comfortable. It was handy, and it was the least costly probably of any entertainment. It was Americana.

Will Henry wrote in *The Los Angeles Times* on May 20, 1974:

> The marshal is good. His enemies are bad. And we all know the difference on *Gunsmoke*. We believe Marshal Dillon, and we believe in him... Who ever really thought there was, or even might have been, a *Bonanza?* Or a *High Chaparral?* Or a *Big Valley?* But, ah! there is a Dodge City, and we are all Marshal Dillons. We come out on that screen with him at main title time and we spread our great bowed legs and plant our size-13 boots and we have our hand brushing the worn walnut butt of our big Colt and, by God! nobody had better kick a stray dog, betray a lost maiden, deceive a brave widow woman, bully a weakling, make poor of a fallen angel, brutalize a child, whip a horse or mistreat a mule or even so much as look sideways at any such temptation in Dodge City... while we are guarding her. And that, companeros, is why there are only one *Gunsmoke* and one Marshal Dillon—because they are us—and we are in the right. And anyone who messes with Dodge City will have to deal with all of us.[174]

PART II.
PHOTOGRAPHS

MY LAKE

I call it My Lake, and why is it not?
Didn't God put it there to be forgot
Till some young wanderer should come and find
Near it—peace for his tired mind?

I in my turn, came upon it today,
And now it's my turn to rest and grow grey
Besides its quiet and langurous shore,
And never be vexed with cares any more.

Some think it's all wrong; some think I'm a fool;
They are but a part of that old Sophist school;
Because in the end, don't they all try to make
Something that somehow resembles My Lake?

Top: A young John Meston. (Courtesy of Mary Ann Meston.) *Bottom:* "My Lake," written by John Meston, a budding writer at the age of 10. (Courtesy of Mary Ann Meston.)

Photographs

Top: Meston, the young cowboy. (Courtesy of Mary Ann Meston.) *Bottom:* "There was never a horse that couldn't be rode, and never a man that couldn't be throw'd." (Courtesy of Mary Ann Meston.)

The creators of *Gunsmoke*. Norman Macdonnell and John Meston (seated). (Courtesy of Mary Ann Meston.)

Photographs

Top: John Meston. (Courtesy of Mary Ann Meston.) *Bottom:* Meston... Was he the real Matt Dillon? (Courtesy of Mary Ann Meston.)

Director-producer Norman Macdonnell and his star William Conrad. (Courtesy of John Hickman.)

Photographs

Top: Rehearsal with Norman Macdonnell, Howard McNear (standing), Parley Baer, and William Conrad. (Courtesy of John Hickman.) *Bottom, left:* Vic Perrin, a member of radio *Gunsmoke's* "stock company" and a guest on the television show. Perrin wrote several radio scripts with his close friend Harry Bartell. (Courtesy of Vic Perrin.) *Bottom, right:* Harry Bartell, a member of radio *Gunsmoke's* elite company and an occasional visitor to television's *Gunsmoke*. To this day a stock line in the Bartell household is, "Be careful, Matt." (Courtesy of Harry Bartell.)

GUNSMOKE — II. PHOTOGRAPHS

Top: Left to right, Parley Baer, Antony Ellis, George Walsh (at the microphone), Charlotte Lawrence, Larry Dobkin (standing), and Herb Ellis. (Provided by S.P.E.R.D.V.A.C. courtesy of Jan Ellis O'Hare.) *Bottom:* Actor Larry Dobkin gets a light from writer Antony Ellis. (Provided by S.P.E.R.D.V.A.C. courtesy of Jan Ellis O'Hare.)

Photographs

An example of a typical "dirty Saturday" morning rehearsal. Howard McNear has accidentally spilled coffee all over Georgia Ellis. The photo is courtesy of Miss Ellis and her caption reads: Left to right, "A drenched and indignant Miss Kitty, an apologetic Doc, a horrified director Norm Macdonnell — face in hands —, Bill Conrad almost delighted, Parley Baer not believing, and Virginia Gregg, Hollywood radio great, disassociating herself from it all."

GUNSMOKE — II. PHOTOGRAPHS

Top: An early photo of Virginia Gregg, character actress extraordinaire, at the mike at station **KHJ**. *Bottom, left:* Gregg in an early publicity photo. *Bottom, right:* Virginia Gregg was considered to be one of Hollywood's "great radio voices." (Photos courtesy of Gregg del Valle.)

Photographs

Top: Left to right, Director Bill Robson, with radio performer Elliott Lewis and Barton Yarborough as Hawk Larabee. *Hawk Larabee,* an adult radio Western and unsuccessful forerunner to *Gunsmoke,* aired in 1947. Robson proudly observed that at least, "Hawk didn't kiss his horse." (Courtesy of John Hickman.) *Bottom, left:* Helen Kleeb, a member of the radio company. She also appeared on several of the television episodes. (Courtesy of Helen Kleeb.) *Bottom, right:* Richard Beals, a member of the "stock company" had the distinction of having played Billy the Kid in the radio premiere of *Gunsmoke.* (Courtesy of Richard Beals.)

Top: William Conrad, composer Rex Koury and Norman Macdonnell. (Provided by S.P.E.R.D.V.A.C. courtesy of Rex Koury.) *Bottom:* A round table rehearsal with Parley Baer, Georgia Ellis, William Conrad and Howard McNear. (Courtesy of John Hickman.)

Photographs

William Conrad, Howard McNear, Georgia Ellis and Parley Baer. (Provided by John Hickman courtesy of CBS, Inc.)

GUNSMOKE — II. PHOTOGRAPHS

Top, left: **Gunsmoke** radio and television announcer George Walsh. (Courtesy of John Hickman.) *Top, right:* Rex Koury, composer of the *Gunsmoke* theme. Koury travels widely today as a concert organist and despite the intervening years, hardly a concert goes by that someone in the audience does not request the theme from *Gunsmoke*. (Courtesy of Rex Koury.) *Bottom, left:* Ray Kemper, one of the brilliant sound artists of radio's *Gunsmoke*. Kemper even penned a few scripts. (Courtesy of Ray Kemper.) *Bottom, right:* Lou Krugman, frequently cast in radio as the villain because of his rough and heavy voice, is seen here in one of his more menacing television roles. (Courtesy of Lou Krugman.)

Photographs

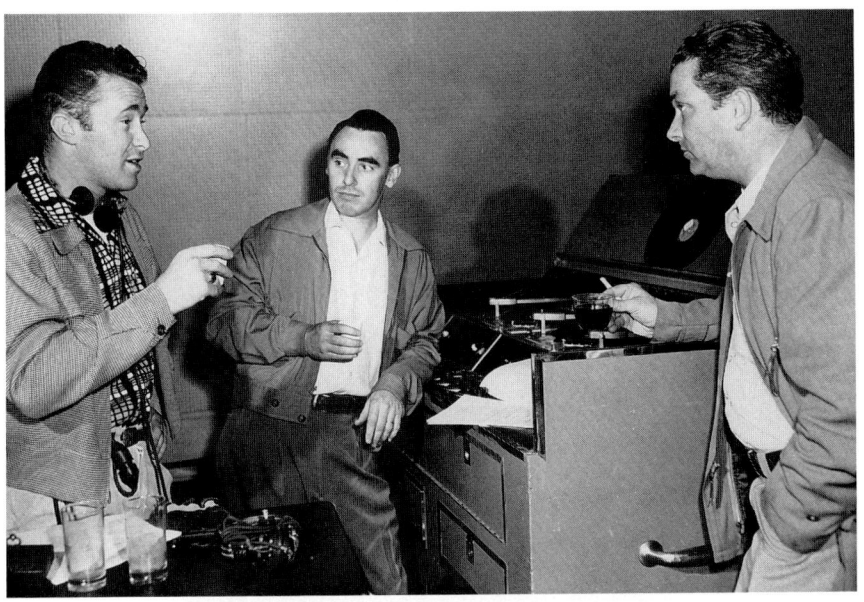

Top: Sound effects masters Ray Kemper and Tom Hanley with director Norman Macdonnell. (Courtesy of John Hickman.) *Bottom:* Actor Herb Ellis and writer Antony Ellis, not related. (Provided by S.P.E.R.D.V.A.C. courtesy of Jan Ellis O'Hare.)

GUNSMOKE — II. PHOTOGRAPHS

Parley Baer, Georgia Ellis and Howard McNear. (Provided by Georgia Ellis courtesy of CBS, Inc.)

[244]

Photographs

Top, left: Sam Edwards was a regular on the radio program and occasionally guest starred on television's *Gunsmoke*. (Courtesy of Sam Edwards.) *Top, right:* Jeanne Bates started in radio soaps and played Nurse Wills on television's *Ben Casey*. (Courtesy of Jeanne Bates.) *Bottom, left:* Herb Purdum wrote for *Romance* and *Suspense* and was one of the first writers on *Gunsmoke*. (Courtesy of Herb Purdum.) *Bottom, right:* Ben Wright considered himself a "dialectician." He played many roles on radio's *Gunsmoke* and provided the voice of "Hey Boy" on *Have Gun, Will Travel*. (Courtesy of Ben Wright.)

Top: Antony Ellis, William Conrad and Ben Wright. (Provided by S.P.E.R.D.V.A.C. courtesy of Jan Ellis O'Hare.) *Bottom:* William Conrad walks the dusty old streets of "Dodge," A.K.A. Knotts Berry Farm, as Matt Dillon. (Photographed by and courtesy of Harry Bartell.)

Photographs

Top, left: Jeannie Bates. (Courtesy of Jeannie Bates.) *Top, right:* Harry Bartell. (Courtesy of Harry Bartell.) *Bottom, left:* Larry Dobkin. (Courtesy of Larry Dobkin.) *Bottom, right:* Lou Krugman. (Courtesy of Lou Krugman.) The actors in more recent years.

Georgia Ellis as Kitty Russell. (Photographed by and courtesy of Harry Bartell.)

Photographs

William Conrad and Parley Baer decked out as Matt and Chester. (Photographed by and courtesy of Harry Bartell.)

Top and bottom: Howard McNear as radio's Doc Adams. (Photographed by and courtesy of Harry Bartell.)

Photographs

Howard McNear, Georgia Ellis and Parley Baer stroll through the streets of Knotts Berry Farm. (Photographed by and courtesy of Harry Bartell.)

Parley Baer, 1986. (Courtesy of Parley Baer.)

Parley Baer as Chester, 1955. (Photographed by and courtesy of Harry Bartell.)

Top: William Conrad being attacked by Lita Milan from the United Artists film *The Ride Back,* 1957, written by Antony Ellis and originally aired on *Gunsmoke* June 28, 1952. (Author's collection.) *Bottom:* William Conrad as *Cannon.* The successful detective program ran on CBS television from 1971 to 1976. In 1980 a made-for-television movie *The Return of Frank Cannon* brought the famous crime fighter out of retirement one last time. (Courtesy of Viacom Enterprises.)

Photographs

William Conrad as Matt Dillon. (Photographed by and courtesy of Harry Bartell.)

The radio cast in Western garb looking like a daguerreotype right out of the 1870s taken at Knotts Berry Farm. (Photographed by and courtesy of Harry Bartell.)

Photographs

Their television counterparts: Doc (Milburn Stone), Chester (Dennis Weaver), Kitty (Amanda Blake), and Matt (James Arness). (Courtesy of Viacom Enterprises.)

Beauty—Amanda Blake as she appeared in MGM's *The Glass Slipper*, 1954. (Author's collection.)

Photographs

And the Beast—James Arness as *The Thing*, 1951. (Author's collection.)

Milburn Stone played the villain in at least 100 B Westerns before he landed the role that was to make him famous. Here he appears in a 1946 Universal Pictures film. (Author's collection.)

Photographs

Top: James Arness with his mentor John Wayne and co-star Nancy Olson in *Big Jim McLain*, a Warner Bros. feature, 1952. (Author's collection.) *Bottom:* Huntz Hall, Amanda Blake, and Leo Gorcey in *High Society,* Warner Bros., 1955. (Author's collection.)

Top: Lisa Daniels, Elsa Lanchester, and Amanda Blake in *The Glass Slipper*. (Author's collection.) *Bottom:* Lisa Daniels and Amanda Blake as the "pretty but poisonous" step-sisters tormenting Leslie Caron as Cinderella in *The Glass Slipper*. (Author's collection.)

Photographs

Amanda Blake, billed early in her career as the "young Greer Garson," is seen here in an early cheesecake publicity photo. (Author's collection.)

James Arness, an early publicity photo. (Author's collection.)

Milburn Stone, 1944. (Author's collection).

Top: James Arness, Amanda Blake, Leo Gordon, Harry Ackerman and Hal Hudson on the set of *Hack Prine,* 1955. (Courtesy of Harry Ackerman.) *Bottom:* Kitty (Amanda Blake) wants Matt (James Arness) to offer Steve Elser (Brett Halsey) a *Helping Hand,* but Matt has a bad feeling about the youth. (March 17, 1956). (Courtesy of Viacom Enterprises.)

Photographs

Writer John Meston and his star James Arness. (Courtesy of Mary Ann Meston.)

GUNSMOKE — II. PHOTOGRAPHS

Amanda Blake as Kitty and James Arness as Matt, 1955. (Courtesy of CBS, Inc.)

Photographs

Dennis Weaver as Chester Goode. (Courtesy of Dennis Weaver.)

GUNSMOKE — II. PHOTOGRAPHS

Top, left: Emmy winner Edward Asner guest starred in two episodes, both times as the heavy. (Photographed by Dana Gluckstein courtesy of Edward Asner.) *Top, right:* Salome Jens guest starred in *Captain Sligo* (January 4, 1971) and *Talbot* (February 26, 1973). (Courtesy of Salome Jens.) *Bottom, left:* Bonnie Bartlett appeared in *The Foundling* (February 11, 1974) and *In Performance of Duty* (November 18, 1974). (Courtesy of Bonnie Bartlett.) *Bottom, right:* Steve Carlson appeared in *The Cage* (March 23, 1970). (Courtesy of Steve Carlson.)

Photographs

Top, left: Harry Carey, Jr., appeared in over ten *Gunsmokes*. (Courtesy of Harry Carey, Jr.) *Top, right:* George Kennedy appeared in several episodes including *The Blacksmith, Kitty Shot, Big Man, The Boys, Harvest, The Warden,* and *Crooked Mile.* (Courtesy of George Kennedy.) *Bottom, left:* Robert Easton played the part of Chester's brother *Magnus* on both the radio and television program. (Courtesy of Robert Easton.) *Bottom, right:* Cloris Leachman guest starred in two of the early half-hour episodes, *Legal Revenge* and *The Love of Money*. (Courtesy of Cloris Leachman.)

Kitty (Amanda Blake) awaiting words of wisdom from Doc (Milburn Stone). (Courtesy of Viacom Enterprises.)

Photographs

Matt Dillon (James Arness) and his faithful friend Chester (Dennis Weaver). (Courtesy of Viacom Enterprises.)

Crego (Charles Bronson) accosts Kitty in *The Killer* (May 26, 1956). (Courtesy of CBS, Inc.)

Photographs

Top, left: Alex Cord was featured in *The Sodbusters* (November 20, 1972). (Courtesy of Alex Cord.) *Top, right:* Lieux Dressler appeared in the two-parter *Women for Sale* (September 10 & 17, 1973) and *Alias Festus Haggen* (March 6, 1972). (Courtesy of Lieux Dressler.) *Bottom, left:* Mariette Hartley was the guest star in *Cotter's Girl, Big Man, Big Target, The Judgement,* and *Iron Blood of Courage.* (Courtesy of Mariette Hartley.) *Bottom, right:* Med Flory appeared in *Sergeant Holly* (December 14, 1970) and *A Town in Chains* (September 16, 1974). (Courtesy Med Flory.)

Kitty (Amanda Blake) and Matt (James Arness) in one of their famous "eyeball scenes." (Courtesy of CBS, Inc.)

Photographs

Top: James Arness, Milburn Stone, and Amanda Blake help rename Walnut Street, "Gunsmoke" in Dodge City, Kansas, 1958. (Courtesy of Boot Hill Museum, Inc.) *Bottom:* Amanda Blake, Chill Wills, David Janssen and Mrs. Janssen in Dodge City for the dedication of Front Street, 1958. (Courtesy of Boot Hill Museum, Inc.)

Top, left: Peter Mark Richman appeared in *Mr. Sam'l* with Ed Begley. (Courtesy of Peter Mark Richman.) *Top, right:* Laurie Prange guest starred in *The Lost* (September 13, 1971). (Courtesy of Laurie Prange.) *Bottom, left:* Loretta Swit starred in *The Pack Rat* (January 12, 1970) and *Snow Train* Parts I and II (October 19 & 26, 1970). (Courtesy of Loretta Swit.) *Bottom, right:* Brendon Boone guest starred in *Hawk,* playing the title role (October 20, 1969). (Courtesy of Brendon Boone.)

Photographs

Top, left: Nina Foch starred in *Coreyville* (October 6, 1969). (Courtesy of Nina Foch.) *Top, right:* Robert Lansing was a guest star in *The Bounty Hunter* (October 30, 1965) and *The Devil's Outpost* (September 22, 1969). (Courtesy of Robert Lansing.) *Bottom, left:* Charles Aidman appeared in *Stage Hold-Up, Unwanted Deputy, About Chester, The Money Store,* and *The Intruders.* (Courtesy of Charles Aidman.) *Bottom, right:* Louise Latham has played "a wide range of ladies from the wife of a lawyer who lived in town, to one who scraped by with her family in a sod house." (Courtesy of Louise Latham.)

Dennis Weaver, Milburn Stone, and Amanda Blake sing and kick up their heels as they tour the rodeo circuits, 1960. (Courtesy of CBS, Inc.)

Photographs

Chester (Dennis Weaver), Matt (James Arness) and Doc (Milburn Stone) congregate outside of the marshal's office. (Courtesy of CBS, Inc.)

Top: James Arness, Glenn Strange and Vic Perrin in *The Promoter* (April 25, 1964). (Provided by Vic Perrin courtesy of CBS, Inc.) *Bottom, left:* June Lockhart as "crazy" Beulah, a woman scorned, in *Dirt* (March 1, 1958). (Courtesy of Viacom Enterprises.) *Bottom, right:* Michael Fox appeared in *Carter Caper* (November 16, 1963), *Wishbone* (February 19, 1966), and *Hard Luck Henry* (October 23, 1967). (Courtesy of Michael Fox.)

Photographs

The inimitable James Nusser as Louie Pheeters, Dodge City's resident drunk. (Courtesy of CBS, Inc.)

Cara (Jorga Curtwright) a former girl friend of Matt's (James Arness) tries to lure him away from her outlaw boyfriend in *Cara* (July 28, 1956). (Courtesy of Viacom Enterprises.)

Photographs

Three other women in Matt's life who almost hooked him. *Top:* Michael Learned, who has the unique distinction of being the only woman Matt ever "kissed" and more, in *Matt's Love Story* (September 24, 1973). He was amnesiac at the time. (Courtesy of Michael Learned.) *Bottom, left:* Anne Francis, who starred as *Sarah* (October, 1972), an old flame of Matt's who winds up running a way-station for outlaws. (Courtesy of Anne Francis.) *Bottom, right:* Beverly Garland guest starred in four episodes. As Leona in *Time of the Jackals* (January 13, 1969), after being abandoned by Matt she went straight downhill and through a long succession of outlaw boyfriends. (Courtesy of Beverly Garland.)

Glenn Strange as Sam, the barkeep of the Long Branch saloon. (Courtesy of Min Strange.)

Photographs

The many faces of Glenn Strange from monster to cowboy. (Courtesy of Min Strange.)

GUNSMOKE — II. PHOTOGRAPHS

Director and actor, Robert Totten. (Courtesy of Robert Totten.)

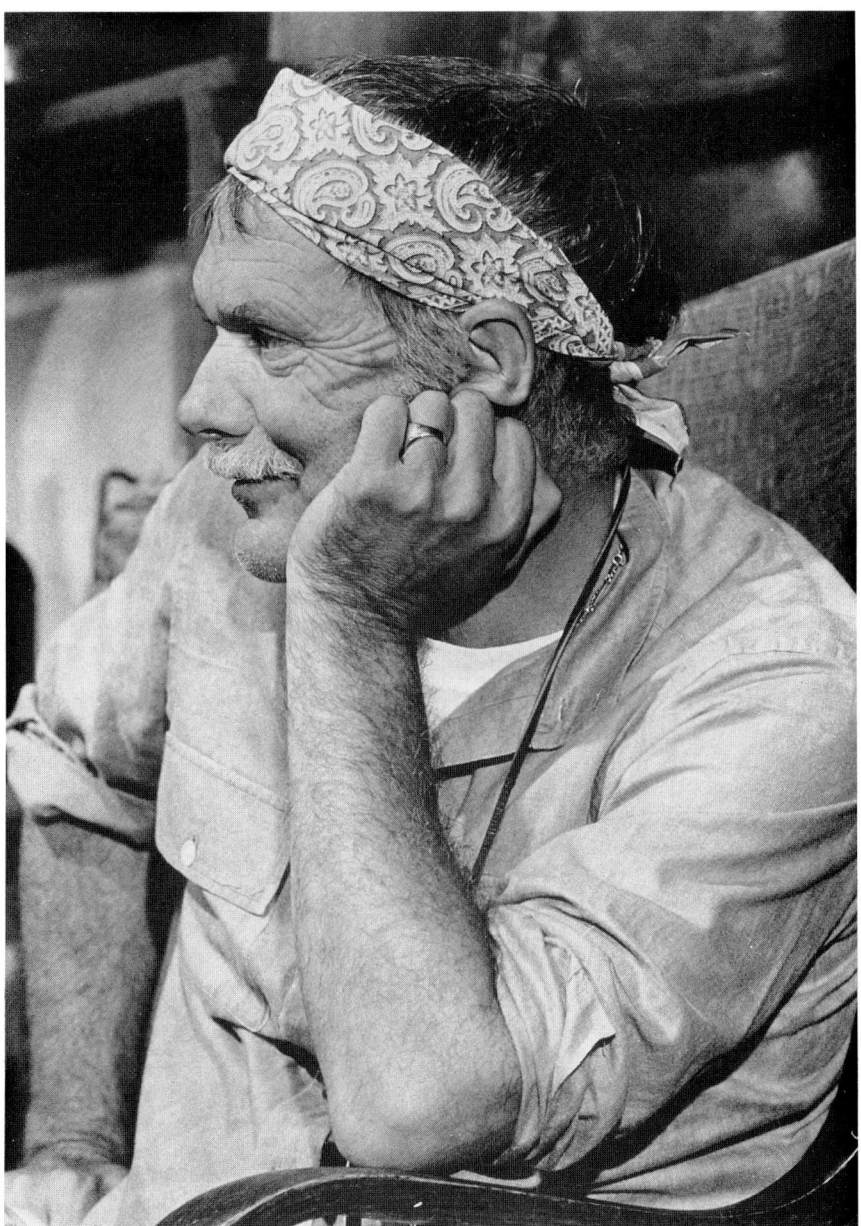

Sam Peckinpah on the set of his film, *Pat Garrett and Billy the Kid,* 1973. Peckinpah wrote nine scripts for *Gunsmoke* in the early years, then went on to fame as the director of films such as *Straw Dogs* and *The Wild Bunch.* (Author's collection.)

Quint Asper (Burt Reynolds) courts Susan Degler (Katharine Ross) while her father (George Kennedy) watches with dismay in *Crooked Mile* (October 3, 1964). (Courtesy of CBS, Inc.)

Photographs

Burt Reynolds as half-breed blacksmith Quint Asper. (Courtesy CBS, Inc.)

Top: Matt (Jim Arness) visits Doc (Milburn Stone) in his office. (Courtesy of Viacom Enterprises.) *Bottom, left:* Actor-director Victor French was one of the most frequently seen guest stars. (Author's collection.) *Bottom, right:* Denver Pyle guest starred in more than a dozen *Gunsmoke* episodes and was one of 26 actors who auditioned for the role of Matt Dillon. (Courtesy of Denver Pyle.)

Photographs

Top: James Arness and Amanda Blake in Dodge City for the dedication of Front Street, 1958. (Courtesy of Boot Hill Museum, Inc.) *Bottom:* James Arness being greeted by Deputy U.S. Marshal Ramon K. House of Dodge City, Kansas, 1958. (Courtesy of Boot Hill Museum, Inc.)

James Arness and Forrest Tucker in *Double Entry* (January 2, 1965). (Courtesy of CBS, Inc.)

Photographs

Kitty (Amanda Blake) explains to Sweet Billy (Warren Oates) and his Pa (Taylor McPeters) that she will not marry into their family in *Marry Me* (December 23, 1961). (Courtesy CBS, Inc.)

GUNSMOKE — II. PHOTOGRAPHS

Top, left: John Fiedler appeared in *Hammerhead* (December 26, 1964) and eight years later *A Quiet Day in Dodge* (January 29, 1973). (Courtesy of John Fiedler.) *Top, right:* Foster Brooks appeared in *Quint Asper Comes Home* (September 29, 1962) and *The Gun* (November 9, 1970). (Courtesy of Foster Brooks.) *Bottom, left:* Lois Nettleton appeared in *Nina's Revenge* (December 16, 1961). Most recently she was a regular on the NBC series *In the Heat of the Night* which stars another *Gunsmoke* alumnus Carroll O'Connor. (Courtesy of Lois Nettleton.) *Bottom, right:* John Saxon appeared in *Dry Road to Nowhere*, *The Avenger*, *The Whispering Tree*, *The Pillagers*, and *The Squaw*. (Courtesy of John Saxon.)

Photographs

Top, left: Paul Carr appeared in *The Squaw* (November 11, 1961) and *Gold Mine* (December 25, 1965). (Courtesy of Paul Carr.) *Top, right:* Jeanne Cooper guest starred in *Ex-Con* (November 30, 1963). (Courtesy of Jeanne Cooper). *Bottom, left:* William Windom, "Mr. Flip Flop," appeared in three episodes of *Gunsmoke*. (Courtesy of William Windom.) *Bottom, right:* Ben Cooper appeared in *Apprentice Doc* (December 9, 1961), *Breckenridge* (March 13, 1965) and *Two Tall Men* (May 8, 1965). (Courtesy of Ben Cooper.)

Matt Dillon (James Arness) warning an adversary to lay down his gun. (Courtesy of Viacom Enterprises.)

Photographs

The famous opening scene where Matt shoots the mysterious man in black. This time, however, James Arness, as a joke, let the gunman beat him to the draw. (Courtesy of Viacom Enterprises.)

Kitty (Amanda Blake) comforts Cooter (Strother Martin) in a scene from *Cooter* (May 19, 1956). (Courtesy of CBS, Inc.)

Photographs

Amanda Blake in the Long Branch Saloon in Dodge City, Kansas, 1958. (Courtesy of Boot Hill Museum, Inc.)

Chester (Dennis Weaver) and Matt (James Arness) riding the prairie tracking outlaws. (Courtesy of Viacom Enterprises.)

Ken Curtis frequently appeared as a singing cowboy in low-budget Westerns. His early films included *Song of the Prairie* (1945) and *Singing on the Trail* (1946). (Author's collection.)

Ken Curtis and Larry Pennell on the set of *Ripcord*. Curtis played skydiver Jim Buckley (1962). (Author's collection.)

Photographs

Jeanette Nolan as Aunt Thede dances with her nephew Festus (Ken Curtis) in *Aunt Thede* (December 19, 1964). In 1974 she starred in the *Gunsmoke* spin-off *Dirty Sally*. Nolan was one of the regulars on radio's *Gunsmoke*. (Courtesy of CBS, Inc.)

Matt (James Arness), Quint (Burt Reynolds), Doc (Milburn Stone), Kitty (Amanda Blake), and Festus (Ken Curtis). (Courtesy CBS, Inc.)

Photographs

Top, left: Hal Smith appeared in *Old Flame* as Mr. Dobie the hotel manager. (Courtesy of Hal Smith.) *Top, right:* Mayf Nutter was Festus' cousin Heathcliff in *Hard Luck Henry*. The hat that he was given to wear was Clark Gable's from *Gone with the Wind*. (Courtesy of Mayf Nutter.) *Bottom, left:* Joseph Campanella in Western regalia. Campanella guest starred in *The Hide Cutters* (September 30, 1968) and *Milligan* (November 6, 1972). (Courtesy of Joseph Campanella.) *Bottom, right:* Character actor R.G. Armstrong guest starred in several episodes. He poses here as a colorful buffalo hunter. (Courtesy of R.G. Armstrong.)

Festus (Ken Curtis) helps *Malachi* (Harry Townes) masquerade as the marshal (November 13, 1965). (Provided by Wisconsin Center for Film and Theater Research courtesy of CBS, Inc.)

Photographs

James Arness and Amanda Blake in front with Glenn Strange, Ken Curtis, Roger Ewing and Milburn Stone in back. (Courtesy of CBS, Inc.)

Top: Lou Stone (Bruce Dern) holds Kitty (Amanda Blake) while his mother (Bette Davis) pulls a ring from Kitty's finger in *The Jailer* (October 1, 1966). (Courtesy of CBS, Inc.) *Bottom:* Amanda Blake, Liam Redmond and J. Pat O'Malley in *The Dreamers* (April 28, 1962). (Courtesy of Viacom Enterprises.)

Photographs

Okey Cathcart (Don Dubbins) has "chosen" Kitty (Amanda Blake) to be his bride. But Kitty is not very cooperative in *Marry Me* (December 23, 1961). (Provided by Don Dubbins courtesy of CBS, Inc.)

GUNSMOKE — II. PHOTOGRAPHS

Top, left: Jeff Corey appeared in *The Night Riders* (February 24, 1969). (Courtesy of Jeff Corey.) *Top, right:* Eunice Christopher was featured in *The Reprisal* (February 10, 1969) and *The Bassops* (February 22, 1964). (Courtesy of Eunice Christopher.) *Bottom, left:* Joshua Bryant appeared in *Twisted Heritage* (January 6, 1969). (Courtesy of Joshua Bryant.) *Bottom, right:* Richard Anderson was in *Jonah Hutchinson, The War Priest,* and *Guns of Cibola Blanca* I and II. (Courtesy of Richard Anderson.)

Photographs

Top, left: Character actor Lonny Chapman appeared in *Tell Chester* (April 20, 1963), *Outlaw's Woman* (December 11, 1965), and *Parson Comes to Town* (April 30, 1966). (Courtesy of Lonny Chapman). *Top, right:* Julie Sommars appeared in *The Jailer* (October 1, 1966). (Courtesy of Julie Sommars.) *Bottom, left:* Clifton James appeared in *Letter of the Law, The Lady, The Wrong Man,* and *Snow Train* Parts I & II. (Courtesy of Clifton James.) *Bottom, right:* Richard Evans appeared in *Moo Moo Raid, The Storm, The Prodigal,* and *Death Watch.* (Courtesy of Richard Evans.)

Ken Curtis as Festus and Royal Dano as Praylie in a scene from *Crooked Mile* (October 3, 1964). (Courtesy of CBS, Inc.)

Photographs

Top, left: John Anderson appeared in over a dozen *Gunsmoke* episodes playing a wide variety of characters. (Courtesy of John Anderson.) *Top, right:* At the 1988 S.P.E.R.D.V.A.C. Salute to CBS Radio, Tyler McVey played Doc in the *Gunsmoke* re-creation. On television he guest starred in several episodes. (Courtesy of Tyler McVey.) *Bottom, left:* Graham Jarvis was featured in the last *Gunsmoke*, *The Sharecroppers* (March 31, 1975). (Courtesy of Graham Jarvis.) *Bottom, right:* Beau Bridges starred in *My Father's Guitar* (February 12, 1966). (Courtesy of Beau Bridges.)

Milburn Stone as Doctor Galen Adams, M.D. (Provided by Wisconsin Center for Film and Theater Research courtesy of CBS, Inc.)

Photographs

Top: Ken Curtis as Festus enjoys a heaping helping of beans. (Courtesy of Viacom Enterprises.) *Bottom:* Festus whispers sweet nothings to his faithful friend, Ruth. (Provided by Wisconsin Center for Film and Theater Research courtesy of CBS, Inc.)

GUNSMOKE — II. PHOTOGRAPHS

Top: Morgan Woodward as Abraham and James Arness as Matt in a scene from the final season *Matt Dillon Must Die*. (Courtesy of Viacom Enterprises.)
Bottom: Morgan Woodward appeared in approximately 20 episodes. He has probably guest starred in more shows than anyone. (Courtesy of Morgan Woodward.)

Photographs

Morgan Woodward and Wayne Rogers help Ed Begley take a bath in *Taps for Old Jeb* (October 16, 1965). (Provided by Wisconsin Center for Film and Theater Research courtesy of CBS, Inc.)

James Arness as Matt Dillon, U.S. Marshal. (Provided by Wisconsin Center for Film and Theater Research courtesy of CBS, Inc.)

Photographs

Milburn Stone, Amanda Blake, and James Arness on the set of *Marry Me* (1961). (Courtesy of CBS, Inc.)

GUNSMOKE — II. PHOTOGRAPHS

Amanda Blake as Kitty Russell. (Provided by Wisconsin Center for Film and Theater Research courtesy of CBS, Inc.)

Photographs

The *Gunsmoke* family: Milburn Stone, James Arness, Amanda Blake, and Ken Curtis. (Courtesy of Viacom Enterprises.)

Top, left: Academy Award winner Eileen Heckart appeared in *The Lady* and *The Innocent*. (Courtesy of Eileen Heckart.) *Top, right:* Character actor Jack Weston appeared in *Sunday Supplement* (February 8, 1958). (Courtesy of Jack Weston.) *Bottom, left:* Tige Andrews appeared in *Gone Straight* (February 9, 1957) and *The Jackals* (February 12, 1968). (Courtesy of Tige Andrews.) *Bottom, right:* John Chandler was featured in *Cowtown Hustler*. He stated that, "In the pool playing episode Jack Albertson played the older champ and he shot a good stick!" (Courtesy of John Chandler.)

Photographs

Rack played by John Dehner has wounded Matt (James Arness) and taken him prisoner in *The Badge* (November 12, 1960). Dehner was a member of radio *Gunsmoke's* elite repertory company. (Courtesy of CBS, Inc.)

Top, left: Writer Paul F. Edwards in the Sierras at 14,000 feet. Edwards wrote memorable *Gunsmoke* episodes including *Chato* and *Hostage!*, that dealt with the American Indian. (Courtesy of Paul F. Edwards.) *Top, right:* Writer Paul Savage whose association with *Gunsmoke* was one of the longest, started as a young actor when Macdonnell hired him as an "off-mike-ad-lib-head-nod" radio performer. (Courtesy of Paul Savage.) *Bottom, left:* Writer Clyde Ware wrote during the final decade of television's *Gunsmoke*. (Courtesy Clyde Ware.) *Bottom, right:* Writer Ron Bishop whose stories were Western parables rich with the vernacular of the time, wrote such classic episodes as *Mannon* and *A Hat*. (Courtesy of Mrs. Ron Bishop.)

Photographs

Producer John Mantley guided *Gunsmoke* through its final decade on television. (Courtesy of John Mantley.)

Ken Curtis as U.S. Deputy Marshal Festus Haggen, the only white sheep in a family of black sheep. (Courtesy of Ken Curtis.)

Photographs

Buck Taylor as Newly O'Brien, U.S. Marshal, 1987. (Courtesy of Buck Taylor.)

GUNSMOKE — II. PHOTOGRAPHS

The *Gunsmoke* cast in the later years: Doc (Milburn Stone), Matt (James Arness), Kitty (Amanda Blake), Festus (Ken Curtis), Newly (Buck Taylor), Sam (Glenn Strange). (Provided by Neil Summers courtesy of CBS, Inc.)

Photographs

Top, left: Michael Constantine appeared in *Old York* which also featured Edgar Buchanan. "He literally had me laughing from morning till night everyday we worked together," Constantine said of his co-star. (Courtesy Michael Constantine.) *Top, right:* Comedian Morey Amsterdam helped Matt Dillon foil a phony marshal in *Joe Phy*. (Courtesy of Morey Amsterdam.) *Bottom, left:* Julie Cobb was featured in *Lynch Town* (November 19, 1973) and *The Colonel* (December 16, 1974). (Courtesy of Julie Cobb.) *Bottom, right:* Fionnula Flanagan guest starred in *The Drummer* (October 9, 1972). In 1978 Flanagan co-starred as James Arness' sister-in-law in *How the West Was Won*. (Courtesy of Fionnula Flanagan.)

GUNSMOKE — II. PHOTOGRAPHS

Top: James Stacy met his second wife, Kim Darby, during a two-part *Gunsmoke* episode, *Vengeance* in 1967. (Courtesy of James Stacy.) *Bottom, left:* Tom Reese appeared in over a dozen episodes playing "mostly villains." (Courtesy of Tom Reese.) *Bottom, right:* Jack Ging appeared in *Stage Stop* (November 26, 1966). (Courtesy of Jack Ging.)

Photographs

After a stage hold-up Kitty (Amanda Blake) helps an ailing unwed mother (Betty Conner) in *Help Me, Kitty* (November 7, 1964). (Provided by Wisconsin Center for Film and Theater Research courtesy of CBS, Inc.)

GUNSMOKE — II. PHOTOGRAPHS

Top: Ken Curtis and Ned Beatty in a scene from *The Hiders* (January 13, 1975). (Courtesy of Viacom Enterprises.) *Bottom, left:* Madlyn Rhue was featured in *Tag, You're It* (December 19, 1959). (Courtesy of Madlyn Rhue.) *Bottom, right:* Robert Pine guest starred in *Lyle's Kid, The Night Riders, Gentry's Law,* and *Jesse.* (Courtesy of Robert Pine.)

Photographs

Gilbert Roland and Anna Navarro in the two parter *Extradition*, 1963. (Provided by Wisconsin Center for Film and Theater Research courtesy of CBS, Inc.)

GUNSMOKE — II. PHOTOGRAPHS

Top: Matt (James Arness), Anne (Julie Cobb) and Josiah (Lee J. Cobb) in *The Colonel* (December 16, 1974.) (Courtesy of CBS, Inc.) *Bottom, left:* DeForest Kelley guest starred in an episode of *Gunsmoke* before *Star Trek* made him famous. Here he is in a scene from *Tension at Table Rock,* 1956. (Courtesy of DeForest Kelley.) *Bottom, right:* Val Dufour's first job in Hollywood was for *Gunsmoke.* (Courtesy of Val Dufour.)

Photographs

Top, left: Academy Award winner Kim Hunter starred in *The Legend*. (Courtesy of Kim Hunter.) *Top, right:* Allen Garfield starred in *The Fires of Ignorance* as a teacher who goes to court to fight for compulsory education in Dodge. (Courtesy of Allen Garfield.) *Bottom, left:* William Schallert made several appearances on *Gunsmoke* including *Daddy Went Away*, *Albert*, and *The Money Store*. (Courtesy of William Schallert.) *Bottom, right:* Katherine Helmond appeared in *The Judgement* (October 2, 1972). (Courtesy of Katherine Helmond.)

GUNSMOKE — II. PHOTOGRAPHS

Top: Ken Curtis and Van Williams in *Thirty a Month and Found* (October 7, 1974). (Courtesy of Viacom Enterprises.) *Bottom, left:* **Donna Bacalla** was featured in *Blood Money* (January 22, 1968). "When you walked onto the *Gunsmoke* stage one really got transported to the Old West...Towering over everyone was this warm gentle man, Jim Arness, whose blue eyes always seemed to sparkle." (Courtesy of Donna Bacalla.) *Bottom, right:* Michael Ansara appeared in *Honor Before Justice* (March 5, 1966) and *The Returning* (February 18, 1967). (Courtesy of Michael Ansara.)

Photographs

Top: Gene Evans as Shaw Anderson and James Arness as Matt Dillon in *The Iron Blood of Courage* (February 18, 1974.) (Courtesy Viacom Enterprises.) *Bottom, left:* Darryl Hickman played a "Billy the Kid type" in *The Choice* and a young man in love with a gypsy girl in *Target.* (Courtesy of Darryl Hickman.) *Bottom, right:* Jane Dulo appeared in *Champion of the World* (December 24, 1966). (Courtesy of Jane Dulo.)

GUNSMOKE — II. PHOTOGRAPHS

Top, left: Before playing "Trapper John" on *M.A.S.H.*, Wayne Rogers guest starred on several television shows including *Gunsmoke*. (Courtesy of Wayne Rogers.) *Top, right:* Val Avery appeared in *Cows and Cribs, The Lure,* and *A Man Called Smith*. (Courtesy of Val Avery.) *Bottom, left:* Don Dubbins played "country or hillbilly" types in four episodes. (Courtesy of Don Dubbins.) *Bottom, right:* Herb Armstrong appeared in *The Drummer* (October 9, 1972). (Courtesy of Herb Armstrong.)

Photographs

Amanda Blake and Andy Devine in *Stryker* (September 29, 1969). (Courtesy of Viacom Enterprises.)

GUNSMOKE — II. PHOTOGRAPHS

Top, left: Ruta Lee guest starred in *Carmen* (May 24, 1958) and *Jenny* (October 13, 1962). (Courtesy of Ruta Lee.) *Top, right:* Leonard Stone appeared in *Jesse* (February 19, 1973) and *The Fourth Victim* (November 4, 1974). (Courtesy of Leonard Stone.) *Bottom, left:* Eddie Firestone appeared in several episodes including *The Brothers*, *Nitro* I and II, *Lobo*, and the three-part *Gold Train*. (Courtesy of Eddie Firestone.) *Bottom, right:* Ralph Bellamy guest starred in *Rope Fever* (December 4, 1967). (Courtesy of Ralph Bellamy.)

Photographs

Top, left: Character actor John Brandon appeared in such films a *Scarface, Serpico* and *Racing with the Moon*. On *Gunsmoke* he appeared in *The Good Samaritans*. (Courtesy of John Brandon.) *Top, right:* James Griffith was in *Kite's Reward, Twelfth Night, The Bassops, Quint's Indian,* and *The Gunrunners*. (Courtesy of James Griffith.) *Bottom, left:* Guy Stockwell was cast in his first starring role in *The Cook* (December 17, 1960). (Courtesy of Guy Stockwell.) *Bottom, right:* Paul Picerni appeared in *The Lure, The Pillagers, Kitty's Love Affair,* and *Disciple*. (Courtesy of Paul Picerni.)

GUNSMOKE — II. PHOTOGRAPHS

Top: Jack Elam and his daughter Jackie visit with James Arness during the filming of *The River*, 1972. (Courtesy of Jack Elam.) *Bottom:* Character actor Jack Elam was a frequent guest star on *Gunsmoke*. (Courtesy of Jack Elam.)

Pernell Roberts is the *Stranger in Town* (November 20, 1967) seen here with Amanda Blake as Kitty. (Courtesy of Viacom Enterprises.)

Top: Fran Ryan was a guest performer in only two episodes, but she was brought in to run the Long Branch after Blake's departure as Miss Hannah. (Courtesy of Fran Ryan.) *Bottom:* Pat Hingle filled in for Milburn Stone as Dr. John Chapman. (Courtesy of Pat Hingle.)

Photographs

Top: Ted Jordan played the regular role of Nathan Burke the gossipy freight agent. (Courtesy of Ted Jordan.) *Bottom:* In addition to the role of Jonas, Dabbs Greer was featured in *Marshal Proudfoot* and *Cowtown Hustler*. (Courtesy of Dabbs Greer.)

GUNSMOKE — II. PHOTOGRAPHS

Top: Fran Ryan as Miss Hannah and James Arness as Matt Dillon. (Courtesy of Viacom Enterprises.) *Bottom:* Ben Stack (Rory Calhoun) and Honey Dare (Joanna Moore) are deadly lovers in *Honey Pot* (May 15, 1965). (Provided by Wisconsin Center of Film and Theater Research courtesy of CBS, Inc.)

Photographs

Top, left: Gary Busey guest starred in *The Busters* (March 10, 1975). (Courtesy of Gary Busey.) *Top, right:* Owen Bush appeared in *A Noose for Dobie Price* and the two-parter *A Game of Death...An Act of Love.* (Courtesy Owen Bush.) *Bottom, left:* Sue Ane Langdon appeared in *Catawomper* (February 10, 1962). (Courtesy of Sue Ane Langdon.) *Bottom, right:* Anne Jackson played Phoebe, a lonely spinster in *Blind Man's Buff* (February 21, 1972). (Courtesy of Anne Jackson.)

GUNSMOKE — II. PHOTOGRAPHS

Top: Milburn Stone at Boot Hill Cemetery accepting an Honorary Marshal of Dodge City Award, 1958. (Courtesy of Boot Hill Museum, Inc.) *Bottom:* Actor-director Gunnar Hellstrom with Milburn Stone. (Courtesy of Viacom Enterprises.)

Photographs

Top, left: A seasoned Matt Dillon. *Top, right:* His younger counterpart. (Courtesy of Viacom Enterprises.) *Bottom:* Gretchen Corbett as Arlene with James Arness in a scene from the final season *A Town in Chains*. (Courtesy of Viacom Enterprises.)

GUNSMOKE — II. PHOTOGRAPHS

Top: A recent photo of William Conrad from his hit television series *Jake and the Fat Man.* (Courtesy of CBS, Inc.) *Bottom, left:* James Arness as he appeared in *How the West Was Won.* (Courtesy of CBS, Inc.) *Bottom, right:* Dennis Weaver in recent years. (Courtesy of Dennis Weaver.)

John Mantley, *Gunsmoke's* executive producer, outside his home, March 1988. (Author's collection).

James Arness as Matt and Amanda Blake as Kitty in *Gunsmoke: Return to Dodge*, 1987. (Courtesy of CBS, Inc.)

Amanda Blake and James Arness at a *Gunsmoke* retrospective held at the Los Angeles County Museum of Art, March 1988. (Author's collection.)

One of John Meston's favorite photos. As Matt might say, "It's a dirty job, but someone has to do it." (Courtesy of Mary Ann Meston.)

PART III.
THE PROGRAMS, EPISODE-BY-EPISODE

THE RADIO PROGRAMS

Gunsmoke was on radio from April 26, 1952, to June 18, 1961. The actors that graced its sound stage were the best in the industry.

The radio principals were William Conrad as Matt Dillon, Georgia Ellis as Kitty Russell, Howard McNear as Doctor Charles Adams, and Parley Baer as Chester Wesley Proudfoot.

A strong supporting cast included John Dehner, Sam Edwards, Harry Bartell, Vic Perrin, Lou Krugman, Lawrence Dobkin, Barney Phillips, Jack Kruschen, Ralph Moody, Ben Wright, James Nusser, Virginia Gregg, Jeanette Nolan, Virginia Christine, Helen Kleeb, Lillian Buyeff, Vivi Janiss, and Jeanne Bates. They became part of the close-knit radio family because the same guest actors were used in almost all of the shows.

During the nine years on the air there were 413 radio stories. Many of the shows were later adapted to the television series. This chapter is a comprehensive list of the radio shows with a brief synopsis of all available stories.

The scripts were titled when submitted, but the titles were not announced on the air. John Meston once commented that his titles were to amuse himself or to cue the cast.

FIRST SEASON

Billy the Kid. April 26, 1952. Written by Walter Brown Newman. Guest cast: Don Diamond, Parley Baer, Georgia Ellis, Howard McNear, Harry Bartell, Richard Beals, Paul DuBov, Mary Lansing.

Clay Richards is wanted for murder, but before the wanted posters are up, he is brought to town draped over his saddle like a "sack of wheat" by Pete "the Dutchman" Ziegler. Ziegler swears he found Clay dead, but when it is discovered that Clay was unarmed, the citizens of Dodge and Clay's brother suspect that Ziegler is lying. They speculate that Clay was murdered to get the $400 reward on his head. In the midst of all this, a 12-year-old runaway from Cottonwood, William Bonnie, has been

GUNSMOKE — III. THE PROGRAMS

eagerly hanging around Matt, listening to his every word and watching his every move.

Georgia Ellis, who in later episodes played Kitty, plays Clay's widow, Francie, in this segment. Don Diamond appeared as a regular in three television Westerns *The Adventures of Kit Carson, Zorro,* and *F Troop.* Mary Lansing was featured on the television series *Mayberry, R.F.D.*

Ben Thompson. May 3, 1952. Written by Herb Purdum. Guest cast: Larry Dobkin, Michael Ann Barrett, Harry Bartell, Sam Edwards, Don Diamond, Bob Griffin.

This episode is often confused with *Jaliscoe.* In *Jaliscoe* Will Thompson is the character referred to, not Ben Thompson. There is no known version of this episode available. Even its author Herb Purdum does not possess a copy, nor does he know of any in existence. In addition to radio drama, Purdum has over 200 television credits. He has written for such series as *Rawhide* and *Crossroads.* Purdum was especially active in the early days when television was mostly half-hour shows. "I wrote for everything," he recalls, "Including *The Cisco Kid, Boston Blackie,* you name it. I even wrote some *Tarzan* and *Sheena, Queen of the Jungle."* His first novel, a Western titled *My Brother, John,* was awarded the Golden Spur Award for Best Western Novel.

Jaliscoe. May 10, 1952. Written by Les Crutchfield. Guest cast: Harry Bartell, Lou Krugman, Barney Phillips, Georgia Ellis, Jack Kruschen, Vivi Janiss, Johnny McGovern.

Homesteader Will Thompson's house is burned to the ground and his family is massacred. The attack is made to look as if Indians are responsible. However, the real evidence points to a cowboy who wears Mexican spurs. The man in question, Jaliscoe Pete, and his three accomplices, work for cattlerancher Ben Roark. The cattleranchers hate the homesteaders for bringing plows and fences into the wide open country. Ezra Hawkins, who represents the other homesteaders in the county, warns Matt of an impending range war if justice is not served.

On television Barney Phillips was a regular on several series including *Dragnet, Twelve O'Clock High, Felony Squad,* and *The Betty White Show.* Les Crutchfield wrote for television's *Rawhide.*

Dodge City Killer. May 17, 1952. Written by Herb Purdum. Guest cast: Ben Wright, Vici Raaf, Paul DuBov, Larry Dobkin, Lillian Buyeff, Lou Krugman, Ralph Moody.

A ruthless killer stalks Dodge and it is up to Matt to discover his identity before he strikes again.

Ben Slade's Saloon. May 24, 1952. Written by Norman Macdonnell. Guest cast: Georgia Ellis, Hy Averbach, Jack Kruschen, Richard Beals, Anne Morrison, Herb Ellis.

Ben Ramaris and Tad Slade are partners in the Ben-Slade Saloon. Les Jones is robbed of $3000 and is found stabbed to death, after a lucky evening at their faro table. This is not the first time that a customer of the Slade Saloon has been found robbed and murdered. After confronting Slade without success, Matt rides over to his ranch to investigate further and meets seductive Evalita, Ben's "sister" and Tad's fiancee.

Hy Averbach was a regular on several television programs including *Our Miss Brooks.* He later became a producer and director for such television comedies as *F Troop, The Real McCoys,* and *M.A.S.H.,* for which he received two Emmy nominations as Best Director. Averbach's film credits as an actor include *The Benny Goodman Story.*

The Radio Programs

He also directed several films among them *The Great Train Robbery* (1968) and *Chamber of Horrors,* in which he also served as producer.

Carmen. May 31, 1952. Written by John Meston. Guest star: Michael Ann Barrett, Jeanette Nolan, Harry Bartell, Don Diamond. Aired on television May 24, 1958.

Two soldiers are murdered and a government payroll is stolen. Meanwhile, Connie Dell, a new girl at Big Kate's saloon, has been very chummy with a Corporal Bowers. After checking on her, Matt discovers she has come from Hayes City, where she was involved with Billy Grounds, "a wild one." After Private Bone, a friend of Corporal Bowers, is murdered, Matt's suspicions fall on Bowers. Both soldiers worked in the army accounting department, giving them access to payroll information. Meanwhile, Connie lures Matt out of town for a moonlight ride. Matt accepts, knowing full well that he is going to be ambushed.

Jeanette Nolan is a superb character actress of radio, films and television. Her films include *Tribute to a Badman,* and *The Man Who Shot Liberty Valance.* She played Lady Macbeth in Orson Welles' *Macbeth.* On television she played the title role in the series *Dirty Sally,* which was a *Gunsmoke* spin-off. She also co-starred with her husband John McIntire in *The Virginian.* John Meston was the preeminent *Gunsmoke* writer on both radio and television. In addition to his various radio credits, he also wrote scripts for television's *Little House on the Prairie.*

Buffalo Killers. June 7, 1952. Written by Joel Murcott. Guest cast: Stan Waxman, John Dehner, Larry Dobkins, Sam Edwards, Lillian Buyeff, Tom Holland, Mary Lansing.

Mr. Biggs' two sons are killed in an apparent Arapahoe raid. Their buffalo skins are stolen, including the skin of a rare white buffalo. However, something is not quite right. The horses and guns were not taken. Matt believes whitemen, not Indians, were responsible for the killings. He decides to watch the unloading barns, looking for the white buffalo skin. When word leaks out that Matt is looking for the killers, two gunmen, Chuck Kell and Tennessee, stage a phoney confrontation to keep Matt from suspecting them.

John Dehner was the voice of Paladin on radio's *Have Gun, Will Travel.* He has been a regular on numerous television and radio shows and has guest starred hundreds of times. His film credits include *The Left-Handed Gun* and *The Boys from Brazil.* Larry Dobkin was a regular on such radio shows as *Suspense* and *Lux Radio Theatre.* He appeared on television during the early days of live programming on *Playhouse 90* and *The Red Skelton Show.* In recent years Dobkin has moved into the field of television directing for such shows as *The Munsters, Barnaby Jones* and *Cannon,* which starred William Conrad. Writer Joel Murcott wrote for such television programs as *Alfred Hitchcock Presents, Barnaby Jones, Cannon, Little House on the Prairie,* and *Perry Mason.*

Jailbait Janet. June 14, 1952. Written by Les Crutchfield. Guest cast: John Dehner, Sammie Hill, Harry Bartell, Paul DuBov. Aired on television February 27, 1960.

A man and his two teenaged children rob a train. During the hold-up the baggage clerk is killed. When Matt arrests the bandits, he discovers that one of the culprits is a young girl.

Heat Spell. June 21, 1952. Written by Lou Houston. Guest cast: John Stephenson, John Dehner, Paul Frees, Nestor Paiva, Jack Kruschen.

GUNSMOKE — III. THE PROGRAMS

The Ride Back. June 28, 1952. Written by Antony Ellis. Guest cast: Larry Dobkin.
Matt is on his way back to Dodge after having captured his prisoner. During the long, dirty ride back they encounter several adventures in which each man, at various times, gets the upper hand. However, through it all a mutual respect and admiration develops between them.
This two man episode is unusual and interesting as a character study. It was later developed into a screenplay and was released as *The Ride Back*. William Conrad produced and starred in the film along with Anthony Quinn. Antony Ellis wrote for television's *Zane Grey Theater* and for *Black Saddle*, which he also produced. Ellis was formerly married to Georgia Ellis, Miss Kitty.

Never Pester Chester. July 5, 1952. Written by John Meston. Guest cast: Paul DuBov, Lou Krugman, Don Diamond, Jack Kruschen, Gil Stratton, Jr. Aired on television November 16, 1957.
Chester is dragged through town by two bullies and is left out on the prairie, all because he tried to do "Matt's job." Matt, feeling terribly guilty about the incident, goes after the two men with a vengeance.

The Boughten Bride. July 12, 1952. Written by John Meston. Guest cast: John Stephenson, Herb Ellis, Jonathan Hole, Mary Lansing, Jim Nusser, Frank Gerstle, Larry Dobkin, Patricia Walter.

Doc Holliday. July 19, 1952. Written by Herb Purdum. Guest cast: Harry Bartell, Lee Millar, Nestor Paiva, Ralph Moody, Tom Tully.
Doc Holliday, a deadly gunman, arrives in Dodge. The town is tense anticipating a showdown between Matt and Holliday. Although Matt is an excellent draw, Holliday is a master. Matt knows that if forced to face Holliday in a gunfight, he stands no chance.

Gentlemen's Disagreement. July 26, 1952. Written by Les Crutchfield. Guest cast: Larry Dobkin, Tom Tully, Lynn Allen, Barney Phillips. Aired on television April 30, 1960.
Jeanne Wells' one time suitor, gunslinger Ed Beaudry, is back in town. When Beaudry discovers Jeanne is married, he threatens to kill her blacksmith husband. Later, when Beaudry is found murdered, suspicion falls on the blacksmith.

Renegade White. August 2, 1952. Written by John Meston. Guest cast: Harry Bartell, Jack Kruschen, Larry Dobkin, Herb Vigran. Aired on television April 11, 1959.
While trying to track down the whiteman who has been selling 44-caliber rifles to the Indians, Matt is captured by hostile Indians.

The Kentucky Tolmans. August 9, 1952. Written by Herb Purdum. Guest cast: Virginia Gregg, Joseph Kearns, Junius Matthews, Harry Bartell, Lou Krugman, Peter Leeds.
Mountain girl Hannah Tolman asks Matt to arrest her father Jed for his own protection. It seems someone has been trying to kill him. Matt has no grounds to lock him up, so Hannah lures Jed into a brief display of his shooting prowess, forcing Matt to arrest him for disorderly behavior. Back at the jailhouse, Chester discovers a wanted poster on Vic Tolman, Jed's son. Matt becomes embroiled in a search for the convict, his hidden money, and the bushwacker who tried to kill Jed.

The Radio Programs

Joseph Kearns appeared on television as a regular on *Our Miss Brooks* and on *Dennis the Menace* as Mr. Wilson. Virginia Gregg guest-starred on numerous radio and television programs. Amongst her many credits she played the voice of Maggie Belle on the children's cartoon *Calvin and the Colonel,* as well as the role of Hannah in the dramatic series *Little Women.*

The Lynching. August 16, 1952. Written by John Meston. Guest cast: John Dehner, Paul DuBov, Tom Tully, Ralph Moody, Lee Millar, Joan Danton.

Billy Saxton is lynched by Ken Powell for allegedly shooting Ken's brother Jobe. Matt discovers that the only witness to Jobe's killing is cook, Hank Ashford. Hank supposedly told Ken that Billy was the murderer and Ken took it from there.

Shakespeare. August 23, 1952. Written by Antony Ellis. Guest cast: Hans Conried, Mary Lansing.

Matt, Chester, and Doc happen upon a man lying by the roadside. Felled by the heat, the stranger hallucinates and recites Shakespeare. Upon recovering he claims he is "O'Irving Henry, Thespian Supreme, Disciple of the Immortal Bard." When a murdered man is found in Henry's wagon, Matt sets out to solve the mystery.

On radio Hans Conried was a regular on *My Friend Irma, Burns and Allen,* and *The Great Gildersleeve.* On television, he played Danny Thomas' Uncle Tonoose on *The Danny Thomas Show,* as well as regulars on numerous other programs. He was also the voice of Snidley Whiplash on *The Bullwinkle Show.* On television Mary Lansing made guest appearances on such programs as *The Andy Griffith Show, The Brothers,* and *Mayberry R.F.D.*

The Juniper Tree. August 30, 1952. Written by Herb Purdum. Guest cast: Vivi Janiss, Paul DuBov, Bill Lally, John Dehner, Michael Ann Barrett.

Jim Stanley, a simple-minded horse rancher, is accused by gambler Mingo of trying to steal money from his roulette table, and then of attempting to kill him. Matt must jail Jim, even though he knows that Jim is most likely innocent. Dixie, a greedy gold digger, adds to Jim's troubles.

Vivi Janiss was seen on television as Myrtle Davis of *Father Knows Best.* Bill Lally played Tommy Clifford on television in the comedy *My Son Jeep.* Actor Paul DuBov turned his sights to writing for such television programs as *Eight Is Enough, Wonder Woman, Backstairs at the Whitehouse* and *Honey West,* which he created with his wife Gwen Bagni.

The Brothers. September 6, 1952. Written by Les Crutchfield. Guest cast: Harry Bartell, Vic Perrin, Paul DuBov, Joe DuVal, Lou Krugman.

Jim and Will Thompson come to Dodge to sell 2,000 head of cattle. Matt becomes suspicious when he finds that they are accompanied by Huston, a gunfighter he ran out of town the previous year.

Home Surgery. September 13, 1952. Written by John Meston. Guest cast: John Dehner, Larry Dobkin, Sammie Hill. Aired on television October 8, 1955.

Tara Hantree's father has gangrene of the leg, and Matt is drafted into performing the amputation. However, the disease has spread too far and Hantree dies. Matt then discovers that the accident that led to Mr. Hantree's condition was actually caused by Ben Walling, who has his sights on Tara.

GUNSMOKE — III. THE PROGRAMS

Drop Dead. September 20, 1952. Written by Les Crutchfield. Guest cast: Harry Bartell, Lou Krugman, Joe DuVal, Barney Phillips.

Jack Jackson must find water for his herd of cattle, for his animals are dying "like flies." He comes to within several yards of a pond, but finds that it is fenced in by barbed wire. Howard, who owns the land, is not above taking advantage of a man in trouble and asks an exorbitant amount to allow the cattle to drink. Matt finds he is caught between the desperate Jackson and the greedy Howard.

The Railroad. September 27, 1952. Written by David Ellis. Guest cast: John Dehner, Jeanette Nolan, Tom Tully.

The railroad is about to run widow Libby Sager off her land. They offer her three times what it is worth, but she refuses. The affair ends in tragedy despite Matt's attempts at keeping the peace, when Libby decides to fight to the death rather than be run off.

Cain. October 3, 1952. Written by John Meston. Guest cast: Harry Bartell, Larry Dobkin. Aired on television March 9, 1957.

The past catches up with Adams, a former riverboat gambler now living in Dodge, when Cain Vestal, a guitar-playing migrant appears. Cain threatens revenge because the girl he loved ran off with Adams, and then killed herself when Adams abandoned her. Adams laughs at the threats, but is unaware that Cain is dying of consumption and is not to be dissuaded.

Hinka-Do. October 10, 1952. Written by Les Crutchfield. Guest cast: Jeanette Nolan, Ralph Moody, John Dehner, Byron Kane. Aired on television January 30, 1960.

Pistol-toting, 190-pound Mamie, is the new owner of the Longhorn saloon. Matt suspects foul play when he discovers that Herman Bleeker, the former owner, has disappeared without saying a word to anyone. When Bleeker's bloody vest is found, Matt attempts to arrest Mamie.

Byron Kane guest starred on television's *The Hardy Boys*.

Lochinvar. October 17, 1952. Written by Les Crutchfield. Guest cast: Herb Ellis, Barney Phillips, Tom Tully, Vivi Janiss.

Ardis Nash and Ben Martin are preparing to get married. In the midst of the preparations, Francis Craig arrives in town. Ardis is Craig's former girlfriend, and he makes it plain that she is still "his girl." Craig insists he will stop the marriage and threatens to kill anyone who stands in his way.

Herb Ellis played Officer Frank Smith on television's *Dragnet,* Frank La Valle on *The D.A.'s Man,* and Dr. Wagner on *Hennesey.* Tom Tully appeared on television as Inspector Grebb of *The Lineup* and Tom Starett of *Shane.* In addition, he appeared regularly on such television dramas as *Zane Grey Theater* and *Ford Theater.* Tully played character roles in numerous films including *The Caine Mutiny,* for which he was nominated for an Academy Award as Best Supporting Actor.

The Mortgage. October 24, 1952. Written by Les Crutchfield. Guest cast: Paula Winslow, Richard Beals, Harry Bartell, Jim Nusser, Joe DuVal, Lawrence Dobkin.

Caleb Andrews plans to foreclose on Ed Blake, who has been unable to make his mortgage payments since he broke his leg. Blake's wife and daughter try desperately to bring in a crop, but fail. When sympathetic townspeople raise the money to pay the debt off, Andrews refuses for he wants Ed's land. Matt and Chester hatch a plan to frustrate Caleb's greedy designs.

The Radio Programs

Jim Nusser appeared in the *Gunsmoke* television series as Louie Pheeters, the town drunk.

Overland Express. October 31, 1952. Written by John Meston. Guest cast: Lawrence Dobkin, Vic Perrin, Jim Nusser, Lou Krugman, Junius Matthews, Ralph Moody. Aired on television May 31, 1958.

After their horses are killed, Matt and Chester are forced to travel with their prisoner Jim Beaudry by stagecoach. Beaudry recognizes one of the stage passengers to be a wanted man, Ches Ryan, and he alerts Matt. When the stage is held up by Ryan's men, Beaudry is enlisted by the bandits. He then faces the dilemma of securing his escape, or helping Matt and the other passengers out of a tight spot.

Tara. November 7, 1952. Written by Norman Macdonnell. Guest cast: Sammie Hill, John Dehner, Vivi Janiss, Ralph Moody, Joe DuVal.

Tara Hantree, a young girl who was orphaned in a previous episode, "Home Surgery," is taken in by the Kells, a kindly couple. Kitty discovers that Tara has been keeping company with Jack Grace and asks Matt to intervene for Grace is a dangerous man. Matt tries to warn Tara, but he only succeeds in incurring her wrath. When the Kells voice their objection, Grace guns them down without remorse.

The Square Triangle. November 14, 1952. Written by Les Crutchfield. Guest cast: Lillian Buyeff, Harry Bartell, Lawrence Dobkin, Jack Kruschen.

Eva Morley is a married woman with her sights on other men. When she flirts with Red Larsen, Matt warns her to return to her husband and avoid trouble. He also confronts Larsen, but Larsen tells Matt that he feels sorry for how Eva is treated by her husband Hal. When Hal is found murdered, Red is the prime suspect. Matt finds, however, that Eva has another suitor who may be the culprit.

On television, Jack Kruschen was a regular on *Hong Kong*, *Busting Loose*, and *Webster*. His film career includes *The War of the Worlds*, *Lover Come Back*, and *McLintock*. In 1960 Kruschen was nominated for an Academy Award for Best Supporting Actor for his performance in *The Apartment*.

Fingered. November 21, 1952. Written by John Meston. Guest cast: Jeanette Nolan, Harry Bartell, Jack Kruschen, Paul DuBov, John McIntire. Aired on television November 23, 1957.

It seems that Jim Corbett's loneliness is over when he marries Lyla. When Lyla disappears Jim tells Matt that a party of Indians abducted her. Foul play is suspected when Matt sees a newly planted garden of columbines near Jim's house, especially since Jim's first wife also disappeared.

John McIntire appeared as a regular on such television programs as *Naked City*, *Wagon Train*, and *The Virginian*. On radio, he often performed with his wife Jeanette Nolan. His films include *The Asphalt Jungle, The Tin Star, Psycho, Elmer Gantry, Summer and Smoke,* and *Rooster Cogburn*.

Kitty. November 29, 1952. Written by Antony Ellis. Guest cast: John Dehner, Vivi Janiss, Mary Lansing, Bob Sweeney, Lawrence Dobkin.

Matt invites Kitty to a dance, however, she refuses for fear that the townsfolk would object. Matt is persistent and she relents. Kitty accompanies him to the dance, but is humiliated when the "good" people of Dodge insist that she leave. Matt takes off his badge to confront those who insulted her.

[365]

GUNSMOKE — III. THE PROGRAMS

Bob Sweeney was part of a comedy team with Hal March in the late 40s. On television Sweeney was a regular on *My Favorite Husband, Our Miss Brooks,* and *Fibber McGee and Molly,* where he played Fibber. In later years Sweeney went into producing and directing for such television series as *Hawaii Five-O, The Love Boat, Dynasty,* and *Fantasy Island.*

I Don't Know. December 6, 1952. Written by Antony Ellis. Guest cast: Richard Beals, John Dehner, Larry Dobkin, Lee Millar, Michael Ann Barrett.

Danny Birch is sent to town by his sister Lily to get Matt because their father has been shooting cattle and acting crazy. Upon arriving at the isolated cabin, Matt and Chester are met by the elder Birch brothers, Dave and Donald, who are angry with Lily for involving the law in their personal problems. The brothers disarm Matt and Chester, and send them on their way back to Dodge. En route the two encounter a dead man, and Matt and Chester set out to find the killer.

On television Richard Beals did voices for several animated series including *Frankenstein Jr. and the Impossibles, Birdman and the Galaxy Trio,* and *The Richie Rich Show.*

Post Martin. December 13, 1952. Written by Les Crutchfield. Guest cast: Sam Edwards, Ralph Moody, Jeanne Bates.

Catherine Blair arrives in Dodge from the East looking for her brother Martin. Matt denies knowing where Martin is, because Martin is also known as Boston Jack, and is awaiting trial for murder and cattle-rustling.

Sam Edwards appeared on television in the PBS children's series, *Villa Alegre.* Jeanne Bates played Nurse Wills on *Ben Casey* and Anne Peters on *Days of Our Lives.*

Christmas Story. December 20, 1952. Written by Antony Ellis. Guest cast: Larry Dobkin, Harry Bartell, John Dehner.

Forty miles from Dodge, Matt's horse breaks its leg. Matt is forced to walk and it looks like he will not make it back in time to spend Christmas Eve with Doc, Chester, and Kitty. Along the way, he meets a stranger on a sickly old nag, who offers Matt the opportunity of riding together. When it is apparent that Matt will be late, the stranger offers Matt his horse saying he will walk. Matt refuses and when they camp for the night, the stranger recounts his tragic story.

The Cabin. December 27, 1952. Written by John Meston. Guest cast: John Dehner, Harry Bartell, Vivi Janiss. Aired on television February 22, 1958.

Matt is caught in a severe blizzard and seeks refuge in a cabin. He is greeted not with hospitality, but by two killers, Hack and Alvie. The two men have been keeping Belle a prisoner in her own home, and have been terribly abusing her. They have already murdered her father and plan the same for Matt.

Westbound. January 3, 1953. Written by Les Crutchfield. Guest cast: Sam Edwards, Barney Phillips, Jim Nusser, John Dehner, Larry Dobkin, Tom Tully.

Chester and Matt go to Abilene to arrest murderer Jack Daggett. Matt is hoping to enlist the aid of his friend, sheriff Wild Bill Hickock. Unfortunately, Hickock is away on business and they must confront a hostile town, as well as a less than sympathetic constable who "is the law" in Hickock's absence. When they finally capture their quarry, Matt and Chester must still face the Dagget brothers, who are determined not to let their brother hang.

The Radio Programs

Word of Honor. January 10, 1953. Written by John Meston. Guest cast: John Dehner, Larry Dobkin, Harry Bartell. Aired on television October 1, 1955.

Jake Worth's son is kidnapped and held for ransom. The kidnappers call Doc to aid the young victim, after he is shot in the back while trying to escape. Unfortunately he dies, but Doc's life is spared when he gives his "word of honor" that he will not reveal the killers' identities. The distraught father gets wind of this, and accuses Doc and Matt of shielding the murderers.

Paid Killer. January 17, 1952. Written by Les Crutchfield. Guest cast: Harry Bartell, Larry Dobkin, Jack Kruschen, Ralph Moody.

Lawson Hale had been a big man in Abilene setting up illegal enterprises. When he comes to Dodge, Hale finds that Matt cannot be bought or intimidated. In response, Hale hires Ed Granger to assassinate Matt for $5000 in gold. The pressure on Matt is intense as he seeks his would-be assailant.

The Old Lady. January 24, 1953. Written by Kathleen Hite. Guest cast: Jeanette Nolan, Sam Edwards, Harry Bartell, John Dehner, Herb Vigran.

Ellen Henry lives alone on the prairie with her no-good son Luther. She is a mean woman, who shoots at Matt and Chester when they approach her homestead to water their horses. Since her husband died, Ellen has become "dried up, dead inside." She and Luther hate one another and when Luther is found dead, Matt suspects Ellen of the deed.

Herb Vibran played the semi-regular role of Judge Brooker on television's *Gunsmoke*. He was also a regular on *The Ed Wynn Show*. Kathleen Hite wrote for numerous television shows including *Falcon Crest, The Guns of Will Sonnett, Wagon Train,* and *The Waltons*.

Cavalcade. January 31, 1953. Written by Les Crutchfield. Guest cast: Larry Dobkin, Lou Krugman, Paul DuBov, Vivi Janiss.

Ed Hunter a sheriff from Virginia rides into town. He has in his possession a warrant for the arrest of Calvin Moore, who has finally been traced to Dodge. Moore killed a wealthy man, Roger Beauregard, 17 years ago in a duel over a young woman. When Hunter tells Matt that Moore was a physician and shows him the man's photograph, Matt is caught in an ethical dilemma. The photograph is of Doc Adams as a young man. The dumbfounded Matt denies ever having seen the wanted man. When Matt confronts Doc with the tale, his friend's secret past unfolds. Doc shot Beauregard in a fair duel but ran because he was an outsider and a Yankee. The young girl fled after him, and they were married in St. Louis. She died two months later of typhus. Matt realizes that despite Doc's innocence, the resolute sheriff from Richmond is bent on finding his man.

Cain. February 7, 1953. Rerun. First aired October 3, 1952. Guest cast: Harry Bartell, Larry Dobkin.

The Round-Up. February 14, 1953. Written by John Meston. Guest cast: James Nusser, Larry Dobkin, Lou Krugman, John Dehner, Harry Bartell. Aired on television September 29, 1956.

Matt wants to close down Front Street to prevent a swarm of rowdy cowhands from taking over the town. However, this move is very unpopular with the local merchants who want the cowboys' money. Matt calls in his old friend Zall Matlock to help him fend off the celebrating mob. In a mass of confusion and gunfire, Matt accidentally shoots Zall.

Meshougah. February 21, 1953. Written by Antony Ellis. Guest cast: Larry Dobkin, Lou Krugman, John Dehner, Vic Perrin, Bob Sweeney, Michael Ann Barrett, Ted Bliss.

Matt is delivering government papers to the little town of Pearceville, which has a population of 50. He and Chester find the town deserted and discover, too late, that it has been taken over by 11 desperadoes. Disarmed, Matt and Chester are imprisoned in the warehouse with the rest of the townsfolk and await their fate.

The title *Meshougah* is a Jewish word that means "crazy."

Trojan War. February 28, 1953. Written by Les Crutchfield. Guest cast: Lawrence Dobkin, Tom Tully, Paul DuBov, John Dehner, Harry Bartell, Louise (Lewis) Fitch.

Matt and Chester are having a quiet breakfast at Delmonico's when Matt recognizes the Pueblo Gang. Ed and Rio Parks and their companion Chuck Evans have been terrorizing the Arizona Territory, but since they have committed no crime in Dodge, Matt can only wait for the inevitable confrontation.

Louise Lewis appeared on the anthology series *Front Row Center.*

Absalom. March 7, 1953. Written by Les Crutchfield. Guest cast: Sam Edwards, John Dehner, Lawrence Dobkin, Harry Bartell, Charlotte Lawrence, Barney Phillips.

Texas cattleman King Mallor and his reckless son Billy ride into Dodge. Billy shoots up half the town and threatens to shoot up the rest before midnight. Matt intends to put a stop to Billy before any real trouble occurs by putting him in jail. However, he gets flack from businessman Kelby, who fears a loss in revenue. When King Mallor causes a ruckus after he finds Billy has been imprisoned, Matt jails him as well. Meddlesome Kelby steps in and has the mayor fix bail on the Mallors. When they are released, Billy storms through town with vengeance in his heart. He tries to shoot Matt, but instead, his stray bullets kill Nora Beal, a sweet young singer from Chicago.

Cyclone. March 14, 1953. Written by Les Crutchfield. Guest cast: Vivi Janiss, Harry Bartell, Lawrence Dobkin, Joe Cranston, Jerry Hausner.

Matt suspects foul play, when old man Bartlett's foreman, Ed, tells him that the Cyclone Ranch was sold to Jed Wade, a stranger from Texas. Although Ed did not actually see the Bartletts leave, he was told they left the county. Everybody knows that Bartlett put half his life into that ranch, so it seems unlikely he would sell. Matt decides to do some digging around, and he unearths more than he bargained for.

Joe Cranston was a regular on the television comedy, *Oh! Susanna.* Jerry Hausner appeared on television as O.D. Dunstall of *Valentine's Day* and Ricky Ricardo's agent on *I Love Lucy.* When asked at a recent radio convention of his experience with *Gunsmoke,* Hausner said he had never appeared on it owing to a conflict with Macdonnell. When this episode was brought to his attention he replied, "Maybe I'm wrong. Send me a copy."

Pussy Cats. March 21, 1953. Written by Antony Ellis. Guest cast: John Dehner, Tom Tully, Michael Ann Barrett, Jack Kruschen, Lawrence Dobkin.

A stranger named Jack Ferra is at the bar drinking heavily. The "lean, almost stringy man" with grey eyes and skin as dry as flint is accompanied by his wife Martha Lou. The two have been eluding someone, but have decided to face their nemesis in

The Radio Programs

Dodge. When the gunsmoke clears, Jack and Martha Lou are gone, and four men are left on the floor of the Texas Trail. Only Brad Acton is still breathing. With his dying words Acton tells Matt about the hold-up that he, Ferra, and the other men staged in California. Ferra and Martha Lou took off with the money, and the four dead men were out to stop them.

Quarter-Horse. March 28, 1953. Written by Norman Macdonnell. Guest cast: Lawrence Dobkin, Joe Kearns, Johnny McGovern, Harry Bartell, Lou Krugman.

While having some drinks at the Texas Trail, Ed Butler torments old man Thatcher about his new breed of quarter-horse. Thatcher has come up from Missouri with his new, funny-looking colts and Butler enjoys ribbing the old man saying his stock is "one-quarter horse and three-quarters what else?" Fed up with Butler's constant harranguing, Thatcher challenges him to a grudge race, and puts up his ranch against $4000 of Butler's money. Matt tries to dissuade the old man, but Thatcher insists that his horse might be funny looking and, "He's sleepy and he's quiet, but he can unwind like lightning."

Jayhawkers. April 4, 1953. Written by John Meston. Guest cast: Lawrence Dobkin, Harry Bartell, Sam Edwards, Jack Kruschen, Jim Nusser. Aired on television January 31, 1959.

Dolph Quince, an old friend of Matt's who is moving a herd of cattle from Texas to Kansas, has been having trouble with a vicious band of jayhawkers. Understandably his men are jittery, so he sends his foreman Phil Jacks to get Matt.

Gonif. April 11, 1953. Written by Antony Ellis. Guest cast: John Dehner, Lawrence Dobkin, Barney Phillips, Jack Kruschen.

Outlaw Frank Bissell and his gang are in Dodge and Matt wants them out. He gives them until sundown, but Bissell just laughs at Matt's threats and flings a five dollar gold piece his way. Bissell is an evil killer who has the "smile of the man who says one thing with his mouth and another with his eyes." Later, at the Texas Trail Kitty introduces a brand new song, "Home, Home on the Range," and Matt sits listening to it, waiting for the inevitable showdown.

Gonif is a Jewish word that means "thief."

Bum's Rush. April 18, 1953. Written by John Meston. Guest cast: John Dehner, Harry Bartell, Lawrence Dobkin, Lou Krugman.

Matt captures William Gorse and Orlo, and leads them back to Dodge to stand trial for the murder of a store clerk. The two men readily admit their guilt and head back peacefully. Matt realizes that Gorse and Orlo are a "couple of not very bright men who have had too much war." The two are not really bad men, but they are dangerous. After he locks them up, Matt is greeted at the Texas Trail by George Blaine, who swears the men are innocent. Blaine insists that he and his friends saw Orlo and Gorse leaving Kelly's stable at the time of the shooting, and that they could not possibly be guilty. Matt does not know what to make of the situation, but he feels that Blaine is up to no good.

The Soldier. April 25, 1953. Written by John Meston. Guest cast: Lawrence Dobkin, Harry Bartell, Vic Perrin, Paul Frees.

Over at the Texas Trail a soldier named Gallagher gets drunk and his friend Spear arrives to bring him back to the Fort. However, Gallagher will have nothing of it. He

GUNSMOKE — III. THE PROGRAMS

wants to stay and drink. Spear insists that if they are late, Captain Shaw will be furious and punish them severely. Gallagher reacts by starting a fight with Spear. Matt breaks up the fight and throws both of the men in jail, even though Kitty assures him that Spear was not responsible. The next morning, feeling somewhat guilty about his hasty judgement of Spear, Matt releases the two soldiers. He promises to ride over to the Fort the next day to straighten things out with Captain Shaw. However, Spear feels it is already too late to do anything. Spear's foreboding proves right, for when the men return to Shaw, he fines them two months pay and sentences them to one month of hard labor, which is only the beginning of the soldiers' troubles.

This show marked the show's first anniversary. Paul Frees was the "voice of doom" announcer on the radio shows *Suspense* and *Escape.* On television Frees played the voice of John Beresford Tipton, in *The Millionaire,* Boris Badenov on *The Bullwinkle Show,* John Lennon and George Harrison on *The Beatles* cartoon series, and Professor Ludwig Von Drake on *Disney.*

Tacetta. May 2, 1953. Written by John Meston. Guest cast: Tom Tully, Lawrence Dobkin, Paul DuBov, Lillian Buyeff.

Tacetta, a new dance hall hostess at the Texas Trail, is "shy as a flower," according to Kitty. Dorgan, a tough cowboy who has been buying Tacetta drinks all night, decides she is his personal property and will not let anyone else dance with her. However, two gunmen, Horn and Watson, want their turn on the dance floor with the new girl. Matt believes the men are just looking for an excuse to draw Dorgan into a gunfight, so he puts a stop to it. The three men are disarmed and told to leave town in the morning. When Tacetta is missing the next day, Matt suspects that Dorgan has abducted her against her will.

The Buffalo Hunter. May 9, 1953. Written by John Meston. Guest cast: Lawrence Dobkin, John Dehner, Harry Bartell, Richard Beals, William Oiler. Aired on television May 2, 1959.

Buffalo hunter Gatluf brings his skinner, Billy, into town. According to Gatluf, Billy fell into 60 pounds of hot lead, but Matt does not like the sound of Gatluf's story. After Billy dies, Gatluf refuses to pay for his burial. Upon talking to Tobe, one of Gatluf's men, Matt realizes Billy was murdered so that Gatluf would not have to pay him the $800 in wages he was due. Without proof, however, Matt can do nothing. Although Matt feels helpless, he believes a man like Gatluf, "would someday overplay his hand," and get his due. Gatluf is a big man with speckled eyes like turkey eggs, greedy, and "downright wicked about money." When young Yorky Kelly witnesses a grisly stabbing committed by Gatluf, Matt finally has the proof he has been waiting for. He and Chester ride out and follow a trail of death left by Gatluf. However, Indians find Gatluf first and when he is found dead, Matt comments that they left Gatluf to die, "Harder than any man I have ever seen."

The Big Con. May 16, 1953. Written by John Meston. Guest cast: Lawrence Dobkin, Harry Bartell, Ralph Moody, James Nusser, Joe Cranston, Peter Leeds, Paul DuBov. Aired on television May 3, 1958.

Banker Mr. Papp is duped into loaning Mr. Hook $20,000 for his poker hand: four aces and a ten. Unfortunately for Mr. Papp, the pot goes to a straight flush. Unable to recover the money, the distraught banker commits suicide. Since there is no proof that confidence man, Hook, and his two accomplices got the money by trickery, Matt bluffs them into running. Unfortunately, however, they take Doc hostage.

[370]

The Radio Programs

A 1966 film starring Joanne Woodward and Jason Robards, *Big Hand for the Little Lady*, originally titled *Big Deal at Dodge City*, uses a similar premise. Peter Leeds played the role of George Colton on the television comedy *Pete and Gladys*. He was also a regular on *The Betty White Show*, along with John Dehner.

Print Asper. May 23, 1953. Written by John Meston. Guest cast: Joseph Kearns, John Dehner, Sam Edwards. Aired on television May 23, 1959.

Old John Asper, a rancher who "knew the land the way a preacher knew the bible," asks attorney Rabb to transfer the title of his ranch to his two sons, Print and Will. However, the dishonest lawyer puts the title in his own name, and when Asper discovers the double-cross, he threatens to kill Rabb. The thief quickly corrects the transfer, and everything appears to have been resolved. Later, when Rabb is found murdered, Asper is the natural suspect. After Asper's alibi is confirmed, Matt surmises that Will or Print might be the culprit.

Fall Semester. May 30, 1953. Written by John Meston. Guest cast: John McIntire, Harry Bartell, John Dehner.

Lee Dorgen hands over his gun to Matt and asks to be locked up overnight. Lee believes he is just drunk enough to kill his foreman Jim Salter, but sober enough to know it. To prevent a killing, Matt obliges the rancher. Lee has lost over 150 head of cattle since last year, and he suspects Salter and his two helpers, Adams and Smith, of the crime. Matt decides to investigate the allegations.

Sundown. June 6, 1953. Written by William Conrad. Guest cast: John McIntire, Michael Ann Barrett, Lawrence Dobkin, John Dehner.

After several days of terrible weather the sky begins to clear. Matt and Chester decide to take a brisk ride over to old man Johnson's. On the way, they encounter a beautiful Indian woman racked with fever lying under an old Hackberry tree. The two manage to get her to Doc, but unfortunately, she dies. Matt discovers that she is wearing a gold wedding band, something an Arapahoe never wears. He decides to visit his friend Great Eagle, also of the Arapahoe tribe, to identify the girl, and to uncover the mystery surrounding her untimely demise.

William Conrad, radio's Matt Dillon, wrote this episode.

Spring Term. June 13, 1953. Written by John Meston. Guest cast: John Dehner, Vic Perrin, Harry Bartell, Lou Krugman. Aired on television December 15, 1956.

Shaw, an innocent man without an enemy in the world, is shot down on Front Street. After uttering the name "Stone," the assailant escapes down a dark alley. Shaw was similar in build to Matt and wore a hat of the same shape and color. Since it was dark, Matt surmises that Shaw was shot by mistake. He remembers a man named Stone who was hung a while back. Stone's partner Danch swore to get Matt, even though he had nothing to do with the lynching. Matt finds that a man answering Danch's description was seen hanging around the Texas Trail, a tall thin man, who once during a fight had his left ear chewed off.

Wind. June 20, 1953. Written by John Meston. Guest cast: Virginia Gregg, John Dehner, James Griffith. Aired on television March 21, 1959.

Matt returns to Dodge only to discover there was a killing at the Texas Trail the night before. Although the killing was in "self-defense," Matt decides to investigate. He finds out there is a new saloon girl in town, Dolly Varden, who claims to be from

St. Louis. Dolly has been making a great deal of money at the faro table lately. Not that she gambles herself, but Dolly is good luck to anyone she sits next to. Naturally, all the men want her to sit by them, and they are willing to pay her handsomely for this favor. Matt discovers that the fatal fight started when one cowboy offered Dolly more money than the man she was already sitting next to. Matt starts to piece the story together, and does not like what he hears. He suspects that Dolly and the new faro dealer, Frank Paris are in cahoots.

Flashback. June 27, 1953. Written by Les Crutchfield. Guest cast: Lawrence Dobkin, Sam Edwards, Joe DuVal, Lou Krugman.

Eighteen-year-old Brian Beck goes to see Matt. It seems his father Colonel Beck, who is a retired cavalry officer, runs the Lazy-B-Bar Ranch like the army. The colonel has been rough on his cowboys and, as a result, one of his men, Bud Stark, has threatened to kill the old commander. Brian wants to get a gun to protect his father, but Matt tells the youth to stay out of it. After a high-stakes poker game with gambler Cottonmouth, Stark is found dead, shot in the back and robbed of his $4000 winnings. Matt has several suspects to contend with: Cottonmouth, Brian, and the old colonel himself.

Dirt. July 4, 1953. Written by John Meston. Guest cast: Lawrence Dobkin, Sam Edwards, Joyce McCluskey, Joe Cranston, Elaine Williams, Pat McGeehan. Aired on television March 1, 1958.

Nat Siebert, a wealthy but raucous rancher, plans to marry Polly, a lady of refinement from Virginia. Although Polly truly has affection for Nat, her father and brother see Siebert merely as their chance to regain some of the luxury they once knew. Shortly before the wedding, Nat receives a note threatening his life, should he proceed with his plans to marry Polly. Matt tries to find someone with a motive, but comes up empty. After the ceremony Siebert is indeed shot in the back. As Matt trails the sniper, he comes upon a rundown cabin, inhabited by Crazy Beulah, a woman once scorned by Nat.

Elaine Williams played a beautiful but troubled nightclub singer in the pilot episode of *Trouble, Inc.*

Grass. July 11, 1953. Written by John Meston. Guest cast: Lawrence Dobkin, Ralph Moody, Harry Bartell. Aired on television November 29, 1958.

Harry Pope, a simple pig farmer who left Boston after the death of his wife, is convinced that Indians have been harrassing him. Matt believes otherwise and advises Pope to arm himself for the next "Indian" raid. Pope takes Matt's advice and when the "Indians" descend upon his ranch, he is prepared. However, after the hooting and hollering stop, trailhand Joe Carter, not an Indian, is left dead. It appears that Carter and Earl Brandt, under the misguided direction of their boss Honeyman, have been trying to scare Pope off his land. Now Brandt claims Pope shot Carter in cold-blood.

Wild West. July 18, 1953. Written by John Meston. Guest cast: Michael Ann Barrett, John McGovern, John Dehner, Joseph Kearns, Nestor Paiva. Aired on television February 15, 1958.

Matt finds young Yorky Kelly out on the prairie. The boy tells Matt a wild story about his father being abducted by two strangers in the middle of the night. Yorky further adds that his recently acquired stepmother Hattie is at the bottom of the plot. Matt sends for Chester and they search for Kelly. When they find the old man, he is near

The Radio Programs

death. Matt suspects that Hattie and two men, Webb and Cutter, plotted to kill Kelly for his ranch.

Character actor Nestor Paiva appeared in such films as *The Song of Bernadette, Humoresque, Mighty Joe Young, The Creature from the Black Lagoon, Les Girls, The Left-Handed Gun, Can-Can,* and *The Four Horsemen of the Apocalypse.*

Hickock. July 25, 1953. Written by John Meston. Guest cast: John Dehner, John McIntire, Lawrence Dobkin, Joe DuVal, Harry Bartell.

Matt's old friend from Abilene, sheriff Bill Hickock, sends him a telegram to make sure two gunmen, Teeters and Gridler, stay in Dodge until he arrives. Hickock is bringing Mr. Trimble, an eyewitness to a murder presumably committed by Teeters and Gridler. However, Matt finds it increasingly difficult to keep the gunmen in Dodge, since he cannot arrest them without evidence.

Boy. August 1, 1953. Written by Norman Macdonnell. Guest cast: Lawrence Dobkin, John Dehner, Charlotte Lawrence.

Webb Johnson buys the Long Horn Saloon. The new owner stocks it full of pretty girls straight from St. Louis, including Miss Olive Hasty, who Chester takes a particular interest in. Webb tries to convince Miss Kitty to work for him too, but she refuses. Matt has a bad feeling about Webb. He does not like the man, and his intuition proves correct. Old Sy Cook rides into Dodge looking for a man he calls Sam Williams. It seems this Williams was a Missouri raider who robbed Cook's farm and raped his daughter. Webb fits Williams' description to a tee.

Sky. August 8, 1953. Written by John Meston. Guest cast: Vivi Janiss, Mary Lansing, Jim Nusser, Helen Kleeb, Ralph Moody, Lou Krugman, Sam Edwards. Aired on television February 14, 1959.

Saloon girl Frog-mouth Kate is sweet on young Billy Daunt, however, the feeling is not quite mutual. Kate is old enough to be his mother, but keeps talking about her plans to go to St. Louis with Billy, once she saves up enough money. Unfortunately, her plan never comes to fruition. Poor Kate is robbed of her life savings and is fatally shot. Billy claims he is innocent and leaves town, but Matt and Chester are in close pursuit. Billy's panic makes him "as near brainless as a man can get," and when Matt finally catches up with him, there is another murder for Billy to account for.

Helen Kleeb appeared on television as Miss Claridge of *Harrigan and Son* and as Mamie Baldwin of *The Waltons.*

Moon. August 15, 1953. Written by John Meston. Guest cast: Vic Perrin, John Dehner, Harry Bartell, Vivi Janiss. Aired on television May 11, 1957.

Charlie Brewer wins $750 from dealer Vint James at the Black Jack table. Vint is usually a crooked dealer but was forced to play straight due to the presence of Brewer's good friend, gunman Jack Saulter. However, Vint is not one to sit idly by and watch his money walk out the door. He convinces his girlfriend, saloon girl Nan Mellor, to lure Brewer into the alley. Once there, Vint clubs him to death and steals back the money. Vint has assured Nan that with this money he will take her to St. Louis. Nan is desperate to escape her life as a saloon girl. Burdened with a worthless husband and a six-year-old daughter she sees Vint as her only way out. As Matt investigates the murder, he realizes what has transpired. However, Matt's hands are tied, since there are no witnesses. He also has to contend with Brewer's buddy Saulter, who is itching for revenge.

Gone Straight. August 22, 1953. Written by John Meston. Guest cast: John Dehner, Tom Tully, Harry Bartell, Paul DuBov, Helen Kleeb, James Nusser. Aired on television February 9, 1957.

Parker arrives in Dodge from New Mexico with a warrant for the arrest of Dane Shaw. Shaw rode with Billy the Kid, but left the gang two years ago. Rumor has it that Shaw is living in Tascosa where he is presumably starting his own gang. When Matt and Chester ride out there they meet the owner of the Red Bear saloon, Nat Trimble. Trimble is a good man, and a respectable citizen, husband and father. He is the man responsible for the new school house that is being built, the first one in Tascosa. He is also Dane Shaw.

Jesse. August 29, 1953. Written by John Meston. Guest cast: Sam Edwards, Larry Dobkin, Harry Bartell, John Dehner. Aired on television October 19, 1957.

Young Jesse Pruitt makes a poor choice in traveling companions when he teams up with Billy Stapp. Along the way to Dodge the two stop to have dinner with a lonely old prairie trapper. After partaking of the old man's hospitality, Billy shoots him in the face. Jesse is appalled, but stays with the murderer, who promises to help young Jesse find his father's killer. Unbeknownst to Jesse, the man responsible for his father's death is Matt Dillon.

SECOND SEASON

The Sutler. September 5, 1953. Written by John Meston. Guest cast: John Dehner, Harry Bartell, Joseph Kearns, James Nusser, Juli Conger.

Jim Vail and his partner Sy plan to steal rifles from the army. Vail has so ingratiated himself with the major of Fort Dodge, that the major plans to fire the fort's current sutler, Will Jonas, in favor of Vail. A sutler is to the army what a general storekeeper is to civilization. While in Dodge unloading supplies, Jonas meets Matt and explains the difficulties he has been having. He also relates that Vail in reality is Jim Lindsa, a renegade who sold weapons to the Indians. Matt goes to the fort and tries to intercede on Jonas' behalf, however, the major doubts Jonas' tale.

Prairie Happy. September 12, 1953. Written by John Meston. Guest cast: John Dehner, Lawrence Dobkin, James Nusser, Vic Perrin, Lillian Buyeff. Aired on television June 30, 1956.

Matt and Chester return to Dodge after a brief absence and find the citizens up in arms over an impending Pawnee attack. Mr. Green has sold more ammunition in one week, than he sells in a whole month. Everyone is buzzing about the Indians and demanding that Matt organize the townsfolk, so that they will be prepared for the onslaught. When Matt tries to find out about the imminent raid, the only answer he gets is, "It's common knowledge." As he digs further into the mystery he discovers that Tewksbury, a crazy old man who has lived with the Indians most of his life, has been spreading false rumors of Indian atrocities.

There Was Never a Horse. September 19, 1953. Written by John Meston. Guest cast: Lawrence Dobkin, John Dehner, Ralph Moody. Aired on television May 16, 1959.

Gunfighter Kin Creed gets into a fight with a drunken pig-farmer and kills him in "self-defense." Matt is aware of Creed's reputation, but is unable to arrest him. Creed would like to advance his reputation by killing a U.S. Marshal, but Matt refuses to

The Radio Programs

allow Creed to goad him into a fight, and the townsfolk begin to think he is afraid to stand up to the killer.

Fawn. September 26, 1953. Written by John Meston. Guest cast: Helen Kleeb, John Dehner, Lawrence Dobkin, Edgar Barrier, Leo Curley. Aired on television April 4, 1959.

Matt and Chester journey to Fort Dodge to pick up a "prisoner" to be held in Dodge until a Mr. Roger Phillips from back East arrives. Matt is surprised to find that there is no prisoner, but only a Mrs. Phillips, who has been a captive of the Cheyennes for the past ten years. She is accompanied by an eight-year-old Indian girl, Gray Fawn, the daughter of chief Black Horn. Dillon brings Mrs. Phillips and Fawn back to Dodge, where he must defend them from the town's prejudice.

Edgar Barrier is a veteran of radio, stage and screen. His film credits include *The Phantom of the Opera, Macbeth,* and *Irma La Douce.*

How to Kill a Friend. October 3, 1953. Written by John Meston. Guest cast: John Dehner, Harry Bartell, Lawrence Dobkin. Aired on television November 22, 1958.

Two crooked gamblers, Ben Corder and Harry Duggan, arrive in Dodge and attempt to bribe Matt. Having failed, one of them takes a pot-shot at Matt, but misses. Although Matt did not see his assailant, he has little doubt as to his identity and he orders Corder and Duggan to take the next stage out of town. Several weeks later, however, the gamblers return accompanied by a paid assassin, Toque Morlan, who was once a good friend of Matt's.

How to Die for Nothing. October 10, 1953. Written by John Meston. Guest cast: John Dehner, Vic Perrin, Harry Bartell, Lawrence Dobkin. Aired on television June 23, 1956.

Two drunken trailhands, Ned and Zack, ride into Dodge for an evening of revelry. Their idea of a good time is to shoot up the town, and when Matt tries to disarm them, Ned makes the mistake of drawing and Matt is forced to kill him. Howard Bulow, Ned's brother, arrives sometime later bent on revenge. Matt jails him to prevent further bloodshed but trail-boss, Will Jacklin demands his release. He gives Matt an ultimatum: if Bulow is not released he and his boys will tear the town apart.

Yorky. October 17, 1953. Written by John Meston. Guest cast: Richard Beals, Lawrence Dobkin, John Dehner. Aired on television February 18, 1956.

Yorky, a young white boy who was raised by Arapahoes, is victimized by horse thieves. The young brave decides to seek vengeance outside the law, which results in his being shot by Abe Brandt. Matt aids the boy, realizing that Yorky's actions were the result of ignorance of the white man's law, rather than criminal intent.

The Buffalo Hunter. October 24, 1953. Rerun. Guest cast: John Dehner, Tom Tully, Jack Edwards, Richard Beals, Louis Jean Heydt.

How to Kill a Woman (Road Ranch). October 31, 1953. Written by John Meston. Guest cast: John Dehner, Lawrence Dobkin, Jack Edwards. Aired on television November 30, 1957.

The stage is robbed and a passenger is shot. Stage driver Jim Buck tells Matt that he suspects gunman Nat Pilcher of the crime. Nat was seen talking to Jesse Dagget, the owner of the waystation, shortly before the robbery and Jim adds that he believes

GUNSMOKE — III. THE PROGRAMS

Dagget may also have been involved in the hold-up. Matt gets nowhere with Dagget who tells him, "Everyman's got to kill his own snakes." He is a man with a past and Matt intends to get to the bottom of the mystery.

Stolen Horses. November 7, 1953. Written by Norman Macdonnell. Guest cast: Helen Kleeb, Ralph Moody, James Nusser, Paul Frees. Aired on television April 8, 1961.

After an evening of steaks, beer, and catfish stew, Matt and Chester ride over to Jim Redigo's ranch. Matt plans on buying a horse from young Jim. They arrive to find the ranch deserted. Old Jed Cuff, who worked for Jim, informs Matt that two men murdered the young rancher and stole his horses.

Professor Lute Bone. November 14, 1953. Written by John Meston. Guest cast: John Dehner, Barney Phillips, Lawrence Dobkin, Paul DuBov. Aired on television January 7, 1956.

Doc campaigns to have quack medicine-man Lute Bone run out of town. The cure-all tonic Bone sold nearly kills a baby. In addition, Doc discovers that the elixir contains alcohol and opium, making it addictive and lethal.

Custer. November 21, 1953. Written by John Meston. Guest cast: Sam Edwards, John Dehner. Aired on television September 22, 1956.

Matt and Chester track rustler Joe Trimble, who has tortured and hung an innocent old rancher named Granby. When Trimble turns out to be a deserter from the army, his major arrives to put him under military arrest. Matt insists on having Trimble tried in Hayes City first, and although the major vehemently opposes the action, Matt is adamant. Due to lack of evidence, Trimble is found innocent of the civil charges, and due to a shortage of manpower, the major is forced to reenlist the scoundrel instead of courtmartialing him.

Kick Me. November 28, 1953. Written by John Meston. Guest cast: Lawrence Dobkin, Ralph Moody, Harry Bartell, Byron Kane, Frank Gerstle. Aired on television January 26, 1957.

A bank robber masquerading as a respectable citizen of Dodge is thwarted in his plans by Tobeel, an embittered Indian upon whom he perpetrated a cruel joke. As a result, the robber kills Tobeel, but the Indian's death is the catalyst for his own doom.

The Lamb. December 5, 1953. Written by John Meston. Guest cast: Vic Perrin, Lawrence Dobkin, Harry Bartell, Herb Ellis.

Dubie Coots, a poor, polite, soft-spoken drifter arrives in Dodge and old Casey mistakes him for notorious gunfighter, Lou Medallon. Once word gets around that Medallon is in town, the drifter is treated with the utmost respect. All goes well for Coots, until Ab Fisher arrives to claim the $1000 bounty on Medallon's head, dead or alive.

The Cast. December 12, 1953. Written by John Meston. Guest cast: Paul Frees, Sam Edwards, Tom Tully. Aired on television December 6, 1958.

Sheeley Tucker hates doctors. When his wife dies after Doc operates to remove a nail from her stomach, Sheeley tries to shoot him. As a consequence, Matt steps in to arrest Sheeley. Fate, however, plays a strange twist when Sheeley's favorite horse breaks a leg. Instead of shooting the animal, Doc offers to cast the broken limb.

The Radio Programs

In this episode Doc, normally played by Howard McNear, was played by Paul Frees.

Big Girl Lost. December 19, 1953. Written by John Meston. Guest cast: Joyce McCluskey, Harry Bartell, Vic Perrin, Lawrence Dobkin. Aired on television April 20, 1957.
Phillip Locke comes to Dodge looking for his ex-fiancee Laura Simmons. Matt runs some interference when Laura chooses not to see Locke. However, Locke does not take too kindly to this and threatens to kill Matt unless Laura's whereabouts are revealed. When Matt refuses to heed his warnings, Locke hires a gunman named Noonan to do his dirty work.

The Guitar. December 26, 1953. Written by John Meston. Guest cast: Vic Perrin, John Dehner, Lawrence Dobkin, Harry Bartell. Aired on television July 21, 1956.
Weed Pindle, a simple-minded, guitar strumming wanderer, plucks his way into the hearts of Dodge City's barflies. Pindle, an ex-soldier who cared not which side he fought on, is set upon by two sadistic cowboys who decide that he fought on the wrong side during the Civil War. The bullies torment poor Pindle, mutilate his beloved burro, break his guitar, and attempt to lynch him.
The special guitar music for this episode was played by Al Hendrickson.

Stage Holdup. January 2, 1954. Written by John Meston. Guest cast: Vic Perrin, John Dehner, Lawrence Dobkin. Aired on television October 25, 1958.
Two masked men, Charlie and Jermo, steal $2000 from the stage on which Matt is a passenger. One of the victims draws a derringer and wounds Charlie, but Charlie returns his fire and kills the man. In addition to the two, a third accomplice is hiding in the bushes with a rifle waiting to assist his partners. Matt makes it a personal, as well as a professional project, to capture the three bandits.

Joke's on Us. January 9, 1954. Written by John Meston. Guest cast: John Dehner, Helen Kleeb, Sam Edwards, Ted Bliss, Herb Ellis. Aired on television March 15, 1958.
Ranchers Jake, Duval, and Benson have been missing horses lately, so when they come upon Tillman with some of Jake's horses, they assume the worst. Tillman explains that he found the horses roaming loose and was rounding them up to return to their rightful owners. His friends, however, say he is lying and lynch him. Moments later, another rancher arrives and corroborates Tillman's story. The men are upset, but take it in their stride saying, "The joke's on us." Mrs. Tillman and her son, Cleb, however, are not so willing to ignore this great injustice and revenge is on their agenda.

The Bear. January 16, 1954. Written by John Meston. Guest cast: Lawrence Dobkin, John Dehner, Lou Krugman, James Nusser. Aired on television February 28, 1959.
Dillon tries unsuccessfully to avert bloodshed when Mike Blocker, a good natured bear of a man, finally loses his temper with Joe Plummer. Plummer has been playing a series of harmful practical jokes on Blocker and his fiancee Tilda, owing to the fact that Plummer once dated her.

Nina. January 23, 1954. Written by Norman Macdonnell. Guest cast: Vic Perrin, Lawrence Dobkin, Lillian Buyeff, James Eagle.

Army scout Cuff Peters arrives in Dodge with Nina his Mexican wife. They have come up from Texas and are headed for Fort Wallace. The couple stop at the Long Horn Saloon, where Nina retires to the ladies parlor and Cuff sidles up to the bar for a drink. Unfortunately, trouble rears its ugly head in the form of Hank Lawson, who resents Mexicans in Dodge. A fight ensues and Hank is roughed up a bit. Although Matt suggests that Peters move on to Fort Dodge to avoid further trouble, the couple is forced to remain in town due to Nina's ill health. Doc discovers the cause of Nina's ailment: she is expecting a baby. Knowing that Nina will be well enough to travel in a few weeks, Cuff heads to Fort Wallace leaving Nina in the care of widow Helgassen. When Hank sees Nina in town buying supplies, he spooks her horses, causing her to miscarry.

Gunsmuggler. January 30, 1954. Written by John Meston. Guest cast: John Dehner, Lawrence Dobkin, Harry Bartell, Barney Phillips, Jack Edwards. Aired on television September 27, 1958.

A family of homesteaders is massacred by the Pawnees with illegal arms bought from white men. Matt and a stubborn army officer Major Evans lock horns when they cannot agree on who should be responsible for tracking the smugglers.

Jack Edwards appeared as Johnny Roberts in the television series, *One Man's Family*.

Big Broad. February 6, 1954. Written by John Meston. Guest cast: Virginia Gregg, Vic Perrin, John Dehner. Aired on television April 21, 1956.

Matt has his share of trouble when Lena Wave arrives in town accompanied by mousy gambler Emmett Fitzgerald. Lena uses her six-foot frame, her 200 pounds of uninhibited strength, and her quick gun to create quite a problem in Dodge.

The Killer. February 13, 1954. Written by John Meston. Guest cast: Lawrence Dobkin, Howard Culver, Vic Perrin, Richard Deacon. Aired on television May 19, 1956.

Crego, an unscrupulous frontier vagrant has a reputation for inciting people to violence and then killing them in "self-defense." While in Dodge, Crego continues with his strange penchant for bloodshed. He crosses paths with a young cowboy named Jesse Hill and ultimately with Matt Dillon.

Howard Culver played Mark Dillon in the original pilot program, *Mark Dillon Goes to Gouge Eye,* broadcast July 15, 1949. In addition, Mr. Culver was frequently seen as Howie, the Dodge House hotel clerk on television's *Gunsmoke*. Richard Deacon is a familiar face on television. He appeared in such series as *The Charlie Farrell Show, Leave It to Beaver,* and *B.J. and the Bear.* However, he is probably best recognized as the bald headed, bespectacled Melvin Cooley of *The Dick Van Dyke Show.* His long list of film credits include *My Sister Eileen, My Man Godfrey, The Solid Gold Cadillac,* and *Enter Laughing.*

Last Fling. February 20, 1954. Written by John Meston. Guest cast: John Dehner, Ralph Moody, Helen Kleeb. Aired on television March 23, 1957.

Two aging sodbusters, John Peavy and Nelligan Rives, come to Dodge for a last fling. The two old sots proceed to annoy Kitty, who threatens to shoot them if they do not leave her alone. When John Peavy is shot in the neck, he accuses Kitty of the deed and threatens retribution. However, Kitty denies any involvement in the shooting. When someone takes a pot-shot at Kitty, Matt decides to investigate the seemingly harmless old cronies.

The Radio Programs

Bad Boy. February 27, 1954. Written by John Meston. Guest cast: John Dehner, Paul DuBov, Sam Edwards, Charles Bastin.

Twenty-year-old Tom Vickers and his hired hand, Blade, get good and drunk. The two men have a brawl over Kitty, and Tom winds up in jail. Matt breaks the news to Dolph Vickers, Tom's father, who takes it in his stride. Although Dolph is a good man, his son is easily led astray. In the company of shifty Blade, Tom is headed for trouble. Dolph is a cattleman who has been losing a lot of stock, and when his men kill a rustler, Matt sets out to investigate.

The Gentleman. March 6, 1954. Written by John Meston. Guest cast: John Dehner, Harry Bartell, Eleanore Tanin. Aired on television June 7, 1958.

Matt tries to prevent trouble when a gambler from Philadelphia named Marcus France falls in love with saloon girl Mavis McCloud. Tiller Evans, a bully who makes a habit of beating poor Mavis, considers her his personal property. Since Mavis is in love with France and not Tiller, Matt suggests the couple leave town to avoid bloodshed. However, France refuses to leave and insists on meeting his opponent head on.

Confederate Money. March 13, 1954. Written by John Meston. Guest cast: Vic Perrin, James Ogg, Harry Bartell, Barney Phillips.

Young Neil Butler is on a drinking binge. Egged on by a stranger, Lee Shinn, Neil is knocked out by Sam the barkeep. When Neil's boss Fate Ender finds out about the boy's drinking spree, he fires him. Unbeknownst to all involved, Lee Shinn is out to settle an old grudge with Ender.

Old Friend. March 20, 1954. Written by John Meston. Guest cast: John Dehner, Lawrence Dobkin, Vic Perrin.

Gambler Ben Corder arrives in Dodge and tries to bribe Matt with one quarter of his gambling profits. Matt refuses and Ben attempts to assassinate him. Having failed at both bribery and murder, Ben is run out of town. However, a few weeks later he returns accompanied by Toque Morlan, a paid killer who at one time was Matt's friend. Ben has paid Toque $300 to kill the lawman.

This is the same plot and characters as in *How to Kill a Friend* aired October 3, 1953, but in the original there were two gamblers.

Blood Money. March 27, 1954. Written by John Meston. Guest cast: Harry Bartell, James Nusser, John Dehner. Aired on television September 28, 1957.

Joe Harp finds Harry Speener out on the prairie, after he is thrown by his horse. Speener has a broken leg and Joe drags him to safety. Matt and Chester happen upon the two men and help them back to Dodge. After six weeks in town, the concensus is that there is no finer man around than Joe Harp and no meaner one than Harry Speener. When Speener discovers that Harp is a wanted man, he repays Harp's kindness by killing him for the $500 reward.

Mr. and Mrs. Amber. April 3, 1954. Written by John Meston. Guest cast: John Dehner, Ralph Moody, Larry Dobkin, Harry Bartell, James Nusser, Helen Kleeb, Frances Drew. Aired on television August 4, 1956.

Neil Amber is caught stealing a sack of seeds from Jonas' store. The poor sodbuster is trying to eke out a meager existence after a run of bad luck. Matt pays for the seeds and sends the weary farmer on his way. Later, cattleman Pete Fletcher accuses Mrs. Amber of stealing a calf. Mrs. Amber denies the accusation, but the whole experience leaves her a shattered woman. The truth is that Jim Baird, under the direction of Fletcher, tried to frame Mrs. Amber because Fletcher wants the couple's land.

Greater Love. April 10, 1954. Written by John Meston. Guest cast: John Dehner, Joyce McCluskey, Frank Gerstle, Ralph Moody. Aired on television December 1, 1956.

Three men hold up the stage and kill a passenger. While attempting to escape, two of the bandits are wounded, Howard Brand and Blake. Blake and a third robber, Jed Butler, drop Brand off at his farm. While Mrs. Brand tends to her fatally wounded husband, Butler kidnaps Doc to treat Blake.

What the Whiskey Drummer Heard. April 17, 1954. Written by John Meston. Guest cast: Edgar Barrier, John Dehner, Vic Perrin. Aired on television April 27, 1957.

Whiskey salesman Wilbur Hawkins who "even when he's standing still you got the feeling he was walking sideways like a crab," tells Matt a bizarre story. Hawkins claims that he overheard one man offer another man $300 to kill Matt. This leaves Matt rather jumpy, especially after someone takes a pot-shot at him. To bring the assailant out into the open, he sends Chester around town spreading the news that Matt Dillon is dead.

Murder Warrant. April 24, 1954. Written by John Meston. Guest cast: John Dehner, Sam Edwards, Lawrence Dobkin, Joe DuVal, James Nusser. Aired on television April 18, 1959.

Jake Harbin arrives in Dodge with a warrant from Sheriff Ben Goddard of Baker City for the arrest of Lee Prentice. Lee is wanted dead or alive for the murder of Jim Turner. Old man Turner, Jim's father, runs Baker City as well as Sheriff Goddard, and even though Lee killed Jim in self-defense, there is no way he could have a fair trial there. Although, Lee has lived in Dodge only for a short time, he is well-liked and has become a respected member of the community. Matt formulates a plan, aided by the connivance of some leading citizens, to save Lee.

Cara. May 1, 1954. Written by John Meston. Guest cast: Harry Bartell, Jill Jarmyn, Vic Perrin, John Dehner. Aired on television July 28, 1956.

Cara, an old girlfriend of Matt's, arrives from St. Louis and takes a job at the Texas Trail. Soon after her arrival Sheriff Benson from Wichita warns Matt that Jack Tolliver and his gang are headed for Dodge. Tolliver usually sends a member of his gang to "look things over for a week or two." The accomplice is 5'7" tall with black hair and hazel eyes, "a right pretty woman," a description that fits Cara to a tee. Matt realizes that Cara's visit to Dodge is not to rekindle an old romance, but to case the town for her current boyfriend, Tolliver.

The Constable. May 8, 1954. Written by John Meston. Guest cast: Jack Kruschen, John Dehner, Joseph Kearns, Fred MacKaye, Vic Perrin. Aired on television May 30, 1959.

Dodge's businessmen hire Willard, an ill-equipped constable, to handle the law in Dodge when they disagree with Matt's policy regarding some rowdy Texas cowboys. Fearful that Matt will destroy the town's economy with his tough tactics, they curtail his activities to matters outside the town limits. When word gets out that Dodge is now an "open town" all the scum and riff-raff within a hundred miles arrive to have a grand old time.

The Radio Programs

The Indian Horse. May 15, 1954. Written by Norman Macdonnell. Guest cast: Harry Bartell, Ralph Moody, Paul Savage, John Dehner.

Colonel Benson sends Lt. Flagg into Dodge to extend an official invitation to Matt to attend the horse races. The Colonel feels that having a peace officer on hand will discourage the civilian element from shooting one another. The object of the race is to win money, and the horses of the cavalry are seldom beaten. Sy Pilcher loses everything, when he bets $500 in silver that his mare can outrace Lt. Flagg's horse. Flagg is beating everyone in sight and there is but one more challenger: an old Indian named Howling Dog who is riding stark naked on a mangy old nag.

Paul Savage, one of the actors in this segment, went on to become a script consultant for the television show as well as one of its most prominent writers.

Monopoly. May 22, 1954. Written by John Meston. Guest cast: Joseph Kearns, Jack Kruschen, Herb Ellis, Vic Perrin. Aired on television October 4, 1958.

Bob Adams is jailed for drunkenness and is released the next morning. He and the other freighters were celebrating their selling out to a man named Ivy, who arrived from St. Louis. Ivy bought them all out, at a price they could not refuse. The only man who ignored Ivy's generous offer was Joe Trimble. This ruins Ivy's plans to eliminate all competition, and his bodyguard, Cam Spiegel, is getting trigger happy.

Feud. May 29, 1954. Written by John Meston. Guest cast: Virginia Gregg, John Dehner, Lawrence Dobkin.

Ozark mountain man Luke Humberg arrives in Dodge looking for Hank Witherspoon. Luke and Hank are the only remaining members of two feuding families and Luke plans to kill Hank. When Matt finds out, he tries to prevent a killing. However, both men are determined to settle their differences despite Matt's interference.

The same story was aired December 25, 1955 under the title *Twelfth Night.*

The Blacksmith. June 5, 1954. Written by Norman Macdonnell. Guest cast: John Dehner, Jeanne Bates, Lou Krugman, Vic Perrin. Aired on television September 17, 1960.

Dodge's good-natured German blacksmith, Emil, takes a mail-order bride named Gretchen. During the wedding ceremony a local rancher named Tolman disrupts the party. Later that evening Tolman lures Emil away from his home and burns it to the ground. Infruriated, the slow to anger blacksmith finally explodes.

The Cover Up. June 12, 1954. Written by John Meston. Guest cast: Joseph Kearns, Paul Savage, Helen Kleeb, Clayton Post. Aired on television January 12, 1957.

Defenseless homesteaders are being murdered in their isolated cabins by a mysterious shot-gun wielding killer on wealthy Sam Baxter's land. When Matt arrests Baxter for the murders, another homesteader is slain, and Matt must reassess the situation.

Going Bad. June 19, 1954. Written by John Meston. Guest cast: Sam Edwards, Harry Bartell, Edmund Penney, Vivi Janiss.

Young Dave Robbins holds a grudge against all lawmen. His father was killed by a dishonest sheriff, so Dave decides that all lawmen are bad. While in Teeter's barber shop, Dave threatens Matt. Matt calls his bluff, and things settle down. However, Teeters tells the story all over town, making the boy a laughing stock. When Dave hooks up with ruffian Luke Quiller, Matt foresees trouble. It comes sooner than Matt expects, when poor Teeters is found murdered.

GUNSMOKE — III. THE PROGRAMS

Claustrophobia. June 26, 1954. Written by John Meston. Guest cast: Vic Perrin, Lawrence Dobkin, Jack Kruschen, John Dehner. Aired on television January 25, 1958.

Hog-farmer Olie Ridger is being driven off his land by greedy, murderous cattlemen. They have already killed Bob Riley and now they intend on getting rid of Olie. While Olie and his best friend Jim Branch are enjoying the pleasures of Dodge, the killers burn Olie's wagon, and shoot all his hogs and his mule. Olie is not one to stand by after such an incident, and violence erupts.

Word of Honor. July 3, 1954. Rerun. Guest cast: Harry Bartell, Larry Dobkin, John Dehner.

This episode marked the end of *Gunsmoke* as a sustaining series.

Hack Prine. July 5, 1954. Written by John Meston. Guest cast: John Dehner, Lawrence Dobkin, Vic Perrin, Harry Bartell. Aired on television April 28, 1956.

After being away from Dodge for almost a month, Matt returns with his prisoner Lee Trumbull. They are greeted by Dolph Trumbull who vows to free his brother. Later, at the Alaferganza, Dolph buys drinks for the crowd in the hope of inciting a mob to break his brother out of jail. Matt quells the riot and closes the saloon for the night. The next day he sees Dolph in the company of Hack Prine, a hired gun and an old friend of Matt's, who had once saved his life.

Gunsmoke is now a commercial series sponsored by Liggett & Myers Tobacco Company for Chesterfield. *Hack Prine* was the pilot episode for the television series.

Texas Cowboys. July 12, 1954. Written by John Meston. Guest cast: Harry Bartell, Vic Perrin, John Dehner, Lawrence Dobkin. Aired on television April 5, 1958.

Matt threatens to close Front Street, when 17 unruly Texan cowboys headed by Tulley their trail boss, refuse to identify the murderer of Bud Collin. Realizing that Matt is serious about keeping the juiced-up cowboys from Dodge's pleasure palaces, Tulley hands over his cook Sam Peeples, swearing that he is the killer. Sam has been beaten into a confession by the rowdy cowboys, and unless Matt can prove otherwise, the innocent old man will hang.

The Queue. July 19, 1954. Written by John Meston. Guest cast: Edgar Barrier, Lawrence Dobkin, Paul DuBov, John Dehner. Aired on television December 3, 1955.

Two ruffians, Cliff Braden and Howard Rabb, take it upon themselves to torment Chen Wong, a young Chinese man who is new to Dodge. When the two cut off Chen's pigtail (queue), Chen is terribly disgraced and he has but two choices. He can wait until it grows back before returning to China to claim his bride, or he can take revenge upon the men who dishonored him.

Matt for Murder (How to Catch a Marshal). July 26, 1954. Written by John Meston. Guest cast: John Dehner, Vic Perrin, James Nusser. Aired on television September 13, 1958.

Matt is framed on a murder charge by crooked gambler Red Samples, and finds that his old friend Wild Bill Hickock is being sent to arrest him. He is accused of killing Samples' partner, Lou Price. Samples has gone to the trouble of paying Jim Huggins $500 to swear that Matt murdered Price and has also promised the perjurer an additional $500 after he testifies at the trial. Matt is relieved of his badge, but Hickock's trust in him plus Doc's old-fashioned truth serum pentathol in the form of whiskey, give Matt the edge he needs to crack Samples' case.

The Radio Programs

No Indians. August 2, 1954. Written by John Meston. Guest cast: Lawrence Dobkin, Joseph Kearns, Harry Bartell, Vic Perrin, John Dehner. Aired on television December 8, 1956.

Three settler families are massacred, including women and children. Captain Starr believes it to be the work of Pawnees, since the victims were scalped and robbed of their horses. However, Matt believes otherwise. All the victims were shot outside their cabins and if Indians had been around they would have taken cover. In addition, Pawnees do not waste ammunition, and would have used arrows if possible. Finally, of the boys killed, two were 12-year-olds, and it is a Pawnee custom to raise young boys to become braves. Matt surmises that the forays were made by white men masquerading as Indians, and he and Chester set a trap for the killers.

Joe Phy. August 9, 1954. Written by John Meston. Guest cast: Ralph Moody, Vic Perrin, John Dehner. Aired on television January 4, 1958.

Matt and Chester journey to Elkader in search of outlaw Carey Post. When they arrive they discover that the town is run by a tough, phoney, marshal Joe Phy. Matt is concerned that Post will not return to Elkader as long as Phy is in charge and devises a scheme to eliminate Phy, aided by an old-timer named Cicero Grimes.

Mavis McCloud. August 16, 1954. Written by John Meston. Guest cast: Harry Bartell, Eleanore Tanin, Sam Edwards, John Dehner. Aired on television October 26, 1957.

Mavis McCloud a pretty 18-year-old from St. Louis, arrives in Dodge eager to find a husband. Barney Wales, a young hard working cowboy who has a little spread outside of Dodge, falls in love and marries Mavis. Soon after the marriage Lou Staley, also from St. Louis, comes to town. Staley tells Matt that he plans on killing Barney. When Matt tells the newlyweds about Staley's threat, Mavis admits that she made up the name McCloud, and that her real name is Staley.

Young Man with a Gun. August 23, 1954. Written by John Meston. Guest cast: Sam Edwards, Lawrence Dobkin, Vivi Janiss, John Dehner. Aired on television October 20, 1956.

Gunman Sam Kertcher comes to town to advance his reputation by killing a lawman. He challenges Matt to meet him at sundown. Matt obliges, but draws first. According to Matt, killers like Kertcher do not deserve a fair chance. A couple of months later, a 16-year-old boy arrives in town. Matt befriends him, only to learn that he is Peyt Kertcher, Sam's brother. Peyt gets a job punching cattle for Emmett Bowers, but quits as soon as he has saved enough to buy a gun.

Obie Tater. August 30, 1954. Written by John Meston. Guest cast: Joseph Kearns, Virginia Gregg, Vic Perrin, Barney Phillips. Aired on television October 15, 1955.

Obie Tater denies the rumors that he is hoarding gold. Not everyone believes him, however, and he is beaten and dragged over the prairie by two unsavory characters. Some time later, after recovering from his near fatal injuries, Obie marries saloon girl Ella. Matt is greatly disturbed by the union for he suspects, and rightly so, that Ella is a gold-digger.

GUNSMOKE — III. THE PROGRAMS

THIRD SEASON

The Handcuffs (The Promise). September 6, 1954. Written by John Meston. Guest cast: Lawrence Dobkin, Jack Kruschen, John Dehner, Joe Forte, Irene Tedrow. Aired on television January 21, 1956.

Deputy Brake arrives from Mingo looking for accused murderer Hank Springer. Springer tells Matt that the charge is unfounded, and that he is being framed by Mingo's dishonest sheriff. Matt decides to unravel the mystery himself, and in the meantime locks Springer up for his own protection. Unfortunately in Matt's absence, Brake enters the jail to remove Springer. A struggle ensues and Brake is hit over the head with his handcuffs. Fearing that Brake has been killed, Springer escapes vowing to kill the crooked sheriff who turned him into a killer.

Irene Tedrow has had a long radio career that included the series, *Meet Corliss Archer,* which she later recreated on television. In addition, Ms. Tedrow was a regular on *The Ruggles, Dennis the Menace,* and *Mr. Novak.* She has also guest-starred on numerous programs including *L.A. Law.* Joe Forte played Horowitz on the television ethnic comedy series, *Life with Luigi,* a role he had previously played on radio.

Dooley Surrenders. September 13, 1954. Written by John Meston. Guest cast: Vic Perrin, Harry Bartell, James Nusser. Aired on television March 8, 1958.

A young buffalo skinner named Emmett Dooley wakes up after a drunken binge, only to be told by his boss that he murdered a fellow worker. Not remembering what happened, Dooley goes into Dodge and turns himself over to Matt. However, the medical evidence that Doc unearths points to a different killer. Matt turns Dooley loose, hoping to lure the guilty party into Dodge.

The F.U. September 20, 1954. Written by John Meston. Guest cast: John Dehner, Lawrence Dobkin. Aired on television March 14, 1959.

Al Clovis cleverly lures Matt and Chester away from Dodge after he is suspected of shooting Onie Becker. Once Matt is out of town, Al's accomplices are free to rob the bank of $25,000. Things go from bad to worse, as Matt is forced to follow the difficult trail of deception left by Clovis and his men.

F.U. stands for exactly what you think it stands for.

Helping Hand. September 27, 1954. Written by John Meston. Guest cast: John Dehner, Sam Edwards, Lawrence Dobkin, Joe Cranston. Aired on television March 17, 1956.

Matt saves Steve Elser from a lynching at the hand of foreman Bill Pence for rustling Emmet Bowers' cattle. Steve has had a hard life with an abusive alcoholic father, so rather than put the boy in jail, Matt decides to give Steve a break. He allows him to go free, provided the young man finds an honest job within the week. When Steve starts carrying a gun and emulating two-bit crook Ben Hander, Matt realizes his helping hand was wasted and that it was "already too late to help him."

This marks the end of the Chesterfield series of commercials.

Matt Gets It. October 2, 1954. Written by John Meston. Guest cast: Vic Perrin, Paul DuBov, Harry Bartell, John Dehner. Aired on television September 10, 1955 as the premiere episode.

Formidable gunman Dan Grat comes to town after killing an unarmed man in Amarillo. The sheriff of Amarillo, Jim Hill, arrives in Dodge looking for Grat, however Grat outdraws Hill, and Matt as well. After Matt recovers from his wounds, he meets the desperado in a final gun duel.

Love of a Good Woman. October 9, 1954. Written by John Meston. Guest cast: John Dehner, Vivi Janiss, James Nusser. Aired on television January 24, 1959.

Coney Thorn, a paroled convict, returns to Dodge City and threatens to kill Matt. Although Matt had thought Coney innocent of the charges against him, he had been forced to arrest him. Matt had always thought Coney to be a good man, but prison and his desire for revenge have changed him. Before Coney can act on his threat, he succumbs to "brain fever." He is nursed back to health, body and soul by an old friend of Doc's, Abby Twilly, a pretty widowed nurse who had worked in the same hospital as Doc during the war.

Kitty Caught. October 16, 1954. Written by John Meston. Guest cast: John Dehner, Lawrence Dobkin, Joe DuVal. Aired on television January 18, 1958.

Matt gets word that bank robbers, Joe Karp and his brother, are headed toward Dodge. On his way to warn Mr. Botkin, Matt runs into Kitty who invites him to breakfast. The two of them venture over to the bank together. While Matt is talking to Mr. Botkin, the Karp brothers rob the bank, shoot the teller, and take Kitty as a hostage. They warn Matt that they will kill her if they are followed.

Ma Tennis. October 23, 1954. Written by John Meston. Guest cast: Virginia Gregg, Sam Edwards, Harry Bartell, Lee Millar. Aired on television February 1, 1958.

Young, hot-tempered Andy Tennis kills an unarmed gambler whom he believed was cheating at cards. Matt arrests the boy, but Andy's brother Ben, feels that Matt is asking for trouble. Ben's premonition is right when Ma Tennis their shotgun wielding mother arrives at the jail demanding her son's release.

The Patsy. October 30, 1954. Written by John Meston. Guest cast: Vic Perrin, Lawrence Dobkin, Jack Kruschen, Jill Jarmyn, James Nusser. Aired on television September 20, 1958.

Saloon girl Holly Fanshaw lures Dave Thorpe into an alley where he is shot in the back and killed. Dave's distraught brother Joe demands that Matt tear Dodge apart to find the killer, or else he will take the law into his own hands. Holly claims that Fly Hoyt, a cowboy who Dave had an argument with is the murderer. Matt and Chester journey to the X-T camp to arrest Fly. When they arrive they find Fly protected by a group of Texan cattle-drivers headed by Jim Cavanaugh. Even though his friends insist that Fly is not subject to Kansas law, Fly agrees to return to Dodge with Matt. He assures Matt he is innocent and wants to confront Holly with her lies.

Smoking Out the Beedles. November 6, 1954. Written by John Meston. Guest cast: Lawrence Dobkin, Harry Bartell, Jeanette Nolan, Joe Cranston. Aired on television November 5, 1955.

Pat Clay tells Matt that Jim Beedle and his wife are squatters on his land. He had given permission for the couple to live in a small sod hut for a few months, but now that their time is up, they refuse to leave. In addition, they have threatened to kill Clay if he bothers them further. Matt and Chester present a court order signed by Judge Miller to the Beedles, ordering them to vacate the premises. Jim insists that he bought the 40 acres around Stone Point from Clay for $60. He cannot produce the deed, however, because Clay kept it, saying that he would register it. Without proof the law is on Clay's side, and Matt is forced to do his duty. He has Chester climb on top of the hut and pour sulfur down the chimney to smoke the Beedles out. Having accomplished his repulsive job, Matt returns to Dodge, knowing full well that Jim will retaliate.

When this show aired on television it was titled *Smoking Out the Nolans*.

Wrong Man. November 13, 1954. Written by John Meston. Guest cast: John Dehner, Vivi Janiss, Vic Perrin, Lawrence Dobkin. Aired on television April 13, 1957.

Homesteader Sam Rickers boastfully claims his $1000 reward for shooting outlaw Bob Hulburt. Rickers later discovers that he has taken the life of an innocent man. The man he shot twice in the chest and once in the back was Jake Haney. Unfortunately Matt cannot arrest Rickers, who along with his wife Letty, swears it was self-defense. Nevertheless, one homicide leads to another when the trigger-happy Rickers finds that he is marked for death by Haney's partner Catlin.

How to Kill a Woman. November 20, 1954. Rerun. Guest cast: Clayton Post, Larry Dobkin, Vic Perrin.

Cooter. November 27, 1954. Written by John Meston. Guest cast: Vic Perrin, John Dehner, Harry Bartell. Aired on television May 12, 1956.

A crooked cowardly gambler named Ben Sisle hires gunfighter Pate to be his body guard. Since Sisle does not carry a gun, Pate kills anyone who draws against the gambler, claiming "self-defense." Having discovered the scam, Matt runs Pate out of town, leaving Sisle unprotected, which forces him to run an honest game. When Cooter Smith, a simple-minded man who had been kicked in the head by a horse, is seen wearing a six-gun, Matt learns he is in Sisle's employ.

Kitty, who has been a free agent until now, frequenting all of the Dodge City saloons: the Long Horn, the Texas Trail, the Alaferganza, etc., has started working at the Long Branch. "Maybe I'll stay here a while," she announces.

Cholera. December 4, 1954. Written by John Meston. Guest cast: Ralph Moody, Virginia Christine, Sam Edwards, Vic Perrin, Clayton Post. Aired on television December 29, 1956.

Old man McReady and his son Billy, are determined to run Jim Gabriel and his family off their land. The Gabriels have a spring well and McReady wants their water. When Gabriel's son becomes deathly ill, McReady prevents Doc from treating the boy, an action that results in personal disaster for both families.

Bone Hunters. December 11, 1954. Written by John Meston. Guest cast: John Dehner, Herb Ellis, Frank Cady.

When bone hunter Bill Zant gets drunk, he loses control and becomes violent. After getting good and plastered, the normally pleasant Zant cuts Nooley Meeker with a bowie knife. Fortunately for Zant, Meeker survives the attack. Some time later, Ezra Marcy, the man who Meeker and Zant collect buffalo bones for, arrives in Dodge. Ezra tells Matt that Meeker has been shot and that Zant is the murderer. Zant admits to being drunk on corn whiskey, but insists that he is innocent. Unfortunately, his only alibi is an old Cheyenne Indian, who has disappeared into the hills.

Magnus. December 18, 1954. Written by John Meston. Guest cast: Robert Easton. Aired on television December 24, 1955.

The Radio Programs

Chester's uncivilized brother Magnus Proudfoot, arrives in Dodge for a visit. Chester is appalled when he learns that his brother plans on staying in Dodge, and decides to civilize Magnus by teaching him to drink, gamble and talk to women. But Magnus has some surprises for his brother that earn him Chester's admiration.

In addition to numerous radio and television performances, Robert Easton has appeared in such films as *The Red Badge of Courage, When You Coming Back Red Ryder, Tai-Pan,* and most recently in *Working Girl.* Easton has the unique distinction of recreating his role of Magnus on the television version. In recent years Easton has taken on the role of "dialect doctor" and taught television's Chester, Dennis Weaver, the Lithuanian dialect he used in *The Pete Gray Story.*

Kitty Lost. December 25, 1954. Written by John Meston. Guest cast: John Dehner, James Nusser, Barney Phillips, Vic Perrin. Aired on television December 21, 1957.

Kitty takes a moonlight ride on the prairie with an Eastern dude named Jim Rachmil. When she fails to show up for several appointments the next day, Matt and Chester decide to look for her.

The Bottle Man. January 1, 1955. Written by John Meston. Guest cast: Lawrence Dobkin, Eleanore Tanin, Ralph Moody. Aired on television March 22, 1958.

Matt is tracking Jim Kelly, a man accused of burning down a hotel in Wichita. Outsmarted by Kelly, however, Matt loses his trail and is forced to give up the search. During Matt's absence all is quiet in Dodge except for one very unusual incident. Old Tom Cassidy a poor, harmless drunk, apparently attacked gambler Bill Clell. Clell, a stranger to Dodge, had arrived with his 18-year-old wife Flora, a girl he had adopted at the age of five after her mother died. Matt and the citizens of Dodge are astonished, for Cassidy is a peaceful man. The act sets off a chain of events culminating in murder.

Robin Hood. January 8, 1955. Written by John Meston. Guest cast: Lawrence Dobkin, Harry Bartell, Helen Kleeb, Joe Cranston, Frank Cady. Aired on television February 4, 1956.

Kitty arrives in Dodge after a visit to Elsworth, with the news that the stage she was traveling on had been robbed. The modus operandi fits Teddy Blue Fish, a modern Robin Hood who robs from the rich, while sparing the women and the poor. As in Kitty's case, the robber stole the strong box containing $500 and took all of banker Botkin's money, but left the other two passengers and Kitty alone. He was a perfect gentleman and well disguised, wearing a flour sack over his head. Matt is in a quandary since no one has been able to get enough evidence to get Fish, and being sort of a gentleman bandit, people feel obliged to protect him.

Frank Cady is best known for his portrayal of storekeeper Sam Drucker on *Green Acres* and *Petticoat Junction.*

Chester's Murder. January 15, 1955. Written by John Meston. Guest cast: Vic Perrin, Lawrence Dobkin, James Nusser, Joyce McCluskey. Aired on television March 30, 1957.

Jealous Charlie Pickard publicly threatens Chester, when he sees him with his girl Nita Tucker. When Pickard is found murdered, circumstantial evidence points to Chester. Matt is forced to take his friend into custody, and then quell the threat of mob violence as irate townspeople demand a conviction. When Nita Tucker announces she plans on marrying horse trader Jake Buley, Matt gets an idea that might save Chester from a hanging.

Sins of the Father. January 22, 1955. Written by John Meston. Guest cast: Lawrence Dobkin. Harry Bartell, Lillian Buyeff, Clayton Post, Joe DuVal. Aired on television January 19, 1957.

Mountain man Big Dan Daggit arrives in Dodge City with his wife Rose, the daughter of notorious Kiowa Indian Chief Yellow Horse. Two years ago Yellow Horse attacked some homesteaders outside of Dodge, killing 18 settlers. Feelings against the Kiowa Indians are running high in Dodge, and when the Daggits take a room at the Dodge House, Mr. Dobie sends for Matt to remove them. Matt refuses, however, much to the consternation of Dobie, who stirs up trouble for Mrs. Daggit with wild stories of Indian uprisings.

Young Love. January 29, 1955. Written by John Meston. Guest cast: Sam Edwards, Eleanore Tanin, Vic Perrin, Don Diamond, Frank Cady. Aired on television January 3, 1959.

Jim Box shoots his boss Jesse Wheat in cold blood, while young Rod Allison looks on in disbelief. Believing he is an accomplice to the murder, Rod joins forces with Box. Anna, Wheat's grieving widow had been more like a daughter to the old man than a wife, for he was almost 30 years her senior. While investigating the murder, Matt discovers that Anna and Rod plan on getting married, which makes Rod a prime suspect.

Cheyennes. February 5, 1955. Written by John Meston. Guest cast: Harry Bartell, Ralph Moody, Lawrence Dobkin, Vic Perrin, Barney Phillips. Aired on television June 13, 1959.

Matt and Chester are forced to circumvent an overeager new army commander, in order to prevent a Cheyenne uprising. Gunrunners have been supplying Spenser repeating rifles to a band of renegade Indians lead by Stone Eagle. After meeting with his Indian friend Long Robe, Matt realizes he must catch the gunrunners before the army commander kills any Cheyennes. If not, there will be a full scale Indian war.

Georgia Ellis and Howard McNear doubled as Indians in this episode.

Chester's Hanging. February 12, 1955. Written by John Meston. Guest cast: James Nusser, Paul DuBov, Clayton Post, Joe Cranston. Aired on television May 17, 1958.

Matt jails Jim Candow, a man wanted for robbery and murder, after Chester recognizes the criminal from a circular. Candow's friend Lee Binders is desperate to free him, so as to prevent Candow from implicating him in the crimes. Being "more weasel than lion," Binders is forced to hire gunman Jack Haney to help him. The two men overpower Chester and threaten to hang him, if Matt does not release Candow.

Poor Pearl. February 19, 1955. Written by John Meston. Guest cast: Vic Perrin, Harry Bartell, Virginia Christine. Aired on television December 22, 1956.

Matt intervenes when two men, farmer Willie Calhoun and gambler Webb Thorne, prepare to shoot it out over saloon girl Pearl Bender. Although a showdown is averted, the embittered Calhoun brings tragedy to the lives of all concerned.

Virginia Christine is familiar to television viewers as Mrs. Olson of the Folger coffee commercials. Her film credits include *High Noon, Judgement at Nuremberg,* and *The Prize.*

The Radio Programs

Crack-Up. February 26, 1955. Written by John Meston. Guest cast: John Dehner, Harry Bartell. Aired on television September 14, 1957.

Gunslinger Nate Springer arrives in Dodge after serving two years in Yuma prison. Springer has the reputation of being a notorious "man of ice" and "the most nerveless there ever was." Matt finds that Nate is unusually jumpy and before he runs him out of town he wants to learn who Nate has been paid to kill, and who hired him.

Kite's Reward. March 5, 1955. Written by John Meston. Guest cast: Vic Perrin, Joe DuVal, Sam Edwards, John Dehner. Aired on television November 12, 1955.

Young Andy Travis kills Jake Kroal in self-defense. Having witnessed the killing, Matt realizes that Andy had no choice. Matt has also observed that Andy is an incredibly fast draw. In order to prevent an unwanted reputation, Matt has Andy remove his gun permanently. After Matt helps Andy get a job with Moss Grimmick, the likeable youth becomes a popular citizen of Dodge. However, Andy's past catches up with him when a mangy bar bum Joe Kite learns that Andy's real name is Haycocks, and that there is a $1000 price on Andy Haycocks' head, dead or alive.

The Trial. March 12, 1955. Written by John Meston. Guest cast: Lawrence Dobkin, Vic Perrin, John Dehner, Harry Bartell.

Homer Tisdale admits to stealing a few potatoes from Van Wallcott's store, but Matt refuses to jail the starving man. Instead, Matt gets Homer a job with Sam Noonan over at the Long Branch. Wallcott, an Easterner who has been in Dodge for only a month, is furious when justice is not served. Wallcott is full of "I told you so's" when he and his friend Jay Bradford accuse Homer of robbing the freight office of $10,000 and of killing Charley Reynolds. The innocent Homer is whisked off to be tried by new circuit judge Stokes, who makes the saying "sober as a judge" take on a whole new meaning.

The Mistake. March 19, 1955. Written by John Meston. Guest cast: Lou Krugman, James Nusser, John Dehner. Aired on television November 24, 1956.

Faro dealer Earl Haney is robbed and fatally beaten. Just before his demise, Haney tells Matt that a tall, red haired man was his assailant. The only man that fits that description is gambler Jim Bostick, a man who did not think very much of Haney. When Matt confronts Bostick with the crime, he denies the charges. In addition, Bostick claims that he was with Doc at the time of the murder. However, Matt does not believe Bostick and with Doc away at the Tewksbury ranch, Bostick has no way of corroborating his alibi. When Bostick escapes from custody, Matt is obligated to go after him.

Lou Krugman worked in radio since 1929 in such shows as *The Shadow, Escape, Suspense,* and *Fort Laramie.* He guest-starred on numerous television programs including *Gunsmoke, Maverick, I Spy,* and *The Rockford Files.* His film credits include *I Want to Live,* which starred Susan Hayward.

Horse Deal. March 26, 1955. Written by John Meston. Guest cast: Harry Bartell, James Nusser, Vic Perrin, Sam Edwards, Joe Cranston. Aired on television September 26, 1959.

Drifter Charlie Deesha accuses wealthy rancher Emmett Bowers of horse theft. Emmett claims he bought the six horses in question from Vic Lowry for $30 a piece. When Deesha shows the certificate of title for the Bar S brand, Emmett realizes that the horses are indeed Deesha's and that he has been robbed by Lowry. The angry rancher threatens to form a lynching party, however, Matt comes up with his own plan for capturing the culprit.

Bloody Hands. April 2, 1955. Written by John Meston. Guest cast: John Dehner, Lawrence Dobkin. Aired on television February 16, 1957.

Matt goes after outlaw Jack Brand and his three accomplices. He returns with Brand and three dead bodies. Brand says it is just "a wagon load of meat" to Matt, who is the "bloodiest marshal" he has ever seen. This violent taking of human life is too much for Matt to shake. He removes his gun and hands in his badge. Unfortunately, Matt's respite from a life of violence proves short-lived, when a friend of Brand, Joe Stanger arrives in Dodge anxious to take advantage of the absence of law and order.

Skid Row. April 9, 1955. Written by John Meston. Guest cast: Eleanore Tanin, Harry Bartell, Barney Phillips. Aired on television February 23, 1957.

Ann Cabot leaves her home in Connecticut to marry prosperous homesteader Jack Shomer. Now destitute and little more than a shell of a man because of land failure, Shomer refuses to see her. However, he lives to regret his decision when Ann, naive, alone, and unfamiliar with the loose way of life in Dodge, becomes the victim of Hank Groat, a man who "ain't fit for a hog pen."

The Gypsum Hill Feud. April 16, 1955. Written by John Meston. Guest cast: Vivi Janiss, John Dehner, Vic Perrin. Aired on television December 27, 1958.

Matt and Chester while en route to Medicine Lodge, stop to hunt antelope in the hill country. Wandering through the gypsum and shale hills, Matt is shot at by a bushwacker. Matt and Chester track the sniper to the home of Alvin and Liza Peavy, where they soon become embroiled in a blood feud between the Peavy clan and the Cades.

Born to Hang. April 23, 1955. Written by John Meston. Guest cast: Joseph Kearns, James Nusser, John Dehner, Lawrence Dobkin. Aired on television November 2, 1957.

Three ranchers Glick, Pate, and Robbo catch drifter Joe Digger with some stolen horses. Glick and Pate want to hang Digger, but Robbo rides away, wanting nothing to do with a lynching. After the men string Digger up, Robbo returns to cut him down. Fortunately for Digger, Robbo is in time and Digger is saved from hanging. As he plots his revenge against Glick and Pate, however, it appears that Digger may be destined to hang after all.

Reward for Matt. April 30, 1955. Written by John Meston. Guest cast: Jeanette Nolan, Sam Edwards, Helen Kleeb. Aired on television January 28, 1956.

Matt rides out to the Hornsby ranch, determined to arrest Mel Hornsby for the murder of homesteader Jake Reeves. Hornsby readily admits his guilt, but self-righteously adds that he was justified because all homesteaders deserve to be killed. Matt does not share Hornsby's warped perspective on the matter and when Hornsby draws his gun resisting arrest, Matt is forced to kill him. Hornsby's wife discovers what has transpired, and to avenge his death she places a $1000 bounty on Matt's life. The hunger for easy money draws all the local scum to Dodge, gunning for the lawman.

Potato Road. May 7, 1955. Written by John Meston. Guest cast: John McIntire, Virginia Gregg, Vic Perrin. Aired on television October 12, 1957.

The Radio Programs

Budge Grilk, a strange looking man with long yellow hair and long yellow teeth who is so thin that it would "take two of him to make a shadow," tells Matt to arrest Pa Grilk for murder. Matt and Chester follow Budge back to his sod hut where the two meet Budge's half-starved mother and his crazy father. Before they are aware of what is transpiring, Matt and Chester are imprisoned in the potato shed. Then the elder Grilk reveals his insane plan to rob the Dodge bank after Matt and Chester are "dead and buried."

Robber Bridegroom. May 14, 1955. Written by John Meston. Guest cast: Larry Dobkin, Harry Bartell, Frank Gerstle, Jeanne Bates, Clayton Post. Aired on television December 13, 1958.

New Yorker Franklin J. Reeves arrives in Dodge, planning to invest in cattle and land. His fiancee Laura is traveling from Denver by stage. Jim Buck the stagecoach driver tells Matt that not only was the stage held up and robbed of $50,000, but the bandit Jack Fitch also kidnapped Laura. Matt's case against the kidnapper is dealt a blow when Laura falls in love with Fitch and refuses to testify against him. Meanwhile Reeves, the jilted fiance, organizes a lynching party to hang his rival.

The Liar from Blackhawk. May 21, 1955. Written by John Meston. Guest cast: Vic Perrin, Paul DuBov, Barney Phillips, John Dehner. Aired on television June 22, 1957.

Hank Shinn comes to Dodge and starts to throw his weight around, bragging that he is a ruthless gunfighter from the Dakota Territory. Although he has much of the town hoodwinked and intimidated, Matt suspects that Hank is mostly talk. When Al James, a gunman from New Mexico arrives to check Hank out, Hank decides to tell Matt the truth and takes off his gun.

Cow Doctor. May 28, 1955. Written by John Meston. Guest cast: John Dehner, Vivi Janiss, Sam Edwards. Aired on television September 8, 1956.

Ben Pitcher, who makes no bones about hating doctors, sends his son Jerry to fetch Doc to treat his ailing cow. In Doc's absence, Mrs. Hill falls into a window because of heat prostration and bleeds to death. When Doc hears this he and Ben get into a fight that ends with Doc being knifed. Matt and Kitty nurse him back to health, and while Doc is still recovering, Jerry calls upon him saying his dad is dying. Despite Matt's warning, Doc insists on going to Ben.

Jealousy. June 4, 1955. Written by John Meston. Guest cast: Vic Perrin, Virginia Gregg, Harry Bartell, Don Diamond. Aired on television July 6, 1957.

An old friend of Matt's, Cam Durbin, arrives in Dodge with his new wife Tilda. Cam plans on running the faro table at the Long Branch. However, Lonny Pike, a conniving card dealer who has a grudge to settle with Matt, starts to spread stories about Tilda and Matt. Cam who has a long history of jealousy, succumbs to the rumors and starts to lose control.

Trust. July 11, 1955. Written by John Meston. Guest cast: Vic Perrin, Joseph Kearns, John Dehner, Clayton Post, James Nusser.

Matt and Chester capture James Nation near the Smokey Hill River almost ninety miles from Dodge. It has been a hard chase and all three horses die, either from exhaustion or from being wounded, and they are forced to return to Dodge via stagecoach. Matt distrusts Nation, but when the fugitive tells him that their companion on the stagecoach is outlaw Art Carp, Matt does not know what to make of his prisoner. Nation is accused of having killed a man in Dodge, although he claims it was self-defense. Matt makes the difficult decision of giving Nation back his gun when the stage is held up by Carp's cronies, hoping the accused man will help.

This story is similar to *Overland Express,* broadcast October 31, 1952.

The Reed Survives. June 18, 1955. Written by Les Crutchfield. Guest cast: Michael Ann Barrett, Sam Edwards, Ralph Moody, Edgar Barrier. Aired on television December 31, 1955.

A hot dry wind is blowing from the panhandle and Matt senses trouble. Sure enough, Lucy Hunt arrives saying she fears for her life because her husband is threatening to kill her. Lucy is the young and beautiful wife of Efram Hunt, an elderly farmer who likes to quote the scripture. Matt suspects that Lucy, an ex-dance hall girl, is actually plotting Efram's death. She lures her lover Booth Rider, a young hired hand, into a scheme that culminates in an ironic twist of fate.

The Army Trial. June 25, 1955. Written by Norman Macdonnell. Guest cast: Vivi Janiss, Larry Dobkin, Harry Bartell, James Nusser.

Matt and Chester come across a broken wagon, but their offers to assist are refused by the man and woman trying to fix the wheel. Matt understands why, when he recognizes the man to be Jed Cook a deserter from the 26th Cavalry in Fort Dodge. Jed and Della were planning to flee to Colorado and get married. It was Della's impatience that prompted Jed to leave his post. Jed had had a distinguished career as a soldier, and only one more year to serve when he foolishly deserted.

General Parcley Smith. July 2, 1955. Written by John Meston. Guest cast: John Dehner, Joe DuVal, Vic Perrin. Aired on television December 10, 1955.

Old-timer Parcley Smith, a former regimental butcher, has a reputation for telling tall tales. He arrives in Dodge and proceeds to spread rumors about the new bank manager Drew Holt. Parcley warns Matt that Holt is a crook and should be run out of town. Matt becomes suspicious when he discovers that Holt has hired ex-con Ed Nash to guard the bank. However, after checking Holt's credentials, Matt believes him to be beyond reproach. In addition, he asks Smith to stop slandering Holt's reputation or suffer the consequences.

Uncle Oliver. July 9, 1955. Written by John Meston. Guest cast: Vic Perrin, Harry Bartell. Aired on television May 25, 1957.

Two men arrive in Dodge, an aged plainsman Oliver Strang and his half-witted nephew Viney. After an argument involves Matt, Strang decides that Viney should become a marshal. The only way to learn how to be a marshal, however, would be to be Matt's helper, a job already taken by Chester. When Chester is ambushed and shot by an unseen assailant, Matt stalks the streets in search of the gunman, certain that Oliver or Viney is responsible.

Twenty-Twenty. July 16, 1955. Written by John Meston. Guest cast: Vic Perrin, Joseph Cranston, James Nusser. Aired on television February 25, 1956.

Ex-lawman Troy Carver, who has been Matt's inspiration for becoming a U.S. Marshal, arrives in Dodge on his way to the ranch he has purchased for his retirement. Matt senses that Carver is especially jumpy, and discovers that Lee Polen, a simple "dirt-farmer," plans to kill Carver to avenge the death of his brother. Matt is confident

The Radio Programs

that the inexperienced Polen poses no threat to a seasoned gunman like Carver, until he discovers his friend's secret, he is going blind.

Ben Tolliver's Stud. July 23, 1955. Written by Norman Macdonnell. Guest cast: Sam Edwards, Eleanore Tanin, James Nusser. Aired on television November 26, 1960.

Jake Creed is a cruel, stingy old rancher who has a history of hiring young cowboys for a few months, then picking a fight and firing them before he has to pay them for their work. Creed's scheme backfires when he tries to cheat his current hand Ben Tolliver. The young man reacts by taking a stud horse and leaves for Dodge. Ben feels the horse is his, since he found it while out on the prairie and broke it during his spare time. Creed, however, claims that the horse belongs to him, since it was fed and housed on his ranch. Creed's pretty, but slow-thinking daughter Nancy, tells Matt that Creed is going to kill Ben. In order to prevent bloodshed, Matt jails the cowboy for his own protection, and rides out to the Creed ranch to uncover the truth.

Tap Day for Kitty. July 30, 1955. Written by John Meston. Guest cast: John Dehner, Michael Ann Barrett, Virginia Gregg. Aired on television March 24, 1956.

Nip Cullers, a weathered old rancher, comes to town for the express purpose of choosing a wife. His journey takes him to the Long Branch where he selects an unwilling Kitty for his bride. When Nip is the victim of an attempted homicide, Kitty is the prime suspect.

Innocent Broad. August 6, 1955. Written by John Meston. Guest cast: Eleanore Tanin, Vic Perrin, Lawrence Dobkin, Paul DuBov. Aired on television April 26, 1958.

While traveling on a stage bound for Dodge, Matt encounters two other passengers, 17-year-old Linda Belle and an annoying stranger. Linda is making the journey to meet her fiancee Lou Paxton, while the stranger seems to have some darker reasons for his pilgrimage. When the three arrive at their destination, it becomes obvious that Paxton knows the stranger, something that bothers Matt.

Johnny Red. August 13, 1955. Written by Les Crutchfield. Guest cast: Sam Edwards, Virginia Gregg, Vic Perrin, Lawrence Dobkin, Paul DuBov. Aired on television October 3, 1959.

A criminal known to Matt as Johnny Red arrives in Dodge posing as Billy Crail the long lost son of a widow. According to army records, Billy was killed in action at the battle of Shiloh, but Matt does not have the heart to tell Mrs. Crail. Matt watches as Johnny ingratiates himself with the old woman, while he stands ready to pounce on anything that indicates trouble.

Indian Scout. August 20, 1955. Written by John Dunkel. Guest cast: Lawrence Dobkin, Harry Bartell, Barney Phillips, Joseph Kearns. Aired on television March 31, 1956.

Comanche scout Amos Cartwright leads a cavalry troop into an ambush where everyone is slaughtered except Amos. Will Bailey, the brother of one of the massacred soldiers, believes that Amos intentionally led the troop into a trap and is determined to avenge the act.

Doc Quits. August 27, 1955. Written by John Meston. Guest cast: Lawrence Dobkin, James Nusser, Anne Morrison, Frank Cady. Aired on television February 21, 1959.

After Joe Crumley dies, Doc begins to question his effectiveness as a physician. A week after the unfortunate incident, Dr. Jamison Betchel arrives in Dodge and approaches Doc with the proposition of a partnership. Doc, who is still extremely agitated by the recent tragedy, is vehemently against the new doctor because Betchel's motives have only to do with avarice. Doc quits his practice in anger when his patients start going to Betchel, whom Doc considers to be a quack and a charlatan.

Anne Morrison appeared as Dr. Margaret Kleeb in the 1950s comedy series, *The Brothers*.

FOURTH SEASON

Change of Heart. September 3, 1955. Written by John Meston. Guest cast: Sam Edwards, Virginia Christine, Vic Perrin, Joe DuVal. Aired on television April 25, 1959.

Bella Grant a dance hall girl from the Long Branch is partners with Brisco Cass. Their plan is to trick Brisco's brother, Jerry, out of his land. The Cass brothers lost their father three months ago, and according to his will, Jerry and Brisco own the ranch jointly. However, if either one leaves the ranch for longer than four months, the entire estate reverts to the other brother. Bella's job is to marry Jerry and lure him away from the ranch. The tables are turned when Bella falls in love with Jerry.

Alarm at Pleasant Valley. September 10, 1955. Written by John Dunkel. Guest cast: John Dehner, Vic Perrin, Helen Kleeb, Eleanore Tanin, Sam Edwards, John James, Jr. Aired on television August 25, 1956.

The Fraser family's happiness at settling in Pleasant Valley is shattered by renegade Kiowa Indians who have been attacking local homesteaders. The Clayburn family is the most recent victim and, Sam Fraser decides to pack up his family and leave. Matt and Chester try to convince the Frasers that they should stand their ground for only a few Indians are involved, but Sam prepares to depart, until his wife Alice goes into labor forcing his hand.

September 10, 1955 marked the premiere of the television show.

Thoroughbreds. September 17, 1955. Written by John Meston. Guest cast: John Dehner, Lawrence Dobkin, Harry Bartell. Aired on television October 18, 1958.

Jack Portis, a well-groomed stranger, rides into Dodge with two beautiful horses bearing the wineglass brand. Although Matt has no proof, he believes that Portis stole the horses. In addition, Portis is very free with his money. He buys drinks for everyone, which makes Portis very popular with the local citizens.

Indian White. September 24, 1955. Written by Tom Hanley. Guest cast: Sammy Ogg, Virginia Gregg, Joseph Kearns, Harry Bartell, John Dehner, Ralph Moody. Aired on television October 27, 1956.

Born of white parents, Dennis must decide whether to return to the Cheyennes who raised him, or journey into the unfamiliar society of his birthright. The boy goes to live with Mrs. Cullen, whose own son had been kidnapped by the Cheyennes, but Dennis' longing to return to the Indians and the prejudice he encounters amongst the townsfolk, make his "rehabilitation" impossible.

Tom Hanley who wrote this script was also the sound effects engineer for many of the radio programs along with Bill James and Ray Kemper.

The Barton Boy. October 1, 1955. Written by Les Crutchfield. Guest cast: Virginia Christine, Lawrence Dobkin, Richard Beals.

The Radio Programs

The train is robbed just three miles outside of Walnut Creek Crossing. The thief escaped with a strongbox containing $20,000 and in the process, killed baggage clerk Ed Barton and wounded Ed's ten-year-old son Billy. Laura, a Long Branch saloon girl, is terribly broken up by the news, since she and Ed were engaged. However, Matt is more concerned about the welfare and safety of Billy, who is the only witness.

Good Girl—Bad Company. October 8, 1955. Written by John Meston. Guest cast: Virginia Christine, John Dehner.

Major Harris from Fort Dodge confronts Matt with the news that two soldiers were murdered and the government payroll stolen. Harris suspects that some Dodge City ruffians are responsible and threatens to put Dodge under marshal law unless Matt can solve the crime. Matt believes the presence of the military would provoke the citizens to violence. When Private Ravage is murdered outside of the Texas Trail, Matt is given 48 hours to find the killer. The only leads Matt has are centered around a new saloon girl from Hayes City, Jenny Lane, who has been keeping company with Corporal Hayes, a friend of the late Private Ravage. In addition, when Jenny left Hayes City she was accompanied by Nat Brand, considered to be a "wild one." However, this Brand fellow has not been seen in Dodge.

This show uses the same plot as *Carmen,* broadcast May 31, 1952, however the characters' names are different.

The Coward. October 9, 1955. Written by John Meston. Guest cast: Vic Perrin, John Dehner, Jack Edwards. Aired on television March 7, 1959.

When Jack Massey is shot in the back, everything points to Matt being the intended target. Massey had been waiting in Matt's office, sitting in his chair. In addition, Massey wears a hat similar to Matt's and has the same build as the marshal. Ed Ebbe, the new Faro dealer at the Long Branch, further confirms Matt's suspicions, when he admits he overheard two men plotting Matt's demise. Not knowing who the assailant is or when, or where he will strike, makes Matt jumpy and wary of every drifter.

The plot is similar to *What the Whiskey Drummer Heard,* broadcast April 17, 1954.

Trouble in Kansas. October 16, 1955. Written by John Meston. Guest cast: Lawrence Dobkin, Barney Phillips, Harry Bartell.

Texan Jim Hoyt brags about how his pack horse is loaded down with ammunition to use against Kansans. Matt does not like the sound of this, so he and Chester accompany Hoyt back to the Cross R herd to talk with cattle boss Jack Raven. Raven admits that they plan on slaughtering as many Kansans as possible, due to the raids and stampedes attributed to Kansas jayhawkers. In order to prevent needless bloodshed, Matt stays on to trap the troublemakers.

Harry Bartell was a free lance actor and announcer on radio from 1943-1962. He was heard on *Dear Abby* on CBS radio from 1962 to 1974. In addition to his radio credits, Bartell made guest appearances in over 70 different television series including *Gunsmoke* and *Dragnet,* and was featured in fifteen movies. He also co-penned a few *Gunsmoke* scripts along with his good friend Vic Perrin.

Brush at Elkader. October 23, 1955. Written by John Meston. Guest cast: James Nusser, Harry Bartell, Vic Perrin, Paul DuBov, Larry Dobkin. Aired on television September 15, 1956.

Matt and Chester journey to Elkader to arrest the murderer of Ben Williams, a man without an enemy in the world. However, Matt's chore is not an easy one. All he knows of the murderer is his name, Lou Shippen. When the two arrive in Elkader they soon realize that the citizens are afraid of Shippen and, therefore, fearing retaliation from the killer, refuse to cooperate in any way.

The Choice. October 30, 1955. Written by John Meston. Guest cast: Sam Edwards, Harry Bartell, Barney Phillips, Lawrence Dobkin. Aired on television May 9, 1959.

Andy Hill, a young stranger to Dodge City, kills a drunk who had been annoying Kitty. Although the shooting was in self-defense, Matt does not like having a gunman in his town. At Kitty's insistence, however, Matt gives Andy a chance by getting him a job riding shotgun for Jim Buck, a decision Matt hopes he will not regret.

Second Choice. November 6, 1955. Written by John Meston. Guest cast: Sam Edwards, Vic Perrin, Joseph Kearns.

Now that Andy Hill has gone straight and has actually helped catch a murderer, Matt wants the former criminal's minor burglary charge dropped. He telegrams sheriff Bob Catlin of the Oklahoma territory, where Andy is wanted, and waits for an answer. Unfortunately, the answer Matt receives is not the one he expected. Catlin is sending deputy Jack Hall to Dodge to return Andy to stand trial for murder.

The Preacher. November 13, 1955. Written by John Meston. Guest cast: Lawrence Dobkin, John Dehner, Joe Cranston. Aired on television June 16, 1956.

The peace and quiet of Dodge is disrupted when Sam Keeler, a big "bearcat" with "hands like shovels," beats up poor old Seth Tandy, a sorrowful looking newcomer to Dodge who has "eyes like a blind horse." Matt hits the bully over the head to stop the fight, an act that leaves Keeler a laughing stock and bent on revenge.

Dutch George. November 20, 1955. Written by John Dunkel. Guest cast: James Nusser, John Dehner, Vic Perrin. Aired on television June 30, 1956.

In his youth, Matt struck up a friendship with Dutch George. Now Dutch is known as the "biggest horse thief West of the Mississippi." Dutch is a bit of a celebrity in Dodge, living high on the hog, and although everybody knows he is a notorious criminal, no one has been able to prove it. However, when Dutch victimizes a young cowboy named Jimmy McQueen, both he and Matt underestimate the cowboy and his ability for revenge.

As with many of these radio shows even the principal performers play additional roles. In this particular episode Howard McNear (Doc) plays Sam Noonan the barkeep.

Amy's Good Deed. November 27, 1955. Written by John Meston. Guest cast: Virginia Gregg, Harry Bartell. Aired on television April 12, 1958.

Amy Slater arrives in Dodge and boldly announces that Matt is going to kill her. The 50-year-old woman, who looks 60 because of what prairie life has done to her, is determined to disgrace Matt by goading him into killing her. Unbeknownst to Matt, Amy is the sister of Jim Band, a bandit he supposedly killed while out in Dakota territory. In addition, Band's former partner, Emmett Gold, has also arrived in Dodge presumably to kill Matt.

Sunny Afternoon. December 4, 1955. Written by Les Crutchfield. Guest cast: Ralph Moody, John Dehner, Virginia Christine.

Matt finds Ned Crater and Josh Sidrow, "the meanest man in town," arguing at the

The Radio Programs

Long Branch. Josh has stashed away five times the hay he needs to feed his stock while the other farmers, Ned included, have watched their crops fail. Ned knows it is but a matter of time until his livestock starve to death. Josh is willing to sell his hay, but with one small stipulation, that he receive at least twice what it is worth. When Josh's son is murdered while guarding the hay-barn, Ned becomes the prime suspect.

Land Deal. December 11, 1955. Written by John Meston. Guest cast: Larry Dobkin, Vivi Janiss, Vic Perrin, John Dehner. Aired on television November 8, 1958.

Ten immigrant families arrive in Dodge escorted by Mr. Trumbull, who has been paid over $400 by each family to procure railroad land for them. When Matt hears the details of the transaction, he suspects that Trumbull is a swindler. To add to his concerns, Matt fears that violence will break out when immigrant Jim Calhoun suspects that his wife Sydney has been unfaithful.

Scared Kid. December 18, 1955. Written by John Meston. Guest cast: Sam Edwards, Anne Morrison, Eleanore Tanin, John Dehner.

Gil Barden is a 20-year-old "kid" who has been spending time with Ida Stewart, one of the new saloon-girls. When Henry Gant insults Ida, Gil threatens to kill him. Gant is later found shot in the back, which forces Matt and Chester to pursue Gil.

Twelfth Night. December 25, 1955. Written by John Meston. Guest cast: John Dehner, Vic Perrin, Helen Kleeb. Aired on television December 28, 1957.

Eban Hakes is a "squirrel huntin', Southern mountain-man" from the Ozarks who has his own ideas about the law. The mountain-man is looking for Joff Monger to settle a "family matter," which turns out to be a deadly family feud that is about to be transplanted to Dodge. Eban and Joff are the last survivors of this violent ritual and Matt tries to prevent further bloodshed. Time may be on Matt's side, for when Eban finally catches up with his opponent it is Sunday, and Eban and Josh, being principaled men, never kill on Sunday.

The title *Twelfth Night* is derived from the Ozark custom of celebrating Christmas on January 6.

Pucket's New Year. January 1, 1956. Written by John Meston. Guest cast: Ralph Moody, James Nusser. Aired on television January 5, 1957.

During a blizzard, old buffalo hunter Ira Pucket is injured and is left to die on the prairie by his skinner Jed Larner. Matt and Chester find Pucket and bring him back to Dodge. His leg wound is quite severe, and although Doc saves Pucket's life, he is forced to walk with a cane and give up buffalo hunting. All that the embittered Pucket wants now, is to kill Larner for deserting him.

Doc's Revenge. January 8, 1956. Written by John Dunkel. Guest cast: Vic Perrin, John Dehner. Aired on television June 9, 1956.

Clem Maddow rides into town and Doc runs to get his gun. Chester and Matt are bewildered as Doc threatens to kill Maddow, whether the man defends himself or not. When questioned, Doc refuses to tell Matt the reason for his strange behavior. Later on, Maddow is found shot in the back. Although Doc is the obvious suspect, as a physician he must try to save the gravely wounded man.

How to Cure a Friend. January 15, 1956. Written by John Meston. Guest cast: Larry Dobkin, Harry Bartell, John Dehner, Ralph Moody. Aired on television November 10, 1956.

GUNSMOKE — III. THE PROGRAMS

Nick Search is an old friend of Matt's who has earned the reputation of being a notorious gambler. He arrives in Dodge with the intent of using Matt's influence with the local townspeople to lure them into a crooked card game. However, Nick must first convince Matt that he has gone straight.

Romeo. January 22, 1956. Written by John Meston. Guest cast: Sam Edwards, John Dehner, James Nusser, Joyce McCluskey. Aired on television November 9, 1957.

When Andy Bowers and Judy Worth, the children of two rival cattlemen, fall in love, it looks like there will be a range war. Matt's problems are further compounded, when a romantic Doc decides to goad Andy into proving his love by running away with Judy.

Bureaucrat. January 29, 1956. Written by John Meston. Guest cast: Vic Perrin, John Dehner, Harry Bartell. Aired on television March 16, 1957.

Claiming a woeful lack of law enforcement, a high-minded Washington official arrives in Dodge bent on reforming this wild and raucous frontier community. Refusing to heed Matt's warnings, the totally inept Rex Procter attempts to impose his strict reforms on the hard-living residents.

Legal Revenge. February 5, 1956. Written by John Meston. Guest cast: Helen Kleeb, Lawrence Dobkin, Stacy Harris. Aired on television November 17, 1956.

Matt and Chester investigate a bizarre story told by Doc. It seems that while returning from a professional visit, Doc stopped at an isolated cabin. There he discovered a wounded man being tended by a strange woman, each obviously struggling to stay awake after days and nights of sleeplessness. Doc surmises that the wound might have been inflicted by the woman after he notices a gun hidden under the man's cover.

Stacy Harris appeared on television as Doug Carter on the dramatic series, *Doorway to Danger,* Detective Beaujac on *N.O.P.D.,* and Mayor Clum of *The Life and Legend of Wyatt Earp.*

Kitty's Outlaw. February 12, 1956. Written by John Meston. Guest cast: Vic Perrin, Barney Phillips. Aired on television October 5, 1957.

An old friend of Kitty's, Cole Yankton, arrives in Dodge and he appears to be more than just a casual acquaintance. While Kitty has dinner with Matt at a restaurant of her choosing on the outskirts of town, Yankton and his accomplices rob the bank. Matt, Chester and Doc fear that Kitty has betrayed them.

New Hotel. February 19, 1956. Written by John Meston. Guest cast: Larry Dobkin, Vic Perrin, John Dehner, Joe DuVal, Harry Bartell.

Enoch Mills is a well-to-do rancher and a bit of an entrepreneur. He decides to put up a new hotel in town much to the consternation of Jim Dobie, the owner of the Dodge House. Dobie tells Mills he will do everything he can to stop him and advises him to "stay up nights." When the new hotel is burned to the ground Matt has his hands full trying to prevent violence.

There is an infamous recording of a "rehearsal" for this show in circulation. It is an excellent example of the "dirty Saturday" rehearsals *Gunsmoke* was notorious for. Everyone was quick to ad-lib, including musical director Rex Koury who played "I Don't Want to Set the World on Fire," while the new hotel was burning. Koury topped off the show with "There's a Small Hotel" from the musical *Pal Joey.* Not to be outdone, the sound effects technicians made sure that they were part of the fun, as dogs barked,

The Radio Programs

frogs croaked, birds sang, horses rode endlessly, guns misfired, and a melange of other sundry and suggestive noises echoed through the sound studio. No one was immune from the insanity, and no one was able to get through the rehearsal without breaking character and laughing.

Who Lives by the Sword. February 26, 1956. Written by John Meston. Guest cast: John Dehner, Sam Edwards, Clayton Post. Aired on television May 18, 1957.

Joe Delk is a calculating gunman whose ruthless stock and trade is shooting down men he goads into drawing against him. Despite his cold-blooded ways, Delk enjoys immunity from the law, something that Matt wants to put a stop to. Through Matt's intervention, Delk learns that the courts are not the only means by which justice can be served.

The Hunter. March 4, 1956. Written by John Dunkel. Guest cast: Sam Edwards, Harry Bartell, Nestor Paiva. Aired on television November 26, 1955.

Jase Murdock is a cruel and crazed buffalo hunter who fears no one, not the Indians, not the cavalry, and certainly not Matt Dillon, whom he once beat mercilessly and left for dead. Murdock and his Blackfoot skinner Golden Calf head for Indian territory to hunt buffalo, even though they have been warned that a treaty has made it off limits. Matt sets out to stop Murdock if he attempts to cross the line.

The Hunter was seen on television before it was aired on radio.

Bringing Down Father. March 11, 1956. Written by John Meston. Guest cast: Larry Dobkin, Vic Perrin, William Idelson.

Harley Burke is the tough trail boss of the Star M herd. When one of his men is killed, Burke is accused and jailed. Andy Gillan, the bitter young son of the owner of the herd, has been accompanying Burke to learn about the family business. When Kitty tells Matt she overheard Andy talking about how he would do anything to get back at his father, Matt suspects that there is much more to the crime.

William Idelson began in the 30s as a juvenile star of such radio programs as *Vic and Sade*. On television, he was a regular on *Mixed Doubles* and *One Man's Family* before shifting into producing. As a producer he was responsible for such series as *The Bob Newhart Show* and *Love American Style*.

The Man Who Would Be Marshal. March 18, 1956. Written by John Meston. Guest cast: John Dehner, James Nusser, Harry Bartell. Aired on television June 15, 1957.

Emmett Egan is a retired army officer who comes to Dodge determined to have Matt's job. Egan is searching for the excitement he once knew in the military and demands to have the opportunity of proving himself. He persuades Matt to deputize him, but when trouble develops Egan learns too late that the law of the military commands little respect among the frontier denizens of Dodge.

Hanging Man. March 25, 1956. Written by John Meston. Guest cast: Lawrence Dobkin, Virginia Gregg, John Dehner. Aired on television April 19, 1958.

When Mr. Sawyer is found hung in his store, everyone thinks it is suicide, except Matt. Sawyer is not the kind of man to kill himself and besides, his cashbox is missing. Matt waits patiently for the killer to show his hand, and when the normally penniless Mel Tucker starts spending money freely, Matt jails him. Mel has been courting saloon girl Cora Belle, and Matt suspects that he killed Sawyer so they could get married.

GUNSMOKE — III. THE PROGRAMS

How to Sell a Ranch. April 1, 1956. Written by John Meston. Guest cast: Ralph Moody, Harry Bartell, Kathy Marlowe, Joe DuVal.

Matt learns that Tupp Quaver is about to sell his ranch but is worried that the old man is so senile that he will be swindled out of his property. When Wayne Rudman arrives from Kansas City and expresses a genuine interest in purchasing the ranch, it appears that Matt has been needlessly concerned and that Tupp will get his asking price. When the deal turns sour Tupp surprises everyone as he outwits Rudman.

Widow's Mite. April 8, 1956. Written by John Meston. Guest cast: Virginia Christine, John Dehner. Aired on television May 10, 1958.

Ada Morton has "lost pride" in her husband Zack who has become an outlaw. When Matt kills Zack during a robbery attempt, a rumor circulates about town that Zack hid his money somewhere on his property. Leach Fields, a smooth-talkin' gambler, arrives in Dodge and starts to court Ada, causing Matt to suspect that he is motivated by more than just love for the widow.

The Executioner. April 15, 1956. Written by John Meston. Guest cast: Sam Edwards, John Dehner, Vic Perrin. Aired on television February 2, 1957.

Tom Clegg is a young itinerant proud of his reputation as a ruthless gunfighter. He goads Abe Curry into a gunfight knowing that the man is no match for him. When Abe's brother Morgan comes to Matt and demands justice, Matt tells him that he is unable to do anything because Abe drew first. Morgan takes off his gun and decides he will hound Clegg until his brother is avenged.

Indian Crazy. April 22, 1956. Written by John Meston. Guest cast: Larry Dobkin, Helen Kleeb.

Mr. and Mrs. Jallup arrive in town to settle on a piece of land they just purchased. However, they are greatly concerned because of rumors that Comanche renegades have been active near their isolated property. When their neighbor Bob Orin and Matt reassure them that the rumor is in fact fiction, they ride out to their land. Chester warns Matt that he took an awful "big responsibility" in reassuring the couple and weeks later when he and Matt ride out to visit the Jallup's, Chester's premonition is realized. The cabin is burned to the ground, and in a freshly dug grave they find Mrs. Jallup. When they ride out to Orin's place, he is found scalped, but Matt suspects that this time it was not the Indians.

Doc's Reward. April 29, 1956. Written by John Meston. Guest cast: John Dehner, Vic Perrin. Aired on television December 14, 1957.

Cam Seaton has been badly injured by a horse and Doc is rushing to his side to tend to his wounds. En route Doc is stopped by a man who threatens to shoot his horse if he continues. Doc responds by telling the man he will shoot him, explaining, "...Nobody keeps me from being where I'm needed." Unfortunately, the man calls Doc's bluff and shoots his horse but is killed in turn. By the time Doc arrives, Cam is dead. Matt is confronted by an awkward situation in Dodge when he refuses to jail Doc. Some of the townsfolk, and the dead man's brother, demand justice.

The Photographer. May 6, 1956. Written by John Dunkel. Guest cast: Larry Dobkin, Harry Bartell, James Nusser. Aired on television April 6, 1957.

Professor Jacoby, an "artist of the camera," arrives in Dodge to photograph the "violence of the West" which is what folks back East will pay for. He is disappointed,

The Radio Programs

however, for it just happens to be a "quiet" time in Dodge. When Old Toad, a harmless old man, is found scalped, Matt investigates. He is convinced that the man could not have been killed by Indians, and when he finds the imprint of a tripod near the killing, he suspects a terrible truth.

Cows and Cribs. May 13, 1956. Written by John Meston. Guest cast: Vic Perrin, John Dehner, Virginia Christine, Frank Cady, Jeanette Nolan. Aired on television December 7, 1957.

Joe Nadler is a homesteader who neglects his farm and his wife. The two are starving and have no more credit in town with which to buy seed. Matt finds Joe slaughtering one of Emmet Bowers' calves but Bowers refuses to press charges against a starving man. Nadler crosses the line, however, when he continues to rustle Emmet's beef and starts to sell the meat in Dodge. In another part of town, Ed Thorpe and his wife have succumbed to "spotted fever" leaving their infant to be tended to by Ma Smalley. When Nadler is killed the fates of his widowed wife and of the orphaned infant converge.

Buffalo Man. May 20, 1956. Written by John Meston. Guest cast: Vic Perrin, John Dehner, Larry Dobkin, Helen Kleeb. Aired on television January 11, 1958.

Matt and Chester are held captive by crazed buffalo hunter Ben Siple and his partner Earl Ticks. Accompanying them is Abby, a young woman who "belongs" to Ben and who is terribly abused. Plans to kill Matt and Chester are thwarted when Ben and Earl are forced to flee to avoid being captured by the Pawnee Indians. They leave Matt and Chester tied up for the Pawnee to finish, but the Indians are only after buffalo hunters and free Matt and Chester who, in turn, rescue Abby and set out after her tormentors.

Man Hunter. May 27, 1956. Written by John Meston. Guest cast: Lawrence Dobkin, John Dehner, Ken Lynch.

Ben Quillan, deputy sheriff from Prescott Arizona, arrives in Dodge City with a warrant for the arrest of Ike Abbott. Abbott is wanted for a murder he committed three years ago. When Matt looks at the warrant, the man described sounds surprisingly like Hank Young, Emmett Bowers' hired hand who has been living in Dodge for three years. Hank is a likeable sort who never wears a gun, but when Quillan's presence makes Hank take his gun out of mothballs, Matt suspects he may have misjudged the young man.

The Pacifist. June 3, 1956. Written by John Meston. Guest cast: James Nusser, Vic Perrin, Harry Bartell, Paul DuBov.

Matt and Chester run into Jeb Wingate, who was about to act as a good samaritan for Hardin Hook, a "poor half starved pilgrim." The two take over for Jeb and help Hook rescue his pathetic wagon. Hook is a scared looking little man from Montana territory who hopes to get a job laying tracks for the Santa Fe. In the meantime, however, he gets a job from Sam Noonan cleaning up at the Long Branch. Missourians, Bill Centers and Ed Hogler, see Hook at the Long Branch and decide they have some unfinished business with their old war buddy. They aim to kill him.

Daddy-O. June 10, 1956. Written by John Meston. Guest cast: John McIntire, Lawrence Dobkin. Aired on television June 1, 1957.

Kitty's father Wayne Russell shows up in Dodge under the pretext of being concerned about her welfare. Although Kitty has not seen him since childhood, Wayne Russell wants her to sell her share in the Long Branch, withdraw all her savings, and leave Dodge to join him in New Orleans.

Cheap Labor. June 17, 1956. Written by John Meston. Guest cast: Lawrence Dobkin, Vic Perrin, Barney Phillips, Harry Bartell, Jeanne Bates. Aired on television May 4, 1957.

Fos Capper has given up his life as a gunman. He meets and falls in love with Kerry Stancil, but her brother Ben forbids the courtship. Ben does not want to lose Kerry. He needs her to do the cooking, cleaning, and all the other chores he would rather not have to pay someone to do. Fos continues to see Kerry despite Ben's objections. However, no matter how hard Fos tries to avoid violence, he is finally forced to meet Ben in a gunfight as a last resort in settling their differences.

Sunday Supplement. June 24, 1956. Written by John Meston. Guest cast: John Dehner, Harry Bartell, Joseph Kearns, Lou Krugman, Ralph Moody. Aired on television February 8, 1958.

Two New York writers, Samuel Sprague and Clifton Bunker, come to Dodge to get a story to thrill their Eastern readers. Disappointed by the lack of gunfights and Indian massacres, they create their own drama. They disturb a Pawnee burial ground and steal a sacred Fox Clan totem from Little Hawk, causing an Indian uprising that is brutally suppressed by the cavalry.

Gun for Chester. July 1, 1956. Written by John Meston. Guest cast: Lawrence Dobkin. Aired on television September 21, 1957.

A stranger arrives in Dodge and Chester recognizes him to be Asa Ledbetter, the man who once vowed to kill him should they ever meet again. Chester claims Ledbetter comes from Live Oak County in South Texas, known as a hideout for bandits where "if the law ever did catch any of them, there ain't enough good men around to act as a jury to try the bad ones." Chester lives in fear of imminent death as all his friends, Matt included, think his story is an exaggeration, especially since Ledbetter denies any knowledge of Chester, and Chester refuses to say why the stranger wants to kill him.

Passive Resistance. July 8, 1956. Written by John Meston. Guest cast: Ralph Moody, John Dehner, Harry Bartell, Jack Moyles. Aired on television January 17, 1959.

Dillon sets out to find the persons responsible for beating up gentle Gideon Seek and slaughtering his sheep. His efforts to seek justice are frustrated, however, when the non-violent Seek refuses to identify two cattlemen, Kell and Boyles, as his assailants.

Letter of the Law. July 15, 1956. Written by John Meston. Guest cast: Joseph Kearns, Vic Perrin, Paul DuBov, Helen Kleeb, Will Wright. Aired on television October 11, 1958.

Matt is ordered by Judge Rambaugh of Wichita to evict ex-gunman Brandon Teek and his wife Sarah from their home. Due to a loop-hole in the law, the Teeks lose all rights to their claim since they did not file their deed within a year's time. Lee Sprague, a wealthy landowner files for the land and Rambaugh determines that Sprague is the rightful owner. When Matt refuses to remove the Teeks, due to the impending birth of Sarah's first child, Rambaugh sends deputy sheriff Jim Haley to do his dirty work.

The Radio Programs

Lynching Man. July 22, 1956. Written by John Meston. Guest cast: Vic Perrin, James Nusser, Harry Bartell, Lawrence Dobkin, John Dehner, Jack Moyles. Aired on television November 15, 1958.

The lynching of homesteader Hank Blinnis by two transients, Shelby and Kringle, starts a chain of grim events. Charlie Drain, a fanatic who bears the scars of seeing his father lynched, is positive that rancher Gil Mather, who recently complained about having some horses stolen, is responsible for the killing. Drain threatens to take the matter into his own hands unless Matt brings the criminal to justice.

Lost Rifle. July 29, 1956. Written by John Meston. Guest cast: John Dehner, Vic Perrin, Jack Kruschen, Richard Beals. Aired on television November 1, 1958.

Frank Paris and Ben Tiple get into an argument and Matt breaks it up just in time. However, Matt fears that the two men are bound for violence. His suspicions unfortunately come true, when he finds Paris shot in the back. There are no witnesses to the crime except young Andy Spangler, who claims he only heard the shot. Everyone in town, including Andy's father Joe wants to see Tiple arrested. Matt is reluctant to arrest his friend, however, for he is convinced Ben would not shoot a man in the back.

Sweet and Sour. August 5, 1956. Written by John Meston. Guest cast: Lynn Allen, Lawrence Dobkin, Harry Bartell. Aired on television March 2, 1957.

Frontier violence explodes in Dodge when newly-arrived saloon girl Rena Decker purposely goads admirers into fights over her affections. In spite of Kitty's shrewd appraisal of the new girl, Matt befriends Rena and arranges for her to work at the Long Branch. Blazing street fights bring death to four men as a result of the girl's strange compulsion to have men fight over her.

Snakebite. August 12, 1956. Written by John Meston. Guest cast: Joseph Kearns, Vic Perrin, Lawrence Dobkin. Aired on television December 20, 1958.

Old Pony Thompson arrives in Dodge for his annual drunk. The scraggly prairie loner who peers over his bushy eyebrows "like an old grey wolf," is accompanied by his little dog. However, Pony soon realizes that Dodge is a bad enough place for humans let alone a poor little pup, when Walt Gorman indiscriminately shoots the puppy down. Walt and his cohort John Hakes are two unsavory fellows that Matt wants out of town, and Matt makes no "bones" about his hostile feelings towards them.

Annie Oakley. August 19, 1956. Written by John Meston. Guest cast: Jeanette Nolan, Harry Bartell, Paul DuBov. Aired on television October 24, 1959.

Matt intercedes in an effort to prevent bloodshed when Kate Kinsman, a romance starved wife, goads her husband Jeff into a fight with their neighbor Ed Dolliver. Kate insists that Dolliver has been flirting with her. Later, when Jeff is found murdered, Dolliver is the prime suspect.

No Sale. August 26, 1956. Written by John Meston. Guest cast: John Dehner, Lawrence Dobkin, Vic Perrin, Harry Bartell.

Tom Breese and Red Temple offer Sam Noonan and Kitty $20,000 for the Long Branch. The terms of the sale would be $10,000 cash and $5000 a year for the next two years. Sam is excited by the prospects, but Kitty is wary of the offer. After thinking it over, Kitty decides not to sell. Breese, however, is determined to own the saloon no matter what he has to do to get it, even if he has to turn his hired gun Temple loose on Sam and Kitty.

GUNSMOKE — III. THE PROGRAMS

FIFTH SEASON

Old Pal. September 2, 1956. Written by Les Crutchfield. Guest cast: Lynn Allen, Tim Graham, Lawrence Dobkin, John Dehner.
   Will Borgler tells Matt that Miss Lily, a Long Branch hostess, bought a ticket on the Santa Fe bound for Kansas City. There is nothing unusual about this, except for the fact that Lily paid for it with two $10 bank notes whose serial numbers match those of a recent Wells Fargo robbery. Matt's good friend Jim Rankin was murdered and in the heist $60,000 in bank notes had been stolen. Neither Jim's body nor the money had been recovered. Matt questions Lily, but she denies any knowledge of who gave her the notes. When Lily later disappears with gambler Deuce McCoy, Matt believes the two know more about the crime then they are saying.

Belle's Back. September 9, 1956. Written by Les Crutchfield. Guest cast: Virginia Christine, Ralph Moody, Sammie Hill. Aired on television May 14, 1960.
   Belle Ainsley, who ran away with wanted criminal Jess Crider, returns to Dodge. She wants to pick up the pieces of her life and make peace with the good people of town who condemned her. Matt is one of the people who need convincing, for before Belle's departure he spent quite a bit of time in her company. Belle confesses to Matt that when she left with Crider three years ago, she was gagged, tied, and draped across the back of his saddle. Three months later when she returned home, she was ostracized by the citizens of Dodge, and returned to her abductor. As bad as Jess was, he was her man. Belle denies any knowledge of Crider's current whereabouts, saying she left him for good back in Durango. However, the actions of Belle's embittered younger sister, Phyllis, make Matt suspect otherwise.

Thick 'n' Thin. September 16, 1956. Written by Les Crutchfield. Guest cast: Vic Perrin, Barney Phillips, Peggy Rea. Aired on television December 26, 1959.
   Odie Perkins and Brace McCoy, who have been friends and partners for over fifteen years, threaten to dissolve their partnership. The two men refuse to tell Matt what set off this sudden feud, but since they jointly own their homestead, Matt has the men draw cards to determine who lives in the house and who gets the barn. That being resolved, the two embittered ranchers leave, but Matt fears the situation will escalate into violence.
   Peggy Rea was a regular on *The Red Skelton Show, The Waltons,* and *The Dukes of Hazzard.*

Box O' Rocks. September 23, 1956. Written by Les Crutchfield. Guest cast: Ralph Moody, Paul DuBov, Joseph Kearns. Aired on television December 5, 1959.
   Matt finds an empty coffin when he interrupts the burial of shiftless old Packy Roundtree. The discovery leads Matt to a confrontation with three men, a sadistic bully who would shatter a man's legs to gain title to a flock of sheep, Reverend Blouze an unordained parson who would mislead but not lie, and an admitted coward who finds a strange and effective manner to wreak revenge.

The Brothers. September 30, 1956. Written by William Leicester. Guest cast: Vic Perrin, Sam Edwards.
   Gunman Leif Tugwell arrives in Dodge from Sweetwater. The one-time marshal of San Antonio is a sad-faced grey haired fellow, with a "face like a hound dog." At one time Leif was a friend of Matt's, but having a gunman in town is not something

The Radio Programs

Matt relishes. When 18-year-old Trace Gore announces he is going to kill Leif, Matt intervenes. Matt feels responsible for Leif since they are really "brothers under the skin." Even so, Matt wants Leif out of town at once, until Doc informs him that the ex-gunman is suffering from a degenerative neurologic disease and "can't hold a gun much less pull a trigger."

The Gambler. October 7, 1956. Written by John Dunkel. Guest cast: Lawrence Dobkin, Ralph Moody.

Clint Ascombe an Ohio Riverboat gambler arrives in Dodge looking for Jamison Cass. Clint is "a man eaten up by hate." He has a look in his eye that Matt has seen too often, and Matt knows Clint's purpose is to kill old Cass. Clint does not deny this, and it is a mystery to Matt and to Cass, as well, why Clint, who has never even met the old man, wants to kill him so desperately.

Gunshot Wound. October 14, 1956. Written by Gil Doud. Guest cast: Harry Bartell, Vic Perrin, Lawrence Dobkin, Jess Kirkpatrick.

Dr. Clay from Abelene tells Jim Neilson that the bullet he caught a few months ago cannot be removed. Even though Jim appears to be healing nicely, the bullet is moving around in his body and the young man will soon die. Hearing this, Jim heads back to Dodge, determined to kill the two men responsible for his "death," Tom and Charley Mahler.

'Til Death Do Us. October 21, 1956. Written by Les Crutchfield. Guest cast: John Dehner, Virginia Gregg, Ralph Moody, Don Diamond. Aired on television January 16, 1960.

A mysterious gunman takes a potshot at miserly Jezra Cobb on Dodge City's Main Street. When Matt investigates, he is shocked to learn that the shooting might be the result of Jezra's attempts to "reform" several of the local saloon girls. Upon further investigation Matt unearths evidence that a drifter was paid $300 to accomplish the deed.

Dirty Bill's Girl. October 28, 1956. Written by Les Crutchfield. Guest cast: Virginia Christine, Vic Perrin, John Dehner.

Rose, a lady gambler, arrives from down South and takes over the Black Jack table at the Long Branch. She is quite an attraction, for Dodge has never seen a female Black Jack dealer before. Matt notices that after three weeks of operation, Rose has not lost yet. He watches her game with intense interest, but cannot determine if she is cheating. Rose's philosophy is simple, "You can't cheat an honest man, but a crook is fair game any day." However, Young Slim Raddick who has taken a shine to Rose, is not a crook and has already lost $2642. Rose informs Matt that she is going to return all of Slim's losings when she leaves Dodge, but professional gambler Elco Dean is another story altogether. Dean has lost over $200 to Rose and she is not through with him yet, not by a long shot.

Crowbait Bob. Preempted November 4, 1956 for a United Nations special session. Aired November 10, 1956 only. Written by Les Crutchfield. Guest cast: Ralph Moody, Larry Dobkin, Virginia Gregg. Aired on television March 26, 1960.

Crowbait Bob, an aged prospector who is suffering from ill health, touches off trouble when he asks Matt to draw up a will naming Kitty as his sole heir. When Elbin and Ruth Cutler, Bob's miserly relatives, learn of the will, they conclude that Crowbait has struck it rich, and plot to get their hands on the estate.

GUNSMOKE — III. THE PROGRAMS

Pretty Mama. November 11, 1956. Written by Les Crutchfield. Guest cast: Jeanne Bates, Butch Bernard, John Dehner.

Hank Marble's son Beenie comes to town to tell Matt that his dad has been shot and killed. When Matt rides out to investigate, he questions June Marble about her husband's death. At first, June tells Matt that Hank was without enemies, but later she admits that Hank had had a recent argument with Jack Teeg, a cowboy known to be a woman chaser. It appears that Teeg had been paying some attention to June and Hank ordered him off his land. Although, things look bad for Teeg, Matt is not convinced and his investigation leads him to the truth.

Brother Whelp. November 18, 1956. Written by Les Crutchfield. Guest cast: Larry Dobkin, Vic Perrin, Lillian Buyeff. Aired on television November 7, 1959.

Sted Rudker returns to Dodge after being away for six years. He finds that, in his absence, his father has died and has left the family ranch to his brother Tom. Adding insult to injury, his "intended," Tessie, has married Tom. Sted vows to kill Tom who "made a clean sweep for hisself." Formalities aside he tells Tessie, "As far as I'm concerned you're still my girl." Matt is caught in the middle trying to avert a tragedy.

Tail to the Wind. November 25, 1956. Written by Les Crutchfield. Guest cast: Ralph Moody, John Dehner, Helen Kleeb. Aired on television October 17, 1959.

Doc drives into town from Meadow Flats with the news that Burke Reese and his "ornery" son Spike are terrorizing peaceful Pezzie Nellor and his wife Cora. Matt is frustrated when his offers of assistance are refused and Pezzie explains that he is a mild man who has learned from cattle, "When a storm comes up they just turn their tail to the wind and wait it out." Unfortunately, Reese wants Pezzie's land and Matt knows that he and his son are not above killing for it. The situation looks grave for Pezzie for he refuses to sign a complaint and Matt is waiting to attend his funeral. An unexpected turn of events, however, shows that sometimes "a couple of babes" can confront a "forest of wolves" without resorting to violence.

Speak Me Fair. December 2, 1956. Written by Les Crutchfield. Guest cast: John Dehner, Harry Bartell, Vic Perrin. Aired on television May 7, 1960.

Old Silas Treach is losing cattle and asks Matt to find the rustlers. He has a great hatred for Indians and suspects that they are the ones responsible. When a young Indian boy is found half dead with his tongue cut out, Matt suspects that the two events are somehow related.

Braggart's Boy. December 9, 1956. Written by Les Crutchfield. Guest cast: John Dehner, Larry Dobkin, Sam Edwards.

Old man Cleveland's son Tom has arrived from Philadelphia. Tom has never known his father and at the train depot everyone laughs at his outfit which he thought was "correct Western attire." Cleveland decides to teach the boy how to use a gun so that he can be a "man." Matt warns Cleveland not to push his boy, but when Tom confronts Brawley Star in the Long Branch, it seems that the warning has come too late.

Cherry Red. December 16, 1956. Written by Les Crutchfield. Guest cast: Sammie Hill, Vic Perrin, Bill Lally. Aired on television June 11, 1960.

Cherry O'Dell's husband Slim has turned outlaw, but she denies the truth. When Slim is killed during a hold-up, Cherry vows revenge. When Red Larnard, a Wells Fargo agent, is wounded by an unknown assailant, Matt suspects Cherry of the deed.

The Radio Programs

Beeker's Barn. December 23, 1956. Written by Les Crutchfield. Guest cast: Ralph Moody, Vic Perrin, Virginia Gregg.

Jethro Beeker comes to Matt demanding that he arrest a couple who have taken over his barn. He claims that they entered during a blizzard and shot at him. It turns out that the "couple" happens to be his daughter Harmony and her husband Will Ross. Jethro disowned Harmony when she married Will and Jethro wants Matt to treat them "like any other criminals." Matt reluctantly goes to evict the young couple, but Will is bent on keeping his wife sheltered during the snow storm.

Hound Dog. December 30, 1956. Written by Les Crutchfield. Guest cast: John Dehner, Vic Perrin, Richard Beals.

Karpas Daig lives alone with his hound Danny Boy. The old hound is going blind and can no longer hunt but he is "everything" to Daig. When Danny Boy is found wounded and dies Karpas suspects his neighbor Pete Rainer. The embittered old man threatens to settle matters in his own way, and Matt must intervene to avoid bloodshed.

Devil's Hindmost. January 6, 1957. Written by Les Crutchfield. Guest cast: Vic Perrin, Harry Bartell, Virginia Christine.

Rancy Weber has left her husband Buck. After seven years of loneliness, drudgery, and abuse on the prairie, she finds the Long Branch a better place than the farm. When an enraged Buck storms into the saloon and tries to drag her back, Matt intervenes. Buck learns that Frisco Bates, a handsome gambler, has been courting Rancy, and he vows revenge.

Ozymandias. January 13, 1957. Written by Les Crutchfield. Guest cast: Vic Perrin, John Dehner, Larry Dobkin.

Burke Krager has finally succeeded in getting papers from Washington evicting Slope Carson from his land. Slope has labored day and night on his homestead for the past three years and is a peaceful man. Krager has over 30,000 acres and Matt wonders what he wants with Slope's 360. An indignant Matt confronts Krager with his avarice, but Krager explains that he set out to own every piece of land between Briar Ridge and Walnut Creek and rename it the Krager Ranch. When a desperate Slope threatens to fight for his land, violence seems inevitable. Help arrives in the unexpected form of Burke's son Crowdy, who has grown to hate his father.

This story is named after Shelley's famous poem that deals with mortality and the transience of power and fame.

Categorical Imperative. January 20, 1957. Written by Les Crutchfield. Guest cast: John Dehner, Ben Wright.

Matt has jailed Clay Macklin for cattle rustling. However, everyone knows, including Judge Bent, that the evidence is not enough to hold him. Clay has little respect for the law and escapes after outwitting Chester. A stubborn Matt pursues him insisting that Macklin have his day in court, even though he and Chester may lose their lives in the blizzard that is currently raging outside.

Woman Called Mary. January 27, 1957. Written by Les Crutchfield. Guest cast: Virginia Gregg, Vic Perrin.

Buffalo Mary is a hard working old woman who struggles alone to maintain her farm. When Matt and Chester ride up to water their horses, they find Mary bruised and with a black eye. She tells them that Reb Sutter, a town bully, beat her and stole her life savings of $48. Matt sets out to bring Reb to justice.

Cold Fire. February 3, 1957. Written by Les Crutchfield. Guest cast: Helen Kleeb, Sam Edwards, Harry Bartell.

Mr. Botkin accuses his bank teller Marvin Goss of stealing $20,000 in gold reserves. When Matt arrives with a warrant for his arrest Goss pulls a gun and Matt is forced to kill him. Mrs. Goss, a nice old lady who was very close to her son, denies that Marvin could have committed such a crime. Matt and Chester search her house, but find no sign of the stolen gold. Several weeks later Mrs. Goss announces that she is going back East to visit with relatives, and tells Matt that he was not to blame for Marvin's death. As Chester keeps reflecting on how close mother and son were, Matt has a revelation.

Hellbent Harriet. February 10, 1957. Written by Les Crutchfield. Guest cast: Virginia Christine, John Dehner.

Jim Morning is found dead and it appears that he was thrown by his horse and dragged. When his wife Harriet is told, she reveals that Jim was probably killed by their neighbor Berle Albin, who covets their land and Harriet as well. After Doc re-examines the body, he declares that Jim's death was indeed accidental, and believes that Harriet is just a hysterical widow. Matt, however, suspects that there might be some truth to what Harriet has been saying.

Doubtful Zone. February 17, 1957. Written by Les Crutchfield. Guest cast: Ben Wright, Sammie Hill, Larry Dobkin.

Miles' store is robbed of some clothes, a pair of boots, a gun, and a bottle of perfume. Matt suspects that the culprit may have been a boy or a woman, for the boots were a very small size. Another store is robbed, and the only things taken are 44-caliber cartridges. When Matt gets to the bottom of things he finds 16-year-old Willy Deaver responsible. The young girl ran away from her abusive stepfather and right into a world of crime. When Matt attempts to arrest her, she escapes, an act that ultimately leads to tragedy.

Impact. February 23, 1957. Written by Les Crutchfield. Guest cast: Sam Edwards, Ben Wright.

Doc goes to see Miss Larkin who has been injured by a bull, and Matt and Chester come along. Miss Larkin tells Matt that the bull's nose-ring broke and that she was most fortunate. Just a few weeks back a horse had thrown her as well, and she was unscathed. To add to her good fortune, Miss Larkin has Lonnie Welsh helping her. She had been alone since her husband and son died and Lonnie is like a son to her. In reality Lonnie is a "shifty-eyed cuss" and Matt tells Mrs. Larkin to be careful. Miss Larkin is offended by Matt's sharp criticism of Lonnie, and in response, orders the lawman off her land.

Colleen So Green. March 3, 1957. Written by Les Crutchfield. Guest cast: John Dehner, Jeanne Bates, Ben Wright.

Pretty orphan Colleen Tawny arrives in Dodge. She informs Matt and Chester that she is from San Francisco and is on her way South to live with relatives. Colleen claims that someone stole her handbag and she is totally broke. Chester is the first of many men to fall for her beauty and Southern drawl. Doc falls victim to her charms as well,

The Radio Programs

explaining that she is "wide-eyed and helpless like a newborn babe," which is exactly why Matt does not trust her. Within three days Colleen has a full larder of groceries sent to her by her admirers. Tough old Bull Rager has even signed over his house to Colleen in the hopes of marrying her. The ever astute Kitty warns Matt to be prepared for trouble.

Grebb Hassle. March 10, 1957. Written by Les Crutchfield. Guest cast: Vic Perrin, Vivi Janiss, Sam Edwards.

Alvin Grebb returns to town after getting out of jail and strikes up a conversation with Matt. The marshal greets Grebb with the warning he should leave town and that his mother and brother are better off without him. While Grebb continues his strained dialogue with Matt, his two accomplices rob the bank.

Spring Freshet. March 17, 1957. Written by Les Crutchfield. Guest cast: John Dehner, Larry Dobkin, Ben Wright.

Saddle Sore Sal. March 24, 1957. Written by Les Crutchfield. Guest cast: Vic Perrin, Virginia Gregg, Ben Wright.

Sal has come to Dodge from the Panhandle pursuing Bricoff Docker who has swindled her. She claims that he sold her a hundred head of cattle knowing full well that they had cowpox. Three days after Docker left the cattle started dying. Sal is handy with a gun and Matt tries to avert violence.

Chicken Smith. March 31, 1957. Written by Les Crutchfield. Guest cast: Larry Dobkin, Virginia Christine, John Dehner.

Prag Looner is the new owner of the Lady Gay Saloon. He sets his sights on pretty Ellie, a young and reckless woman, who just happens to be married to Chicken Smith. When Kitty tells Matt that Ellie has been slipping into Dodge late at night, Matt prepares for trouble.

Rock Bottom. April 7, 1957. Written by Les Crutchfield. Guest cast: Harry Bartell, Jeanne Bates, Ben Wright, Barney Phillips.

Van Tover is an ex-gunman who surrendered his gun to Matt years ago, when he settled in Dodge and married Edna. Unfortunately, Tover's past has caught up with him in the form of Largo Greeland, who swore to kill him after Tover showed him up in a gunfight. Tover wants his gun back but Matt points out that he is too rusty to stand up to Greeland, who has been searching for him for 12 years. When Tover insists on meeting his nemesis, Matt searches for a way to avoid the inevitable.

Saludos. April 14, 1957. Written by Les Crutchfield. Guest cast: Larry Dobkin, John Dehner, Jim Nusser. Aired on television October 31, 1959.

Souchee travels 50 miles with a bullet wound, after her husband Walking Deer is killed. Unfortunately, she does not survive. Matt and Chester track down three suspects Peggar, Steed and Foss. Not knowing which one is the murderer, Matt heads them all back toward Dodge, with the story that Souchee can identify the murderer. In reality, Matt is just waiting for one of them to make a wrong move.

This episode is often confused with *Odd Man Out* and *Spring Freshet.*

Bear Trap. April 21, 1957. Written by Les Crutchfield. Guest cast: Ralph Moody.

Hod Logan returns to Dodge after having been in jail for a robbery. He is looking for Andy who was "downright brave" in identifying him during the trial. Matt gets caught up in the affair and tries to prevent Andy's death. Andy, however, has a few thoughts on how to confront Logan.

Medicine Man. April 28, 1957. Written by Les Crutchfield. Guest cast: John Dehner, Vic Perrin, Virginia Gregg.

Hart Finney and his wife Meg have left Virginia to start a new life out West. On their way they stop in Dodge to sell "Old Doctor Walker's muscle, bone, blood and nerve tonic." They set their wagon on what appears to be the only vacant lot in Dodge. However, Matt must evict them when Grant Medford files a legal complaint that they are trespassing. Finney finds a loophole because land that has been unimproved for five years reverts to public land. Medford does not take kindly to this and when he shows up with nine of his men Matt realizes that violence cannot be avoided.

How to Kill a Friend. May 5, 1957. Rerun.

Sheep Dog. May 12, 1957. Written by Les Crutchfield.

Jeb Barkas and his dog are herding sheep when Matt and Chester ride up. They are looking for Jeb's son Orlin, who has shot Will Peterson. The unarmed Peterson was shot when he rightly accused Orlin of cheating in poker. Jeb informs Matt that his son is one of his "flock" and he will handle matters in his own way.

One Night Stand. May 19, 1957. Written by Les Crutchfield.

When Ben Argo shows up in Dodge with $15,000 in gold in his saddle bags, he tells Matt that he plans on staying one day and wants to deposit his gold overnight. He fears that some men are after him, for there are many parasitic characters hanging around the prospectors who have been mining on Gold Hill. When Pete Wells and Rocky Martin show up in town it seems that Argo's fears are well founded. However, Matt suspects that Argo is not quite telling the truth.

Pal. May 26, 1957. Written by Tom Hanley.

Chester brings in a sick dog for Doc to look at. The dog, which looks more like a wolf, is Spiny Murphy's protection against his wife Moll. Moll has little respect for her runt of a husband and has the charming habit of beating him. Doc finally agrees to "prostitute his talents" and treat Pal, who appears to have strychnine poisoning. Matt suspects that Moll poisoned the dog to get rid of Spiny's defender.

Ben Tolliver's Stud. June 2, 1957. Rerun.

Dodge Podge. June 9, 1957. Written by Les Crutchfield.

Packy Sutter is frequently beaten by his brutal father Lafe, who wants to make a man and cattleman of the boy. Packy, however, loves to read and is befriended by Jason Roll, who raises sheep and shares Packy's interests. In Sutter's eyes this makes Roll a fair target for his hatred. When Packy runs away Sutter comes looking for Jason and Matt is forced to intervene.

Summer Night. June 16, 1957. Written by Tom Hanley.

A wagon train passes through Dodge on its way from Ohio to California. The pioneers are befriended by the townspeople, but when they leave Kitty and Doc plummet into a depression because they know that the naive settlers are unaware of the

The Radio Programs

dangers lying before them. This provides the setting for a reunion between Jennie Bailey, one of the women in the caravan, and her husband Clint, who has been chasing the wagons since he was discharged from the army.

Home Surgery. June 23, 1957. Rerun.

The Buffalo Hunter. June 30, 1957. Rerun.

Word of Honor. July 7, 1957. Rerun.

Bloody Hands. July 14, 1957. Rerun.

Kitty Caught. July 21, 1957. Rerun.

Cow Doctor. July 28, 1957. Rerun.

Big Hands. August 4, 1957. Written by Les Crutchfield. Guest cast: Vic Perrin.
   Martha Rudker drives into town with her husband's body in the back of her wagon. She claims that Hank was shot by some stranger who wanted to water his horse. Martha eulogizes Hank saying that although he did not treat her good "at least he was always there." Matt suspects that there is more to the story and when Bull Logan becomes her hired hand he investigates the man's background.

Jayhawkers. August 11, 1957. Rerun.

The Peace Officer. August 18, 1957. Written by Norman Macdonnell. Aired on television October 15, 1960.
   The Citizen's Committee of nearby Tascosa sends for Matt because they want him to get rid of their crooked sheriff. Cleg Rawlins cleaned up their town like they asked, but now he has taken to victimizing the populace. When Matt tells Rawlins that he plans to replace him with a peace officer from Dodge, he is threatened. On his way back to Dodge, Matt is joined by Stella Harkney, Rawlins' ex-girlfriend who is running away from him. It is evident that Matt will not reach Dodge without a fight. If he makes it back to Dodge, his plans are to send a new peace officer, Bill Hickock, to Tascosa.

Grass. August 25, 1957. Rerun.

SIXTH SEASON

Jobe's Son. September 1, 1957. Written by Marian Clark. Guest cast: Vic Perrin, John Dehner.
   Tad Harley returns home after being away for four years. His father Jobe is ailing, but Doc feels that with Tad's support he will regain his health. However, Tad has no intention of taking care of the farm or the "broken down old man." When he starts to cause trouble in town, it becomes evident that Tad was up to no good during his four year absence. When Jobe discovers that Tad is planning to rob the Dodge bank he plans to keep the family name "clean."

GUNSMOKE — III. THE PROGRAMS

Loony McCluny. September 8, 1957. Written by Les Crutchfield. Guest cast: Virginia Gregg, Larry Dobkin, Jess Kirkpatrick.

Old Pop McCluny is a prospector little seen but well liked in Dodge. He comes to Doc asking that he assay his gold. Doc relents, even though he is resentful of his office being used as a "metallurgical laboratory." Once again Doc finds that Pop's strike is nothing more than fool's gold. When the "confounded lunatic" is murdered, Matt suspects that Pop's strikes may be more than pyrite.

Child Labor. September 15, 1957. Written by Robert Mitchell.

Orin Sybert is a rancher with a bad reputation. Not only is he mean, but he is known to renege on promises. When Buss and Howie Chaney, two orphaned boys arrive in Dodge, Matt befriends them and gets them jobs and shelter. When Sybert hires the boys to break broncos for him, trouble is assured.

Custer. September 22, 1957. Rerun.

Another Man's Poison. September 29, 1957. Written by Les Crutchfield. Guest cast: Vic Perrin.

Sally Bogan is seen running down the boardwalk as if she has just seen a ghost. Matt and Chester discover that she has just encountered her first husband, who has been a sailor on a clipper that went down four years before in a typhoon. Sally has since remarried, and Matt is caught between the two husbands who plan to settle matters like "men."

The Rooks. October 6, 1957. Written by Marian Clark. Guest cast: John Dehner, Jim Nusser, Vic Perrin, Harry Bartell, Barney Phillips, Don Diamond, Larry Dobkin.

Jess and Clate, the Rook brothers, show up in Dodge and start to tear up the town. Matt has just returned from Wichita and is sick with the ague and is not in the mood to take care of a couple of rowdy cowhands. He must finally leave his sickbed when the boys shoot a man without provocation.

The Margin. October 13, 1957. Written by Les Crutchfield. Guest cast: Vic Perrin, John Dehner.

Young Grody Beck has been accused by Flagg Miller's daughter of rustling her father's cattle. He is released from jail by Judge Beck because the girl is "too bashful" to appear in court and testify. Doc likes Grody and tells Matt that he thinks that Flagg's daughter lied because Grody scorned her. When Flagg loses another hundred head of cattle, he decides to take the law into his own hands.

Professor Lute Bone. October 20, 1957. Rerun.

Man and Boy. October 27, 1957. Written by Les Crutchfield. Guest cast: Vic Perrin.

Crowley Tobin, a special deputy from California, arrives in Dodge looking for Jess Richer. When Matt offers to help him capture the criminal, the young hot-headed Tobin refuses. Matt is concerned that this may turn out to be the deputy's first and last assignment.

Bull. November 3, 1957. Written by Robert Mitchell. Guest cast: John Dehner, Sam Edwards.

Buffalo hunter Bull Hogan causes a ruckus at the Long Branch, all in fun, of course.

The Radio Programs

He and his partner Delwin Casper have been working hard and have not had the opportunity to kick up their heels for quite a while. Matt warns Bull to "leave a little of the town for the people who live there," and although it cramps his style, Bull promises to try. Unfortunately, Bull gets into a fist fight with a young cowboy, Frank Wilkins, but leaves Frank still breathing. When Frank is found dead, however, everyone is sure Bull is responsible, and the boy's father puts a $1000 bounty on Bull's head.

Gunshy. November 10, 1957. Written by Marian Clark. Guest cast: Vic Perrin.

Rafe Mayfield believes that someone has been trespassing on his land. He suspects that it is Tom Wilson, who used to work for him. Rafe fired Tom because he was not good at his work and brought nothing but trouble. Tom is "purely out of place on the prairie" and "never should have left Baltimore in the first place." Rafe tells his wife that if he finds Tom hanging around, he will fill the outcast full of buckshot. Mrs. Mayfield finds the boy in the barn, wounded. It seems that Tom accidentally shot himself while trying to shoot a rabbit.

The Queue. November 17, 1957. Rerun.

Odd Man Out. November 24, 1957. Written by Les Crutchfield. Guest cast: John Dehner, Larry Dobkin, Harry Bartell. Aired on television November 21, 1959.

Elderly Cyrus reports to Matt that his wife has left him after 37 years of marriage. Matt decides to investigate and suspects foul play, when a drifter is caught trying to sell the missing woman's clothes.

Jud's Woman. December 1, 1957. Written by Marian Clark. Guest cast: Vic Perrin.

Chester and Matt are caught out on the prairie during a storm. When they seek refuge in a lonely cabin, they are turned away by a frightened woman holding a rifle. It turns out that she is Jennie, Jud Barton's "woman." Barton has forbidden her to talk to any men and is unbearably brutal. When Jennie finally escapes she seeks Matt's help. Doc examines her after she faints and finds that she has been beaten savagely and often, and will not survive another encounter with the crazed Jud.

Long As I Live. December 8, 1957. Written by Les Crutchfield. Guest cast: John Dehner.

While Doc is out of town on his first vacation in two years, Hod Bricker's daughter comes down with the "chokes" and dies. The embittered Hod blames Doc, and in retaliation shoots him in an ambush. With no doctor available for a hundred miles, Matt is forced to operate on Doc to remove the bullet.

Ugly. December 15, 1957. Written by Les Crutchfield. Guest cast: John Dehner, Vic Perrin.

Twenty-six-year-old Bruno Thayer, horribly deformed as a youth when he tried to outrace a herd of buffalo, is trying to make a go of the old Jenk's farm. Only his horse and dog are able to look at him without turning away in fear. Because of Bruno's terrifying appearance, wild stories are spread about him. When he saves Hazel Perkins from a wolf, the frightened woman claims that Thayer tried to attack her. An outspoken Frisbee has no trouble in inciting a mob to take care of the "monster" in their midst once and for all.

Twelfth Night. December 28, 1957. Rerun.

GUNSMOKE — III. THE PROGRAMS

Where'd They Go? December 29, 1957. Written by Les Crutchfield. Guest cast: Joseph Kearns, Virginia Gregg, Ralph Moody.

Wilbur Jonas accuses Clint Dodie of robbing the general store of $68. Although Jonas did not actually see his assailant, he is sure he recognized Dodie's voice. On that bit of flimsy testimony, Matt and Chester head out to Dodie's farm. When they arrive, Dodie assures them that he did not rob the store, but does not furnish an alibi. Matt has no choice, but to arrest Dodie. However, before they take the long trip back to Dodge, Dodie manages to persuade Matt and Chester to help him with all his chores, so as not to burden his pregnant wife Medora, while he is in jail.

Pucket's New Year. January 5, 1958. Rerun.

Second Son. January 12, 1958. Written by Marian Clark. Guest cast: John Dehner, Vic Perrin, Ben Wright.

Englishman Sedgley Carstairs loses his horse in a poker game to gambler Newston. Sedgley spends all his time and money trying to learn the game in preparation to win back his horse when Newston returns. Although, Sedge does not mean to, he gives the impression of having a lot of money, when in reality he has only a small allowance that has seriously dwindled down to a mere $3.00. Nevertheless, when Newston returns to town, he is convinced Sedge has money and he is determined to get it.

Moo Moo Raid. January 19, 1958. Written by Les Crutchfield. Guest cast: John Dehner, Vic Perrin.

Oney Hager has a special cow that is able to lead a herd of cattle through water. Tush Lee, who is depending on Hager's cow to bring his cattle into Dodge, accuses fellow cattleman Bert Collins of foul play, when Hager and his cow are missing.

One for Lee. January 26, 1958. Written by Les Crutchfield. Guest cast: John Dehner, Ralph Moody.

Senator Hooper arrives in Dodge to find he is the object of a vengeful assassin. The murder attempt fails, and the assassin turns out to be mild sheep farmer Willie Angel, who lost two brothers to Hooper during the Civil War.

Kitty's Killing. February 2, 1958. Written by Marian Clark. Guest cast: John Dehner.

Fanatic Jacob Leach asks Matt to put him in jail so that he does not kill Ollie Radford. Ollie was married to Jacob's sister, who died in childbirth. Now, unbeknownst to Jacob, Ollie's new wife Molly is expecting. When Jacob is released from jail and finds out that Molly is in labor, he wants revenge. Kitty tries to lure Jacob away from the Radfords, who are staying at Ma Smalley's.

Joke's On Us. February 9, 1958. Rerun.

Bruger's Folly. February 16, 1958. Written by Les Crutchfield.

Sam Bruger, paroled from prison after serving three years for a murder he did not commit, returns to Dodge hoping to clear his name. As a homecoming surprise, Sam finds that his wife Holly, whose testimony, or lack of it, helped to put him behind bars, has divorced him to marry Jack Dean.

The Surgery. February 23, 1958. Written by Marian Clark. Guest cast: John Dehner.

Lucy Middleton needs an operation or she will die, but her husband Aaron refuses

The Radio Programs

to let Doc perform the experimental surgery. Doc gets Matt to step in and the surgery is performed despite Aaron's attempts to prevent it.

The Guitar. March 2, 1958. Rerun.

Laughing Gas. March 9, 1958. Written by James Fonda & Norman Macdonnell. Guest cast: John Dehner, Ralph Moody, Vic Perrin. Aired on television March 29, 1958.
Stafford, a reformed gunman who now runs a laughing gas medicine show, wants to keep his promise to his wife to stay out of gunfights. The job is complicated after Stafford is mauled by three town bullies.

Real Sent Sonny. March 16, 1958. Written by Les Crutchfield.
Young Sonny Garnett tries to kill Matt, but fails and is arrested. Matt releases him with the hopes of finding Nate Skyler, a notorious outlaw, who put Sonny up to the deed.

Indian. March 23, 1958. Written by Les Crutchfield.
While traveling back to Dodge, Matt and Chester stumble upon a Pawnee Indian who has been brutally murdered. When Matt painfully recounts the story at the Long Branch, Egert, a man listening to the conversation, finds it amusing. Egert admits he has been killing Indians for the past 16 years, ever since his wife was murdered and his two-year-old son was captured by Pawnees. The wife of the murdered Pawnee comes to town to talk to Matt. Her 18-year-old "brother," Little White Wolf, saw a man fitting Egert's description leaving the scene of the crime.

Why Not. March 30, 1958. Written by Les Crutchfield. Guest cast: John Dehner.
Wealthy Cyrus Taggert arrives in Dodge searching for his runaway daughter Evie. Evie ran away from New York over a year ago and is living in town with part-time blackjack dealer Burl Alden and is working at the Long Branch. Since Evie is over the age of 21, Matt feels he should speak to "Patsy" before revealing her whereabouts to her determined father. Once Taggert is aware of Evie's situation, he puts the squeeze on Kitty by way of the bank, to have Patsy fired. Taggert will stop at nothing to make Evie return with him, even if it means hiring a hit man named Bill Jacks to kill Burl.

Yorky. April 6, 1958. Rerun.

Livvie's Loss. April 13, 1958. Written by Marian Clark. Guest cast: John Dehner, Vic Perrin, Jeanette Nolan.
Horatio Redgate, a philandering no-good, wanderer, returns to his wife Livvie and his son Ben. Livvie wants to keep Ben away from Horatio's evil influence, but Ben feels boxed in by his mother's over-protectiveness, claiming she keeps him tied to her like a "tethered calf." Ben and Horatio ride into Dodge for a night of drinking and free-living. Livvie stands outside the door of the Long Branch witnessing the corruption of her son. She responds by smashing Ben's bottle of whiskey and wishing that every saloon in Dodge be burned to the ground. "I'd even strike the matches," she declares, "If it would keep Ben out of the saloons." When The Prairie Wagon Saloon is burned to the ground, Livvie is accused of the incendiary deed.

GUNSMOKE — III. THE PROGRAMS

The Partners. April 20, 1958. Written by John Dunkel. Guest cast: James Nusser, Barney Phillips, John Dehner, Sam Edwards, Virginia Christine.

Little Maury Smith and Cranston P. Grover are partners in a "William Tell" exhibition. Cranston places a tin can on his head and Maury counts to three and shoots the can off. In return Cranston shoots one off Maury's head. When Matt stops the show, claiming a stray bullet could kill an innocent bystander, the two gamblers move their act outside of town. While in Dodge, Maury and Cranston stay at widow Effie Gans' boarding house and both men fall for her. According to Doc, "She's real pretty, too, but so's a rattlesnake, if you want to look at it that way."

The Squaw. April 27, 1958. Written by John Dunkel. Guest cast: Vic Perrin, Dick Crenna, Ralph Moody, Lillian Buyeff, Frank Cady.

While Chester blames President Grant for letting men take out a patent on barbed wire, which he believes will be the ruination of this country, a fight is in full progress at the Long Branch between Culley Tate and Ambrose. Matt breaks it up and Kitty buys him a drink for saving her place. It seems the fight began when Ambrose called Culley's father "squaw man" for marrying an Arapahoe woman. Culley's mother has been dead for some years and his new Indian stepmother is closer to his age than his father's. Culley is full of anger and bitterness over the "marriage," which has not been sanctioned by benefit of clergy. The boy is pious like his mother, who came from a long line of Puritan ministers. Matt fears that Culley might cause trouble for Hardie Tate and his young wife.

How to Die for Nothing. May 10, 1958. Preempted May 14, 1958. Rerun.

Little Bird. May 11, 1958. Written by Les Crutchfield. Guest cast: Harry Bartell, John McIntire, Lillian Buyeff.

Big, mean, 280-pound buffalo hunter Bull Taggert is "mean as sin and twice as ugly." When he arrives in town with a young frightened woman who is dark, beautiful and small "like a little bird," Bull claims she is his "Indian wife." In reality the woman is a Mexican named Maria Velazquez, who was kidnapped from her husband, Don Marco, by Bull.

The Stallion. May 18, 1958. Written by Marian Clark. Guest cast: Larry Dobkin, Ralph Moody, James Nusser.

Dan Stokes has borrowed money from Harker. When Harker's son, Oat, takes over his father's business, he demands repayment. Stokes is unable to pay because his crops have been damaged by fire, so Oat takes Stokes' prize stud horse as payment. The law is with Oat, so Stokes can do nothing, however, he threatens to kill Oat if the boy mistreats the horse in anyway.

Blue Horse. May 25, 1958. Written by Marian Clark. Guest cast: Dick Crenna, Vic Perrin, Harry Bartell. Aired on television June 6, 1959.

While returning to Dodge with a prisoner, Matt's horse accidentally stumbles injuring itself and Matt. Chester is forced to shoot the horse and to leave Matt with the prisoner, while he journeys to Dodge for Doc. Feverish and weak, Matt is overpowered by his prisoner and is left to die. He is saved, however, by Blue Horse, a fugitive Indian hunted by the cavalry.

Quarter-Horse. June 1, 1958. Rerun.

The Radio Programs

Hot Horse Hyatt. June 8, 1958. Written by Les Crutchfield. Guest cast: Jack Moyles, John Dehner, Richard Beals.

Del Braggen and some of his men are "fixin' to hang a stranger" for horse thieving. Doc gets Matt and he puts a stop to the lynching. Braggen claims he caught saddle bum Jesse Hyatt red handed with two of his best horses. When Jesse recovers from his injuries he denies the accusation. He claims he bought the horses from a trader in Wichita, but without proof he will probably be found guilty. Young Tommy Braggen, who does not think too much of his father and believes that "someday the devil's gonna get him," visits Jesse in his cell to apologize for his father's brutal ways. Before Tommy leaves, he gives Jesse a gun and promises to help him escape.

Old Flame. June 15, 1958. Written by Marian Clark. Guest cast: Joseph Kearns, Jeanne Bates, John Dehner. Aired on television May 28, 1960.

Dolly, an old girlfriend of Matt's seeks him out in Dodge City. Dolly claims she is running away from her philandering husband who wants to kill her. Kitty is wary of Dolly's behavior and points it out to Matt. Thinking that Kitty is too cynical, Matt checks Dolly's story and soon discovers that she may have other motives for her erratic actions.

Target. June 22, 1958. Written by Les Crutchfield. Guest cast: Tommy Cook, Ralph Moody, John Dehner. Aired on television September 5, 1959.

Trouble is imminent when gypsies camp on land owned by an unfriendly rancher. The problem is magnified by an attachment that grows between the rancher's son Danny and a gypsy girl named Nayomi.

What the Whiskey Drummer Heard. June 29, 1958. Rerun.

Chester's Choice. July 6, 1958. Written by Marian Clark. Guest cast: Harry Bartell, Larry Dobkin, Jess Kirkpatrick.

Chester overhears two men planning to rob the Dodge City bank. When the men discover him, they threaten to kill Doc and Kitty unless he cooperates with them. Chester is told to lure Matt out of town, leaving the two free to commit the robbery.

The Proving Kid. July 13, 1958. Written by Les Crutchfield. Guest cast: Vic Perrin, Virginia Christine, John Dehner.

A young upstart known only as Bravo, causes trouble for Matt when he tries to prove he is a man. First, he attempts to get Kitty's attention, but she rebuffs his advances and Matt is forced to cut Bravo down to size. When his girlfriend joins forces with her old partner in crime, Big Red, the jealous Bravo plots his revenge against Matt and Big Red.

Marshal Proudfoot. July 20, 1958. Written by Tom Hanley. Guest cast: John Dehner. Aired on television January 10, 1959.

Chester's father Wesley Proudfoot comes to town with the impression that Chester is the marshal. Not wanting to embarrass Chester in front of his father, Matt, Doc and Kitty pretend it is true. Trouble occurs however, when despite Matt's warning, Doc and Kitty stage a fake hold-up to make Chester look like a hero.

Parley Baer plays the parts of Chester and Chester's father in this episode.

The Cast. July 27, 1958. Rerun.

GUNSMOKE — III. THE PROGRAMS

Miguel's Daughter. August 3, 1958. Written by Marian Clark. Guest cast: Dick Crenna, Vic Perrin, Lynn Allen, Lawrence Dobkin. Aired on television November 28, 1959.

Josephina Ramirez, a young Mexican girl, is harrassed by two cowboys. When her proud father Miguel finds out, he seeks to avenge her honor. Matt attempts to track down the ruffians before Miguel gets to them.

A House Ain't a Home. August 10, 1958. Written by Les Crutchfield. Guest cast: Ralph Moody, Vic Perrin, John Dehner, Sammie Hill.

Old Jedro Higg, a rancher who does not come to town too often, is hanging out at the Long Branch drinking heavily and sporting a gun. Matt knows something is wrong. It appears that Jedro's son Raney has returned "like a bad penny." Gunslingers, Harden and King, who have "the wild bunch look to them" have accompanied Raney and taken over the ranch. The three men threw the old man out of his house and told him to cut wood and do chores if he wants to return. Now Jedro, a normally peaceful man, is wearing a gun, not so much for himself, but he is worried about his daughter Diane's safety.

The Piano. August 17, 1958. Written by Marian Clark. Guest cast: Vic Perrin, Virginia Gregg.

While pursuing Rack Miller and his brother, who have robbed the stage of $20,000 and killed the driver, Chester and Matt impose upon an elderly southern belle, Mrs. Hamford. The old lady is reluctant to allow the lawman and his assistant to enter her "elegant" home which contains all her precious treasures including an ancient upright cherry-wood piano. Mrs. Hamford and her home, which is no more than a tumbled-down shack, have seen better days. However, in her mind's eye she still lives in the grand style she has always been accustomed to. She has trained herself "not to see or hear the ugly things in life."

The Blacksmith. August 24, 1958. Rerun.

I Thee Wed. August 31, 1958. Written by Les Crutchfield. Guest cast: John Dehner, Virginia Christine, Harry Bartell. Aired on television April 16, 1960.

Matt tangles with a cowardly wife beater named Sam Lacket. Lacket's long-suffering wife Hester finally testifies against Lacket after he almost kills her, and Matt throws the brute in jail. Unfortunately, Lacket's term is shortened, when Hester produces the necessary money for his release.

SEVENTH SEASON

Tried It — Didn't Like It. September 7, 1958. Written by Les Crutchfield. Guest cast: Vic Perrin, Jeanne Bates, Richard Beals.

Hank Jurgen calls on Matt to intercede when he discovers twelve-year-old Eddie Kates has been taking pot shots at his prize turkeys. Unaccustomed to having the law step in, Hank feels the necessity because of his old romance with Alma, Eddie's mother. Alma was once Hank's girlfriend, but has since married Grover Kates. Hank would rather have Matt handle the situation then get into a personal stew with Grover over the problem.

False Witness. September 14, 1958. Written by Marian Clark. Guest cast: Harry Bartell, Sam Edwards, James Nusser. Aired on television December 12, 1959.

The Radio Programs

Young Tom Maury is found guilty of murder because of the "eye witness" testimony of Romy Hawkins, a weasel of a man who enjoys the notoriety of his day in court. According to Kitty, Romy "should have been born a buzzard feeding on another man's killing." Tom insists that he is innocent and although Matt likes young Tom, the lawman is "bound by the court" to do his duty. As soon as he is well, Matt must bring Tom to Hayes City to be hanged. The young man has been quite feverish all through his trial and Doc has been nursing him back to health. Even though it is quite ironic to mend him for his funeral, Matt insists that Tom be able to "stand straight" for his execution. No one minds the delay except Romy, who feels it is his citizen's duty to demand that the sentence be carried out swiftly.

Big Girl Lost. September 21, 1958. Rerun.

Kitty's Rebellion. September 28, 1958. Written by Marian Clark. Guest cast: John Dehner, Vic Perrin, Sam Edwards. Aired on television February 7, 1959.

Billy Kret, the brother of a childhood friend of Kitty's, comes to Dodge for a visit. When Billy discovers the life Kitty leads, he decides to "rescue" her. The young Southern gentleman does not think it fitting for a refined lady like Miss Kitty to be in a saloon, much less run such an establishment. However, his good intentions are leading him to a showdown with all the cowboys he feels are "insulting" Kitty's honor. Kitty is rightly concerned that Billy is going to be killed.

Tag, You're It. October 5, 1958. Written by Les Crutchfield. Guest cast: Vic Perrin, Dick Crenna, Virginia Christine. Aired on television December 19, 1959.

When Karl Killian, a notorious killer, drifts into Dodge City residents reach near panic speculating about his intended victim. Killian, who Chester claims has the "coldest pair of eyes...ever seen in a man's head," was once an old friend of Matt's. He became a paid killer after his wife was murdered by some fence cutters, and after Killian avenged her death, he kept on with the slaughter. Matt swings into action when it appears that Rusty, a hostess at the Long Branch, is the target.

Doc's Showdown. October 12, 1958. Written by Marian Clark. Guest cast: Sam Edwards, Helen Kleeb, Irene Andres, John Dehner, Lawrence Dobkin.

Doc tries to save the life of young Lem Woods after the boy is fatally shot in the back. Unfortunately, Lem dies without revealing his killer. Sara, his grief-stricken mother, tells Doc that the killer sent her boy home "tied to the back of his horse like a butchered hog." It seems Lem was sent home as a warning to his mother in case she knew anything about her son's affairs. Despite Matt's disapproval, Doc decides to flush out the murderer by pretending the boy made a deathbed statement that only he was witness to.

Kick Me. October 19, 1958. Rerun.

The Tragedian. October 26, 1958. Written by Les Crutchfield. Guest cast: John Dehner, James Nusser, Vic Perrin, James Westerfield. Aired on television January 23, 1960.

Matt runs into double trouble in the form of Ray and Brad Kyler. After he jails Ray, he searches Dodge for Ray's cowardly brother Brad, who would not hesitate to shoot Matt in the back. Matt's problems are further compounded when he befriends Edward Vanderman, a penniless Shakespearian actor who turns out to be a thief and a card shark.

James Westerfield appeared regularly on television as John Murrel in the Western series, *The Travels of Jaimie McPheeters.*

Old Man's Gold. November 2, 1958. Written by Marian Clark. Guest cast: Ralph Moody, John Dehner, Harry Bartell.

Cassius Mayhew's journey westward is interrupted by the illness of his wife. The Mayhews are heading West to find a more suitable climate for Mrs. Mayhew's failing health, but are forced to stay in Dodge so Doc can minister to her. While in town, Cassius intrusts a suitcase to Matt, which he claims contains all their family treasures. Matt locks up the suitcase as per Cassius' request, but is then ordered to open it by Henry Brails, Cassius' greedy brother-in-law.

Target: Chester. November 9, 1958. Written by Marian Clark. Guest cast: Lawrence Dobkin, Vic Perrin, Sam Edwards, John Dehner.

Purd and Jabe Leach decide to have some fun by tormenting and terrorizing an old drunk. When Matt intervenes and grabs for Jabe's gun, it goes off wounding Purd in the wrist. Although Purd recovers from the minor injury, Jabe is determined to make Matt pay for the deed. Doc believes there is something wrong with Jabe and that Matt should not take his threat lightly. The old doctor's hunch proves correct when Jabe kidnaps Chester and tricks Matt into shooting his loyal friend.

Brush at Elkader. November 16, 1958. Rerun.

The Correspondent. November 23, 1958. Written by Marian Clark. Guest cast: Larry Thor, Harry Bartell, Sam Edwards.

Newspaper correspondent Reed Norton arrives in town from St. Louis anxious to find a story on the recent stage hold-up. Reed wants the real facts not the romanticized version or exaggerated accounts. He believes all the stories about the wild West are tall tales concocted by people like Matt Dillon, and he taunts Matt for not going after the bandits. When Joe Porter returns from a trip claiming that two people were firing at him near the old Hutchinson place, Matt and Chester investigate. Reed follows them to watch Matt "single-handedly bring in the desperadoes" and learns a powerful lesson from the experience.

Burning Wagon. November 30, 1958. Written by Marian Clark. Guest cast: Virginia Gregg, Lawrence Dobkin, Tom Hanley.

While traveling to Hayes City, Matt and Chester happen upon a burning wagon. As they approach, shots ring out. At first the men think they are being shot at, but Matt realizes that cartridges are going off inside the wagon as it burns. When they take a closer look they discover that whiskey has been poured over everything and they find a dead man who has been shot in the back. The contents of the wagon indicate that a woman was there, so Matt and Chester set out to find her.

The Grass Asp. December 7, 1958. Written by Les Crutchfield. Guest cast: Vic Perrin, Harry Bartell, James Nusser.

As winter approaches, "another bunch of cowboys come to eat up the town." This time it is Carl Willet and his drovers from the Lazy T ranch. The boys arrive hooting and shooting, but Matt lets them be. He figures they are just letting off steam and will soon settle down to spending their money. When Red Bastion's wife is discovered shot, Red claims that one of the "half-wit, drunken cowboys" did it. Carl says if one of his

The Radio Programs

men did it he will find out and turn him in. Matt hopes Carl acts fast because, although Red "treats his wife like a dog," he sure seems determined to take the law into his own hands.

Kitty's Injury. December 14, 1958. Written by Marian Clark. Guest cast: John Dehner, Jeanne Bates, Vic Perrin. Aired on television September 19, 1959.

While returning from a trip with Matt, Kitty is thrown by her horse and is badly injured. Afraid to leave her with the hostile occupants of a nearby shack, Matt finds himself in the position of relying upon the uncooperative inhabitants to summon Doc.

Where'd They Go? December 21, 1958. Rerun.

The Choice. December 28, 1958. Rerun.

The Coward. January 4, 1959. Rerun.

The Wolfer. January 11, 1959. Written by John Dunkel. Guest cast: Lawrence Dobkin, Vic Perrin, Tom Hanley.

Rancher Nate Guthrie pays a call on his hired hand, wolfer Webb. However, Guthrie has not left his warm ranch to brave the freezing cold to pay Webb a social call. He is there to order the wolfer off his land. Guthrie hired Webb to clean the wolves off his land, however, just this morning five of his best colts were found with their bellies slit open, apparently the work of a pack of wolves. Webb claims that there is no pack of wolves, only one wolf, a big, mean, white one with a splayed foot. Guthrie does not believe Webb, in fact he even accuses the wolfer of killing the colts to prolong his employment. Webb is a man with cold eyes "wide open like a snake's" whose very stare makes "you think he's just measuring you for your grave." "More injun than white," he has lived with the Cheyennes for over 20 years and believes as the Cheyenne do that the white wolves are "big medicine" and hard to catch. Guthrie decides to call on Matt to remove the stinking wolfer from his land once and for all.

Tom Hanley was one of the brilliant sound technicians responsible for *Gunsmoke*. He not only had the opportunity to act in some of the episodes, but also wrote a few of the scripts.

Kangaroo. January 18, 1959. Written by John Meston. Guest cast: Joseph Kearns, Harry Bartell, Sam Edwards, Jack Edwards. Aired on television October 10, 1959.

About five miles outside of town, Matt and Chester come across an old cottonwood grove, where they spy a long, lean, bearded old patriarch with "pale jumpy eyes" who, along with two young men, is brutally whipping a cowboy. Matt orders the beating to stop and has Chester release the young man from his bondage. The release of the "sinner" causes religious fanatic Ira Scurlock to swear vengeance. Soon after, Chester is kidnapped by Scurlock and his two sons and is tried in a kangaroo court for his actions. The crazy old man finds Chester guilty of interferring with the hand of God and sentences Chester to amputation of his right hand, the sinful instrument of evil that led the "sinner" free.

The Boots. January 25, 1959. Written by John Meston. Guest cast: Lawrence Dobkin, Vic Perrin, Richard Beals. Aired on television November 14, 1959.

Zeno Smith, a 45-year-old drunk, and Tommy, a 13-year-old orphan make a strange couple. Little Tommy worships old Zeno and makes sure he gets to the General Store on time for work, whenever Zeno is sober enough that is. Zeno, a former gunman who lost his nerve ten years ago, turned to drink to forget his cowardice. He has been drinking ever since. The man who made the great Zeno Smith crawl like a snake was a young upstart gunslinger named Hank Fergus. When Hank rides into Dodge, Zeno tries to keep Tommy from disillusionment and heartbreak and is blackmailed into helping Hank commit a robbery.

The Bobsy Twins. February 1, 1959. Written by John Meston. Guest cast: Joseph Kearns, Ralph Moody, Sam Edwards, Jeanne Bates, Jack Moyles, James Nusser. Aired on television May 21, 1960.

Two elderly, pathetically amoral brothers, Merle and Harvey Finney, wander into Dodge looking for Indians to kill. Their strange behavior is a joke to the entire town, until Matt learns that beneath their amusing eccentric exterior they are cold-blooded, insane killers.

Groat's Grudge. February 8, 1959. Written by Marian Clark. Guest cast: Harry Bartell, Lawrence Dobkin, Jess Kirkpatrick, Frank Cady. Aired on television January 2, 1960.

A former Confederate soldier, Yancy Groat, arrives in Dodge. He asks gunsmith Walt Dow to repair an old confederate pistol so he can even an old score. Next he asks Jonas to make a coffin "just like the ones they buried the Yankees in." Finally, he asks Chester to line up a preacher to read the service over a body. As yet, there is no body, but Groat plans to remedy that as soon as he meets Tom Hasket. Groat believes Hasket was responsible for his wife's death during Sherman's march through Georgia.

Body Snatch. February 15, 1959. Written by Marian Clark. Guest cast: Jack Moyles, Howard Culver, James Nusser, Vic Perrin, Ralph Moody.

Matt jails Joe Red for robbing a Pawnee grave. During the arrest Joe hurts his leg and in Doc's absence Dr. Milford Brand treats the criminal. Brand is from Philadelphia where they have the newest and most up to date medical equipment. He intends on settling down in Dodge to "practice medicine in a professional and scientific manner." At first Doc Adams welcomes Brand's much needed assistance. However, Brand makes it clear that he is not in any way, shape, or form Doc's "assistant." Doc begins to feel Brand's intrusion when he asks Zack Willard about his wife Myrtle. According to Doc, Myrtle has been suffering from a common Kansas ailment "too much dust, too much loneliness, too much prairie." However, Zack says she is feeling much better now that Dr. Brand has been stopping by. When Doc discovers that the new doctor keeps a corpse in his back room, Matt decides to investigate.

Sarah's Search. February 22, 1959. Written by Marian Clark. Guest cast: Vic Perrin, Clark Gordon, Anne Morrison.

While returning from Park City, Matt and Chester happen upon a buggy by the side of the road. The rear wheel has given way and Miss Sarah Howell is stranded. Miss Sarah, a lonely middle-aged spinster, left Wichita to find her fiancee Guy Porter. She believes that Guy was headed for Dodge and that he may be in trouble. Unfortunately for Sarah, the description of her boyfriend fits that of one of two men who robbed a bank in Wichita.

Big Tom. March 1, 1959. Written by Marian Clark. Aired on television January 9, 1960.

The Radio Programs

Big Tom Burr, a former fighter, is challenged to a match by Hack Creel, a professional prize fighter who once beat Tom "blue 'til he was crawling away" in a "foul dirty fight." So as not to be considered a coward, Big Tom accepts the challenge and then visits Doc for a pill to discourage his "gitty spells." Upon examining his patient, Doc discovers that Big Tom is not healthy enough to undergo any strenuous activity, in fact, a fight might kill him.

Maw Hawkins. March 8, 1959. Written by Tom Hanley. Guest cast: Jeanette Nolan, Sam Edwards, Vic Perrin.

Maw Hawkins wants her son Raze to follow in her husband's footsteps. Now that he is old enough, she wants him to make something of himself. The first assignment Maw chooses for Raze is for him to rob the stage. Although he "ain't got the juice for it" Raze reluctantly agrees to obey his mother. The stage he happens to rob is laden down with $20,000 and Chester is a passenger.

Incident at Indian Ford. March 15, 1959. Written by John Dunkel. Guest cast: Jeanne Bates, Jack Moyles, Vic Perrin. Aired on television December 2, 1961.

While Matt and Chester are returning from Hayes City, Kitty and Doc are keeping themselves amused by playing checkers. Although there has been Indian trouble in the region of Hayes, Kitty is not concerned about their safety, but is more worried about the Hayes City women. Matt and Chester, however, have been loyally heading back to Dodge and have not partaken of the pleasures of Hayes. En route the two stumble upon a cavalry troop headed by an over-cautious new Lt. Dick and an old friend Sergeant Cromwell. The troop recently rescued a young woman, Mary Tabor, from the Arapahoes. Mary's father gave the Indians a wagon load of supplies to trade for her safe return. Mary confesses to Matt that she was captured by the Cheyennes and sold to Two Eagle, an Arapahoe, for ten horses. She further reveals that in her two months with the Arapahoes, Two Eagles has never laid a hand on her. Mary has been treated like a member of the family. Lt. Dick does not trust Indians and believes the Arapahoes are following them, but in reality only one Indian is following the troop, Two Eagles.

This aired on television under the title *Indian Ford.*

The Trial. March 22, 1959. Rerun.

Laurie's Suitor. March 29, 1959. Written by Marian Clark. Guest cast: Sam Edwards, Eleanore Barry, Vic Perrin, Larry Dobkin.

Rad Dawson and his partner Bone head into Dodge for an evening of fun at the Long Branch. The fun turns sour when Rad finds Easterner Andy Scott spending time with Miss Laurie Benson, who he considers his girl. Andy is vacationing in Dodge, enjoying his adventure on the plains because of the generosity of his wealthy father. Once his graduation present is over, he plans to return to Philadelphia with Miss Laurie as his wife. Rad threatens to "hurt" the "young wet earred dude" if Laurie continues to see him. However, Bone comes up with an even better plan that might result in a windfall for him and Rad, kidnap the youth and ask his wealthy old man for ransom money.

Trapper's Revenge. April 5, 1959. Written by John Dunkel. Guest cast: Vic Perrin, Ralph Moody, Lawrence Dobkin. Aired on television November 3, 1962.

While taking a moonlight buggy ride down by the river, Tom Kyles hears something thrashing around in the willows under the bank. He reports this and Matt, Chester, and Doc investigate. When they arrive they find a half dead Tug Marsh who has been wounded by a grizzly bear. Tug was left for dead by his partner Billy Adams, when hostile Indians approached. Adams did not even leave Tug a knife with which to kill himself. Tug crawled five days on his hands and knees, and the only thing keeping him alive was his desire for revenge. Once he recovers he wants to kill his former partner, "slow...real slow."

This aired on television under the title *The Trappers.*

Chester's Mistake. April 12, 1959. Written by Marian Clark. Guest cast: James Nusser.

After taking a trip to visit his family Chester returns and his stagecoach is greeted by Matt. Matt is anxious to obtain some important papers that Chester was to pick up in Dalhart, Texas upon his return. Unfortunately, with the excitement of seeing his family, the assignment completely slipped Chester's mind. Matt reprimands Chester and asks Joe Frees to pick up the papers. This incident causes Chester to reflect on his position or lack of it. Frees tells everyone how Chester goofed and with the help of a rowdy barfly named Lud Holt, Chester becomes a laughing stock. Doc adds insult to injury when he, with his casual quips, calls Chester "a sieve-headed, no-account excuse for a helper." Finally Chester overhears Matt and Kitty laughing about him and he is totally dejected. When Chester intercepts a telegraph message from Frees telling Matt that he is heading for Arizona and is unable to stop in Dalhart, Chester decides to redeem himself by braving the inclement weather and journeying to Dalhart without telling anyone.

Third Son. April 19, 1959. Written by Marian Clark. Guest cast: Sam Edwards, Ralph Moody, Barney Phillips, Ken Lynch.

Shots ring out on the streets as Burns and York ride out of Dodge, leaving Rob Crandall behind, dead drunk. Matt jails young Rob for disorderly conduct. Unfortunately, sleeping it off does not help Rob's disposition. The young man is ornery and rude when he awakens the next morning. His father Josea Crandall arrives and Matt releases Rob in the old man's custody. Josea has lost two sons because of violence, one because of the war and the other because of a barroom brawl. Josea has no intention of losing a third son. He wants the boy to stay on the ranch and stay out of Dodge, which he believes is a "town of sin and violence." However, Rob seems drawn to trouble no matter what Josea does. Rob joins his two friends, Burns and York, and listens to their plans of an early morning stage hold-up. Although Rob seeks adventure, he does not want to hurt anyone and he reveals the plans to Matt.

The Badge. April 26, 1959. Written by Marian Clark. Guest cast: Harry Bartell, Vic Perrin. Aired on television November 12, 1960.

Bandits Rack and Augie stage a hold-up and flee with the money. On their way to the border they cross paths with Matt, who is returning from Larned. Augie, who is somewhat simpleminded, spots Matt's badge and decides he wants it. Augie believes that if he wears the badge "people will think he amounts to something." Augie's desire for the badge is so great, that he shoots Matt in the shoulder, and Rack decides to keep Matt as a hostage for the remainder of their journey. He promises Augie that once they cross the border, he can finish Matt off and keep the badge.

Unwanted Deputy. May 3, 1959. Written by Marian Clark. Guest cast: Jeanne Bates, Vic Perrin, Paul DuBov, Howard Culver. Aired on television March 5, 1960.

The Radio Programs

In an attempt at vengeance Vince "Wiley," the brother of Billy Wilson a killer brought to justice by Matt, tries to unseat Matt as marshal. Vince arrives in Dodge and offers his services to Matt as an assistant. Matt promptly refuses, causing Vince to settle disputes, keep the peace, and serve the citizens of Dodge on his own time. By turning the townsfolk against Matt, Vince believes he will be able to get Matt to draw on him and kill the marshal in a fair fight.

Dowager's Visit. May 10, 1959. Written by Marian Clark. Guest cast: Sam Edwards, Jess Kirkpatrick, Joseph Kearns, Vic Perrin, Jeanette Nolan.

Mrs. Junius Chamberlain, the wife of the late senator Chamberlain, arrives in Dodge in search of her wayward grandson Junius. Mrs. Chamberlain promptly approaches Matt for assistance in her endeavor to return the young man to Yale College. Matt refuses to go out of his way to help the old woman, so she insists on staying put in Dodge, until the young man turns up.

Scared Boy. May 17, 1959. Written by Marian Clark. Guest cast: Richard Beals, Virginia Christine, Lawrence Dobkin, Ben Wright.

Tad Meadows and his mother Cora witness the murder of a gambler whose name is Roark. The man is shot in the back by a stranger in the kitchen of the Meadows' farm. The murderer threatens to kill Tad and Cora if they tell anyone what has happened. When Mrs. Meadows promises to keep his secret, the man leaves. However, when Tad is missing the next morning, Mrs. Meadows is afraid that the boy might have gone after the killer. Afraid to tell anyone and afraid not to, Cora finally confides in Matt.

Wagon Show. May 24, 1959. Written by Tom Hanley. Guest cast: Ralph Moody, Jeanette Nolan, James Nusser, Vic Perrin.

The Bannock Circus arrives in Dodge much to the delight of the townspeople. However, Matt does not share their amusement. In the last town the circus played, a riot caused the death of two people. Trouble seems to follow Maggie Bannock, who was once billed as "dainty Margarita, the strongest lady in the world," but she and her husband Jim Conger, "the human fly," are not concerned. They intend to put on their show in Dodge, with or without Matt's consent.

The Deserter. May 31, 1959. Written by Marian Clark. Guest cast: Ben Wright, Joseph Kearns, Virginia Christine, Vic Perrin. Aired on television June 4, 1960.

Soldier Lurie Morton and civilian Joe Rawley steal an army payroll. Lurie is wounded in the robbery, but escapes to Dodge. There he is given refuge by his parents, Jed and Maddie, who wound Chester and hold Matt at gunpoint, while they figure out a way to help their son escape retribution.

Doc's Indians. June 7, 1959. Written by Marian Clark. Guest cast: Howard Culver, Lawrence Dobkin, James Nusser, Harry Bartell.

While returning from a house call, Doc and Kitty are captured by Indians. The Indians take them to their camp where chief Little Wolf insists that Doc cure his critically ill son. Doc agrees to try provided that Kitty is sent home. Once Kitty swears not to reveal Doc's whereabouts, she is released. Back in Dodge, Hudd Perkins has been waiting for Doc to treat him for an imagined illness. When Doc does not return, Hudd enlists a group of volunteers to go hunting for him. Kitty, afraid that the Indians will misconstrue the search party and kill Doc, finally confides in Matt.

GUNSMOKE — III. THE PROGRAMS

Kitty's Kidnap. June 14, 1959. Written by Marian Clark. Guest cast: Ken Lynch, Harry Bartell, Vic Perrin, James Nusser.

Matt and Chester happen upon a lynching and save Pete Brass from a swift death. Matt quickly discovers that Brass is wanted in three states for robbery and murder, the most recent being a Wichita hold-up. Although Brass is arrested, he swears that his men, Milt and Jess, will not let him stay in jail. Brass is correct. The men kidnap Kitty and send Doc into Dodge with the message, "I'm in the mood to do some horse trading."

Carmen. June 21, 1959. Rerun.

Jailbait Janet. June 28, 1959. Rerun.

Emma's Departure. July 5, 1959. Written by Marian Clark. Guest cast: Virginia Christine, Lawrence Dobkin, Harry Bartell.

Ben and Emma Hyde live out on the prairie. Ben is a man who does not take to company, nor does he take to keeping his wife company. "Farmin' ain't talkin'" is his frequent response when Emma pleads for some companionship. She spends her life "getting old and drying up and losing babies." When Matt and Chester stop by on their way to pick up a prisoner, Emma is all aglow with the opportunity to talk to someone. She insists that the men stop in again on their way back to Dodge, and they do. This time Matt and Chester are accompanied by Joe Bursey, their prisoner. Emma is in all her glory. She lavishes food on the men and even confides in them that Ben and she need not live the life they do. In fact, they have a considerable amount of money in a box, more than enough to send her back home to Philadelphia for a visit. However, Ben does not allow it. The three men return to Dodge, but Matt is forced to release Bursey when his alibi pans out. Soon after his release, Ben is murdered and robbed of his money box.

Friend's Payoff. July 12, 1959. Written by Marian Clark. Guest cast: Richard Beals, Lawrence Dobkin, Barney Phillips, Joseph Kearns. Aired on television September 3, 1960.

A young boy arrives with a cryptic message for Matt. Upon reading it, the marshal takes off, leaving behind a bewildered Chester. Matt rides out of town to find his old friend Ab Butler, who has been shot in the back. He helps his friend back to Dodge, where Doc treats Ab's wound. Ab tells Matt that he had been ambushed on the trail up from Texas and was unable to see his assailant. He further reveals that he has to stay hidden, or he will be killed. Matt is afraid that his old friend might be in trouble with the law. When Joe Leeds arrives in Dodge asking for Ab Butler, Matt questions the stranger. Leeds tells Matt not to interfere because, "It's a personal matter."

Second Arrest. July 19, 1959. Written by Marian Clark. Guest cast: Jeanette Nolan, Frank Cady, Vic Perrin, Lawrence Dobkin.

Mort Sealy is on trial for stealing one of Will Hunter's horses. When Will does not show up to testify, the judge is forced to release Mort for lack of evidence. Matt soon discovers the reason for Will's absence, he had been critically beaten by Mort's brother.

Old Beller. July 26, 1959. Written by Marian Clark. Guest cast: Harry Bartell, Ken Lynch, Ralph Moody.

The Radio Programs

Doc is called to cure a sick drover in a trail herd, but it turns out to be Old Beller the lead steer. Although unaccustomed to doctoring cattle, Doc acquiesces because Old Beller is known throughout the county to be worth his weight in gold. The steer "has a human brain betwixt those long horns" allowing him to lead a herd as no one else can. He gets herds across streams that even a horse would refuse to ford and keeps them calm when ordinarily they would be spooked. Doc pulls the animal through, explaining it was just a simple case of bloat, or food poisoning. When trail boss Hod Wydell hears this he fires Charlie the cook who has been feeding Old Beller scraps from the chuck wagon. Charlie is devastated, for he loves the old steer and would never do anything to harm it. When Ab Slate hears what has transpired, he tricks Charlie into stealing Old Beller, then beats the old man senseless, and runs off with the steer.

Ball Nine, Take Your Base. August 2, 1959. Written by Vic Perrin. Guest cast: Ralph Moody, Barney Phillips, Joseph Kearns, Sam Edwards, Vic Perrin, Harry Bartell.

Doc is chosen as umpire in a baseball game to be played in Dodge between the citizens, managed by Mr. Lindstrum, and the Eastern All-Star Professional Baseball Club, managed by Asa Granville. Although the game is supposed to be a friendly exhibition, Matt is expecting trouble.

Mavis McCloud. August 9, 1959. Rerun.

Pokey Pete. August 16, 1959. Written by Marian Clark. Guest cast: Bart Robinson, Richard Beals, Barney Phillips, Vic Perrin, Jeanne Bates.

"Pete, Pete, pokey Pete he wears boxes on his feet" is the chant echoed by little Tad. Silent Pete, is a funny looking, "strange old coot." He drags his leg as he walks and has never been known to utter a word. Although he is often tormented by the youngsters, he is always gentle with them. Chester puts Tad straight about teasing the old man. He even goes so far as to say, "Pete don't sleep a wink...he just sets there guarding his buried treasure." Tad's eyes light up as he fantasizes about pirate ships and pieces of eight. Most people would not believe Chester's tall tale, but Tad believes it and so do Mort and Reese, two no-good vagrants.

The Reed Survives. August 23, 1959. Rerun.

Shooting Stopover. August 30, 1959. Written by Marian Clark. Guest cast: Barney Phillips, Jeanne Bates, Harry Bartell, Vic Perrin. Aired on television October 8, 1960.

Gurney, Matt's prisoner, turns out to be wanted on two counts of murder back in Wichita. After receiving a telegram asking for Gurney's extradition, Matt and Chester board the morning stage with their prisoner. Driver Jim Buck is glad to have the marshal aboard, since he is carrying a large gold shipment. Also on board is a reverend and Miss Randall, a pretty, young schoolmarm. When the stage stops at old man Miller's for coffee and a change of horses, the old man is no where to be found. Instead, a team of bandits attack. The robbers wound Jim and keep the passengers penned up in the relay station, cut off from their water supply.

EIGHTH SEASON

Matt's Decision. September 6, 1959. Written by Marian Clark. Guest cast: Ben Wright, Virginia Christine, Vic Perrin, Ralph Moody, Lawrence Dobkin, Joseph Kearns, Richard Perkins.

GUNSMOKE — III. THE PROGRAMS

A series of annoyances make Matt rethink his position as marshal of Dodge. Chester complains about having to clean up after a couple of drunks, the drunks complain about not getting breakfast, Doc complains about having his buggy turned over by a drunken drover, Dobie wants Matt to keep the town loafers off his hotel chairs, and Miss Bagley is disturbed about bottles all over the streets, the noise, and the wild gunshots of the celebrating cowboys. An old buddy of Matt's, Luke Gilmore, offers him an escape. Luke has his eye on the far West and he believes it is time for Matt to move on. According to Luke, Matt spends his time "frying in the summer...freezing in the winter and nurse maiding a town that doesn't appreciate him."

Johnny Red. September 13, 1959. Rerun.

Gentlemen's Disagreement. September 20, 1959. Rerun.

Personal Justice. September 27, 1959. Written by Marian Clark. Guest cast: Jack Moyles, Harry Bartell, Vic Perrin.

Matt and Chester bring young Reed Morley to Wichita to stand trial for the murder of a woman. While in town, Matt is confronted by Reed's brother Clayt, a Southern gentleman who does not want a "stain on the family name." In fact, Clayt goes so far as to make a "simple appeal" to Matt's "sense of justice and honor," and threatens that if Reed is found guilty, the marshal will not live to see the boy hung. As chance would have it, Reed is found not guilty and is released. Although Clayt is relieved that the family honor has been upheld, he will not be satisfied until everyone else believes in Reed's innocence, including Matt.

Hinka-Do. October 4, 1959. Rerun.

Kitty's Quandary. October 11, 1959. Written by Marian Clark. Guest cast: Vic Perrin, Harry Bartell, Lawrence Dobkin.

Shave Murdock and his partner have been entertaining themselves in Dodge for a few days. Matt considers them a couple of no-good drifters, but Kitty is taken in by the smooth talking Shave. She enjoys his company and flowery compliments in contrast to Matt who "wastes as many compliments as he does bullets." During an evening's conversation Kitty inadvertently tells Shave that Matt is having a tooth extracted at midnight. Since Matt will need a lot of liquoring up to kill the pain, he obviously will not be up and around the next morning. Shave uses this information to his advantage. He and his partner rob the bank and shoot teller Tom Johnson while Matt is incapacitated.

The Mortgage. October 18, 1959. Rerun.

Old Gunfighter. October 25, 1959. Written by Marian Clark. Guest cast: Jack Moyles, Ralph Moody, Vic Perrin, Sam Edwards, Larry Dobkin, Dick Beals.

According to old Charlie, infamous gunfighter Rio Joe "could hit anything that he could see." Charlie has a reputation for telling tall tales about his riding buddy Rio Joe, the notorious gunman. Most people do not believe the old man, but they humor him. However, Rasp and his friends are annoyed by Charlie and his stories and want to put a stop to it. Rasp plans to scare the man out of town by calling him out. Their plan turns sour when old Charlie takes out his ancient horse pistols, despite Matt's warning.

The Radio Programs

Westbound. November 1, 1959. Rerun.

Cavalcade. November 8, 1959. Rerun.

The Square Triangle. November 15, 1959. Rerun.

Paid Killer. November 22, 1959. Rerun.

Hard Lesson. November 29, 1959. Written by Marian Clark. Guest cast: Lawrence Dobkin, Vic Perrin, Sam Edwards, Harry Bartell.
Pete Belvin returns to his family ranch in need of his mother's "healing hands." He is greeted by his younger brother Joe who informs the fugitive that Ma died a year ago. Pete's injury is the result of a hold up in which his accomplices were Riley and Lowe. Although Pete was wounded, he managed to escape with all the money, including his partner's shares. Joe is naturally concerned about his brother's welfare and wants to get Doc. Pete, however, is afraid that the law will be brought in. Joe's solution is to return the stolen money and all will be forgiven.

Georgia Ellis, Miss Kitty, used the name Georgia Hawkins on and off for the next few months.

Big Chugg Wilson. December 6, 1959. Written by Ray Kemper. Guest cast: Barney Phillips, Virginia Christine, Lawrence Dobkin, James Nusser.
Laurie, a saloon girl at the Long Branch, is in love with a young cowboy named Roke. Although Roke seems to be equally attracted to her, Laurie muses, "Men don't ask saloon girls to marry them." In order to get Roke jealous, Laurie makes up to Chugg Wilson, a buffalo hunter who "probably ain't seen a woman in six months." Chugg is taken aback by Laurie's attention, and makes a date to meet her later that evening. When Chugg leaves to sell his hides, Laurie returns to Roke. She thinks the whole interaction is a big joke, but as Roke warns her, Chugg may have taken it seriously.

Don Matteo. December 13, 1959. Written by Marian Clark. Guest cast: Don Diamond, Vic Perrin, Barney Phillips, James Nusser. Aired on television October 22, 1960.
Estaban, an old range riding comrade of Matt's arrives in Dodge seeking his friend's assistance. Estaban wants "Don Matteo" to join him as in the old days to track down a man. According to Estaban, Rollo, the drifter in question, is "a nothing," an "insect" that has become bothersome. The insect hurt his Maria and must be killed. Matt attempts to dissuade his friend from breaking the law. When Estaban persists in his actions, "Don Matteo" realizes he must use force to stop his amigo.

Beeker's Barn. December 20, 1959. Rerun.

Pucket's New Year. December 27, 1959. Rerun.

Trojan War. January 3, 1960. Rerun.

Luke's Law. January 10, 1960. Written by Marian Clark. Guest cast: Dick Crenna, Ralph Moody, Lawrence Dobkin.

GUNSMOKE — III. THE PROGRAMS

Luke Burris is a stubborn old man. When Smed Moley beats him half to death, old Luke refuses to allow the law to step in. He insists that he "ain't never had no need for the law." Luke wants to handle the matter on his own. His resistance results in the death of his son, Jess, at the hands of the cowardly Moley. However, even after Jess' murder, Luke is determined to settle with Moley himself.

Fiery Arrest. January 17, 1960. Written by Marian Clark. Guest cast: Vic Perrin, Harry Bartell, Sam Edwards, Barney Phillips, Jeanne Bates.

During a severe storm, Matt and Chester take shelter in an abandoned shack. While they are sound asleep, they are surprised by Hod and Mosley, two would-be hold-up men. Even though Matt stumbled upon the cabin by happenstance, Hod, the meaner of the two outlaws, believes that his woman, Millie, sent for the law. He ties her up along with Matt and Chester and he and Mosley ride off to rob the stage. After Matt frees himself and sends Chester back to town with Millie, he hunts for Hod and Mosley. He finally catches up with the bandits and apprehends Mosley, but Hod escapes. Back in Dodge, Millie is under Doc's care and Kitty's watchful eye. The frightened woman has been frequently beaten by Mosley and she is terrified that he will kill her.

Bless Me Till I Die. January 24, 1960. Written by Ray Kemper. Guest cast: Harry Bartell, Virginia Christine, Lawrence Dobkin, Ralph Moody. Aired on television April 22, 1961.

Parson Cole Treadwell and his wife Beth Ann settle, temporarily, in Dodge. No sooner do the Treadwells arrive that Nate Bush a no-good saddle tramp, accosts Mrs. Treadwell, provoking a fight with Cole. This is just the beginning, however, of the young couples' troubles. The vagrant informs Matt that he recognizes Treadwell to be Cole Trankin, who escaped from Arizona territorial prison.

Chester's Dilemma. January 31, 1960. Written by Vic Perrin. Guest cast: Vic Perrin, Joseph Kearns, Barbara Eiler, John Dehner. Aired on television May 20, 1961.

Chester becomes infatuated with pretty Edna Wallstrom. However, the feelings may not be mutual. Although the lovely lady spends considerable time with Chester, she appears to be inordinately interested in his delivery of Matt's official mail.

At the 1988 SPERDVAC Convention's "Salute to CBS Radio" this episode was chosen for the *Gunsmoke* re-creation. Parley Baer played Chester, Tyler McVey was Doc, Lillian Buyeff played Kitty, and Michael Rye (Rye Billsbury) played Matt. Rye played "Mark" Dillon in the original pilot *Mark Dillon Goes to Gouge Eye*. The principal cast was supported by Jeanne Bates, Vic Perrin, Herb Ellis, and announcer George Walsh. It was directed at the convention by William Froug and sound effects were provided by Ray Erlenborn.

Delia's Father. February 7, 1960. Written by Marian Clark. Guest cast: Virginia Christine, Lawrence Dobkin, Bartlett Robinson.

While heading to testify at a trial in Hayes City, Matt and Chester capture a wanted criminal named Keel. The three men brave the tempestuous weather as they continue to journey toward Hayes, until Keel's horse goes lame. Circumstances force the men to take shelter in a small ranch inhabited by Delia Robbin. When Delia realizes that Matt Dillon is her guest, she brags about how her late father was Matt's good friend. What Delia is not aware of is that Matt was somehow responsible for Ben Robbins' death.

The Radio Programs

Distant Drummer. February 14, 1960. Written by Marian Clark. Guest cast: Vic Perrin, Joseph Kearns, Barney Phillips, Harry Bartell, Ralph Moody, James Nusser. Aired on television November 19, 1960.

Two mule skinners, Bull Ramsey and Slope, torment and terrorize Raffie, a young army drummer. The simpleminded Raffie is the brunt of many a joke as he walks around town always wearing his drum. Doc surmises that Raffie's lack of mental growth is due to "too much war." Raffie wears his drum proudly because it was entrusted to him by his army captain. But no matter how proudly he displays his drum, "folks give me misery" he claims. When Bull and Slope go at Raffie a bit too hard, the boy takes a serious tumble. "Them folks that hurt me, they got to be taught different," the confused Raffie pieces together. When Bull is found dead with a drumstick by his side, Raffie is the prime suspect.

Mr. and Mrs. Amber. February 21, 1960. Rerun.

Prescribed Killing. February 28, 1960. Written by Marian Clark. Guest cast: Lawrence Dobkin, Virginia Christine, Jeanne Bates.

When Myra Kirby calls her husband Luke in for supper she "might as well be calling a hog, only a hog would come faster." According to Myra their life together is pure misery. "Ain't nothing in his life but horses" and Joe Holland's widow. The bitter Mrs. Kirby is determined to make Luke pay for her unhappiness. Myra is so full of hatred that she is willing to die as long as Luke is blamed for her death.

Blood Money. March 6, 1960. Rerun.

Unloaded Gun. March 13, 1960. Written by Marian Clark. Guest cast: Vic Perrin, Barney Phillips, Sam Edwards, Harry Bartell, Richard Beals. Aired on television January 14, 1961.

Matt tracks the murderous Lime brothers, fatally wounding Red Lime. Before he is able to apprehend Joe Lime, the lawman is stricken with a raging fever and is forced to return to Dodge. While still desperately ill, Matt must face the vengeful gun of Joe, who has tracked him back to town.

The Constable. March 20, 1960. Rerun.

Indian Baby. March 27, 1960. Written by Marian Clark. Guest cast: Jeanne Bates, Ralph Moody, Vic Perrin.

Returning from bringing a new life into the world, Doc and Kitty find a woman lying unconscious on the prairie. Upon closer examination they find that the young woman, Dory, is clutching a baby. However, Dory is white and the baby is an Indian. The two manage to bring Dory and the infant back to Dodge, where Matt tries to question the delirious woman. What he surmises is that Dory's baby died and she kidnapped this one to take its place. Matt is afraid that there will be an Indian uprising if the baby is not returned. He is also worried about what the Indians will do to Dory for her actions.

Greater Love. April 3, 1960. Rerun.

Dave's Lesson. April 10, 1960. Written by Marian Clark. Guest cast: Sam Edwards, Ralph Moody, Harry Bartell, Joseph Kearns.

GUNSMOKE — III. THE PROGRAMS

Matt receives news that two of his friends, Joe and Lida Barrett, have died. The two had lived through the war, survived a riverboat disaster, and lived in renegade Indian country, only to be stricken and taken by fever. They leave behind a sixteen-year-old son, Dave, who has a fascination for guns. Will Barrett, Joe's brother, sends young Dave to spend the summer with Matt. While Matt is in Hayes City, Chester is left in charge of the boy. Unfortunately, Dave does not think pushing a broom is the kind of help a lawman needs. He is anxious to prove himself with a gun and sees his chance when old Hob Frank gets himself liquored up and shoots off his gun. Dave wants to help by shooting Hob.

Solomon River. April 17, 1960. Written by Kathleen Hite. Guest cast: Virginia Christine, Vic Perrin.

While returning with prisoner Ben Crown, Matt and Chester happen upon Lettie Thatcher trying to dig a grave. She collapses in the process and Matt carries the careworn woman into her modest home. Inside he finds her husband Luther dead. Lettie laments, "He was a long time dying and a long time lying there dead." After Matt sees that Luther is properly buried, Lettie shows him five more graves along the Solomon River, her babies, one for each year she has been out there. Although Lettie is 25 she looks like 50. "The sun, the land, the life it's all punishing." It is hard out there in the middle of nowhere. Still, Lettie refuses to accompany them back to Dodge. She does not want to leave for it is all she knows. In the meantime, Matt and Chester discover that Crown is innocent of wrong doing and release him. Chester has been collecting a care package for Lettie, and since Crown will be heading in her general direction, he reluctantly agrees to bring it to her. However, when Crown arrives he takes more than he gives.

Stage Snatch. April 24, 1960. Written by Marian Clark. Guest cast: Vic Perrin, Ralph Moody, Lawrence Dobkin.

Matt and his prisoner Rowse are headed for Hayes City via stagecoach when they are stopped by two Indians. Big Foot and his son Young Hawk want Matt to relinquish Rowse to their custody. According to Big Foot, Rowse murdered his father, therefore, the killer's life belongs to him. Matt explains that Rowse is being taken to Hayes to stand trial for murder and will most likely hang. However, the Indians are not satisfied. Matt and Rowse are removed from the stage, their fate in the hands of their captors.

Nettie Sitton. May 1, 1960. Written by Kathleen Hite. Guest cast: Virginia Gregg.

Kitty and Doc are enjoying a game of checkers in the Long Branch, while Matt and Chester are skirting renegade Indians outside of Pueblo. Matt is hit in the leg and Chester brings him to a cabin for shelter. The house is occupied by a feisty, rifle-toting, old lady named Nettie Sitton, who demands payment before allowing the wounded marshal and his assistant to enter.

Wrong Man. May 8, 1960. Written by Marian Clark. Guest cast: Harry Bartell, Sam Edwards, Lawrence Dobkin, Vic Perrin, Jack Moyles.

Old man Wydell and his son Ruff have settled outside of Dodge City. Wydell's other son Jim is a wanted outlaw whose stock and trade is his handy use of a knife. Sheriff Blair arrives in Dodge with information regarding the fugitive. When a sweet talking Jack Norman glides into town and into Miss Kitty's favor, Matt soon realizes that he fits Jim Wydell's description. Matt arrests Wydell, much to the consternation of Kitty, and awaits Blair's return to identify the criminal.

The Radio Programs

The title *Wrong Man* was used by John Meston for an episode broadcast November 13, 1954. The stories were not the same.

Tall Trapper. May 15, 1960. Written by Marian Clark. Guest cast: Vic Perrin, Barney Phillips. Aired on television January 21, 1961.

Ben, a lonely trapper, offers a night's hospitality to Rowley and his wife Tassie. The trapper is smitten by Tassie, who is obviously in a bad marriage. The next day Rowley arrives in Dodge claiming that Tassie is in desperate need of a doctor. When Doc and Matt arrive they find that Tassie has been brutally beaten to death. The grief stricken husband accuses Ben of the deed.

Marryin' Bertha. May 22, 1960. Written by Tom Hanley. Guest cast: Virginia Gregg, Joseph Kearns, Ben Wright, Vic Perrin.

Chester is in the dog house for not doing his chores due to a whopping case of spring fever. However, that is just the beginning of Chester's troubles. A widow woman from St. Louis who Chester has been corresponding with, Coreen Gatesly, is over at the Dodge House awaiting her "fiance's" arrival. Chester is in quite a pickle. He has stretched the truth a bit implying he has money and even went so far as to send Coreen a picture of Matt as himself. The lovely Coreen is no beauty, however. She is taller than Chester and weighs more than Matt. If all this is not enough, Kitty suspects that the widow is really Bertha Housecavitz, a woman who marries wealthy men and then has them murdered.

Bad Seed. May 29, 1960. Written by Norman Macdonnell. Guest cast: John Dehner, Eve McVeigh, Sam Edwards. Aired on television February 4, 1961.

Matt has a long hard ride to Fort Larned to pick up a prisoner, but his trip is fruitless. The prisoner dies before he arrives. Matt's trip back is more pleasant. It is cooler due to a breeze from the Rockies. However, he is awakened in the middle of the night by a young, hungry, runaway Trudy Trent. Trudy wants to go to Dodge, but Matt insists on taking her back home. Once there the lawman realizes why Trudy left. He rescues her from Asa, her abusive and incestuous father, but in the struggle Matt is forced to kill him. Matt brings Trudy to Dodge, only to find that she has her mind set on marrying him. When Matt rebuffs Trudy's advances, she reacts by slandering his good name.

Fabulous Silver Extender. June 5, 1960. Written by Vic Perrin. Guest cast: Vic Perrin, Jack Moyles, Joseph Kearns, Harry Bartell.

While Matt is heading for Hayes City with his prisoner Scaglow, Chester is left in charge of things. No sooner is Matt out of town, that Chester is approached by professor Albert Cramston. Cramston claims he is a professor of metallurgial research and is in terrible danger. The silver syndicate has put a $10,000 price on his head and no fewer than eight assassins are stalking him because he claims to have invented a machine that extends silver in size and weight in multiples of ten. If Cramston puts a silver dime in the funnel, counts to three, cranks it four times, adds three drops of quick silver, turns the spiggot and pulls the lever, out pops a silver dollar. Chester, Wilburt Gatsby, and Mr. Dergin witness the results of the "fabulous silver extender" and are astounded. The men are then drawn into a scam that results in deception and death.

Kitty Accused. June 12, 1960. Written by Marian Clark. Guest cast: Barney Phillips, Vic Perrin, Virginia Christine, Richard Beals.

Arnie and Hattie Grimes live on one of the most fertile plots of land in Dodge. However, it takes more than good land to make a good marriage. A sore point in their frequent and bitter arguments is Kitty, who Arnie is sweet on. Kitty, however, does not share his feelings. In fact, Arnie gives her "the creeps." Ironically, Kitty finds Mr. and Mrs. Grimes her traveling companions on the stage to Fort Larned. Kitty plans on staying a few days with her friends Sally and Hank, who are expecting their eighth child. Upon their return, Hattie Grimes marches into Matt's office declaring that Kitty be arrested for the theft of her diamond pin.

Homely Girl. June 19, 1960. Written by Kathleen Hite. Guest cast: Vic Perrin, Virginia Gregg, John Dehner.

Miss Erma Crown, a rather homely looking woman, arrives in Dodge. Erma is under the impression that Dodge City is full of lonely, desperate men, one of whom should be lonely and desperate enough to want her. Another sorrowful soul in Dodge, Hook, a tormented man who was jilted by a two-timing woman, takes it upon himself to break apart the Long Branch. Eventually Hook's and Erma's paths cross.

Line Trouble. June 26, 1960. Written by Marian Clark. Guest cast: Harry Bartell, Joseph Kearns, Lawrence Dobkin, Ralph Moody, Jack Moyles.

Jasper Foss tells Matt that the telegraph line just west of town has been cut. When the marshal investigates he finds the Army already on the scene. In custody is a friend of Matt's, Small Hawk, who confesses that his knife cut the wire. Small Hawk believes the wire is "bad magic" for it "carries bad sounds across the land for his people." Matt convinces Colonel Hooper to release the Indian to his custody. Matt then proceeds to prove that the wire is not bad magic.

Little Girl. July 3, 1960. Written by Kathleen Hite. Guest cast: Lawrence Dobkin, Anne Whitfield, Joseph Kearns. Aired on television April 1, 1961.

Matt and Chester find a little girl in the ruins of a burned down cabin. It appears that her stepfather fell asleep while drinking a jug of whiskey and knocked over the kerosene lamp that started the blaze. All that is left of the man is "just a cinder." Matt takes ten-year-old Charity Gil back to Dodge with him to find her a good home. However, Charity wants to live with Matt. "She tags along like a little stray." To add to Matt's trouble, all the women of Dodge are in Wichita for a women's suffrage meeting. The only woman left in town is Kitty, who refuses to keep a little girl in a saloon and Matt does not know what to do with little Charity.

Reluctant Violence. July 10, 1960. Written by Marian Clark. Guest cast: John Dehner, Sam Edwards, Joseph Kearns, Lawrence Dobkin, Barney Phillips.

Homer Ladely is in Dodge preaching the seriousness and destructiveness of violence, and trying to get the citizens to give up their guns. Zack and his buddy do not take kindly to Homer's suggestion and knock down the old man and kick him senseless. Matt steps in and sends the culprits on their way. Homer recovers and is determined to continue his anti-gun campaign, but Matt is afraid the old man will be greeted by violent opposition.

Busted-Up Guns. July 17, 1960. Written by Kathleen Hite. Guest cast: Ralph Moody, Vic Perrin, Virginia Christine.

Matt and Chester decide to visit their friends Whip and Gladys on the Sioux reservation. Whip is the Indian agent for the Government and has always been good to

The Radio Programs

his charges. When Matt and Chester arrive, they are greeted by Big Feather, who insists on searching their packs. Matt is confused by the strange behavior of the Indians. When he finally encounters Whip and Gladys, Matt learns that the Indians are being deprived of their hunting ground, rations, and their guns. Unsatisfied with the answers he gets from Whip and Gladys, Matt is determined to learn what is at the bottom of the trouble.

The Imposter. July 24, 1960. Written by Kathleen Hite. Guest cast: Jeanne Bates, Vic Perrin, Lawrence Dobkin. Aired on television May 13, 1961.

Ab Stringer arrives in Dodge claiming to be a sheriff from the small town of Miami, Texas. The pleasant, easy going, gentle natured lawman tells Matt that he is searching for Sam Frazer, a murderer who has eluded him. Matt gives Stringer run of the town and all the assistance he has available. However, Rob and Sara Curtin, a respected and well-liked couple, run into serious trouble when Stringer meets them.

Stage Smash. July 31, 1960. Written by Marian Clark. Guest cast: John Dehner, Barney Phillips, Vic Perrin, James Nusser, Richard Beals.

Matt arrests killer Cleary Small. However, Cleary insists that his brother Nort will find a way to free him. Sure enough, Nort approaches Matt with a proposition. Being a gambling man, Nort wants to play poker for Cleary's release. Matt reacts by throwing Nort out. Undaunted, Nort's play comes a few days later when he causes the wreck of a stagecoach that Kitty is a passenger on. He removes the seriously injured Kitty from the scene of the accident, which is strewn with dead bodies. Next he contacts Matt with a new proposition. He will trade Miss Kitty for his brother.

Old Fool. August 7, 1960. Written by John Meston. Guest cast: Virginia Gregg, Joseph Kearns, Sam Edwards, Peggy Webber. Aired on television December 24, 1960.

Hannibal and Della Bass have been married for 45 years. The old couple have a lovely farm that they built up from nothing. When Dunk Hedgepeth tries to steal a pig from the Bass' farm, Old Hannibal is lead down the garden path. He confronts Dunk's widowed mother with the attempted theft and she responds by stealing his heart.

The Noose. August 14, 1960. Written by Marian Clark. Guest cast: Vic Perrin, Harry Bartell, John Dehner, Bartlett Robinson, Lawrence Dobkin, Ben Wright, Barney Phillips.

A strange young man known only as Claude arrives in Dodge "wearing a rope like he was sent from the devil." His bizarre behavior and appearance has the townsfolk spooked. The noose around Claude's neck is for Creole, whom Claude blames for the death of a woman he loved. When Claude finally finds Creole, he sticks to him "like a leech," all the while waiting for him to confess his crime. According to Claude, "a man should speak his guilt" before he is hung.

Georgia Ellis plays the part of Mrs. C.

Dangerous Bath. August 21, 1960. Written by Marian Clark. Guest cast: Sam Edwards, Lawrence Dobkin, Jeanne Bates.

While Matt and Chester are taking a refreshing bath in a stream, outlaws Harve and Ollie steal their horses, guns, and boots. The two are left to walk back to Dodge. Luckily, after a night and a day of hard walking they encounter Doc, who gives them a ride home. When Matt sees his boots on a young cowboy at the Long Branch, the cowboy confesses his crime. However, he wants Matt to accompany him to find his brother Ollie. It seems that Ollie took off with their stolen gold and Harve's girl Molly. Harve does not care about the money, all he wants back is his girlfriend.

The Tumbleweed. August 28, 1960. Written by Tom Hanley. Guest cast: Vic Perrin, Joseph Kearns, Virginia Christine, Barney Phillips.

Chester releases Bood Wilson from jail, but Bood does not want to leave. Wilson enjoys staying in prison. He gets fed regularly and likes the company of Matt and Chester. Bood is "kinda like a tumbleweed" wandering about here and there. He was run off by his father and most people run him off after a while. When hangman Henry Maples arrives in town with his gallows being pulled by three oxen, Bood attaches himself to the self-proclaimed lawman. He helps Maples settle his gallows outside of Dodge, where Maples plans to hang the deserving scum of the lawless city.

FINAL SEASON

Peace Officer. September 4, 1960. Rerun.

About Chester. September 11, 1960. Written by Frank Paris. Guest cast: Bartlett Robinson, Harry Bartell, Lynn Allen, Vic Perrin, John Dehner. Aired on television February 25, 1961.

Matt and Chester set out to look for Doc, who has been missing for several days. They split up to follow two different paths. Matt's trail leads to Doc, who is recovering from an illness at a friend's ranch. Chester's path leads to Lilly Mae and her husband Dack, a horse thief who ties Chester up and threatens to kill him.

Bartlett Robinson was radio's original Perry Mason. On television he appeared as a regular on *Wendy and Me* and *Mona McCluskey.*

Two Mothers. September 18, 1960. Written by Marian Clark. Guest cast: John Dehner, Jeanne Bates, Virginia Christine.

Jake Meisner murders Mrs. Henshaw's son and must pay the consequences. Jake is sentenced to hang. While Mrs. Henshaw grieves for the loss of her boy, Hattie Meisner, Jake's mother, who is normally a good woman is "thrown off balance" by the imminent death of her son. Each woman reacts differently to the tragedy. Mrs. Henshaw locks herself in her home avoiding all visitors, and Mrs. Meisner threatens to kill Matt if her son's sentence is carried out.

Doc Judge. September 25, 1960. Written by John Meston. Adapted for radio by Norman Macdonnell. Guest cast: Harry Bartell, James Nusser, John Dehner. Aired on television February 6, 1960.

Brice Harp, a gunman who served seven years in state prison arrives in Dodge and mistakes Doc for Judge Kenabrew, who sentenced him. The embittered Harp declares openly that he intends to kill Doc. Since Matt is out of town, it is up to Chester to prevent Doc's murder.

The Big Itch. October 2, 1960. Written by Marian Clark. Guest cast: Lynn Allen, Sam Edwards.

Samantha Church reports to Matt that her husband George has been missing for

The Radio Programs

two days. The Churches had done well with their cattle sale and George was bringing the money into Dodge to pay off the note on their house. The only people who knew about the money were Ben Stanley, who worked for the Churches since childhood, and Hobie Price, who rode off with George the day he disappeared. It takes a case of poison ivy to help Matt solve the mystery.

Born to Hang. October 9, 1960. Rerun.

Crack-Up. October 16, 1960. Rerun.

Newsma'am. October 23, 1960. Written by Marian Clark. Guest cast: Harry Bartell, Jeanne Bates, Barney Phillips, Vic Perrin.
  Trail boss Finn dumps journalist Phoebe Appleby on Matt's doorstep, and tells him to put the "unwomanly woman" in jail. Finn has been trying to run a cattle drive and Phoebe has "hung on like a stray cat" being "pesty as a tick." Phoebe maintains she was only observing so she could have a true picture of the West to send back to her Philadelphia newspaper. Nevertheless, Matt locks Phoebe up for her own protection, while he decides what to do with her.

Never Pester Chester. October 30, 1960. Rerun.

Jedro's Woman. November 6, 1960. Written by Marian Clark. Guest cast: James Nusser, Lawrence Dobkin, Virginia Christine.
  Matt and Chester make camp and prepare to eat a sumptuous dinner of beans. While the beans are simmering, the two leave to check on something for old man Goss. When they return, they are surprised to find the beans are missing. The mysterious theft leads them to Hallie, a bruised and beaten, half-starved woman. Matt and Chester manage to get Hallie to Dodge to see Doc. Barely clinging to life, Hallie is left in Doc's able hands.

The Big Con. November 13, 1960. Rerun.

The Professor. November 20, 1960. Written by Marian Clark. Guest cast: Vic Perrin, Barney Phillips, Lawrence Dobkin, Ralph Moody.
  Two robbers, who have eluded capture, bury their gold and head for Dodge. At about the same time, professor Otis Milford journeys to Dodge to study the Indians. Eventually Milford's path crosses that of the thieves.

Dirt. November 27, 1960. Rerun.

Kitty's Good Neighboring. December 4, 1960. Written by Marian Clark. Guest cast: John Dehner, Virginia Christine, Vic Perrin, Barney Phillips.
  Matt has been unsuccessful in his search for Joe Gans, a murderous back-shooter. While Kitty is staying at the Marby ranch nursing Nettie Marby back to health, Lucas Marby returns home with a stranger. The stranger turns out to be none other than Gans.

The Cook. December 11, 1960. Written by John Meston. Adapted for radio by Frank Paris. Guest cast: Sam Edwards, Bart Robinson, Vic Perrin, John Dehner, Jeanne Bates, Harry Bartell, Ben Wright, Larry Dobkin. Aired on television December 17, 1960.

GUNSMOKE — III. THE PROGRAMS

In order to pay off a debt, Sandy King becomes the new cook at Delmonico's. Business begins to boom for the restaurant, as word spreads that the food is finally palatable. During one of Sandy's busy moments, buffalo hunter Ed Fisher storms into the kitchen and the two lock horns. Sandy hits Fisher on the head with a skillet during the scuffle, and unfortunately, Fisher dies. Sandy panics and flees town. When Matt captures the young man, the hungry townspeople try to prevent Matt from bringing him to trial. Sandy's the best cook Dodge has ever had.

Hero's Departure. December 18, 1960. Written by Marian Clark. Guest cast: John Dehner, Vic Perrin, Jack Moyles, Sam Edwards.

Jonathan Wood announces that he intends to settle down in Dodge. The residents are thrilled because Wood is "a bigger hero than Molly Pitcher." Wood single-handedly fought off the enemy at the Battle of Hog Back, during the Civil War. At least, that is the story Wood is spreading. In reality, he is a coward and a liar. Jake Roe, whose father died as a result of Wood's actions, is determined to make him pay dearly for his deeds.

Minnie. December 25, 1960. Written by John Meston. Guest cast: John Dehner, Virginia Gregg, Vic Perrin. Aired on television April 15, 1961.

Minnie, the wife of a jealous buffalo hunter, arrives in town nursing a suspicious gunshot wound. Doc treats her and immediately becomes her romantic prey. The triangle in which Doc is unwittingly involved, is left for Chester to manage, since Matt is out of town.

Spring Term. January 1, 1961. Rerun.

Old Faces. January 8, 1961. Written by John Meston. Adapted for radio by Frank Paris. Guest cast: Harry Bartell, Vic Perrin, Jeanne Bates, John Dehner, Lawrence Dobkin. Aired on television March 18, 1961.

Tilda, a pretty young bride, fails in her efforts to hide her checkered past from her husband Tom. Ed Ivers, a Dodge City cattleman, recognizes Tilda as an entertainer from the Memphis Queen River boat and makes insulting remarks, forcing her naive husband to challenge the ex-gunman to a showdown.

Georgia Ellis plays an extra role in this episode.

The Wake. January 15, 1961. Written by John Meston. Adapted for radio by Norman Macdonnell. Guest cast: John Dehner, Virginia Gregg. Aired on television December 10, 1960.

Gus Mather brings a coffin into town claiming that it contains the body of his good buddy, Orson Boggs. Gus proceeds to invite everyone to Orson's wake, which turns out to be quite an event. Matt suspects foul play and tracks down Orson's "widow," who claims she has never heard of Gus Mather.

This episode appeared on television before it was aired on radio.

Hard Virtue. January 22, 1961. Written by John Meston. Adapted for radio by Norman Macdonnell. Guest cast: Jeanne Bates, Vic Perrin, John Dehner, Harry Bartell. Aired on television May 6, 1961.

Lovely Millie Coe and her hot-tempered husband Andy arrive in Dodge. Andy attempts to sell their wagon, for they are penniless and without work. Before he can transact the deal, however, the wagon is accidentally wrecked by Ed Fallon. Andy flies

The Radio Programs

off the handle, but Millie calms him down. To make amends, Fallon gives them $20 for the wagon and offers Andy a job. The gesture seems genuine, until Millie realizes that Fallon is really interested in her.

Harriet. January 29, 1961. Written by John Meston. Adapted for radio by Frank Paris. Guest cast: Eve McVeigh, Ben Wright, John Dehner, Barney Phillips. Aired on television March 4, 1961.

Harriet Horn and her father are on their way to Pueblo. Mr. Horn has a position waiting for him at the mission school. A "withering, pallid school teacher," Horn is no match for the two beasts that ride up to their wagon. Harriet, well hidden in the brush, witnesses the brutal murder of her father by the two strangers. After a 40 mile walk to Dodge, Harriet takes a job at the Long Branch, hoping that the killers will eventually appear there.

In 1946, Eve McVeigh appeared as a regular on *Faraway Hill,* an early television drama.

Love of Money. February 5, 1961. Written by John Meston. Adapted for radio by Norman Macdonnell. Guest cast: John Dehner, Virginia Christine, Lawrence Dobkin. Aired on television May 27, 1961.

Nate Tatum, an old friend of Matt's, arrives in Dodge en route to California. The former marshal of Oklahoma recently quit his position because over the years he had made so many enemies, he had the feeling his number was up. Nate's foreboding proves correct. The once proud lawman is shot in the back and killed. The only witness to the brutal murder is Bonnie, a money-hungry saloon girl. Motivated by greed, Bonnie cooperates after she learns of a $500 reward for the killer.

Daddy-O. February 12, 1961. Rerun.

Kitty Love. February 19, 1961. Written by Frank Paris. Guest cast: John Dehner.

Matt reneges on his promise to take Kitty to the Dodge City sociable, when he is called to Springville to pick up bank robber Blake Grant. The disappointment leaves Kitty vulnerable to her emotions. When she and Doc stumble upon a wounded stranger out in the prairie, Kitty eagerly volunteers to nurse him back to health. The man turns out to be Dean Murdock, handsome, charming, and the murderous partner of Blake Grant.

Joe Sleet. February 26, 1961. Written by Marian Clark. Guest cast: Vic Perrin, Harry Bartell.

"Hard talking gunfighter" Joe Sleet is in town blowing off steam at the Long Branch. He gets into a fight with Meeker, but Matt steps in to break it up. After Matt leaves the saloon he is summoned back by gunshots. Joe is lying on the floor with two bullets in him from Meeker's gun. Matt knows if Joe dies, he will have to go after Meeker.

Melinda Miles. March 5, 1961. Written by John Meston. Guest cast: John Dehner, Anne Whitfield, Sam Edwards, Vic Perrin. Aired on television June 3, 1961.

Melinda Miles and Tom Potter plan on getting married. However, Melinda's father, Harry, strongly objects to the union, as does their hired hand, Roy Tayloe. Tom loses all his money to Tayloe in a poker game and when Tayloe is found murdered and robbed, Matt suspects Potter of the crime.

Sweet and Sour. March 12, 1961. Rerun.

Joe Phy. March 19, 1961. Rerun.

No Indians. March 26, 1961. Rerun.

Chester's Inheritance. April 2, 1961. Written by Vic Perrin & Harry Bartell. Guest cast: Harry Bartell, Vic Perrin, Ralph Moody, Jack Moyles.
  Farmer Ed Grinds is given ten days to come up with the money he owes Bert Donald or he will lose his farm. Donald, who is a prosperous cattlebroker, refuses to give Grinds more time, even though the two men were once good friends. Grinds believes, and rightly so, that Donald has become, "something slimy that ought to be stepped on." While Grinds is coping with his share of trouble, Chester's luck seems to have changed for the better. The demise of Chester's cousin Clarence makes him heir to $368.63.

Hangman's Mistake. April 9, 1961. Written by Marian Clark. Guest cast: Ken Lynch, Lawrence Dobkin, Vic Perrin.
  Although Matt believes Art Burney is guilty of robbery and murder, he is forced to release him when another man is arrested for the crime in Abelene. The man turns out to be Art's brother Junius, an innocent man who is a victim of circumstances. Both Art and Matt know Junius is not guilty, but unless Art confesses to the charges, Junius will suffer the consequences.
  Ken Lynch appeared as the lieutenant on *The Plainclothesman* from 1949 to 1954. He was also seen as Sgt. Grover of *McCloud,* which starred Dennis Weaver.

Cooter. April 16, 1961. Rerun.

Father and Son. April 23, 1961. Written by Vic Perrin & Harry Bartell. Guest cast: Harry Bartell, Vic Perrin, Ralph Moody, Lillian Buyeff.
  Zachery Wilkins wants to teach his son Buford how to be a man. His methods include torturing and raping Reyna, a young Indian bride, and beating her husband Adam near to death. Matt and Chester rescue Reyna from a wagon they thought to be abandoned, and back in Dodge she tells how her husband was setting up camp when the man arrived. Reyna offered them coffee and they took what they wanted. When Adam tried to protect her, they beat him to the ground. She heard a shot and passed out, and when she came to Adam was nowhere to be found.

Ex-Urbanites. April 30, 1961. Written by John Meston. Adapted by Frank Paris. Guest cast: Vic Perrin, Harry Bartell, John Dehner. Aired on television April 9, 1960.
  While returning from Hayes City, Doc and Chester happen upon a wounded man. Nate Guillot will surely die, unless Doc can treat him. Complications arise when the wounded man's partners, Jesse Turnbull and Pitt Guillot, arrive. They are concerned that Nate might have informed on them, and try to kill him. In the process they seriously wound Doc. Chester faces the grim responsibility of attempting to feed and nurse Doc, while fending off the two outlaws.
  This episode appeared on television before it was aired on radio.

Ma's Justice. May 7, 1961. Written by Marian Clark. Guest cast: Sam Edwards, Richard Crenna, Virginia Christine, John Dehner, Vic Perrin.
  Reed and Jakey Sayle round-up two wild colts and bring them back to their ranch. However, old man Sloat wants the horses for himself and descends upon the Sayles'

The Radio Programs

ranch with his son Jase. Sloat shoots both Reed and Jakey before Ma Sayles blasts Sloat's son with a shotgun. Sloat retreats, but swears vengeance. Fortunately, Jakey is not seriously hurt. He heads for Dodge to summon Doc and Matt.

Richard Crenna began on radio as a squeaky-voiced juvenile in such programs as *The Great Gildersleeve, A Date with Judy, Burns and Allen,* and *Our Miss Brooks,* the later being the vehicle to bring him to television as Walter Denton for three years. Crenna was quite prolific on television and appeared as a regular on several series including *The Real McCoys, Slattery's People, All's Fair, Centennial,* and *It Takes Two.* In 1985 Crenna won an Emmy Award as Best Actor in a Special for *The Rape of Richard Beck.* He is equally familiar for his films and has appeared in such movies as *The Sand Pebbles, Wait Until Dark, Marooned, Body Heat, Summer Rental, The Flamingo Kid,* and *Rambo.*

The Lady Killer. May 14, 1961. Written by John Meston. Adapted by Frank Paris. Guest cast: Harry Bartell, Lynn Allen, Lawrence Dobkin, John Dehner. Aired on television April 23, 1960.

Grant Lucas arrives in town to testify at Cy Welsh's trial. Both he and Matt are key witnesses for the prosecution. While in the Long Branch, Grant is introduced to Mae Talme, a new hostess. She invites Grant back to her hotel room later that night and when he appears at her window, she shoots him. Mae claims Grant was attempting to steal her valuable brooch, and that the killing was justified. Matt doubts her story, but has no evidence to prove otherwise.

This episode appeared on television before it was aired on radio.

Chester's Rendevous. May 21, 1961. Written by Marian Clark. Guest cast: Jeanne Bates, John Dehner, James Nusser.

A dry windy day in Dodge causes fortune to smile upon Chester, when a lady's bonnet blows his way. Chester rescues the little hat and is immediately smitten by its owner Miss Em Feeney. It looks like Chester's romance is working out quite well as he calls upon Miss Feeney day after day. But Chester realizes his happiness is short-lived, when he spies a wanted poster for Rupe Feeney, Em's brother.

The Sod-Buster. May 28, 1961. Written by Ray Kemper. Guest cast: Ralph Moody, Jeanne Bates, John Dehner, Barney Phillips.

While Matt is out of town searching for murderer Cliff Meadows, Chester is left in charge of things. Two people who "look like they both came off a hog farm" arrive in Dodge, Sedge Wilker a "scrawny old coot" and his daughter Bessie Mae, whose looks, according to Chester, are rivaled only by "wart hogs." When the old sodbuster mistakes Chester for the marshal, he sets Bessie Mae to gussie herself up and try to romance the unwilling victim.

Cows and Cribs. June 4, 1961. Rerun.

Doc's Visitor. June 11, 1961. Written by Marian Clark. Guest cast: John Dehner, Virginia Gregg, Vic Perrin, Ralph Moody, James Nusser, Sam Edwards.

Doctor William Weber, who according to Mr. Dobie, "looks like a doctor ought ta look," arrives in Dodge City. Dr. Weber is the bearer of unfortunate news. One of Doc Adams' old friends, Dr. Henry Wilson, has passed away, and Wilson's final wish was for Doc Adams to take over his successful clinic in Philadelphia. Doc is faced with a difficult decision. If he stays in Dodge, he gives up the opportunity to learn new techniques and work with up-to-date equipment in a comfortable surrounding. If he goes to Philadelphia, he leaves a town that desperately needs him.

Letter of the Law. June 18, 1961. Rerun. Last Show.

THE TELEVISION PROGRAMS

During its 20 year run, 635 episodes of *Gunsmoke* were filmed. There were 233 half-hour episodes and 402 one-hour episodes.

This chapter lists and summarizes all the television episodes. The air dates are given and in some cases the rerun dates are also provided. In addition, production numbers, guest cast, production staff, and other information are presented.

PRINCIPAL AND SUPPORTING CAST

Matt Dillon	James Arness
Doctor Galen Adams	Milburn Stone
Chester Goode	Dennis Weaver
Kitty Russell	Amanda Blake
Festus Haggen	Ken Curtis
Newly O'Brien	Buck Taylor
Quint Asper	Burt Reynolds
Thaddeus Greenwood	Roger Ewing
Sam the bartender	Glenn Strange
Louie Pheeters, the town drunk	James Nusser
Nathan Burke, freight agent	Ted Jordan
Mr. Jonas, general storekeeper	Dabbs Greer
Roy and Mr. Jonas	Roy Barcroft
Barney, the telegraph agent	Charles Seel
Moss Grimmick	George Selk
Hank, the stableman	Hank Patterson
Howie, the hotel clerk	Howard Culver
Ma Smalley	Sarah Selby
Mr. Lathrop	Woody Chambliss
Mr. Bodkin, bank manager (first season)	Wilfred Knapp

Mr. Bodkin, bank manager .... Roy Roberts
Ed O'Connor .... Tom Brown
Halligan .... Charles Wagenheim
Percy Crump, the undertaker.................... John Harper
Judge Brooker .... Herb Vigran
Clem .... Clem Fuller
Mr. Dobie, the hotel manager .... Gage Clark
Jim Buck .... Robert Brubaker
Dr. John Chapman .... Pat Hingle
Miss Hannah .... Fran Ryan

FIRST SEASON

Matt Gets It. September 10, 1955. Premiere Episode. Production #502.

Dan Grat, a formidable gunslinger with a reputation for provoking violence, arrives in Dodge after killing an unarmed man in Amarillo. Grat is determined to prove that lawmen are expendable, and defies everything that smacks of law-and-order. He ruthlessly shoots down anyone who dares upset the chip on his shoulder, including the sheriff of Amarillo and even Matt Dillon. After Matt recovers from his wounds, he meets the desperado in a final gun duel.

    Dan Grat.................................... Paul Richards
    Jim Hill .... Robert Anderson
    Bird.................................... Malcolm Atterbury
    Hotel Clerk .... Howard Culver
    Story .... John Meston
    Script, Director, Producer .... Charles Marquis Warren

This episode was introduced by John Wayne. Howard Culver was the voice of Mark Dillon in the 1949 radio pilot, *Mark Dillon Goes to Gouge Eye*. Paul Richards appeared on television as Dr. McKinley Thompson in the dramatic series *Breaking Point*. Robert Anderson was a regular on *Court of Last Resort*. Malcolm Atterbury has played a wide variety of character roles, appearing in such films as *North by Northwest*, *Summer and Smoke*, and *The Birds*. In addition, he appeared on two television series, *Thicker Than Water* and *Apple's Way*.

Hot Spell. September 17, 1955. Production #503.

Matt intercedes on behalf of ex-con Cope Borden, when Rance Bradley accuses Cope of horse theft and attempts to lynch him. Cope is proven innocent of the charge, but later kills Bradley's nephew in a fair fight during a gambling dispute. Matt is caught in an awkward situation when he must defend the unsavory Cope against the decent people of Dodge.

    Cope Borden................................ John Dehner
    Rance Bradley .... James Westerfield
    Jason Bradley............................... Marvin Bryan
    Writer...................................... E. Jack Neuman
    Director, Producer .... Charles Marquis Warren

John Dehner was a frequent guest on radio's *Gunsmoke*, as well as on the television version. He was a regular in such television series as *The Roaring Twenties*, *The Doris Day Show*, and *Young Maverick*. On radio his credits include *Frontier Gentleman* and *Have Gun, Will Travel*. Dehner has also appeared in numerous films including *The Left-*

The Television Programs

Handed Gun and *The Boys from Brazil*. In addition to television, character actor James Westerfield was active in films and on Broadway. He won the New York Drama Critics Award as Best Supporting Actor in 1948 for *The Madwoman of Chaillot* and in 1949 for *Detective Story*. Westerfield's films include *On the Waterfront* and *True Grit*.

Word of Honor. October 1, 1955. Production #504. Rerun September 1, 1956.

Hank Worth, son of wealthy rancher Jake Worth, is kidnapped and held for $20,000 ransom by three men. The kidnappers call on Doc to aid young Hank, who has been shot in the back while trying to escape. Unfortunately, Hank dies. The killers decide to let Doc go because he is the only doctor within 400 miles and they fear they might need his services some day. Before sparing his life and freeing him, however, they force the reluctant Doc to give his word of honor that he will never reveal their identities.

```
Jake Worth ............................... Robert Middleton
Harry .......................................... Claude Akins
Jeff Worth ........................................ Ray Boyle
Ed Worth ..................................... Will J. Wright
Rudy ............................................. Dick Paxton
Jack ............................................. Thom Carney
Story ........................................... John Meston
Script, Director, Producer ............... Charles Marquis Warren
```

Husky character actor Robert Middleton has had a memorable career playing nasty villains on television and in films. His credits include *The Desperate Hours*, *Friendly Persuasion* and *The Lonely Man*.

Home Surgery. October 8, 1955. Production #505. Rerun June 29, 1957.

While returning to Dodge, Chester and Matt are confronted by Holly Hawtree, whose father is desperately ill with gangrene. His only hope for survival is amputation of the affected leg. Matt performs the surgery, but the gangrene has spread too far and the old man dies. Matt later discovers that the presumed accident leading to Mr. Hawtree's condition was actually caused by Ben Walling, who has his sights on Holly.

```
Holly Hawtree .............................. Gloria Talbott
Mr. Hawtree ................................. Joe De Santis
Ben Walling ................................. Wright King
Writer ........................................ John Meston
Director, Producer ..................... Charles Marquis Warren
```

Gloria Talbott played Abbie Crandall on the television Western *The Life and Legend of Wyatt Earp*. On television Joe De Santis was a regular on *Photocrime* and was the narrator of *The Trap*. Wright King was featured on the television Western *Wanted: Dead or Alive*.

Obie Tater. October 15, 1955. Production #507. Rerun August 11, 1956.

Rumor has it that Obie Tater is hoarding gold. After he denies the gossip, two unsavory characters, Mitch and Quade, beat Obie and drag him across the prairie. Several weeks later, Obie marries Ella, a saloon girl from the Long Branch. Matt is greatly disturbed by the union, for he suspects that Ella is just a gold-digger. His concerns prove justified when it becomes apparent that Ella is involved with the two men who attacked Obie.

```
Obie Tater .................................... Royal Dano
Ella .......................................... Kathy Adams
```

GUNSMOKE — III. THE PROGRAMS

Mitch	John Shepodd
Quade	Pat Conway
Story	John Meston
Script, Director, Producer	Charles Marquis Warren

Character actor Royal Dano has an impressive list of television and film credits. Dano has cast his "evil shadow" in such features as *Tribute to a Bad Man, The Outlaw Josey Wales,* and *Welcome to Hard Times.* Jon Shepodd appeared as Paul Martin in the television series *Lassie.* Pat Conway was Sheriff Clay Hollister on the television Western *Tombstone Territory.*

October 22, 1955, preempted for *Ford Star Jubilee.*

Night Incident. October 29, 1955. Production #511.

Little Timmy Wyatt has been witness to a series of bizarre robberies. When his teacher and schoolmates accuse him of telling tall tales, his mother asks Matt to straighten the boy out. Timmy confesses to Matt that he has been playing with White Fawn Hinton, and has watched her parents "jump from the sky" onto passerbys, robbing and killing them. Matt is incredulous but decides to check out the story as he accompanies Timmy to their hideout.

Timmy Wyatt	Peter Votrian
Hinton	Robert Foulk
Mrs. Hinton	Amzie Strickland
White Fawn	Anne Warren
Maggie	Lance Warren
Mrs. Wyatt	Jeanne Bates
Cal Ross	Lou Vernon
Writer, Director, Producer	Charles Marquis Warren

In addition to being a frequent performer on radio's *Gunsmoke,* Jeanne Bates played Nurse Wills on the television series *Ben Casey.* Robert Foulk was seen regularly on *Father Knows Best* and *Wichita Town.* Amzie Strickland was Julia Mobley on the comedy series *Carter Country.*

Smoking Out the Nolans. November 5, 1955. Production #506.

Mr. Burgess, a wealthy man from St. Louis, offers Clay a large sum of money for the land known as Stone Point. Josh Nolan and his wife, however, claim they bought the land from Clay for $170, and that Clay had promised to register the title in their name. Clay insists the Nolans are lying squatters, and forces Matt to serve them an eviction notice. The Nolans refuse to budge from their rightful place, and Matt and Chester must resort to pouring sulfur down their chimney to smoke them out. After the eviction, Matt provides the Nolans with a room at the Dodge House at his own expense. He fears, however, that Josh will not let matters rest, and unfortunately, Matt's suspicions prove correct.

Clay	John Larch
Josh Nolan	Ainslie Pryor
Mrs. Nolan	Jeanne Bates
Mr. Burgess	Ed Platt
Story	John Meston
Script, Director, Producer	Charles Marquis Warren

The title of the radio version was called *Smoking Out the Beedles.* Ed Platt played the ever-frustrated "Chief" on the popular comedy series *Get Smart.* On television, John Larch was a regular on *Arrest and Trial* and *Convoy.*

The Television Programs

Kite's Reward. November 12, 1955. Production #508. Rerun June 8, 1957.

Andy Travers is a penitent outlaw trying to go straight. His past catches up with him, however, when Joe Kite learns that there is still a price on Andy's head — dead or alive. Kite frustrates Andy's attempts at becoming a respected member of the community, and ignores Matt's warnings to leave Andy alone. He schemes to get the reward by tricking Andy into a showdown.

    Andy Travers .... Adam Kennedy
    Joe Kite .... James Griffith
    Writer .... John Meston
    Director, Producer .... Charles Marquis Warren

James Griffith played in many Westerns in the 1950s including *Tribute to a Badman* and *How the West Was Won*. Adam Kennedy appeared as Dion Patrick in the television Western *The Californians*.

November 19, 1955, preempted for *Ford Star Jubilee*.

The Hunter. November 26, 1955. Production #510.

Jase Murdock is a cruel and crazed buffalo hunter who fears no one, not the Indians, not the cavalry, and certainly not Matt Dillon, who he once beat mercilessly and left for dead. Murdock and his skinner, Golden Calf, head for the high country, even though they have been warned that it is off-limits because of a treaty with the Indians. Matt sets out to stop Murdock if he attempts to cross the line.

    Jase Murdock .... Peter Whitney
    Golden Calf .... Richard Gilden
    Cal Ross .... Lou Vernon
    Dude .... Robert Keene
    Writer .... John Dunkel
    Director, Producer .... Charles Marquis Warren

Peter Whitney was born in Long Branch, N.J., the town for which the real Long Branch Saloon of Dodge City, Kansas was named. On television he was a regular on *The Rough Riders*.

The Queue. December 3, 1955. Production #513.

Two ruffians, Rabb and Howard, take it upon themselves to torment Chen, a young Chinese man who is new to Dodge. They hold a grudge against all Chinese, blaming them for the death of their brother. When Rabb and Howard cut off Chen's pig-tail (queue), Chen is terribly disgraced. He has only two choices: either to wait until it grows back before returning to China, or to take revenge upon the men who dishonored him.

    Chen .... Keye Luke
    Ed Bailey .... Sebastian Cabot
    Rabb .... Robert Gist
    Howard .... Devlin McCarthy
    Story .... John Meston
    Script .... Sam Peckinpah
    Director, Producer .... Charles Marquis Warren

Sam Peckinpah began his career as a writer for *Gunsmoke*. He later became a prominent film director in the 1960s with *The Wild Bunch*. His reputation grew with such films as *Straw Dogs, Junior Bonner* and *The Getaway*. Peckinpah's films are known for their graphic violence, complex characters, and ambiguous moral values. Sebastian Cabot is probably best remembered as the portly English butler Mr. French of *Family*

GUNSMOKE — III. THE PROGRAMS

Affair. Keye Luke is best known as "Number One Son" from a series of nine *Charlie Chan* films produced in the 1930s. On television he was a regular on *Kentucky Jones,* which starred Dennis Weaver, as well as on *Anna and the King, Kung Fu,* and *Harry-O.* He was the voice of Charlie Chan on the Saturday morning cartoon series *Amazing Chan and the Chan Clan.* Robert Gist was seen on the comedy series *Hennesey* that starred Jackie Cooper and Abby Dalton.

General Parcley Smith. December 10, 1955. Production #517. Rerun July 19, 1958.

Old-timer Parcley Smith is a former regimental butcher who has a reputation for telling tall tales. He arrives in Dodge and immediately starts to spread rumors about Drew Holt, the manager of Dodge's newest bank. Smith warns Matt that Holt is a crook and should be run out of town. Matt is also concerned, after he discovers that Holt has hired ex-con Ed Nash to guard the bank. However, once Holt's credentials are checked, it is Smith who is asked to leave town.

   Parcley Smith . . . . Raymond Bailey
   Drew Holt . . . . James O'Rear
   Ed Nash . . . . John Alderson
   Mr. Botkin . . . . Wilfred Knapp
   Story . . . . John Meston
   Script . . . . John Dunkel
   Director, Producer . . . . Charles Marquis Warren

John Alderson appeared as Sergeant Bullock in the television Western *Boots and Saddles.* Raymond Bailey was a regular on *My Sister Eileen, The Many Loves of Dobie Gillis,* and *The Beverly Hillbillies.*

December 17, 1955, preempted for *Ford Star Jubilee.*

Magnus. December 24, 1955. Production #512.

Chester's uncivilized brother, Magnus, arrives in town just in time for Christmas. Chester is far from brotherly and tries to avoid Magnus like the plague. Magnus has been living on the prairie with only animals for company since the age of ten, and Chester is afraid his brother will embarrass him. To avoid having his friends think he was raised in a cave, Chester launches a campaign to "civilize" Magnus by teaching him to gamble, drink and talk to women. However, it is Chester who gets the education. He learns just what type of person his long-lost brother is, when bible-spouting madman Lucifer Jones storms into the Long Branch with a shotgun, threatening to kill Miss Kitty.

   Magnus Goode . . . . Robert Easton
   Lucifer Jones . . . . James Anderson
   Dealer . . . . Than Wyenn
   Cowboy . . . . Tim Graham
   Olive . . . . Dorothy Schuyler
   Writer . . . . John Meston
   Director, Producer . . . . Charles Marquis Warren

Robert Easton had the distinction of playing Magnus in the radio version as well. He was recently featured in the block-buster movie, *Working Girl.* Than Wyenn was featured on the television series *Pete Kelly's Blues.*

Reed Survives. December 31, 1955. Production #520. Rerun August 10, 1957.

Lucy, the young and beautiful wife of elderly farmer Ephram Hunt, plots her husband's death. The ex-dance hall entertainer professes her love for handsome Booth

The Television Programs

Rider, and concocts a scheme in which Ephram is the intended victim. Booth becomes the unwitting pawn in a homicide that culminates in an ironic twist of fate

    Lucy Hunt . . . . Lola Albright
    Ephram Hunt . . . . John Carradine
    Booth Rider . . . . James Drury
    Gypsy . . . . Virginia Arness
    Writer . . . . Les Crutchfield
    Director, Producer . . . . Charles Marquis Warren

Virginia Arness, former wife of James Arness, has a cameo role in this episode. James Drury went on to become the star of the television series *The Virginian*. John Carradine has had an impressive career as a character actor with over 170 film credits. He was featured as a villain in such grade-B horror classics as *House of Frankenstein*, *House of Dracula*, and *The Bride of Frankenstein*. Carradine has also appeared in numerous Westerns including *The Man Who Shot Liberty Valance* and *Cheyenne Autumn*. In 1985 Carradine won an Emmy for Best Performance in a Children's Program for *Umbrella Jack*. His sons David, Keith, and Robert Carradine are also actors. Lola Albright was a regular on the television series *Peter Gunn*. Her film credits include *The Tender Trap* and *The Champion*.

Professor Lute Bone. January 7, 1956. Production #515.

Doc insists that quack medicine man, Professor Lute Bone, be run out of town. His fears prove justified when the cure-all tonic Bone sells to Mr. and Mrs. Ringle almost kills their infant. When Doc discovers that the elixir contains opium as well as alcohol, he demands that Matt take action. Doc confronts Matt and accuses him of "protecting" an opium peddler. Frustrated by Matt's inaction, Doc finally decides to take the law into his own hands and gets his gun.

    Professor Lute Bone . . . . John Abbott
    Wellington . . . . Jester Hairston
    Mrs. Ringle . . . . Gloria Castillo
    Mr. Ringle . . . . Don Gardner
    Mr. Stooler . . . . Strother Martin
    Mrs. Stooler . . . . Sally Corner
    Story . . . . John Meston
    Script . . . . David Victor & Herbert Little
    Director, Producer . . . . Charles Marquis Warren

Strother Martin was a character actor extraordinaire. Martin had many memorable performances in television and film. His credits include *The Asphalt Jungle*, *The Wild Bunch*, and *True Grit*. He is probably best remembered for his brilliant portrayal in *Cool Hand Luke* where he coined the phrase, "What we got here is a failure to communicate." Jester Hairston was the first black actor to appear on *Gunsmoke*.

January 14, 1956, preempted for *Ford Star Jubilee*.

No Handcuffs. January 21, 1956. Production #519. Rerun July 13, 1957.

Deputy August Brake arrives in Dodge from Mingo, gunning for Hank Springer who has been accused of murder. Hank, who does not even carry a gun, informs Matt that the charges are unjustified and that he has been framed by the dishonest sheriff of Mingo. Matt decides to journey to Mingo to unravel the mystery. While he is out of town, Brake enters the jail to get Hank. In the ensuing struggle, Brake is hit on the head with Hank's handcuffs. Fearing that Brake has been killed, Hank escapes and vows to kill the crooked sheriff who turned him into a killer.

GUNSMOKE — III. THE PROGRAMS

Hank Springer	Vic Perrin
Sheriff	Charles Gray
Brake	Mort Mills
Woman	Marjorie Owens
Hunter	Herbert Lytton
Turnkey	Cyril Delevanti
Story	John Meston
Script	Les Crutchfield
Director, Producer	Charles Marquis Warren

Vic Perrin was a frequent performer on radio's *Gunsmoke*. Although he was born in England, Charles Gray was a regular on two television Westerns, *Gunslinger* and *Rawhide*. Mort Mills appeared as Marshal Tallman of *Man Without a Gun*. Another Western television regular was Cyril Delevanti who appeared on *Jefferson Drum*.

Reward for Matt. January 28, 1956. Production #516.

Matt rides out to Jeremy Stoner's ranch to arrest him for the murder of Jake Reeves. Stoner readily admits his guilt, but self-righteously states that he was justified in his action because homesteaders deserve to be killed. Stoner draws his gun to resist arrest, and Matt is forced to shoot. When Stoner's wife Sarah discovers what has transpired, she places a $1000 bounty on Matt's life. Matt faces death at every turn as the local scum have a field day. In the forefront is Day Barrett, who already holds a grudge against Matt for ousting him and his friends from Dodge for rowdiness.

Sarah Stoner	Helen Wallace
Jeremy Stoner	Paul Newlan
Day Barrett	Val Dufour
Mrs. Reeves	Jean Inness
Young Farmer	John G. Lee
Story	John Meston
Script	David Victor & Herbert Little
Director, Producer	Charles Marquis Warren

Paul Newlan played Captain Grey on the television series *M Squad*.

Robin Hood. February 4, 1956. Production #518. Rerun June 20, 1959.

John Henry Jordan has 19 arrests to his credit, ranging from robbery to murder, but he consistently confounds the law by avoiding convictions. The secret of his success is that he robs from the rich and not the poor. Henry is no altruist, however, but rather a scheming criminal who buys the loyalty of potential witnesses in this manner. Every time he goes to trial they give conflicting testimony to protect him. Jordan enjoys his bounties in Dodge until Matt discovers a way to turn the tables against the so-called Robin Hood.

John Henry Jordan	William Hopper
Mrs. Bowen	Nora Marlowe
Mr. Bowen	Barty Atwater
Vince Butler	James McCallion
Mr. Botkin	Wilfred Knapp
Judge	S. John Launer
Story	John Meston
Script	Dan Ullman
Director, Producer	Charles Marquis Warren

The Television Programs

The son of columnist Hedda Hopper, William Hopper is best known for his portrayal of detective Paul Drake on *Perry Mason*.

February 11, 1956, preempted for *Ford Star Jubilee* "The Day Lincoln Was Shot."

Yorky. February 18, 1956. Production #514. This episode was originally scheduled for December 10, 1955, but was postponed.

Yorky, a white boy raised by Arapahoes, is victimized by horse thieves. The young brave decides to seek vengeance which results in his being shot by Abe Brandt and his son. They claim that Yorky was attempting to steal "their" horses. The wounded boy escapes from the Brandts and is found by Mr. Seldon. Matt arrives and treats the injured boy whose criminal actions were more the result of ignorance of the white man's laws than of criminal intent. In the process of aiding Yorky, Matt becomes the target of the real horse thieves.

Yorky	Jeff Silver
Brandt	Howard Petrie
Tom	Dennis Cross
Seldon	Malcolm Atterbury
Mrs. Seldon	Mary Gregory
Story	John Meston
Script	Sam Peckinpah
Director, Producer	Charles Marquis Warren

Character actor Howard Petrie began his career in radio working for NBC. Eventually he moved on to television and films. His movies include *Carbine Williams*, which featured Arness in a minor role, and *The Tin Star*. Jeff Silver was a regular on *The Charlie Farrell Show*. Dennis Cross appeared on the television series *The Blue Angels*. Mary Gregory was a regular on *The Wacky World of Jonathan Winters*.

20-20. February 25, 1956. Production #522.

Ex-lawman Troy Carver, has been Matt's inspiration for becoming a U.S. Marshal. He arrives in Dodge on his way to a ranch he has purchased for his retirement. Matt senses that Carver is especially jumpy and discovers that "dirt-farmer" Lee Polen plans to kill Carver to avenge the death of his brother. Matt is confident that the inexperienced Polen poses no threat to a seasoned gunman like Carver, until he discovers his friend's secret.

Troy Carver	Wilton Graff
Lee Polen	Martin Kingsley
Dealer	Pitt Herbert
Moss Grimmick	George Selk
Story	John Meston
Script	David Victor & Herbert Little
Director, Producer	Charles Marquis Warren

Reunion '78. March 3, 1956. Production #526. Rerun July 20, 1957.

Jerry Shand arrives in Dodge City looking for Andy Culley. His plan is to kill Andy for a murder committed ten years ago. Matt intervenes and jails Shand, but in a strange turn of events Andy posts his bail. Later that night Andy offers Shand $600 hush money to forget the past, but Shand refuses and demands that Andy leave Kansas. Andy draws his gun but Shand is faster. Matt has a hard time believing Shand's story of self-defense, especially after the threats he made. Unfortunately for Shand the only witness to the shooting is Belle, a saloon girl who refuses to come forward.

GUNSMOKE — III. THE PROGRAMS

Jerry Shand	Val Dufour
Belle Archer	Marian Brash
Andy Culley	Maurice Manson
Witness	Joe Perry
Marty	Mason Curry
Writer	Harold Swanton
Director, Producer	Charles Marquis Warren

Maurice Manson was a regular on the television series *One Man's Family*. Joe Perry was seen as Max Waltz on *The Bill Cosby Show*.

March 10, 1956, preempted for *Ford Star Jubilee*.

Helping Hand. March 17, 1956. Production #509.

Steve Elser enters the Long Branch expecting trouble from cattle foreman Bill Pence and his boys. They arrive shortly and accuse Steve of cattle rustling, and threaten to lynch him. Kitty, who has taken a fancy to the young man, rescues him by locking him in her room and getting Matt. Her hunch about Steve turns sour, however, when he starts carrying a gun and emulating Hander, a cheap outlaw.

Steve Elser	Brett Halsey
Pence	Ken L. Smith
Wilkins	James Nusser
Emmett Bowers	Russ Thorson
Hander	Michael Granger
Story	John Meston
Script	David Victor & Herbert Little
Director, Producer	Charles Marquis Warren

James Nusser was a frequent performer on radio's *Gunsmoke*. Nusser went on to play Louie Pheeters, Dodge's resident drunk on the television series. Brett Halsey was a regular on the television series *Follow the Sun*. Russ Thorson was a radio performer often heard on mysteries of the 1940s. On television, Thorson was a regular on *One Man's Family* and *The Detectives*.

Tap Day for Kitty. March 24, 1956. Production #521. Rerun June 14, 1958.

Nip Cullers, a weathered old rancher who lives near Crooked Creek with his housekeeper and an Indian girl named Blossom, comes to Dodge to find a wife. His journey takes him to the Long Branch, where he selects an unwilling Kitty to be his bride. When Nip becomes the victim of an attempted homicide, Kitty is the prime suspect.

Nip Cullers	John Dehner
Nettie	Mary Adams
Jonas	John Patrick
Olive	Evelyn Scott
Kate	Dorothy Schuyler
Blossom	Charlene Brooks
Story	John Meston
Script	John Dunkel
Director, Producer	Charles Marquis Warren

Evelyn Scott was a regular on *Bachelor Father* and *Peyton Place*.

Indian Scout. March 31, 1956. Production #524. Rerun July 5, 1958.

In order to circumvent an Indian uprising, Matt and Chester take off to find Amos

The Television Programs

Cartwright, an Indian scout accused of leading a troop of cavalrymen into an ambush. The chase finally leads them to Cartwright and into renegade Comanche territory.

　　Amos Cartwright .... Eduard Franz
　　Will Bailey .... DeForest Kelley
　　Twitchell .... William Vaughn
　　Buffalo Tongue .... Pat Hogan
　　Clay .... Tommy Hart
　　Writer .... John Dunkel
　　Director, Producer .... Charles Marquis Warren

　　DeForest Kelley is best known for his role as Dr. Leonard "Bones" McCoy of the popular science fiction series *Star Trek*. His films include *Gunfight at the O.K. Corral*, *Raintree County*, and the *Star Trek* sequels. Eduard Franz appeared as a regular on *Zorro* and *Breaking Point*.

April 7, 1956, preempted for *Ford Star Jubilee*.

The Pest Hole. April 14, 1956. Production #525.
　　When several members of Dodge's German population come down with typhoid, Doc and Matt race against time to determine the cause. Meanwhile, much to the chagrin of the town's businessmen, the citizens of Dodge start to panic and leave town. Backed into a corner, Doc takes drastic measures to find the carrier, a decision that puts his life and Chester's in grave danger.

　　Cast .... Patrick O'Moore, Howard McNear,
　　............................... Norbert Schiller, Evelyn Scott
　　Writers .... David Victor & Herbert Little
　　Director, Producer .... Charles Marquis Warren

　　Howard McNear, radio's Doc, plays a businessman in this episode.

April 21, 1956, preempted for President Eisenhower's Address to the Nation.

The Big Broad. April 28, 1956. Production #523. Originally scheduled for April 21. Rerun July 12, 1958.
　　Matt has his share of trouble when Lena Wave arrives in town accompanied by mousy gambler Emmett Fitzgerald. Lena uses her six-foot frame, her great strength, and her quick gun to create quite a problem in Dodge, especially after she shoots a man who tried to kiss her.

　　Lena Wave .... Dee J. Thompson
　　Nate Bannister .... Joel Ashley
　　Emmett Fitzgerald .... Terry Becker
　　Mr. Uzzel .... Howard Culver
　　Drummer .... Heinie Brock
　　Story .... John Meston
　　Script .... David Victor & Herbert Little
　　Director, Producer .... Charles Marquis Warren

　　Terry Becker was seen on television as Chief Sharkey on the sci-fi series *Voyage to the Bottom of the Sea*.

May 5, 1956, preempted for *Ford Star Jubilee*.

Hack Prine. May 12, 1956. Production #501. Originally scheduled for April 28, 1956.
　　Hack Prine, a former friend of Matt's, arrives in Dodge. However, his purpose is

GUNSMOKE — III. THE PROGRAMS

not to rekindle old friendships. Hack has been offered $800 to assassinate Matt, whose life he once saved.

Hack Prine	Leo Gordon
Dolph Trimble	George Wallace
Lee Trimble	Hal Baylor
Oley	Wally Cassell
Additional Cast	Tyler McVey
Writer	John Meston
Director, Producer	Charles Marquis Warren

Hack Prine was the pilot episode filmed for the series. Hal Baylor was a regular on *The Life and Legend of Wyatt Earp*.

Cooter. May 19, 1956. Production #527. Originally scheduled for May 12, 1956. Rerun August 3, 1957.

Sissle, a crooked gambler, is foiled by Matt in his activities in Dodge. To get back at the lawman, he hires Cooter, a simple-minded young man to work for him. Sissle deliberately arms the unstable Cooter in an attempt to lure him into a gunfight against Matt. When Cooter realizes that he has been used as a pawn by the unscrupulous Sissle, he loses control.

Cooter	Strother Martin
Sissle	Vinton Hayworth
Pate	Brett King
Additional Cast	Robert Vaughn
Story	John Meston
Script	Sam Peckinpah
Director	Robert Stevenson
Producer	Charles Marquis Warren

Robert Vaughn won an Emmy in 1978 for *Washington: Behind Closed Doors*, however, it was his role as Napoleon Solo in *The Man from U.N.C.L.E.* that first brought him into prominence. Vinton Hayworth starred as Jack Arnold in the *Myrt and Marge* radio series. He was also a founder of the American Federation of Radio Actors, now known as AFTRA. On television he was a regular on *Zorro* and *I Dream of Jeannie*. British born Robert Stevenson directed such classic films as *Jane Eyre* and *Mary Poppins*.

The Killer. May 26, 1956. Production #528. Originally scheduled for May 19, 1956. Rerun August 17, 1957.

Crego is an unscrupulous frontier vagrant who has a reputation for inciting people to violence and then killing them in "self-defense." After murdering an unsuspecting saddle tramp, Crego arrives in Dodge and continues his strange preoccupation with provoking bloodshed.

Crego	Charles Bronson
Jesse Hill	David Chapman
Man	James Nusser
Jonas	Dabbs Greer
Story	John Meston
Script	John Dunkel
Director	Robert Stevenson
Associate Producer	Norman Macdonnell
Producer	Charles Marquis Warren

Charles Bronson soared to super-stardom in such films as *Death Wish, The Mag-*

The Television Programs

ficent Seven, and *The Dirty Dozen.* In 1971 he received the Golden Globe Award as the World's Most Popular Actor.

June 2, 1956, preempted for *Ford Star Jubilee.*

Doc's Revenge. June 9, 1956. Production #530. Rerun July 27, 1957.

A stranger rides into town and Doc gets his gun. When the man is shot Doc is the obvious suspect.

Cast	Ainslie Pryor, Harry Bartell, Chris Alcaide
Writer	John Dunkel
Director	Ted Post
Producer	Charles Marquis Warren

Harry Bartell was a frequent performer on radio's *Gunsmoke.*

The Preacher. June 16, 1956. Production #529. Rerun June 28, 1958.

Seth Tandy, a helpless newcomer to Dodge, is bullied by boxer "Roaring" Sam Keeler. Keeler continues to torment Tandy until Matt steps in and meets him on his own terms: hand-to-hand combat.

Sam Keeler	Chuck Connors
Seth Tandy	Royal Dano
Humbert	Paul DuBov
Stage Driver	Jim Hyland
Story	John Meston
Script	John Dunkel
Director	Robert Stevenson
Producer	Charles Marquis Warren

Fame came to Chuck Connors when he played Lucas McCain on *The Rifleman.* He also starred in the Western *Branded* and was most recently featured in the short-lived television series *Werewolf.* Paul DuBov was a frequent guest star on radio's *Gunsmoke.*

How to Die for Nothing. June 23, 1956. Production #531. Rerun June 21, 1958.

Ned and Zack share a bottle and ride into Dodge ready to tear it apart. When Matt tries to disarm the trailhands he is forced to kill Ned.

Howard Bulow	Mort Mills
Zack	James Nolan
Reisling	Maurice Manson
Jacklin	Larry Dobkin
Ned	Bill White, Jr.
Stranger	Herbert Lytton
Story	John Meston
Script	Sam Peckinpah
Director	Ted Post
Producer	Charles Marquis Warren

Larry Dobkin was a frequent guest star on radio's *Gunsmoke.* James Nolan was a regular on the television series *Dante.*

Dutch George. June 30, 1956. Production #532.

During his childhood Matt idolized Dutch George who has since become the leader of a notorious gang of horse thieves. Dutch victimizes Jimmy McQueen, a young cowboy, but both Dutch and Matt underestimate the seemingly naive cowboy.

GUNSMOKE — III. THE PROGRAMS

Dutch George	Robert Middleton
Jimmy McQueen	Tom Pittman
Story	John Dunkel
Script	John Dunkel
Director	Robert Stevenson
Producer	Charles Marquis Warren

Prairie Happy. July 7, 1956. Production #534.

An embittered old man deliberately incites the Dodge City populace to riot by spreading fear with fabricated stories of an impending Indian raid. When a young boy shoots at Matt and Chester, mistaking them for Pawnee, the fires are fanned further. Matt and Chester return to Dodge to find the town's panic-stricken citizens arming themselves, and preparing for the Indian uprising.

Tewksbury	Robert Ellenstein
Quiet One	Anne Barton
Mr. Botkin	Wilfred Knapp
Father	Tyler McVey
Boy	Bruce Holland
Danvers	Jack Holland
Citizen	Roy Engle
Story	John Meston
Script	David Victor & Herbert Little
Director	Ted Post
Associate Producer	Norman Macdonnell
Producer	Charles Marquis Warren

Roy Engle appeared on *Date with the Angels* and *My Favorite Martian*.

Chester's Mail Order Bride. July 14, 1956. Production #535. Rerun August 31, 1957.

Chester becomes an unwilling bridegroom when his innocent correspondence with Miss Ann Smithwright is misconstrued to be a serious marriage proposal. Ann leaves her home in Philadelphia to travel to Dodge. Chester's embarrassment is further heightened by the fact that she expects to meet Matt, whose picture Chester had sent to her as his own.

Ann Smithwright	Mary Carver
Linus	Joel Ashley
Brady	Russ Thorson
Writers	David Victor & Herbert Little
Director	Robert Stevenson
Producer	Charles Marquis Warren

Mary Carver played Celia Simon on the television series *Simon and Simon*.

The Guitar. July 21, 1956. Production #533. Rerun September 7, 1957.

Weed Pindle is a simple-minded, guitar-strumming wanderer who travels aimlessly from town to town with his burro, Rainbow. After arriving in Dodge, he finds that he has become the object of ridicule for two sadistic cowboys, Short and Tyler. When the two discover that Weed is a Texan who served in the Union Army, they decide to lynch him. Although the lynching is averted, they are undaunted. They paint Weed's beloved burro and break his guitar. When Weed leaves Dodge, the two bullies follow him to finish the hanging they were robbed of.

Weed Pindle	Aaron Spelling
Short	Jacques Aubuchon

The Television Programs

Tyler	Charles Gray
Delmer	Duane Thorsen
Tom	Bill Hale
Pence	Joseph Mell
Story	John Meston
Script	Sam Peckinpah
Director	Harry Horner
Associate Producer	Norman Macdonnell
Producer	Charles Marquis Warren

Harry Horner started as an assistant to Max Reinhardt. When he accompanied Reinhardt to the United States, Horner became a production designer and art director, winning Academy Awards for *The Heiress* and *The Hustler*. As a director, Horner's films include *Beware My Lovely* and *The Red Planet Mars*. Although Aaron Spelling began his career as an actor, he became a successful producer of such programs as *Zane Grey Theater, Burke's Law, The Rookies, S.W.A.T., Family, Charlie's Angels,* and numerous made-for-television movies. Jacques Aubuchon was a regular on the adventure series *Paris 7000*.

Cara. July 28, 1956. Production #536.

Cara, an old girlfriend of Matt's, feigns suicide in an attempt to throw Matt off the trail of her new love Jack Tolliver. Cara has become a member of a gang of outlaws headed by Tolliver that plans on robbing Dodge's bank. Cara's job is to arrive a few days early to case the town.

Cara	Jorja Curtwright
Sheriff Benson	Charles Webster
Tolliver	Douglas Odney
Botkin	Wilfrid Knapp
Mr. Uzzel	Howard Culver
Story	John Meston
Script	David Victor & Herbert Little
Director	Robert Stevenson
Associate Producer	Norman Macdonnell
Producer	Charles Marquis Warren

Mr. and Mrs. Amber. August 4, 1956. Production #537. Rerun August 24, 1957.

Neil Amber is a poverty-stricken farmer struggling to eke out a meager existence. In his desperate state he is driven to violence against his father-in-law, Peak Fletcher. Fletcher is a self-proclaimed prophet who harasses Amber mercilessly for marrying his daughter Sarah against his will.

Sarah Amber	Gloria McGhee
Peak Fletcher	Ainslie Pryor
Neil Amber	Paul Richards
Simon	Bing Russell
Story	John Meston
Script	David Victor & Herbert Little
Director	Ted Post
Producer	Charles Marquis Warren

Former baseball player Bing Russell played the deputy sheriff on *Bonanza*. Russell was seen in the feature film *Sunset*. His son is film star Kurt Russell.

GUNSMOKE — III. THE PROGRAMS

Obie Tater. August 11, 1956, rerun. First aired October 15, 1955.

Unmarked Grave. August 18, 1956. Production #538. Rerun August 2, 1958.
    Blackie, an unscrupulous outlaw, is taken into custody by Matt. The opportunistic young man befriends Mrs. Randolph, a sympathetic older woman who has recently lost her own son. Mrs. Randolph, unaware of Blackie's shady past, feels that he is being victimized. Blackie seizes the moment to use her in an attempt to secure his freedom.

Rusty (Blackie)	Ron Hagerthy
Mrs. Randolph	Helen Kleeb
Tasker Sloan	William Hopper
Darcy	Than Wyenn
Munro	Joe Scudero
Stage Driver	Boyd Stockman
Writers	David Victor & Herbert Little
Director	Ted Post
Associate Producer	Norman Macdonnell
Producer	Charles Marquis Warren

Although Ron Hagerthy's character was named Rusty in the credits, he was called Blackie in the episode. Hagerthy played Clipper on the kiddie television Western *Sky King*. Helen Kleeb was a frequent guest star on radio's *Gunsmoke*. On television, Ms. Kleeb was a regular on *Harrigan and Son* and *The Waltons*.

Alarm at Pleasant Valley. August 25, 1956. Production #539.
    En route to Dodge, Chester and Matt encounter a fleeing homestead family. The Fraser family's happiness in their little paradise, Pleasant Valley, has been shattered by renegade Indians who have been murdering homesteaders. Matt tries to convince the Frasers that only a few Kiowas are responsible, and that the family should not evacuate. Sam Fraser is skeptical and prepares to leave, but he is forced to remain and fight when his wife goes into labor.

Sam Fraser	Lew Brown
Ma Fraser	Helen Wallace
Alice Fraser	Dorothy Schuyler
Tad Fraser	Bill White, Jr.
Lieutenant	Dan Blocker
Writer	John Dunkel
Director	Ted Post
Associate Producer	Norman Macdonnell
Producer	Charles Marquis Warren

Dan Blocker is best remembered for his portrayal of Hoss Cartwright on the television Western *Bonanza*.

Word of Honor. September 1, 1956 rerun. First aired October 1, 1955.

SECOND SEASON

Cow Doctor. September 8, 1956. Production #541. Rerun July 26, 1958.
    Doc is summoned to the home of Ben Pitcher, a doctor-hating farmer, and discovers that he has been called to treat an ailing cow. Matt, who has escorted Doc, tries

The Television Programs

unsuccessfully to stop a scuffle that erupts between the two men leaving Doc seriously wounded. To add to Doc's resentment of Pitcher, a patient who really needed his help died while he was away. Some time later, while still recovering from his knife wounds, Doc is once again summoned to the farmer's home. Although Kitty and Matt try to discourage him from going the irascible physician ignores their advice.

Ben Pitcher	Robert H. Harris
Mrs. Pitcher	Dorothy Adams
Jerry Pitcher	Tommy Kirk
Story	John Meston
Script	John Dunkel
Director	Andrew McLaglen
Associate Producer	Norman Macdonnell
Producer	Charles Marquis Warren

Robert Harris was a regular on *The Goldbergs* and *Court of Last Resort*.

Brush at Elkader. September 15, 1956. Production #542. Rerun July 1, 1961.

Matt and Chester journey to Elkader to arrest the murderer of Ben Williams, a man without an enemy in the world. But Matt's chore is not an easy one. All he knows of the murderer is his name, and the townspeople of Elkader are exceptionally uncooperative when it comes to identifying the suspect.

Hinkle	Gage Clark
Lou Shippen	Paul Lambert
Clerk	Alfred Linder
Bartender	Dennis Cross
Liveryman	Malcolm Atterbury
Story	John Meston
Script	Les Crutchfield
Director	Ted Post
Associate Producer	Norman Macdonnell
Producer	Charles Marquis Warren

On television, Gage Clark appeared as a regular on *The Hartmans*, *Mr. Peeper*, and *Date with the Angels*. Paul Lambert was featured as Tom Dalessio on the dramatic series, *Executive Suite*.

Custer. September 22, 1956. Production #540.

While tracking rustler Joe Trimble, Matt and Chester encounter a fatally beaten rancher. Major Banker, who has also been tracking Trimble, plans to court-marshal him for desertion. Matt, however, refuses to release Trimble to Banker, insisting on a civil trial. Unfortunately for Matt a jury finds Trimble "not guilty" for lack of evidence. Trimble is then released to Major Banker, who due to a shortage of soldiers is forced to re-recruit him.

Joe Trimble	Brian Hutton
Major Banker	Richard Keith
Judge	Herbert Lytton
Story	John Meston
Script	Gil Doud
Director	Ted Post
Associate Producer	Norman Macdonnell
Producer	Charles Marquis Warren

GUNSMOKE — III. THE PROGRAMS

The Round Up. September 29, 1956. Production #544. Rerun August 9, 1958.
 To avoid bloodshed, Matt "closes" Front Street to a rowdy group of celebrating cowboys. His edict proves to be very unpopular with Dodge's businessmen, who have been counting on the trailhands' revenue to line their pockets. The cowboys are also resentful of having their activities curtailed.

Ed Summers	Barney Phillips
Ray Torp	Jacques Aubuchon
Sam Rydell	John Dierkes
Zel Blatnick	Michael Hinn
Jake	Mason Curry
Dad	John Patrick
Ted Hightower	Sam Schwartz
Story	John Meston
Script	Sam Peckinpah
Director	Ted Post
Associate Producer	Norman Macdonnell
Producer	Charles Marquis Warren

 Rugged character actor John Dierkes is probably best known for his performance in the classic Western, *Shane*. Barney Phillips was a frequent guest-star on radio's *Gunsmoke*. On television, Mr. Phillips was a regular on several programs including *Dragnet, Twelve O'Clock High,* and *The Felony Squad.*

October 6, 1956, preempted.

October 13, 1956, preempted for President Eisenhower's Birthday.

Young Man with a Gun. October 20, 1956. Production #545.
 After his outlaw brother is killed in what he perceives to have been an unfair fight, young Peyt Kertcher vows vengeance. Harboring a warped sense of duty because of the bad influence of his brother, Peyt saves up his money to buy a gun. He then practices daily, while he devises a plan to take Matt's life.

Peyt Kertcher	Jack Diamond
Sam Kertcher	Fredd Wayne
Jack Rynning	Clegg Hoyt
Spencer	Sid Clute
Bartender	Bert Rumsey
Story	John Meston
Script	Winston Miller
Director	Christian Nyby
Associate Producer	Norman Macdonnell
Producer	Charles Marquis Warren

 Christian Nyby directed James Arness in the cult classic *The Thing*. Sid Clute appeared as a regular on *Lou Grant* and *Cagney and Lacey.*

Indian White. October 27, 1956. Production #546.
 A white boy who was raised by the Cheyennes is found by the cavalry. Christened "Dennis" the young boy goes to live with Mary Cullen, whose own son had been kidnapped by the Cheyennes many years ago. Unfortunately, the prejudice Dennis encounters and his longing to return to the Indians make it impossible for him to adjust to his new life.

The Television Programs

Dennis	Peter Votrian
Mrs. Mary Cullen	Marian Seldes
Colonel Honeyman	Alexander Lockwood
Little Wolf	Abel Fernandez
Ross	Stanley Adams
Dutchholder	Clegg Hoyt
Cowboy	Kenneth Alton
Citizen	George Archambeault
Story	Tom Hanley
Script	David Victor & Herbert Little
Director	Ted Post
Associate Producer	Norman Macdonnell
Producer	Charles Marquis Warren

Tom Hanley was one of the audio magicians on radio's *Gunsmoke*. Abel Fernandez appeared regularly on *Steve Canyon* and *The Untouchables*.

November 3, 1956, preempted for *Ford Star Jubilee*.

How to Cure a Friend. November 10, 1956. Production #550.

Nick Search is an old friend of Matt's who has earned the reputation of being a notorious gambler. He arrives in Dodge with the intent of using Matt's influence with the local townspeople to lure them into a crooked card game. However, Nick first must convince Matt that he has gone straight.

Nick Search	Andrew Duggan
Enoch Mills	Simon Oakland
Bill Pence	Joseph Mell
Mr. Teeters	Jess Kirkpatrick
Story	John Meston
Script	Winston Miller
Director	Ted Post
Producer	Charles Marquis Warren

Jess Kirkpatrick was a performer on radio's *Gunsmoke*. Andrew Duggan is a familiar face to television audiences. He starred in several series including *Bourbon Street Beat*, *Room for One More*, *Twelve O'Clock High*, and *Lancer*.

Legal Revenge. November 17, 1956. Production #547. Rerun August 30, 1958.

Matt and Chester ride onto the prairie to investigate a bizarre story told by Doc. It seems that while returning from a professional visit, Doc stopped at an isolated cabin where he discovered a sick man tended by a strange woman. Both the man and woman were exhausted, each obviously struggling to stay awake after days and nights of watchfulness. The man had a knife wound that might have been inflicted by the woman, and under his bedcover he held a gun. Doc surmises that the first to fall asleep will be murdered by the other.

Flory Tibbs	Cloris Leachman
George Bassett	Philip Bourneuf
Clerk	Robert Strong
Story	John Meston
Script	Sam Peckinpah
Director	Andrew McLaglen
Associate Producer	Norman Macdonnell
Producer	Charles Marquis Warren

GUNSMOKE — III. THE PROGRAMS

Cloris Leachman has a long list of television and film credits. She won an Academy Award for Best Supporting Actress for *The Last Picture Show,* Emmy Awards for *A Brand New Life, The Mary Tyler Moore Show, The Woman Who Willed a Miracle, The Screen Actor's Guild 50th Anniversary Celebration,* and for her appearance on *Cher.* The versatile actress is equally at home in comedy or drama and has appeared as a regular on numerous television programs including, *The Mary Tyler Moore Show, Phyllis,* and *The Facts of Life.* Among her credits are two Mel Brooks' films, *Young Frankenstein* and *High Anxiety.*

The Mistake. November 24, 1956. Production #543.

When a gambler is murdered, the prime suspect claims he was with Doc at the time of the crime. Unfortunately, Doc is absent from town and cannot corroborate his alibi. When he escapes, Matt is forced to pursue him, leaving the town at the mercy of the real killer.

Jim Bostick . . . . Touch Connors
Haney . . . . Gene O'Donnell
Driver . . . . Cyril Delevanti
Rider . . . . Robert Hinkle
Bartender . . . . Bert Rumsey
Story . . . . John Meston
Script . . . . Gil Doud
Director . . . . Andrew McLaglen
Associate Producer . . . . Norman Macdonnell
Producer . . . . Charles Marquis Warren

Although born in London, Andrew V. McLaglen specialized mostly in Westerns. In addition to being one of *Gunsmoke's* most frequent directors, McLaglen directed such films as *McLintock, Shenandoah,* and *The Rare Breed.* Mike "Touch" Connors struck television gold when he portrayed Joe Mannix on the dramatic series, *Mannix.* Gene O'Donnell played the role of Barney Blake in the 1948 television series, *Barney Blake, Police Reporter.*

Greater Love. December 1, 1956. Production #548. Rerun August 23, 1958.

With his buddy close to death after being wounded in a hold-up, Jed Butler threatens to kill Doc if he fails to save the injured man. In an attempt to rescue Doc, Matt deliberately puts himself at the mercy of the shotgun-wielding Butler who realizes that he can only shoot one of the men.

Jed Butler . . . . Claude Akins
Hank . . . . Ray Bennett
Mrs. Brant . . . . Amzie Strickland
Tobeel . . . . Frank DeKova
Story . . . . John Meston
Script . . . . Winston Miller
Director . . . . Ted Post
Associate Producer . . . . Norman Macdonnell
Producer . . . . Charles Marquis Warren

Ted Post, who directed numerous *Gunsmoke* episodes, also directed stage plays, made for television movies, and feature films including *Hang 'Em High, Beneath the Planet of the Apes,* and *Good Guys Wear Black.* Burly Claude Akins has had his share of film and television credits. Although he started out playing mostly villains, his most memorable performances in recent years have been in two television comedy shows

The Television Programs

B.J. and the Bear and *Lobo*. On both programs he played "Sheriff Elroy P. Lobo." His movie credits include *From Here to Eternity, The Caine Mutiny,* and *Inherit the Wind.* Frank DeKova played Chief Wild Eagle on the television comedy, *F Troop.*

No Indians. December 8, 1956. Production #554. Rerun June 27, 1959.

A series of brutal Indian attacks on homesteads outside of Dodge anger the townspeople, and drive one family out of the territory completely. Matt investigates the raids and unearths evidence showing that the forays were not by Indians, but by white men masquerading as Indians.

Sam Butler .... Dick Rich
Captain Starr .... Herbert Rudley
Arie O'Dell .... Fintan Meyler
Jake .... Joel Ashley
Cran .... K.L. Smith
Stapp .... Mickey Simpson
Story .... John Meston
Script .... John Dunkel
Director .... Ted Post
Producer .... Norman Macdonnell

Herbert Rudley was a regular on several television series including *The Californians* and *The Mothers-In-Law*.

Spring Term. December 15, 1956. Production #552. Rerun July 11, 1959.

Dane Shaw is shot down on Dodge City's Front Street. When Matt tries to discover the reason, he learns that it was a case of mistaken identity. The bullet that killed Dane was meant for him.

Barker .... H.M. Wynant
Mr. Uzzell .... Howard Culver
Bill Lee .... Harry Townes
Jed .... Jack Kruschen
Danch .... Paul Newlan
Dane Shaw .... Ross Ford
Bartender .... Stanley Adams
Citizen .... Clayton Post
Story .... John Meston
Script .... William F. Leicester
Director .... Ted Post
Associate Producer .... Norman Macdonnell
Producer .... Charles Marquis Warren

Jack Kruschen and Clayton Post were both frequent performers on radio's *Gunsmoke*. Jack Kruschen was a television regular on *Hong Kong, Busting Loose,* and *Webster*. He has also had a successful film career and was nominated for an Academy Award for Best Supporting Actor for his superb performance in *The Apartment*. Ross Ford appeared regularly in the television comedy, *Meet Millie*.

Poor Pearl. December 22, 1956. Production #551.

Matt intervenes when two men, farmer Willie Calhoun and gambler Webb Thorne, prepare to shoot it out. They are both in love with the same saloon girl, Pearl Bender. The showdown is averted when Pearl chooses to marry Webb. Calhoun believes, however, that Pearl made her choice under duress and his bitterness finally brings tragedy to the lives of all concerned.

GUNSMOKE — III. THE PROGRAMS

Pearl Bender	Constance Ford
Willie Calhoun	Denver Pyle
Webb Thorne	Michael Emmet
Frank Teeters	Jess Kirkpatrick
Bartender	Bert Rumsey
Big John	John Hamilton
Jimmie	John McGough
Story	John Meston
Script	Sam Peckinpah
Director	Andrew McLaglen
Associate Producer	Norman Macdonnell
Producer	Charles Marquis Warren

Denver Pyle guest starred frequently on *Gunsmoke*. He was also a regular on *The Doris Day Show*, *The Life and Times of Grizzly Adams*, and *The Dukes of Hazzard* where he played Uncle Jesse Duke. In addition, Denver has played a wide variety of character roles in such major films as *Bonnie and Clyde* and *The Man Who Shot Liberty Valance*. John Hamilton is familiar to television viewers as Perry White of *The Adventures of Superman*.

Cholera. December 29, 1956. Production #553. Rerun July 4, 1959.

Despite the threats of landowner McCready and his gang, homesteader Gabriel and his wife Jenny courageously refuse to give up their rightful land. When McCready hatches a heartless plot to evict Gabriel and his family, the scheme backfires and results in a personal disaster of his own. Matt attempts to preserve justice in a struggle that is eventually marked by tragedy and death.

McCready	Paul Fix
Gabriel	Bartlett Robinson
Jenny	Peg Hillias
Bart	Stuart Whitman
Billy	Gordon Gebert
David	John Smith
Story	John Meston
Script	Les Crutchfield
Director	Andrew McLaglen
Producer	Norman Macdonnell

Bartlett Robinson was radio's *Perry Mason*. Stuart Whitman appeared as U.S. Marshal Jim Crown in the short-lived Western *Cimarron Strip*. John Smith went on to become the star of two television Westerns *Cimarron City* and *Laramie*. Paul Fix is familiar to television viewers as Marshal Torrance of *The Rifleman*. However, the mild-mannered, character actor has also had a successful film career, appearing in *Red River*, *Giant*, and *To Kill a Mockingbird*.

Pucket's New Year. January 5, 1957. Production #555.

Matt and Chester come upon aged buffalo-hunter Ira Pucket lying near death on a freezing Kansas plain. Left there to die by his cowardly partner Jed Larner, Pucket is permanently crippled by exposure to sub-zero temperatures. The embittered Pucket stalks the streets of Dodge in search of his hated partner while Matt tries to rehabilitate the old man and prevent a senseless killing.

Ira Pucket	Edgar Stehli
Jed Larner	Grant Withers

The Television Programs

Botkin	Richard Deacon
Jim	Rocky Shahan
Bartender	Bert Rumsey
Story, Script	John Meston
Director	Andrew McLaglen
Producer	Norman Macdonnell

Richard Deacon is probably best known for his role as the bald, bewildered, bespectacled, Melvin Cooley of *The Dick Van Dyke Show*. Rocky Shahan played Joe Scarlett on *Rawhide*. The character Mr. Botkin, is sometimes spelled Bodkin. This is not a typo; in the television credits the name is spelled both ways.

The Cover Up. January 12, 1957. Production #558.

One by one, defenseless homesteaders meet their deaths behind the doors of their remote cabins, as a mysterious shotgun-wielding killer stalks the land of wealthy rancher Sam Baxter. When Matt finally arrests Baxter for the killings, another murder with a similar pattern is committed, forcing Matt to reinvestigate the situation.

Hoffer	Roy Engle
Sara Baxton	Vivi Janiss
Sam Baxton	Tyler McVey
Zack Ritter	Ted Marcuse
Jed Bates	Malcolm Atterbury
Story	John Meston
Script	William Robson
Director	William D. Russell
Producer	Norman Macdonnell

Vivi Janiss was a frequent guest performer on radio's *Gunsmoke*. On television she appeared regularly on *Father Knows Best*. William Robson was known to radio listeners as "the master of mystery and adventure" for producing and directing such classic radio shows as *Suspense* and *Escape*.

Sins of the Father. January 19, 1957. Production #557. Rerun July 25, 1959.

Dan Daggit arrives in Dodge with Rose, his Indian wife. They take a room at the Dodge House, much to the consternation of Mr. Dobie who stirs up trouble for Rose by telling wild stories of Indian uprisings.

Dan Daggit	Peter Whitney
Rose Daggit	Angie Dickinson
Mr. Dobie	Gage Clark
Rodin	Paul Wexler
Story	John Meston
Script	John Dunkel
Director	Andrew McLaglen
Producer	Norman Macdonnell

Angie Dickinson is familiar to television viewers as Sgt. Suzanne "Pepper" Anderson of *Police Woman*. Her film career includes Howard Hawk's *Rio Bravo*, and Brian DePalma's *Dressed to Kill*.

Kick Me. January 26, 1957. Production #549.

Bank robber Fred Myers eludes justice by posing as a respectable citizen in Dodge, until Matt discovers his true identity. When Myers gets wind of this he attempts to escape by taking Miss Kitty hostage. Tobeel, an illiterate Indian guide on whom Myers had played a cruel joke, repays the hoax with violence as he halts Myers in his bid for freedom.

Fred Myers	Robert H. Harris
Tobeel	Frank DeKova
Jennifer Myers	Julie Van Zandt
Harry Bent	Paul Lambert
Story	John Meston
Script	Endre Bohem & Lou Vittes
Director	Andrew McLaglen
Associate Producer	Norman Macdonnell
Producer	Charles Marquis Warren

Executioner. February 2, 1957. Production #559. Rerun July 18, 1959.

Tom Clegg, a ruthless young gunfighter, goads farmer Abe Curry into a senseless duel and kills him. Since Abe drew first, Matt is unable to arrest Clegg. However, the dead man's brother plots his own method of revenge. Morgan Curry, who is unarmed, follows Clegg everywhere. Eventually the gunman grows weary of his unwanted shadow.

Abe Curry	Robert Keys
Morgan Curry	Michael Hinn
Tom Clegg	Liam Sullivan
Story	John Meston
Script	Gil Doud
Director	Andrew V. McLaglen
Producer	Norman Macdonnell

Liam Sullivan appeared on the television Western, *The Monroes.*

Gone Straight. February 9, 1957. Production #562.

An ex-gunman and one-time member of a notorious outlaw band attempts to go straight but faces threats from his former companions. When Matt and Chester learn that the wanted man is living in a nearby frontier community, they set out to arrest him armed only with a sketchy description. Matt and Chester are thwarted in their attempts to apprehend the reformed outlaw when the townspeople refuse to identify him. Matt finally discovers his true identity after a vicious ambush where the suspect and his former partners battle it out.

Nate Timble	Carl Betz
Mike Postil	Tige Andrews
Gunter	Joe De Santis
Mrs. Timble	Marianne Stewart
Parker	Ward Wood
Ace	John Dierkes
Story	John Meston
Script	Les Crutchfield
Director	Ted Post
Producer	Norman Macdonnell

Carl Betz played the perfect husband and father, Dr. Alex Stone, in *The Donna Reed Show.* In 1969 he won an Emmy for Best Actor in a Dramatic Series for *Judd, For the Defense,* in which he starred as Clinton Judd. Tige Andrews co-starred in two television adventure series, *The Detectives* as Lt. John Russo, and *The Mod Squad* as Captain Adam Greer.

The Television Programs

Bloody Hands. February 16, 1957. Production #561. Rerun August 8, 1959.

Matt decides to turn in his badge after a violent gunfight in which he is forced to take the lives of three men. Having to kill time and time again has taken its toll on Matt, and he is unable to shake this latest experience. With his lawman days over, Matt can at long last breathe easy and enjoy life. He spends time with the local children, teaching them to track, and has time to go fishing with Kitty. Unfortunately, his respite from a life of violence proves short-lived. Chester makes an impassioned plea for his return when Dodge is terrorized by a notorious outlaw who takes advantage of the absence of law and order.

  Jack Brand . . . . Lawrence Dobkin
  Joe Stranger . . . . Russell Johnson
  Linda Hawkins . . . . Gloria Marshall
  Billy . . . . Harvey Grant
  Tom . . . . David Saber
  Story, Script . . . . John Meston
  Director . . . . Andrew McLaglen
  Producer . . . . Norman Macdonnell

Russell Johnson is best known for his role as "The Professor" on *Gilligan's Island*. He also appeared in several films including *Tumbleweed, This Island Earth,* and *The Greatest Story Ever Told*. Gloria Marshall was a regular on *The Bob Cummings Show*.

Skid Row. February 23, 1957. Production #564.

Ann Cabot leaves her home back East to marry a promising homesteader. However, Jack Shomer has become destitute because of land failure. Shomer refuses to see Ann despite Doc's and Matt's urgings, but lives to regret his decision when Ann, naive and unfamiliar with the loose ways of life in Dodge, becomes the victim of the brutal Hank Groat.

  Ann Cabot . . . . Susan Morrow
  Jack Shomer . . . . Joseph Sargent
  Hank Groat . . . . Guinn Williams
  Story . . . . John Meston
  Script . . . . Gil Doud
  Director . . . . Ted Post
  Producer . . . . Norman Macdonnell

Joseph Sargent turned his career to directing, first on television with *The Man from U.N.C.L.E.* and then to feature films such as *The Taking of Pelham One-Two-Three* and *MacArthur*. Guinn Williams was nicknamed "Big Boy" by Will Rogers. Williams appeared in over 80 movies including, *Dodge City, A Star Is Born, Billy the Kid,* and *The Alamo*. In Western films he played mostly heavy toughs and dim-witted cowboys.

Sweet and Sour. March 2, 1957. Production #569. Rerun August 22, 1959.

Frontier violence explodes in Dodge when newly-arrived dance hall girl, Rena Decker, purposely goads admirers into fighting over her affections. Despite Kitty's shrewd appraisal of the girl, Matt befriends Rena and arranges for her to work at the Long Branch. Blistering street fights bring death to four men as a result of Rena's strange compulsion.

  Rena Decker . . . . Karen Sharpe
  Ab Laster . . . . John Alderson
  Joe Garrett . . . . Walter Reed

GUNSMOKE — III. THE PROGRAMS

Hank	Ken Mayer
Joe	Joe Mitchum
Story, Script	John Meston
Director	Andrew McLaglen
Producer	Norman Macdonnell

Karen Sharpe appeared as a regular on *Johnny Ringo* and *I Dream of Jeannie*. Ken Mayer was a regular on the kiddie series, *Space Patrol*.

Cain. March 9, 1957. Production #566. Rerun August 15, 1959.

Former gunslinger Joel Adams has become a wealthy rancher. His past catches up with him when Cain Vestal, a frontier migrant, appears and vows to take his life. Adams is not one to be easily intimidated, and he is convinced that Cain will never carry out his threat. In a showdown at the Long Branch, Adams learns too late, just how determined and embittered Cain really is.

Cain Vestal	Harry Bartell
Joel Adams	Mark Roberts
Pritchard	Paul DuBov
Story, Script	John Meston
Director	Ted Post
Producer	Norman Macdonnell

Mark Roberts appeared as Hildy Johnson in the television series, *Front Page* and as Bob Brannagan in *The Brothers Brannagan*.

Bureaucrat. March 16, 1957. Production #570.

Claiming a woeful lack of law enforcement, Rex Procter, a high-minded Washington official arrives in Dodge bent on reforming the wild frontier community. Refusing to heed Dillon's warnings, the totally inept Procter attempts to impose his strict reforms on the hard-living residents, but is attacked by a riotous mob that openly rebels against his unrealistic edicts.

Rex Procter	John Hoyt
Husk	Ned Glass
Will Stroud	Ken Lynch
Story	John Meston
Script	William F. Leicester
Director	Ted Post
Producer	Norman Macdonnell

John Hoyt appeared on two comedy series, *Tom, Dick and Mary* and *Gimme a Break*. Character actor Ned Glass appeared regularly on *Julia* and *Bridget Loves Bernie*. On television, Ken Lynch was a regular on *The Plainclothesman* and *McCloud*, which starred Dennis Weaver.

Last Fling. March 23, 1957. Production #571. Rerun June 18, 1960.

Two aging sodbusters, John Peavy and Mulligan Rives, come to Dodge for a last fling. They proceed to pester Kitty who warns them to leave her alone. Later, when one of them is shot in the neck, Kitty is accused but she denies any involvement. When someone mysteriously takes a shot at Kitty, Matt investigates the two seemingly harmless cronies.

John Peavy	Florenz Ames
Sabina Peavy	Anne O'Neal
Mulligan Rives	Frank DeKova

The Television Programs

Melanie	Susan Morrow
Story, Script	John Meston
Director	Andrew McLaglen
Producer	Norman Macdonnell

Florenz Ames portrayed Ellery Queen's father in two dramatic television series, and played Dagwood's overbearing boss in *Blondie*.

Chester's Murder. March 30, 1957. Production #568.
A jealous cowhand publicly threatens Chester when he sees him with his girlfriend, Nita Tucker. When the cowhand is found slain, circumstantial evidence points to Chester. Matt is forced to take his friend into custody, and then must quell the threat of mob violence as irate townspeople demand a conviction.

Jake Buley	Murray Hamilton
Nita Tucker	Peggie Castle
Ned Pickard	Tom Greenway
Jim Dobie	Gage Clark
Man	Charles Conrad
Jonas	Tim Graham
Story, Script	John Meston
Director	Ted Post
Producer	Norman Macdonnell

In addition to playing in numerous B-pictures in the 1950s, Peggie Castle played saloon keeper Lily Merrill on the television Western *Lawman*. Murray Hamilton is familiar to television audiences. He appeared as a regular in such series as *Hail to the Chief*, *Rich Man Poor Man—Book I*, and *B.J. and the Bear*.

The Photographer. April 6, 1957. Production #556. Originally scheduled for February 23, 1957. Rerun August 1, 1959.
Professor Jacoby is a photographer from the East who arrives in Dodge to satisfy a morbid curiosity about the violent ways of the West. Heedless of Matt's warnings, Jacoby foolishly wanders into an area held sacred by an Indian tribe.

Professor Jacoby	Sebastian Cabot
Gart	Norman Frederic
Grubby	Ned Glass
Left Hand	Charles Horvath
Citizen	Howard Culver
Kate	Dorothy Schuyler
Story, Script	John Dunkel
Director	William D. Russell
Producer	Norman Macdonnell

Wrong Man. April 13, 1957. Production #563.
Sam Rickers boastfully claims his reward for shooting Bob Hulburt, a wanted criminal. Rickers later discovers that he has taken the life of Jake Haney, an innocent man. One homicide leads to another when the trigger-happy Rickers finds that he is marked for revenge by Jake's partner, Catlin.

Sam Rickers	Don Keefer
Letty	Catherine McLeod
Catlin	Robert Griffin
Story, Script	John Meston

Director .... Andrew V. McLaglen
Producer .... Norman Macdonnell

The title *The Wrong Man* was used again October 27, 1966. Don Keefer appeared in the situation comedy, *Angel*.

Big Girl Lost. April 20, 1957. Production #560.

Philadelphian Philip Locke arrives in Dodge inquiring after the whereabouts of his ex-fiancee Laura Simmons. Matt pretends to have no knowledge of her, even though he is aware that she works at the Long Branch. When Matt asks Laura if she wants to see Locke, she confesses that Locke's family had disapproved of their proposed marriage, and as a consequence, he had broken their engagement. Laura does not want Locke to see her in a saloon. Meanwhile, Locke suspects that Matt has been lying to him and threatens to have him killed.

Laura Simmons .... Gloria McGhee
Philip Locke .... Michael Pate
Bill Pence .... Judson Pratt
Ed Doolin .... Gerald Milton
Story, Script .... John Meston
Director .... Ted Post
Producer .... Norman Macdonnell

Actor-writer-producer Michael Pate is Australian born. His films include *Hondo, All the Brothers Were Valiant, PT-109,* and *McLintock*.

What the Whiskey Drummer Heard. April 27, 1957. Production #572.

Marked for death by an unknown sniper, Matt is defenseless against an attempt on his life. Hoping to bring the assailant out into the open, Matt feigns death by disappearing. Unfortunately, Matt's plan is foiled by the loose talk of the town braggard, and he is forced to resurrect himself and await the next attack.

Wilbur Hawkins .... Vic Perrin
Roberts .... Robert Karnes
Sheriff Tom Smith .... Robert Burton
Story .... John Meston
Script .... Gil Doud
Director .... Andrew McLaglen
Producer .... Norman Macdonnell

Robert Burton played Dr. Gordon on the dramatic series, *Kings Row*. Robert Karnes was a regular on *The Lawless Years*.

Cheap Labor. May 4, 1957. Production #567. Rerun August 29, 1959.

Fos Capper gives up the life of a gunman and settles in Dodge. When he meets lovely Flora Stancil, they fall in love. Unfortunately, Flora's brother Ben does not like anyone paying attention to her. Ben fears that Flora might be persuaded to leave him and he would have to pay someone to do the cooking, housekeeping, and other chores he burdens her with. Ben tries to bully and intimidate Fos and Flora, but despite insults and threats, Fos continues his courtship. Fos does everything to avoid violence, but is finally forced into a gunfight.

Fos Capper .... Andrew Duggan
Ben Stancil .... Robert F. Simon
Flora Stancil .... Peggy Webber
Joe .... Alan Emerson

The Television Programs

Pete	Tom Gleason
Melanie	Susan Morrow
Bum	James Nusser
Story, Script	John Meston
Director	Andrew V. McLaglen
Producer	Norman Macdonnell

On television, Robert Simon appeared as a regular of several series including *Nancy, M.A.S.H.,* and *The Amazing Spider-Man.* Peggy Webber is a veteran of numerous radio shows including *Gunsmoke.*

Moon. May 11, 1957. Production #575.

Card dealer Vint is accused of fatally beating Charlie Brewer, who had won a fortune from him at the card table. The unfortunate Brewer had fallen into a trap set by Vint and Nan Mellors, a hostess at the Long Branch. Since there are no witnesses, Vint is free. Trouble befalls Vint when he finds himself caught between the law and Brewer's good friend Jack Salter, a notorious gunman.

Nan Mellors	Rebecca Welles
Vint	Phil Pine
Charlie Brewer	Stafford Repp
Jack Salter	Thomas Palmer
Vickie	Jane Ray
Story, Script	John Meston
Director	William D. Russell
Producer	Norman Macdonnell

Phil Pine was seen as Sgt. Newman on the television series, *The Blue Knight.* Stafford Repp was a regular on *The Thin Man,* and *The New Phil Silvers Show.* In the cult series, *Batman,* he played Chief O'Hara.

Who Lives by the Sword. May 18, 1957. Production #573.

Joe Delk is a calculating gunman whose ruthless stock and trade is shooting down men he goads into drawing. Despite his cold-blooded ways, Delk enjoys immunity from the law because of his unique methods. When Matt finds that he is powerless in stopping Delk legally, he challenges him to a fist fight to mete out justice. Delk learns the hard way that the courts are not the only means by which justice can be served.

Joe Delk	Harold J. Stone
Billy Baxter	Steve Terrell
Lew Baxter	Robert C. Ross
Snyder	Harry Wood
Story, Script	John Meston
Director	Andrew McLaglen
Producer	Norman Macdonnell

Harold J. Stone appeared as a regular on several television programs including *The Goldbergs, My World and Welcome to It,* and *Bridget Loves Bernie.* Steven Terrell was seen as Clarence Day, Jr., on the comedy series, *Life with Father.*

Uncle Oliver. May 25, 1957. Production #574.

Chester fights for his life after being shot in an ambush as Matt searches for the gunman. Matt is certain that aged plainsman Oliver Stang or his half-witted nephew Viney was the assailant. He is unable to make an arrest, however, because there were no witnesses. Matt has no choice but to risk the lives of Doc and Chester, who serve as decoys in a final desperate attempt to trap the sniper.

  Oliver Stang . . . . Earle Hodgins
  Viney Stang . . . . Paul Wexler
  Story, Script . . . . John Meston
  Director . . . . Andrew McLaglen
  Producer . . . . Norman Macdonnell

Daddy-O. June 1, 1957. Production #565.

 Wayne Russell, Kitty's wayward father, shows up in Dodge under the pretext of being concerned about her welfare. Although Kitty has not seen her father since childhood, Russell wants his daughter to sell her share in the Long Branch, withdraw all her savings, and leave town and accompany him to New Orleans.

  Wayne Russell . . . . John Dehner
  Additional Cast . . . . Judson Pratt
  Story, Script . . . . John Meston
  Director . . . . Andrew McLaglen
  Producer . . . . Norman Macdonnell

Kite's Reward. June 8, 1957 rerun. First aired November 12, 1955.

The Man Who Would Be Marshal. June 15, 1957. Production #577.

 Emmett Egan is a retired army officer who comes to Dodge intent on having Matt's job. Emmett has been searching for the excitement he once knew in the military, and demands the opportunity to prove himself. The determined Emmett persuades Matt to deputize him. When trouble finally develops, Emmett learns that the law of the military commands little respect amongst the frontier migrants of Dodge.

  Emmett Egan . . . . Herbert Rudley
  Jeff Willoughby . . . . Alex Sharp
  Gere . . . . Rusty Westcoat
  Bozeman . . . . Clancy Cooper
  Story, Script . . . . John Meston
  Director . . . . William B. Russell
  Producer . . . . Norman Macdonnell

Liar from Blackhawk. June 22, 1957. Production #576.

 Hank Shinn has the reputation of being a ruthless gunfighter, and the citizens of Dodge cower under his threat. When Shinn goes too far with his boasting, a man finally calls his bluff.

  Hank Shinn . . . . Denver Pyle
  Additional Cast . . . . Strother Martin, John Doucette
  Story . . . . John Meston
  Script . . . . David Victor & Herbert Little
  Director . . . . Andrew McLaglen
  Producer . . . . Norman Macdonnell

John Doucette was a regular on *Big Town, Lock Up,* and *The Partners.*

Home Surgery. June 29, 1957 rerun. First aired October 8, 1955.

Jealousy. July 6, 1957. Production #578.

 Cam Durban, an old friend of Matt's, arrives in Dodge with his new wife Tilda. Cam plans on running the faro table at the Long Branch. Lonnie Pike, a conniving

The Television Programs

faro dealer who holds a grudge against Matt, hopes to cause trouble between Matt and Cam by spreading rumors about Matt's relationship with Tilda. Unfortunately Cam has a long history of jealousy, and the gossip causes him to lose control.

Cam Durbin	Jack Kelly
Tilda	Joan Tetzel
Lonnie Pike	Than Wyenn
Jack Davis	Jack Mann
Cowboy	Ken Drake
Waitress	Barbara Dodd
Story	John Meston
Script	Sam Peckinpah
Director	Andrew McLaglen
Producer	Norman Macdonnell

Jack Kelly is probably best known for his role as the amiable gambler, Bart Maverick, from the popular Western *Maverick*.

No Handcuffs. July 13, 1957, rerun. First aired January 21, 1956.

Reunion '78. July 20, 1957, rerun. First aired March 3, 1956.

Doc's Revenge. July 27, 1957, rerun. First aired June 9, 1956.

Cooter. August 3, 1957, rerun. First aired May 19, 1956.

The Reed Survives. August 10, 1957, rerun. First aired December 31, 1955.

The Killer. August 17, 1957, rerun. First aired May 26, 1956.

Mr. and Mrs. Amber. August 24, 1957, rerun. First aired August 4, 1956.

Chester's Mail Order Bride. August 31, 1957, rerun. First aired July 14, 1956.

The Guitar. September 7, 1957, rerun. First aired July 21, 1956.

THIRD SEASON

Crack-Up. September 14, 1957. Production #585. Rerun July 30, 1960.

Nate Springer has the reputation of being a hired assassin. When he arrives in Dodge, Matt is determined to learn the identity of the man who sent for Springer. Inevitably Matt and Springer meet in a final showdown, where Matt makes a surprising discovery.

Nate Springer	John Dehner
Mr. Peters	Jess Kirkpatrick
Girl	Jean Vaughn
Story, Script	John Meston
Director	Ted Post
Producer	Norman Macdonnell

Gun for Chester. September 21, 1957. Production #579. Rerun July 23, 1960.

When a stranger arrives in Dodge, Chester recognizes him to be Asa Ledbetter, a

GUNSMOKE — III. THE PROGRAMS

man who once vowed to kill him should they ever meet again. All his friends, Matt included, believe that he is mistaken, especially after Ledbetter denies any knowledge of Chester, and Chester refuses to explain why Ledbetter wants to kill him.

> Asa Ledbetter .... Thomas Coley
> Moss Grimmick .... George Selk
> Hotel Clerk .... Howard Culver
> Man .... Clayton Post
> *Story, Script* .... John Meston
> *Director* .... Louis King
> *Producer* .... Norman Macdonnell

Blood Money. September 28, 1957. Production #580. Rerun August 13, 1960.

When Harry Spencer falls from his horse, he is rescued by Joe Harpe, who turns out to be a wanted bank robber with a price on his head. Spencer shows his gratitude by claiming the reward for Harpe's capture.

> Harry Spencer .... Vinton Hayworth
> Joe Harpe .... James Dobson
> Smith .... Lawrence Green
> *Story, Script* .... John Meston
> *Director* .... Louis King
> *Producer* .... Norman Macdonnell

The title *Blood Money* was used again for the episode broadcast January 22, 1968. The plots were not similar.

Kitty's Outlaw. October 5, 1957. Production #582.

Outlaw Cole Yankton arrives in Dodge. It is apparent that he is more than just a casual acquaintance of Miss Kitty's, and their "friendship" has Chester and Doc concerned. To add fuel to the fire, while Kitty and Matt have dinner on the outskirts of Dodge, Yankton and two accomplices rob the bank. Matt, Chester, and Doc all feel that Kitty has betrayed them.

> Cole Yankton .... Ainslie Pryor
> Mr. Jonas .... Dabbs Greer
> Cowboy .... Chris Alcaide
> Hotel Clerk .... Howard Culver
> First Man .... Jack Mann
> *Story* .... John Meston
> *Script* .... Kathleen Hite
> *Director* .... Andrew McLaglen
> *Producer* .... Norman Macdonnell

Potato Road. October 12, 1957. Production #586. Rerun August 6, 1960.

Budge Grilk asks Matt to investigate an alleged murder committed by his father. While checking on the story, Matt and Chester encounter Pa Grilk who is ready for a showdown. Matt soon realizes that Budge's allegations were a hoax invented by the elder Grilk to lure him out of town so he could rob the bank. Grilk threatens to eliminate anyone who stands in his way, and he proves it when he shoots down two people, one of them his son.

> Pa Grilk .... Robert F. Simon
> Ma Grilk .... Jeanette Nolan
> Budge Grilk .... Tom Pittman

The Television Programs

Story, Script	John Meston
Director	Ted Post
Producer	Norman Macdonnell

Jeanette Nolan was a frequent guest-star on radio's *Gunsmoke*. On television she was a regular on *The Richard Boone Show*, *The Virginian*, and played the title role in the *Gunsmoke* spin-off series, *Dirty Sally*. She recently was hailed for her bravura performance on an episode of *Cagney and Lacey*. Miss Nolan has an impressive stage and film career as well, and is married to actor John McIntire.

Jesse. October 19, 1957. Production #581.

Jesse Pruett rides into Dodge bent on avenging the death of his father by an unknown assailant. He comes under the influence of a tough gunslinger named Bill Stapp. In his search to find the murderer, Pruett befriends Matt and makes a startling discovery.

Jesse Pruett	George Brenlin
Bill Stapp	Edward Binns
Karl	James Maloney
Story, Script	John Meston
Director	Andrew McLaglen
Producer	Norman Macdonnell

The title *Jesse* was used again February 19, 1973, however, the plots were not related. Edward Binns appeared on television as a regular of several programs including *Brenner*, *The Nurses*, and *It Takes a Thief*. James Maloney was a regular on the dramatic series *21 Beacon Street*.

Mavis McCloud. October 26, 1957. Production #584. Rerun August 27, 1960.

Pretty Mavis McCloud leaves her home back East for a taste of frontier life. She arrives in Dodge with the hope of finding a husband. At Matt's suggestion she is put under Kitty's protective wing. Mavis finally meets and marries Barney Wales, a respected rancher. Unfortunately, her plans for living happily ever after are frustrated when Lou Staley, a man who once swore vengeance on Mavis for leaving him, comes gunning for her.

Mavis McCloud	Fay Spain
Barney Wales	Casey Adams
Lou Staley	Robert Cornthwaite
Story, Script	John Meston
Director	Buzz Kulik
Producer	Norman Macdonnell

Buzz Kulik went on to direct the highly acclaimed television movie *Brian's Song* starring James Caan.

Born to Hang. November 2, 1957. Production #583. Rerun August 20, 1960.

Drifter Joe Digger is saved by Matt from being lynched by two ranchers who label him a horse thief. However, Digger seems determined to face the hangman's noose when he carries out a plan of revenge against the men who tried to lynch him.

Joe Digger	Wright King
Hank	Anthony Caruso
Robie	Mort Mills
Ed Glick	Ken Lynch
Mrs. Glick	Dorothy Adams

GUNSMOKE — III. THE PROGRAMS

Story, Script .... John Meston
Director .... Buzz Kulik
Producer .... Norman Macdonnell

John Meston was nominated for an Emmy for Best Half-hour Teleplay for this episode. He lost to Paul Monash for "Lonely Wizard," *Schlitz Playhouse.* Anthony Caruso is a familiar face in numerous films primarily as the villain. He appeared in such features as *Johnny Apollo, Watch on the Rhine,* and *The Asphalt Jungle.*

Romeo. November 9, 1957. Production #588.

Andy Bowers and Judy Pierce are in love, but their fathers are rival cattlemen who threaten bloodshed if the young couple continue their courtship. When Andy tells his story to Doc, Doc goads him into running away with Judy. This places Matt in the untenable position of having to stave off a range war.

Jake Pierce .... Barry Kelly
Andy Bowers .... Robert Vaughn
Judy Pierce .... Barbara Eden
Emmett Bowers .... Tyler McVey
Pete Knight .... Robert McQueeney
Ab Drain .... Bill McGraw
Preacher .... William Erwin
Story, Script .... John Meston
Director .... Ted Post
Producer .... Norman Macdonnell

Barbara Eden is known to television viewers as Jeannie from the comedy series *I Dream of Jeannie.* William Erwin was a regular on the comedy *Struck by Lightning.*

Never Pester Chester. November 16, 1957. Production #590. Rerun June 10, 1961.

Chester is dragged behind a horse and is left for dead by two ruffians, Stobo and Treavitt, after he asks them to stop bothering the local ladies. Doc feels his condition is critical and Matt blames himself for sending Chester to do his job. Not knowing whether Chester will live or die, Matt goes after the two men with a vengeance.

Stobo .... Buddy Baer
Treavitt .... Tom Greenway
Shiloh .... Woodrow Chambliss
Boss .... Paul Birch
Jim .... Gary Vinson
Story, Script .... John Meston
Director .... Richard Whorf
Producer .... Norman Macdonnell

Actor-director-producer Richard Whorf directed the comedy *Champagne for Caesar* starring Ronald Coleman. As an actor he appeared in such films as *Yankee Doodle Dandy* with James Cagney and *Keeper of the Flame* with Katharine Hepburn and Spencer Tracy. Woodrow Chambliss, who in later years played the continuing character of Lathrop, has the role of Shiloh in this episode. Buddy Baer is the brother of former heavy-weight champion of the world, Max Baer. Like his brother, Buddy was a veritable giant, which is why he was cast as the titan in such films as *Quo Vadis* and *Jack and the Beanstalk.* Paul Birch appeared as a regular on *Court of Last Resort* and *Cannonball.* Gary Vinson was a member of *The Roaring Twenties, McHale's Navy,* and *Pistols 'n' Petticoats.*

The Television Programs

Fingered. November 23, 1957. Production #589.

Jim Cobbett is accused of being a homicidal maniac by his neighbor Hank Luz when the disappearance of Jim's wife goes unexplained. When Jim's second bride Lila also vanishes under strange circumstances, he claims she was captured by Indians. When Matt discovers a freshly dug grave under some newly planted columbines, he cross-examines the distraught homesteader who painfully reveals the truth.

Jim Cobbett	John Larch
Hank Luz	Karl Swenson
Lila	Virginia Christine
Story, Script	John Meston
Director	James Sheldon
Producer	Norman Macdonnell

Virginia Christine was a frequent performer on radio's *Gunsmoke*. To television fans, Ms. Christine is familiar as Mrs. Olson of the Folger's coffee commercials. Her films include *High Noon* and *Judgement at Nuremberg*.

How to Kill a Woman. November 30, 1957. Production #591.

When two stagecoach passengers are robbed and killed, Matt and Chester set out to investigate. They maintain a lonely vigil in a remote waystation in an effort to catch the ruthless gunman responsible for the crime.

Jim Buck	Robert Brubaker
Jesse Daggett	Barry Atwater
Nat Pilcher	Pernell Roberts
Story, Script	John Meston
Director	John Rich
Producer	Norman Macdonnell

Mike Pozen won an Emmy for Best Editing of a Film for Television for this episode. Pernell Roberts appeared on two long running television series. He was Adam Cartwright on *Bonanza* and Dr. "Trapper" John McIntyre on *Trapper John, M.D.* John Rich won an Emmy in 1963 for Outstanding Directorial Achievement in Comedy for *The Dick Van Dyke Show* and two more Emmy Awards for directing and producing segments of *All in the Family*. Robert Brubaker played Deputy Blake on *The Sheriff of Cochise*.

Cows and Cribs. December 7, 1957. Production #592.

Drunken dirt farmer Joe Nadler refuses to provide for his destitute family, despite Matt's threats of imprisonment. Although Nadler claims to have no money, he inadvertently reveals that he does have an unexplained income. When cattle rustling and homicide are discovered on a nearby ranch, Matt faces Nadler in a violent confrontation.

Pa Thorpe	Judson Taylor
Joe Nadler	Val Avery
Mrs. Thorpe	Cathy Browne
Story	John Meston
Script	Kathleen Hite
Director	Richard Whorf
Producer	Norman Macdonnell

Doc's Reward. December 14, 1957. Production #593. Rerun June 24, 1961.

On route to an emergency, Doc is stopped by Myles Brandell who threatens to shoot

Doc's horse. Doc tells Myles that he will retaliate by shooting him. Myles calls Doc's bluff and shoots the horse. Doc responds by killing Myles. This precipitates an awkward situation back in Dodge. Matt refuses to jail Doc, but the townsfolk and Nate Brandell, the dead man's brother, demand justice.

   Myles/Nate Brandell .... Jack Lord
   Joe .... Bruce Wendell
   1st Lady .... Netta Packer
   2nd Lady .... Jean Fenwick
   Bartender .... Brick Sullivan
   Story, Script .... John Meston
   Director .... Richard Whorf
   Producer .... Norman Macdonnell

 Jack Lord played Stoney Burke in the series of the same name and Detective Steve McGarrett in *Hawaii Five-O*.

Kitty Lost. December 21, 1957. Production #404.

 Rachmil, an Eastern dude who has his sights on Miss Kitty, convinces her to accompany him on a romantic moonlight buggy ride. When Rachmil's advances are rebuffed, Kitty finds herself in dire peril after he deserts her, leaving her alone on the desolate Kansas plain. When the two are missing the next day, Matt and Chester set out to find them.

   Rachmil .... Warren Stevens
   Dobie .... Gage Clark
   Pete .... Brett King
   Pence .... Steve Ellsworth
   Moss Grimmick .... George Selk
   Story, Script .... John Meston
   Director .... Ted Post
   Producer .... Norman Macdonnell

 Warren Stevens was a regular on such programs as *Tales of the 77th Bengal Lancers*, *The Richard Boone Show*, and *Behind the Screen*.

Twelfth Night. December 28, 1957. Production #403.

 Hillbilly farmer Eben Hakes arrives in Dodge to "do in" Joth Monger. Hakes and Monger are the only two surviving members of rival families from the Ozarks. Ironically, Hakes no longer recalls the reason for their bitter feud. Monger accepts Hakes' challenge despite Matt's protestations. Since the code of the Ozark's prohibits killing on Sundays, Monger and Hakes put down their guns and lift their jugs when the Sabbath commences. The 40-year rivalry between the two families culminates in a strange discovery.

   Eben Hakes .... William Schallert
   Mrs. Monger .... Rose Marie
   Joth Monger .... James Griffith
   Farmer .... Dick Rich
   Story, Script .... John Meston
   Director .... John Rich
   Producer .... Norman Macdonnell

 William Schallert played Martin Lane, Patty Duke's ever-patient father, on *The Patty Duke Show*. Rose Marie is best known for her comic portrayal of the man-hungry, wisecracking Sally Rogers of *The Dick Van Dyke Show*.

The Television Programs

Joe Phy. January 4, 1958. Production #402.

Carey Post arrives in Dodge and ambushes Matt. Matt is wounded, and Post gets away. When Matt recovers, he and Chester head for Elkader to arrest Post. They discover that the town is run by a tough "marshal" Joe Phy, who has everyone towing the line. Matt is convinced that Post will not return to Elkader as long as Phy is in charge, and devises a scheme to rid the town of the phoney marshal.

Cicero Grimes	Morey Amsterdam
Joe Phy	Paul Richards
Carey Post	William Kendis
Bartender	Jack Reitzen
Cowboy	Ken Becker
Story, Script	John Meston
Director	Ted Post
Producer	Norman Macdonnell

Morey Amsterdam was popular with early radio and television audiences because of his one-line gags and his rapid-fire jokes. He is probably best remembered for his role as comedy writer Buddy Sorrell from *The Dick Van Dyke Show*.

Buffalo Man. January 11, 1958. Production #594.

Matt and Chester are held captive by crazed buffalo hunter Ben Siple and his partner, Earl Ticks. The two criminals have in their company, Abby, a young woman that they have been terrorizing. The vicious Siple plans to kill Matt and Chester, but his plans are frustrated when he and Ticks are forced to desert their camp to avoid an Indian attack. They leave Matt and Chester tied up for the Indians, and leave Abby unconscious after a savage beating.

Abby	Patricia Smith
Ben Siple	John Anderson
Earl Ticks	Jack Klugman
Indian	Abel Fernandez
Story	John Meston
Script	Les Crutchfield
Director	Ted Post
Producer	Norman Macdonnell

Jack Klugman played sports writer, Oscar Madison, on *The Odd Couple* for which he won two Emmy Awards. Previously, Klugman won an Emmy for *The Defenders*. He was also seen as the irascible Dr. Quincy. John Anderson appeared in hundreds of television programs and feature films, many of which were Westerns. For his great achievement in this field, he was honored by the National Cowboy Hall of Fame and was presented a Western Heritage Award in 1967. Some of his most recent credits include the film *Tucker, The Man and His Dream* and the television mini-series *North and South*. The long fight sequence between John Anderson and Jim Arness was used by the U.S.C. Film School as well as many other film schools around the country to train student film editors. Patricia Smith was a regular on *The Debbie Reynolds Show* and *The Bob Newhart Show*.

Kitty Caught. January 18, 1958. Production #595. Rerun July 22, 1961.

Kitty is taken hostage during a bank hold-up by the ruthless Gunter brothers, who have no qualms about killing her if they are followed. Matt and Chester carefully trail the fugitives to an abandoned cabin, where they are forced to wait until daybreak to make their move.

GUNSMOKE — III. THE PROGRAMS

Jed Gunter	Bruce Gordon
Billy Gunter	Pat Conway
Blain	John Compton
Mr. Botkin	William Keene
Cashier	Charles Tannen
Story, Script	John Meston
Director	Richard Whorf
Producer	Norman Macdonnell

Bruce Gordon was a regular on several television series including *The Untouchables*, *Peyton Place*, and *Run, Buddy, Run*. John Compton appeared on the police series *The D.A.'s Man*.

Claustrophobia. January 25, 1958. Production #596. Rerun August 5, 1961.

Pig farmer Olie Ridgers is being driven off his land by cattlemen Dever and Giles. The two men have already killed farmer Bob Riley for his land, and now plan on removing Olie. While Olie and his best friend Jim Branch are enjoying a well-earned holiday in Dodge, Olie receives word that someone has shot his mule and all his pigs. Olie is not one to stand for this and reacts violently against the culprits. Matt is forced to arrest Olie. Branch, knowing what jail would mean to his claustrophobic friend, takes drastic steps to prevent his incarceration.

Jim Branch	Joe Maross
Olie Ridgers	Vaughn Taylor
Dever	Willard Sage
Giles	James Winslow
Hank	Lynn Shubert
Judge	Jason Johnson
Story, Script	John Meston
Director	Ted Post
Producer	Norman Macdonnell

Joe Maross was a regular on *Peyton Place* and *Code Red*. Vaughn Taylor was very active during the golden age of live television drama in the 40s and 50s. He appeared as a regular on *Robert Montgomery Presents* and on the children's series, *Johnny Jupiter*. His film credits include *Psycho*, *In Cold Blood*, and *Cat on a Hot Tin Roof*.

Ma Tennis. February 1, 1958. Production #598.

Matt encounters problems when he tries to arrest Andy Tennis for the cold-blooded murder of a gambler. Ma Tennis, an aging but iron-willed widow, defends her wayward son and tries to prevent Matt from bringing him to justice.

Ma Tennis	Nina Varela
Andy Tennis	Ron Hagerthy
Ben Tennis	Corey Allen
Story, Script	John Meston
Director	Buzz Kulik
Producer	Norman Macdonnell

Sunday Supplement. February 8, 1958. Production #599. Rerun August 19, 1961.

Two Eastern journalists arrive in Dodge to get stories of the lawless West. Impatient when the stories do not materialize fast enough, they create some of their own. Their meddling triggers problems with the Pawnee Indians when they steal a sacred totem.

Clifton Bunker	Werner Klemperer

The Television Programs

Samuel Spring	Jack Weston
Jack	David Whorf
Major	Theodore Newton
Moss Grimmick	George Selk
Chief Little Hawk	Eddie Little
Karl	K.L. Smith
Story, Script	John Meston
Director	Richard Whorf
Producer	Norman Macdonnell

Werner Klemperer was Col. Wilhelm Klink in the comedy series *Hogan's Heroes* for which he won two Emmy Awards for Best Supporting Actor in a Comedy. Jack Weston has an impressive film career that includes *Wait Until Dark*, *The Ritz*, and *The Four Seasons*.

Wild West. February 15, 1958. Production #597. Rerun July 29, 1961.

Yorky Kelly tells Matt that his elderly father was abducted by two men in the middle of the night, and that his pretty stepmother, Hattie, is at the bottom of the plot. Matt decides to investigate Yorky's strange story.

Mr. Kelly	Philip Bourneuf
Hattie Kelly	Phyllis Coates
Yorky Kelly	Paul Engle
Cutter	Murray Hamilton
Rourke	Robert Gist
Story, Script	John Meston
Director	Richard Whorf
Producer	Norman Macdonnell

Phyllis Coates played Lois Lane on *The Adventures of Superman*.

The Cabin. February 22, 1958. Production #417.

While returning from Hayes City, Matt is caught in a blinding snowstorm. He takes refuge in a cabin occupied by two desperate outlaws and their even more desperate young victim, Belle. The outlaws have killed Belle's father, and have been abusing her for over a month. When Matt enters the picture they decide to kill him to keep their whereabouts secret.

Belle	Patricia Barry
Hack	Claude Akins
Alvy	Dean Stanton
Story, Script	John Meston
Director	John Rich
Producer	Norman Macdonnell

Dean Stanton, also known as Harry Dean Stanton, appeared in numerous feature films including *Cool Hand Luke*, *Alien*, and *Paris Texas*.

Dirt. March 1, 1958. Production #400.

Nat, a wealthy rancher, celebrates his last night as a single man. While in the throes of the festivities at the Long Branch, his ex-lover Beulah enters. She is a girl from the wrong side of the tracks, very much in love with Nat, and unaware of his plans to marry a lady of refinement from the old South. When Beulah is finally told, she is surprised, but exits gracefully. However, Nat's future brother-in-law disapproves of Nat's free-living life style, and when Nat is shot leaving his wedding, there are several suspects for Matt to contend with.

GUNSMOKE — III. THE PROGRAMS

Beulah	June Lockhart
Nat	Wayne Morris
Mr. Troyman	Ian MacDonald
Polly Troyman	Gail Kobe
Henry Troyman	Barry McGuire
Additional Cast	Tyler McVey
Story	John Meston
Script	Sam Peckinpah
Director	Ted Post
Producer	Norman Macdonnell

June Lockhart appeared on television as Ruth Martin in *Lassie*, Maureen Robinson in *Lost in Space*, and Dr. Janet Craig in *Petticoat Junction*. Gail Kobe became the star of such soap operas as *Peyton Place* and *Bright Promise*. She then later graduated to the role of producer of daytime serials including *Peyton Place* and *Guiding Light*.

Dooley Surrenders. March 8, 1958. Production #401.

Buffalo skinner Emmett Dooley wakes up after a drunken binge only to be told he shot a man. Not remembering what happened, Dooley rides into Dodge and turns himself over to Matt. After investigating the story and examining the dead man, Matt realizes that Dooley is not the murderer. The victim was stabbed, not shot. Matt suspects that Dooley's boss is the real killer, so he turns Dooley loose hoping to lure the real culprit into Dodge.

Emmett Dooley	Strother Martin
Colpitt	Ken Lynch
Faber	James Maloney
Mr. Ross	Ben Wright
Moss Grimmick	George Selk
Nelson	James Nusser
Story, Script	John Meston
Director	John Rich
Producer	Norman Macdonnell

Ben Wright was a frequent performer on radio's *Gunsmoke*.

Joke's on Us. March 15, 1958. Production #406. Rerun August 12, 1961.

Jake Kaiser, Jim Duval, and Tom Benson find Frank Tilman with some of their horses and accuse him of theft. Frank claims he was only rounding them up and that Bill Jennings was a witness. When Bill returns he corroborates the story, but he is too late to save Frank from the noose. The ranchers consider the lynching an honest mistake, but Mrs. Tilman and her son plan their revenge.

Mrs. Tilman	Virginia Gregg
Jake Kaiser	Bartlett Robinson
Frank Tilman	Michael Hinn
Clabe Tilman	James Kevin
Bill Jennings	Kevin Hagen
Tom Benson	Herbert C. Lytton
Jim Duval	Craig Duncan
Story, Script	John Meston
Director	Ted Post
Producer	Norman Macdonnell

Virginia Gregg was one of Hollywood's great radio voices and a frequent guest

The Television Programs

performer on radio's *Gunsmoke*. Her numerous film credits include *Body and Soul, Love Is a Many Splendored Thing, I'll Cry Tomorrow,* and *Little Women.* Kevin Hagen was a regular on *Yancy Derringer, Land of the Giants,* and *Little House on the Prairie.*

Bottleman. March 22, 1958. Production #413.

Matt and the citizens of Dodge are astonished when town drunk Tom Cassidy, who is normally harmless, tries to attack Dan Clell, a stranger in town. This act starts a chain of events that culminates in murder, and Matt, Chester, and Kitty attempt to unravel a mystery from Cassidy's whiskey-fogged past.

Tom Cassidy	John Dehner
Dan Clell	Ross Martin
Fiora Clell	Peggy McKay
Story, Script	John Meston
Director	John Rich
Producer	Norman Macdonnell

Ross Martin played Andamo in the television series *Mr. Lucky* and Artemus Gordon in the popular Western series *The Wild Wild West.* His most acclaimed film role was that of the asthmatic psychopath in *Experiment in Terror.* Peggy McKay appeared as a regular on *The Lazarus Syndrome.*

Laughing Gas. March 29, 1958. Production #414. Rerun August 26, 1961.

Matt, Chester, and Doc attempt to help Stafford, a reformed gunman who runs a laughing-gas medicine show. Stafford has promised his wife that he would stay out of gunfights, but finds the vow difficult to keep after he is mauled by the Marsh brothers. Further complications arise when Mrs. Stafford refuses to press charges against the assailants.

Mrs. Stafford	June Dayton
Stafford	Dean Harens
Cloud Marsh	Val Benedict
Old Man	Cyril Delevanti
Mr. Teeters	Jess Kirkpatrick
Story, Script	James Fonda
Director	Ted Post
Producer	Norman Macdonnell

Although his name did not appear in the closing credits, James Nusser had a cameo role as a barfly who helps Matt with some investigative snooping.

Texas Cowboys. April 5, 1958. Production #407.

Matt tangles with 18 Texan cowboys after one of them shoots a man in the back. To force the cowboys to give up the murderer, Matt threatens to close Dodge's pleasure palaces, arousing the greed and ire of the town's businessmen. Finally the cowboys turn over their cook, whom they have battered into confessing.

Kin Talley	Allan Lane
Gil Choate	Clark Gordon
Sam Peeples	Ned Glass
Mr. Hightower	Stafford Repp
Bob	John Mitchum
Story, Script	John Meston
Director	John Rich
Producer	Norman Macdonnell

GUNSMOKE — III. THE PROGRAMS

Allan "Rocky" Lane was a big Western star of the 1940s, appearing in over 100 films and serials. On television Rocky was the voice of *Mister Ed* the talking horse.

Amy's Good Deed. April 12, 1958. Production #411.

Matt has an unusual and dangerous problem when Amy Slater arrives in Dodge determined to shoot him for having killed her brother. Matt knows that if he shoots or arrests Amy his authority as marshal will be damaged. In addition, the "deadman's" former partner, Gold, has also arrived presumably to kill Matt.

    Amy Slater . . . . Jeanette Nolan
    Gold . . . . Lou Krugman
    Story . . . . John Meston
    Script . . . . Kathleen Hite
    Director . . . . John Rich
    Producer . . . . Norman Macdonnell

Lou Krugman was a frequent performer on radio's *Gunsmoke*.

Hanging Man. April 19, 1958. Production #415.

Cattlebuyer Harp Sawyer is found hanged in his office, an apparent suicide. Further investigation reveals that Sawyer was robbed and murdered. Matt arrests drifter Mel Tucker for the crime when he spies Tucker spending large amounts of money. Matt's conviction that he has found the killer is shaken when Joe Dabney is murdered in a similar way and he is forced to release Tucker. In order to solve the murders, Matt tries a ruse that might put Kitty in an uncomfortable position if it fails.

    Mel Tucker . . . . Luis Van Rooten
    Dan Dresslar . . . . Robert Osterloh
    Cora Bell . . . . Zina Provendie
    Mrs. Sawyer . . . . Helen Kleeb
    Hank . . . . Dick Rich
    Jim . . . . K.L. Smith
    Story, Script . . . . John Meston
    Director . . . . John Rich
    Producer . . . . Norman Macdonnell

Innocent Broad. April 26, 1958. Production #405.

Matt oversteps his authority as marshal when he tries to save 17-year-old Linda Bell from disaster. He first senses trouble when he rides a stagecoach into Dodge with Linda and an annoying stranger named Joe Bassett. When the three finally arrive at their destination, it becomes apparent that Bassett is in cahoots with Lou Paxton, Linda's fiance.

    Lou Paxton . . . . Ed Kemmer
    Linda Bell . . . . Myrna Fahey
    Joe Bassett . . . . Aaron Saxon
    Story . . . . John Meston
    Script . . . . Kathleen Hite
    Director . . . . John Rich
    Producer . . . . Norman Macdonnell

Myrna Fahey played Kay on the television series, *Father of the Bride*.

The Big Con. May 3, 1958. Production #409.

After duping an assistant bank manager into "lending" them $20,000, three

The Television Programs

confidence men, Hook, Varden, and Shane, are safe from the law. There is no proof they got the money by trickery, until Matt bluffs them into running. As they attempt to flee Dodge, they take Doc hostage, threatening to kill him if Matt follows.

    Banker Papp . . . . Joe Kearns
    Hook . . . . Alan Dexter
    Varden . . . . Gordon Mills
    Shane . . . . Raymond Bailey
    Story, Script . . . . John Meston
    Director . . . . John Rich
    Producer . . . . Norman Macdonnell

Joe Kearns was a frequent performer on radio's *Gunsmoke*. On television he was a regular on *Our Miss Brooks* and *Dennis the Menace*.

Widow's Mite. May 10, 1958. Production #408.

Matt is suspicious of gambler Leach Fields after Fields shoots bank robber Zack Morton. His suspicions are confirmed when he finds Fields harrassing Ada, Morton's destitute widow, hoping she will reveal the location of some missing bank money. After rescuing Ada, Matt is forced into a gunfight with the despicable Fields.

    Ada Morton . . . . Katharine Bard
    Leach Fields . . . . Marshall Thompson
    Zack Morton . . . . Ken Mayer
    Story, Script . . . . John Meston
    Director . . . . Ted Post
    Producer . . . . Norman Macdonnell

Marshall Thompson played Dr. Marsh Tracy the veterinarian on *Daktari*.

Chester's Hanging. May 17, 1958. Production #412.

Matt imprisons a murderer and then has to face the killer's accomplices. The men threaten to hang Chester unless Matt agrees to cooperate with them. Matt has to think and shoot his way out of the stalemate.

    Jim Cando . . . . Charles Cooper
    Lee Binders . . . . Sam Edwards
    Jack Haney . . . . Walter Barnes
    Story, Script . . . . John Meston
    Director . . . . Ted Post
    Producer . . . . Norman Macdonnell

Sam Edwards was a frequent performer on radio's *Gunsmoke*. Charles Cooper played the sheriff on *Father Murphy*. Walter Barnes appeared as Carl Pusser in the television series, *Walking Tall*.

Carmen. May 24, 1958. Production #410.

The murder of three cavalry men and the theft of an army payroll puts Matt on the spot. The Fort Dodge commandant threatens to put Dodge under marshal law, unless Matt apprehends the culprit within 48 hours. Knowing that the presence of the military could disrupt the peace in Dodge, Matt takes a gamble and knowingly rides into an ambush to meet the murderer.

    Jennie Lane . . . . Ruta Lee
    Nate Brand . . . . Robert Patten
    Pfc. Atwood . . . . Tommy Farrell
    Sgt. Jones . . . . Ray Teal

GUNSMOKE — III. THE PROGRAMS

Major Harris .... Alan Gifford
Story, Script .... John Meston
Director .... Ted Post
Producer .... Norman Macdonnell

Ray Teal was sheriff Roy Coffee on the television Western, *Bonanza*. His film credits include *The Men*, *Carrie*, and *Inherit the Wind*.

Overland Express. May 31, 1958. Production #587.

During a scuffle with suspected murderer Jim Nation, Matt's and Chester's horses are killed. The lawmen are forced to escort their prisoner via the stage. On route the stage is held up by highwayman Art Carp. Nation, enlisted by Carp as an ally, faces a dilemma: to secure his escape, or to help Matt, Chester, and a stagecoach full of passengers out of a tight spot.

Jim Nation .... Simon Oakland
Art Carp .... Peter Mamakos
Fly .... Clem Bevens
Wells .... James Gavin
Griffin .... Forrest Stanley
Station Man .... Jan Arvan
Hank .... Jimmy Cross
Bill .... Alfred Hopson
Story, Script .... John Meston
Director .... Seymour Berns
Producer .... Norman Macdonnell

Versatile character actor Simon Oakland appeared in such films as *Psycho*, *West Side Story* and *Bullitt*. His television credits include Inspector Spooner on *Toma* and Tony Vincenzo on *Kolchak: The Night Stalker*.

The Gentleman. June 7, 1958. Production #416.

Gambler Marcus France falls in love with Boni Damon, despite Tiller Evans' threat to kill anyone who associates with her. Matt tries to avert trouble by sending Boni and Marcus out of town. However, Marcus refuses to leave and insists on meeting Tiller head-on.

Marcus France .... Jack Cassidy
Boni Damon .... Virginia Baker
Tiller Evans .... Timothy Carey
Butler .... Henry Corden
Story, Script .... John Meston
Director .... Ted Post
Producer .... Norman Macdonnell

Jack Cassidy was an established star of the musical stage, winning a Tony Award in 1963 for *She Loves Me*. He was an accomplished actor, singer and dancer, and in addition to his stage credits, appeared in films and on television.

Tap Day for Kitty. June 14, 1958, rerun. First aired March 24, 1956.

How to Die for Nothing. June 21, 1958, rerun. First aired June 24, 1956.

The Preacher. June 28, 1958, rerun. First aired June 16, 1956.

Indian Scout. July 5, 1958, rerun. First aired March 31, 1956.

The Television Programs

Big Broad. July 12, 1958, rerun. First aired April 28, 1956.

General Parcley Smith. July 19, 1958, rerun. First aired December 10, 1955.

Cow Doctor. July 26, 1958, rerun. First aired September 8, 1956.

Unmarked Grave. August 2, 1958, rerun. First aired August 18, 1956.

The Round-Up. August 9, 1958, rerun. First aired September 29, 1956.

Greater Love. August 23, 1958, rerun. First aired December 1, 1956.

Legal Revenge. August 30, 1958, rerun. First aired November 17, 1956.

September 6, 1958, preempted.

FOURTH SEASON

Matt for Murder. September 13, 1958. Production #418.
 Matt is framed on a murder charge by Red Samples, a crooked gambler who hopes to open a game in Dodge. Wild Bill Hickock, Matt's old friend, is sent to arrest him and relieve him of his badge. However, Hickock's trust in Matt gives him enough time out of jail to investigate the iron-clad case developed by Samples.

  Wild Bill Hickock . . . . Robert Wilke
  Red Samples . . . . Bruce Gordon
  Henchman . . . . Elisha Cook
  Story, Script . . . . John Meston
  Director . . . . Richard Whorf
  Producer . . . . Norman Macdonnell

 Wild Bill Hickock, an actual figure from history, is depicted on the program. Although historic persons are often referred to in the series, it is unusual for one to be portrayed. Elisha Cook is a character actor par excellence. Although tiny in stature, Cook made a success of playing heavies and bizarre characters in a wide range of films including *The Maltese Falcon, Shane,* and *Rosemary's Baby*. On television, Cook played Francis "Ice Pick" Hofstetler on *Magnum, P.I.* Robert Wilke played Marshal Sam Corbett in the television Western, *The Legend of Jesse James*.

The Patsy. September 20, 1958. Production #419.
 Holly Fanshaw, a dance-hall hostess at the Long Branch, claims she saw Fly Hoyt shoot hide-merchant Dave Thorp. Dave's brother incites a mob to lynch Hoyt and only a perilous bluff and some quick thinking by Matt, prevent the mob from carrying out their plan.

  Holly Fanshaw . . . . Jan Harrison
  Fly Hoyt . . . . Peter Breck
  Thorp . . . . Martin Landau
  Dave Thorp . . . . John Alderman
  Additional Cast . . . . Ken Lynch
  Story . . . . John Meston
  Script . . . . Les Crutchfield

GUNSMOKE — III. THE PROGRAMS

Director . . . . Richard Whorf
Producer . . . . Norman Macdonnell

Peter Breck played Nick Barkley, Barbara Stanwyck's son and Linda Evans' and Lee Majors' brother in *The Big Valley*. Martin Landau starred with his wife Barbara Bain, in the hit television series *Mission: Impossible*. He was also Commander John Koenig in the ill-fated *Space 1999* in which his wife also starred. Landau was nominated for an Academy Award for his performance in *Tucker*.

Gunsmuggler. September 27, 1958. Production #423.

A homestead family is massacred by Indians who have been sold weapons by white men. Problems continue when Matt locks horns with an Army major who feels the military, and not a U.S. marshal, should find the gun-smugglers.

Tobeel . . . . Frank De Kova
Major Evans . . . . Paul Langton
Story . . . . John Meston
Script . . . . Les Crutchfield
Director . . . . Richard Whorf
Producer . . . . Norman Macdonnell

Paul Langton played Leslie Harrington on *Peyton Place* from 1964–1968.

Monopoly. October 4, 1958. Production #426. Rerun aired July 8, 1961.

Bob Adams is thrown into jail for drunkenness after he and other celebrating freighters sell out to Ivy, a shady operator from St. Louis. Ivy plans to eliminate all competition in the freight business and establish a monopoly by paying the freighters more than they are worth. Ivy's plans turn deadly when two people resist his very generous offer, and he hires a gunman to intervene on his behalf.

Joe Trimble . . . . J. Pat O'Malley
Ivy . . . . Harry Townes
Speegle . . . . Robert Gist
Story . . . . John Meston
Script . . . . Les Crutchfield
Director . . . . Seymour Berns
Producer . . . . Norman Macdonnell

J. Pat O'Malley started his career as the romantic lead of many silent films. He went on to play character roles in numerous features, including the 1956 sci-fi classic *Invasion of the Body Snatchers*. The cherubic Irishman's television credits include Bert Beasley on *Maude*, and Harry Burns on *My Favorite Martian*.

Letter of the Law. October 11, 1958. Production #422.

Matt is ordered to adhere strictly to the "letter of the law" when he is told to evict ex-gunman Brandon Teek, and his wife Sarah, from their home. Brandon refuses to leave, however, and Matt decides to investigate the legal ramifications with District Judge Rambeau.

Sarah Teek . . . . Mary Carver
Judge Rambeau . . . . Harold J. Stone
Brandon Teek . . . . Clifton James
Additional Cast . . . . Bartlett Robinson
Story . . . . John Meston
Script . . . . Les Crutchfield
Director . . . . Richard Whorf
Producer . . . . Norman Macdonnell

The Television Programs

Thoroughbreds. October 18, 1958. Production #420.

Portis, a well-groomed stranger, arrives in Dodge with a pair of thoroughbred horses. He promptly becomes one of the town's most popular residents with his generosity and free spending. Matt goes out on a limb when he suspects that Portis is a thief.

Portis	Ron Randell
Burke	Walter Barnes
Keller	Dan Blocker
Story, Script	John Meston
Director	Richard Whorf
Producer	Norman Macdonnell

Stage Hold-Up. October 25, 1958. Production #421.

Matt makes it a personal, as well as a professional project, to capture the three bandits who killed a passenger and held up the stagecoach in which he and Chester were riding.

Yermo	John Anderson
Verd	Charles Aidman
Green	Sandy Kenyon
Jim Buck	Robert Brubaker
Charley	Bob Morgan
Story	John Meston
Script	Les Crutchfield
Director	Ted Post
Producer	Norman Macdonnell

Sandy Kenyon was seen as Reverend Kathrun on *Knots Landing*. In addition to his acting talents, Charles Aidman is an accomplished director and composer. He has appeared extensively on television and was the narrator in the return of *Twilight Zone* in 1985. Aidman also appeared in one of the original *Twilight Zone* episodes, *And When the Sky Was Opened*, in 1959.

Lost Rifle. November 1, 1958. Production #430.

Ben Tiple gets into an argument with a cowboy and when the cowboy is later found shot in the back, suspicion falls on Tiple. There are no witnesses to the crime except young Andy Spangler who claims he only heard the shot. Although Tiple insists that he did not do it, everyone in town wants to see him brought to justice.

Ben Tiple	Charles Bronson
Andy Spangler	Paul Engle
Joe Spangler	Lew Gallo
Will Gibbs	Tom Greenway
Story, Script	John Meston
Director	Richard Whorf
Producer	Norman Macdonnell

Lew Gallo played Major Joe Cobb on the dramatic series, *Twelve O'Clock High*.

Land Deal. November 8, 1958. Production #428.

A confidence man promises to provide immigrant homesteaders with railroad land, at a cost. When Matt hears the details of the transaction, he suspects a swindle. To add to his concerns, Sidna, the wife of immigrant Jim Calhoun, is discontent with her marriage. She is more flirtatious than her husband will tolerate, which may soon erupt in violence.

GUNSMOKE — III. THE PROGRAMS

Sidna ....Nita Talbot
Calhoun ....Murray Hamilton
Keppert ....Ross Martin
Trumbill..Dennis Patrick
Story ....John Meston
Script ....Les Crutchfield
Director ....Ted Post
Producer.....................................Norman Macdonnell

Nita Talbot was seen on television frequently. She was nominated for an Emmy for her appearances on *Hogan's Heroes* and was a regular on several shows including *The Thin Man* starring Peter Lawford and Phyllis Kirk.

Lynching Man. November 15, 1958. Production #438.

Charlie Drain witnessed his father's lynching when he was a child. Forever scarred by the incident, the lynching of a suspected horse thief sends Drain on a mission to catch the killers. Drain's blind hatred of lynchers forces him into doing the very thing he abhors.

Charlie Drain ....George MacReady
Ed Shelby ....Bing Russell
Bob Gringle ....Charles Gray
Hank Blenis ..................................O.Z. Whitehead
Jake ....Chuck Hayward
Story, Script ....John Meston
Director ....Richard Whorf
Producer.....................................Norman Macdonnell

George MacReady was one of Hollywood's most colorful villains. He portrayed Rita Hayworth's ruthless husband in *Gilda*, as well as numerous other screen evildoers. On television MacReady appeared as Martin Peyton of *Peyton Place*.

How to Kill a Friend. November 22, 1958. Production #429.

Two crooked gamblers, Ben Corder and Harry Duggan, attempt to bribe Matt. Having failed, one of them takes a potshot at the lawman but misses. Although Matt did not see his assailant, he orders the two gamblers out of town. Some time later they return to Dodge accompanied by Toque Morlan, a hired killer who was once Matt's good friend.

Ben Corder ....Philip Abbott
Toque Morlan ....Pat Conway
Harry Duggan ....James Westerfield
Story, Script ....John Meston
Director ....Richard Whorf
Producer.....................................Norman Macdonnell

Philip Abbott played Arthur Ward on television's *The F.B.I.*

Grass. November 29, 1958. Production #434.

Farmer Harry Pope is convinced that he is being harrassed by Indians. Matt thinks otherwise, and suggests that Pope arm and protect himself. Pope takes Matt's advice and when the "Indians" return hooting, hollering, and shooting, Pope returns their fire and kills trailhand Joe Carter. A so-called witness to the shooting, Earl Brant, claims that Pope killed Carter in cold blood.

Harry Pope ....Phil Coolidge

The Television Programs

Ned Curry	Chris Alcaide
Earl Brant	Charles Fredericks
Story, Script	John Meston
Director	Richard Whorf
Producer	Norman Macdonnell

Phil Coolidge played Cooper on the television comedy, *The Farmer's Daughter*. His films include *I Want to Live!* and *The Tingler*.

The Cast. December 6, 1958. Production #433.

Doc faces the wrath of Shell Tucker, a man who hates doctors, after he tries, without success, to operate on Mrs. Tucker to remove a nail she had swallowed. When despite Doc's efforts, Mrs. Tucker dies, Shell vows vengeance.

Shell Tucker	Robert F. Simon
Additional Cast	Ben Carruthers
Story, Script	John Meston
Director	Jesse Hibbs
Producer	Norman Macdonnell

Robber Bridegroom. December 13, 1958. Production #439.

Matt's case against kidnapper Jack Fitch is dealt a blow when Laura Church, the abducted young lady, refuses to testify against her captor. When Laura tells Matt that she is in love with Fitch, the marshal is forced to confront Reeves, Laura's jilted fiancee, who organizes a lynching party to hang his rival.

Jack Fitch	Burt Douglas
Laura Church	Jan Harrison
Reeves	Donald Randolph
Stage Driver	Frank Maxwell
Hank	Dan Sheridan
Joe	Clem Fuller
Pete	Tex Terry
Story, Script	John Meston
Director	Richard Whorf
Producer	Norman Macdonnell

Snakebite. December 20, 1958. Production #437.

Poney Thompson is an old prairie man who is suspected of killing the man who shot his dog. He flees when Matt attempts to apprehend him, and the lonely old man meets his doom before Matt can learn the identity of the real killer.

Poney Thompson	Andy Clyde
Jed Hakes	Warren Oates
Walt Moorman	Charles Maxwell
Story, Script	John Meston
Director	Ted Post
Producer	Norman Macdonnell

Warren Oates played villains in numerous television and movie Westerns. A superb character actor, Oates gained star status with his brilliant performance in *In the Heat of the Night*. His films include *The Wild Bunch, Dillinger,* and *Stripes*. Charles Maxwell was an occasional regular on the television series, *I Led Three Lives*.

Gypsum Hills Feud. December 27, 1958. Production #424.

While tracking antelope in the hill country, a sniper shoots at Matt. Chester and

Matt return the fire and are caught in the middle of a blood feud between the Peavy and Cade families.

　　　　Lize Peavy . . . . Anne Barton
　　　　Alben Peavy . . . . William Schallert
　　　　Jack Cade . . . . Albert Linville
　　　　Ellen Cade . . . . Hope Summers
　　　　Ben Cade . . . . Sam Edwards
　　　　Story . . . . John Meston
　　　　Script . . . . Les Crutchfield
　　　　Director . . . . Richard Whorf
　　　　Producer . . . . Norman Macdonnell

Actress Hope Summers was seen on television as Hattie Denton on *The Rifleman* and Clara Edwards on *The Andy Griffith Show*.

Young Love. January 3, 1959. Production #425.

Elderly rancher Jesse Wheat is murdered by one of his hired hands. It looks bad for "young love" when Matt finds that Anna Wheat, Jesse's pretty widow, is in love with one of two men Matt suspects of the murder.

　　　　Anna Wheat . . . . Joan Taylor
　　　　Jesse Wheat . . . . Jon Lormer
　　　　Rod Allison . . . . Wesley Lau
　　　　Jim Box . . . . Charles Cooper
　　　　Enoch Miller . . . . Stephen Chase
　　　　Story, Script . . . . John Meston
　　　　Director . . . . Seymour Berns
　　　　Producer . . . . Norman Macdonnell

Wesley Lau was Lt. Anderson on *Perry Mason*. Charles Cooper played the sheriff on *Father Murphy*. Joan Taylor appeared on *The Rifleman*.

Marshal Proudfoot. January 10, 1959. Production #445. Rerun September 16, 1961.

Chester's uncle Wesley arrives in Dodge for a visit. Unfortunately, Wesley is under the assumption that Chester is the marshal of Dodge, and that Matt is his able-bodied assistant. Chester is terribly embarrassed by the misunderstanding, and tries to keep a low profile. In the meantime, Matt is sick in bed. Trouble arises when Doc and Kitty decide to stage a fake hold-up to make "Marshal" Chester look like a hero.

　　　　Uncle Wesley . . . . Dabbs Greer
　　　　Jack Pargo . . . . Charles Fredericks
　　　　Ben . . . . Earl Parker
　　　　Jim Buck . . . . Robert Brubaker
　　　　Story . . . . Tom Hanley
　　　　Script . . . . John Meston
　　　　Director . . . . Jesse Hibbs
　　　　Producer . . . . Norman Macdonnell

Dabbs Greer is familiar as Mr. Jonas the proprietor of Dodge City's General Store. His other television credits include regular appearances on *Hank*, a sit-com, and on *Little House on the Prairie*, where for nine years he played Rev. Alden.

Passive Resistance. January 17, 1959. Production #427.

Matt sets out to find two cattlemen, Kell and Boyles, who have injured Gideon Seek and slaughtered his sheep. His problem is intensified when Seek, a firm believer in non-violence, refuses to identify the men.

The Television Programs

Gideon Seek	Carl Benton Reid
Hank Boyles	Alfred Ryder
Joe Kell	Read Morgan
Story, Script	John Meston
Director	Ted Post
Producer	Norman Macdonnell

Carl Benton Reid was memorable as Oscar Hubbard in both the film and Broadway productions of Lillian Hellman's *The Little Foxes*. On television he was a regular on *Burke's Law*. Read Morgan played Sgt. Tasker on the television Western, *The Deputy*.

Love of a Good Woman. January 24, 1959. Production #447.

Embittered convict Coney Thorn breaks his parole and returns to Dodge to kill Matt, who he holds responsible for his imprisonment. Before Thorn can complete his mission, however, he is stricken with brain fever. Doc puts him under the care of Abby, a pretty widow, who nurses Thorn back to health, body and soul.

Coney Thorn	Kevin Hagen
Abby	Jacqueline Scott
Story	John Meston
Script	Les Crutchfield
Director	Arthur Hiller
Producer	Norman Macdonnell

Jacqueline Scott played David Janssen's sister on *The Fugitive*. In addition to directing *Gunsmoke,* Arthur Hiller directed other prestigious television shows including *Playhouse 90* and *Alfred Hitchcock Presents*. He moved on to the big screen to direct such features as *Love Story, The Americanization of Emily,* and *The In-Laws*.

Jayhawkers. January 31, 1959. Production #441. Rerun September 23, 1961.

Dolph Quince, an old friend of Matt's is moving a herd of cattle from Texas to Kansas and has been having trouble. Jayhawkers have been stampeding his cattle and his men are understandably jittery. Matt is called upon to help them elude the vicious band of jayhawkers.

Phil Jacks	Ken Curtis
Dolph Quince	Jack Elam
Jay	Lane Bradford
Studer	Chuck Hayward
Snyder	Earl Parker
Cowboy	Cliff Ketchum
Cook	Brad Payne
Story, Script	John Meston
Director	Andrew McLaglen
Producer	Norman Macdonnell

Ken Curtis, who later appears in the series as Festus Haggen, plays the part of a cattle drover who falls victim to the jayhawkers.

Kitty's Rebellion. February 7, 1959. Production #446. Rerun September 2, 1961.

Billy Chrit, brother of a childhood friend of Kitty's, arrives in town, and is shocked to find that Miss Kitty is half-owner of a saloon. Billy feels that a saloon is no place for a proper lady. A real Southern gentleman, Billy is intent on defending Kitty's honor from every trail bum and drunken cowpuncher that approaches her. Kitty is afraid the young man is going to succeed in getting himself killed.

GUNSMOKE — III. THE PROGRAMS

Billy Chrit	Barry McGuire
Tal	Addison Powell
Jim Buck	Robert Brubaker
Additional Cast	Richard Rust
Story	Marian Clark
Script	John Meston
Director	Jesse Hibbs
Producer	Norman Macdonnell

Richard Rust played Hank Tabor on the television series *Sam Benedict*.

Sky. February 14, 1959. Production #443.

Billy Daunt is accused of killing his girlfriend Frog-Mouth Kate for her life savings. The panic-stricken young man flees Dodge in terror with Matt and Chester in hot pursuit.

Billy Daunt	Allen Case
Clabe	Charles Thompson
Frog-Mouth Kate	Linda Watkins
Additional Cast	Olive Blakeney, Patricia Huston
Story	John Meston
Script	Les Crutchfield
Director	Ted Post
Producer	Norman Macdonnell

Linda Watkins starred in several Hollywood films in the 1930s. In later years she played character roles on television and in films such as *The Parent Trap* and *Huckleberry Finn*. Allen Case was a regular on two television Westerns, *The Deputy* and *The Legend of Jesse James*.

Doc Quits. February 21, 1959. Production #442.

Dr. Betchel arrives in Dodge and approaches Doc with the proposition of a partnership. Doc is vehemently against Betchel because his motives have only to do with avarice. Doc quits his practice in anger when his patients start going to Betchel, whom Doc considers to be a quack and a charlatan.

Dr. Betchel	Wendell Holmes
Mrs. Crumley	Fionna Hale
Jake Wirth	Bartlett Robinson
Cullen	Jack Younger
Andy Wirth	Jack Grinnage
Sam	Bert Rumsey
Story, Script	John Meston
Director	Edward Ludlum
Producer	Norman Macdonnell

Jack Grinnage was a regular on *The Bob Newhart Show* and on *Kolchak: The Night Stalker*.

The Bear. February 28, 1959. Production #432.

Joe Plummer and Harry Webb have been playing a series of harmful practical jokes on their boss Mike Blocker and his fiancee Tilda, whom Joe once dated. Blocker, a big, good-natured bear of a man, finally loses his temper with Plummer and beats him to within an inch of his life. When Plummer is later discovered bludgeoned to death, Blocker is the prime suspect.

The Television Programs

Mike Blocker	Denver Pyle
Tilda	Norma Crane
Joe Plummer	Grant Williams
Harry Webb	Russell Johnson
Pete Wilkins	Guy Wilkerson
Story, Script	John Meston
Director	Jesse Hibbs
Producer	Norman Macdonnell

Grant Williams played Greg MacKenzie on television in *Hawaiian Eye* and the title role in the cult film *The Incredible Shrinking Man*.

The Coward. March 7, 1959. Production #448.

Ed Eby wants Matt dead, but is too cowardly to kill Matt himself or hire someone to do it. Instead, he spreads a rumor that someone is gunning for Matt, which makes Matt jumpy and suspicious of every drifter.

Ed Eby	Barry Atwater
Jack Massey	Jim Beck
Nat Swan	House Peters, Jr.
Lou	William Phipps
Pence	Barney Phillips
Pete	John Close
Bill	Sheldon Allman
Story, Script	John Meston
Director	Jesse Hibbs
Producer	Norman Macdonnell

William Phipps was a regular in another adult Western, *The Life and Legend of Wyatt Earp*.

The F.U. March 14, 1959. Production #440.

Al Clovis is suspected of shooting Onie Becker and Matt and Chester are lured out of town in pursuit, while Clovis' accomplices rob the bank of $25,000. Things go from bad to worse, as Matt and Chester are forced to follow the difficult trail cleverly laid out by Clovis.

Al Clovis	Bert Freed
Onie Becker	Joe Flynn
Mr. Botkin	Fay Roope
First Cowboy	Steve Raines
Second Cowboy	Ed Faulkner
Story, Script	John Meston
Director	Andrew McLaglen
Producer	Norman Macdonnell

Joe Flynn is best known to television viewers as Captain Binghamton of *McHale's Navy*. Steve Raines portrayed Jim Quince on *Rawhide*.

Wind. March 21, 1959. Production #449.

Frank Paris is a crooked blackjack dealer who teams up with Dolly Varden, a hostess at the Long Branch. Whoever Dolly stands next to at the blackjack table comes away a winner, and men are willing to pay handsomely to have her as their good luck charm. The problem is most of them wind up shooting each other for the privilege of her company. Dolly becomes a personal problem for Matt when she tries to shoot him in the back, after he asks her to leave town.

GUNSMOKE — III. THE PROGRAMS

Frank Paris	Mark Miller
Dolly Varden	Whitney Blake
Jed Garvey	Roy Engle
Jonas	Dabbs Greer
Bystander	Walter Burke
Singer	Allen Lurie
Hank	Stephen Roberts
Man	George Douglas
Norman	Guy Teague
John	Robert Swan
Story, Script	John Meston
Director	Arthur Hiller
Producer	Norman Macdonnell

Mark Miller was a regular on several television series including *Please Don't Eat the Daisies* and *The Name of the Game*. Whitney Blake played Dorothy Baxter on the comedy series *Hazel*.

March 28, 1959, preempted for *DuPont Show of the Month*.

Fawn. April 4, 1959. Production #451.

Mrs. Philips is a white woman who had been a captive of the Cherokees for years. She is finally released by the chief, but is captured by buffalo hunters headed by Jack Band. Matt rescues her and her half-Indian daughter Fawn from the abusive Band, but when Mrs. Philips and Fawn arrive in Dodge, Matt must defend them from a more subtle enemy.

Mrs. Philips	Peggy Stewart
Fawn	Wendy Stuart
Jep Hunter	Robert Karnes
Roger Philips	Robert Rockwell
Band	Charles Fredericks
Henry	Phil Harvey
Lou	Raymond Guth
Bert	Mike Gibson
Dobie	Joe Kearns
Story, Script	John Meston
Director	Andrew McLaglen
Producer	Norman Macdonnell

Peggy Stewart co-starred in numerous B-Westerns with such screen cowboys as Gene Autry and Sunset Carson. Robert Rockwell is probably best remembered on television as Mr. Boynton, the object of Eve Arden's ardor, in *Our Miss Brooks*.

Renegade White. April 11, 1959. Production #455.

Matt is captured by hostile Indians while tracking Ord Spencer, a renegade white man who has been selling 44-caliber rifles to the Indians.

Wild Hog	Michael Pate
Ord Spencer	Barney Phillips
Jim Buck	Robert Brubaker
Jake	Hank Patterson
Story	John Meston
Script	Les Crutchfield

The Television Programs

Director ....Andrew McLaglen
Producer ....Norman Macdonnell

Hank Paterson became a regular on *Gunsmoke* as Hank the stableman. He also played Fred Ziffel on the television comedy *Green Acres*. Robert Brubaker played the recurring role of Jim Buck the stagecoach driver. After the death of Glenn Strange, Brubaker played the role of Floyd, a bartender at the Long Branch.

Murder Warrant. April 18, 1959. Production #454.

Jake Harbin arrives in Dodge with an arrest warrant for Lee Prentice. Lee is wanted, dead or alive, in Baker City for the murder of Jim Turner. Even though Lee acted in self-defense, Jim's father runs the town so there is no way he can have a fair trial. Lee has lived in Dodge but a short time, yet he is so well-liked that Matt and the leading citizens formulate a plan to save him.

Lee Prentice ....Ed Nelson
Jake Harbin ....Mort Mills
Sheriff Ben Goddard ....Onslow Stevens
Botkin ....Fay Roope
Dobie ....Joe Kearns
Moss Grimmick ....George Selk
Story, Script ....John Meston
Director ....Andrew McLaglen
Producer ....Norman Macdonnell

Ed Nelson played Dr. Michael Rossi on *Peyton Place*. Onslow Stevens appeared in numerous films including *All the Fine Young Cannibals* and the cult horror classic, *Them*, which co-starred James Arness.

Change of Heart. April 25, 1959. Production #452.

Bella Grant, a saloon girl at the Long Branch, plans on tricking young rancher Jerry Cass out of his land. Her accomplice is Jerry's brother, Briscoe Cass. All is going according to plan until Bella falls in love with her victim, and tries to double-cross her partner.

Bella Grant ....Lucy Marlowe
Jerry Cass ....James Drury
Briscoe Cass ....Ken Curtis
Botkin ....Fay Roope
Story, Script ....John Meston
Director ....Andrew McLaglen
Producer ....Norman Macdonnell

Ken Curtis makes another guest appearance, this time as a villain.

Buffalo Hunter. May 2, 1959. Production #444.

Matt and Chester follow the bloody trail of buffalo hunter Jim Gatluf. Gatluf is a "greedy, downright wicked" man, who prefers to kill his men rather than pay them for their work.

Jim Gatluf ....Harold J. Stone
Tobe ....Garry Walberg
Tom Mercer ....Lou Krugman
Agent ....William Meigs
Cook ....Sam Buffington
Alvin ....Tom Holland

GUNSMOKE — III. THE PROGRAMS

>   Duff .... Brett King
>   Pete .... Scott Stevens
>   *Story, Script* .... John Meston
>   *Director* .... Ted Post
>   *Producer* .... Norman Macdonnell

Garry Walberg appeared as a regular on two Jack Klugman television shows. He played Speed on *The Odd Couple* and Lt. Monahan on *Quincy*.

The Choice. May 9, 1959. Production #431.

Andy Hill, a young stranger, gets into a fight with a drunk who has been annoying Kitty and kills the man in self-defense. Matt does not like having a gunman in his town, but decides to give Andy a chance by getting him a job riding shotgun on the stage with Jim Buck. Matt has to sweat it out when it appears that Andy has betrayed his confidence.

>   Andy Hill .... Darryl Hickman
>   Jim Buck .... Robert Brubaker
>   Kerrick .... Charles Maxwell
>   Tough .... Dick Rich
>   Additional Cast .... Tyler McVey
>   *Story, Script* .... John Meston
>   *Director* .... Ted Post
>   *Producer* .... Norman Macdonnel

Darryl Hickman began a film career at the age of four and appeared in almost 200 films including *The Grapes of Wrath* with Henry Fonda. Before he moved into television production he appeared on the *The Many Loves of Dobie Gillis* as Dwayne Hickman's fictional brother. Dwayne is his brother off camera as well.

There Was Never a Horse. May 16, 1959. Production #453.

Gunfighter Kin Creed gets into a fight with a drunk at the Long Branch and kills him in "self-defense." Matt is aware of Creed's reputation, but is unable to arrest him. Creed would like to advance his reputation by killing a U.S. marshal, but Matt refuses to be goaded into a gunfight.

>   Kin Creed .... Jack Lambert
>   Drunk .... Joe Sargent
>   Roy .... Bill Wellman, Jr.
>   *Story, Script* .... John Meston
>   *Director* .... Andrew McLaglen
>   *Producer* .... Norman Macdonnell

Jack Lambert played Joshua on the adventure series, *Riverboat*.

Print Asper. May 23, 1959. Production #435.

Print Asper asks attorney Jay Rabb to transfer title of his ranch to his sons, Will and Johnny. The ruthless Rabb tricks the illiterate Print and puts the title in his own name. Print threatens the dishonest lawyer with violence when he discovers the treachery and Rabb correctly transfers the title. A few days later Rabb is shot and Print is the natural suspect. When Print's alibi is confirmed, Matt surmises that Johnny or Will might be the guilty party.

>   Print Asper .... J. Pat O'Malley
>   Jay Rabb .... Ted Knight
>   Will Asper .... Lew Brown

The Television Programs

Johnny Asper	Robert Ivers
Story, Script	John Meston
Director	Ted Post
Producer	Norman Macdonnell

Ted Knight was Ted Baxter on *The Mary Tyler Moore Show* and Henry Rush on *Too Close for Comfort*. He won two Emmy Awards for his work on *The Mary Tyler Moore Show*.

The Constable. May 30, 1959. Production #450.

Dodge's businessmen hire an ill-equipped constable to handle the law in town when they disagree with Matt's policy regarding some rowdy Texas cowboys. Fearful that Matt will destroy the economy with his tough tactics, the businessmen decide that Matt will have jurisdiction only outside the city limits. When word gets out that Dodge is an "open town" all the scum and riff-raff within a hundred miles arrive to have a good time. Constable Dillard Band is unable to cope with the ruffians and the businessmen learn a hard lesson.

Rance	John Larch
Dillard Band	Strother Martin
Green	Pitt Herbert
First Cowboy	William Bryant
Second Cowboy	Joel Ashley
Pete	Scott Peters
Botkin	Joe Kearns
Mike	Joseph Breen
Dobie	Dan Sheridan
Joe	John Mitchum
Bob	Lee Winters
Hank	Vic Lundin
Carl	Robert DeCost
Story, Script	John Meston
Director	Arthur Hiller
Producer	Norman Macdonnell

Blue Horse. June 6, 1959. Production #456.

While returning to Dodge with murderer Hob Cannon, Matt's horse stumbles, causing Matt to break his leg. Chester shoots the horse and leaves Matt with the prisoner while he goes for help. Feverish and weak, Matt is overpowered by Hob, and is left to die. Fortunately, he is saved by a fugitive Indian, Blue Horse, who is being hunted by the cavalry. Blue Horse's selfless act forces Matt to choose between his duty to report Blue Horse's escape from the reservation, and his sense of justice.

Blue Horse	Michael Pate
Hob Cannon	Gene Nelson
Sergeant	Monte Hale
Lt. Eldridge	Bill Murphy
Story	Marian Clark
Script	John Meston
Director	Andrew McLaglen
Producer	Norman Macdonnell

Cheyennes. June 13, 1959. Production #436.

Matt and Chester are forced to circumvent an overeager new army commander,

GUNSMOKE — III. THE PROGRAMS

Captain Nichols, in order to avoid a Cheyenne uprising. Gunrunners have been supplying 44-caliber Spenser rifles to the Indians and Matt wants to stop the gunrunners before Nichols kills any Cheyennes. According to Matt's friend Long Robe, if any Cheyennes are killed, the act would trigger a full-fledged war against the white man.

    Captain Nichols .... Walter Brooke
    Long Robe .... Ralph Moody
    Sgt. Keller .... Chuck Roberson
    Major .... Tom Brown
    Warrior .... Eddie Little Sky
    Jim .... Dennis Cross
    Daughter .... Connie Buck
    Brown .... Edward Robinson, Jr.
    Story, Script .... John Meston
    Director .... Ted Post
    Producer .... Norman Macdonnell

 Walter Brooke whispered the immortal word "plastics" to Dustin Hoffman in *The Graduate*. Ralph Moody was a frequent guest on radio's *Gunsmoke*. Tom Brown played Ed O'Connor on *Gunsmoke* and Al Weeks on *General Hospital*. Chuck Roberson was for many years, John Wayne's stuntman. He is also the author of *Fall Guy*.

Robin Hood. June 20, 1959, rerun. First aired February 4, 1956.

No Indians. June 27, 1959, rerun. First aired December 8, 1956.

Cholera. July 4, 1959, rerun. First aired December 29, 1956.

Spring Term. July 11, 1959, rerun. First aired December 15, 1956.

Executioner. July 18, 1959, rerun. First aired February 2, 1957.

Sins of the Father. July 25, 1959, rerun. First aired January 19, 1957.

The Photographer. August 1, 1959, rerun. First aired April 6, 1957.

Bloody Hands. August 8, 1959, rerun. First aired February 16, 1957.

Cain. August 15, 1959, rerun. First aired March 9, 1957.

Sweet and Sour. August 22, 1959, rerun. First aired March 2, 1957.

Cheap Labor. August 29, 1959, rerun. First aired May 4, 1957.

FIFTH SEASON

Target. September 5, 1959. Production #160.
 Matt steps in to prevent bloodshed when a group of gypsies camp on land owned by old man Kater, a trigger-happy rancher. Kater is unpleasantly surprised when he finds that his son Danny, has fallen in love with Nayomi the daughter of the gypsy chief, who is equally displeased with the situation.

The Television Programs

```
Danny . . . . . . . . . . . . . . . . . . . . . . . . . . . . . . . . . . . Darryl Hickman
Nayomi . . . . . . . . . . . . . . . . . . . . . . . . . . . . . . . . . . Suzanne Lloyd
Kater. . . . . . . . . . . . . . . . . . . . . . . . . . . . . . . . . . . . John Carradine
Gypsy Chief . . . . . . . . . . . . . . . . . . . . . . . . . . . . . . . Frank De Kova
Story . . . . . . . . . . . . . . . . . . . . . . . . . . . . . . . . . . . . Les Crutchfield
Script . . . . . . . . . . . . . . . . . . . . . . . . . . . . . . . . . . . . John Meston
Director . . . . . . . . . . . . . . . . . . . . . . . . . . . . . . . . . . Andrew McLaglen
Producer . . . . . . . . . . . . . . . . . . . . . . . . . . . . . . . . . Norman Macdonnell
```

September 12, 1959, preempted for *The Miss America Pageant.*

Kitty's Injury. September 19, 1959. Production #161.

While riding with Matt, Kitty is thrown from her horse and is badly injured. Afraid to leave her alone with the hostile occupants of a nearby shack, Matt finds himself in the uncomfortable position of having to rely on them to summon Doc.

```
Lutie Judson . . . . . . . . . . . . . . . . . . . . . . . . . . . . . Don Dubbins
Raff Judson . . . . . . . . . . . . . . . . . . . . . . . . . . . . . . Karl Swenson
Cora Judson . . . . . . . . . . . . . . . . . . . . . . . . . . . . . Anne Seymour
Story . . . . . . . . . . . . . . . . . . . . . . . . . . . . . . . . . . . Marian Clark
Script . . . . . . . . . . . . . . . . . . . . . . . . . . . . . . . . . . John Meston
Director . . . . . . . . . . . . . . . . . . . . . . . . . . . . . . . . Buzz Kulik
Producer . . . . . . . . . . . . . . . . . . . . . . . . . . . . . . . Norman Macdonnell
```

Karl Swenson played Lars Hanson on *Little House on the Prairie,* but he is best known for his delightful character Lorenzo Jones, inventor of impractical, whimsical gadgets. Anne Seymour played character roles in films, as well as on television. She appeared in such classic movies as *All the King's Men* and *Desire Under the Elms.*

Horse Deal. September 26, 1959. Production #159.

A group of ranchers threaten to form a lynching party when Matt is reluctant to track down a horse thief. Matt has his own plan for capturing the culprit, a plan that also results in a spending spree for Chester.

```
Bowers . . . . . . . . . . . . . . . . . . . . . . . . . . . . . . . . . Bart Robinson
Deesha . . . . . . . . . . . . . . . . . . . . . . . . . . . . . . . . . Harry Carey, Jr.
Slim . . . . . . . . . . . . . . . . . . . . . . . . . . . . . . . . . . . Trevor Bardette
Worth . . . . . . . . . . . . . . . . . . . . . . . . . . . . . . . . . Michael Hinn
Harper . . . . . . . . . . . . . . . . . . . . . . . . . . . . . . . . . Fred Grossinger
Joe . . . . . . . . . . . . . . . . . . . . . . . . . . . . . . . . . . . . Bill Catching
Story, Script . . . . . . . . . . . . . . . . . . . . . . . . . . . . . John Meston
Director . . . . . . . . . . . . . . . . . . . . . . . . . . . . . . . . Andrew McLaglen
Producer . . . . . . . . . . . . . . . . . . . . . . . . . . . . . . . Norman Macdonnell
```

Harry Carey, Jr. appeared in such films as *Red River, Three Godfathers,* and *Gentlemen Prefer Blondes.* Trevor Bardette played Old Man Clayton on *The Life and Legend of Wyatt Earp.* His film credits include *The Sea of Grass, The Big Sleep,* and *Destry.*

Johnny Red. October 3, 1959. Production #162.

Johnny Red arrives in Dodge, claiming to be the long lost son of widow Crale. Matt believes the young man may be a criminal, but lacks evidence. He watches closely as the bandit ingratiates himself with the old woman.

```
Johnny Red . . . . . . . . . . . . . . . . . . . . . . . . . . . . . James Drury
Mrs. Crale . . . . . . . . . . . . . . . . . . . . . . . . . . . . . . Josephine Hutchinson
```

GUNSMOKE — III. THE PROGRAMS

Nate	Abel Fernandez
Ponca City Kid	Dennis McMullen
Jim Buck	Robert Brubaker
Story	Les Crutchfield
Script	John Meston
Director	Buzz Kulik
Producer	Norman Macdonnell

Kangaroo. October 10, 1959. Production #164.

Matt and Chester come across a crazy religious fanatic, Ira Scurlock, and his sons who are whipping a cowboy for being a "sinner." Chester releases the cowboy, which sets Scurlock into a flurry of threats. Later, Chester is kidnapped by Scurlock, who conducts a kangaroo court, finds Chester guilty, and sentences him to amputation of the right hand.

Ira Scurlock	Peter Whitney
Hod	John Crawford
Dal	Richard Rust
Jim Bride	Lew Brown
Clem	Clem Fuller
Story, Script	John Meston
Director	Andrew McLaglen
Associate Producer	James Arness
Producer	Norman Macdonnell

John Crawford appeared on television as Sheriff Ep Bridges on *The Waltons* from 1972 to 1981.

Tail to the Wind. October 17, 1959. Production #166.

Matt is frustrated when his offers of assistance are refused by rancher Pezzy Neller, who is constantly being harrassed by Burke and Harlow Reese, a bullying father and son. The Reeses intend to drive Pezzy and his wife, Cora, off their land. Matt knows the persecution will continue until Pezzy either leaves or is killed, but he is unable to help when the rancher refuses to sign a complaint.

Pezzy Neller	Harry Townes
Cora	Alice Backes
Burke Reese	Harry Swoger
Harlow Reese	Alan Reed, Jr.
Story	Les Crutchfield
Script	John Meston
Director	Christian Nyby
Associate Producer	James Arness
Producer	Norman Macdonnell

Annie Oakley. October 24, 1959. Production #158.

Matt intercedes in an effort to prevent bloodshed when Kate Kinsman, a romance-starved wife, goads her husband, Jeff, into a fight with their neighbor, Mr. Dolliver. When Jeff is murdered, Kate insists the killer is Dolliver. Matt plays his own hunch and sets a trap for the murderer.

Kate Kinsman	Florence MacMichael
Jeff Kinsman	George Mitchell
Dolliver	John Anderson

The Television Programs

Story, Script	John Meston
Director	Jesse Hibbs
Associate Producer	James Arness
Producer	Norman Macdonnell

Florence MacMichael is familiar to television viewers as Winnie Kirkwood from the comedy *Mister Ed*.

Saludos. October 31, 1959. Production #163.

Sochi, an Indian girl, is gravely wounded after her husband is murdered. She manages to drag herself to Dodge, where Doc tries to save her. Matt rounds up three suspects and heads back to Dodge, hoping that the gunman who shot the girl will make a break for freedom en route.

Sochi	Connie Buck
Joe Foss	Gene Nelson
Clem Steed	Jack Elam
Pegger	Robert J. Wilke
Story	Les Crutchfield
Script	John Meston
Director	Andrew McLaglen
Associate Producer	James Arness
Producer	Norman Macdonnell

Jack Elam is one of the "meanest hombres" ever to "cast a shadow across a movie-lot cowtown." *The Sundowners* launched his successful screen career as a back-shooting bad guy, but the dark, scowling heavy with the wandering left eye eventually proved he could play sympathetic and comedic characters as well. His most recent venture has been a television sit-com *Easy Street* with Loni Anderson.

Brother Whelp. November 7, 1959. Production #169.

Sted Rutger returns to Dodge after having served three years in prison. During his absence, his father has died, and has left the family ranch to his younger brother, Tom. Adding insult to injury, Tassy, Sted's girlfriend, has married Tom. Sted believes his only recourse is to set matters straight by calling out his brother.

Sted Rutger	Lew Gallo
Tassy	Ellen Clark
Tom	John Clarke
Clem	Clem Fuller
Jonas	Dabbs Greer
Story	Les Crutchfield
Script	John Meston
Director	R.G. Springsteen
Associate Producer	James Arness
Producer	Norman Macdonnell

John Clarke is probably best known for his role as Mickey Horton on the soap opera *Days of Our Lives*.

The Boots. November 14, 1959. Production #157.

Young Tommy and Zeno, the town drunk, make an odd pair. Tommy looks up to the old man and takes care of him after his binges. The boy is faced with heartbreak when gunslinger Hank Fergus rides into Dodge. He threatens to expose Zeno as a former gunman who became a coward. In order to prevent Tommy's disillusionment, Zeno agrees to help Fergus rob the general store.

GUNSMOKE — III. THE PROGRAMS

Zeno	John Larch
Tommy	Richard Eyer
Hank Fergus	Wynn Pearce
Story, Script	John Meston
Director	Jesse Hibbs
Associate Producer	James Arness
Producer	Norman Macdonnell

Odd Man Out. November 21, 1959. Production #168.

Elderly farmer Cyrus Tucker reports to Matt that his wife has left him after 37 years. Matt suspects foul play when Hody Peel tries to sell Mrs. Tucker's clothes to Jonas.

Cyrus Tucker	Elisha Cook
Hody Peel	William Phipps
Mrs. Peel	Elizabeth York
Cowboy	Dallas Mitchell
Jonas	Dabbs Greer
Moss Grimmick	George Selk
Clem	Clem Fuller
Story	Les Crutchfield
Script	John Meston
Director	Andrew McLaglen
Associate Producer	James Arness
Producer	Norman Macdonnell

Miguel's Daughter. November 28, 1959. Production #171.

Two rowdy trail hands, Ab Cole and Rusk Davis, annoy Chavela Ramerez, a pretty Mexican girl. Kitty intervenes and Chavela goes her merry way selling eggs. Later, however, the men once again run into Chavela. This time Kitty is not there to protect her, and she is injured while fighting off her assailants. Matt sets out to find Ab and Rusk before Chavela's outraged father does.

Chavela Ramerez	Fintan Meyler
Miguel Ramerez	Simon Oakland
Ab Cole	Wesley Lau
Rusk Davis	Ed Nelson
Story	Marian Clark
Script	John Meston
Director	Andrew McLaglen
Associate Producer	James Arness
Producer	Norman Macdonnell

Box O' Rocks. December 5, 1959. Production #173.

Matt interrupts the burial of Packy Roundtree and finds an empty coffin. While trying to solve the mystery, he encounters Jeb Crooder, a sadistic bully, and Reverend Blouze, an unordained parson. The solution eventually points to Preston Hawkins, an admitted coward, who has invented an unusual way to wreak revenge against his brutal ex-partner.

Pete	Howard McNear
Rev. Blouze	Vaughn Taylor
Jed Crooder	Larry Blake

The Television Programs

Packy Roundtree	William Fawcett
Mrs. Blouze	Gertrude Flynn
Story, Script	Les Crutchfield
Director	R.G. Springsteen
Associate Producer	James Arness
Producer	Norman Macdonnell

R.G. "Bud" Springsteen started out his directing career in B-Westerns for Republic. His films include *Come Next Spring*.

False Witness. December 12, 1959. Production #179.

Matt has good reason to believe that an innocent man was hanged, when he proves that an "eyewitness" to the murder has committed willful perjury.

Romey Crep	Wright King
Tom Morey	Wayne Rogers
Judge	Robert Griffin
Hank	Len Hendry
Bob	Richard Sinatra
Clem	Clem Fuller
Jake	Norman Sturgis
Sawyer	Brad Trumbull
Clerk	Harold Goodwin
Story	Marian Clark
Script	John Meston
Director	Ted Post
Associate Producer	James Arness
Producer	Norman Macdonnell

Wayne Rogers was Captain "Trapper" John McIntyre on *M.A.S.H.* and Dr. Charley Michaels on the sit-com *House Calls*.

Tag, You're It. December 19, 1959. Production #176.

Karl Killion is a hired gun who drifts into town. Dodge's residents are in a near-panic as they speculate about who his intended victim may be. Matt swings into action when it becomes apparent that Rusty, a new hostess at the Long Branch, is Killion's target.

Karl Killion	Paul Langton
Rusty	Madlyn Rhue
Tex	Gregg Stewart
Clem	Clem Fuller
Clerk	Harold Goodwin
Story, Script	Les Crutchfield
Director	Jesse Hibbs
Associate Producer	James Arness
Producer	Norman Macdonnell

Madlyn Rhue appeared as Marjorie Grant on *Bracken's World* and as Hilary Madison on *Executive Suite*.

Thick 'N' Thin. December 26, 1959. Production #165.

Brace McCoy and Otie Perkins have been partners for years, but now a silly dispute threatens to destroy their longtime friendship. Since the two elderly ranchers own their farm jointly, neither one of them wants to vacate. Matt mediates and has the two men draw cards to determine who gets the farmhouse and who gets the barn.

Brace McCoy	Robert Emhardt
Otie Perkins	Percy Helton
Summer Dove	Tina Menard
Story	Les Crutchfield
Script	John Meston
Director	Stuart Heisler
Associate Producer	James Arness
Producer	Norman Macdonnell

Stuart Heisler directed such films as *Tulsa* with Susan Hayward, *Tokyo Joe* starring Humphrey Bogart, and *Storm Warning* with Ronald Reagan. Percy Helton was Homer Cratchit on *The Beverly Hillbillies*.

Groat's Grudge. January 2, 1960. Production #172.

Lee Grayson, who fought with the Confederates during the Civil War, vows to avenge the death of his wife, killed during Sherman's march through Georgia. Grayson rides to intercept Tom Haskett, a cowboy who he believes responsible for her death. Matt and Chester follow, hoping to avert violence.

Lee Grayson	Ross Elliott
Tom Haskett	Thomas Coley
Additional Cast	Ben Wright
Story	Marian Clark
Script	John Meston
Director	Andrew McLaglen
Associate Producer	James Arness
Producer	Norman Macdonnell

Ross Elliott played Sheriff Abbott on the television Western *The Virginian*.

Big Tom. January 9, 1960. Production #180.

Professional prize fighter Hob Creel challenges Big Tom Burr, a former fighter, to a match. Creel and his associates have hatched a scheme to raise money. Not wanting to appear the coward, Tom accepts the challenge, but Doc finds that he is not fit enough to fight. Matt engages in a knock-down battle with Creel, to put an end to the insinuations that Tom is afraid to fight.

Hob Creel	Don Megowan
Tom Burr	Robert J. Wilke
Clay Cran	Harry Lauter
Brady	Howard Caine
Harry	Gregg Palmer
Jim	Rand Harper
Story	Marian Clark
Script	John Meston
Director	Andrew McLaglen
Associate Producer	James Arness
Producer	Norman Macdonnell

Harry Lauter was Jim Herrick on the television series, *Waterfront* and Ranger Clay Morgan on *Tales of the Texas Rangers*. His film credits include *I Was a Male War Bride*, with Cary Grant and *Hellcats of the Navy* with Ronald and Nancy Reagan.

Till Death Do Us. January 16, 1960. Production #178.

A mysterious gunman takes a shot at miserly Jezra Cobb and his wife Minerva on

The Television Programs

Dodge's Main Street. Matt suspects the shooting may be the result of Jezra's attempts to "reform" several of the town's dancehall girls.

Jezra Cobb	Milton Selzer
Minerva Cobb	Mary Field
Puggy Rado	Rayford Barnes
Story, Script	Les Crutchfield
Director	Jean Yarbrough
Associate Producer	James Arness
Producer	Norman Macdonnell

Jean Yarbrough began his career in films as a prop man for Hal Roach. He went on to direct several Abbott and Costello comedies along with other budget features. Milton Selzer appeared on television as Julius Singer on the sit-com, *Needles and Pins* and as Sid Amos on the dramatic series, *Scruples*.

The Tragedian. January 23, 1960. Production #182.

Matt jails Brad, a murderer who claims that his brother Vince will not let him go to trial. Matt searches Dodge for Vince, a cowardly killer who would not hesitate to shoot him in the back. In the process, Matt befriends Edward Vanderman, a down-and-out Shakespearian actor who turns out to be a thief and a card cheat.

Edward Vanderman	John Abbott
Joe	Howard McNear
Ben	Harry Woods
Brad	Stanley Clements
Story	Les Crutchfield
Script	John Meston
Director	Arthur Hiller
Associate Producer	James Arness
Producer	Norman Macdonnell

British character actor John Abbott appeared in such films as *Mrs. Miniver*, *Jane Eyre* and *Gigi*. Harry Woods is credited with playing some of the meanest villains in the history of film. His features include *I Am a Fugitive from a Chain Gang* and *The Ten Commandments*.

Hinka Do. January 30, 1960. Production #177.

Mamie, a tough-as-nails, fast-shooting cowlady, takes over the Lady Gay Saloon, and Dodge's residents are intrigued by the brawny, gravel-voiced proprietress. Matt suspects Mamie of foul play when the former owner, wimpy Herman Bleeker, mysteriously disappears, and his boots and vest are found buried, and covered with blood.

Mamie	Nina Varela
Herman Bleeker	Walter Burke
Cowboy	Mike Green
Drunk	Richard Reeves
Manuel	Ric Roman
Pete	Bob Hopkins
Story, Script	Les Crutchfield
Director	Andrew McLaglen
Associate Producer	James Arness
Producer	Norman Macdonnell

GUNSMOKE — III. THE PROGRAMS

Doc Judge. February 6, 1960. Production #183.

Gunman Brice Harp arrives in Dodge and mistakes Doc for the Wyoming Judge who sentenced him to seven years in prison. While Doc and Chester are dining at Delmonico's, Brice enters and openly swears to kill Doc. Since Matt is away on Government business, it is up to Chester to protect his irascible friend.

Brice Harp	Barry Atwater
Bob	Dennis Cross
Moss	George Selk
Jonas	Dabbs Greer
Story, Script	John Meston
Director	Arthur Hiller
Associate Producer	James Arness
Producer	Norman Macdonnell

Moo Moo Raid. February 13, 1960. Production #167.

Onie Tucker owns a valuable old cow that is used to lead herds of cattle through water. When Onie and the cow disappear, it sets off a series of events that threaten a range war.

Onie	Raymond Hatton
Bert	Robert Karnes
Tush	Lane Bradford
Pete	Richard Evans
Gib	Tyler McVey
Cary	Ron Hayes
Joe	John Close
Clem	Clem Fuller
Story	Les Crutchfield
Script	John Meston
Director	Andrew McLaglen
Associate Producer	James Arness
Producer	Norman Macdonnell

Kitty's Killing. February 20, 1960. Production #186.

Jacob Leech arrives in Dodge bent on murdering rancher Ollie Radford. Radford was married to Leech's daughter, who died during childbirth and out of a warped sense of justice, Leech has sworn vengeance. Radford has since remarried and settled outside of Dodge. When Leech discovers that Radford's wife is expecting, he tries to find the couple by forcing Kitty to lead the way. Kitty lures the madman in the wrong direction and in doing so she endangers her life.

Jacob Leech	Abraham Sofaer
Ollie Radford	John Pickard
Clem	Clem Fuller
Story	Marian Clark
Script	John Meston
Director	Arthur Hiller
Associate Producer	James Arness
Producer	Norman Macdonnell

John Pickard was one of 26 actors who auditioned for the role of Matt Dillon. According to producer Charles Marquis Warren, Pickard lost the part when he "floundered in a love scene with Kitty." Warren mused that Pickard never knew

The Television Programs

how close to immortality he had come. Abraham Sofaer often played sinister, exotic characters. Primarily a film actor, Sofaer's credits include *Taras Bulba*.

Jailbait Janet. February 27, 1960. Production #175.
After a bandit and his two teenage children rob a train and kill the baggage clerk, Matt and Chester set out to capture them. When Matt discovers that one of the bandits is a young girl, he puts her in Kitty's custody. This angers Krocker, a bitter railroad agent.

Dan	John Larch
Janet	Nan Peterson
Krocker	Bartlett Robinson
Jerry	Steve Terrell
Clerk	Jon Lormer
Story, Script	Les Crutchfield
Director	Jesse Hibbs
Associate Producer	James Arness
Producer	Norman Macdonnell

Unwanted Deputy. March 5, 1960. Production #181.
Vince Walsh is the brother of Dave Walsh who was brought to justice by Matt. Bent on vengeance, he plans on killing Matt in a "fair fight." The first step in his scheme is to take Matt's job by turning the townsfolk against the marshal.

Vince Walsh	Charles Aidman
Maise	Mary Carver
Dave Walsh	Marlowe Jenson
Rudd	Dick Rich
Harry	Ed Faulkner
Tourney	Dick London
Lee	Craig Fox
Bob	Bob Wiensko
Charlie	Joe Haworth
Story	Marian Clark
Script	John Meston
Director	Andrew V. McLaglen
Associate Producer	James Arness
Producer	Norman Macdonnell

Where'd They Go. March 12, 1960. Production #187.
Matt and Chester set out to arrest Clint Dodie for allegedly robbing Mr. Jonas' store. When the two arrive at Dodie's ranch, the foxy farmer outwits them and they wind up doing all his chores. Dodie implies that his wife Medora is expecting any day, and that if he is imprisoned with the farmwork undone, she will be left destitute.

Clint Dodie	Jack Elam
Medora	Betty Harford
Jonas	Dabbs Greer
Story	Les Crutchfield
Script	John Meston
Director	Jesse Hibbs
Associate Producer	James Arness
Producer	Norman Macdonnell

GUNSMOKE — III. THE PROGRAMS

March 19, 1960, preempted for *Jack Benny Special*.

Crowbait Bob. March 26, 1960. Production #191.
   Aged prospector Crowbait Bob touches off trouble when he asks Matt to draw up a will naming Kitty as his sole heir. When miserly relatives learn of the will, they conclude that Bob has struck it rich, and plot to get their hands on the estate.

Crowbait Bob	Hank Patterson
Elbin	Ned Glass
Martha	Shirley O'Hara
Ace	John Apone
Story, Script	Les Crutchfield
Director	Andrew McLaglen
Associate Producer	James Arness

Colleen So Green. April 2, 1960. Production #188.
   Chester, Doc, and wealthy buffalo skinner Bull Reeger turn themselves and their purses inside out when Colleen Tawny, a helpless and beautiful Southern belle, arrives in Dodge.

Colleen Tawny	Joanna Moore
Bull Reeger	Harry Swoger
Jonas	Dabbs Greer
Jim Buck	Robert Brubaker
Clerk	Harold Goodwin
Clem	Clem Fuller
Employee	Perry Ivins
Story	Les Crutchfield
Script	John Meston
Director	Jean Yarbrough
Associate Producer	James Arness
Producer	Norman Macdonnell

The Ex-Urbanites. April 9, 1960. Production #195.
   Doc is shot while tending to a wounded man on the open prairie. Chester faces the grim responsibility of attempting to nurse and feed him, while fending off two desperados. Their long-established antagonism goes out the window as Doc's life hangs in the balance.

Jesse	Ken Curtis
Pitt	Robert Wilke
Nate	Lew Brown
Story	John Meston
Script	John Meston
Director	Andrew McLaglen
Associate Producer	James Arness
Producer	Norman Macdonnell

   Ken Curtis (Festus) once again plays an outlaw in this segment.

I Thee Wed. April 16, 1960. Production #184.
   Matt is wounded when he tangles with wife beater Sam Lacket. After Lacket is jailed, his long suffering wife, Hester, pays his fine and obtains his release, only to be abused once again by her brutal husband.

The Television Programs

Sam Lacket	Allyn Joslyn
Hester Lacket	Alice Frost
Judge	Hank Patterson
Story	Les Crutchfield
Script	John Meston
Director	Jesse Hibbs
Associate Producer	James Arness
Producer	Norman Macdonnell

From 1949 to 1957 Alice Frost played the part of Aunt Trina Gunnerson on the television series *Mama*.

The Lady Killer. April 23, 1960. Production #193.

Mae is a new girl at the Long Branch who has her sights on cowboy Grant Lucas, a key witness in a pending robbery trial. She invites him to her room late at night, telling him to arrive by her bedroom window. When the unsuspecting Lucas taps on her window pane, she responds by killing him. When Matt investigates, Mae claims she shot Lucas because he tried to kill her for her brooch. Matt, however, doubts her story.

Mae Talmey	Jan Harrison
Grant Lucas	Ross Elliott
Sy	Harry Lauter
Cowboy	Charles Sterrett
Story, Script	John Meston
Director	Andrew McLaglen
Associate Producer	James Arness
Producer	Norman Macdonnell

Gentleman's Disagreement. April 30, 1960. Production #189.

Jeanne Wells asks Matt to protect her blacksmith husband Bert, who has been threatened by Jeanne's one-time suitor, Ed Beaudry. When Beaudry is found slain with a hammer the evidence points to Bert, and Matt is forced to arrest him.

Bert Wells	Adam Kennedy
Jeanne Wells	Fintan Meyler
Ed Beaudry	Val Dufour
Tulsa	Tom Reese
Pete	Joseph Hamilton
Story, Script	Les Crutchfield
Director	Jesse Hibbs
Associate Producer	James Arness
Producer	Norman Macdonnell

Speak Me Fair. May 7, 1960. Production #194.

After rancher Traych complains about cattle rustlers, Matt encounters a badly beaten Indian boy. An angry Matt sets out to determine if the two incidents are connected, and to find those responsible.

Traych	Douglas Kennedy
Scout	Ken Curtis
Driver	Chuck Roberson
Gunner	Perry Cook
Story, Script	Les Crutchfield

GUNSMOKE — III. THE PROGRAMS

Director .... Andrew McLaglen
Associate Producer .... James Arness
Producer .... Norman Macdonnell

Ken Curtis (Festus) has the role of an Indian in this episode.

Belle's Back. May 14, 1960. Production #185.

Belle Ainsley is ostracized after she runs away with a wanted criminal. She returns to Dodge and denies any knowledge of his whereabouts, but the actions of Belle's embittered younger sister, Phyllis, makes Matt suspect otherwise.

Belle Ainsley .... Nita Talbot
Phyllis .... Nancy Rennick
Mr. Ainsley .... Daniel White
Dobie .... Gage Clark
Story, Script .... Les Crutchfield
Director .... Jesse Hibbs
Associate Producer .... James Arness
Producer .... Norman Macdonnell

Nancy Rennick appeared as Edith Thorncroft on *Kentucky Jones* which starred Dennis Weaver.

The Bobsy Twins. May 21, 1960. Production #170.

Merle and Harvey, two psychopathic, illiterate, and totally amoral brothers, wander into Dodge looking for Indians to kill. Their strange behavior is a joke to the entire town, until Matt learns that their eccentricities make them unreasoning killers.

Merle .... Morris Ankrum
Harvey .... Ralph Moody
Buck Grant .... Buck Young
Lavinia .... Jean Howell
Man .... John O'Malley
Taylor .... Charles McArthur
Pete .... Richard Chamberlain
Les .... Paul Hahn
Carl .... Hank Patterson
Clem .... Clem Fuller
Story, Script .... John Meston
Director .... Jesse Hibbs
Associate Producer .... James Arness
Producer .... Norman Macdonnell

Richard Chamberlain rose to television stardom as *Dr. Kildare*. In recent years he has become the king of television mini-series with the success of *Centennial*, *Shogun* and *The Thorn Birds*. His film credits include *The Three Musketeers* and *King Solomon's Mines*.

Old Flame. May 28, 1960. Production #190.

Dolly Winters, an old girlfriend of Matt's, arrives in Dodge seeking his assistance in a rather personal matter. Rad Meadow, the man Dolly calls her husband, allegedly stole all of Dolly's money and ran off with another woman. Dolly insists that her life is in danger and Matt is naturally concerned for his friend's safety. However, Kitty suspects that Dolly's motives are not entirely sincere, and she is willing to bet a "barrel of whiskey" that her hunch is right.

Dolly Winters .... Marilyn Maxwell

The Television Programs

Rad Meadows	Lee Van Cleef
Mary	Peggy Stewart
Dobie	Hal Smith
Story	Marian Clark
Script	John Meston
Director	Jesse Hibbs
Associate Producer	James Arness
Producer	Norman Macdonnell

This episode is *Gunsmoke's* answer to the 1987 blockbuster movie *Fatal Attraction*. Blonde sex symbol Marilyn Maxwell appeared in several films of the 40s and 50s including *Rock-a-Bye Baby*. She also guest-starred on numerous television shows and was a regular on *Bus Stop*. Lee Van Cleef appeared as a heavy in many popular "spaghetti Westerns" and feature films including *High Noon, The Good, the Bad, and the Ugly*, and *For a Few Dollars More*. Hal Smith is best known for his portrayal of Otis Campbell, the town drunk, of *The Andy Griffith Show*.

The Deserter. June 4, 1960. Production #174.

Corporal Lurie deserts from the army and hooks up with Radin, a civilian. The two men rob an army payroll, but as they are making their escape Lurie is wounded. The young man heads toward Dodge and finds refuge on his parents' farm. When Matt and Chester arrive, Lurie's desperate father shoots Chester and holds Matt at gunpoint so that his son can escape.

Cpl. Lurie	Rudy Solari
Radin	Joe Perry
Major	Henry Brandon
Sgt. Strate	Charles Fredericks
Jed	Harry Bartell
Maddie	Jean Inness
Story	Marian Clark
Script	John Meston
Director	Arthur Hiller
Associate Producer	James Arness
Producer	Norman Macdonnell

Cherry Red. June 11, 1960. Production #192.

Beautiful and spirited Cherry O'Dell rebuffs the attentions of Red Larned. However, Larned is not easily put off and continues to pursue the young widow. Matt suspects that Larned is involved with the recent stage coach robbery that took the life of Cherry's outlaw husband, and so does Cherry.

Cherry O'Dell	Joanna Moore
Red Larned	Arthur Franz
Yancey	Douglas Kennedy
Nightshirt	Cliff Ketchum
Story, Script	Les Crutchfield
Director	Andrew McLaglen
Associate Producer	James Arness
Producer	Norman Macdonnell

Last Fling. June 18, 1960, rerun. Originally aired March 23, 1957.

GUNSMOKE — III. THE PROGRAMS

What the Whiskey Drummer Heard. July 2, 1960, rerun. First aired April 27, 1957.

The Bureaucrat. July 9, 1960, rerun. First aired March 16, 1957.

Who Lives by the Sword. July 16, 1960, rerun. First aired May 18, 1957.

Gun for Chester. July 23, 1960, rerun. First aired September 21, 1957.

Crack-Up. July 30, 1960, rerun. First aired September 14, 1957.

Potato Road. August 6, 1960, rerun. First aired October 12, 1957.

Blood Money. August 13, 1960, rerun. First aired September 28, 1957.

Born to Hang. August 20, 1960, rerun. First aired November 2, 1957.

Mavis McCloud. August 27, 1960, rerun. First aired October 26, 1957.

SIXTH SEASON

Friend's Pay-Off. September 3, 1960. Production #30156 (154-201).
   Matt faces a difficult situation when he kills Joe Leeds to save his old friend Ab Butler. On his death-bed, Leeds tells Matt that Ab is a wanted bank robber and killer. Unless Matt can prove the statement false, he knows he must arrest Ab for murder.

Ab Butler	Mike Road
Joe Leeds	Tom Reese
Moss	George Selk
Boy	Jay Hector
Clem	Clem Fuller
Story	Marian Clark
Script	John Meston
Director	Jesse Hibbs
Associate Producer	James Arness
Producer	Norman Macdonnell

September 10, 1960, preempted for *The Miss America Pageant.*

The Blacksmith. September 17, 1960. Production #30161 (154-206).
   Emil, Dodge City's good natured German blacksmith, marries Gretchen, a mail-order bride. During the wedding ceremony, Tolman, a local rancher and bully, disrupts the festivities. Later that evening, Tolman lures Emil away from his home and burns it. Infuriated, the slow to anger Emil finally lets Tolman have it.

Emil	George Kennedy
Tolman	Bob Anderson
Gretchen	Anna-Lisa
Willy	Wesley Lau
Spooner	Herb Patterson
Story	Norman Macdonnell
Script	John Meston

The Television Programs

Director	Andrew McLaglen
Associate Producer	James Arness
Producer	Norman Macdonnell

George Kennedy has appeared in numerous films and starred in the television series, *The Blue Knight*. He is an Oscar winner for *Cool Hand Luke*.

Small Water. September 24, 1960. Production #30162 (154-207).

Matt arrests Finn Pickett for murder and he and Chester head back to Dodge with their prisoner. On their long trip back, Matt and Chester encounter the vengeful Pickett brothers, who want to free their father.

Finn Pickett	Trevor Bardette
Leroy Pickett	Rex Holman
Seth Pickett	Warren Oates
Story, Script	John Meston
Director	Andrew McLaglen
Associate Producer	James Arness
Producer	Norman Macdonnell

Say Uncle. October 1, 1960. Production #30152 (154-197).

Young Lee Nagel believes that his shiftless Uncle Hutch deliberately caused the death of his father through a contrived accident. Since Lee's suspicions are unsubstantiated, Matt can do nothing. When Hutch begins courting Lee's widowed mother, Lee sets about to prove his theory.

Lee Nagel	Richard Rust
Hutch	Gene Nelson
Martin Nagel	Harry Lauter
Nancy Nagel	Dorothy Green
Story, Script	John Meston
Director	Andrew McLaglen
Associate Producer	James Arness
Producer	Norman Macdonnell

Shooting Stopover. October 8, 1960. Production #30157 (154-202).

Matt and Chester are on board when a gold-laden stagecoach is attacked by armed gunmen. The passengers, a young school teacher, a wanted killer, and a minister, are trapped by the bandits in a waystation without water.

Laura	Patricia Barry
Gurney	Anthony Caruso
Reverend	Paul Guilfoyle
Jim Buck	Robert Brubaker
Story	Marian Clark
Script	John Meston
Director	Andrew McLaglen
Associate Producer	James Arness
Producer	Norman Macdonnell

The Peace Officer. October 15, 1960. Production #30160 (154-205).

After Matt receives complaints about a corrupt sheriff in nearby Tascosa, he journeys to the town to investigate the allegations. When he confirms the reports of misconduct, he strips Clegg Rawlins of his badge. On his trip home, Matt is confronted by Stella, Rawlins' runaway girlfriend, who begs for protection from her ex-lover. The two set out for Dodge, and await the inevitable ambush by Rawlins and his men.

Stella	Susan Cummings
Clegg Rawlins	Lane Bradford
Ponce	John Zaccaro
Parks	Arthur Peterson, Jr.
Lighter	John Close
Shay	Gilman Rankin
Styles	Stafford Repp
Crowe	James Nusser
Story	Norman Macdonnell
Script	John Meston
Director	Jesse Hibbs
Associate Producer	James Arness
Producer	Norman Macdonnell

In 1957 Gilman Rankin played Deputy Riggs on the short-lived television Western *Tombstone Territory*.

Don Matteo. October 22, 1960. Production #30155 (154-200).

Matt attempts to dissuade Esteban Garcia, an old range-riding comrade, from gunning down the man who stole his wife. When Garcia persists in his actions, Matt realizes he must use force against his old friend.

Esteban Garcia	Lawrence Dobkin
Grave Tabor	Bing Russell
Calmers	Ben Wright
Trudy	Anne Whitfield
Bill Pence	Barney Phillips
Grimes	Roy Engle
Story	Marian Clark
Script	John Meston
Director	Jesse Hibbs
Associate Producer	James Arness
Producer	Norman Macdonnell

The Worm. October 29, 1960. Production #30158 (154-203).

Spadden, a brutish buffalo hunter, gets into a fight with a Dodge resident and Matt is forced to jail him. When Spadden is released, Ritchie, his badly abused cook, devises a scheme to rid himself of his monstrous boss once and for all. Unfortunately for Ritchie, his plans backfire.

Spadden	Kenneth Tobey
Cornet	H.M. Wynant
Ritchie	Ned Glass
Archer	Stewart Bradley
Judge	Gage Clark
Clerk	Howard Culver
Story, Script	John Meston
Director	Arthur Hiller
Associate Producer	James Arness
Producer	Norman Macdonnell

The Television Programs

Kenneth Tobey is familiar to television audiences as Chuck Martin of the adventure series *The Whirlybirds*.

November 5, 1960, preempted for a paid political broadcast.

The Badge. November 12, 1960. Production #30151 (154-196).
Matt is wounded, captured, and then is taken on a forced march by a madman named Rack and a simpleton named Augie, who are trying to elude a posse.

Rack	John Dehner
Augie	Conlan Carter
Mac	Allan Lane
Additional Cast	Harry Swoger, Michael Mikler
Story	Marian Clark
Script	John Meston
Director	Andrew McLaglen
Associate Producer	James Arness
Producer	Norman Macdonnell

The title *The Badge* was used again for an episode broadcast on February 2, 1970. The plots were not related. Conlan Carter has been seen on television as C.E. Carruthers on *The Law and Mr. Jones* and as Doc on *Combat*.

Distant Drummer. November 19, 1960. Production #30164 (154-209).
Two mule skinners have a grand old time tormenting a young army drummer named Raffie. They embarrass the young boy by forcing him to beat his drums on the streets of Dodge. When Raffie turns to Matt for help, the two skinners swear to get even with the boy. Later, when one skinner winds up dead, Raffie is held as a suspect.

Sloat	Bruce Gordon
Raffie	Jack Grinnage
Grade	George Mitchell
Moss	George Selk
Green	William Newell
Hugo	Phil Chambers
Story	Marian Clark
Script	John Meston
Director	Arthur Hiller
Associate Producer	James Arness
Producer	Norman Macdonnell

Ben Tolliver's Stud. November 26, 1960. Production #30154 (154-199).
Local rancher Jake Creed accuses Ben Tolliver, his young hired hand, of horse theft. The accusation follows an argument between Jake and Ben involving Creed's daughter Nancy, and Ben's refusal to use unnecessary roughness in breaking horses.

Ben Tolliver	John Lupton
Nancy Creed	Jean Ingram
Jake Creed	Roy Barcroft
Carl	Hank Patterson
Story	Norman Macdonnell
Script	John Meston
Director	Andrew McLaglen

GUNSMOKE — III. THE PROGRAMS

  Associate Producer .... James Arness
  Producer .... Norman Macdonnell

  John Lupton appeared on television in the Western *Broken Arrow* and as Dr. Tommy Horton on the soap opera *Days of Our Lives.* Roy Barcroft was featured on the popular *Mickey Mouse Club* serial, *The Adventures of Spin and Marty.*

No Chip. December 3, 1960. Production #30167 (154-212).
  The vicious Dolan brothers move in on tough cattle rancher Jeff Mossman and his non-violent son Pete. Mossman is a hard-as-nails rancher when it comes to the Dolan's cattle grazing on his property. Pete, on the other hand, does not believe in fighting. When the Dolans destroy Mossman's supplies and pour flour all over Pete, the boy refuses to put up a struggle. When the elder Mossman seeks retribution, he is shot. While he is recovering from his injury, the Dolans burn down his barn with Pete in it.

  Jeff Mossman .... John Hoyt
  Pete Mossman .... Rex Holman
  Hutch Dolan .... Leo Gordon
  Lee Dolan .... Guy Stockwell
  Grant .... Mark Allen
  Story, Script .... John Meston
  Director .... Jean Yarbrough
  Associate Producer .... James Arness
  Producer .... Norman Macdonnell

  Leo Gordon played Hank Miller in the television series *Circus Boy* and more recently, General Benton in the mini-series *The Winds of War.* In addition to his television credits, Gordon played character roles in numerous films including *Seven Angry Men,* which was directed by Charles Marquis Warren and featured Dennis Weaver in a supporting role. Gordon is also credited for writing a number of screenplays including *Tobruk,* in which he also played a part.

The Wake. December 10, 1960. Production #30165 (154-210). Originally scheduled for November 5, 1960.
  A drifter who calls himself Gus Mather brings Orson Boggs' corpse into Dodge for burial on Boot Hill and invites everyone to the wake. When questioned, Gus tells Doc that poor Orson died of "chills and ague." Matt senses that something is wrong and locates Mrs. Boggs who claims she has never heard of Mather. Concerned that there might have been foul play, Matt, Chester, and Doc exhume the body and are astounded by what they find.

  Gus Mather .... Denver Pyle
  Mrs. Boggs .... Anne Seymour
  Moss Grimmick .... George Selk
  Joe Brant .... Michael Hinn
  Story, Script .... John Meston
  Director .... Gerald H. Mayer
  Associate Producer .... James Arness
  Producer .... Norman Macdonnell

The Cook. December 17, 1960. Production #30171 (154-216).
  Drifter Sandy King takes a job at Delmonico's as a cook and suddenly business is booming. The young man has a natural ability and people begin lining up around the block to eat his tasty morsels. Everything seems to be going splendidly, until Sandy

The Television Programs

accidentally kills a crazy buffalo hunter named Ed Fisher. Frightened by the incident, Sandy flees. Matt catches the frightened youth and brings him back to Dodge for trial. However, some rowdy cowboys demand Sandy's release. He is the best cook Dodge has ever had and they will not be cheated of his cooking.

Sandy King	Guy Stockwell
Waiter	Gene Benton
Hank Green	Harry Swoger
Effie	Sue Randall
Jack Purdy	John Pickard
Ed Fisher	Ken Mayer
Gus	Tom Greenway
Joe Grisim	John Milford
Pete	Brad Trumbull
Joe	Craig Duncan
Cowboy	Sam Woody
Story, Script	John Meston
Director	Ted Post
Associate Producer	James Arness
Producer	Norman Macdonnell

Sue Randall played the recurring role of Miss Landers on *Leave It to Beaver*. Guy Stockwell was a regular on *Adventures in Paradise* and *The Richard Boone Show*.

Old Fool. December 24, 1960. Production #30166 (154-211).

Middle-aged widow Elsie Hedgepeth seeks to break up the marriage of Hannibal and Della Bass, an elderly couple living on a comfortable ranch on the outskirts of Dodge. When Hannibal asks Della for a divorce, she takes a surprisingly drastic step.

Hannibal Bass	Buddy Ebsen
Della Bass	Hope Summers
Elsie Hedgepeth	Linda Watkins
Additional Cast	Hampton Fancher
Story, Script	John Meston
Director	Ted Post
Associate Producer	James Arness
Producer	Norman Macdonnell

Buddy Ebsen is a familiar face on television having played Jed Clampett of *The Beverly Hillbillies* and the title role in *Barnaby Jones*.

Brother Love. December 31, 1960. Production #30163 (154-208).

A fatally wounded shopkeeper identifies his murderer by his last name only. Mrs. Cumbers, the mother of two brothers who bear that name is determined that the guilty son shall pay the death penalty, but not at the hands of an outsider.

Mrs. Cumbers	Lurene Tuttle
Nate Cumbers	Kevin Hagen
Frank Cumbers	Gene Lyons
Gus	Jack Grinnage
Polly	Jan Harrison
Jonas	Dabbs Greer
Clem	Clem Fuller
Story, Script	John Meston
Director	Franklin Adreon

GUNSMOKE — III. THE PROGRAMS

Associate Producer .... James Arness
Producer .... Norman Macdonnell

Gene Lyons is best remembered for his role as Commissioner Dennis Randall on the television series *Ironside*.

Bad Sheriff. January 7, 1961. Production #30153 (154-198).

Hark and Turloe ambush and capture a stage coach bandit named Gance, hoping to steal his loot. When Matt and Chester, who have been trailing Gance come across the ambushers, Hark and Turloe pose as a lawman and his deputy.

Hark .... Russell Arms
Turloe .... Harry Carey, Jr.
Gance .... Kenneth Lynch
Chet .... Don Keefer
Sam .... Lane Chandler
Story, Script .... John Meston
Director .... Andrew McLaglen
Associate Producer .... James Arness
Producer .... Norman Macdonnell

Russell Arms is best known as the singer for *Your Hit Parade*.

Unloaded Gun. January 14, 1961. Production #30159 (154-204).

Matt sets out to catch the murderous Lime brothers but is successful in killing only one. Before he is able to bring the second brother to justice, Matt is stricken with a raging fever and must return to Dodge. While in Dodge, and still desperately ill, Matt must face the vengeful gun of the surviving brother.

Joe Lime .... William Redfield
Red Lime .... Lew Brown
Bob Carter .... Greg Dunn
Carl Miller .... Hank Patterson
Harry .... James Malcolm
Clem .... Clem Fuller
Boy .... Bobby Goodwins
Townsman .... Rik Nervik
Story .... Marian Clark
Script .... John Meston
Director .... Jesse Hibbs
Associate Producer .... James Arness
Producer .... Norman Macdonnell

William Redfield had quite a diversified show business career. He was active on the Broadway stage, appearing in such productions as *Hamlet* with Richard Burton and John Gielgud. His film credits include *One Flew Over the Cuckoo's Nest*. In addition, he was a founding member of the Actor's Studio.

Tall Trapper. January 21, 1961. Production #30175 (154-220).

Ben, a solitary trapper, offers a night's hospitality to Rowley and his wife Tassie. Ben and Tassie seem to have an affinity towards each other, something that Tassie's gruff husband objects to. Ben is jailed on suspicion of murder when Tassie is found brutally beaten to death.

Ben .... Tom Reese
Rowley .... Strother Martin

The Television Programs

Tassie	Jan Shepard
Story	Marian Clark
Script	John Meston
Director	Harry Harris, Jr.
Associate Producer	James Arness
Producer	Norman Macdonnell

Love Thy Neighbor. January 28, 1961. Production #30169 (154-214).

A misunderstanding regarding a sack of stolen potatoes results in a feud that ends in tragedy for two families.

Rose	Jeanette Nolan
Ben	Jack Elam
Leroy	Kenneth Lynch
Harley	Dean Stanton
Jep	Warren Oates
Jennie	Nora Marlowe
Peter	David Kent
Sy Tewksbury	Cyril Delevanti
Man	Wayne West
Story, Script	John Meston
Director	Dennis Weaver
Associate Producer	James Arness
Producer	Norman Macdonnell

Dennis Weaver made his directorial debut with this episode.

Bad Seed. February 4, 1961. Production #30177 (154-222).

Matt rescues Trudy, a beautiful young girl, from an incestuous and abusive father. He brings Trudy back to Dodge with him, only to find she has her mind set on marrying him. When Matt scorns Trudy's advances she reacts by slandering his good name.

Trudy	Anne Helm
Asa	Roy Barcroft
Gar	Burt Douglas
Story	Norman Macdonnell
Script	John Meston
Director	Harry Harris, Jr.
Associate Producer	James Arness
Producer	Norman Macdonnell

Kitty Shot. February 11, 1961. Production #30170 (154-215).

Kitty is seriously wounded by a stray bullet during a gunfight between Jake Baylor and his partner. With his partner dead, Baylor flees and Matt sets out in cold fury to find him. In his pursuit, Matt discovers that he is not the only one gunning for Baylor.

Jake Baylor	George Kennedy
Bill Pence	Joseph Mell
Helm	Rayford Barnes
Additional Cast	Lew Brown
Story, Script	John Meston
Director	Andrew McLaglen

GUNSMOKE — III. THE PROGRAMS

Associate Producer .... James Arness
Producer .... Norman Macdonnell

February 18, 1961, preempted for *Dupont Show of the Month*, "Lincoln Murder Case."

About Chester. February 25, 1961. Production #30176 (154-221).

Matt and Chester set out to find Doc, who has been missing for four days. They split up to follow two different paths. Matt's path leads him to Doc, who has been ill and is recovering at a friend's ranch. Chester's trail leads him to a horse thief, who ties Chester up and plans to kill him.

   Lilymae .... Mary Munday
   Dack .... Charles Aidman
   Cluney .... George Eldridge
   Jake .... House Peters, Jr.
   Bowers .... Harry Shannon
   Story .... Frank Paris
   Script .... John Meston
   Director .... Alan Crosland, Jr.
   Associate Producer .... James Arness
   Producer .... Norman Macdonnell

Frank Paris was an assistant to Norman Macdonnell in the radio version of *Gunsmoke* and in later years he became an associate producer for the television show.

Harriet. March 4, 1961. Production #30172 (154-217).

Harriet Horne is a young woman who watched helplessly as her father was murdered. She vows vengeance and takes a job at the Long Branch, hoping that the killers will eventually appear.

   Harriet Horne .... Suzanne Lloyd
   Dan Scorp .... Tom Reese
   Hoagler .... Ron Hayes
   Howard .... Howard Culver
   James Horne .... Joseph Hamilton
   Story, Script .... John Meston
   Director .... Gene Fowler, Jr.
   Associate Producer .... James Arness
   Producer .... Norman Macdonnell

Potshot. March 11, 1961. Production #30185 (154-230).

Chester is seriously wounded by an unseen rifleman. Matt suspects a pair of bank robbers who have been expected in Dodge, but he is baffled when he learns that neither of the men was in town at the time of the shooting.

   Hutch Dawkins .... Karl Swenson
   Mr. Botkin .... Gage Clark
   Bill Pence .... Joseph Mell
   Bert .... Dallas Mitchell
   Additional Cast .... Barton Heyman, Wallace Rooney,
   .... Michael Harris, John Harmon
   Story, Script .... John Meston
   Director .... Harry Harris, Jr.
   Associate Producer .... James Arness
   Producer .... Norman Macdonnell

The Television Programs

Old Faces. March 18, 1961. Production #30184 (154-229).

Tilda Cook is a pretty young bride with a secret past that she has kept hidden from her husband Tom. When a cattleman recognizes Tilda to be an ex-entertainer from a Mississippi River boat, he makes insulting remarks to Tom. The scandalized husband reacts by challenging the man to a gunfight to defend his wife's honor.

Tom Cook	James Drury
Tilda Cook	Jan Shepard
Ed Ivers	George Keymas
Milt Varden	Ron Hayes
Jim Buck	Robert Brubaker
Sam	Glenn Strange
Story, Script	John Meston
Director	Harry Harris
Associate Producer	James Arness
Producer	Norman Macdonnell

Although Glenn Strange plays Sam the bartender in this episode, it is not until the following season that Sam becomes a regular.

Big Man. March 25, 1961. Production #30188 (154-233).

Matt is accused of murder when Pat Swarner, a tough, raw-boned cowpuncher who has designs on Kitty, is found beaten to death in an alley. A down-and-out farmer, whom Matt had befriended, is the only witness to the murder. Ironically, he points to Matt as the killer.

Pat Swarner	George Kennedy
Jud Sloan	John McLiam
Mike	Chris Alcaide
Ak	Sandy Kenyon
Harry	Rayford Barnes
Pence	Barney Phillips
Cowboy	Steve Warren
Dick	James Nusser
Joe	Mathew McCue
Story, Script	John Meston
Director	Gerald Mayer
Associate Producer	James Arness
Producer	Norman Macdonnell

Big Man was the last half-hour episode filmed.

Little Girl. April 1, 1961. Production #30179(89) (154-224).

Matt and Chester stumble upon an orphaned ten-year-old girl in the ruins of a burned down cabin. Matt takes little Charity Gill back to Dodge with him, hoping to find her a good home. However, his efforts are complicated by the fact that nearly the entire female population of Dodge has gone on a pilgrimage to Wichita to a women's suffrage meeting. Undaunted by the situation, little Charity adopts Matt as her temporary father.

Charity Gill	Susan Gordon
Hi Stevens	Wright King
Rafe	Bill McLean
Albie	Doc Douglas
Story	Kathleen Hite

GUNSMOKE — III. THE PROGRAMS

Script	John Meston
Director	Dennis Weaver
Associate Producer	James Arness
Producer	Norman Macdonnell

Dennis Weaver's children Ricky, Bobby and Rusty, and Wright King's children Megan, Michael, and Rip play the Stevens' children. Dennis Weaver once again sat in the director's chair for this episode.

Stolen Horses. April 8, 1961. Production #30174 (154-219).

Matt and Chester trail a horse thief and killer. The job of tracking the murderer becomes more difficult after the killer takes a poor farmer hostage.

Jim Redigo	Buck Young
Mrs. Kurtch	Shirley O'Hara
Tebow	Jack Lambert
Abe	Guy Raymond
Chief Quick Knife	Henry Brandon
Jed Cuff	Charles Seel
Acker	Alex Sharp
Brave	Eddie Little Sky
Story	Norman Macdonnell
Script	John Meston
Director	Andrew McLaglen
Associate Producer	James Arness
Producer	Norman Macdonnell

Charles Seel is known to viewers in later episodes as Barney the telegraph agent. Guy Raymond portrayed Martin Perkins on the comedy *Ichabod and Me.*

Minnie. April 15, 1961. Production #30183 (154-228).

Minnie Higgins, the wife of a jealous buffalo skinner, arrives in Dodge with a suspicious gunshot wound. After Doc treats Minnie she falls in love with him, and begins courting the unwilling Doc. An unusual triangle develops while Matt is out of town, as the "wronged" husband arrives on the scene and vows to kill Doc. It is up to Chester to avert the violence.

Minnie Higgins	Virginia Gregg
Jake Higgins	Alan Hale, Jr.
Moss Grimmick	George Selk
Pence	Joseph Mell
Pete	Barry Cahill
Hank	Robert Human
Joe	Mathew McCue
Story, Script	John Meston
Director	Harry Harris, Jr.
Associate Producer	James Arness
Producer	Norman Macdonnell

Alan Hale, Jr. is best known for his portrayal of the Skipper on the television comedy *Gilligan's Island.*

Bless Me Till I Die. April 22, 1961. Production #30186 (154-231).

Cole Treadwell, a young would-be doctor, runs into trouble when he and his wife Beth settle temporarily in Dodge. No sooner does the couple arrive, that a drunken

The Television Programs

saddle tramp, Nate Bush, spooks their horses by firing his gun recklessly into the streets. However, that is just the beginning of their troubles, for Nate informs Matt that he recognizes Treadwell to be the escaped convict Cole Trankin. When Matt follows up on Nate's story, it proves to be correct.

Cole Treadwell	Ronald Foster
Beth Treadwell	Phyllis Love
Nate Bush	Vic Perrin
Jonas	Dabbs Greer
Story	Ray Kemper
Script	John Meston
Director	Ted Post
Associate Producer	James Arness
Producer	Norman Macdonnell

Ray Kemper was integrally involved in radio's *Gunsmoke* as a master sound technician.

Long Hours, Short Pay. April 29, 1961. Production #30173 (154-218).

While attempting to capture Serpa, a man who has been selling guns to the Indians, Matt is taken prisoner by the same Indians.

Serpa	John Larch
Little Fox	Lalo Rios
Crooked Knife	Frank Sentry
Captain Graves	Allan Lane
Squaw	Dawn Little Sky
Sergeant	Steve Warren
Tracker	Fred McDougall
Story, Script	John Meston
Director	Andrew McLaglen
Associate Producer	James Arness
Producer	Norman Macdonnell

Hard Virtue. May 6, 1961. Production #30178 (154-223).

Andy Coe, a jealous husband, vows to kill the man he suspects has been seeing his pretty wife Millie. In an attempt to prevent bloodshed, Matt tries to discover the identity of the man before Andy does.

Andy Coe	Lew Brown
Millie Coe	Lia Waggner
Ed Fallon	Robert Karnes
Jenkins	James Maloney
Moss	George Selk
Story, Script	John Meston
Director	Dennis Weaver
Associate Producer	James Arness
Producer	Norman Macdonnell

The Imposter. May 13, 1961. Production #30180(90) (154-225).

Ab Stringer arrives in Dodge claiming to be a sheriff from Texas trailing a wanted killer. Matt agrees to assist the stranger, but becomes concerned when the case involves Rob Curtin, a respected Dodge citizen.

Mrs. Curtin	Virginia Gregg

GUNSMOKE — III. THE PROGRAMS

Ab Stringer .... Harp McGuire
Rob Curtin .... Paul Langton
Harve Peters .... Garry Walberg
Story .... Kathleen Hite
Script .... John Meston
Director .... Byron Paul
Associate Producer .... James Arness
Producer .... Norman Macdonnell

Chester's Dilemma. May 20, 1961. Production #30187 (154-232).

Chester becomes infatuated with pretty Edna Walstrom. Unfortunately for Chester, Edna's interests are not reciprocal. She is only concerned with Chester's daily deliveries of Matt's official mail. When a letter from Hans Gruber arrives and mysteriously disappears, Chester is forced to confront Edna.

Edna Walstrom .... Patricia Smith
Hans Gruber .... John Van Dreelen
Story .... Vic Perrin
Script .... John Meston
Director .... Ted Post
Associate Producer .... James Arness
Producer .... Norman Macdonnell

Vic Perrin, an actor who appeared on both the radio and television versions of *Gunsmoke,* created the scenario for this episode.

The Love of Money. May 27, 1961. Production #30182 (154-227).

An ex-marshal who turned in his badge because of fear, is murdered by an unseen assassin. Motivated only by her "love of money," Boni Van Deman, a hostess at the Long Branch, aids Matt in his search to find the killer.

Boni Van Deman .... Cloris Leachman
Nate Tatham .... Warren Kemmerling
Myles Cody .... Tod Andrews
Story, Script .... John Meston
Director .... Ted Post
Associate Producer .... James Arness
Producer .... Norman Macdonnell

Melinda Miles. June 3, 1961. Production #30181 (154-226).

Melinda Miles and Tom Potter plan on marrying. However, their marriage is opposed by Melinda's father Harry, and Harry's foreman Ray Tayloe, who wants Melinda for himself. When Tayloe is murdered, Matt considers Potter a suspect with a strong motive.

Tom Potter .... Burt Douglas
Melinda Miles .... Diana Millay
Harry Miles .... Walter Sande
Ray Tayloe .... Charles Gray
Rand .... Rand Brooks
Moss .... George Selk
Man .... Glenn Strange
Story, Script .... John Meston
Director .... William Dario Faralla

The Television Programs

```
Associate Producer ............................. James Arness
Producer ...................................... Norman Macdonnell
```

Glenn Strange, who in later shows played Sam the barkeep, plays the part of a disgruntled poker player. Rand Brooks played Scarlett O'Hara's unfortunate first husband in *Gone With the Wind*. After that blockbuster he went on to perform in mostly B-movies, several of which were "Hopalong Cassidy" features. On television Rand played Corporal Boone on *The Adventures of Rin Tin Tin*.

Never Pester Chester. June 10, 1961, rerun. First aired November 16, 1957.

Colorado Sheriff. June 17, 1961. Production #30168 (154-213).

Matt locks horns with a stubborn sheriff from Colorado. The man is determined to arrest a wounded cowboy, even though he has no warrant. Matt feels obligated to stop the sheriff, unless he can come up with the appropriate papers to prove his allegations.

```
Ben Witter .................................... Robert Karnes
Rod Ellison ................................... Wright King
Sam Jones ..................................... Kelton Garwood
Milton Myles .................................. Wayne West
Story, Script ................................. John Meston
Director ...................................... Jesse Hibbs
Associate Producer ............................ James Arness
Producer ...................................... Norman Macdonnell
```

Kelton Garwood is also known as John Harper, who portrayed Percy Crump, Dodge City's busy undertaker.

Doc's Reward. June 24, 1961, rerun. First aired December 14, 1957.

Brush at Elkader. July 1, 1961, rerun. First aired September 15, 1956.

Monopoly. July 8, 1961, rerun. First aired October 4, 1958.

July 15, 1961, preempted for "The Miss Universe Pageant."

Kitty Caught. July 22, 1961, rerun. First aired January 18, 1958.

Wild West. July 29, 1961, rerun. First aired February 15, 1958.

Claustrophobia. August 5, 1961, rerun. First aired January 25, 1958.

Joke's On Us. August 12, 1961, rerun. First aired March 15, 1958.

Sunday Supplement. August 19, 1961, rerun. First aired February 8, 1958.

Laughing Gas. August 26, 1961, rerun. First aired March 29, 1958.

Kitty's Rebellion. September 2, 1961, rerun. First aired February 7, 1959.

Marshal Proudfoot. September 16, 1961, rerun. First aired January 10, 1959.

Jayhawkers. September 23, 1961, rerun. First aired January 31, 1959.

GUNSMOKE — III. THE PROGRAMS

SEVENTH SEASON

Now an hour

Perce. September 30, 1961. Production #31004. Rerun August 11, 1962.

Reformed hold-up man Perce McCall falls in love with Ida, a saloon girl with an eye for easy money. Matt attempts to dissuade Perce from pursuing Ida, but when his advice is ignored, violence erupts.

Perce McCall	Ed Nelson
Withers	Chuck Bail
Ida	Norma Crane
Seeber	Kenneth Lynch
Jim Buck	Robert Brubaker
Louie Pheeters	James Nusser
Norm	John Mitchum
Kemp	Chuck Hayward
Vicks	Baynes Barron
Nickels	Alex Sharp
Del	Ted Jordan
Story, Script	John Meston
Director	Harry Harris, Jr.
Associate Producer	Frank Paris
Producer	Norman Macdonnell

Ted Jordan, who plays the part of freight agent Nathan Burke in later episodes, has a cameo role. James Nusser appears as Louie Pheeters, Dodge's resident town drunk, for the first time.

Old Yellow Boots. October 7, 1961. Production #31005. Rerun October 10, 1962.

A young rancher named Leroy Parker is murdered and the only clue Matt has is the heel print from an old boot. Parker's sister Beulah inherits the ranch after his death, and when drifter Frank Cassidy suddenly displays a romantic interest in Beulah, Matt becomes suspicious.

Cassidy	Warren Stevens
Beulah Parker	Joanne Linville
Leroy Parker	Dean Stanton
Additional Cast	Steve Brodie, Bing Russell
Story, Script	John Meston
Director	Ted Post
Associate Producer	Frank Paris
Producer	Norman Macdonnell

Both Warren Stevens and Joanne Linville were regulars on the short-lived television series *Behind the Screen*. Steve Brodie played Sheriff Behan on *The Life and Legend of Wyatt Earp*.

Miss Kitty. October 14, 1961. Production #31002. Rerun June 16, 1962.

Kitty rides out of Dodge at three in the morning, and keeps her destination a secret, completely mystifying Matt, Chester, and Doc. Their bewilderment and concern is further intensified when they learn that a woman answering Kitty's description was seen at a stagecoach relay station a short distance from Dodge, and then rode off accompanied by a small boy.

[528]

The Television Programs

Thad	Roger Mobley
Horace	Harold Stone
Mattie	Linda Watkins
Tucker	John Lasell
Charlie	Frank Sutton
Driver	Joseph Breen
Proprietor	Andy Albin
Story, Script	Kathleen Hite
Director	Harry Harris, Jr.
Associate Producer	Frank Paris
Producer	Norman Macdonnell

Frank Sutton is best remembered for his portrayal of Sgt. Vince Carter of *Gomer Pyle, U.S.M.C.*

Harper's Blood. October 21, 1961. Production #31007.

A father believes that his two sons have inherited the bad blood of their great-grandfather, who was a notorious killer. His revelation leads to an unexpected hanging.

Gip Cooley	Peter Whitney
Kyle Cooley	Dan Stafford
Jeff Cooley	Conlan Carter
Sarah Cooley	Moira Turner
Additional Cast	Evan Evans, Warren Kemmerling
Story, Script	John Meston
Director	Andrew McLaglen
Associate Producer	Frank Paris
Producer	Norman Macdonnell

Peter Whitney is another actor with the dubious honor of having been born in Long Branch, New Jersey, for which the real Long Branch saloon was named.

All That. October 28, 1961. Production #31013. Rerun July 7, 1962.

Rancher Cliff Shanks is forced into the rough, uncertain life of gold prospecting after he loses his cattle, his land and his wife. He returns to Dodge with his buddy Print Quimby, and tries an old ruse, which tests the friendship of the people who think he has struck it rich.

Cliff Shanks	John Larch
Print Quimby	Buddy Ebsen
Clara Shanks	Frances Helm
Additional Cast	Harry Lauter, Guy Raymond
Story, Script	John Meston
Director	Harry Harris, Jr.
Associate Producer	Frank Paris
Producer	Norman Macdonnell

Long, Long Trail November 4, 1961. Production #31015. Rerun June 23, 1962.

Sarah Drew, a beautiful young woman from Boston, pursuades Matt to take her on a perilous journey to meet her fiance. Along the way the dangers include a prairie fire, an Indian attack, and a very strong mutual attraction.

Sarah Drew	Barbara Lord
Farmer	Alan Baxter

GUNSMOKE — III. THE PROGRAMS

Gody	Mabel Albertson
Additional Cast	Peggy Stewart
Story, Script	Kathleen Hite
Director	Andrew McLaglen
Associate Producer	Frank Paris
Producer	Norman Macdonnell

Mabel Albertson, the sister of character actor Jack Albertson, was a great character actor in her own right. She appeared in numerous television programs and films, primarily as a wisecracking mother or grandmother.

The Squaw. November 11, 1961. Production #31008. Rerun August 4, 1962.

Well-to-do widower Hardy Tate takes for his second wife a young Indian woman named Natacea. Cully, Tate's son from his first wife, is taken aback by his father's marriage to this "heathen," and the hot-tempered youth reacts violently.

Hardy Tate	John Dehner
Natacea	Vitina Marcus
Cully Tate	Paul Carr
Story, Script	John Dunkel
Director	Gerald H. Mayer
Associate Producer	Frank Paris
Producer	Norman Macdonnell

The title *The Squaw* was used again January 6, 1975.

Chesterland. November 18, 1961. Production #31006.

Chester falls in love with pretty Daisy Fair and decides to get married. Before his bride will say "I do," however, Chester must provide a home and prove that he can earn a decent living. The love-smitten suitor digs an underground home and takes up farming on an arid unyielding piece of Kansas ground. Daisy does not take very kindly to living underground and Chester's rosy view of the future is dimmed, until he strikes water. It appears that Chester will become a man of means, and Daisy's ardor is fanned until the well dries up.

Daisy Fair	Sondra Kerr
Tubby	Earle Hodgins
William	Harold Innocent
Arny	Arthur Peterson, Jr.
Ma Smalley	Sarah Selby
Story, Script	Kathleen Hite
Director	Ted Post
Associate Producer	Frank Paris
Producer	Norman Macdonnell

Chesterland is one of Dennis Weaver's favorite episodes, and rightly so. It is a tour-de-force for Chester fans. Sarah Selby plays the recurring character of Ma Smalley, the owner of a clean, modest, affordable boarding house in Dodge, a sensible alternative to the more expensive Dodge House. Selby was also featured as Miss Thomas on *Father Knows Best*.

Milly. November 25, 1961. Production #31003. Rerun July 27, 1963.

Seventeen-year-old Milly Glover decides to marry the first available man. Her father has been negligent and Milly is determined to provide for herself and her younger brother Joey, and marriage seems the only solution. Milly heads for Dodge

The Television Programs

where she finds several eligible, but undesirable candidates. When they reject her advances Milly vows to get even.

Milly	Jena Engstrom
Joey	Billy Hughes
Bart Glover	Malcolm Atterbury
Additional Cast	Sue Randall, Don Dubbins
Story	Hal Moffett
Script	John Meston
Director	Richard Whorf
Associate Producer	Frank Paris
Producer	Norman Macdonnell

Indian Ford. December 2, 1961. Production #31001.

Matt and Chester accompany a cavalry troop to negotiate for the freedom of Mary Tabor, a white woman who has been held captive by Arapahoe Indians. Negotiations are difficult, however, because Spotted Wolf, Mary's "owner," refuses to give her up.

Captain Benter	R.G. Armstrong
Mary Tabor	Pippa Scott
Spotted Wolf	Robert Dix
Tabor	Roy Roberts
Lone Eagle	Anthony Caruso
Sgt. Cromwell	John Newton
Trumbull	Lane Chandler
Indian Woman	Dawn Little Sky
Story, Script	John Dunkel
Director	Andrew McLaglen
Associate Producer	Frank Paris
Producer	Norman Macdonnell

Roy Roberts is no stranger to television. In addition to playing the recurring role of Mr. Bodkin for the final ten years of *Gunsmoke,* Roberts played regulars in numerous other television programs including Captain Huxley on *The Gale Storm Show* and Harrison Cheever of *The Lucy Show*. R.G. Armstrong, burly character actor and frequent visitor on *Gunsmoke,* has been featured on various television programs and feature films including *The Fugitive Kid* and *Heaven Can Wait*.

Apprentice Doc. December 9, 1961. Production #31009. Rerun June 30, 1962.

Doc is kidnapped to treat a wounded outlaw. In the process, he befriends one of his abductors, Pitt, a bright young man who wants to study medicine. After the incident, Pitt approaches Doc to become his apprentice. Doc agrees to the arrangement and is impressed by Pitt's skill. However, tragedy threatens when the youth's former companions seek him out.

Pitt	Ben Cooper
Clint	Crahan Denton
Augie	Robert Sorrells
Story, Script	Kathleen Hite
Director	Harry Harris, Jr.
Associate Producer	Frank Paris
Producer	Norman Macdonnell

Ben Cooper's film career includes *The Rose Tattoo* and *Support Your Local Gunfighter*.

GUNSMOKE — III. THE PROGRAMS

Nina's Revenge. December 16, 1961. Production #31010. Rerun July 25, 1964.

Rancher Lee Sharky tries to frame his wife Nina and Jim Garza, his hired-hand, in a plot to extort money from Nina's wealthy father. However, his plan backfires when he learns that Nina and Jim have fallen in love.

Nina Sharky	Lois Nettleton
Lee Sharky	William Windom
Jim Garza	Ron Foster
Sam	Glenn Strange
Friend	Quentin Sondergaard
Harry Blucher	Johnny Seven
Story, Script	John Meston
Director	Tay Garnett
Associate Producer	Frank Paris
Producer	Norman Macdonnell

Lois Nettleton won an Emmy in 1977 for *The American Woman: Portraits of Courage* and another in 1983 for *Insight*. William Windom, also an Emmy Award recipient won his in 1970 for *My World and Welcome to It*. Johnny Seven played Lt. Carl Reese on *Ironside*. Screenwriter-director Tay Garnett began his career writing jokes for Mack Sennett and Hal Roach. His films include *The Postman Always Rings Twice* with Lana Turner and John Garfield.

Marry Me. December 23, 1961. Production #31016. Rerun July 28, 1962.

Orkey Cathcart heads into Dodge to find a bride, and winds up at the Long Branch. Much to Kitty's astonishment, she learns that Orkey has "chosen" her to be his wife. Since his younger brother, Sweet Billy, is already engaged, family custom demands that the eldest son marry first. When Kitty refuses his proposal, she is abducted by the Cathcart clan and is whisked away to be courted.

Orkey Cathcart	Don Dubbins
Sweet Billy	Warren Oates
Pa Cathcart	Taylor McPeters
Sam	Glenn Strange
Story, Script	Kathleen Hite
Director	Dennis Weaver
Associate Producer	Frank Paris
Producer	Norman Macdonnell

This episode is one of writer Kathleen Hite's favorites and one of Amanda Blake's and Dennis Weaver's favorites as well.

A Man a Day. December 30, 1961. Production #31019. Rerun July 21, 1962.

A band of ruthless outlaws try to lure Matt away from Dodge so that they can steal a large gold shipment. When Matt refuses to leave, the gang begins to carry out a brutal ultimatum. They will kill a man a day until the marshal departs.

Cooner	Val Dufour
Bessie	Fay Spain
Grice	Leonard Nimoy
Story, Script	John Meston
Director	Harry Harris, Jr.
Associate Producer	Frank Paris
Producer	Norman Macdonnell

Leonard Nimoy has been praised for his directorial skills for such films as *Three Men*

The Television Programs

and a Baby. However, he will always be known for his role as the Vulcan, Mr. Spock, in *Star Trek.*

The Do-Badder. January 6, 1962. Production #31012.

Gold prospector Harvey Easter takes it upon himself to reform the citizens of Dodge. His crusading efforts, however, lead to unhappy results for saloon girl Mary Picket, two cowboys, Bunch and Kelly, and finally for Easter as well.

Harvey Easter	Abraham Sofaer
Gene Bunch	Strother Martin
Chris Kelly	Warren Oates
Mary Picket	Mercedes Shirley
Additional Cast	Adam Williams, Roy Engle, Harry Bartell
Story, Script	John Meston
Director	Andrew McLaglen
Associate Producer	Frank Paris
Producer	Norman Macdonnell

Lacey. January 13, 1962. Production #31017. Rerun August 25, 1962.

Beautiful Lacey Parcher has her mind set on marrying a handsome farmhand, but her father objects vehemently to the union. When Cyrus Parcher is found murdered, Lacey confesses to the killing. Matt is forced to jail the young woman, who soon finds that she has even greater trouble to look forward to.

Lacey Parcher	Sherry Jackson
Jess Ayley	Jeremy Slate
Ellen Parcher	Dorothy Green
Cyrus Parcher	Oliver McGowan
Additional Cast	Norah Hayden
Story, Script	Kathleen Hite
Director	Harry Harris, Jr.
Associate Producer	Frank Paris
Producer	Norman Macdonnell

Sherry Jackson played Danny Thomas' daughter in *Make Room for Daddy.*

Cody's Code. January 20, 1962. Production #31023.

Cody Durham is considered to be one of Dodge's most respected citizens. When he harbors a wounded outlaw who Matt has been trailing, Cody receives bitter repayment for his kindness. The outlaw sets his sights on Rose Loring, Cody's girlfriend.

Cody Durham	Anthony Caruso
Sam Dukes	Robert Knapp
Rose Loring	Gloria Talbott
Brach	Wayne Rogers
Story, Script	John Meston
Director	Andrew McLaglen
Associate Producer	Frank Paris
Producer	Norman Macdonnell

Character actor Anthony Caruso appeared in such films as *Johnny Apollo, Watch on the Rhine,* and *The Asphalt Jungle.*

Old Dan. January 27, 1962. Production #31022.

Doc tackles the difficult task of trying to rehabilitate Dan Witter, a long time

GUNSMOKE — III. THE PROGRAMS

alcoholic. Old Dan makes a determined effort. He takes a job as a hired hand on Lem Petch's ranch, and life begins to take on a new meaning for him. In his struggle for sobriety, however, Dan runs into an obstacle in the form of Luke Petch, Lem's no-good son.

Dan Witter	Edgar Buchanan
Lem Petch	Philip Coolidge
Luke Petch	William Campbell
Mr. Jonas	Dabbs Greer
Thede	Hugh Sanders
Mrs. Bales	Dorothy Neumann
Gates	Joe Haworth
Story, Script	Kathleen Hite
Director	Andrew McLaglen
Associate Producer	Frank Paris
Producer	Norman Macdonnell

Old-timer Edgar Buchanan is a familiar face in films and television. Among his many credits he played Red Connors, Hopalong Cassidy's sidekick. In later years he was seen as kindly old Uncle Joe in *Petticoat Junction*. Few people know, however, that he started out as a dentist. For a time, William Campbell played the role of Luke Fuller on *Dynasty*. He moved on to the part of Detective Joey Indelli on *Crime Story*.

February 3, 1962, preempted for *Westinghouse Presents*.

Catawomper. February 10, 1962. Production #31020. Rerun August 18, 1962.

Headstrong Kate Tassel quarrels with her boyfriend Bud Bones during a "sociable," after which Kate invites suitors to come calling. Bud tries to discourage the young men from courting her, but eventually frustrated by his lack of success, he gives up. This happens just about the same time that Chester learns about Kate's home cooking. Encouraged by Kate, Chester starts to court her, but the young woman is not interested in Chester romantically. She wants him to teach her to play the guitar. This way she can run away, become a saloon entertainer, and teach Bud a lesson.

Kate Tassel	Sue Ane Langdon
Bud Bones	Dick Sargent
Bert Tassel	Roy Wright
Olie	Frank Sutton
Lt.	Robert Brubaker
George	Harold Innocent
Hank	Quentin Sondergaard
Pete	Warren Vanders
Jester	Joe Devlin
Sgt.	Jay Overholts
Wit	Robert Gravage
Story	Gil Favor
Script	John Meston
Director	Harry Harris, Jr.
Associate Producer	Frank Paris
Producer	Norman Macdonnell

Dick Sargent played Samantha's befuddled husband, Darrin, on *Bewitched*. Sue Ane Langdon appeared as a regular on a number of series including *Bachelor Father*, *The Jackie Gleason Show*, and *Arnie*.

The Television Programs

Half Straight. February 17, 1962. Production #31026. Rerun June 15, 1963.

Gunslinger Lute Willis has been employed to kill Matt. However, plans go awry when Lute falls in love with Fanny Fields. Further complications arise when Lute hires someone else to do the job for him.

Lute Willis	John Kerr
Fanny Fields	Elizabeth MacRae
Hank Browder	William Bramley
Additional Cast	J. Edward McKinley
Story, Script	John Meston
Director	Ted Post
Associate Producer	Frank Paris
Producer	Norman Macdonnell

John Kerr played the sensitive young man opposite Deborah Kerr in the film *Tea and Sympathy.* His other film credits include that of Lt. Cable in *South Pacific.* Among Elizabeth MacRae's television credits are several daytime dramas including *General Hospital,* where she played nurse Meg Baldwin. Her films include *The Conversation.*

He Learned About Women. February 24, 1962. Production #31014. Rerun September 9, 1962.

Chester is taken prisoner by a ruthless gang of comancheros. With the help of a beautiful half-breed named Chavela, the two manage to escape. However, Solis, the leader of the renegades hunts them down. When Chester and Chavela are finally cornered, Chester learns a dramatic lesson about love and self-sacrifice.

Chavela	Barbara Luna
Solis	Claude Akins
Ab Rankin	Robert Wilke
Kisla	Miriam Colin
Garvey	Ted de Corsia
Red	Jeff De Benning
Ru	Susan Petrone
Guard	Val Ruffino
Jose	Andy Romano
Juan	Joseph Ferrante
Pepe	Miguel d'Anda
Story	John Rosser
Script	John Meston
Director	Tay Garnett
Associate Producer	Frank Paris
Producer	Norman Macdonnell

Being of Hungarian-Phillippine descent, Barbara Luna has played primarily exotic beauties in films. Her credits include *Ship of Fools* and *The Devil at 4 O'Clock.* She was married to television actor Doug McClure of *The Virginian* and screen actor Alan Arkin. Character actor Ted de Corsia appeared in such films as *The Naked City* and *A Place in the Sun.*

The Gallows. March 3, 1962. Production #31028. Rerun September 14, 1963.

In this particularly dark and disturbing tale, Pruit Dover, a down-on-his-luck cowboy accused of murder, saves Matt's life. Matt, however, is obligated to return Dover to Dodge for trial. Despite Matt's intervention, and despite circumstantial evidence, Dover is sentenced to hang. Matt has the difficult task of escorting Dover to his place of execution. Along the way, Matt grapples with his conscience and whether or not to let Dover escape.

Pruit Dover	Jeremy Slate
Judge	Joseph Ruskin
Ax Parsons	Robert J. Stevenson
Gamer	Richard Shannon
Louie Pheeters	James Nusser
Sheriff	Orville Sherman
Feist	William Chamlee
Gal	Nancy Walters
Hangman	Robert Gravage
Milt	Ollie O'Toole
Story, Script	John Meston
Director	Andrew McLaglen
Associate Producer	Frank Paris
Producer	Norman Macdonnell

Reprisal. March 10, 1962. Production #31027. Rerun June 20, 1964.

Oren Conrad is slain in a gunfight with Matt and his widow Cornelia swears vengeance. Cornelia's attempt at reprisal backfires, however, when she falls in love with the man she persuades to help her.

Cornelia Conrad	Dianne Foster
Ben Harden	Jason Evers
Oren Conrad	George Lambert
Pearl	Grace Lee Whitney
Additional Cast	Tom Reese, Brad Trumbull
Story, Script	John Meston
Director	Harry Harris, Jr.
Associate Producer	Frank Paris
Producer	Norman Macdonnell

The title *Reprisal* was used again February 10, 1969. The stories were not related. Grace Lee Whitney was Yeoman Janice Rand on *Star Trek*. Tom Reese played Sgt. Velie on *The Adventures of Ellery Queen*.

Coventry. March 17, 1962. Production #31021. Rerun August 22, 1964.

When Matt is unable to get a conviction against Dean Beard, a hardened killer who knows how to circumvent the law, he pursuades the citizens of Dodge to give Beard the "silent treatment." The unusual punishment proves to be effective.

Dean Beard	Joe Maross
Jessie Ott	Paul Birch
Clara Ott	Mary Field
Additional Cast	Don Keefer
Story, Script	John Meston
Director	Chris Nyby
Associate Producer	Frank Paris
Producer	Norman Macdonnell

The Widow. March 24, 1962. Production #31025.

Mady Arthur, an attractive widow whose husband was killed in an Indian massacre, arrives in Dodge. She has journeyed there in search of his missing body.

The Television Programs

Despite Matt's severe warnings, Mady insists on pursuing her plans to enter hostile Indian territory. To assist her, Mady hires Emil Peck, an unscrupulous lush who during a recent ruckus knocked Doc out and threw Miss Kitty in a horse trough.

Mady Arthur	Joan Hackett
Emil Peck	J. Edward McKinley
Corporal Jennings	Alan Reed, Jr.
Story, Script	John Dunkel
Director	Ted Post
Producer	Norman Macdonnell
Associate Producer	Frank Paris

Joan Hackett's film credits include *The Group, Support Your Local Sheriff*, and *Only When I Laugh*, for which she was nominated for an Academy Award. In addition to numerous guest appearances and made-for-television movies, she appeared as a regular on *The Defenders* and briefly on *Another Day*.

Durham Bull. March 31, 1962. Production #31011.

It looks like an uneven match when four outlaws try to rob Henry Squires and his grandson, Little Bit, of their prize cattle. But tough old Henry and Little Bit have some surprises of their own for the desperados.

Henry Squires	Andy Clyde
Little Bit	Ricky Kelman
Silva	John Kellogg
Rudd	Gilbert Green
Polk	George Keymas
Kearny	Ted Jordan
Dan Binny	Richard Keene
Cowboy	Hank Patterson
Moss Grimmick	George Selk
Howard	Howard Culver
Brakeman	Ted Jacques
Downey	Roger Torrey
Story	Jack Shettlesworth
Script	John Meston
Director	Harry Harris, Jr.
Associate Producer	Frank Paris
Producer	Norman Macdonnell

Hank Patterson played Hank the stableman. In films, Andy Clyde played William Boyd's grizzled old sidekick, California. On television Clyde appeared as a regular on *The Real McCoys, Lassie* and *No Time for Sergeants*. Roger Torrey was featured on *The Iron Horse* and *The Beverly Hillbillies*.

Wagon Girls. April 7, 1962. Production #31018.

A group of girls prospecting for rich gold miners, get hitched up with an unscrupulous wagon master. Matt steps in and escorts the women through dangerous Indian territory. He then tries to find a way to stop them from continuing their journey toward disappointment.

Karl Feester	Arch Johnson
Kelly Bowman	Kevin Hagen
Polly	Ellen McRae
Additional Cast	Joan Marshall, Constance Ford

GUNSMOKE — III. THE PROGRAMS

Story, Script .... John Meston
Director .... Andrew McLaglen
Associate Producer .... Frank Paris
Producer .... Norman Macdonnell

Ellen McRae is better known as Ellen Burstyn. Burstyn appeared frequently on television before moving on to films. She won the New York and the National Film Critics Awards for *The Last Picture Show,* for which she was also nominated for an Academy Award. She was also nominated for *The Exorcist.* In 1975 she won the Academy Award for her performance in *Alice Doesn't Live Here Anymore.* That same year she received the Tony Award for *Same Time Next Year,* and then received an Oscar nomination for the film version.

The Dealer. April 14, 1962. Production #31029.

Despite Matt's warnings that she is inviting trouble, Kitty hires a woman faro dealer. The men folk of Dodge are attracted to pretty Lily Baskin's card table like bees to honey. Matt's predictions prove true when Johnny Cole, who killed Lily's father in self-defense, comes to town. He now wants to soften her hatred for him.

Lily Baskin .... Judi Meredith
Johnny Cole .... Gary Clarke
Billy Baskin .... Roy Roberts
Additional Cast .... George Mathews
Story, Script .... John Dunkel
Director .... Harry Harris, Jr.
Associate Producer .... Frank Paris
Producer .... Norman Macdonnell

Judi Meredith played Ronnie Burns' girlfriend on *The George Burns and Gracie Allen Show.* Gary Clarke was a regular on *The Virginian* for two seasons.

The Summons. April 21, 1962. Production #31030. Rerun August 17, 1963.

Loy Bishop, a vicious, unscrupulous gunfighter, kills one of his fellow outlaws to collect the $1000 bounty. When he is unable to obtain the reward, Bishop holds Matt responsible. To get back at him, Bishop has his girlfriend Rose-Ellen, lure Matt into an ambush, and into one of the toughest fights of his career.

Rose-Ellen .... Bethel Leslie
Loy Bishop .... John Crawford
Dawkins .... Cal Bolder
Cape .... Robert J. Stevenson
Story .... Marian Clark
Script .... Kathleen Hite
Director .... Andrew McLaglen
Associate Producer .... Frank Paris
Producer .... Norman Macdonnell

Bethel Leslie appeared on television quite frequently in the 50s and 60s. She became a regular on the daytime series *The Doctors* and then became headwriter for *The Secret Storm.* She also wrote a script for *Gunsmoke* called *Sam McTavish, M.D.,* which aired October 5, 1970.

The Dreamers. April 28, 1962. Production #31032.

When Kitty turns down the marriage proposal of scroungy old miner Henry Cairn, he takes drastic steps to change her mind. Cairn decides to put Kitty and the Long

The Television Programs

Branch out of business. He buys the competing Lady Gay Saloon, and then sells beer at cut-throat prices.

Henry Cairn	Liam Redford
Jake Fogle	J. Pat O'Malley
Annie	Valerie Allen
Story, Script	John Meston
Director	Andrew McLaglen
Associate Producer	Frank Paris
Producer	Norman Macdonnell

Cale. May 5, 1962. Production #31034. Rerun aired July 13, 1963.

Matt finds Cale out on the prairie. Although wounded, the stubborn young man refuses Matt's help. Cale feels he has a score to settle with Sterret, the man responsible for his injuries.

Cale	Carl Reindel
Tate Gifford	Ford Rainey
Sterret	Robert Karnes
Nick Archer	Joseph Hamilton
Additional Cast	Peter Ashley
Story, Script	Kathleen Hite
Director	Harry Harris, Jr.
Producer	Norman Macdonnell
Associate Producer	Frank Paris

Carl Reindel recreated his role as Cale in a sequel called *The Search*, which aired September 15, 1962. Ford Rainey was a regular on a number of television shows including *The Richard Boone Show*, *The Manhunter*, and *The Bionic Woman*.

Chester's Indian. May 12, 1962. Production #31024. Rerun June 8, 1963.

Callie Dill, a pretty young woman whose father prevents her from associating with men, befriends a fugitive Indian. After Chester accidentally wounds the Indian, Callie insists that he be responsible for the Indian's health and safety until he has recovered. Chester faces the dilemma of trying to please Callie, and at the same time evade her father and brother who are hunting for the runaway. In the meantime, Callie is falling in love with the Indian.

Callie Dill	Jena Engstrom
Adam Dill	Karl Swenson
Indian	Eddie Little Sky
Miss Peggity	Peggy Rea
Frank Dill	Lew Brown
Simeon	Garry Walberg
Cowboy	Michael Barrier
Obie	Shug Fisher
Waiter	Gene Benton
Story, Script	Kathleen Hite
Director	Richard Sargent
Associate Producer	Frank Paris
Producer	Norman Macdonnell

Peggy Rea appeared on radio's *Gunsmoke*. On television Peggy Rea appeared as a regular on *The Red Skelton Show*, *The Waltons*, and *The Dukes of Hazzard*.

GUNSMOKE — III. THE PROGRAMS

The Prisoner. May 19, 1962. Production #31033.

Major Emerson Owen blames Billy Joe Arlen for the death of his son Ham, and is determined to take the law into his own hands. Matt, however, feels obliged to protect Arlen, since he is a federal prisoner and must stand trial on an earlier federal account. Matt's interference causes the Major and his remaining son Seth, to swear vengeance.

  Billy Joe Arlen .... Andrew Prine
  Sarah .... Nancy Gates
  Major Emerson Owen .... Conrad Nagel
  Seth .... Ed Nelson
  Ham Owen .... William Phipps
  Story, Script .... Tommy Thompson
  Director .... Andrew McLaglen
  Associate Producer .... Frank Paris
  Producer .... Norman Macdonnell

The title *The Prisoner* was used again March 17, 1969. Andrew Prine was a regular on two short-lived series *The Wide Country* and *The Road West,* both Westerns. In recent years he appeared in the made-for-television movie and miniseries, *V.* Conrad Nagel was a romantic lead in numerous Hollywood flicks of the 20s and 30s. A co-founder of the Academy of Motion Picture Arts and Sciences, Nagel helped create the Academy Awards. He, himself, was awarded a special Academy Award for his philanthropic efforts on behalf of the Motion Picture Relief Fund. His films include *Stage Struck* and *All That Heaven Allows.*

The Boys. May 26, 1962. Production #31031.

Professor Eliot is a medical charlatan who tries to ply his phoney wares in Dodge. However, the residents refuse to buy his story or his merchandise. Angered by the treatment he receives, Eliot orders Hug, Nate, and Park, his three worthless sons, to rob a stagecoach. Disguised as Indians, the boys attack the stage and murder a young girl. Then they offer Matt their services to help hunt down the killers, for a price.

  Professor Eliot .... Malcolm Atterbury
  Hug .... George Kennedy
  Nate .... Dean Stanton
  Park .... Michael Parks
  Molly .... May Heatherly
  Farnum .... Arthur Malet
  Story, Script .... John Meston
  Director .... Harry Harris, Jr.
  Associate Producer .... Frank Paris
  Producer .... Norman Macdonnell

Michael Parks played the brooding anti-hero of the television series *Then Came Bronson* and was a regular on *The Young Lawyers.* In films his credits include John Huston's, *The Bible.* Arthur Malet was most recently seen as Bobby the butler on the sit-com *Easy Street.*

Miss Kitty. June 16, 1962, rerun. First aired October 14, 1961.

Long, Long Trail. June 23, 1962, rerun. First aired November 4, 1961.

Apprentice Doc. June 30, 1962, rerun. First aired December 9, 1961.

The Television Programs

All That. July 7, 1962, rerun. First aired October 28, 1961.

A Man a Day. July 21, 1962, rerun. First aired December 30, 1961.

Marry Me. July 28, 1962, rerun. First aired December 23, 1961.

The Squaw. August 4, 1962, rerun. First aired November 11, 1961.

Perce. August 11, 1962, rerun. First aired September 30, 1961.

Catawomper. August 18, 1962, rerun. First aired February 10, 1962.

Lacey. August 25, 1962, rerun. First aired January 13, 1962.

He Learned About Women. September 1, 1962, rerun. First aired March 24, 1962.

EIGHTH SEASON

The Search. September 15, 1962. Production #31208.

Matt rides out after Cale, a young man suspected of horse theft, and finds him seriously wounded after a fall from his horse. Trouble follows Matt as he tries to find a way of bringing Cale back to safety, including a rendezvous with three trigger-happy outlaws and an encounter with Ess Cutler, a desperately lonely woman. Finally, Matt brings Cale to Mr. Tate, the rancher whose horse was reported stolen. There the young man is able to recuperate from his injuries.

Cale . . . . Carl Reindel
Tate . . . . Ford Rainey
Ess Cutler . . . . Virginia Gregg
Hank Miller . . . . Hank Patterson
Sam Cutler . . . . Raymond Guth
Arnie . . . . Leonard Nimoy
Frank . . . . Mike Ragan
Horn . . . . Fred Coby
Coot . . . . Mickey Morton
Story, Script . . . . Kathleen Hite
Director . . . . Harry Harris, Jr.
Associate Producer . . . . Frank Paris
Producer . . . . Norman Macdonnell

The Search is a sequel to *Cale,* which aired May 5, 1962.

Call Me Dodie. September 22, 1962. Production #31206. Rerun August 10, 1963.

Dodie runs away from the orphanage where she has been brutally treated. She arrives in Dodge and creates quite a stir amongst the local barflies, who try to take advantage of her innocence. Dodie holds her own, however, and proves to be more than a match for the men folk. In addition, she helps Matt bring Addie and Floyd Bagge, the villainous brother and sister due who run the orphanage, to justice.

Dodie . . . . Kathy Nolan
Addie Bagge . . . . Mary Patten
Floyd Bagge . . . . Jack Searl

GUNSMOKE — III. THE PROGRAMS

Lady	Dianne Mountford
Martha	Carol Seflinger
Additional Cast	Joby Baker
Story, Script	Kathleen Hite
Director	Harry Harris, Jr.
Associate Producer	Frank Paris
Producer	Norman Macdonnell

Kathy Nolan appeared as Kate McCoy in *The Real McCoys*. In 1975 she was the first woman elected president of the Screen Actors Guild, a position that Ronald Reagan once held. Jack Searl started out on radio when he was only three. He moved on to become a child star in films of the 30s. His films include *Tom Sawyer, Peck's Bad Boy,* and *My Little Chickadee*.

Quint Asper Comes Home. September 29, 1962. Production #31035. Rerun September 21, 1963.

After white men slay his father, half-breed Quint Asper joins the Comanche tribe of his mother so he can avenge the killing. Quint is wounded during a raid, and Matt brings him back to Dodge to recover. Matt bears not only the brunt of Quint's bitterness but also the wrath of Dodge's townfolk, when he befriends Quint.

Quint Asper	Burt Reynolds
Topsanah	Angela Clarke
John Asper	William Zuckert
Jim Grant	Harry Carey, Jr.
Chief	Michael Keep
Bob	Lane Bradford
Mike	Myron Healey
Dobie	Earle Hodgins
Cowboy	Robert Hinkle
Ed	Foster Brooks
Brave	Michael Barrier
Duff	Henry Beckman
Leader	John Vari
Davit	James Doohan
Semple	Ed Peck
Charlie	Robert Gravage
Story, Script	John Meston
Director	Andrew McLaglen
Associate Producer	Frank Paris
Producer	Norman Macdonnell

This episode introduces Burt Reynolds as Quint Asper. On television he appeared as *Hawk* and *Dan August* before moving into films. His films include *Deliverance, The Longest Yard,* and *Smokey and the Bandit.* Henry Beckman was a regular in about a half-dozen television shows. Most recently he has been seen as Alf Scully on *Check It Out.* Although James Doohan has appeared in such films as *The Wheeler Dealers* and *The Satan Bug,* he is best known as Scotty, the chief engineer of the Starship Enterprise, on *Star Trek.*

Root Down. October 6, 1962. Production #31210. Rerun August 29, 1964.

Pretty Aggie Dutton is so anxious to settle down that she lies to her father Luke, telling him Chester wants to marry her. Aggie stretches the truth even more, when

The Television Programs

she implies Chester has spent the night with her. When the bewildered Chester balks, Luke and his son Grudie kidnap him. The unwilling bridegroom is bound and gagged, and the Dutton's set out to fetch a preacher.

Aggie Dutton	Sherry Jackson
Luke Dutton	John Dehner
Grudie Dutton	Robert Doyle
Howard	Howard McNear
Moss Grimmick	George Selk
Cowboy	Michael Carr
Clerk	Ollie O'Toole
Story, Script	Kathleen Hite
Director	Charles Martin
Associate Producer	Frank Paris
Producer	Norman Macdonnell

Jenny. October 13, 1962. Production #31207.

Matt jails an outlaw and winds up battling with Jenny, the man's girlfriend. Jenny lures Matt up to her hotel room with the intention of seducing the steadfast lawman. When he spurns her advances, Matt finds out about the fury of a woman scorned.

Jenny	Ruta Lee
Zel Meyers	Ron Hayes
Al Flack	John Duke
Louie Pheeters	James Nusser
Chuck	Barry Cahill
Pete	Ken Hudgins
Joe	Monte Montana, Jr.
Story, Script	John Meston
Director	Andrew McLaglen
Associate Producer	Frank Paris
Producer	Norman Macdonnell

The title *Jenny* was used again December 28, 1970.

Collie's Free. October 20, 1962. Production #31204. Rerun September 5, 1964.

After eight years in prison, embittered Collie Patten is unable to adjust to the changes he finds when he finally comes home. Collie blames everyone, including Matt, for his troubles, and he is especially upset to find that his young son Rob is afraid of him.

Collie Patten	Jason Evans
Francie Patten	Jacqueline Scott
Rob Patten	James Halferty
Additional Cast	William Bramley
Story, Script	Kathleen Hite
Director	Harry Harris, Jr.
Associate Producer	Frank Paris
Producer	Norman Macdonnell

The Ditch. October 27, 1962. Production #31212.

Headstrong Susan Bart plans to divert a creek on her ranch. The problem is that this will cut off the water supply of some neighboring homesteaders, who vehemently protest the action. Tempers begin to flare and Susan hires gunman Lafe Crider to protect her workmen. Although unintentional on Susan's part, Crider's presence threatens to provoke a range war.

Susan Bart	Joanne Linville
Lafe Crider	Christopher Dark
Trent Hawkins	Jay Lanin
Waco	Dehl Berti
Peckett	Hardie Albright
Foreman	Ted Jordan
Mrs. Hawkins	Gail Bonney
Boss	Miguel deAnda
Story, Script	Les Crutchfield
Director	Harry Harris, Jr.
Associate Producer	Frank Paris
Producer	Norman Macdonnell

Hardie Albright appeared in such films as *White Heat, The Scarlet Letter,* and the 1957 sex exploitation film, *Mom and Dad.* He also taught drama at U.C.L.A. and wrote several textbooks on acting and stage direction.

The Trappers. November 3, 1962. Production #31209. Rerun July 4, 1964.

Fur trapper Billy Logan leaves his partner Tug Marsh for dead, after Tug is attacked by a bear in hostile Indian territory. However, Tug survives and swears to settle the score. Logan has additional problems in store in the pleasing form of two-timing Irma Watkins. Irma schemes, with the assistance of conman Idaho Smith, to relieve Logan of his fur trading money.

Billy Logan	Strother Martin
Tug Marsh	Richard Shannon
Irma Watkins	Doris Singleton
Idaho Smith	Robert Lowery
Luke	Lane Chandler
Tom	Chal Johnson
Jim Buck	Robert Brubaker
Story, Script	John Dunkel
Director	Andrew McLaglen
Associate Producer	Frank Paris
Producer	Norman Macdonnell

Robert Lowery played Big Tim Champion on the series *Circus Boy.*

Phoebe Strunk. November 10, 1962. Production #31213.

Vicious Phoebe Strunk and her four criminal sons climax a round of murder and robbery by kidnapping a young girl. Matt and Quint set out to find the Strunks, and to hopefully bring the girl back unharmed.

Phoebe Strunk	Virginia Gregg
Annie	Joan Freeman
Oliver Strunk	Don Megowan
Simsie	Dick Peabody
Hulett	Gregg Palmer
Casper	Harry Raybould
Story, Script	John Meston
Director	Andrew McLaglen
Associate Producer	Frank Paris
Producer	Norman Macdonnell

The Television Programs

Dick Peabody played Littlejohn on television's *Combat*. Joan Freeman was featured as Elma Gahringer on the dramatic series, *Bus Stop*.

The Hunger. November 17, 1962. Production #31036.

Althea Dorf is a quiet, unassuming young woman, who is the victim of a brutal father. After rescuing Althea from her father's cellar, where she had been imprisoned without food, Doc realizes she has fallen in love with him. Doc is genuinely touched by the young lady's affection. However, Doc has to make it clear to Althea that this misplaced "love" for him is more filial than romantic.

Althea Dorf	Elen Willard
Claude Dorf	Robert Middleton
Clem Dorf	Hampton Fancher
Mrs. Dorf	Linda Watkins
Drummer	Joe Flynn
Ma Smalley	Sarah Selby
Dooley	Byron Foulger
Fred	Kelton Garwood
Dolly	Henrietta Moore
Cowboy	Robert McQuain
Martha	Sue Casey
Story, Script	Jack Curtis
Director	Harry Harris, Jr.
Associate Producer	Frank Paris
Producer	Norman Macdonnell

Byron Foulger was a regular on *Petticoat Junction*.

Abe Blocker. November 24, 1962. Production #31215. Rerun July 6, 1963.

An old friend of Matt's, Abe Blocker, has become mentally deranged. Blocker is a kind of free spirit who believes the land should be untouched and unsettled. He is bent on driving ranchers off their land by any means, including murder. Matt refuses to believe that Blocker is responsible for the deaths of several homesteaders and journeys up to the hills to meet with him. Despite Matt's warning to stop harrassing the settlers, Blocker persists in his campaign of killings, and a grim posse sets out to hunt him down.

Abe Blocker	Chill Wills
Bud Groves	Wright King
Mary Groves	Miranda Jones
Jake	Harry Carey, Jr.
Emmett	Robert Adler
Sam Vestal	Marshall Reed
Gant	Lane Bradford
Dan Binney	Wallace Rooney
Joe	Chuck Roberson
Story, Script	John Meston
Director	Andrew McLaglen
Associate Producer	Frank Paris
Producer	Norman Macdonnell

Chill Wills made numerous films including *Honky Tonk* and *The Alamo*, for which he was nominated for an Academy Award. He was also the voice of Francis, Hollywood's talking mule.

GUNSMOKE — III. THE PROGRAMS

The Way It Is. December 1, 1962. Production #31214. Rerun August 31, 1963.

Angered when Matt breaks an important date, Kitty storms off to visit friends. On her journey she encounters a stranger, Ad Bellem, who has been seriously injured after a fall from his horse. Kitty nurses Ad back to health, and a romance develops. There is a strong attraction between the two, but Kitty soon learns that Ad has a hot temper, especially when other men are attentive to her.

Ad Bellem	Claude Akins
Bent Dillard	Garry Walberg
Annie	Virginia Lewis
Rancher	Duane Grey
Moss Grimmick	George Selk
Slim	Bob Murphy
Story, Associate Producer	Frank Paris
Script	Kathleen Hite
Director	Harry Harris, Jr.
Producer	Norman Macdonnell

Us Haggens. December 8, 1962. Production #31205. Rerun August 24, 1963.

Black Jack Haggen is Festus Haggen's uncle and a murderous scoundrel. Whether blood is thicker than water is put to the test, when Matt asks Festus to help track his uncle. Festus is torn between his liking for Matt, and the motto of his villainous uncle, that Haggens stick together, especially when it comes to the law.

Festus Haggen	Ken Curtis
Black Jack Haggen	Denver Pyle
April	Elizabeth MacRae
Timmy	Billy Hughes
Dietzer	Howard Wright
Story, Script	Les Crutchfield
Director	Andrew McLaglen
Associate Producer	Frank Paris
Producer	Norman Macdonnell

This episode introduces Festus Haggen. However, Festus does not become a regular until the following season.

Uncle Sunday. December 15, 1962. Production #31218. Rerun June 27, 1964.

Nothing goes right for Chester when he tries to earn extra money to keep his crooked uncle, Sunday Meachem, out of Dodge. Despite Chester's efforts, Sunday and his pretty "niece" Ellie come to town, obviously up to no good. Chester has to find a way of foiling their plot to rob the bank.

Uncle Sunday Meachem	Henry Beckman
Ellie	Joyce Bulifant
Burt Cury	Ed Nelson
Story, Script	John Meston
Director	Joseph Sargent
Associate Producer	Frank Paris
Producer	Norman Macdonnell

Perky blonde, Joyce Bulifant, has appeared as a regular on numerous programs including *The Mary Tyler Moore Show* where she played Marie Slaughter.

False Front. December 22, 1962. Production #31201.

Crafty journalist Paul Hill bets $1000 that Clay Tatun, who has never fired a shot,

[546]

The Television Programs

can pose as a hardened gunman without getting himself killed. The whole scheme smacks of trouble for Matt, whose job is endangered by an economy minded U.S. Senator, who does not think that Dodge needs a marshal.

Paul Hill	William Windom
Clay Tatum	Andrew Prine
Nick Heber	Art Lund
Senator	Charles Fredericks
Rita	Shary Marshall
Dan Binney	Wallace Rooney
Ray Costa	Robert Fortier
Hank	Brett King
Pete	K.L. Smith
Joe	William Bryant
Harry	Roy Thinnes
Bill	Michael Mikler
Story	Hal Moffett
Script	John Meston
Director	Andrew McLaglen
Associate Producer	Frank Paris
Producer	Norman Macdonnell

William Bryant was a regular on *Switch*. Roy Thinnes is probably best known on television for his role as David Vincent on the sci-fi series *The Invaders*.

Old Comrade. December 29, 1962. Production #31217.

To please war hero, General Kip Marston, Colonel Gabe Wilson agrees to look up Marston's son Billy. However, Wilson is unprepared for what he finds. Billy turns out to be an object of ridicule in Dodge, and Wilson is concerned about the effect this will have on his ailing friend.

Col. Gabe Wilson	J. Pat O'Malley
Billy	Frank Sutton
General Kip Marston	Ralph Moody
Story, Script	John Dunkel
Director	Harry Harris, Jr.
Associate Producer	Frank Paris
Producer	Norman Macdonnell

Louie Pheeters. January 5, 1963. Production #31202.

Louie Pheeters is witness to a murder that he believes to be an alcoholic fantasy. Unfortunately, Louie tells his "dream" to the killers and becomes the target of a deadly plot.

Murph Moody	John Larkin
Bart Felder	Larry Ward
Clara Felder	Gloria McGhee
Louie Pheeters	James Nusser
Additional Cast	Woodrow Parfrey
Story, Script	John Meston
Director	Harry Harris, Jr.
Associate Producer	Frank Paris
Producer	Norman Macdonnell

John Larkin was the voice of *Perry Mason* on radio in the late 40s and 50s. He appeared on television in *Twelve O'Clock High*.

GUNSMOKE — III. THE PROGRAMS

The Renegades. January 12, 1963. Production #31211.

Lavinia Pate, the haughty daughter of an army colonel, has a low opinion of Quint and Indians in general. When she and Quint find themselves pursued by renegade whites, she finds herself in the disagreeable position of having to disguise herself as an Indian to escape capture. The pair then find themselves being hunted, not only by the renegade whites, but by army troops who blame the Indians for the renegades' actions.

Lavinia Pate	Audrey Dalton
Colonel Pate	Ben Wright
Brice	Jack Lambert
McIver	Donald Barry
Additional Cast	John Pickard
Story, Script	John Meston
Director	Andrew McLaglen
Associate Producer	Frank Paris
Producer	Norman Macdonnell

Cotter's Girl. January 19, 1963. Production #31219. Rerun June 13, 1964.

Matt goes on a mission to find Clarey Cotter, the daughter of an old drunk, to give her her inheritance. What Matt finds is more than he bargained for. Clarey is an unpredictable nature-girl who is almost too much for him to handle. She is uncertain as to whether she likes the constraints of civilization, but knows she likes Matt and is not at all shy about showing it. Matt's chore is to civilize the free-spirited Clarey before sending her to live with relatives.

Clarey	Mariette Hartley
Cotter	Roy Barcroft
Mackle	John Clarke
Proprietress	Jesslyn Fax
Ma Smalley	Sarah Selby
Story, Script	Kathleen Hite
Director	Harry Harris, Jr.
Associate Producer	Frank Paris
Producer	Norman Macdonnell

Mariette Hartley won an Emmy Award for Best Actress in a Single Performance in a Drama Series for *The Incredible Hulk*. She has appeared frequently on television and in commercials, most notably with James Garner for Polaroid. John Clarke is best known for his role as Mickey Horton on the daytime drama *Days of Our Lives*. Jesslyn Fax played Angela on *Our Miss Brooks*.

The Bad One. January 26, 1963. Production #31216.

Willie Jett seems set on proving that he is worse than his convict father, until he meets convent raised Jenny Anne Parker. Jenny takes a fancy to Willie, when he kisses her after holding up the stage that she is a passenger on. When questioned by Matt, Jenny does not identify Willie as the robber. However, trouble rears its ugly head when Jenny's strict father threatens to kill Willie for courting her.

Willie Jett	Chris Robinson
Jenny Anne Parker	Dolores Sutton
Gant Parker	Booth Colman
Mr. Jonas	Dabbs Greer
Cowpoke	Michael Mikler

The Television Programs

Clancy	Ken Kenopka
Porter	Gil Lamb
Saloon Girl	Sue Casey
Telegrapher	Robert Gravage
Story, Script	Gwen Bagni Gielgud
Director	Charles Martin
Associate Producer	Frank Paris
Producer	Norman Macdonnell

Chris Robinson is familiar to television viewers as Dr. Rick Webber of the soap opera *General Hospital*. Gwen Bagni Gielgud and her husband Paul DuBov created the television series *Honey West*, that starred Anne Francis.

The Cousin. February 2, 1963. Production #31221.

This episode offers a glimpse into Matt's childhood, when ex-convict Chance Hopper, who was raised with Matt by the same foster parents, arrives in Dodge. Chance breaks his leg while trying to set up a robbery, and the injury gives him time to test Matt's strength against that of his own.

Chance Hopper	Michael Forest
Hallie	Gloria Talbott
Cheevers	John Anderson
Moran	Joseph Perry
Story	Marian Clark
Script	Kathleen Hite
Director	Harry Harris, Jr.
Associate Producer	Frank Paris
Producer	Norman Macdonnell

Shona. February 9, 1963. Production #31220.

A friend of Quint's brings his Indian wife Shona to Dodge for medical treatment. With Matt away, Quint is faced with the dangerous job of guarding Shona from the angry, prejudiced citizens of Dodge, who want her out of town. Kitty joins Quint in befriending Shona, and the two find themselves targets of a vicious racial boycott.

Shona	Miriam Colon
Gib	Robert Bray
Forbert	John Crawford
Additional Cast	Robert Palmer, Bart Burns
Story, Script	John Meston
Director	Ted Post
Associate Producer	Frank Paris
Producer	Norman Macdonnell

Robert Bray played Corey Stuart on *Lassie*. Bart Burns appeared as Captain Chambers on *Mickey Spillane's Mike Hammer*.

Ash. February 16, 1963. Production #31223. Rerun July 18, 1964.

Kindly Ben Galt turns into a murderous troublemaker, after he suffers a head injury. When Galt goes after Tillie, another man's girl, his best friend and partner, Ash Farior, sets out to stop him.

Ben Galt	John Dehner
Ash Farior	Anthony Caruso
Tillie	Dee Hartford

[549]

GUNSMOKE — III. THE PROGRAMS

Emmett Hall	Adam West
Murdock	Sheldon Allman
Hawkins	William Fawcett
Driver	Robert Bice
Harry	Richard Bartell
Frank	Michael Mikler
Story, Script	John Meston
Director	Harry Harris, Jr.
Associate Producer	Frank Paris
Producer	Norman Macdonnell

Adam West was *Batman* in the cult television series.

Blind Man's Bluff. February 23, 1963. Production #31222.

When his eyesight is impaired because of an attack, Matt gets assistance from Billy Poe, a prisoner accused of murder. Later Matt has to bring Poe in for trial, but convinced of Poe's innocence, he sets out to help him clear his name.

Billy Poe	Will Hutchins
Frank Walker	Crahan Denton
Bud Hays	Herbert Lytton
Additional Cast	John Alderson, Gregg Palmer, Judson Pratt
Story, Script	John Meston
Director	Ted Post
Associate Producer	Frank Paris
Producer	Norman Macdonnell

Will Hutchins played *Sugarfoot* on the popular television Western.

Quint's Indian. March 2, 1963. Production #31224.

Quint is beaten up by some townsfolk for a crime he did not commit. Angered by the incident, he leaves town. Matt rides out to bring Quint back, and runs into danger from a band of hostile Indians.

Stope	Will Corry
Feeney	James Brown
Houser	Patrick McVey
Bettis	James Griffith
Story	Marian Clark
Script	John Meston
Director	Fred H. Jackman
Associate Producer	Frank Paris
Producer	Norman Macdonnell

James Brown played Lt. Rip Masters on the kiddie Western, *Rin Tin Tin*. Patrick McVey appeared as a regular on *Big Town, Boots and Saddles — The Story of the 5th Cavalry,* and *Manhunt*.

Anybody Can Kill a Marshal. March 9, 1963. Production #31225.

When two outlaws fail in their efforts to kill Matt, a meek little man named Painter volunteers to do the job for $200. When Painter is killed by Matt in a gunfight, he sets out to learn who wants him dead, and why Painter made the attempt.

Painter	Milton Selzer
Lucas	Warren Stevens
Cleed	James Westerfield

[550]

The Television Programs

Betsy	Brenda Scott
Additional Cast	Joyce Van Patten
Story, Script	Kathleen Hite
Director	Harry Harris, Jr.
Associate Producer	Frank Paris
Producer	Norman Macdonnell

Joyce Van Patten appeared as a regular on many television shows including *The Danny Kaye Show*. She is the younger sister of actor Dick Van Patten.

Two of a Kind. March 16, 1963. Production #31226.

To quell a feud between two Irish business partners, Matt gets a court order saying that each is to be responsible for the other's life. The ruling inspires a plot by four men to kill one of the partners and claim his land, in the hope that the other partner will hang for murder.

Sean O'Ryan	Richard Jaeckel
Tim Finnegan	Michael Higgins
Clay Bealton	Kent Smith
Anson	Garry Walberg
Harris	Ben Wright
Wills	John Mitchum
Judge	Earle Hodgins
Girl	Bee Tompkins
Story, Script	Merwin Gerard
Director	Andrew McLaglen
Associate Producer	Frank Paris
Producer	Norman Macdonnell

Richard Jaekel has appeared as a regular on numerous television programs, the most recent being, *Spencer for Hire*. His films include *Come Back Little Sheba, The Dirty Dozen, Wing and a Prayer, Sands of Iwo Jima,* and *Battleground,* in which James Arness and Amanda Blake had small parts. In addition, Jaekel was nominated for an Academy Award for Best Supporting Actor for *Sometimes a Great Notion*. Michael Higgins played the part of Johnny Roberts in the television dramatic series, *One Man's Family*. Kent Smith's film credits include *Cat People, My Foolish Heart, The Spiral Staircase, Strangers When We Meet,* and *Sayonara*. On television he appeared in the documentary series, *Profiles in Courage* and the sci-fi adventure, *The Invaders*.

I Call Him Wonder. March 23, 1963. Production #31227.

Jud Sorrell, a poker playing drifter, reluctantly finds himself looking after a small Indian boy he names Wonder. His problem is compounded by the fact that nobody else likes Wonder, who in turn takes a violent dislike to anyone who tries to help him, including Matt.

Jud Sorrell	Ron Hayes
Wonder	Edmund Vargus
Docker	Sandy Kenyon
Holt	Leonard Nimoy
Keogh	Duane Grey
Colonel	Harry Bartell
Enock	William Zuckert
Charlie	Eddie Little Sky

GUNSMOKE — III. THE PROGRAMS

                Cook .... Alex Sharp
                Moss Grimmick .... George Selk
                Waiter .... Gilman Rankin
                Story, Script .... Kathleen Hite
                Director .... Harry Harris
                Associate Producer .... Frank Paris
                Producer .... Norman Macdonnell

The title *Wonder* was used again on December 18, 1967. The story revolved around the same characters.

With a Smile. March 30, 1963. Production #31228. Rerun August 8, 1964.

Dal Creed brutally murders a woman and his father, Major Creed, tries desperately to save him from execution. The Major is driven to drastic action when he finally realizes his worthless son is a cowardly murderer.

                Major Creed .... R.G. Armstrong
                Dal .... James Best
                Sheriff Ben Carver .... Dick Foran
                Pat Cain .... Linden Chiles
                Lottie Foy .... Sharon Farrell
                Additional Cast .... Dan Stafford
                Story .... Bud Furillo
                Script .... John Meston
                Director .... Andrew McLaglen
                Associate Producer .... Frank Paris
                Producer .... Norman Macdonnell

James Best played Sheriff Coltrane on *The Dukes of Hazzard*. He appeared in such films as *The Caine Mutiny* with Humphrey Bogart and *Seven Angry Men*, which featured Dennis Weaver. Sharon Farrell appeared as a regular on *Hawaii Five-O*. Dick Foran became the singing hero of a number of B-Westerns. His film credits include *Song of the Saddle, The Mummy's Hand,* and *Fort Apache*.

The Far Places. April 6, 1963. Production #31229. Rerun August 15, 1964.

Domineering Carrie Newcomb wants a better life for her son Jeff. Realizing that she is dying, Carrie stubbornly resolves to sell the ranch. Jeff is vehemently opposed to her plan. He wants to marry his sweetheart Millie Smith and continue working the ranch. When a potential buyer approaches the Newcombs, Jeff drives him off at gunpoint, which forces Matt to intervene.

                Carrie Newcomb .... Angela Clarke
                Jeff Newcomb .... Rees Vaughn
                Millie Smith .... Bennye Gatteys
                Story, Script .... John Dunkel
                Director .... Harry Harris, Jr.
                Associate Producer .... Frank Paris
                Producer .... Norman Macdonnell

Panacea Sykes. April 13, 1963. Production #31203.

Panacea Sykes boards a stagecoach heading for Dodge, well aware that she does not have any money. When asked for her fare, she replies that her "daughter" Kitty Russell will reimburse the driver. A larcenous pickpocket, but otherwise likeable lady, Panacea arrives in Dodge and proceeds to create her own brand of confusion.

The Television Programs

Although not really Kitty's mother, the old con artist did raise her. Kitty happily puts Panacea up at the Long Branch, but encounters difficulties when she realizes that Panacea has been robbing her and running a poker game in her room.

Panacea Sykes	Nellie Burt
Foote	Dan Tobin
Little	Charles Watts
Station Agent	Lindsay Workman
Driver	Charlie Briggs
Young Man	John Clarke
Ethel	Jan Brooks
Agent	Carl Prickett
One	Charles Seel
Two	Robert Nash
Other	John Lawrence
Telegrapher	Ollie O'Toole
Story, Script	Kathleen Hite
Director	William Conrad
Associate Producer	Frank Paris
Producer	Norman Macdonnell

Dan Tobin was a regular on *I Married Joan, Perry Mason* and *My Favorite Husband*. Radio's Matt Dillon, William Conrad, directed this episode.

Tell Chester. April 20, 1963. Production #31231.

Chester becomes involved in a deadly love triangle when a former girlfriend, Polly Donahue, marries a man who already has a wife.

Polly Donahue	Mitzi Hoag
Wade Stringer	Lonny Chapman
Wendy Stringer	Jo Helton
Story, Script, Associate Producer	Frank Paris
Director	Joseph Sargent
Producer	Norman Macdonnell

Mitzi Hoag played Essie Gillis on the television series *Here Come the Brides*.

Quint-Cident. April 27, 1963. Production #31230. Rerun July 11, 1964.

Lonely widow Willa Devlin takes bitter revenge after realizing she has mistaken Quint's kindness for romantic interest. Willa claims that Quint attacked her, and Matt has the difficult task of confronting his friend with the accusation.

Willa Devlin	Mary La Roche
Ben Crown	Ben Johnson
Nally	Don Keefer
Additional Cast	Catherine McLeod
Story, Script	Kathleen Hite
Director	Andrew McLaglen
Associate Producer	Frank Paris
Producer	Norman Macdonnell

Ben Johnson appeared in such films as *Shane, Mighty Joe Young*, and John Ford's *Wagonmaster*. In 1971 he won the Academy Award as Best Supporting Actor and the New York Film Critics Award for *The Last Picture Show*.

Old York. May 4, 1963. Production #31233.

At the ripe young age of 18, Matt was taken hostage during a bank hold-up. One of the outlaws responsible for the robbery was Dan York. Although the ruthless leader of the gang planned on killing the future marshal, York stopped him dead in his tracks. Old York arrives in Dodge to renew his acquaintance with Matt and cash in on the marshal's debt. Dan figures that Matt's gratitude will give him the edge he and his accomplice, Baca, need to stage a bank robbery.

Dan York	Edgar Buchanan
Sage	H.M. Wynant
Clayton	Robert Knapp
Baca	Michael Constantine
Mr. Botkin	Roy Roberts
Taylor	Edward Madden
Clerk	Howard Culver
Mrs. Finney	Dorothy Neumann
Barkeep	Lou Krugman
Jim	Don Spruance
Milt	Robert S. White
Story, Script	John Meston
Director	Harry Harris, Jr.
Associate Producer	Frank Paris
Producer	Norman Macdonnell

This episode starts with a flashback to 1858 and one gets a rare glimpse into Matt's past. Michael Constantine won an Emmy Award for Best Supporting Actor for the situation comedy *Room 222*.

Daddy Went Away. May 11, 1963. Production #31232.

Chester falls for penniless seamstress Lucy Damon, when he sympathetically lends a helping hand to the pretty, young "widow" and her daughter Jessica. Lucy presents him with a new shirt and suit, and Chester considers matrimony.

Lucy Damon	Mary Carver
Jessica Damon	Suzanne Cupito
Jess Damon	William Schallert
Story	John Rosser
Script	Kathleen Hite
Director	Joseph Sargent
Associate Producer	Frank Paris
Producer	Norman Macdonnell

The Odyssey of Jubal Tanner. May 18, 1963. Production #31234.

Saloon girl Leah Brunson accepts a proposal of marriage from farmer Aaron Larker. Unfortunately, Colie Fletcher, angered at being spurned by Leah, kills Aaron and flees Dodge. Leah withdraws into bitterness and resumes her false carefree attitude, until she meets drifter Jubal Tanner. Jubal has much in common with Leah. While out on the prairie, Fletcher shot Jubal and stole his horse. The two victims are ultimately drawn together by their misfortunes.

Leah Brunson	Beverly Garland
Jubal Tanner	Peter Breck
Aaron Larker	Denver Pyle
Colie Fletcher	Gregg Palmer
Additional Cast	Kevin Hagen
Story, Script	Paul Savage

The Television Programs

Director	Andrew McLaglen
Associate Producer	Frank Paris
Producer	Norman Macdonnell

Beverly Garland is a familiar face to television audiences. She appeared as the first liberated female detective, Casey Jones, in *Decoy,* as well as Fred MacMurray's wife on *My Three Sons* and Kate Jackson's mother on *Scarecrow and Mrs. King.* Her film credits include *D.O.A., The Desperate Hours,* and *The Joker Is Wild.* Paul Savage began his long association with *Gunsmoke* on the radio show as an actor. He later wrote and became story consultant for the television program.

Jeb. May 25, 1963. Production #31235.

Jeb Willis finds a horse loose on the prairie and appropriates it as his own to ride into Dodge. While in town, Jeb is befriended by Ab Singleton, who buys the horse from him. Later, Ab is accused of stealing the horse and as a result, is killed.

Jeb Willis	Jim Hampton
Ab Singleton	Roy Thinnes
Chouteau	Emile Genest
Story, Script	Paul Savage
Director	Harry Harris, Jr.
Associate Producer	Frank Paris
Producer	Norman Macdonnell

In addition to his other television credits, Jim Hampton appeared as a regular on *F Troop* and *The Doris Day Show.*

The Quest for Asa Janin. June 1, 1963. Production #31236.

Matt is forced to send his friend Dave Ingalls to prison, even though he believes Dave to be innocent of the crime. Dave has been found guilty of murdering his girlfriend and is sentenced to hang. A deputy arrives to take Dave to Hayes City for execution, leaving Matt one week to find the real killer, and save his friend's life.

Macklin	Anthony Caruso
Asa Janin	Richard Devon
Dave Ingalls	Gene Darfler
Pardee	George Keymas
Additional Cast	Jack Lambert
Story, Script	Paul Savage
Director	Andrew McLaglen
Associate Producer	Frank Paris
Producer	Norman Macdonnell

Chester's Indian. June 8, 1963, rerun. First aired May 12, 1962.

Half Straight. June 15, 1963, rerun. First aired February 17, 1962.

Old Yellow Boots. June 29, 1963, rerun. First aired October 10, 1961.

Abe Blocker. July 6, 1963, rerun. First aired November 24, 1962.

Cale. July 13, 1963, rerun. First aired May 5, 1962.

Milly. July 27, 1963, rerun. First aired November 25, 1961.

GUNSMOKE — III. THE PROGRAMS

Cody's Code. August 3, 1963, rerun. First aired January 20, 1962.

Call Me Dodie. August 10, 1963, rerun. First aired September 22, 1962.

The Summons. August 17, 1963, rerun. First aired April 21, 1962.

Us Haggens. August 24, 1963, rerun. First aired December 8, 1962.

The Way It Is. August 31, 1963, rerun. First aired December 1, 1962.

The Gallows. September 14, 1963, rerun. First aired March 3, 1962.

Quint Asper Comes Home. September 21, 1963, rerun. First aired September 29, 1962.

NINTH SEASON

Kate Heller. September 28, 1963. Production #7102.

The lure of easy money is too much for teenaged Andy Heller, who plans to run away from his grandmother's relay station. Andy's greed drives him to murder, when he is surprised by his victim as he breaks into a cash box. Matt sets out after the killer without knowing his identity, and is shot in an ambush by Andy. He is rescued by a passing stage, only to be taken unconscious to the home of the young fugitive.

```
Kate Heller .................................. Mabel Albertson
Andy Heller .................................. Tom Lowell
Tess ......................................... Betsy Jones-Moreland
Story, Script ................................ Kathleen Hite
Director ..................................... Harry Harris, Jr.
Associate Producer ........................... Frank Paris
Producer ..................................... Norman Macdonnell
```

Tom Lowell was a regular on the television series *Combat*.

Lover Boy. October 5, 1963. Production #7107.

Frontier philanderer Kyle Kelly has an affair with a married woman named Avis Fisher. When her husband Ab is made aware of the romance, the stage is set for tragedy.

```
Avis Fisher .................................. Sheree North
Ab Fisher .................................... Alan Baxter
Kyle Kelly ................................... Ken Curtis
Mom .......................................... Dorothy Konrad
Additional Cast .............................. Richard Coogan
Story, Script ................................ John Meston
Director ..................................... Andrew McLaglen
Associate Producer ........................... Frank Paris
Producer ..................................... Norman Macdonnell
```

Even though Ken Curtis played Festus Haggen in a previous episode, he did not become a principle member of the cast until *Prairie Wolfer,* January 18, 1964. Ken Curtis plays the suave Kyle Kelly in this episode. Sheree North was a regular on several television shows. She was nominated for Emmy Awards for guest-starring roles on *Marcus Welby, M.D.,* and *Archie Bunker's Place.* Her film credits include *No Down*

The Television Programs

Payment, Madigan, and *The Shootist.* North is at her best playing once-glamorous tough women who are "a little past their prime, but not their pride." Dorothy Konrad was a regular on the television comedy *The Last Resort.* On television, Richard Coogan was the original Captain Video of *Captain Video and His Video Rangers* and Matthew Wayne of *The Californians.* Coogan's radio credits include *Abie's Irish Rose* and *Young Doctor Malone.*

Legends Don't Sleep. October 12, 1963. Production #7106.
Notorious gunman Race Fallon returns to Dodge after serving five years in prison. Frustrated in his attempts to convince anyone he has reformed his ways, Fallon is further hampered by Britt, a young would-be-bad-man, who admires Fallon's darker deeds.

Race Fallon	William Talman
Britt	Scott Marlowe
Aunt Jen	Hope Summers
Filler	Robert Bice
Sheriff	Don Haggerty
Louie Pheeters	James Nusser
Grosset	Alan Dexter
Barkeep	Ken Kenopka
Story, Script	Kathleen Hite
Director	Harry Harris, Jr.
Associate Producer	Frank Paris
Producer	Norman Macdonnell

On television William Talman is best remembered as Hamilton Burger, the district attorney on *Perry Mason* who never won a case. Don Haggerty appeared as a regular on several television programs including *The Life and Legend of Wyatt Earp.*

Tobe. October 19, 1963. Production #7109.
Tobe Hostader loses his farm to creditors and takes a job in Dodge. His new life brings him in contact with Hanna Young, one of Kitty's saloon girls. Tobe falls in love with Hanna, not realizing she has run away from gambler Frank Ebels. When Ebels catches up with Hanna, he threatens to do harm to her boyfriend, unless she returns to him.

Tobe Hostader	Harry Townes
Hanna Young	Mary La Roche
Frank Ebels	Philip Abbott
Skinner	L.Q. Jones
Ma Smalley	Sarah Selby
Story, Script	Paul Savage
Director	John W. English
Associate Producer	Frank Paris
Producer	Norman Macdonnell

Philip Abbott appeared on television as Arthur Ward of *The F.B.I.* and John Franklin in *Rich Man, Poor Man—Book II.* L.Q. Jones appeared as a regular on two television Westerns, *Cheyenne* and *The Virginian.* John English directed many serials and B-Westerns starring such cowboys as Roy Rogers and Gene Autry.

Easy Come. October 26, 1963. Production #7103.
A mild appearing, bespectacled cowboy named Elmo Sippy leads Matt on a trail

GUNSMOKE — III. THE PROGRAMS

of senseless killings, all committed because Sippy needs gambling money. Along the way, Sippy enlists an unwitting partner, which leads to further tragedy.

Elmo Sippy	Andrew Prine
Emmett Calhoun	Carl Reindel
Tobin	George Wallace
Riley	Charles Briggs
Story, Script	John Meston
Director	Andrew McLaglen
Associate Producer	Frank Paris
Producer	Norman Macdonnell

My Sister's Keeper. November 2, 1963. Production #7110.

Widower Pete Sievers finds solace by accepting a job at a ranch owned by spinster Nell Shuler and her spirited younger sister Leah. Leah's fascination with Sievers creates trouble when it is discovered by Nell.

Nell Shuler	Nancy Wickwire
Pete Sievers	James Broderick
Leah Shuler	Jennifer Billingsley
Story, Script	Kathleen Hite
Director	Harry Harris, Jr.
Associate Producer	Frank Paris
Producer	Norman Macdonnell

James Broderick is best remembered as Doug Lawrence on the television program *Family.* His son is film star Matthew Broderick.

Quint's Trail. November 9, 1963. Production #7112.

Cyrus Neff, his wife Flora, and his daughter Belle decide to flee from a tragedy in their past by starting a new life in Oregon. On their way they are bilked out of a large sum of money by a fast talking trail guide, who fails to show up with their promised supplies. While Chester tracks the crook's trail, Quint is pursuaded to act as Neff's guide. In the course of their journey, Quint finds that Belle has fallen for him.

Cyrus Neff	Everett Sloane
Belle Neff	Sharon Farrell
Florie Neff	Shirley O'Hara
Clardy	Don Haggerty
Finch	Charles Seel
Story, Script	Kathleen Hite
Director	Harry Harris, Jr.
Associate Producer	Frank Paris
Producer	Norman Macdonnell

Charles Seel, who in later years played the part of Barney the telegraph agent, plays Finch in this episode. Seel was also a regular on *The Road West* and was seen as Mr. Kringle on *Dennis the Menace.* Everett Sloan was a member of Orson Welles' Mercury Theatre. His films include *Citizen Kane, The Lady from Shanghai,* and *The Men.*

Carter Caper. November 16, 1963. Production #7111.

Billy Hargis stops shiftless Joe Stark from stealing his horse and gives Stark a beating. Stark follows Hargis into Dodge and retaliates by spreading the rumor that Hargis killed the fast-gun artist of Armarillo. Hargis' plans for marrying Cara Miles are thwarted by his new unwanted reputation.

The Television Programs

Billy Hargis	Jeremy Slate
Joe Stark	William Phipps
Cara Miles	Anjanette Comer
Flack	Rayford Barnes
Mims	I. Stanford Jolley
Smith	Barney Phillips
Moss Grimmick	George Selk
Waiter	Michael Fox
Turner	William Fawcett
Carter	Jacque Shelton
Bud	Dennis Cross
Story, Script	John Meston
Director	Jerry Hopper
Associate Producer	Frank Paris
Producer	Norman Macdonnell

Anjanette Comer's screen credits include *The Loved One*. Michael Fox appeared as a regular on the television series *Casablanca*. Director Jerry Hopper originally wrote for radio before moving on to films and then television. His film credits include *Hurricane Smith* and *Never Say Goodbye*.

Ex-Con. November 30, 1963. Production #7117.

After serving a prison term, ex-convict Leo Pitts returns to Dodge with his saloon girl bride Lily and $5000 in stolen gold. Pitts intends to start a new life, but only after he settles with Matt. When Pitts is discovered shot dead in a cabin, Matt is also found there unconscious from a raging fever. When Matt awakens he does not remember anything about the incident, and adding to the complications, Pitts was unarmed.

Lily Pitts	Jeanne Cooper
Leo Pitts	John Kellogg
Pitts	Richard Devon
Clabe	Raymund Guth
Judge	Howard Wendell
Mr. Botkin	Roy Roberts
Kelly	Harry Lauter
Kid	Tommy Alexander
Story, Script	John Meston
Director	Thomas Carr
Associate Producer	Frank Paris
Producer	Norman Macdonnell

Jeanne Cooper played Grace Douglas on the television series *Bracken's World* and Kay Chancellor on the soap opera *The Young and the Restless*. Cooper is the mother of Corbin Bernsen of *L.A. Law*. Thomas Carr directed B-features in the 1940s, primarily Westerns. On television he often directed for *Rawhide*.

Extradition [Part I]. December 7, 1963. Production #7115.

Matt tracks murderer Charlie Hacker as far as the Mexican border. Greedy Lt. Julio Chavez allows Matt to continue through Mexico on one condition, that he accompany the marshal and perhaps share in the reward money. Chavez has one further demand, he insists on taking his sweetheart Marguerita.

Extradition [Part II]. December 14, 1963. Production #7116.

Matt and his prisoner Charlie Hacker are behind bars as guests of a Mexican army captain named Diaz. The corrupt Diaz would like a share of the reward money for Hacker. To add to Matt's problems, waiting along the desolate route back to the U.S. is El Pinon and his ruthless band of desperados.

>   Julio Chavez .... Gilbert Roland
>   Charlie Hacker .... Gene Evans
>   Marguerita .... Anna Navarro
>   El Pinon .... Rico Alaniz
>   Captain Diaz .... Alex Montoya
>   Willie .... Walter Burke
>   Rivera .... Miguel Landa
>   Miguel .... Pepe Hern
>   Girl .... Lisa Seagram
>   Boy .... Ricky Vera
>   *Story, Script* .... Antony Ellis
>   *Director* .... John W. English
>   *Associate Producer* .... Frank Paris
>   *Producer* .... Norman Macdonnell

Gilbert Roland parlayed his Latin looks into a lucrative film career as a dashing romantic lead. He began in silent movies and made a successful transition into "talkies." His credits include *Camille, Captain Kidd,* and *Cheyenne Autumn*. Character actor Gene Evans appeared in such films as *Operation Petticoat, Support Your Local Sheriff* and *There Was a Crooked Man*. On television he was a regular on *My Friend Flicka, Matt Helm* and *Spencer's Pilot*. Antony Ellis wrote for radio's *Gunsmoke*. He also produced the television Western *Black Saddle*.

The Magician. December 21, 1963. Production #7104.

Medicine man Jeremiah Dark and his daughter Alice find only tragedy when they attempt to sell their wares in Dodge. Dark's hopes for starting a new life are shattered by an influential rancher, after Dark is accused of being a card shark.

>   Jeremiah Dark .... Lloyd Corrigan
>   Alice Dark .... Brooke Bundy
>   Wells .... Barry Kelley
>   Tom Wells .... Tom Simcox
>   Banks .... Sheldon Allman
>   Ned .... William Zuckert
>   Sy .... Ken Tyles
>   *Story, Script* .... John Kneubuhl
>   *Director* .... Harry Harris, Jr.
>   *Associate Producer* .... Frank Paris
>   *Producer* .... Norman Macdonnell

Lloyd Corrigan appeared as a regular on a number of television programs including *The Life and Legend of Wyatt Earp*. Barry Kelley appeared as Charlie Anderson in the dramatic series *Big Town*. Tom Simcox played Walt Robinson on the short-lived adventure series *Code R*. Sheldon Allman was seen as Norm Miller in the television comedy series *Harris Against the World*. On television William Zuckert was a regular on three series, *Mr. Novak, The Wackiest Ship in the Army,* and *Captain Nice*.

Pa Hack's Brood. December 28, 1963. Production #7108.

Eccentric transient, Pa Hack, has never done an honest day's work in his life. Still, he is determined to acquire a ranch for himself and his motley brood of three.

The Television Programs

Unfortunately, the ranch he sets his sights on belongs to Jeb Willis. This does not pose a problem to old Hack, however, who plans to abduct Willis and force him into a marriage with his daughter Maybelle.

Pa Hack	Milton Selzer
Maybelle Hack	Lynn Loring
Jeb Willis	Jim Hampton
Lonnie Hack	Charles Kuenstle
Orville Hack	George Lindsey
Pa Willis	Russell Thorson
Annie	Marianna Hill
Story, Script	Paul Savage
Director	Jerry Hopper
Associate Producer	Frank Paris
Producer	Norman Macdonnell

Lynn Loring is a familiar face to television viewers. As a child she started on daytime television in *Search for Tomorrow*. She grew into prime time with such series as *Fair Exchange*. In recent years she has moved into producing films that include *Sizzle* and *Mr. Mom*. George Lindsey is best known to television audiences as Goober Pyle of *The Andy Griffith Show* and *Mayberry R.F.D.* Radio veteran Russell Thorson's voice was heard on numerous mystery programs. On television he played on *One Man's Family* and *The Detectives*.

The Glory and the Mud. January 4, 1964. Production #7113.

Jack Dakota, a retired gunfighter and star of a wild west show, returns to Dodge to rekindle a 20-year romance with Sarah Carr. Although Dakota is unable to escape his own legendary deeds, his former sweetheart is tempted to foresake her dress shop to start a new life with him.

Jack Dakota	Kent Smith
Sarah Carr	Marsha Hunt
Sam Beal	James Best
Cloudy	Robert Sorrells
Dan Binney	Joseph Hamilton
Young Buck	Rick Murray
Amy	Jenny Lee Arness
Story, Script	Gwen Bagni Gielgud
Director	Jerry Hopper
Associate Producer	Frank Paris
Producer	Norman Macdonnell

Jenny Lee Arness is James Arness' daughter. Marsha Hunt is the former wife of director Jerry Hopper. Hunt's films include *Pride and Prejudice, Blossoms in the Dust,* and *Smash-Up*. Her career suffered a setback when she was blacklisted because of the House on Un-American Activities hearings. On television she appeared as Jennifer Peck in *Peck's Bad Girl*.

Dry Well. January 11, 1964. Production #7120.

Vain Yuma Linz enjoys the attention of Web Vickers and Jeff Daly, her husband's cowhands. When her husband Dave is shot by one of the two men, Quint is the only witness. In an attempt to clear his son of the murder, Ira Vickers kidnaps Quint, hoping to terrorize him into testifying on his son's behalf.

Yuma Linz	Karen Sharpe

GUNSMOKE — III. THE PROGRAMS

Web Vickers	Tom Simcox
Ira Vickers	Ned Glass
Jeff Daly	John Hanek
Dave Yuma	Bill Henry
Story, Script	John Meston
Director	Harry Harris, Jr.
Associate Producer	Frank Paris
Producer	Norman Macdonnell

Prairie Wolfer. January 18, 1964. Production #7119.

Drifter Festus Haggen, the only honest member of an outlaw family, has turned to the disreputable trade of wolf hunter to make a living. He surprises rancher Nate Guthrie, and his partner-in-crime, Rolly Wendt, in the act of butchering stolen cattle. Later, when Festus is hired by the cattlemen's association to take care of wolves supposedly killing the cattle, Guthrie fears Festus will betray his operation and plots to frame him.

Nate Guthrie	Noah Beery, Jr.
Rolly Wendt	Don Dubbins
Sarah Guthrie	Holly McIntire
Charlie	Fred Coby
Dude	James Drake
Story, Script	John Dunkel
Director	Andrew V. McLaglen
Associate Producer	Frank Paris
Producer	Norman Macdonnell

Prairie Wolfer introduces Festus as a regular. This is a rare episode because James Arness, Dennis Weaver, Milburn Stone, Amanda Blake, Burt Reynolds, Ken Curtis, and Glenn Strange all appear. The title *Prairie Wolfer* was used again November 13, 1967. Noah Beery, Jr., is probably best known as Rocky of *The Rockford Files.* In addition, he appeared as a regular on several other series including *Circus Boy.* His films include *Of Mice and Men, Red River,* and *Inherit the Wind.*

Friend. January 25, 1964. Production #7122.

Judd Nellis, who saved Matt's life ten years earlier, turns up in Dodge once again in the role of the good samaritan. Frank Gore has been beaten and robbed of his life savings and Judd has managed to carry Gore into Dodge for help. After a brief reunion with Matt, Judd returns to his ranch in the town of Friend. Three weeks later Matt receives news that Judd is dead. Matt rides out to Friend, and tries to unravel the baffling circumstances surrounding Judd's mysterious demise.

Judd Nellis	Tom Reese
Frank Gore	George Keymas
Marge	Jan Shepard
Father Tom	Ben Wright
Runt	Butch Patrick
Barkeep	Frank Kreig
Finley	Ralph Moody
Story, Script	Kathleen Hite
Director	Harry Harris, Jr.
Associate Producer	Frank Paris
Producer	Norman Macdonnell

The Television Programs

On television, child performer Butch Patrick was a regular on *The Real McCoys*, but Butch is probably best known for his role as pointy-eared Eddie Munster on *The Munsters*.

Once a Haggen. February 1, 1964. Production #7118.
Festus and his partner Bucko Taos lose all their money in a poker game. Self-pity sends the two to drown their sorrows in drink. When the winner is later found stabbed to death, Bucko is charged with the crime. Festus claims his buddy is innocent and must find a way to prove it.

Bucko Taos	Slim Pickens
April	Elizabeth MacRae
Fickett	Kenneth Tobey
Pop	Roy Barcroft
Additional Cast	John Hudson
Story, Script	Les Crutchfield
Director	Andrew McLaglen
Associate Producer	Frank Paris
Producer	Norman Macdonnell

Slim Pickens was a character actor of note appearing regularly on television and in films. The former rodeo star's movie credits include *Dr. Strangelove*, where he was seen riding a bomb as if it was a bucking bronco.

No Hands. February 8, 1964. Production #7101.
Pa Ginnis and his four worthless sons burst into Doc's office, after Lon Ginnis breaks his leg. Doc is busy treating carpenter Will Timble for an eye injury and the Ginnis' take offense at being kept waiting. Later that evening, they vent their anger by assaulting the harmless Timble, injuring his hand and jeopardizing his livelihood.

Will Timble	Strother Martin
Pa Ginnis	Denver Pyle
Emmett Ginnis	Kevin Hagen
Jess Ginnis	Rayford Barnes
Ben Ginnis	Conlan Carter
Lon Ginnis	Wright King
Wib Smith	Orville Sherman
Barkeep	Shug Fisher
Boy	Mark Murray
Story, Script	John Meston
Director	Andrew McLaglen
Associate Producer	Frank Paris
Producer	Norman Macdonnell

Shug Fisher appeared regularly on television on *Ozark Jubilee, Ripcord,* which starred Ken Curtis, and *The Beverly Hillbillies*.

May Blossoms. February 15, 1964. Production #7123. Rerun September 19, 1964.
Marriage-shy Festus faces the threat of matrimony, when his pretty cousin May Blossoms arrives in Dodge. May Blossoms has travelled all the way from Texas to make good the marriage promise their fathers made the day she was born. The comic atmosphere of the show takes a serious turn, when May Blossoms is molested by Lon Harder while Festus is away. Upon learning of the incident, Festus goes after Harder with a vengeance.

GUNSMOKE — III. THE PROGRAMS

May Blossoms	Lauri Peters
Lon	Charles Gray
Greer	Richard X. Slattery
Feeder	Roger Torrey
Ma Smalley	Sarah Selby
Story, Script	Kathleen Hite
Director	Andrew McLaglen
Associate Producer	Frank Paris
Producer	Norman Macdonnell

Richard X. Slattery appeared as a regular on such programs as *The Gallant Men, Mr. Roberts, Switch,* and *C.P.O. Sharkey.* Roger Torrey is familiar to television audiences from his appearances on *The Iron Horse* and *The Beverly Hillbillies.*

The Bassops. February 22, 1964. Production #7121.

While Matt is bringing Wayne Kelby back to trial, Kelby attacks him. In the struggle Matt loses his badge and gunbelt, but manages to handcuff Kelby to his own wrist before losing consciousness. The two are found by Deke and Mellie Bassop and their son Tommy. Mellie is pregnant and in bad need of water. Kelby, who regains consciousness first, tries to convince the Bassops that he, not Matt, is the lawman.

Wayne Kelby	Robert Wilke
Deke Bassop	Warren Oates
Mellie Bassop	Eunice Pollis Christopher
Tommy Bassop	Mickey Sholdar
Harford	James Griffith
Telegrapher	Ollie O'Toole
Wilson	Robert Bice
Donna Lee	Patricia Joyce
Story, Script	Tom Hanley
Director	Andrew McLaglen
Associate Producer	Frank Paris
Producer	Norman Macdonnell

Mickey Sholdar played Steve Morley on the television comedy *The Farmer's Daughter.* Robert Bice was a regular on the dramatic series, *Mysteries of Chinatown.*

The Kite. February 29, 1964. Production #7124.

Young Letty Cassidy is alone with her mother Clara, when outlaw Ed Polk rides up to the lonely ranch. Clara reaches for a rifle to defend herself and Polk shoots her down, unaware that Letty is hiding in the bushes. When Letty's father returns, he insists on revenge for his wife's death. He drags Letty all over Dodge looking for the killer, all the while making her a target for the murderer.

Ed Polk	Lyle Bettger
Rod Cassidy	Michael Higgins
Letty Cassidy	Betsy Hale
Clara Cassidy	Allyson Ames
Story, Script	John Meston
Director	Andrew McLaglen
Associate Producer	Frank Paris
Producer	Norman Macdonnell

Character actor Lyle Bettger played mostly heavies. His film credits include *The Greatest Show on Earth, Destry,* and *Gunfight at the OK Corral.* He guest starred in

The Television Programs

numerous television programs and was a regular on two unsuccessful series, *Court of Last Resort* and *The Grand Jury*. Michael Higgins appeared on television as Johnny Roberts of *One Man's Family*.

Comanches Is Soft. March 7, 1964. Production #7126.

In a playfull scuffle between Quint and Festus, Quint's bellows are smashed beyond repair. When no replacement is available in Dodge, Quint heads for Wichita, accompanied by Festus. When they arrive, the boys celebrate with a big night in a local saloon. The next morning, Liz, a pretty saloon girl, informs the two that they had invited her to accompany them back to Dodge. Both are so enamored with Liz, that neither remembers that she already has a boyfriend, a bruiser of a man by the name of Big Hardy, who is not about to give her up without a fight.

Liz	Kathy Nolan
Big Hardy	Don Megowan
One	Ted Jordan
Additional Cast	Dean Stanton, Rex Holman
Story, Script	Kathleen Hite
Director	Harry Harris, Jr.
Associate Producer	Frank Paris
Producer	Norman Macdonnell

Father's Love. March 14, 1964. Production #7125.

When saloon girl Cora Prell rebuffs Jesse Price's advances, he vows he will get even with her. Sometime later Cora marries Tom King and when she arrives at Tom's ranch, she is shocked to learn that Price is Tom's uncle.

Tom King	Ed Nelson
Cora Prell	Shary Marshall
Jesse Price	Robert F. Simon
Simms	Anthony Caruso
Story, Script	John Meston
Director	Harry Harris, Jr.
Associate Producer	Frank Paris
Producer	Norman Macdonnell

Now That April's Here. March 21, 1964. Production #7127.

Festus' girlfriend April tries to convince him and Quint that she has witnessed a murder. The two believe that she is trying to play each for a fool, but the murderers heed April's statement.

April	Elizabeth MacRae
Bender	Royal Dano
Grody	Hal Baylor
Story, Script	Les Crutchfield
Director	Andrew McLaglen
Associate Producer	Frank Paris
Producer	Norman Macdonnell

Caleb. March 28, 1964. Production #7128.

Caleb Marr, a poor dirt farmer with only 14 bushels of potatoes to show for his latest crop, decides to leave his farm and his work-worn wife Dorcas for a new life in Dodge. Caleb becomes acquainted with the intricacies of city life through an

GUNSMOKE — III. THE PROGRAMS

innocent relationship with saloon girl Julie. Unfortunately, this puts him in the awkward position of having to stand up to gunman Lige Follett, Julie's boyfriend. The incident with Lige is blown totally out of proportion by the townfolk and Caleb is considered a hero, something that Lige feels he must put a stop to.

Caleb Marr	John Dehner
Dorcas Marr	Ann Loos
Lige Follett	Lane Bradford
Julie	Dorothy Green
Betsy	Vickie Cos
George	Christopher Barrey
Stable Boy	Dennis Robertson
Chad	Ted Jordan
Story, Script	Paul Savage
Director	Harry Harris, Jr.
Associate Producer	Frank Paris
Producer	Norman Macdonnell

Dennis Robertson appeared as a regular in two short-lived television comedies, *Tammy* and *The Tim Conway Show*.

Owney Tupper Had a Daughter. April 4, 1964. Production #7105.

Elderly widower Owney Tupper loses the custody of his only child to the girl's aunt. The judge decrees that Owney can have Amity back when he is able to maintain a fit home for her. In his desperation, Owney accepts the job of hangman, so he can buy seed for a crop. As a result, the lonely old farmer faces the scorn of his neighbors.

Owney Tupper	Jay C. Flippen
Amity Tupper	Andrea Darvi
Ellen	Noreen Corcoran
Jay	James Seay
Judge	Howard Wendell
Wib Smith	Orville Sherman
Hank Miller	Hank Patterson
Clara	Dolores Quinton
Art	Vernon Rich
Mal	Berkeley Harris
Clay	Steve Gaynor
Story, Script	Paul Savage
Director	Jerry Hopper
Associate Producer	Frank Paris
Producer	Norman Macdonnell

Character actor Jay C. Flippen appeared as a regular on *Ensign O'Toole*. His film credits include *The Wild One*, *How the West Was Won*, and *Cat Ballou*. Noreen Corcoran appeared as niece Kelly on *Bachelor Father*. Paul Savage was nominated for a Writer's Guild Award for this episode.

Bently. April 11, 1964. Production #7114.

Clara Wright is scorned by townfolk after her husband Ned is acquitted or murder. Strangely, Clara is befriended by the same people who scorned her, after Ned gives a deathbed confession. Chester, however, refuses to believe Ned was capable of murder. The plot thickens when well-to-do Emily and Albert Calvin, close friends of the man Ned was accused of killing, bring Clara into their home to live.

The Television Programs

```
Clara Wright ................................. Jan Clayton
Albert Calvin ............................. Charles McGraw
Emily Calvin ................................. June Dayton
Ned Wright .................................... Bill Erwin
Additional Cast .............................. Gene Lyons
Story, Script ............................. John Kneubuhl
Director ................................ Harry Harris, Jr.
Associate Producer ........................... Frank Paris
Producer ............................... Norman Macdonnell
```

This episode marks Dennis Weaver's final appearance on *Gunsmoke*. Jan Clayton is best remembered as the mother on *Lassie*. Tough-guy character actor Charles McGraw appeared on television as a regular on *The Falcon*, *Casablanca*, and *The Smith Family*. Included in his film credits are *The Birds*, *In Cold Blood*, and *Hang 'Em High*. On television, June Dayton was a regular on *The Aldrich Family*.

Kitty Cornered. April 18, 1964. Production #7131.

The future of the Long Branch is threatened, when brash Stella Damon flounces into Dodge with the intention of putting Kitty out of business. Stella has come to Dodge from Pueblo, after her establishment there was destroyed by fire. When Kitty refuses to sell, Stella puts up the fanciest saloon in Dodge history, complete with dancing girls and a runway.

```
Stella Damon ........................... Jacqueline Scott
Harry Oble .................................. Shug Fisher
Eddie Fitch ................................ Joseph Sirola
Story, Script ............................. Kathleen Hite
Director .................................... John Brahm
Associate Producer ........................... Frank Paris
Producer ............................... Norman Macdonnell
```

Joseph Sirola appeared as a regular on *The Magician* and *The Montefuscos*. John Brahm directed such films as *The Lodger* and *Hangover Square*. On television, in addition to *Gunsmoke*, he directed for such suspense series as *Thriller*, *Alfred Hitchcock Presents*, and *The Twilight Zone*.

The Promoter. April 25, 1964. Production #7129.

When Henry Huckaby arrives in Dodge he is unable to land a job. After professional boxer Otto Gundlach is involved in a fist fight, Huckaby hits upon an idea to make his fortune. He is going to promote a prize fight in Dodge.

```
Henry Huckaby ................................ Vic Perrin
Lt. Gibbins .................................. Allen Case
Sgt. Clyde ................................ Robert Fortier
Otto Gundlach ...................... Wilheim Von Homburg
Daisy Huckaby ............................. Peggy Stewart
Johnny Towers ............................... John Newman
Story, Script ............................... John Meston
Director ................................ Andrew McLaglen
Associate Producer ........................... Frank Paris
Producer ............................... Norman Macdonnell
```

This episode required more extras than any other *Gunsmoke* episode up to that time.

Trip West. May 2, 1964. Production #7132.

Professor Ramsey convinces timid Elwood Hardacre that unless Hardacre partakes of the professor's special elixir, he has only three months to live. Before Hardacre learns otherwise, Ramsey is run out of town by the law. Believing he has only months to live, Hardacre throws caution to the wind. He quits his 15 year position as bank clerk and takes up with saloon girl Annie Gilroy. Annie leaves her ruthless boyfriend Meade Agate for Hardacre, who draws all his savings out of the bank and joins Annie to seek adventure.

>   Elwood Hardacre .... Herbert Anderson
>   Professor Ramsey .... Vinton Hayworth
>   Annie Gilroy .... Sharon Farrell
>   Meade Agate .... H.M. Wynant
>   Arbuckle .... Percy Helton
>   Lucille .... Elizabeth Shaw
>   Frank .... Henry Rowland
>   Mrs. Crabbe .... Angela Clarke
>   *Story, Script* .... John Dunkel
>   *Director* .... Harry Harris, Jr.
>   *Associate Producer* .... Frank Paris
>   *Producer* .... Norman Macdonnell

Herbert Anderson is well known to television viewers as Henry Mitchell, the long-suffering father of *Dennis the Menace*.

Scot Free. May 9, 1964. Production #7130.

Matt and Festus find a body near the old Whitaker place, now owned by beautiful newcomer Nora Brand. Nora claims no knowledge of the incident. She tells Matt she is a widow and lives alone except for her hired hand. What Matt does not know is that the so-called hired hand is her lover, Rob Scot, and that the body is that of her husband.

>   Nora Brand .... Patricia Owens
>   Rob Scot .... Jay Lanin
>   Millie Scot .... Anne Barton
>   *Story, Script* .... Kathleen Hite
>   *Director* .... Harry Harris, Jr.
>   *Associate Producer* .... Frank Paris
>   *Producer* .... Norman Macdonnell

The Warden. May 16, 1964. Production #7133.

A sly Indian named Bull Foot sells his beautiful daughter Cool Dawn to a man named Stark. The man places his lovely bounty in a wagon and leaves. En route to Dodge, Festus' path crosses that of Stark's wagon and Cool Dawn leaps out. Stark angrily demands her return, but she refuses. Instead she accompanies Festus back toward Dodge. During their journey Cool Dawn gives Festus the slip as well, and steals his horse.

>   Cool Dawn .... Julie Parrish
>   Bull Foot .... Anthony Caruso
>   Stark .... George Kennedy
>   Trainey .... Christopher Connelly
>   *Story, Script* .... Les Crutchfield
>   *Director* .... Andrew McLaglen
>   *Associate Producer* .... Frank Paris
>   *Producer* .... Norman Macdonnell

The Television Programs

Julie Parrish was a regular on the comedy series, *Good Morning, World.* Christopher Connelly played Norman Harrington in *Peyton Place* and Moze Pray in the comedy series *Paper Moon.*

Homecoming. May 23, 1964. Production #7134.

Orval Bass returns home after serving seven years in prison. He learns that his wife Edna has had him declared dead and has remarried so she can cash in on Bass' home and harness shop. Bass is determined to take back what is his, but the struggle will be a difficult one. His former wife has even turned his son Ethan against him, and the emnity between Orval, and Edna's new husband, Hector Lowell, threatens to turn into bloodshed.

Orval Bass	Harold J. Stone
Edna Lowell	Phyllis Coates
Hector Lowell	Jack Elam
Additional Cast	Tom Lowell
Story	Shimon Wincelberg
Script	John Meston
Director	Harry Harris, Jr.
Associate Producer	Frank Paris
Producer	Norman Macdonnell

The title *Homecoming* was used again January 8, 1973. Tom Lowell was a regular on the television series *Combat.*

The Other Half. May 30, 1964. Production #7135.

Twins, Jess and Jay Bartell, have joint responsibility for their handicapped father's feed and fuel store. Both boys are also in love with the same girl, Nancy Otis. Jay begins to display signs of jealousy and chaffs at the fact that Jess appears to be the more popular of the two. When Jess is murdered in cold blood while working alone in the office, Jay appears to have the motive and the means.

Jess/Jay Bartell	Lee Kinsolving
Nancy Otis	Donna J. Anderson
Sam Bartell	Paul Fix
Story, Script	John Dunkel
Director	Andrew McLaglen
Associate Producer	Frank Paris
Producer	Norman Macdonnell

Journey for Three. June 6, 1964. Production #7136.

While en route to California, Adam Gifford tries to warn his younger brother Cyrus about their traveling companion, a young ruffian named Boyd Lambert. However, Cyrus refuses to heed Adam, even after Lambert accidentally kills a girl he attempted to molest. Cyrus' misplaced admiration for Lambert could spell serious trouble for both brothers.

Adam Gifford	William Arvin
Cyrus Gifford	Michael J. Pollard
Boyd Lambert	Mark Goddard
Girl	Margaret Bly
Telegrapher	Ollie O'Toole
Story, Script	Frank Paris
Director	Harry Harris, Jr.

GUNSMOKE — III. THE PROGRAMS

  Associate Producer .... Frank Paris
  Producer .... Norman Macdonnell

 Michael J. Pollard appeared as Leonard in the television comedy series *Leo and Liz in Beverly Hills*. The offbeat character actor appeared in such films as *Bonnie and Clyde*, for which he was nominated for an Academy Award as Best Supporting Actor, and *Little Fauss and Big Halsy*. Mark Goddard appeared as a regular in such television series as *The Detectives* and *Lost in Space*.

Cotter's Girl. June 13, 1964, rerun. First aired January 19, 1963.

Reprisal. June 20, 1964, rerun. First aired March 10, 1962.

Uncle Sunday. June 27, 1964, rerun. First aired December 15, 1962.

The Trappers. July 4, 1964, rerun. First aired November 3, 1962.

Quint-Cident. July 11, 1964, rerun. First aired April 27, 1963.

Ash. July 18, 1964, rerun. First aired February 16, 1963.

Nina's Revenge. July 25, 1964, rerun. First aired December 16, 1961.

With a Smile. August 8, 1964, rerun. First aired March 30, 1963.

The Far Places. August 15, 1964, rerun. First aired April 6, 1963.

Coventry. August 22, 1964, rerun. First aired March 17, 1962.

Root Down. August 29, 1964, rerun. First aired October 6, 1962.

Collie's Free. September 5, 1964, rerun. First aired October 20, 1962.

May Blossoms. September 19, 1964, rerun. First aired February 15, 1964.

TENTH SEASON

Blue Heaven. September 26, 1964. Production #0410.
 Although wanted for murder, Kip Gilman risks capture to help a runaway boy find his estranged mother. Matt and Festus recognize Gilman from a wanted poster, but they are not convinced that the charge is legitimate. While Gilman, posing as the father of ragamuffin Packy Kerlin, arranges a homecoming for the boy and his alcoholic mother, the evidence mounts that the three men trailing Gilman have a hidden purpose.
  Kip Gilman .... Tom O'Connor
  Packy Kerlin .... Kurt Russell
  Elena .... Diane Ladd
  Tabe .... Karl Swenson
  Sykes .... Jan Merlin
  Duster .... Eddie Hice

The Television Programs

Story, Script	Les Crutchfield
Director	Michael O'Herlihy
Associate Producer	Frank Paris
Producer	Norman Macdonnell

Tim O'Connor appeared as a regular on *Peyton Place*, *Wheels*, and *Buck Rogers in the 25th Century*. Before moving on to films, Kurt Russell starred in three television series, *The Travels of Jaimie McPheeters*, *The New Land*, and *Quest*. His movie credits include *Swing Shift*, *Overboard*, and the 1982 remake of *The Thing*. James Arness appeared in the original version of *The Thing*. Diane Ladd played in both the film and television versions of *Alice Doesn't Live Here Anymore*, renamed *Alice* on television. She was nominated for an Academy Award for Best Supporting Actress for her performance. Jan Merlin was a regular on *Tom Corbett, Space Cadet* and *The Rough Riders*. He expanded his horizons to include writing and in 1975 won an Emmy for Best Writing for a Daytime Drama Series for *Another World*.

Crooked Mile. October 3, 1964. Production #0401.

Quint falls in love with Susan Degler, but her domineering father Cyrus is vehemently opposed to the relationship. Cyrus threatens reprisals against Quint unless he stops seeing his daughter. When Quint ignores the threats, Cyrus ambushes him at the blacksmith's shop with a bullwhip. Finally, Cyrus sends for the family's hatchet man cousin Praylie to figure out a way to remove Quint permanently.

Susan Degler	Katharine Ross
Cyrus Degler	George Kennedy
Praylie	Royal Dano
Story, Script	Les Crutchfield
Director	Andrew V. McLaglen
Associate Producer	Frank Paris
Producer	Norman Macdonnell

Known primarily as a film actress, Katharine Ross began on television and has since come back to the little screen. *The Colbys* marked her return to television in the role of Francesca Scott Colby Hamilton. Her film credits include *Games*, *Butch Cassidy and the Sundance Kid*, *The Stepford Wives*, and *The Graduate*, for which she was nominated for an Academy Award.

Old Man. October 10, 1964. Production #0409.

Alone on the prairie, a gravely ill, nameless old man is brought back to health by a young drifter named Danny Adams. While recuperating in Dodge, the man is dragged into an argument during a drinking spree with Joe Silva. Joe's rival Harve Litton grasps the opportunity to murder Joe and to frame the old man for the crime. Matt suspects that the old man is innocent but all the evidence points in his direction.

Old Man	Ned Glass
Danny Adams	Robert Hogan
Joe Silva	Ed Peck
Harve Litton	Rayford Barnes
Story, Script	John Meston
Director	Harry Harris, Jr.
Associate Producer	Frank Paris
Producer	Norman Macdonnell

Robert Hogan was a regular on several television shows including *Peyton Place*, *The Manhunter*, *Operation Petticoat*, and *Secrets of Midland Heights*.

GUNSMOKE — III. THE PROGRAMS

The Violators. October 17, 1964. Production #0413. Rerun June 12, 1965.

The Indian style scalping of ne'er-do-well Will Scroggs causes his companions, George Hewitt and Harve Foster, to run scared. The men's panic stirs the Dodge populace to the brink of retaliation against the Cheyenne nation. Matt insists the Indians are innocent, and steers his investigation towards an old mountain man Caleb Nash, who is a friend of the Indians.

Caleb Nash	Denver Pyle
George Hewitt	James Anderson
Harve Foster	Art Batanides
Willy Scroggs	Garry Walberg
Additional Cast	Michael Pate
Story, Script	John Dunkel
Director	Harry Harris, Jr.
Associate Producer	Frank Paris
Producer	Norman Macdonnell

Art Batanides was featured in the crime show, *Johnny Midnight* that starred Edmond O'Brien.

Doctor's Wife. October 24, 1964. Production #0406.

When young Doctor Wesley May hangs out his shingle in Dodge, his ambitious wife Jennifer tries to steal patients away from Doc Adams. She starts by spreading gossip that Doc is drinking and is no longer capable of practicing medicine. Doc tries at first to befriend the young couple, and turns a deaf ear to the malicious gossip. Finally, when it poses a threat to his reputation, he pays a visit to Jennifer and teaches her a dramatic lesson about the medical profession in Dodge.

Dr. Wesley May	James Broderick
Jennifer May	Phyllis Love
Boake	Harold Gould
Mrs. Boake	Anne Barton
Mrs. Gort	Helen Kleeb
Louie Pheeters	James Nusser
Jared	Robert Biheller
Old Woman	Dorothy Neumann
Clerk	Howard Culver
Martha Lou	Jewel Jaffe
Carney	Buck Young
Story, Script	George Eckstein
Director	Harry Harris, Jr.
Associate Producer	Frank Paris
Producer	Norman Macdonnell

Writer George Eckstein sat in the producer's seat for two short-lived television series, a situation comedy called *Sunshine* and *Sara,* and a Western that starred Brenda Vaccaro.

Take Her, She's Cheap. October 31, 1964. Production #0411. Rerun June 19, 1965.

Shiftless Duggan Carp father of a rag-tag family of seven, tries to repay a favor by offering his teenaged daughter Allie to Matt for a wife. Although Matt declines the offer, Allie is smitten by his kindness and follows him to Dodge. En route, she is molested by Mel Billings, who has been run out of town along with his brother Loren for shooting up the Long Branch and Matt's office.

The Television Programs

Duggan Carp	Malcolm Atterbury
Allie	Lauri Peters
Mel Billings	Willard Sage
Loren Billings	Mort Mills
Ma Carp	Linda Watkins
Story, Script	Kathleen Hite
Director	Harry Harris, Jr.
Associate Producer	Frank Paris
Producer	Norman Macdonnell

Help Me Kitty. November 7, 1964. Production #0414.
When 18-year-old Hope Farmer learns she is going to have a baby, she asks Kitty to take her home to her mother. Along the way their stage is attacked by a pair of outlaws, Spector and Furnes, who kill the driver and leave the passengers for dead. Kitty and Hope survive, however, and continue their journey on foot. They finally reach a relay station, where their host turns out to be one of the men who attacked the stage.

Hope Farmer	Betty Conner
Spector	Jack Elam
Furnes	James Frawley
Mrs. Farmer	Peggy Stewart
Story, Script	Kathleen Hite
Director	Harry Harris, Jr.
Producer	Norman Macdonnell
Associate Producer	Frank Paris

James Frawley turned his sights toward directing for television. In 1967 he won an Emmy Award for Outstanding Directorial Achievement in Comedy.

Hung High. November 14, 1964. Production #0416. Rerun June 26, 1965.
Matt tracks and arrests Tony Serpa for killing his good friend retired Cavalry Col. Jim Downey. Joe Costa seizes the opportunity to get even with Matt. While the marshal and his prisoner are heading back to Dodge, Costa ambushes them. He then takes Serpa from Matt, hangs him, and makes it appear that the marshal is guilty of the deed.

Joe Costa	Robert Culp
Jim Downey	Harold J. Stone
Tony Serpa	Scott Marlowe
Sargent Wilks	Ed Asner
Bud	George Lindsey
George	Elisha Cook
Dick	Michael Conrad
Story, Script	John Meston
Story Consultant	John Mantley
Director	Mark Rydell
Producer	Philip Leacock

Robert Culp played Hoby Gilman in the television Western, *Trackdown*. Then he teamed with Bill Cosby for the successful adventure series, *I Spy*. In the 1980s he appeared as Bill Maxwell on *The Greatest American Hero*. His films include *Bob and Carol and Ted and Alice* and *Breaking Point*. Ed Asner became a television superstar with such hit series as *The Mary Tyler Moore Show*, *Lou Grant*, and *The Bronx Zoo*. He won Emmy

Awards in 1971, '72, '75 for *The Mary Tyler Moore Show*. In 1976 he won the Emmy for *Roots*. He took home Best Actor in a Drama for *Lou Grant* in 1978 and 1980. Mr. Asner is politically active and was elected president of the Screen Actors Guild. Michael Conrad is best remembered for his role as Sgt. Phil Esterhaus of *Hill Street Blues*, for which he won two Emmy Awards for Best Supporting Actor. Director Mark Rydell moved into films with *The Fox*, based on a D.H. Lawrence novel. His subsequent films include *The Reivers, Cinderella Liberty, The Rose*, and *The River*. In 1981 he directed the highly acclaimed film, *On Golden Pond*, which starred Katherine Hepburn, Henry Fonda, and Jane Fonda.

Jonah Hutchinson. November 21, 1964. Production #0404.

Jonah Hutchinson returns to Dodge after serving a prison term. Jonah is determined to pick up where he left off in the ruthless rebuilding of his crumbling cattle empire. Embittered by the loss of years and of the possessions which his son has allowed to dwindle, Jonah enlists the aid of his teenaged grandsons to reconstruct the Hutchinson holdings. Careful always to stay within the letter of the law, Jonah is ultimately forced to shift his emphasis to violence.

> Jonah Hutchinson .... Robert F. Simon
> Samuel Hutchinson .... Richard Anderson
> Phoebe .... June Dayton
> *Story, Script* .... Calvin Clements
> *Director* .... Harry Harris, Jr.
> *Associate Producer* .... Frank Paris
> *Producer* .... Norman Macdonnell

Big Man, Big Target. November 28, 1964. Production #0417.

Pike Beechum, a man wanted for murder and robbery, has his sights set on beautiful Ellie Merchant. The only thing standing in Beechum's way is Joe Merchant, Ellie's husband. Beechum takes care of that slight problem by framing the young dirt farmer on a horse stealing charge. Matt is forced to arrest Joe, leaving the way clear for Beechum to move in on Ellie.

> Joe Merchant .... Mike Road
> Ellie Merchant .... Mariette Hartley
> Pike Beechum .... J.D. Cannon
> *Story, Script, Story Consultant* .... John Mantley
> *Director* .... Michael O'Herlihy
> *Producer* .... Philip Leacock

John Mantley, who eventually took over as producer and then executive producer of *Gunsmoke*, wrote this episode. J.D. Cannon is probably best known as Peter Clifford, Dennis Weaver's tough boss on *McCloud*. Producer Philip Leacock is also an accomplished director for films and television. His film credits include *The Little Kidnappers, Let No Man Write My Epitaph*, and *The War Lover*. In later seasons he directed for *Gunsmoke*.

Chicken. December 5, 1964. Production #0403.

Peaceful cowboy Dan Collins is found at a relay station where four outlaws and a stage agent have killed each other during a gun battle. The assumption is that Collins killed the four bandits. Acclaimed, "the greatest gunfighter who ever lived," Collins, at first, tries to explain that he was just an innocent bystander. However, when his protests seem futile, he decides to enjoy his new status. Collins' false reputation eventually leads to a showdown.

The Television Programs

Dan Collins	Glenn Corbett
Lucy Benton	Gigi Perreau
Brady	L.Q. Jones
Additional Cast	Bob Anderson, John Lupton
Story, Script	John Meston
Director	Andrew V. McLaglen
Associate Producer	Frank Paris
Producer	Norman Macdonnell

Glenn Corbett is familiar to television viewers as Linc from *Route 66* and more recently as Paul Morgan of *Dallas*. Gigi Perreau was featured on two short-lived television series, *The Betty Hutton Show* and *Follow the Sun*.

Innocence. December 12, 1964. Production #0418.

Pretty Elsa Poe perks up the social life at the Long Branch. However, gaiety turns to violence, when the new hostess becomes the innocent victim of a dispute between two jealous cowboys, Art McClain and Bob Sullins. Art and Bob feel they have a right to interfere, when Elsa takes a romantic interest in businessman Charlie Ross.

Elsa Poe	Bethel Leslie
Art McClain	Claude Akins
Bob Sullins	Michael Forest
Charlie Ross	Jason Evers
Story, Script	John Meston
Story Consultant	John Mantley
Director	Harry Harris, Jr.
Producer	Philip Leacock

Aunt Thede. December 19, 1964. Production #0412. Rerun June 5, 1965.

Festus' gun-toting Aunt Thede arrives in Dodge to get herself a husband. What she does get is trouble. Aunt Thede wants to marry another Haggen, but one look at Festus tells her that he is not the one. Discouraged, but undaunted, she sets up a moonshining camp on the outskirts of Dodge, the site of a trysting place for George Rider and Ivy Norton. After Aunt Thede tries to marry the couple against the wishes of Ivy's mean tempered domineering father, the moonshine and marriage operation is investigated by Matt.

Aunt Thede	Jeanette Nolan
George Rider	James Stacy
Ivy Norton	Dyan Cannon
Webb Norton	Frank Cady
Howard	Howard McNear
Townsman	Hap Glaudi
Laurie	Jenny Lee Aurness
Story, Script	Kathleen Hite
Director	Sutton Roley
Associate Producer	Frank Paris
Producer	Norman Macdonnell

Jenny Lee Aurness, James Arness' daughter, has a cameo role in this episode. Three of the cast members of radio's *Gunsmoke* appeared in this episode: Howard McNear, Jeanette Nolan, and Frank Cady. Frank Cady appeared on television as a regular on *Ozzie and Harriet*. He is probably best known, however, for his portrayal of storekeeper Sam Drucker on *Green Acres* and *Petticoat Junction*. His films include *The*

GUNSMOKE — III. THE PROGRAMS

Big Carnival, Rear Window and *The Bad Seed*. James Stacy was the star of his own television Western, *Lancer*. Although she guest-starred on numerous television programs in the 60s, Dyan Cannon is primarily a film actress. Her movies include *Bob and Carol and Ted and Alice* and *Heaven Can Wait*.

Hammerhead. December 26, 1964. Production #0408.

Rich gambler Big Jim Ponder comes to Dodge to buy a horse from Fitch Tallman. Instead, Festus steers Big Jim to his horse trader friend Wohaw Simmons. Festus then proceeds to rave about Hammerhead, a puny looking quarter horse, claiming he is the fastest animal afoot. Surprisingly, Carrie, Jim's daughter, buys the horse. Then Festus attempts to prove his boast by riding Hammerhead in a 350 mile race from Dodge City to Cheyenne. His bragging leads to a three-way race with gambling stakes of more than $50,000. Matt fears that the heavy betting will lead to foul play.

Big Jim Ponder	Arch Johnson
Carrie	Linda Foster
Wohaw Simmons	Chubby Johnson
Fitch Tallman	John Fiedler
Feeney	William Henry
Squatty	Peter Dunn
Deggers	Don Briggs
Gambler	Tommy Richards
Tom	Ray Hemphill
Gambler	Gene Redfern
Stomp	Bill Catching
Attendant	Daniel M. White
Cowhand	Chuck Hayward
Story, Script	Antony Ellis
Director	Chris Nyby
Associate Producer	Frank Paris
Producer	Norman Macdonnell

On television, Linda Foster appeared as Doris Royal in the situation comedy, *Hank*. Peter Dunn played Dody Hamer in the television Western, *Cimarron City*.

Double Entry. January 2, 1965. Production #0419.

Upon arriving in Dodge, Brad McClain renews his old friendship with Matt, and gains the confidence of the people of Dodge. When Brad announces an interest in buying the stage coach line and settling in Dodge, he is given confidential information about the stage operation. It soon becomes apparent that Brad has more than a business interest in the gold shipments of the stage coach line. He is given carte blanche to ride shotgun on an important shipment and when the stage is held-up, a page from Brad's past comes back to haunt him.

Brad McClain	Forrest Tucker
Jake	Cyril Delevanti
Yuma Joe	Mel Gallagher
Pete Elder	Lew Brown
Woman Passenger	Nora Marlowe
Story, Script	Les Crutchfield
Story Consultant	John Mantley
Director	Joe Sargent
Producer	Philip Leacock

The Television Programs

Forrest Tucker is best remembered as the unscrupulous entrepreneur Sgt. Morgan O'Rourke of the comedy western series, *F Troop*.

Run, Sheep, Run. January 9, 1965. Production #0420.

Tom Stocker needs money to take his wife to California, so he sells his ranch to grain store owner, Dan Braden. Under the terms of the contract, however, Braden need not pay for a year, so he refuses to pay Tom anything. Tom's desperation for money leads to a showdown in which Braden is killed. Although it is uncertain whether Tom is guilty, the incident sends him and his terrified wife on a panic stricken flight.

Tom Stocker	Burt Brinckerhoff
Dan Braden	Peter Whitney
Mary Stocker	Davey Davison
Cox	Arthur Malet
Story, Script	John Meston
Story Consultant	John Mantley
Director	Harry Harris, Jr.
Producer	Philip Leacock

Arthur Malet was a regular on two television series, *Casablanca* and *Easy Street*.

Deputy Festus. January 16, 1965. Production #0422. Rerun July 3, 1965.

After locking up three trappers for starting a brawl at the Long Branch, Matt has to leave town to attend a trial. He leaves Festus in charge and instructs him to release the men in the morning. The men turn out to be Festus' country cousins, which leaves Festus with a moral dilemma. His cousins insist on being freed immediately.

Lambert	Royal Dano
Emery	Shug Fisher
Claudius	Denver Pyle
Dave Carson	Carl Reindel
Halligan	Don Beddoe
Mr. Jacobsen	Bill Zuckert
Glen	Michael Petit
Tiplett	Ken Mayer
Waiter	Harold Ensley
Story, Script	Calvin Clements
Story Consultant	John Mantley
Director	Harry Harris, Jr.
Producer	Philip Leacock

Don Beddoe was a character actor on television, stage, and films. His numerous movie credits include, *The Best Years of Our Lives*, *Carrie*, and *The Farmer's Daughter*, in which James Arness had a featured role.

One Killer on Ice. January 23, 1965. Production #0421. Rerun July 10, 1965.

Afraid of being ambushed, Anderson, a bounty hunter, asks Matt to help him bring in a wanted man. He claims his partner is holding the killer in a shack near Timberline, and he is unable to bring him in alone. Matt knows better than to trust Anderson, but he feels obligated to see the alleged murderer brought to justice.

Anderson	John Drew Barrymore
Owney Dales	Philip Coolidge
Helena Dales	Anne Helm

GUNSMOKE — III. THE PROGRAMS

Billy Kimbro	Dennis Hopper
Story, Script	Richard Carr
Story Consultant	John Mantley
Director	Joseph Lewis
Producer	Philip Leacock

John Drew Barrymore is a descendant of one of the most prominent theatrical families. The son of John Barrymore and Dolores Costello, John Jr. did not quite live up to the "Fabulous Barrymores" reputation and was frequently in trouble with the law. His film credits include *The Sundowners* and *High School Confidential*. Multifaceted Dennis Hopper has been both actor and director of numerous films. His acting credits include *Rebel Without a Cause, Giant,* and *Gunfight at the OK Corral.* In 1969 he directed and starred in the phenomenally successful, *Easy Rider,* which he also co-authored. In more recent years he was featured as the sadistic villain in *Blue Velvet.* Joseph Lewis directed a number of B-movies in the 40s and 50s. *Gun Crazy,* a gangster film he directed in 1949, was considered "a tone poem of camera movement."

Chief Joseph. January 30, 1965. Production #0424.

Chief Joseph, the spiritual leader of the Nez Pez Indians, stops in Dodge while on route to a peace conference with President Ulysses S. Grant. Joseph is suffering from pneumonia and cannot continue his journey to Washington. His military escort, Lt. Cal Tripp, uses subterfuge to get the ailing Joseph a room at the Dodge House. The powerful Indian leader encounters the hostility of the residents, many of whom have lost relatives in Indian wars. They threaten violence, in spite of Matt's vow to protect the Chief. Meanwhile, thousands of Indians are secretly arming themselves, while they await the developments that could lead either to peace or an uprising.

Chief Joseph	Victor Jory
Lt. Cal Tripp	Robert Loggia
Charlie Britton	Joe Maross
Wiley	Leonard Stone
Story	Thomas Warner
Script	Clyde Ware
Story Consultant	John Mantley
Director	Mark Rydell
Producer	Philip Leacock

Character actor Victor Jory has played heavies in numerous feature films. The former boxer and wrestler appeared as Oberon in *A Midsummer Night's Dream* in the 1938 Reinhardt-Dieterle production. His other films include *Gone With the Wind, The Miracle Worker* and *Papillon.* In addition, Jory guest starred in over 200 television shows. On television Robert Loggia starred in two series *T.H.E. Cat* and *Emerald Point N.A.S.* His film credits include *Somebody Up There Likes Me,* with Paul Newman, and *An Officer and a Gentleman,* with Richard Gere. Leonard Stone was a regular on the comedies, *Camp Runamuck* and *The Jean Arthur Show.* In addition to writing 25 *Gunsmoke* episodes, Clyde Ware has written for several other programs including *Rawhide, Bonanza,* and *The Alfred Hitchcock Hour.* His television movies include *Coward of the County,* which starred Kenny Rogers, and *The Alamo: 13 Days to Glory,* which starred James Arness.

Circus Trick. February 6, 1965. Production #0407.

Matt expects trouble when a travel worn carnival arrives in Dodge. Suspecting a link between the circus' travels and a string of bank robberies, Matt closely watches

The Television Programs

the Dodge City bank. Festus' girlfriend, April, joins the magician's sword throwing act and stumbles onto a crime that Matt was not prepared for.

April	Ellizabeth MacRae
Big Eddie	Ken Scott
Speeler	Warren Oates
Elko	Walter Burke
Additional	Isabelle Jewell
Story, Script	Les Crutchfield
Director	William F. Claxton
Associate Producer	Frank Paris
Producer	Norman Macdonnell

Isabelle Jewell's film credits include *A Tale of Two Cities, Lost Horizon,* and *The Snake Pit.*

Song for Dying. February 13, 1965. Production #0425.

A wandering balladeer known only as "the singer," refuses to explain his mysterious past, or why he expects to be killed. The only one with a clue to his mystery is Doc, who remembers the singer as Doctor Martin Kellums. When Dave Lukens takes a shot at Kellums, Doc confronts the ex-physician for an explanation.

Martin Kellums	Theodore Bikel
Will Lukens	Robert F. Simon
Dave Lukens	Lee Majors
Ben Lukens	Rogert Ewing
Mace	Russell Thorson
Cory Lukens	Sheldon Allman
Sam	Glenn Strange
Hode Embry	Ford Rainey
Story, Script	Harry Kronman
Story Consultant	John Mantley
Director	Allen Reisner
Producer	Philip Leacock

Roger Ewing, who plays Ben Lukens, was seen in later episodes in the role of Thad. Theodore Bikel's film credits include *The African Queen,* which starred Katherine Hepburn and Humphrey Bogart, *The Little Kidnappers,* which was directed by Philip Leacock, and *My Fair Lady,* which starred Audrey Hepburn and Rex Harrison. In 1958 Bikel was nominated for an Academy Award for *The Defiant Ones.* Bikel is also an accomplished folk singer and guitarist. In this episode he has the opportunity to display these talents. Lee Majors starred in several television series including, *Big Valley, The Six Million Dollar Man,* and *The Fall Guy.*

Winner Take All. February 20, 1965. Production #0415.

Matt tries to end a feud between the two hot-tempered Renner brothers, Curly and Pinto. Unable to offer more than friendly advice, he finally steps in when an argument threatens to escalate over a cattle sale and a saloon girl.

Curly Renner	Tom Simcox
Pinto Renner	John Milford
Karen	Margaret Bly
Story, Script	Les Crutchfield
Story Consultant	John Mantley
Director	Vincent McEveety
Producer	Philip Leacock

GUNSMOKE — III. THE PROGRAMS

Eliab's Alm. February 27, 1965. Production #0423. Rerun July 17, 1965.

Festus Haggen's hillbilly nephew Eliab comes to Dodge to even an old score with Festus. Although Festus is his favorite uncle, Eliab figures he owes him some bodily damage. Eliab's father still bears a scar from a scuffle the two had long ago. In the struggle Festus bit off part of his ear. Festus leads his nephew in a spirited chase, until Quint and Doc, who have taken a liking to Eliab, decide to help the two out of their predicament.

Eliab	James Hampton
Pearl	Dee J. Thompson
Dealer	Donald O'Kelly
Jake	Gregg Palmer
Story, Script	Will Corry
Story Consultant	John Mantley
Director	Richard Sarafian
Producer	Philip Leacock

This story was inspired by Burt Reynolds and Ken Curtis. Richard Sarafian directed such films as *The Man Who Loved Cat Dancing,* which starred Burt Reynolds and Sarah Miles.

Thursday's Child. March 6, 1965. Production #0426. Rerun August 14, 1965.

While en route to Wichita to see her son and help bring her grandchild into the world, Julie Blane stops in Dodge for an unexpected visit with her old friend Kitty. There is an air of mystery about Julie's travels, however, as she slips out of town in the middle of the night without even a good-bye.

Julie Blane	Jean Arthur
Lon Blane	Scott Marlowe
Vardis	Joe Raciti
Amy Blane	Suzanne Benoit
Roy	Roy Barcroft
Hank	Hank Patterson
Clint Marston	Fred Coby
Story, Script	Robert Lewin
Story Consultant	John Mantley
Director	Joseph H. Lewis
Producer	Philip Leacock

Jean Arthur's films include *Mr. Smith Goes to Washington, You Can't Take It with You,* and *The Whole Town's Talking.* She was nominated for an Academy Award for *The More the Merrier.* In 1956 she won critical praise for her performance as *Peter Pan* on Broadway. Her last film was the classic Western, *Shane,* with Alan Ladd. She came out of retirement to film this episode and enjoyed the experience so much that she agreed to do her own series, *The Jean Arthur Show.*

Breckinridge. March 13, 1965. Production #0427.

Breck Taylor, an ambitious Eastern lawyer, witnesses a ruckus at the Long Branch involving troublemaker Sled Grady and bartender Jocko. When Matt orders Grady out of town, Breck challenges Matt's authority to take such steps without first preferring charges. Breck takes Grady on as a client and gets a restraining order, keeping Matt from further action. Breck soon regrets his action, as he learns a practical lesson in the law of the West.

Breck Taylor	Ben Cooper

The Television Programs

Sled Grady	Robert Sorrells
Jocko	Elisha Cook
Judge Danby	John Warburton
Story, Script	Les Crutchfield
Story Consultant	John Mantley
Director	Vincent McEveety
Producer	Philip Leacock

Bank Baby. March 20, 1965. Production #0405.

Clum, a no-good thief, kidnaps a baby from a pilgrim camp so he can masquerade as a respectable family man. The pilgrims blame Indians for the kidnapping and accuse Quint of a cover-up. Meanwhile, Clum drives into Dodge with the baby, his wife Bess, and his son Milton. Posing as a law abiding citizen who is looking for a place to settle and invest his life savings, Clum plots to rob the bank.

Clum	Jacques Aubuchon
Grace Fisher	Gail Kobe
Bess	Virginia Christine
Milton	Hampton Fancher
Mr. Botkin	Roy Roberts
Additional Cast	Harry Carey, Jr.
Story, Script	John Meston
Director	Andrew V. McLaglen
Associate Producer	Frank Paris
Producer	Norman Macdonnell

The Lady. March 27, 1965. Production #0430. Rerun July 31, 1965.

Hattie Silks runs out of money while en route to California with her pretty niece Liz Beaumont. The sophisticated Miss Silks swallows her pride and takes a temporary job at the Long Branch. Her new employment brings her in contact with a charming widower, Jud Briar, who takes an immediate and sincere interest in her welfare. The relationship blossoms into a full-fledged romance, which shatters Liz's selfish dream of a more elegant life in San Francisco. To assure her own future happiness, Liz hires someone to do away with Jud.

Hattie Silks	Eileen Heckart
Liz Beaumont	Katharine Ross
Jud Briar	R.G. Armstrong
Charlie	Walter Sande
Hank	Hank Patterson
Sam Hare	Clifton James
Ray Pate	Michael Forest
Story, Script, Story Consultant	John Mantley
Director	Mark Rydell
Producer	Philip Leacock

Highly acclaimed actress of stage, screen, and television, Eileen Heckart received the Drama Critics Award in 1958 for *The Dark at the Top of the Stairs*. In 1967 she was awarded an Emmy for her performance in *Save Me a Place at Forest Lawn*. In 1972 she won the Academy Award for *Butterflies Are Free*. Her other film credits include *Bus Stop*, *The Bad Seed*, and *The Color of Money*.

Dry Road to Nowhere. April 3, 1965. Production #0429. Rerun August 28, 1965.

Amos Campbell, a persuasive, self-ordained temperance preacher, sets out to dry up Dodge. Amos, a man whose fists are as convincing as his sermons, uses both to protect his pretty young daughter Bess from the advances of Dingo Tebbets. When Campbell brings his temperance campaign to Dodge he runs into stubborn resistance from a group of celebrating cowhands and from Kitty. Their opposition is peaceful until Tebbetts tries to organize a riot.

    Amos Campbell . . . . James Whitmore
    Bess Campbell . . . . Julie Sommars
    Dingo Tebbetts . . . . John Saxon
    Pete Moreland . . . . Read Morgan
    Howie . . . . Howard Culver
    Wally . . . . L.Q. Jones
    Story, Script . . . . Harry Kronman
    Story Consultant . . . . .John Mantley
    Director . . . . Vincent McEveety
    Producer . . . . Philip Leacock

Character actor James Whitmore starred in several television movies and series including *The Law and Mr. Jones*. As a stage performer he is known for his one man shows, most notably *Give 'Em Hell Harry!*, which was later released as a feature film for which he was nominated for an Academy Award. In 1949 he was nominated for an Academy Award for his performance in *Battleground*, a film in which Jim Arness and Amanda Blake had bit parts. His other films include *The Next Voice You Hear*, *Black Like Me*, and *Bully*. On television, Julie Sommars was a regular on *The Governor and J.J.* John Saxon starred in the series *The Doctors*. His film credits include *The Cardinal*, *Portrait in Black*, and *The Electric Horseman*.

Twenty Miles from Dodge. April 10, 1965. Production #0428. Rerun August 21, 1965.

 Kitty, along with gambler Will Helmick, railroad executive Follansbee, and a young widow Eleanor Starkey, is kidnapped from the stage by a band of outlaws and is held for ransom.

    Will Helmick . . . . Darren McGavin
    Follansbee . . . . Everett Sloane
    Eleanor Starkey . . . . Aneta Corsault
    Story, Script . . . . Clyde Ware
    Story Consultant . . . . John Mantley
    Director . . . . Mark Rydell
    Producer . . . . Philip Leacock

Darren McGavin appeared in *Riverboat*, with Burt Reynolds, played the monster chasing reporter, Carl Kolchak, on *Kolchak: The Night Stalker* and was the original Mike Hammer in *Mickey Spillane's Mike Hammer*. His films include *Summertime* and *The Man with the Golden Arm*. Aneta Corsault appeared regularly on *The Gertrude Berg Show*, *The Andy Griffith Show*, and *House Calls*.

The Pariah. April 17, 1965. Production #0432. Rerun August 7, 1965.

 Paolo Scanzano, a poor immigrant farmer, kills wanted outlaw John Hooker to protect his family. At first the Dodge City townsfolk toast Paolo's bravery, however, when the poor farmer accepts a reward for his deed, his friends turn on him. Paolo is labeled a coward and is shunned, all because his actions are misunderstood. Mocked by the townspeople and threatened by Hooker's brothers, Paolo risks his life to clear his name and to prove he is not a coward.

    Paolo Scanzano . . . . John Dehner

The Television Programs

Rosita Scanzano	Ilka Windish
Thomas Scanzano	Donald Losby
Ben Hooker	Steve Ihnat
Wayne Hooker	Tom Reese
John Hooker	Lee Van Cleef
Newspaper Editor	Don Keefer
Story, Script	Calvin Clements, Sr.
Director	Harry Harris, Jr.
Story Consultant	John Mantley
Producer	Philip Leacock

Gilt Guilt. April 24, 1965. Production #0402.

Mary Rice is poverty stricken. Her farm has turned to dust from drought and she is left without fresh fruit or vegetables. She and her son, Sully develop scurvy and by the time they are discovered by Doc it is almost too late. When Doc manages to locate a few jars of preserved food, Mary gives her portion to her desperately ill son.

Mary Rice	Jan Clayton
Sully	Peter Brooks
John Crail	Andrew Duggen
Story, Script	Kathleen Hite
Director	Harry Harris, Jr.
Associate Producer	Frank Paris
Producer	Norman Macdonnell

Bad Lady from Brookline. May 1, 1965. Production #0431.

Molly McConnell, a rather sheltered and refined Easterner, arrives in Dodge with her young son in tow. Once there she discovers that her husband has been killed by Matt. Unaware that her husband was an outlaw and that the shooting was justified, Molly decides to avenge his death. Not knowing her intentions, Kitty gives Molly a job at the Long Branch as a saloon-singer and teaches her how to break out of her genteel shell. In the meantime, her husband's ex-business partner, Sy Sherne, reluctantly teaches Molly to handle a gun so she can kill Matt.

Molly McConnell	Betty Hutton
Sy Sherne	Claude Akins
Willie McConnell	Billy Bowles
LaFarge	John Hubbard
Harper	Jonathan Kidd
Herb	Ollie O'Toole
Curley	Jan Peters
Cowboy	Eddie Hice
Ben	Tom McCauley
Story, Script	Gustave Field
Story Consultant	John Mantley
Director	Michael O'Herlihy
Producer	Philip Leacock

Betty Hutton, the energetic performer known as "The Blonde Bombshell" starred in such movies as *Annie Get Your Gun, The Greatest Show on Earth,* and *The Perils of Pauline.* On television she starred in *The Betty Hutton Show.* Miss Hutton sings several songs in this episode. John Hubbard was a regular on two television comedies, *The Mickey Rooney Show* and *Don't Call Me Charlie.*

GUNSMOKE — III. THE PROGRAMS

Two Tall Men. May 8, 1965. Production #0435.

Festus Haggen and lawyer Breck Taylor take the law into their own hands, when buffalo hunter Abihu Howell accuses two hard bitten saddle bums, Billy Yager and Ned Moore, of beating and robbing Doc. With Matt out of town and Doc's life hanging in the balance, Festus and Breck track down the suspects and lock them in jail without a trial. Meanwhile, Howell incites a lynch mob with his drunken accusations.

Billy Yager	George Lindsey
Ned Moore	Jay Ripley
Abihu Howell	Harry Townes
Breck Taylor	Ben Cooper
Story, Script	Frank Q. Dobbs & Robert C. Stewart
Story Consultant	John Mantley
Director	Vincent McEveety
Producer	Phillip Leacock

Honey Pot. May 15, 1965. Production #0434.

Ben Stack, an old friend of Matt's, falls in love with saloon hostess Honey Dare and kills her jealous husband. To cover up the killing, Ben and Honey conspire to blame the crime on someone else. They are successful in diverting suspicion until they reveal their love for one another. When they finally tip their hand, Matt is forced into a decision involving his reponsibilities to the law and to his old friend.

Ben Stack	Rory Calhoun
Honey Dare	Joanna Moore
Hal Biggs	John Crawford
Sol Durham	Dick Wessel
James Riley	Harry Bartell
Gregory Bellow	Harry Lauter
Hank	Hank Patterson
Roy	Roy Barcroft
Hy Evers	Charles Maxwell
Story, Script	Clyde Ware
Story Consultant	John Mantley
Director	Vincent McEveety
Producer	Philip Leacock

Rory Calhoun starred in his own Western on CBS, *The Texan.* Recently he co-starred with Amanda Blake in an episode on the anthology series, *Modern Romance* hosted by Bill Bixby. Mr. Calhoun's film credits include *I'd Climb the Highest Mountain, With a Song in My Heart,* and *How to Marry a Millionaire.* Dick Wessel played Carney on the adventure series, *Riverboat,* which featured Burt Reynolds.

The New Society. May 22, 1965. Production #0436. Rerun September 4, 1965.

Matt is greeted with fright, suspicion, and hostility from nervous citizens, when he travels to a town to solve a 12-year-old murder mystery. Matt's investigation leads him to the sheriff's wife, and then to a jail attendant, where he discovers the surprising truth.

John Scanlon	James Gregory
Tom Scanlon	Jeremy Slate
Vera Scanlon	Elizabeth Perry
Additional Cast	Jack Weston
Story, Script	Calvin Clements, Sr.

The Television Programs

    Story Consultant .... John Mantley
    Director .... Joseph Sargent
    Producer .... Philip Leacock

Veteran character actor James Gregory is familiar to television audiences as Inspector Luger of *Barney Miller*. His movie credits include *The Naked City, The Manchurian Candidate,* and *PT-109*.

He Who Steals. May 29, 1965. Production #0451.

Cowboy Billy Walters sacrifices his job and the respect of his friends, when he defends an old buffalo hunter he idolizes, after the old man is charged with stealing one of his boss' calves.

    Billy Walters .... Russ Tamblyn
    Jeff Sutro .... Harold J. Stone
    Jim Donner .... Len Wayland
    Charlie .... Stanley Adams
    Story, Script .... John Meston
    Story Consultant .... John Mantley
    Director .... Harry Harris, Jr.
    Producer .... Philip Leacock

Russ Tamblyn appeared in such films as *Seven Brides for Seven Brothers, West Side Story,* and *Peyton Place,* for which he was nominated for an Academy Award for Best Supporting Actor. Len Wayland played Captain Tom Clagett in the police series, *Sam*.

Aunt Thede. June 5, 1965, rerun. First aired December 19, 1964.

The Violators. June 12, 1965, rerun. First aired October 17, 1964.

Take Her, She's Cheap. June 19, 1965, rerun. First aired October 31, 1964.

Hung High. June 26, 1965, rerun. First aired November 14, 1964.

Deputy Festus. July 3, 1965, rerun. First aired January 16, 1965.

One Killer on Ice. July 10, 1965, rerun. First aired January 23, 1965.

Eliab's Arm. July 17, 1965, rerun. First aired February 27, 1965.

The Lady. July 31, 1965, rerun. First aired March 27, 1965.

The Pariah. August 7, 1965, rerun. First aired April 17, 1965.

Thursday's Child. August 14, 1965, rerun. First aired March 6, 1965.

Twenty Miles from Dodge. August 21, 1965, rerun. First aired April 10, 1965.

Dry Road to Nowhere. August 28, 1965, rerun. First aired April 3, 1965.

The New Society. September 4, 1965, rerun. First aired May 22, 1965.

GUNSMOKE — III. THE PROGRAMS

ELEVENTH SEASON

Seven Hours to Dawn. September 18, 1965. Production #0433.
A gang of outlaws terrorize the inhabitants of Dodge. Matt is disarmed and is forced to stand by helplessly, as they pillage and ransack the town. Unable to stand the atrocities, Matt risks his life to save Dodge.

Mace Gore	John Drew Barrymore
Raider	Michael Vandever
Smitty	Al Lettier
Jack Down	Allen Jaffe
Barney	Charles Seel
Deeks	Morgan Woodward
Clark	Jerry Douglas
Barens	Johnny Seven
Story, Script	Clyde Ware
Director	Vincent McEveety
Associate Producer	John Mantley
Producer	Philip Leacock

Morgan Woodward is a familiar face to television audiences. Besides being a frequent guest star on *Gunsmoke,* he appeared on numerous television series and was a regular on *The Life and Legend of Wyatt Earp* and *Dallas.*

The Storm. September 25, 1965. Production #0456.
Ranchers Adam and Clara Benteen are close friends of Matt's. The friendship is tested, however, when their two sons, Claude and Ab, accidentally kill a British hide-hunter and let another man face the noose for their crime.

Adam Benteen	Forrest Tucker
Clara Benteen	Ruth Warrick
Claude Benteen	Tim McIntyre
Ab Benteen	Richard Evans
Mel Woodley	Kelly Thordsen
Cantrell	Willard Sage
Hope Woodley	Mary Lou Taylor
Cowboy	Lincoln Demyan
Barney	Charles Seel
Judge	Steven Darrell
Sheriff	Stuart Margolin
Bartender	Victor Izay
Hank Cooters	Shug Fisher
Rudy	Rudy Sooter
Story, Script	Paul Savage
Director	Joseph Sargent
Associate Producer	John Mantley
Producer	Philip Leacock

Ruth Warrick made her movie debut in Orson Welles' classic film, *Citizen Kane.* On television, she was a regular on *Father of the Bride* and *Peyton Place.* However, television viewers know Miss Warrick best as the cunning conniving Phoebe Tyler of the daytime drama, *All My Children.* Tim McIntyre, also spelled McIntire, was the son of Jeanette Nolan and John McIntire. He appeared as Bob Younger on the Western series, *The Legend of Jesse James,* and Brad Knight on *Rich Man, Poor Man.* Stuart

The Television Programs

Margolin was a regular on many series including *Love, American Style, Nichols,* and *The Rockford Files,* for which he won an Emmy. Margolin is also an accomplished writer and director. Ken Curtis, once famous for his mellifluous voice, regales viewers with a tune in this episode.

Clayton Thaddeus Greenwood. October 2, 1965. Production #0454. Rerun April 2, 1966.
    Four cowboys bully an elderly man until he dies of a heart attack. Thad Greenwood, his son, seeks to avenge his death and tracks the culprits to Dodge. Once there, Thad waits for the men to commit a crime for which they can be punished. Although Thad's cause arouses the sympathy of Matt, the marshal is legally helpless.

    Clayton Thaddeus Greenwood .... Roger Ewing
    Sam Band .... Jack Elam
    Waiter .... William Henry
    Greenwood, Sr. .... Paul Fix
    Frank Brand .... Sherwood Price
    Zachary .... Robert Sorrells
    Webster .... Allen Jaffe
    Story, Script .... Calvin Clements
    Director .... Joseph Sargent
    Associate Producer .... John Mantley
    Producer .... Philip Leacock

This episode introduces the character Thad Greenwood to the series.

Ten Little Indians. October 9, 1965. Production #0452. Rerun August 13, 1966.
    In Matt's absence, a group of gunfighters converge on Dodge. The killers arrive thinking that someone has put a $25,000 price on Matt's head. The rumors of the $25,000 bounty grow, when an old friend of Matt's becomes involved. While the gunmen start to kill each other off, a mysterious visitor begins counting the survivors.

    Jack Pinto .... Nehemiah Persoff
    Al Tresh .... Warren Oates
    Doyle Phleger .... Bruce Dern
    Billy Coe .... Zalman King
    Miguel Samando .... Rafael Campos
    Ben Pringle .... John Marley
    Eddie Cannon .... Stanja Lowe
    Lafe Cannon .... Don Ross
    Nancy .... Nina Roman
    Story, Script .... George Eckstein
    Director .... Mark Rydell
    Associate Producer .... John Mantley
    Producer .... Philip Leacock

Noted character actor Nehemiah Persoff guest starred on numerous television series. His films include *On the Waterfront, Some Like It Hot,* and *Voyage of the Damned.* Bruce Dern has played a wide variety of roles. His moves include *The King of Marvin Gardens, They Shoot Horses Don't They,* and *The Great Gatsby.* In 1978 he was nominated for an Academy Award for his performance in *Coming Home.* On television, Zalman King played Aaron Silverman in the dramatic series, *The Young Lawyers.* Raphael Campos was a regular on *Rhoda* and *Centennial.*

Taps for Old Jeb. October 16, 1965. Production #0463.

Jeb, a shaggy old prospector, brags about striking it rich and indulges in a spending spree. Jeb's celebration, the likes of which Dodge has rarely seen, is a spirited affair. But there is a hint of trouble beneath the gaiety, when Jeb's boasts of wealth make him an easy target for robbery.

  Jeb Crater .... Ed Begley
  Stretch Morgan .... Wayne Rogers
  Sholo .... Morgan Woodward
  Feeter Kreb .... Arthur Batanides
  Milty Sims .... Don Keefer
  Rudy .... Rudy Sooter
  Story, Script .... Les Crutchfield
  Director .... James Sheldon
  Associate Producer .... John Mantley
  Producer .... Philip Leacock

Character actor Ed Begley began his career in network radio drama. On Broadway he starred in such productions as Arthur Miller's, *All My Sons*, and *Inherit the Wind*, which he later recreated for television. His films include *12 Angry Men* and *Sweet Bird of Youth*, for which he won the Academy Award in 1962. His son is actor Ed Begley, Jr.

Kioga. October 23, 1965. Production #0453.

A young Indian named Kioga is relentlessly pursuing fur trader Jayce McCaw, who robbed his family and killed his father. When Kioga shows up in Dodge, after traveling 200 miles on foot, Matt tries to befriend him. Kioga refuses to cooperate with the law, however, determined to administer his own brand of justice.

  Jayce McCaw .... Neville Brand
  Kioga .... Teno Pollick
  Howie .... Howard Culver
  Katawa .... John War Eagle
  Hank .... Hank Patterson
  Bodkin .... Roy Roberts
  Father Kioga .... Ken Renard
  Storekeeper .... John Hubbard
  Nancy .... Nina Roman
  Sister Kioga .... Catherine Wyles
  Story, Script .... Robert Lewin
  Director .... Harry Harris, Jr.
  Associate Producer .... John Mantley
  Producer .... Philip Leacock

Although Neville Brand played hundreds of tough-guy villains on television, the character he portrayed on his Western series, *Laredo*, was played with a hard head and a soft heart. His film credits include *D.O.A.*, *Stalag 17*, and *Birdman of Alcatraz*.

The Bounty Hunter. October 30, 1965. Production #0457. Rerun May 14, 1966.

Luke Frazer, a reformed bounty hunter, has a lifelong dream to own a ranch. When wealthy rancher Chris Thornton offers Frazer a 1000-acre reward for one last job, Frazer accepts the challenge. Thornton wants Frazer to kill the man who "murdered" his son. In Dodge, Frazer arouses more suspicion than cooperation when he produces a "wanted" poster of the accused to Matt. The marshal wonders why he has never seen the poster before, and to add to the mystery, Matt recognizes the man pictured as Lon Jensen, a respected farmer who lives near Dodge.

The Television Programs

Luke Frazer	Robert Lansing
Chris Thornton	Bert Freed
Doak	Gregg Palmer
Cowboy	Hal Lynch
Rancher	Jon Kowal
Lon Jensen	Wright King
Mal Jensen	Lisabeth Hush
Amy Jensen	Amber Flower
Barney Danches	Charles Seel
Cowboy	James Anderson
Bartender	Victor Izay
Homesteader	Jason Johnson
Story, Script	Paul Savage
Director	Harry Harris, Jr.
Associate Producer	John Mantley
Producer	Philip Leacock

Robert Lansing has had a diversified career on Broadway, screen, and television. The star of numerous series his list includes *87th Precinct* and *Twelve O'Clock High*. Most recently he has appeared as Control on *The Equalizer*. His films include *Namu, the Killer Whale, Under the Yum Yum Tree,* and *Empire of the Ants*.

The Reward. November 6, 1965. Production #0462.

Jim Forbes, sent to prison because of a gold-mine swindle, returns after serving his time. Forbes comes back to Dodge determined to prove that he is not a thief and a coward. Of all the obstacles he must overcome, the most difficult is that his son Brian is ashamed of him.

Jim Forbes	James Whitmore
Brian Forbes	David Ladd
Jason Holt	Peter Whitney
Pedro	Julio Medina
Clint Fisher	Fred J. Scollay
Hank Purvis	Gil Rankin
Banker	Roy Roberts
Farmer	Berkeley Harris
Ed	Normann Burton
Story	Gilbert Ralston
Script	Beth Keele & Scott Hunt
Director	Marc Daniels
Associate Producer	John Mantley
Producer	Philip Leacock

David Ladd, the son of actor Alan Ladd, appeared in such films as *A Dog of Flanders* and *The Day of the Locust*. Normann Burton appeared regularly on *The New Adventures of Wonder Woman* and *The Ted Knight Show*. Marc Daniels produced and directed *Ford Theater* on CBS and he directed the first season of *I Love Lucy*. He was also credited for suggesting Vivian Vance for the part of Ethel Mertz on *I Love Lucy*.

Malachi. November 13, 1965. Production #0461.

Buffalo-bone hunter Malachi Harper tries to conceal the fact that he is a drunken bum from his well-to-do brother, Ethan, by posing as the marshal of Dodge. Festus, Doc, and Kitty help Malachi with his masquerade while Ethan is visiting. The likeable vagrant enjoys his new role until a stranger, Del Ordman, arrives in town determined to lay to rest the marshal who killed his brother.

Malachi Harper	Harry Townes
Ethan Harper	Edward Andrews
Del Ordman	Jack Elam
Cowboy	Robert Sorrells
Knowles	Woodrow Chambliss
Boy	Joey Wilcox
Shobin	Rex Holman
Hank	Hank Patterson
Story, Script	Paul Savage
Director	Gene Nelson
Associate Producer	John Mantley
Producer	Philip Leacock

Character actor Edward Andrews appeared as a regular on the comedy series, *Broadside* and the dramatic series, *Supertrain*. His films include *Tea and Sympathy*, *Elmer Gantry*, and *Avanti!* Director Gene Nelson is also an actor and dancer. The one time skater in Sonja Henie's ice shows appeared in such films as *Apartment for Peggy*, *Tea for Two*, and *Lullaby of Broadway*. His directorial credits include *Your Cheatin' Heart*, *Harum Scarum*, and *Kissin' Cousins*. Woodrow Chambliss is best known as Mr. Lathrop on *Gunsmoke*.

The Pretender. November 20, 1965. Production #0465. Rerun May 28, 1966.

Edmund and Frank Dano return to their father's ranch after serving a prison term for cattle rustling. Their father holds a bitter resentment against Frank for corrupting his younger brother. Frank also blames himself and tries to make amends by covering up for Edmund's new adventures in crime.

Frank Dano	Tom Simcox
Edmund Dano	Tom Skerritt
Sheriff Jackson	Gregg Palmer
Elsie Howell	Julie Sommars
Will Baker	Rusty Lane
Rudy	Rudy Sooter
Mr. Dano	Nehemiah Persoff
Mrs. Dano	Athena Lorde
Albert	Sam Edwards
Daniels	Harry Davis
Waiter	Ed McCready
John Neers	Allen Jaffe
Story, Script	Calvin Clements
Director	Vincent McEveety
Producer	Philip Leacock
Associate Producer	John Mantley

Rusty Lane was a regular on *Crime with Father*, *Jimmy Hughes, Rookie Cop*, and *Operation Neptune*. Tom Skerritt played Dr. Thomas Ryan in the dramatic series, *Ryan's Four*. Skerritt appeared in such films as *M.A.S.H.*, *Alien*, *Top Gun*, and *Poltergeist III*. Athena Lorde played Judith Richardson in the dramatic series, *One Man's Family*.

South Wind. November 27, 1965. Production #0460. Rerun June 4, 1966.

Twelve-year-old Homer Bonney is orphaned when his father is killed on the prairie.

The Television Programs

Homer is rescued by Doc who cures his physical ills, but is not able to quell Homer's desire for revenge.

Homer Bonney	Pat Cardi
Judd Print	Bruce Dern
Verlyn Print	Bob Random
Coy Print	Michael Davis
Wade Bonney	Ryan Hayes
Cavalry Captain	Michael Whitney
Blacksmith	Gregg Palmer
Bar Girl	Michelle Breeze
Story, Script	Jack Bartlett
Director	Allen Reisner
Associate Producer	John Mantley
Producer	Philip Leacock

Pat Cardi played Breer on the television comedy, *It's About Time*. Bob Random was a regular on the television Western, *The Iron Horse*.

The Hostage. December 4, 1965. Production #0455. Rerun June 11, 1966.

Four escaped convicts capture Matt and hold him hostage. The desperados are headed for the Mexican border. Lon Gorman the leader of the outlaws threatens to kill Matt if their bid for freedom is interfered with. Despite the threat, Festus and Thad trail them, hoping to find a way to free Matt without endangering his life.

Lon Gorman	Darren McGavin
Carl Mandee	Simon Oakland
Wade Keys	Tom Reese
Torreon	Vito Scotti
Sheriff Foley	I. Stanford Jolley
Sheriff Hockley	Willis Bouchey
Arly Phillips	Jimmy Cross
Barney	Charles Seel
Story	Joe Ann Johnson
Script	Clyde Ware
Director	Vincent McEveety
Associate Producer	John Mantley
Producer	Philip Leacock

The title *Hostage* was used again December 11, 1972. Vito Scotti was a regular on several situation comedies including *The Flying Nun*.

Outlaw's Woman. December 11, 1965. Production #0468. Rerun July 2, 1966.

Allie Sommers, a pretty young woman traveling with an outlaw gang, tries to leave her companions for a new life in Dodge. Allie is befriended by Matt, Doc, Kitty, and Festus during her convalescence from a bullet wound. However, she has a change of heart when outlaw Harve Kane convinces her that Matt killed her brother. With vengeance in mind, Allie leads Matt into an ambush.

Allie Sommers	Lane Bradbury
Harve Kane	Lou Antonio
Coley Martin	Vincent Beck
Dove Bailey	Lonny Chapman
Eddie	Gene Tyburn
Hank Wheeler	Ted Jordan

Dress Shop Owner	Peggy Rea
Jonas	Roy Barcroft
Story, Script	Clyde Ware
Director	Mark Rydell
Associate Producer	John Mantley
Producer	Philip Leacock

Lou Antonio is a successful actor-director. His acting credits include *The Snoop Sisters, Dog and Cat,* and *Makin' It.* His directing credits include episodes of *McCloud,* starring Dennis Weaver. Antonio was nominated for an Emmy Award for Best Direction for *Something for Joey* in 1978 and *Silent Victory: The Kitty O'Neill Story* in 1979.

The Avengers. December 18, 1965. Production #0467. Rerun July 9, 1966.

Kitty is attacked by Judge Calvin Strom's son and Festus is forced to kill him. The Judge does not take his loss well and accuses Kitty and Festus of conspiracy and murder. To avenge his son's death he plans on crippling Matt, kidnapping Kitty and Festus, and trying them in a kangaroo court. Certain that the killing was premeditated, Strom sets himself up to act as judge, jury and executioner.

Judge Calvin Strom	James Gregory
Cal Strom, Jr.	John Saxon
Mark Strom	Les Brown, Jr.
Barber	Olan Soule
Hotel Clerk	Howard Culver
Freight Agent	Ed McCready
Story, Script	Don Mullally
Director	Vincent McEveety
Associate Producer	John Mantley
Producer	Philip Leacock

Les Brown, Jr., was a regular on the comedy *Baileys of Balboa*. Olan Soule was seen as Mr. Pfeiffer on *My Three Sons* and Fred Springer on *Arnie*. Soule was also the voice of *Batman* on the Saturday morning cartoons.

Gold Mine. December 25, 1965. Production #0464.

Kitty inherits a gold mine and sets out alone to claim it. Matt is unable to accompany her and is naturally concerned about her welfare. To insure her safety he sends Thad to keep an eye on her. During her journey she is confronted by renegades, leering loafers, quicksand, and a brawling backwoods clan. Thad, with the help of a local boy named Richard Danby, aids Kitty in her struggle for her claim.

Pa Gibbijohn	John Anderson
Jud Gibbijohn	Paul Carr
Ed Gibbijohn	Michael Vandever
Richard Danby	Tom Nardini
Louise Danby	Argentina Brunetti
Sheriff	Russ Bender
Story, Script	Scott Hunt & Beth Keele
Director	Abner Biberman
Associate Producer	John Mantley
Producer	Philip Leacock

Tom Nardini was a regular on the short-lived series, *Cowboy in Africa*. Primarily a television director for such series as *Ben Casey, Ironside,* and *The Virginian,* Abner Biberman began his show business career as an actor in such films as *Gunga Din* and *His*

The Television Programs

Girl Friday. As a director his credits include *Running Wild* and *The Price of Fear*.

One Killer on Ice. January 1, 1966, rerun. First aired January 23, 1965.

Death Watch. January 8, 1966. Production #0466. Rerun August 20, 1966.

Matt forces two bounty hunters to postpone their attempt to claim a $30,000 Mexican reward until their prisoner, John Drago, is well enough to travel to the border with them. It is a tough predicament for the bounty hunters, who can only stand by and wait as the wounded Drago struggles for his life under Matt's watchful eye. If Drago dies, there is a chance his captors will lose their bounty. If he survives, the bounty hunters may have to fight others along the way for the reward money.

Holly	Albert Salmi
Walker	Willard Sage
John Drago	Frank Silvera
Austin Boyle	Richard Evans
Story, Script	Calvin Clements
Director	Mark Rydell
Associate Producer	John Mantley
Producer	Philip Leacock

This episode won the Western Heritage award for Outstanding Fictional Television Western Episode of 1966 by the National Cowboy Hall of Fame and Western Heritage Center in Oklahoma City. Character actor Albert Salmi appeared in such films as *The Brothers Karamazov, The Unforgiven,* and *Brubaker*. On television Salmi was a regular on *Daniel Boone, Petrocelli,* and *79 Park Avenue*. Frank Silvera played Don Sebastian Montoya on the television Western, *High Chaparral*.

Sweet Billy, Singer of Songs. January 15, 1966. Production #0469. Rerun June 18, 1966.

Sweet Billy, Festus' young nephew, arrives in Dodge to marry Orabelle Beal. However, Pony Beal, Orabelle's father, is a shrewd businessman and demands a dowery. The hard bargain forces Sweet Billy and some backwoods cousins to go to work to raise enough money to fullfill Pony's requirements.

Sweet Billy	Bob Random
Orabelle Beal	Brooke Bundy
Lambert	Royal Dano
Pony Beal	Slim Pickens
Story, Script	Gustave Field
Director	Alvin Ganzer
Associate Producer	John Mantley
Producer	Philip Leacock

Brooke Bundy was a regular on the daytime dramas *Days of Our Lives* and *General Hospital*. Her film credits include *Firecreek, The Young Runaways* and *M.A.S.H.*

The Raid [Part I]. January 22, 1966. Production #0458. Rerun August 27, 1966.

Outlaws on a bank robbing spree led by Jim Stark head for Dodge. Matt faces one of his toughest battles and one of his greatest crises.

The Raid [Part II]. January 29, 1966. Production #0459. Rerun September 3, 1966.

Stark's band of outlaws rob the bank, kidnap Doc, and set fire to the town to cover their getaway. The desperadoes who are tired, wounded, and fighting amongst themselves, leave a trail of blood for Matt's posse to follow. There are not many men left on either side when the final showdown is reached.

Jim Stark	Gary Lockwood
T.R. Stark	John Kellogg
Tence Fraley	Richard Jaeckel
Web Fraley	Jeremy Slate
Jeff Fraley	Preston Pierce
Les McConnell	John Anderson
Clell Williams	Jim Davis
Shilo	Ted Jordan
Cash McLean	Michael Conrad
Mr. Early	Percy Helton
Story, Script	Clyde Ware
Director	Vincent McEveety
Associate Producer	John Mantley
Producer	Philip Leacock

Gary Lockwood starred in *Follow the Sun* and *The Lieutenant*. His films include *Tall Story* and *2001: A Space Odyssey*. Jim Davis appeared on numerous television shows most notably as Jock Ewing of *Dallas*. His film credits include *Winter Meeting* with Bette Davis.

Killer at Large. February 5, 1966. Production #0471.

Festus flees Dodge after being bullied into killing a drunken sharpshooter from a traveling medicine show. Esther Harris, a widow whom Festus meets during his flight, helps him regain his courage and teaches him he cannot solve his troubles by running away from them.

Esther Harris	Geraldine Brooks
Grange	Robert Ballew
James Harris	Craig Hundley
Sandy	Tim O'Kelly
Storekeeper	Hardie Albright
Grandpa Harris	Cyril Delevanti
Gabin	John Pickard
Doc Brown	Stuart Erwin
Jace	James Beggs
Horsetrader	Gilman Rankin
Ira	Jonathan Lippe
Coor	Morgan Jones
Story, Script	Calvin Clements
Director	Marc Daniels
Associate Producer	John Mantley
Producer	Philip Leacock

Geraldine Brooks was a regular on *Faraday and Company* and *The Dumplings*. Her films include *Possessed* and *Volcano*. An accomplished photographer, in 1975 Brooks published a book called *Swan Watch*, which was a compilation of her bird photographs. "Bumbling" but appealing Stu Erwin appeared on *The Stu Erwin Show* and *The Greatest Show on Earth*. His films include *It Could Happen to You* and *Pigskin Parade,* for which he was nominated for an Academy Award in 1936. Morgan Jones played Commander Donovan in the series *The Blue Angels.*

The Television Programs

My Father's Guitar. February 12, 1966. Production #0474. Rerun July 23, 1966.
All that Jason has to remind him of his father is his guitar, something that the young man treasures more than anything else in the world. When a rancher threatens to destroy Jason's beloved instrument, the boy loses his temper and kills him. Panic stricken after the incident, Jason rides into Dodge and gets a job playing guitar at the Long Branch.

Jason	Beau Bridges
Dan	Charles Dierkop
Jack	Steve Ihnat
Jeb	William Bramley
Sonny Starr	Dub Taylor
Saloon Girl	Robin Blake
Story, Script	Hal Sitowitz
Director	Robert Totten
Associate Producer	John Mantley
Producer	Philip Leacock

Beau Bridges is the son of actor Lloyd Bridges of *Seahunt* fame and the older brother of film actor Jeff Bridges. Beau's movie career includes such films as *Gaily, Gaily, The Landlord, The Hotel New Hampshire,* and *The Fabulous Baker Boys*. In addition to numerous made-for-television movies Mr. Bridges was a regular on *Ensign O'Toole* and *United States.* Dub "Cannonball" Taylor is the father of Buck Taylor who played gunsmith Newly O'Brien. A favorite cowboy sidekick of the B-Western circuit, Cannonball appeared in such films as *Saddle and Sagebrush, Song of the Drifter,* and *Pardon My Gun*. After the 30s and 40s serials and B-Westerns died down, the multi-talented character actor shifted gears toward television and feature films that included *Bonnie and Clyde, A Man Called Horse,* and *Support Your Local Sheriff.* Charles Dierkop played Detective Pete Royster on television's *Police Woman.*

Wishbone. February 19, 1966. Production #0473.
Matt tracks three killers who have robbed a stagecoach, while at the same time, Festus is following Doc's trail. Their paths cross when Festus is forced to kill one of the robbers, while fighting to save Doc's life after a rattlesnake bite.

Spellman	Lew Gallo
Travers	Victor French
Aiken	Lyle Waggoner
Tomkin	Billy Beck
Buffalo Hunter	Michael Fox
Stage Driver	Don Happy
Passengers	Adar Jameson, Natalie Masters,
	William Meader, Joan Granville
Story, Script	Paul Savage
Director	Marc Daniels
Producer	Philip Leacock
Associate Producer	John Mantley

This story was inspired by an incident that happened to Ken Curtis' mother and is his favorite episode. Victor French guest starred on numerous episodes of *Gunsmoke* and even directed several. On television French is a familiar face. His many roles included Agent 44 on *Get Smart,* Mr. Edwards of *Little House on the Prairie,* and most recently Mark Gordon of *Highway to Heaven*. His film credits include *An Officer and a Gentleman.* Lyle Waggoner was a regular on *The Carol Burnett Show* and *Wonder Woman.*

On television, Billy Beck played the photo editor on *Lou Grant*. Natalie Masters played Wilma Clemson on the comedy series *Date with the Angels*.

Sanctuary. February 26, 1966. Production #0472.
   A wounded outlaw fleeing a bank robbery takes sanctuary in a church where he holds Reverend John Porter, Porter's fiancee and another woman hostage, while Doc treats his injury. The tense situation tests the pastor's courage, as he questions his own motives for not resisting the bandit.

Reverend John Porter	Sean Garrison
Paul Wiley	Richard Bradford
Phyllis Bowman	Joan Blackman
Miss Holland	Virginia Gregg
Ayers	Larry Wood
Wiley's Friend	Bill Hart
Baker	Martin Place
Gorman	Jack Grinnage
Halligan	Charles Wagenheim
Mrs. Ayers	Marsha Blakesley
Porter	Woodrow Chambliss
Story, Script	Calvin Clements
Director	Harry Harris, Jr.
Associate Producer	John Mantley
Producer	Philip Leacock

   Sean Garrison appeared as Culhane on the television Western, *Dundee and the Culhane*, and as Yannuck on the dramatic series, *The Secret Empire*. On television Richard Bradford played McGill on *Man in a Suitcase*. Joan Blackman was a regular on television's *Peyton Place*. Bill Hart appeared on the Western series, *Stoney Burke*. Charles Wagenheim played the part of Halligan through the next nine seasons.

Honor Before Justice. March 5, 1966. Production #0475.
   Sarah, a pretty Indian girl, defies a tribal consul when she tries to prove her father innocent of a crime. The consul has found her father guilty and has decreed that he should die. A desperate Sarah goes to Dodge for help but Matt is out of town. Despite Doc's warnings that he stay out of Indian affairs, Thad agrees to help her.

Sarah	France Nuyen
John-Two-Bears	Noah Beery
Grey Horse	Michael Ansara
Herkimer Crawford	Barton MacLane
Elias Franklin	Harry Bartell
Thunderman	George Keymas
Little Walker	Richard Gilden
Blacksmith	Ken Renard
Barking Dog	James Almanzar
Policeman	Ted Jordan
Story, Script	Frank Q. Dobbs & Robert C. Stewart
Director	Harry Harris, Jr.
Associate Producer	John Mantley
Producer	Philip Leacock

   Although primarily a film actress, France Nuyen was a regular on television's *St. Elsewhere*. The French-Chinese actress appeared in such films as *South Pacific*, *A Girl*

The Television Programs

Named Tamiko, and *Diamond Head*. On Broadway she starred in *The World of Suzie Wong*. Michael Ansara is best known for his Indian roles. He appeared in several television shows including *Broken Arrow*, *Law of the Plainsman*, and the mini-series *Centennial*. Ansara's film credits include *The Robe*, *The Greatest Story Ever Told*, and *The Manitou*. He was married to *I Dream of Jeannie* actress, Barbara Eden. Barton MacLane played Marshal Frank Caine on *The Outlaws* and General Martin Peterson on *I Dream of Jeannie*. MacLane appeared in over 200 films including *Dr. Jekyll and Mr. Hyde*, *The Prince and the Pauper*, and *The Maltese Falcon*. James Almanzar was a regular on *Doctor's Hospital*.

The Brothers. March 12, 1966. Production #0470.

An outlaw vows to free his younger brother from jail by threatening violence against Matt's friends. Although, the outlaw's actions are aimed at intimidating Matt into releasing his brother, they only serve to make the marshal more determined to bring the brothers to justice.

Ed	Scott Marlowe
Billy	Bobby Crawford
Dave Crandall	Joseph Hoover
Will Taylor	Mark Sturges
Carl Wilkins	Eddie Firestone
Okie	Tom Reese
Wat	Warren Vanders
Durgen	Edmund Hashim
Story, Script	Tom Hanley
Director	Tay Garnett
Associate Producer	John Mantley
Producer	Philip Leacock

The title *The Brothers* was used again November 27, 1972. Bobby Crawford played Andy Sherman on *Laramie*. Crawford is the older brother of Johnny Crawford of *The Rifleman*. Eddie Firestone appeared on the dramatic series, *Mixed Doubles*.

Which Dr. March 19, 1966. Production #0476.

While on a fishing trip, Doc and Festus get caught up in a sticky situation. A clan of scruffy buffalo hunters capture them, and want to keep Doc as their camp doctor. They also think Doc will make a suitable husband for their leader's spinster daughter.

Skeeter	George Lindsey
Argonaut	R.G. Armstrong
Addie	Shelley Morrison
Herk	Gregg Palmer
Piney	Claire Wilcox
Daisy Lou	Elizabeth Frazer
Story, Script	Les Crutchfield
Director	Peter Graves
Associate Producer	John Mantley
Producer	Philip Leacock

Director Peter Graves is James Arness' brother. Graves was a regular on such series as *Fury*, and *Mission: Impossible*. His film credits include *Stalag 17*, *Red Planet Mars*, and *Airplane*. Shelley Morrison played Sister Sixto on *The Flying Nun*.

Harvest. March 26, 1966. Production #0477.

Betsy Payson, a rancher's daughter, falls in love with David McGovern, a Scottish homesteader's son. Their liason only serves to stir up more trouble between their fathers, who have already been quarreling over a land dispute. The feud developed when Ian McGovern settled on land wrongfully claimed by Ben Payson.

David McGovern	James MacArthur
Betsy Payson	Leslie Ann Warren
Ben Payson	George Kennedy
Cran McGovern	Alma Platt
Leemer	Ted Jordan
Marty	Fred Coby
Ian McGovern	Karl Swenson
Story, Script	Les Crutchfield
Director	Harry Harris, Jr.
Associate Producer	John Mantley
Producer	Philip Leacock

James MacArthur, the son of Helen Hayes and Charles MacArthur, was a regular on television's *Hawaii Five-O*. Before moving into feature films, Leslie Ann Warren played a number of television roles and was featured in several series including *Mission: Impossible*. She was nominated for an Academy Award for Best Supporting Actress for *Victor/Victoria*. Her other film credits include *The Happiest Millionaire, A Night in Heaven, Choose Me* and *Clue*.

Clayton Thaddeus Greenwood. April 2, 1966, rerun. First aired October 2, 1965.

By Line. April 9, 1966. Production #0479. Rerun July 30, 1966.
Festus gets a job working for Dodge City's newspaper, which is amazing, since he can neither read nor write. Nevertheless, he stirs up a mess of trouble digging up gossip and advertising for the paper. Festus is so adept at getting the inside stories on Dodge's citizens and starting price wars between advertisers, that he and the paper's editors are on the verge of being run out of town.

Angus McTabbott	Chips Rafferty
Clab Chummer	Denver Pyle
Jock	Stefan Arngrim
Story, Script	Les Crutchfield
Director	Allen Reisner
Associate Producer	John Mantley
Producer	Philip Leacock

Stefan Arngrim was featured in the sci-fi series, *Land of the Giants*.

Treasure of John Walking Fox. April 16, 1966. Production #0480.
Comanche John Walking Fox pays for the funeral of his hide hunter friend with a $50 gold piece. The money is from a long lost treasure, which causes gold fever to break out in Dodge. Fox is silent as to the source of the gold, which further fans everyone's curiosity, including that of Matt and the man who murdered the hide hunter.

John Walking Fox	Leonard Nimoy
Aaron Tigue	Richard Webb
Gainer	Jim Davis
Jacob Beamus	Lloyd Gough
Holtz	Ted Gehring
Banjo	Tom McCauley

The Television Programs

Story	Gwen Bagni
Script	Clyde Ware
Director	Marc Daniels
Associate Producer	John Mantley
Producer	Philip Leacock

Lloyd Gough appeared in the 1966 television series *The Green Hornet*. Ted Gehring was a regular on several television shows including *Little House on the Prairie, Alice,* and *Dallas*.

My Father, My Son. April 23, 1966. Production #0478. Rerun August 6, 1966.

Gunman Jim Barrett kills a young challenger and becomes a target for revenge from the victim's family. Unbeknownst to Barrett, another young man is determined to avenge the killing, David Barrett, Jim's son.

Jim Barrett	Jack Elam
David Barrett	Teno Pollick
Ike Jeffords	Lee Van Cleef
Story, Script	Hal Sitowitz
Director	Robert Totten
Associate Producer	John Mantley
Producer	Philip Leacock

Parson Comes to Town. April 30, 1966. Production #0482.

Asa Longworth arrives in Dodge dressed in the frock coat of his dead brother. Longworth then proceeds to employ a scare campaign to avenge the preacher's death. The war of nerves begins when Longworth asks to see three people Matt, Doc, and an undertaker. He then announces that he has come to Dodge to watch a man die.

Asa Longworth	Sam Wanamaker
Sipes	Lonny Chapman
Dougherty	John McLiam
Mother	Joan Granville
Boy	Kevin Burchett
Percy Crump	Kelton Garwood
Story, Script	Verne Jay
Director	Marc Daniels
Associate Producer	John Mantley
Producer	Philip Leacock

Character actor Sam Wanamaker appeared on television as Moses Weiss in *Holocaust,* and Simon Berrenger on the dramatic series, *Berrengers*. His film credits include *Taras Bulba, The Spy Who Came in from the Cold,* and *Voyage of the Damned*.

Prime of Life. May 7, 1966. Production #0481.

Kyle and Woody Stoner are two trouble making sons of John Stoner, an ex-lawman. Although the brothers are involved in a killing and stage hold-up, their father refuses to believe they are outlaws until it is too late to stop them. When Matt and Festus step in, they become the targets for revenge.

John Stoner	Douglas Kennedy
Kyle Stoner	Jonathan Lippe
Joe Smith	Victor French
Woody Stoner	Joe Don Baker
Brown	Martin West

GUNSMOKE — III. THE PROGRAMS

Wilma	Lyn Edgington
Brad	Cal Naylor
Barkeep	Ted French
Story, Script	Dan Ullman
Director	Robert Totten
Associate Producer	John Mantley
Producer	Philip Leacock

Joe Don Baker's film credits include *Cool Hand Luke, Junior Bonner,* and *Walking Tall.*

The Bounty Hunter. May 14, 1966, rerun. First aired October 30, 1965.

The Pretender. May 28, 1966, rerun. First aired November 20, 1965.

South Wind. June 4, 1966, rerun. First aired November 27, 1965.

The Hostage. June 11, 1966, rerun. First aired December 4, 1965.

Sweet Billy, Singer of Songs. June 18, 1966, rerun. First aired January 15, 1966.

Outlaw's Woman. July 2, 1966, rerun. First aired December 11, 1965.

The Avengers. July 9, 1966, rerun. First aired December 18, 1965.

My Father's Guitar. July 23, 1966, rerun. First aired February 12, 1966.

By Line. July 30, 1966, rerun. First aired April 9, 1966.

The Raid [Part I]. August 27, 1966, rerun. First aired January 22, 1966.

The Raid [Part II]. September 3, 1966, rerun. First aired January 29, 1966.

TWELFTH SEASON

Now in color

Snap Decision. September 17, 1966. Production #0203. Rerun May 6, 1967 and July 26, 1971.

Matt is forced to kill a man who was once his friend. The incident forces Matt to rethink his position as a lawman. The burden has always been great, but Matt no longer wants to shoulder it. He resigns his post and turns his badge over to a new marshal, Clint Tucker. However, he begins to reconsider his "snap decision," when a bounty hunter and a man claiming to be the dead man's son arrive in Dodge and join forces.

Marshal Clint Tucker	Claude Akins
Shaver	Michael Strong
Kipp	Michael Cole
Gilcher	Sam Gilman
Preacher	Orville Sherman
Story, Script	Richard Carr
Story Consultant	Paul Savage

[600]

The Television Programs

Director	Mark Rydell
Producer	John Mantley
Executive Producer	Philip Leacock

Michael Cole played Pete Cochrane on *The Mod Squad*. Sam Gilman appeared in the short-lived television Western, *Shane*.

The Goldtakers. September 24, 1966. Production #0304. Rerun September 9, 1967.

Britton, the leader of a notorious gang of outlaws, steals an enormous bar of gold. He then impersonates a cavalry captain and commandeers the Dodge blacksmith shop in an attempt to divide the loot. As a cover-up, Britton claims that his troops are preparing to test a new rapid fire weapon. He succeeds in diverting suspicion from their true purpose, until a fire breaks out in the shop forcing Matt to investigate.

Britton	Martin Landau
Caleb Nash	Denver Pyle
Troy	Roy Jenson
Jenkins	Brad Weston
Kale	Charles Francisco
Holcroft	Michael Greene
Jake Struck	William Bramley
Warner	John Boyer
Garvey	Woodrow Chambliss
Halligan	Charles Wagenheim
Story, Script	Clyde Ware
Story Consultant	Paul Savage
Director	Vincent McEveety
Producer	John Mantley
Executive Producer	Philip Leacock

Roy Jenson appeared as Pete Tierney on *Rich Man, Poor Man—Book I*.

The Jailer. October 1, 1966. Production #0206. Rerun April 29, 1967 and June 28, 1971.

Etta Stone has waited six years to avenge the death of her husband. As soon as her sons are released from prison, she has them kidnap Kitty. This is the first step in her diabolical plan to lure Matt into a trap. Once caught, Etta imprisons Matt and prepares to hang him. She plans for him to die on the "morning of the second day" with Kitty watching, just like Etta had to watch her husband hang six years earlier.

Etta Stone	Bette Davis
Lou Stone	Bruce Dern
Mike Stone	Robert Sorrells
Jack Stone	Zalman King
Ben Stone	Tom Skerritt
Sara Stone	Julie Sommars
Story, Script	Hal Sitowitz
Story Consultant	Paul Savage
Director	Vincent McEveety
Producer	John Mantley
Executive Producer	Philip Leacock

The Jailer was one of Amanda Blake's favorite episodes because it allowed her the opportunity to work with Bette Davis, one of Hollywood's true superstars. A winner of two Academy Awards, Davis starred in such classics as *Dangerous, Jezebel, Of Human*

GUNSMOKE — III. THE PROGRAMS

Bondage, The Petrified Forest, Dark Victory, All About Eve, and most recently *The Whales of August.* An indomitable queen of cinema, Davis weathered the ups and downs of her career, always winding up on top. In recent years she made numerous made-for-television movies. In 1977 she was honored by the American Film Institute and was presented with the coveted Life's Achievement Award, which has been given to only four other individuals. Davis was the first woman to receive this honor.

The Mission. October 8, 1966. Production #0205. Rerun August 26, 1967.

Matt travels into Mexico to take custody of a convict and tangles with three American drifters. The men steal his horses, his credentials, and his prisoner. In the struggle Matt is wounded and is given refuge by Amos Jessup, an ex-confederate colonel. The colonel turns out to be the convict's father, a man who lives in the past, and refuses to accept the truth about himself or his son.

Colonel Amos Jessup	Robert F. Simon
Reb Jessup	Bob Random
Lafe	Warren Oates
Ashe	Steve Ihnat
Sergeant Macklin	Arch Johnson
Jim Basset	Jim Davis
Young Soldier	Rafael Campos
Colonel Romero	Robert Tafur
Captain	Ruben Moreno
Soldier	Mike Avelar
Blacksmith	Bert Madrid
Story, Script	Richard Carr
Story Consultant	Paul Savage
Director	Mark Rydell
Producer	John Mantley
Executive Producer	Philip Leacock

The Good People. October 15, 1966. Production #0210. Rerun August 19, 1967 and May 10, 1971.

Against the protests of his son, Ben Rucker hangs an innocent man and lets a bounty hunter take the blame. All of the evidence points to a conviction for the accused, while the guilty hide behind their reputation as respectable, law abiding citizens. Matt plays a hunch and gets the conscience-stricken son to serve on the jury.

Ben Rucker	Morgan Woodward
Gabe Rucker	Allen Case
Seth Rucker	Tom Simcox
Silas Shute	Shug Fisher
Judge Evers	Frederic Downs
Sutton	James O'Hara
Henry Biggs	Clyde Howdy
Halligan	Charles Wagenheim
Jed Bailey	Steve Gravers
Story, Script	James Landis
Story Consultant	Paul Savage
Director	Robert Totten
Producer	John Mantley
Executive Producer	Philip Leacock

The Television Programs

Gunfighter, R.I.P. October 22, 1966. Production #0215. Rerun April 1, 1967, September 16, 1968 and May 18, 1970.

Gunfighter Joe Bascome is inadvertantly drawn into a fight and tries to save the life of an old Chinese man, Ching Fa. In the process, he is seriously wounded. Ching Fa dies, but his daughter Ching Lee is forever indebted to Bascome. She nurses the ailing gunman back to health and a romance develops between the two. The romance troubles Mark and Paul Douglas who have hired Bascome to kill Matt, and they start to worry that Bascome will not live up to his contract.

Joe Bascome	Darren McGavin
Ching Lee	France Nuyen
Burt	Allen Emerson
Mark Douglas	Stefan Gierasch
Paul Douglas	Michael Conrad
Ching Fa	H.T. Tsiang
Barber	Don Hanmer
Story	Michael Fisher
Script	Hal Sitowitz
Story Consultant	Paul Savage
Director	Mark Rydell
Producer	John Mantley
Executive Producer	Philip Leacock

Stefan Gierasch appeared in the comedy series, *A.E.S. Hudson Street.* Director Mark Rydell stepped out from behind the camera and into the spotlight for a featured role in *Punchline* that starred Sally Field and Tom Hanks.

The Wrong Man. October 29, 1966. Production #0208. Rerun May 27, 1967 and August 9, 1971.

Hootie Kyle, a farmer whose credit has run out, gets a loan from Matt and Festus and then loses the money in a poker game with a professional gambler. Later, when the gambler is found robbed and murdered, the evidence points to Hootie. Although Hootie admits getting his money back, he denies the killing.

Hootie Kyle	Carroll O'Connor
Tenner Jackson	Clifton James
James Kyle	Kevin O'Neal
Wilton Kyle	Charles Kuenstle
Harmon	James Anderson
Morell	James Almanzar
Squeak	Mel Gaines
Purvis	Gilman Rankin
Dutch	Victor Izay
Stage Driver	Terry Frost
Story, Script	Clyde Ware
Story Consultant	Paul Savage
Director	Robert Totten
Producer	John Mantley
Executive Producer	Philip Leacock

The title *The Wrong Man* was first used April 13, 1957. Carroll O'Connor went on to achieve superstar fame as Archie Bunker of *All in the Family* and *Archie Bunker's Place.* He won the Emmy in 1972, 1977, 1978, and 1979 for his portrayal. Most recently he starred in the series *In the Heat of the Night*. Kevin O'Neal is the younger brother of actor Ryan O'Neal. He appeared in the television series *No Time for Sergeants*. Terry Frost appeared in over 200 films in the 1940s and 1950s, many of them serials and Westerns where he played the villain. They include *Dillinger, Apache Rose,* and *Left Handed Gun*. In 1988 Frost was honored for his achievements by The Riders of the Silver Screen in Knoxville, Tennessee.

November 5, 1966, preempted for *Miss Teenage America*.

The Whispering Tree. November 12, 1966. Production #0201. Rerun April 22, 1967 and March 22, 1971.

Virgil Stanley returns home after serving eight years in prison for theft, only to discover his wife Ada has completely changed the face of their ranch. Ordinarily this would be no problem, however, Virgil hid the stolen fortune under a tree he can no longer find. Furthermore, he is hounded by his ex-partner who wants a share of the money, and by a tough range detective who wants it all.

Virgil Stanley	John Saxon
Ada Stanley	Jacqueline Scott
Redmond	Edward Asner
Mother	Kathleen O'Malley
Boy	Stephen McEveety
Earl Miller	Morgan Woodward
Bryant	Donald Losby
Curtis	Christopher Pate
Garr	Rex Holman
Ryan	Allen Jaffe
Station Attendant	Fred Coby
Guard	Lane Chandler
Story, Script	Calvin Clements, Sr.
Story Consultant	Paul Savage
Director	Vincent McEveety
Producer	John Mantley
Executive Producer	Philip Leacock

Vincent McEveety's son Stephen has a cameo role.

The Well. November 19, 1966. Production #0209. Rerun August 12, 1968.

A rainmaker arrives in drought-ridden Dodge and Matt permits the conman to operate. The marshal feels it will give the suffering people something to hope for, while he looks for more conventional means to help end the critical water shortage.

Dr. Tobias	Guy Raymond
Janie	Joan Payne
Jim Libby	Lawrence Casey
Mrs. Davis	Elizabeth Rogers
Lathrop	Woodrow Chambliss
Halligan	Charles Wagenheim
Boyd	Ted Gehring
Lake	Karl Lucas
Monk	Pete Kellett
Jim Grady	Robert Ballew
Story, Script	Francis Cockrell

The Television Programs

Story Consultant	Paul Savage
Director	Marc Daniels
Producer	John Mantley
Executive Producer	Philip Leacock

Lawrence Casey played Private Mark Hitchcock on *The Rat Patrol*.

Stage Stop. November 26, 1966. Production #0212.

Doc takes up arms to defend a gold shipment from bandits, first during a stagecoach ambush, and then at a waystation where his host Jed Coombs is in cahoots with the outlaws. Doc's problems are compounded by the plight of his fellow companions, a wounded stage driver, an injured bandit, a blind passenger, and a cruel station master who mistreats his pregnant wife.

Jed Coombs	John Ireland
Lori Coombs	Anne Whitfield
Simon Dobbs	Jack Ging
Trivers	Steve Raines
Lingo	Michael Vandever
Curt Hanson	Joseph Ruskin
Wade Hanson	Sid Haig
Charley Woodson	Andy Albin
Story, Script	Hal Sitowitz
Story Consultant	Paul Savage
Director	Irving Moore
Producer	John Mantley
Executive Producer	Philip Leacock

John Ireland was a regular on *The Cheaters, Cassie and Company*, and *Rawhide*. His impressive screen credits include *A Walk in the Sun, Red River*, and *All the King's Men*, for which he was nominated for an Academy Award. Jack Ging was featured on several television series including *Tales of Wells Fargo, The Eleventh Hour*, and *Riptide*. His film credits include *Desire in the Dust* and *Sniper's Ridge*. Sid Haig played Drago, the arch villain, in the Saturday morning television series, *Jason of Star Command*.

The Newcomers. December 3, 1966. Production #0218. Rerun June 24, 1967 and June 7, 1971.

A Scandinavian immigrant and his teenaged son, find the West even wilder than they had imagined when they settle in Dodge. Before they have a chance to get used to their new environment, the boy is forced into a deadly fight by a hired hand. Because of fear and shock, the father and son delay telling Matt about the killing. Meanwhile, they are visited by a blackmailer, who claims to be the only eyewitness to the incident.

Dirger Engdahl	Ben Wright
Pony	James Murdock
Joey	Laurence Aten
Lars Karlgren	Karl Swenson
Tetter Karlgren	Jon Voight
Handley	Robert Sorrells
Silvee	Charles Dierkop
Vigilante	John Pickard
Vasquez	Daniel Ades
Story, Script	Calvin Clements, Sr.

GUNSMOKE — III. THE PROGRAMS

Story Consultant .... Paul Savage
Director .... Robert Totten
Producer .... John Mantley
Executive Producer .... Philip Leacock

James Murdock played Mushy on *Rawhide*. Jon Voight received the Academy Award for his performance in *Coming Home*. His other film credits include *Midnight Cowboy, Deliverance,* and *Runaway Train*.

Quaker Girl. December 10, 1966. Production #0202.

Criminal Fred Bateman's identity is confused with that of Thad's, when a Quaker family rescues the pair after a do-or-die fight. Recovering from their wounds in the Quaker settlement, Thad and Bateman offer conflicting stories about their identities. Bateman seems more convincing, until Thad begins to make friends with a pretty Quaker girl, Cora Ellis.

Fred Bateman .... William Shatner
Cora Ellis .... Ariane Quinn
Benjamin Ellis .... Liam Sullivan
Vern Morland .... Ben Johnson
John Thenly .... Warren Vanders
Charles "Buster" Rilla .... Timothy Carey
Woman #1 .... Anna Karen
Woman #2 .... Nancy Marshall
Henry .... Ed McCready
Kesler .... William Bryant
George .... Joseph Breen
Dave Westerfield .... Tom Reese
Story, Script .... Preston Wood
Story Consultant .... Paul Savage
Director .... Bernard Kowalski
Producer .... John Mantley
Executive Producer .... Philip Leacock

On television, William Shatner was a regular on *For the People, The Barbary Coast* and *T.J. Hooker*. However, he will be forever known as Captain James T. Kirk of *Star Trek*.

The Moonstone. December 17, 1966. Production #0216.

When Del Philips is released from prison, he goes gunning for Chad Timpson. Chad, Del's former partner in crime, is now a respectable farmer. Although Del loses the showdown, he leaves behind a faded wanted poster revealing Chad's forgotten past. When Orv, Chad's mentally retarded brother, discovers the poster, it proves to be his undoing.

Chad Timpson .... Michael Kellin
Orv Timpson .... Tom Skerritt
Madge .... Gail Kobe
Del Philips .... Warren Kemmerling
Todd .... Jeff Palmer
Bartender .... Larry Barton
Rankin .... Fred Coby
Cowboy #1 .... Fred Dale
Cowboy #2 .... Chick Sheridan
Story, Script .... Paul Savage

The Television Programs

Story Consultant .... Paul Savage
Director .... Dick Colla
Producer .... John Mantley
Executive Producer .... Philip Leacock

Michael Kellin was a regular on several television shows including *The Wackiest Ship in the Army, Seventh Avenue,* and *Fitz and Bones.*

Champion of the World. December 24, 1966. Production #0214. Rerun July 8, 1968.

Bull Bannock, an ex-heavy weight champion, arrives in Dodge and tries to buy Kitty's Long Branch Saloon. When Kitty tells the ex-champ that she is not selling, the former boxer refuses to take "no" for an answer. Bull makes the mistake of aligning himself with a swindler called the Professor, who advises him to build a grand saloon to force Kitty out of business.

Bull Bannock .... Alan Hale
Professor .... Dan Tobin
Gopher Freely .... Ralph Rose
Cora Argyle .... Jane Dulo
Maude .... Gale Robbins
Drunk .... Arthur Peterson
Dougherty .... John McLiam, Jr.
Wally .... Don Keefer
Mac .... Pete Kellett
Zac .... Troy Melton
Burke .... Ted Jordan
Halligan .... Charles Wagenheim
Story, Script .... Les Crutchfield
Story Consultant .... Paul Savage
Director .... Marc Daniels
Producer .... John Mantley
Executive Producer .... Philip Leacock

Jane Dulo was a regular in several television series including, *McHale's Navy, Get Smart, Medical Center, Sha Na Na,* and *Gimme a Break.* Gale Robbins appeared regularly on the television variety program, *Hollywood House.*

The Hanging. December 31, 1966. Production #0207.

A desperado vows he will never climb the gallows that are being built especially for him in Dodge. His promise seems a certainty, for enemies and friends alike come gunning for him at the Dodge jail.

Billy Boles .... Tom Stern
Ivy .... Kit Smythe
Warren .... Robert Knapp
Oro .... Henry Darrow
Maria Oro .... Anna Navarro
Teems .... Richard Bakalyan
Saline .... Edmund Hashim
Preston .... Larry Ward
Beaumont .... Morgan Woodward
Ollie .... Byron Foulger
Story, Script .... Calvin Clements, Jr.
Story Consultant .... Paul Savage

GUNSMOKE — III. THE PROGRAMS

Director .... Bernard Kowalski
Producer .... John Mantley
Executive Producer .... Philip Leacock

Henry Darrow was a regular on several television programs including *The High Chaparral* and *Harry-O*. Richard Bakalyan appeared in such films as *The Delicate Delinquent, Up Periscope,* and *Von Ryan's Express*. On television he was a regular on *The Bobby Darin Show*.

Saturday Night. January 7, 1967. Production #0220. Rerun May 13, 1967 and May 24, 1971.

Matt and his prisoner Carl Craddock, drink poisonous water while out on the prairie. The two are rescued from certain death by trail boss, Virgil Powell, who gives Matt and Craddock passage back to Dodge. Matt owes his life to Powell, but a new set of problems arise when Powell's celebrating cowboys hit town. The drovers tear up the town in a Saturday night free-for-all, and Matt has to stop them.

Virgil Powell .... Leif Erickson
Carl Craddock .... William C. Watson
C.K. Ross .... Victor French
Cook .... Dub Taylor
Lucky .... Link Harget
Rudy .... Rudy Sooter
Storekeeper .... Frederick Downs
Story, Script .... Clyde Ware
Story Consultant .... Paul Savage
Director .... Robert Totten
Producer .... John Mantley
Executive Producer .... Philip Leacock

Leif Erickson appeared in such films as, *The Snake Pit, Sorry, Wrong Number,* and *On the Waterfront*. On television he guest starred on several shows and was the patriarch, Big John Cannon, of *The High Chapparral*. William C. Watson played Garner on *Roots* and Andy in the dramatic series *The Contender*.

Mad Dog. January 14, 1967. Production #0217. Rerun June 10, 1967.

The three surly Watson brothers mistake Festus for a hired gunman and try to goad the deputy into a fight. Festus wants no part of the troublesome Watsons until he is attacked by a "mad dog." Advised by doctor Rand that the dog bite could prove fatal, Festus decides he has nothing to lose, and challenges the Watsons to a shootout.

Doctor Rand .... Denver Pyle
Jim Travers .... George Murdock
Mayor Wheeler .... Iggie Wolfington
Roan Watson .... Hoke Howell
Pinto Watson .... George Lindsey
Buff Watson .... Sammy Reese
Tom John .... Butch Patrick
Bartender .... Dub Taylor
Story, Script .... Jay Simms
Story Consultant .... Paul Savage
Director .... Charles Rondeau
Producer .... John Mantley
Executive Producer .... Philip Leacock

The Television Programs

George Murdock appeared as a regular on *No Time for Sergeants, Barney Miller,* and *The Winds of War.* Hoke Howell played Ben Jenkins on the adventure-comedy, *Here Come the Brides.*

Muley. January 21, 1967. Production #0213. Rerun August 5, 1967.

A young gunman named Muley wounds Matt. While waiting in Dodge, preparing to finish Matt off and rob the bank, Muley falls for Lucy, one of Kitty's saloon girls. In the meantime, his partners grow restless, especially when Lucy appears to have softened Muley's desire to kill Matt.

Muley	Zalman King
Lucy	Lane Bradbury
Tell	Anthony Call
Arky	Marc Cavell
Kay Cee	Ross Hagen
Howie	Howard Culver
Story, Script	Les Crutchfield
Story Consultant	Paul Savage
Director	Allen Reisner
Producer	John Mantley
Executive Producer	Philip Leacock

Marc Cavell was a regular on the television comedy, *Pistols 'n' Petticoats.* Ross Hagen played Bart Jason on *Daktari.*

Mail Drop. January 28, 1967. Production #0222. Rerun July 8, 1967 and July 22, 1968.

Billy, a runaway school boy, makes friends with Festus when he comes to Dodge looking for his father. After Billy spots a wanted poster in Matt's office with his father's picture on it, his attitude toward Festus and Matt turns bitter. He assumes that they are using his friendship as a means of tracking down his father. Eventually Billy has to choose between his father and the law.

Billy	Eddie Hodges
Roberts	John Anderson
Walsh	Bing Russell
Lathrop	Woodrow Chambliss
Steve	Steve Raines
Drover	Ted French
Al	Pete Kellett
Gabe	Fred McDougall
Sherm	Chick Sheridan
Chuck	Robert Miles, Jr.
Story, Script	Calvin Clements
Story Consultant	Paul Savage
Director	Robert Totten
Producer	John Mantley
Executive Producer	Philip Leacock

Child star, Eddie Hodges, appeared in such films as *A Hole in the Head, The Adventures of Huckleberry Finn,* and *Summer Magic.*

Old Friend. February 4, 1967. Production #0211. Rerun July 1, 1967.

Burl Master, a quick triggered Arizona marshal and an old friend of Matt's, comes to Dodge looking for the outlaw gang that burned his town and stole his woman. Master is driven by vengeance and pursues the bandits with an obsession that reaches beyond his duties as a lawman and threatens his renewed friendship with Matt.

Marshal Burl Master	Fritz Weaver
Willa	Delphi Lawrence
Gus	William Benedict
Cheeno	Valentin de Vargas
Trail	Carlos Rivas
Boley	David Renard
Fred	Lew Brown
Tod	Pat Cadi
Charley	Robert B. Williams
Story, Script	Clyde Ware
Story Consultant	Paul Savage
Director	Allen Reisner
Producer	John Mantley
Executive Producer	Philip Leacock

On television, veteran character actor Fritz Weaver guest starred on numerous series and movies. In the mini-series *Holocaust* he played Joseff Weiss. His film credits include *Fail Safe*, *The Day of the Dolphin*, and *Marathon Man*. On Broadway Weaver starred as Sherlock Holmes in the musical, *Baker Street*. Robert B. Williams played Garth Gimble, Sr. on the comedy, *Fernwood 2-Night*.

Fandango. February 11, 1967. Production #0219.

Matt captures Lorca, a fugitive wanted for killing three men. On the trip back to Dodge, John Tyson, the brother of one of the victims, trails the two men. Tyson hopes to do away with Lorca, and threatens to kill anyone who stands in his way, including his own daughter.

Lorca	Mario Alcade
John Tyson	Torin Thatcher
Laurel Tyson	Diana Muldaur
Doc Lacey	Paul Fix
Chongra	Shug Fisher
Smithy	Joe Higgins
Old Man	Walter Baldwin
Ben Tyson	Fletcher Brian
Story, Script	Don Ingalls
Story Consultant	Paul Savage
Director	James Landis
Producer	John Mantley
Executive Producer	Philip Leacock

Diana Muldaur was a regular on several series including *Born Free*, *The Tony Randall Show*, and *McCloud*, on which she played Chris Coughlin, Dennis Weaver's girlfriend. Joe Higgins was a regular on *Arrest and Trial* and *Johnny Cash Presents the Everly Brothers Show*.

The Returning. February 18, 1967. Production #0221.

After eight years as a struggling farmer, reformed outlaw Luke Todd rejoins his old gang to rob the Dodge freight office of $20,000. While fleeing from the law, Todd leaves the stolen money behind in a hatbox. His law-abiding wife, Amy, discovers the money and wrestles with her conscience. Faced with the dilemma of feeding her sons and staving off a foreclosure on her home, she must make a difficult decision.

Luke Todd .... Michael Ansara
Amy Todd .... Lois Nettleton
Ethan Todd .... Steve Sanders
Shem Todd .... Johnnie Whitaker
Billy Judd .... Jonathan Lippe
Will Hayes .... Richard Webb
Clyde Hayes .... Kenneth Mars
Jonas .... Roy Barcroft
Mr. Bodkin .... Roy Roberts
Barney .... Billy Halop
Barton .... Troy Melton
Story, Script .... James Landis
Story Consultant .... Paul Savage
Director .... Marc Daniels
Producer .... John Mantley
Executive Producer .... Philip Leacock

Johnnie Whitaker had a successful career as a child star of the television series *Family Affair*. In addition to frequent parts in other television shows, Whitaker played in such films as *The Russians Are Coming, The Russians Are Coming*. Kenneth Mars was a regular on several programs including *He & She*, *The Don Knotts Show*, and *Sha Na Na*. His flair for comedy was highlighted in such films as *The Producers* and *Young Frankenstein*. Billy Halop, one of the original Dead End Kids, was a regular on *All in the Family*.

The Lure. February 25, 1967. Production #0224.

Kitty is in the wrong place at the wrong time, when private detectives remove her and Carrie Neely, the daughter of a notorious outlaw, from their stage. The detectives are forced to take Kitty along to protect their plan of using Carrie as a lure to trap her fugitive father. The bait attracts outlaw Dal Neely, but he escapes taking Kitty and his daughter with him. Neely vows to give up his lawless life for a fresh start with Carrie, after pulling one more bank robbery.

Dal Neely .... Stephen McNally
Carrie Neely .... Kim Darby
Boles .... Warren Vanders
John Vanner .... John Pickard
William McGee .... Paul Picerni
Driver .... Fred Coby
Station Master .... Len Wayland
Young .... Martin Brooks
Trent .... Val Avery
Swiger .... Woodrow Chambliss
Hemmington .... Troy Melton
Story, Script .... Clyde Ware
Story Consultant .... Paul Savage
Director .... Marc Daniels
Producer .... John Mantley
Executive Producer .... Philip Leacock

Stephen McNally, a former lawyer who turned to acting, appeared as a regular on *Target: The Corruptors*. His numerous film credits include *Johnny Belinda* and *Tribute to a Bad Man*. Kim Darby appeared in *Rich Man, Poor Man,* and *The Last Convertible,* in addition to a number of made-for-television movies. Her film credits include *True Grit, The Grissom Gang,* and *Better Off Dead.* Paul Picerni was agent Lee Hobson of *The Untouchables.*

Noose of Gold. March 4, 1967. Production #0226. Rerun June 3, 1967.

Charles Shepard is an ambitious assistant attorney-general. He uses his old friendship with Matt to capture John Farron, a fugitive. He falsely uses Matt's name to convince Edna Farron that the state will make a deal with her husband if he turns himself in. In reality, however, Shepherd plans to ambush the unsuspecting Farron. When Matt discovers the plan, he prepares to risk everything, including his job, to prevent the showdown.

> Charles Shepherd .... Vincent Gardenia
> John Farron .... Steve Ihnat
> Jim Gunther .... Sam Gilman
> Edna Farron .... Jan Shepard
> Willard F. Kerner .... Barton MacLane
> Harry Barnes .... Michael Preece
> Ben Leary .... Jack Bailey
> Milt Agnew .... Harry Basch
> Sheriff Porter .... Robert B. Williams
> Halligan .... Charles Wagenheim
> *Story, Script* .... Clyde Ware
> *Story Consultant* .... Paul Savage
> *Director* .... Irving Moore
> *Producer* .... John Mantley
> *Executive Producer* .... Philip Leacock

Character actor Vincent Gardenia was a regular on *All in the Family* and *Breaking Away*. His films include *The Hustler, Death Wish,* and *Heaven Can Wait.* He was nominated for Academy Awards for *Bang the Drum Slowly* and *Moonstruck*. On Broadway, Gardenia received a Tony Award for his performance in *The Prisoner of Second Avenue*. Jack Bailey was a popular game show host best remembered as the emcee of the incredibly bizarre *Queen for a Day*. Harry Basch played Vince Caproni on *Falcon Crest*.

The Favor. March 11, 1967. Production #0223.

Fellow stagecoach passenger, John Crowley, saves Kitty's life when they are attacked by Indians at a waystation. When Crowley is later wounded in a gunfight in which he kills a man, he comes to Kitty for help. Kitty is faced with an ethical decision and is torn between her gratitude for Crowley and her concern for the law and Matt.

> John Crowley .... James Daly
> Adam Haley .... William Bramley
> Bonnie Mae Haley .... Diane Ladd
> Stage Driver .... Troy Melton
> Townswoman .... Shirley Wilson
> Morgan Haley .... Fred J. Scollay
> Kelly Bates .... Lew Gallo
> *Story, Script* .... Don Ingalls
> *Story Consultant* .... Paul Savage
> *Director* .... Marc Daniels

The Television Programs

Producer . . . . John Mantley
Executive Producer . . . . Philip Leacock

James Daly starred on *Foreign Intrigue* and *Medical Center*. In 1966 Daly won an Emmy for his performance in the Hallmark Hall of Fame production of *Eagle in a Cage*. His daughter is Tyne Daly of *Cagney and Lacey* fame.

Mistaken Identity. March 18, 1967. Production #0277. Rerun June 17, 1967.

Fugitive Ed Carstairs switches identities with Mel Gates after the latter is apparently fatally bitten by a rattlesnake. He decides to settle in Dodge where he is unknown but Matt and Thad find Gates alive and bring him back to town. Due to his serious injury, Gates is suffering from amnesia and Carstairs realizes he must get rid of Gates before he recovers his memory.

Ed Carstairs . . . . Albert Salmi
Mel Gates . . . . Hal Lynch
Timmons . . . . Ken Mayer
Dunsters . . . . Sam Melville
Story, Script . . . . Les Crutchfield & Paul Savage
Story Consultant . . . . Paul Savage
Director . . . . Robert Totten
Producer . . . . John Mantley
Executive Producer . . . . Philip Leacock

Sam Melville played Officer Mike Danko of *The Rookies*. Second to John Meston, writer Les Crutchfield wrote the most radio scripts for *Gunsmoke*.

Ladies from St. Louis. March 25, 1967. Production #0228. Rerun August 12, 1967.

A group of nuns from St. Louis bring wounded outlaw Worth Sweeney into Dodge. However, they are reluctant to turn Sweeney over to Matt because they believe Sweeney saved their lives. As Sweeney begins to recover from his wounds, he threatens violence if the sisters do not let him escape.

Worth Sweeney . . . . Claude Akins
Sister Ellen . . . . Josephine Hutchinson
Sister Ruth . . . . Aneta Corsault
Sister John . . . . Kelly Jean Peters
Sister Margaret . . . . Venita Wolf
Sister Louise . . . . Lois Roberts
Segurra . . . . Henry Darrow
Doyle . . . . John Carter
Williams . . . . Ralph Roberts
Outlaw . . . . Lew Brown
Gaines . . . . Vic Tayback
Story, Script . . . . Clyde Ware
Story Consultant . . . . Paul Savage
Director . . . . Irving Moore
Producer . . . . John Mantley
Executive Producer . . . . Philip Leacock

Kelly Jean Peters was a regular on *Hank* and *M.A.S.H*. Lois Roberts was seen as Molly McGuire on *Broadside*. Henry Darrow was a regular on several series including *The High Chaparral* and *Harry-O*. John Carter played a regular on numerous dramatic series including *Barnaby Jones* and *Falcon Crest*. Vic Tayback is best recognized as Mel from the sitcom, *Alice*.

GUNSMOKE — III. THE PROGRAMS

Gunfighter, R.I.P. April 1, 1967, rerun. First aired October 22, 1966.

Nitro [Part I]. April 8, 1967. Production #0225. Rerun July 22, 1967 and April 12, 1971.

George McClaney, a penniless, lovesick transient, takes a dangerous job with a gang of bank robbers. The robbers pay George handsomely for making nitroglycerine for them to blow up bank safes. George's life changes for the better. He has money in his pocket and the love of Anne Gilchrist, the girl he wants to marry.

Nitro [Part II]. April 15, 1967. Production #0230. Rerun July 29, 1967 and April 19, 1971.

Matt hunts a gang that has blown-up one safe after another with nitroglycerine. Meanwhile, McClaney, who makes the nitroglycerine, is about to invest his earnings in oil stock and go straight. Ironically, the bank where his money is deposited is blown up and McClaney is once again left destitute. Needing cash in order to marry Anne, McClaney returns to the gang to make nitroglycerine once more.

George McClaney	David Canary
Anne Gilchrist	Bonnie Beecher
Ben Stearman	Tom Reese
Reb Bailey	Eddie Firestone
Joe Keller	Robert Rothwell
Farnum	Dub Taylor
Saloon girl	Sue Collier
Saloon girl	Michelle Breeze
Rudy	Rudy Scoter
Bank Teller	Anthony Redondo
Waiter	John Breen
Dying Man	Scott Hale
Hotel Clerk	Howard Culver
Story, Script	Preston Wood
Story Consultant	Paul Savage
Director	Robert Totten
Producer	John Mantley
Executive Producer	Philip Leacock

Nitro ended the season with a "bang." David Canary was a regular on *Peyton Place, Bonanza, Another World,* and *All My Children,* for which he won the Emmy for Best Actor in a Daytime Drama. Canary claims to be a descendant of Western folklore heroine, Martha Jane Canary, better known as Calamity Jane. Just before the final scene of this episode was filmed, *Gunsmoke* was unexpectedly cancelled. The last scene to be shot shows Matt racing furiously on horseback to reach McClaney. Under the emotional trauma of the cancellation, Arness rode like the wind. Three weeks later the program was reinstated. The following season Arness' dramatic race was incorporated into the new opening title.

Whispering Tree. April 22, 1967, rerun. First aired November 12, 1966.

The Jailer. April 29, 1967, rerun. First aired October 1, 1966.

Snap Decision. May 6, 1967, rerun. First aired September 17, 1966.

Saturday Night. May 13, 1967, rerun. First aired January 7, 1967.

The Television Programs

The Wrong Man. May 27, 1967, rerun. First aired October 29, 1966.

Noose of Gold. June 3, 1967, rerun. First aired March 4, 1967.

Mad Dog. June 10, 1967, rerun. First aired January 14, 1967.

Mistaken Identity. June 17, 1967, rerun. First aired March 18, 1967.

The Newcomers. June 24, 1967, rerun. First aired December 3, 1966.

Old Friend. July 1, 1967, rerun. First aired February 4, 1967.

Mail Drop. July 8, 1967, rerun. First aired January 28, 1967.

Nitro! [Part I]. July 22, 1967, rerun. First aired April 8, 1967.

Nitro! [Part II]. July 29, 1967, rerun. First aired April 15, 1967.

Muley. August 5, 1967, rerun. First aired January 21, 1967.

Ladies from St. Louis. August 12, 1967, rerun. First aired March 25, 1967.

The Good People. August 19, 1967, rerun. First aired October 15, 1966.

The Mission. August 26, 1967, rerun. First aired October 8, 1966.

The Goldtakers. September 9, 1967, rerun. First aired September 24, 1966.

THIRTEENTH SEASON

Now shown on Monday nights

The Wreckers. September 11, 1967. Production #0251. Rerun May 6, 1968.
   Outlaws wreck a stage carrying Matt, Kitty, and convict Monk Wiley. Matt is knocked unconscious and it appears as if Wiley has been killed. Kitty handcuffs Matt and pins his badge on Wiley, hoping to save Matt's life. The three are brought to the gang's hideout, where Kitty discovers Wiley is not dead after all, and may in fact, betray her ruse.

```
        Monk Wiley .............................. Edmund Hashim
        Tate Crocker ............................. Warren Oates
        Reb ...................................... Warren Vanders
        Frankie .................................. Rex Holman
        Jud ...................................... Gene Rutherford
        Luke ..................................... Charles Kuenstle
        Eli ...................................... Charles Seel
        Clete Walker ............................. Trevor Bardette
        Indio .................................... James Almanzar
        Ben Paisley .............................. Lew Brown
        Halligan ................................. Charles Wagenheim
        Townsman ................................. Joe Haworth
```

GUNSMOKE — III. THE PROGRAMS

Stage Attendant	Bobby E. Clark
Shotgun Rider	Jerry Brown
Stage Driver	Joe Yrigoyen, Sr.
Man	Bob Duggan
Story, Script	Hal Sitowitz
Story Consultant	Paul Savage
Director	Robert Totten
Associate Producer	Joseph Dackow
Producer	John Mantley

Bob Duggan was a regular on *The Red Skelton Show*.

Cattle Barons. September 18, 1967. Production #0261. Rerun April 1, 1968.

Matt is caught in the middle of a cattle war when feuding cattle lords, John Charron and Luke Cumberledge, bring their struggle for power to Dodge during a massive cattle drive. Matt's problem is further compounded when Charron, an old friend, appears to be on the wrong side of the law.

John Charron	Forrest Tucker
Luke Cumberledge	Robert Wilke
Laskin	Brad Johnson
Blair Smith	John Milford
Frank Holtz	Lew Brown
McKenny	Robert Sampson
Tooley	Fred Colby
Lathrop	Woodrow Chambliss
Halligan	Charles Wagenheim
Roy	Roy Barcroft
Boy	Steve Liss
Drovers	Mike Howden
Cowboy	Clyde Howdy
Townsman	Hank Wise
Story, Script	Clyde Ware
Story Consultant	Paul Savage
Director	Gunnar Hellstrom
Associate Producer	Joseph Dackow
Producer	John Mantley

Brad Johnson played deputy sheriff Lofty Craig on the kiddie Western, *Annie Oakley*. Robert Sampson was a regular on *Bridget Loves Bernie* and *Falcon Crest*.

The Prodigal. September 25, 1967. Production #0229. Rerun April 15, 1968.

Two brothers, Amos and William Cole, return to Dodge to join their grandfather in taking care of his ranch, and to find the person who shot their father in the back 12 years earlier. According to questionable statements made by a sensation seeking-newsman named Stoner, the evidence seems to indicate that Matt was the killer. Everybody in town, including Kitty and Doc, appear to be covering up something and Matt claims that the case should remain closed. In addition, the brothers learn that no one claimed the $15,000 bounty for their father's death.

Jonathan Cole	Lew Ayers
Amos Cole	Charles Robinson
William Cole	Richard Evans
Stoner	Lamont Johnson

The Television Programs

Eli	Lee Krieger
Lemuel	Ted Gehring
Regal	Kelly Thordsen
Story, Script	Calvin Clements
Story Consultant	Paul Savage
Director	Bernard McEveety
Producer	John Mantley
Executive Producer	Philip Leacock

This episode was shot the previous season. Lew Ayers was a regular on *Lime Street* and the host of *Frontier Justice*. In addition to his other films, Ayers played Dr. Kildare in the 1930s movie series and the pacifist hero of *All Quiet on the Western Front*.

Vengeance [Part I]. October 2, 1967. Production #0252. Rerun March 11, 1968.
Three drifters are accused by wealthy rancher Parker of stealing a calf and are attacked by Parker's men. The lone survivor, Bob Johnson, heads into Dodge determined to take justice into his own hands. Once there, he meets a young girl appropriately named Angel. The two immediately hit it off and make plans to go to a dance together. However, Johnson's romance does not sway him from his path of vengeance. He succeeds in provoking Parker's boastful son Leonard into a shootout.

Vengeance [Part II]. October 9, 1967. Production #0253. Rerun March 18, 1968.
Johnson is ordered out of Dodge by Matt after a gunfight with Leonard Parker. The young drifter heads for the town Parker owns, where he is captured and sentenced to hang. However, Johnson manages to escape and sets fire to the town.

Parker	John Ireland
Bob Johnson	James Stacy
Zack Johnson	Morgan Woodward
Hiller	James Anderson
Leonard Parker	Buck Taylor
Angel	Kim Darby
Sloan	Paul Fix
Rory Luken	Royal Dano
Eben Luken	Victor French
Floyd Binnes	Sandy Kevin
Rudy	Rudy Sooter
Story, Script	Calvin Clements
Story Consultant	Paul Savage
Director	Richard Sarafian
Associate Producer	Joseph Dackow
Producer	John Mantley

Buck Taylor, who is better known as *Gunsmoke's* Newly O'Brien, plays a heavy in this episode. James Stacy met his second wife, Kim Darby, while filming this episode.

A Hat. October 16, 1967. Production #0254. Rerun April 22, 1968 and July 13, 1970.
Cattle baron Red Connisdon and frontiersman Clint Sorils involve Matt in their life and death dispute over a hat. The hat is more than a hat to Clint. It represents property, principle, and his rights as a rugged individualist. When Red and one of his twin sons try to take Clint's hat away, Clint shoots back killing the boy. Wounded himself in the exchange, Clint flees to Dodge. Although the killing was in self-defense, Red convinces his other son to go after Clint.

GUNSMOKE — III. THE PROGRAMS

Red Connisdon	Chill Wills
Clint Sorils	Gene Evans
Jed/Ben Connisdon	Tom Simcox
Martin Brewer	H.M. Wynant
Louisville	Robert Sorrells
Hank	Hank Patterson
Clem	Scott Hale
Waiter	Gene O'Donnell
Townsman	Bill Erwin
Villager	Ed McCready
Cowpuncher	Lee De Broux
Storekeeper	Don Happy
Wife	Shirley Wilson
Story, Script	Ron Bishop
Story Consultant	Paul Savage
Director	Robert Totten
Associate Producer	Joseph Dackow
Producer	John Mantley

Ron Bishop wrote for several television series including *Combat, Father Murphy, How the West Was Won,* and *Kung Fu.* Lee De Broux was a regular on *Salvage 1* and *MacGruder and Loud.*

Hard Luck Henry. October 23, 1967. Production #0262. Rerun May 13, 1968.

Hard-Luck Henry Haggen, Festus' clumsy hillbilly cousin, involves Festus in a heavy footed feud with the Dooley clan. Hard-Luck finds a box of confederate gold and Festus talks him into turning it over to Matt. In their mission to do the right thing, Festus and Hard-Luck have a difficult time keeping the gold away from the greedy Dooleys.

Hard-Luck Henry	John Astin
Jefferson Dooley	Royal Dano
Sheriff	Ken Drake
Jed Walsh	Michael Fox
Martha Walsh	Mary Lou Taylor
Charlie Walsh	Bobby Riha
Reb Dooley	Anthony James
Truly Dooley	John Shank
Homer Haggen	Charles Kuenstle
Harper Haggen	Bo Hopkins
Heathcliff Haggen	Mayf Nutter
Story, Script	Warren Douglas
Director	John Rich
Associate Producer	Joseph Dackow
Producer	John Mantley

John Astin is best known for his role as Gomez of *The Addams Family.* Bobby Riha played the role of little Bruce Landers on *The Debbie Reynolds Show.* Bo Hopkins was a regular on several programs including *The Rockford Files* and *Dynasty.*

Major Glory. October 30, 1967. Production #0257. Rerun June 3, 1968 and June 21, 1971.

Rather than tarnish the glorious record of his hero Major Vanscoy, Sergeant Spear

The Television Programs

does not report two deserters. Instead, he captures them and forces them into hard labor. The deserters are anxious to get out from under Spear's heavy thumb. They know, too well, that as soon as they get into a battle the Sergeant will make sure they are in the front line ready to die as heroes. When the men see their chance, they stab Spear and frame Festus. The incident results in a head on confrontation between Matt and Major Vanscoy, who threatens to put Dodge under marshal law unless Festus is delivered into his custody.

Major Vanscoy	Carroll O'Connor
Sergeant Spear	Victor French
Maxwell	Robert F. Lyons
Doak	Link Wyler
Lanny	Lawrence Mann
Cobb	Don G. Ross
Corporal	Cal Naylor
Corporal of Guard	Chris Stephens
Guard	Russ Siler
Soldier	William L. Sumper
Story	Dick Carr & Clyde Ware
Script	Dick Carr
Story Consultant	Paul Savage
Director	Robert Totten
Associate Producer	Joseph Dackow
Producer	John Mantley

Morton Stevens was nominated for an Emmy for Outstanding Achievement in Musical Composition for *Major Glory*. He lost to Earle Hagen for *I Spy*.

The Pillagers. November 6, 1967. Production #0259. Rerun May 20, 1968.

While traveling to Dodge, Kitty and a young gunsmith from the East, Newly O'Brien, are abducted from their stagecoach. The two are held prisoner in the lair of border cut-throat, Manez. Because O'Brien carries his blacksmith tools in the medical bag of his late uncle, Manez is convinced that O'Brien is a doctor. Manez orders him, on the threat of death, to treat his gravely wounded brother Juan.

Newly O'Brien	Buck Taylor
Manez	John Saxon
Juan	Joseph Schneider
Savrin	Vito Scotti
Ganns	Paul Picerni
Turner	William Bramley
Johns	Allen Jaffe
Eli	Harry Harvey, Sr.
Story, Script	Calvin Clements
Story Consultant	Paul Savage
Director	Vincent McEveety
Associate Producer	Joseph Dackow
Producer	John Mantley

This episode introduces Buck Taylor as Newly O'Brien. Harry Harvey, Sr. was a regular on *Man Without a Gun* and *It's a Man's World*.

Prairie Wolfer. November 13, 1967. Production #0255. Rerun March 25, 1968 and April 26, 1971.

GUNSMOKE — III. THE PROGRAMS

Two hard working trappers bring their wolf pelts over to Matt's office to collect their bounty. They need the money for their journey West. Unfortunately, Matt is out of town and Festus is in charge. Festus has been misinformed about the wolf bounty and believes it has been removed. This sets off a chain of events that leads to a $20,000 robbery.

Cory	Jon Voight
Rich	Lou Antonio
Adele	Kelly Jean Peters
Dolen	Charles McGraw
Grandpa	I. Stanford Jolley
Trail Boss	Matt Emery
Story, Script	Calvin Clements
Story Consultant	Paul Savage
Director	Robert Butler
Associate Producer	Joseph Dackow
Producer	John Mantley

This is the second time the title *Prairie Wolfer* has been used. The first time was January 18, 1964.

Stranger in Town. November 20, 1967. Production #0263. Rerun June 10, 1968.

Gunfighter Dave Reeves is hired to kill Carl Anderson by Anderson's business partner, Harvey Cagle. When Reeves arrives in Dodge, he discovers that Anderson has been courting his estranged wife Anne. His former wife has been posing as a widow to cover-up her past and to protect her young son from harrassment. Reeves' assignment takes an unexpected turn when he discovers that eight-year-old Billy Madison is his son.

Dave Reeves	Pernell Roberts
Anne Madison	Jacqueline Scott
Carl C. Anderson	R.G. Armstrong
Harvey Cagle	Henry Jones
Billy Madison	Eric Shea
Shamrock Casey	Jon Kowal
Story	John Dunkel & Emily Mosher
Script	John Dunkel
Story Consultant	Paul Savage
Director	Daryl Hallenbeck
Associate Producer	Joseph Dackow
Producer	John Mantley

Character actor Henry Jones has guest starred in hundreds of television programs over the years. He was also featured in several series including *Phyllis* and *Falcon Crest*. Eric Shea played young Louis on the television program *Anna and the King*.

Death Train. November 27, 1967. Production #0264. Rerun June 17, 1968.

The butler of wealthy Harl and Isabel Townsend is stricken with spotted-fever, and Doc is forced to quarantine their luxury railroad car. Doc tends to the gravely ill man, while Matt tries to hold off the panicky townspeople. Matt's job is made more difficult by the impatient Townsend who wants to continue his journey, and by the terrified citizens who threaten to destroy the train if it remains in Dodge.

Isabel Townsend	Dana Wynter
Harl Townsend	Morgan Woodward

The Television Programs

Purlie Loftus	Norman Alden
Reverend Bright	Ed Bakey
Jack Marple	Mort Mills
Conductor	Trevor Bardette
Willie Groom	Zalman King
Zack Hodges	Sam Melville
Story, Script	Ken Trevey
Story Consultant	Paul Savage
Director	Gunnar Hellstrom
Associate Producer	Joseph Dackow
Producer	John Mantley

Although primarily a film actress, Dana Wynter starred in the television dramatic series *The Man Who Never Was*. Born in England, Miss Wynter starred in such films as *Invasion of the Body Snatchers*, *The List of Adrian Messenger*, and *Fraulein*. Character actor, Norman Alden was a regular on several television shows including *Not for Hire*, *Hennesey*, and *Fay*. Mort Mills played Marshal Frank Tallman on the television Western, *Man Without a Gun*.

Rope Fever. December 4, 1967. Production #0260. Rerun May 27, 1968.

Sheriff Bassett, an aging lawman who appears to have reached the end of his usefulness, gains new glory by killing a bank robber. The lawman then proceeds to jail Festus as an accomplice to the robbery. Festus' efforts to prove that he was on the scene only to tend to the outlaw's gunshot wound fails to move the Sheriff.

Sheriff Bassett	Ralph Bellamy
Amy Bassett	Anna Lee
Bret Gruber	George Murdock
Bates	Sam Gilman
Shad	Ken Mayer
Keno	Ted Gehring
Zeb Butler	Dennis Cross
Luke Summers	Hal Baylor
Hank	Hank Patterson
Woman	Gertrude Flynn
Story, Script	Chris Rellas
Story Consultant	Paul Savage
Director	David Alexander
Associate Producer	Joseph Dackow
Producer	John Mantley

Ralph Bellamy has enjoyed a successful film and stage career. His movie credits include *His Girl Friday*, *Rosemary's Baby*, *Trading Places*, *Sunrise at Campobello*, and *The Awful Truth*, for which he was nominated for an Academy Award. His stage credits include *State of the Union*, *Detective Story*, and *Sunrise at Campobello* for which he received the Tony Award and the New York Drama Critic Award. On television Bellamy starred in a number of series including *Man Against Crime*, *The Eleventh Hour*, and *The Most Deadly Game*. Anna Lee was a panelist on the quiz show, *It's News to Me*, and played Aunt Wilhelmina on the television drama, *Scruples*.

December 11, 1967, preempted for *Winged World*.

Wonder. December 18, 1967. Production #0258. Rerun April 29, 1968.

Drifter Jud Pryor is adopted by a young Indian boy who Jud has named "Wonder."

When Jud becomes the target of some dubious cowboys, Wonder enlists Matt's aid.

Jud Pryor	Richard Mulligan
Wonder	Tony Davis
Deke Franklin	Norman Alden
Ed Franklin	Warren Berlinger
Annie Franklin	Jackie Russell
Willy	Fay Spain
Bo Warrick	Ken Swofford
Story	William Blinn & Mary Worell
Script	William Blinn
Story Consultant	Paul Savage
Director	Irving J. Moore
Associate Producer	Joseph Dackow
Producer	John Mantley

I Call Him Wonder, broadcast March 23, 1963, makes use of the same characters. Richard Mulligan is familiar to television audiences as Burt Campbell of *Soap* for which he received an Emmy for Best Actor in a Comedy Series. His films include *One Potato, Two Potato* and *S.O.B.* With more than 300 roles to his credit, Warren Berlinger has appeared on television since he was a child. In addition, Berlinger was a regular on several shows including *The Secret Storm, The Joey Bishop Show,* and *Operation Petticoat.* Ken Swofford was a regular on such shows as *Switch, The Adventures of Ellery Queen,* and *Fame.*

Baker's Dozen. December 25, 1967. Production #0265. Rerun April 8, 1968 and December 21, 1970.

After a stagecoach hold-up, Doc delivers the triplets of one of the passengers. He then has his hands full taking care of the infants when they are orphaned. Matt, Kitty, and Festus try to help Doc in finding a home for the babies. It proves difficult, however, once it is known that their father was an outlaw. When Judge Blent arrives in Dodge and discovers that the babies have not yet been placed, he decides to put them in the state orphanage. Doc objects vehemently, however, and the Judge agrees to hold a hearing to determine the babies' fate.

Judge Blent	Denver Pyle
Mrs. Roniger	Peggy Rea
Will Roniger	Harry Carey, Jr.
Henry Rucker	Harry Lauter
Clara Remick	Mitzi Hoag
Fred Remick	Ed McCready
Robber	Sam Greene
Old Lady	Phyllis Coghlan
Halligan	Charles Wagenheim
Bailiff	Tyler MacDuff
Monk	William Murphy
Mary	Dana Dillaway
Timothy	Keith Schultz
Bede	Gary Grimes
Story, Script	Charles Joseph Stone
Story Consultant	Paul Savage
Director	Irving J. Moore

The Television Programs

    Associate Producer .... Joseph Dackow
    Producer .... John Mantley

Writer Charles Joseph Stone is Milburn Stone's brother. In 1968 Milburn Stone won an Emmy for Best Supporting Actor in a Drama. The idea for this episode, originally titled *The Triplets,* was first conceived as a vehicle for Chester, but it was abandoned and picked up in later years for Doc. Keith Schultz appeared on the television Western, *The Monroes.*

The Victim. January 1, 1968. Production #0268. Rerun August 3, 1970.

This episode takes place in the town of Martin's Bend where we encounter Bo Remick, a powerful man with the mentality of a small child. The simpleminded Bo is devoted to pretty saloon owner Lee Stark and accidentally kills young Billy Martin during a fight over her. Unfortunately for all involved, Billy is the son of Wes Martin, the powerful rancher for whom the town is named. Lee is the only eyewitness to the killing and Bo's fate hangs on her testimony, despite her avowed loyalty to Martin. Matt steps in to prevent a lynching and to maintain a fair trial.

    Lee Stark .... Beverly Garland
    Wes Martin .... James Gregory
    Bo Remick .... Cliff Osmond
    Sheriff Wood .... John Kellogg
    Judge Pike .... Kevin Hagen
    Lefty .... Warren Vanders
    Brock .... Edmund Hashim
    Crow .... Roy Jenson
    Deputy Reed .... Gregg Palmer
    Billy Martin .... Tim O'Kelly
    Jim Stark .... Willis Bouchey
    Story .... Hal Sitowitz
    Script .... Arthur Rowe
    Story Consultant .... Paul Savage
    Director .... Vincent McEveety
    Associate Producer .... Joseph Dackow
    Producer .... John Mantley

Deadman's Law. January 8, 1968. Production #0269. Rerun July 1, 1968.

While pursuing an outlaw, Matt is wounded and rescued by an Indian. The outlaw Matt had been tracking is killed and an immigrant family finds the dead fugitive, buries him and brings Matt's horse back to Dodge. The assumption is that Matt has been buried, but Doc, Kitty and Festus refuse to believe this. Nevertheless, greedy cattlemen seize the opportunity to take over the town. In addition, Eriksson, a hard nosed Swede, joins forces with the head of the cattlemen's cooperative to try to gain control of the marshal's office. The men underestimate, however, the power of Matt's friends, who block the cattlemen's efforts.

    Sam Wall .... John Dehner
    Eriksson .... Gunnar Hellstrom
    Indian .... Eddie Little Sky
    Sonny .... Craig Curtis
    Marco .... Ralph Manza
    Fry .... Gregg Palmer
    Wrangler .... Robert Brubaker

GUNSMOKE — III. THE PROGRAMS

Trail Boss .... Steve Raines
Newt .... Baynes Barron
Lathrop .... Woodrow Chambliss
Rustler .... Alex Sharp
Hank .... Hank Patterson
Percy Crump .... Jonathan Harper
Story, Script .... Calvin Clements, Jr.
Story Consultant .... Paul Savage
Director .... John Rich
Associate Producer .... Joseph Dackow
Producer .... John Mantley

Swedish actor-director, Gunnar Helstrom, is a frequent director for *Gunsmoke*. Ralph Manza was a regular on several programs including *Banacek* and *Newhart*. Calvin Clements, Jr., is the son of Calvin Clements, one of *Gunsmoke's* most important writers.

Nowhere to Run. January 15, 1968. Production #0270. Rerun June 29, 1970.

Young Mark Stonecipher gets mixed up with the wrong crowd. His friends Bishop and Honker involve the teenager in a robbery that results in a death and in Mark being wounded. Mark's two partners escape and leave him behind to die. However, he manages to return to his father's ranch. In trying to retrieve some water from his well, Mark loses his footing and falls in. The whole town of Dodge turns out to rescue him. Bishop and Honker are afraid that they will arouse suspicion if they do not help. If Mark is freed, however, the two fear he will implicate them in the crime.

Mark Stonecipher .... J. Robert Porter
Bishop .... Bob Random
Honker .... Dan Ferrone
Ira Stonecipher .... Mark Lenard
Vera Stonecipher .... Ilka Windish
Dale Stonecipher .... Michael Burns
Ed O'Connor .... Tom Brown
Storekeeper .... Harry Harvey, Sr.
John Hirschbeck .... William Tannen
Story .... Robert Totten
Script .... Ron Honthaner
Story Consultant .... Paul Savage
Director .... Vincent McEveety
Associate Producer .... Joseph Dackow
Producer .... John Mantley

Actor-director, Robert Totten, developed the story for this episode. Ron Honthaner, who wrote the script, became *Gunsmoke's* associate producer starting in the 17th season. Mark Lenard was a regular on *Here Come the Brides, The Planet of the Apes*, and *The Secret Empire*. Michael Burns was a regular on *It's a Man's World* and *Wagon Train*. William Tannen played deputy Hal Norton on *The Life and Legend of Wyatt Earp*.

Blood Money. January 22, 1968. Production #0267. Rerun May 31, 1971.

Alex Skouras, the father of gunfighter Nick Skouras, decides to end his son's violent career by wounding his gunhand. While Nick is recovering from his injury under the watchful eyes of Doc, Alex and his daughter Elenya become pawns in a plot to lure Nick out of Dodge for a showdown.

The Television Programs

Alex Skouras	Nehemiah Persoff
Nick Skouras	Anthony Zerbe
Elenya Skouras	Donna Baccala
Jesse Hill	James Anderson
Hank	Hank Brandt
Brent	Mills Watson
Stu	Lee De Broux
Jake Walker	Troy Melton
Story, Script	Hal Sitowitz
Story Consultant	Paul Savage
Director	Robert Totten
Associate Producer	Joseph Dackow
Producer	John Mantley

Anthony Zerbe played Captain Martin Grey on the television mini-series, *How the West Was Won*, Melvin Wendell of *Centennial*, and Lt. K.C. Trench on *Harry-O*, for which he won the Emmy as Best Supporting Actor in 1976. Zerbe was most recently featured in the James Bond film *License to Kill*. Donna Baccala was a regular on the dramatic series, *The Survivors*. Hank Brandt played Len Waggendorn on the comedy *Julia*. Mills Watson was seen as deputy Perkins of *B.J. and the Bear* and *Lobo*, and as Uncle Buster on *Harper Valley P.T.A.*

Hill Girl. January 29, 1968. Production #0273. Rerun June 1, 1970.

While away on a hunting trip, Newly gets involved with a pretty hillbilly girl named Merry Florence and her two half-brothers Roland and Elbert. Merry has run away from the hills seeking a better life, but her kin want her to return. At first Roland and Elbert suspect that Newly and Merry are sweethearts and the men tie Newly up while they try to get up the courage to shoot him. After drinking enough moonshine to kill a horse, the hill men fall asleep. Merry, who is already sweet on Newly, frees him under the condition that he take her to Dodge. Unfortunately, her bullying brothers follow close behind. Back in Dodge, Newly gets Merry a job clerking for Jonas at the general store. When Roland and Elbert arrive in town, they size up the situation and decide to rob the store enlisting Merry's reluctant help.

Merry Florene	Lane Bradbury
Roland Daniel	Victor French
Elbert Moses	Anthony James
Story, Script	Calvin Clements
Story Consultant	Paul Savage
Director	Robert Totten
Associate Producer	Joseph Dackow
Producer	John Mantley

Lane Bradbury, Victor French, and Anthony James had previously played the roles of Merry Florene, Roland, and Elbert in *Uncle Finney*, broadcast October 14, 1968. In addition, Ms. Bradbury and Mr. James recreated their characters in *Gold Town* (January 27, 1969) and *The Still* (November 10, 1969).

The Gunrunners. February 5, 1968. Production #0272.

Tahrohon, the adopted Indian son of fur trapper Noah Meek, is severely beaten and left to die by a gang of vicious gunrunners. Noah brings Tahrohon to Dodge, where Doc helps the injured boy fight for his life. In the meantime, Noah sets out to find the assailants.

GUNSMOKE — III. THE PROGRAMS

Noah Meek	Michael Constantine
Tahrohon	Dan Ferrone
Jubal Gray	Jim Davis
Patch	Dick Peabody
Wade Lester	James Griffith
Bender	John McLiam
Reese	Lane Bradford
Singleton	X Brands
Story, Script	Hal Sitowitz
Story Consultant	Paul Savage
Director	Irving J. Moore
Associate Producer	Joseph Dackow
Producer	John Mantley

X Brands played Pahoo-Ka-Ta-Wah on the television Western, *Yancy Derringer*.

The Jackals. February 12, 1968. Production #0256. Rerun June 24, 1968.

Matt heads into Mexico in pursuit of four fugitives wanted for killing his friend, Sheriff Handlin. The trail, infested with Mexican banditos who are allies of the outlaws, leads to a showdown at an old mission.

Mel Deever	Paul Richards
Santillo	Tige Andrews
Sheriff Mark Handlin	Joe De Santis
Emilio	Felice Orlandi
Bates	Ward Wood
Poorly	Michael Vandever
Bandito	Alex Montoya
Policeman	David Renard
Older Padre	Martin Garralaga
Young Padre	Rico Alaniz
Perino	Jorge Moreno
2nd Bandito	Ruben Moreno
Wife	Ellen Davalos
Mexican Girl	Carmen Austin
Juanita	Olga Velez
Story, Script	Calvin Clements, Jr.
Story Consultant	Paul Savage
Director	Alvin Ganzer
Associate Producer	Joseph Dackow
Producer	John Mantley

The First People. February 19, 1968. Production #0271.

John Eagle Wing, successor to the chief of the Wichita Indians, gets into a dispute with a tyrannical Indian agent, Thomas Evans. When Matt is called in, instead of taking the agent's case, he sides with young Eagle Wing. He is then suspended as marshal and is framed for a killing on the reservation.

John Eagle Wing	Todd Armstrong
Thomas Evans	Gene Evans
William Prange	Jack Elam
Mako	James Almanzar
Baines	James Lydon

The Television Programs

White Buffalo	Richard Hale
Grey Feather	Felix Locher
Captain	Bill Erwin
Policeman	Eddie Little Sky
Story, Script	Calvin Clements
Director	Robert Totten
Associate Producer	Joseph Dackow
Producer	John Mantley

Todd Armstrong starred in the police series *Manhunt*. His films include *Jason and the Argonauts* and *King Rat*.

Mr. Sam'l. February 26, 1968. Production #0274.

Mr. Sam'l, a bewhiskered water witch, shows up in Dodge during a drought, and promises to find water. His embittered daughter Marcie, hostile skeptics, and threats on his life fail to stop Mr. Sam'l, who has a mystical religious zeal for his witchery.

Mr. Sam'l	Ed Begley
Norm Trainer	Mark Richman
Marcie	Sandra Smith
Ben Akins	Larry Pennell
Dave Akins	Duke Hobbie
Ed O'Connor	Tom Brown
Story, Script	Harry Kronman
Story Consultant	Paul Savage
Director	Gunnar Hellstrom
Associate Producer	Joseph Dackow
Producer	John Mantley

Mark Richman, better known as Peter Mark Richman, was a regular on *Cain's Hundred*, *Longstreet*, and *Dynasty*. Sandra Smith appeared on *Our Private World* and *The Interns*. Larry Pennell was a regular on *Ripcord*, *The Beverly Hillbillies*, and *Lassie*.

A Noose for Dobie Price. March 4, 1968. Production #0266.

While on the trail of two escapees from the Dodge City jail, Matt is forced to enlist the assistance of ex-outlaw Elihu Gorman. The likeable conman is deputized by Matt, but Elihu's former bad habits keep cropping up and getting in Matt's way.

Elihu Gorman	Chill Wills
Dobie Price	Shug Fisher
Skeets Walden	Sheldon Allman
Gil Boylan	Robert Donner
Joe Katcher	E.J. Andre
Melanie Katcher	Rose Hobart
Jackson Narramore	Owen Bush
Corny Tate	Michael Greene
Harry Walden	Raymond Mayo
Mick Smith	John "Bear" Hudkins
Jabez	Bob Herron
Story, Script	Antony Ellis
Story Consultant	Paul Savage
Director	Richard C. Sarafian
Associate Producer	Joseph Dackow
Producer	John Mantley

Sheldon Allman appeared on *Harris Against the World*. E.J. Andre was seen as Eugene Bullock on *Dallas*. Robert Donner entered show business upon the insistance of Clint Eastwood. Donner appeared in numerous television shows and was a regular on *The Waltons* and *Mork and Mindy*. His film credits include *Cool Hand Luke, Damnation Alley,* and *Chisum*. Owen Bush played Bailiff John Bellson on *Sirota's Court*.

Vengeance [Part I]. March 11, 1968, rerun. First aired October 2, 1967.

Vengeance [Part II]. March 18, 1968, rerun. First aired October 9, 1967.

Prairie Wolfer. March 25, 1968, rerun. First aired November 13, 1967.

Cattle Barons. April 1, 1968, rerun. First aired September 18, 1967.

Baker's Dozen. April 8, 1968, rerun. First aired December 25, 1967.

The Prodigal. April 15, 1968, rerun. First aired September 25, 1967.

A Hat. April 22, 1968, rerun. First aired October 16, 1967.

Wonder. April 29, 1968, rerun. First aired December 18, 1967.

The Wreckers. May 6, 1968, rerun. First aired September 11, 1967.

Hard Luck Henry. May 13, 1968, rerun. First aired October 23, 1967.

The Pillagers. May 20, 1968, rerun. First aired November 6, 1967.

Rope Fever. May 27, 1968, rerun. First aired December 4, 1967.

Major Glory. June 3, 1968, rerun. First aired October 30, 1967.

Stranger in Town. June 10, 1968, rerun. First aired November 20, 1967.

Death Train. June 17, 1968, rerun. First aired November 27, 1967.

The Jackals. June 24, 1968, rerun. First aired February 12, 1968.

Deadman's Law. July 1, 1968, rerun. First aired January 8, 1968.

FOURTEENTH SEASON

Lyle's Kid. September 23, 1968. Production #0302. Rerun April 28, 1969 and August 16, 1971.

Grant Lyle, a former Sheriff and friend of Matt's, arrives in Dodge with his son Jeffrey. Grant's purpose in Dodge is to confront a one-time outlaw about to be released from prison. The former lawman comes seeking vengeance for an injury done to his hands ten years earlier, and Jeffrey is his instrument of vengeance. Matt finds an ally in Iris, a childhood friend of Jeffrey's. Through the advice of Kitty, Iris marries Jeffrey in an attempt to stave off trouble.

The Television Programs

Grant Lyle	Morgan Woodward
Iris	Charlotte Considine
Jeffrey Lyle	Robert Pine
Jack Garvin	Sam Melville
Tuttle	Ken Mayer
Drover	Mills Watson
Hillman	Lew Palter
Hoxy	Joe De Santis
Attendant	I. Stanford Jolley
Percy Crump	Jonathan Harper
Story, Script	Calvin Clements
Story Consultant	Paul Savage
Director	Bernard McEveety
Associate Producer	Joseph Dackow
Producer	John Mantley

Robert Pine was a regular on *Dert D'Angelo/Superstar* and *CHiPs*.

The Hide Cutters. September 30, 1968. Production #0305. Rerun May 12, 1969 and August 2, 1971.

Festus is injured in an avalanche while on a hunting trip with Matt. The two are given passage back to Dodge by the not-too-friendly trail boss of a cattle drive, Amos McKee, who is being pursued by a group of hide cutters. Matt tries to ward off impending trouble between the drovers and the hide cutters, a job made more difficult by McKee, who holds an old time grudge against Matt.

Amos McKee	Joseph Campanella
Arlie Joe	Michael Burns
Chunk	Cliff Osmond
Weevil	Eddie Firestone
Sugar John	Ken Swofford
Bodiddly	Conlan Carter
Clete Davis	Gregg Palmer
Lawson	Steve Raines
Colton	Mike Howden
Story, Script	Jack Turley
Story Consultant	Paul Savage
Director	Bernard McEveety
Associate Producer	Joseph Dackow
Producer	John Mantley

Joseph Campanella has been a frequent guest star on numerous television programs and a regular on *The Nurses, Mannix,* and *The Lawyers*. He is also the host of *The Undersea World of Jacques Cousteau* and was the host of the 1983 version of *This Is Your Life*.

Zavala. October 7, 1968. Production #0301. Rerun January 18, 1971.

Matt tracks the Rawlins brothers to the little town of Zavala in Mexico, and is befriended by a 13-year-old boy named Paco. Paco sees Matt as a man who can rid his village of all its bandits. The marshal, injured by one of the fugitives, accepts shelter from Paco and his mother. While waiting for the final showdown with the outlaws, Matt becomes the bait in Paco's trap for the bandit who killed his father.

Amelita Avila	Miriam Colon
Paco Avila	Manuel Padilla, Jr.

Ben Rawlins	Jim Davis
Alex Rawlins	Jonathan Lippe
Bakman	Larry D. Mann
Smitty	Rex Holman
Blacksmith	Rico Alaniz
Oakes	Robert Sorrells
Densen	Warren Vanders
Rojas	Nacho Galindo
Gurato	Jose Chavez
Doriat	Elizabeth Germaine
Colton	Bobby E. Clark
Story, Script, Story Consultant	Paul Savage
Director	Vincent McEveety
Associate Producer	Joseph Dackow
Producer	John Mantley

Manuel Padilla, Jr., was featured in *Tarzan* and *The Flying Nun*. Canadian actor Larry D. Mann was a regular on *Accidental Family* and *Dr. Simon Locke*.

Uncle Finney. October 14, 1968. Production #0311. Rerun May 26, 1969 and July 19, 1971.

Two hillbilly brothers, Roland Daniel and Elbert Moses, turn their 103-year-old Uncle Finney over to Festus for an old horse stealing charge. They collect the $50 reward, and leave Festus with the job of caring for their ancient uncle. In the meantime, the two sly characters scheme to rob the Dodge freight office.

Roland Daniel	Victor French
Elbert Moses	Anthony James
Merry Florene	Lane Bradbury
Uncle Finney	Burt Mustin
Mr. Bodkin	Roy Roberts
Wagon Driver	Steve Raines
Frank	John Dolan
Bank Teller	Monte Hale
Joe	Pete Kellett
Woman in Bank	Margaret Bacon
Story, Script	Calvin Clements
Story Consultant	Paul Savage
Director	Bernard McEveety
Producer	John Mantley
Associate Producer	Joseph Dackow

The characters of Roland Daniel, Elbert Moses, and Merry Florene were first introduced in the episode called *Hill Girl*, broadcast January 29, 1968. Burt Mustin was a regular on several television series including *The Andy Griffith Show, All in the Family*, and *Phyllis*. He has the honor of being the oldest actor featured as a regular on a television series. He was in his nineties when he worked on *Phyllis*.

Slocum. October 21, 1968. Production #0396. Rerun April 14, 1969.

Matt stops an argument between an unarmed frontiersman named Slocum, and one of Noah Riker's sons. Noah and his other four sons do not take kindly to Matt's interference, and seek him out. Meanwhile Slocum, who figures he owes the marshall for possibly saving his life, shadows Matt at every turn, protecting him from Riker and his family.

The Television Programs

Noah Riker	Dub Taylor
Slocum	Will Geer
Mark Riker	James Wainwright
Luke Riker	Ross Hagen
Paul Riker	Lee Lambert
Peter Riker	Mills Watson
John Riker	Steve Sandor
Judge	Bill Erwin
1st Cowboy	Lew Brown
2nd Cowboy	Charles Kuenstle
Story, Script	Ron Bishop
Story Consultant	Paul Savage
Director	Leo Penn
Associate Producer	Joseph Dackow
Producer	John Mantley

Will Geer is best known for his role as Grandpa Zeb of *The Waltons*, for which he received the Emmy in 1975. James Wainwright was featured on two television series, *Jigsaw* and *Beyond Westworld*. Steve Sandor was seen on the police drama, *Amy Prentiss*.

O'Quillian. October 28, 1968. Production #0304. Rerun June 16, 1969.

A fight erupts when Leary O'Quillian catches Curt Tynan cheating at poker. While Curt is deciding whether to cut off O'Quillian's left or right ear, the Irishman grabs a gun and shoots him. After being found not guilty of murder, O'Quillian goes his merry way. The likeable troublemaker and teller of tall tales, drifts into Dodge, where he causes a free-for-all at the Long Branch reminiscent of the Battle of Bull Run. He then proceeds to stir up even more trouble when he tells Kitty's saloon girls to ask for higher wages, complains that the general store is too expensive, and implies that Doc is bilking his patients. Eventually O'Quillian winds up in jail for bottling illegal liquor. Finally, when everyone has had enough of him, Clay Tynan, Curt's brother, rides into town seeking revenge.

Leary O'Quillian	John McLiam
Clay Tynan	Victor French
Curt Tynan	Lou Antonio
Judge Fletcher Anderson	Vaughn Taylor
Parker	Ken Drake
Chickenfoot	Anthony James
Brigs	Steve Raines
Indian	Iron Eyes Cody
Rosey	Peggy Rea
Lathrop	Woodrow Chambliss
Breed	Jerry Summers
Roy	Roy Barcroft
Story, Script	Ron Bishop
Story Consultant	Paul Savage
Director	John Rich
Associate Producer	Josph Dackow
Producer	John Mantley

Native American, Iron Eyes Cody, appeared in such films as *The Paleface, Red Mountain,* and *Gun for a Coward.* However, he is probably best known for a television commercial, where he is seen with a tear trickling down his cheek, crying because of the pollution of his country.

November 4, 1968, preempted for a paid political program — Humphrey and Muskie.

9:12 to Dodge. November 11, 1968. Production #0308. Rerun June 6, 1969 and May 3, 1971.

Matt and Doc escort a prisoner, Johnny August, on a tense train trip to Dodge. During the journey they are beset by problems, first from a meddling passenger and then by hijackers who want to free August. Elizabeth Devlin, the well-meaning wife of a territorial Governor, thinks August, who has a minor leg wound, is being mistreated. The would-be hijackers, lose their identity amongst the other passengers and make it difficult for Matt to spot them.

           Johnny August.............................Todd Armstrong
           Elizabeth Devlin............................Joanne Linville
           Leitner......................................Frank Marth
           Fox...Tom Water
           Conductor..................................Robert Emhardt
           Michael Drennen ....Harry Lauter
           Miles......................................Troy Melton
           Peter Frye ....Link Wyler
           Mokey......................................Fred Coby
           Tim ....Lee De Broux
           Hugh ....William Murphy
           Dispatcher.................................Harry Harvey, Sr.
           Karns ....Ed Long
           Devlin ....Dan Terranova
           Williams...................................Rush Williams
           Ned Stallcup ....Johnny Haymer
           Barstow...................................Bobby E. Clark
           Joe ....Pete Kellett
           Story, Script ....Preston Wood
           Story Consultant ....Paul Savage
           Director ....Marvin Chomsky
           Associate Producer ....Joseph Dackow
           Producer ....John Mantley

Johnny Haymer was featured on *M.A.S.H.* and *Madame's Place.*

Abelia. November 18, 1968. Production #0312. Rerun April 7, 1969.

A gang of outlaws led by Judd Ward is trying to elude Matt's posse. Ward's brother is seriously wounded and the gang takes refuge at the home of a young farm widow named Abelia. Circumstances force Festus to pose as Abelia's husband, to protect her and her two children against the outlaws.

           Abelia ....Jacqueline Scott
           Judd Ward ....Jeremy Slate
           Tom Cole ....Tom Stern
           Gar ....Jack Lambert
           Wales ....Gregg Palmer
           Jonathan ....Mike Durkin
           Marieanne ....Susan Olsen

The Television Programs

Deeter Ward	Jack Chaplain
Story, Script	Calvin Clements
Story Consultant	Paul Savage
Director	Vincent McEveety
Associate Producer	Joseph Dackow
Producer	John Mantley

Sequels to *Abelia* were *A Man Called Smith* (October 27, 1969) and *The Predators* (January 31, 1972). Jacqueline Scott played Abelia in all three episodes. In an article from the *Journal of Popular Film and Television*, Kristine Fredriksson states that the role of Abelia was originally written for Faye Dunaway at Ms. Dunaway's request. Child actress Susan Olsen played curly-locked Cindy on *The Brady Bunch*.

Railroad. November 25, 1968. Production #0314. Rerun June 23, 1969.

Matt blocks a railroad company's efforts to force Jim Graham off his land. The right-of-way dispute halts progress on a new track which would link Omaha and Dodge. When the irascible old sodbuster refuses to sell his land, Matt supports his stand. The railroad does not take too kindly to Matt's reaction, and threatens to run him and Graham out of town.

Jim Graham	Shug Fisher
Wes Cameron	Jim Davis
O'Shay	Buck Holland
Forbes	Ramon Bieri
Larnen	Roy Jenson
Lindsey	Don Hanmer
Amos Billings	James McCallion
Story, Script	Arthur Rowe
Story Consultant	Paul Savage
Director	Marvin Chomsky
Associate Producer	Joseph Dackow
Producer	John Mantley

Ramon Bieri appeared as a regular on three television series, *Sarge*, *Joe's World*, and *Bret Maverick*.

The Miracle Man. December 2, 1968. Production #0313. Rerun May 19, 1969 and May 17, 1971.

Slick talking Bob Sullivan is confronted by a mob of dissatisfied customers after hawking his overpriced goods in Dodge. He is rescued by widow Lorna Wright, who takes Sullivan on as a hired hand. Although Festus tries to warn Lorna that Sullivan is a liar and a crook, she and her three children are charmed by the suave thief. He is thought of as some sort of a "miracle man," especially by Lorna's daughter Nettie, who is gravely ill. Sullivan stays on, all the while planning to swindle Lorna out of her property.

Bob Sullivan	Don Chastain
Lorna Wright	Sandra Smith
Miller	William Bramley
Gerard	Joey Walsh
Howard	Bruce Watson
Prudence	Margie De Meyer
Nettie	Lisa Gerritsen
Jacob	Kevin Cooper

GUNSMOKE — III. THE PROGRAMS

Drunk	John Crawford
Boy	Christopher Knight
Story, Script	Calvin Clements
Story Consultant	Paul Savage
Director	Bernard McEveety
Associate Producer	Joseph Dackow
Producer	John Mantley

Don Chastain was a regular on *The Edie Adams Show* and *The Debbie Reynolds Show*. Joey Walsh was featured on *The Frank Sinatra Show*. Lisa Gerritsen grew up in front of the television viewing audience as a young member of *My World and Welcome to It, The Mary Tyler Moore Show,* and *Phyllis*. Christopher Knight also grew up on television as Peter from *The Brady Bunch*.

Waco. December 9, 1968. Production #0316. Rerun March 31, 1969 and March 15, 1971.

Matt journeys to the ghost town of Spivey, Kansas, to arrest Waco Thompson. Waco goes along with Matt peacefully, but tells him that there are four reasons why they will never make it to Dodge: Slick, Fuller, Hood and Gamble, Waco's partners. "Them old boys, they stick closer to a trail than the hair on your head," snickers Waco. Matt, however, is able to avoid Waco's men, until he happens upon a pregnant Indian in need of medical attention. Matt takes the woman along, which slows them down considerably.

Waco Thompson	Victor French
Nathan Cade	Harry Carey, Jr.
Polly Cade	Louise Latham
Slick Ragan	Tom Reese
Fuller	Lee De Broux
Hood	Mills Watson
Gamble	Lawrence Mann
One Moon	Pat Thompson
Ann Cade	Joy Fielding
Lillie	Liz Marshall
Town Drunk	Fred McDougall
Story, Script	Ron Bishop
Story Consultant	Paul Savage
Director	Robert Totten
Producer	Joseph Dackow
Executive Producer	John Mantley

Louise Latham was a regular on *Sara, The Contender,* and *Scruples*.

Lobo. December 16, 1968. Production #0315. Rerun September 8, 1969 and June 14, 1971.

Weathered mountain man, Luke Brazo, persuades Matt to help him track an elusive renegade wolf before it is destroyed by a pack of bounty hunters. Brazo would prefer the wolf to remain free, but realizes the animal must be killed because of all the destruction it has caused. Like Brazo, the wolf is a free spirit of the land and, therefore, Brazo feels he must be the one to kill it.

Luke Brazo	Morgan Woodward
Branch Nelson	David Brian
Badger	Sheldon Allman

The Television Programs

  Catlin .... Sandy Kenyon
  Guffy .... Ken Swofford
  Riney .... Eddie Firestone
  Wes Flood .... Fred Coby
  Ethen .... William Murphy
  Story, Script .... Jim Byrnes
  Story Consultant .... Paul Savage
  Director .... Bernard McEveety
  Producer .... Joseph Dackow
  Executive Producer .... John Mantley

David Brian was featured on *Mr. District Attorney* and *The Immortal*.

Johnny Cross. December 23, 1968. Production #0309. Rerun May 5, 1969.

  A young fugitive, Johnny Cross, returns to his grandfather's ranch, hoping to clear his name in connection with a stagecoach robbery. The only eyewitness to the robbery, an old squatter named Franks, has identified Johnny as the man he saw leaving the scene of the crime. Both Johnny and Newly believe the change to be a case of mistaken identity. However, Johnny is being tracked by two bounty hunters, who force Franks to stick to his original story, so they can collect the reward.

  Johnny Cross .... Jeff Pomerantz
  Hodge .... Dean Stanton
  Yates .... John Crawford
  Franks .... Shug Fisher
  Mr. Cross .... Charles Thompson
  Vera Cross .... Kelly Jean Peters
  Story, Script .... Calvin Clements
  Story Consultant .... Paul Savage
  Director .... Herschel Daugherty
  Associate Producer .... Joseph Dackow
  Producer .... John Mantley

The Money Store. December 30, 1968. Production #0303. Rerun August 25, 1969 and March 29, 1971.

  Mike and Annie Jarvis, the children of a poor, but honest, dirt farmer, try to get a loan for him by putting up as collateral their most precious possession, their dog Poorely. Poorely upsets the banker's desk, and in the confusion, Annie and Mike run away with some of the spilled cash. Later when the money is discovered on the farm, their father accepts the blame.

  Mike Jarvis .... Eric Shea
  Annie Jarvis .... Pamelyn Ferdin
  Ezra Thorpe .... William Schallert
  Ray Jarvis .... Charles Aidman
  Louise Thorpe .... Virginia Vincent
  Story, Script .... William Blinn
  Story Consultant .... Paul Savage
  Director .... Vincent McEveety
  Associate Producer .... Joseph Dackow
  Producer .... John Mantley

  A successful child performer, Pamelyn Ferdin was a regular on several television shows including *Blondie*, *The Paul Lynde Show*, and *Lassie*. She was also the voice of

GUNSMOKE — III. THE PROGRAMS

numerous television cartoon characters as well as that of Charlotte's human friend in the animated film *Charlotte's Web*. Virginia Vincent was featured on such series as *Meet Millie*, *The Joey Bishop Show*, and *Eight Is Enough*.

The Twisted Heritage. January 6, 1969. Production #0317. Rerun September 1, 1969 and July 12, 1971.

On her way home to Dodge, Kitty's stage is attacked and the driver is killed. In a desperate race across the prairie, Kitty takes the reins to save the life of wounded passenger Blaine Copperton. She manages to make it to the Copperton ranch, much to the amazement and admiration of Jesse Copperton, Blaine's domineering mother. Jesse sees Kitty as a potential mate for her widower son and as a mother for Tracey, Blaine's lonely little daughter. However, Kitty is not quite ready to settle down.

Jesse Copperton	Virginia Gregg
Tracey	Lisa Gerritsen
Blaine Copperton	John Ericson
Ma Dagget	Nora Marlowe
Logan Dagget	Conlan Carter
Elan Dagget	Charles Kuenstle
Simpson	Richard O'Brien
Webb	David McLean
Cookie	Robert Luster
Driver #1	Steve Raines
Driver #2	Robert Karnes
Young	Joshua Bryant
Story	Robert Haverly & Jack Turley
Script	Paul Savage & Arthur Rowe
Story Consultant	Paul Savage
Director	Bernard McEveety
Producer	Joseph Dackow
Executive Producer	John Mantley

John Ericson played Sam Bolt on the television series *Honey West*. David McLean starred in the short-lived television Western, *Tate*. Joshua Bryant was featured on the television show *Behind the Screen*.

Time of the Jackals. January 13, 1969. Production #0310. Rerun July 21, 1969.

While tracking escaped prisoner Jess Trevor, Matt battles with one of his gang members at a desolate relay station. After the gunsmoke clears, Matt finds one dead outlaw and one wounded woman. The woman turns out to be Leona, an old girlfriend of Matt's. Feeling responsible for her injury, Matt brings Leona back to Dodge anxious for her to recover. The years have not been kind to Leona. She has a dead ex-boyfriend, another ex-boyfriend who Matt is tracking, and a spineless ex-husband. The one good man in her life was Matt, and for a while she almost hooked him.

Jess Trevor	Leslie Nielson
Leona	Beverly Garland
Lucas Brant	Jonathan Lippe
Tim Jackson	Edmund Hashim
Dan Foley	Robert Knapp
Del Rainey	Charles Maxwell
Cawkins	Sid Haig
Trail Hand	Art Stewart

The Television Programs

Daggett	Kip Whitman
Story	Richard Fielder
Script	Paul Savage & Richad Fielder
Story Consultant	Paul Savage
Director	Vincent McEveety
Associate Producer	Joseph Dackow
Producer	John Mantley

Leslie Nielson has been featured in numerous television series including *The New Breed, Peyton Place, The Protectors,* and *Police Squad*. His film credits include *The Poseidon Adventure* and *Airplane*.

Mannon. January 20, 1969. Production #0319. Rerun April 21, 1969 and September 9, 1971.

One of the most menacing villains to walk the dusty boardwalks of Dodge is Will Mannon. Mannon, who used to ride with Quantrill and was, "Quantrill's killing arm more than any of the others," takes over the town during Matt's absence. The mysterious man dressed in black and reminiscent of Matt's nemesis in *Gunsmoke's* classic opening scene, begins by wounding Festus and stealing his mule, Ruth. Then, when Mannon rides into town on "Old Tanglefoot," no one can arrest him because he is too fast a gun. Mannon remains in Dodge waiting for Matt to return. He hopes to increase his reputation and to gain respect once he has "Matt Dillon's toes pointing to the clouds." Festus, having seen Mannon in action, thinks he can do it. While waiting for the inevitable showdown, Mannon helps himself to all the comforts of Dodge, free food, drinks and lodging. As a final affront he turns his attention towards Kitty, the only one in town he has not "shrunk down to size."

Mannon	Steve Forrest
Barney	Charles Seel
Howie	Howard Culver
Halligan	Charles Wagenheim
Chris	Michelle Breeze
Lathrop	Woodrow Chambliss
O'Connor	Tom Brown
Story, Script	Ron Bishop
Story Consultant	Paul Savage
Director	Robert Butler
Producer	Joseph Dackow
Executive Producer	John Mantley

Will Mannon is one of *Gunsmoke's* greatest villains. He is pure evil, with no shades of gray. Segments of *Mannon* were used as flashbacks for the two-hour special, *Gunsmoke: Return to Dodge*, which aired September 26, 1987. Although Will Mannon was killed in the original episode, he was miraculously resurrected for the made-for-television movie. Steve Forrest recreated the role of Will Mannon for the special. In addition to playing various and sundry villains on *Gunsmoke* over the years, Forrest was a regular on *The Baron, S.W.A.T.,* and *Dallas*. The younger brother of actor Dana Andrews, Forrest followed in his footsteps and made a number of films including *The Longest Day* and *Spies Like Us*.

Gold Town. January 27, 1969. Production #0318. Rerun July 14, 1969.

After Matt runs hillbillies Elbert Moses and Smiley out of Dodge for creating a shell game, the two concoct another swindle. They take over an old mine, and salt it with

[637]

gold dust. Next they open their own town complete with a school operated by Merry Florene, and a saloon managed by their 70-year-old grandmother. The gold fever they create causes a rush from Dodge to their worthless gold mine. The only ones who manage to strike it rich are Elbert and Smiley, until a couple of outlaws decide to hone in on the bounty.

   Elbert Moses . . . . Anthony James
   Merry Florene . . . . Lane Bradbury
   Smiley . . . . Lou Antonio
   Grandmother . . . . Kathryn Minner
   Shorty . . . . Harry Davis
   Oldtimer . . . . Chubby Johnson
   Stone . . . . Paul Wexler
   Hale . . . . Jack Searl
   Spectator . . . . Pete Kellett
   John . . . . Jimmy Bracken
   Sue . . . . Eve Plumb
   Story, Script . . . . Calvin Clements
   Story Consultant . . . . Paul Savage
   Director . . . . Gunnar Hellstrom
   Producer . . . . Joseph Dackow
   Executive Producer . . . . John Mantley

  On television, Eve Plumb played Jan on *The Brady Bunch* and Melissa Jane Driscoll on *Little Women*.

The Mark of Cain. February 3, 1969. Production #0322. Rerun September 15, 1969 and August 30, 1971.

  Driscoll, a respected rancher, is giving a lecture on ancient Greek culture, when his son Tom tangles with two buffalo hunters. In the scuffle, the hunters discover that the elder Driscoll bears the mark they once branded on their hated commandant's chest. The discovery exposes Driscoll as the once notorious commander of a Civil War camp.

   Driscoll . . . . Nehemiah Persoff
   Louise . . . . Louise Latham
   Corley . . . . Robert Totten
   Tom . . . . Kevin Coughlin
   McInnerny . . . . Stanley Clements
   Waiter . . . . Olan Soule
   Sadler . . . . Robert DoQui
   Roy . . . . Roy Barcroft
   Story, Script . . . . Ron Bishop
   Story Consultant . . . . Paul Savage
   Director . . . . Vincent McEveety
   Producer . . . . Joseph Dackow
   Executive Producer . . . . John Mantley

  In addition, to being one of *Gunsmoke's* prominent directors, Robert Totten also acted in several episodes. As a child, Kevin Coughlin was a regular on the comedy *Mama*. Robert DoQui was featured on the police drama, *Felony Squad*.

The Reprisal. February 10, 1969. Production #0321. Rerun July 28, 1969.

  When Matt is forced to shoot Garth, a convicted outlaw, Doc must choose between staying to treat the wounded man, or leaving to deliver a baby. Doc saves Garth's life,

The Television Programs

but reaches Tom Butler's farm too late, and his wife Sarah loses the baby. Butler blames Doc for the infant's death, and swears vengeance.

Tom Butler	Joe Don Baker
Sarah	Eunice Christopher
Jeb	I. Stanford Jolley
Forbes	John Pickard
Jinks	Dennis Cross
Garth	Jack Lambert
Story, Script	Jack Hawn
Story Consultant	Paul Savage
Director	Bernard McEveety
Producer	Joseph Dackow
Executive Producer	John Mantley

This is the second use of the title *The Reprisal*. It was first used March 10, 1962.

The Long Night. February 17, 1969. Production #0275. Rerun August 18, 1969 and April 5, 1971.

Bounty hunters hold Doc, Kitty, Sam, and Louie hostage at the Long Branch. The men hope to trade their captives to Matt in return for cowhand, Ben Miller, on whose head there is a $10,000 reward. Miller has turned himself over the Matt, however, and Matt has no intention of releasing him to the blood thirsty headhunters.

Guerin	Bruce Dern
Mace	Lou Antonio
Diggs	Russell Johnson
Rita Lane	Susan Silo
Ben Miller	Robert Totten
Henry Wade	Robert Brubaker
Broker	Rex Holman
Keever	Matt Emery
Rawlins	Victor Tayback
Story	Dick Carr
Script, Story Consultant	Paul Savage
Director	John Rich
Associate Producer	Joseph Dackow
Producer	John Mantley

Fans of James Nusser will be impressed by his poignant scene with Bruce Dern. "Louie Pheeters" is forced to beg for a drink by "Guerin," who despises drunks because his father was one. In front of Doc, Kitty, and Sam, Louie painfully crawls across the floor as commanded by Guerin. When finally rewarded with his glass of whiskey, Louie picks it up, but just as he is about to put it to his lips, he dramatically slams it down. When the scene was completed the cast and crew broke into spontaneous applause. Susan Silo was a regular on *The Sammy Kaye Show, Harry's Girls*, and *Occasional Wife*.

The Night Riders. February 24, 1969. Production #0323. Rerun June 2, 1969.

Fanatical Judge Procter and his notorious band of Missouri freebooters, travel the West burning farms and sacking towns, to avenge property lost during the Civil War. When they hit Dodge, they meet stubborn resistance from acting Deputy Festus. Procter also faces challenges from his power hungry lieutenant and his own two sons. One son, Jay, wants to prove he is a bigger man than his father, and the other, Eliot, questions the meaning of his father's insane crusade.

GUNSMOKE — III. THE PROGRAMS

Judge Procter	Jeff Corey
Eliot Procter	Robert Pine
Jay Procter	Bob Random
Berber	Norman Alden
Williams	Warren Vanders
Ross	Robert Karnes
Bernaby	Scott Hale
Farmer	Ed Bakey
Story, Script	Calvin Clements
Story Consultant	Paul Savage
Director	Irving J. Moore
Producer	Joseph Dackow
Executive Producer	John Mantley

Jeff Corey was a regular on *Hell's Town* and *Morningstar/Eveningstar*. He also directed for several television series including *Night Gallery*, *Police Story*, and *The Bob Newhart Show*.

The Intruders. March 3, 1969. Production #0325. Rerun June 30, 1969.

Festus and a wounded prisoner named Riley Sharp, find refuge at a nearby ranch. The ranch turns out to be owned by Henry and Ellie Decker and their young son, Timmy. Unbeknownst to Festus, Ellie and Timmy are the wife and son Riley left behind eight years earlier. Ellie, believing Riley had died, married Henry, who would give her up in a minute, if Riley would reveal to him where the $25,000 he stole is hidden.

Riley Sharp	Charles Aidman
Henry Decker	John Kellogg
Ellie Decker	Gail Kobe
Timmy	Eric Shea
Hall	Ralph James
Ennis	Robert Gravage
Story, Script	Jim Byrnes
Story Consultant	Paul Savage
Director	Vincent McEveety
Producer	Joseph Dackow
Executive Producer	John Mantley

Ralph James supplied the booming voice of Orson for the comedy *Mork and Mindy*.

The Good Samaritans. March 10, 1969. Production #0324. Rerun August 11, 1969 and July 5, 1971.

While on route to Dodge with crucial evidence for a trial, Matt is wounded by bounty hunters searching for the papers. He finds refuge in the camp of an ex-slave family, who risk their lives to protect Matt from further harm. However, one member of the group tries to steal the vital documents and sell them to the bounty hunters.

Cato	Brock Peters
Juba	Rex Ingram
Kittridge	L.Q. Jones
Croyden	Sam Melville
Erlene	Hazel Medina
Mama Olabelle	Paulene Myers
Benji	Robert DoQui

The Television Programs

Ike	Davis Roberts
Reba	Lynn Hamilton
Jeb	Dan Ferrone
Timmons	John Brandon
Heck	Pepe Brown
Willa	Alycia Gardner
Story, Script, Story Consultant	Paul Savage
Director	Bernard McEveety
Producer	Joseph Dackow
Executive Producer	John Mantley

Brock Peters has appeared in such films as *To Kill a Mockingbird*, *The L-Shaped Room*, and *The Pawnbroker*. Pauline Myers played Gloria Byrd on the dramatic series, *Storefront Lawyers*. Davis Roberts was a regular on the series *Boone*. Lynn Hamilton was featured on *Sanford and Son*, *The Waltons*, and *Roots: The Next Generations*. Pepe Brown was seen on *Pat Paulsen's Half a Comedy Hour*.

The Prisoner. March 17, 1969. Production #0320. Rerun July 7, 1969.

Steven Downing, a convicted murderer brought to Dodge by bounty hunter Garvis, saves Kitty's life by pushing her out of the way of an overturning load of freight. The grateful Kitty sets out to repay the favor by winning young Steven from his brutal captor in a poker game. She then learns the seriousness of Steven's crime. He has been convicted of killing the wife of an influential Missouri county boss.

Steven Downing	Jon Voight
Jarvis	Ramon Bieri
Bob Mathison	Kenneth Tobey
Pink Simmons	Ned Glass
Sheriff	Paul Bryar
Ed O'Connor	Tom Brown
Cardplayer	Jan Peters
Barber	David Fresco
Freighter	Don Happy
Story, Script	Calvin Clements
Story Consultant	Paul Savage
Director	Leo Penn
Producer	Joseph Dackow
Executive Producer	John Mantley

Exodus 21:22. March 24, 1969. Production #0307. Rerun August 4, 1969.

Frank Reardon, an old friend of Matt's, is relentless in his pursuit of the seven men responsible for the death of his pregnant Indian wife. Only three members of the gang are left alive by the time Reardon reaches Dodge, where Matt tries to put a stop to his friend's crusade.

Frank Reardon	Steve Ihnat
Keith	Kaz Garas
Lloyd	Brandon Carroll
Cane	William Bramley
Bradford	Lane Bradford
Farm Girl	Sarah Hardy
Additional Cast	Hank Brandt
Story, Script	Arthur Rowe

GUNSMOKE — III. THE PROGRAMS

Story Consultant ....Paul Savage
Director ....Herschel Daugherty
Associate Producer ....Joseph Dackow
Producer ....John Mantley

Kaz Garas was featured on the dramatic series *Strange Report*.

Waco. March 31, 1969, rerun. First aired December 9, 1968.

Abelia. April 7, 1969, rerun. First aired November 18, 1968.

Slocum. April 14, 1969, rerun. First aired October 21, 1968.

Mannon. April 21, 1969, rerun. First aired January 20, 1969.

Lyle's Kid. April 28, 1969, rerun. First aired September 23, 1968.

Johnny Cross. May 5, 1969, rerun. First aired December 23, 1968.

The Hide Cutters. May 12, 1969, rerun. First aired September 30, 1968.

The Miracle Man. May 19, 1969, rerun. First aired December 2, 1968.

Uncle Finney. May 26, 1969, rerun. First aired October 14, 1968.

The Night Riders. June 2, 1969, rerun. First aired February 24, 1969.

9:12 to Dodge. June 9, 1969, rerun. First aired November 11, 1968.

O'Quillian. June 16, 1969, rerun. First aired October 28, 1969.

Railroad. June 23, 1969, rerun. First aired November 25, 1968.

The Intruder. June 30, 1969, rerun. First aired March 3, 1969.

The Prisoner. July 7, 1969, rerun. First aired March 17, 1969.

Gold Town. July 14, 1969, rerun. First aired January 27, 1969.

Time of the Jackals. July 21, 1969, rerun. First aired January 13, 1969.

The Reprisal. July 28, 1969, rerun. First aired February 10, 1969.

Exodus 21:22. August 4, 1969, rerun. First aired March 24, 1969.

The Good Samaritans. August 11, 1969, rerun. First aired March 10, 1969.

The Long Night. August 18, 1969, rerun. First aired February 17, 1969.

The Money Store. August 25, 1969, rerun. First aired December 30, 1968.

The Twisted Heritage. September 1, 1969, rerun. First aired January 6, 1969.

The Television Programs

Lobo. September 8, 1969, rerun. First aired December 16, 1968.

The Mark of Cain. September 15, 1969, rerun. First aired February 10, 1969.

FIFTEENTH SEASON

The Devil's Outpost. September 22, 1969. Production #0356. Rerun May 4, 1970.

Matt captures outlaw Cody Tyce in a stage holdup, and is pursued on the trail back to Dodge by Cody's brother, Yancy, and his gang of renegades. The case leads to a showdown at a waystation where Yancy and his men hope to ambush Matt and free Cody.

Yancy Tyce	Robert Lansing
Cody Tyce	Jonathan Lippe
McGruder	Karl Swenson
Abby Tillman	Sheila Larkin
Loomis	Ken Swofford
Bo Harper	Warren Vanders
Pacos	Val de Vargas
Kelly	Charles Kuenstle
Tillman	I. Stanford Jolley
Lora	Sabrina Scharf
Mike Lennox	Troy Melton
George Miller	Joe Higgins
Telegrapher	Sam Edwards
Townsman	William Tannen
Cowboy	Joe Haworth
Farley	Ed Long
Story	Robert Barbash
Script	Jim Byrnes & Robert Barbash
Executive Story Consultant	Calvin Clements
Director	Philip Leacock
Producer	Joseph Dackow
Executive Producer	John Mantley

Sheila Larkin played Deborah Sullivan on the dramatic series, *Storefront Lawyers.*

Stryker. September 29, 1969. Production #0352. Rerun May 25, 1970.

Former Dodge marshal Josh Stryker returns to town after 15 years in prison. Stryker is seeking revenge against his successor, Matt, whose testimony helped convict him for killing an unarmed man. While in prison, Stryker lost an arm, for which he also blames Matt.

Josh Stryker	Morgan Woodward
Sara Jean Stryker	Joan Van Ark
Jessup	Royal Dano
Jed Whitlow	Andy Devine
Reager	Mills Watson
Cal Hoskins	Walter Sande
Dish	Ted French
Cowboy #1	Don Happy
Story, Script	Herman Groves

GUNSMOKE — III. THE PROGRAMS

    Executive Story Consultant .... Calvin Clements
    Director .... Robert Totten
    Producer .... Joseph Dackow
    Executive Producer .... John Mantley

Joan Van Ark was a regular on *Temperatures Rising, We've Got Each Other, Dallas,* and *Knots Landing.* With his raspy voice, the distinctive Andy Devine played mostly second fiddle in films and on television. He was Jingles on *The Adventures of Wild Bill Hickok* and Hap Gorman on *Flipper.* He was also the host of a Saturday morning children's show called *Andy's Gang,* where he uttered the immortal words, "Plunk your magic twanger, Froggy."

Coreyville. October 6, 1969. Production #0361. Rerun August 24, 1970.

In the decaying town of Coreyville, rawhider Titus Wylie is accused of murdering saloon girl Mary Elizabeth. Titus is framed on the homicide charge due to the influence of a wealthy widow, Agatha Corey, for whom the town is named. Agatha owns almost everything and everyone in the aging town. The sole exclusion is the Saloon and its proprietress Flo Watson, Agatha's bitter enemy. When Titus' sister Ellie sees that her brother is fighting a no-win situation, she goes to Dodge to get Matt. Matt arrives in time for a mock trial. With the judge and jury intoxicated and no one appointed to defend Titus, Matt declares a mistrial and attempts to unravel the bizarre mystery. His investigation reveals that the real culprit is being protected for different reasons by both Agatha and Flo.

    Agatha Corey .... Nina Foch
    Flo Watson .... Ruth Roman
    Ellie Wylie .... Jo Ann Harris
    Titus Wylie .... Bruce Glover
    Billy Joe Corey .... Kevin Coughlin
    Frank Corey .... Thomas Hunter
    Amos Blake .... John Schuck
    Rankin .... James Almanzar
    Clel Wilson .... Charles Fredericks
    Juror .... Bill Erwin
    Guard #1 .... Pete Kellett
    Guard #2 .... Bill Catching
    Guard #3 .... Gary Combs
    Story, Script .... Herman Groves
    Executive Story Consultant .... Calvin Clements
    Director .... Bernard McEveety
    Producer .... Joseph Dackow
    Executive Producer .... John Mantley

Nina Foch appeared in such films as *A Song to Remember, An American in Paris, Johnny Allegro,* and *The Ten Commandments.* On television she appeared in most of the major dramatic series in the 50s and 60s, and was a regular on *Two Girls Named Smith* and *Shadow Chasers.* In 1979 she was nominated for an Emmy for her performance on *Lou Grant.* Ruth Roman's movie credits include *Good Sam, Strangers on a Train,* and *The Far Country.* On television she played Minnie Littlejohn on *The Long Hot Summer* and Sylvia Lean on *Knots Landing.* Jo Ann Harris was featured on *Rich Man, Poor Man, Most Wanted,* and *Detective School.* Bruce Glover was a regular on *Hawk.* John Schuck appeared as a regular on such series as *McMillan and Wife, Holmes and Yoyo,* and *The New Odd Couple.* His film credits include *M.A.S.H.*

The Television Programs

Danny. October 13, 1969. Production #0354. Rerun April 13, 1970.

Loveable old conman Danny Wilson is quite philosophical when he suspects he is reaching the end of the line. When Doc confirms his suspicions, Danny does not let it get him down. He simply starts to plan his swan song. Danny arranges for the biggest funeral and the most extravagant wake the West has ever seen, and then organizes the greatest con game of his dubious career to pay for it.

Danny Wilson	Jack Albertson
Heenan	Scott Brady
Indiana	Vito Scotti
Ed Wickes	Frank Marth
Carl Dahlman	Rayford Barnes
Percy Crump	Jonathan Harper
Ed O'Connor	Tom Brown
Stage Driver	Steve Raines
Story, Script	Preston Wood
Executive Story Consultant	Calvin Clements
Director	Bernard McEveety
Producer	Joseph Dackow
Executive Producer	John Mantley

Famed character actor Jack Albertson had an illustrious career on the Broadway stage, in cinema, and on television. His television credits include Lt. Harry Evans on *The Thin Man*, Walter Burton of *Room for One More*, and Senator Joe Kelley from *Grandpa Goes to Washington*. But he is probably best known for his portrayal of Ed Brown on *Chico and the Man*, for which he received an Emmy in 1976. By 1975 he had already received an Emmy for his guest appearance on *Cher*. In 1965 he won a Tony for his performance in *The Subject Was Roses* and in 1968 when it was made into a film he won an Academy Award. Scott Brady was the star of the television Western, *Shotgun Slade* and was also featured in the television drama *The Winds of War*. His film credits include *Johnny Guitar*, *Gentlemen Marry Brunettes*, and *John Goldfarb, Please Come Home*.

Hawk. October 20, 1969. Production #0360. Rerun April 20, 1970.

While trailing four renegade Indians, police Sergeant Hawk happens upon the home of his mother Phoebe Clifford. Phoebe had been a captive of the Apaches when she was 16 and gave birth to Hawk during her two-year imprisonment. When she escaped, Phoebe abandoned her half-breed son. Now 20 years later, Phoebe still rejects Hawk and sees him as a threat to the happiness she now has with her husband and two children, who know nothing about her experience.

Hawk	Brendon Boone
Phoebe Clifford	Louise Latham
Amos Clifford	Michael-James Wixted
Rachel Clifford	Hilarie Thompson
Dave Clifford	Robert Brubaker
Renegade Indian	X Brands
Renegade #2	Bill Hart
Renegade #3	Hal Needham
Renegade #4	Glen Randal, Jr.
Story, Script	Kay Lenard & Jess Carneol
Executive Story Consultant	Calvin Clements
Director	Gunnar Hellstrom

GUNSMOKE — III. THE PROGRAMS

Producer .... Joseph Dackow
Executive Producer .... John Mantley

Brendon Boone was featured as Chief on the dramatic series, *Garrison's Gorillas*. Michael-James Wixted was a regular on *The Smith Family*. Hilarie Thompson appeared as a regular on several series including *The Young Rebels*, *The Manhunter*, and *Operation Petticoat*.

A Man Called "Smith." October 27, 1969. Production #0351. Rerun April 27, 1970.

Abelia is forced into a compromising situation, when her husband Will "Smith" returns after years of desertion. Abelia has been living the respectable life of a widow all these years, with no knowledge of her outlaw husband. Not even her children know their father's identity. Will promises to remain anonymous and disappear, if Abelia will sell his stolen gold for him. Reluctantly she agrees and meets with Bull Landers, the corrupt owner of the Bull's Head Saloon, to exchange the gold for paper money.

Will .... Earl Holliman
Abelia .... Jacqueline Scott
Marieanne .... Susan Olsen
Jonathan .... Michael Durkin
Bull .... Val Avery
Mr. Bodkin .... Roy Roberts
Buffalo Hunter .... Sid Haig
Old Prospector .... William Fawcett
Saloon Girl .... Margarita Cordova
Story, Script, Executive Story Consultant .... Calvin Clements
Director .... Vincent McEveety
Producer .... Joseph Dackow
Executive Producer .... John Mantley

A Man Called Smith is a sequel to last season's *Abelia*. Jacqueline Scott, Susan Olsen, and Michael Durkin recreate their roles. Earl Holliman was a regular on several series including *Hotel de Paree*, *The Wide Country*, and *Police Woman*. He also appeared in *Gunsmoke: Return to Dodge*.

Charlie Noon. November 3, 1969. Production #0363. Rerun March 30, 1970 and August 12, 1974.

While Matt crosses the desert with condemned prisoner Charlie Noon, an Indian widow and her white stepson Jamie join his entourage. A band of Comanches led by Lone Wolf is after the woman. Lone Wolf seeks vengeance because two years earlier she jilted him to marry Jeremiah Parker, a white man. Lone Wolf has been pursuing her ever since. Unaware that Parker died, the Comanches mistakenly believe that Noon is her husband and plan on killing them both.

Charlie Noon .... James Best
The Woman .... Miriam Colon
Jamie .... Ronny Howard
Lone Wolf .... Edmund Hashim
Takawa .... Kip Whitman
Story, Script .... Jim Byrnes
Executive Story Consultant .... Calvin Clements
Director .... Vincent McEveety
Producer .... Joseph Dackow
Executive Producer .... John Mantley

The Television Programs

Richard E. Raderman and Norman Karlin won Emmy Awards for Outstanding Achievement in Film Sound Editing for *Charlie Noon*. A teenaged Ronny Howard is seen in this episode of *Gunsmoke*. Howard played Opie on *The Andy Griffith Show* and Ritchie Cunningham on *Happy Days*. He has appeared in numerous feature films and made-for-television movies. In recent years he has turned his sights to producing and directing such hit movies as *Cocoon* and *Splash*.

The Still. November 10, 1969. Production #0362.

Once again hillbillies wreak havoc upon Dodge. This time Elbert Moses and Uncle Titus hide a moonshining still and a prize bull in the cellar of a school. Festus suspects the scoundrels are up to something when they come into Dodge celebrating Thomas Jefferson's birthday on the wrong day. The two men con Festus out of the $50 reward money for information about the stolen bull and the deputy has trouble following the right clues to their logical conclusion.

Merry Florene	Lane Bradbury
Elbert Moses	Anthony James
Uncle Titus	Shug Fisher
Franks	James Westerfield
Mr. Bishop	J. Edward McKinley
Chester	Trent Lehman
Story, Script, Executive Story Consultant	Calvin Clements
Director	Gunnar Hellstrom
Producer	Joseph Dackow
Executive Producer	John Mantley

Trent Lehman appeared on the comedy series *Nanny and the Professor*.

A Matter of Honor. November 17, 1969. Production #0355. Rerun April 6, 1970.

C.V. and Otis Fletcher get into a fight with Billy Holland after Billy pays a little too much attention to their sister Lydia. The confrontation takes place in the stable and during the scuffle the brothers accidentally kill Billy. Unbeknownst to them, Louie Pheeters is sleeping off a binge in a buggy and has been witness to the whole incident. When the body is discovered, however, Louie is charged with the homicide. He had the opportunity and the motive. Holland had swindled Louie out of his most prized possession, his father's watch. Unfortunately, in Louie's intoxicated state he cannot remember a thing about the previous evening, nor does he remember how he recovered his watch. Although the boys are conscience stricken, they allow Louie to go to trial, rationalizing that he will not be convicted.

Jess Fletcher	John Anderson
Lydia Fletcher	Katherine Justice
C.V. Fletcher	Tom Simcox
Otis Fletcher	Dan Ferrone
Billy Holland	Richard Bakalyan
Cal Haines	Walter Sande
Judge Brooker	Jack Bailey
Prosecutor	Lawrence Mann
Ranch Hand	Bob Burrows
Story, Script	Joy Dexter
Executive Story Consultant	Calvin Clements
Director	Robert Totten
Producer	Joseph Dackow
Executive Producer	John Mantley

GUNSMOKE — III. THE PROGRAMS

The Innocent. November 24, 1969. Production #0353.

Frontier teacher, Athena Partridge Royce, and Festus are captured by a family of hillbilly desperadoes when their wagon breaks down while hauling supplies to an Indian Mission school. Yewker and his sons, Zeal and Loyal, have their eye on the wagon and the supplies, and put Festus to work fixing the wheel. Fearing harm to Athena and himself when the job is completed, Festus stretches it out as long as he dares.

Athena Partridge Royce	Eileen Heckart
Yewker	Barry Atwater
Zeal	Lee de Broux
Loyal	Anthony James
Phelps	Robert B. Williams
Indian Chief	Eddie Little Sky
Indian Boy	Manuel Padilla, Jr.
Sonny	Tom Nolan
Stage Driver	Rush Williams
Story, Script	Walter Black
Executive Story Consultant	Calvin Clements
Director	Marvin Chomsky
Producer	Joseph Dackow
Executive Producer	John Mantley

Tom Nolan appeared as Officer Hubbell on *Jessie*.

Ring of Darkness. December 1, 1969. Production #0359. Rerun May 11, 1970.

Ben Hurley is a decent farmer who has been blackmailed into stealing some horses by three outlaws. When Newly arrives to check into the matter, he meets Susan, Ben's blind daughter. Concerned for her well-being, Newly offers Ben another chance, provided he returns the stolen horses. Ben, however, rejects Newly's offer and makes the deputy his prisoner. Susan is in the dark, not only because of her blindness, but because Ben tells her that Newly is the horse thief. Not wanting to destroy the girl's image of her father, Newly goes along with Ben's decree.

Susan Hurley	Pamela Dunlap
Ben Hurley	Tom Drake
Pinto	John Crawford
Gulley	Anthony Caruso
Carr	Rex Holman
Story, Script	Arthur Dales
Executive Story Consultant	Calvin Clements
Director	Bernard McEveety
Producer	Joseph Dackow
Executive Producer	John Mantley

MacGraw. December 8, 1969. Production #0364.

Ex-gunfighter Jake MacGraw arrives in Dodge after completing a 20-year prison term. The citizens are still in awe of his reputation with a gun and speculate about what his business is in Dodge. MacGraw claims to be rehabilitated and takes a job at the Long Branch as a piano player. However, when he starts to show particular attention to a young buck named Dave Wilson and to Dave's girlfriend Ella Horton, Matt wonders about MacGraw's intentions.

Jake MacGraw	J.D. Cannon

[648]

The Television Programs

Dave Wilson	Michael Larrain
Ella Horton	Diana Ewing
Garvey	Sam Melville
Wilkes	Charles Kuenstle
Jed Douglas	Ned Wertimer
Ed O'Connor	Tom Brown
Eli Crawford	Sid Haig
Ed Crawford	Allen Jaffe
Hamilton	Bobby Hall
Barfly	Sam Edwards
Story, Script	Kay Lenard & Jess Carneol
Executive Story Consultant	Calvin Clements
Director	Philip Leacock
Producer	Joseph Dackow
Executive Producer	John Mantley

Michael Larrain was featured on the dramatic series *Matt Lincoln*. Ned Wertimer appeared as Ralph the doorman on *The Jeffersons*.

Roots of Fear. December 15, 1969. Production #0366.

The Dodge City bank is forced to close its doors after a run on the bank. The citizens are naturally shaken, especially Amos Sadler, a dirt farmer faced with losing his farm. The desperate Sadler breaks into the bank wanting only the money that is rightfully his. Unfortunately, his accomplices, a ne'er do well cousin and a slow witted brother, complicate matters.

Amos Sadler	John Anderson
Emilie Sadler	Louise Latham
Ridge Sadler	Warren Vanders
Daniel Sadler	Cliff Osmond
Susan Sadler	Jody Foster
George Acton	Walter Burke
Judge Brooker	Arthur Peterson
Charlie	Robert Karnes
Assistant Teller	Paul Micale
Townsman	Hank Wise
Mr. Bodkin	Roy Roberts
Story	Arthur Browne, Jr.
Script	Jim Byrnes & Arthur Browne, Jr.
Executive Story Consultant	Calvin Clements
Director	Philip Leacock
Producer	Joseph Dackow
Executive Producer	John Mantley

Primarily a film actress, Jody (later spelled Jodie) Foster's movies include *Alice Doesn't Live Here Anymore*, *Foxes*, and *Taxi Driver*, for which she was nominated for an Academy Award. Most recently she received an Academy Award for Best Actress for *The Accused*. As a child she appeared on numerous television series and was a regular on *Bob and Carol and Ted and Alice* and *Paper Moon*.

The Sisters. December 29, 1969. Production #0348. Rerun July 20, 1970.

Pack Landers, a contemptable drunken brute, pretends to have a change of heart, when three black nuns deliver into his custody his two motherless children. It soon becomes apparent, however, that Landers is more interested in the money the nuns are taking to Cimarron to build a school, than he is in becoming a fit father for his children.

Pack Landers	Jack Elam
Mother Tabitha	Lynn Hamilton
Sister Blanche	Susan Batson
Sister Charles	Gloria Calomee
Gail	Erica Petal
Toby	Chris Hundley
Ivy Landers	Cece Whitney
Story, Script	William Kelley
Executive Story Consultant	Calvin Clements
Director	Philip Leacock
Producer	Joseph Dackow
Executive Producer	John Mantley

Eric Petal was featured on *The Bob Crane Show*.

The War Priest. January 5, 1970. Production #0367. Rerun August 10, 1970.

On route from Owl Flats to Dodge by buckboard, Kitty is kidnapped and held hostage by wounded Apache war priest, Gregario. Gregario is an escaped cavalry prisoner, who is being pursued by a drunken cavalry sergeant named Emmet Holly. While Kitty is Gregario's bait in a showdown between the two men, the Apache seems less of a menace to her than the inebriated sergeant, whose stretch in the Army ends at sundown.

Gregario	Richard Anderson
Sergeant Emmet Holly	Forrest Tucker
Amos Strange	John Crawford
El Cuerno	Richard Hale
Lt. Snell	Sam Melville
1st Sentry	Link Wyler
2nd Sentry	Tom Sutton
Shotgun	Pete Kellett
1st Trooper	Vincent Deadrick
Story, Script	William Kelley
Executive Story Consultant	Calvin Clements
Director	Bernard McEveety
Producer	Joseph Dackow
Executive Producer	John Mantley

Forrest Tucker recreates his role as Emmet Holly in the episode titled *Sergeant Holly* broadcast December 14, 1970.

The Pack Rat. January 12, 1970. Production #0369.

While out on the prairie, Matt and his wounded prisoner Sam Danton meet up with a little Mexican thief named Sancho. They stop off in Dodge to have Doc check Danton's leg and to drop Sancho off with Kitty before continuing on to Fort Union. The stagecoach arrives with two passengers, Belle Clark and Martha Mason, who are also headed for Fort Union. Martha is about eight months pregnant and Doc will not allow her to continue her journey to meet her husband. When Matt and Danton leave, Belle and Newly accompany them. Martha, desperate to be with her husband, stows away in Matt's wagon. Meanwhile back in Dodge, Sancho forages through Belle's jewelry

The Television Programs

box and discovers a daguerreotype of her husband Sam Danton. Fearful that Matt is in grave danger, Sancho steals Ruth and rides to warn him.

Sam Danton	William C. Watson
Belle Clark	Loretta Swit
Sancho	Manuel Padilla, Jr.
Martha Mason	Heidi Vaughn
Shotgun	Robert Rothwell
Jake Hawkins	Robert Brubaker
Trapp	Bill Catching
Shockley	Tom Sutton
Story	Arthur Browne, Jr.
Script	Jim Byrnes & Arthur Browne, Jr.
Executive Story Consultant	Calvin Clements
Director	Philip Leacock
Producer	Joseph Dackow
Executive Producer	John Mantley

Loretta Swit is best known for her performance as Major Margaret "Hot Lips" Houlihan of *M.A.S.H.* for which she won an Emmy in 1980 and 1982.

The Judas Gun. January 19, 1970. Production #0365. Rerun June 15, 1970.

The longtime feud of ranchers Noah Haimes and Clete Bolden is rekindled by the romance of Cully, Haimes' only son, and Janie, Clete's only daughter. The matter takes an unexpected turn when Boyd Avery, a hired gunman, enters the dispute. Ironically, the family feud evolves into a personal showdown between Avery and Cully.

Boyd Avery	Ron Hayes
Cully Haimes	Peter Jason
Noah Haimes	Richard X. Slattery
Janie Bolden	Laurie Mock
Clete Bolden	Sean McClory
Ed O'Connor	Tom Brown
Bargirl	Margarita Cordova
Liveryman	William Fawcett
Teddy	Brad David
Town Bum	Ralph Neff
Story, Script	Harry Kronman
Executive Story Consultant	Calvin Clements
Director	Vincent McEveety
Producer	Joseph Dackow
Executive Producer	John Mantley

Sean McClory was a regular on *The Californians*, *Kate McShane*, and *Bring 'Em Back Alive*. Brad Davis was featured on *Firehouse*.

Doctor Herman Schultz, M.D. January 26, 1970. Production #0370. Rerun August 17, 1970.

Dr. Herman Schultz, an old friend of Doc's, arrives in Dodge. The German doctor has been dabbling in hypnosis and appears to have a special interest in hypnotizing Festus. Schultz gains Doc's approval first by hypnotizing Festus for a painless tooth extraction, and then for a practical joke in which Festus is made to crow like a rooster. It soon becomes evident, however, that Schultz's interest in Festus may be of a darker nature, and that he may be betraying his old friend Doc.

GUNSMOKE — III. THE PROGRAMS

Doctor Herman Schultz ....Benny Rubin
Stoney ....Pete Kellett
Howie ....Howard Culver
Story...Benny Rubin
Script, Executive Story Consultant ....Calvin Clements
Director ....Bernard McEveety
Producer ....Joseph Dackow
Executive Producer ....John Mantley

The story for this episode was suggested by Benny Rubin, who also stars as Dr. Schultz. Rubin started in show business as a vaudeville comic and later drifted into movies. In the 1940s he was a panelist on a television quiz show, *Stop Me If You've Heard This One,* and was the host of his own program, *The Benny Rubin Show.* His films include *Here Comes Mr. Jordan, Thoroughly Modern Millie* and *Coma.*

The Badge. February 2, 1970. Production #0374. Rerun September 7, 1970.

Kitty, stunned at seeing Matt wounded once again in the line of duty, decides to leave Dodge for good. She puts the Long Branch up for sale and joins her old friend Claire Hollis in running another establishment far from Dodge City and Matt Dillon. Kitty's problems begin anew, however, when she challenges the authority of a despotic man known as "Papa." Papa Steiffer controls the town and everyone in it. Kitty insists that she and Claire fight Steiffer's corruption, and when Matt shows up unexpectedly, Kitty resents his interference.

Claire Hollis ....Beverly Garland
Papa Steiffer ....Henry Jones
John Dawson ....John Milford
Keller ....Roy Jenson
Locke ....Jack Lambert
Jackson ....William O'Connell
Bea ....Mary Angela
Worden ....John Flinn
Sloan ....Fred Coby
Story, Script ....Jim Byrnes
Executive Story Consultant ....Calvin Clements
Director ....Vincent McEveety
Producer ....Joseph Dackow
Executive Producer ....John Mantley

Flashbacks from this episode were used in the made-for-television movie, *Gunsmoke: Return to Dodge.* The flashbacks were used to explain why Kitty left Matt and moved to New Orleans. However, in the original episode Kitty did return at the end.

Albert. February 9, 1970. Production #0368. Rerun June 8, 1970.

Albert Schiller has been a loyal employee of the Dodge City Bank. After 15 years of devoted service he is given his notice from the main office. Albert is extremely disheartened by the turn of events, but blythly goes about his duties as teller. Then fate steps in affording Albert his just dues. Albert foils a bank robbery, and although the outlaws escape empty handed, Albert impulsively takes $5000 for himself. No one suspects him of the theft except the outlaws. Certain of Albert's guilt, the bandits return to town and force him to help them restage the robbery.

Albert Schiller ....Milton Selzer
Kate Schiller ....Patricia Barry

The Television Programs

Nix	L.Q. Jones
Tom Clark	Bob Random
Jake Spence	William Schallert
Emily Cushing	Dorothy Neumann
Mrs. Bodkin	Natalie Masters
Mr. Bodkin	Roy Roberts
Story, Script	Jim Byrnes
Executive Story Consultant	Calvin Clements
Director	Vincent McEveety
Producer	Joseph Dackow
Executive Producer	John Mantley

Kiowa. February 16, 1970. Production #0372. Rerun aired July 27, 1970.

Melissa Vail is abducted from her home by a Kiowa Indian party. Her father and her two brothers reluctantly accept the assistance of Reverend Cox and Matt, as they set out to find her. The men carefully track the Indians, but Matt soon realizes that the Kiowa's are laying a deliberate trail for them to follow. He suspects that Vail knows why, but it all remains a mystery until they reach their final destination.

Reverend Cox	Dub Taylor
Ed Vail	Victor French
Albert Vail	John Beck
Russ Vail	Lucas White
Melissa Vail	Joyce Ames
Martha Vail	Jean Allison
Tomani	Richard Lapp
Quichero	Richard Angarola
Indian woman	Angela Carroll
Story, Script	Ron Bishop
Executive Story Consultant	Calvin Clements
Director	Bernard McEveety
Producer	Joseph Dackow
Executive Producer	John Mantley

John Beck was a regular on *Nichols, Flamingo Road,* and *Dallas.* Joyce Ames was seen on *Dean Martin Presents the Golddiggers.* Richard Angarola played Chief Claw on *How the West Was Won.*

Celia. February 23, 1970. Production #0373. Rerun June 22, 1970.

Ben Sommars, Dodge's blacksmith, advertises in a newspaper for a bride. When a pretty girl named Celia answers the ad, Newly suspects that she is after Ben's money. Celia claims to be a Missouri farm girl, but Newly sizes her up as a big city girl. He has a hard time convincing Ben, however, even after another man shows up claiming Celia bilked him out of $1500.

Ben Sommars	Cliff Osmond
Celia Madden	Melissa Murphy
Martin Blake	Frank Marth
Mr. Bodkin	Roy Roberts
Barney	Charles Seel
Cashier	George Petrie
Burnett	Walker Edmiston
Story, Script	Harry Kronman

GUNSMOKE — III. THE PROGRAMS

Executive Story Consultant .... Calvin Clements
Director .... Philip Leacock
Producer .... Joseph Dackow
Executive Producer .... John Mantley

Walker Edmiston played Regan on *The Rounders*.

Morgan. March 2, 1970. Production #0375.

Outlaw Cole Morgan and his gang invade Dodge in Matt's absence. Morgan, shot in the face by Kitty, holds her hostage along with Doc, Festus, and Newly. It is a race against the clock for Morgan, who orders his captives to heal his wounds and repair his gatling gun overnight. A gold shipment is due to arrive on a train guarded by Matt and a cavalry patrol, and Morgan plans on being ready for them. The vain Morgan also plans on paying Kitty back for disfiguring his face.

Morgan .... Steve Forrest
Clint .... Hank Brandt
Jenny .... Charlotte Stewart
Trent .... Ed Long
Greer .... Mills Watson
Carter .... Jonathan Lippe
Barney .... Charles Seel
Telegrapher .... Jack Garner
Zack .... I. Stanford Jolley
Hawkins .... Fletcher Bryant
Lt. .... Read Morgan
Story, Script .... Kay Lenard & Jess Carneol
Executive Story Consultant .... Calvin Clements
Director .... Bernard McEveety
Producer .... Joseph Dackow
Executive Producer .... John Mantley

Charlotte Stewart was featured as Eva Beadle Simms on *Little House on the Prairie*. Jack Garner played Jack, the bartender on *Bret Maverick*, which starred his brother James Garner.

The Thieves. March 9, 1970. Production #0371. Rerun July 6, 1970.

Three boys, Eric Tabray, Shuffles Jones, and Billy Clarke are given probation from county jail. They are taken to Dodge where Shuffles and Billy get jobs working for Mr. and Mrs. Hale, a gentle Quaker couple. Something about young Eric touches Sam's heart, and through his insistance, the boy gets a job at the Long Branch. According to Sam, Eric reminds him of how he was as a reckless youth. He, too, had faced a jail sentence, but fortunately, a kind small town marshal gave him a chance and let him go. Sam is hoping that Eric will choose to follow a straight path, rather than hang from a rope like his outlaw father. The boys soon get into trouble, however, by robbing the Long Branch of $400. Undaunted, Sam covers for them, offering them still another chance to redeem themselves.

Eric Tabray .... Michael Burns
Claude "Shuffles" Jones .... Bill Callaway
Billy Clarke .... Timothy Burns
Gideon Hale .... Royal Dano
Mrs. Hale .... Daphne Field
Burt Tilden .... John Schuck

The Television Programs

Story, Script	Thomas Thompson
Executive Story Consultant	Calvin Clements
Director	Philip Leacock
Producer	Joseph Dackow
Executive Producer	John Mantley

This episode offers a rare glimpse into the character of Sam. In addition to being a regular on *Love, American Style,* Bill Callaway did the voices for several cartoon characters on such Saturday morning fare as *The Drak Pack, Cattanooga Cats,* and *Richie Rich.*

Hackett. March 16, 1970. Production #0376. Rerun August 31, 1970.

Hackett, a vengeful ex-convict, seeks reprisal against Quentin Sargent, a former partner in crime who is now a poor dirt farmer. Sargent had backed down from participating in a train holdup that sent Hackett and the others to prison for ten years. Hackett taunts the guilt-ridden Sargent for his cowardice, and threatens to tell Sargent's wife about his secret past. Finally, Hackett forces Sargent into staging another train robbery.

Hackett	Earl Holliman
Quentin Sargent	Morgan Woodward
Geneva Sargent	Jennifer West
Alvin Bronk	Ken Swofford
Phelps Tulley	Robert Totten
Businessman	Bill Erwin
Chinese Proprietor	Allen Jung
Story, Script	William Kelley
Executive Story Consultant	Calvin Clements
Director	Vincent McEveety
Producer	Joseph Dackow
Executive Producer	John Mantley

The Cage. March 23, 1970. Production #0357.

Matt and Festus rescue Roy Stewart from a prison van in which his brother is killed by his own gang of gold robbers. Roy offers to help Matt trap the bandits and restore the gold. Matt understands Roy's desire for vengeance, but what he does not realize is that Roy has another motive for recovering the gold. He wants to keep it to pay for medical treatment for his mute Mexican wife.

Roy Stewart	Steve Carlson
Maria	Laura Figueroa
Luke Stewart	Hank Brandt
Alfonso	Jorge Moreno
Sanders	Paul Stewart
Benson	Gregg Palmer
Blake	Ken Mayer
Weden	Robert Swan
Gresley	Allen Jaffe
Pepe	Joaquin Martinez
Mrs. Ramos	Renata Vanni
Elderly Mexican	Pedro Vegas
Elderly Mexican Woman	Araceli Rey
Story, Script, Executive Story Consultant	Calvin Clements

GUNSMOKE — III. THE PROGRAMS

Director .... Bernard McEveety
Producer .... Josep Dackow
Executive Producer .... John Mantley

Paul Stewart was featured on such television series as *Top Secret U.S.A.*, *Deadline* and *The Man Who Never Was*. Stewart, a veteran radio performer, was heard frequently on Orson Welles' *Mercury Theater*. In addition, Stewart was an active television director for numerous series including *Peter Gunn*, *Philip Marlowe*, and *The Twilight Zone*.

Charlie Noon. March 30, 1970, rerun. First aired November 3, 1969.

A Matter of Honor. April 6, 1970, rerun. First aired November 17, 1969.

Danny. April 13, 1970, rerun. First aired October 13, 1969.

Hawk. April 20, 1970, rerun. First aired October 20, 1969.

A Man Called Smith. April 27, 1970, rerun. First aired October 27, 1969.

The Devil's Outpost. May 4, 1970, rerun. First aired September 22, 1969.

Ring of Darkness. May 11, 1970, rerun. First aired December 1, 1969.

Gunfighter, R.I.P. May 18, 1970, rerun. First aired October 22, 1966.

Stryker. May 25, 1970, rerun. First aired September 29, 1969.

Hill Girl. June 1, 1970, rerun. First aired January 29, 1968.

Albert. June 8, 1970, rerun. First aired February 9, 1970.

The Judas Gun. June 15, 1970, rerun. First aired January 19, 1970.

Celia. June 22, 1970, rerun. First aired February 23, 1970.

Nowhere to Run. June 29, 1970, rerun. First aired January 15, 1968.

The Thieves. July 6, 1970, rerun. First aired March 9, 1970.

A Hat. July 13, 1970, rerun. First aired October 16, 1967.

The Sisters. July 20, 1970, rerun. First aired December 29, 1969.

Kiowa. July 27, 1970, rerun. First aired February 16, 1970.

The Victim. August 3, 1970, rerun. First aired January 1, 1968.

The War Priest. August 10, 1970, rerun. First aired January 5, 1970.

Doctor Herman Schultz, M.D. August 17, 1970, rerun. First aired January 26, 1970.

Coreyville. August 24, 1970, rerun. First aired October 6, 1969.

The Television Programs

Hackett. August 31, 1970, rerun. First aired March 16, 1970.

The Badge. September 7, 1970, rerun. First aired February 2, 1970.

SIXTEENTH SEASON
In 1970 Gunsmoke *won an award from the Western Writers of America for 15 years of quality Western drama*

Chato. September 14, 1970. Production #0409. Rerun May 1, 1972 and September 2, 1974.

Matt tracks a fugitive named Chato, for personal as well as professional reasons. He travels from Kansas to New Mexico in his quest to catch the man who murdered one of his friends. Hoping to lure the killer out of hiding, Matt takes Chato's woman into custody. When Chato materializes, a twist of fate forces the two men into an uncomfortable alliance in order to save themselves from death at the hands of desperados.

Chato	Ricardo Montalban
Mora	Miriam Colon
Sheriff Cooter	William Bryant
Mrs. Cooter	Peggy McCay
Old Man	Pedro Regas
Juanito	Rodolfo Hoyos
Surgeon	Robert Knapp
Case	Jim Sheppard
Story, Script	Paul F. Edwards
Executive Story Consultant	Calvin Clements
Director	Vincent McEveety
Producer	Joseph Dackow
Executive Producer	John Mantley

Chato won the Western Writers of America's Golden Spur Award for Paul F. Edwards. Latin actor Ricardo Montalban is best known for his role as Mr. Roarke of *Fantasy Island*. He also appeared as Zachery Powers on *The Colbys* and won an Emmy for *How the West Was Won*. In the movies he played the menacing Khan of *Star Trek: The Wrath of Khan*. Peggy McCay was a regular on *Room for One More, Gibbsville, Love of Life, General Hospital*, and *Days of Our Lives*. Pedro Regas was seen regularly on *Pat Paulsen's Half a Comedy Hour*. Rodolfo Hoyos appeared as Luis Valdez on the comedy series, *Viva Valdez*.

The Noose. September 21, 1970. Production #0401. Rerun June 12, 1972.

Fred Garth returns to Dodge after a 15 year absence. He was only a boy when he left town, and Kitty does not recognize him when he enters the Long Branch. Garth forces Kitty at gunpoint to accompany him to Old Dodge Town and later lures Festus and Doc out there as well. Once there, Garth locks them in the old jail and waits for Matt to come looking for his friends. The young man has an old score to settle. Fifteen years earlier, when the young Garth tried to interfere with his father's hanging, Matt was forced to shoot him in the leg and chain him to a post. Certain of his father's innocence, Garth struggled, clawing at the chains, as he watched his father's execution. Now he intends to repay the kindness and justice he was accorded. When Matt arrives, Garth shoots him in the leg and chains him to a post. Then he prepares to hang an innocent victim, Doc.

GUNSMOKE — III. THE PROGRAMS

Fred Garth	Tom Skerritt
Hank	Hank Patterson
Nebs	William Fawcett
Story, Script	Arthur Browne, Jr.
Executive Story Consultant	Calvin Clements
Director	Vincent McEveety
Producer	Joseph Dackow
Executive Producer	John Mantley

Stark. September 28, 1970. Production #0403. Rerun May 8, 1972.

Stark, a shrewd and ruthless bounty hunter, captures an escaped prisoner in Dodge. When Stark learns that his prisoner is Adam Bramley, the brother of wealthy Glory Bramley, his bounty dreams transform into schemes of blackmail.

Stark	Richard Kiley
Glory Bramley	Suzanne Pleshette
John Bramley	Henry Wilcoxon
Adam Bramley	Shelly Novack
Charlie	Bob Burrows
Bo	Rusty Lane
Story, Script	Donald S. Sanford
Executive Story Consultant	Calvin Clements
Assistant Story Consultant	Paul F. Edwards
Director	Robert Totten
Producer	Joseph Dackow
Executive Producer	John Mantley

Richard Kiley most recently appeared in the critically acclaimed series *A Year in the Life*. He was Paddy Cleary on *The Thorn Birds*, for which he won an Emmy, and starred along with Joanne Woodward in the made-for-television movie, *Do You Remember Love?* Kiley's stage credits include *Man of La Mancha*, for which he won a Tony Award. His films include *The Blackboard Jungle*, *The Little Prince*, and *Looking for Mr. Goodbar*. Suzanne Pleshette is best known as Emily Hartley of *The Bob Newhart Show*. Her films include *Rome Adventure*, *40 Pounds of Trouble* and *The Birds*. Ex-football professional, Shelly Novak, was a regular on *The F.B.I.* and *Most Wanted*.

Sam McTavish, M.D. October 5, 1970. Production #0410. Rerun December 20, 1971.

Doc is planning a well-earned vacation and the replacement he hires turns out to be Sam McTavish, a woman doctor. Hesitant at leaving a woman to handle a man's job, the chauvinistic Doc soon learns that Dr. McTavish is not only an extremely competent professional, but is also a very warm and loving woman. Having been assured of Sam's ability, Doc prepares to leave. However, a plague breaks out in Dodge and forces Doc to cancel his trip. Both doctors work together hand in hand. Realizing he has finally found a kindred spirit, Doc falls in love and decides to marry.

Dr. Samuel McTavish	Vera Miles
Barn Bascomb	Arch Johnson
Ellen	Dee Carroll
Christina	Lisa Gerritsen
Minnie Carver	Amzie Strickland
Harley	Tom Fadden
Bridget O'Reilly	Kathleen O'Malley
Johnson	Harry Harvey, Sr.

The Television Programs

Dan Slade	Read Morgan
Joe Slade	Robert Rothwell
Tom Slade	Lance Thomas
Frank O'Reilly	Glenn Redding
Story, Script	Gerry Day & Bethel Leslie
Executive Story Consultant	Calvin Clements
Director	Bernard McEveety
Producer	Joseph Dackow
Executive Producer	John Mantley

Vera Miles appeared in such films as John Ford's *The Searchers,* and Alfred Hitchcock's *The Wrong Man* and *Psycho.* Arch Johnson was a regular on *Peter Loves Mary, The Asphalt Jungle,* and *Camp Runamuck.* Tom Fadden appeared in two television Westerns, *Broken Arrow* and *Cimarron City.* Bethel Leslie, who co-wrote this episode, switches back and forth between writer and actress. In addition to appearing in films and made-for-television movies, she was a regular on *The Girls, The Richard Boone Show,* and *The Doctors.* Leslie was also headwriter for *The Secret Storm.*

Gentry's Law. October 12, 1970. Production #0404. Rerun June 19, 1972.

Amos Gentry, a heavy handed land baron, has two reckless and free-wheeling sons, Colt and Ben. When the boys catch Floyd Babcock in the act of cattlerustling, they decide to put a scare into the harmless drifter. Unfortunately, their practical joke ends in tragedy. Babcock's body is discovered by a friend, who calls in Matt. When Matt pieces the puzzle together, he asks Gentry to hand his sons over for trial, but Gentry refuses to cooperate.

Amos Gentry	John Payne
Colt Gentry	Peter Jason
Ben Gentry	Robert Pine
Floyd Babcock	Don Keefer
Claire Gentry	Louise Latham
Orly Grimes	Shug Fisher
Leelah Case	Darlene Conley
Buel	John Flinn
Abner	Robert Totten
Story, Script	Jack Miller
Executive Story Consultant	Calvin Clements
Director	Vincent McEveety
Producer	Joseph Dackow
Executive Producer	John Mantley

John Payne, rugged, handsome leading man of the 40s and 50s starred in his own Western series, *The Restless Gun.* His movies include *Miracle on 34th Street.*

Snow Train [Part I]. October 19, 1970. Production #0406. Rerun May 15, 1972 and July 22, 1974.

A train is stopped and Matt is given an ultimatum to release two men to the Sioux Indians, or face the consequences for himself and the other passengers. Indian Chief, Red Willow, is demanding custody of the pair responsible for the death of two braves from poison whiskey. While Matt tries to explain that the guilty will be punished by the law, the Indians attack the train and two passengers are wounded.

Snow Train [Part II]. October 26, 1970. Production #0407. Rerun May 22, 1972 and July 29, 1974.

GUNSMOKE — III. THE PROGRAMS

Matt is cornered by three Sioux after he escapes from the train in an effort to seek help. While Matt is having his problems with the Indians, Festus is overpowered by the passengers, who decide to turn over the wanted men to Chief Red Willow.

Sam Wickes	Clifton James
Billy	Gene Evans
Lucas	Ken Lynch
Tibbett	Roy Engel
Ada Coleman	Pamela Dunlap
Little Nose	Richard Lapp
Donna	Loretta Swit
Scott Coleman	Tim Considine
Bud	Richard D. Kelton
Clay Foreman	John Milford
Pennigrath	Dana Elcar
Lloyd Coleman	Ron Hayes
Chief Red Willow	X Brands
Story, Script	Preston Wood
Executive Story Consultant	Calvin Clements
Director	Gunnar Hellstrom
Producer	Joseph Dackow
Executive Producer	John Mantley

The score for *Snow Train* won a Western Heritage Wrangler Award for John Parker. Tim Considine was a regular on *My Three Sons*. Dana Elcar appeared on *Baretta, Baa Baa Black Sheep,* and *MacGyver*.

Luke. November 2, 1970. Production #0412. Rerun April 3, 1972.

Luke Dangerfield deserts his wife and daughter to pursue a life of crime. Fourteen years later, while still trying to evade a posse, Luke is shot in the back by Moses Reedy, a bounty hunter. Luke's young friend Austin Keep manages to bring the seriously injured Luke to Dodge. Thinking he is dying, Luke wants to see his daughter Kathy, who he has not seen in 14 years. To Austin, Luke is like a father, and he would do anything to make Luke's final days happy ones. All Luke knows of his estranged daughter is that she is a school teacher in Dodge. However, Austin soon discovers that Kathy was a cheap saloon girl who was shot and killed by a jealous lover. Unable to face his friend with the grim news, Austin hires another saloon girl, Doris Prebble, to impersonate Luke's daughter.

Luke Dangerfield	Morgan Woodward
Austin Keep	Anthony Costello
Howie	Howard Culver
Doris Prebble	Katherine Justice
Moses Reedy	Rex Holman
Bull	Victor Izay
Story, Script	Jack Miller
Executive Story Consultant	Calvin Clements
Director	Bernard McEveety
Producer	Joseph Dackow
Executive Producer	John Mantley

The Gun. November 9, 1970. Production #0408. Rerun June 11, 1973.

Randy Gogan, a young dreamer, accidentally outdraws a famous gunfighter and becomes the hero of Dodge. Randy, who gets most of his excitement from reading pulp fiction, is unaccustomed to such notoriety and is soon drawn into real danger by an unscrupulous newspaper man. The journalist plans on exploiting Randy's new reputation by molding the young man into a slick gunman and hence a moneymaker.

Randy Gogan	Kevin Coughlin
Sumner Pendleton	L.Q. Jones
Stella Felton	Patricia Morrow
Vance Jessop	Robert Phillips
Wade Pasco	Sam Melville
Greenwood	Ken Mayer
Ed Jacobi	Stanley Clements
Kemble	Jack Garner
Tom	Jon Jason Mantley
Anne	Marie Mantley
Sporting Gentleman #1	Foster Brooks
Sporting Gentlemen #2	Frank Biro
Townsman #1	Henry Wise
Townsman #2	Bert Madrid
Joseph	Eric Chase
Story, Script	Donald S. Sanford
Executive Story Consultant	Calvin Clements
Director	Bernard McEveety
Producer	Joseph Dackow
Executive Producer	John Mantley

Patricia Morrow was a regular on *I Led Three Lives* and *Peyton Place*. Morrow later gave up acting to become an attorney. Jon Jason and Marie Mantley, John Mantley's children, are seen in this episode. Eric Chase played Christopher Pruitt on *Here Come the Brides*.

The Scavengers. November 16, 1970. Production #0411. Rerun May 29, 1972.

Piney Biggs, a hungry traveler, arrives on the scene after an Indian massacre and begins to scavenge about. He is soon interrupted by three Indians, who are also scavenging for food, money, and jewelry. Out of fear, Piney stabs himself with an arrow and feigns death. The Indians collect a few items and move on. Piney is eventually rescued and brought to Dodge, where he is reunited with his little daughter and pregnant wife. When questioned about the massacre, Piney lies to Matt about his role in the attack. After bragging about his courageous deeds, Biggs is considered a hero by the citizens of Dodge, but is soon faced with a dilemma. Three buffalo hunters bring in the three "guilty" Indians for the reward money. If Biggs tells the truth, the bounty hunters will shoot him, if he continues to lie, the innocent Indians will be executed.

Piney Biggs	Yaphet Kotto
Rachel Biggs	Cicely Tyson
Colley	Slim Pickens
Rath	Roy Jenson
Logan	Link Wyler
Lieutenant	Victor Holchak
Driver	Steve Raines
Ogana	James Almanzar
Scarface	Eddie Little Sky
Barkeep	Victor Izay

GUNSMOKE — III. THE PROGRAMS

Merrilee Biggs	Jerelyn Fields
Livery Man	Henry Wise
Story, Script	Jack Miller
Executive Story Consultant	Calvin Clements
Director	Bernard McEveety
Producer	Joseph Dackow
Executive Producer	John Mantley

The Scavengers won the prestigious Black Image Award. On television, Yaphet Kotto played Sgt. James "China" Bell on *For Love and Honor*. His films include *The Thomas Crown Affair, Alien, Brubaker,* and *The Star Chamber*. Cicely Tyson was a regular on *East Side/West Side*. In addition, she appeared in the mini-series *Roots* and played the title role in the much acclaimed *The Autobiography of Miss Jane Pittman*. Her films have included *The Heart Is a Lonely Hunter* and *Sounder,* for which she was nominated for an Academy Award.

The Witness. November 23, 1970. Production #0405. Rerun June 5, 1972.

While aboard a train heading for Dodge, Arnie Sprague and his neighbor Beecher witness a cold-blooded shooting committed by a young gunfighter named Ira Pickett. Matt arrests Ira after Sprague and Beecher give their statements. However, when Ira's father and brother arrive in Dodge the situation changes. Beecher is "accidentally" killed when he is crushed while fixing his wagon. Osgood Pickett, Ira's father, soon pays Sprague a visit as well. Osgood is a man whose words are like honey and who smiles as he "puts in the knife." Sprague is quickly coerced into changing his testimony, and Matt is forced to release Ira.

Osgood Pickett	Harry Morgan
Arnie Sprague	Tim O'Connor
Beecher	I. Sanford Jolley
Ira Pickett	Dack Rambo
Jared Sprague	Barry Brown
Texan	Robert Swan
Martha Sprague	June Dayton
Edda Sprague	Annette O'Toole
Joseph	Ray Young
Judge Brooker	Herb Vigran
Story, Script	Shimon Wincelberg
Executive Story Consultant	Calvin Clements
Director	Philip Leacock
Producer	Joseph Dackow
Executive Producer	John Mantley

Gunsmoke has a long line of colorful villains and Osgood Pickett, as played by Harry Morgan, ranks right up there as one of the most perverse and wicked portrayals. Morgan has had a long and successful career on television. He was a regular on several series including *December Bride, Pete and Gladys, The Richard Boone Show, Kentucky Jones, Dragnet,* and *Hec Ramsey*. Today he is probably most familiar for his portrayal of Col. Sherman Potter on *M.A.S.H.* for which he won an Emmy in 1980. Dack Rambo was a regular on numerous television shows including *The New Loretta Young Show, The Guns of Will Sonnett, Dallas,* and *Dirty Sally,* which was a spin-off of a two-part *Gunsmoke* called *Pike*. Annette O'Toole appeared in such films as *King of the Gypsies, Cat People,* and *48 Hours*. Herb Vigran was featured on *The Ed Wynn Show*.

The Television Programs

McCabe. November 30, 1970. Production #0402.
While Matt is trying to arrest him, a bank robber named McCabe grabs a hostage and forces Matt into a compromise. McCabe will let the hostage go, if Matt will let him visit the family he deserted 11 years ago. What McCabe discovers, however, is not what he had hoped for. His wife Amy has died, and his son Dobie is full of resentment. McCabe escapes from Matt's custody, only to be caught by the local townspeople. Then, with the aid of their biased judge, the citizens convict and sentence McCabe to hang.

McCabe	Dan Kemp
Amy	Tani Phelps
Dobie	Mitch Vogel
Sheriff Shackwood	Jim Davis
Clay White	David Brian
Judge Claireborne	Jon Lormer
J.W. Hicks	Robert Sorrells
Kipp	Mills Watson
Weaver	Lew Brown
Abigail Hartly	Marie Cheatham
Conductor	Trevor Bardette
Lennie	Tom Sutton
Bartender	Pete Kellett
Story, Script	Jim Byrnes
Executive Story Consultant	Calvin Clements
Director	Bernard McEveety
Producer	Joseph Dackow
Executive Producer	John Mantley

Mitch Vogel appeared as Jamie Hunter on *Bonanza*.

The Noon Day Devil. December 7, 1970. Production #0413. Rerun May 21, 1973.
Matt is baffled when he learns that Father Hernando Cantrell of Mission El Santuario de Chimayo, has been identified as one of the two men who stole a gold shipment and killed deputy marshal Bones Cunningham. Matt later discovers that the crime was actually committed by Father Cantrell's twin brother Heraclio. However, Heraclio has been given sanctuary at the mission, and is seeking forgiveness for his sins.

Hernando/Heraclio Cantrell	Anthony Zerbe
Actor Double	John Dullaghan
Bones Cunningham	Warren Vanders
Quito Vega	Ernest Sarracino
Rita	Annette Cardona
Diego	Natividad Vacio
Carlos	Bert Madrid
John Hike	Pepe Callahan
Brother Antonio	Anthony Cordova
Doctor	Fred Coby
Indian Boy	Tony Davis
Rodriguez	Julio Medina
Story, Script	William Kelley
Director	Philip Leacock
Executive Story Consultant	Calvin Clements

GUNSMOKE — III. THE PROGRAMS

Producer .... Joseph Dackow
Executive Producer .... John Mantley

Sergeant Holly. December 14, 1970. Production #0414.

While waiting in Dodge for further orders, Sergeant Holly decides to continue his efforts to court Miss Kitty. Holly stops by the Long Branch to have a drink and gets happily drunk. Later he wakes up missing his uniform and horse, and discovers that a trigger happy army patrol is looking for him in connection with a payroll robbery. The only way for Holly to clear himself of the charges, is to recover the money and catch the bandits responsible. Although Kitty wants nothing more to do with the inebriated sergeant, she feels obligated to help save him, and in the process, she becomes his reluctant "bride."

Sergeant Holly .... Forrest Tucker
Willis Jeeter .... Albert Salmi
Corporal Steckey .... Med Flory
Roy Gast .... Read Morgan
Chico Fuentes .... David Renard
Luke Pinero .... Victor Eberg
Bodine .... Gregg Palmer
The Indian .... Vito Scotti
Lomax .... Bob Morgan
Corp. Tuttle .... Frank Hotchkiss
Story, Script .... William Kelley
Executive Story Consultant .... Calvin Clements
Director .... Bernard McEveety
Producer .... Leonard Katzman
Executive Producer .... John Mantley

The character of Sergeant Holly first appeared in *The War Priest* which aired January 5, 1970. Med Flory was a regular on *The Ray Anthony Show*.

Baker's Dozen. December 21, 1970, rerun. First aired December 25, 1967.

Jenny. December 28, 1970. Production #0415.

After her mother dies, ten-year-old Jenny Pritchard arrives in Dodge looking for her father, unaware that he is a wanted criminal. In Matt's absence, Newly captures Lucas Pritchard. However, the precocious little girl has touched Newly's heart and he releases Pritchard to visit with Jenny, with the understanding that he return to jail afterwards. Pritchard, unfortunately, does not stick to his part of the bargain and escapes, an act which costs Newly his badge.

Jenny .... Lisa Gerritsen
Lucas Pritchard .... Steve Ihnat
Judge Franklin .... Rance Howard
Ed Reilly .... Steve Raines
Driver .... Bob Burrows
Story, Script .... Jack Miller
Executive Story Consultant .... Calvin Clements
Director .... Robert Totten
Producer .... Leonard Katzman
Executive Producer .... John Mantley

Rance Howard played Henry Boomhauer on *Gentle Ben* and Doc Wilson on *The*

The Television Programs

Thorn Birds. He is also the father of Clint Howard, who was also featured on *Gentle Ben*, and of actor-producer-director Ron Howard. Leonard Katzman went on to produce several other television series including *Logan's Run, Hawaii Five-O, Petrocelli, The Wild Wild West, Dallas*, and *Dirty Sally*, a *Gunsmoke* spin-off.

Captain Sligo. January 4, 1971. Production #0416. Rerun July 2, 1973.

A rugged seaman, Captain Sligo, decides to retire to Dodge and make a home for himself and his pet buffalo. In addition, the Captain reveals that he plans on marrying his new neighbor Josephine Burney, a feisty, attractive widow with two children. Unfortunately, Josephine does not wish to share his life or his company, especially after Sligo announces that he expects her to bear him ten sons.

Captain Aron Sligo	Richard Basehart
Josephine Burney	Salome Jens
Watney	Royal Dano
Leonard	Stacy Harris
Blacksmith	Robert Totten
Tim Burney	Bob Eilbacher
Anne Burney	Geri Reischl
Bartender	Larry Finley
Trail Boss	Matt Emery
Cowboy	Brian Foley
Tanner	Boyd "Red" Morgan
Tobin	Fred Stromsoe
Rackley	Troy Melton
Vern	Bob Herron
Story, Script	William Kelley
Executive Story Consultant	Calvin Clements
Director	William Conrad
Producer	Leonard Katzman
Executive Producer	John Mantley

Radio's Matt Dillon, William Conrad, directed this episode. On television Richard Basehart starred in *Voyage to the Bottom of the Sea* and *W.E.B.* In 1965 he won an Emmy for Best Narration for *Let My People Go*. His film credits include *He Walked by Night, La Strada*, and *Moby Dick*. On television Salome Jens appeared as Mrs. Kipfer in *From Here to Eternity*. Her films include *Angel Baby, Seconds*, and *Me, Natalie*. Stacy Harris was featured on *Doorway to Danger, N.O.P.D.*, and *The Life and Legend of Wyatt Earp*. Boyd Morgan appeared in the film *Violent Saturday*. Fred Stromsoe played Officer Woods on *Adam 12*.

Mirage. January 11, 1971. Production #0417.

The chase after an outlaw named Eli Maddox leads Festus far into the desert. Before Festus kills Maddox, the outlaw manages to put a bullet into the deputy's water canteen. Days of wandering in the desert without water causes Festus to hallucinate. Eventually, he and Ruth drift into a "deserted" ghost town. When shots ring out from one of the broken down buildings, Festus responds in kind, but by this time he no longer knows what is real or imagined. However, he is sure he has killed someone. After burying the unknown victim, Festus and Ruth continue their journey until Mr. Stocker finds the deputy near death. Once in Dodge, Festus cannot remember what happened, and the only clue to the identity of the dead man is a saddle inscribed "Adam Cleary, Ridge Tree." What Matt wants to know is why Adam was in the ghost town and why he was shooting at Festus. Lemuel Cleary, the young man's father, wants answers, too, for according to him his son was on his way to buy a milk cow, and "Adam never shot a living soul."

Lemuel	John Anderson
Tom	Gary Wood
Elsie	Mary Rings
Hotel Clerk	Bill Zuckert
Maddox	Harry Raybould
Deputy	Robert Knapp
Stocker	Dan White
Adam	Kevin Burchett
Story, Script	Jack Miller
Executive Story Consultant	Calvin Clements
Director	Vincent McEveety
Producer	Leonard Katzman
Executive Producer	John Mantley

Zavala. January 18, 1971, rerun. First aired October 7, 1968.

The Tycoon. January 25, 1971. Production #0418.

Festus becomes heir to $500 from an old friend and with the help of his friend Titus, is immediately transformed into Dodge's newest business tycoon. Titus, Festus' new business associate, convinces him to invest in the freight business and uses the money to buy two fancy circus wagons, and to outfit Festus as elegantly as Mr. Jonas' store allows. Festus is soon considered Dodge's most eligible bachelor and is regarded as a prime catch by a local widow.

Titus	Shug Fisher
Moody Fowler	John Beck
Ma Fowler	Nora Marlowe
Amos Fowler	James Minotto
Dora Lou	Gwynne Gilford
Clarence Carver	Herman Poppe
Henry Folsom	Walker Edmiston
Parson Mueller	Charles Wagenheim
Story, Script	Robert Vincent Wright
Executive Story Consultant	Calvin Clements
Director	Bernard McEveety
Producer	Leonard Katzman
Executive Producer	John Mantley

Charles Wagenheim, who usually plays Halligan, is seen in this episode as Parson Mueller. Gwynne Gilford was a regular on *The Waverly Wonders* and *A New Kind of Family*. She is the wife of actor Robert Pine of *CHiPs* and played his wife on the series. Robert Vincent Wright wrote scripts for *Bonanza, Little House on the Prairie,* and *Voyage to the Bottom of the Sea*.

Jaekel. February 1, 1971. Production #0420. Rerun June 26, 1972.

Carl Jaekel is paroled from prison, only to find that his fiancee, Beth, is married and is the mother of a little girl. Not knowing how to break it off, Beth Wilson wrote to Carl every day for ten years telling him she loved him and would wait for his return. When Carl discovers the truth of the situation, he threatens the lives of Beth's daughter and her husband, unless she agrees to go away with him.

The Television Programs

Carl Jaekel	Eric Braeden
Beth Wilson	Julie Gregg
Penny Wilson	Mia Bendixen
Norman Wilson	John Crawford
Dirks	Victor Tayback
Warden	James Chandler
Doctor	Scott Edmonds
Guard	Bob Golden
Story	True Boardman
Script, Executive Story Consultant	Calvin Clements
Director	Bernard McEveety
Producer	Leonard Katzman
Executive Producer	John Mantley

Eric Braeden (formerly Hans Gudegast) was a regular on *The Rat Patrol* and *The Young and the Restless*. Julie Gregg was featured on *Banyon* and *Mobile One*. James Chandler appeared in the comedy pilot of *The Miss and the Missiles*. He also starred in the syndicated drama *The Tracer*, back in 1957. On television, Bob Golden appeared in *Fools, Female and Fun: I've Gotta Be Me*. True Boardman wrote scripts for *Perry Mason*. His father, True Boardman, Sr., was the star of early action films and serials from 1915–1918 and his mother, Virginia True Boardman, was also a film star.

Murdock. February 8, 1971. Production #0419. Rerun June 25, 1973.

Lucas Murdock is a raw, self-assured U.S. marshal. His quest to capture a gang of outlaws leads him to Dodge, where Matt agrees to help him. Murdock spreads information about a large gold shipment, in an effort to smoke out the bandits. The two marshals work together preparing the capture, until Murdock discovers that his son, Scott, is one of the outlaws.

Lucas Murdock	Jack Elam
Scott	Bob Random
Amos Carver	Jim Davis
Townsend	Anthony Caruso
Lonny	Clint Howard
Morris	Tom Waters
Braly	Tim Burns
Ruth	Liz Marshall
Gatlin	Bobby Clark
Fairchild	Gary Combs
Story, Script	Jack Miller
Executive Story Consultant	Calvin Clements
Director	Robert Totten
Producer	Leonard Katzman
Executive Producer	John Mantley

As a child, Clint Howard was featured on *The Baileys of Balboa, Gentle Ben,* and *The Cowboys*. His older brother is actor-director-producer Ron Howard.

Cleavus. February 15, 1971. Production #0424. Rerun March 20, 1972.

Cleavus Lukens, a tired and weary vagabond, accidentally kills prospector Uriah Spessard. Cleavus then relieves old Uriah of his gold and his mule, and then journeys to Dodge where he poses as a rich prospector. While in town, Cleavus gets reacquainted with his childhood friend, Festus, and decides to court Miss Kitty. However, Kitty is not interested in Cleavus, no matter how wealthy he claims to be.

GUNSMOKE — III. THE PROGRAMS

Cleavus Lukens	Robert Totten
Uriah Spessard	Arthur Hunnicutt
Baylock	William Challee
Clerk	Robert Cornthwaite
Woody	Robert B. Williams
Waiter	Henry Wise
Story, Script	Donald Z. Koplowitz & Richard D. Scott
Executive Story Consultant	Calvin Clements
Director	Vincent McEveety
Producer	Leonard Katzman
Executive Producer	John Mantley

Arthur Hunnicutt appeared on *Elfego Baca*, a ten episode segment of *Walt Disney Presents*, and *Kilroy*, a four-part *Walt Disney Presents*. In films Hunnicutt played numerous character roles in such features as *The Red Badge of Courage*, *The Cardinal*, *Cat Ballou*, and *Harry and Tonto*.

Lavery. February 22, 1971. Production #0421.

While heading to Dodge, Keith Lavery's horse goes lame. He takes Mr. Arno's old broken down work horse and leaves his $80 mare behind in trade. However, Arno does not perceive it to be a trade. He shoots Lavery for being a horse thief. Lavery gets away and takes refuge with his wife April. With five years of probation hanging over his head, the last thing Lavery needs is to be caught for being a horse thief. While recovering in April's room Lavery sees a man about to ambush Matt. Without thinking, the young parolee shoots, thus saving Matt's life. Feeling naturally grateful for the rescue, Matt squares things away with Arno and gets Lavery a job in a tannery. The young man's life starts to look bright. His pregnant wife can stop working at the Long Branch and they can finally settle down. However, when his ex-partners arrive in town, his luck starts to fade. Lavery, always a dreamer, wants a better life than a "nickel and dime existence," and his friends fill his mind full of empty promises. Later when the tannery is robbed, Lavery is charged with the crime.

Keith Lavery	Anthony Costello
April	Judi West
Clint	David Carradine
Mr. Hubert	Karl Swenson
Harry	Ken Swofford
Arno	David Huddleston
Verna	Chanin Hale
Trapper	Jack Perkins
Hank	Hank Patterson
Story, Script	Donald S. Sanford
Executive Story Consultant	Calvin Clements
Director	Vincent McEveety
Producer	Leonard Katzman
Executive Producer	John Mantley

David Carradine is part of a famous show business family. His father is actor John Carradine and his half-brothers Keith and Robert are also prominent actors. On television Carradine starred in *Shane*, *Kung Fu*, and *North and South*. His films include *Bus Riley's Back in Town*, *Bound for Glory*, and *The Serpent's Egg*. Character actor David Huddleston was featured in *Tenafly*, *Petrocelli*, and *How the West Was Won*. His films include *All the Way Home*, *A Lovely Way to Die*, and *Rio Lobo*. Chanin Hale was a regular

The Television Programs

on *The Red Skelton Show*. Jack Perkins appeared on *The Circle Family* and the short-lived comedy series, *The Hero*. Writer Donald S. Sanford also scripted for *Bonanza*, *The F.B.I.*, *The Outer Limits*, *Perry Mason*, and *Wagon Train*.

Pike [Part I]. March 1, 1971. Production #0422. Rerun April 10, 1972 and December 31, 1973.

Pike, wounded while robbing a freight office in Dodge, steals the money from his fellow outlaws, and escapes into the desert. Whiskey swigging, dirty Sally Fergus, finds Pike unconscious and near death. She brings him back to her shack and tries to nurse the young outlaw back to health.

Pike [Part II]. March 8, 1971. Production #0423. Rerun April 17, 1972 and January 7, 1974.

Sally removes two bullets from Pike's shoulder, but is forced to go to Dodge to seek medical advice. Once there she learns that Pike is an escaped convict. When Sally returns home she finds Pike desperately ill. She continues caring for him despite her new knowledge. Having barely escaped death and still quite weak, Pike takes off. When his former partners discover Sally's shack and one of Pike's shirts, they threaten her with death, unless she tells them Pike's whereabouts.

Sally Fergus	Jeanette Nolan
Cyrus Pike	Dack Rambo
Tom Macomb	Cliff Osmond
Loomis	William Murphy
Hicks	Ross Hagen
Hawkins	William Mims
Sutro	Jim Boles
Billy	Jon Jason Mantley
Girl #1	Maria Mantley
Boy #1	John Puglia
Girl #2	Susan Newmark
Boy #2	Billy McMickle
Story, Script	Jack Miller
Executive Story Consultant	Calvin Clements
Director	Bernard McEveety
Producer	Leonard Katzman
Executive Producer	John Mantley

This two-parter received the greatest mail response in *Gunsmoke* history and spurred the spin-off series, *Dirty Sally,* which aired on CBS-TV January 1974. Jeanette Nolan recreated the role of Sally Fergus in another *Gunsmoke* episode *One for the Road* January 24, 1972. *Pike* won an award for Outstanding Western Episode from the Cowboy Hall of Fame. It also won for Jack Miller an award for Best Western Television Script from the Western Writers of America. Jim Boles played Joe Yarborough on *One Man's Family* and was a regular on *Kraft Music Hall Presents: The Dave King Show*.

Waco. March 15, 1971, rerun. First aired December 9, 1968.

The Whispering Tree. March 22, 1971, rerun. First aired November 12, 1966.

The Money Store. March 29, 1971, rerun. First aired December 30, 1968.

The Long Night. April 5, 1971, rerun. First aired February 17, 1969.

GUNSMOKE — III. THE PROGRAMS

Nitro [Part I]. April 12, 1971, rerun. First aired April 8, 1967.

Nitro [Part II]. April 19, 1971, rerun. First aired April 15, 1967.

Prairie Wolfer. April 26, 1971, rerun. First aired November 13, 1967.

9:12 to Dodge. May 3, 1971, rerun. First aired November 11, 1968.

The Good People. May 10, 1971, rerun. First aired October 15, 1966.

The Miracle Man. May 17, 1971, rerun. First aired December 2, 1968.

Saturday Night. May 24, 1971, rerun. First aired January 7, 1967.

Blood Money. May 31, 1971, rerun. First aired January 22, 1968.

The Newcomers. June 7, 1971, rerun. First aired December 3, 1966.

Lobo. June 14, 1971, rerun. First aired December 16, 1968.

Major Glory. June 21, 1971, rerun. First aired October 30, 1967.

The Jailor. June 28, 1971, rerun. First aired October 1, 1966.

The Good Samaritans. July 5, 1971, rerun. First aired March 10, 1969.

The Twisted Heritage. July 12, 1971, rerun. First aired January 6, 1969.

Uncle Finney. July 19, 1971, rerun. First aired October 14, 1968.

Snap Decision. July 26, 1971, rerun. First aired September 17, 1966.

The Hidecutters. August 2, 1971, rerun. First aired September 30, 1968.

The Wrong Man. August 9, 1971, rerun. First aired October 29, 1966.

Lyle's Kid. August 16, 1971, rerun. First aired September 23, 1968.

Abelia. August 23, 1971, rerun. First aired November 18, 1968.

The Mark of Cain. August 30, 1971, rerun. First aired February 3, 1969.

Mannon. September 6, 1971, rerun. First aired January 20, 1969.

SEVENTEENTH SEASON

New time Monday nights at 8:00 p.m.

The Lost. September 13, 1971. Production #0512. Rerun June 4, 1973.
   Kitty is injured in a stagecoach accident and is forced to rely on a strange feral child

The Television Programs

to help her survive. When they finally reach civilization, new perils await them. They arrive at the Mather ranch, where the two encounter Mrs. Mather, an opportunistic frontier woman, and her bizarre family.

Mrs. Mather	Mercedes McCambridge
Girl	Laurie Prange
Henry Mather	Royal Dano
Lamond Mather	Link Wyler
Valjean Mather	Charles Kuenstle
Mrs. Grayson	Dee Carroll
Will Roniger	Harry Carey, Jr.
Mrs. Roniger	Peggy Rea
Stage Driver	Jerry Brown
Boy Jon	Jon Jason Mantley
Girls	Maria Mantley, Heather Cotton
Story	Warren Vanders
Script, Executive Story Consultant	Jack Miller
Director	Robert Totten
Associate Producer	Ron Honthaner
Producer	Leonard Katzman
Executive Producer	John Mantley

The story for this episode, originally titled *The Wild Child*, was suggested by Warren Vanders, who had been a frequent performer on *Gunsmoke*. Mercedes McCambridge, had an active career on radio in the 40s. On television she appeared as a regular on *One Man's Family* and *Wire Service*. Her film credits include *All the King's Men*, *Giant*, *A Farewell to Arms*, *Angel Baby*, *Suddenly Last Summer*, and the voice of Regan in *The Exorcist*. Laurie Prange appeared on numerous programs including *Night Gallery* and *Testimony of Two Men*.

Phoenix. September 20, 1971. Production #0503. Rerun May 14, 1973.

Upon his release from prison, Phoenix accepts a contract from a fellow inmate to take the life of Jesse Hume. Hume, a man Phoenix has never even met, is a retired lawman who is living a quiet life with his young wife. Phoenix manages to get a job at Hume's ranch, but finds his position as executioner compromised as he becomes friends with his intended victim and his wife.

Phoenix	Glenn Corbett
Kate Hume	Mariette Hartley
Jesse Hume	Gene Evans
Sontag	Ramon Bieri
Fraker	Frank Corsentino
Story, Script	Anthony Lawrence
Executive Story Consultant	Jack Miller
Director	Paul Stanley
Associate Producer	Ron Honthaner
Producer	Leonard Katzman
Executive Producer	John Mantley

Writer Anthony Lawrence contributed scripts to such television series as *Ben Casey*, *Bonanza*, *Hawaii Five-O*, *Naked City*, and *Route 66*.

Waste [Part I]. September 27, 1971. Production #0511. Rerun March 12, 1973 and August 19, 1974.

GUNSMOKE — III. THE PROGRAMS

Fugitive Ben Rodman is being pursued by Matt through the desert. Before meeting up with his gang, Ben stops for water and shoots an old man. Matt arrives in time to hear the old man's last request and promises to take Willie Hubbard, his young grandson, to find his mother who he has not seen in six years. The two meet up with a wagon load of Maggie Blaisedell's saloon women and, unbeknownst to Maggie's girls, several sacks of gold dust. One of the women, Amy Waters, claims that she knew Willie's mother back in Table Flats, and that she is "dead."

Waste [Part II]. October 4, 1971. Production #0511. Rerun aired March 19, 1973 and August 26, 1974.

Ben and his outlaw gang find out about the gold dust and track the wagon. Maggie, who was once in love with Ben does not know if she could shoot him if it came to that. In the meantime, Matt discovers that Amy is really Sarah Hubbard, Willie's mother. When the outlaws finally meet up with the wagon, Matt and his charges are held up in a dusty old fort without food or water. Ben and his men decide to play a waiting game, "perched out there like a bunch of buzzards."

Maggie Blaisedell	Ruth Roman
Ben Rodman	Jeremy Slate
Amy Waters	Ellen Burstyn
Willie Hubbard	Johnnie Whitaker
Preacher	David Sheiner
Victoria	Lieux Dressler
Jed Rascoe	Shug Fisher
Oakley	Rex Holman
Additional Cast	Merry Anders
Story, Script	Jim Byrnes
Executive Story Consultant	Jack Miller
Director	Vincent McEveety
Associate Producer	Ron Honthaner
Producer	Leonard Katzman
Executive Producer	John Mantley

David Sheiner was a regular on *Mr. Novak* and *Diana.* Lieux Dressler appeared on such television shows as *The Blue Knight, Return of the World's Greatest Detective,* and *General Hospital.* On television Merry Anders was a regular on *The Stu Erwin Show, It's Always Jan,* and *How to Marry a Millionaire.*

New Doctor in Town. October 11, 1971. Production #0505. Rerun July 3, 1972.

Doc leaves Dodge unexpectedly, without even a good-bye. His sudden departure follows the death of a little girl Doc thinks he could have saved. Unable to shake his guilt, Doc returns to medical school. During his absence, he sends Dr. Chapman to fill his shoes. However, Chapman is not welcomed with open arms. He faces suspicion and mistrust from the townspeople and especially from Festus. The new doctor is soon confronted with a severe test when Newly is badly injured in an accident.

Dr. John Chapman	Pat Hingle
Dump Hart	Lane Bradford
Cody Sims	Jon Lormer
Sam	Glenn Strange
Burke	Ted Jordan
Lathrop	Woodrow Chambliss
Ma Smalley	Sarah Selby

The Television Programs

Halligan	Charles Wagenheim
Story, Script	Jack Miller
Executive Story Consultant	Jack Miller
Director	Philip Leacock
Producer	Leonard Katzman
Executive Producer	John Mantley

Pat Hingle filled in for Milburn Stone, while Stone was recovering from open heart surgery. This episode introduces the character of Dr. Chapman as played by Hingle. Interestingly, there was a Dr. Chapman that practiced medicine in Kansas in the late 1880s, who was a pioneer of new methodology and was instrumental in up-grading the level of medical care in the area. On television Hingle played Chief Paulton on the police drama, *Stone*. Hingle, an excellent character actor, appeared frequently on the Broadway stage. His film credits include *On the Waterfront, Splendor in the Grass, The Ugly American, Norma Rae,* and most recently *Batman*.

The Legend. October 18, 1971. Production #0507. Rerun August 7, 1972.

Bea Colter, the mother of two notorious outlaws, tries to steer her youngest son, Travis, into a law-abiding life. However, Bea is up against great odds. Her late husband, also a notorious outlaw, is the subject of numerous tabloids and songs. Keeping the legend alive, also keeps the fear alive. Although he attempts to get an honest job, young Travis finds that the prejudices of the people of Dodge force him into seeking out his fugitive brothers.

Bea Colter	Kim Hunter
Travis Colter	Jan-Michael Vincent
Clayt Colter	Richard D. Kelton
Virgil Colter	Greg Mullavey
Slater	Lloyd Nelson
Prairie Scavenger	Pat Dennis-Leigh
Bull	Victor Izay
Dr. Chapman	Pat Hingle
Slim	Michael Greene
Eddie	Read Morgan
Mr. Palmer	Bryan O'Byrne
Farmer	Ken Mayer
Carro	Red Currie
Workman	Dick Cangey
Story, Script	Calvin Clements, Jr.
Executive Story Consultant	Jack Miller
Director	Philip Leacock
Associate Producer	Ron Honthaner
Producer	Leonard Katzman
Executive Producer	John Mantley

On television Kim Hunter played Ellen Wilson on *Backstairs at the White House*. Primarily a movie actress, Hunter appeared in such films as *Planet of the Apes, Storm Center,* and *Streetcar Named Desire,* for which she won an Academy Award for her performance as Stella. Jan-Michael Vincent appeared in *The Survivors, The Winds of War,* and *Airwolf*. His films include *Buster and Billie, Baby Blue Marine,* and *Hooper*. Greg Mullavey was a regular on *Mary Hartman, Mary Hartman, Number 96,* and *Rituals*. Bryan O'Byrne appeared on the comedy, *Occasional Wife*.

GUNSMOKE — III. THE PROGRAMS

Trafton. October 25, 1971. Production #0504. Rerun September 4, 1972.

Trafton, a gunslinger, attempts to rob the freight office of Cascabelle, New Mexico. When the safe turns out to be empty, Trafton heads for the church where he steals the gold chalices and crosses from the altar. Interrupted in the act by the priest, Trafton turns and shoots. "I forgive you," the priest utters, and with his own blood he makes the sign of the cross on Trafton's forehead before he dies. Upon his exit from town Trafton kills sheriff Niles and continues his trail of bloodshed. However, he soon begins to lose his edge. Trafton, who used to kill a man with no more thought than "squashing a beetle" now realizes his killing days are over, and that he is "not going to last very long." Not understanding what is happening to him, Trafton touches his forehead and turns his trail toward Dodge for final retribution. Once there he comes face to face with the woman he raped 12 years earlier and the little girl he fathered.

Trafton	Victor French
Capps	Clay Tapper
Brant	Bill Catching
Prew	Fred Stromoe
Tereese Farrell	Sharon Acker
Priest	John Dullaghan
Whale	Mike Mazurki
Mary K	Marie Windsor
Bannion	Philip Carey
Storekeeper	Jon Lormer
Reverend English	Paul Stevens
Maria Farrell	Patti Cohoon
Manuel	Manuel Padilla, Jr.
Story, Script	Ron Bishop
Executive Story Consultant	Jack Miller
Director	Bernard McEveety
Associate Producer	Ron Honthaner
Producer	Leonard Katzman
Executive Producer	John Mantley

Sharon Acker was on *The Senator, Executive Suite,* and the *Perry Mason* 1973 revival series. Former wrestler Mike Mazurki appeared on television in *It's About Time* and *Chicago Teddy Bears.* Marie Windsor starred in numerous B-features and Westerns including *Dakota Lil, Hellfire,* and *Cat Women of the Moon.* Philip Carey was a regular on several television shows including *Tales of the 77th Bengal Lancers, Philip Marlowe, Laredo,* and more recently, *One Life to Live.* Patti Cohoon was featured on *Here Comes the Brides, Apple's Way,* and *The Runaways.*

Lynott. November 1, 1971. Production #0509. Rerun August 14, 1972.

Ex-marshal, Tom Lynott, saves Matt's life. While Matt is confined to bed recovering from his wounds, Lynott agrees to fill in as marshal. However, he takes a permissive attitude toward lawlessness in town and Matt must ultimately leave his sickbed, when a gang threatens Lynott and the safety of Dodge.

Tom Lynott	Richard Kiley
Pene Lynott	Peggy McCay
Talley	Anthony Caruso
Additional Cast	Jonathan Lippe
Story, Script	Ron Bishop
Executive Story Consultant	Jack Miller

The Television Programs

Director	Gunnar Hellstrom
Associate Producer	Ron Honthaner
Producer	Leonard Katzman
Executive Producer	John Mantley

Lijah. November 8, 1971. Production #0506. Rerun July 24, 1972.

Lijah, a stern but gentle mountain man, is accused of three brutal murders. When brought to trial, Lijah says nothing in his defense. In fact, he spends all his time staring at one member of the jury, Doctor Chapman. Although Chapman does not recall ever seeing Lijah before, his silent plea for help forces Chapman to do some investigating on his own.

Lijah	Denny Miller
Howie	Howard Culver
Ed O'Connor	Tom Brown
Dump Hart	Lane Bradford
Rachel	Erin Moran
Dr. Chapman	Pat Hingle
Hale Parker	Harry Townes
Will Standish	William Wintersole
Judge Brooker	Herb Vigran
Frank	Pete Kellett
Tack	Dan Flynn, Jr.
Hank	Henry Wise
Story, Script	William Blinn
Executive Story Consultant	Jack Miller
Director	Irving J. Moore
Associate Producer	Ron Honthaner
Producer	Leonard Katzman
Executive Producer	John Mantley

Denny (Scott) Miller played Duke Shannon on *Wagon Train* and Mike McCluskey on *Mona McCluskey*. Erin Moran grew up on front of the television camera in such shows as *Daktari*, *Happy Days*, and *Joanie Loves Chachi*. William Wintersole was featured in the short-lived series *Sara*.

My Brother's Keeper. November 15, 1971. Production #0508. Rerun July 31, 1972.

Seeking refuge from a storm, Festus stumbles into a cave where he encounters an old Indian who has obviously been brought there to die. After the storm abates, Festus brings the Indian back to Dodge. Matt and Doctor Chapman strongly object to Festus' interference, however, Kitty is proud of his actions. Despite the apprehensions of Matt and Chapman, the constitution of the old Indian seems to improve, until an angry buffalo hunter goes after him with a knife.

Indian	John Dierkes
Cobb	Malcolm Atterbury
Sarah	Pippa Scott
Squaw Man	Charles McGraw
Dr. Chapman	Pat Hingle
Story, Script	Arthur Dales
Executive Story Consultant	Jack Miller
Director	Paul Stanley
Associate Producer	Ron Honthaner

GUNSMOKE — III. THE PROGRAMS

Producer .... Leonard Katzman
Executive Producer .... John Mantley

Drago. November 22, 1971. Production #0510. Rerun July 17, 1972.

For the past two years Drago, an old trail blazing mountain man, has been working as a hired hand for Miss Clara and her little boy. While Drago is off fishing, a gang of horse thieves kill Clara and seriously injure the boy. Matt, obliged to go to Hayes City, deputizes Drago to head a posse to track down the murderers. However, according to Drago, "posses are slow and noisy," so he branches off from the rest of the men with only his dog, Hound. One by one he picks off the outlaws. Newly, afraid that Drago is taking the law into his own hands, joins the old scout in his pursuit.

Drago .... Buddy Ebsen
Hannon .... Ben Johnson
Ruben .... Mitchell Silberman
Flagg .... Del Monroe
Trask .... Edward Faulkner
Gillis .... Rick Gates
Dr. Chapman .... Pat Hingle
Clara .... Tani Phelps Guthrie
Sheepherder .... Jim Skaggs
Larry .... Larry Randles
Story, Script .... Jim Brynes
Executive Story Consultant .... Jack Miller
Director .... Paul Stanley
Associate Producer .... Ron Honthaner
Producer .... Leonard Katzman
Executive Producer .... John Mantley

Del Monroe was a regular on *Voyage to the Bottom of the Sea*. Jim Skaggs appeared on television in *The Best of Friends*. Rick Gates appeared on *The Hardy Boys*. Featured in this episode was Rote, a six-year-old rottweiler. Rote's trainer, Ralph McCutcheon said, "He's very sensitive. If you do anything to reproach him, it breaks his heart."

Gold Train: The Bullet [Part I]. November 29, 1971. Production #0514. Rerun aired July 16, 1973.

Matt is bushwhacked on the streets of Dodge and is wounded. He will either die or become paralyzed, unless the bullet is removed from an area near his spine. It is too delicate an operation to be done in Doc's office so Matt is put on a train for Denver. Festus, Newly, and Kitty accompany Doc and Matt on the perilous journey. While he lies helpless in a railroad car, an outlaw band stops the train in an effort to steal an army gold shipment.

Gold Train: The Bullet [Part II]. December 6, 1971. Production #0515. Rerun July 23, 1973.

Festus and Newly overpower the outlaws guarding the stolen gold and ride off with a wagon load of the loot. The decoy leads the gang away from the railroad car, where Matt lies critically wounded. While the outlaws battle Festus and Newly, Doc fears Matt is losing his battle against death and Kitty is afraid that Matt's identity will be revealed, which would put him in additional peril.

Gold Train: The Bullet [Part III]. December 13, 1971. Production #0516. Rerun July 30, 1973.

The Television Programs

The band of outlaws learn that Matt is aboard the train and go gunning for the gravely wounded marshal. Doc faces a critical decision as to whether he should operate on Matt. Unable to avoid the inevitable, Doc operates to remove the bullet as Kitty assists.

Sinclaire	Eric Braeden
Father Sanchez	Alejandro Rey
Beth	Katherine Justice
Captain Darnell	Robert Hogan
Secos	Pepe Callahan
Allie	Sian Barbara Allen
Conductor	Warren Kemmerling
Caldwell	Walter Sande
Kelliher	Harry Carey, Jr.
Nebo	Sam Melville
Orley	Eddie Firestone
Concho	Robert Sorrells
Blanchard	John Crawford
Roper	Jonathan Lippe
Pony	Mills Watson
Drummer	Harry Harvey, Sr.
Harper	Dan Ferrone
Story, Script	Jim Byrnes
Executive Story Consultant	Jack Miller
Director	Bernard McEveety
Associate Producer	Ron Honthaner
Producer	Leonard Katzman
Executive Producer	John Mantley

This three-parter marks the return of Milburn Stone as Doc Adams. Alejandro Rey was a regular on *Slattery's People*, *The Flying Nun*, and *Dallas*. Sian Barbara Allen appeared in numerous made-for-television movies including *The Lindbergh Kidnapping Case* and *Smash-Up on Interstate 5*. *Gold Train* used a 19th-century train that once hauled millions in gold out of the great Comstock Lode in California. In 1971 it was operated by the Sierra Railway Company.

Sam McTavish, M.D. December 20, 1971, rerun. First aired October 5, 1970.

P.S. Murry Christmas. December 27, 1971. Production #0513.

When their only grown-up advocate, Titus Spangler, is fired "for flagrant immorality," seven children run away from their Kansas orphanage. The children accompany Titus and get as far as Dodge City. The youngsters are cold and hungry, so Titus goes into town to steal some food. Festus catches the culprit and locks him up. In the meantime, stern Emma Grundy, the head of the orphanage, arrives in town with legal documents to reclaim her charges. According to Miss Grundy, Titus is an "insensitive, ne'er-do-well" and a kidnapper. According to Titus, Miss Grundy is an "abominable wretch" who refuses to let the children celebrate Christmas. At any rate, the people of Dodge are determined to give the children a Christmas that they will never forget. Kitty plans a special party at the Long Branch, but Grundy refuses to give permission for the children to attend. Undaunted, Kitty discovers Miss Grundy's weakness for brandy, and gets her intoxicated, an act she later regrets.

Emma Grundy	Jeanette Nolan

GUNSMOKE — III. THE PROGRAMS

Titus Spangler	Jack Elam
Mary	Patti Cohoon
Patricia	Jodie Foster
Jenny	Eric Moran
Michael	Josh Albee
Owen	Brian Morrison
Tom	Willie Aames
Jake	Todd Lookinland
Story, Script	William Kelley
Executive Story Consultant	Jack Miller
Director	Herb Wallerstein
Associate Producer	Ron Honthaner
Producer	Leonard Katzman
Executive Producer	John Mantley

Although it's only a Christmas peck on the cheek, Matt finally gets an on screen kiss from Kitty. Josh Albee appeared on *Lassie*. Brian Morrison was a regular on *Maude*. Willie Aames was featured on several series including *Swiss Family Robinson*, *Eight Is Enough*, and *Charles in Charge*. Todd Lookinland appeared in *The New Land*.

No Tomorrow. January 3, 1972. Production #0517. Rerun May 28, 1973.

Ben Justin, an honest, hardworking rancher, with a baby on the way, is framed by a neighbor for horse stealing. Hoping to take over Justin's land, the greedy rancher testifies against Justin at the trial. Convicted and sent to prison, Justin overpowers a sadistic guard and escapes. While the guard is still groggy from the attack, another prisoner stabs him. A tyrannical prosecutor vows to catch Justin, who now has a murder charge hanging over him. Although Matt believes he is innocent, he and Festus are forced to track down Justin and his family.

Ben Justin	Sam Groom
Elizabeth	Pamela McMyler
Morris Cragin	H.M. Wynant
Garth Brantley	Steve Brodie
J. Luther Cross	Henry Jones
Old Luke	Richard Hale
Judge Brooker	Herb Vigran
Eli Bruder	Liam Dunn
Warden	Robert Nichols
Rider	Joe Haworth
Hargis	Leo Gordon
Kyle Brantley	Dan Flynn
Bailiff	Allan Fudge
Story, Script	Richard Fielder
Executive Story Consultant	Jack Miller
Director	Irving J. Moore
Associate Producer	Ron Honthaner
Producer	Leonard Katzman
Executive Producer	John Mantley

On television Sam Groom starred in *Our Private World*, *Dr. Simon Locke*, and *Otherworld*. Liam Dunn appeared as a regular on *Captain Nice*, *The Queen and I*, and *Diana*. Allan Fudge was featured on *Man from Atlantis*, *Eischied*, and *Paper Dolls*.

The Television Programs

Hidalgo. January 10, 1972. Production #0501.
After trailing fugitive Mando from Kansas to Chihuahua, Matt is gunned down by Mando's gang and left to die. Critically injured, Matt is found by little Lucho. The boy and his old grandfather bring Matt to their home and try to nurse him back to health. Without medicine Matt is certain to die, so Lucho goes into town to ask his sister Lucero for money. Lucero helps her little brother, despite the fact that she is Mando's woman. When Mando learns that Matt is alive and being cared for, he prepares to kill them all.

Mando	Alfonso Arau
Augustin	Thomas Gomez
Lucho	Fabian Gregory
Lucero	Linda Marsh
Chona	Stella Garcia
Gorio	David Renard
Fermin	Julio Medina
Cuero	Edward Colmans
Story, Script	Colley Cibber
Executive Story Consultant	Jack Miller
Director	Paul Stanley
Associate Producer	Ron Honthaner
Producer	Leonard Katzman
Executive Producer	John Mantley

On television Thomas Gomez was seen in *Caesar and Cleopatra, Life With Luigi,* and *The Rifleman.* Stella Garcia appeared on the television show *Kraft Suspense Theater: Rapture at Two-Forty,* which was the pilot film for *Run for Your Life.* Linda Marsh appeared on *The Facts of Life.* Edward Colmans was seen in the television pilot *Tonight in Havana* for *Colgate Theater,* which starred Ricardo Montalban. Colley Cibber also wrote for *The Mississippi* and *The Yellow Rose,* which starred Ken Curtis.

Tara. January 17, 1972. Production #0522. Rerun April 9, 1973.
Newly is attracted to a vivacious young woman named Tara. Unaware that the lovely lady has a crimson past, which includes a husband in jail for robbery, Newly attempts to court her. However, Tara's past closes in on her in the form of Gecko Ridley, who has murdered her husband and is now looking for the missing money. Tara, anxious to keep the money herself, turns to Newly for protection.

Tara Hutson	Michele Carey
Gecko Ridley	L.Q. Jones
Roy Hutson	Laurence Delaney
Story, Script	William Kelley
Executive Story Consultant	Jack Miller
Director	Bernard McEveety
Associate Producer	Ron Honthaner
Producer	Leonard Katzman
Executive Producer	John Mantley

Michele Carey was the voice of Effie the computer on the dramatic program *A Man Called Sloane.* She also appeared on such programs as *Death Ray 2000, Mission: Impossible,* and *The Six Million Dollar Man.*

One for the Road. January 24, 1972. Production #0520.
Eccentric millionaire Lucius Prince, a drunken old wanderer, tries to elude his

GUNSMOKE — III. THE PROGRAMS

granddaughter Elsie and her trigger happy boyfriend, Tom Rickaby. While escaping from their clutches, he meets up with salty old Sally Fergus. In the course of their inebriated journey, Prince suffers the twin indignities of a sanity hearing and an attempt on his life at the hands of Rickaby, who wants the old man's money.

Lucius Prince................................Jack Albertson
Sally Fergus.................................Jeanette Nolan
Tom Rickaby................................Victor Holchak
Miss Elsie..................................Melissa Murphy
Judge Brooker..............................Herb Vigran
Old Woman................................Dorothy Neumann
Bouncer....................................Jack Perkins
Story, Script................................Jack Miller
Executive Story Consultant....................Jack Miller
Director...................................Bernard McEveety
Associate Producer..........................Ron Honthaner
Producer...................................Leonard Katzman
Executive Producer..........................John Mantley

Jeanette Nolan recreates her role as Sally Fergus, originally seen in the two-part episode *Pike*.

The Predators. January 31, 1972. Production #0518.

Two predators converge on Abelia's ranch almost simultaneously. First, her children's dog Dobie, who was a pup when he ran away, is back three years later. After living in the wild all these years, he has become a killer. The other is Howard Kane, an ex-gunman seeking revenge. Kane has spent the past four years hunting for Cole Matson, who double-crossed him back in Midland during a savage range war.

Howard Kane...............................Claude Akins
Abelia.....................................Jacqueline Scott
Ed O'Connor...............................Tom Brown
Marieanne.................................Jodie Foster
Jonathan..................................Brian Morrison
Cole Matson...............................George Murdock
Currie.....................................Mills Watson
Smith.....................................Lew Brown
Brown.....................................Read Morgan
Story, Script................................Calvin Clements
Executive Story Consultant....................Jack Miller
Director...................................Bernard McEveety
Associate Producer..........................Ron Honthaner
Producer...................................Leonard Katzman
Executive Producer..........................John Mantley

This is the third time the character of Abelia has appeared. The previous episodes were *Abelia*, and *A Man Called Smith*. Once again Jacqueline Scott plays Abelia.

Yankton. February 7, 1972. Production #0521. Rerun August 28, 1972.

A young drifter named Yankton swears to get revenge on wealthy rancher Donovan, for wiping him out in a poker game. Yankton plans on wooing Donovan's daughter, a plain looking, vulnerable young woman. The tables are turned, however, as Yankton falls in love with his prey.

Yankton...................................James Stacy

[680]

The Television Programs

Will Donavan	Forrest Tucker
Henrietta Donavan	Nancy Olson
Emma Donavan	Pamela Payton-Wright
Hank	Hank Patterson
Dressmaker	Margaret Bacon
Pete	Tom Sutton
Cowboy #1	Bill Hart
Cowboy #2	Bennie Dobbins
Story, Script	Jim Byrnes
Executive Story Consultant	Jack Miller
Director	Vincent McEveety
Associate Producer	Ron Honthaner
Producer	Leonard Katzman
Executive Producer	John Mantley

Nancy Olson was a regular on *Kingston: Confidential* and *Paper Dolls*.

Blind Man's Buff. February 21, 1972. Production #0519.

Two drifters, Charlie and Hank, ambush a man for his money, horse, and boots. Thinking him dead, the two leave him for the buzzards. Phoebe Preston, a lonely spinster, finds the wounded stranger, who has lost his memory due to the attack. Phoebe is used to caring for a man, having lost her father only last year, and she savors the chance to feel needed again. Phoebe takes this opportunity, probably the only one she will ever have, to obtain a husband. She tells the stranger that he is Jed Frazer, and that they are newlyweds.

Phoebe Preston	Anne Jackson
Jed Frazer	Victor French
Charlie Clavin	George Lindsey
Hank McCall	Charles Kuenstle
Story, Script	Ron Honthaner
Executive Story Consultant	Jack Miller
Director	Herb Wallerstein
Associate Producer	Ron Honthaner
Producer	Leonard Katzman
Executive Producer	John Mantley

Ron Honthaner, who wrote this episode, was an associate producer for *Gunsmoke*. He also produced the *Gunsmoke* spin-off, *Dirty Sally*.

February 28, 1972, preempted for *Appointment with Destiny*.

Alias Festus Haggin. March 6, 1972. Production #0523.

Because Festus bears an uncanny likeness to wanted murderer Frank Eaton, the deputy is arrested and deported for trial to a neighboring town. Believing that the real Frank Eaton is dead, Matt hunts down Eaton's supposed "widow," to testify at Festus' trial. Unexpectedly, Mrs. Eaton quickly identifies Festus as the husband she thought dead, and an angry lynch mob gathers outside the jail.

Doyle	Ramon Bieri
Susie	Lieux Dressler
Walker	Robert Totten
Rand	Booth Colman
Guthrie	Gregg Palmer

GUNSMOKE — III. THE PROGRAMS

Bennett . . . . William Bryant
Grebbs . . . . Rayford Barnes
Judge Brooker . . . . Herb Vigran
Judge Clayborne . . . . Jon Lormer
Bailiff . . . . Bill Erwin
Luke . . . . Tom McFadden
Sheriff Buckley . . . . Rusty Lane
Scotty . . . . Ed McCready
Cowboy . . . . Louie Elias
Shorty . . . . Lloyd Nelson
Story, Script . . . . Calvin Clements
Executive Story Consultant . . . . Jack Miller
Director . . . . Vincent McEveety
Associate Producer . . . . Ron Honthaner
Producer . . . . Leonard Katzman
Executive Producer . . . . John Mantley

Tom McFadden played Hugh Cleveland on *The Winds of War*.

The Wedding. March 13, 1972. Production #0502.

Cory Soames and Donna Clayton are in love and want to marry. However, Donna's father is dead set against the union. Walt Clayton even goes so far as to accuse Soames of horse stealing, in an effort to eliminate the young man from his daughter's life. Soames is arrested on the trumped up charge and Matt is summoned to the town of Salt Flat to see that "justice" is served. When Clayton discovers that his daughter is in the "family way," he allows the marriage to proceed. Thinking that all is well, Soames tries to make peace with his new father-in-law. However, Clayton has no intention of letting Soames play the role of new husband. He informs the bridegroom that he is still going to jail for horse theft. The two argue and violence erupts. When Matt finally arrives, he finds himself enmeshed in the fiery vendetta. Soames, having escaped, is being hunted by Clayton's men, and Matt must keep them from killing the young man.

Walt Clayton . . . . Morgan Woodward
Cory Soames . . . . Sam Elliott
Donna Clayton . . . . Melissa Murphy
Reverend Keller . . . . James Chandler
Joe Eggers . . . . Lane Bradford
Mrs. Keller . . . . Fran Ryan
Townsman . . . . Larry Barton
Sheriff Henning . . . . George Wallace
Sandy Carr . . . . Byron Mabe
Pete Calder . . . . Troy Melton
Dr. Cleery . . . . Jason Wingreen
Story, Script . . . . Harry Kronman
Executive Story Consultant . . . . Jack Miller
Director . . . . Bernard McEveety
Associate Producer . . . . Ron Honthaner
Producer . . . . Leonard Katzman
Executive Producer . . . . John Mantley

Sam Elliot was featured in several television series including *Mission: Impossible, Once an Eagle, Aspen,* and *The Yellow Rose,* which also starred Ken Curtis. Fran Ryan,

The Television Programs

who plays the part of Mrs. Keller, was Miss Hannah, the owner of the Long Branch during the show's final season. Her other regular television appearances include *Green Acres, The Doris Day Show,* and *The Wizard.* Jason Wingreen was a regular on *The Rounders* and *All in the Family.*

Cleavus. March 20, 1972, rerun. First aired February 15, 1971.

March 27, 1972, preempted for *The Lost Vikings.*

Luke. April 3, 1972, rerun. First aired November 2, 1970.

Pike [Part I]. April 10, 1972, rerun. First aired March 1, 1971.

Pike [Part II]. April 17, 1972, rerun. First aired March 8, 1971.

April 24, 1972, preempted for *Appointment with Destiny.*

Chato. May 1, 1972, rerun. First aired September 14, 1970.

Stark. May 8, 1972, rerun. First aired September 28, 1970.

Snow Train [Part I]. May 15, 1972, rerun. First aired October 19, 1970.

Snow Train [Part II]. May 22, 1972, rerun. First aired October 26, 1970.

The Scavengers. May 29, 1972, rerun. First aired November 16, 1970.

The Witness. June 5, 1972, rerun. First aired November 23, 1970.

The Noose. June 12, 1972, rerun. First aired September 21, 1970.

Gentry's Law. June 19, 1972, rerun. First aired October 12, 1970.

Jaekel. June 26, 1972, rerun. First aired February 1, 1971.

New Doctor in Town. July 3, 1972, rerun. First aired October 11, 1971.

July 10, 1972, preempted for the Democratic National Convention.

Drago. July 17, 1972, rerun. First aired November 22, 1971.

Lijah. July 24, 1972, rerun. First aired November 8, 1971.

My Brother's Keeper. July 31, 1972, rerun. First aired November 15, 1971.

The Legend. August 7, 1972, rerun. First aired October 18, 1971.

Lynott. August 14, 1972, rerun. First aired November 1, 1971.

Yankton. August 28, 1972, rerun. First aired February 7, 1972.

Trafton. September 4, 1972, rerun. First aired October 25, 1971.

GUNSMOKE — III. THE PROGRAMS

EIGHTEENTH SEASON

The River [Part I]. September 11, 1972. Production #0560. Rerun April 16, 1972.

Charley Utter and his hard riding gang of outlaws have pulled a series or robberies. Having recovered the stolen money, Matt is forced into a shootout with the bandits once again. With hopeless odds, Matt makes a dangerous dive off a cliff into a turbulent river. He is pulled to safety by two runaway children aboard a raft.

The River [Part II]. September 18, 1972. Production #0561. Rerun April 23, 1972.

Utter and his notorious gang try to stop Matt and reclaim the stolen money by blocking his passage down the river. As the gang closes in, Matt faces a new threat. A Frenchman Matt had saved from a lynch mob, is signaling an unseen band of accomplices.

Charley Utter	Slim Pickens
Paulette	Miriam Colon
Tuttle Kinkaid	Clay O'Brien
Hannah Kinkaid	Patti Cohoon
Finn MacCool	Roger Torrey
Suggs	Read Morgan
Lapin	Jerry Gatlin
Additional Cast	Jack Elam
Story, Script	Jack Miller
Executive Story Consultant	Jack Miller
Director	Herb Wallerstein
Associate Producer	Ron Honthaner
Producer	Leonard Katzman
Executive Producer	John Mantley

Jerry Gatlin played Weedy in the television Western, *The Cowboys*.

Bohannan. September 25, 1972. Production #0555. Rerun March 26, 1972.

A faith healer named Bohannan travels the West ministering to a stream of supplicants and curing an occasional bout of colic or sciatica. At first, Doc considers Bohannan to be just another miracle worker, "the last refuge of an incurable scoundrel." But, as Doc soon discovers, Bohannan is different. He gives his followers the "ability to believe so strongly, that they can forget their pain." Although Doc does not encourage Bohannan's method of "laying on of hands," he does realize that the man is sincere and is not just trying to bilk the populace. In fact, Bohannan wishes that the Lord would "find someone else for this here job." His sojourn in Dodge brings the healer a most difficult challenge in the form of a charming youngster, Heck, who has taken a particular liking to Bohannan. Heck is suffering from the same hereditary, degenerative neuro-muscular disorder that killed his father seven years ago. Lydia Walden, Heck's desperate mother, begs Bohannan to try to weave his magic and cure her son but Bohannan refuses. Even her offer of $1200 does not sway him, for despite all of Bohannan's posturing and preaching, he "doesn't have the courage to risk failing."

Bohannan	Richard Kiley
Lydia Walden	Linda Marsh
Heck	Vincent Van Patten
Goody Stackpole	Ed Bakey
Dorcas Wentzel	Helen Kleeb

The Television Programs

Reverend	Rege Cordic
Story, Script	William Kelley
Executive Story Consultant	Jack Miller
Director	Alf Kjellin
Associate Producer	Ron Honthaner
Producer	Leonard Katzman
Executive Producer	John Mantley

Bohannan won for writer William Kelley the Spur Award for Best Western TV Script from the Western Writers of America. Vincent Van Patten, the son of actor Dick Van Patten, appeared on television on *Apple's Way* and *Three for the Road*.

The Judgement. October 2, 1972. Production #0553.

Musgrov is a man who "carries an awful powerful grudge." He arrives in Dodge looking for Ira Spratt. Spratt, a "little no account scum" who Musgrov considers to be "one of nature's mistakes," was Musgrov's Judas. When Musgrov deserted from the army, Spratt turned him in for a $25 reward. As a result, Musgrov was sentenced to five years in prison and had his chest branded. Now he is back to reap his revenge. He has already killed his judge and prosecutor and is willing to kill anyone else who stands in the way of Spratt's "judgement." Newly and Festus are in charge during Matt's absence, and when they attempt to intervene, Musgrov shoots them down "like they was tin cans." Spratt escapes Musgrov's clutches and takes refuge in rancher Gideon's barn. When Musgrov corners him, he once again gets away. Tired of tracking, Musgrov takes the good rancher hostage and issues an ultimatum. Unless Spratt is delivered to him by eight o'clock that evening, Gideon will be killed. Gideon, however, being a principled man, does not want the ransom to be paid.

Musgrov	Ramon Bieri
Ira Spratt	William Windom
Ena Spratt	Katherine Helmond
Gideon	Tim O'Connor
Fiona Gideon	Mariette Hartley
Ab Craddock	Richard Kelton
Orval	Jon Locke
Spratt's Child	Melissa Gilbert
Story, Script	Shimon Wincelberg
Executive Story Consultant	Jack Miller
Director	Philip Leacock
Associate Producer	Ron Honthaner
Producer	Leonard Katzman
Executive Producer	John Mantley

William Windom starred in several series including *The Farmer's Daughter* and *My World and Welcome to It,* for which he won an Emmy in 1970. In recent years he has been very successful in his one man shows based on the writings and the life of Thurber. Katherine Helmond struggled for years in show business and finally won fame in the series *Soap.* She also appeared in *Sally* and most recently in, *Who's the Boss?* Her films include *Baby Blue Marine, Time Bandits,* and *Overboard.* Melissa Gilbert is best known for her performance as Laura Ingalls Wilder of *Little House on the Prairie.* She has also made a number of made-for-television movies including remakes of *The Miracle Worker, The Diary of Anne Frank,* and *Splendor in the Grass.* Gilbert recently starred in the off-Broadway play, *A Shayna Maidel.*

GUNSMOKE — III. THE PROGRAMS

The Drummer. October 9, 1972. Production #0554. Rerun April 30, 1972.

Mouse trap salesman, Daniel Shay, arrives in Dodge plying his wares. The ex-army officer, meets an emotional challenge when he encounters Sarah Morgan, a young widow, and her half-breed son, Jimmy. Shay is trying to escape his past, but running into some of his ex-army companions, painfully restores his memories of a brutal massacre on an Indian village. Ironically, Sarah's husband had been killed in the raid and Jimmy was crippled as a result of the attack. When Sarah discovers Shay was the officer in charge, she blames him for the senseless slaughter.

Daniel Shay	Victor French
Sarah Morgan	Fionnula Flanagan
Jimmy Morgan	Brandon Cruz
Enoch Brandt	Bruce Glover
Ike Daggett	Kiel Martin
Sayers	Herb Armstrong
Liveryman	Hank Patterson
Trent	Paul Sorensen
Story, Script	Richard Fielder
Executive Story Consultant	Jack Miller
Director	Bernard McEveety
Associate Producer	Ron Honthaner
Producer	Leonard Katzman
Executive Producer	John Mantley

Fionnula Flanagan was featured on *How the West Was Won* and *Rich Man, Poor Man*, for which she won an Emmy Award. Her films include *James Joyce's Women*. Brandon Cruz is best known for his portrayal of little Eddie Corbett on *The Courtship of Eddie's Father*. Kiel Martin played Detective LaRue on *Hill Street Blues*. Richard Fielder wrote for such shows as *Marcus Welby, M.D.*, *Rawhide*, and *The Waltons*.

Sarah. October 16, 1972. Production #0558. Rerun April 2, 1972 and July 15, 1974.

Matt tracks Vesco, a wanted killer, to a bandit waystation called "The Roost." When cornered, Vesco draws and is killed. Matt then discovers that the outlaw sanctuary is run by an old girlfriend of his. Sarah and Matt knew each other back in San Antonio, when he was still a deputy, just before he left for Dodge to become marshal. The only thing Sarah regrets is that she never told Matt that she loved him, but "that was a long time ago," as Matt delicately reminds her. For "old time's sake," however, he agrees to help Sarah out of a jam. Pappy Quinn and his gang arrive at "The Roost," hootin' and hollering and pawing Sarah as usual, until she declares that she is married. She then introduces Matt as Dakota Charlie, her "husband." Having never met the notorious Dakota Charlie, Pappy invites Matt to join the gang in hijacking a gold shipment. What Matt, Sarah, Pappy, and the rest are unaware of is that the real Dakota Charlie was buried two weeks ago.

Sarah	Anne Francis
Pappy Quinn	Anthony Caruso
Sonny	Jonathan Lippe
Digby	Michael Lane
Taylor	John Orchard
Warren	Kay E. Kuter
Ed	Rex Holman
Deering	George Keymas
Vesco	Larry Duran

The Television Programs

Engels	Ronald Manning
Liveryman	Alberto Pina
Story, Script	Calvin Clements
Executive Story Consultant	Jack Miller
Director	Gunnar Hellstrom
Associate Producer	Ron Honthaner
Producer	Leonard Katzman
Executive Producer	John Mantley

On television, Anne Francis appeared on *My Three Sons*, *Dallas*, *Riptide*, and starred in *Honey West*. Her films include *Bad Day at Black Rock*, *Forbidden Planet*, and *Funny Girl*. John Orchard was Ugly John on *M.A.S.H.* Kay E. Kuter appeared on *Petticoat Junction* and *Green Acres* as Newt Kiley.

The Fugitives. October 23, 1972. Production #0551.

Doc and Festus are abducted by a gang of outlaws headed by Bede Stalcup. Doc is then forced to minister to Bede's younger brother, Danny, who was impaled by a stick during a fall from his horse. Festus manages to escape and gets Matt. When they return, a gun battle ensues, and Festus, worried about Doc's safety, rushes the fugitives to save him. Although he succeeds, he is wounded. Meanwhile, Bede escapes and rides into Dodge in an attempt to free his gravely injured brother. Unbeknownst to Bede, Danny has died of his mortal wound.

Bede Stalcup	James Olson
Danny Stalcup	Darrell Larson
Bill Hankins	Victor Tayback
Link Parrin	Russell Johnson
Curley Danzig	Troy Melton
Story, Script	Charles Joseph Stone
Executive Story Consultant	Jack Miller
Director	Irving J. Moore
Associate Producer	Ron Honthaner
Producer	Leonard Katzman
Executive Producer	John Mantley

James Olson played Custer in *The Hallmark Hall of Fame* dramatization *The Court Martial of General George Armstrong Custer*. His films include *Rachel Rachel* and *The Andromeda Strain*. Darrell Larson was featured on *Morningstar/Eveningstar*.

Eleven Dollars. October 30, 1972. Production #0559.

Festus rides across Kansas to deliver a small inheritance to the daughter of a farmer who had befriended him. He soon finds that he must defend the legacy from two young children, as well as a band of hide hunters.

Sarah Elkins	Susan Oliver
Chad	Josh Albee
Clay	Ike Eisenmann
Charity Spenser	Diane Shalet
Story, Script	Paul Savage
Executive Story Consultant	Jack Miller
Director	Irving J. Moore
Associate Producer	Ron Honthaner
Producer	Leonard Katzman
Executive Producer	John Mantley

GUNSMOKE — III. THE PROGRAMS

Susan Oliver played Ann Howard on *Peyton Place* and was a regular on *Days of Our Lives*. Her films include *The Green Eyed Blonde* and *The Disorderly Orderly*. Ike Eisenmann was featured on *Fantastic Journey*.

Milligan. November 6, 1972. Production #0552. Rerun July 9, 1973.

Milligan, a quiet farmer, is enlisted to be a member of a posse tracking notorious Jack Norcross. Norcross and his gang had just robbed the Dodge bank and are happily making their getaway in Matt's absence. The posse is reluctant to track Norcross even though he is wanted for murder, for he has a Robin Hood reputation of robbing from rich banks and insurance companies. There are even rumors that Norcross has given money to needy people from time to time. Even so, Festus and Newly insist that the hunt go on. Milligan, lagging behind, branches off in his search, and gets lost. While trying to find his way back to the posse he spies a small shack where Norcross and one of the wounded outlaws are hiding. In his panic, Milligan closes his eyes and shoots through the window, hitting Norcross in the back and killing him. The other outlaw is also hit in the back by a stray bullet. Back in Dodge, the townsfolk are outraged and treat Milligan and his family like outcasts.

John Milligan	Harry Morgan
Jack Norcross	Joseph Campanella
Janet Milligan	Lynn Carlin
Gerald Pandy	Sorrell Booke
Wendy Milligan	Patti Cohoon
Mattis	Scott Walker
Bob Power	John Pickard
Reeves	Lew Brown
Potter	Read Morgan
Logan	Gene Tyburn
Looter	Robert Swan
Dofeny	Charles Magaulay
Tom	Todd Bass
Girl	Sammee Lee Jones
Story, Script	Ron Bishop
Executive Story Consultant	Jack Miller
Director	Bernard McEveety
Associate Producer	Ron Honthaner
Producer	Leonard Katzman
Executive Producer	John Mantley

Character actor, Sorrell Booke, has appeared in such films as *Fail Safe, Up the Down Staircase,* and *The Iceman Cometh*. Lynn Carlin's films include *Tick Tick Tick* and *Wild Rover*. On television she appeared as Joan Hunter on *James at 15*. Todd Bass was a regular on *Rowan and Martin's Laugh-In*.

Tatum. November 13, 1972. Production #0556. Rerun August 6, 1973.

When an angry bear menaces his Indian wife and infant son, Bodie Tatum challenges the animal with his bare hands. The former outlaw is a giant of a man, but he is no match for the ferocious beast. Tatum, dying of mortal wounds, wants to be reunited with his three grown daughters and to be brought home for burial next to his first wife. Unfortunately, Tatum meets opposition in the form of angry townfolk, who do not want him in their town. He also encounters difficulties with his estranged daughters. Undaunted, Tatum continues his journey with the assistance of Matt and the four women.

The Television Programs

Bodie Tatum	Gene Evans
Kata	Ana Korita
Maddy	Sandra Smith
Gwenn	Jay MacIntosh
Marion	Sheila Larkin
Dirk Mitchell	Jeff Pomerantz
Ed Terrall	Ken Tobey
Clergyman	Lloyd Nelson
Joe Beel	Neil Summers
Man #1	Robert Tindall
Man #2	Duncan Inches
Story, Script	Jim Byrnes
Executive Story Consultant	Jack Miller
Director	Gunnar Hellstrom
Associate Producer	Ron Honthaner
Producer	Leonard Katzman
Executive Producer	John Mantley

The bear used in this episode was Bruno, who co-starred with Dennis Weaver in *Gentle Ben*. Stuntman Neil Summers appeared in numerous television series and movies. His experiences led him to write a book on television Westerns, *The First Official T.V. Western Book*.

The Sodbusters. November 20, 1972. Production #0557. Rerun May 7, 1973.

Matt rides into the middle of a range war while pursuing an outlaw. A group of cattlemen prepare to gun down farmer Pete Brown over a dispute for water rights, and Matt appears on the scene just in time.

Lamoor Underwood	Morgan Woodward
Pete Brown	Alex Cord
Clarabelle Callahan	Katherine Justice
John Callahan	Leif Garrett
Maria Callahan	Dawn Lyn
Print	Harrison Ford
Dick Shaw	Robert Viharo
Deems	Richard Bull
Navin	Joe di Reda
Kestin	Jim Boles
Gene Hill	Colin Male
Dan	Paul Prokop
Darga	Norman Bartold
Murphy	Evans Thornton
Story, Script	Ron Bishop
Executive Story Consultant	Jack Miller
Director	Robert Butler
Associate Producer	Ron Honthaner
Producer	Leonard Katzman
Executive Producer	John Mantley

Alex Cord appeared on *W.E.B.*, *Cassie and Company*, and *Airwolf*. Leif Garrett was a regular on the short-lived series *Three for the Road*. Dawn Lyn played Dodie on *My Three Sons*. Super-star Harrison Ford appeared in such blockbuster films as *Raiders of the Lost Ark*, *Star Wars*, *Witness*, and *Working Girl*. Robert Viharo was a regular on *The*

GUNSMOKE — III. THE PROGRAMS

Survivors. Richard Bull appeared on *Voyage to the Bottom of the Sea* and *Little House on the Prairie*. Colin Male was a regular on *The Dotty Mack Show*. Norman Bartold was featured on *Adam's Rib* and *Teachers Only*.

The Brothers. November 27, 1972. Production #0564.

Stopping at a waystation on route to Dodge, Kitty is annoyed by a fellow passenger. The man turns out to be wanted killer Jay Wrecken. In a strange turn of events, Kitty shoots Jay in the stomach with her derringer, just as slimy Beal Brown shoots him in the back. Although Brown is anxious to partake in the reward, Kitty refuses her share of the $7000 bounty and just wants to shake the experience from her memory. This becomes increasingly difficult as Cord Wrecken sets out to discover and kill all those involved in his brother's death. Wrecken is suave, debonaire, and deadly. As he begins to unravel the mystery, Wrecken leaves a trail of bodies that eventually lead to Dodge and to Kitty.

Cord Wrecken	Steve Forrest
Beal Brown	Joe Silver
Jay Wrecken	Angus Duncan
Carter	Richard O'Brien
Sheriff Crane	Regis J. Cordic
The Undertaker	Eddie Ryder
Drummer	Edward Faulkner
Mr. Denton	Reid Cruickshanks
Liveryman	Terry Wilson
Alf	Daniel Thorpe
Percy Crump	John Harper
Howie	Howard Culver
Flo	Nancy Fisher
Barfly Joe	Jon Kowal
Barfly Bob	Al Berry
Oldtimer	Daniel M. White
Shotgun	Phil Chambers
Story, Script	Calvin Clements
Executive Story Consultant	Jack Miller
Director	Gunnar Hellstrom
Associate Producer	Ron Honthaner
Producer	Leonard Katzman
Executive Producer	John Mantley

The title *The Brothers* was used March 12, 1966. Once again Steve Forrest plays a classic villain, Cord Wrecken. Joe Silver appeared as a regular on several television series including *The Red Buttons Show* and *Fay*. Angus Duncan played Len Ralston on *Aspen*. Eddie Ryder was featured on *The Dennis O'Keefe Show* and *Dr. Kildare*. Terry Wilson was Bill Hawks on *Wagon Train*.

December 4, 1972, preempted for Dr. Seuss' *How the Grinch Stole Christmas*.

Hostage! December 11, 1972. Production #0566. Rerun September 3, 1973.

Sociopathic killer Jude Bonner and his gang of "dog soldiers" invade Dodge and abduct Kitty. This is their last ditch attempt to free Jude's younger brother, Virgil, who has been convicted of murder and is sentenced to hang. Jude leaves Matt an ultimatum that if Virgil hangs, Kitty will be killed. The Governor refuses to grant Matt a stay

The Television Programs

of execution, and the sentence is carried out on schedule. When Jude and his gang realize their threats went unheeded, they savagely abuse Kitty, deposit her dazed and battered in front of the Long Branch, and shoot her down. Matt returns to Dodge confronted with the news that Kitty's life hangs in the balance. After an all night vigil at her side, Matt takes off his badge and goes after Jude Bonner.

Jude Bonner	William Smith
Lafitte	Geoffrey Lewis
Virgil Bonner	Marco St. John
Amy Lee	Nina Roman
Governor	James Chandler
Toke	Hal Baylor
Martha	Sandra Kent
Sheriff Tanner	Stafford Repp
Story, Script	Paul F. Edwards
Executive Story Consultant	Jack Miller
Director	Gunnar Hellstrom
Associate Producer	Ron Honthaner
Producer	Leonard Katzman
Executive Producer	John Mantley

The title, *The Hostage*, was used December 4, 1965. *Gunsmoke* has always had its share of wonderful badmen, but Jude and Virgil Bonner are two of the best. Written by Paul F. Edwards and masterfully played by William Smith and Marco St. John, these brothers are evil incarnate. In a recent interview Edwards recalled that they were fashioned after real life brothers. They were, "...based loosely on old man Bent, who had a bunch of half-breed sons with a Comanche woman...and a couple of them hooked up with a society called the 'dog soldiers'...one of the sons was a real maniac...a very psychotic and savage guy." William Smith appeared in several shows including *Laredo, Hawaii Five-O,* and *Rich Man, Poor Man.* Marco St. John was a regular on the comedy *Ball Four.* Geoffrey Lewis appeared in *Flo* and *Gun Shy.*

Jubilee. December 18, 1972. Production #0565.

Tuck Frye, a poor Kansas farmer, dreams of striking it rich with his quarter horse, Jubilee. Obsessed with this desire, Tuck pursues his quest at the expense of everything else in his life. He neglects his farm and fails to provide for his family as well.

Ed Wells	Scott Brady
Dave Chaney	Alan Hale
Tuck Frye	Tom Skerritt
Bess Frye	Collin Wilcox-Horne
Annie Frye	Lori Rutherford
Caleb Frye	Todd Cameron
Billy Banner	Whitey Hughes
Story	Jack Freeman
Script	Paul Savage
Executive Story Consultant	Jack Miller
Director	Herb Wallerstein
Associate Producer	Ron Honthaner
Producer	Leonard Katzman
Executive Producer	John Mantley

Lori Rutherford was a regular on *The New Andy Griffith Show.*

GUNSMOKE — III. THE PROGRAMS

December 25, 1972, pre-empted for *Opening Night: U.S.A.*

Arizona Midnight. January 1, 1973. Production #0563.

A little cowboy who calls himself, Arizona, rides into Dodge astride a giant horse. He storms into the Long Branch huffing and panting with a tale of turning himself into a "were-elephant" when the moon is full. Desperate to find someone to care for him when he is in this awkward state, Arizona offers $50 to anyone who will feed and look after him and his horse for the night. Despite a great amount of skepticism, the residents of Dodge are stupefied, when a great lumbering elephant, wearing the midget's tiny hat on his huge head, appears in the streets of the dusty cowtown.

Arizona	Billy Curtis
Red	Stanley Clements
Fred	Mills Watson
Ed	Ken Mayer
Beatrice	Sandye Powell
Story, Script	Dudley Bromley
Executive Story Consultant	Jack Miller
Director	Irving J. Moore
Associate Producer	Ron Honthaner
Producer	Leonard Katzman
Executive Producer	John Mantley

Kitty confesses to Arizona, "My real name's Kathleen. Kitty is just a nickname."

Homecoming. January 8, 1973. Production #0568. Rerun June 18, 1973.

Rick and Raymond Wilson, two outlaw brothers, return to Dodge to visit their dying mother. They had planned to briefly stop in and see her and then escape to Mexico. However, their plans fall through when they discover their mother is not alone. Doc is there administering to her in her final hours. The men take Doc hostage and plan on bringing him with them to insure their safe journey. Newly goes to the ranch where they are holding Doc hoping to rescue him by faking a broken arm and hiding a gun in the cast.

Rick Wilson	Richard Kelton
Raymond Wilson	Robert Pratt
Martha Beal	Ivy Jones
John Mophet	Stuart Margolin
Anna Wilson	Lurene Tuttle
Prudence	Lynn Marta
Mrs. Bronson	Claudia Bryar
Story, Script	Calvin Clements
Executive Story Consultant	Jack Miller
Director	Gunnar Hellstrom
Associate Producer	Ron Honthaner
Producer	Leonard Katzman
Executive Producer	John Mantley

The title, *The Homecoming*, was used May 23, 1964. Lynn Marta was frequently seen on *Love, American Style*. Claudia Bryar was a regular on the dramatic series, *The Manhunter*.

Shadler. January 15, 1973. Production #0567.

Boone Shadler escapes from prison after masquerading as a priest. He journeys to

The Television Programs

the town where his mother is living, looking for the money he had the old woman hide for him. While still in his holy attire, Shadler encounters Newly. Believing Shadler to be a priest, Newly enlists his aid. The two are forced into an uneasy alliance to save the small town from being overrun by a gang of outlaws.

Boone Shadler	Earl Holliman
Dallas Fair	Diana Hyland
Cyrus Himes	Denver Pyle
Abby Shadler	Linda Watkins
Reno	Alex Sharp
Varnum	Pat Conway
McKee	Ken Lynch
Rogers	John Davis Chandler
Dobson	Donald Barry
Creech	James Jeeter
Father Walsh	John Carter
Mr. Jonas	Bill Erwin
Mrs. Evans	Meg Wyllie
Elmer	Tom Pittman
Walters	Barry Cahill
Farina	Wallace Earl
Story, Script	Jim Byrnes
Executive Story Consultant	Jack Miller
Director	Arnold Lathan
Associate Producer	Ron Honthaner
Producer	Leonard Katzman
Executive Producer	John Mantley

Diana Hyland was a regular on *Peyton Place* and *Eight Is Enough*. In 1977 she won an Emmy for *The Boy in the Plastic Bubble*. Meg Wyllie was featured on *Hennesey* and *The Travels of Jamie McPheeters*.

Patricia. January 22, 1973. Production #0569. Rerun August 20, 1973.

Romance blossoms in Dodge when Newly marries a beautiful young governess from the East, Patricia Colby. The two meet on a stagecoach headed for Dodge, and although they are immediately attracted to one another, the courtship comes as a result of their surviving a Kansas tornado and working side-by-side administering to the victims. Tragically, Newly's happiness is short-lived when Doc confirms that Patricia is suffering from a blood disease which could take her life.

Patricia Colby	Jess Walton
Johnny	Ike Eisenmann
Johnny's Father	John Baer
Mrs. Peary	Gail Bonney
Brown	Donald Elson
Stage Driver	Richard Lundin
Story, Script	Calvin Clements
Executive Story Consultant	Jack Miller
Director	Alf Kjellin
Associate Producer	Ron Honthaner
Producer	Leonard Katzman
Executive Producer	John Mantley

GUNSMOKE — III. THE PROGRAMS

A Quiet Day in Dodge. January 29, 1973. Production #0571.
   Matt returns to Dodge after tracking and catching Job Snelling, a dangerous fugitive. Not having slept for two days, Matt has to face another unbelievable 24-hour period before he gets any rest. He no sooner gets his prisoner locked up, that he is faced with a nine-year-old runaway boy, a brawl in the Long Branch, and an old woman locked in a safe. To top it all off, Kitty is furious with him for standing her up on a date.

Edsel Pry	Margaret Hamilton
Job Snelling	Leo Gordon
Dobie Crimps	Shug Fisher
Buck Doolin	Douglas V. Fowley
Mr. Ballou	John Fiedler
Mrs. Ballou	Helen Page Camp
Drummer	J. Pat O'Malley
Ludlow	Walker Edmiston
Judge Brooker	Herb Vigran
Andy Ballou	Willie Ames
Hank	Henry Wise
Sadie	Michelle Breeze
Story, Script, Executive Story Consultant	Jack Miller
Director	Alf Kjellin
Associate Producer	Ron Honthaner
Producer	Leonard Katzman
Executive Producer	John Mantley

Margaret Hamilton will always be remembered for her role as the Wicked Witch of the West in *The Wizard of Oz*. In more recent years she was seen as Cora on the Maxwell House Coffee commercials. John Fiedler was a regular on *The Bob Newhart Show, Kolchak: The Night Stalker,* and *Buffalo Bill*. Douglas Fowley appeared on several programs including *The Life and Legend of Wyatt Earp, Pistols 'n' Petticoats,* and *Detective School*. Helen Page Camp was featured on *13 Queens Boulevard*.

Whelan's Men. February 5, 1973. Production #0562.
   An outlaw gang led by a vengeance seeking ex-lawman named Dan Whelan, invades Dodge during Matt's absence. They rob the bank, the freight office, and every citizen in the town. Then the men sit around playing poker while waiting for Matt to return. Whelan plans to burn down the town and kill Matt on sight. When one of the gang is caught cheating and is shot, Miss Kitty is asked to join the game. After she cleans everyone out, Kitty boldly challenges Whelan to a game, with Matt's life as the stake.

Dan Whelan	Robert Burr
Loomis	William Bramley
Tuck	Noble Willingham
Hobey	Harrison Ford
Breed	Frank Ramirez
Gentry	Gerald McRaney
Musgrove	Bobby Hall
Acker	Seamon Glass
Partridge	Ed Craig
Miner	Richard Hale
Story, Script	Ron Bishop

The Television Programs

Executive Story Consultant	Jack Miller
Director	Paul Edwards
Associate Producer	Ron Honthaner
Producer	Leonard Katzman
Executive Producer	John Mantley

Noble Willingham was a regular on *When the Whistle Blows* and *Cutter to Houston*. Frank Ramirez was featured on the police series *Paris*. Gerald McRaney starred as Rick Simon on the successful series *Simon and Simon*. According to Tim Brooks in his book *The Complete Directory to Prime Time TV Stars*, McRaney "holds the distinction of having been the last guest star on *Gunsmoke* to have a face to face shoot-out with Matt Dillon." The episode Brooks was referring to was *Hard Labor,* which aired February 24, 1975.

Kimbro. February 12, 1973. Production #0570.

Matt learns that the man who taught him everything he knows, Adam Kimbro, is now an itinerant drunk reduced to sweeping out stables for whiskey money. Hoping to rehabilitate Adam, who used to be the best lawman in the West, Matt deputizes him to go out on a dangerous job protecting a gold shipment. Matt does a lot of soul searching while in Adam's company, for in Adam he can see his own past and possibly his future.

Adam Kimbro	John Anderson
Mary Bentley	Doreen Long
Peak Stratton	Michael Strong
Moss Stratton	William DeVane
Turkey Stratton	Rick Weaver
Billy Stratton	Tom Falk
Melody	Lisa Eilbacher
John	Wendell Baker
Story, Script	Jim Byrnes
Executive Story Consultant	Jack Miller
Director	Gunnar Hellstrom
Associate Producer	Ron Honthaner
Producer	Leonard Katzman
Executive Producer	John Mantley

The part of Turkey Stratton is played by Rick Weaver, Dennis Weaver's son. William DeVane's television credits include *From Here to Eternity, The Missiles of October,* and *Knots Landing*. His film credits include *McCabe and Mrs. Miller, Marathon Man,* and *Testament*. Lisa Eilbacher appeared in such television programs as *The Ordeal of Patty Hearst, Wheels,* and *The Winds of War*. Her films include *An Officer and a Gentleman* and *Beverly Hills Cop*.

Jesse. February 19, 1973. Production #0572. Rerun August 27, 1973.

Festus' old friend Jesse is in trouble with the law. Festus and Newly must face the decision of whether to free Jesse, or deliver him to the appropriate authorities. The situation comes to a head when a band of cattle drovers, determined to decide the fate of Jesse among themselves, descend upon the two deputies.

Jesse Dillard	Brock Peters
Pete Murphy	Don Stroud
Dave Carpenter	Jim Davis
Marshal Halstead	Regis J. Cordic

GUNSMOKE — III. THE PROGRAMS

Abel Glass	Leonard Stone
Sheriff	Norman Bartold
Dr. Miller	Lloyd Nelson
Link	Robert Pine
Sheriff Bradley	Ted Gehring
Barkeep	Larry Finley
Drucker	Pete Kellett
Agner	Karen Welch
Story, Script	Jim Byrnes
Executive Story Consultant	Jack Miller
Director	Bernard McEveety
Associate Producer	Ron Honthaner
Producer	Leonard Katzman
Executive Producer	John Mantley

The title *Jesse* was used October 19, 1957. A black belt and former stunt man, Don Stroud was featured in *Kate Loves a Mystery* and *Mickey Spillane's Mike Hammer*.

Talbot. February 26, 1973. Production #0574.

Talbot and his associates are planning a daring bank robbery in Dodge. In the midst of planning the hold-up, Talbot meets Katherine, an attractive young woman. As fate would have it, Talbot is forced into a lethal fight with Katherine's abusive husband. Leaving her a widow, Talbot suddenly feels responsible for Katherine. The two fall in love, which alters his plans for the robbery. However, his partners are not happy with the new situation and insist that Talbot go ahead with his original scheme.

Talbot	Anthony Zerbe
Katherine	Salome Jens
Bob Pope	Peter Jason
Eli Snider	Robert Totten
Story, Script	Jim Byrnes
Executive Story Consultant	Jack Miller
Director	Vincent McEveety
Associate Producer	Ron Honthaner
Producer	Leonard Katzman
Executive Producer	John Mantley

This Golden Land. March 5, 1973. Production #0573. Rerun August 13, 1973.

The Gorofskys, a family of Jewish immigrants, have purchased a farm in Kansas. They have journeyed to the American frontier to escape the pogroms and harrassment of their homeland. Unfortunately, their dream of the promised land turns into a nightmare when Semel, the youngest son, dies after an incident involving three ruffians. Although Moshe Gorofsky saw the men drag Semel away, he did not witness the fatal blow. Because of this, Talmudic Law prohibits Moshe from pointing the finger of accusation at the culprints. Since Moshe will not testify, Matt is unable to act on behalf of the grieving family. Moshe must come to terms with himself, his grieving family, and his Talmudic beliefs.

Moshe Gorofsky	Paul Stevens
Ruxton	Victor French
Gearshon	Richard Dreyfuss
Zisha	Bettye Ackerman
Calvin	Kevin Coughlin

The Television Programs

Laibel	Joseph Hindy
Homer	Wayne McLaren
Semel	Scott Selles
Barkeep	Robert Nichols
Story, Script	Hal Sitowitz
Executive Story Consultant	Jack Miller
Director	Gunnar Hellstrom
Associate Producer	Ron Honthaner
Producer	Leonard Katzman
Executive Producer	John Mantley

This episode won the prestigious Mass Media Award from the National Conference of Christians and Jews. Film star Richard Dreyfuss appeared in such blockbuster hits as *Close Encounters of the Third Kind, Nuts, Whose Life Is It Anyway?, Down and Out in Beverly Hills,* and *The Goodbye Girl,* for which he won the Academy Award. Bettye Ackerman co-starred with her husband, Sam Jaffe, on the popular doctor series, *Ben Casey.*

Waste [Part I]. March 12, 1973, rerun. First aired September 27, 1971.

Waste [Part II]. March 19, 1973, rerun. First aired October 4, 1971.

Bohannan. March 26, 1973, rerun. First aired September 25, 1972.

Sarah. April 2, 1973, rerun. First aired October 16, 1972.

Tara. April 9, 1973, rerun. First aired January 17, 1972.

The River [Part I]. April 16, 1973, rerun. First aired September 11, 1972.

The River [Part II]. April 23, 1973, rerun. First aired September 18, 1972.

The Drummer. April 30, 1973, rerun. First aired October 9, 1972.

The Sodbusters. May 7, 1973, rerun. First aired November 20, 1972.

Phoenix. May 14, 1973, rerun. First aired September 20, 1971.

The Noon Day Devil. May 21, 1973, rerun. First aired December 7, 1970.

No Tomorrow. May 28, 1973, rerun. First aired January 3, 1972.

The Lost. June 4, 1973, rerun. First aired September 13, 1971.

The Gun. June 11, 1973, rerun. First aired November 9, 1970.

The Homecoming. June 18, 1973, rerun. First aired January 8, 1973.

Murdock. June 25, 1973, rerun. First aired February 8, 1971.

Captain Sligo. July 2, 1973, rerun. First aired January 4, 1971.

Milligan. July 9, 1973, rerun. First aired November 6, 1972.

GUNSMOKE — III. THE PROGRAMS

Gold Train [Part I]. July 16, 1973, rerun. First aired November 29, 1971.

Gold Train [Part II]. July 23, 1973, rerun. First aired December 6, 1971.

Gold Train [Part III]. July 30, 1973, rerun. First aired December 13, 1971.

Tatum. August 6, 1973, rerun. First aired November 13, 1972.

This Golden Land. August 13, 1973, rerun. First aired March 5, 1973.

Patricia. August 20, 1973, rerun. First aired January 22, 1973.

Jesse. August 27, 1973, rerun. First aired February 19, 1973.

Hostage! September 3, 1973, rerun. First aired December 11, 1972.

NINETEENTH SEASON

Women for Sale [Part I]. September 10, 1973. Production #0607.
   Comanche renegades kidnap several women and children for the purpose of selling them to white slaver, Fitzpatrick, who plans to send them into Mexico. Among the prisoners is outspoken, hard-as-nails Stella, a feisty saloon girl, who is rejected by Fitzpatrick because she is too independent and troublesome. Stella then finds herself stuck with her Indian captor, Blue Jacket, along with another captive named Rachel, and Rachel's young daughter, Marcy. Matt tracks Blue Jacket and his captives, who depart in one direction, while Fitzpatrick and his slaves head toward Mexico.

Women for Sale [Part II]. September 17, 1973. Production #0607.
   Matt rescues Stella and Marcy, now motherless, and they accompany him as he attempts to stop Fitzpatrick. While Stella is trying to escape the responsibility of caring for Marcy, Fitzpatrick also has problems. Britt, his young protege, begins to fall in love with Cynthia, one of his captives.

Blue Jacket	Gregory Sierra
Stella	Shani Wallis
Fitzpatrick	James Whitmore
Cynthia	Kathleen Cody
Marcy	Dawn Lynn
Britt	Nicholas Hammond
Liz	Lieux Dressler
Dan Ross	Dan Ferrone
Rachel	Sally Kemp
Story, Script	Jim Byrnes
Executive Story Consultant	Jack Miller
Director	Vincent McEveety
Associate Producer	Ron Honthaner
Producer	Leonard Katzman
Executive Producer	John Mantley

   William Conrad, radio's Matt Dillon, narrates. Gregory Sierra was a regular on several series including *Sanford and Son, Barney Miller,* and *Soap.* British film star and

The Television Programs

singer, Shani Wallis, appeared in such movies as *Oliver!*, *Terror in the Wax Museum*, and *Arnold*. Nicholas Hammond played the title role in the television series *The Amazing Spider-Man*.

Matt's Love Story. September 24, 1973. Production #0609. Rerun April 15, 1974.

An attractive widow, Mike Yardner, finds Matt wounded and suffering from amnesia, after he is ambushed by murder suspect, Les "Favorite" Dean. Matt does not remember anything, not his name, nor where he is from, or how he got shot. Mike christens him "Dan" and the two fall in love during his recuperation. The courtship is playful and sweet, and just as everything seems to be falling into place, Hasty Starcourt, a land hungry rancher, hires Favorite to "remove" Mike from her property.

Mike Yardner	Michael Learned
Les Dean	Victor French
Starcourt	Keith Andes
Monte Rupert	Jonathan Lippe
Cordelius	William Schallert
Canoot	Richard Lundin
Mio	S. Michael De France
Man	Neil Summers
Story, Script	Ron Bishop
Executive Story Consultant	Jack Miller
Director	Gunnar Hellstrom
Associate Producer	Ron Honthaner
Producer	Leonard Katzman
Executive Producer	John Mantley

Matt gives his first television kiss and it is not to Miss Kitty. Of course, he is suffering from amnesia at the time. The object of his affection is "Mike" Yardner played by Michael Learned. Throughout the 19 years that Kitty and Matt were paramours, sex was always left to the imagination of the viewers. However, in this episode it is made quite plain that Matt and Mike are intimate. Although Victor French's character was called "Favorite," Jim Arness and Michael Learned both make the mistake of calling him "Fortunate." Michael Learned played Olivia on *The Waltons*, for which she won Emmy Awards as Best Actress in 1973, 1974, and 1976. On the television series *Nurse* she starred as Nurse Mary Benjamin and won an Emmy in 1982 for her portrayal. Keith Andes appeared on several series including *This Man Dawson*, *Glynis*, and *Search*.

The Boy and the Sinner. October 1, 1973. Production #0604. Rerun July 1, 1974.

A drunken beggar, Noah Beal, accepts an offer from two gunfighters to stake a false land claim in exchange for whiskey. Soon afterwards a young neighbor, Colby Eaton, befriends Beal. The boy teaches the old man to farm, giving Beal hope for the future. Beal begins to realize that he will soon have to make a decision, either give up the farm and the boy's friendship, or stay and jeopardize his own personal safety.

Noah Beal	Ron Moody
Colby Eaton	Vincent Van Patten
Otis Miller	Warren Vanders
Hugh Eaton	John Crawford
Jess Bradman	Ken Lynch
Jack Beaver	Read Morgan
Mrs. Travers	Florida Friebus

GUNSMOKE — III. THE PROGRAMS

Boomer .... Hal Baylor
Story, Script .... Hal Sitowitz
Executive Story Consultant .... Jack Miller
Director .... Bernard McEveety
Associate Producer .... Ron Honthaner
Producer .... Leonard Katzman
Executive Producer .... John Mantley

British character actor, Ron Moody, appeared in such films as *The Twelve Chairs*, *David Copperfield*, and *Oliver!*, which he also played on Broadway. On television he was featured in the comedy *Nobody's Perfect*. Florida Friebus played Winnie Gillis, Dobie's scatterbrained mother, on *The Many Loves of Dobie Gillis* and Mrs. Bakerman on *The Bob Newhart Show*.

The Widow-Maker. October 8, 1973. Production #0610. Rerun April 29, 1974.

Legendary gunfighter, Scott Coltrane, is trying to live a quiet non-violent life with the woman he loves. The presence of Coltrane in Dodge, however, draws numerous young challengers who are seeking an instant reputation. Although sympathetic with Coltrane's desire for a life of his own, Matt is forced to order him to leave town.

Scott Coltrane .... Steve Forrest
Teresa .... Barra Grant
Dad Goodpaster .... David Huddleston
Kid Chama .... Randolph Roberts
Buck Lennart .... Jerry Gatlin
Preacher .... James Chandler
Boy .... Don Carter
Deak Towler .... Rand Bridges
Sundog Wheeler .... J.R. Clark
Story, Script .... Paul F. Edwards
Executive Story Consultant .... Jack Miller
Director .... Bernard McEveety
Associate Producer .... Ron Honthaner
Producer .... Leonard Katzman
Executive Producer .... John Mantley

Randolph Roberts played Chuck, the eldest brother, on *Happy Days*.

Kitty's Love Affair. October 22, 1973. Production #0611.

On route to St. Louis with Kitty, Matt is called back to Dodge on business. Kitty is furious and decides to go on alone. Ex-gunman, Will Stambridge, joins the stage, and rescues Kitty when they are attacked by outlaws. Although Kitty questions the direction of her future with Matt, and is somewhat drawn to Will, she is never-the-less uneasy when Will decides to settle down in Dodge. Will indicates that he wants to start a new life with her by his side. Despite her disquiet Kitty is willing to give him a chance. However, as they start seeing more of each other, they become the targets of vicious gossip. The problems escalate when Will finds himself facing a lynch mob, after he is falsely accused of murder.

Will Stambridge .... Richard Kiley
Corley Deems .... Leonard Stone
Sheb Deems .... Christopher Connelly
Grimes .... Paul Picerni
Turner .... Don Keefer

The Television Programs

Drummer	Jack Perkins
Lonnie Colby	Gerald McRaney
Coots	Del Monroe
Mrs. Colby	Virginia Baker
Mayhew	Richard D. Hurst
Morg	Ed Long
Dowel	Rayford Barnes
Clel	James Almanzar
Curt	Pete Kellett
Station Master	Ken Kenopka
Hank	Phil Chambers
R.J.	Louis Elias
Zeke	Jeff Parks
Story	Susan Kotar & Joan E. Gessler
Script	Paul Savage
Executive Story Consultant	Jack Miller
Director	Vincent McEveety
Associate Producer	Ron Honthaner
Producer	Leonard Katzman
Executive Producer	John Mantley

The Widow and the Rogue. October 29, 1973. Production #0606. Rerun April 8, 1974.

J.J. Honegger, a personable thief who does not relish the thought of a two year jail sentence, seeks to escape from Festus while on route to Dodge. Festus is injured during one of J.J.'s escape attempts, and they lose their only horse during a storm. The deputy handcuffs himself to J.J. and tries to cross the desert on foot. However, after encountering a mother and son stranded in the desert and a band of comancheros, their chances for survival appear slim.

J.J. Honegger	James Stacy
Martha Cunningham	Beth Brickell
Caleb Cunningham	Clay O'Brien
Woman	Helen Page Camp
Daughter	Monica Svensson
Station Master	Walker Edmiston
Farmer	Paul Sorensen
Stage Driver	Richard Lundin
Story	Harvey Marlowe & Paul Savage
Script	Paul Savage
Executive Story Consultant	Jack Miller
Director	Bernard McEveety
Associate Producer	Ron Honthaner
Producer	Leonard Katzman
Executive Producer	John Mantley

Beth Brickell was featured as Ellen Wedloe on *Gentle Ben*.

A Game of Death...An Act of Love [Part I]. November 5, 1973. Production #0602. Rerun June 17, 1974.

Bear Sanderson seeks his own revenge when outlaw Indians kill his wife and burn his home. Matt attempts to find an attorney to defend the Indian suspects, but he is unsuccessful. He is even refused help by a traveling lawyer, Cicero Wolfe. However, Matt forces Wolfe to stay in Dodge until the situation is resolved.

GUNSMOKE — III. THE PROGRAMS

A Game of Death...An Act of Love [Part II]. November 12, 1973. Production #0602. Rerun June 24, 1974.

Wolfe, after much deliberation, accepts Matt's plea to defend the Indians accused of murdering the wife of Bear Sanderson. The lawyer warns Matt that he will do everything he can to win an acquittal for his clients. Tempers are fanned even further when Sanderson and his daughter, Paula, learn that Wolfe is part Indian himself.

May Lassiter	Michael Learned
Bear Sanderson	Morgan Woodward
Cicero Wolfe	Paul Stevens
Paula Sanderson	Donna Mills
Lavinia Sanderson	Whitney Blake
Captain Sykes	John Pickard
Lt. Briggs	Geoffrey Horne
Dekker	Garry Walberg
Bailiff	Owen Bush
Story, Script	Paul F. Edwards
Executive Story Consultant	Jack Miller
Director	Gunnar Hellstrom
Associate Producer	Ron Honthaner
Producer	Leonard Katzman
Executive Producer	John Mantley

Donna Mills is best known for her portrayal of sexy, villainous Abby Cunningham Ewing on *Knots Landing*.

Lynch Town. November 19, 1973. Production #0601.

Rob Fielder's father is arrested for the murder of a lady saloon owner, and is lynched before circuit judge Warfield arrives to try him. Matt insists that drunken judge Warfield hold an inquest. However, John King, the town boss, has a strong influence over Warfield, and even with Matt's assurance, Rob has little hope of clearing his father's name.

Judge Warfield	David Wayne
Rob Fielder	Mitch Vogel
John King	Scott Brady
Sheriff Ridder	Warren Kemmerling
Jake Fielder	Ken Swofford
Tom Hart	Norman Alden
Minnie Nolen	Julie Cobb
Story	Joann Carlino & Anne Snyder
Script	Calvin Clements
Executive Story Consultant	Jack Miller
Director	Bernard McEveety
Associate Producer	Ron Honthaner
Producer	Leonard Katzman
Executive Producer	John Mantley

David Wayne appeared on the Broadway stage and won Tony Awards for *Finian's Rainbow* and *Teahouse of the August Moon*. His film credits include *Adam's Rib* and *How to Marry a Millionaire*. On television he was featured in several series including *The Adventures of Ellery Queen, Dallas,* and *House Calls*. The daughter of actor Lee J. Cobb, Julie Cobb, appeared as a regular on *The D.A., A Year at the Top,* and *Charles in Charge*.

The Television Programs

The Hanging of Newly O'Brien. November 26, 1973. Production #0605.
 Newly's skill with medicine is put to the test when Doc sends him out to check on some families in the back country. At first, Newly is frustrated by the poor response he receives from his patients. Later, however, his own life is threatened after an emergency operation results in the death of a patient. Doc and Festus arrive as Newly is about to be hung, and in an ensuing battle Doc is shot. The only one left to save him is Newly, who the mountain folk have locked in their jail along with Festus.

    Kermit . . . . Billy Green Bush
    Tim . . . . Jimmy Van Patten
    Grandma . . . . Jessamine Milner
    Grandpa . . . . Rusty Lane
    Anna . . . . Jan Burrell
    Ronda . . . . Deborah Dozier
    John . . . . Walter Scott
    Adrian . . . . Bobby Hall
    Farmer Buey . . . . Donald Elson
    Old Woman . . . . Billie Bird
    Oldtimer . . . . Arthur Malet
    Little Girl . . . . Erica Hunton
    Story, Script . . . . Calvin Clements
    Executive Story Consultant . . . . Jack Miller
    Director . . . . Alf Kjellin
    Associate Producer . . . . Ron Honthaner
    Producer . . . . Leonard Katzman
    Executive Producer . . . . John Mantley

 Billie Bird was featured on *It Takes Two* and *Benson.*

Susan Was Evil. December 3, 1973. Production #0613.
 Nellie, a widow who has sold her waystation and has promised to take her niece, Susan, to St. Louis, has to postpone their plans when Matt arrives with a wounded prisoner. Susan is furious at the delay and makes her feelings known to all. However, Nellie feels obligated to care for Norman Boswell, who turns out to be a gentle, sensitive man. As fate would have it, Nellie and Boswell fall in love. Susan, perceiving Boswell to be a threat to her future happiness, vows to eliminate him.

    Nellie . . . . Kathleen Nolan
    Norman Boswell . . . . Art Lund
    Susan . . . . Kathy Cannon
    Newt . . . . George Di Cenzo
    Sam . . . . Henry Olek
    Dudley . . . . Jim Gammon
    Glenn Murphy . . . . Robert Brubaker
    Story, Script . . . . William Keys
    Executive Story Consultant . . . . Jack Miller
    Director . . . . Bernard McEveety
    Associate Producer . . . . Ron Honthaner
    Producer . . . . Leonard Katzman
    Executive Producer . . . . John Mantley

 George Di Cenzo was a regular on *Aspen, Dynasty,* and *McClain's Law,* which starred James Arness.

 December 10, 1973, preempted for *Frosty the Snowman.*

GUNSMOKE — III. THE PROGRAMS

The Deadly Innocent. December 17, 1973. Production #0617. Rerun April 22, 1974.

Billy is a powerful young man with the mind of a child, who erupts into uncontrollable violence when he sees anyone or anything being hurt. Billy leaves the sheltered valley where he grew up, and comes to Dodge to visit his long time friend Festus. When the life of a cat is threatened by some town toughs, Billy gets into a fight and nearly kills one of them. Doc is afraid that Billy, not knowing his own strength, could eventually kill someone, and Judge Brooker agrees. Therefore, Billy is ordered to be delivered to the Kansas asylum for the mentally disturbed. It is Festus' task to bring Billy to his new home, a job he does not look forward to.

Billy	Russell Wiggins
Barnett	Charles Dierkop
Judge Brooker	Herb Vigran
Pete	Jack Garner
Crooms	William Shriver
Annie	Erica Hunton
Slim	Denny Arnold
Story, Script	Calvin Clements
Executive Story Consultant	Jack Miller
Director	Bernard McEveety
Associate Producer	Ron Honthaner
Producer	Leonard Katzman
Executive Producer	John Mantley

The Deadly Innocent won the Golden Spur Award from the Western Writers of America and an award from the President's Council on Mental Retardation.

The Child Between. December 24, 1973. Production #0612.

Fugitive, Lew Harrod, and his Indian wife frustrate Newly by first seeking medical help for their child and then refusing to take his advice. Harrod has kidnapped Newly at gunpoint to treat his sick baby, but Harrod's wife Makesha wants Newly shot after she learns he is a deputy. Makesha further endangers her baby's life by taking him to a Comanche camp and seeking help from a shaman.

Lew Harrod	Sam Groom
Makesha	Alexandra Morgan
Dahoma	John Dierkes
Goriko	Eddie Little Sky
First Hide Cutter	Pete Kellett
Second Hide Cutter	Bill Hart
Third Hide Cutter	Alex Sharp
Story, Script	Harry Kronman
Executive Story Consultant	Jack Miller
Director	Irving Moore
Associate Producer	Ron Honthaner
Producer	Leonard Katzman
Executive Producer	John Mantley

Pike [Part I]. December 31, 1973, rerun. First aired March 1, 1971.

Pike [Part II]. January 7, 1974, rerun. First aired March 8, 1971.

A Family of Killers. January 14, 1974. Production #0616. Rerun May 13, 1974.

The Sutterfield family is a vicious outlaw band. They are reunited during a daring

The Television Programs

jail break, during which Marshal Hargraves is wounded and his deputy killed. Enranged over his deputy's sadistic murder, Hargraves wants instant justice as he sets out to track down Elton Sutterfield, his brothers, and his cousins. Matt insists on joining the search, anxious that the wanted men be brought back alive.

Hargraves	Glenn Corbett
Elton Sutterfield	Anthony Caruso
Crazy Harley	Mills Watson
Ham	Morgan Paull
Jonnalee Simpson	Zina Bethune
Brownie	Stuart Margolin
Tobin	George Keymas
Jacob	Frank Corsentino
Story, Script	William Keys
Executive Story Consultant	Jack Miller
Director	Gunnar Hellstrom
Associate Producer	Ron Honthaner
Producer	Leonard Katzman
Executive Producer	John Mantley

Mills Watson was called Harley in the story but Charley in the credits. Matt tells sheriff Hargraves that he looks like he "tangled with a buzz-saw," which is something of an anachronism for the 1870s. Zina Bethune played Gail Lucas in the dramatic television series, *The Nurses*. She also appeared on the daytime soaps, *The Guiding Light, Young Doctor Malone,* and *Love of Life.*

Like Old Times. January 21, 1974. Production #0619. Rerun May 20, 1974.

Benjamin Franklin Rando, "the greatest safecracker in the history of Kansas," returns to Dodge after serving 12 years in jail. He hopes to renew his romance with saloon girl, Carrie Thompson, but finds that the years have wrought many changes. They have been especially unkind to Carrie, who now works at the Bull's Head saloon, a rather unfashionable establishment. She has also become bitter over the 12 years of hard living. However, Rando is persistent and gets a job at the Adams' Express Office to prove that he has gone straight. Rando's attempt to pick up the threads of his life and win back his girl is threatened by a pair of crooks who want the former safe cracker to help them in a robbery.

Ben Rando	Nehemiah Persoff
Carrie Louise Thompson	Gloria de Haven
Aaron Barker	Dan Travanty
Lem Hargis	Charles Haid
Bull	Victor Izay
Bartender	Robert Brubaker
Mrs. Hopewell	Rhodie Cogan
Clay	Hal Bokar
Stage Drive	Richard Lundin
Story, Script	Richard Fielder
Executive Story Consultant	Jack Miller
Director	Irving Moore
Associate Producer	Ron Honthaner
Producer	Leonard Katzman
Executive Producer	John Mantley

Floyd played by Robert Brubaker has replaced Sam, Glenn Strange, who died in

GUNSMOKE — III. THE PROGRAMS

September of 1973. Ben Rando asks Floyd about the whereabouts of Sam, and Floyd replies, "We lost him awhile back...everybody around here misses him alot." Festus holds up a poster of Frank Eaton, describing him as an ugly looking criminal sort. Eaton looks exactly like Festus, which is reminiscent of another episode *Alias Festus Haggen* (March 6, 1972), in which Festus was mistaken for outlaw Frank Eaton. Gloria de Haven appeared in numerous films including *Modern Times, Three Little Words,* and *Summer Stock.* Dan Travanty (Daniel Travanti) and Charles Haid were reunited years later when they co-starred on *Hill Street Blues.*

The Town Tamers. January 28, 1974. Production #0614. Rerun May 27, 1974.

Matt and Marshal Luke Rumbaugh are sent to tame Hilt, a lawless Kansas town. After things quiet down in Hilt, Matt returns to Dodge, leaving Luke behind to keep the town in order. However, love and marriage soon interfere with Rumbaugh's ability to function as a lawman. Rumbaugh's new lifestyle makes him reluctant to continue facing gunfighters set on eliminating him and as he loses his edge he also loses his new stepson's respect.

Luke Rumbaugh	Jim Davis
Martha	Jean Allison
Caleb	Ike Eisenmann
Aikens	Rex Holman
Badger	Leo Gordon
Sham	Sean McClory
Barker	James Jeter
McCurdy	Kay Kuter
Preacher	James Chandler
Kate	Julie Bennett
Michael	Don Megowan
Texan Leader	Clay Tanner
Farmer	Ed Call
Farmer's Wife	Mary Betten
Texan Rider	Larry Randles
Story, Script	Paul Savage
Executive Story Consultant	Jack Miller
Director	Gunnar Hellstrom
Associate Producer	Ron Honthaner
Producer	Leonard Katzman
Executive Producer	John Mantley

February 4, 1974, preempted for *The Little Mermaid.*

The Foundling. February 11, 1974. Production #0621. Rerun June 3, 1974.

Matt is full of remorse after shooting Eli Baines, a farmer who was on a drunken rampage. He leaves Dodge and goes up to the hills to get over his depression. During a rain storm, Matt takes shelter in a cave and finds a young girl, Lettie, who has just given birth to a baby. When Matt brings Lettie back to her bible-spouting parents, they take their daughter in, but reject the illegitimate child. Matt returns to Dodge with the abandoned baby and puts the little girl in Kitty's charge, until he can find her a good home. Maylee Baines, Eli's widow, wants the homeless baby. Both Matt and Doc think that Maylee would be a wise choice. However, caring for the infant triggers Kitty's maternal instincts and she decides to keep little Mary.

The Television Programs

Lettie	Kay Lenz
Joseph Graham	Donald Moffat
Agnes Graham	Dran Hamilton
Maylee Baines	Bonnie Bartlett
Eli Baines	Don Collier
Bob Ranger	Jerry Hardin
Burke	Ted Jordan
Lathrop	Woodrow Chambliss
Bartender	Robert Brubaker
Story, Script	Jim Byrnes
Executive Story Consultant	Jack Miller
Director	Bernard McEveety
Associate Producer	Ron Honthaner
Producer	Leonard Katzman
Executive Producer	John Mantley

Kay Lenz appeared in *Rich Man, Poor Man* and won an Emmy for *Heart in Hiding*. Her films include *Breezy* and *The Great Scout and Cathouse Thursday*. On television Donald Moffat was featured on *The New Land* and *Logan's Run*. Bonnie Bartlett was a regular on *Little House on the Prairie* and *St. Elsewhere,* for which she won an Emmy in 1986.

The Iron Blood of Courage. February 18, 1974. Production #0622. Rerun June 10, 1974.

Lawyer Colie Burdette incites a group of small ranchers to fight for their water rights against powerful rancher Shaw Anderson. To ensure their success, Burdette hires gunman William Talley. Talley arrives in Dodge accompanied by his wife and daughter, for this is to be his last assignment. Fearing for the lives of their husbands, Mrs. Talley and Mrs. Anderson take drastic steps. They arrange a potentially dangerous rendezvous between their mates. Matt is certain that there will be bloodshed, until something remarkable happens.

Colie Burdette	Lloyd Bochner
William Talley	Eric Braeden
Ellie Talley	Mariette Hartley
Ronilou Talley	Patti Cohoon
Mignon Anderson	Miriam Colon
Shaw Anderson	Gene Evans
Hutchinson	John Milford
Rolfing	Bing Russell
Chandler	Robert Karnes
Nichols	John Baer
Morris	Lloyd Nelson
Toey	Jerry Gatlin
Mrs. O'Roarke	Elizabeth Harrower
Lynit	Nick Ramus
Story, Script	Ron Bishop
Executive Story Consultant	Jack Miller
Director	Gunnar Hellstrom
Associate Producer	Ron Honthaner
Producer	Leonard Katzman
Executive Producer	John Mantley

GUNSMOKE — III. THE PROGRAMS

Lloyd Bochner was featured in several series including *Hong Kong*, *The Richard Boone Show*, and *Dynasty*. Nick Ramus was a regular on *The Chisholms* and *Falcon Crest*.

The Schoolmarm. February 25, 1974. Production #0623.

Sarah Merkle fears that her position as Dodge City's school teacher is at an end. After having been raped by a drunken salesman named Stokes, Sarah discovers that she is pregnant. Widower Carl Pruitt suspects her secret and puts his own admiration for Sarah aside to force Stokes into marrying her. He confronts Stokes, who is less than agreeable, and a fight ensues. Stokes trips and falls down the stairs, fatally injuring himself. When Pruitt refuses to explain the circumstances surrounding the incident, he is charged with murder.

Sarah Merkle	Charlotte Stewart
Carl Pruitt	Lin McCarthy
Stokes	Scott Walker
Lester Pruitt	Todd Lookinland
Howie	Howard Culver
Eliza	Laura Nichols
Thomas	Kevin C. McEveety
Story, Script	Dick Nelson
Executive Story Consultant	Jack Miller
Director	Bernard McEveety
Associate Producer	Ron Honthaner
Producer	Leonard Katzman
Executive Producer	John Mantley

Trail of Bloodshed. March 4, 1974. Production #0615.

Festus is in pursuit of escaped convict, Rance Woolfe, who has robbed and beaten Lathrop. While trying to make his getaway, Woolfe guns down his own brother and wounds his nephew. The young man, Buck Henry, sets out to find Woolfe to settle the score.

Gambler	Craig Stevens
Buck Henry	Kurt Russell
Rance Woolfe	Tom Simcox
Amos Brody	Harry Carey, Jr.
Joanie	Janit Baldin
John Woolfe	Larry Pennell
Lathrop	Woodrow Chambliss
Rita	Nina Roman
Bartender	Read Morgan
Lady Card Dealer	Gloria Dixon
Story	Earl W. Wallace
Script	Paul Savage
Executive Story Consultant	Jack Miller
Director	Bernard McEveety
Associate Producer	Ron Honthaner
Producer	Leonard Katzman
Executive Producer	John Mantley

Craig Stevens is familiar to television audiences as *Peter Gunn*. Stevens has been featured on several other series including *Mr. Broadway*, *The Invisible Man*, and *Dallas*.

The Television Programs

Cowtown Hustler. March 11, 1974. Production #0618. Rerun July 8, 1974.

Moses Darby, a down-and-out pool player, meets up with an ambitious young gambler, Dave Rope. Moses reluctantly takes young Dave as his partner in a hustling scheme. Dave's girlfriend Sally accompanies the two men to Dodge with the hope that after a big win, Dave will finally settle down. Darby is also ready to settle down and is "tired of drifting and tired of being alone." He wants roots and hopes to open a little billiard parlor in a small Colorado town. After Darby wins $1000 from Adam Kearney, Kearney vows to get even. He imports Willie Tomsen, a young expert, to settle the score. Darby sees the high-stakes match as the chance to regain his self respect. Dave, however, sees it as a means to more money. He bets all their savings on Tomsen and then tells Darby to lose.

Moses Darby	Jack Albertson
Dave Rope	Jonathan Goldsmith Lippe
Sally	Nellie Bellflower
Joe Bean	Dabbs Greer
Thaddius McKay	Henry Beckman
Beeton	Lew Brown
Willie Tomsen	John Davis Chandler
Adam Kearney	Richard O'Brien
Cox	Robert Swan
Turner	Chuck Hicks
Story, Script	Jim Byrnes
Executive Story Consultant	Jack Miller
Director	Gunnar Hellstrom
Producer	Leonard Katzman
Associate Producer	Ron Honthaner
Executive Producer	John Mantley

In previous seasons, Dabbs Greer played Mr. Jonas, the owner of Dodge's General Store. Nellie Bellflower was featured on *The Keith Monteith Show* and *East of Eden*. Henry Beckman was a regular on several television series including *McHale's Navy*, *Here Come the Brides*, and *Check It Out*.

To Ride a Yellow Horse. March 18, 1974. Production #0624.

Joan Shepard, an ambitious mother does not consider either Newly or Orlo, "a bone poor dirt farmer," suitable enough to court her daughter. Joan, haunted by memories of her own girlhood, does not want her children to marry the wrong person. After disastrously interfering in her son's life, she tries to manipulate her daughter, Anna May. Although Mrs. Shepard allows Newly to escort Anna May to a dance, once there she maneuvers her daughter into the arms of young Steven Rogers, a wealthy rancher's son.

Joan Shepard	Louise Latham
Anna May	Kathleen Cody
Chester	Thomas Leopold
Orlo	John Reilly
Steven	Parker Stevenson
Judge Brooker	Herb Vigran
Mr. Rogers	Simon Scott
Mrs. O'Roarke	Elizabeth Harrower
Story, Script	Calvin Clements
Executive Story Consultant	Jack Miller

GUNSMOKE — III. THE PROGRAMS

Director .... Vincent McEveety
Associate Producer .... Ron Honthaner
Producer .... Leonard Katzman
Executive Producer .... John Mantley

Thomas Leopold was a regular on *The Ted Knight Show* and *The Steve Allen Variety Hour*. John Reilly was featured on *Dallas*, *As the World Turns*, and *General Hospital*. Simon Scott appeared on *Markham*, *McHale's Navy*, and *Trapper John, M.D.*

Disciple. April 1, 1974. Production #0620.

Matt is shot in his right arm trying to stop a robbery. After Doc removes the bullet, Matt is left without the use of his shooting arm and Doc does not know if Matt will ever be able to shoot as before. Feeling he can no longer protect and serve the residents of Dodge, Matt turns in his badge. He leaves Dodge to learn to live with his handicap. As always, Kitty takes it the hardest. Her fear is that Matt may never return. Matt's journey is interrupted when he must defend himself and Lem, a young army deserter, first from a bounty hunter and then from the gang of outlaws that robbed Dodge. The job is complicated because Lem does not believe in killing, and since Matt is forced to shoot with his left hand, they are at a considerable disadvantage. Meanwhile, back in Dodge, the new marshal arrives and is coldly received by all the residents.

Lew Rawlins .... Dennis Redfield
Loveday .... Frank Marth
Darcy .... Marco St. John
The New Marshal .... Paul Picerni
Bill Jim .... Robert Phillips
Ransom .... R.L. Armstrong
Asa .... David Huddleston
Sissy .... Claire Brennen
Burke .... Ted Jordan
Bartender .... Robert Brubaker
Lathrop .... Woodrow Chambliss
Halligan .... Charles Wagenheim
Barney .... Charles Seel
Junior .... Bobby E. Clark
Story, Script .... Shimon Wincelberg
Executive Story Consultant .... Jack Miller
Director .... Gunnar Hellstrom
Associate Producer .... Ron Honthaner
Producer .... Leonard Katzman
Executive Producer .... John Mantley

Dennis Redfield played Charley Wilks in the comedy series, *Friends*. During his journey Matt departs from wearing his usual "bugger red" shirt and uncharacteristically wears a blue one. The reason that Arness almost always wore the same outfit was so that the editors, if they needed more footage of Matt, could splice segments from any episode and the continuity would flow. *The Disciple* was Amanda Blake's last appearance on the series.

The Widow and the Rogue. April 8, 1974, rerun. First aired October 29, 1973.

Matt's Love Story. April 15, 1974, rerun. First aired September 24, 1973.

The Deadly Innocent. April 22, 1974, rerun. First aired December 17, 1973.

The Television Programs

The Widow-Maker. April 29, 1974, rerun. First aired October 8, 1973.

A Family of Killers. May 13, 1974, rerun. First aired January 14, 1974.

Like Old Times. May 20, 1974, rerun. First aired January 21, 1974.

The Town Tamers. May 27, 1974, rerun. First aired January 28, 1974.

The Foundling. June 3, 1974, rerun. First aired February 11, 1974.

The Iron Blood of Courage. June 10, 1974, rerun. First aired February 18, 1974.

A Game of Death...An Act of Love [Part I]. June 17, 1974, rerun. First aired November 5, 1973.

A Game of Death...An Act of Love [Part II]. June 24, 1974, rerun. First aired November 12, 1973.

The Boy and the Sinner. July 1, 1974, rerun. First aired October 1, 1973.

Cowtown Hustler. July 8, 1974, rerun. First aired March 11, 1974.

Sarah. July 15, 1974, rerun. First aired October 16, 1972.

Snow Train [Part I]. July 22, 1974, rerun. First aired October 19, 1970.

Snow Train [Part II]. July 29, 1974, rerun. First aired October 26, 1970.

Charlie Noon. August 12, 1974, rerun. First aired November 3, 1969.

Waste [Part I]. August 19, 1974, rerun. First aired September 27, 1971.

Waste [Part II]. August 26, 1974, rerun. First aired October 4, 1971.

Chato. September 2, 1974, rerun. First aired September 14, 1970.

TWENTIETH SEASON

The final season

Matt Dillon Must Die. September 9, 1974. Production #0661. Rerun December 30, 1974.

Matt finds himself in the dangerous hands of a half-crazed widower, Abraham Wakefield. Out of a deranged sense of fair play, Abraham releases Matt and gives him an hour's head start. Abraham plans, with the aid of his four sons, to hunt Matt down like an animal and kill him to revenge the death of his son Laban, a wanted murderer. Matt tries to make his escape on foot in freezing mountains while the Wakefields pursue him on horseback.

  Abraham Wakefield .... Morgan Woodward
  Jacob .... Joseph Hindy

GUNSMOKE — III. THE PROGRAMS

Esau	Bill Lucking
Isaac	Henry Olek
Abel	Douglas Dirkson
Laban	Frederick Herrick
Annabelle	Elaine Fulkerson
Story, Script	Roy Goldrup
Executive Story Consultant	Jack Miller
Director	Victor French
Associate Producer	Ron Honthaner
Producer	Leonard Katzman
Executive Producer	John Mantley

Bill Lucking was a regular on several series including *Shannon* and *The A-Team*.

A Town in Chains. September 16, 1974. Production #0656. Rerun June 9, 1975.

Fleeing after a robbery in Dodge and not concerned about Matt being on their trail, five outlaws decide they need one more big heist before retiring to become legitimate businessmen. Posing as Union officers, they declare marshal law on a small town. They easily eliminate their problems with Matt by telling the local sheriff that he is a wanted man. When Matt rides into town to warn the inhabitants the outlaws are prepared for him.

Big Thicket	Ramon Bieri
Arlene	Gretchen Corbett
Oregon	Lance Le Gault
Clatch	Ron Soble
Foss	Don Stroud
Pryor	Russell Wiggins
Sheriff Van Berkle	Med Flory
Muller	John Crawford
Shields	Thad Hall
Welch	Lloyd Nelson
Townsman	Neil Summers
Mr. Burry	Paul C. Thomas
Martha	Francesca Jarvis
Helen	Bernice Smith
Dorothy	Mari Martin
Mary	Margaret L. Kingman
Story, Script	Ron Bishop
Executive Story Consultant	Jack Miller
Director	Bernard McEveety
Associate Producer	Ron Honthaner
Producer	Leonard Katzman
Executive Producer	John Mantley

Gretchen Corbett was featured on *The Rockford Files* and *Otherworld*. Lance Le Gault played Col. Decker on *The A-Team*. Ron Soble was a regular on the television Western, *The Monroes*.

The Guns of Cibola Blanca [Part I]. September 23, 1974. Production #0654. Rerun July 14, 1975.

On route to Dodge, Doc and pretty saloon owner, Lyla Ross, are unfortunate enough to share a stagecoach with a man wanted by comanchero leader, Lucius

The Television Programs

Shindrow. When the stage is attacked, Doc and Lyla become captives in the outlaw's desert fortress. With no hope of escape, Doc and Lyla find themselves virtual slaves.

The Guns of Cibola Blanca [Part II]. September 30, 1974. Production #0654. Rerun July 21, 1975.

With Doc overdue and a stage coach with three passengers missing, Matt and Festus set out to try to find their friend. They pose as outlaws selling guns to the Indians, in order to gain entrance into the desert fortress where Doc and Lyla are being held prisoner. Doc is faced with an ethical dilemma when Ben, the dying son of the comanchero leader, overhears their escape plan. Ben threatens to expose everyone, unless Doc puts him out of his misery by killing him.

Lucius Shindrow	Harold Gould
Lyla	Dorothy Tristan
Coltrain	Richard Anderson
Ben	Michael Christofer
Ivers	James Luisi
Sheriff Stoudenaire	Jackie Coogan
Dr. Rhodes	Henry Beckman
Mady	Gloria Le Roy
Mule Skinner	Shug Fisher
Story, Script	Paul Savage
Executive Story Consultant	Jack Miller
Director	Gunnar Hellstrom
Associate Producer	Ron Honthaner
Producer	Leonard Katzman
Executive Producer	John Mantley

Harold Gould was a regular on several television shows including *Rhoda*. His films include *Love and Death* and *Silent Movie*. James Luisi was featured on *The Rockford Files* and won an Emmy Award in 1976 for *First Ladies' Diaries: Martha Washington*. Jackie Coogan was one of the most famous child stars. He co-starred in *The Kid* with Charlie Chaplin. In more recent years, however, he is recognized as Uncle Fester of *The Addams Family*. Gloria Le Roy appeared regularly on *Hot L Baltimore* and *Kaz*.

Thirty a Month and Found. October 7, 1974. Production 50653. Rerun April 14, 1975.

Three cowboys are frustrated when they find their way of life coming to an end. Losing all their earnings in a drunken evening in Dodge, the cowboys steal what they believe is their money from a bar owner.

Will Parmalee	Gene Evans
Doak	Nicholas Hammond
Quincy	Van Williams
Tait Cavanaugh	David Brian
Storekeeper	Ford Rainey
Katherine	Kim O'Brien
Bull	Victor Izay
Railroader	Hal Baylor
Delilah	Bonnie Jedell
Sheriff	Hank Kendrick
Story, Script	Jim Byrnes
Executive Story Consultant	Jack Miller
Director	Bernard McEveety

GUNSMOKE — III. THE PROGRAMS

Associate Producer .... Ron Honthaner
Producer .... Leonard Katzman
Executive Producer .... John Mantley

Thirty a Month and Found won the Writer's Guild of America Award for Best Episodic Drama and the Spur Award for Best Western Television Script from the Western Writers of America. Van Williams played the title role in *The Green Hornet* and Ken Madison on both *Bourbon Street Beat* and *Surfside Six*.

The Wiving. October 14, 1974. Production #0652. Rerun April 21, 1975.

Farmer Jed Hockett orders his three sons to go to town, and not to return unless they find their future brides. When the three brothers arrive in Dodge, they find that the women do not take too readily to their country ways. Remembering their father's directive, they arrive at what seems to be a simple solution, kidnapping.

Jed Hockett .... Harry Morgan
Ike .... John Reilly
Luke .... Herman Poppe
Sarah Lynn .... Michele Marsh
Shep .... Dennis Redfield
Fran .... Karen Grassle
Emily .... Linda Sublette
Hannah .... Fran Ryan
Floyd .... Robert Brubaker
Cowboy #1 .... Rod McGaughy
Cowboy #2 .... Bobby E. Clark
Story, Script .... Earl Wallace
Executive Story Consultant .... Jack Miller
Director .... Victor French
Associate Producer .... Ron Honthaner
Producer .... Leonard Katzman
Executive Producer .... John Mantley

Actor Victor French directed this episode. According to French this episode spurred a record amount of fan mail and led to the sequel, *Brides and Grooms*, which aired February 10, 1975. Fran Ryan appears as Miss Hannah the new owner of the Long Branch. Karen Grassle is best known for her portrayal of Caroline Ingalls on *Little House on the Prairie*. Linda Sublette was a regular on *The John Byner Comedy Hour*.

The Iron Man. October 21, 1974. Production #0660. Rerun April 7, 1975.

Chauncey Demon, once a highly respected Sheriff, has let himself deteriorate into a saloon bum. However, his old friend Matt will not accept the situation as final. Matt tries to get Demon to give up the bottle and to help him face Ryker, a ruthless cattle baron.

Chauncey Demon .... Cameron Mitchell
Carl Ryker .... John Russell
Kathy Carter .... Barbara Colby
Luke .... George Murdock
Sheriff .... William Bryant
Kane .... Marc Alaimo
Dubbins .... Paul Gehrman
Johnny Carter .... Eric Olson
Mace .... Alec Murdock

The Television Programs

Story, Script, Executive Producer	John Mantley
Executive Story Consultant	Jack Miller
Director	Gunnar Hellstrom
Associate Producer	Ron Honthaner
Producer	Leonard Katzman

Cameron Mitchell played John Lackman on *The Beachcomber*, Buck Cannon on *High Chaparral*, and Jeremiah Worth on *Swiss Family Robinson*. John Russell is best known on television as marshal Dan Troop of *The Lawman*. Marc Alaimo was featured on the short-lived comedy, *Billy*. Eric Olson was a regular on *Apple's Way* and *Swiss Family Robinson*.

The Fourth Victim. November 4, 1974. Production #0659. Rerun April 28, 1975.

A series of seemingly random killings have the citizens of Dodge in a panic, but Matt believes they are part of a pattern in which Doc is slated to be the next victim. Matt is unsuccessful in trying to force Doc to stay in hiding until the murderer is caught. Instead, Doc decides to set a trap using himself as bait.

Potter	Biff McGuire
Ray Price	Leonard Stone
Lathrop	Woodrow Chambliss
Bill Saxbe	Paul Sorensen
Howie	Howard Culver
Homer Jones	Victor Killian
Henry Meeker	Lloyd Perryman
Jeb Nelson	Frank K. Janson
Earl Haines	Al Wyatt
Second Matt	Ben Bates
Third Matt	Alex Sharp
Story, Script	Jim Byrnes
Executive Story Consultant	Jack Miller
Director	Bernard McEveety
Associate Producer	Ron Honthaner
Producer	Leonard Katzman
Executive Producer	John Mantley

While going over a jury list from 15 years ago, Matt makes references to both Quint Asper and Chester Goode. Biff McGuire appeared on *Gibbsville*.

The Tarnished Badge. November 11, 1974. Production #0657. Rerun June 2, 1975.

Sheriff Beau Harker is a town tamer who keeps the citizens of Ludlow in line by using a heavy hand. The townsfolk convince Matt to fire his old friend Harker, but Harker angrily resents Matt's interference, and a showdown seems inevitable.

Sheriff Harker	Victor French
Grandma Boggs	Ruth McDevitt
Jenny Blair	Pamela McMyler
Barney Austin	Nick Nolte
Story, Script	Robert Vincent Wright
Executive Story Consultant	Jack Miller
Director	Michael O'Herlihy
Associate Producer	Ron Honthaner
Producer	Leonard Katzman
Executive Producer	John Mantley

GUNSMOKE — III. THE PROGRAMS

Ruth McDevitt was a regular on several television shows including *Mr. Peepers, Kolchak: The Night Stalker,* and *All in the Family.* Before zooming into superstardom with such hits as *48 Hours* and *Down and Out in Beverly Hills,* Nick Nolte made a splash in the mini-series *Rich Man, Poor Man.*

In Performance of Duty. November 18, 1974. Production #0658.

Emmett Kaysinger and his gang kill Frank Benton and seriously injure Benton's wife. Matt arrests the Kaysingers but is unable to find the stolen money, or other incriminating evidence. This leaves only Mrs. Benton's identification of them as means for conviction, and the chances of her recovery are slim. Matt is frustrated by Judge Kendall's insistence that Kaysinger and his gang, all known outlaws, be set free unless there is solid evidence to hold them.

Judge Kendall	Eduard Franz
Emmett	David Huddleston
Agnes Benton	Bonnie Bartlett
Frank Benton	Rance Howard
Story, Script	William Keys
Executive Story Consultant	Jack Miller
Director	Gunnar Hellstrom
Associate Producer	Ron Honthaner
Producer	Leonard Katzman
Executive Producer	John Mantley

Island in the Desert [Part I]. December 2, 1974. Production #0662. Rerun May 12, 1975.

After Matt and Festus capture fugitive Gard Dixon, Matt heads for Dodge leaving Festus in charge of bringing Dixon back. Unfortunately, Dixon manages to escape and shoots Festus. The wounded deputy, certain to die in the barren desert, is saved by Ben Snow, a half-crazed desert hermit. However, Snow's motives are far from altruistic. As soon as Festus is able, Snow forces him to become a human pack animal.

Island in the Desert [Part II]. December 9, 1974. Production #0662. Rerun May 19, 1975.

Snow forces Festus to carry his long hidden gold back to civilization. As Festus carries Snow's treasure across the barren desert, they encounter Dixon, the killer who shot Festus and left him for dead. The old hermit makes Dixon another unwilling participant in his compulsive drive to satisfy an old grudge.

Ben Snow	Strother Martin
Gard Dixon	William C. Watson
Sheriff Grimes	Regis J. Cordic
Sheriff Lipon	Hank Brandt
Story, Script	Jim Byrnes
Executive Story Consultant	Jack Miller
Director	Gunnar Hellstrom
Associate Producer	Ron Honthaner
Producer	Leonad Katzman
Executive Producer	John Mantley

The Colonel. December 16, 1974. Production #0651.

Colonel Josiah Johnson, a once proud military officer, faces a painful and un-

The Television Programs

planned reunion with his daughter, Anne. Josiah, now the town drunk, decides to keep their relationship secret, due to Anne's impending marriage. When the groom-to-be forbids Josiah to attend the wedding, he tries to leave town quietly, but a gang of outlaws frustrates his plan.

Josiah	Lee J. Cobb
Anne	Julie Cobb
Bill Higgins	Richard Ely
Obie	Randolph Roberts
Jeff Higgins	Roy Jenson
Floyd	Robert Brubaker
Corporal	Todd Lookinland
Carl	Dan Travanty
Biggs	Pete Kellett
Story, Script	Arthur Dales
Executive Story Consultant	Jack Miller
Director	Bernard McEveety
Associate Producer	Ron Honthaner
Producer	Leonard Katzman
Executive Producer	John Mantley

Veteran actor Lee J. Cobb starred in such classic films as *On the Waterfront* and *The Brothers Karamazov*, both of which won him Oscar nominations. His other films include *Exodus, The Three Faces of Eve,* and *The Exorcist.* Julie Cobb is his daughter.

Matt Dillon Must Die. December 30, 1974, rerun. First aired September 9, 1974.

The Squaw. January 6, 1975. Production #0665. Rerun June 16, 1975.

Gristy Calhoun double-crosses his partner in crime and takes off. Both his ex-partner and Matt track Gristy through the Badlands. Gristy soon discovers that his survival depends on the help of Quahnah, an Indian woman. Although Quahnah is necessary for Gristy's escape, she later proves to be the key to his capture.

Gristy Calhoun	John Saxon
Quahnah	Arlene Martel
Charlie Dent	Tom Reese
Brinker	Morgan Paull
Story, Script	Jim Byrnes
Executive Story Consultant	Jack Miller
Director	Gunnar Hellstrom
Associate Producer	Ron Honthaner
Producer	Leonard Katzman
Executive Producer	John Mantley

The title *The Squaw* was used November 11, 1961.

The Hiders. January 13, 1975. Production #0666. Rerun June 30, 1975.

Karp and his associates are cattle skinners, who make their living lawfully by scavenging skins from range cattle. When they overstep their legal boundaries, they find themselves confronted by the law. Karp's desire for revenge is particularly directed toward Festus, who has tried to help young Dink leave the hiders for a more decent life.

Karp	Ned Beatty
Dink	Mitch Vogel

GUNSMOKE — III. THE PROGRAMS

Quincannon	Lee de Broux
Story, Script	Paul Savage
Executive Story Consultant	Jack Miller
Director	Victor French
Associate Producer	Ron Honthaner
Producer	Leonard Katzman
Executive Producer	John Mantley

Ned Beatty has appeared in such movies as *Deliverance, All the President's Men, Network,* and *Superman.* He has starred in numerous made-for-television movies including *Friendly Fire.*

Larkin. January 20, 1975. Production #0667. Rerun June 23, 1975.

Even after being wounded by bounty hunters, Newly refuses to arm his prisoner Larkin. The deputy tries to fight impossible odds and his strength quickly fades. Fate tosses Newly into a strange alliance with Larkin, as he tries to get him to Dodge before they are both killed by the bounty hunters.

Larkin	Richard Jaeckel
Lon Toomes	Anthony Caruso
Tucker	Robert Gentry
Hickory	Robert Sorrells
Melissa Cass	Kathleen Cody
Woman	Maggie Malooly
Jess	Michael Le Clair
Angus	Jack Rader
Farmer	Elliot Lindsay
Waiter	Gilman W. Rankin
Story, Script	Jim Byrnes
Executive Story Consultant	Jack Miller
Director	Gunnar Hellstrom
Associate Producer	Ron Honthaner
Producer	Leonard Katzman
Executive Producer	John Mantley

Maggie Malooly was featured on television's *Little Women.*

The Fires of Ignorance. January 27, 1975. Production #0668. Rerun August 18, 1975.

Oliver Harker, having decided that his son Tommy is spending too much time reading books, takes the boy out of school to concentrate on farm work. However, Tommy's desire to learn cannot be quelled. He goes back to his teacher, Henry Decory, on the sly. When Harker discovers this, he is livid. Decory tries to intercede on behalf of Tommy, but soon finds that his views on education provoke strong, even violent, feelings on the part of Harker. Decory's belief in compulsory education leads to a trial, and heated clashes with the irate townsfolk, who feel Decory is interfering with a father's rights.

Henry Decory	Allen Garfield
Oliver Harker	John Vernon
Tommy Harker	Lance Kerwin
Ami Harker	Diane Shalet
Judge Brooker	Herb Vigran
Mr. Bruce	George DiCenzo
Sallie	Karen Oberdiear

The Television Programs

Bud	John Pickard
Halligan	Charles Wagenheim
Floyd	Robert Brubaker
Lucy	Janet Nichols
Burke	Ted Jordan
Story, Script	Jim Byrnes
Executive Story Consultant	Jack Miller
Director	Victor French
Associate Producer	Ron Honthaner
Producer	Leonard Katzman
Executive Producer	John Mantley

The Fires of Ignorance won the National Education Award. Character actor Allen Garfield appeared in such films as *The Long Goodbye, Nashville,* and *The Stunt Man.* John Vernon was featured in National Lampoon's *Animal House* and on television on the spin-off series, *Delta House.* Lance Kerwin played the title role in the television series, *James at 15.* Karen Oberdiear appeared in the series *Texas Wheelers.*

The Angry Land. February 3, 1975. Production #0669. Rerun August 11, 1975.

Matt brings a young orphan, Bessie Sutherland, to live with her Aunt Rachel, only to discover that she is not wanted. Rachel recently buried both her young son and her husband, and views Bessie as someone she is afraid to love. Rachel fears that Bessie, too, might be taken from her.

Rachel	Carol Vogel
Bessie	Eileen McDonough
Mr. Holmby	Dayton Lummis
Man	Bruce M. Fischer
Story	Herman Groves
Script	Jim Byrnes
Executive Story Consultant	Jack Miller
Director	Bernard McEveety
Associate Producer	Ron Honthaner
Producer	Leonard Katzman
Executive Producer	John Mantley

Dayton Lummis was Marshal Andy Morrison on the television Western series, *Law of the Plainsman.*

Brides and Grooms. February 10, 1975. Production #0673.

Jed Hockett decides that a wedding for his three sons is the only way he is going to get their minds back to farm work. Jed sets the date for the multiple weddings, but a trio of rowdy cowboys and some last minute cold feet complicate the plan.

Jed Hockett	Harry Morgan
Ike	David Soul
Fran	Amanda McBroom
Sarah	Michele Marsh
Shep	Dennis Redfield
Jinx	Spencer Milligan
Cliff Tobin	Ray Girardin
Rev. Mr. Sims	Jim Backus
Miss Hannah	Fran Ryan
Story, Script	Earl W. Wallace

GUNSMOKE — III. THE PROGRAMS

Executive Story Consultant .... Jack Miller
Director .... Victor French
Associate Producer .... Ron Honthaner
Producer .... Leonard Katzman
Executive Producer .... John Mantley

The characters from a previous episode *The Wiving* are reunited in this sequel. David Soul is best known as detective Ken "Hutch" Hutchinson of *Starsky and Hutch*. Ray Girardin was featured in the television comedy, *Charlie and Company*. Jim Backus has starred in numerous television shows including *I Married Joan, The Jim Backus Show,* and *Blondie*. However, he is probably best known for two other television roles, Thurston Howell, III, from *Gilligan's Island* and the voice of the near sighted cartoon character, Mr. Magoo. His film credits include the classic, *Rebel Without a Cause*.

Hard Labor. February 24, 1975. Production #0674. Rerun August 25, 1975.

While in the town of Bedrock, Matt is forced to shoot a fugitive. Judge Flood finds Matt guilty of murder and sentences him to life imprisonment at hard labor. Unless he can escape, Matt will spend the rest of his life underground, digging in Judge Flood's silver mine. Matt's chances of a getaway are slim, since no other prisoner has ever succeeded in escaping.

Judge Flood .... John Colicos
Widge .... Hal Williams
Latch .... William Smith
Elton Prine .... Kevin Coughlin
Fifer .... Ben Piazza
Osuna .... Gregory Sierra
Pete Murphy .... Gerald McRaney
Mike .... Don Megowan
Bar Girl .... Jackie Russell
Jury Foreman .... Lloyd Nelson
Guard .... Fred Lerner
Story .... Hal Sitowitz
Script .... Earl W. Wallace
Executive Story Consultant .... Jack Miller
Director .... Bernard McEveety
Associate Producer .... Ron Honthaner
Producer .... Leonard Katzman
Executive Producer .... John Mantley

John Colicos appeared as Count Baltar on *Battlestar Galactica* and Mikkos Cassadine on *General Hospital*. Hal Williams was featured in numerous television series including *Sanford and Son, Private Benjamin,* and *227*. Ben Piazza was a regular on such shows as *Ben Casey* and *Dallas*.

I Have Promises to Keep. March 3, 1975. Production #0671. Rerun August 4, 1975.

When an Eastern preacher sets out to build a church that is open to both the Indians and the townspeople, he encounters prejudice. He ignores the many obstacles in his way, and Festus is inadvertently made a part of his crusade.

Reverend Byrne .... David Wayne
Reverend Atkins .... Tom lacy
Dunbar .... Ken Swofford
Tonkowa .... Ken Renard

The Television Programs

Meala	Trini Tellez
Hannah	Fran Ryan
Waiter	John Wheeler
Freight Angel	Ed McCready
Story	William Putnam
Script	William Putnam & Earl W. Wallace
Executive Story Consultant	Jack Miller
Director	Vincent McEveety
Associate Producer	Ron Honthaner
Producer	Leonard Katzman
Executive Producer	John Mantley

William Putnam is writer Paul Savage's pseudonym.

The Busters. March 10, 1975. Production #0672. Rerun September 1, 1975.

Two bronco busters, Harve Daley and Mitch Hansen, risk their necks to raise money to buy a ranch in Montana. Unfortunately, their dream is shattered by a wild stallion when Harve is thrown by the horse and is gravely injured. However, he dismisses his injury, and prepares to leave for the big sky country with his fiancee Zoe. Burdened with the truth about Harve's condition, Mitch is frustrated when Zoe comes between them.

Harve Daley	Gary Busey
Mitch Hansen	John Beck
Zoe	Lynn Benesch
Story, Script	Jim Byrnes
Executive Story Consultant	Jack Miller
Director	Bernard McEveety
Associate Producer	Ron Honthaner
Producer	Leonard Katzman
Executive Producer	John Mantley

This was the last episode to air on *Gunsmoke* as a rerun. In a September 1, 1975, *Los Angeles Times* article, John Mantley said of the episode, "It's a Captain Ahab kind of story, the bronc is the White Whale the boy must conquer. Maybe it is significant as the last *Gunsmoke*. It's going out with all your flags flying, not slinking out like a thief in the night. That's the proper way for *Gunsmoke* to end." This episode won for Jim Byrnes an award for Best Western Television Script from the Western Writers of America. Gary Busey won critical praise for his performance in *The Buddy Holly Story*. His other films include *Silver Bullet* and *Straight Time*.

Manolo. March 17, 1975. Production #0670. Rerun July 28, 1975.

Manolo is not recognized as a man in the eyes of his people because he refuses to fight his father Alejo. The fight is a traditional Basque custom to prove one's manhood. Manolo's fear is not for his own safety, but for his father's. He is afraid he might kill the proud old man.

Manolo	Robert Urich
Alejo	Nehemiah Persoff
Joachim	Mark Shera
Hannah	Fran Ryan
Joe Barnes	Brian James
Story	Harriet Charles & Earl W. Wallace
Script	Earl W. Wallace

GUNSMOKE — III. THE PROGRAMS

Executive Story Consultant .... Jack Miller
Director .... Gunnar Hellstrom
Associate Producer .... Ron Honthaner
Producer .... Leonard Katzman
Executive Producer .... John Mantley

Among his television credits, Robert Urich has starred in *Spenser: For Hire* and as Dan Tanna on *Vega$*. Mark Shera played Jedediah on *Barnaby Jones*. Both Urich and Shera were featured on *S.W.A.T.*

The Sharecroppers. March 31, 1975. Production #0663.

Av Marie Pugh is a young lady who has her hands full trying to get her lazy family to plant a crop. If Av Marie is unsuccessful their landlord will have them evicted, but her father Dibble Pugh does not take kindly to working. In desperation, Av Marie pulls together all her savings to buy a mule. When her brother Abel is wounded, Festus and the mule find themselves working a plow on the Pugh farm.

Abel .... Terry Williams
Av Marie .... Suzanne Benton
Dibble Pugh .... Victor French
Linder Hogue .... Jacque Aubuchon
Tobe Hogue .... Bruce Boxleitner
Additional Cast .... Lisa Eilbacher, Graham Jarvis
Story, Script .... Earl W. Wallace
Executive Story Consultant .... Jack Miller
Director .... Leonard Katzman
Associate Producer .... Ron Honthaner
Producer .... Leonard Katzman
Executive Producer .... John Mantley

Bruce Boxleitner has always held a fondness for Westerns and has appeared on several. He was featured as Luke Macahan in *How the West Was Won,* which starred James Arness, and in the recent television remake of *Red River,* also with Arness. Boxleitner's other television credits include the popular adventure series, *Scarecrow and Mrs. King* and the ambitious, but unsuccessful, adventure-comedy, *Bring 'Em Back Alive.* Graham Jarvis was a regular on *Mary Hartman, Mary Hartman, Making the Grade,* and *Fame.*

The Iron Man. April 7, 1975, rerun. First aired October 21, 1974.

Thirty a Month and Found. April 14, 1975, rerun. First aired October 7, 1974.

The Wiving. April 21, 1975, rerun. First aired October 14, 1974.

The Fourth Victim. April 28, 1975, rerun. First aired November 4, 1974.

Island in the Desert [Part I]. May 12, 1975, rerun. First aired December 2, 1974.

Island in the Desert [Part II]. May 19, 1975, rerun. First aired December 9, 1974.

The Tarnished Badge. June 2, 1975, rerun. First aired November 11, 1974.

Town in Chains. June 9, 1975, rerun. First aired September 16, 1974.

The Television Programs

The Squaw. June 16, 1975, rerun. First aired January 6, 1975.

Larkin. June 23, 1975, rerun. First aired January 20, 1975.

The Hiders. June 30, 1975, rerun. First aired January 13, 1975.

Guns of Cibola Blanca [Part I]. July 14, 1975, rerun. First aired September 23, 1974.

Guns of Cibola Blanca [Part II]. July 21, 1975, rerun. First aired September 30, 1974.

Manolo. July 28, 1975, rerun. First aired March 17, 1975.

I Have Promises to Keep. August 4, 1975, rerun. First aired March 3, 1975.

The Angry Land. August 11, 1975, rerun. First aired February 3, 1975.

The Fires of Ignorance. August 18, 1975, rerun. First aired January 27, 1975.

Hard Labor. August 25, 1975, rerun. First aired February 24, 1975.

The Busters. September 1, 1975, rerun. First aired March 10, 1975.

Gunsmoke: Return to Dodge. September 26, 1987. Two-hour, made-for-television movie.

It is 15 years since we have seen the residents of Dodge. Matt Dillon is retired and is living the life of a mountain man. He is a trapper and plays "uncle" to a bunch of Indian children. Newly O'Brien is the marshal of Dodge, and Miss Hannah still runs the Long Branch. Miss Kitty, having gotten Matt out of her system, lives in New Orleans. Matt's life of tranquility is interrupted when an ex-con, Logan, arrives to settle an old grudge. Matt, still quick on the trigger, outdraws Logan, and feels it is his duty to bring the man back to Dodge. On route, the two are attacked by some seedy mountain folks, who want Matt's skins and rifle. They kill Matt's prisoner and stab the ex-lawman. Matt is not expected to live. However, he pulls through, and when he opens his eyes, Kitty is there beside him, and explains, "Old habits die hard." Meanwhile, back in territorial prison, Matt's arch-nemesis, Will Mannon, is being released. Mannon has just one thing on his mind, revenge. Jack Flagg, an old friend of Matt's who is also in the territorial prison, escapes to warn him. This sets off a chain of events that lead to confrontations with the mountain men, a young inexperienced army officer, and some friendly Indians. The final showdown, however is between Matt and Mannon.

Matt Dillon	James Arness
Kitty Russell	Amanda Blake
Will Mannon	Steve Forrest
Jake Flagg	Earl Holliman
Newly O'Brien	Buck Taylor
Miss Hannah	Fran Ryan
Lieutenant Dexter	Ken Olandt
Digger	W. Morgan Sheppard
Bright Water	Patrice Martinez
Little Doe	Tantoo Cardinal

GUNSMOKE — III. THE PROGRAMS

Oakum	Mickey Jones
Logan	Frank M. Totino
Warden Brown	Robert Koons
Judge Collins	Walter Kaasa
Mrs. Collins	Georgie Collins
Farnum	Tony Epper
Bubba	Louie Ellias
Potts	Ken Kirzinger
Clyman	Denny Arnold
The Flogger	Alex Green
Harry	Paul Daniel Wood
Wilber	Larry Musser
Guard	Robert Clinton
Watt	Frank Huish
Hutter	Jacob Rupp
Indian Woman	Mary Jane Wildman
Writer	Jim Byrnes
Director	Vincent McEveety
Producer	John Mantley

CBS had been planning a sequel to *Gunsmoke* for several years. It was originally projected to air in November 1985 but it took two more years to develop a script and produce the special. After a 12-year absence, it brought together James Arness, Amanda Blake, Buck Taylor and John Mantley. The movie was dedicated to the memory of Milburn Stone, Glenn Strange, James Nusser, Woodrow Chambliss, Charles Wagenheim, Charles Seel, and Roy Barcroft. Mantley explained that he "never considered having a new Doc" and Milburn Stone was incorporated into the story from flashbacks. Dennis Weaver had been approached for the special, but his agent said that he was unavailable. Weaver was getting ready to shoot his new television series, *Buck James*. Ken Curtis expressed an interest but the financial details could not be agreed upon. "Festus," "Sam" and "Burke" were also seen from flash-backs from *The Badge* (February 2, 1970) and *Mannon* (January 20, 1969). The two-hour special was filmed in Calgary, Alberta, which caused a great deal of hard feelings from fans who wanted the show filmed in the States. The show cost $3.5 million and was filmed in Canada because filming in the States would have demanded a budget of $4.2 million. It was a very emotional time for the cast. They were going home after all the intervening years, back to Dodge. Mantley explained that it was like "Joe Louis climbing back into the ring after all those years. And we saw Joe Louis get the hell kicked out of him." He recalls the reaction when Blake walked on the set of the Long Branch Saloon after a 13-year-absence:

> When she walked on the set, I introduced her to the people as the first lady of the Long Branch. All the extras were there and they all stood on their feet and applauded and she began to cry...

In a recent interview, Blake remembered the experience:

> It was just wonderful. It felt like stepping into an old pair of bedroom slippers. The first day for me on the set was...well, I was just a mess the whole day. I couldn't stop crying. I just kept bubbling up...I hadn't seen Jim for several years...The last time I'd seen him, we had been at Oklahoma City at the Cowboy Hall of Fame...It was just incredible...And Buck Taylor, I had done Buck's test with him when he tested for the role of Newly...It was a

very, very emotional thing for me, it really was and I was just a blubbering fool the whole first day... And of course, I got all sentimental and we talked about Milburn and I cried over him, "The only thing that's wrong here is Milly isn't here." And then I thought, "Well he is really, he is here viewing things, he's going to change this."... It was fabulous. It was a most, most happy experience. I just hope that CBS gets their act together and does another one... I'd be delighted.

James Arness reflected about making the special:

There had been some talk about it. I know John Mantley had spoken about it over the years... It turned out to be a great experience. I had a lot of hesitation about doing it. It was difficult to think of coming back and trying to resurrect this guy after all this time. I felt a little uneasy about it because of the fact that there were so many people still out there that had this memory of the show and of us. I was afraid that if we didn't bring it off right, instead of having given all those old fans a wonderful evening, we would leave them hanging out to dry with a disappointed feeling about the whole thing. I was concerned about that. But I felt it was a good show and I think the reaction to it was good. And so we seemed to get away with it, anyway.

PART IV.
APPENDICES

APPENDIX A
QUOTES FROM
GUNSMOKE

The writers for *Gunsmoke* were among the finest on radio and television. Many followed Meston's lead and strove for authenticity, researching their subject in great depth. They sought to capture the Western "idiom" and heighten realism. The principal actors were tough judges, for they had lived in Dodge City so long they knew when a phrase rang false and were quick to point it out. Over the years there was a great deal of wisdom offered on the show, and a lot of humor. Here is a collection of classic quotes.

HANK: They got a saying down there, when the sheriff handcuffs a man, you can start diggin' his grave. — *No Handcuffs,* written by Les Crutchfield/story by John Meston.

YERMO: You sure ain't one to let a man die happy, are ya marshal? MATT: A man makes his dying by the way he lives, Yermo. — *Stage Hold-Up,* written by Les Crutchfield/story by John Meston.

CHESTER: Mister Dillon, you've heard me talk about Stone County? MATT: ...Yeah. According to you that's a hideout for bandits. CHESTER: Yes, sir, that's right... You know they got a saying down there that if the law ever did catch any of them, there wouldn't be enough good men there to act as a jury to try the bad ones. — *Gun for Chester,* by John Meston.

MATT: Chester, Kitty knows a lot of men. — *Kitty's Outlaw,* written by Kathleen Hite/story by John Meston.

MATT: Well, it's like I was telling Chester, Doc. Kitty knows a lot of men. — *Kitty's Outlaw,* written by Kathleen Hite/story by John Meston.

NAT: You don't understand, Marshal. I got nothin' against you. MATT: Then why did you try to shoot me for then? NAT: Well, I came into town and I heard all that talk about how somebody was gonna kill you, and I thought... I figured that I could make a name for myself if *I* did it. I swear there wasn't any more to it than that. DOC: No more to it than that, eh? NAT: Well, nothin' personal. — *The Coward*, by John Meston.

PANACEA: *(To Doc)* You doctor animals or people? MATT: Well, now, there's been some questions about that, ma'am. DOC: People, mostly. — *Panacea Sykes*, by Kathleen Hite.

PANACEA: Mercy, I'm as weak as a kitten, Marshal. FOOTE: That's a trick. Watch it, Marshal. She'll pry the gold right out of your teeth. MATT: Would you like some coffee, Panacea? PANACEA: Mercy, no. FOOTE: Half a bottle of whiskey will bring her around. — *Panacea Sykes*, by Kathleen Hite.

MATT: Now why did you pass the word all around town that you were leaving today on a train? CLOVIS: Did I say that? MATT: You know, I can always kick you in the head and take you back to Dodge in a sack. — *The F. U.*, by John Meston.

CLOVIS: Let me have a gun. I can help you. You can trust me. MATT: Clovis, I wouldn't trust you if you were in church praying. — *The F. U.*, by John Meston.

WILKS: *(To Matt, as he is being locked up)* ... You know what you've cost me? For the last two years I've had a post job at Fort Dodge. An easy one. No horses, no chasing around on the prairie. No nothin'. What do you think the colonel's going to do with me, now? MATT: If he does what I think he will, he'll send you out on the longest patrol he's got. WILKS: And all because I was protecting myself against a guy who was trying to beat my brains out. MATT: He never laid a hand on you. WILKS: I suppose I got these bruises from chewing taffy? — *Hung High*, by John Meston.

MATT: ... I always thought of you as being indestructable. I figured you'd go on forever. JIM: No one is indestructable, Matt. A man could be shot at or knifed up just so many times. The law of averages is bound to close in on him. I wanted to turn in my badge myself. Not have some coroner do it for me. — *Hung High*, by John Meston.

MATT: ... Jim, you always took more chances than most. JIM: Is there any other way to do this job? MATT: That's what you taught me. Along with about everything else I learned. JIM: You were the best student I ever had. MATT: I don't know about that. JIM: Well, you have to be. All the others are dead. — *Hung High*, by John Meston.

MATT: He's gonna make it? DOC: No. He never had a chance. — *Hung High*, by John Meston.

Quotes from Gunsmoke

CHESTER: What is it, Doc? Huh? What is it? DOC: Ah, Chester, he never had a chance. — *The F.U.*, by John Meston.

MATT: Anything I can get you? LEONA: What in the world would I need? I have a jelly-spined ex-husband downstairs who wouldn't lift a hand to preserve the sanctity of our marriage. I have another slow-drawing ex-boyfriend who's lying on a board at the undertakers. I also have another ex-boyfriend who just broke jail and is probably ready to wring my neck. Now what else could a good woman want, Marshal? — *A Time for the Jackals*, by Paul Savage.

KITTY: Matt, you can't account for everything that happens to people who touch you. You know I learned a long time ago there's some things in this life you just accept the way they are. MATT: Pretty deep for a redhead. KITTY: I'm a pretty deep redhead. — *A Time for the Jackals*, by Paul Savage.

JESSE: I got it all worked out. One, two, three. You, me, and my friends are going to be richer than we ever figured. Yessir, three hundred thousand dollars. BRANT: You know, that man's got a light in his eyes. And I'm gonna find out if that light means you've gotta be the smartest fella I ever met or flat out the craziest, or what. JESSE: *(Laughing, takes a rifle and shoots Brant in the stomach)* Well, which is it, Brant? Smart or flat out crazy. Take a good look before the light goes out. — *A Time for the Jackals*, by Paul Savage.

MATT: *(On Boot Hill)* I try to remember that if they'd argued a little they might not be here. Arguing doesn't fill any graves. Take me, I'm a U.S. Marshal. How many times I'd rather have argued than gone for guns. Take Dodge City over there, Gomorrah of the plains they call it. Jump-off spot. People coming and going all the time. Good, bad and worse. Tempers high. A man'll draw a gun quicker to prove a point than he'll draw on his logic. That's where I come in. Whether they like it or not. When they draw their guns somebody's got to be around. Somebody on the law's side. And the Lord knows they hate that. — Prologue to *Matt Gets It*, written by Charles Marquis Warren/story by John Meston.

NIP: You hold your tongue for twenty years and then you blow me up with a shotgun? You're quite a woman, Nettie, quite a woman... Funny I never noticed that. NETTIE: You ain't looked at me in twenty years. NIP: I'm looking at you now. — *Tap Day for Kitty*, written by John Dunkel/story by John Meston.

MATT: ...It took her twenty years and a little buckshot, but she finally landed him. KITTY: Twenty years?... That's an awfully long time. I don't know whether I could wait that long... A little buckshot, huh? MATT: Hey now, wait a minute. KITTY: What's a matter, you scared? — *Tap Day for Kitty*, written by John Dunkel/story by John Meston.

MATT: *(On Boot Hill)* Out here I remind myself how violence ends. Buried on the rim of a nation. The edge of a wild frontier. Some of these Boot Hill men are the victims of aimless slaughter. The rest I killed myself. I'm a lawman, United States Marshal. The law comes hard to the frontier. Men like these didn't want it... And more men still alive, in Dodge City... They don't want it. They're the drifters, the killers and the spoilers, and they have to be met. It's a chancey job. It makes a man watchful and a little lonely, but somebody has to do it. — Prologue to *Hack Prine*, by John Meston.

KITTY: Men, they're gabbier than women. MATT: Maybe they are, when they're with you. KITTY: Matt, do you think that if I closed my eyes and prayed real hard that they'd all go away? MATT: Then what would you do for a living? — *Hack Prine*, by John Meston.

MATT: You're killing days are over, Crego. This time *you're* gonna die. CREGO: I ain't gonna fight you. I'm taking off my gun right now. Now, Marshal, you can't shoot an unarmed man. MATT: That's not gonna save you, Crego. You put that gun back on and you come out in the street. I'm gonna give you just one minute. And then I'm coming back in after you. And armed or unarmed, I'm gonna kill you. — *The Killer*, written by John Dunkel/story by John Meston.

MATT: The lawman's got a full-time job out here that spans the whole field of human problems. One man came to me because his sister'd stopped going to church. And just recently another complained that somebody'd blown his neighbor's head off with a shotgun and left the rest lying on the road for the hawks to eat. That one I solved. But the girl is still spending her Sundays out picking berries. Sometimes I think I'd be better off clerking in a Philadelphia bank. But that's not the way it is. Matt Dillon, U.S. Marshal. — Prologue to *Buffalo Man*, written by Les Crutchfield/story by John Meston.

MATT: The law says you can't murder people, Steed. STEED: Indians is people, huh? MATT: That's right. STEED: How 'bout that. — *Saludos*, written by John Meston/story by Les Crutchfield.

MATT: Peggar, hanging's too good for a man like you. — *Saludos*, written by John Meston/story by Les Crutchfield.

FAVORITE: *(To his horse, while concealed and taking aim at Matt through his gunsight)* Yessir, Slick. I'll be a gelded rooster if I figure out why they do it. All on account of I gutted me a gambler crooked as a gulley. You figure they'd be right glad to get rid of him. But no. Got them laws tattooed on their eyeballs... They don't never learn. Just keep comin' after you bigger than a skinned mule. Fool doin's. There aught to be a law about the law. Listen here, though. He's got sand to him. Most of 'em don't have. Still and all, gonna lose his life. They don't never learn. — *Matt's Love Story*, by Ron Bishop.

Quotes from Gunsmoke

FAVORITE: *(To Miss Mike)* ...I come to kill you ma'am. Starcourt, he wants this valley short grass and long. He's paid me a hundred eagles, full feather. Hundred more in a bank in town. I done bent low in recent times...But not this low. A man could pound dreams to iron with a woman like you... — *Matt's Love Story*, by Ron Bishop.

DOC: Good morning, Chester. CHESTER: Oh, good morning, Doc. What's the matter? Somebody sick today or something? DOC: Somebody's always sick, Chester. That's why I'm rich. CHESTER: Yeah, well you know I ain't been feelin' too good myself lately. I got them shootin' pains back here again. You know, like when you breathe deep. It's like itchy right here. DOC: Yep. CHESTER: Well, what would you prescribe for somethin' like that? DOC: An office call...Two dollars. — *Young Man with a Gun*, written by Winston Miller/story by John Meston.

DOC: *(To Peyt)* You miserable young whelp...I'm going to tell you something, son. I don't know why I bother to do it. But Matt Dillon can let you practice with that gun for the next ten years. He can let you aim it right at him, and he can still draw and kill you before you can squeeze the trigger. Now you quit your foolin' around. Throw that thing away and get out of Dodge before somebody carries you out. You hear? — *Young Man with a Gun*, written by Winston Miller/story by John Meston.

LOUIE PHEETERS: Me...I'm a bum... Like you say, I ain't even got the courage of a night-moth banging on the window. — *O'Quillian*, by Ron Bishop.

O'QUILLIAN: Louie, you and me are dreamers. *(Pointing to bottle)* And here is the birthplace of dreams, if we can capture them... The world needs dreamers, and the world owes us, the dreamers, a meal when we come to its doors. It does, Louie. It owes us. — *O'Quillian*, by Ron Bishop.

O'QUILLIAN: *(As Matt locks him up)* Turn the key, Marshal. Oh, turn the key. And lock me mortal composition in your hellish dungeon. But know that when you do, the spirit of O'Quillian soars beyond your grasp and reach. MATT: Why don't you lie down and get some sleep. O'QUILLIAN: Sleep? Sleep, indeed. Sleep...sleep you say? The time will come when aught but sleep will be my fate. Oh, sleep. The very cousin of death itself. When death's cold arms will be around me...Sleep! Sleep, indeed! — *O'Quillian*, by Ron Bishop.

MATT: O'Quillian, what I understand is that when you dig a hole in this earth, you owe it to the earth to fill it back with something better. That's called work. O'QUILLIAN: Work? Why should I work? I've committed no crime. I hate work! I hate work the same way the good Lord hates Dodge City! — *O'Quillian*, by Ron Bishop.

CLAY: *(Shot and dying)* I never did get my bath. — *O'Quillian*, by Ron Bishop.

MATT: There was never a horse that couldn't be rode, and never a man that couldn't be throw'd. — *There Was Never a Horse*, by John Meston.

PRINT ASPER: Well, Chester, life's always uncertain and full of boils. — *Print Asper*, by John Meston.

MATT: Trouble just keeps hangin' on to them like a burr in a horse's mane. — *Cara*, written by David Victor and Herbert Little/story by John Meston.

CHESTER: My Ma always said, the best thing for healing was a pure heart and a lot a sleep. — *Yorky*, written by Sam Peckinpah/story by John Meston.

DAY BARRETT: Now don't this beat all... Now just last night, me and the other boys in the Double Bar outfit, was thrown out of town by Mister Dillon for being a little noisy in the street. And we were shooting it up some, yeah, but he called it disturbing the peace, even though we didn't hit nobody. *Him!*... Making every day in Dodge like Sunday in Philadelphia. — *Reward for Matt*, written by David Victor and Herbert Little/story by John Meston.

DOC: I'm losing too many patients... Lost one yesterday. MATT: Died, huh? DOC: Oh no, cured. MATT: Cured? Say, I bet that did come as a surprise, huh? — *Johnny Red*, written by John Meston/story by Les Crutchfield.

KITTY: There wasn't one of those Texans that could have ever known a mother. They all acted like they'd been raised in caves. — *20/20*, written by David Victor and Herbert Little/story by John Meston.

PEZZY: I believe in nature... Like with cattle. When there's a big storm coming they just turn their tails to the wind and wait it out. Yes, a man can learn a lot by just watching animals. — *Tail to the Wind*, written by John Meston/story by Les Crutchfield.

FESTUS: She's slicker than possum-fat and getting better every day. — *Bad Lady from Brookline*, by Gustave Field.

KITTY: Matt's a man with no strings on him. Let's just say he's more mine than anybody else's. — *Bad Lady from Brookline*, by Gustave Field.

FESTUS: Matt, you fixin' to just set there like a boll weevil on a corncob and wait for her to come and get ye? — *Bad Lady from Brookline*, by Gustave Field.

AMOS GENTRY: Matt's got a poker face that'd take the skin off a rattler. — *Gentry's Law*, by Jack Miller.

UNDERWOOD: ...Wived an Arapaho woman, best human being God used his clay fer. Made two sons, that woman did. One of 'em ain't worth spit in winter. The other 'un tries, but he got a brain belongs under a hen. — *The Sodbusters*, by Ron Bishop.

Quotes from Gunsmoke

PETE BROWN: Never put a lock on nothin' but your heart. — *The Sodbusters,* by Ron Bishop.

UNDERWOOD: ...Sodpounders. Juiceless, hymn-singin', tea-drinkin' virgins with hoes. I hate 'em. I'm goin' to drive 'em out. — *The Sodbusters,* by Ron Bishop.

FESTUS: You see, it's like pushin' water upstream... Well, there's men in this town that ain't never tasted water. Men that was weaned on whiskey right straight from milk to red-eye. — *Dry Road to Nowhere,* by Harry Kronman.

CAMPBELL: Everyday you put in some man's hand the means to his own destruction. KITTY: I don't force anybody to drink. CAMPBELL: When a man's lookin' at an angel's face, he ain't apt to know when a devil grabs him. — *Dry Road to Nowhere,* by Harry Kronman.

FESTUS: Have you ever saw the hair on an old dog's neck git all stand-uppity and stickity-out, kinda slow and scared like...And then he start grumbling, and growl way down deep, did you ever see that? — *The Judas Gun,* by Harry Kronman.

TUSH LEE: What kind of a man would murder a cow? — *Moo Moo Raid,* written by John Meston/story by Les Crutchfield.

LOU STONE: You know, I'll bet tomorrow night at this time you're knocking on the pearly gates and hollering up at Saint Peter saying, "Open up the gates, Saint Peter. I'm the Marshal." — *The Jailer,* by Hal Sitowitz.

KITTY: ...I can tell you a little bit about life, but I can't tell you anything about war. I don't think any woman can explain to another woman about war. It's an insanity that women just can't understand... It's like falling down a hill, you can't stop and you can't change directions and you're bound to get hurt. — *The Mark of Cain,* by Ron Bishop.

DOC: ...I'll tell you something else, Burke, it's my own personal and private opinion that if they put your brains in a mustard seed they'd rattle like a peanut in a boxcar. Now shut up! — *The Mark of Cain,* by Ron Bishop.

KITTY: ...A man's strength doesn't make him a man, it's his heart. — *The Mark of Cain,* by Ron Bishop.

SAM DANTON: You're a hard man, Marshal, harder than a landlord's heart. — *The Pack Rat,* written by Jim Byrnes and Arthur Browne/story by Arthur Browne.

TEWKSBURY: It's better to die fighting then to rot old age. — *Prairie Happy,* written by David Victor and Herbert Little/story by John Meston.

BEN: Lucky for you fellows I wasn't riding shotgun for them jackasses. The crows would be pickin' at your eyeballs by now. — *Waste,* Part I, by Jim Byrnes.

MATT: Marge, my name's Matt Dillon. I'm a friend of Judd's. MARGE: Any friend of Judd's is a friend of Judd's. — *Friend*, by Kathleen Hite.

KITTY: You didn't do him justice, Matt. It'd take two of him to be simple-minded. — *Uncle Oliver*, by John Meston.

KITTY: What do you want here, Mr. Mannon? MANNON: Nothin' much. KITTY: Then move on. MANNON: I figure Matt Dillon is nothin' much...ma'am. I'm gonna walk across Matt Dillon like you walk across short grass. — *Mannon*, by Ron Bishop.

MANNON: (To Newly) Friend, I'm going to kill that barkeep before he pulls the trigger, and him with his finger on it... Then I'm going to kill you. SAM: You'll pay up first. — *Mannon*, by Ron Bishop.

FESTUS: You wanna talk about a fast gunhand? If you wuz to take a snake's tongue an' grease it an' tie it to a bolt of lightnin', you couldn't get nothin' as fast as his gun hand... This Mannon is twice as fast as Mathew is. — *Mannon*, by Ron Bishop.

CHESTER: Mister Dillon, here's your coffee...is it strong enough? MATT: If it were any stronger I'd deputize it. — *Greater Love*, written by Winston Miller/story by John Meston.

VIRGIL BONNER: (On his way to his execution, to the sheriff of Hayes City) Okay fat man, let's go to the party. — *Hostage!*, by Paul F. Edwards.

MATT: Bonner, Jude Bonner! JUDE: You're talkin', law. MATT: I'm here to kill ya. JUDE: What are ya gonna do, talk me to death, Dillon? — *Hostage!*, by Paul F. Edwards.

KELLY: ...She tried to kill me, least she had a hand in it. If she was a man, I'd shoot her. But, she's a woman. Good or bad, she's a woman. So I'm sending her back to Abilene, back to what she was when I found her. — *Wild West*, by John Meston.

RAWLINS: You know, it always seems too bad when a man dies for something he ain't concerned with. MATT: ...If I was worried about dying, I'd a quit this job a long time ago. — *The Peace Officer*, written by John Meston/story by Norman Macdonnell.

CHESTER: Dang, golly, Mister Dillon, these doggone Eastern newspapers will print just about anything... It pretty near chokes you up in your craw the things in here that they expects you to believe. You listening? MATT: Huh, something choking you up? Is that it? CHESTER: Well, it says here that they got a train over in England that'll do 150 miles in three hours flat. MATT: Pretty fast. CHESTER: You don't believe that, do you? MATT: It's possible, I guess. CHESTER: Oh, human beings wasn't meant to go that fast, Mister

Quotes from Gunsmoke

Dillon... Why that'd get a person's innards all out of whack... Why a person'd choke to death tryin' to breathe going that fast... It just...it...no...if a person was meant to go that fast, Mister Dillon, the good Lord'd put wheels on him to begin with. — *Crowbait Bob,* by Les Crutchfield.

DOC: The words out of his mouth were smoother than butter, but war was in his heart. — *The Bobsy Twins,* by John Meston.

MERLE: Marshal, I think I'd sooner not be hung if I had my sooners. MATT: You're gonna hang, both of you. HARVEY: Wait a minute, Merle. I know what we done wrong. MERLE: What? HARVEY: We plain forgot as how it wuz Sunday, both times, and you know Pa never did hold with killing on Sunday. MERLE: By golly, you're right! — *The Bobsy Twins,* by John Meston.

DAN: What town is this, Doc? DOC: Dodge City, Kansas. DAN: Well, I declare. I don't recollect ever being here before. Of course, I don't recollect being here now. How'd I get up the stairs, fly? — *Old Dan,* by Kathleen Hite.

DAN: You know I'm a drunk, don't ya? Of course, you understand, I'm not proud of it. Ain't ashamed either. It's just the way it is. DOC: Well, somethin' like my cooking. I'm not proud of it. I'm not ashamed of it either. That's the way it is. — *Old Dan,* by Kathleen Hite.

MATT: All right, who's next? Anybody else wanna die in here? — *Texas Cowboys,* by John Meston.

MATT: Now you men break it up and get out of that door right now! GIL: You talkin' to ten men, Marshal. You figure on whippin! us all? ...'Course not. So we gonna whip you. We gonna beat you half to death. Ain't we men? — *Texas Cowboys,* by John Meston.

DOOLEY: *(To Matt)* Well, can I come see ya sometime, maybe? You, Chester... pass the time a day sorta? *Matt*: Sure. Sure ya can, Dooley. DOOLEY: Jus' once in a while. I wouldn't feel right otherwise, Marshal, me bein' a murderer an' all. — *Dooley Surrenders,* by John Meston.

MATT: Well, come on, Chester. We got three men to bury. — *Dooley Surrenders,* by John Meston.

MATT: You know, there must be easier ways to die then most of the men up here took, like passing away in one's sleep, or gently dissolving in old age, or even being carried off by some disease of some kind. But getting stabbed, shot, hung, kicked to death, all the violent ways we have of dying out here, they leave a man without any dignity at all. And, it's worse when it happens suddenly, when a man hasn't time to prepare himself, It's something I, myself, have to face everyday— Matt Dillon, United States Marshal. — Prologue for *Young Love,* by John Meston.

NEWLY: Dedicated ain't he? MATT: He may be dedicated, but you can put his brains in a teacup. He's got to be stopped. — *Gunsmoke: Return to Dodge,* by Jim Byrnes.

FOS: All you need's just a little sunnin' out.... You've been livin' in the shade too long, Miss Flora. Nothin' can grow good like that. A body needs space, air, a chance to breathe. — *Cheap Labor,* by John Meston.

CHESTER: Melanie, you're jest as pretty as you can be. But you jest don't realize how little it takes to get yourself killed around here. — *Cheap Labor,* by John Meston.

STANCIL: You leave now and you're fired, both of you. COWBOY: It beats gettin' buried. — *Cheap Labor,* by John Meston.

KITTY: No woman ever loved a man more than I loved Matt Dillon, but I had to make a decision. So I moved to New Orleans and thought I was cured. HANNAH: Until you heard he was stabbed. KITTY: Yeah. I should a known he wouldn't die. — *Gunsmoke: Return to Dodge,* by Jim Byrnes.

CHESTER: ...When a woman's been churched she's got a duty to her husband. It don't make no difference whether he's good or bad. — *Minnie,* by John Meston.

CHESTER: Doc, you can spit at bad weather, but you sure enough can't change it. — *Minnie,* by John Meston.

JEFF: For your sake Pete, I hope they don't kill me. If they did, they'd wash you off this place like you wuz made of paper. — *No Chip,* by John Meston.

MATT: Sure is making friends, isn't he? KITTY: That bunch would drink with a hangman if it was free. — *The Tragedian,* written by John Meston/story by Les Crutchfield.

MRS. BOGGS: The earth'll open up one day and swallow this sinful town. MATT: Well, I'm afraid they'd just build another one like it, ma'am. — *The Wake,* by John Meston.

CHESTER: That's about the cold-bloodedest woman that I'd ever seen. MATT: Well, I think she's hiding something, Chester. CHESTER: Too bad it ain't her face, if ya ask me. — *The Wake,* by John Meston.

FESTUS: It's hotter than a jug full a red ants, ain't she? — *Whelan's Men,* by Ron Bishop.

HOBEY: *(Looking at Sam)* Ya know, I had me a blue tick hound once, had a face like that. Seen himself lookin' back at him from a pond surface and went into a thicket and died a shame. — *Whelan's Men,* by Ron Bishop.

Quotes from Gunsmoke

TUCK: *(To Kitty)* Hold on woman. We may steal a little from time to time, and we killed a few folks that got in our way. But we don't cheat or welsh. Now if you've got somethin' to bet, Red, sit down. — *Whelan's Men,* by Ron Bishop.

MAMIE: I aim to give the squarest deal in town here. All the liquor's gonna be aged over thirty days, and the dancin' girls aged under thirty years. The liquor's straight, and the girls are grateful. The decks only have four aces, and all the cards read only from the front side. — *Hinka-Do,* by Les Crutchfield.

NATE: Oh, another thing, how come I didn't get no breakfast this morning? CHESTER: Well, we jest don't feed common ordinary drunks around here. But if you'll go out and git yourself arrested on a murder charge, why we'll give ya a whole banquet. — *Bless Me Till I Die,* written by John Meston/story by Ray Kemper.

COWBOY: Marshal, you got ten minutes. If that cook ain't out here, then we're gonna start shooting up this town... MATT: That would be kinda foolish wouldn't it? Start a shoot-out over a cook? Lot of other good restaurants around, boys. COWBOY: Well now, we tried all those other places when we wuz here last year, Marshal. And from what folks tell us, they're no better now then they wuz then. Swill, jest pig swill. BOSS: Make a man sick, Marshal. MATT: All right now, let me tell you something, all of you. It's a whole lot better to have a little bad food then it is a belly full a buckshot. — *The Cook,* by John Meston.

MATT: I've seen a lot of men buried up here on Boot Hill and most of them really earned what they got. They cheated at cards, robbed banks, stole horses, murdered innocent men, picked fights with friend and enemy alike. They lived and died as though they'd never heard of the law, and they treated me like a trespasser, like someone who had no right to interfere with their bloody little games. But I shot it out with them anyway. I guess I'll go right on doing it long as I last. Matt Dillon, U.S. Marshal. — Prologue to *Stage Hold-Up,* written by Les Crutchfield/story by John Meston.

FESTUS: Well now, them Sutterfield's, they're a hair trigger outfit just meaner than a four-headed rattlesnake. — *A Family of Killers,* by William Keys.

FESTUS: Them Injuns send out peace bells when there's a high muckety-muck comin' through, so's he'll get fit treatment and everything. KITTY: Well, I see you know as much about Indians as you do about muskrats. — *Chief Joseph,* written by Clyde Ware/story by Thomas Warner.

MATT: Law comes hard to a young country and especially out here in the frontier. I know just how hard. I'm Matt Dillon, U.S. marshal out a Dodge City. It's a roaring town filled to overflowing with cowmen, gamblers, buffalo hunters and killers. And this is Boot Hill. There aren't many tears lost for these men lying here, not back there in Dodge. Most men can look at the result of their job and say, "I did that pretty well." And they can be proud of their handy work. But not me, because part of this is my handy work. I put some of these men here and I take no pride in killing. It's just that sometimes it's a part of my job, a job that has to be done. — Prologue to *The Hunter,* by John Dunkel.

Doc: *(After removing a bullet from Matt)* Kitty, I know this has been harder on you than on anybody... He's gonna be all right. I promise you.   Kitty: *(After a belt of whiskey)* What about next time, Doc? What can you promise me about that? — *The Badge,* by Jim Byrnes.

Raff: Ain't been nothin' clean here in a mule's age, Marshal. — *Kitty's Injury,* written by John Meston/story by Marian Clark.

Osgood: Now I always say, a boy don't need to measure his manhood by the amount of iron on him. It's the iron in the soul that counts. — *The Witness,* by Shimon Wincelberg.

Osgood: Nice day for a hanging, as my old daddy used to say. — *The Witness,* by Shimon Wincelberg.

Favorite: ...Never thought I'd be taking bait under a roof tonight. No sir, not after that pass up yonder with the wind howling like lost souls hunting for graves... — *Matt's Love Story,* by Ron Bishop.

Favorite: You, Junior boy, pour a drink.   Monte: Go to hell.   Favorite: Been there. Pour a drink! — *Matt's Love Story,* by Ron Bishop.

Favorite: (To Starcourt) I ain't saying you won't kill me. I'm saying I don't care. Done my living, money-pockets. I done it all. You ain't licked your lip, come the first bullet. I'm gonna put a hole in you low. You gonna shout out loud...And a long time praying, even longer dying. — *Matt's Love Story,* by Ron Bishop.

Favorite: *(Dying)* I'll be made of milk...I'll be made of milk... — *Matt's Love Story,* by Ron Bishop.

Kimbro: ...A man should have a chance to die with his boots on. — *Kimbro,* by Jim Byrnes.

Kitty: I need some answers. The scales are getting all out of whack. It's hard to throw away eighteen years.   Matt: Yeah.   Kitty: I know what that badge means to you, to this town, to everyone. But I'm thinking of us. I was just a kid when we met, Matt, and I was gonna live forever. I knew how things had to be with us, and it was all right. But I thought that someday, some far off someday, that things would change. Well, Matt my somedays are almost gone. I guess what I'm asking is for you to tell me to say "no" to Will Stambridge.   Matt: Kitty you know how I feel. But that's a decision you're gonna have to make yourself.   Kitty: I know, Matt. I know. — *Kitty's Love Affair,* written by Paul Savage/story by Susan Kotar and Joan E. Gressler.

Quotes from Gunsmoke

MATT: *(To Kitty)* ...You know most of the time I've got about one second to decide whether or not to kill a man. Sometimes that's a weight that gets a little heavy to carry around and I just want to get away from it.... — *The Foundling,* by Jim Byrnes.

MATT: Ya still fixed all right for money to get home? WILLY: Where's home? Once there was the smell of wild strawberries... Home? I'll never get home. — *Extradition,* by Antony Ellis.

APPENDIX B
THE TELEVISION DIRECTORS

YEAR	1	2	3	4	5	6	7	8	9	10	11	12	13	14	15	16	17	18	19	20	TOTAL
A. McLaglen	0	20	2	8	16	10	11	13	12	3	0	0	0	0	0	0	0	0	0	0	95
H. Harris	0	0	0	0	0	5	12	16	15	12	5	0	0	0	0	0	0	0	0	0	65
T. Post	6	14	14	9	1	5	4	2	0	0	0	0	0	0	0	0	0	0	0	0	55
B. McEveety	0	0	0	0	0	0	0	0	0	0	0	0	1	8	8	9	8	3	9	7	53
V. McEveety	0	0	0	0	0	0	0	0	0	5	6	3	3	6	6	8	4	1	4	1	47
G. Hellstrom	0	0	0	0	0	0	0	0	0	0	0	0	3	1	2	1	1	7	8	9	32
C. Warren	26	0	0	0	0	0	0	0	0	0	0	0	0	0	0	0	0	0	0	0	26
R. Totten	0	0	0	0	0	0	0	0	0	3	8	6	1	2	3	1	0	0	0	0	24
J. Hibbs	0	0	0	5	10	5	0	0	0	0	0	0	0	0	0	0	0	0	0	0	20
R. Whorf	0	0	6	11	0	0	1	0	0	0	0	0	0	0	0	0	0	0	0	0	18
J. Rich	0	0	10	0	0	0	0	0	0	0	0	0	2	2	0	0	0	0	0	0	14
I. Moore	0	0	0	0	0	0	0	0	0	0	3	3	1	0	0	2	3	2	0	0	14
P. Leacock	0	0	0	0	0	0	0	0	0	0	0	0	0	7	2	2	1	0	0	0	12
M. Rydell	0	0	0	0	0	0	0	0	0	4	3	3	0	0	0	0	0	0	0	0	10
M. Daniels	0	0	0	0	0	0	0	0	0	5	5	0	0	0	0	0	0	0	0	0	10
A. Hiller	0	0	0	3	4	2	0	0	0	0	0	0	0	0	0	0	0	0	0	0	9
J. Sargent	0	0	0	0	0	0	0	3	0	2	2	0	0	0	0	0	0	0	0	0	7
R. Stevenson	6	0	0	0	0	0	0	0	0	0	0	0	0	0	0	0	0	0	0	0	6
V. French	0	0	0	0	0	0	0	0	0	0	0	0	0	0	0	0	0	0	0	5	5
B. Kulik	0	0	3	0	2	0	0	0	0	0	0	0	0	0	0	0	0	0	0	0	5
A. Reisner	0	0	0	0	0	0	0	0	1	2	2	0	0	0	0	0	0	0	0	0	5
H. Wallerstein	0	0	0	0	0	0	0	0	0	0	0	0	0	0	0	0	2	3	0	0	5
A. Kjellin	0	0	0	0	0	0	0	0	0	0	0	0	0	0	0	0	0	3	1	0	4
P. Stanley	0	0	0	0	0	0	0	0	0	0	0	0	0	0	0	0	4	0	0	0	4
J. Hopper	0	0	0	0	0	0	0	0	4	0	0	0	0	0	0	0	0	0	0	0	4
D. Weaver	0	0	0	0	0	3	1	0	0	0	0	0	0	0	0	0	0	0	0	0	4
C. Nyby	0	1	0	0	1	0	1	0	0	1	0	0	0	0	0	0	0	0	0	0	4
W. Russell	0	4	0	0	0	0	0	0	0	0	0	0	0	0	0	0	0	0	0	0	4
R. Sarafian	0	0	0	0	0	0	0	0	0	1	0	0	3	0	0	0	0	0	0	0	4
M. O'Herlihy	0	0	0	0	0	0	0	0	0	3	0	0	0	0	0	0	0	0	0	1	4
R. Butler	0	0	0	0	0	0	0	0	0	0	0	0	1	1	0	0	0	1	0	0	3

Television Directors

YEAR	1	2	3	4	5	6	7	8	9	10	11	12	13	14	15	16	17	18	19	20	TOTAL
J. Yarbrough	0	0	0	0	2	1	0	0	0	0	0	0	0	0	0	0	0	0	0	0	3
M. Chomsky	0	0	0	0	0	0	0	0	0	0	0	0	2	1	0	0	0	0	0	0	3
G. Mayer	0	0	0	0	0	2	1	0	0	0	0	0	0	0	0	0	0	0	0	0	3
S. Berns	0	0	1	2	0	0	0	0	0	0	0	0	0	0	0	0	0	0	0	0	3
T. Garnett	0	0	0	0	0	0	2	0	0	0	1	0	0	0	0	0	0	0	0	0	3
A. Ganzer	0	0	0	0	0	0	0	0	0	0	1	0	1	0	0	0	0	0	0	0	2
J. Lewis	0	0	0	0	0	0	0	0	0	2	0	0	0	0	0	0	0	0	0	0	2
B. Kowalski	0	0	0	0	0	0	0	0	0	0	0	2	0	0	0	0	0	0	0	0	2
H. Daugherty	0	0	0	0	0	0	0	0	0	0	0	0	0	2	0	0	0	0	0	0	2
L. King	0	0	2	0	0	0	0	0	0	0	0	0	0	0	0	0	0	0	0	0	2
R. Springsteen	0	0	0	0	2	0	0	0	0	0	0	0	0	0	0	0	0	0	0	0	2
C. Martin	0	0	0	0	0	0	0	2	0	0	0	0	0	0	0	0	0	0	0	0	2
W. Conrad	0	0	0	0	0	0	0	1	0	0	0	0	0	0	0	0	1	0	0	0	2
L. Penn	0	0	0	0	0	0	0	0	0	0	0	0	0	2	0	0	0	0	0	0	2
J. English	0	0	0	0	0	0	0	0	2	0	0	0	0	0	0	0	0	0	0	0	2
J. Sheldon	0	0	1	0	0	0	0	0	0	0	1	0	0	0	0	0	0	0	0	0	2
E. Ludlum	0	0	0	1	0	0	0	0	0	0	0	0	0	0	0	0	0	0	0	0	1
S. Heisler	0	0	0	0	1	0	0	0	0	0	0	0	0	0	0	0	0	0	0	0	1
F. Andreon	0	0	0	0	0	1	0	0	0	0	0	0	0	0	0	0	0	0	0	0	1
A. Crosland	0	0	0	0	0	1	0	0	0	0	0	0	0	0	0	0	0	0	0	0	1
G. Fowler	0	0	0	0	0	1	0	0	0	0	0	0	0	0	0	0	0	0	0	0	1
B. Paul	0	0	0	0	0	1	0	0	0	0	0	0	0	0	0	0	0	0	0	0	1
T. Carr	0	0	0	0	0	0	0	0	1	0	0	0	0	0	0	0	0	0	0	0	1
J. Brahm	0	0	0	0	0	0	0	0	1	0	0	0	0	0	0	0	0	0	0	0	1
W. Faralla	0	0	0	0	0	1	0	0	0	0	0	0	0	0	0	0	0	0	0	0	1
R. Sargent	0	0	0	0	0	0	1	0	0	0	0	0	0	0	0	0	0	0	0	0	1
F. Jackman	0	0	0	0	0	0	0	1	0	0	0	0	0	0	0	0	0	0	0	0	1
S. Roley	0	0	0	0	0	0	0	0	0	1	0	0	0	0	0	0	0	0	0	0	1
W. Claxton	0	0	0	0	0	0	0	0	1	0	0	0	0	0	0	0	0	0	0	0	1
H. Horner	1	0	0	0	0	0	0	0	0	0	0	0	0	0	0	0	0	0	0	0	1
G. Nelson	0	0	0	0	0	0	0	0	0	1	0	0	0	0	0	0	0	0	0	0	1
A. Biberman	0	0	0	0	0	0	0	0	0	1	0	0	0	0	0	0	0	0	0	0	1
P. Graves	0	0	0	0	0	0	0	0	0	1	0	0	0	0	0	0	0	0	0	0	1
D. Colla	0	0	0	0	0	0	0	0	0	0	0	1	0	0	0	0	0	0	0	0	1
C. Rondeau	0	0	0	0	0	0	0	0	0	0	1	0	0	0	0	0	0	0	0	0	1
J. Landis	0	0	0	0	0	0	0	0	0	0	1	0	0	0	0	0	0	0	0	0	1
D. Hallenbeck	0	0	0	0	0	0	0	0	0	0	0	1	0	0	0	0	0	0	0	0	1
D. Alexander	0	0	0	0	0	0	0	0	0	0	0	1	0	0	0	0	0	0	0	0	1
A. Lathan	0	0	0	0	0	0	0	0	0	0	0	0	0	0	0	0	0	1	0	0	1
P. Edwards	0	0	0	0	0	0	0	0	0	0	0	0	0	0	0	0	0	1	0	0	1
L. Katzman	0	0	0	0	0	0	0	0	0	0	0	0	0	0	0	0	0	0	1	1	1

The Directors

Franklin Adreon
David Alexander
Seymour Berns
Abner Biberman
John Brahm
Robert Butler
Thomas Carr
Marvin Chomsky
William F. Claxton
Dick Colla
William Conrad
Alan Crosland, Jr.
Marc Daniels
Herschel Daugherty
Paul F. Edwards
John W. English
William Dario Faralla
Gene Fowler, Jr.
Victor French
Alvin Ganzer
Tay Garnett
Peter Graves
Daryl Hallenbeck
Harry Harris, Jr.
Stuart Heisler
Gunnar Hellstrom
Jesse Hibbs

GUNSMOKE — IV. APPENDIX B

Arthur Hiller
Jerry Hopper
Harry Horner
Fred H. Jackman
Leonard Katzman
Louis King
Alf Kjellin
Bernard Kowalski
Buzz Kulik
James Landis
Arnold Lathan
Philip Leacock
Joseph H. Lewis
Edward Ludlum
Norman Macdonnell (Radio)
Charles Martin

Gerald H. Mayer
Bernard McEveety
Vincent McEveety
Andrew V. McLaglen
Irving J. Moore
Gene Nelson
Christian Nyby
Michael O'Herlihy
Byron Paul
Leo Penn
Ted Post
Allen Reisner
John Rich
Sutton Roley
Charles Rondeau

William D. Russell
Mark Rydell
Richard C. Sarafian
Joseph Sargent
Richard Sargent
James Sheldon
R.G. Springsteen
Paul Stanley
Robert Stevenson
Robert Totten
Herb Wallerstein
Charles Marquis Warren
Dennis Weaver
Richard Whorf
Jean Yarbrough

APPENDIX C
THE RADIO
AND TELEVISION
WRITERS

Individuals marked (R) wrote scripts for radio only; those with an * wrote for both radio and television; the others wrote only for television.

Robert Barbash
Harry Bartell (R)
Jack Bartlett
Ron Bishop
Walter Black
William Blinn
Dudley Bromley
Arthur Browne, Jr.
Jim Byrnes
Endre Bohem
Joann Carlino
Jess Carneol
Richard Carr
Colley Cibber
Marian Clark (R)
Calvin Clements
Calvin Clements, Jr.
Francis Cockrell
William Conrad (R)
Will Corry
Les Crutchfield*
Arthur Dales
Gerry Day
Joy Dexter

Frank Q. Dobbs
Gil Doud*
Warren Douglas
John Dunkel*
George Eckstein
Paul F. Edwards
Antony Ellis*
David Ellis (R)
Gustave Field
Richard Fielder
James Fonda*
Merwin Gerard
Gwen Bagni Gielgud
Roy Goldrup
Herman Groves
Tom Hanley*
Jack Hawn
Kathleen Hite*
Ron Honthaner
Lou Houston (R)
Scott Hunt
Don Ingalls
Verne Jay
Beth Keele

GUNSMOKE — IV. APPENDIX C

William Kelley	Vic Perrin (R)
Ray Kemper (R)	Herb Purdum (R)
William Keys	William Putnam
John Kneubuhl	Chris Rellas
Donald Z. Koplowitz	William Robson
Harry Kronman	Arthur Rowe
James Landis	Donald S. Sanford
Anthony Lawrence	Paul Savage
William F. Leicester*	Richard D. Scott
Kay Lenard	Jay Simms
Bethel Leslie	Hal Sitowitz
Robert Lewin	Anne Snyder
Herbert Little	Robert C. Stewart
Norman Macdonnell (R)	Charles Joseph Stone
John Mantley	Harold Swanton
Harvey Marlowe	Thomas Thompson
John Meston*	Ken Trevey
Jack Miller	Jack Turley
Winston Miller	David Victor
Robert Mitchell (R)	Dan Ullman
Don Mullally	Lou Vittes
Joel Murcott (R)	Earl W. Wallace
Dick Nelson	Clyde Ware
E. Jack Neuman	Charles Marquis Warren
Walter B. Newman (R)	Shimon Wincelberg
Frank Paris*	Preston Wood
Sam Peckinpah	Robert Vincent Wright

In addition to the writers listed above, the following contributed stories to *Gunsmoke* on television but did not write any of the television scripts:

True Boardman	Norman Macdonnell
Harriet Charles	Hal Moffett
Marian Clark	Emily Mosher
Gil Favor	Vic Perrin
Michael Fisher	Gilbert Ralston
Jack Freeman	John Rosser
Bud Furillo	Benny Rubin
Joan E. Gessler	Jack Shettlesworth
Robert Heverly	Robert Totten
Joe Ann Johnson	Warren Vanders
Ray Kemper	Thomas Warner
Susan Kotar	Mary Worell

APPENDIX D
THE TELEVISION PRODUCERS

	Executive Producer	Producer	Associate Producer
1955-56		Warren	Macdonnell
1956-57		Warren/Macdonnell	
1957-58		Macdonnell	
1958-59		Macdonnell	
1959-60		Macdonnell	Arness
1960-61		Macdonnell	Arness
1961-62		Macdonnell	Paris
1962-63		Macdonnell	Paris
1963-64		Macdonnell	Paris
1964-65		Macdonnell/Leacock	
1965-66		Leacock	Mantley
1966-67	Leacock	Mantley	
1967-68		Mantley	Dackow
1968-69	Mantley	Mantley	Dackow
1969-70	Mantley	Dackow	
1970-71	Mantley	Dackow/Katzman	
1971-72	Mantley	Katzman	Honthaner
1972-73	Mantley	Katzman	Honthaner
1973-74	Mantley	Katzman	Honthaner
1974-75	Mantley	Katzman	Honthaner

1. Macdonnell became producer in December 1956 with *Cholera* (Prod. #553).
2. Mantley became executive producer during the 1968-69 season with *Waco*.
3. Katzman became producer midway through 1970-71 season.
4. Arness was associate producer for several years, during which time he was part owner of the show. He later sold his share back to CBS.
5. CBS utilized Bob Stabler and his production staff in the first several years to help produce the show.

APPENDIX E
THE RADIO
AND TELEVISION
AWARDS

Awards: Radio (Selected)

1954–55	TV-Radio Mirror Award for Favorite Radio Mystery-Adventure
1955–56	TV-Radio Mirror Award for Favorite Radio Western
1956–57	TV-Radio Mirror Award for Favorite Radio Western
1956–57	TV-Radio Mirror Award for Favorite Radio Western Star to William Conrad
1957–58	TV-Radio Mirror Award for Favorite Radio Western
1957–58	TV-Radio Mirror Award for Favorite Radio Western Star to William Conrad
1957	Radio-Television Daily All-American Favorites: Dramatic Show of the Year
1958	Radio-Television Daily All-American Favorites: Dramatic Show of the Year
1960	Radio-Television Daily All-American Favorites: Dramatic Show of the Year

Awards and Nominations: Television (Selected)

1955

Emmy nomination for *Gunsmoke* for Best Action or Adventure Series. (Winner: *Disneyland*, ABC.)

Radio and Television Awards

1956

Emmy nomination to James Arness for Best Actor in a Dramatic Series. (Winner: Robert Young, for *Father Knows Best,* NBC.)

1957

Emmy Award for Best Dramatic Series with Continuing Characters to *Gunsmoke*. (Other nominees: *Lassie,* CBS; *Maverick,* ABC; *Perry Mason,* CBS; *Wagon Train,* NBC.)
Emmy nomination for James Arness for Best Actor. (Winner: Robert Young, for *Father Knows Best,* NBC.)
Emmy nomination for Dennis Weaver for Best Supporting Actor. (Winner: Carl Reiner, for *Caesar's Hour,* NBC.)
Emmy nomination for John Meston for Best Teleplay Writing (Half Hour or Less, for *Born to Hang.* (Winner: Paul Monash, for *The Lonely Wizard, Schlitz Playhouse of Stars,* CBS.)
Emmy Award for Best Editing of a Film for Television to Mike Pozen, for *How to Kill a Woman.* (Other nominees: Samuel Beetley, *The Tinhorn, Schlitz Playhouse of Stars,* CBS; Danny Landres, *The Lonely Wizard, Schlitz Playhouse of Stars,* CBS; Michael McAdam, *Trail to Christmas, G.E. Theater,* CBS; Robert Sparr, *The Quick and the Dead, Maverick,* ABC.)

1958

Emmy nomination for *Gunsmoke* for Best Western Series. (Winner: *Maverick,* ABC.)
Emmy Award for Best Supporting Actor in a Dramatic Series to Dennis Weaver. (Other nominees: Herschel Bernardi, for *Peter Gunn,* NBC; Johnny Crawford, for *The Rifleman,* ABC; William Hopper, for *Perry Mason,* CBS.)
Emmy nomination to James Arness for Best Actor. (Winner: Raymond Burr, for *Perry Mason,* CBS.)
Emmy nomination to Amanda Blake for Best Supporting Actress. (Winner: Barbara Hale, for *Perry Mason,* CBS.)
LOOK Magazine's Annual Television Awards — Best Action Series to *Gunsmoke.*
Radio-Television Daily All-American Favorites: Western Show of the Year.

1959

Television Champion Awards (Quigley Publications) — Best Western: *Gunsmoke.*

1960

10th Annual Silver Spurs Award to James Arness for Outstanding Western Actor of the Year. (Conferred by the motion picture editors in a nationwide poll conducted by the Reno, Nevada, Chamber of Commerce; first television star to win the award; previous winners were Gary Cooper and John Wayne.)

1965

Emmy nomination to Morton Stevens for Achievement in Music Composition, for *Seven Hours to Dawn*. (Winner: Laurence Rosenthal, for *Michelangelo: The Last Giant*, NBC.)

1966

Western Heritage Award for Outstanding Fictional Television Western Episode, for *Death Watch*, written by Calvin Clements, Sr.

1967

Emmy Award for Outstanding Performance by an Actor in a Supporting Role in a Drama to Milburn Stone. (Other nominees: Joseph Campanella, *Mannix*, CBS; Lawrence Dobkin, *Do Not Go Gentle Into That Good Night*, CBS Playhouse, CBS; Leonard Nimoy, *Star Trek*, NBC.)
Emmy nomination to Morton Stevens for Outstanding Achievement in Musical Composition, for *Major Glory*. (Winner: Earle Hagen, for *Laya, I Spy*, NBC.)

1969

Emmy Award for Outstanding Achievement in Film Sound Editing to Richard E. Radarman and Norman Karlin, for *Charlie Noon*. (Other nominees: Douglas Grindstaff, Alex Bamattre, Michael Colgan, Bill Lee, Joe Kavigan, Josef Von Stroheim, for *The Immortal, Movie of the Week*, ABC; Don Hall, Jr., Larry Meek, William Howard, John Kline, Robert Cornett, Frank White, for *A Small War, Land of the Giants*, ABC.)
Television Champion Awards (Quigley Publications) — Best Western

1971

Television Champion Awards (Quigley Publications) — Best Western
National Cowboy Hall of Fame Wrangler Award — Outstanding Western Music Composition to Composer/Conductor John Parker, for two-part *Snow Train;* John Mantley cited as executive producer.
Western Writers of America Golden Spur Award for *Chato*, written by Paul F. Edwards.
The Black Image Award for *The Scavengers*, by Jack Miller.

1972

Television Champion Awards (Quigley Publications) — Best Western
National Cowboy Hall of Fame Award for Outstanding Western Episode for *Pike*, by Jack Miller.
Writers Guild of America Award for Best Western Television Script for *Pike*, by Jack Miller.

Radio and Television Awards

1973

Mass Media Award from the National Conference of Christians and Jews for *This Golden Land*—for "the unusual and provocative concept of the universality of the Jewish traditions that the program depicted."

Western Writers of America Spur Award for Best Western Television Script, for *Bohannan,* by William Kelley.

1974

Writer's Guild of America Award for Best Episodic Drama to Jim Byrnes, for *Thirty a Month and Found.*

Western Writers of America Spur Award for Best Western Television Script, for *Thirty a Month and Found,* by Jim Byrnes.

Award from the President's Council on Mental Retardation to *The Deadly Innocent,* by Calvin Clements, Sr.

Western Writers of America Golden Spur Award for *The Deadly Innocent,* by Calvin Clements, Sr.

1975

Western Writers of America Spur Award for Best Western Television Script for *The Busters,* by Jim Byrnes.

National Education Award for *The Fires of Ignorance,* by Jim Byrnes.

APPENDIX F
THE TELEVISION TIME SCHEDULE

Season	Time Slot	NBC	ABC
1955–56	Sat. 10–10:30	George Gobel	Tomorrow's Careers
1956–57		George Gobel	Masquerade Party
1957–58		What's It For	Mike Wallace Interviews
1958–59		Cimarron City	Sammy Kaye's Music
1959–60		Five Fingers	Jubilee U.S.A.
1960–61		The Nation's Future	The Fight of the Week
1961–62	Sat. 10–11	NBC Movies	The Fight of the Week
1962–63		NBC Movies	The Fight of the Week
1963–64		NBC Movies	Jerry Lewis
1964–65		NBC Movies	Hollywood Palace / Show Street
1965–66		NBC Movies	Hollywood Palace / ABC Scope
1966–67		NBC Movies	Hollywood Palace
1967–68	Mon. 7:30–8:30	The Monkees / The Man from Uncle	Cowboy in Africa
1968–69		I Dream of Jeannie / Laugh-In	The Avengers
1969–70		My World and Welcome to It / Laugh-In	The Music Scene / The New People
1970–71		Red Skelton Show / Laugh-In	The Young Lawyers
1971–72	Mon. 8–9	Laugh-In	Nanny and the Professor / In the Game
1972–73		Laugh-In	The Rookies
1973–74		Lotsa Luck / Diana	The Rookies
1974–75		Born Free	The Rookies

APPENDIX G
THE TELEVISION ACTORS*

Willie Aames
John Abbott
Philip Abbott
Sharon Acker
Bettye Ackerman
Casey Adams
Dorothy Adams
Kathy Adams
Mary Adams
Stanley Adams
Daniel Ades
Robert Adler
Charles Aidman
Claude Akins
Marc Alaimo
Rico Alaniz
Josh Albee
Jack Albertson
Mabel Albertson
Andy Albin
Hardie Albright
Lola Albright
Chris Alcaide
Mario Alcaide
Norman Alden
John Alderman

John Alderson
Tommy Alexander
Corey Allen
Mark Allen
Sean Barbara Allen
Valery Allen
Jean Allison
Sheldon Allman
James Almanzar
Kenneth Alton
Allyson Ames
Florenz Ames
Joyce Ames
Morey Amsterdam
Merry Anders
Donna Anderson
Herbert Anderson
James Anderson
John Anderson
Richard Anderson
Robert Anderson
Keith Andes
E.J. Andre
Edward Andrews
Tige Andrews
Tod Andrews

Richard Angarola
Mary Angela
Morris Ankrum
Anna-Lisa
Michael Ansara
Lou Antonio
John Apone
Alfonso Arau
George Archambeault
Russell Arms
Herb Armstrong
R.G. Armstrong
R.L. Armstrong
Todd Armstrong
James Arness
Virginia Arness
Stefan Arngrim
Denny Arnold
Jean Arthur
Jan Arvan
William Arvin
Joel Ashley
Peter Ashley
Edward Asner
John Astin
Laurence Aten

*Credits were obtained primarily by viewing TV episodes. Some were obtained through CBS news releases, and logs of Macdonnell and Mantley. These provided only a partial listing. Therefore, some actors may have been omitted.

Malcolm Atterbury
Barry Atwater
Jacque Aubuchon
Jenny Lee Arness
Carmen Austin
Mike Avelar
Val Avery
Lew Ayers

Donna Bacalla
Alice Backes
Jim Backus
Margaret Bacon
Buddy Baer
John Baer
Chuck Bail
Jack Bailey
Raymond Bailey
Richard Bakalyan
Joby Baker
Joe Don Baker
Virginia Baker
Wendell Baker
Ed Bakey
Janit Baldin
Walter Baldwin
Robert Ballew
Roy Barcroft
Katherine Bard
Trevor Bardette
Rayford Barnes
Walter Barnes
Christopher Barrey
Michael Barrier
Baynes Barron
Donald Barry
Patricia Barry
John Drew Barrymore
Harry Bartell
Richard Bartell
Bonnie Bartlett
Norman Bartold
Anne Barton
Larry Barton
Harry Basch
Richard Basehart
Todd Bass
Art Batanides
Ben Bates

Jeanne Bates
Susan Batson
Alan Baxter
Hal Baylor
Ned Beatty
Billy Beck
Jim Beck
John Beck
Vincent Beck
Ken Becker
Terry Becker
Henry Beckman
Don Beddoe
Bonnie Beecher
Noah Beery, Jr.
James Beggs
Ed Begley
Ralph Bellamy
Nellie Bellflower
Russ Bender
Mia Bendixen
Val Benedict
William Benedict
Lynn Benesch
Ray Bennet
Julie Bennett
Suzanne Benoit
Gene Benton
Suzanne Benton
Warren Berlinger
Al Berry
Dehl Berti
James Best
Zina Bethune
Mary Betten
Lyle Bettger
Carl Betz
Clem Bevens
Robert Bice
Ramon Bieri
Robert Biheller
Theodore Bikel
Jennifer Billingsly
Ed Binns
Paul Birch
Billie Bird
Frank Biro
Joan Blackman
Amanda Blake
Larry Blake

Robin Blake
Whitney Blake
Olive Blakeney
Marsha Blakesley
Dan Blocker
Margaret Bly
Lloyd Bochner
Hal Bokar
Cal Bolder
Jim Boles
Gail Bonney
Sorrell Booke
Brendon Boone
Willis Bouchey
Philip Bourneuf
Billy Bowles
Bruce Boxleitner
John Boyer
Ray Boyle
Jimmy Bracken
Lane Bradbury
Lane Bradford
Richard Bradford
Stewart Bradley
Scott Brady
Eric Braeden
William Bramley
Neville Brand
Henry Brandon
John Brandon
X Brands
Hank Brandt
Marian Brash
Robert Bray
Peter Breck
John Breen
Joseph Breen
Michelle Breeze
George Brenlin
Claire Brennen
David Brian
Fletcher Brian
Beth Brickell
Beau Bridges
Rand Bridges
Charlie Briggs
Don Briggs
Burt Brinckerhoff
Heinie Brock
James Broderick

Television Actors

Steve Brodie
Charles Bronson
Walter Brooke
Charlene Brooks
Foster Brooks
Geraldine Brooks
Jan Brooks
Martin Brooks
Peter Brooks
Rand Brooks
Barry Brown
James Brown
Jerry Brown
Les Brown, Jr.
Lew Brown
Pepe Brown
Tom Brown
Cathy Browne
Robert Brubaker
Argentina Brunetti
Marvin Bryan
Fletcher Bryant
Joshua Bryant
William Bryant
Claudia Bryar
Paul Bryar
Edgar Buchanan
Connie Buck
Sam Buffington
Joyce Bulifant
Richard Bull
Brooke Bundy
Kevin Burchette
Walter Burke
Bart Burns
Michael Burns
Timothy Burns
Robert Burr
Jan Burrell
Bob Burrows
Ellen Burstyn
Nellie Burt
Normann Burton
Robert Burton
Gary Busey
Billie Green Bush
Owen Bush

Sebastian Cabot

Frank Cady
Barry Cahill
Howard Caine
Rory Calhoun
Anthony Call
Ed Call
Pepe Callahan
Bill Callaway
Gloria Calomee
Todd Cameron
Helen Page Camp
Joseph Campanella
William Campbell
Raphael Campos
David Canary
Dick Cangey
Dyan Cannon
J.D. Cannon
Kathy Cannon
Pat Cardi
Tantoo Cardinal
Annette Cardona
Harry Carey, Jr.
Michele Carey
Philip Carey
Tim Carey
Lynn Carlin
Steve Carlson
Thom Carney
Michael Carr
Paul Carr
David Carradine
John Carradine
Angela Carroll
Brandon Carroll
Dee Carroll
Ben Carruthers
Conlan Carter
Don Carter
John Carter
Anthony Caruso
Mary Carver
Allen Case
Lawrence Casey
Sue Casey
Wally Cassell
Jack Cassidy
Gloria Castillo
Peggie Castle
Bill Catching

Marc Cavell
William Challee
Phil Chambers
Richard Chamberlain
Woodrow Chambliss
James Chandler
John Davis Chandler
Lane Chandler
Jack Chaplain
David Chapman
Lonny Chapman
Eric Chase
Stephen Chase
Don Chastain
Jose Chavez
Marie Cheatham
Linden Chiles
Virginia Christine
Michael Christofer
Eunice Christopher
Ellen Clark
Bobby E. Clark
Gage Clark
J.R. Clark
Angela Clarke
Gary Clarke
John Clarke
Jan Clayton
Stanley Clements
Robert Clinton
John Close
Sid Clute
Andy Clyde
Phyllis Coates
Julie Cobb
Lee J. Cobb
Fred Coby
Iron Eyes Cody
Kathleen Cody
Rhodie Cogan
Phyllis Coghlan
Patti Cohoon
Barbara Colby
Fred Colby
Michael Cole
Thomas Coley
John Colicos
Don Collier
Sue Collier
Booth Colman

Edward Colmans
Miriam Colon
Gary Combs
Anjanette Comer
John Compton
Darlene Conley
Christopher Connelly
Betty Conner
Chuck Connors
Touch (Mike) Connors
Charles Conrad
Michael Conrad
Charlotte Considine
Tim Considine
Michael Constantine
Pat Conway
Jackie Coogan
Richard Coogan
Elisha Cook
Perry Cook
Philip Coolidge
Ben Cooper
Charles Cooper
Clancy Cooper
Jeanne Cooper
Kevin Cooper
Glenn Corbett
Gretchen Corbett
Noreen Corcoran
Alex Cord
Henry Corden
Rege Cordic
Anthony Cordova
Margarita Cordova
Jeff Corey
Sally Corner
Robert Cornthwaite
Lloyd Corrigan
Will Corry
Aneta Corsault
Frank Corsentino
Vickie Cos
Anthony Costello
Heather Cotton
Kevin Coughlin
Ed Craig
Norma Crane
Bobby Crawford
John Crawford
Dennis Cross

Jimmy Cross
Reid Cruickshanks
Brandon Cruz
Howard Culver
Robert Culp
Susan Cummings
Suzanne Cupito
Red Currie
Mason Curry
Billy Curtis
Craig Curtis
Ken Curtis
Jorga Curtwright

Fred Dale
Audrey Dalton
James Daly
Michael D'Anda
Royal Dano
Kim Darby
Gene Darfler
Christopher Dark
Steven Darrell
Henry Darrow
Andrea Darvi
Ellen Davalos
Brad David
Bette Davis
Harry Davis
Jim Davis
Michael Davis
Tony Davis
Davey Davidson
June Dayton
Richard Deacon
Vincent Deadrick
Jeff DeBenning
Lee De Broux
Ted deCorsia
Robert DeCost
S. Michael De France
Gloria de Haven
John Dehner
Frank DeKova
Laurence Delaney
Cyril Delevanti
Margie De Meyer
Lincoln Demyan
Pat Dennis-Leigh

Crahan Denton
Bruce Dern
Joe DeSantis
William Devane
Valentin De Vargas
Andy Devine
Joe Devlin
Richard Devon
Alan Dexter
Jack Diamond
George Di Cenzo
Angie Dickinson
John Dierkes
Charles Dierkop
Dana Dillaway
Joe di Reda
Douglas Dirkson
Robert Dix
Gloria Dixon
Bennie Dobbins
Lawrence Dobkin
James Dobson
Barbara Dodd
John Dolan
Robert Donner
James Doohan
Robert DoQui
John Doucette
Burt Douglas
Doc Douglas
George Douglas
Jerry Douglas
Frederic Downs
Robert Doyle
Deborah Dozier
James Drake
Ken Drake
Tom Drake
Lieux Dressler
Richard Dreyfuss
James Drury
Don Dubbins
Paul DuBov
Val Dufour
Andrew Duggan
Bob Duggan
John Duke
John Dullaghan
Jane Dulo
Angus Duncan

Television Actors

Craig Duncan
Pamela Dunlap
Gregg Dunn
Liam Dunn
Peter Dunn
Larry Duran
Mike Durkin

Wallace Earl
Robert Easton
Victor Eberg
Buddy Ebsen
Barbara Eden
Lyn Edington
Walker Edmiston
Scott Edmonds
Sam Edwards
Bob Eilbacher
Lisa Eilbacher
Ike Eisenmann
Jack Elam
Dana Elcar
George Eldridge
Louis Elias
Robert Ellenstein
Ross Elliot
Sam Elliot
Steve Ellsworth
Donald Elson
Richard Ely
Alan Emerson
Matt Emery
Robert Emhardt
Michael Emmett
Paul Engle
Roy Engle
Jena Engstrom
Harold Ensley
Tony Epper
Leif Erickson
John Ericson
Stuart Erwin
William Erwin
Evan Evans
Gene Evans
Richard Evans
Jason Evers
Diana Ewing
Roger Ewing

Richard Eyer

Tom Fadden
Myrna Fahey
Tom Falk
Hampton Fancher
Sharon Farrell
Tommy Farrell
Edward (Ed) Faulkner
William Fawcett
Jesslyn Fax
Jean Fenwick
Pamelyn Ferdin
Abel Fernandez
Joseph Ferrante
Dan Ferrone
John Fiedler
Daphne Field
Mary Field
Joy Fielding
Jerelyn Fields
Laura Figueroa
Larry Finley
Eddie Firestone
Bruce M. Fischer
Nancy Fisher
Shug Fisher
Paul Fix
Fionnuala Flanagan
John Flinn
Jay C. Flippen
Med Flory
Amber Flower
Dan Flynn, Jr.
Gertrude Flynn
Joe Flynn
Nina Foch
Brian Foley
Dick Foran
Constance Ford
Harrison Ford
Ross Ford
Michael Forest
Steve Forrest
Robert Fortier
Diane Foster
Jodi Foster
Linda Foster
Ron Foster

Byron Foulger
Robert Foulk
Douglas V. Fowley
Craig Fox
Michael Fox
Anne Francis
Charles Francisco
Arthur Franz
Eduard Franz
James Frawley
Elizabeth Frazer
Norman Frederic
Charles Fredericks
Bert Freed
Joan Freeman
Ted French
Victor French
David Fresco
Florida Friebus
Alice Frost
Terry Frost
Allan Fudge
Elaine Fulkerson
Clem Fuller

Mel Gaines
Nacho Galindo
Mel Gallagher
Lew Gallo
Jim Gammon
Kaz Garas
Stella Garcia
Vincent Gardenia
Alycia Gardner
Allen Garfield
Beverly Garland
Don Garner
Jack Garner
Martin Garralaga
Leif Garrett
Sean Garrison
Kelton Garwood
Nancy Gates
Rick Gates
Jerry Gatlin
Bennye Gatteys
James Gavin
Steve Gaynor
Gordon Gebert

[757]

Will Geer
Ted Gehring
Paul Gehrman
Emile Genest
Robert Gentry
Elizabeth Germaine
Lisa Gerritsen
Mike Gibson
Stefan Gierasch
Alan Gifford
Melissa Gilbert
Richard Gilden
Gwynne Gilford
Sam Gilman
Jack Gilman
Jack Ging
Ray Girardin
Robert Gist
Ned Glass
Seamon Glass
Hap Glaudi
Tom Gleason
Bruce Glover
Mark Goddard
Bob Golden
Thomas Gomez
Harold Goodwin
Bobby Goodwins
Bruce Gordon
Clark Gordon
Leo Gordon
Susan Gordon
Lloyd Gough
Harold Gould
Wilton Graff
Tim Graham
Michael Granger
Barbara Grant
Harvey Grant
Joan Granville
Karen Grassle
Robert Gravage
Steve Gravers
Charles Gray
Alex Green
Dorothy Green
Gilbert Green
Lawrence Green
Michael Greene
Sam Greene

Tom Greenway
Dabbs Greer
Julie Gregg
Virginia Gregg
Fabian Gregory
James Gregory
Mary Gregory
Duane Grey
Robert Griffin
James Griffith
Gary Grimes
Jack Grinnage
Sam Groom
Fred Grossinger
Paul Guilfoyle
Raymond Guth
Tani Phelps Guthrie

Joan Hackett
Kevin Hagen
Ross Hagen
Ron Hagerthy
Don Haggerty
Paul Hahn
Charles Haid
Sid Haig
Jester Hairston
Alan Hale
Betsy Hale
Bill Hale
Chanin Hale
Fiona Hale
Monte Hale
Richard Hale
Scott Hale
James Halferty
Bobby Hall
Thad Hall
Billy Halop
Brett Halsey
Dran Hamilton
John Hamilton
Joseph Hamilton
Lynn Hamilton
Margaret Hamilton
Murray Hamilton
Nicholas Hammond
Jim Hampton
John Hanek

Don Hanmer
Don Happy
Jerry Hardin
Sarah Hardy
Dean Harens
Betty Harford
Link Harget
John Harmon
Jonathan Harper
Rand Harper
Berkeley Harris
Jo Ann Harris
Michael Harris
Robert H. Harris
Stacy Harris
Jan Harrison
Elizabeth Harrower
Bill Hart
Tommy Hart
Dee Hartford
Mariette Hartley
Edmund Hashim
Raymond Hatton
Harry Harvey, Sr.
Phil Harvey
Joe Haworth
Norah Hayden
Ron Hayes
Johnny Haymer
Chuck Hayward
Vinton Hayworth
Myron Healey
May Heatherly
Eileen Heckart
Jay Hector
Gunnar Hellstrom
Anne Helm
Frances Helm
Katharine Helmond
Joe Helton
Percy Helton
Ray Hemphill
Len Hendry
William Henry
Pitt Herbert
Pepe Hern
Frederick Herrick
Bob Herron
Barton Heyman
Eddie Hice

Television Actors

Darryl Hickman
Harry Hickox
Chuck Hicks
Joe Higgins
Michael Higgins
Marianna Hill
Peg Hillias
Joseph Hindy
Pat Hingle
Robert Hinkle
Michael Hinn
Mitzi Hoag
Rose Hobart
Duke Hobbie
Eddie Hodges
Earle Hodgins
Pat Hogan
Robert Hogan
Victor Holchak
Bruce Holland
Buck Holland
Jack Holland
Tom Holland
Earl Holliman
Rex Holman
Wendell Holmes
Joseph Hoover
Bo Hopkins
Bob Hopkins
Dennis Hopper
William Hopper
Alfred Hopson
Geoffrey Horne
Charles Horvath
Frank Hotchkiss
Clint Howard
Rance Howard
Ronny Howard
Mike Howden
Clyde Howdy
Hoke Howell
Jean Howell
Rodolfo Hoyos
Clegg Hoyt
John Hoyt
John Hubbard
David Huddleston
Ken Hudgins
John "Bear" Hudkins
John Hudson

Billy Hughes
Whitey Hughes
Frank Huish
Robert Human
Chris Hundley
Craig Hundley
Arthur Hunnicutt
Marsha Hunt
Kim Hunter
Thomas Hunter
Erica Hunton
Richard D. Hurst
Lisabeth Hush
Patricia Huston
Will Hutchins
Josephine Hutchinson
Betty Hutton
Brian Hutton
Diana Hyland
Jim Hyland

Steve Ihnat
Duncan Inches
Jean Ingram
Rex Ingram
Jean Inness
Harold Innocent
John Ireland
Robert Ivers
Perry Ivins
Victor Izay

Anne Jackson
Sherry Jackson
Ted Jacques
Richard Jaeckel
Allen Jaffe
Jewel Jaffee
Anthony James
Brian James
Clifton James
Ralph James
Adar Jameson
Vivi Janiss
Frank K. Janson
Francesca Jarvis
Graham Jarvis
Peter Jason
Bonnie Jedell

Salome Jens
Marlowe Jenson
Roy Jenson
James Jeter
Isabelle Jewell
Arch Johnson
Ben Johnson
Brad Johnson
Chal Johnson
Chubby Johnson
Jason Johnson
Lamont Johnson
Russell Johnson
I. Sanford Jolley
Henry Jones
Ivy Jones
L.Q. Jones
Mickey Jones
Miranda Jones
Morgan Jones
Samee Lee Jones
Betsy Jones-Moreland
Ted Jordan
Victor Jory
Allyn Joslyn
Patricia Joyce
Allen Jung
Katherine Justice

Walter Kaasa
Anna Karen
Robert Karnes
Joseph Kearns
Don Keefer
Richard Keene
Robert Keene
William Keene
Michael Keep
Richard Keith
Pete Kellett
Michael Kellin
John Kellogg
Barry Kelley
DeForest Kelley
Jack Kelly
Rick Kelman
Richard D. Kelton
Ed Kemmer
Warren Kemmerling

Dan Kemp
Sally Kemp
William Kendis
Hank Kendrick
Adam Kennedy
Douglas Kennedy
George Kennedy
Ken Kenopka
David Kent
Sandra Kent
Sandy Kenyon
John Kerr
Sondra Kerr
Lance Kerwin
Cliff Ketchum
James Kevin
Sandy Kevin
George Keymas
Robert Keys
Jonathan Kidd
Richard Kiley
Victor Killian
Brett King
Wright King
Zalman King
Margaret L. Kingman
Martin Kingsley
Lee Kinsolving
Tommy Kirk
Jess Kirkpatrick
Ken Kirzenger
Helen Kleeb
Werner Klemperer
Jack Klugman
Robert Knapp
Wilfred Knapp
Christopher Knight
Ted Knight
Gail Kobe
Dorothy Konrad
Robert Koons
Ana Korita
Yaphet Kotto
Jon Kowal
Frank Kreig
Lee Krieger
Lou Krugman
Jack Kruschen
Charles Kuenstle
Kay E. Kuter

Tom Lacy
David Ladd
Diane Ladd
Gil Lamb
George Lambert
Jack Lambert
Lee Lambert
Paul Lambert
Miguel Landa
Martin Landau
Allen Lane
Michael Lane
Rusty Lane
Sue Ane Langdon
Paul Langton
Jay Lanin
Robert Lansing
Richard Lapp
John Larch
John Larkin
Sheila Larkin
Mary LaRoche
Michael Larrain
Darrell Larson
John Lasell
Louise Latham
Wesley Lau
S. John Launer
Harry Lauter
Delphi Lawrence
John Lawrence
Cloris Leachman
Michael Learned
Michael Le Clair
Anna Lee
John G. Lee
Ruta Lee
Lance Le Gault
Trent Lehman
Mark Lenard
Kay Lenz
Thomas Leopold
Fred Lerner
Gloria LeRoy
Bethel Leslie
Al Lettier
Jeffrey Lewis
Virginia Lewis
Alfred Linder
Elliot Lindsay

George Lindsey
Albert Linville
Joanne Linville
Jonathan Lippe
Steve Liss
Dawn Little Sky
Eddie Little Sky
Suzanne Lloyd
Felix Locher
Jon Locke
June Lockhart
Alexander Lockwood
Gary Lockwood
Robert Loggia
Doreen Long
Ed Long
Dick London
Todd Lookinland
Ann Loos
Barbara Lord
Jack Lord
Athena Lorde
Lynn Loring
Jon Lormer
Donald Losby
Phyllis Love
Stanja Lowe
Tom Lowell
Robert Lowry
Karl Lucas
Bill Lucking
James Luisi
Keye Luke
Dayton Lummis
Barbara Luna
Art Lund
Richard Lundin
Vic Lundin
John Lupton
Allen Lurie
Robert Luster
James Lydon
Dawn Lyn
Hal Lynch
Ken Lynch
Gene Lyons
Robert F. Lyons
Herbert Lytton

Television Actors

Byron Mabe
James MacArthur
Ian MacDonald
Tyler MacDuff
Biff McGuire
Jay MacIntoshe
Barton MacLane
Florence MacMichael
Elizabeth MacRae
George Macready
Edward Madden
Bert Madrid
Charles Magaulay
Lee Majors
James Malcolm
Colin Male
Arthur Malet
James Maloney
Maggie Malooly
Peter Mamakos
Larry Mann
Lawrence Mann
Jack Mann
Ronald Manning
Maurice Manson
Jon Jason Mantley
Marie Mantley
Ralph Manza
Vitina Marcus
Ted Marcuse
Stuart Margolin
Marie Rose
John Marley
Lucy Marlowe
Nora Marlowe
Scott Marlowe
Joe Maross
Kenneth Mars
Linda Marsh
Michele Marsh
Gloria Marshall
Joan Marshall
Liz Marshall
Nancy Marshall
Shary Marshall
Lynn Marta
Arlene Martel
Frank Marth
Kiel Martin
Mari Martin
Ross Martin
Strother Martin
Joaquin Martinez
Patrice Martinez
Natalie Masters
George Mathews
Charles Maxwell
Frank Maxwell
Marilyn Maxwell
Ken Mayer
Raymond Mayo
Mike Mazurki
Charles McArthur
Amanda McBroom
James McCallion
Mercedes McCambridge
Devlin McCarthy
Lin McCarthy
Tom McCauley
Peggy McCay
Sean McClory
Ed McCready
Mathew McCue
Ruth McDevitt
Eileen McDonough
Fred McDougall
Kevin C. McEveety
Stephen McEveety
Tom McFadden
Rod McGaughy
Darren McGavin
Gloria McGhee
John McGough
Oliver McGowan
Bill McGraw
Charles McGraw
Robert McGraw
Barry McGuire
Harp McGuire
Rod McGuire
Holly McIntire
Tim McIntyre
J. Edward McKinley
Wayne McLaren
Bill McLean
David McLean
Catherine McLeod
John McLiam
Billy McMickle
Dennis McMullen
Pamela McMyler
Stephen McNally
Howard McNear
Taylor McPeters
Ellen McRae
Gerald McRaney
Robert McQuain
Robert McQueeney
Patrick McVey
Tyler McVey
William Meader
Hazel Medina
Julio Medina
Don Megowan
William Meigs
Joseph Mell
Troy Melton
Sam Melville
Tina Menard
William Menard
Judi Meredith
Jan Merlin
Fintan Meyler
Paul Micale
Robert Middleton
Michael Mikler
Robert Miles, Jr.
Vera Miles
John Milford
Diana Millay
Denny Miller
Mark Miller
Spencer Milligan
Donna Mills
Gordon Mills
Mort Mills
Jessamine Milner
Gerald Milton
William Mims
Kathryn Minner
James Minotto
Cameron Mitchell
Dallas Mitchell
George Mitchell
Joe Mitchum
John Mitchum
Roger Mobley
Laurie Mock
Donald Moffat
Del Monroe

GUNSMOKE — IV. APPENDIX G

Ricardo Montalban
Monte Montana, Jr.
Alex Montoya
Ralph Moody
Ron Moody
Henrietta Moore
Joanna Moore
Erin Moran
Jorge Moreno
Ruben Moreno
Alexandra Morgan
Bob Morgan
Boyd "Red" Morgan
Harry Morgan
Read Morgan
Mickey Morton
Wayne Morris
Brian Morrison
Shelley Morrison
Patricia Morrow
Susan Morrow
Dianne Mountford
Diana Muldaur
Greg Mullavey
Richard Mulligan
Mary Munday
Alec Murdock
George Murdock
James Murdock
Bob Murphy
Melissa Murphy
William Murphy
Mark Murray
Rick Murray
Larry Musser
Burt Mustin
Pauline Myers

Conrad Nagel
Tom Nardini
Robert Nash
Anna Navarro
Cal Naylor
Hal Needham
Brad Neff
Ed Nelson
Gene Nelson
Lloyd Nelson
Rik Nervik
Lois Nettleton

Dorothy Neumann
William Newell
Paul Newlan
John Newman
Susan Newmark
John Newton
Theodore Newton
Janet Nichols
Laura Nichols
Robert Nichols
Leslie Nielson
Leonard Nimoy
James Nolan
Jeanette Nolan
Kathy Nolan
Tom Nolan
Nick Nolte
Sheree North
Shelly Novak
James Nusser
Mayf Nutter
France Nuyen

Simon Oakland
Warren Oates
Karen Oberdiear
Clay O'Brien
Kim O'Brien
Richard O'Brien
Bryan O'Byrne
William O'Connell
Carroll O'Connor
Tim O'Connor
Doug Odney
Gene O'Donnell
James O'Hara
Shirley O'Hara
Donald O'Kelly
Tim O'Kelly
Ken Olandt
Henry Olek
Susan Oliver
Susan Olsen
Eric Olson
James Olson
Nancy Olson
J. Pat O'Malley
John O'Malley
Kathleen O'Malley
Pat O'Moore

Anne O'Neal
Kevin O'Neal
John Orchard
James O'Rear
Felice Orlandi
Cliff Osmond
Robert Osterloh
Annette O'Toole
Ollie O'Toole
Jay Overholts
Marjorie Owens
Patricia Owens

Netta Packer
Manuel Padilla, Jr.
Gregg Palmer
Jeff Palmer
Robert Palmer
Thomas Palmer
Lew Palter
Woodrow Parfrey
Earl Parker
Jeff Parks
Michael Parks
Julie Parrish
Christoper Pate
Michael Pate
Butch Patrick
Dennis Patrick
John Patrick
Mary Patten
Robert Patten
Hank Patterson
Herb Patterson
Morgan Paull
Dick Paxton
Brad Payne
Joan Payne
John Payne
Pamela Payton-Wright
Dick Peabody
Wynn Pearce
Ed Peck
Larry Pennell
Jack Perkins
Gigi Perreau
Vic Perrin
Elizabeth Perry
Joseph Perry
Lloyd Perryman

Television Actors

Nehemiah Persoff
Erica Petal
Brock Peters
House Peters, Jr.
Jan Peters
Kelly Jean Peters
Lauri Peters
Scott Peters
Arthur Peterson, Jr.
Nan Peterson
Michael Petit
George Petrie
Howard Petrie
Susan Petrone
Tani Phelps
Barney Phillips
Robert Phillips
William Phipps
Ben Piazza
Paul Picerni
John Pickard
Slim Pickens
Preston Pierce
Alberto Pina
Philip Pine
Robert Pine
Tom Pittman
Martin Place
Alma Platt
Ed Platt
Suzanne Pleshette
Eve Plumb
Michael J. Pollard
Teno Pollick
Eunice Pollis
Jeff Pomerantz
Herman Poppe
J. Robert Porter
Clayton Post
Addison Powell
Sandye Powell
Laurie Prange
Judson Pratt
Robert Pratt
Michael Preece
Sherwood Price
Carl Prickett
Andrew Prine
Paul Prokop
Zina Provendie

Ainslie Pryor
John Puglia
Don Pulford
Denver Pyle

Ariane Quinn
Dolores Quinton

Joe Raciti
Jack Rader
Chip Rafferty
Mike Ragan
Steve Raines
Ford Rainey
Dack Rambo
Frank Ramirez
Nick Ramus
Glen Randall, Jr.
Sue Randall
Ron Randell
Larry Randles
Donald Randolph
Bob Random
Gilman Rankin
Jane Ray
Harry Raybould
Guy Raymond
Peggy Rea
Glenn Redding
Gene Redfern
Dennis Redfield
William Redfield
Liam Redmond
Anthony Redondo
Alan Reed, Jr.
Marshall Reed
Walter Reed
Sammy Reese
Tom Reese
Richard Reeves
Pedro Regas
Carl Benton Reid
John Reilly
Carl Reindel
Geri Reische
Jack Reitzen
David Renard
Ken Renard
Nancy Rennick
Stafford Repp

Alejandro Rey
Araceli Rey
Burt Reynolds
Madlyn Rhue
Dick Rich
Vernon Rich
Mark Richman
Paul Richards
Tommy Richards
Bobby Riha
Mary Rings
Lalo Rios
Jay Ripley
Carlos Rivas
Mike Road
Gale Robbins
Chuck Roberson
Davis Roberts
Lois Roberts
Mark Roberts
Pernell Roberts
Ralph Roberts
Randolph Roberts
Roy Roberts
Stephen Roberts
Dennis Robertson
Bartlett Robinson
Charles Robinson
Chris Robinson
Edward Robinson, Jr.
Robert Rockwell
Elizabeth Rogers
Wayne Rogers
Gilbert Roland
Nina Roman
Ric Roman
Ruth Roman
Andy Romano
Wallace Rooney
Fay Roope
Ralph Rose
Don G. Ross
Katherine Ross
Robert C. Ross
Robert Rothwell
Henry Rowland
Benny Rubin
Herbert Rudley
Val Ruffino
Burt Rumsey

Jack Rupp
Joseph Ruskin
Bing Russell
Jackie Russell
John Russell
Kurt Russell
Richard Rust
Gene Rutherford
Lori Rutherford
Fran Ryan
Alfred Ryder
Eddie Ryder

David Saber
Lee Sabinson
Will Sage
Marco St. John
Albert Salmi
Robert Sampson
Walter Sande
Hugh Sanders
Steve Sanders
Steve Sandor
Dick Sargent
Joe Sargent
Ernest Sarracino
Aaron Saxon
John Saxon
William Schallert
Sabrina Scharf
Norbert Schiller
Joseph Schneider
John Schuck
Keith Schultz
Dorothy Schuyler
Sam Schwartz
Fred J. Scollay
Brenda Scott
Evelyn Scott
Jacqueline Scott
Ken Scott
Pippa Scott
Simon Scott
Walter Scott
Vito Scotti
Joe Scudero
Lisa Seagram
Jack Searl
James Seay
Charles Seel

Carol Seflinger
Sarah Selby
Marian Seldes
George Selk
Scott Selles
Milton Selzer
Frank Sentry
John Seven
Anne Seymour
Rocky Shahan
Diane Shalet
John Shank
Harry Shannon
Richard Shannon
Alex Sharp
Karen Sharpe
William Shatner
Elizabeth Shaw
Eric Shea
David Sheiner
Jacque Shelton
Jan Shepard
Jim Sheppard
W. Morgan Sheppard
Jon Sheppodd
Mark Shera
Chick Sheridan
Dab Sheridan
Orville Sherman
Mercedes Shirley
Mickey Sholdar
William Shriver
Lynn Shubert
Gregory Sierra
Mitchell Silberman
Russ Siler
Susan Silo
Jeff Silver
Joe Silver
Frank Silvera
Tom Simcox
Robert F. Simon
Mickey Simpson
Richard Sinatra
Doris Singleton
Joseph Sirola
Jim Skaggs
Tom Skerritt
Jeremy Slate
Richard X. Slattery

Everett Sloane
Bernice Smith
Hal Smith
John Smith
Ken L. Smith
Kent Smith
Pat Smith
Sandra Smith
William Smith
Kit Smythe
Ron Soble
Abraham Sofaer
Rudy Solari
Julie Sommars
Quentin Sondergaard
Rudy Sooter
Paul Sorenson
Robert Sorrells
David Soul
Olan Soule
Fay Spain
Aaron Spelling
Don Spruance
James Stacy
Dan Stafford
Forrest Stanley
Harry Dean Stanton
Edgar Stehli
Chris Stephens
Tom Stern
Charles Sterrett
Craig Stevens
Onslow Stevens
Paul Stevens
Scott Stevens
Warren Stevens
Parker Stevenson
Robert Stevenson
Robert J. Stevenson
Art Stewart
Charlotte Stewart
Gregg Stewart
Marianne Stewart
Paul Stewart
Peggy Stewart
Boyd Stockman
Guy Stockwell
Harold J. Stone
Leonard Stone
Milburn Stone

Television Actors

Glenn Strange
Amzie Strickland
Fred Stromsoe
Michael Strong
Robert Strong
Don Stroud
Wendy Stuart
Mark Stuges
Norman Sturgis
Linda Sublette
Brick Sullivan
Liam Sullivan
Hope Summers
Jerry Summers
Neil Summers
William L. Sumper
Dolores Sutton
Frank Sutton
Tom Sutton
Monica Svensson
Robert Swan
Karl Swenson
Loretta Swit
Ken Swofford
Harry Swoger

Robert Tafur
Nita Talbot
Gloria Talbott
William Talman
Russ Tamblyn
Charles Tannen
William Tannen
Clay Tanner
Vic Tayback
Buck Taylor
Dub "Cannonball" Taylor
Joan Taylor
Judson Taylor
Mary Lou Taylor
Vaughn Taylor
Guy Teague
Ray Teal
Trini Tellez
Dan Terranova
Steve Terrell
Tex Terry
Joan Tetzel
Torin Thatcher
Roy Thinnes

Lance Thomas
Paul C. Thomas
Charles Thompson
Dee J. Thompson
Hilarie Thompson
Marshall Thompson
Pat Thompson
Kelly Thordsen
Evans Thornton
Daniel Thorpe
Duane Thorsen
Russ Thorson
Robert Tindall
Kenneth Tobey
Dan Tobin
Bee Tompkins
Roger Torrey
Frank M. Totino
Robert Totten
Harry Townes
Daniel Travanti
Dorothy Tristin
Brad Trumbull
H.T. Tsiang
Forrest Tucker
Moira Turner
Lurene Tuttle
Gene Tyburn
Ken Tyles
Cicely Tyson

Robert Urich

Nitividad Vacio
Joan Van Ark
Lee Van Cleef
Warren Vanders
Michael Vandever
John Van Dreelen
Renata Vanni
Jimmy Van Patten
Joyce Van Patten
Vincent Van Patten
Luis Van Rooten
Julie Van Zandt
Nina Varela
Edmund Vargas
John Vari
Heidi Vaughn
Jean Vaughn

Rees Vaughn
Robert Vaughn
William Vaughn
Pedro Vegas
Olga Velez
Ricky Vera
John Vernon
Lou Vernon
Herb Vigran
Robert Viharo
Jan-Michael Vincent
Virginia Vincent
Gary Vinson
Karen Vogel
Mitch Vogel
Jon Voight
Wilheim Von Homburg
Peter Votrian

Charles Wagenheim
Lia Waggner
Lyle Waggoner
James Wainwright
Garry Walberg
Scott Walker
George Wallace
Helen Wallace
Shani Wallis
Joey Walsh
Nancy Walters
Jess Walton
Sam Wanamaker
John War Eagle
John Warburton
Larry Ward
Anne Warren
Lance Warren
Leslie Ann Warren
Steve Warren
Ruth Warrick
Tom Water
Linda Watkins
Bruce Watson
Mills Watson
William C. Watson
Charles Watts
Len Wayland
David Wayne
Fred Wayne
Dennis Weaver

[7 6 5]

Fritz Weaver
Rick Weaver
Richard Webb
Peggy Webber
Charles Webster
Karen Welch
Rebecca Welles
Bill Wellman, Jr.
Bruce Wendell
Howard Wendell
Ned Wertimer
Dick Wessel
Adam West
Jennifer West
Judi West
Martin West
Wayne West
Rusty Westcoat
James Westerfield
Brad Weston
Jack Weston
Paul Wexler
John Wheeler
Johnnie Whitaker
Bill White, Jr.
Daniel M. White
Lucas White
Robert S. White
O.Z. Whitehead
Anne Whitfield
Kip Whitman
Stuart Whitman
James Whitmore
Cece Whitney
Grace Lee Whitney
Michael Whitney

Peter Whitney
David Whorf
Nancy Wickwire
Bob Wiensko
Russell Wiggins
Claire Wilcox
Joey Wilcox
Collin Wilcox-Horne
Henry Wilcoxon
Mary Jane Wildman
Robert Wilke
Guy Wilkerson
Elen Willard
Adam Williams
Grant Williams
Guinne Williams
Hal Williams
Robert B. Williams
Rush Williams
Terry Williams
Van Williams
Noble Willingham
Chill Wills
Shirley Wilson
Terry Wilson
Ilka Windish
William Windom
Marie Windsor
Jason Wingreen
Jim Winslow
Lee Winters
William Wintersole
Henry Wise
Grant Withers
Michael-James Wixted

Venita Wolf
Iggie Wolfington
Gary Wood
Harry Wood
Larry Wood
Paul Daniel Wood
Ward Wood
Morgan Woodward
Sam Woody
Lindsey Workman
Ben Wright
Howard Wright
Roy Wright
Will Wright
Al Wyatt
Than Wyenn
Link Wyler
Catherine Wyles
Meg Wyllie
H.M. Wynant
Dana Wynter

Elizabeth York
Buck Young
Ray Young
Jack Younger
Joe Yrigoyen, Sr.

John Zaccaro
Anthony Zerbe
William Zuckert

APPENDIX H
THE RADIO PERFORMERS

Lynn Allen
Irene Andres
Hy Averbach
Parley Baer
Michael Ann Barrett
Edgar Barrier
Eleanore Barry
Harry Bartell
Charles Bastin
Jeanne Bates
Richard Beals
Butch Bernard
Ted Bliss
Lillian Buyeff
Frank Cady
Virginia Christine
Juli Conger
William Conrad
Hans Conried
Tommy Cook
Joe Cranston
Richard Crenna
Howard Culver
Leo Curley
Joan Danton
Richard Deacon
John Dehner
Don Diamond
Lawrence Dobkin
Frances Drew

Paul DuBov
Joe DuVal
James Eagle
Robert Easton
Jack Edwards
Sam Edwards
Barbara Eiler
Georgia Ellis
Herb Ellis
Richard Fields
Joe Forte
Paul Frees
Frank Gerstle
Clark Gordon
Tim Graham
Virginia Gregg
Bob Griffin
James Griffith
Tom Hanley
Stacy Harris
Jerry Hausner
Louis Jean Heydt
Sammie Hill
Jonathan Hole
Tom Holland
William Idelson
John James, Jr.
Vivi Janiss
Jill Jarmyn
Byron Kane

Joseph Kearns
Jess Kirkpatrick
Helen Kleeb
Lou Krugman
Jack Kruschen
Bill Lally
Mary Lansing
Charlotte Lawrence
Peter Leeds
Louise Lewis
Ken Lynch
Joyce McCluskey
Pat McGeehan
Johnny McGovern
John McIntire
Fred MacKaye
Howard McNear
Eve McVeigh
Kathy Marlowe
Junius Matthews
Lee Millar
Ralph Moody
Anne Morrison
Jack Moyles
Jeanette Nolan
James Nusser
James Ogg
Sammy Ogg
William Oiler
Nestor Paiva

Edmund Penney
Richard Perkins
Vic Perrin
Barney Phillips
Clayton Post
Vici Raaf
Peggy Rea
Bart Robinson
Paul Savage

John Stephenson
Gil Stratton, Jr.
Bob Sweeney
Eleanore Tanin
Irene Tedrow
Larry Thor
Tom Tully
Herb Vigran
Patricia Walter

Stan Waxman
Peggy Webber
James Westerfield
Anne Whitfield
Elaine Williams
Paula Winslow
Ben Wright
Will Wright

APPENDIX I
THE TELEVISION PRODUCTION STAFF

First Season: *Assistant Director* Glenn Cook *Director of Photography* Ernest Miller, A.S.C., Fleet Southcott, Elsworth Fredericks *Art Director* Nicolai Remisoff *Property Master* Mike Gordon *Supervising Editor* Fred W. Berger, A.C.E. *Editor* Michael Luciano, A.C.E., Leslie Vidor *Makeup* Glen Alden *Hairdresser* Pat Whiffing *Wardrobe* John E. Dowsing, Jr. *Script Supervisor* Mary Chaffee *Optical Effects* Jack Rabin and Louis DeWitt *Sound* Roderick Sound, Inc. *Casting* Lynn Stalmaster *Filmed in Hollywood by* Filmaster Productions, Inc.

Second Season: *Production Manager* Glenn Cook *Assistant Director* William Dario Faralla, Howard Joslin *Director of Photography* Fleet Southcott *Art Director* Nicolai Remisoff *Property Master* Mike Gordon *Supervising Editor* Fred W. Berger, A.C.E. *Editor* Leslie Vidor, Sam Gold *Makeup* Glen Alden *Hairdresser* Pat Whiffing *Wardrobe* John E. Dowsing, Jr. *Script Supervisor* Mary Chaffee *Set Decorator* G.W. Berntsen *Special Photographic Effects* Jack Rabin and Louis DeWitt *Sound* Roderick Sound, Inc. *Casting* Lynn Stalmaster *Filmed in Hollywood by* Filmaster Productions, Inc.

Third Season: *Production Manager* Glenn Cook *Assistant Director* Howard Joslin, Robert Beche, W.B. (Mike) Eason *Director of Photography* Fleet Southcott *Art Director* James W. Sullivan *Property Master* Mike Gordon, Ted Cooper *Supervising Editor* Fred W. Berger, A.C.E. *Editor* Harry Coswick, Samuel Gold, Mike Pozen *Makeup* Glen Alden *Hairdresser* Pat Whiffing *Wardrobe* Robert Odell *Script Supervisor* Mary Chaffee *Set Decorator* G.W. Berntsen, Raymond Boltz, Jr. *Optical Effects* Jack Rabin & Louis DeWitt *Sound* Roderick Sound *Casting* Lynn Stalmaster and Assoc. *Filmed in Hollywood by* Filmaster Productions, Inc.

Fourth Season: *Production Manager* Glenn Cook *Assistant Director* Nathan Barragar *Director of Photography* Fleet Southcott *Supervising Editor* Fred W. Berger, A.C.E. *Editor* Leslie Vidor, A.C.E., Al Joseph *Set Designer* Paul Sylos, Jr. *Property Master* Mike Gordon, Ted Cooper *Makeup* Glen Alden *Hairstylist* Pat Whiffing, C.H.S. *Wardrobe*

GUNSMOKE — IV. APPENDIX I

Robert Odell *Script Supervisor* Mary Chaffee *Set Decorator* Raymond Boltz, Jr. *Optical Effects* Jack Rabin & Louis Dewitt *Sound* Roderick Sound, Inc. *Casting* Stalmaster-Lister, Co. *Filmed in Hollywood by* Filmaster Productions, Inc.

Fifth Season: *Production Supervisor* Dewey Starkey *Unit Production Manager* Howard Joslin *Director of Photography* Fleet Southcott *Music by* Fred Steiner, Jerry Goldsmith *Art Director* Walter E. Keller *Film Editor* Otto Meyer, A.C.E., Al Joseph *Assistant Director* Robert Beche *Set Decorators* Charles Vassar, Herman N. Schoenbrun *Sound Effects Editor* Gene Eliot, M.P.S.E. *Music Editor* Gene Feldman *Script Supervisor* Adele Cannon *Property Master* Clem R. Widrig *Casting* Stalmaster-Lister Co. *Costumer* Alexander Velcoff *Makeup Artist* Glen Alden *Hairstylist* Pat Whiffing, C.H.S. *Sound* Roderick Sound, Inc.

Sixth Season: *Production Supervisor* Dewey Starkey *Director of Photography* Fleet Southcott *Music by* Fred Steiner, Jerry Goldsmith, Lynn Murray *Art Director* Walter E. Keller *Assistant Director* Robert Beche *Film Editor* Al Joseph, A.C.E. *Set Decorator* Herman N. Schoenbrun *Sound Effects Editor* Gene Eliot, M.P.S.E. *Music Editor* Gene Feldman *Production Sound Mixer* Vernon W. Kramer *Script Supervisor* Adele Cannon *Casting* Stalmaster-Lister Co. *Property Master* Clem R. Widrig *Costumers* Alexander Velcoff, Ruth Stella, Glenita Dinneen *Makeup Artist* Glen Alden *Hairstylist* Pat Whiffing, C.H.S. *Rerecording* Joel Moss *Titles and Opticals* Pacific Title *Filmed at* Paramount Studios

Seventh Season: *Director of Photography* Fleet Southcott *Music by* Fred Steiner, Wilbur Hatch, Lucien Moraweck, Rene Garriguenc *Music Conducted by* Lud Gluskin *Art Director* Albert Heschong *Assistant Director* Robert Beche, Wes McAfee *Film Editor* Otto Meyer, A.C.E., Al Joseph, A.C.E. *Set Decorator* Herman Schoenbrun *Sound Effects Editor* Gene Eliot, M.P.S.E. *Music Editor* Gene Feldman *Script Supervisor* Edla Bakke, Gana Jones, Adele Cannon *Production Sound Mixer* Vernon W. Kramer *Rerecording* Joel Moss *Casting* Stalmaster-Lister Co. *Property Master* Clem R. Widrig *Costumers* Alexander Velcoff, Thelma Hilborn *Makeup* Greg Alden *Hairstylist* Pat Whiffing *Titles and Opticals* Pacific Title *Filmed at* Paramount Studios

Eighth Season: *Director of Photography* Fleet Southcott, Robert Pittack, A.S.C., Frank Phillips *Art Director* Albert Heschong *Assistant Director* Robert L. Rosen, Al Joseph, Wes McAfee, Robert Beche *Film Editor* Otto Meyer, A.C.E. *Set Decorator* Herman Schoenbrun *Sound Effects Editor* Gene Eliot, M.P.S.E. *Music Editor* Gene Feldman *Script Supervisor* Edla Bakke *Production Sound Mixer* Vernon W. Kramer *Rerecording* Joel Moss *Casting* Stalmaster-Lister Co. *Property Master* Clem R. Widrig *Costumers* Alexander Velcoff, Thelma Hilborn *Makeup Artist* Glen Alden *Hairstylist* Pat Whiffing, C.H.S. *Filmed at* Paramount Studios

Ninth Season: *Director of Photography* Frank Phillips, A.S.C. *Music by* Fred Steiner, Richard Shores *Production Manager* Robert M. Beche *Art Director* James D. Vance *Assistant Director* Wes McAfee, Robert L. Rosen *Set Decorator* Herman Schoenbrun *Script Supervisor* Edla Bakke *Film Editor* Otto Meyer, A.C.E., Al Joseph, A.C.E. *Sound Effects Editor* Gene Eliot, M.P.S.E. *Music Editor* Gene Feldman *Production Sound Mixer* Vernon W. Kramer *Casting* Stalmaster-Lister Co. *Property Master* Clem R. Widrig *Costumers* Alexander Velcoff, Thelma Hilborn *Makeup* Glen Alden *Hairstylist* Pat Whiffing, C.H.S. *Filmed at* CBS Studio Center

The Television Production Staff

Tenth Season: *Director of Photography* Fleet Southcott, Frank Phillips, A.S.C., Harry Stradling, Jr. *Music by* Rudy Schrager *Music Supervised by* Herschel Burke Gilbert *Art Director* Albert Heschong *Assistant Director* Wes McAfee, Robert Beche, Christopher Seiter *Assistant to Producer* Herbert DuFine *Film Editor* Al Joseph, Otto Meyer, A.C.E. *Set Decorator* Herman N. Schoenbrun *Script Supervisor* Edla Bakke, Adele Cannon *Sound Effects Editor* Gene Eliot, M.P.S.E. *Music Editor* Gene Feldman *Production Sound Mixer* Vernon W. Kramer *Casting* Stalmaster-Lister Co., James Lister *Property Master* Clem R. Widrig *Costumers* Alexander Velcoff, Thelma Hilborn *Makeup Artist* Glen Alden *Hairstylist* Pat Whiffing, C.H.S., Betty Pedretti *Rerecording* Joel Moss *Titles and Opticals* Pacific Title *Filmed at* CBS Studio Center

Eleventh Season: *Director of Photography* Harry Stradling, Jr. *Music by* Leon Klatzkin, Morton Stevens, Harry Zimmerman, Willis H. Schaefer *Production Manager* Robert M. Beche *Assistant to the Producer* Herbert DuFine *Art Director* Raymond Beal *Assistant Director* Christopher Seiter *Set Decorator* Herman N. Schoenbrun *Script Supervisor* Edla Bakke *Film Editor* Otto Meyer, A.C.E., Al Joseph, A.C.E., Howard A. Smith, A.C.E. *Sound Effects Editor* Jack A. Finlay *Music Editor* Gene Feldman *Production Sound Mixer* Vernon W. Kramer *Casting* James Lister *Property Manager* Clem R. Widrig *Costumer* Alexander Velcoff *Makeup* Glen Alden *Hairstylist* Pat Whiffing, C.H.S., Kay Shea *Filmed at* CBS Studio Center

Twelfth Season: *Director of Photography* Harry Stradling, Jr. *Music by* Morton Stevens, Irwin Kostal *Art Director* John B. Goodman *Film Editor* Otto Meyer, A.C.E., Al Joseph, A.C.E. *Production Manager* Robert M. Beche *Assistant to the Producer* Herbert DuFine *Assistant Director* Paul Nichols, Al Kraus *Casting* Pam Polifroni *Music Editor* Gene Feldman *Sound Effects Editor* Jack A. Finlay *Production Sound Mixer* Vernon W. Kramer *Script Supervisor* Edla Bakke *Set Decorator* Herman N. Schoenbrun *Property Master* Clem R. Widrig *Costumer* Alexander Velcoff *Makeup* Glen Alden *Hairstylist* Pat Whiffing, C.H.S. *Filmed at* CBS Studio Center

Thirteenth Season: *Director of Photography* Monroe Askins, A.S.C. *Music by* Leon Klatzkin, Allyn Ferguson, Morton Stevens, Johnny Parker *Art Director* Joseph R. Jennings *Film Editor* Gerard Wilson, Bill Mosher, A.C.E., Grant Smith, A.C.E. *Production Manager* Robert M. Beche *Assistant to the Producer* Herbert DuFine *Assistant Director* Al Kraus, Paul Nichols *Casting* Pam Polifroni *Music Editor* Gene Feldman *Sound Effects Editor* Jack A. Finlay *Production Sound Mixer* Vernon W. Kramer *Script Supervisor* Edla Bakke *Set Decorator* Herman N. Schoenbrun *Property Master* Clem R. Widrig *Costumer* Alexander Velcoff *Makeup* Glen Alden, Newton Jones *Hairstylist* Helen Young *Filmed at* CBS Studio Center

Fourteenth Season: *Director of Photography* Monroe Askins, A.S.C. *Music by* Leon Klatzkin *Art Director* Joseph R. Jennings *Film Editor* Gerard Wilson, Thomas McCarthy, Donald W. Ernst *Production Manager* Robert M. Beche *Assistant Director* Al Kraus, Paul Nichols, Robert R. Shue *Assistant to the Producer* Ron Honthaner *Casting* Pam Polifroni *Music Editor* Gene Feldman *Sound Effects Editor* Jack A. Finlay *Production Sound Mixer* Vernon W. Kramer *Script Supervisor* Edla Bakke, Erika Werner *Set Decorator* Herman N. Schoenbrun *Property Master* Clem R. Widrig *Costumer* Alexander Velcoff *Makeup* Glen Alden, Newton Jones *Hairstylist* Gertrude Wheeler, Helen Young *Filmed at* CBS Studio Center

GUNSMOKE — IV. APPENDIX I

Fifteenth Season: *Director of Photography* Monroe Askins, A.S.C. *Music by* Leon Klatzkin, John Parker *Art Director* Joseph R. Jennings *Film Editor* Donald W. Ernst, Thomas McCarthy, Gerard Wilson *Production Manager* Robert M. Beche *Assistant Director* Paul Nichols, Al Kraus *Post Production Executive* Ron Honthaner *Casting* Pam Polifroni *Music Editor* Gene Feldman *Sound Effects Editor* Jack A. Finlay *Production Sound Mixer* Andrew Gilmore *Script Supervisor* Edle Bakke *Set Decorator* Herman N. Schoenbrun *Property Master* Clem R. Widrig *Costumer* Alexander Velcoff *Makeup Artists* Glen Alden, Newton Jones *Hairstylist* Gertrude Wheeler *Filmed at* CBS Studio Center

Sixteenth Season: *Director of Photography* Monroe Askins, A.S.C., Charles F. Wheeler, A.S.C. *Music by* Leon Klatzkin, John Parker *Art Director* Joseph R. Jennings, Albert Heschong, Craig Smith *Set Decorator* Herman N. Schoenbrun *Property Master* Clem R. Widrig *Film Editor* Thomas McCarthy, A.C.E., Gerard Wilson, A.C.E., Donald W. Ernst *Supervising Music Editor* Gene Feldman *Sound Effects Supervisor* Jerry Rosenthal *Production Sound Mixer* Andrew Gilmore *Production Manager* Paul Nichols *Assistant Director* Robert Beche, Paul Nichols, Christopher Seiter, Bob White, Martin Cohan *Script Supervisor* Lloyd Nelson *Casting* Pam Polifroni *Post Production Executive* Ron Honthaner *Costumer* Alexander Velcoff *Makeup Artists* Glen Alden, Irving Pringle *Hairstylists* Gertrude Wheeler, Cheri Banks *Filmed at* CBS Studio Center

Seventeenth Season: *Director of Photography* Monroe Askins, A.S.C. *Music by* Leon Klatzkin, John Parker, Richard Shores, Harry Geller *Art Director* Albert Heschong, Craig Smith *Set Decorator* Herman N. Schoenbrun *Property Master* Clem R. Widrig, Howard Cole *Film Editor* Thomas McCarthy, Gerard Wilson, A.C.E., Howard Smith *Supervising Music Editor* Gene Feldman *Sound Effects Editor* Jerry Rosenthal *Production Sound Mixer* Andrew Gilmore *Production Manager* Paul Nichols *Script Supervisor* Lloyd Nelson, Terry Terrill *Assistant Director* Austen Jewell, Gordon Webb, Max Stein, Robert R. Shue *Casting* Pam Polifroni *Costumer* Alexander Velcoff *Makeup Artists* Glen Alden, Irving Pringle, George Lane *Hairstylists* Gertrude Wheeler, Esperanza Corona *Filmed at* CBS Studio Center

Eighteenth Season: *Director of Photography* Monroe Askins, A.S.C. *Music by* John Parker, Elmer Bernstein, Bruce Broughton, Jerrold Immel *Art Director* Albert Heschong, Craig Smith *Set Decorator* Herman N. Schoenbrun *Property Master* Earl Huntoon *Film Editor* Gerard Wilson, A.C.E., Howard Smith, A.C.E., Thomas McCarthy, A.C.E. *Supervising Music Editor* Gene Feldman *Sound Effects Supervisor* Jack A. Finlay *Production Manager* Paul Nichols *Assistant Director* Robert R. Shue, Bob White *Production Sound Mixer* Andrew Gilmore *Casting* Pam Polifroni *Script Supervisor* Lloyd Nelson *Costumer* Alexander Velcoff *Makeup* Glen Alden, Kenneth Chase *Hairstylists* Gertrude Wheeler, Esperanza Corona *Filmed at* CBS Studio Center

Nineteenth Season: *Director of Photography* Ted D. Landon *Music by* John Parker, Jerrold Immel *Film Editor* Howard Smith, A.C.E., Roland Gross, A.C.E., Tom Stevens *Art Director* Joseph R. Jennings *Set Decorator* Herman N. Schoenbrun *Property Master* Earl Huntoon, Craig Binkley *Production Manager* Paul Nichols *Assistant Director* Don Torpin, Gordon A. Webb *Script Supervisor* Lloyd Nelson *Production Sound Mixer* Andrew Gilmore *Supervising Music Editor* Gene Feldman *Sound Effects Supervisor* Jack A. Finlay *Casting* Pam Polifroni *Costumers* Alexander Velcoff, Aida Swinson *Makeup Artists* Glen Alden, George Lane, Richard Cobos, Lynn Reynolds *Hairstylists* Gertrude Wheeler, Esperanza Corona *Filmed at* CBS Studio Center

The Television Production Staff

Twentieth Season: *Director of Photography* Edward R. Plante *Music by* John Parker, Jerrold Immel, Bruce Broughton, Martin L. Klein *Film Editor* Gerard Wilson, A.C.E., Howard Smith, A.C.E., Carroll Sax *Art Director* Joseph R. Jennings *Set Decorator* Herman N. Schoenbrun *Property Master* Earl Huntoon *Production Manager* Abby Singer *Assistant Director* Gordon A. Webb, Paul Nichols *Script Supervisor* Lloyd Nelson *Production Sound Mixer* Alan Bernard *Supervising Music Editor* Robert Y. Takagi *Sound Effects Supervisor* Jack A. Finlay *Casting* Pam Polifroni *Costumers* Alexander Velcoff, Aida Swinson *Makeup Artists* Glen Alden, George Lane *Hairstylist* Esperanza Corona *Filmed at* CBS Studio Center

Gunsmoke: Return to Dodge: *Casting* Pam Polifroni, C.S.A. *Unit Production Manager* Shirley J. Gill *First Assistant Director* Bud Grace *Second Assistant Director* E. Joseph Thornton *Costume Supervisor* Frances Hays *Make-up Artist* Al Magallon *James Arness' Make-up* Byrd Holland *Hairstylist* Iloe Flewelling *Casting (Edmonton)* Bette Chadwick *Casting (Calgary)* Diane Rogers *Set Decorator* Bruce Sinski *Property Master* D. Brent Lane *Script Supervision* Temple Anderson *Key Grip* Jerry Bertolami *Gaffer* Jim Gregor *Production Sound Mixer* George Tarrant *Sound Editor* G. Michael Graham *Music Editor* Robert Takagi *Music Supervision* Robert Drasnin *Stunt Co-ordinator (U.S.)* Bill Burton *Stunt Co-ordinator (Canada)* Brent Woolsey *Production Executive* Paul Tucker *Post Production Executive* Cosmas Bolger *Executive in Charge of Production* Norman S. Powell

APPENDIX J
THE PRINCIPAL PERFORMERS' CREDITS

James Arness

Born James Aurness on May 26, 1923, in Minneapolis, Minnesota. Played Matt Dillon on television from 1955 to 1975.
Films: *The Farmer's Daughter* (1947), *Man from Texas* (1947), *Roses Are Red* (1947), *Battleground* (1949), *Wagonmaster* (1950), *Sierra* (1950), *Two Lost Worlds* (1950), *Double Crossbones* (1950), *Stars in My Crown* (1950), *Wyoming Mail* (1950), *Cavalry Scout* (1951), *Belle le Grand* (1951), *Iron Man* (1951), *The Thing* (1951), *The People Against O'Hara* (1951), *Carbine Williams* (1952), *Hellgate* (1952), *The Girl in White* (1952), *Big Jim McLain* (1952), *Horizons West* (1952), *Lone Hand* (1953), *Hondo* (1953), *Ride the Man Down* (1953), *Island in the Sky* (1953), *Veils of Bagdad* (1953), *Hondo* (1954), *Her Twelve Men* (1954), *Them* (1954), *Flame of the Islands* (1955), *Many Rivers to Cross* (1955), *The Sea Chase* (1955), *Arizona Mission* (1956), *Gun the Man Down* (1956), *The First Traveling Saleslady* (1956).
Television: *The Lone Ranger* (1950), *Lux Video Theatre:* "The Chase" (1954), *Front Row Center* (1956), *The Red Skelton Chevy Special* (1959), *The Chevrolet Golden Anniversary Show* (1961), *A Salute to Television's 25th Anniversary* (1972), *The Macahans* (1976), *How the West Was Won* (1976-79), *McLain's Law* (1981), *The Alamo: 13 Days to Glory* (1987), *Gunsmoke: Return to Dodge* (1987), *Red River* (1988), *Gunsmoke 2: The Last Apache* (1990).

Parley Baer

Played Chester Wesley Proudfoot on radio from 1952 to 1961.
Radio: *Tales of the Texas Rangers*, *The Six Shooter*, *Suspense*, *Escape*, *The Lux Radio Theatre*, *Screen Guild Theatre*, *The Man Called X*, *Dr. Christian*, *Fort Laramie*, *Frontier Gentleman*, *Nero Wolfe*, *The Count of Monte Cristo*, *Granby's Green Acres*, *The Hal Peary Show — Honest Harold*, *Rogers of the Gazette*, *Yours Truly, Johnny Dollar*, *The Adventures of Philip Marlowe*, *Pat Novak for Hire*, *This Is Your F.B.I.*, *The First Nighter*, *Shorty Bell*, *Tell It Again*, *Romance*, *Barry Crane, Confidential Investigator*, *Dr. Kildare*, *Let George Do It*, *My Little Margie*, *The Whistler*, *Have Gun, Will Travel*, *The C.B.S. Radio Workshop*, *Those Websters*.

The Principal Performers' Credits

Films: *Comanche Territory* (1950), *Union Station* (1950), *Air Cadet* (1951), *People Will Talk* (1951), *Elopement* (1951), *The Frogmen* (1951), *Deadline, U.S.A.* (1952), *Fearless Fagan* (1952), *Pickup on South Street* (1953), *Vicki* (1953), *D Day, the Sixth of June* (1956), *Drango* (1957), *The Young Lions* (1958), *The F.B.I. Story* (1959), *Cash McCall* (1960), *The Adventures of Huckleberry Finn* (1960), *Wake Me When It's Over* (1960), *A Fever in the Blood* (1961), *Gypsy* (1962), *The Spiral Road* (1962), *The Brass Bottle* (1963), *Bedtime Story* (1964), *Bus Riley's Back in Town* (1965), *Two on a Guillotine* (1965), *Fluffy* (1965), *Those Callaways* (1965), *Follow Me, Boys!* (1966), *The Ugly Dachshund* (1966), *The Adventures of Bullwhip Griffin* (1967), *The Gnome-Mobile* (1967), *Day of the Evil Gun* (1968), *Where Were You When the Lights Went Out?* (1968), *Young Billy Young* (1968), *Counterpoint* (1968), *The Amazing Dobermans* (1976), *White Dog* (1982), *Dr. Detroit* (1983), *Chattanooga Choo, Choo* (1984), *License to Drive* (1988), *Pray, The Boy Who Stole the Elephant, Bristle Face.*

Television: *The Addams Family, Bachelor Father, Bewitched, The Bill Cosby Show, December Bride, Dennis the Menace, F Troop, Farmer's Daughter, Father Knows Best, Gomer Pyle, U.S.M.C., Hazel, Here's Lucy, I Love Lucy, The Joey Bishop Show, The Lucy Show, Night Court, Newhart, Sledgehammer, One Big Family, Twilight Zone, Simon and Simon, Stolen Dreams, Flag, The A-Team, Children of Alcoholics, Shadow Chasers, This Is the Life, Father Murphy, The Dukes of Hazzard, Doc, The Don Rickles Show, Gallagher, Hello, Larry, Three's Company, Charlie's Angels, Archie Bunker's Place, Burns and Allen, Our Miss Brooks, The Jack Benny Show, Eisenhower and Lutz, The Golden Girls, Hunter, Mr. President, Mrs. G Goes to College/The Gertrude Berg Show, Petticoat Junction, Rango, Room for One More, The Adventures of Ozzie and Harriet* (1955–61), *Carolyn* (1956), *Sneak Preview* (1956), *The Marriage Broker* (1957), *The Andy Griffith Show* (1962–63), *The Slowest Gun in the West* (1963), *Perry Mason:* "The Case of the Telltale Tap" (1965), *Perry Mason:* "The Case of the Positive Negative" (1966), *The Double Life of Henry Phyfe* (1966), *The Over-the-Hill Gang Rides Again* (1970), *The Plot to Overthrow Christmas* (1971), *Punch and Jody* (1974), *True Grit* (1978), *Norman Rockwell's Breaking Home Ties* (1987).

Amanda Blake

Born Beverly Louise Neill on February 20, 1929, in Buffalo, N.Y. Died: August 16, 1989. Played Kitty Russell on television from 1955 to 1974.

Films: *Duchess of Idaho* (1950), *Stars in My Crown* (1950), *Counterspy Meets Scotland Yard* (1950), *On the Sunnyside of the Street* (1951), *Smuggler's Gold* (1951), *Battleground* (1951), *Scarlet Angel* (1952), *Cattle Town* (1952), *Lili* (1953), *Sabre Jet* (1953), *Miss Robin Crusoe* (1953), *Adventures of Hajji Baba* (1954), *A Star Is Born* (1954), *About Mrs. Leslie* (1954), *The Glass Slipper* (1955), *High Society* (1955), *The Boost* (1988), *B.O.R.N.* (1989).

Television: *Lux Video Playhouse, My Favorite Husband, Professional Father, The Red Skelton Show, Climax, Schlitz Playhouse of Stars:* "Double Exposure" (1952), *Schlitz Playhouse of Stars:* "Crossroads" (1952), *Calvalcade of America:* "Breakfast at Nancy's" (1953), *Fireside Theatre:* "Nine Quarts of Water" (1954), *Four Star Playhouse:* "Vote of Confidence," (1954), *Matinee Theatre:* "Sound of Fear" (1956), *Studio One:* "Tide of Corruption" (1958), *G.E. Theatre:* "Night Club" (1959), *Clown Alley* (1966), *Betrayal* (1974), *The Quest:* "Day of Outrage" (1976), *The Love Boat* (1979), *The Best Little Special in Texas* (1982), *Hart to Hart:* "The Wayward Hart" (1983), *The Edge of Night* (1984), *Gunsmoke: Return to Dodge* (1987), *Brothers* (1987), *Modern Romance* (1988), *Divorce Court* (1988), *Dragnet* (1989).

William Conrad

Born on September 27, 1920, in Louisville, Kentucky. Played Matt Dillon on radio from 1952 to 1961.

Radio: *Escape, Jason and His Golden Fleece, Pete Kelly's Blues, Dragnet, This Is Your F.B.I., Suspense, Romance, On Stage, The C.B.S. Radio Workshop, Yours Truly, Johnny Dollar, Night Beat, Dangerous Assignment, Hollywood Star Playhouse, The Lux Radio Theatre, The Man Called X, The Adventures of Philip Marlowe, Johnny Madero, Pier 23, The Hermit's Cave, Favorite Story, The Whistler, The Count of Monte Cristo, The Voyage of the Scarlet Queen, Hawk Larabee, Screen Director's Playhouse, Pat Novak for Hire, Richard Diamond, Private Detective, Sam Spade, The Halls of Ivy, The Man from Homicide, Crime Classics, Rogers of the Gazette, Screen Guild Theatre, Dr. Kildare, Tums Hollywood Theatre, The Green Lama, Michael Shayne, Private Detective, Let George Do It, Bold Venture; Rocky Jordan, Dark Venture, The Whisperer, Hollywood Star Time, The Saint, Box 13, Damon Runyon Theatre, Frontier Gentleman, The Six Shooter, The First Nighter.*

Films: *The Killers* (1946), *Body and Soul* (1947), *To the Victor* (1948), *Sorry, Wrong Number* (1948), *Arch of Triumph* (1948), *Joan of Arc* (1948), *Four Faces West* (1948), *East Side, West Side* (1949), *Any Number Can Play* (1949), *Dial 1119* (1950), *Tension* (1950), *One Way Street* (1950), *The Milkman* (1951), *Cry Danger* (1951), *The Sword of Monte Cristo* (1951), *The Racket* (1951), *Lone Star* (1952), *The Desert Song* (1953), *Cry of the Hunted* (1953), *The Naked Jungle* (1954), *Five Against the House* (1955), *The Conqueror* (1956), *Johnny Concho* (1956), *The Ride Back* (1957), *30* (1959), *Moonshine County Express* (1977), *Killing Cars* (1986). As narrator: *The Naked Sea* (1955), *The Cowboy* (1955). As director: *The Man from Galveston* (1964), *Two on a Guillotine* (1965), *My Blood Runs Cold* (1965), *Brainstorm* (1965). As producer: *The Ride Back* (1957), *Two on a Guillotine* (1965), *My Blood Runs Cold* (1965), *Brainstorm* (1965), *An American Dream* (1966), *Chamber of Horrors* (1966), *A Covenant with Death* (1967), *First to Fight* (1967), *The Cool Ones* (1967), *Countdown* (1968), *Chubasco* (1968), *Assignment to Kill* (1969).

Television: *Bat Masterson:* "Stampede at Tent City" (1958), *Aquanauts* (1961), *Bat Masterson:* "Terror on the Trinity" (1961), *Cain's Hundred* (1961), *Have Gun, Will Travel* (1962), *G.E. True:* "Circle of Death" (1962), *Alfred Hitchcock Presents:* "The Thirty-First of February" (1963), *Have Gun, Will Travel* (1963), *Name of the Game:* "The Skin Game" (1970), *The Brotherhood of the Bell* (1970), *Storefront Lawyers:* "Survivors Will Be Prosecuted" (1970), *Conspiracy to Kill* (1971), *O'Hara, U.S. Treasury* (1971), *Cannon* (1971–76), *The Flip Wilson Special* (1975), *Keefer* (1979), *The Return of Frank Cannon* (1980), *Battles: The Murder That Wouldn't Die* (1980), *Turnover Smith* (1980), *Nero Wolfe* (1981), *The Mikado* (1982), *Shock-Trauma* (1982), *Police Squad* (1982), *In Like Flynn* (1985), *Vengeance: The Story of Tony Cimo* (1986), *Jake and the Fatman* (1987–). As narrator: *Escape* (1950), *Rocky and His Friends* (1959–61), *The Bullwinkle Show, The Fugitive* (1963–67), *George of the Jungle* (1967–70), *The Dudley Do-Right Show* (1969–70), *The Wild, Wild World of Animals* (1973–78), *Night Cries* (1977), *Tales of the Unexpected* (1977), *How the West Was Won* (1977), *Buck Rogers in the 25th Century* (1979–80), *The Lone Ranger Adventure Hour* (1981–82), *Manimal* (1983). As director: *Bat Masterson* (1957–59), *This Man Dawson* (1959), *Klondike* (1960), *General Electric True Theatre* (1962–63), *Side Show* (1981), *Naked City, Temple Houston, Gunsmoke.* As producer: *Bat Masterson* (1957–59), *This Man Dawson* (1959), *Klondike* (1960), *77 Sunset Strip* (1963–64).

Ken Curtis

Born Curtis Gates on July 2, 1916, in Lamar, Colorado. Played Festus Haggen on television from 1964 to 1975.

Films: *Song of the Prairie* (1945), *Rhythm Roundup* (1945), *Out of Depths* (1946), *Singing on the Trail* (1946), *That Texas Jamboree* (1946), *Throw a Saddle on a Star* (1946), *Cowboy Blues* (1946), *Lone Star Moonlight* (1946), *Over the Sante Fe Trail* (1947), *Stallion Canyon* (1949), *Call of the Forest* (1949), *Rio Grande* (1950), *Don Daredevil Rides Again* (1951), *The*

The Principal Performers' Credits

Quiet Man (1952), *Mister Roberts* (1955), *The Searchers* (1956), *Spring Reunion* (1957), *The Wings of Eagles* (1957), *The Missouri Traveler* (1958), *The Last Hurrah* (1958), *The Horse Soldiers* (1959), *Escort West* (1959), *The Giant Gila Monster* (1959), *The Young Land* (1959), *The Killer Shrews* (1959), *Freckles* (1960), *My Dog, Buddy* (1960), *The Alamo* (1960), *Two Rode Together* (1961), *How the West Was Won* (1962), *Cheyenne Autumn* (1964), *Robin Hood* (1973), *Pony Express Rider* (1976). As producer: *The Giant Gila Monster* (1959), *The Killer Shrews* (1959), *My Dog, Buddy* (1960).
Television: *Perry Mason, Rawhide, Have Gun, Will Travel, Ripcord* (1961–63), *When the West Was Fun: A Western Reunion* (1979), *California Gold Rush* (1981), *The Yellow Rose* (1983–84), *Once Upon a Texas Train* (1988).

Georgia Ellis

Born Georgia Hawkins. Died: April 1988. Played Kitty Russell on radio from 1952 to 1961.
Radio: *Suspense, Romance, Dr. Kildare, Fort Laramie, I Fly Anything, The Baby Snooks Show, Crime Classics, Rogers of the Gazette, The Adventures of Philip Marlowe, Escape, The Six Shooter, Night Beat, The Whistler, Yours Truly, Johnny Dollar.*
Films: *Doomed Caravan* (1941), *Dragnet* (1954).

Roger Ewing

Played Clayton Thaddeus Greenwood on television from 1965 to 1967.
Films: *Ensign Pulver* (1964), *None But the Brave* (1965), *Play It as It Lays* (1972).
Television: *Bewitched.*

Howard McNear

Born in 1905 in Los Angeles, California. Died in 1969. Played Doctor Charles Addams on radio from 1952 to 1961.
Radio: *The Whistler, Romance of the Ranchos, Calling All Cars, I Was There, Richard Diamond, Private Detective, The Six Shooter, Yours Truly, Johnny Dollar, Suspense, Escape, Night Beat, Rogers of the Gazette, The Lux Radio Theatre, Fort Laramie, Frontier Gentleman, Nero Wolfe, Screen Guild Theatre, The Man Called X, Screen Director's Playhouse, The Smiths of Hollywood, The Adventures of Philip Marlowe, On Stage, Barry Crane, Confidential Investigator, The Line-up, Crime Classics, The Count of Monte Cristo, Speed Gibson of the International Secret Police, The Cinnamon Bear, Jerry of the Circus, Bill Lance, One Man's Family, The Casebook of Gregory Hood, The C.B.S. Radio Workshop, The Story of Sandra Martin, Twelve Players.*
Films: *Drums Across the River* (1954), *The Long, Long Trailer* (1954), *Bundle of Joy* (1956), *You Can't Run Away from It* (1956), *Public Pigeon No. 1* (1957), *Affair in Reno* (1957), *Bell, Book and Candle* (1958), *The Big Circus* (1959), *Anatomy of a Murder* (1959), *Good Day for a Hanging* (1959), *Voyage to the Bottom of the Sea* (1961), *The Errand Boy* (1961), *Follow That Dream* (1962), *Bachelor Flat* (1962), *Blue Hawaii* (1962), *Irma La Douce* (1963), *The Wheeler Dealers* (1963), *Kiss Me, Stupid* (1964), *Love and Kisses* (1965), *My Blood Runs Cold* (1965), *The Fortune Cookie* (1966).
Television: *Bachelor Father, The Burns and Allen Show, December Bride, The Many Loves of Dobie Gillis, The Donna Reed Show, Hennesey, I Love Lucy, The Joey Bishop Show, The People's Choice, The Jetsons, Pete and Gladys, Room for One More, The Tab Hunter Show, The Brothers* (1956–58), *The Many Sides of Mickey Rooney* (1960), *Tom, Dick, and Harry* (1960), *The Andy Griffith Show* (1960–68).

Burt Reynolds

Born on February 11, 1936, in Waycross, Georgia. Played Quint Asper on television from 1962 to 1965.

Films: *Armored Command* (1961), *Angel Baby* (1961), *Operation C.I.A.* (1965), *Navajo Joe* (1967), *Fade-In* (1968), *Sam Whiskey* (1969), *100 Rifles* (1969), *Impasse* (1969), *Shark!* (1969), *Skull Duggery* (1970), *Deliverance* (1972), *Everything You Always Wanted to Know About Sex...* (1972), *Fuzz* (1972), *The Man Who Loved Cat Dancing* (1973), *Shamus* (1973), *White Lightning* (1973), *The Longest Yard* (1974), *W.W. and the Dixie Dancekings* (1975), *At Long Last Love* (1975), *Hustle* (1975), *Lucky Lady* (1975), *Gator* (1976), *Silent Movie* (1976), *Nickelodeon* (1976), *Smokey and the Bandit* (1977), *Semi-Tough* (1977), *Hooper* (1978), *The End* (1978), *Starting Over* (1979), *Smokey and the Bandit II* (1980), *Rough Cut* (1980), *Sharky's Machine* (1981), *The Cannonball Run* (1981), *The Best Little Whorehouse in Texas* (1982), *Best Friends* (1982), *Stroker Ace* (1983), *Smokey and the Bandit III* (1983), *The Man Who Loved Women* (1983), *Cannonball Run II* (1984), *City Heat* (1984), *Stick* (1985), *Heat* (1987), *Physical Evidence* (1988). As director: *Gator* (1976), *The End* (1978), *Sharky's Machine* (1981), *Stick* (1985).

Television: *The Twilight Zone*, *M Squad:* "The Teacher" (1959), *Schlitz Playhouse of the Stars:* "You Can't Win 'Em All" (1959), *Riverboat* (1959), *Lawless Years:* "The Payoff" (1959), *Playhouse 90:* "Alas, Babylon" (1960), *Johnny Ringo:* "The Stranger" (1960), *Aquanauts:* "The Big Swim" (1960), *Michael Shayne:* "The Boat Caper" (1961), *Zane Grey Theatre:* "Man from Everywhere" (1961), *Malibu Run:* "Kidnap Adventure" (1961), *Perry Mason:* "The Case of the Counterfeit Crank" (1962), *Route 66:* "Love Is a Skinny Kid" (1962), *Branded:* "Now Join the Human Race" (1965), *Flipper* (1965), *The F.B.I.:* "All the Streets Are Silent" (1965), *12 O'Clock High:* "The Jones Boy" (1965), *Hawk* (1966), *Gentle Ben* (1967), *The F.B.I.* (1968), *Lassiter* (1968), *Run, Simon, Run* (1970), *Love American Style* (1970), *Hunters Are for Killing* (1970), *Dan August* (1970), *How to Handle a Woman* (1972), *Super Comedy Bowl 2* (1972), *Burt and the Girls* (1973), *The Burt Reynolds Late Show* (1973), *The Very First Glen Campbell Special* (1973), *Dinah in Search of the Ideal Man* (1973), *The Wayne Newton Special* (1974), *The Celebrity Football Classic* (1979), *Jerry Reed and Special Friends* (1982), *The Best Little Special in Texas* (1982), *Celebrity Daredevils* (1983), *Steve Martin's The Winds of Whoopie* (1983), *Dom Deluise and Friends* (1983), *Win, Lose, or Draw*.

Milburn Stone

Born on July 5, 1904, in Burton, Kansas. Died on June 12, 1980. Played Doctor Galen Adams on television from 1955 to 1975.

Films: *The Fighting Marines* (1935), *Ladies Crave Excitement* (1935), *Rendezvous* (1935), *The Three Mesquiteers* (1935), *The Milky Way* (1936), *China Clipper* (1936), *The Princess Comes Across* (1936), *Two in a Crowd* (1936), *A Doctor's Diary* (1937), *Wings Over Honolulu* (1937), *Blazing Barriers* (1937), *Music for Madame* (1937), *Swing It, Professor* (1937), *Youth on Parole* (1937), *The Thirteenth Man* (1937), *The Man in Blue* (1937), *Mr. Boggs Steps Out* (1937), *Atlantic Flight* (1937), *Federal Bullets* (1937), *The Port of Missing Girls* (1938), *Wives Under Suspicion* (1938), *The Storm* (1938), *Paroled from the Big House* (1938), *California Frontier* (1938), *Crime School* (1938), *Sinners in Paradise* (1938), *Tail Spin* (1939), *Mystery Plane/Sky Pilot* (1939), *King of the Turf* (1939), *Society Smugglers* (1939), *Fighting Mad* (1939), *Blind Alley* (1939), *Stunt Pilot* (1939), *When Tomorrow Comes* (1939), *Sky Patrol* (1939), *Made for Each Other* (1939), *Danger Flight* (1939), *Crashing Through* (1939), *Charlie McCarthy, Detective* (1939), *Young Mr. Lincoln* (1939), *Tropic Fury* (1939), *Nick Carter, Master Detective* (1939), *Chasing Trouble* (1940), *Johnny Apollo* (1940), *An Angel from Texas*

The Principal Performers' Credits

(1940), *Framed* (1940), *Lillian Russell* (1940), *Colorado* (1940), *The Great Plane Robbery* (1940), *Enemy Agent/Secret Enemy* (1940), *Give Us Wings* (1940), *The Great Train Robbery* (1941), *The Phantom Cowboy* (1941), *Death Valley Outlaws* (1941), *Frisco Lil* (1942), *Eyes in the Night* (1942), *Rubber Racketeers* (1942), *Invisible Agent* (1942), *Police Bullets* (1942), *Pacific Rendezvous* (1942), *Reap the Wild Wind* (1942), *Captive Wild Woman* (1943), *Sherlock Holmes Faces Death* (1943), *Keep 'Em Slugging* (1943), *You Can't Beat the Law* (1943), *Get Going* (1943), *Corvette K-225/The Nelson Touch* (1943), *The Mad Ghoul* (1943), *Gung Ho!* (1943), *The Imposter* (1944), *Hi, Good Looking* (1944), *Hat Check Honey* (1944), *Moon Over Las Vegas* (1944), *Twilight on the Prairie* (1944), *Jungle Woman* (1944), *The Great Alaskan Mystery* (1944), *Phantom Lady* (1944), *The Master Key* (1945), *She Gets Her Man* (1945), *The Frozen Ghost* (1945), *The Beautiful Cheat/What a Woman* (1945), *The Daltons Ride Again* (1945), *I'll Remember April* (1945), *On Stage, Everybody* (1945), *Swing Out, Sister* (1945), *The Royal Mounted Rides Again* (1945), *Strange Confession* (1945), *The Spider Woman Strikes Back* (1946), *Danger Woman* (1946), *Smooth as Silk* (1946), *Little Miss Big/Baxter's Millions* (1946), *Strange Conquest* (1946), *Her Adventurous Night* (1946), *Inside Job* (1946), *Cass Timberlane* (1947), *Killer Dill* (1947), *The Michigan Kid* (1947), *Headin' for Heaven* (1947), *Buck Privates Come Home/Rookies Come Home* (1947), *Train to Alcatraz* (1948), *The Judge/The Gamblers* (1948), *Sky Dragon* (1949), *The Green Promise/Raging Waters* (1949), *Calamity Jane and Sam Bass* (1949), *No Man of Her Own* (1950), *The Fireball* (1950), *Snow Dog* (1950), *Branded* (1950), *The Racket* (1951), *Road Block* (1951), *Flying Leathernecks* (1951), *The Savage* (1952), *The Atomic City* (1952), *Pickup on South Street* (1953), *Arrowhead* (1953), *The Sun Shines Bright* (1953), *Invaders from Mars* (1953), *Second Chance* (1953), *The Siege at Red River* (1954), *Black Tuesday* (1954), *The Long Gray Line* (1955), *White Feather* (1955), *Smoke Signal* (1955), *The Private War of Major Benson* (1955), *Drango* (1957), *The World of Sport Fishing* (1972).

Television: *Dragnet:* "The Big Jump" (1952), *The Adventures of Wild Bill Hickock:* "The Silver Mine Protection Story" (1952), *T.V. Readers Digest:* "A Million Dollar Story" (1955), *Front Row Center:* "Morals Squad" (1956), *Climax:* "The Great World and Timothy Colt" (1958), *When the West Was Fun: A Western Reunion* (1979).

Buck Taylor

Born Walter Clarence Taylor, III, on May 13, 1938, in Hollywood, California. Played Newly O'Brien on television from 1967 to 1975.

Films: *Ensign Pulver* (1964), *And Now Miguel* (1966), *The Wild Angels* (1966), *The Devil's Angels* (1967).

Television: *Ben Casey, The Fugitive, Big Valley, The Rebel, Alfred Hitchcock Presents, Death Valley Days, Crazy Like a Fox, The Monroes* (1966-67), *The Busters* (1978), *Kate Bliss and the Ticker Tape Kid* (1978), *The Sacketts* (1979), *Wild Times* (1980), *The Cherokee Trail* (1981), *No Man's Land* (1984), *Gunsmoke: Return to Dodge* (1987).

Dennis Weaver

Born on June 4, 1924, in Joplin, Missouri. Played Chester Goode on television from 1955 to 1964.

Films: *Horizons West* (1952), *The Raiders* (1952), *The Lawless Breed* (1952), *The Redhead from Wyoming* (1952), *Column South* (1953), *Mississippi Gambler* (1953), *Law and Order* (1953), *The Nebraskan* (1953), *War Arrow* (1954), *Dangerous Mission* (1954), *The Bridges at Toko-Ri* (1954), *Chief Crazy Horse* (1955), *10 Wanted Men* (1955), *Storm Fear* (1955), *Seven Angry Men* (1955), *Touch of Evil* (1958), *The Gallant Hours* (1960), *Way... Way Out* (1966), *Duel at Diablo* (1966), *Gentle Giant* (1968), *Mission Bantangas* (1969), *What's the Matter with Helen* (1971).

Television: *Dragnet:* "The Big Bible" (1954), *Schlitz Playhouse of the Stars:* "Underground" (1955), *Dragnet:* "The Big Screen" (1955), *Big Town:* "Crime in the City Room" (1956), *The Silent Service:* "Two Davids and Goliath" (1957), *Climax:* "Burst of Fire" (1958), *Playhouse 90:* "The Dungeon" (1958), *Alfred Hitchcock Presents:* "Insomnia" (1960), *The Twilight Zone:* "Shadow Play" (1961), *That Girl, Kentucky Jones* (1964-65), *Dr. Kildare:* "A Reverence for Life" (1965), *Combat:* "The Farmer" (1965), *World of Disney:* "Showdown with the Sundown Kid" (1966), *Gentle Ben* (1967-69), *Judd, for the Defense:* "The View from the Ivy Tower" (1969), *Name of the Game:* "Play Till It Hurts" (1969), *The Virginian:* "Train of Darkness" (1970), *McCloud,* (1970-77), *The Great Man's Whiskers* (1971), *The Forgotten Man* (1971), *Duel* (1971), *Rolling Man* (1972), *Female Artillery* (1973), *Terror on the Beach* (1973), *Opryland U.S.A.* (1975), *Intimate Strangers* (1977), *The Hardy Boys/Nancy Drew Mysteries:* "The Mystery of the Hollywood Phantom" (1977), *Pearl* (1978), *The Islander* (1978), *Centennial* (1978), *Ishi: The Last of His Tribe* (1978), *The Ordeal of Patty Hearst* (1979), *Stone* (1979-80), *Amber Waves* (1980), *The Ordeal of Dr. Mudd* (1980), *The Day the Loving Stopped* (1981), *Don't Go to Sleep* (1982), *Cocaine: One Man's Seduction* (1983), *Go for the Gold, Emerald Point, N.A.S.* (1983-84), *Bluffing It* (1987), *Buck James* (1987-88).

APPENDIX K
GUNSMOKE 2

Gunsmoke 2: The Last Apache. Scheduled for release March, 1990.
    This second made-for-television movie had been in the works since 1988. Filmed in Texas, *The Last Apache,* is based on the true story of the decimation of the Apaches directed by General Nelson Appleton Miles and dutifully carried out by General Philip Henry Sheridan.
    Once again James Arness recreates his role as Matt Dillon. Michael Learned returns as Mike Yardner (*Matt's Love Story,* September 24, 1973), and it is discovered that after their brief affair, she bore Matt a daughter. The young lady, who is now grown up, is played by Amy Stock-Pointon.

    Cast: James Arness, Richard Kiley, Michael Learned, Geoffrey Lewis, Hugh O'Brian, Joe Lara, Amy Stock-Pointon.

    Producer .... John Mantley
    Writer .... Earl Wallace
    Director .... Charles Correll

    Hugh O'Brian appeared as Hugh Lockwood in *Search* and on several television anthologies. He is best known, however, as Wyatt Earp in *The Life and Legend of Wyatt Earp.* Geoffrey Lewis played Earl Tucker on *Flo* and Amos Tucker on *Gun Shy.* Former *Star Search* winner Amy Stock-Pointon played Lisa Alden on *Dallas.*

REFERENCES

Unless otherwise noted, all quotes have been obtained by the authors through interviews collected between 1986 and 1989. During that period of time many individuals were interviewed who had been involved in the radio and television programs. Most of the synopses of the radio programs were obtained by listening to original tapes. A few were obtained by reading scripts, and through the recollections of authors and actors. The majority of the synopses of the television programs were obtained through private viewings. Additional synopses were obtained through CBS news releases and original scripts. The television credits were obtained through private viewings, CBS releases, and the logs of Norman Macdonnell and John Mantley. The radio credits were obtained from original tapes, scripts, and Norman Macdonnell's log.

1-2. "47 Weeks of Prestige," *Time*, March 23, 1953, pp. 104, 106.
3. Young, Fredric R., *Dodge City*, Boot Hill Museum, 1972, p. 45.
4. Young, *Dodge City*, 1972, pp. 15-38.
5. Vestal, Stanley, *Queen of the Cowtowns*, Harper and Bros., New York, 1952, p. 3.
6. Young, *Dodge City*, 1972, p. 41.
7. Young, *Dodge City*, 1972, p. 40.
8. Vestal, *Queen of the Cowtowns?*, 1952, pp. 1-2.
9. Meston, John, Letter to the *New York Tribune*, original copy.
10. "This Is Marshal Dillon," *CBS Television Features News Release*, Aug. 12, 1955.
11. Young, *Dodge City*, 1972, p. 47.
12. Young, *Dodge City*, 1972, p. 40.
13-14. MacDonald, J.F., *Who Shot the Sheriff? The Rise and Fall of the Television Western*, Praeger Pub., New York, 1987, p. 1.
15. Cawelti, J.G., *The Six-Gun Mystique*, Bowling Green State University Press, Bowling Green, Ohio, 1984, p. 121.
16. Adams, Les, and Rainey, Buck, *Shoot-Em Ups: The Complete Reference Guide to Westerns of the Sound Era*, Arlington House, New Rochelle, N.Y., 1978.
17. Autry, Gene, "Gene Autry's Prize Round-Up," *Radio-Television Mirror*, July 1951, p. 46.
18. Horwitz, James, *They Went Thataway*, Ballantine Books, New York, 1978, pp. 141-142.
19. Lardner, John, "Decline and Fall Possible," *New Yorker*, Feb. 28, 1959, p. 97.
20. Amory, Cleveland, "The Dakotas," *TV Guide*, April 6, 1963, p. 1.
21-26. Hickman, John, WAMU-FM Broadcast: *Gunsmoke*, Washington, D.C., April 25, 1976.

REFERENCES

27. "47 Weeks," *Time,* 3/53.
28-34. Hickman, J., WAMU-FM Broadcast.
35. Meston, John, Letter to *New York Tribune,* original copy.
36-45. Hickman, J., WAMU-FM Broadcast.
46. "47 Weeks," *Time,* 3/53.
47-56. Hickman, J., WAMU-FM Broadcast.
57. Hickman, J. (personal interview tapes never aired)
58-66. Hickman, J., WAMU-FM Broadcast.
67. Hickman, J. (personal interview tapes never aired)
68. Humphreys, Hal, "Can Gunsmoke Stay Legit?" *Mirror-News,* Feb. 9, 1955.
69-80. Hickman, J., WAMU-FM Broadcast.
81. Metz, Robert, *CBS—Reflections in a Bloodshot Eye,* Playboy Press, Chicago, 1975, p. 200.
82-85. Scott, Vernon, "Gunsmoke's Mysterious James Arness," *Ladies' Home Journal,* May 1971, pp. 90-92, 186-187.
86. de Roos, Robert, "Private Life of Gunsmoke's Star," *Saturday Evening Post,* April 12, 1958, 32-33.
87-90. Davidson, Muriel, "Unlikely Brothers: James Arness and Peter Graves," *Good Housekeeping,* April 1973, 48-56.
91. de Roos, "Private Life," 4/58.
92. "Famed Gunsmoke Series Makes Its Television Debut," *CBS Television Feature News Release,* Aug. 11, 1955.
93. de Roos, Robert, "The Greta Garbo of Dodge City," *TV Guide,* Dec. 10, 1966.
94. Russell, Dick, "I Can't Live Up to What People Think I Am," *TV Guide,* Feb. 24, 1979.
95-98. de Roos, "The Greta Garbo," 12/66.
99. Scott, "Gunsmoke's Mysterious," 5/71.
100-101. de Roos, "Private Life," 4/58.
102-103. Russell, "I Can't Live Up," 2/79.
104. de Roos, "The Greta Garbo," 12/66.
105. Hickman, J., WAMU-FM Broadcast.
106. Amory, Cleveland, "Review," *TV Guide,* March 14, 1964, p. 3.
107. "Chester Limps Off into the Sun-Set Again," *TV Guide,* Jan. 4, 1964, pp. 4-5.
108. Lewis, Richard W. "Dodge City's Medicine Man," *TV Guide,* Nov. 24, 1962, pp. 22-24.
109. "Milburn Stone—His Fans Like Him Grouchy," *CBS News Release,* Sept. 9, 1965.
110-111. Lewis, "Dodge City's Medicine," 11/62.
112. O'Hallaran, Bill, "When Chester Forgot to Limp," *TV Guide,* August 23, 1975.
113. Lewis, "Dodge City's Medicine," 11/62.
114. "Milburn Stone," *CBS News Release,* 9/65.
115. Amory, "Review," *TV Guide,* 3/64.
116. Raddatz, Leslie, "Look What's Happened to These Dodge City Citizens," *TV Guide,* Aug. 17, 1968, 16-19.
117-118. de Roos, "Private Life," 4/58.
119. Raddatz, "Look What's Happened," 8/68.
120. de Roos, "Private Life," 4/58.
121-123. Morhaim, Joe, "She Who Never Gets Kissed," *TV Guide,* March 15, 1958, pp. 8-11.
124. de Roos, "Private Life," 4/58.
125. Raddatz, Leslie, "An Open Letter to My Wife," *TV Guide,* June 6, 1964, pp. 15-19.
126. Amory, "Review," *TV Guide,* 3/64.
127. Becker, Joyce, "New Directions for Miss Kitty," *Los Angeles Times,* July 5, 1974, p. 19.
128. Henry, Will, "Dodge City Could Bite the Dust," *Los Angeles Times,* May 20, 1974.
129. "After 19 Years Kitty Dropping Out of Gunsmoke," *Los Angeles Times,* March 6, 1974, p. 3.
130. Russell, "I Can't Live Up," 2/79.
131. Morhaim, "She Who Never," 3/58.
132. Kaufman, David, "Gunsmoke, Matt Gets It," *Daily Variety,* Sept. 12, 1955, p. 7.
133-135. Whitney, Dwight, "Why Gunsmoke Keeps Blazing Away," *TV Guide,* Dec. 1958.
136. *House and Garden,* Sept. 1957, 32-33.
137. Whitney, "Why Gunsmoke," 12/58.
138. Morhaim, "She Who Never," 3/58.
139. Streetback, Nancy, *The Films of Burt Reynolds,* Citadel Press, Secaucus, N.J., 1981.
140. "Festus Still Has Hankering for Gunsmoke," *The Register* (Tucson, Ariz.), Feb. 15, 1978.
141. "Hot as a Pistol," *Newsweek,* Nov. 20, 1967, p. 96.
142. Smith, Cecil, "Legend Goes Down the Tubes," *Los Angeles Times,* Sept. 1, 1975.
143-144. Whitney, Dwight, "When Gunslinger Nielsen Hit Town," *TV Guide,* Aug. 22, 1970.
145. Dallos, Robert E., "Stations' Pleas Save

References

Gunsmoke," *New York Times*, March 8, 1967.

146–149. Whitney, "When Gunslinger," 8/70.

150–151. "Hot as a Pistol," *Newsweek*, 11/67.

152. Buck, Jerry, "Anti-Violence Pressure Keeps Marshal's Gun in Holster," *Oklahoma City Times*, June 23, 1972, p. 21.

153. Smith, Cecil. "Gunsmoke Wins Without Shootout," *Los Angeles Times*, Dec. 8, 1969.

154. Scott, Vernon, "The Indestructible Western," *New York Times*, Jan. 11, 1971.

155. Deeb, Gary, "The Jig Is Up for Marshal Dillon," *Chicago Tribune*, July 3, 1974, p. 11.

156. Smith, "Gunsmoke Wins," 12/69.

157. Kleiner, Dick, "Gunsmoke Is Better Without Violence," *Miami Herald*, July 5, 1971.

158. Folkart, Burt A., "Obituary, Ron Bishop," *Los Angeles Times*, Feb. 5, 1988.

159. Cyclops, "Sex on Gunsmoke? Right, Pardner," *Variety*, Oct. 12, 1973.

160. Folkart, "Obituary, Ron Bishop," *Los Angeles Times*, Feb. 5, 1988.

161. Witbeck, Charles, "Town Drunk of TV," *Honolulu Advertiser*, Feb. 17, 1969.

162. "Looking at Dodge City with an Eye Toward Relevance," *Washington Post*, March 5, 1973.

163. Gardella, Kay. "It's Off to Boot Hill for Matt Dillon's Gang," *Daily News*, May 2, 1975.

164. Zito, Tom, "The Death of Gunsmoke," *Honolulu Advertiser*, Sept. 1, 1975.

165–166. Smith, "Legend Goes," 9/75.

167. "Jim Arness, Hero of Gunsmoke," *Look*, Oct. 29, 1957, p. 115.

168. Smith, "Legend Goes," 9/75.

169. Summers, Neil, *The First Official TV Western Book*, Old West Shop Publishing, Vienna, W.V., 1987, p. 25.

170. Adams, and Rainey, *Shoot-Em Ups*, 1978.

171. "Westerns on the Comeback Trail," *TV Guide*, June 18, 1988, p. A-60.

172. "Hot as a Pistol," *Newsweek*, 11/67.

173. Lasson, Robert, "Still Hotter Than a Pistol, Why?" *New York Times*, Jan. 11, 1970, p. 19 D.

174. Henry, Will, "Dodge City Could Bite the Dust with Kitty Gone, Will the Guns Fall Silent?" *Los Angeles Times*, May 20, 1974.

BIBLIOGRAPHY

Articles

"After 19 Years Kitty Dropping Out of Gunsmoke," *Los Angeles Times,* March 6, 1974, pp. 3, 24.
Amory, Cleveland. "The Dakotas," *TV Guide,* April 6, 1963, p. 1.
———. "Review." *TV Guide,* March 14, 1964, p. 3.
Atkinson, Brooks. "The Dedicated World of Gunsmoke Has Values That Mere Ratings Transcend," *New York Times,* November 10, 1964, p. 44.
Autry, Gene. "Gene Autry's Prize Round-Up." *Radio-Television Mirror,* July 1951, p. 46.
"Award Winners." *TV Radio Mirror,* May 1955, p. 35.
"Award Winners." *TV Radio Mirror,* May 1956, p. 34.
"Award Winners." *TV Radio Mirror,* 1958, p. 50.
Becker, Joyce. "New Direction for Miss Kitty." *Los Angeles Times,* July 5, 1974, p. 19.
Benson, Ray. "Smoke Crew Called Extraordinary Pros." *Columbia Record* (South Carolina), April 17, 1971.
Bensoua, Joe. "Gunsmoke Still a Blast." *The Outlook* (Santa Monica, Calif.), September 26, 1987.
"The Best Limp in the West Is a Fake, But It's the Trade Mark of Gunsmoke's Chester." *Look,* September 12, 1961, pp. 55–57.
"Bette Davis Goes West... With a Wallop." *TV Guide,* July 30, 1966, pp. 3–5.
Bianculli, David. "Return to Dodge," *New York Post,* September 26, 1987, p. 25.
Brown, Les, "CBS Will Drop Gunsmoke and Introduce Nine Series for the Fall," *New York Times,* April 30, 1975.
Buck, Jerry. *Anti-Violence Pressure Keeps Marshal's Gun in Holster, Oklahoma City Times,* June 23, 1972, p. 21.
———. *Gunsmoke Survives as TV Phenomenon, Globe* (Joplin, Mo.), July 6, 1974.
———. "No Miss Kitty in 20th Year of Gunsmoke," *The Courier Journal and Times* (Louisville, Ky.), September 1, 1974, p. H-8.
Budd, Millie. "The Duke Started It," *Houston Post,* January 11, 1972.
———. "Emmy, Are You Even Watching?" *Houston Post,* April 26, 1971.
———. "The Man Got Ouchy," *Houston Post,* January 10, 1972.
"Busy Day at the Office." *TV Guide,* January 30, 1971.
CBS Television Feature News Release. "Famed Gunsmoke Series Makes Its Television Debut" (news release), August 11, 1955.
———. *Milburn Stone—His Fans Like Him Grouchy,* September 9, 1955.
———. [News Release]. September 9, 1965.
———. "This Is Marshal Dillon" (news release). August 12, 1955.
"CBS Will Drop Gunsmoke and Introduce Nine Series for the Fall," *New York Times,* April 30, 1975, p. 82.

[787]

BIBLIOGRAPHY

"Chester, Kitty, and Doc: Dances, Songs and Snappy Patter." *TV Guide,* January 2, 1960, pp. 20-23.
"Chester Limps Off Into the Sun-Set Again." *TV Guide,* January 4, 1964, pp. 4-5.
Clepper, P.M. "The Brothers Aurness." *TV Guide,* July 18, 1970, pp. 16-18.
"Cutting Capers with Mistuh Dillon." *TV Guide,* September 12, 1959, pp. 24-27.
Cyclops, "Sex on Gunsmoke? Right, Pardner." *Variety,* October 12, 1973.
Dallos, Robert E. "Stations' Pleas Save Gunsmoke." *New York Times,* March 8, 1967.
Davidson, Muriel. "Unlikely Brothers: James Arness and Peter Graves." *Good Housekeeping,* April 1973, pp. 48-56.
Deeb, Gary. "The Jib Is Up for Marshal Dillon." *Chicago Tribune,* July 3, 1974, p. 11.
de Roos, Robert. "The Greta Garbo of Dodge City." *TV Guide,* December 10, 1966, pp. 19-21.
———. "Private Life of Gunsmoke's Star." *Saturday Evening Post,* April 12, 1958, pp. 32-33, 108, 110.
"Dodge City...8 Years Later." *TV Guide,* October 24, 1964, pp. 8-9.
DuBrow, Rick. "CBS Monday Night Lineup Is Tops." *Tucson Daily Citizen,* March 26, 1969.
———. "Gunsmoke Still One of Television's Finest Hours." *Ventura County (Calif.) Star-Free Press,* November 12, 1968.
"18 Years Later...And the Game's Still Not Over." *TV Guide,* September 29, 1973, pp. 12-13.
"Festus Still Has Hankering for Gunsmoke." *The Register,* Tucson, Arizona, February 15, 1978.
Finnigan, Joseph. "TV Teletype: Hollywood." *TV Guide,* April 14, 1973, p. 42.
Folkart, Burt A. "Obituary, Ron Bishop, 66, War Hero, TV Western Scriptwriter." *Los Angeles Times,* February 5, 1988.
"For the Record." *TV Guide,* December 2, 1961, p. A-1.
"47 Weeks of Prestige." *Time,* March 23, 1953, p. 104, 106.
Francis, Barbara. "The Great Shows: Gunsmoke." *Emmy Magazine,* Winter 1979, pp. 32-49.
Fredriksson, Kristine. "Gunsmoke: Twenty-Year Videography, Part I." *Journal of Popular Film & Television,* Vol. 12:1, Spring 1984.
———. "Gunsmoke: Twenty-Year Videography, Part II." *Journal of Popular Film & Television,* Vol. 12:3, Fall 1984.
———. "Gunsmoke: Twenty-Year Videography, Part III." *Journal of Popular Film & Television,* Vol. 12:4, Winter 1984-85.
———. "Gunsmoke: Twenty-Year Videography, Part IV." *Journal of Popular Film & Television,* Vol. 13:1, Spring 1985.
Freeman, Don. "Gunsmoke...After 17 Years It's Still a Red-Hot Show." *San Diego Union,* February 13, 1972.
———. "Point of View." *San Diego Union,* September 25, 1987.
———. [Review.] *San Diego Union,* October 11, 1974.
Gardella, Kay. "It's Off to Boot Hill for Matt Dillon's Gang." *Daily News,* May 2, 1975.
Gould, Jack. "Radio in Review: Gunsmoke, a Western Well Off the Beaten Path, Presented by CBS," *New York Times,* May 6, 1953.
———. [Review.] *New York Times,* September 14, 1955, p. 63.
"Gunsmoke." *TV Guide,* November 26, 1955, p. 19.
"Gunsmoke." *Variety,* September 19, 1973, p. 32.
"Gunsmoke." *Variety,* September 11, 1974, p. 56.
"Gunsmoke." *Variety,* February 19, 1975, p. 40.
"Gunsmoke Wins Without Shootout," *Los Angeles Times,* March 6, 1974, pp. 3, 24.
"Gunsmoke's Miss Kitty Wins a Showdown to Keep Her Exotic Cats." *People,* January 27, 1975, p. 24.
Hennessee, Judith. "The Woman from Dodge," Letter to the Editor. *New York Times,* July 27, 1975.
Henry, Will. "Dodge City Could Bite the Dust with Kitty Gone, Will The Guns Fall Silent?" *Los Angeles Times,* May 20, 1974.
"Home Home in the Clink." *TV Guide,* July 20, 1963, pp. 6-9.
"Hot as a Pistol." *Newsweek,* November 20, 1967, p. 96.
House and Garden, September 1957, pp. 32-33.
House, Ramon (as told to Bob Lardine). "You Wouldn't Recognize the Place," *Sunday News,* February 25, 1962, p. 8.

Bibliography

Humphreys, Hal. "Can Gunsmoke Stay Legit?" *Mirror-News,* February 9, 1955.
"Jim Arness, Hero of Gunsmoke." *Look,* October 29, 1957, p. 115.
Kaufman, Dave. "Gunsmoke, Matt Gets It." *Daily Variety,* September 12, 1955.
Kleiner, Dick. "Gunsmoke Is Better Without Violence." *The Miami Herald,* July 5, 1971.
LaCamera, Anthony. "Gunsmoke Thrives Without Emmy Help." *Record American* (Boston), November 2, 1971.
Lardner, John. "Decline and Fall Possible." *New Yorker,* February 28, 1959, p. 97.
Lasson, Robert. "Still Hotter Than a Pistol, Why?" *New York Times,* (Arts and Leisure), January 11, 1970, p. 19 D.
Laurent, Lawrence. "Arness Won't Quit Gunsmoke Now, But Maybe in Two Years," *The Courier-Journal and Times* (Louisville, Ky.), April 1, 1973, p. H-6.
Lewis, Richard W. "Dodge City's Medicine Man." *TV Guide,* November 24, 1962, pp. 22-24.
"Looking at Dodge City with an Eye Toward Relevance." *Washington Post,* March 5, 1973.
McHarry, Charles. "On the Town," *Daily News,* September 6, 1975, p. 28.
Maksian, George. "Gunsmoke Riding Back to TV," *Daily News,* February 27, 1987, p. 74.
Markield, Wallace. "A Fond Farewell to Matt Dillon, Dodge City and Gunsmoke." *New York Times,* July 3, 1975.
"Marshal from Minneapolis." *TV Guide,* May 11, 1957, pp. 24-26.
Meston, John. Letter to the *New York Tribune,* original copy.
"Mona Lisa of the Long Branch." *TV Guide,* December 1960, pp. 24-27.
Morhaim, Joe. "She Who Never Gets Kissed." *TV Guide,* March 15, 1958, pp. 8-11.
Morrison, Bill. "Matt Dillon Gets New Image." *News and Observer* (Raleigh, N.C.), September 26, 1973.
Nachman, Gerald. "Gunsmoke Still at Home on Range." *Variety,* March 27, 1973.
Newton, Dwight. "Revived Show Tops Original." *San Francisco Examiner and Chronicle,* February 16, 1969.
"Notes on People." *New York Times,* March 7, 1974, p. 78.
O'Hallarin, Bill. "Holy Gunsmoke, It's Matt Dillon and Miss Kitty Back at the Long Branch." *TV Guide,* September 26, 1987.
_____. "When Chester Forgot to Limp." *TV Guide,* August 23, 1975, pp. 11-12.
"On Saturday Night What Do You Expect." *TV Guide,* February 10, 1962.
Page, Don. "Everything Jells in Gunsmoke Episode." *Los Angeles Times,* January 23, 1969.
Phillips, D., and Copeland, B. "Riding High on the Waves of Indignation." *TV Guide,* July 12, 1965, pp. 24-27.
Post, Kathleen. "Dennis Weaver of Gunsmoke." *TV Radio Mirror,* March 1958, pp. 46-47.
"The Private Life of Gunsmoke's Kitty." *Look,* November 25, 1958, pp. 60-64.
Raddatz, Leslie. "Biggest Voice in the West." *TV Guide,* February 21, 1976, pp. 8-11.
_____. "The Dodge City Gang." *TV Guide,* March 18, 1972, pp. 14-17.
_____. "Gunsmoke's Designated Hitter." *TV Guide,* December 8, 1973, pp. 17-20.
_____. "Look What's Happened to These Dodge City Citizens." *TV Guide,* August 17, 1968, pp. 16-19.
_____. "An Open Letter to My Wife." *TV Guide,* 1964, pp. 15-19.
Russell, Dick. "I Can't Live Up to What People Think I Am." *TV Guide,* February 24, 1979, pp. 18-22.
Sanders, Coyne Steven. "Kinescope," *Emmy,* July/August, 1985, vol. vii, No. 4, p. 90.
Scott, Vernon. "Gunsmoke Keeps Riding On." *Virginian Pilot,* April 12, 1969.
_____. "Gunsmoke's Mysterious James Arness." *Ladies' Home Journal,* May 1971.
Smith, Cecil. "Gunsmoke Wins Without a Shootout." *Los Angeles Times,* December 12, 1969.
_____. "Legend Goes Down the Tubes." *Los Angeles Times,* September 1, 1975.
"Special TV-Radio Report." *Newsweek,* July 22, 1957, pp. 51-54.
Steiner, Robert. "Gunsmoke's Chester Recalls He Played Stock at Ivoryton," *The New Era,* (Rhinebeck, N.Y.), October 6, 1960.
"Tall in the Saddle, Part I." *TV Guide,* November 25, 1961, pp. 6-9.
"Tall in the Saddle, Part II." *TV Guide,* December 2, 1961, pp. 22-25.
"This Man Kissed a Girl." *TV Guide,* June 27, 1964, pp. 12-13.
"TV Goes Wild Over Westerns," *Life,* October 28, 1957, pp. 99-101.

BIBLIOGRAPHY

"Westerns on the Comeback Trail." *TV Guide,* June 18, 1988, p. A-60.
Whitney, Dwight. "When Gunslinger Nielsen Hit Town." *TV Guide,* August 22, 1970, pp. 20-25.
———. "Why Gunsmoke Keeps Blazing Away." *TV Guide,* December 6, 1958, pp. 8-11.
"Who Set Dodge City Afire? He Did." *TV Guide,* October 23, 1965, pp. 28-29.
"Who's Who on Gunsmoke." *TV Radio Mirror,* May 1955, pp. 64-65.
"Wild Old West." *TV Radio Mirror,* May 1957, p. 65.
Witbeck, Charles. "Town Drunk of TV." *Honolulu Advertiser,* February 17, 1969.
Zito, Tom. "The Death of Gunsmoke." *Honolulu Advertiser,* September 1, 1975.

Books

Adams, Les, and Rainey, Buck. *Shoot-Em Ups: The Complete Reference Guide to Westerns of the Sound Era.* New Rochelle, N.Y.: Arlington House, 1978.
Alicoate, Charles, ed. *Radio Annual and Television Year Book,* N.Y., N.Y.: 1953-1964.
Aros, Andrew A. *An Actor Guide to the Talkies, 1965-1974.* Metuchen, New Jersey: Scarecrow Press, 1977.
Aylesworth, T.G., and Bowman, J.S. *The World Almanac Who's Who of Film.* New York: World Almanac, 1987.
Bergan, R.; Fuller, G.; and Malcolm, D. *Academy Award Winners.* New York: Crown Publishers, 1986.
Brooks, T. *The Complete Directory to Prime Time TV Stars.* New York: Ballantine Books, 1987.
———, and Marsh, E. *The Complete Directory to Prime Time Network TV Shows, 1946-Present.* New York: Ballantine Books, 1979.
Broughton, I. *Producers on Producing.* Jefferson, N.C.: McFarland, 1986.
Brown, L. *Encyclopedia of Television.* New York: New York Zoetrope, 1977.
———. *The New York Times Encyclopedia of Television.* Times Books, 1977.
———. *Television: The Business Behind the Box.* New York: Harcourt Brace Jovanovich, 1971.
Buxton, Frank, and Owen, Bill. *The Big Broadcast, 1920-1950.* New York: Viking Press, 1972.
Castleman, H., and Podrazik, W.J. *The Schedule Book.* New York: McGraw-Hill, 1984.
Cawelti, J.G. *The Six-Gun Mystique.* Bowling Green, Ohio: Bowling Green State University Press, 1984.
Coursodon, Jean-Pierre, and Sauvage, Pierre. *American Directors, Vol. I and II.* New York: McGraw-Hill Book Co., 1983.
Dimmitt, Richard Bertrand. *An Actor Guide to the Talkies,* vol. I. Metuchen, New Jersey: Scarecrow Press, 1967.
———. *An Actor Guide to the Talkies,* vol. II. Metuchen, New Jersey: Scarecrow Press, 1968.
Dunning, John. *Tune In Yesterday: The Ultimate Encyclopedia of Old-Time Radio.* Englewood Cliffs, N.J.: Prentice-Hall, 1976.
Eliot, M. *American Television.* New York: Anchor Press, 1981.
Fenin, G.N., and Everson, W.K. *The Western.* New York: Orion Press, 1962.
Gianakos, L.J. *Television Drama Series Programming: A Comprehensive Chronicle, 1975-1980.* Metuchen, N.J.: Scarecrow Press, 1981.
———. *Television Drama Series Programming: 1980-82.* Metuchen, N.J.: Scarecrow Press, 1983.
Gitlin, T. *Inside Prime Time.* New York: Pantheon Books, 1983.
Goldrup, T., and Goldrup, J. *Feature Players, The Stories Behind the Faces,* Volume 1. Goldrup and Goldrup, 1986.
Goldsen, R.K. *The Show and Tell Machine.* New York: Dial Press, 1975.
Halliwell, L. *Halliwell's Film Guide.* New York: Charles Scribner's Sons, 1977.
———. *Halliwell's Filmgoer's Companion.* New York: Charles Scribner's Sons, 1983.
———. *Halliwell's Filmgoer's Companion.* New York: Charles Scribner's Sons, 1988.
———. *Halliwell's Film and Video Guide.* New York: Charles Scribner's Sons, 1987.
Himmelstein, H. *Television Myth and the American Mind.* New York: Praeger Publishers, 1984.
Horwitz, James. *They Went Thataway.* New York: E.P. Dutton and Co., 1976.
International Television Almanac. New York: Quigley Publishing, 1982.

Bibliography

International Television Almanac. New York: Quigley Publishing, 1985.
International Television Almanac. New York: Quigley Publishing, 1986.
Jones, K.D.; McClure, A.F.; and Twomey, A.E. *Character People.* Secaucus, N.J.: Citadel Press, 1976.
Katz, E. *The Film Encyclopedia.* New York: Putnam Publishing Co., 1979.
Langman, Larry. *A Guide to American Film Directors,* Vol. I and II. Metuchen, N.J.: Scarecrow Press, 1981.
Lloyd, A.; Fuller, G.; and Desser. A. *The Illustrated Who's Who of the Cinema.* New York: Portland House, 1987.
McDonald, Archie P. *Shooting Stars.* Bloomington, Ind.: Indiana University Press, 1987.
McNeil, A. *Total Television.* New York: Viking Penguin, 1980.
MacDonald, J.F. *Who Shot the Sheriff? The Rise and Fall of the Television Western.* New York: Praeger Pub., 1987.
Maltin, Leonard. *TV Movies and Video Guide, 1990 Edition.* New York: New American Library, 1989.
Metz, R. *Reflections in a Bloodshot Eye.* Chicago: Playboy Press, 1975.
Meehan, D.M. *Ladies of the Evening: Women Characters of Prime-Time Television.* Metuchen, N.J.: Scarecrow Press, 1983.
Michael, P., and Parish, J.R. *The Emmy Awards.* New York: Crown Publishers, 1970.
Morrow, L.A. *The Tony Award Book: Four Decades of Great American Theater.* New York: Abbeville Press, 1987.
Newcomb, H., and Alley, R.S. *The Producer's Medium.* New York: Oxford University Press, 1983.
The New York Times Directory of the Film. New York: Arno Press/Random House, 1971.
The New York Times Film Reviews Appendix Index, 1913-1968. New York: New York Times and Arno Press, 1970.
Paper, L.J. *Empire: William S. Paley and the Making of CBS.* New York: St. Martin's Press, 1987.
Parks, Rita. *The Western Hero in Film and Television: Mass Media Mythology.* Ann Arbor: UMI Research Press, 1982.
Parish, James Robert. *Actors' Television Credits, 1950-72.* Metuchen, N.J.: Scarecrow Press, 1973.
_____, and Trost, Mark. *Actors' Television Credits, Supp. I.* Metuchen, N.J.: Scarecrow Pres, 1978.
_____, and Terrace, Vincent. *Actors' Television Credits, Supp. II.* Metuchen, N.J.: Scarecrow Press, 1982.
_____, and _____. *Actor's Television Credits, Supp III.* Metuchen, N.J.: Scarecrow Press, 1986.
Perry, J.H. *Variety Obits: An Index to Obituaries in Variety, 1905-1978.* Metuchen, N.J.: Scarecrow Press, 1980.
Quinlan, D. *The Illustrated Encyclopedia of Movie Character Actors.* New York: Harmony, 1985.
_____. *Quinlan's Illustrated Directory of Film Stars.* New York: Hippocrene Books, 1986.
Ragan, David. *Who's Who in Hollywood, 1900-1976.* New Rochelle, N.Y.: Arlington House, 1976.
Rothel, D. *Those Great Cowboy Sidekicks.* Waynesville, N.C.: WOY Publications, 1984.
Scheuer, Steven H. *Movies on TV and Videocassette, 1990.* New York: Bantam Books, 1989.
Sennett, T. *Great Movie Directors.* New York: Harry N. Abrams, Inc., 1986.
Shale, R. *Academy Awards.* New York: Ungar Publishing Co., 1978.
Smith, H. *Saturdays Forever.* Knoxville, Tenn.: National Paperback Books, 1985.
Steinberg, C.S. *TV Facts.* New York: Facts on File, 1980.
Streetback, N. *The Films of Burt Reynolds.* Secaucus, N.J.: Citadel Press, 1981.
Summers, N. *The First Official TV Western Book.* Vienna, W.V.: Old West Shop Publishing, 1987.
Swarthout, M. "Hey, Mister Dillon! A History of Gunsmoke—America's Most Successful Dramatic Television Series." Master's thesis. University of Southern California, 1973.
Terrace, V. *Encyclopedia of Television Series, Pilots and Specials, 1937-1973.* New York: New York Zoetrope, 1986.
_____. _____. *1937-1984.* New York: New York Zoetrope, 1986.
_____. _____. *1974-1984.* New York: New York Zoetrope, 1985.
_____. *Radio's Golden Years.* San Diego: A.S. Barnes and Co., 1981.
Vestal, Stanley. *Queen of the Cowtowns.* New York: Harper and Brothers, 1952.

BIBLIOGRAPHY

Weaver, J.T. *Forty Years of Screen Credits, 1929-1969,* Volume 1: A-J, Volume 2: K-Z. Metuchen, N.J.: Scarecrow Press, 1970.
West, R. *Television Westerns: Major and Minor Series, 1946-1978,* Jefferson, N.C.: McFarland, 1987.
Young, F.R. *Dodge City.* High Plains Publishers, Boot Hill Museum, 1972.

INDEX

A.E.S. Hudson Street 603
The A-Team 43, 144, 712
Aames, Willie 678, 694
Abandoned 52
Abbott, John 449, 507
Abbott, Philip 490, 557
Abbott and Costello Meet Frankenstein 149
Abe Blocker 545, 555
Abelia 141, 632, 633, 642, 646, 670, 680
Abie's Irish Rose 557
Abilene Town 150
About Chester 279, 436, 522
Absalom 368
Academy Award 14, 50, 135, 364, 365, 457, 462, 463, 515, 537, 538, 540, 545, 551, 553, 570, 571, 579, 580, 581, 582, 585, 587, 588, 594, 598, 601, 605, 606, 612, 621, 645, 649, 662, 673, 697
Accidental Family 630
The Accused 649
Acker, Sharon 674
Ackerman, Bettye 696, 697
Ackerman, Harry 25, 65, 67, 68, 74, 76, 78, 89, 214–215, 266
Adam 12 665
Adams, Casey 475
Adams, Charles 44, 223
Adams, Dorothy 459, 475
Adams, Kathy 445
Adams, Les 19
Adams, Mary 452

Adams, Stanley 461, 463, 585
Adam's Rib 690, 702
The Addams Family 43, 618, 713
Ades, Daniel 605
Adler, Robert 545
Adreon, Franklin 519
Adventures in Paradise 519
The Adventures of Ellery Queen 536, 622, 702
The Adventures of Huckleberry Finn 609
The Adventures of Kit Carson 19, 360
The Adventures of Ozzie and Harriet 43
The Adventures of Philip Marlowe 25, 44, 59, 215
The Adventures of Rin Tin Tin 20, 527
The Adventures of Sonny and Buddy 51
The Adventures of Spin and Marty 58
The Adventures of Superman 464, 481
The Adventures of Wild Bill Hickock 19, 644
An Affair to Remember 151
The African Queen 579
Aidman, Charles 157, 279, 489, 509, 522, 635, 640
Airplane 597, 637
Airport 150
Airwolf 143, 673, 689
Akins, Claude 445, 462, 481, 535, 546, 575, 583, 600, 613, 680
Alaimo, Marc 714, 715
The Alamo 467, 545
The Alamo: 13 Days to Glory 578
Alaniz, Rico 560, 626, 630
Alarm at Pleasant Valley 394, 458
Albee, Josh 678, 687
Albert 377, 652, 656
Albertson, Jack 160, 324, 530, 645, 680, 709
Albertson, Mabel 530, 556
Albin, Andy 529, 605
Albright, Hardie 544, 594
Albright, Lola 449
Alcaide, Chris 455, 474, 491, 523
Alcaide, Mario 610
Alden, Norman 621, 622, 640, 702
Alderman, John 487
Alderson, John 448, 467, 550
The Aldrich Family 567
Alexander, David 621
Alexander, Tommy 559
The Alfred Hitchcock Hour 121, 578
Alfred Hitchcock Presents 114, 143, 361, 493, 567
Alias Festus Haggin 275, 681, 706
Alice 599, 613
Alice Doesn't Live Here Anymore 538, 571, 649
Alien 481, 590, 662
All About Eve 602

[793]

INDEX

All in the Family 113, 477, 603, 611, 612, 630, 683, 716
All My Children 586, 614
All My Sons 588
All Quiet on the Western Front 617
All That 529, 541
All That Heaven Allows 540
All the Brothers Were Valiant 470
All the Fine Young Cannibals 497
All the King's Men 501, 605, 671
All the President's Men 718
All the Way Home 668
Allen, Corey 480
Allen, Lynn 362, 403, 404, 418, 436, 441
Allen, Mark 518
Allen, Sean Barbara 677
Allen, Steve 108, 154
Allen, Valery 539
Allison, Clay 34
Allison, Jean 653, 706
Allman, Sheldon 495, 550, 560, 579, 627, 628, 634
All's Fair 441
Almanzar, James 596, 597, 603, 615, 626, 644, 661, 701
Alton, Kenneth 461
Amazing Chan and the Chan Clan 448
The Amazing Spiderman 471, 699
An American in Paris 644
An American Werewolf in London 603
The American Woman: Portraits of Courage 532
The Americanization of Emily 114, 493
Ames, Allyson 564
Ames, Florenz 468, 469
Ames, Joyce 653
Amory, Cleveland 21, 91, 94, 99
Amsterdam, Morey 157, 331, 479
Amy Prentiss 631
Amy's Good Deed 396, 484
Anatomy of a Murder 43, 54
Anders, Merry 672
Anderson, Donna 569

Anderson, Gilbert 14
Anderson, Herbert 568
Anderson, James 448, 572, 589, 603, 617, 625
Anderson, John 158, 164, 315, 479, 489, 502, 549, 592, 594, 609, 647, 649, 666, 695
Anderson, Loni 503
Anderson, Michael 211
Anderson, Richard 158-159, 312, 574, 650, 713
Anderson, Robert 102, 444, 514, 575
Andes, Keith 81, 195, 699
Andre, E.J. 627, 628
Andres, Irene 419
Andrews, Dana 637
Andrews, Edward 590
Andrews, Tige 159, 324, 466, 626
Andrews, Tod 526
The Andromeda Strain 687
The Andy Griffith Show 43, 363, 492, 513, 561, 582, 630, 647
Andy's Gang 644
Angarola, Richard 653
Angel 470
Angel Baby 665, 671
Angela, Mary 652
The Angry Land 719, 723
The Angry Red Planet 50
Animal House 719
Ankrum, Morris 512
Anna and the King 448, 620
Anna-Lisa 514
Annie Get Your Gun 583
Annie Oakley 19, 403, 502, 616
Another Day 537
Another Man's Poison 412
Another World 571, 614
Ansara, Michael 108, 159, 338, 596, 597, 611
Anthony, Mrs. Calvina 7
Antiviolence movement 130-132, 136, 151
Antonio, Lou 591, 592, 620, 631, 638, 639
Anybody Can Kill a Marshal 550
Apache Rose 604
The Apartment 50, 365, 463
Apartment for Peggy 590
Apone, John 510

The Apostle of Vengeance 14
The Apple Dumpling Gang Rides Again 225
Apple's Way 444, 674, 685, 715
Appointment with Destiny 681, 683
Apprentice Doc 167, 219, 220, 297, 531, 540
Arau, Alfonso 679
Archambeault, George 461
Archie Bunker's Place 556, 603
Arden, Eve 496
Arizona Midnight 133, 692
Arkin, Alan 535
Arms, Russell 520
Armstrong, Herb 159, 340, 686
Armstrong, R.G. 159, 307, 531, 552, 581, 597, 620
Armstrong, R.L. 710
Armstrong, Todd 626, 627, 632
The Army Trial 392
Arn, Edward F. 28
Arness, James 3, 5, 10, 41, 67, 74, 77, 78, 79, 80-87, 88, 91, 96, 98, 100, 103, 104, 106, 107, 110, 115, 116, 119, 120, 121, 122, 123, 124, 131, 134, 149, 154, 158, 159, 160, 161, 162, 163, 165, 166, 167, 168, 169, 170, 171, 172, 174, 175, 176, 177, 178, 179, 180, 181, 183, 184, 185, 186, 187, 189, 191, 192, 193, 194, 195, 196, 197, 201-204, 207, 209, 210, 212, 214, 217, 227, 257, 259, 261, 264, 266, 267, 268, 273, 276, 277, 281, 282, 284, 292, 293, 294, 298, 299, 302, 306, 309, 318, 320, 321, 323, 325, 330, 331, 336, 338, 339, 344, 348, 351, 352, 354, 355, 443, 449, 451, 460, 479, 497, 502, 503, 504, 505, 506, 507, 508, 509, 510, 511, 512, 513, 514, 515, 516, 517, 518, 519, 520, 521, 522, 523, 524, 525, 526, 527,

Index

551, 561, 562, 571, 575, 577, 578, 582, 597, 614, 699, 703, 710, 723, 724, 725
Arness, Virginia 449
Arngrim, Stefan 598
Arnie 534, 592
Arnold 699
Arnold, Denny 704, 724
Around the Corner 93
Arrest and Trial 446, 610
Arthur, Jean 133, 134, 212, 580
Arrowhead 75, 92
Arvan, Jan 486
Arvin, William 469
As the World Turns 710
Ash 549, 570
Ashley, Joel 453, 456, 463, 499
Ashley, Peter 539
Asner, Edward 132, 160, 193, 270, 573, 574, 604
Aspen 682, 690, 703
The Asphalt Jungle 365, 449, 476, 533, 659
The Assassin 151
Astaire, Fred 74
Astin, John 618
Aten, Laurence 605
Atterbury, Malcolm 102, 444, 451, 459, 465, 531, 540, 573, 675
Atwater, Barry 450, 477, 495, 508, 648
Aubrey, James 119, 130
Aubuchon, Jacque 456, 457, 460, 581, 722
Aunt Mary 47
Aunt Thede 305, 575, 585
Aurness, Jenny Lee 561, 575
Austin, Carmen 626
The Autobiography of Miss Jane Pittman 662
Autry, Gene 18, 19, 20, 109, 173, 207, 219, 496, 557
Avanti 590
Avelar, Mike 602
The Avengers 296, 592, 600
Averbach, Hy 360
Avery, Val 160, 340, 477, 611, 646
The Awful Truth 621
Ayres, Lew 174, 616, 617

B

B.J. and the Bear 378, 463, 469, 625
Baa Baa Black Sheep 660
Baby Blue Marine 673, 685
Bacalla, Donna 338, 625
Bachelor Father 452, 534, 566
Backes, Alice 502
Backstairs at the Whitehouse 363, 673
Backus, Jim 719, 720
Bacon, Margaret 630, 681
Bad Boy 379
Bad Day at Black Rock 687
Bad Lady from Brookline 583
Bad Man of Deadwood 226
The Bad One 548
Bad Seed 433, 521, 581
The Bad Seed 576
Bad Sheriff 520
The Badge 141, 325, 424, 517, 652, 657, 724
Baer, Buddy 476
Baer, John 693, 707
Baer, Max 476
Baer, Parley 3, 24, 26, 31, 41, 42-43, 44, 45, 56, 58, 60, 61, 62, 66, 68, 70, 89-90, 107, 209, 216, 223, 235, 236, 237, 240, 241, 244, 249, 251, 252, 253, 256, 359, 417, 430
Bail, Chuck 528
Bailey, Jack 612, 647
Bailey, Raymond 448, 485
Baileys of Balboa 592, 667
Bain, Barbara 488
Bakalyan, Richard 607, 608, 647
Baker, Joby 542
Baker, Joe Don 599, 600, 639
Baker, Virginia 486, 701
Baker, Wendell 695
Baker Street 610
Baker's Dozen 94, 622, 628, 664
Bakey, Ed 621, 640, 684
Baldin, Janit 708
Baldwin, Walter 610
Ball, Lucille 48, 212
Ball Four 691
Ball Nine, Take Your Base 427
The Ballad of Cable Hogue 112

The Ballad of Josie 226
Ballew, Robert 594, 604
Balls, Bullets, and Bonnets, and in That Order 138
Bambi 46
Banacek 624
The Bandit Makes Good 14
Bang the Drum Slowly 612
Bank Baby 581
Banyon 667
The Barbary Coast 606
Barbash, Robert 643
Barcroft, Roy 443, 517, 518, 521, 548, 563, 580, 584, 592, 611, 616, 631, 638, 724
Bard, Katherine 485
Bardette, Trevor 501, 515, 615, 621, 663
Baretta 113, 660
Barker, Lex 81
Barnaby Jones 361, 519, 613, 722
Barnes, Rayford 77, 507, 521, 523, 559, 563, 571, 645, 682, 701
Barnes, Walter 485, 489
Barney Blake, Police Reporter 462
Barney Miller 585, 609, 698
The Baron 637
Barrett, Michael Ann 360, 361, 363, 366, 368, 371, 372, 392, 393
Barrey, Christopher 566
Barrier, Edgar 375, 380, 382, 392
Barrier, Michael 539, 542
Barron, Baynes 528, 624
Barry, Donald 548, 693
Barry, Eleanore 423
Barry, Patricia 481, 515, 652
Barrymore, John 578
Barrymore, John Drew 143, 577, 578, 586
Bartell, Harry 16, 25, 36, 39, 46, 47, 49, 50, 52, 53, 60, 66, 121, 215, 216, 235, 247, 359, 360, 361, 362, 363, 364, 365, 366, 367, 368, 369, 370, 371, 372, 373, 374, 375, 376, 377, 378, 379, 380, 381, 382, 383, 384, 385, 386, 387, 388, 389, 390, 391,

[795]

INDEX

392, 393, 394, 395, 396,
397, 398, 399, 400, 401,
402, 403, 405, 406, 407,
408, 409, 412, 413, 416,
417, 418, 420, 421, 422,
424, 425, 426, 427, 428,
429, 430, 431, 432, 433,
434, 435, 436, 437, 438,
439, 440, 441, 455, 468,
513, 533, 551, 584, 596
Bartell, Richard 550
Bartlett, Bonnie 160, 270,
  707, 716
Bartlett, Jack 591
Bartold, Norman 696,
  689, 690
Barton, Anne 456, 477,
  492, 568, 572
Barton, Larry 606, 682
The Barton Boy 394
Basch, Harry 612
Basehart, Richard 183, 665
Bass, Todd 688
Bassett, Charles 10
The Bassops 312, 343, 564
Bastin, Charles 379
Bat Masterson 40, 226
Batanides, Art 572, 588
Bates, Ben 715
Bates, Jeanne 53, 54, 55,
  245, 247, 359, 366, 381,
  391, 402, 406, 408, 409,
  417, 418, 421, 422, 423,
  424, 427, 430, 431, 435,
  436, 437, 438, 441, 446
Batman 471, 550, 592
Batson, Susan 650
Battleground 82, 96, 551, 582
Battlestar Galactica 720
Baxter, Alan 529, 556
Baylor, Hal 102, 454, 565,
  621, 691, 700, 713
Beal's, Richard 52, 239,
  359, 360, 364, 366, 370,
  375, 394, 403, 407, 417,
  418, 421, 425; 426, 427,
  428, 431, 433, 435
The Beachcomber 715
The Bear 377, 494
Bear Trap 409
The Beatles 370
Beatty, Ned 334, 717, 718
Beck, Billy 595, 596
Beck, Jim 495
Beck, John 162, 653, 666, 721

Beck, Vincent 591
Becker, Ken 479
Becker, Terry 453
Beckman, Henry 542,
  546, 709, 713
Beddoe, Don 577
Beebee, Lucius 34
Beecher, Bonnie 614
Beeker's Barn 407, 429
Beery, Noah, Jr. 562, 596
Beeson, Chalk 9
Beggs, James 594
Begley, Ed 192, 197, 278,
  319, 588, 627
Begley, Ed, Jr. 588
Behind the Screen 478, 528, 636
Bell, Book, and Candle 43
Bellamy, Ralph 160, 342, 621
Belle's Back 404, 512
Bellflower, Nellie 160, 709
Ben Casey 55, 143, 245,
  366, 446, 592, 671, 697, 720
Ben-Hur 14
Ben Slade's Saloon 360
Ben Thompson 360
Ben Tolliver's Stud 393, 410, 517
Bender, Russ 592
Bendixen, Mia 667
Beneath the Planet of the Apes 462
Benedict, Val 483
Benedict, William 610
Benesch, Lynn 721
Benjamin, Richard 177
Bennet, Ray 462
Bennett, Julie 706
The Benny Goodman Story 360
The Benny Rubin Show 652
Benoit, Suzanne 580
Benson 113, 703
Bently 566
Benton, Gene 519, 539
Benton, Suzanne 722
Berlinger, Warren 622
Bernard, Butch 406
Berns, Seymour 486, 488, 492
Berrengers 599
Berry, Al 690
Berti, Dehl 544
Best, James 162, 552, 561, 646

The Best Little Whorehouse in Texas 115
The Best of Friends 676
The Best Years of Our Lives 577
Bethune, Zina 705
Betten, Mary 706
Better Off Dead 612
Bettger, Lyle 564
The Betty Hutton Show 575, 583
The Betty White Show 54, 360, 371
Betz, Carl 466
Bevens, Clem 486
The Beverly Hillbillies 151,
  448, 506, 519, 563, 564, 627
Beverly Hills Cop 695
Beware My Lovely 457
Bewitched 151, 534
Beyond Glory 74
Beyond Westworld 631
Biberman, Abner 164, 592
The Bible 540
Bice, Robert 550, 557, 564
Bieri, Ramon 633, 641,
  671, 681, 685, 712
Big Broad 378, 453, 487
The Big Carnival 576
Big Chugg Wilson 429
The Big Con 370, 437, 484
The Big Country 226
Big Deal at Dodge City 371
Big Girl Lost 377, 419, 470
Big Hand for the Little Lady 371
Big Hands 411
The Big Heat 52
The Big Itch 436
Big Jim McLain 82, 261
The Big Land 226
Big Man 271, 523
Big Man, Big Target 275, 574
The Big Show 226
The Big Sleep 501
Big Tom 422, 506
Big Town 472, 550, 560
The Big Trail 15
The Big Valley 47, 144, 226,
  228, 488, 579
Biheller, Robert 572
Bikel, Theodore 126, 211, 579
The Bill Cosby Show 452

Index

Billingsly, Jennifer 558
Billsbury, Rye 25
Billy 715
Billy the Kid 26, 27, 49, 52, 359
Billy the Kid Returns 18
Binns, Ed 475
The Bionic Woman 539
Birch, Paul 476, 536
Bird, Billie 703
Birdman and the Galaxy Trio 366
Birdman of Alcatraz 588
The Birds 444, 567, 658
Biro, Frank 661
Bishop, Ron 3, 137–140, 142, 202, 217, 326, 618, 631, 634, 637, 638, 653, 674, 688, 689, 694, 699, 707, 712
Bixby, Bill 584
Black, Walter 648
Black Image Award 133, 662
"Black Jack" Bill 12
Black Like Me 582
Black Saddle 38, 362, 560
The Blackboard Jungle 658
Blackman, Joan 596
The Blacksmith 271, 381, 418, 514
Blake, Amanda 3, 5, 45, 77, 83, 93, 95-102, 107, 111, 119, 121, 148, 151, 159, 170, 179, 185, 189, 191, 192, 194, 198, 199, 204-206, 207, 209, 210, 214, 257, 258, 261, 263, 266, 268, 272, 274, 276, 277, 280, 293, 295, 300, 301, 306, 309, 310, 311, 321, 322, 323, 330, 333, 341, 345, 346, 354, 355, 443, 532, 551, 562, 582, 584, 601, 710, 723, 724, 725
Blake, Larry 504
Blake, Robin 595
Blake, Whitney 496, 702
Blakeney, Olive 494
Blakesley, Marsha 596
Bless Me Till I Die 430, 524
Blind Man's Bluff 550
Blind Man's Buff 349, 681
Blinn, William 622, 635, 675

Bliss, Ted 368, 377
Blocker, Dan 458, 489
Blondie 469, 635, 720
Blood Money 338, 379, 431, 474, 514, 624, 670
Bloody Hands 206, 390, 411, 467, 500
Blossoms in the Dust 561
The Blue Angels 451, 594
Blue Heaven 570
Blue Horse 416, 499
The Blue Hotel 14
The Blue Knight 471, 515, 672
Blue Velvet 578
Blueprint for Murder 54
The Blues Brothers 603
Blues in the Night 113
Bly, Margaret 569, 579
Boardman, True 667
Bob and Carol and Ted and Alice 573, 576, 649
The Bob Crane Show 650
The Bob Cummings Show 467
The Bob Newhart Show 399, 479, 494, 640, 658, 694, 700
The Bobby Darin Show 608
The Bobsy Twins 422, 512
Bochner, Lloyd 707, 708
Body Heat 441
Body and Soul 26, 53, 483
Body Snatch 422
Bogart, Humphrey 86, 506, 552, 579
Bohannan 684, 685, 697
Bohem, Endre 466
Bokar, Hal 705
Bolder, Cal 538
Boles, Jim 669, 689
Bonanza 141, 162, 180, 190, 226, 228, 457, 458, 477, 486, 578, 614, 663, 666, 669, 671
Bond, Ward 108
Bone Hunters 386
Bonney, Gail 544, 693
Bonnie and Clyde 464, 570, 595
Booke, Sorrell 688
Boone 641
Boone, Brendon 278, 645, 646
Boone, Richard 17, 77, 165
The Boost 101
Boot Hill 10, 11, 12, 102

The Boots 421, 503
Boots and Saddles — The Story of the 5th Cavalry 448, 550
Borgnine, Ernest 108
Born Free 610
Born to Hang 390, 437, 475, 514
Boston Blackie 360
The Bottle Man 387, 483
Bouchey, Willis 591, 623
The Boughton Bride 362
Bound for Glory 668
The Bounty Hunter 279, 588, 600
Bourbon Street Beat 461, 714
Bourneuf, Philip 461, 481
Bowers, William 16
Bowles, Billy 583
Box O' Rocks 404, 504
Boxleitner, Bruce 722
Boy 373
The Boy in the Plastic Bubble 693
The Boy and the Sinner 699, 711
Boyd, William 17, 18, 537
Boyer, John 601
Boyle, Ray 445
The Boys 271, 540
The Boys from Brazil 46, 361, 445
Bracken, Jimmy 638
Bracken's World 505, 550
Bradbury, Lane 591, 609, 625, 630, 638, 647
Bradford, Lane 493, 508, 516, 542, 545, 566, 626, 641, 672, 675, 682
Bradford, Richard 160-161, 596
Bradley, Stewart 516
Brady, Scott 645, 691, 702
The Brady Bunch 113, 633, 634, 638
Braeden, Eric 667, 677, 707
Braggart's Boy 406
Brahm, John 567
Bramley, William 535, 543, 595, 601, 612, 619, 633, 641, 694
Brand, Neville 588
A Brand New Life 462
Branded 455
Brandon, Henry 513, 524

[797]

INDEX

Brandon, John 161, 343, 641
Brands, X 626, 645, 660
Brandt, Hank 625, 641, 654, 655, 716
Brash, Marian 452
The Brave Don't Cry 121
Bray, Robert 549
Breaking Away 612
Breaking Point 444, 453, 573
Breck, Peter 487, 488, 554
Breckinridge 297, 580
Breen, John 614
Breen, Joseph 499, 529, 606
Breeze, Michelle 591, 614, 637, 694
Breezy 707
Bremicker, Dick 81
Brenlin, George 475
Brennen, Claire 710
Brenner 475
Bret Maverick 633, 654
Brian, David 634, 635, 663, 713
Brian, Fletcher 610
Brian's Song 475
Brickell, Beth 701
The Bride Comes to Yellow Sky 14
The Bride of Frankenstein 449
Brides and Grooms 714, 719
Bridges, Beau 100, 190, 315, 595
Bridges, Jeff 595
Bridges, Lloyd 595
Bridges, Rand 700
Bridget Loves Bernie 468, 471, 616
Briggs, Charlie 553, 558
Briggs, Don 576
Bright Promise 482
Brinckerhoff, Burt 577
Bring 'Em Back Alive 651, 722
Bringing Down Father 399
Broadside 590, 613
Brock, Heinie 453
Broderick, James 558, 572
Brodie, Steve 528, 678
Broken Arrow 16, 108, 110, 518, 597, 659
Bromley, Dudley 692
Broncho Billy 14
Bronco 108

Bronson, Charles 274, 454, 489
The Bronx Zoo 573
Brooke, Walter 500
Brooker, Judge 444
Brooks, Charlene 452
Brooks, Foster 161, 296, 542, 661
Brooks, Geraldine 594
Brooks, Jan 553
Brooks, Martin 611
Brooks, Mel 462
Brooks, Peter 583
Brooks, Rand 526, 527
Brooks, Tim 695
Brother Love 519
Brother Whelp 406, 503
Brotherhood Award 133
Brothers 101
The Brothers 342, 363, 394, 404, 597, 690
The Brothers Brannagan 468
The Brothers Karamazov 593, 717
Brown, Barry 662
Brown, George "Hoodoo" 8
Brown, James 550
Brown, Jerry 616, 671
Brown, John 87
Brown, Johnny Mack 168
Brown, Les, Jr. 592
Brown, Lew 458, 498, 502, 510, 520, 521, 525, 539, 576, 610, 613, 615, 616, 631, 663, 680, 688, 709
Brown, Mack 21
Brown, Pepe 641
Brown, Tom 151, 500, 624, 627, 637, 641, 645, 649, 651, 675, 680
Browne, Arthur, Jr. 649, 651, 658
Browne, Cathy 477
Brubaker 593, 662
Brubaker, Robert 150, 444, 477, 489, 492, 494, 496, 497, 498, 502, 510, 515, 523, 528, 534, 544, 623, 639, 645, 651, 703, 705, 707, 710, 714, 717, 719
Bruger's Folly 414
Brunetti, Argentina 592
Brush at Elkader 395, 420, 459, 527

Bryan, Marvin 444
Bryant, Fletcher 654
Bryant, Joshua 161–162, 312, 636
Bryant, William 499, 547, 606, 657, 682, 714
Bryar, Claudia 692
Bryar, Paul 641
Buchanan, Edgar 331, 534, 554
Buck, Connie 500, 503
Buck, Jim 150, 444, 497
Buck James 91, 724
Buck Rogers in the 25th Century 129, 571
The Buddy Holly Story 721
Buffalo Bill 14, 694
The Buffalo Hunter 370, 375, 411, 497
Buffalo Killers 361
Buffalo Man 158, 401, 479
Buffington, Sam 16, 497
Bulifant, Joyce 546
Bull 412
Bull, Richard 689, 690
Bullitt 486
The Bullwinkle Show 40, 363, 370
Bully 582
Bum's Rush 369
Bundy, Brooke 560, 593
Burchett, Kevin 599, 666
Bureaucrat 398, 468, 514
Burke, Walter 496, 507, 560, 579, 649
Burke's Law 457, 493
Burning Wagon 420
Burns, Bart 549
Burns, Michael 624, 629, 654
Burns, Timothy 654, 667
Burns and Allen 363, 441
Burr, Raymond 16, 26, 38, 47, 77
Burr, Robert 694
Burrell, Jan 703
Burrows, Bob 647, 658, 664
Burstyn, Ellen 132, 538, 672
Burt, Nellie 553
Burton, Normann 589
Burton, Richard 520
Burton, Robert 470
Bus Riley's Back in Town 668

[798]

Index

Bus Stop 513, 545, 581
Busey, Gary 162, 349, 721
Bush, Billie Green 703
Bush, George 190
Bush, Owen 162, 349, 627, 628, 702
Busted-Up Guns 434
Buster and Billy 673
The Busters 135, 154, 349, 721, 723
Busting Loose 50, 365, 463
Butch Cassidy and the Sundance Kid 571
Butler, Robert 620, 637, 689
Butterflies Are Free 581
Buttram, Pat 18
Buyeff, Lillian 53, 54, 55–56, 359, 360, 361, 365, 370, 374, 377, 388, 406, 416, 430
By Line 598, 600
Byrd, Senator 124
Byrnes, Jim 3, 5, 95, 135, 141–143, 195, 635, 640, 643, 646, 652, 653, 663, 672, 676, 677, 681, 689, 693, 695, 696, 698, 707, 709, 713, 715, 716, 717, 718, 719, 721, 724

C

C.B.S. Radio Workshop 40
C.P.O. Sharkey 564
Caan, James 475
The Cabin 105, 366, 481
Cabot, Sebastian 447, 469
Cady, Frank 386, 387, 388, 393, 401, 416, 422, 426, 575
Caesar and Cleopatra 679
The Cage 270, 655
Cagney, James 476
Cagney and Lacey 113, 460, 475, 613
Cahill, Barry 524, 543, 693
Cain 364, 367, 468, 500
Caine, Howard 506
The Caine Mutiny 364, 463, 552
The Caine Mutiny Court Martial 149, 175
Cain's Hundred 192, 627

Cale 539, 541, 555
Caleb 565
Calhoun, Rory 348, 584
The Californians 447, 463, 557, 651
Call, Anthony 609
Call, Ed 707
Call Me Dodie 541, 556
Call of the Forest 117
Callahan, Pepe 663, 677
Callaway, Bill 654, 655
Calomee, Gloria 650
Calvin and the Colonel 363
Cameron, Todd 691
Camile 560
Camp, Helen Page 694, 701
Camp Runamuck 578, 659
Campanella, Joseph 163, 307, 629, 688
Campbell, William 534
Campos, Raphael 587, 602
Canary, David 614
Can Can 373
Cangey, Dick 673
Cannon 40, 254, 361
Cannon, Dyan 575, 576
Cannon, J.D. 574, 648
Cannon, Kathy 703
Cannonball 476
The Cannonball Run 115
Captain Kidd 560
Captain Nice 560, 678
Captain Sligo 183, 270, 665, 697
Captain Video and His Video Rangers 557
Captive 139
Cara 284, 380, 457
Carbine Williams 451
Cardi, Pat 591, 610
The Cardinal 582, 668
Cardinal, Tantoo 723
Cardona, Annette 663
Carey, Harry, Jr. 163, 271, 501, 520, 542, 545, 581, 622, 634, 671, 677, 708
Carey, Michele 679
Carey, Philip 674
Carey, Tim 486, 606
Carlin, Lynn 688
Carlino, Joann 702
Carlson, Steve 163–164, 270, 655

Carmen 342, 361, 426, 485
Carneol, Jess 645, 649, 654
Carney, Thom 445
The Carol Burnett Show 595
Caron, Leslie 262
Carr, Michael 543
Carr, Paul 164–165, 297, 530, 592
Carr, Richard 578, 600, 602, 619, 639
Carr, Thomas 559
Carradine, David 165, 668
Carradine, John 449, 501, 668
Carrie 486, 577
Carrillo, Leo 19
Carroll, Angela 653
Carroll, Brandon 641
Carroll, Dee 658, 671
Carruthers, Ben 491
Carson, Sunset 496
Carter, Conlan 517, 529, 563, 629, 636
Carter, Don 700
Carter, John 613, 693
Carter Caper 282, 558
Carter Country 446
Caruso, Anthony 169, 475, 476, 515, 531, 533, 549, 555, 565, 568, 648, 667, 674, 686, 705, 718
Carver, Mary 165–166, 456, 488, 509, 554
Casablanca 559, 567, 577
Case, Allen 494, 567, 602
Casey, Lawrence 604, 605
Casey, Sue 545, 549
Cassell, Wally 102, 454
Cassidy, Jack 486
Cassie and Company 605, 689
The Cast 376, 417, 491
Cast a Long Shadow 46
Castillo, Gloria 449
Castle, Peggie 469
Cat Ballou 566, 668
Cat on a Hot Tin Roof 480
Cat People 551, 662
Cat Women of the Moon 674
Catawomper 349, 534, 541
Catching, Bill 501, 576, 644, 651, 674
Categorical Imperative 407
Cather, Willa 14
Cattanooga Cats 655

[799]

INDEX

Cattle Barons 616, 628
Cattle Town 96
Cavalcade 367, 429
Cavell, Marc 609
Cawelti, John G. 13
Celia 653, 656
Centennial 441, 512, 587, 597, 625
Challee, William 536, 668
The Challenge of the Yukon 52
Chamber of Horrors 361
Chambers, Phil 517, 690, 701
Chamberlain, Richard 512
Chambliss, Woodrow 150, 443, 476, 590, 596, 601, 604, 609, 611, 616, 624, 631, 637, 672, 707, 708, 710, 715, 724
Champagne for Caesar 476
The Champion 449
Champion of the World 339, 607
Chandler, James 667, 682, 691, 700, 706
Chandler, John Davis 324, 693, 709
Chandler, Lane 520, 531, 544, 604
Chaney, Lon, Jr. 54
Change of Heart 394, 497
Chaplain, Jack 633
Chaplin, Charlie 713
Chapman, David 454
Chapman, Lonny 313, 553, 591, 599
Charles, Harriet 721
Charles in Charge 678, 702
Charlie and Company 720
The Charlie Farrell Show 378, 451
Charlie Noon 135, 162, 646, 647, 656, 711
Charlie's Angels 144, 457
Charlotte's Web 636
Chase, Eric 661
Chase, Stephen 492
Chastain, Don 633, 634
Chato 135, 326, 657, 683, 711
Chavez, Jose 630
Cheap Labor 402, 470, 500
The Cheaters 605
Cheatham, Marie 663
Check It Out 542, 709
Chekhov, Michael 150

Cher 462, 645
Cherry Red 406, 513
Chesterland 206, 530
Chester's Choice 417
Chester's Dilemma 430, 526
Chester's Hanging 388, 485
Chester's Indian 539, 555
Chester's Inheritance 440
Chester's Mail Order Bride 165, 456, 473
Chester's Mistake 424
Chester's Murder 387, 469
Chester's Rendezvous 441
Cheyenne 17, 21, 108, 110, 209, 557
Cheyenne Autumn 449, 560
Cheyennes 388, 499
Chicago Teddy Bears 674
Chicken 574
Chicken Smith 409
Chico and the Man 645
Chief Joseph 578
The Child Between 704
Child Labor 412
Chiles, Linden 552
CHiPs 629, 666
The Chisholms 708
Chism 628
The Choice 339, 396, 421, 498
Cholera 386, 464, 500
Chomsky, Marvin 632, 633, 648
Choose Me 598
Christine, Virginia 53, 54, 359, 386, 388, 394, 395, 396, 400, 401, 404, 405, 407, 408, 409, 416, 417, 418, 419, 425, 426, 427, 429, 430, 431, 432, 433, 434, 436, 437, 439, 440, 477, 581
Christmas Story 38, 366
Christofer, Michael 713
Christopher, Eunice 166, 312, 564, 639
Cibber, Colley 679
Cimarron City 464, 576, 659
Cimarron Strip 144, 464
Cinderella Liberty 144, 574
The Circle Family 669
Circus Boy 518, 544, 562
Circus Trick 578
The Cisco Kid 15, 19, 226, 360
Citizen Kane 558, 586

City Heat 115
Clark, Bobby E. 616, 630, 632, 667, 710, 714
Clark, Ellen 503
Clark, Gage 444, 459, 465, 469, 478, 512, 516, 522
Clark, J.R. 700
Clark, Marian 3, 29, 35, 37, 39, 411, 412, 413, 414, 415, 416, 417, 418, 419, 420, 421, 422, 423, 424, 425, 426, 427, 428, 429, 430, 431, 432, 433, 434, 435, 436, 437, 438, 439, 440, 441, 494, 499, 501, 504, 505, 506, 508, 509, 513, 514, 515, 516, 517, 520, 521, 538, 549, 550
Clark, Walter Van Tilburg 16
Clarke, Angela 542, 552, 568
Clarke, Gary 538
Clarke, John 503, 548, 553
Claustrophobia 382, 480, 527
Claxton, William F. 579
Clayton, Jan 567, 583
Clayton Thaddeus Greenwood 587, 598
Cleavus 667, 683
Clements, Calvin 3, 113, 126, 135, 137, 141, 142, 147, 574, 577, 583, 584, 587, 590, 593, 594, 596, 604, 605, 609, 617, 619, 620, 624, 625, 627, 629, 630, 633, 634, 635, 638, 640, 641, 643, 644, 645, 646, 647, 648, 649, 650, 651, 652, 653, 654, 655, 657, 658, 659, 660, 661, 662, 663, 664, 665, 666, 667, 668, 669, 680, 682, 687, 690, 692, 693, 702, 703, 704, 709
Clements, Calvin, Jr. 607, 624, 626, 673
Clements, Stanley 507, 638, 661, 692
Clinton, Robert 724
Climax 48
Close, John 495, 508, 516

[800]

Index

Close Encounters of the Third Kind 697
Clue 598
Clute, Sid 460
Clyde, Andy 491, 537
The Clyde Beatty Show 47
Coates, Phyllis 481, 569
Cobb, Julie 166-167, 331, 336, 702, 717
Cobb, Lee J. 166, 167, 336, 702, 717
Coby, Fred 541, 562, 580, 598, 604, 606, 611, 632, 635, 652, 663
Cockrell, Francis 604
Cocoon 647
Code R 560
Code Red 480
Cody, Iron Eyes 631
Cody, Kathleen 698, 709, 718
Cody, William F. 14
Cody's Code 533, 556
Cogan, Rhodie 705
Coghlan, Phyllis 622
Cohoon, Patti 674, 678, 684, 688, 707
Colby, Barbara 714
Colby, Fred 616
The Colbys 571, 657
Cold Fire 408
Cole, Michael 600, 601
Coleman, Ronald 476
Coley, Thomas 474, 506
Colgate Theater 679
Colicos, John 720
Colla, Dick 607
Colleen So Green 36, 408, 510
Collier, Don 707
Collier, Sue 614
Collie's Free 543, 570
Collins, Georgie 724
Colman, Booth 548, 681
Colmans, Edward 679
Colon, Miriam 535, 549, 629, 646, 657, 684, 707
The Colonel 167, 331, 716
The Color of Money 581
Colorado Sheriff 527
Colt .45 109
Columbia Radio Players 59
Columbo 113
Coma 652
Comanches Is Soft 565

Combat 517, 545, 556, 569, 618
Combs, Gary 644, 667
Come Back Little Sheba 551
Come Next Spring 505
Comer, Anjanette 559
Coming Home 587, 606
Compton, John 480
Confederate Money 379
Conger, Juli 374
Congressional Record 28
Conley, Darlene 659
Connelly, Christopher 568, 569, 700
Conner, Betty 333, 573
Connors, Chuck 455
Connors, Mike (Touch) 462
Conrad, Charles 469
Conrad, Joseph 24
Conrad, Michael 573, 574, 594, 603
Conrad, William 3, 11, 23, 24, 25, 26, 27, 28, 31, 33, 36, 39, 40-42, 43, 44, 45, 51, 52, 53, 60, 62, 63, 65, 66, 67, 76, 83, 106, 107, 180, 209, 220, 221, 222-223, 234, 235, 237, 240, 241, 246, 249, 254, 255, 256, 352, 359, 361, 362, 371, 553, 665, 698
Conried, Hans 56, 71, 363
Considine, Charlotte 629
Considine, Tim 660
The Constable 380, 431, 499
Constantine, Michael 331, 554, 626
The Contender 608, 634
The Conversation 535
Convoy 446
Conway, Pat 446, 480, 490, 693
Coogan, Jackie 713
Coogan, Richard 556, 557
The Cook 195, 343, 437, 518
Cook, Elisha 175, 487, 504, 573, 581
Cook, Perry 511
Cook, Tommy 417
Cool Hand Luke 449, 481, 515, 600, 628
Coolidge, Philip 490, 491, 534, 577

Cooper, Ben 167, 297, 531, 580, 584
Cooper, Charles 485, 492
Cooper, Clancy 472
Cooper, Gary 74, 76, 86
Cooper, Jackie 448
Cooper, James Fenimore 13
Cooper, Jeanne 167-168, 297, 559
Cooper, Kevin 633
Cooter 300, 386, 440, 454, 473
Corbett, Glenn 571, 671, 705
Corbett, Gretchen 351, 712
Corcoran, Noreen 566
Cord, Alex 168, 275, 689
Corden, Henry 486
Cordic, Rege 685, 690, 695, 716
Cordova, Anthony 663
Cordova, Margarita 646, 651
Corey, Jeff 168-169, 190, 312, 640
Coreyville 279, 644, 656
Corner, Sally 449
Cornthwaite, Robert 475, 668
The Correspondent 420
Corrigan, Lloyd 560
Corry, Will 550, 580
Corsault, Aneta 582, 613
Corsentino, Frank 671, 705
Cos, Vickie 566
Costello, Anthony 660, 668
Costello, Dolores 578
Cotter's Girl 180, 275, 548, 570
Cotton, Heather 671
Coughlin, Kevin 638, 644, 661, 696, 720
Courage Is a Gun 109
The Court Martial of General George Armstrong Custer 687
Court of Last Resort 444, 459, 476, 565
The Courtship of Eddie's Father 686
The Cousin 549
Coventry 536, 570
The Cover Up 381, 465

[801]

INDEX

The Covered Wagon 15
Covered Wagon Days 55
Cow Doctor 391, 411, 458, 487
The Coward 395, 421, 495
Coward of the County 578
The Cowboy in Africa 592
Cowboy Serenade 18
The Cowboys 667, 684
Cows and Cribs 340, 401, 441, 477
Cowtown Hustler 324, 347, 709, 711
Crack-Up 389, 437, 473, 514
Craig, Ed 694
Crane, Norma 495, 528
Crane, Stephen 14
Cranston, Joe 368, 370, 372, 384, 385, 387, 388, 389, 392, 396
Crawford, Bobby 597
Crawford, John 502, 538, 549, 584, 634, 635, 648, 650, 667, 677, 699, 712
Crawford, Johnny 597
Crazy Beulah 186
The Creature from the Black Lagoon 373
Crenna, Richard 56, 59, 416, 418, 419, 429, 440, 441
Crime Story 534
Crime with Father 590
Crooked Mile 271, 290, 314, 571
Crosland, Alan, Jr. 522
Cross, Dennis 451, 459, 500, 508, 559, 621, 639
Cross, Jimmy 486, 591
Crossing Paris 24, 29
Crossroads 360
Crowbait Bob 405, 510
Cruickshanks, Reid 690
Crump, Percy 150, 444, 527
Crutchfield, Les 3, 11, 24, 29, 35, 36–37, 39, 111, 113, 116, 120, 142, 193, 360, 361, 362, 363, 364, 365, 366, 367, 368, 372, 392, 393, 394, 396, 404, 405, 406, 407, 408, 409, 410, 411, 412, 413, 414, 415, 416, 417, 418, 419, 420, 449, 450, 459, 464,
466, 479, 487, 488, 489, 490, 492, 493, 494, 496, 501, 502, 503, 504, 505, 506, 507, 508, 509, 510, 511, 512, 513, 544, 546, 563, 565, 568, 571, 576, 579, 581, 588, 597, 598, 607, 609, 613
Cruz, Brandon 686
Cruze, James 15
Cry Terror 54
Culp, Robert 573
Culver, Howard 25, 102, 150, 378, 422, 424, 425, 443, 444, 453, 457, 463, 469, 474, 516, 522, 537, 554, 572, 582, 588, 592, 609, 614, 637, 652, 660, 675, 690, 708
Cummings, Susan 516
Cupito, Suzanne 554
Curley, Leo 375
Currie, Red 673
Curry, Mason 452, 460
Curtis, Billy 692
Curtis, Craig 623
Curtis, Jack 545
Curtis, Ken 3, 91, 115, 116–118, 122, 134, 148, 159, 163, 176, 204, 208, 209, 210, 303, 304, 305, 306, 308, 309, 314, 317, 323, 328, 330, 334, 338, 443, 493, 497, 510, 511, 512, 546, 556, 562, 563, 580, 587, 595, 679, 682, 715, 724
Curtwright, Jorga 284, 457
Custer 376, 412, 459
Cutter to Houston 695
Cyclone 368
Cyclops 139
Cyrano de Bergerac 128

D

The D.A. 702
The D.A.'s Man 364, 480
D.O.A. 555, 588
Dackow, Joseph 153, 616, 617, 618, 619, 620, 621, 622, 623, 624, 625, 626, 627, 629, 630, 631, 632, 633, 634, 635, 636, 637,
638, 639, 640, 641, 642, 643, 644, 645, 646, 647, 648, 649, 650, 651, 652, 653, 654, 655, 656, 657, 658, 659, 660, 661, 662, 663, 664
Daddy Went Away 337, 554
Daddy-O 401, 439, 472
Dakota Lil 674
Dakota Story 135
Daktari 485, 609, 675
Dale, Fred 606
Dales, Arthur 648, 675, 717
Dallas 113, 144, 153, 197, 575, 586, 594, 599, 628, 637, 644, 653, 662, 665, 677, 687, 702, 708, 710, 720
Dalton, Abby 448
Dalton, Audrey 548
Daly, James 612, 613
Daly, Tyne 613
D'Anda, Michael 535, 544
Damnation Alley 628
Dan August 542
Dangerous 601
Dangerous Bath 435
Dangerous Mission 88
Daniel Boone 144, 593
Daniels, Lisa 262
Daniels, Marc 589, 594, 595, 599, 605, 607, 611, 612
Dann, Michael 123, 124
Danny 645, 656
The Danny Kaye Show 551
The Danny Thomas Show 363
Dano, Royal 169, 314, 445, 446, 455, 565, 571, 577, 593, 617, 618, 643, 654, 665, 671
Dante 455
Danton, Joan 363
Darby, Kim 194, 211, 332, 611, 612, 617
Darfler, Gene 555
Dark, Christopher 544
The Dark at the Top of the Stairs 581
Dark Victory 602
Darrell, Steven 586
Darrow, Henry 607, 608, 613
Darvi, Andrea 566
A Date with the Angels 456, 459, 596

[802]

Index

A Date with Judy 441
Daugherty, Herschel 635, 642
Davalos, Ellen 626
Dave's Lesson 431
David, Brad 651
David Copperfield 700
Davis, Bette 99, 123, 133, 194, 212, 310, 594, 601, 602
Davis, Gail 19
Davis, Harry 590, 638
Davis, Jim 594, 598, 602, 626, 630, 633, 663, 667, 695, 706
Davis, Michael 591
Davis, Tony 622, 663
Davison, Davey 577
Davy Crockett, Indian Fighter 20
Dawson, Tom 125
Day, Gerry 659
Day of the Dolphin 46, 610
The Day of the Locust 589
Days of Our Lives 55, 366, 503, 518, 548, 593, 657, 688
Dayton, June 169, 483, 567, 574, 662
Deacon, Richard 378, 465
Deadline 656
The Deadly Innocent 133, 704, 710
Deadman's Law 144, 623, 628
Deadrick, Vincent 650
The Dealer 538
Dean Martin Presents the Golddiggers 653
The Death of Billy the Kid 21
Death Ray 2000 679
Death Train 620, 628
Death Valley Days 15
Death Watch 313, 593
Death Wish 454, 612
The Debbie Reynolds Show 479, 618, 634
DeBenning, Jeff 535
De Broux, Lee 618, 625, 632, 634, 648, 718
December Bride 65, 662
The Decks Ran Red 49
DeCorsia, Ted 535
DeCost, Robert 449
Decoy 555
The Deerslayer 13

The Defenders 121, 479, 537
The Defiant Ones 49, 579
De France, Michael S. 699
Deger, Lawrence 10
De Haven, Gloria 705, 706
Dehner, John 16, 17, 24, 25, 46, 51, 59, 70, 164, 169, 216, 325, 359, 361, 363, 364, 365, 366, 367, 368, 369, 370, 371, 372, 373, 374, 375, 376, 377, 378, 379, 380, 381, 382, 383, 384, 385, 386, 387, 388, 389, 390, 391, 392, 393, 394, 395, 396, 397, 398, 399, 400, 401, 402, 403, 404, 405, 406, 407, 408, 409, 410, 411, 412, 413, 414, 415, 416, 417, 418, 419, 420, 421, 430, 433, 434, 435, 436, 437, 438, 439, 440, 441, 452, 472, 473, 483, 543, 549, 566, 582, 623
DeKova, Frank 462, 463, 466, 468, 488, 501, 517, 530
Delaney, Laurence 679
Delevanti, Cyril 450, 462, 483, 521, 576, 594
Delia's Father 430
The Delicate Delinquent 608
Deliverance 115, 542, 606, 718
della Cioppa, Guy 25, 26, 65
Delta House 719
De Meyer, Margie 633
DeMille, Cecil B. 17
Demyan, Lincoln 586
Dennis the Menace 54, 150, 363, 384, 485, 558, 568
Dennis-Leigh, Pat 673
The Dennis O'Keefe Show 690
Denton, Crahan 531, 550
DePalma, Brian 465
The Depression 15, 93, 226
The Deputy 165, 493, 494
Deputy Festus 577, 585
Dern, Bruce 140, 174, 194, 310, 587, 591, 601, 639
Dert D'Angelo/Superstar 629
DeSantis, Joe 445, 466, 626, 629
The Deserter 513

The Desilu Playhouse 113
Desilu-Westinghouse Playhouse 128
Desire in the Dust 605
Desire Under the Elms 501
Desperate Hours 445, 555
Destry 501, 564
Destry Rides Again 17
Detective School 644, 694
Detective Story 445, 621
The Detectives 452, 466, 561, 570
Devane, William 695
De Vargas, Valentin 610, 643
The Devil at 4 O'Clock 535
The Devil's Angels 148
The Devil's Double 14
Devil's Hindmost 407
The Devil's Outpost 279, 643, 656
Devine, Andy 19, 198, 341, 643, 644
Devlin, Joe 534
Devon, Richard 555, 559
Dexter, Alan 485, 557
Dexter, Joy 647
Diamond, Don 19, 359, 360, 361, 362, 388, 391, 405, 412, 429
Diamond, Jack 460
Diamond Head 597
Diana 672, 678
The Diary of Anne Frank 685
Di Cenzo, George 169-170, 703, 718
The Dick Van Dyke Show 113, 378, 465, 477, 478, 479
Dickens, Charles 33
Dickinson, Angie 465
Dierkes, John 460, 466, 675, 704
Dierkop, Charles 595, 605, 704
Dillaway, Dana 622
Dillinger 491, 604
Di Reda, Joe 689
Dirkson, Douglas 712
Dirt 186, 282, 372, 437, 481
Dirty Bill's Girl 405
The Dirty Dozen 455, 551
Dirty Sally 53, 144, 153, 192, 305, 361, 475, 662, 665, 669, 681
Disciple 343, 710

[803]

INDEX

Disneyland 20, 108, 370
Disorderly Orderly 688
Distant Drummer 431, 517
The Ditch 543
Dix, Robert 531
Dixon, Gloria 708
Do Not Go Gentle into That Good Night 49
Do You Remember Love 658
The Do-Badder 533
Dobbins, Bennie 681
Dobbs, Frank Q. 584, 596
Dobie Gillis 150
Dobkin, Lawrence 16, 24, 25, 38, 45, 46, 48–49, 59, 61, 236, 247, 359, 360, 361, 362, 363, 364, 365, 366, 367, 368, 369, 370, 371, 372, 373, 374, 375, 376, 377, 378, 379, 380, 381, 382, 383, 384, 385, 386, 387, 388, 389, 390, 391, 392, 393, 394, 395, 396, 397, 398, 399, 400, 401, 402, 403, 404, 405, 406, 407, 408, 409, 412, 413, 416, 417, 418, 419, 420, 421, 422, 423, 425, 426, 427, 428, 429, 430, 431, 432, 434, 435, 437, 438, 439, 440, 441, 455, 467, 516
Dobson, James 474
Doc 125
Doc Holliday 362
Doc Judge 436, 508
Doc Quits 393, 494
Doc's Indians 425
Doc's Showdown 419
Doc's Revenge 397, 455, 473
Doc's Reward 400, 477, 527
Doc's Visitor 441
Dr. Christian 55
Dr. Detroit 43
Doctor Herman Schultz, M.D. 651, 656
Dr. Jekyll and Mr. Hyde 597
Dr. Kate 55
Dr. Kildare 53, 512, 690
Dr. Paul 47
Dr. Simon Locke 630, 678
Dr. Six-Gun 16
Dr. Strangelove... 563
The Doctors 538, 582, 659
Doctor's Hospital 597
Doctor's Wife 572

Dodd, Barbara 473
Dodd, Thomas J. 130
Dodge City 226, 467
Dodge City Killer 360
Dodge Podge 410
Dog and Cat 592
A Dog of Flanders 589
Dolan, John 630
The Don Knott's Show 46, 611
Don Matteo 429, 516
The Donna Reed Show 466
Donner, Robert 627, 628
Don't Call Me Charlie 583
Doohan, James 542
Dooley Surrenders 384, 482
Doorway to Danger 398, 665
Doorway to Life 59
DoQui, Robert 638, 640
The Doris Day Show 46, 151, 444, 464, 555, 683
Dorsey, Tom 116
The Dotty Mack Show 690
Double Entry 294, 576
The Double Life of Henry Phyfe 43
Doubtful Zone 408
Doucette, John 472
Doud, Gil 39, 405, 459, 462, 466, 467, 470
Douglas, Burt 491, 521, 526
Douglas, Doc 523
Douglas, George 496
Douglas, Jerry 586
Douglas, Warren 618
Dove, Delmer 16
Dowager's Visit 52, 425
Down and Out in Beverly Hills 697
Downs, Frederic 602, 608
Doyle, Robert 543
Dozier, Deborah 703
Dozier, William 76, 77, 79
Dragnet 47, 53, 54, 55, 175, 215, 360, 460, 662
Drago 676, 683
The Drak Pack 655
Drake, James 562
Drake, Ken 473, 618, 631
Drake, Tom 648
The Dreamers 310, 538
Dressed to Kill 465
Dressler, Lieux 170, 275, 672, 681, 698
Drew, Frances 379

Dreyfuss, Richard 132, 696, 697
Drop Dead 364
The Drummer 331, 340, 686, 697
Drury, James 192, 449, 497, 501, 523
Dry Road to Nowhere 296, 581, 585
Dry Well 561
Dubbins, Don 170–171, 311, 340, 501, 531, 532, 562
DuBov, Paul 56, 359, 360, 361, 362, 363, 365, 367, 368, 370, 374, 376, 379, 382, 384, 388, 391, 393, 395, 401, 402, 403, 404, 424, 455, 549
Duel in the Sun 16, 150
Dufour, Val 171–172, 336, 450, 452, 532
Duggan, Andrew 461, 470, 583
Duggan, Bob 616
Duke, John 543
The Dukes of Hazzard 404, 464, 539, 552
Dull Knife 11
Dullaghan, John 663, 674
Dulo, Jane 172, 339, 607
du Maurier, Daphne 24
The Dumplings 594
Dunaway, Faye 633
Duncan, Angus 690
Duncan, Craig 482, 519
Dundee and the Culhane 596
Dunkel, John 3, 24, 29, 35, 37, 39, 41, 56, 59, 66, 69, 111, 113, 120, 393, 394, 396, 397, 399, 400, 405, 416, 421, 423, 447, 448, 452, 453, 454, 455, 456, 458, 459, 463, 465, 469, 530, 531, 537, 538, 544, 552, 562, 568, 569, 572, 620
Dunlap, Pamela 648, 660
Dunn, Gregg 520
Dunn, Liam 678
Dunn, Peter 576
DuPont Show of the Month 496, 522
Duran, Larry 686
Durango Kid 17
Durham Bull 537

Index

Durkin, Mike 632, 646
Dutch George 396, 455
DuVal, Joe 363, 364, 365, 372, 373, 380, 385, 388, 389, 392, 394, 398, 400
Dynasty 366, 534, 618, 627, 703, 708

E

Eagle, James 377
Eagle in a Cage 613
Earl, Wallace 693
Earp, Wyatt 10, 11, 14, 34, 109
East of Eden 709
East Side/West Side 662
Easton, Robert 172-173, 271, 386, 387, 448
Eastwood, Clint 128, 210, 628
Easy Come 557
Easy Come Easy Go 113
Easy Rider 578
Easy Street 503, 540, 577
Eberg, Victor 664
Ebsen, Buddy 519, 529, 676
Eckstein, George 572, 587
The Ed Sullivan Show 110
The Ed Wynn Show 367, 662
Eden, Barbara 476, 597
The Edie Adams Show 634
Edington, Lyn 600
Edmiston, Walker 653, 654, 666, 694, 701
Edmonds, Scott 667
Edwards, Jack 375, 378, 395, 421
Edwards, Paul F. 135-138, 139, 141, 142, 326, 657, 658, 691, 700, 702
Edwards, Sam 24, 51-52, 62, 216, 245, 359, 360, 361, 366, 367, 368, 369, 371, 372, 373, 374, 376, 377, 379, 380, 381, 383, 384, 385, 386, 388, 389, 390, 391, 392, 393, 394, 396, 397, 398, 399, 400, 404, 406, 408, 409, 412, 416, 418, 419, 420, 421, 422, 423, 424, 425, 427, 428, 429, 430, 431, 432, 433, 434, 435, 436, 437, 438, 439, 440, 441, 485, 492, 590, 643, 649
Eight Iron Men 54
Eight Is Enough 113, 363, 636, 678, 693
87th Precinct 589
Eilbacher, Bob 665
Eilbacher, Lisa 695, 722
Eiler, Barbara 430
Eischied 678
Eisenhower, Dwight D. 109
Eisenmann, Ike 687, 688, 693, 706
El Dorado 226
Elam, Jack 173, 198, 344, 493, 503, 509, 521, 569, 573, 587, 590, 599, 626, 650, 667, 678, 684
Elcar, Dana 660
Eldridge, George 522
The Electric Horseman 582
Eleven Dollars 687
Eleventh Hour 126, 605, 621
Elfego Bay 668
Eliab's Aim 580, 585
Elias, Louis 682, 701, 724
Eliasberg, Jay 124
Ellenstein, Robert 456
Ellery Queen 48, 150
Elliot, Ross 506, 511
Elliot, Sam 682
Elliot, Wild Bill 17, 168
Ellis, Antony 16, 24, 25, 29, 35, 37-38, 39, 236, 243, 246, 254, 362, 363, 365, 366, 368, 369, 560, 576, 627
Ellis, David 39, 364
Ellis, Georgia 3, 24, 26, 38, 42, 44-45, 53, 59, 61, 63, 64, 69, 97, 107, 216, 223, 237, 240, 241, 244, 248, 251, 256, 359, 360, 362, 388, 429, 435, 438
Ellis, Herb 236, 243, 360, 362, 364, 376, 377, 381, 386, 430
Ellsworth, Steve 478
Elmer Gantry 365, 590
Elson, Donald 693, 703
Ely, Richard 717
Emerald Point N.A.S. 578
Emerson, Alan 470, 603
Emery, Matt 620, 639, 665
Emhardt, Robert 506, 632
Emma's Departure 426
Emmett, Michael 464
Emmy Award 21, 49, 90, 94, 96, 113, 144, 166, 191, 360, 449, 454, 462, 466, 477, 479, 481, 490, 499, 532, 548, 554, 556, 571, 573, 574, 581, 587, 591, 592, 603, 613, 614, 619, 622, 623, 625, 631, 644, 645, 647, 651, 657, 658, 662, 665, 685, 686, 693, 699, 707, 713
Empire of the Ants 589
Engle, Paul 481, 489
Engle, Roy 456, 465, 496, 516, 533, 660
English, John W. 557, 560
Engstrom, Jena 531, 539
Ensign O'Toole 566, 595
Ensign Pulver 126, 148
Ensley, Harold 577
Enter Laughing 378
Epper, Tony 724
The Equalizer 589
Erickson, Leif 608
Ericson, John 636
Erlenborn, Ray 430
Erwin, Stuart 594
Erwin, William 476, 567, 618, 627, 631, 644, 655, 682, 693
Escape 24, 36, 38, 40, 44, 46, 50, 51, 59, 221, 370, 389, 465
Evans, Dale 18
Evans, Evan 529
Evans, Gene 339, 560, 618, 626, 660, 671, 689, 707, 713
Evans, Linda 488
Evans, Richard 173-174, 313, 508, 586, 593, 616
Evers, Jason 536, 543, 575
Ewing, Diana 649
Ewing, Roger 122, 126-127, 211-213, 309, 443, 579, 587
Ex-Con 297, 559
The Executioner 400, 466, 500
Executive Suite 459, 505, 674
Exodus 717
Exodus 21:22 641, 642

INDEX

The Exorcist 538, 671
Experiment in Terror 483
Extradition 335, 559
Ex-Urbanites 116, 440, 510
Eyer, Richard 504

F

The F.B.I. 114, 490, 557, 658, 669
F Troop 360, 463, 555, 577
The F.U. 384, 495
The Fabulous Baker Boys 595
Fabulous Silver Extender 433
The Facts of Life 462, 679
Fadden, Tom 658, 659
Fahey, Myrna 484
Fail Safe 610, 688
Fair Exchange 561
The Falcon 567
Falcon Crest 113, 367, 612, 613, 616, 620, 708
Falk, Tom 695
The Fall Guy 500, 579
Fall Semester 371
False Front 546
False Witness 418, 505
Fame 113, 622, 722
Family 457, 558
Family Affair 132, 151, 447, 611
A Family of Killers 704, 711
Fancher, Hampton 519, 545, 581
Fandango 610
Fantasia 46
Fantastic Journey 153, 688
Fantasy Island 366, 657
The Far Country 644
The Far Places 552, 570
Faraday and Company 594
Faralla, William Dario 526
Faraway Hill 439
A Farewell to Arms 671
The Farmer's Daughter 81, 126, 491, 564, 577, 685
Farrell, Sharon 552, 558, 568
Farrell, Tommy 485
Fatal Attraction 513
Father and Son 440
Father Knows Best 55, 56, 363, 446, 465, 530
Father Murphy 485, 618

Father of the Bride 484, 492, 586
Father's Love 565
Faulkner, Edward 495, 509, 676, 690
The Favor 612
Favor, Gil 534
Fawcett, William 505, 550, 559, 646, 651, 658
Fawn 375, 496
Fax, Jesslyn 548
Fay 621, 690
Felony Squad 54, 360, 460, 638
Fenneman, George 28
Fenwick, Jean 478
Ferdin, Pamelyn 635
Fernandez, Abel 461, 479, 502
Fernwood 2-Night 610
Ferrante, Joseph 535
Ferrone, Dan 624, 626, 641, 647, 677, 698
Feud 381
Fibber McGee and Molly 366
Fiedler, John 175, 296, 576, 694
Field, Daphne 654
Field, Gustave 583, 593
Field, Mary 507, 536
Field, Sally 603
Fielder, Richard 637, 678, 686, 705
Fielding, Joy 634
Fields, Jerelyn 662
Fiery Arrest 430
Figueroa, Laura 655
Fine, Mort 25
Fingered 365, 477
Finian's Rainbow 702
Finley, Larry 665, 696
Firecreek 123, 125, 129, 593
Firehouse 651
The Fires of Ignorance 133, 178, 337, 718, 719, 723
Firestone, Eddie 175, 342, 597, 614, 629, 635, 677
The First Ladies Diaries: Martha Washington 713
The First People 626
Fischer, Bruce M. 719
Fisher, Michael 603
Fisher, Nancy 690
Fisher, Shug 539, 563, 567, 577, 586, 602, 610, 627, 633, 635, 647, 659,

666, 672, 694, 713
Fitz and Bones 607
Fitzgerald, F. Scott 72
Fix, Paul 464, 569, 587, 610, 617
The Flamingo Kid 441
Flamingo Road 653
Flanagan, Fionnula 175–176, 331, 686
Flashback 372
Fleming, Eric 120
Flight to Tangier 75
Flinn, John 652, 659
Flippen, Jay C. 566
Flipper 644
Flo 691
Flory, Med 176, 275, 664, 712
Flower, Amber 589
The Flying Nun 591, 597, 630, 677
Flynn, Dan, Jr. 675, 678
Flynn, Gertrude 505, 621
Flynn, Joe 495, 545
Foch, Nina 176, 279, 644
Foley, Brian 665
Follow the Sun 452, 575, 594
Fonda, Henry 86, 129, 144, 149, 175, 498, 574
Fonda, James 39, 415, 483
Fonda, Jane 574
Fontaine, Joan 67
For a Few Dollars More 513
For Love and Honor 662
For the People 606
Foran, Dick 552
Forbes, Scott 108
Forbidden Planet 687
Ford, Constance 464, 537
Ford, Harrison 689, 694
Ford, John 15, 16, 113, 117, 659
Ford, Ross 463
Ford Star Jubilee 446, 447, 448, 449, 451, 452, 453, 455
Ford Theater 364, 589
Foreign Intrigue 613
Forest, Michael 549, 575, 581
Forrest, Steve 637, 654, 690, 700, 723
Fort Apache 552
Fort Laramie 16, 38, 47, 389

Index

Forte, Joe 384
Fortier, Robert 547, 567
40 Pounds of Trouble 658
48 Hours 662, 716
Foster, Diane 536
Foster, Jodie 649, 678, 680
Foster, Linda 576
Foster, Ron 525, 532
Foulger, Byron 545, 607
Foulk, Robert 446
The Foundling 143, 270, 706, 711
The Four Horsemen of the Apocalypse 373
The Four Seasons 481
The Fourth Victim 342, 715, 722
Fowler, Gene, Jr. 522
Fowley, Douglas V. 694
The Fox 144, 574
Fox, Craig 509
Fox, Michael 176-177, 282, 559, 595, 618
Foxes 649
Foy, Eddie 9, 210
Francis, Anne 177, 285, 549, 686, 687
Francisco, Charles 601
The Frank Sinatra Show 634
Frankenheimer, Frank 35
Frankenstein, Jr. and the Impossibles 366
Franz, Arthur 513
Franz, Eduard 453, 716
Fraulein 621
Frawley, James 573
Frazer, Elizabeth 597
Frederic, Norman 469
Fredericks, Charles 491, 492, 496, 513, 547, 644
Freebie and the Bean 50
Freed, Bert 495, 589
Freeman, Jack 691
Freeman, Joan 544, 545
Frees, Paul 361, 369, 370, 376, 377
French, Ted 177, 600, 609, 643
French, Victor 86, 145-147, 166, 177-178, 179, 186, 195, 198, 292, 595, 599, 608, 617, 619, 625, 630, 631, 634, 653, 674, 681, 686, 696, 699, 712, 714, 715, 718, 719, 720, 722

Fresco, David 641
Friebus, Florida 699, 700
Friedkin, David 25
Friend 562
Friendly Fire 718
Friendly Persuasion 445
Friends 710
Friends Payoff 426, 514
Frings, Kurt 77
From Here to Eternity 463, 665, 695
Front Page 468
Front Row Center 368
Frontier 21
Frontier Gentleman 16, 38, 46, 444
Frontier Justice 617
Frost, Alice 511
Frost, Terry 603, 604
Frosty the Snowman 703
Froug, William 430
Fudge, Allan 678
The Fugitive 40, 114, 493
The Fugitive Kind 531
The Fugitives 687
Fulkerson, Elaine 712
Fuller, Clem 444, 502, 503, 504, 505, 508, 510, 512, 514, 519, 520
Funny Girl 687
Furillo, Bud 552
Fury 597

G

G.E. Theater 141
Gable, Clark 74
Gaffney, Anne 61
Gaily, Gaily 595
Gaines, Mel 603
The Gale Storm Show 151, 531
Galindo, Nacho 630
Gallagher, Mel 576
The Gallant Men 654
Gallo, Lew 489, 503, 595, 612
Galloping Dynamite 17
The Galloping Kid 17
The Gallows 535, 556
The Gambler 405
A Game of Death...An Act of Love 349, 701, 702, 711
Games 571
Gammon, Jim 703

Ganzer, Alvin 593, 626
Garas, Kaz 641, 642
Garcia, Stella 679
Gardenia, Vincent 612
Gardner, Alycia 641
Gardner, Ava 54
Garfield, Allen 178, 337, 718, 719
Garfield, John 53, 532
Garland, Beverly 178-179, 285, 554, 555, 623, 636, 652
Garner, Don 449
Garner, Jack 654, 661, 704
Garner, James 108, 548, 654
Garnett, Tay 187, 197, 532, 535, 597
Garralaga, Martin 626
Garrett, Leif 689
Garrett, Pat 10
Garrettson, Fannie 9
Garrison, Sean 596
Garrison's Gorillas 646
Garwood, Kelton 527, 545, 599
Gates, Nancy 540
Gates, Rick 676
Gatlin, Jerry 684, 700, 707
Gatteys, Bennye 552
Gavin, James 486
Gaynor, Steve 566
Gebert, Gordon 464
Geer, Will 631
Gehring, Ted 598, 599, 604, 617, 621, 696
Gehrman, Paul 714
The Gene Autry Show 18
General Hospital 151, 170, 500, 535, 549, 593, 657, 672, 710, 720
General Parcley Smith 392, 448, 487
Genest, Emile 555
Gentle Ben 91, 664, 665, 667, 689, 701
The Gentleman 379, 486
Gentlemen Marry Brunettes 645
Gentlemen Prefer Blondes 501
Gentlemen's Disagreement 362, 428, 511
Gentry, Robert 718
Gentry's Law 334, 659, 683
The George Burns and Gracie Allen Show 538

[807]

INDEX

Gerard, Merwin 551
Gere, Richard 578
Germaine, Elizabeth 630
Gerritsen, Lisa 633, 634, 636, 658, 664
Gerstle, Frank 362, 376, 380, 391
The Gertrude Berg Show 582
Gessler, Joan E. 701
Get Smart 446, 595, 607
The Getaway 447
The Ghost and Mrs. Muir 150
Giant 16, 464, 578, 671
The Giant Gila Monster 117
Gimme a Break 468, 607
Gibbsville 657, 715
Gibson, Hoot 17, 149, 168
Gibson, Mel 144
Gibson, Mike 496
Gielgud, Gwen Bagni 363, 549, 561, 599
Gielgud, John 520
Gierasch, Stefan 603
Gifford, Alan 489
The Gift of Love 54
Gigi 507
Gilbert, Melissa 685
Gilda 490
Gilden, Richard 447, 596
Gilford, Gwynne 666
Gilligan's Island 113, 125, 467, 524, 720
Gilman, Sam 600, 601, 612, 621
Gilt Guilt 583
Ging, Jack 179, 332, 605
Girardin, Ray 719, 720
A Girl Named Tamiko 596
The Girls 659
Gist, Robert 447, 448, 481, 488
Give 'Em Hell Harry 582
Glass, Ned 468, 469, 483, 510, 516, 562, 571, 641
Glass, Seamon 694
The Glass Slipper 96, 258, 262
Glaudi, Hap 575
Gleason, Jackie 153
Gleason, Tom 471
The Glory and the Mud 561
Glover, Bruce 644, 686
Glynis 699
Goddard, Mark 569, 570
Going Bad 381

Gold Mine 297, 592
Gold Town 625, 637, 642
Gold Train: The Bullet 95, 141, 342, 676, 677, 698
The Goldbergs 459, 471
Golden, Bob 667
The Golden Girls 43
Golden Globe Award 455
Golden Spur Award 360, 704
Goldrup, Roy 712
The Goldtakers 601, 615
Gomer Pyle, U.S.M.C. 529
Gomez, Thomas 679
Gone Straight 106, 324, 374, 466
Gone with the Wind 307, 527, 578
Gonif 369
The Good, the Bad, and the Ugly 513
Good Girl—Bad Company 395
Good Guys Wear Black 462
Good Men and True 14
Good Morning, World 569
The Good People 602, 615, 670
Good Sam 644
The Good Samaritans 343, 640, 642, 670
The Goodbye Girl 697
Goodwin, Harold 505, 510
Goodwins, Bobby 520
Gorcey, Leo 261
Gordon, Bruce 480, 487, 517
Gordon, Clark 422, 483
Gordon, Leo 102, 179, 266, 454, 518, 678, 694, 706
Gordon, Susan 523
Gough, Lloyd 598, 599
Gould, Harold 572, 713
Gould, Jack 28
The Governor and J.J. 582
The Graduate 500, 571
Graff, Wilton 451
Graham, Tim 404, 448, 469
The Grand Jury 565
Grandpa Goes to Washington 645
Granger, Michael 452
Grant, Barbara 700
Grant, Cary 506

Grant, Harvey 467
Grant, Kirby 19
Granville, Joan 595, 599
The Grapes of Wrath 498
Grass 372, 411, 490
The Grass Asp 420
Grassle, Karen 179–180, 714
Gravage, Robert 534, 536, 542, 549, 640
Gravers, Steve 602
Graves, Peter 80, 597
Gray, Charles 450, 457, 490, 526, 564
The Great Adventure 121, 128, 141
The Great Gatsby 587
The Great Gildersleeve 363, 441
The Great Scout and Cathouse Thursday 707
The Great Train Robbery 14, 17, 361
Greater Love 380, 431, 462, 487
The Greatest American Hero 573
The Greatest Show on Earth 141, 564, 583, 594
The Greatest Story Ever Told 597
Grebb Hassle 409
Green, Alex 724
Green, Dorothy 515, 533, 566
Green, Gilbert 537
Green, Lawrence 474
Green Acres 150, 151, 387, 497, 575, 683, 687
The Green Eyed Blonde 688
The Green Hornet 52, 599, 714
Greene, Michael 507, 601, 627, 673
Greene, Sam 622
Greenway, Tom 469, 476, 489, 519
Greer, Dabbs 150, 180, 347, 443, 454, 474, 492, 496, 503, 504, 508, 509, 510, 519, 525, 534, 548, 709
Gregg, Julie 667
Gregg, Virginia 16, 17, 24, 25, 46, 51, 53, 216, 237, 238, 359, 362, 363, 371,

[808]

Index

378, 381, 383, 385, 390, 391, 393, 394, 396, 399, 405, 407, 409, 410, 412, 414, 418, 420, 432, 433, 434, 435, 438, 441, 482, 483, 524, 525, 541, 544, 596, 636
Gregory, Fabian 679
Gregory, James 584, 585, 592, 623
Gregory, Mary 451
Grey, Duane 546, 551
Grey, Zane 14
Griffin, Robert 360, 469, 505
Griffith, Andy 153
Griffith, James 180, 343, 371, 447, 478, 550, 564, 626
Grimes, Gary 622
Grinnage, Jack 494, 517, 519, 596
The Grissom Gang 612
Groat's Grudge 422, 506
Groom, Sam 678, 704
Grossinger, Fred 501
The Group 537
Groves, Herman 643, 644, 719
Guare, John 181
Guess Who's Coming to Dinner 54
Guiding Light 482, 705
Guilfoyle, Paul 515
The Guitar 105, 377, 415, 456, 473
The Gun 296, 660, 697
Gun Crazy 578
Gun for a Coward 631
Gun for Chester 402, 473, 514
Gun Law 5
Gun Shy 691
Gun the Man Down 113
Gunfight at the OK Corral 184, 453, 564, 578
The Gunfighter 16, 226
Gunfighter, R.I.P. 603, 614, 656
Gung Ho! 93
Gunga Din 592
The Gunrunners 343, 625
The Guns of Cibola Blanca 312, 712, 713, 723
The Guns of Will Sonnett 367, 662

Gunshot Wound 405
Gunshy 108, 413
Gunslinger 450
Gunsmoke: Return to Dodge 5, 141, 152, 354, 637, 646, 652, 723
Gunsmoke Trail 220
Gunsmuggler 378, 488
Guth, Raymond 496, 541, 559
Guthrie, Tani Phelps 676
The Gypsum Hills Feud 390, 491
Gypsy 43

H

Hack Prine 102, 179, 266, 382, 453, 454
Hackett 655, 657
Hackett, Joan 537
Hagen, Earle 619
Hagen, Kevin 482, 483, 493, 519, 537, 554, 563, 623
Hagen, Ross 609, 631, 669
Hagerthy, Ron 458, 480
Haggard, H. Ryder 24
Haggerty, Don 557, 558
Hahn, Paul 512
Haid, Charles 705
Haig, Sid 605, 636, 646, 649
Hail to the Chief 469
Hairston, Jester 449
Hale, Alan 524, 607, 691
Hale, Barbara 96
Hale, Betsy 564
Hale, Bill 457
Hale, Chanin 668
Hale, Fiona 494
Hale, Monte 499, 630
Hale, Richard 627, 650, 678, 694
Hale, Scott 614, 618, 640
Half Straight 535, 555
Halferty, James 543
Hall, Bobby 649, 694, 703
Hall, Huntz 261
Hall, Thad 712
Hallenbeck, Daryl 620
Hallmark Hall of Fame 613, 687
Halls of Ivy 175
Halop, Billy 611

Halsey, Brett 266, 452
Hamilton, Dran 707
Hamilton, John 464
Hamilton, Joseph 511, 522, 539, 561
Hamilton, Lynn 641, 650
Hamilton, Margaret 694
Hamilton, Murray 469, 481, 490
Hamlet 520
Hammerhead 296, 576
Hammond, Nicholas 698, 699, 713
Hampton, Jim 555, 561, 580
Hand, Dora 9, 11
Hand in Hand 128
The Handcuffs 384
Hanek, John 562
Hang 'Em High 462, 567
The Hanging 607
Hanging Man 399, 484
The Hanging of Newly O'Brien 703
The Hanging Tree 53
Hangman's Mistake 440
Hangover Square 567
Hank 492, 576, 613
Hanks, Tom 603
Hanley, Tom 35, 39, 57, 62, 63, 243, 394, 410, 417, 420, 421, 423, 425, 433, 436, 461, 492, 564, 597
Hanmer, Don 603, 633
Happy, Don 595, 618, 641, 643
Happy Days 647, 675, 700
Hard Boiled 17
Hard, Fast and Beautiful 54
Hard Labor 695, 720, 723
Hard Lesson 429
Hard Luck Henry 189, 282, 307, 618, 628
Hard Virtue 438, 525
Hardin, Jerry 707
Hardin, Ty 108
Hardy, Sarah 641
The Hardy Boys 364, 676
Harens, Dean 169, 483
Harford, Betty 509
Harget, Link 608
Harmon, John 522
Harper, Jonathan 150, 444, 527, 624, 629, 645, 690

[809]

INDEX

Harper, Rand 506
Harper Valley, P.T.A. 625
Harper's Blood 529
Harriet 439, 522
Harrigan and Son 55, 373, 458
Harris, Berkeley 566, 589
Harris, Harry, Jr. 3, 113, 114, 146, 187, 202, 521, 522, 523, 524, 528, 529, 531, 532, 533, 534, 536, 537, 538, 539, 540, 541, 542, 543, 544, 545, 546, 547, 548, 549, 550, 551, 552, 554, 555, 556, 557, 558, 560, 562, 565, 566, 567, 568, 569, 571, 572, 573, 574, 575, 577, 583, 585, 588, 589, 596, 598
Harris, Jo Ann 644
Harris, Michael 522
Harris, Robert H. 459, 466
Harris, Stacy 398, 665
Harris Against the World 560, 628
Harrison, Jan 487, 491, 511, 519
Harrison, Rex 579
Harrower, Elizabeth 707, 709
Harry and Tonto 668
Harry-O 448, 608, 613, 625
Harry's Girls 639
Hart, Bill 596, 645, 681, 704
Hart, Tommy 453
Hart, William S. 14
Hart to Hart 101
Harte, Bret 13
Hartford, Dee 549
Hartley, Mariette 180, 275, 548, 574, 671, 685, 707
The Hartmans 459
Harum Scarum 590
Harvest 271, 597
Harvey, Harry, Sr. 619, 624, 632, 658, 677
Harvey, Phil 496
Hashim, Edmund 597, 607, 615, 623, 636, 646
A Hat 138, 217, 326, 617, 628, 656
Hatton, Raymond 508
Hausner, Jerry 368

Have Gun, Will Travel 17, 46, 51, 53, 108, 116, 117, 169, 187, 208, 245, 361, 444
Hawaii Five-O 153, 366, 478, 552, 598, 665, 671, 691
Hawaiian Eye 114, 495
Hawk 278, 542, 644, 645, 656
Hawk, Howard 465
Hawk Larabee 23, 239
Hawkins, Georgia 429
Hawn, Jack 639
Haworth, Joe 509, 534, 615, 643, 678
Hayden, Norah 533
Hayes, Helen 212, 598
Hayes, Ron 508, 522, 523, 543, 551, 591, 651, 660
Haymer, Johnny 632
Hayward, Chuck 490, 493, 528, 576
Hayward, Susan 50, 389, 506
Hayworth, Rita 490
Hayworth, Vinton 454, 474, 568
Hazel 496
He and She 177, 611
He Learned About Women 535, 541
He Walked by Night 665
He Who Steals 585
Healey, Myron 542
Heart in Hiding 707
The Heart Is a Lonely Hunter 662
Heat Spell 361
Heatherly, May 540
Heaven Can Wait 531, 576, 612
Hec Ramsey 662
Heckart, Eileen 180, 324, 581, 648
Hector, Jay 514
Hee Haw 194
The Heiress 457
Heisler, Stuart 506
The Hell with Heroes 114
Hellbent Harriet 408
Hellcats of the Navy 506
Hellfire 674
Hellgate 74, 78, 82
Hellman, Lillian 493

Hell's Town 640
Hellstrom, Gunnar 144, 146, 350, 616, 621, 623, 624, 627, 638, 645, 647, 660, 675, 687, 689, 690, 691, 692, 695, 697, 699, 702, 705, 706, 707, 709, 710, 713, 715, 716, 717, 718, 722
Helm, Anne 521, 577
Helm, Frances 529
Helmond, Katharine 181, 337, 685
Help Me, Kitty 333, 573
Helping Hand 106, 266, 384, 452
Helton, Joe 553
Helton, Percy 506, 568, 594
Hemphill, Ray 576
Hendrickson, Al 377
Hendry, Len 505
Henie, Sonja 590
Hennesey 364, 448, 621, 693
Henry, Will 100, 228
Henry, William 562, 576, 587
Herbert, Pitt 451, 499
Hepburn, Audrey 579
Hepburn, Katharine 144, 574, 579
Here Come the Brides 553, 609, 624, 661, 674, 709
Here Comes Mr. Jordan 652
Herman, Max 220
Hern, Pepe 560
The Hero 669
Hero's Departure 438
Herrick, Frederick 712
Herron, Bob 627, 665
Heston, Charlton 75
Heverly, Robert 636
Heydt, Louis Jean 375
Heyman, Barton 522
Hibbs, Jesse 114, 491, 492, 494, 495, 503, 504, 505, 509, 511, 512, 513, 514, 516, 520, 527
Hice, Eddie 570, 583
Hickman, Darryl 181, 339, 498, 501
Hickman, Dwayne 498
Hickman, John 34
Hickock 373
Hicks, Chuck 709
Hidalgo 679

[810]

Index

The Hide Cutters 307, 629, 642, 670
The Hiders 334, 717, 723
Higgins, Joe 610, 643
Higgins, Michael 551, 564, 565
High Anxiety 462
High Chaparral 113, 228, 593, 608, 613, 715
High Noon 16, 33, 54, 388, 477, 513
High School Confidential 578
High Society 261
Highway to Heaven 198, 595
Hill, Marianna 561
Hill, Sammie 361, 363, 365, 404, 406, 408, 418
Hill Girl 625, 630, 656
Hill Street Blues 574, 686, 706
Hiller, Arthur 114, 493, 496, 499, 507, 508, 513, 516, 517
Hillias, Peg 464
Hindy, Joseph 697, 711
Hingle, Pat 94, 181–182, 346, 444, 672, 673, 675, 676
Hinka-Do 364, 428, 507
Hinkle, Robert 462, 542
Hinn, Michael 460, 466, 482, 501, 518
His Girl Friday 592, 621
Hitchcock, Alfred 659
Hite, Kathleen 3, 24, 25, 29, 35, 37, 38, 39, 49, 94, 97, 111, 113, 120, 180, 193, 219–220, 367, 432, 434, 435, 474, 477, 484, 523, 526, 529, 530, 531, 532, 533, 534, 538, 539, 541, 542, 543, 546, 548, 549, 551, 552, 553, 554, 556, 557, 558, 562, 564, 565, 567, 568, 573, 575, 583
Hoag, Mitzi 553, 622
Hobart, Rose 627
Hobbie, Duke 627
Hodges, Eddie 609
Hodgins, Earle 472, 530, 542, 551
Hoffman, Dustin 500
Hogan, Pat 453
Hogan, Robert 571, 677
Hogan's Heroes 481, 490

Hogroff, George 87
Holchak, Victor 661, 680
Holden, William 74
Hole, Jonathan 362
A Hole in the Head 609
Holland, Bruce 456
Holland, Buck 633
Holland, Jack 456
Holland, Tom 361, 497
Holliday, Cyrus K. 7
Holliman, Earl 646, 655, 693, 723
Hollywood House 607
Holman, Rex 515, 518, 565, 590, 604, 615, 630, 639, 648, 660, 672, 686, 706
Holmes, Wendell 494
Holmes and Yoyo 644
Holocaust 599, 610
Home Surgery 363, 411, 445, 472
Homecoming 445, 569, 692, 697
Homely Girl 53, 434
Hondo 82, 470
Honey Pot 348, 584
Honey West 363, 549, 636, 687
Hong Kong 50, 365, 463, 708
Honky Tonk 545
Honor Before Justice 338, 596
Honthaner, Ron 153, 624, 671, 672, 673, 674, 675, 676, 677, 678, 679, 680, 681, 682, 684, 685, 686, 687, 688, 689, 690, 691, 692, 693, 694, 695, 696, 697, 698, 699, 700, 701, 702, 703, 704, 705, 706, 707, 708, 709, 710, 712, 713, 714, 715, 716, 717, 718, 719, 720, 721, 722
Hooper 115, 673
Hoover, George 8, 9
Hoover, Joseph 597
Hopalong Cassidy 17, 18, 23, 44, 149, 527
Hopkins, Bo 188, 618
Hopkins, Bob 507
Hopper, Dennis 578
Hopper, Hedda 451
Hopper, Jerry 559, 561, 566

Hopper, William 450, 451, 458
Hopson, Alfred 486
Horne, Geoffrey 702
Horner, Harry 457
Horse Deal 389, 501
Horton, Robert 108
Horvath, Charles 469
The Hospital 114
Hostage! 98, 135, 137, 194, 326, 690, 698
The Hostage 591, 600, 691
Hot Horse Hyatt 417
Hot L Baltimore 713
Hot Spell 444
Hotchkiss, Frank 664
Hotel De Paree 646
The Hotel New Hampshire 595
Hough, Emerson 13
Hound Dog 407
House, Ramon K. 293
A House Ain't a Home 418
House Calls 505, 582, 702
House of Blue Leaves 181
House of Dracula 149, 449
House of Frankenstein 149, 449
Houston, Lou 39, 361
How the Grinch Stole Christmas 690
How the West Was Won 176, 203, 226, 331, 352, 447, 566, 618, 625, 653, 657, 668, 686, 722
How to Cure a Friend 397, 461
How to Die for Nothing 375, 416, 455, 486
How to Kill a Friend 375, 379, 410, 490
How to Kill a Woman 375, 386, 477
How to Marry a Millionaire 584, 672, 702
How to Sell a Ranch 400
Howard, Clint 665, 667
Howard, Rance 664, 716
Howard, Ronny 162, 646, 647, 665, 667
Howden, Mike 616, 629
Howdy, Clyde 602, 616
Howdy Doody 18
Howell, Hoke 608, 609
Howell, Jean 612
Hoy, George 11

[811]

INDEX

Hoyos, Rodolfo 657
Hoyt, Clegg 460, 461
Hoyt, John 182, 468, 518, 588
Hubbard, John 583
Huckleberry Finn 144, 494
Huddleston, David 668, 700, 710, 716
Hudgins, Ken 543
Hudkins, John "Bear" 627
Hudson, Hal 78, 266
Hudon, John 563
Hughes, Billy 531, 546
Hughes, Whitey 691
Huish, Frank 724
Human, Robert 524
Humoresque 373
Humphries, Hal 65
Hundley, Charles 650
Hundley, Craig 594
Hung High 573, 585
The Hunger 545
Hunnicutt, Arthur 668
Hunt, Marsha 561
Hunt, Scott 589, 592
The Hunter 399, 447
Hunter, Kim 182, 337, 673
Hunter, Thomas 644
Huntley, Chet 56
Hunton, Erica 703, 704
Hurricane Smith 559
Hurst, Richard D. 701
Hush, Lisabeth 589
The Hustler 457, 612
Huston, John 540
Huston, Patricia 494
Hutchins, Will 108, 550
Hutchinson, Josephine 501, 613
Hutton, Betty 134, 583
Hutton, Brian 459
Hyland, Diana 693
Hyland, Jim 455

I

I Am a Fugitive from a Chain Gang 507
I Call Him Wonder 551, 622
I Died a Thousand Times 54
I Don't Know 366
I Dream of Jeannie 454, 468, 476, 597
I Have Promises to Keep 720, 723

I Led Three Lives 491, 661
I Love Lucy 108, 110, 154, 368, 589
I Married Joan 553, 720
I Spy 143, 389, 573, 619
I Thee Wed 418, 510
I Want to Live 50, 389, 491
I Was a Male War Bride 506
I Was There 55
Ichabod and Me 524
The Iceman Cometh 688
I'd Climb the Highest Mountain 584
Idelson, William 399
Ihnat, Steve 583, 595, 602, 612, 641, 664
The Iliad 154
I'll Cry Tomorrow 53, 483
The Immortal 635
Impact 408
The Imposter 435, 525
In Cold Blood 480, 567
In Old Santa Fe 18
In Performance of Duty 270, 716
In the Heat of the Night 296, 491, 604
Inches, Duncan 689
Incident at Indian Ford 423
The Incredible Hulk 548
The Incredible Shrinking Man 449
Indian 415
Indian Baby 431
Indian Crazy 400
Indian Ford 423, 531
The Indian Horse 381
Indian Scout 184, 393, 452, 486
Indian White 394, 460
Ingalls, Don 610, 612
Ingram, Jean 517
Ingram, Rex 640
Inherit the Wind 463, 486, 562, 588
The In-Laws 493
Inness, Jean 450, 513
Innocence 575
The Innocent 324, 648
Innocent, Harold 530, 534
Innocent Broad 393, 484
Insight 532
The Interns 627
The Intruders 279, 640, 642
The Invaders 114, 547, 551
The Invasion of the Body Snatchers 488, 621
The Invisible Man 708
Ireland, John 211, 605, 617
Irma La Douce 43, 375
The Iron Blood of Courage 275, 339, 707, 711
The Iron Horse 15, 226, 537, 564, 591
The Iron Man 714, 722
The Iron Mistress 151
Ironside 520, 532, 592
Island in the Desert 716, 722
Island in the Sky 82, 163
It Came from Outer Space 150
It Could Happen to You 594
It Takes a Thief 475
It Takes Two 441, 703
It's About Time 591, 674
It's Always Jan 672
It's a Man's World 619, 624
It's News to Me 621
Ivers, Robert 499
Ivins, Perry 510
Izay, Victor 586, 589, 603, 660, 661, 673, 705, 713

J

Jack and the Beanstalk 476
Jack Benny Special 510
The Jackals 324, 626, 628
The Jackie Gleason Show 534
Jackman, Fred H. 550
Jackson, Anne 183, 349, 681
Jackson, Kate 555
Jackson, Sherry 533, 543
Jacques, Ted 537
Jaeckel, Richard 551, 594, 718
Jaekel 666, 683
Jaffe, Allen 586, 587, 590, 604, 619, 649, 655
Jaffe, Sam 697
Jaffee, Jewel 572
Jailbait Janet 361, 426, 509
The Jailer 99, 310, 313, 601, 614, 670
Jake and the Fat Man 40, 352
Jaliscoe 360
James, Anthony 618, 625, 630, 631, 638, 647, 648
James, Bill 57, 69

Index

James, Brian 721
James, Clifton 183, 313, 488, 581, 603, 660
James, John, Jr. 394
James, Ralph 640
James at 15 688, 719
James Joyce's Women 686
Jameson, Adar 595
Jane Eyre 454, 507
Janiss, Vivi 24, 53, 359, 360, 363, 364, 365, 366, 367, 368, 373, 381, 383, 385, 386, 390, 391, 392, 397, 409, 465
Janson, Frank K. 715
Janssen, David 277
Jarmyn, Jill 380, 385
Jarvis, Francesca 712
Jarvis, Graham 183, 315, 722
Jason, Peter 651, 659, 696
Jason and the Argonauts 627
Jason of Star Command 605
Jay, Verne 599
Jayhawkers 116, 190, 369, 411, 493, 527
The Jayhawkers 93
Jealousy 391, 472
The Jean Arthur Show 578, 580
Jeb 555
Jedell, Bonnie 713
Jedro's Woman 437
Jeff Spain 25
Jefferson Drum 194, 450
The Jeffersons 649
Jenny 342, 543, 664
Jens, Salome 183, 270, 665, 696
Jenson, Marlowe 509
Jenson, Roy 601, 623, 633, 652, 661, 717
Jesse 334, 342, 374, 475, 695, 696, 698
Jessie 648
Jeter, James 693, 706
Jewell, Isabelle 579
Jezebel 601
Jigsaw 631
The Jim Backus Show 720
Jim Bowie 108
Jimmy Hughes, Rookie Cop 590
Joanie Love Chachi 675
Jobe's Son 411
Joe Phy 331, 383, 440, 479

Joe Sleet 439
Joe's World 633
The Joey Bishop Show 622, 636
The John Byner Comedy Hour 714
John Goldfarb, Please Come Home 645
Johnny Allegro 644
Johnny Apollo 476, 533
Johnny Belinda 611
Johnny Cash Presents the Everly Brothers Show 610
Johnny Concho 40, 49
Johnny Cross 635, 642
Johnny Guitar 645
Johnny Jupiter 480
Johnny Midnight 54, 572
Johnny Red 393, 428, 501
Johnny Ringo 468
Johnson, Arch 537, 576, 602, 658, 659
Johnson, Ben 553, 606, 676
Johnson, Brad 616
Johnson, Chal 544
Johnson, Chubby 576, 638
Johnson, Jason 480, 589
Johnson, Joe Ann 591
Johnson, Lady Bird 177
Johnson, Lamont 174, 616
Johnson, Lyndon 177
Johnson, Russell 184, 467, 495, 639, 687
The Joker Is Wild 555
Joke's on Us 377, 414, 482, 527
Jolley, I. Sanford 559, 591, 620, 629, 639, 643, 654, 662
Jonah Hutchinson 312, 574
Jones, Buck 149, 178
Jones, Henry 620, 652, 678
Jones, Ivy 692
Jones, L.Q. 557, 575, 582, 640, 653, 661, 679
Jones, Mickey 724
Jones, Miranda 545
Jones, Morgan 594
Jones, Samee Lee 688
Jones-Moreland, Betsy 556
Jordan, Ted 149, 184, 347, 443, 528, 537, 544, 565, 566, 591, 594, 596, 598, 607, 672, 707, 710, 719

Jory, Victor 578
Joslyn, Allyn 511
Journey for Three 569
Joyce, Patricia 564
Jubilee 691
The Judas Gun 651, 656
Judd, for the Defense 466
The Judge 46
The Judgement 275, 337, 685
Judgement at Nuremberg 54, 388, 477
Jud's Woman 413
Julia 468, 625
Jung, Allen 655
Junior Bonner 112, 447, 600
The Juniper Tree 363
Justice, Katherine 647, 660, 677, 689

K

Kaasa, Walter 724
Kane, Byron 24, 364, 376
Kangaroo 421, 502
Kansas Pacific 226
Karen, Anna 606
Karlin, Norman 647
Karloff, Boris 149
Karnes, Robert 470, 496, 508, 525, 527, 539, 636, 640, 649, 707
Kate Heller 556
Kate Loves a Mystery 696
Kate McShane 651
Katzman, Leonard 153, 195, 197, 664, 665, 666, 667, 668, 669, 671, 672, 673, 674, 675, 676, 677, 678, 679, 680, 681, 682, 684, 685, 686, 687, 688, 689, 690, 691, 692, 693, 694, 695, 696, 697, 698, 699, 700, 701, 702, 703, 704, 705, 706, 707, 708, 709, 710, 712, 713, 714, 715, 716, 717, 718, 719, 720, 721, 722
Kaufman, David 108
Kaz 713
Kearns, Joseph 16, 53, 54, 362, 363, 369, 371, 372, 374, 380, 381, 383, 390, 391, 393, 394, 396, 402, 403, 404, 414, 417, 421,

[813]

INDEX

422, 425, 426, 427, 430, 431, 433, 434, 435, 436, 485, 496, 497, 499
Keefer, Don 469, 470, 520, 536, 553, 583, 588, 607, 659, 700
Keele, Beth 589, 592
Keene, Richard 537
Keene, Robert 447
Keene, William 480
Keep, Michael 542
Keeper of the Flame 476
Kefauver, Estes 130
Keith, Richard 459
The Keith Monteith Show 709
Kellett, Pete 604, 607, 609, 630, 632, 638, 644, 650, 652, 663, 675, 696, 701, 704, 717
Kelley, Barry 476, 560
Kelley, DeForest 184, 336, 453
Kelley, William 135, 142, 650, 655, 663, 664, 665, 678, 679, 685
Kellin, Michael 606, 607
Kellogg, John 537, 559, 594, 623, 640
Kelly, Jack 473
Kelman, Rick 537
Kelton, Richard D. 660, 673, 685, 692
Kemmer, Ed 484
Kemmerling, Warren 526, 529, 606, 677, 702
Kemp, Dan 663
Kemp, Sally 698
Kemper, Ray 35, 39, 57, 58, 62, 242, 243, 429, 430, 441, 525
Kendis, William 479
Kendrick, Hank 713
Kennedy, Adam 447, 511
Kennedy, Douglas 511, 513, 599
Kennedy, George 184, 271, 290, 514, 515, 521, 523, 540, 568, 571, 598
Kennedy, John F. 130, 133
Kenopka, Ken 549, 557, 701
Kent, David 521
Kent, Sandra 691
Kentucky Jones 91, 448, 512, 662

The Kentucky Tolmans 362
Kenyon, Sandy 489, 523, 551, 635
Kerr, Deborah 535
Kerr, John 535
Kerr, Sondra 530
Kerwin, Lance 718, 719
Ketchum, Cliff 493, 513
Kevin, James 482
Kevin, Sandy 617
Keymas, George 523, 537, 555, 562, 596, 686, 705
Keys, Robert 466
Keys, William 703, 705, 716
Kick Me 376, 419, 465
The Kid 713
Kidd, Jonathan 583
Kiley, Richard 658, 674, 684, 700
The Killer 274, 378, 454, 473
Killer at Large 594
The Killer Elite 112
The Killer Shrews 117
The Killers 26, 40, 54
Killian, Victor 715
Kilroy 668
Kimbro 143, 695
King, Brett 454, 478, 498, 547
King, Louis 474
King, Martin Luther 130, 133
King, Wright 445, 475, 505, 523, 524, 527, 545, 563, 589
King, Zalman 587, 601, 609, 621
King of Dodge City 17
King of Kings 17
King of Marvin Garden 587
King of the Gypsies 662
King of the Rodeo 17
King Rat 627
King Solomon's Mines 512
Kingman, Margaret L. 712
Kings Row 470
Kingsley, Martin 451
Kingston: Confidential 681
Kinsolving, Lee 569
Kinter, Robert 130
Kioga 588
Kiowa 138, 653, 656
Kipling, Rudyard 24
Kirk, Phyllis 490

Kirk, Tommy 459
Kirkpatrick, Jess 405, 417, 422, 425, 461, 464, 473, 483
Kirzinger, Ken 724
Kissin' Cousins 590
The Kite 564
Kite's Reward 343, 389, 447, 472
Kitty 365
Kitty Accused 433
Kitty Caught 385, 411, 479, 527
Kitty Cornered 567
Kitty Lost 387, 478
Kitty Love 439
Kitty Shot 93, 271, 521
Kitty's Good Neighboring 437
Kitty's Injury 170, 421, 501
Kitty's Kidnap 426
Kitty's Killing 414, 508
Kitty's Love Affair 140, 343, 700
Kitty's Outlaw 398, 474
Kitty's Quandary 428
Kitty's Rebellion 419, 493, 527
Kjellin, Alf 685, 693, 694, 703
Kleeb, Helen 53, 54, 55, 239, 359, 373, 374, 375, 376, 377, 378, 379, 381, 387, 390, 394, 397, 398, 400, 401, 402, 406, 408, 419, 458, 484, 572, 684
Kleiner, Dick 134
Klemperer, Werner 480, 481
Klondike 40
Klugman, Jack 158, 479, 498, 499
Knapp, Robert 533, 554, 607, 636, 657, 666
Knapp, Wilfred 443, 448, 450, 456, 457
Kneubuhl, John 560, 567
Knight, Christopher 634
Knight, Ted 498
Knots Landing 489, 644, 695, 702
Kobe, Gail 482, 581, 606, 640
Kolchak: The Night Stalker 486, 494, 582, 694, 716
Konrad, Dorothy 556, 557
Koons, Robert 724

[814]

Index

Koplowitz, Donald Z. 668
Korita, Ana 689
Kotar, Susan 701
Kotto, Yaphet 661, 662
Koury, Rex 27, 61, 64, 71, 220, 240, 242, 398
Kowal, Jon 589, 620, 690
Kowalski, Bernard 606, 608
Kraft Music Hall Presents 669
Kraft Suspense Theater 679
Kramer, Stanley 54
Kreig, Frank 562
Krieger, Lee 617
Kronman, Harry 579, 582, 627, 651, 653, 682, 704
Krugman, Lou 46, 50, 60, 67, 242, 247, 359, 360, 362, 363, 364, 365, 367, 368, 369, 371, 372, 373, 377, 381, 389, 402, 484, 497, 554
Kruschen, Jack 16, 24, 25, 46, 50, 51, 359, 360, 361, 362, 365, 367, 368, 369, 380, 381, 382, 384, 385, 403, 463
Kuenstle, Charles 561, 603, 615, 618, 631, 636, 643, 649, 671, 681
Kukla, Fran and Ollie 18
Kulik, Buzz 114, 475, 476, 480, 501, 502
Kung Fu 165, 448, 618, 668
Kuter, Kay E. 686, 687, 706

L

L.A. Law 384
The L-Shaped Room 641
Lacey 533, 541
Lacy, Tom 720
Ladd, Alan 74, 580, 589
Ladd, David 589
Ladd, Diane 570, 571, 612
Ladies Crave Excitement 93
Ladies from St. Louis 613, 615
The Lady 313, 324, 581, 585
The Lady Consents 151
The Lady from Shanghai 558

The Lady Killer 441, 511
Lafferty, Perry 126
Lally, Bill 363, 406
The Lamb 376
Lamb, Gil 549
Lambert, George 536
Lambert, Jack 498, 524, 555, 632, 639, 652
Lambert, Lee 631
Lambert, Paul 459, 466
Lance, Leon 81
Lancer 461, 576
Lanchester, Elsa 47, 262
Land Deal 397, 489
Land of the Giants 483, 598
Landa, Miguel 560
Landau, Martin 487, 488, 601
Landis, James 602, 603, 610, 611
The Landlord 595
Lane, Allen "Rocky" 483, 484, 517, 525
Lane, Michael 686
Lane, Rusty 590, 658, 682, 703
Langdon, Sue Ane 184-185, 349, 534
Langton, Paul 488, 505, 526
Lanin, Jay 544, 568
Lansing, Mary 359, 360, 361, 362, 363, 365, 373
Lansing, Robert 185, 279, 589, 634
Lapp, Richard 653, 660
Laramie 114, 165, 464, 597
Larch, John 446, 477, 499, 504, 509, 525, 529
Lardner, John 21
Laredo 226, 588, 674, 691
Larkin 718, 723
Larkin, John 547
Larkin, Sheila 643, 689
LaRoche, Mary 553, 557
Larrain, Michael 649
Larson, Darrell 687
Lasell, John 529
Lassie 150, 446, 482, 537, 549, 567, 627, 635, 678
Lasson, Robert 227
The Last Convertible 612
Last Fling 378, 468, 513
The Last Hunt 54
The Last Hurrah 117
The Last of the Mohicans 13, 226

The Last Picture Show 462, 538, 553
The Last Resort 557
The Last Wagon 226
Latham, Louise 185-186, 279, 634, 638, 645, 649, 659, 709
Lathan, Arnold 693
Lau, Wesley 492, 504, 514
Laugh-In 152
Laughing Gas 169, 415, 483
Laughton, Charles 47, 48, 74, 527
Launer, S. John 450
Laurie's Suitor 423
Lauter, Harry 20, 506, 511, 515, 529, 559, 584, 622, 632
Lavery 668
The Law and Mr. Jones 517, 582
The Law of the Plainsman 597, 719
Lawford, Peter 490
The Lawless Breed 88
The Lawless Years 470
Lawman 469, 715
Lawrence, Anthony 671
Lawrence, Charlotte 236, 368, 373
Lawrence, D.H. 574
Lawrence, Delphi 610
Lawrence, John 553
The Lawyers 629
The Lazarus Syndrome 483
Leachman, Cloris 186, 271, 461, 526
Leacock, Philip 3, 35, 112, 119, 120, 121-123, 125, 126, 128, 129, 130, 143, 144, 146, 174, 196, 197, 205, 216, 573, 574, 575, 576, 577, 578, 579, 580, 581, 582, 583, 584, 585, 586, 587, 588, 589, 590, 591, 592, 593, 594, 595, 596, 597, 598, 599, 600, 601, 602, 603, 604, 605, 606, 607, 608, 609, 610, 611, 612, 613, 614, 617, 643, 649, 650, 651, 654, 655, 662, 663, 673, 685
Learned, Michael 186, 195, 285, 699, 702
Leave It to Beaver 378, 519
Le Clair, Michael 718

[815]

INDEX

Le Gault, Lance 712
Le Roy, Gloria 713
Lee, Anna 621
Lee, John G. 450
Lee, Ruta 186, 342, 485, 543
Leeds, Peter 362, 370, 371
The Left-Handed Gun 46, 361, 373, 444, 604
Legal Revenge 271, 398, 461, 487
The Legend 337, 673, 683
The Legend of Jesse James 487, 494, 586
Legends Don't Sleep 557
Lehman, Trent 647
Leicester, William F. 39, 404, 463, 468
Lenard, Kay 645, 649, 654
Lenard, Mark 624
Lenz, Kay 707
Leo and Liz in Beverly Hills 570
Leopold, Thomas 709, 710
Lerner, Fred 720
Les Girls 373
Leslie, Bethel 538, 575, 659
Let George Do It 53
Let My People Go 665
Let No Man Write My Epitah 121, 574
Letter of the Law 313, 402, 442, 488
Lettier, Al 586
Lewin, Robert 580, 588
Lewis, Elliott 239
Lewis, Geoffrey 691
Lewis, Joseph H. 578, 580
Lewis, Louise 368
Lewis, Virginia 546
The Liar from Blackhawk 391, 472
The Lieutenant 594
The Life and Legend of Wyatt Earp 21, 73, 110, 398, 445, 454, 495, 501, 528, 557, 560, 586, 624, 665, 694
The Life and Times of Grizzly Adams 464
Life with Father 471
Life with Luigi 384, 679
Lijah 675, 683
Like Old Times 705, 711

Lili 96
Lime Street 617
The Lindbergh Kidnapping Case 677
Linder, Alfred 459
Lindsay, Elliot 718
Lindsey, George 561, 573, 584, 597, 608, 681
Line Trouble 434
The Lineup 364
Linville, Albert 492
Linville, Joanne 186, 528, 544, 632
Lippe, Jonathan 594, 599, 611, 630, 636, 643, 654, 674, 677, 686, 699, 709
Liss, Steve 616
The List of Adrian Messenger 621
Lister, James 197
Little, Herbert 449, 450, 451, 452, 453, 456, 457, 458, 461, 472
Little Big Horn 74
Little Bird 416
Little Fauss and Big Halsy 570
The Little Foxes 493
Little Girl 434, 523
Little House on the Prairie 150, 177, 179, 361, 483, 492, 501, 531, 595, 599, 654, 666, 685, 690, 707, 714
The Little Kidnappers 121, 128, 574, 579
The Little Mermaid 706
The Little Prince 658
Little Sky, Dawn 525
Little Sky, Eddie 481, 500, 524, 539, 551, 623, 627, 648, 661, 704
Little Women 53, 363, 483, 638, 718
Livvie's Loss 415
Lloyd, Suzanne 501, 522
Lobo 198, 342, 463, 625, 634, 643, 670
Lochinvar 364
Lochner, Felix 627
Locke, Jon 685
Lockhart, June 186–187, 282, 482
Lockwood, Alexander 461
Lockwood, Gary 594
The Lodger 567

Logan's Run 153, 665, 707
Loggia, Robert 578
London, Dick 509
London, Jack 24
The Lone Ranger 15, 19, 20, 23, 46, 52, 226
The Lonely Man 445
Long, Doreen 695
Long, Ed 632, 643, 654, 701
Long As I Live 413
Long Branch Blues 194
The Long Goodbye 719
The Long Hot Summer 644
Long Hours, Short Pay 525
Long, Long Trail 529, 540
The Long Night 140, 639, 642, 669
The Longest Day 637
The Longest Yard 115, 542
Longstreet 627
Looking for Mr. Goodbar 658
Lookinland, Todd 678, 708, 717
Loony, McCluny 412
Loos, Ann 566
Lord, Barbara 529
Lord, Jack 478
Lorde, Athena 590
Loring, Lynn 561
Lormer, Jon 492, 509, 663, 672, 674, 682
Losby, Donald 583, 604
The Lost 198, 278, 670, 697
Lost Horizon 579
Lost in Space 113, 482, 570
Lost Rifle 403, 489
The Lost Vikings 683
Lou Grant 460, 573, 574, 596, 644
Louie Pheeters 547
Love, Phyllis 525, 572
Love American Style 399, 587, 655, 692
Love and Death 713
The Love Boat 101, 366
Love Is a Many Splendored Thing 483
Love of a Good Woman 385, 493
Love of Life 657, 705
Love of Money 271, 439, 526
Love Story 114, 493
Love Thy Neighbor 521
The Loved One 559
Lover Boy 556

[816]

Index

Lover Come Back 365
Lowe, Stanja 587
Lowell, Tom 556, 569
Lowry, Robert 544
Lucas, Karl 604
The Luck of Roaring Camp and Other Sketches 13
Lucking, Bill 712
Lucky Pup 18
Lucky U Ranch 117
The Lucy Show 151, 531
Ludlum, Edward 494
Luisi, James 713
Luke 660, 683
Luke, Keye 447, 448
Luke Slaughter of Tombstone 16
Luke's Law 429
Lullaby of Broadway 590
Lum and Abner 53
Lummis, Dayton 719
Luna, Barbara 535
Lund, Art 547, 703
Lundin, Richard 693, 699, 701, 705
Lundin, Vic 499
Lupton, John 517, 518, 575
The Lure 340, 343, 611
Lurie, Allen 496
Lust in the Dust 226
Luster, Robert 636
Lux Radio Theatre 361
Lydon, James 626
Lyle's Kid 189, 334, 628, 642, 670
Lyn, Dawn 689, 698
Lynch, Hal 589, 613
Lynch, Ken 401, 424, 426, 440, 468, 475, 482, 487, 520, 521, 528, 660, 693, 699
Lynch Town 331, 702
The Lynching 363
Lynching Man 403, 490
Lynott 674, 683
Lyons, Gene 519, 520, 567
Lyons, Robert F. 619
Lytton, Herbert 450, 455, *459, 482, 550*

M

M Squad 450
Ma Tennis 385, 480

Mabe, Byron 682
MacArthur 114, 467
MacArthur, Charles 598
McArthur, Charles 512
MacArthur, James 212, 598
Macbeth 52, 361, 375
McBroom, Amanda 719
McCabe 663
McCabe and Mrs. Miller 695
McCall, Perce 187
McCallion, James 450, 633
McCambridge, Mercedes 671
McCarthy, Devlin 447
McCarthy, Lin 708
McCarty, H.T. 11
McCauley, Tom 583, 598
McCay, Peggy 483, 657, 674
McClellan, John 109
McClory, Sean 651, 706
McCloud 91, 440, 468, 574, 592, 610
McClure, Doug 535
McCluskey, Joyce 372, 377, 380, 387, 398
McCoy, Tim 17, 109, 149
McCready, Ed 590, 592, 606, 618, 622, 682, 721
McCue, Mathew 523, 524
McCulley, Johnston 21
McDevitt, Ruth 715, 716
MacDonald, Ian 482
MacDonald, J. Fred 13
McDonald, John 8
MacDonnell, Norman 3, 4, 7, 16, 17, 24, 25, 26, 27, 30, 33, 35, 36, 37, 38, 39, 41, 42, 44, 46, 48, 51, 52, 53, 54, 57, 58–60, 61, 62, 63, 64, 65, 66, 67, 68, 71, 74, 75, 79, 82, 83, 84, 86, 90, 94, 95, 96, 97, 98, 99, 108, 111, 112, 113, 114, 115, 116, 119–121, 128, 134, 140, 143, 148, 169, 172, 173, 201, 205, 206, 208, 209, 215, 216, 217, 219, 220, 221, 222, 226, 232, 234, 235, 237, 240, 243, 326, 360, 365, 369, 373, 376, 377, 381, 392, 393, 411, 415, 433, 436,

438, 439, 454, 456, 457, 458, 459, 460, 461, 462, 463, 464, 465, 466, 467, 468, 469, 470, 471, 472, 473, 474, 475, 476, 477, 478, 479, 480, 481, 482, 483, 484, 485, 486, 487, 488, 489, 490, 491, 492, 493, 494, 495, 496, 497, 498, 499, 500, 501, 502, 503, 504, 505, 506, 507, 508, 509, 510, 511, 512, 513, 514, 515, 516, 517, 518, 519, 520, 521, 522, 523, 524, 525, 526, 527, 528, 529, 530, 531, 532, 533, 534, 535, 536, 537, 538, 539, 540, 541, 542, 543, 544, 545, 546, 547, 548, 549, 550, 551, 552, 553, 554, 555, 556, 557, 558, 559, 560, 561, 562, 563, 564, 565, 566, 567, 568, 569, 570, 571, 572, 573, 574, 575, 576, 579, 581, 583
Macdonnell, Judith 120
McDonough, Eileen 719
McDougall, Fred 103, 525, 609, 634
MacDuff, Tyler 622
McEveety, Bernard 3, 144, 146, 169, 176, 202, 617, 629, 630, 634, 635, 636, 639, 641, 644, 645, 648, 650, 652, 653, 654, 656, 659, 660, 661, 662, 663, 664, 666, 667, 669, 674, 677, 679, 680, 682, 686, 688, 696, 700, 701, 702, 703, 704, 707, 708, 712, 713, 715, 717, 719, 720, 721
McEveety, Kevin C. 708
McEveety, Stephen 604
McEveety, Vincent 3, 5, 85, 103, 114, 122, 123, 144, 146, 169, 176, 189, 193, 202, 579, 581, 582, 584, 586, 590, 591, 592, 594, 601, 604, 619, 623, 624, 630, 633, 635, 637, 638, 640, 646, 651, 652, 653, 655, 657, 658, 659, 666, 668, 672, 681, 682, 696, 698, 701, 710, 721, 724

[817]

INDEX

McFadden, Tom 682
McGaughy, Rod 714
McGavin, Darren 582, 591, 603
McGeehan, Pat 372
McGhee, Gloria 457, 470, 547
McGough, John 464
McGovern, John 360, 369, 372
McGowan, Oliver 533
MacGraw 648
McGraw, Bill 476
McGraw, Charles 567, 620, 675
MacGruder and Loud 618
McGuire, Barry 482, 494
McGuire, Biff 715
McGuire, Harp 526
MacGyver 129, 660
McHale's Navy 151, 476, 495, 607, 709, 710
McIntire, Holly 562
McIntire, John 16, 53, 56, 361, 365, 371, 373, 390, 401, 416, 475, 586
MacIntoshe, Jay 689
McIntyre, Tim 586
McKay, Peggy *see* McCay, Peggy
MacKaye, Fred 380
McKinley, J. Edward 535, 537, 647
McLaglen, Andrew V. 3, 112, 114, 116, 120, 173, 187, 202, 208, 459, 461, 462, 464, 465, 466, 467, 468, 469, 470, 471, 472, 473, 474, 475, 493, 495, 496, 497, 498, 499, 501, 502, 503, 504, 506, 507, 508, 509, 510, 511, 512, 513, 515, 517, 520, 521, 524, 525, 529, 530, 531, 533, 534, 536, 538, 539, 540, 542, 543, 544, 545, 546, 547, 548, 551, 552, 553, 555, 556, 558, 562, 563, 564, 565, 567, 568, 569, 571, 575, 581
McLaglen, Victor 112
McLain's Law 170, 204, 703
MacLane, Barton 596, 597, 612
McLaren, Wayne 697

McLean, Bill 523
McLean, David 636
McLeod, Catherine 469, 553
McLiam, John 523, 599, 607, 626, 631
McLintock! 113, 365, 462, 470
MacMichael, Florence 502, 503
McMickle, Billy 669
McMillan and Wife 644
McMullen, Dennis 502
MacMurray, Fred 555
McMyler, Pamela 678, 715
McNally, Stephen 611
McNear, Howard 3, 24, 26, 42, 43-44, 45, 61, 62, 94, 107, 216, 222, 223, 235, 237, 240, 241, 244, 250, 251, 256, 359, 377, 388, 396, 453, 504, 507, 543, 575
McPeters, Taylor 295, 532
McQuain, Robert 545
McQueen, Steve 115
McQueeney, Robert 476
MacRae, Elizabeth 535, 546, 563, 565, 579
McRae, Ellen 537, 538
McRaney, Gerald 694, 695, 701, 720
Macready, George 490
McVeigh, Eve 433, 439
McVey, Patrick 550
McVey, Tyler 187, 315, 430, 454, 456, 465, 476, 482, 498, 508
Mad Dog 608, 615
The Mad Monster 149
Madame's Place 632
Madden, Edward 554
Madigan 557
Madison, Guy 19
Madrid, Bert 602, 661, 663
The Madwoman of Chaillot 445
Magaulay, Charles 688
The Magician 560, 567
The Magnificent Seven 454
Magnum, P.I. 487
Magnus 172, 271, 386, 448
Mahoney, Jock 19
Mail Drop 609, 615

Major Glory 618, 619, 670
Majors, Lee 100, 126, 211, 488, 579, 628
Make Room for Daddy 533
Makin' It 592
Making the Grade 722
Malachi 308, 589
Malcolm, James 520
Male, Colin 689, 690
Malet, Arthur 540, 577, 703
Maloney, James 525
Malooly, Maggie 718
The Maltese Falcon 487, 597
Mama 511, 638
Mamakos, Peter 486
The Man 114
A Man a Day 532, 541
Man Against Crime 621
Man and Boy 412
A Man Called Horse 595
A Man Called Sloan 679
A Man Called Smith 340, 633, 646, 656, 680
The Man from Africa 126
Man from Atlantis 678
The Man from Denver 150
The Man from Nowhere 14
The Man from Sundown 17
The Man from U.N.C.L.E. 126, 454, 467
Man Hunter 401
Man in a Suitcase 596
The Man in the Glass Booth 114
The Man of a Thousand Faces 150
Man of La Mancha 658
The Man Who Loved Cat Dancing 115, 580
The Man Who Never Was 621, 656
The Man Who Shot Liberty Valance 52, 226, 361, 449, 464
The Man Who Would Be King 24
The Man Who Would Be Marshal 399, 472
The Man with the Golden Arm 582
Man Without a Gun 450, 619, 621
The Manchurian Candidate 585
Manhunt 550, 627

Index

The *Manhunter* 539, 571, 646, 692
The Manitou 597
Mann, Jack 473, 474
Mann, Larry D. 630
Mann, Lawrence 619, 634, 647
Manning, Ronald 687
Mannix 196, 462, 629
Mannon 138, 140, 217, 326, 637, 642, 670, 724
Manolo 721, 723
Manson, Maurice 452, 455
Mantley, John 3, 5, 42, 83, 85, 95, 101, 112, 119, 121, 123, 124, 125, 127–134, 135, 139, 140, 142, 147, 151, 152, 154, 174, 175, 176, 181, 183, 184, 189, 191, 192, 193, 195, 197, 199, 206, 209, 213–214, 217, 327, 353, 573, 574, 575, 576, 577, 578, 579, 580, 581, 582, 583, 584, 585, 586, 587, 588, 589, 590, 591, 592, 593, 594, 595, 596, 597, 598, 599, 600, 601, 602, 603, 604, 605, 606, 607, 608, 609, 610, 611, 612, 613, 614, 616, 617, 618, 619, 620, 621, 622, 623, 624, 625, 626, 627, 629, 630, 631, 632, 633, 634, 635, 636, 637, 638, 639, 640, 641, 642, 643, 644, 645, 646, 647, 648, 649, 650, 651, 652, 653, 654, 655, 656, 657, 658, 659, 660, 661, 662, 663, 664, 665, 666, 667, 668, 669, 671, 672, 673, 674, 675, 676, 677, 678, 679, 680, 681, 682, 684, 685, 686, 687, 688, 689, 690, 691, 692, 693, 694, 695, 696, 697, 698, 699, 700, 701, 702, 703, 704, 705, 706, 707, 708, 709, 710, 712, 713, 714, 715, 716, 717, 718, 719, 720, 721, 722, 724, 725
Mantley, Jon Jason 661, 669, 671
Mantley, Marie 661, 669, 671

The Many Loves of Dobie Gillis 448, 498, 700
Manza, Ralph 623, 624
Marathon Man 610, 695
March, Hal 366
Marcus Welby, M.D. 144, 556, 686
Marcus, Vitina 530
Marcuse, Ted 465
The Margin 412
Margolin, Stuart 586, 587, 692, 705
Marie, Rose 478
Mark Dillon Goes to Gouge Eye 25, 102, 150, 378, 430, 444
The Mark of Cain 638, 643, 670
Markham 710
Marley, John 587
Marlowe, Harvey 701
Marlowe, Kathy 400
Marlowe, Lucy 497
Marlowe, Nora 450, 521, 576, 636, 666
Marlowe, Scott 557, 573, 580, 597
Marooned 441
Maross, Joe 480, 536, 578
Marry Me 91, 170, 207, 219, 295, 311, 321, 532, 541
Marryin' Bertha 53, 433
Mars, Kenneth 611
Marsh, Linda 679, 684
Marsh, Michele 714, 719
Marshal Proudfoot 347, 417, 492, 527
Marshall, Gloria 467
Marshall, Joan 537
Marshall, Liz 634, 667
Marshall, Nancy 606
Marshall, Shary 547, 565
Ma's Justice 440
Marta, Lynn 692
Martell, Arlene 717
Marth, Frank 632, 645, 653, 710
Martin, Charles 543, 549
Martin, Dean 153
Martin, Kiel 686
Martin, Mari 712
Martin, Ross 483, 490
Martin, Strother 162, 192, 198, 300, 449, 454, 472, 482, 499, 520, 533, 544, 563, 716

Martinez, Joaquin 655
Martinez, Patrice 723
Marvin, Tony 59
Mary Hartman, Mary Hartman 673, 722
Mary Poppins 454
The Mary Tyler Moore Show 462, 499, 546, 573, 574, 634
M.A.S.H. 340, 360, 471, 505, 590, 593, 613, 632, 644, 651, 662, 687
Mass Media Award 697
Massey, Raymond 75, 87
Masters, Natalie 563, 595, 596
Masterson, Bat 10, 11, 14, 34
Masterson, Ed 11
Mathews, George 538
Mathias, Bob 88
Matinee Theater 48
Matt Dillon Must Die 318, 711, 717
Matt for Murder 382, 487
Matt Gets It 102, 139, 384, 444
Matt Helm 560
Matt Lincoln 649
A Matter of Honor 647, 656
Matthews, Junius 362, 365
Matt's Decision 427
Matt's Love Story 139, 195, 285, 699, 710
Maude 488, 678
Maverick 108, 110, 162, 389, 473
Mavis McCloud 383, 427, 475, 514
Maw Hawkins 52, 423
Maxwell, Charles 491, 498, 584, 636
Maxwell, Frank 491
Maxwell, Marilyn 512, 513
May Blossoms 563, 570
Mayberry R.F.D. 360, 363, 561
Mayer, Gerald H. 518, 523, 530
Mayer, Ken 468, 485, 519, 577, 613, 621, 629, 655, 661, 673, 692
Maynard, Ken 17, 109
Maynard, Kermit 17
Mayo, Raymond 627
Mazurki, Mike 674

INDEX

Me, Natalie 665
Meader, William 595
Medical Center 607, 613
Medicine Man 410
Medina, Hazel 640
Medina, Julio 589, 663, 679
Meet Corliss Archer 384
Meet Millie 463, 636
Megowan, Don 506, 544, 565, 706, 720
Meigs, William 497
Melinda Miles 439, 526
Mell, Joseph 457, 461, 521, 522, 524
Melton, Troy 607, 611, 612, 625, 632, 643, 665, 682, 687
Melville, Sam 613, 621, 629, 640, 649, 650, 661, 677
The Men 486, 558
Menard, Tina 506
Mercer, Johnny 117
Meredith, Judi 538
Merlin, Jan 570, 571
Meshougah 368
Meston, John 3, 7, 10, 12, 24, 25, 26, 27, 29–35, 36, 38, 39, 40, 41, 44, 49, 51, 60, 64, 66, 67, 68, 70 74, 76, 82, 83, 86, 95, 102, 105, 107, 111, 113, 114, 120, 122, 123, 134, 135, 139, 141, 169, 193, 201, 215, 216, 219, 220, 221, 222, 226, 230, 231, 232, 233, 267, 356, 359, 361, 362, 363, 364, 365, 366, 367, 369, 370, 371, 372, 373, 374, 375, 376, 377, 378, 379, 380, 381, 382, 383, 384, 385, 386, 387, 388, 389, 390, 391, 392, 393, 394, 395, 396, 397, 398, 399, 400, 401, 402, 403, 421, 422, 433, 435, 436, 437, 438, 439, 440, 441, 444, 445, 446, 447, 448, 449, 450, 451, 452, 453, 454, 455, 456, 457, 459, 460, 461, 462, 463, 464, 465, 466, 467, 468, 469, 470, 471, 472, 473, 474, 475, 476, 477, 478, 479, 480, 481, 482, 483, 484, 485, 486, 487, 488, 489, 490, 491, 492, 493, 494, 495, 496, 497, 498, 499, 500, 501, 502, 503, 504, 505, 506, 507, 508, 509, 510, 511, 512, 513, 514, 515, 516, 517, 518, 519, 520, 521, 522, 523, 524, 525, 526, 527, 528, 529, 530, 531, 532, 533, 534, 535, 536, 537, 538, 539, 540, 542, 543, 544, 545, 546, 547, 548, 549, 550, 552, 554, 556, 558, 559, 562, 563, 564, 565, 567, 569, 571, 573, 575, 577, 581, 585, 613
Meston, Mary Ann Hopper 29, 34, 35
Meyler, Fintan 463, 504, 511
Micale, Paule 649
Mickey Mouse Club 518
The Mickey Rooney Show 583
Mickey Spillane's Mike Hammer 549, 582, 696
Middleton, Robert 445, 456, 545
Midnight 113
Midnight Cowboy 145, 606
A Midsummer Night's Dream 578
Mighty Joe Young 373, 553
Miguel's Daughter 504
Mikler, Michael 517, 547, 548, 550
Milan, Lita 254
Miles, Robert, Jr. 609
Miles, Sarah 580
Miles, Vera 658, 659
Milford, John 519, 579, 616, 652, 660, 707
Millar, Lee 362, 363, 366, 385
Millay, Diana 526
Miller, Arthur 588
Miller, Denny 675
Miller, Jack 142, 659, 660, 662, 664, 666, 667, 669, 671, 672, 673, 674, 675, 676, 677, 678, 679, 680, 681, 682, 684, 685, 686, 687, 688, 689, 690, 691, 692, 693, 694, 695, 696, 697, 698, 699, 700, 701, 702, 703, 704, 705, 706, 707, 708, 709, 710, 712, 713, 714, 715, 716, 717, 718, 719, 720, 721, 722
Miller, Mark 496
Miller, Winston 460, 461, 462
Milligan 307, 688, 697
Milligan, Spencer 719
The Millionaire 370
Mills, Donna 702
Mills, Gordon 485
Mills, Mort 450, 455, 475, 497, 573, 621
Milly 530, 555
Milner, Jessamine 703
Milton, Gerald 470
The Milton Berle Show 18
Mims, William 669
Minner, Kathryn 638
Minnie 53, 438, 524
Minotto, James 666
Miracle Man 633, 642, 670
Miracle on 34th Street 659
The Miracle Worker 578, 685
Mirage 665
Miss America Pageant 501, 514
The Miss and the Missiles 667
Miss Kitty 528, 540
Miss Teenage America 604
The Miss Universe Pageant 527
Mrs. Miniver 507
The Missiles of October 46, 695
The Mission 602, 615
Mission: Impossible 47, 80, 488, 597, 598, 679, 682
The Mississippi 679
The Mississippi Gambler 88
The Mistake 389, 462
Mistaken Identity 613, 615
Mr. and Mrs. Amber 379, 431, 457, 473
Mr. Broadway 708
Mr. District Attorney 635
Mr. Ed 484, 503
Mr. Lucky 483
Mr. Mom 561
Mr. Novak 384, 560, 672
Mr. Peeper 459, 716

[8 2 0]

Index

Mister Roberts 115, 117, 564
Mr. Sam'l 278, 627
Mr. Smith Goes to
    Washington 580
Mitchell, Cameron 714, 715
Mitchell, Dallas 504, 522
Mitchell, George 502, 517
Mitchell, Robert 39, 412
Mitchum, Joe 468
Mitchum, John 483, 499, 528, 551
Mix, Tom 15, 17, 109
Mixed Doubles 399, 597
Mobile One 667
Mobley, Roger 529
Moby Dick 665
Mock, Laurie 651
The Mod Squad 466, 601
Modern Romance 584
Modern Times 706
Moffat, Donald 707
Moffett, Hal 531, 547
The Mojave Kid 17
Mom and Dad 544
Mona McCluskey 436, 675
Monash, Paul 476
The Money Store 157, 279, 337, 635, 642, 669
The Monkees 126
Monopoly 381, 488, 527
Monroe, Charles S. 24
Monroe, Del 676, 701
The Monroes 466, 211, 226, 623, 712
The Monster Maker 149
Montalban, Ricardo 108, 657, 679
Montana, Monte, Jr. 543
The Montefuscos 567
Montoya, Alex 560, 626
Moo Moo Raid 173, 313, 414, 508
Moody, Ralph 46, 53, 54, 359, 360, 362, 363, 364, 365, 366, 367, 370, 372, 373, 374, 376, 378, 379, 380, 381, 383, 386, 387, 388, 392, 394, 396, 397, 400, 402, 404, 405, 406, 407, 409, 414, 415, 416, 417, 418, 420, 422, 423, 424, 425, 426, 427, 428, 429, 430, 431, 432, 434, 437, 440, 441, 500, 512, 547, 562

Moody, Ron 699, 700
Moon 373, 471
The Moonstone 606
Moonstruck 612
Moore, Clayton 19
Moore, Henrietta 545
Moore, Irving J. 3, 144, 146, 605, 612, 613, 622, 626, 640, 675, 678, 687, 692, 704, 705
Moore, Joanna 348, 510, 513, 584
Moran, Erin 675, 678
The More the Merrier 580
Moreno, Jorge 626, 655
Moreno, Ruben 602, 626
Morgan 654
Morgan, Alexandra 704
Morgan, Bob 489, 664
Morgan, Boyd "Red" 665
Morgan, Harry 662, 688, 714, 719
Morgan, Read 493, 582, 654, 659, 664, 673, 680, 684, 688, 699, 708
Mork and Mindy 628, 640
Morningstar/Eveningstar 640, 687
Morris, Wayne 186, 482
Morrison, Anne 360, 393, 394, 397, 422
Morrison, Brian 678, 680
Morrison, Shelley 597
Morrow, Patricia 661
Morrow, Susan 467, 469, 471
The Mortgage 364, 428
Morton, Mickey 541
Mosher, Emily 620
The Most Deadly Game 621
Most Wanted 644, 658
The Mothers-In-Law 463
Mountford, Dianne 542
Moyles, Jack 16, 402, 403, 417, 422, 423, 428, 432, 433, 434, 438, 440
Muldaur, Diana 610
Muley 609, 615
Mullally, Don 592
Mullavey, Greg 673
Mulligan, Richard 622
The Mummy's Curse 54
The Mummy's Hand 552
Munday, Mary 522
The Munsters 48, 361, 563
Murcott, Joel 39, 361

Murder Warrant 380, 497
Murder Will Out 55
Murdock 667, 697
Murdock, Alec 714
Murdock, George 608, 609, 621, 680, 714
Murdock, James 605, 606
Murphy, Bob 546
Murphy, Melissa 653, 680, 682
Murphy, William 499, 622, 632, 635, 669
Murray, Mark 563
Murray, Rick 561
Musser, Larry 724
Mustin, Burt 530
Mutiny on the Bounty 74
My Blood Runs Cold 53
My Brother, John 360
My Brother's Keeper 675, 683
My Fair Lady 579
My Father, My Son 599
My Father's Guitar 315, 595, 600
My Favorite Husband 96, 366, 553
My Favorite Martian 456, 488
My Foolish Heart 551
My Friend Flicka 560
My Friend Irma 363
My Little Chickadee 542
My Man Godfrey 150, 368
My Pal Trigger 18
My Sister Eileen 378, 448
My Sister's Keeper 558
My Six Convicts 149
My Son Jeep 363
My Three Sons 151, 555, 592, 660, 687, 689
My World and Welcome to It 471, 532, 634, 685
Myers, Pauline 640, 641
Myrt and Marge 454
Mysteries of Chinatown 564

N

N.O.P.D. 398, 665
Nagel, Conrad 540
Naked City 49, 114, 187, 365, 535, 585, 671
The Naked Jungle 40
The Name of the Game 496
Namu, the Killer Whale 589

[8 2 1]

INDEX

Nancy 471
Nanny and the Professor 647
Nardini, Tom 592
The Narrow Trail 14
Nash, Robert 533
Nashville 719
National Conference of Christians and Jews 697
National Cowboy Hall of Fame 18, 133, 144, 593, 669, 724
National Education Award 719
National Film Critics Award 538
Navarro, Anna 335, 560, 607
Naylor, Cal 600, 619
Needham, Hal 162, 645
Needles and Pins 507
Neff, Brad 651
Nelson, Anne 26
Nelson, Dick 708
Nelson, Ed 187, 497, 504, 528, 540, 546, 565
Nelson, Gene 499, 503, 515, 590
Nelson, Lloyd 673, 682, 689, 696, 707, 712, 720
Nero Wolfe 40
Nervik, Rik 520
Nettie Sitton 53, 432
Nettleton, Lois 187-188, 296, 532, 611
Network 718
Neuman, E. Jack 444
Neumann, Dorothy 534, 554, 572, 653, 680
Never Pester Chester 362, 437, 476, 527
Never Say Goodbye 559
The New Adventures of Wonder Woman 589
The New Andy Griffith Show 691
The New Beginning 150
The New Breed 637
New Doctor in Town 672, 683
New Hotel 64, 398
The New Intern 113
A New Kind of Family 666
The New Land 571, 678, 707
The New Loretta Young Show 662

The New Odd Couple 644
The New Phil Silvers Show 471
The New Society 584
New York Drama Critics Award 445, 621
New York Film Critics Award 538, 553
The Newcomers 145, 605, 615, 670
Newell, William 517
Newhart 624
Newlan, Paul 450, 463, 578
Newman, John 567
Newman, Paul 21
Newman, Walter Brown 26, 27, 39, 359
Newmark, Susan 669
Newsma'am 437
Newton, John 531
Newton, Theodore 481
The Next Voice You Hear 582
Nichols 587, 653
Nichols, Janet 719
Nichols, Laura 708
Nichols, Paul 195
Nichols, Robert 678, 697
Nielson, Leslie 636, 637
Nielson ratings 108, 110, 111, 123, 152-153
Night Court 43
Night Gallery 640, 671
Night Incident 446
Night Riders 17, 190, 312, 334, 639, 642
Nimoy, Leonard 532, 541, 551, 598
Nina 377
Nina's Revenge 296, 532, 570
9:12 to Dodge 632, 642, 670
Nitro 175, 342, 614, 615, 670
Nixon, Richard 109
No Chip 518
No Down Payment 556
No Handcuffs 449, 473
No Hands 563
No Indians 383, 440, 463, 500
No Sale 403
No Sun, No Moon 74
No Time for Sergeants 537, 604, 609
No Tomorrow 678, 697

Nobody's Perfect 700
Nolan, James 455
Nolan, Jeanette 16, 46, 52-53, 59, 305, 359, 361, 364, 365, 367, 385, 390, 401, 403, 415, 423, 425, 426, 474, 475, 484, 521, 575, 586, 669, 677, 680
Nolan, Kathy 541, 542, 565, 703
Nolan, Tom 648
Nolte, Nick 715, 716
None But the Brave 126
The Noon Day Devil 663, 697
The Noose 435, 657, 683
A Noose for Dobie Price 349, 627
Noose of Gold 612, 615
Norma Rae 673
Norris, Frank 13
North, Sheree 556
North and South 479, 668
North by Northwest 444
Not for Hire 621
Novak, Shelly 658
Now That April's Here 565
Nowhere to Run 624, 656
Number 96 673
Nurse 699
The Nurses 475, 629, 705
Nusser, James 53-54, 149, 283, 359, 362, 364, 365, 366, 367, 369, 370, 373, 374, 376, 377, 379, 380, 382, 384, 385, 387, 388, 389, 390, 391, 392, 393, 395, 396, 397, 398, 399, 400, 401, 403, 409, 412, 416, 418, 419, 420, 422, 424, 425, 426, 429, 431, 435, 436, 437, 441, 443, 452, 454, 471, 482, 483, 516, 523, 528, 536, 543, 547, 557, 572, 639, 724
Nuts 697
Nutter, Mayf 188-189, 307, 618
Nuyen, France 596, 603
Nyby, Christian 460, 502, 536, 576

O

O Pioneers 14
Oakland, Simon 461, 486, 504, 591

[822]

Index

Oates, Warren 295, 491, 515, 521, 532, 533, 564, 579, 587, 602, 615
Oberdiear, Karen 718, 719
Obie Tater 383, 445, 458
O'Brian, Hugh 73
O'Brien, Clay 684, 701
O'Brien, Edmond 572
O'Brien, Kim 713
O'Brien, Margaret 185
O'Brien, Richard 636, 690, 709
O'Byrne, Bryan 673
Occasional Wife 639, 673
O'Connell, William 652
O'Connor, Carroll 189, 296, 603, 619
O'Connor, Tim 570, 571, 662, 685
The Octopus 13
The Odd Couple 479, 498
Odd Man Out 409, 413, 504
Odney, Doug 457
O'Donnell, Gene 462, 618
The Odyssey 154
The Odyssey of Jubal Tanner 554
Of Human Bondage 601
Of Mice and Men 562
An Officer and a Gentleman 578, 595, 695
Ogg, James 379
Ogg, Sammy 394
Oh! Susanna 368
O'Hara, James 602
O'Hara, Shirley 510, 524, 558
O'Herlihy, Michael 571, 574, 583, 715
Oiler, William 370
Ojala, Arvo 103
O'Kelly, Donald 580
O'Kelly, Tim 594, 623
Olandt, Ken 723
Old Beller 426
Old Comrade 547
Old Dan 533
Old Faces 438, 523
Old Flame 307, 417, 512
Old Fool 53, 435, 519
Old Friend 379, 609, 615
Old Gunfighter 428
The Old Lady 367
Old Man 571
Old Man's Gold 420
Old Pal 404

Old Yellow Boots 528, 555
Old York 331, 553
Olek, Henry 703, 712
Oliver! 699, 700
Oliver, Susan 687, 688
Olsen, Susan 632, 633, 646
Olson, Eric 714, 715
Olson, James 687
Olson, Nancy 261, 681
O'Malley, J. Pat 310, 488, 498, 539, 547, 694
O'Malley, John 512
O'Malley, Kathleen 604, 658
O'Moore, Pat 453
On Golden Pond 144, 574
On the Waterfront 445, 587, 608, 673, 717
Once a Haggen 563
Once an Eagle 682
One Flew Over the Cuckoo's Nest 520
One for Lee 414
One for the Road 669, 679
One Killer on Ice 577, 585, 593
One Life to Live 674
One Man's Family 47, 53, 55, 378, 399, 452, 551, 561, 565, 590, 669, 671
One Night Stand 410
One Potato, Two Potato 622
O'Neal, Anne 468
O'Neal, Kevin 603, 604
O'Neal, Ryan 604
Only the Valiant 74
Only When I Laugh 537
Opening Night: U.S.A. 692
Operation Neptune 590
Operation Petticoat 560, 571, 622, 646
Operation Underground 25
O'Quillian 631, 642
Orchard, John 686, 687
The Ordeal of Patty Hearst 695
O'Rear, James 448
Orlandi, Felice 626
Osmond, Cliff 623, 629, 649, 653, 669
Osterloh, Robert 484
The Other Half 569
Otherworld 678, 712
O'Toole, Annette 662
O'Toole, Ollie 536, 543, 553, 564, 569, 583

Our Miss Brooks 54, 65, 113, 360, 363, 365, 441, 485, 496, 548
Our Private World 627, 678
Outer Limits 47, 669
The Outlaw Josey Wales 226, 446
The Outlaws 153, 597
Outlaw's Woman 313, 591, 600
"The Outriders" 104
The Outsiders 54
Over the Santa Fe Trail 117
Overboard 571, 685
Overholts, Jay 534
The Overland Express 365, 392, 486
Owens, Marjorie 450
Owens, Patricia 568
Owney Tupper Had a Daughter 140, 217, 566
The Oxbow Incident 16
Ozark Jubilee 563
Ozymandias 407
Ozzie and Harriet 575

P

P.S. Murry Christmas 677
P.T.-109 470, 585
Pa Hack's Brood 560
The Pacifist 401
The Pack Rat 196, 278, 650
Packer, Netta 478
Padilla, Manuel, Jr. 629, 630, 648, 651, 674
Pagosa 24, 25, 26
Paid Killer 367, 429
Paiva, Nestor 361, 362, 372, 373, 399
Pal 410
Pal Joey 64, 398
Palance, Jack 75, 119
The Paleface 631
Paley, William 25, 65, 74, 89, 124, 125, 126, 132, 202, 215
Palmer, Gregg 506, 544, 550, 554, 580, 589, 590, 591, 597, 623, 629, 632, 655, 664, 681
Palmer, Jeff 606
Palmer, Robert 549
Palmer, Thomas 471
Palter, Lew 629
Panacea Sykes 552

INDEX

Paper Dolls 678, 681
Paper Moon 569, 649
Papillon 578
Pardon My Gun 17, 595
The Parent Trap 494
Parfrey, Woodrow 547
The Pariah 582, 585
Paris 695
Paris, Frank 36, 39, 61, 436, 437, 438, 439, 440, 441, 522, 528, 529, 530, 531, 532, 533, 534, 535, 536, 537, 538, 539, 540, 541, 542, 543, 544, 545, 546, 547, 548, 549, 550, 551, 552, 553, 554, 555, 556, 557, 558, 559, 560, 561, 562, 563, 564, 565, 566, 567, 568, 569, 570, 571, 572, 573, 574, 575, 576, 579, 581, 583
Paris 7000 457
Paris Texas 481
Parker, Earl 492, 493
Parker, John 660
Parker, Willard 20
Parks, Jeff 701
Parks, Michael 540
Parrish, Julie 568, 569
Parson Comes to Town 313, 599
The Partners 416, 472
Passive Resistance 402, 492
Pastore, John 130, 151
Pat Garrett and Billy the Kid 112, 289
Pat Paulsen's Half a Comedy Hour 641, 657
Pate, Christopher 604
Pate, Michael 470, 496, 499, 572
The Pathfinder 13
Patricia 147, 196, 693, 698
Patrick, Butch 562, 563, 608
Patrick, Dennis 490
Patrick, John 452, 460
The Patsy 385, 487
Patten, Mary 541
Patten, Robert 485
Patterson, Hank 150, 443, 496, 497, 510, 511, 512, 514, 517, 520, 537, 541, 566, 580, 581, 584, 588, 590, 618, 621, 624, 658, 668, 681, 686

Patton 49
The Patty Duke Show 478
Paul, Byron 526
The Paul Lynde Show 635
Paull, Morgan 705, 717
The Pawnbroker 641
Paxton, Dick 445
Payne, Brad 493
Payne, Joan 604
Payne, John 190, 659
Payton-Wright, Pamela 681
Peabody, Dick 544, 545, 626
Peabody Award 23, 144
The Peace Officer 411, 436, 515
Pearce, Wynn 504
Peck, Ed 542, 571
Peck, Gregory 74
Peckinpah, Sam 3, 112, 113, 136, 289, 447, 451, 454, 455, 457, 460, 461, 464, 473, 482
Peck's Bad Boy 542
Peck's Bad Girl 561
Penn, Leo 631, 641
Pennell, Larry 304, 627, 708
Penney, Edmund 381
The People Against O'Hara 82
Perce 528, 541
The Perils of Pauline 583
Perkins, Jack 668, 669, 680, 701
Perkins, Richard 427
Perreau, Gigi 575
Perrin, Vic 16, 35, 39, 46, 47–48, 49, 60, 61, 64, 65, 67, 235, 282, 359, 363, 365, 368, 369, 371, 373, 374, 375, 376, 377, 378, 379, 380, 381, 382, 383, 384, 385, 386, 387, 388, 389, 390, 391, 392, 393, 394, 395, 396, 397, 398, 399, 400, 401, 402, 403, 404, 405, 406, 407, 409, 410, 411, 412, 413, 414, 415, 416, 417, 418, 419, 420, 421, 422, 423, 424, 425, 426, 427, 428, 429, 430, 431, 432, 433, 434, 435, 436, 437, 438, 439, 440, 441, 450, 470, 525, 526, 567
Perry, Elizabeth 584

Perry, Joseph 452, 513, 549
Perry Mason 96, 113, 114, 117, 144, 177, 361, 436, 451, 464, 492, 547, 553, 557, 667, 669, 674
Perryman, Lloyd 715
Persoff, Nehemiah 587, 590, 625, 638, 705, 721
Personal Justice 428
The Pest Hole 453
Petal, Erica 650
Pete and Gladys 371, 662
The Pete Gray Story 387
Pete Kelly's Blues 448
Peter Gun 449, 656, 708
Peter Loves Mary 659
Peter Pan 580
Peters, Brock 640, 641, 695
Peters, House, Jr. 495, 522
Peters, Jan 583, 641
Peters, Kelly Jean 613, 620, 635
Peters, Lauri 564, 573
Peters, Scott 499
Peterson, Arthur, Jr. 516, 530, 607, 649
Peterson, Nan 509
Petit, Michael 577
Petrie, George 653
Petrie, Howard 451
The Petrified Forest 602
Petrocelli 593, 665, 668
Petrone, Susan 535
Petticoat Junction 68, 150, 151, 387, 482, 534, 545, 575, 687
Peyton Place 113, 452, 480, 482, 488, 490, 497, 569, 571, 585, 586, 596, 614, 637, 661, 688, 693
The Phantom of the Opera 375
Phantom Ranger 17
Phelps, Tani 663, 676
Phillips, Barney 53, 54, 359, 360, 362, 364, 366, 368, 369, 376, 378, 379, 383, 387, 388, 390, 391, 393, 395, 396, 398, 402, 404, 409, 412, 416, 424, 426, 427, 429, 430, 431, 433, 435, 436, 437, 439, 441, 460, 495, 496, 516, 523, 559

[824]

Index

Philip Marlowe 656, 674
Phillips, Robert 661, 710
Phipps, William 495, 504, 540, 559
Phoebe Strunk 544
Phoenix 661, 697
Photocrime 445
The Photographer 400, 469, 500
Phyllis 154, 462, 620, 630, 634
The Piano 37, 418
Piazza, Ben 720
Picerni, Paul 189, 343, 611, 612, 619, 700, 710
Pickard, John 77, 508, 519, 548, 594, 605, 611, 639, 688, 702, 719
Pickens, Slim 174, 563, 593, 661, 684
Pickford, Mary 127
Pierce, Preston 594
The Pigman 135
Pigskin Parade 594
Pike 662, 669, 680, 683, 704
The Pillagers 141, 296, 343, 619, 628
Pina, Alberto 687
Pine, Philip 471
Pine, Robert 168, 189–190, 629, 640, 659, 696
The Pioneers 13
Pistols 'n' Petticoats 476, 609, 694
Pittman, Tom 456, 474, 693
Place, Martin 596
A Place in the Sun 535
The Plainclothesman 440, 468
The Planet of the Apes 624, 673
Platt, Alma 598
Platt, Ed 446
Playhouse 90 48, 114, 361, 493
Please Don't Eat the Daisies 496
Pleshette, Suzanne 658
Plumb, Eve 638
Poe, Edgar Allan 24
Pokey Pete 427
Police Squad 637
Police Story 640
Police Woman 465, 595, 646

Polifroni, Pam 160, 161, 175, 188, 196, 197, 199
Pollard, Michael J. 569, 570
Pollick, Teno 588, 599
Pollis, Eunice 564
Poltergeist III 590
Pomerantz, Jeff 635, 689
Pony Express 75
Poor Pearl 388, 463
Poppe, Herman 666, 714
Porter, J. Robert 624
Portrait in Black 582
The Poseidon Adventure 637
Possessed 594
Post, Clayton 381, 386, 388, 391, 399, 463, 474
Post, Ted 86, 113, 114, 187, 202, 455, 456, 457, 458, 459, 460, 461, 462, 463, 466, 467, 468, 469, 470, 473, 476, 478, 479, 480, 482, 483, 485, 486, 489, 490, 491, 493, 494, 498, 499, 500, 505, 519, 525, 526, 528, 530, 535, 537, 549, 550
Post Martin 366
The Postman Always Rings Twice 532
Potato Road 390, 474, 514
Potshot 522
Powell, Addison 494
Powell, Dick 38
Powell, Sandye 692
The Powers of Matthew Star 144
Pozen, Michael 477
Prairie Happy 374, 456
Prairie Wolfer 116, 556, 562, 619, 620, 628, 670
Prange, Laurie 191, 278, 671
Pratt, Judson 470, 472, 550
Pratt, Robert 692
The Preacher 396, 455, 486
The Predators 633, 680
Preece, Michael 612
President's Council on Mental Retardation 133, 704
The Pretender 590, 600
Prescribed Killing 431
Pretty Mama 406
Price, Sherwood 587

The Price of Fear 593
Prickett, Carl 553
Pride and Prejudice 561
Prime of Life 599
The Prince and the Pauper 597
Prine, Andrew 540, 547, 558
Print Asper 371, 498
The Prisoner 540, 641, 642
The Prisoner of Second Avenue 612
Private Benjamin 720
The Prize 54, 388
The Prodigal 313, 616, 628
The Producers 611
Professional Father 96
The Professor 437
Professor Lute Bone 376, 412, 449
Profiles in Courage 551
Prokop, Paul 689
The Promoter 282, 567
The Protectors 637
Provendie, Zina 484
The Proving Kid 417
Pryor, Ainslie 446, 455, 457, 474
Psycho 365, 480, 486, 659
Public Defender 150
Pucket's New Year 397, 414, 429, 464
Puglia, John 669
Punchline 603
Purdum, Herb 26, 35, 38, 39, 48, 111, 245, 360, 362, 363
Pussy Cats 368
Putnam, William 721
Pyle, Denver 77, 191–192, 292, 464, 472, 495, 518, 546, 554, 563, 572, 577, 598, 601, 608, 622, 693

Q

Quaker Girl 606
Quarter-Horse 369, 416
The Queen and I 678
Queen for a Day 612
The Quest 101, 571
The Quest for Asa Janin 555
The Queue 105, 382, 413, 447
A Quiet Day in Dodge 296, 694

[825]

INDEX

Quincy 498
Quinn, Anthony 362
Quinn, Ariane 606
Quinn, Pat 174
Quint Asper Comes Home 115, 296, 542, 556
Quint-Cident 553, 570
Quinton, Dolores 566
Quint's Indian 343, 550
Quint's Trail 558
Quo Vadis 476

R

Raaf, Vici 360
The Rabbit Trap 52
Rachel, Rachel 687
Racing with the Moon 343
Raciti, Joe 580
Raddatz, Leslie 98
Rader, Jack 718
Raderman, Richard E. 647
Radio-Television Mirror Daily Award 23
Rafferty, Chip 598
Ragan, Mike 541
The Raid 593, 600
Raiders of the Lost Ark 689
Railroad 633, 642
The Railroad 364
Raines, Steve 495, 605, 609, 624, 629, 630, 631, 636, 645, 661, 664
Rainey, Buck 19
Rainey, Ford 539, 541, 579, 713
Raintree County 453
Ralston, Gilbert 589
Rambo 441
Rambo, Dack 662, 669
Ramirez, Frank 694, 695
Ramus, Nick 707, 708
Ranch Life in the Great Southwest 15
Randall, Glen, Jr. 645
Randall, Sue 519, 531
Randell, Ron 489
Randles, Larry 676, 706
Randolph, Donald 491
Random, Bob 591, 593, 602, 624, 640, 653, 667
The Range Rider 19
The Range Riders 17
Rankin, Gilman 516, 552, 589, 594, 603, 718

The Rape of Richard Beck 441
The Rare Breed 113, 462
The Rat Patrol 605, 667
Rath, Charles 8
Rawhide 104, 110, 113, 117, 120, 121, 128, 143, 184, 210, 360, 450, 465, 495, 559, 578, 605, 606, 686
Ray, Jane 471
The Ray Anthony Show 664
Raybould, Harry 544, 666
Rayburn, Sam 109
Raymond, Guy 524, 529, 604
Rea, Peggy 404, 539, 592, 622, 631, 671
Reach for Glory 121
Reagan, Nancy 506
Reagan, Ronald 102, 190, 506, 542
The Real McCoys 360, 441, 537, 542, 563
Real Sent Sonny 415
Rear Window 576
Rebel Without a Cause 578, 720
The Red Badge of Courage 387, 668
The Red Button Show 690
Red Mountain 54, 631
The Red Planet Mars 457, 597
Red River 464, 501, 562, 605, 722
Red River Valley 18
Red Ryder 15, 23
The Red Skelton Show 361, 404, 539, 616, 669
Redding, Glenn 659
Redfern, Gene 576
Redfield, Dennis 710, 714, 719
Redfield, William 520
Redmond, Liam 310, 539
Redondo, Anthony 614
Reed, Alan, Jr. 502, 537
Reed, Marshall 545
Reed, Walter 467
The Reed Survives 392, 427, 448, 473
Reese, Sammy 608
Reese, Tom 192, 332, 511, 514, 520, 522, 536, 562, 583, 591, 597, 606, 614, 634, 717
Reeves, Richard 507

Regas, Pedro 657
Reid, Carl Benton 493
Reilly, John 709, 710, 714
Reindel, Carl 539, 541, 558, 577
Reische, Geri 665
Reisner, Allen 144, 146, 579, 591, 598, 609, 610
Reitzen, Jack 479
The Reivers 574
Rellas, Chris 621
Reluctant Violence 434
Renaldo, Duncan 19
Renard, David 610, 626, 679
Renard, Ken 588, 596, 664, 720
Renegade White 362, 496
The Renegades 548
Rennick, Nancy 512
Repp, Stafford 471, 483, 516, 691
Reprisal 536, 570
The Reprisal 312, 638, 639, 642
Restless Gun 109, 659
The Return of Frank Cannon 254
The Return of Frank James 226
The Return of the Beverly Hillbillies 150
The Return of the World's Greatest Detective 672
The Returning 338, 610
Reunion '78 451, 473
The Reward 589
Reward for Matt 390, 450
Rey, Alejandro 677
Rey, Araceli 655
Reynolds, Burt 79, 91, 114–116, 122, 126, 161, 195, 209–210, 211, 290, 291, 306, 443, 542, 562, 580, 582, 584
Rhoda 154, 587, 713
Rhodes, Eugene Manlove 14
Rhue, Madlyn 192, 334, 505
Rich, Dick 463, 478, 484, 498, 509
Rich, John 113, 114, 146, 189, 477, 478, 481, 482, 483, 484, 485, 618, 624, 631, 639

Index

Rich, Vernon 566
Rich Man, Poor Man 113, 469, 557, 586, 601, 612, 644, 686, 691, 707, 716
The Richard Boone Show 53, 475, 478, 519, 539, 659, 662, 708
Richard III 113
Richards, Paul 102, 444, 457, 479, 626
Richards, Tommy 576
The Richie Rich SHow 366, 655
Richman, Peter Mark 192, 278, 627
The Ride Back 37, 48, 254, 362
Ride a Crooked Trail 114
Ride Clear of Diablo 114
Riders of the Purple Sage 14
The Rifleman 112, 226, 455, 464, 492, 597, 670
The Right Stuff 46
Riha, Bobby 618
Rin Tin Tin 550
Ring of Darkness 648, 656
Rings, Mary 666
Rio Bravo 465
Rio Lobo 668
Rios, Lalo 525
Ripcord 117, 304, 563, 627
Ripley, Jay 584
Riptide 605, 687
Rituals 673
The Ritz 481
Rivas, Carlos 610
The River 344, 574, 684, 697
Riverboat 498, 582, 584
Roach, Hal 507, 532
Road, Mike 514, 574
The Road West 540, 558
The Roaring Twenties 46, 444, 476
Robards, Jason 371
Robber Bridegroom 391, 491
Robbins, Gale 607
The Robe 597
Roberson, Chuck 500, 511, 545
Robert Montgomery Presents 480
Robert Taylor Detectives 159
Roberts, Davis 641
Roberts, Lois 613
Roberts, Mark 468

Roberts, Pernell 345, 477, 620
Roberts, Ralph 613
Roberts, Randolph 700, 717
Roberts, Roy 150–151, 444, 531, 538, 554, 559, 581, 588, 589, 611, 630, 646, 649, 653
Roberts, Stephen 496
Robertson, Dennis 566
Robin Hood 387, 450, 500
Robinson, Bartlett 427, 430, 435, 436, 437, 464, 482, 488, 495, 501, 509
Robinson, Charles 616
Robinson, Chris 548, 549
Robinson, Edward, Jr. 500
Robinson, Hubbell, Jr. 25, 73, 76
Robson, William 23, 24, 25, 36, 59, 71, 220–222, 239, 465
Rock-a-Bye Baby 513
Rock Bottom 409
The Rockford Files 389, 562, 587, 618, 712, 713
Rockwell, Robert 496
Rogers, Elizabeth 604
Rogers, Ginger 74
Rogers, Kenny 578
Rogers, Roy 18, 207, 557
Rogers, Wayne 319, 340, 505, 533, 588
Rogers, Will 18, 467
Rogers of the Gazette 44
Roland, Gilbert 335, 560
Roley, Sutton 575
Roman, Nina 587, 588, 691, 708
Roman, Ric 507
Roman, Ruth 644, 672
Romance 24, 36, 38, 46, 51, 245
Romano, Andy 535
Rome Adventure 658
Romeo 398, 476
Rondeau, Charles 608
The Rookies 457, 613
The Rooks 412
Room for One More 461, 645, 657
Room 222 126, 554
Rooney, Wallace 522, 545, 547
Roope, Fay 495, 497

Rooster Cogburn 365
Root Down 542, 570
Roots 574, 608, 662
Roots of Fear 649
Roots: The Next Generation 641
Rope Fever 342, 621, 628
The Rose 144, 574
Rose, Ralph 25, 607
The Rose Tattoo 531
Rosemary's Baby 487, 621
Ross, Don G. 587, 619
Ross, Katherine 290, 571, 581
Ross, Robert C. 471
Rosser, John 535, 554
Rothwell, Robert 614, 651, 659
The Rough Riders 447, 571
Roughing It 13
The Round-Up 367, 460, 487
The Rounders 654, 683
Route 66 113, 1fi1, 575, 671
Rowan and Martin's Laugh-In 688
Rowe, Arthur 623, 633, 636, 641
Rowland, Henry 568
Roy Rogers Show 18, 150
The Royal Hunt of the Sun 165
Rubin, Benny 652
Rudley, Herbert 463, 472
Ruffino, Val 535
The Ruggles 384
Rumsey, Burt 460, 462, 464, 465, 494
Run, Buddy, Run 480
Run for Cover 226
Run for Your Life 679
Run, Sheep, Run 577
Runaway Train 606
Runaways 674
Running Wild 593
Rupp, Jack 724
Ruskin, Joseph 536, 605
Russell, Bing 457, 490, 516, 528, 609, 707
Russell, Jackie 622, 720
Russell, John 714, 715
Russell, Kurt 457, 570, 571, 708
Russell, William D. 465, 469, 471, 472
The Russians Are Coming, the Russians Are Coming 611

INDEX

Rust, Richard 494, 502, 515
Rutherford, Gene 615
Rutherford, Lori 691
Ryan, Fran 101, 151, 192, 346, 348, 444, 682, 714, 719, 721, 723
Ryan, Robert 47
Ryan's Four 590
Rydell, Mark 3, 114, 123, 143, 146, 174, 573, 574, 578, 581, 582, 587, 592, 593, 601, 602, 603
Ryder, Alfred 493
Ryder, Eddie 690
Rye, Michael 430

S

S.O.B. 622
S.P.E.R.D.V.A.C 430
S.W.A.T. 457, 637, 722
Saber, David 467
The Sacketts 144
Saddle and Sagebrush 595
Saddle Sore Sal 409
Sage, Willard 480, 573, 586, 593
St. Elsewhere 596, 707
St. John, Marco 691, 710
Sally 685
Salmi, Albert 593, 613, 664
Saludos 409, 503
Salvage 1 618
Sam 585
Sam McTavish, M.D. 538, 658, 677
Sam Spade 46
Same Time Next Year 538
The Sammy Kaye Show 639
Sampson, Robert 616
San Fernando Valley 226
Sanctuary 596
The Sand Pebbles 441
Sande, Walter 526, 581, 643, 647, 677
Sanders, Hugh 534
Sanders, Steve 611
Sandor, Steve 631
Sanford, Donald S. 658, 661, 668, 669
Sanford and Son 641, 698, 720
Santa Fe Trail 7

Santee 226
Sara 572, 634, 675
Sarafian, Richard C. 580, 617, 627
Sarah 285, 686, 697, 711
Sarah's Search 422
Sarge 633
Sargent, Dick 534
Sargent, Joe 498, 576
Sargent, Joseph 114, 467, 546, 553, 554, 585, 586, 587
Sargent, Richard 539
Sarracino, Ernest 663
The Satan Bug 542
Saturday Night 608, 614, 670
Saturday Night Movies 153
Savage, Paul 3, 113, 118, 119, 135, 140-141, 142, 175, 216-219, 326, 381, 554, 555, 557, 561, 566, 586, 589, 590, 595, 600, 601, 602, 603, 604, 605, 606, 607, 608, 609, 610, 611, 612, 613, 614, 616, 617, 618, 619, 620, 621, 622, 623, 624, 625, 626, 627, 629, 630, 631, 632, 633, 634, 635, 636, 637, 638, 639, 640, 641, 642, 687, 691, 701, 706, 708, 713, 718, 721
Save Me a Place at Forest Lawn 581
Saxon, Aaron 484
Saxon, John 192-193, 296, 582, 592, 604, 619, 717
Say Uncle 515
Sayonara 551
Scarecrow and Mrs. King 555, 722
Scared Boy 425
Scared Kid 397
Scarface 343
The Scarlet Letter 544
The Scavengers 133, 661, 662, 683
Schaefer, Jack 16
Schallert, William 157, 180, 193-194, 337, 478, 492, 554, 635, 699
Scarf, Sabrina 643
Schary, Dore 82
Schiller, Norbert 453
Schlitz Playhouse 476

Schneider, Joseph 619
Schoenberg, Arnold 194
The Schoolmarm 708
Schuck, John 644, 654
Schultz, Keith 622, 623
Schuyler, Dorothy 448, 452, 458, 469
Schwartz, Sam 460
Scollay, Fred J. 589, 612
Scot Free 568
Scott, Brenda 551
Scott, Evelyn 452, 453
Scott, Jacqueline 493, 543, 567, 604, 620, 632, 633, 646, 680
Scott, Ken 579
Scott, Pippa 531, 675
Scott, Richard D. 668
Scott, Simon 709, 710
Scott, Walter 703
Scotti, Vito 591, 619, 645, 664
The Screen Actor's Guild 50th Anniversary Celebration 462
Scruples 507, 621, 634
Scudero, Joe 458
The Sea Chase 82
The Sea of Grass 501
Seagram, Lisa 560
Seahunt 595
Search 699
The Search 539, 541
Search for Tomorrow 561
The Searches 117, 659
Searl, Jack 541, 542, 638
Seay, James 566
Second Arrest 426
Second Choice 396
Second Son 414
Seconds 665
The Secret Empire 596, 624
The Secret Storm 538, 622, 659
Secrets of Midland Heights 571
Seel, Charles 150, 443, 524, 553, 558, 586, 589, 591, 615, 637, 653, 654, 710, 724
Seflinger, Carol 542
Selby, Sarah 151, 443, 530, 545, 548, 557, 564, 672
Seldes, Marian 461
Selk, George 150, 443, 451, 474, 478, 481, 482, 497, 504, 508, 514, 517,

Index

518, 524, 525, 526, 537, 543, 546, 552, 559
Selles, Scott 697
Selzer, Milton 507, 550, 561, 652
The Senator 674
Sennett, Mack 532
Sentry, Frank 525
Sergeant Holly 176, 275, 650, 664
Sergeant Preston of the Yukon 20
The Serpent's Egg 668
Serpico 343
Seven, Johnny 532, 586
Seven Angry Men 75, 87, 518, 552
Seven Brides for Seven Brothers 585
Seven Days in May 55
Seven Hours to Dawn 143, 586
Seventh Avenue 607
79 Park Avenue 593
Seymour, Anne 501, 518
Sha Na Na 607, 611
Shadler 692
The Shadow 389
Shadow Chasers 644
Shadow in the Night 55
Shahan, Rocky 465
Shakespeare 38, 363
Shalet, Diane 687, 718
Shane 16, 33, 165, 168, 226, 460, 487, 553, 580, 601, 668
Shank, John 618
Shannon 712
Shannon, Harry 522
Shannon, Richard 536, 544
The Sharecroppers 54, 315, 722
Sharkey's Machine 115
Sharp, Alex 472, 524, 528, 552, 624, 693, 704, 715
Sharpe, Karen 467, 468, 561
Shatner, William 606
Shaw, Elizabeth 568
A Shayna Maidel 685
She Loves Me 486
Shea, Eric 620, 635, 640
Sheena, Queen of the Jungle 360
Sheep Dog 410

Sheiner, David 672
Sheldon, James 477, 588
Shelton, Jacque 559
Shenandoah 113, 226, 462
Shepard, Jan 521, 523, 562, 612
Sheppard, Jim 657
Sheppard, W. Morgan 723
Sheppodd, Jon 446
Shera, Mark 721, 722
Sheridan, Chick 606, 609
Sheridan, Dan 491, 499
The Sheriff of Cochise 477
Sherman, Orville 536, 563, 566, 600
Shettlesworth, Jack 537
Ship of Fools 535
Shirley, Mercedes 533
Shogun 512
Sholdar, Mickey 564
Shona 549
Shooting Stopover 427, 515
The Shootist 557
Shotgun Slade 645
Shriver, William 704
Sierra, Gregory 698, 720
Silberman, Mitchell 676
Silent Movie 713
Silent Victory: The Kitty O'Neill Story 592
Siler, Russ 619
Silo, Susan 639
Silver, Jeff 451
Silver, Joe 690
Silver Bullet 721
Silver Streak 114
Silvera, Frank 174, 593
Silverado 210
Silverheels, Jay 19
Silverman, Fred 154
Simcox, Tom 560, 562, 579, 590, 602, 618, 647, 708
Simmons, Richard 20
Simms, Jay 608
Simon, Robert F. 470, 471, 474, 491, 565, 574, 579, 602
Simon and Simon 43, 456, 695
Simpson, Mickey 463
Sinatra, Frank 116, 126, 176
Sinatra, Richard 505
The Singing Cowboy 18
Singing on the Trail 117, 303

The Singing Vagabond 18
Singleton, Doris 544
Sins of the Father 388, 465, 500
Sirola, Joseph 567
Sirota's Court 628
The Sisters 649, 656
Sitler, Henry L. 7
Sitowitz, Hal 142, 595, 599, 601, 603, 605, 616, 623, 625, 626, 697, 700, 720
The Six-Gun Mystique 13
The Six Million Dollar Man 579, 679
The Six-Shooter 16
Sizzle 561
Skaggs, Jim 676
Skelton, Red 48
Skerritt, Tom 100, 194, 590, 601, 606, 658, 691
Skid Row 390, 467
Sky 373, 494
Sky King 19, 226, 458
Slate, Jeremy 533, 536, 559, 584, 594, 632, 672
Slattery, Richard X. 564, 651
Slattery's People 441, 677
Slaughterhouse-Five 46
Sloane, Everett 558, 582
Slocum 630, 642
Small Fry Club 18
Small Water 515
Smash-Up 561
Smash-Up on Interstate 5 677
Smith, Bernice 712
Smith, Cecil 119, 134, 154
Smith, Frank 124
Smith, Hal 194, 307, 513
Smith, John 464
Smith, Ken L. 452, 463, 481, 484, 547
Smith, Kent 551, 561
Smith, Pat 479, 526
Smith, Sandra 627, 633, 689
Smith, William 194, 691, 720
The Smith Family 567, 646
Smokey and the Bandit 115, 542
Smoking Out the Beedles 106, 385, 446
Smoking Out the Nolans 106, 386, 446

[829]

INDEX

Smuggler's Gold 96
Smythe, Kit 607
The Snake Pit 579, 608
Snakebite 403, 491
Snap Decision 600, 614, 670
Sniper's Ridge 605
The Snoop Sisters 592
The Snow Birch 128
Snow Train 278, 313, 659, 660, 683, 711
Snyder, Anne 702
Soap 622, 685, 698
Soble, Ron 712
The Sod-buster 441
The Sodbusters 275, 689, 697
Sofaer, Abraham 508, 533
Solari, Rudy 513
The Soldier 369
The Solid Gold Cadillac 378
Solomon River 432
Some Like It Hot 587
Somebody Up There Likes Me 578
Something for Joey 592
Sometimes a Great Notion 551
Sommars, Julie 194, 313, 582, 590, 601
Sondergaard, Quentin 532, 534
Song for Dying 126, 579
Song of Bernadette 373
Song of the Drifter 595
Song of the Prairie 117, 303
Song of the Saddle 552
A Song to Remember 644
Sooter, Rudy 586, 588, 590, 608, 614, 617
Sorenson, Paul 686, 701, 715
Sorrells, Robert 531, 561, 581, 587, 590, 601, 605, 618, 630, 663, 677, 718
Sorry Wrong Number 26, 40, 608
Soul, David 719, 720
The Soul of a Monster 55
Soule, Olan 592, 638
Sounder 662
South of the Border 226
South Pacific 535, 596
South Wind 590, 600
Space 1999 488
Space Patrol 468
Spacek, Sissy 144
Spain, Fay 475, 532, 622

Speak Me Fair 116, 406, 511
Spelling, Aaron 456, 457
Spencer for Hire 551, 722
Spencer's Mountain 53
Spencer's Pilot 560
The Spirit of the Border 14
Splash 647
Splendor in the Grass 673, 685
Spies Like Us 637
Spring Freshet 409
Spring Term 371, 438, 463, 500
Springfield Rifle 74
Springsteen, R.G. 503, 505
Spruance, Don 554
The Spy Who Came in from the Cold 599
The Square Triangle 365, 429
The Squaw 296, 297, 416, 530, 541, 717, 723
Stacy, James 194, 211, 332, 575, 576, 617, 680, 701
Stafford, Dan 529, 552
Stage Holdup 11, 279, 377, 489
Stage Smash 435
Stage Snatch 432
Stage Stop 332, 605
Stage Struck 540
Stagecoach 16, 168
Stalag 17 588, 597
The Stallion 416
Stalmaster, Lynn 171
Stanley 108
Stanley, Forrest 486
Stanley, Paul 671, 675, 676, 679
Stanton, Harry Dean 481, 521, 528, 540, 565, 635
Stanwyck, Barbara 488
A Star Is Born 96
The Star Chamber 662
Star Trek 47, 144, 161, 170, 184, 336, 453, 533, 536, 542, 606
Star Trek: The Wrath of Khan 657
Star Wars 689
Stark 658, 683
Starrett, Charles 17
Stars in My Crown 96
Starsky and Hutch 720
State of the Union 621

Steele, Bob 17, 168
Stehli, Edgar 464
The Stepford Wives 571
Stephens, Chris 619
Stephenson, John 361, 362
Stern, Tom 607, 632
Sterrett, Charles 511
The Steve Allen Variety Hour 710
Steve Canyon 461
Stevens, Craig 195, 708
Stevens, Morton 619
Stevens, Onslow 497
Stevens, Scott 498
Stevens, Paul 674, 696, 702
Stevens, Warren 478, 528, 550
Stevenson, Parker 709
Stevenson, Robert 114, 454, 455, 456, 457
Stevenson, Robert J. 536, 538
Stewart, Art 636
Stewart, Charley 8
Stewart, Charlotte 654, 708
Stewart, Gregg 505
Stewart, James 16, 86, 129
Stewart, Marianne 466
Stewart, Paul 162, 655, 656
Stewart, Peggy 496, 513, 530, 567, 573
Stewart, Robert C. 584, 596
The Still 625, 647
The Sting 150
Stockman, Boyd 458
Stockwell, Guy 195, 343, 518, 519
Stolen Horses 376, 524
Stone 673
Stone, Charles Joseph 622, 623, 687
Stone, Fred 92, 210
Stone, Harold J. 471, 488, 497, 529, 569, 573, 585
Stone, Jack 182
Stone, Leonard 195, 342, 578, 696, 700, 715
Stone, Milburn 3, 75, 84, 85, 86, 92–95, 99, 101, 107, 115, 117, 118, 122, 123, 134, 147, 148, 159, 163, 164, 167, 171, 172,

[830]

Index

176, 181, 184, 192, 196, 205, 207, 209, 217, 257, 260, 265, 272, 277, 280, 281, 292, 306, 309, 316, 321, 323, 330, 346, 350, 443, 562, 623, 673, 677, 724
Stoney Burke 596
Stop Me If You've Heard This One 652
Stopover Tokyo 151
Storefront Lawyers 641, 643
Stories of the Century 21
The Storm 313, 586
Storm Center 673
Storm Fear 88
Storm Warning 506
The Story of Holly Sloan 47
The Story of Temple Drake 150
The Story of the Cowboy 13
Straight Arrow 15
Straight Time 721
Strain, Smokey 92
Strange, Glenn 148, 149, 282, 286, 287, 309, 330, 443, 497, 523, 526, 527, 532, 562, 579, 672, 705, 724
Strange Report 642
Stranger in Town 345, 620, 628
Strangers on a Train 644
Stratton, Gil, Jr. 362
Straw Dogs 112, 289, 447
A Streetcar Named Desire 673
Streets of Laredo 74
Strickland, Amzie 446, 462, 658
Striker, Fran 15
Stripes 491
Stromberg, Hunt 119, 120
Stromsoe, Fred 665, 674
Strong, Michael 600, 695
Strong, Robert 461
Stroud, Don 695, 696, 712
Struck by Lightning 476
Stryker 341, 643, 656
The Stu Erwin Show 594, 672
Stuart, Wendy 496
The Stuntman 719
Sturges, Mark 597
Sturgis, Norman 505
The Subject Was Roses 645
Sublette, Linda 714
Suddenly Last Summer 671
Sugarfoot 108, 550

Sullivan, Brick 478
Sullivan, Ed 108
Sullivan, Liam 466, 606
Summer and Smoke 128, 365, 444
Summer Magic 609
Summer Night 410
Summer Rental 441
Summer Stock 706
Summertime 582
Summers, Hope 492, 519, 557
Summers, Jerry 631
Summers, Neil 195-196, 689, 699, 712
The Summons 538, 556
Sumper, William L. 619
Sunday Supplement 324, 402, 480, 527
Sundown 371
The Sundowners 503, 578
Sunny Afternoon 396
Sunrise at Campobello 621
Sunset 457
Sunshine 572
The Surgery 414
Superman 718
Supertrain 590
Support Your Local Gunfighter 531
Support Your Local Sheriff 537, 560, 595
Surfside Six 714
The Survivors 625, 673, 690
Susan Was Evil 703
Suspense 38, 46, 59, 175, 221, 245, 361, 370, 389, 465
The Sutler 374
Sutton, Dolores 548
Sutton, Frank 529, 534, 547
Sutton, Tom 650, 651, 663, 681
Svensson, Monica 701
Swafford, Tom 152
Swan, Robert 496, 655, 662, 688, 709
Swan Watch 594
Swanton, Harold 452
Sweeney, Bob 365, 366, 368
Sweet and Sour 403, 439, 467, 500
Sweet Billy, Singer of Songs 593, 600

Sweet Bird of Youth 588
Swenson, Karl 145, 477, 501, 522, 539, 570, 598, 605, 643, 668
Swing Shift 571
Swiss Family Robinson 678, 715
Swit, Loretta 100, 196, 278, 651, 660
Switch 547, 564, 622
Swofford, Ken 622, 629, 635, 643, 655, 668, 702, 720
Swoger, Harry 502, 510, 517, 519

T

T.H.E. Cat 578
T.J. Hooker 606
Tacetta 370
Tafur, Robert 602
Tag, You're It 36, 334, 419, 505
Tai-Pan 387
Tail to the Wind 406, 502
Take Her, She's Cheap 572, 585
The Taking of Pelham One-Two-Three 114, 467
Talbot 270, 696
Talbot, Nita 490, 512
Talbott, Gloria 445, 533, 549
A Tale of Two Cities 579
Tales of the 77th Bengal Lancers 478, 674
Tales of the Texas Rangers 20, 506
Tales of the Unexpected 40
Tales of Wells Fargo 108, 110, 605
Tall Story 594
Tall Trapper 433, 520
Talman, William 557
Tamblyn, Russ 585
Taming of the West 17
Tammy 566
Tanin, Eleanore 379, 383, 387, 388, 390, 393, 394, 397
Tannen, Charles 480
Tannen, William 624, 643
Tanner, Clay 674, 706

[831]

INDEX

Tap Day for Kitty 393, 452, 486
Taps for Old Jeb 319, 588
Tara 365, 679, 697
Taras Bulba 509, 599
Target 339, 417, 500
Target: Chester 420
Target: The Corruptors 611
The Tarnished Badge 715, 722
Tarzan 360, 630
Tate 636
Tatum 688, 698
Taxi Driver 649
Tayback, Vic 613, 639, 667, 687
Taylor, Buck 4, 5, 127, 147-148, 211, 329, 330, 443, 595, 617, 619, 723, 724
Taylor, Dub "Cannonball" 148, 595, 608, 614, 631, 653
Taylor, Joan 492
Taylor, Judson 477
Taylor, Mary Lou 586, 618
Taylor, Vaughn 480, 504, 631
Tea and Sympathy 535, 590
Tea for Two 590
Teachers Only 690
Teague, Guy 496
Teahouse of the August Moon 702
Teal, Ray 485, 486
The Ted Knight Show 589, 710
Tedrow, Irene 384
Tell Chester 313, 553
Tellez, Trini 721
Temperatures Rising 644
Temple Houston 153
The Ten Commandments 49, 507, 644
Ten Little Indians 587
Ten Wanted Men 88
Tenafly 668
The Tender Trap 449
Tension at Table Rock 184, 336
Terranova, Dan 632
Terrell, Steve 471, 509
Terror in the Wax Museum 699
Terry, Tex 491

Testament 695
Testimony of Two Men 671
Tetzel, Joan 473
The Texan 584
Texas Cowboys 382, 483
Texas Gunfighter 17
Texas Wheelers 719
Thatcher, Torin 610
Them 497
Then Came Bronson 540
There Was a Crooked Man 560
There Was Never a Horse 374, 498
They Shoot Horses Don't They? 587
Thick 'n' Thin 404, 505
Thicker Than Water 444
The Thieves 654, 656
The Thin Man 471, 490, 645
The Thing 78, 82, 259, 460, 571
Thinnes, Roy 547, 555
Third Son 424
13 Queens Boulevard 694
13 West Street 121
Thirty a Month and Found 338, 713, 714, 722
This Golden Land 133, 696, 698
This Man Dawson 699
This Is Your Life 629
Thomas, Danny 533
Thomas, Lance 659
Thomas, Paul C. 712
The Thomas Crown Affair 662
Thompson, Charles 494, 635
Thompson, Dee J. 453, 580
Thompson, Hilarie 645, 646
Thompson, Marshall 485
Thompson, Pat 634
Thompson, Thomas 540, 655
Thor, Larry 420
Thordsen, Kelly 586, 617
The Thorn Birds 512, 658, 665
Thorton, Evans 689
Thoroughbreds 394, 489
Thorpe, Daniel 690
Thorsen, Duane 457

Thorson, Russell 452, 456, 561, 579
Those Calloways 43
The Three Faces of Eve 717
Three for the Road 685, 689
Three Godfathers 501
Three Little Words 706
Three Men and a Baby 532
The Three Musketeers 512
Thriller 567
Thursday's Child 580, 585
Tick, Tick, Tick 688
A Ticket to Tomahawk 226
Till Death Do Us 405, 506
The Tim Conway Show 566
Time Bandits 685
Time of the Jackals 285, 636, 642
The Tin Star 365, 451
Tindall, Robert 689
The Tingler 491
To the Ends of the Earth 50
To Hell and Back 114
To Kill a Mockingbird 464, 641
To Ride a Yellow Horse 709
Tobe 557
Tobey, Kenneth 516, 517, 563, 641, 689
Tobin, Dan 553, 607
Tobruk 114, 518
Tokyo Joe 506
Tom Corbett, Space Cadet 571
Tom, Dick and Mary 468
Tom Mix 15, 23
Tom Sawyer 542
Toma 486
Tombstone Territory 109, 446, 516
Tompkins, Bee 551
Tonight in Havana 679
Tony Award 486, 538, 612, 621, 645, 658, 702
The Tony Randall Show 610
Too Close for Comfort 499
Top Gun 590
Top Hat 74
Top Secret 656
Torrey, Roger 537, 564, 684
Totino, Frank M. 724
Totten, Robert 123, 131, 140, 144-145, 146, 163, 175, 191, 199, 214, 228, 288, 595, 599, 600, 602, 603, 606, 608, 609, 613,

Index

614, 616, 618, 619, 624, 625, 627, 634, 638, 639, 644, 647, 655, 658, 659, 664, 665, 667, 668, 671, 681, 696
A Town in Chains 275, 351, 712, 722
The Town Tamers 706, 711
Townes, Harry 308, 463, 488, 502, 557, 584, 590, 675
The Tracer 667
Trackdown 573
Tracy, Spencer 85, 86, 476
Trading Places 621
Trafton 674, 683
The Tragedian 419, 507
Trail of Bloodshed 708
The Trail of the Lonesome Pine 14
The Trap 445
Trapper John, M.D. 477, 710
The Trappers 424, 544, 570
Trapper's Revenge 423
Travanti, Daniel 166, 705, 706, 717
The Travels of Jaimie McPheeters 420, 571, 693
Traven, B. 16
Treasure of John Walking Fox 598
The Treasure of Sierra Madre 16
Trendle, George W. 19
Trevy, Ken 621
The Trial 389, 423
The Tribe 146
Tribute to a Badman 52, 361, 446, 447, 611
Tried It—Didn't Like It 418
Trip West 567
The Triplets 623
Tristin, Dorothy 713
Trojan War 368, 429
Trouble in Kansas 395
Trouble, Inc. 372
True Grit 226, 445, 449, 612
Trumbull, Brad 505, 519, 536
The Trumpet Blows 150
Trust 391
Tsiang, H.T. 603
Tucker, Forrest 174, 176,

294, 576, 577, 586, 616, 650, 664, 681
Tucker, the Man and His Dream 479
Tully, Tom 362, 363, 364, 366, 368, 370, 374, 375, 376
Tulsa 506
The Tumbleweed 436
Tumbleweeds 14
Tumbling Tumbleweeds 18
Turley, Jack 629, 636
Turner, Lana 532
Turner, Moira 529
Tuttle, Lurene 519, 692
Twain, Mark 13
Twelfth Night 180, 193, 343, 381, 397, 413, 478
12 Angry Men 588
The Twelve Chairs 700
Twelve O'Clock High 49, 54, 360, 460, 461, 489, 547, 589
Twenty Miles from Dodge 582, 585
21 Beacon Street 475
The 27th Day 128
20-20 392, 451
The Twilight Zone 43, 113, 489, 567, 656
The Twisted Heritage 312, 636, 642, 670
Two Girls Named Smith 644
Two Mothers 436
Two of a Kind 551
Two Tall Men 297, 584, 585
2001: A Space Odyssey 594
227 720
Tyburn, Gene 591, 688
The Tycoon 666
Tyles, Ken 560
Tyson, Cicely 133, 661, 662

U

U.S. Marshal 150
Ugly 413
The Ugly American 673
Ullman, Dan 450, 600
Umbrella Jack 449
Uncle Finney 625, 630, 642, 670
Uncle Oliver 392, 471

Uncle Sunday 546, 570
Under the Yum Yum Tree 589
The Undersea World of Jacques Cousteau 629
The Unforgiven 593
United States 595
Unloaded Gun 431, 520
Unmarked Grave 458, 487
The Untouchables 47, 128, 130, 132, 144, 189, 461, 480, 612
Unwanted Deputy 279, 424, 509
Up Periscope 608
Up the Down Staircase 688
Urich, Robert 721, 722
Us Haggens 116, 546, 556

V

V 540
Vaccaro, Brenda 572
Vacio, Natividad 663
Vajaro, Robert 168
Valentine's Day 368
Van Ark, Joan 643, 644
Van Cleef, Lee 513, 583, 599
Van Dreelen, John 526
Van Patten, Dick 551, 685
Van Patten, Jimmy 703
Van Patten, Joyce 551
Van Patten, Vincent 684, 685, 699
Van Rooten, Luis 484
Van Zandt, Julie 466
Vance, Vivian 589
Vanders, Warren 534, 597, 606, 611, 615, 623, 630, 640, 643, 649, 663, 671, 691
Vandever, Michael 586, 592, 605, 626
Vanni, Renata 655
Varela, Nina 480, 507
Vargus, Edmund 551
Vari, John 542
Vaughn, Heidi 651
Vaughn, Jean 473
Vaughn, Rees 552
Vaughn, Robert 454, 476
Vaughn, William 453
Vega$ 722
Vegas, Pedro 655
Velez, Olga 626

INDEX

Vengeance 147, 332, 617, 628
Vera, Ricky 560
Vernon, John 718, 719
Vernon, Lou 446, 447
Vic and Sade 399
The Victim 623, 656
Victor, David 449, 450, 451, 452, 453, 456, 457, 458, 461, 472
Victor/Victoria 598
Vigran, Herb 362, 367, 444, 662, 675, 678, 680, 682, 694, 704, 709, 718
Viharo, Robert 689
Villa Alegre 366
Vincent, Jan-Michael 673
Vincent, Virginia 635, 636
Vinson, Gary 476
Violent Saturday 665
The Violators 572, 585
The Virginian 13, 14, 53, 104, 113, 188, 192, 361, 365, 449, 475, 506, 535, 538, 557, 592
Vittes, Lou 466
Viva Valdez 657
Vogel, Karen 719
Vogel, Mitch 663, 702, 717
Voice in the Mirror 49
Voight, Jon 132, 145, 194, 197, 605, 606, 620, 641
Volcano 594
The Volga Boatman 17
Von Homburg, Wilheim 567
Von Ryan's Express 608
Votrian, Peter 446, 461
Voyage of the Damned 587, 599
Voyage to the Bottom of the Sea 453, 665, 666, 676, 690

W

The Wackiest Ship in the Army 560, 607
The Wacky World of Jonathan Winters 451
Waco 139, 634, 642, 669
Wagenheim, Charles 151, 444, 596, 601, 602, 604, 607, 612, 615, 616, 622, 637, 666, 673, 710, 719, 724

Waggner, Lia 525
Waggoner, Lyle 595
Wagner, Alan 154
Wagon Girls 537
Wagon Master 163, 553
Wagon Show 52, 425
Wagon Train 108, 113, 226, 365, 367, 624, 669, 675, 690
Wainwright, James 631
Wait Until Dark 441, 481
The Wake 438, 518
Walberg, Garry 497, 526, 539, 546, 551, 572, 702
A Walk in the Sun 605
Walk the Proud Land 114
Walker, Clint 108, 209
Walker, Scott 688, 708
Walking Tall 485, 600
Wallace, Earl W. 135, 708, 714, 719, 720, 721, 722
Wallace, George 102, 454, 558, 682
Wallace, Helen 450, 458
Wallerstein, Herb 678, 681, 684, 691
Wallis, Shani 698, 699
Walsh, George 28, 41, 57, 61, 70, 99, 236, 242, 430
Walsh, Joey 633, 634
Walsh, Raoul 15
Walt Disney Presents 668
Walter, Patricia 362
Walters, Nancy 536
Walton, Jess 196, 693
The Waltons 55, 113, 144, 186, 367, 373, 404, 458, 502, 539, 628, 631, 641, 686, 699
Wanamaker, Sam 599
Wanted: Dead or Alive 445
Wanted: The Sundance Woman 226
War Eagle, John 588
The War Lover 574
The War of the Worlds 50, 365
The War Priest 312, 650, 656, 664
Warburton, John 581
Ward, Albert 24
Ward, Larry 547, 607
The Warden 271, 568
Ware, Clyde 3, 93, 113, 142, 143, 145, 326, 578,

582, 584, 586, 591, 592, 594, 599, 601, 603, 608, 610, 611, 612, 613, 616, 619
Warner, Thomas 578
Warren, Anne 446
Warren, Charles Marquis 3, 11, 65, 74-77, 78, 79, 82, 87, 88, 89, 92, 95-96, 102, 104, 105, 110, 114, 171, 172, 184, 191, 193, 202, 209, 216, 444, 445, 446, 447, 448, 449, 450, 451, 452, 453, 454, 455, 456, 457, 458, 459, 460, 461, 462, 463, 464, 466, 508, 518
Warren, Lance 446
Warren, Leslie Ann 598
Warren, Robert Penn 29
Warren, Steve 523, 525
Warrick, Ruth 586
Washington: Behind Closed Doors 454
Waste 671, 672, 697, 711
Watch on the Rhine 476, 533
Water, Tom 632, 667
Waterfront 506
Watkins, Linda 494, 519, 529, 545, 573, 693
Watson, Bruce 633
Watson, Mills 625, 629, 631, 634, 643, 654, 663, 677, 680, 692, 705
Watson, William C. 608, 651, 716
Watts, Charles 553
The Waverly Wonders 666
Waxman, Stan 361
The Way It Is 546, 556
Wayland, Len 585, 611
Wayne, David 702, 720
Wayne, Fredd 460
Wayne, John 15, 75, 78, 79, 80, 82, 125, 160, 165, 168, 177, 261, 444, 500
Wayne, Pat 78
Weaver, Dennis 3, 87-92, 134, 148, 159, 170, 171, 172, 181, 184, 187, 192, 193, 201, 206-208, 209, 210, 257, 269, 273, 280, 281, 302, 352, 387, 440, 443, 468
Weaver, Fritz 610
Weaver, Rick 695

[834]

Index

W.E.B. 665, 689
Webb, Jack 59, 215
Webb, Richard 598, 611
Webber, Peggy 435, 470, 471
Webster 50, 365, 463
Webster, Charles 457
The Wedding 682
Welch, Karen 696
Welcome to Hard Times 446
Welk, Lawrence 109
The Well 604
Welles, Orson 26, 40, 52, 109, 361, 558, 586, 656
Welles, Rebecca 471
Wells Fargo 54
Wellman, Bill, Jr. 498
Wendell, Bruce 478
Wendell, Howard 559, 566
Wendy and Me 436
Werewolf 455
Wertimer, Ned 649
Wessel, Dick 584
West, Adam 550
West, Jennifer 655
West, Judi 668
West, Martin 599
West, Wayne 521, 527
West Side Story 486, 585
West Is West 14
Westbound 366, 429
Westcoat, Rusty 472
Westerfield, James 419, 420, 444, 445, 490, 550, 647
Western Heritage Awards 133, 479, 593, 660
Western Writers of America 657, 669, 685, 704, 714, 721
The Westerner 17, 46, 112
Westinghouse Presents 534
Weston, Brad 601
Weston, Jack 324, 481, 584
We've Got Each Other 644
Wexler, Paul 465, 472, 638
The Whales of August 602
What the Whiskey Drummer Heard 380, 417, 470, 514
Wheeler, John 721
The Wheeler Dealers 542
Wheels 571, 695
Whelan's Men 694

When the Whistle Blows 695
When You Coming Back Red Ryder 387
Where'd They Go? 414, 421, 509
Which Dr.? 597
The Whirlybirds 517
The Whispering Tree 192, 296, 604, 614, 669
The Whistler 222
Whitaker, Johnnie 611, 672
White, Bill, Jr. 455, 458
White, Daniel M. 512, 576, 666, 690
White, Lucas 653
White, Robert S. 554
White Heat 544
White Lightning 114
Whitehead, O.Z. 490
Whitfield, Anne 434, 439, 516, 605
Whitlock, Albert 213
Whitman, Kip 637, 646
Whitman, Stuart 464
Whitmore, James 134, 582, 589, 698
Whitney, Cece 650
Whitney, Dwight 108
Whitney, Grace Lee 536
Whitney, Michael 591
Whitney, Peter 447, 465, 502, 529, 577, 589
Who Lives by the Sword 399, 471, 514
Who Shot the Sheriff? The Rise and Fall of the Television Western 13
Whodunit 55
The Whole Town's Talking 580
Whorf, David 481
Whorf, Richard 113, 114, 476, 477, 478, 480, 481, 487, 488, 489, 490, 491, 492, 531
Who's the Boss? 685
Whose Life Is It Anyway 697
Why Change Your Wife? 17
Why Not? 415
Wichita Town 446
Wickwire, Nancy 558
The Wide Country 540, 646
The Widow 536
The Widow and the Rogue 701, 710
The Widow-Maker 700, 710

Widow's Mite 400, 485
Wiensko, Bob 509
Wiggins, Russell 704, 712
Wilcox, Claire 597
Wilcox, Joey 590
Wilcox-Horne, Collin 691
Wilcoxon, Henry 658
The Wild Angels 148
The Wild Bunch 112, 289, 447, 449, 491
The Wild Child 198, 671
The Wild Geese 113
Wild Jack Rhett 24, 26, 29
The Wild One 149, 566
Wild Rover 688
Wild West 372, 481, 527
The Wild Wild West 129, 143, 144, 153, 226, 483, 665
Wildman, Mary Jane 724
Wilke, Robert 487, 503, 506, 510, 535, 564, 616
Wilkerson, Guy 495
Will Penny 226
Willard, Elen 545
Williams, Adam 533
Williams, Bill 19
Williams, Elaine 372
Williams, Grant 495
Williams, Guinn 467
Williams, Guy 21
Williams, Hal 720
Williams, Robert B. 610, 612, 648, 668
Williams, Rush 632, 648
Williams, Terry 722
Williams, Van 338, 713, 714
Willingham, Noble 694, 695
Wills, Chill 277, 545, 618, 627
Wilson, Shirley 612, 618
Wilson, Terry 690
Wincelberg, Shimon 569, 662, 685, 710
Wind 371, 495
Windish, Ilka 583, 624
Windom, William 196-197, 297, 532, 547, 685
The Winds of Autumn 53
The Winds of War 46, 518, 609, 645, 673, 682, 695
Windsor, Marie 674
Winged World 621
Wingreen, Jason 682, 683

[835]

INDEX

The Wings of Eagles 117
Winner Take All 579
Winning of the West 226
Winslow, Jim 480
Winslow, Paula 364
Winter Meeting 594
Winters, Lee 499
Winters, Shelley 47, 88, 108
Wintersole, William 675
Wire Service 671
Wise, Henry 616, 649, 661, 662, 668, 675, 694
Wishbone 118, 282, 595
Wister, Owen 13
With a Smile 552, 570
With a Song in My Heart 584
Withers, Grant 464
Witness 135, 689
The Witness 169, 662, 683
Wives and Lovers 113
The Wiving 714, 720, 722
Wixted, Michael-James 645, 646
The Wizard 151, 683
The Wizard of Oz 694
Wolf, Venita 613
The Wolfer 421
Wolfington, Iggie 608
Woman Called Mary 407
The Woman Who Willed a Miracle 462
Women for Sale 275, 698
Wonder 522, 621, 628
Wonder Woman 595
Wood, Gary 666
Wood, Harry 471, 507
Wood, Larry 596
Wood, Paul Daniel 724
Wood, Preston 142, 606, 614, 632, 645, 660
Wood, Ward 466, 626
Woodman, Ruth 15
Woods, James 101
Woodward, Joanne 371, 658
Woodward, Morgan 190, 197-198, 318, 319, 586,
588, 602, 604, 607, 617, 620, 629, 634, 643, 655, 660, 682, 689, 702, 711
Woody, Sam 519
Word of Honor 367, 382, 411, 445, 458
Worell, Mary 622
Working Girl 387, 448, 689
Workman, Lindsey 553
The World of Suzie Wong 597
The Worm 516
The Wreckers 615, 628
Wright, Ben 17, 24, 25, 46, 50-51, 59, 67, 245, 246, 359, 360, 407, 408, 409, 414, 425, 427, 433, 435, 437, 439, 482, 506, 516, 548, 551, 562, 605
Wright, Howard 546
Wright, Robert Vincent 666, 715
Wright, Roy 534
Wright, Will 402, 445
Writer's Guild Award 140, 566, 714
Wrong Man 386, 432, 433, 469
The Wrong Man 313, 470, 603, 615, 659, 670
Wyatt, Al 715
Wyatt, Jane 47
Wyenn, Than 448, 458, 473
Wyler, Link 198-199, 619, 632, 650, 661, 671
Wyles, Catherine 588
Wyllie, Meg 693
Wynant, H.M. 463, 516, 554, 568, 618, 678
Wynter, Dana 620, 621

Y

Yancy Derringer 483, 626
Yankee Doodle Dandy 113, 476
Yankton 680, 683

Yarborough, Barton 23, 239
Yarbrough, Jean 507, 510, 518
A Year at the Top 702
A Year in the Life 658
The Yellow Mountain 114
The Yellow Rose 679, 682
The Yellow Rose of Texas 18
York, Elizabeth 504
Yorky 375, 415, 451
You Are There 184
You Can't Take It with You 580
Young, Buck 512, 524, 572
Young, Isaac 8
Young, Loretta 81
Young, Ray 662
Young, Sean 101
Young Doctor Malone 557, 705
Young Frankenstein 462, 611
The Young Lawyers 540, 587
Young Love 12, 388, 492
Young Man with a Gun 383, 460
Young Maverick 444
The Young and the Restless 559, 667
The Young Rebels 646
The Young Runaways 593
Younger, Jack 494
Your Cheatin' Heart 590
Your Hit Parade 521
Yrigoyen, Joe, Sr. 616

Z

Zaccaro, John 516
Zane Grey Theater 38, 110, 363, 364, 457
Zavala 217, 629, 666
Zerbe, Anthony 625, 663, 696
Zorro 20, 226, 360, 453, 454
Zuckert, William 542, 551, 560, 577, 666